IEEE Standards
Software Engineering, 1999 Edition

Volume Two:
Process Standards

This volume contains the *process* standards of the SESC collection.

Includes an introduction by James W. Moore, Member, SESC Management Board.

(Portions of the introductory material was excerpted from *Software Engineering Standards: A User's Road Map*, James W. Moore, IEEE Computer Society Press. © 1998 IEEE.)

The Institute of Electrical and Electronics Engineers, Inc.
345 East 47th Street, New York, NY 10017-2394, USA

Copyright © 1999 by the Institute of Electrical and Electronics Engineers, Inc.
All rights reserved. Published 5 April 1999. Printed in the United States of America.

Print: ISBN 0-7381-1560-6   SC107

At the time this standards collection was assembled, all the standards included were the latest editions available. However, the reader should understand that standards are reviewed at least every five years to ensure that their content is up-to-date, so standards in this collection may be revised or withdrawn at any time. In addition, new standards may be in preparation that were not available at the time of this edition. For information about the current status of standards in this area, please contact the IEEE Standards Department, 445 Hoes Lane, P.O. Box 1331, Piscataway, NJ 08855-1331, USA.

The Institute of Electrical and Electronics Engineers, Inc.
345 East 47th Street, New York, NY 10017-2394, USA

Copyright © 1999 by the
Institute of Electrical and Electronics Engineers, Inc.
All rights reserved. Published 1999
Printed in the United States of America

ISBN 0-7381-1560-6

March 1999

To: Software Engineering Standards Collection User

Since the last publication of its collected standards, the Software Engineering Standards Committee (SESC) of the IEEE Computer Society has made significant improvements aimed at better satisfying the needs of its users. One important improvement is the transformation of 38 (of the nearly 50 standards in the software engineering collection) vaguely related individual standards into a single integrated edition. The resulting edition

— Fits all of the standards into a single overall framework.
— Aligns the software engineering standards with key international standards on software engineering and quality management.
— Aligns the process and data standards of the collection with the international standard on software life cycle processes.
— Establishes connections with related disciplines such as systems engineering, project management, and quality management.

To better explain the relationships among all of the standards in the software engineering collection, the SESC also commissioned a book, *Software Engineering Standards: A User's Roadmap* by James W. Moore. This book is available as a companion to this four-volume edition.

Another important improvement was the extension and update of the collection. This endeavor produced 17 revised standards and new standards dealing with enterprise modeling, reuse libraries, and concept of operations.

And finally, a user's group has been established to promote uptake and provide feedback to standards writers.

We are very pleased with the results of this tremendous effort to update, integrate, and reorganize a very complicated group of standards.

An update of this magnitude is the result of the work of many people. We wish to acknowledge the following contributors:

Contributors

Special thanks are extended to all working group members, balloting group members, and comment resolution participants.

Working Group chairs

Tom Bruce *(1320.2 addition)*
Perry De Weese *(12207 adoption, 12207.2 addition)*
Richard Fairley *(1058 update)*
Roger Fujii *(1012 update)*

Dennis Lawrence *(1028 update)*
Howard McQuerry *(1320.1 addition)*
Richard Schmidt *(1220 update)*
Norman Schneidewind *(1061 update)*
David Schultz *(1074 update)*

Raghu Singh *(12207 adoption, 12207.2 addition)*
Richard Thayer *(1362 addition)*
Ronald L. Wade *(PMBOK Guide adoption)*

James W. Moore

For leadership in software reuse standards and the preparation of introductory material in each volume.

Peer reviewers of the introductory material

Paul R. Croll
John Harauz

Mark Henley
Tom Kurihara

Peter T. Poon
Peter Voldner

How to Use this Edition

Since 1979, when the IEEE Software Engineering Standards Committee (SESC) published its first standard (IEEE Std 730, Software Quality Assurance), SESC standards have provided a high-quality reference for the best practices for software development. Each standard was carefully written to provide the best possible description of the practice with which it was concerned.

In the intervening 20 years, the practice of software engineering has grown from an individual craft to a highly organized team operation. There has been growing emphasis on the adoption of organization-level processes that are intended to be applied repeatedly to all software engineering projects within the organization. This has presented a new challenge to the SESC. Not only must the standards be technically excellent on an individual basis, but each must also take its place within a suite of standards that can be adopted in totality or in part by interested organizations. In order to accomplish this, the SESC needed to include an organizing framework, uniform terminology, and clear relationships.

Since 1994, SESC has been following a strategy to achieve the desired level of integration within the collection. Complete integration has not yet been achieved, but substantial progress has been made:

— An organizing framework has been selected.
— The collection has been aligned with key international standards.
— The collection has been aligned with key standards in related disciplines such as quality management and project management.
— An umbrella standard for software life cycle processes has been adopted.
— All SESC standards dealing with software processes and the data that they produce have been harmonized with the umbrella standard.

All of these integrating forces play a role in the organization of this four-volume edition.

In addition, SESC decided to provide an overall guide to its collection. For this purpose, it tasked one of the members of its Management Board to write a "road map" describing the integration of the collection. The road map is published as:

James W. Moore, *Software Engineering Standards: A User's Road Map*, IEEE Computer Society Press, Los Alamitos, California, 1997.

The *Road Map* is available as a companion to this four-volume edition of the SESC standards.

Finding the standards in the framework

The organizing framework of the SESC collection is shown in Figure 2 on page v of the general introduction that opens each volume. It depicts seven major parts of the SESC collection:

— The Terminology layer is populated with standards providing terms for use in the entire SESC collection. For convenience, the Terminology portion of the collection is included in *Volume One* of this edition. Additional information regarding terminology standards can be found in Chapters 5 and 11 of the *Road Map*.
— The Overall Guide layer provides a description of the entire collection and how the standards relate to each other and with those of related disciplines. The overall guide is the *Road Map* book.
— The next three layers (the Principles, the Element Standards, and the Application Guides) are subdivided according to the four objects of software engineering: Customer, Processes, Products, and Resources. Each of these objects occupies a separate volume of this edition. Additional information regarding each object can be found in Chapters 11 through 14 of the *Road Map*.
— The Techniques layer contains standards on detailed techniques that may be useful in the context of any of the other layers. For convenience, the Techniques portion of the collection is included in *Volume Four* of this edition. Additional information regarding technique standards can be found in Chapters 5 and 11 of the *Road Map*.

The organizing framework itself is described in *The SESC Framework for Standards* beginning on page iv of each volume. More details can be found in *Organization of the SESC Collection*, pages 43–52 of the *Road Map*.

Finding the standards by object

In order to make a rough classification of nearly 50 standards, SESC developed a model of four objects treated by a software engineering project. These objects are: the Customer, the Processes, the Products and the Resources. Because the four-object classification was developed after many of the standards were written, the assignment of standards to objects is necessarily forced. The fit is not yet perfect and will be improved as the standards are revised.

The four-object classification is the primary organizer for this edition of the SESC standards; each object occupies one of the four volumes of the collection. Further information can be found in Chapters 11 through 14 of the *Road Map*.

Finding the key standards

In order to integrate the SESC collection, it is important to select a few key standards that provide an "umbrella" for the other more detailed standards. These standards are used as the basis for integration. Other standards are revised to become more consistent with the key standards. So far, the SESC has selected three key standards for integration:

— For quality management, SESC has selected ISO 9001 and ISO 9000-3 as the key standards. Quality management activities in other standards will maintain consistency with the two key standards. Further information on this subject can be found in the section *Quality management* on page xvi of the general introduction to each of the volumes. Additional information can be found in the *Road Map* in the discussion of ISO TC176 on pages 72–79 and in Chapter 6.

— For project management, SESC has adopted the *Guide to the Project Management Body of Knowledge* written by the Project Management Institute (PMI) and adopted by SESC as IEEE Std 1490. Further information on this subject can be found in the section *Project management* on page xvi of the general introduction to each of the volumes. Additional information can be found in the *Road Map* in the discussion of PMI on pages 53–54 and in Chapter 7.

— For software engineering processes and for the customer relationship, SESC has adopted ISO/IEC 12207, *Software Life Cycle Processes* as its integrating standard. All other process standards in the SESC collection will maintain consistency with 12207. Furthermore, the SESC standards that describe documents have been revised to be consistent with the data requirements of 12207. The IEEE/EIA 12207 series can be found in *Volume One* of this edition and other SESC process standards can be found in *Volume Two*. Additional information regarding process standards can be found in the *Road Map* in Chapter 13.

Finding the standards by subject areas

Some may prefer to reference a classification of the standards into the traditional subject areas of

— Terminology
— Processes
— Tools
— Reuse
— Project Management
— Plans
— Documentation
— Measurement (including reliability and metrics)

The general introduction that begins each volume contains the section *Alternative ways to organize the SESC collection* beginning on page xiv. This section classifies the standards by the given subject area. More details can be found in *Current Collection of the SESC*, pages 36–39 of the *Road Map*.

Finding the standards in context

Because software engineering is strongly related to other disciplines, its standards are also related to other disciplines. SESC has formulated specific relationships to the six disciplines listed below. For each discipline, more information can be found in the *Road Map* in the chapter cited below.

— Computer Science: Chapter 5
— Quality Management: Chapter 6
— Project Management: Chapter 7
— Systems Engineering: Chapter 8
— Dependability: Chapter 9
— Safety: Chapter 10

SESC user feedback

The SESC has taken steps to organize and integrate its collection because of feedback from its users, the individuals and organizations who apply SESC standards. In order to improve its relationship with its users, SESC has established a Software Engineering Standards Users Group (SESUG). More information about the SESUG can be found at http://computer.org/standard/sesc/.

Contents

IEEE Standards
Software Engineering, 1999 Edition

Volume Two:
Process Standards

This volume contains the *process* standards of the SESC collection.

Introduction to the 1999 Edition

The Institute of Electrical and Electronics Engineers (IEEE) is the world's largest technical professional society. With membership numbering more than 320,000 individuals in nearly 150 countries, the IEEE publishes nearly 25 percent of the world's technical papers in the scope described by its name [IEEE97].[1] The IEEE is organized into 37 Technical Societies, some of which are active in developing standards, including the Computer Society. The Computer Society's Software Engineering Standards Committee (SESC) develops and maintains a collection of nearly 50 standards, which grows at the rate of 5 or so per year. This remarkable record of success also introduces a problem. The sheer number of standards in the collection hampers the intuitive selection of appropriate standards. Instead, guidance is needed to assist in selection.

Fortunately, SESC has prepared itself for this challenge by developing a framework that organizes and integrates its entire collection of standards. At this time, the framework is retrospectively superimposed upon the collection, hence the "fit" of the individual standards into the framework is not perfect. Nevertheless, the framework is already useful for the selection of standards.

This four-volume edition of the SESC standards uses that framework as its organizing principle. To explain and apply that framework, the following material is provided in this introduction:

- ◆ An overview of the IEEE and the SESC
- ◆ Fundamental principles
- ◆ The SESC framework for standards
- ◆ The principles behind the framework

---

[1]Information appearing in brackets corresponds to references, which can be found on page xxviii of this introduction.

i

◆ Applying the framework to the SESC collection
◆ Alternative ways to organize the SESC collection
◆ Organizational conformance

The IEEE Computer Society Software Engineering Standards Committee (SESC)

◆ Institute of Electrical and Electronics Engineers (IEEE)

All standards-making activities within the IEEE are governed by the IEEE Standards Association, often called "IEEE-SA." IEEE produces three types of standards (with a lowercase "s") documents—Standards (with a capital "S"), Recommended Practices, and Guides. The types of standards are differentiated by the degree of prescription in their normative requirements. *Standards* contain requirements for conformance, generally characterized by the use of the verb "shall." *Recommended Practices* (RPs) present procedures and positions preferred by the IEEE; they are characterized by the use of the verb "should." *Guides* suggest alternative approaches to good practice but generally refrain from clear-cut recommendations; they are characterized by the use of the verb "may" [IEEE97a]. It is important to note, though, that any of the three documents can contain any of the three verb forms. Therefore it is possible to claim conformance with any of the three types of documents, although, in the case of a Guide or even an RP, the claim may not be a strong one.

IEEE can produce any of the three types of documents on a "Trial Use" basis. Trial Use standards are approved for a period of two years. At the end of this period, they may be administratively promoted to full use or returned to the sponsor for revision based on comments received during the trial use period.

The numbering of IEEE standards can seem a little complicated. In principle (although there are exceptions), the base number assigned to an IEEE standard has no meaning and is not meant to suggest any relationships among standards. It is possible to suggest relationships among standards by appending a part number to the base number. For example, standard "123.1" would be related to the "123" standard. It is also possible to add a supplement to an existing standard with the intention that the supplement eventually will be merged with the base standard. Supplements are indicated by appending a letter to the number. For example, standard "123a" would be regarded as a supplement, a logical part of, the "123" standard. The number is sometimes followed by an "R" with a year; this indicates the date of the latest reaffirmation of the standard.

Standards development projects that have not yet reached final approval are indicated by the presence of a "P" before the number, indicating that the number denotes a "project" rather than a completed standard. One may also find the notation "(R)" following the number of an IEEE standard; this simply denotes a project to revise an existing standard.

An approved IEEE standard has a life of 5 years. At the end of that time it must be reviewed with one of three results: withdrawal, reaffirmation (without change), or revision. Revision is performed by a working group using a process very similar to that for writing a new standard [IEEE95].

◆ IEEE Computer Society Software Engineering Standards Committee (SESC)

The IEEE Computer Society is the largest association for computer professionals in the world. Founded 50 years ago, it is now the largest of the technical societies of IEEE. Any Computer Society standards project is assigned to one of a dozen or so "sponsors." For software engineering standards, the sponsor is the Software Engineering Standards Committee (SESC).

SESC traces its roots back two decades to the creation in 1976 of the Software Engineering Standards Subcommittee of the Technical Committee on Software Engineering (TCSE). Its first standard, IEEE Std 730, *IEEE Standard for Software Quality Assurance Plans*, was published on a trial use basis three years later. By 1997, the collection had grown to 44 documents. In addition to the development of standards, SESC sponsors or cooperates in annual US or international conferences and workshops in its subject area. SESC also participates in international standards-making as a member of the US Technical Advisory Group (TAG) to ISO/IEC JTC1/SC7.

The *Overview of the SESC* [SESC98] describes the SESC's mission as follows:

> *Our mission is to:*
>
> • *identify and understand user needs in the field of software engineering,*
> • *develop an integrated family of standards that respond effectively to user needs,*
> • *support implementation of these standards, and*
> • *facilitate meaningful evaluation of resulting implementations*
>
> *using the IEEE processes to achieve consensus and compatibility with other IEEE standards.*

Most of the SESC standards are *practice* standards rather than *product* standards, concerned with the regulation of the practice of software engineering rather than the interfaces of the products produced.

Fundamental principles

Unfettered by physical constraints or dominant products, most software engineering practice standards are ad hoc recordings of practices thought to be "best" by a group of practitioners. This is acceptable when the standards are considered individually. When the standards are considered as a body, though, the lack of underlying principles leads to capricious inconsistencies among them. Part of the solution lies in the adoption of vocabulary and key relationships provided by the SESC framework. Perhaps more important, though, would be the development of a set of *fundamental principles* that would unify and motivate the practices of software engineering.

Figure 1 shows a notional depiction of the role of principles. The software engineering principles would be specializations of the general principles of engineering and would motivate practice standards. Viewed in the other direction, experience from implementation would be abstracted in practice standards and eventually generalized as principles. In this model, practice standards exist in the tension between the consolidating and integrating force provided by the principles and the expansive and innovative force provided by implementation.

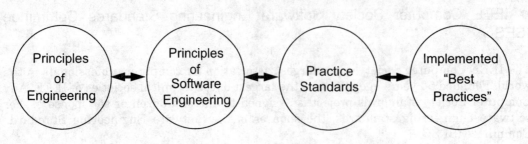

Figure 1—Relationship of principles and practice

In cooperation with the Université du Québec à Montréal, SESC has initiated a project to identify a set of fundamental principles [Dupuis97]. To date the project has completed two rounds of alternating workshops and Delphi studies and has obtained some preliminary results. The following candidate principles have achieved a high degree of consensus:

— *Invest in the understanding of the problem.*
— *Since change is inherent to software, plan for it and manage it.*
— *Uncertainty is unavoidable in software engineering. Identify and manage it.*
— *Minimize software component interaction.*
— *Since tradeoffs are inherent to software engineering, make them explicit and document them.*
— *To improve design, study previous solutions to similar problems.*

The candidates listed below have attracted a high level of support, but not yet consensus. Listed in decreasing order of agreement, they will be the subject of further discussion and refinement.

— *Control complexity with multiple perspectives and multiple levels of abstraction.*
— *Produce software in a stepwise fashion.*
— *Define software artifacts rigorously.*
— *Establish a software process that provides flexibility.*
— *Manage quality throughout the life cycle as formally as possible.*
— *Set quality objectives for each deliverable product.*
— *Implement a disciplined approach and improve it continuously.*
— *Build with and for reuse.*
— *Apply and use quantitative measurements in decision making.*

The SESC framework for standards

The SESC collection has grown large enough that users can no longer be expected to intuitively perceive the relationships among the various component standards. In attempting to articulate overall organizing concepts as well as relationships to other collections of standards, an SESC strategy statement [SESC95] formulated the framework depicted in Figure 2.

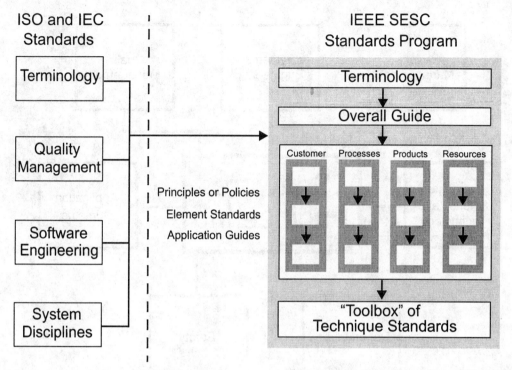

(Source: Adapted from [SESC95].)

Figure 2—Elements of the SESC program plan

Figure 2 is based on the following organizing concepts:

— Context of software engineering
— Normative relationships of standards
— Objects of software engineering

Each of these organizing concepts will be treated in the sections that follow. The framework will then be applied to the overall collection of SESC standards.

The principles behind the framework

◆ Context of software engineering

Software engineering occupies a position intermediate between, on the one hand, the mathematical and physical disciplines of *computer science and technology* and, on the other hand, the requirements of the particular *application domains,* applying the findings of the former to solve problems of the latter. (See Figure 3.) The techniques for the engineering of software can be viewed, in part, as specializations of the techniques of more general disciplines, such as *project management*, *system engineering*, and *quality management.* Furthermore, a software project must often implement requirements imposed by cross-cutting disciplines like *dependability* (a term more general than reliability) and *safety.*

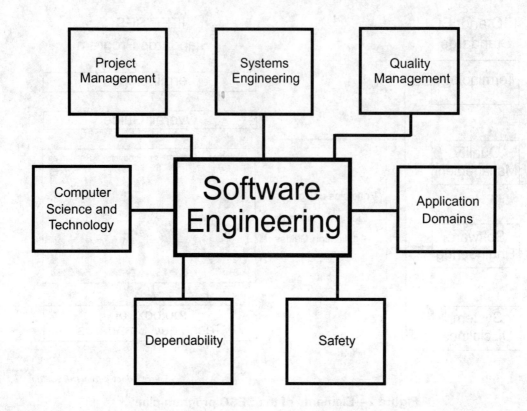

Figure 3—Relationship of software engineering to other disciplines

IEEE SESC recognizes that its standards exist in these contexts. In instances where appropriate coordination and integration have been achieved, SESC has designated contextual standards as integrating standards for its own collection. For example, ISO 9001 and its software guide, ISO 9000-3, have been recognized as the strategic standards relating software engineering to quality management.

◆ Normative relationships of standards

Another way to describe a collection of standards is with a layer diagram that proceeds from general considerations at the top to specific, detailed concerns at the bottom.[2] Each layer is characterized by the nature of the direction given by the standards at that level and their relationships to standards on other levels.

Figure 4 is a layer diagram using a part of the SESC collection of standards as an example. Fundamental concepts are found at the top two levels. The top layer provides essential terminology, vocabulary, and unifying concepts used by other standards in the collection. Typically, the documents in the top layer are standards. In many cases, the documents occupying this level are an integral part of the collection being described; in other cases, they are adopted from related collections. On the other hand, the second layer is typically guides—often a single guide. It provides overall advice on how the other documents of the collection may be applied.

---

[2]This approach to organizing a collection of standards was originally developed by Technical Committee 56 of the International Electrotechnical Commission (IEC TC56).

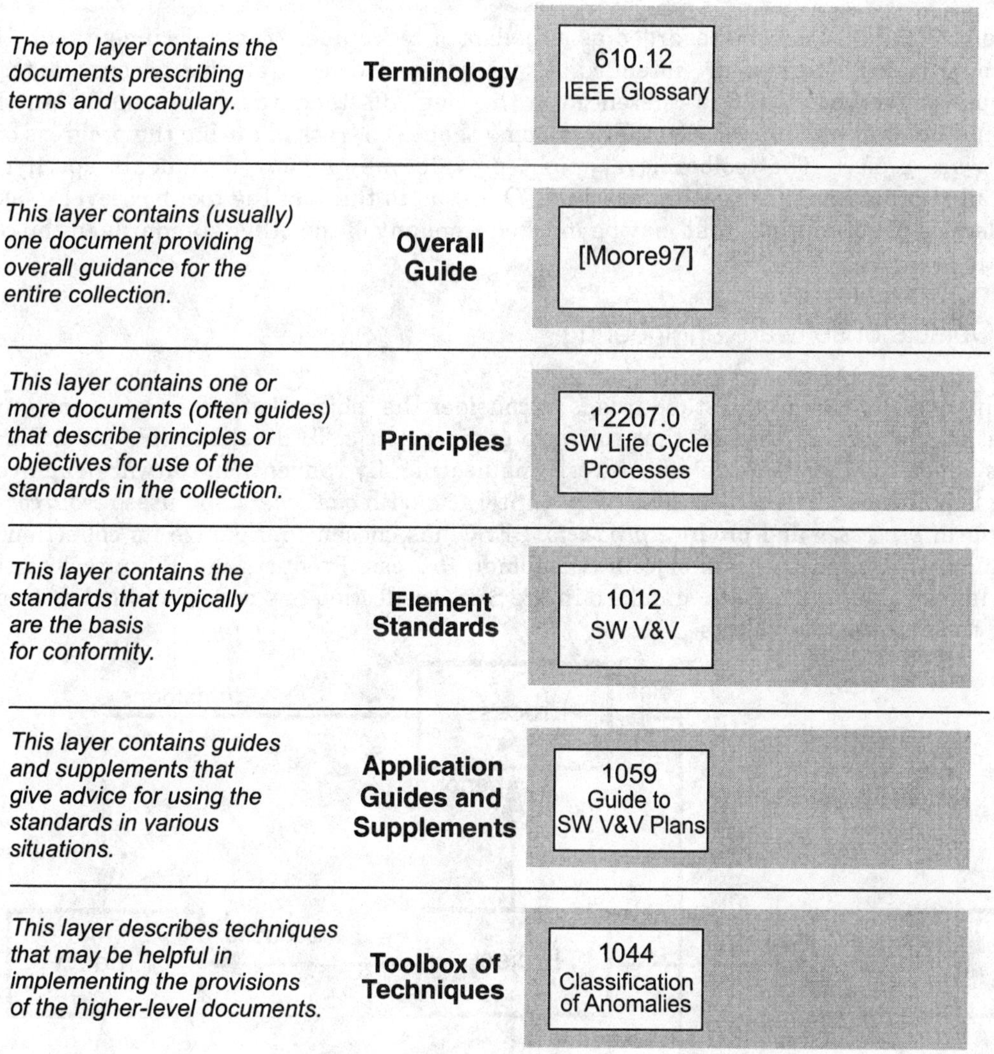

The top layer contains the documents prescribing terms and vocabulary.	**Terminology**	610.12 IEEE Glossary
This layer contains (usually) one document providing overall guidance for the entire collection.	**Overall Guide**	[Moore97]
This layer contains one or more documents (often guides) that describe principles or objectives for use of the standards in the collection.	**Principles**	12207.0 SW Life Cycle Processes
This layer contains the standards that typically are the basis for conformity.	**Element Standards**	1012 SW V&V
This layer contains guides and supplements that give advice for using the standards in various situations.	**Application Guides and Supplements**	1059 Guide to SW V&V Plans
This layer describes techniques that may be helpful in implementing the provisions of the higher-level documents.	**Toolbox of Techniques**	1044 Classification of Anomalies

Figure 4—Format of layer diagram using a part of the SESC collection as an example

The third layer may consist of standards or guides. These documents specify the principles and objectives pursued by the collection being described. There may be several such documents, specific to different subject areas of standards in the collection.

For those assessing conformance, the "meat" of a collection is found at the fourth level. These are the element standards that provide the basis for conformance. Often, there are several of these documents, depending on how the standards organization has chosen to subdivide its area of interest.

The fifth layer is a set of application guides and supplements. These documents interpret and elaborate how the element standards may be applied in various situations. In many cases, they are structured to provide insight regarding the intentions of the standards organization in creating the element standards. Sometimes they are descriptive rather than prescriptive. They should be used cautiously—in some cases, they have been mistakenly applied as replacements of the element standards rather than supplements to them.

The bottom layer may be regarded as a toolbox of techniques. These documents may be standards or guides and are intended to specify detailed requirements for specific techniques or methods that are referenced in the element standards. For example, an element standard might prescribe that problems should be tracked during the progress of a software project. The toolbox level might provide one or more documents specifying detailed procedures for problem tracking. One way to think of the tool box level is as a collection of subroutines that may be invoked from any of the other standards in the collection.

◆ Objects of software engineering

A final way to look at the standards is to consider the "objects" of software engineering, that is, the sorts of "things" that software engineers use. To illustrate this view, SESC has adopted a simple model of software engineering. By convention, software engineering is performed by a *project*. The project interacts with *customers* and uses *resources* to perform *processes* and produce *products*. SESC has chosen to organize its collection of standards around the four objects (Customer, Process, Product, and Resource) at the perimeter of Figure 5. Each standard in the SESC collection has been classified as treating one of these four objects.

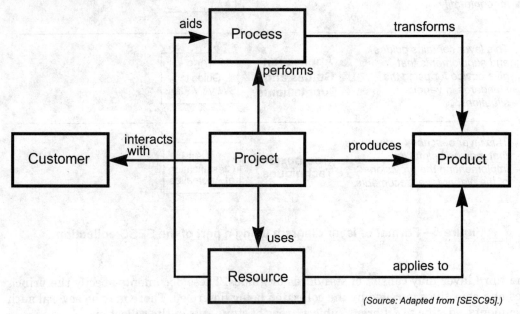

(Source: Adapted from [SESC95].)

Figure 5—Objects of software engineering

Applying the framework to the SESC collection

Again referring to Figure 2, we can see that the SESC framework combines the three organizing concepts depicted in Figures 3, 4, and 5. The collection recognizes the important contextual influences provided by standards from other disciplines, particularly those standards adopted by international organizations. The SESC collection is organized into the six-layer model describing the normative relations among the documents. To more precisely categorize the subjects of the standards, the three "inner" layers are organized into four "stacks" corresponding to the four key objects of software engineering.

This section will explain how the existing SESC standards may be mapped into the framework provided by Figure 2. The organization of this four-volume edition mirrors the mapping. The *terminology* layer is combined with the *customer* stack in one volume. The *process* and *product* stacks each have their own volume. The *resource* stack is combined with the *techniques* layer in the final volume. The overall guide is available as a separate companion book.

Figure 6 provides a look at the outer layers of the collection and the subsequent four figures provide detailed looks at each of the stacks. Some standards might be appropriately classified into more than one stack, but each is described in only one volume of the edition. Figures 7 through 10 show all applicable SESC standards; the ones not included in the corresponding volume are shaded and surrounded by a dotted line.

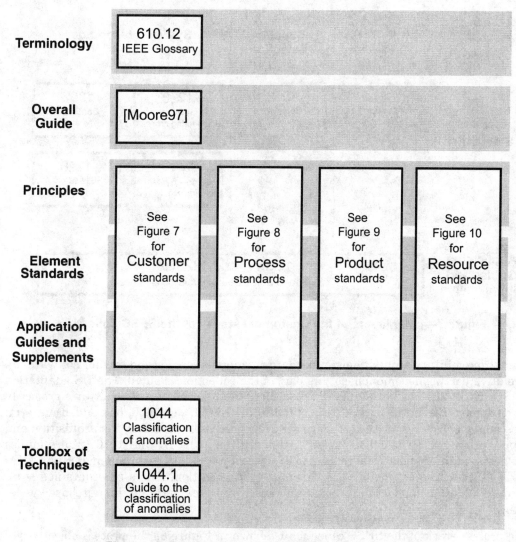

Figure 6—Outer layers of the SESC collection

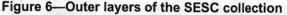

Figure 6 summarizes the outer three layers of the collection. There is a single terminology standard. IEEE Std 610 is a multi-part glossary of engineering terminology; its part 12 is specific to software engineering.

IEEE Std 1044 and its companion guide, IEEE Std 1044.1, provide a method for classifying software anomalies. The method is clearly applicable during software integration and for tracking failures after operational deployment of the software. Some users, though, might find it useful throughout the development and maintenance cycles. Therefore, it is positioned in the "toolbox" of broadly applicable techniques.

The customer "stack" of the SESC collection is depicted in Figure 7. SESC strategy documents, e.g., [SESC96a], subdivide the subject into the following areas: two-party agreement, contractor/supplier selection, and system stakeholders.

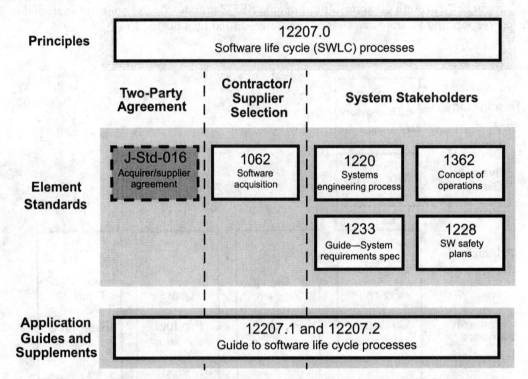

Figure 7—Inner layers of the Customer "stack" of the SESC collection

Aside from military acquisition standards, customer-oriented standards for software are a relatively new phenomenon, so this part of the collection is small. The US adaptation of ISO/IEC 12207 is a key standard prescribing the relationship of a software project to its customer. The initial part of this standard, IEEE/EIA 12207.0, has added material prescribing objectives for the software life cycle processes, including the acquisition and supply processes. Parts 1 and 2 of the standard (i.e., 12207.1 and 12207.2) are guides providing additional material related to life cycle data and process implementation. EIA/ IEEE J-Std-016 is not included in this four-volume edition. It is a self-contained standard suitable for application in legacy defense programs and may be purchased separately.

The process stack of the SESC collection is shown in Figure 8. The process objectives of IEEE/EIA 12207.0 are the source of the principles that many of the standards would detail. For purposes of summary exposition at this point, four categories of process standards have been abstracted from the eight categories used in [SESC96a]. The category of general processes encompasses the overall software life cycle (SWLC) as well as closely related enveloping processes such as systems engineering and project management. The primary processes are those of ISO/IEC 12207—acquisition, supply, development, operation, and maintenance. The supporting processes contribute to the execution of the primary processes. Finally, process measurement cuts across all of these processes.

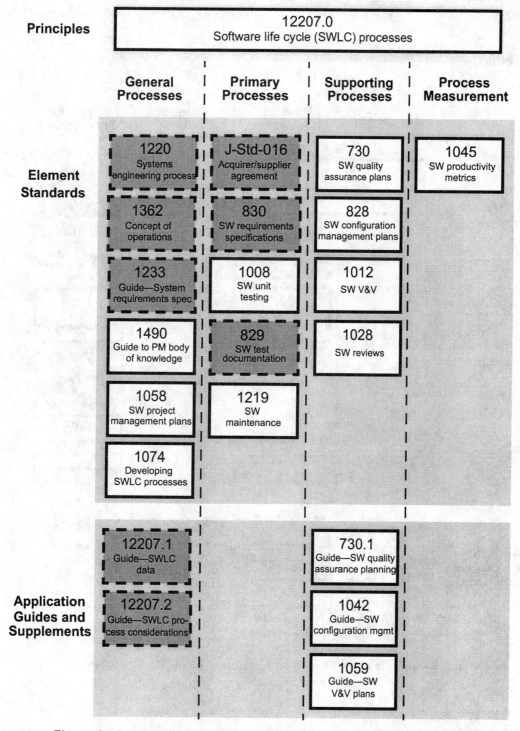

Figure 8—Inner layers of the Process "stack" of the SESC collection

Figure 9 shows the product "stack" of the SESC collection. Software engineering standards have traditionally focused on process rather than product, so it is not surprising that this section of the collection is relatively sparse. There is no standard providing overall principles. The element standards and their guides have been force-fitted into four categories: characteristics, product measurement, product evaluation, and end-item specification. Many of these documents are listed in other stacks, but are also listed here because they have something to contribute to this relatively new area of emphasis.

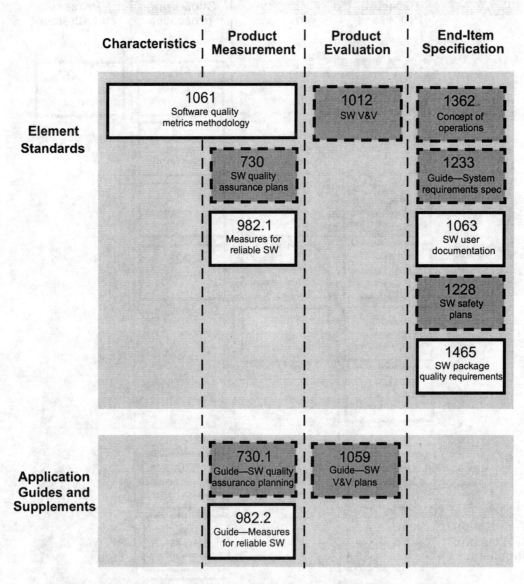

Figure 9—Inner layers of the Product "stack" of the SESC collection

Finally, Figure 10 illustrates the resource "stack" of the SESC collection. This category encompasses several standards that are grouped into the following four sets: process information products, notation, reuse libraries, and tools and environments. Prospects are good for increased integration of these standards. The 1420 family, along with 1430, will provide an integrated collection of standards for the interoperation of software reuse libraries. Similarly, the 1320 family will provide standards and guides for using the IDEF0 and IDEF1X97 notations for both data and process description. The Computer-Aided Software Engineering (CASE) tools standards are being developed in close cooperation with a working group of ISO/IEC JTC1/SC7 with the goal of consistency within the standards and between the two standards organizations.

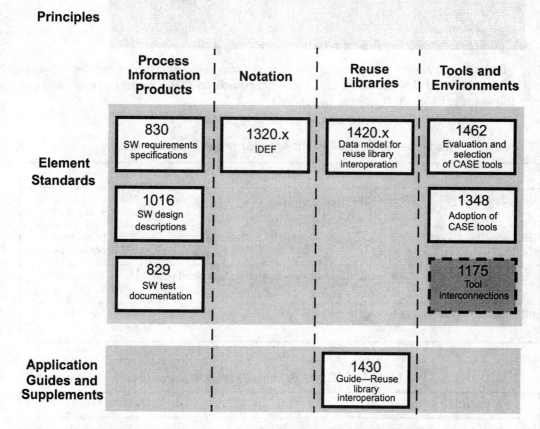

Figure 10—Inner layers of the Resource "stack" of the SESC collection

Alternative ways to organize the SESC collection

Software engineering standards cover a broad scope of subjects related to the responsible and effective practice of the software engineering discipline. The 1997 SESC Program Plan [SESC97] organized the collection by the following subject areas:

— Terminology (Volume One: Customer and Terminology Standards)
— Life cycle processes (Volume Two: Process Standards)
— Tools (Volume Four: Resource and Technique Standards)
— Reuse (Volume Four: Resource and Technique Standards)
— *Project management*
— *Plans*
— *Documentation*
— *Measurement* (including reliability and metrics)

The subject areas shown in italics do not directly correspond with the strategic framework. The tables in this section will list the standards in those subject areas and indicate the volume in which they may be found.

Table 1—IEEE SESC standards for project management

Standard	Title	Volume
IEEE Std 1044-1993	IEEE Standard Classification for Software Anomalies	Volume Four: Resource and Technique Standards
IEEE Std 1044.1-1995	IEEE Guide to Classification for Software Anomalies	Volume Four: Resource and Technique Standards
IEEE Std 1058-1998	IEEE Standard for Software Project Management Plans	Volume Two: Process Standards
IEEE Std 1490-1998	IEEE Guide to the Project Management Body of Knowledge	Volume Two: Process Standards

Table 2—IEEE SESC standards for plans

Standard	Title	Volume
IEEE Std 730-1998	IEEE Standard for Software Quality Assurance Plans	Volume Two: Process Standards
IEEE Std 730.1-1995	IEEE Guide for Software Quality Assurance Planning	Volume Two: Process Standards
IEEE Std 828-1998	IEEE Standard for Software Configuration Management Plans	Volume Two: Process Standards
IEEE Std 1012-1998	IEEE Standard for Software Verification and Validation	Volume Two: Process Standards
IEEE Std 1012a-1998	Supplement to IEEE Standard for Software Verification and Validation	Volume Two: Process Standards
IEEE Std 1228-1994	IEEE Standard for Software Safety Plans	Volume One: Customer and Terminology Standards

NOTE—See also IEEE Std 1058-1998 under project management.

Table 3—IEEE SESC standards for documentation

Standard	Title	Volume
IEEE Std 829-1998	IEEE Standard for Software Test Documentation	Volume Four: Resource and Technique Standards
IEEE Std 830-1998	IEEE Recommended Practice for Software Requirements Specifications	Volume Four: Resource and Technique Standards
IEEE Std 1016-1998	IEEE Recommended Practice for Software Design Descriptions	Volume Four: Resource and Technique Standards
IEEE Std 1063-1987	IEEE Standard for Software User Documentation	Volume Three: Product Standards
IEEE Std 1233, 1998 Edition	IEEE Guide for Developing System Requirements Specifications	Volume One: Customer and Terminology Standards
IEEE Std 1362-1998	IEEE Guide for Information Technology—System Definition—Concept of Operations Document	Volume One: Customer and Terminology Standards

Table 4—IEEE SESC standards for measurement

Standard	Title	Volume
IEEE Std 982.1-1988	IEEE Standard Dictionary of Measures to Produce Reliable Software	Volume Three: Product Standards
IEEE Std 982.2-1988	IEEE Guide for the Use of Standard Dictionary of Measures to Produce Reliable Software	Volume Three: Product Standards
IEEE Std 1045-1992	IEEE Standard for Software Productivity Metrics	Volume Two: Process Standards
IEEE Std 1061-1998	IEEE Standard for a Software Quality Metrics Methodology	Volume Three: Product Standards

Umbrella standards

The preceding material explains how the SESC collection may be *organized*. That does not necessarily imply that it is *integrated*. In general, the various standards were written individually with the overall integration of the collection as only a secondary concern. In recent years, though, SESC has placed greater emphasis on integration.

A first step in achieving integration is the selection of a small number of key standards with broad impact on software engineering. Each of these umbrella standards is designated as a target for integration; each new or revised SESC standard is required to be consistent with the umbrella standards. Umbrella standards have been designated in three areas:

— Quality management: ISO 9001:1994 and ISO 9000-3:1997
— Project management: IEEE Std 1490-1998
— Software engineering process: IEEE/EIA 12207.0-1996

◆ Quality management

ISO 9001:1994, *Quality Systems—Model for Quality Assurance in Design, Development, Production, Installation and Servicing*, includes design and development within its scope. Hence, it is the quality management standard suitable for application to software development. Because its scope is far more general than software, developers may find its provisions difficult to apply directly. ISO 9000-3:1997, *Quality Management and Quality Assurance Standards—Part 3: Guidelines for the Application of ISO 9001:1994 to the Development, Supply, Installation and Maintenance of Computer Software*, is a guidance document specifically written for this purpose.

ISO 9000-3 forms a bridge from ISO 9001 to ISO/IEC 12207. ISO 9000-3 is organized with the same structure as ISO 9001; it quotes each relevant provision of ISO 9001 and provides advice for its application to software. Furthermore, detailed cross-references are provided to 12207 at the subclause level. Because IEEE/EIA 12207 incorporates the entire text of ISO/IEC 12207, the cross-references are equally applicable to the IEEE document.

◆ Project management

IEEE Std 1490, *IEEE Guide to the Project Management Body of Knowledge*, is an adoption of a document written by the Project Management Institute. Its provisions relate to the general discipline of project management. The IEEE standard that is specialized to software engineering project management is IEEE Std 1058 (newly revised and renumbered from the old 1058.1).

◆ Software engineering process

ISO/IEC 12207 provides seventeen processes that are applicable across the entire life cycle of software, from conception to retirement. A project may utilize these processes to deal with acquisition, supply, development, operation, and maintenance of software. When IEEE adopted this standard, it corrected a few errors and added material to create IEEE/EIA 12207.0. Two additional guidance parts, IEEE/EIA 12207.1 and IEEE/EIA 12207.2, covering data and process, respectively, were approved in 1997.

Each of the SESC process standards will be revised to be consistent with IEEE/EIA 12207.0. Furthermore, each of the SESC standards describing plans or other documents will be revised to be consistent with 12207.1. As an interim step, each of the standards describing documents has already been revised to include a table explaining the relationship of its provisions and the provisions of 12207.1.

IEEE Std 1074 also describes processes and is also designated as an integrating standard. Its viewpoint is different than that of IEEE/EIA 12207.0, though. IEEE/EIA 12207.0 can be considered as providing requirements for processes. IEEE Std 1074 can be viewed as providing standardized building blocks for the construction of those processes.

Organizational conformance

Historically, SESC standards have focused on the software project as the entity that would implement conformance to the standards, particularly process standards. In recent years, though, it has become generally accepted that organizations or enterprises should adopt processes and execute them repeatedly in all of their projects. In general, the existing body of standards did not address this possibility. Because they ignored the existence of organization-level resources, they apparently encouraged the form of conformance shown in Figure 11 where the enterprise's resources are, in effect, ignored.

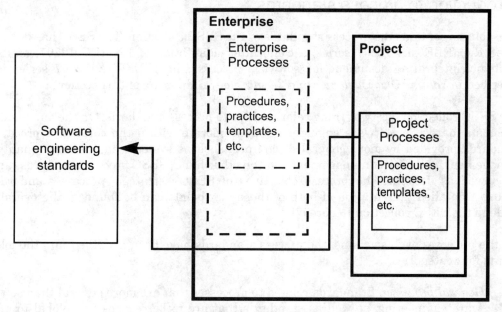

Figure 11—Project-level conformance

SESC addressed this problem when it adopted ISO/IEC 12207. The IEEE/EIA version of the standard includes provisions for additional forms of conformance to the standard. In particular, the standard provides the possibility for conformance at the organizational level. In this case, as shown in Figure 12, an enterprise conforms with the standard by implementing processes, procedures, tools, and other organizational resources. Any particular project adapts the organizational-level processes to fit the scope of the project and applies the organizational resources.

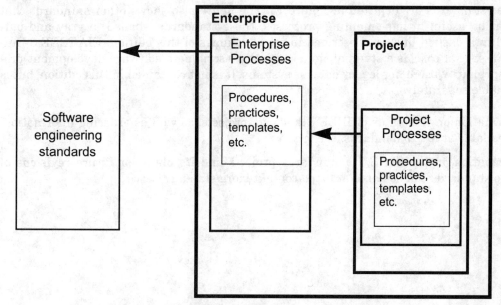

Figure 12—Organization-level conformance

Process standards

Introduction to process standards

This volume contains the process standards of the SESC collection. The SESC has designated the IEEE/EIA 12207 series, a conforming adaptation of ISO/IEC 12207, as its strategic, integrating document for software process. The IEEE/EIA 12207 series is described in *Volume One: Customer and Terminology Standards* of this edition.

The SESC collection has two strong relationships to process standards. On the one hand, SESC standards for software engineering must operate within the context of process standards provided by more general disciplines, such as systems engineering, quality management, and project management. On the other hand, SESC process standards can be viewed as detailing the process objectives of SESC's strategic process standard, 12207. A detailed presentation of both of these viewpoints can be found in the overall guide to the SESC collection [Moore97].

For the purposes of this volume, the process standards have been classified into the following four categories:

— *General processes:* Standards related to processes that are more general than software engineering, as well as standards that are to be regarded as global to all software engineering processes.

— *Primary processes:* Standards that are useful in implementing the primary processes—Acquisition, Supply, Development, Maintenance, and Operations—of the IEEE/EIA 12207 series.

— *Supporting processes:* Standards that are useful in implementing the supporting processes of the IEEE/EIA 12207 series.

— *Process measurement:* Standards that are useful for measuring the execution and results of software processes.

These standards are depicted in Figure 13. The figure also shows other standards that might be useful in implementing processes; these standards, shaded in gray and outlined in a dashed line, are described in other volumes of this edition. EIA/IEEE J-Std-016, a special case, is a stand-alone document prescribing a software development process primarily useful for legacy defense systems. It is not contained in this edition, but is available separately.

Information on the status of IEEE Standards projects, as well as ordering information, is available at http://standards.ieee.org/.

Information on the SESC, its standards projects and its plans for future revisions of these standards can be found at http://computer.org/standard/sesc/.

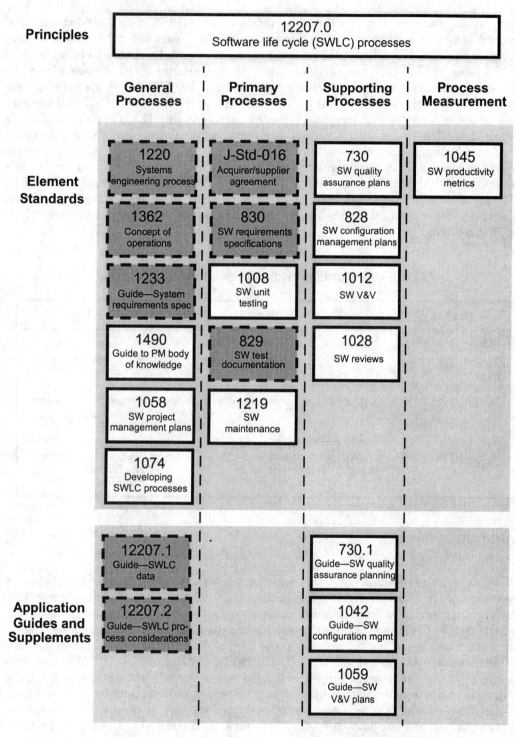

Figure 13—Process "stack" of the SESC collection

Principles

Among other changes, the IEEE/EIA adaptation of ISO/IEC 12207 added material intended to better position it as the integrating document for the SESC process standards. An annex of IEEE/EIA 12207.0 provides a set of high-level objectives for each of the processes of 12207. These objectives can be considered as a set of principles to be pursued by various standards—including the body of 12207.0—in implementing processes. Aside from the objectives, the process descriptions in the body of 12207.0 are generally at a higher level of abstraction than the corresponding IEEE standards. That is because the 12207 processes are viewed as a set of continuing responsibilities assigned to the agent responsible for execution of the process. On the other hand, the process descriptions in the IEEE documents are generally discrete requirements prescribed at a finer level of detail. The two parts added in the adaptation of ISO/IEC 12207, IEEE/EIA 12207.1 and 12207.2, provide guidance on implementing life cycle data and processes, respectively. Table 5 lists these standards and shows the volume of this edition in which they may be found.

Table 5—Standards providing principles for processes

Standard	Title	Volume
IEEE/EIA 12207.0-1996	Software life cycle processes	Volume One: Customer and Terminology Standards
IEEE/EIA 12207.1-1997	Software life cycle processes—Life cycle data	Volume One: Customer and Terminology Standards
IEEE/EIA 12207.1-1997	Software life cycle processes—Implementation considerations	Volume One: Customer and Terminology Standards

General processes

Just as software is incapable of action without a system to provide a context, software projects cannot be executed without the context of the enterprise performing the project. Software engineering processes must integrate into the context of more general processes such as project management, quality management, and systems engineering. In some cases, such as quality management, the appropriate standards organizations have written standards suitable in the context of software. For example, ISO TC176 has written ISO 9001 (on the general subject of quality management) and ISO 9000-3 (on the application of quality management to software). These standards may be cited by SESC. In other cases, though, there is no appropriate standards organization, or the responsible organization has not written a standard suitable in the software context. In these cases, SESC has taken the initiative to extend its own collection to cover the subject. Table 6 lists SESC standards for project management and systems engineering along with one standard, IEEE Std 1074, that should be regarded as general to all software engineering processes. Some of the standards are included in other volumes of this edition—the table indicates the volume.

Table 6—Standards describing general processes

Standard	Title	Volume
IEEE Std 1058-1998	IEEE Standard for Software Project Management Plans	—
IEEE Std 1074-1997	IEEE Standard for Developing Software Life Cycle Processes	—
IEEE Std 1220-1998	IEEE Standard for Application and Management of the Systems Engineering Process	Volume One: Customer and Terminology Standards
IEEE Std 1233, 1998 Edition	IEEE Guide for Developing System Requirements Specifications	Volume One: Customer and Terminology Standards
IEEE Std 1362-1998	IEEE Guide for Information Technology—System Definition—Concept of Operations Document	Volume One: Customer and Terminology Standards
IEEE Std 1490-1998	IEEE Guide to the Project Management Body of Knowledge	—

◆ IEEE Std 1058—Software project management plans

SESC completed this 15-page standard in 1987 and reaffirmed it 6 years later. The 1998 revision was intended to improve the consistency between this document and the recently adopted IEEE Std 1490, IEEE Guide to the Project Management Body of Knowledge. Previous editions of the standard were numbered 1058.1.

IEEE Std 1058 is the key standard in the IEEE SESC collection for project management requirements focusing specifically on software. It specifies the format and content of a software project management plan but does not prescribe the techniques used in developing the plan nor the techniques for managing the project. The standard is addressed to software project managers and personnel who prepare and update plans and control adherence to those plans. It is intended to be applicable to all forms of software projects, not merely those concerned with new product development. Projects of all sizes can make use of this standard although smaller ones may require less formality.

The document could be useful in a variety of contexts, including implementing the management requirements of the ISO 9001 standard, or implementing the management process of the 12207 standard.

There are two forms of conformance provided in the document.

a) *Format conformance*—The project plan conforms in both format and content to the provisions of the standard;
b) *Content conformance*—The content has been rearranged in some way.

An annex (Annex B) was added to the 1998 version of this standard that explains the relationship of the project plan of IEEE Std 1058 to the data provisions of IEEE/EIA 12207.1.

◆ **IEEE Std 1074—Developing software life cycle processes**

SESC originally developed IEEE Std 1074 in 1991, and performed minor revisions in 1995 and a major revision in 1997 to "harmonize" the document with ISO/IEC 12207. The document is a standard for *generating* processes for software development and maintenance. It does not itself provide life cycle processes nor does it provide a life cycle model. The user, a *process architect*, must define the intended life cycle of the software, select a life cycle model, and then apply the standard to define processes suiting those needs. The resource that the standard provides to the architect is a set of 17 predefined and interrelated activity groups, composed from 65 activities, along with specified inputs and outputs, and entry and exit criteria. The architect composes the activity groups to create appropriate processes. (Requirements for those processes may be provided by other standards, notably 12207.) Finally, the processes may be augmented with *organizational* process assets, such as policies, standards, procedures, etc., to create implementable processes.

◆ **IEEE Std 1490—Guide to the project management body of knowledge**

IEEE Std 1490 is a 1998 adoption of a document originally prepared by the Project Management Institute (PMI), an organization that certifies project management professionals. PMI defines the *project management body of knowledge* (PMBOK) as the sum of knowledge within the profession of project management. The PMBOK Guide is intended to describe the subset of the PMBOK that is generally accepted. The guide describes project management as a specialization of general management disciplines. In turn, SESC regards software project management as a specialization of project management.

During the adoption process, IEEE added a two-page foreword explaining the relationship of the document to the SESC collection.

Primary processes

IEEE/EIA 12207 identifies five primary software processes: *acquisition* and *supply* to form the business relationship; and *development*, *maintenance*, and *operations* to perform the technical work. The acquisition and supply processes are treated in Volume One of this edition, leaving the three technical processes for treatment here. The IEEE collection has one standard suitable for implementing the maintenance process and three standards helpful in implementing specific activities of the development process. Those standards are identified in Table 7. The table also lists EIA/IEEE J-Std-016, a stand-alone document suitable for software development in legacy defense systems Some of the standards are included in other volumes of this edition—the table indicates the volume.

Table 7—Standards helpful in implementing primary processes

Standard	Title	Volume
IEEE Std 829-1998	IEEE Standard for Software Test Documentation	Volume Four: Resource and Technique Standards
IEEE Std 830-1998	IEEE Recommended Practice for Software Requirements Specifications	Volume Four: Resource and Technique Standards
IEEE Std 1008-1987	IEEE Standard for Software Unit Testing	—
IEEE Std 1219-1998	IEEE Standard for Software Maintenance	—
EIA/IEEE J-Std-016-1995	EIA/IEEE Interim Standard for Information Technology—Software Life Cycle Processes—Software Development—Acquirer-Supplier Agreement[*]	Available separately

[*]This is an interim EIA standard and a trial-use IEEE standard.

◆ IEEE Std 1008—Software unit testing

The primary objective of IEEE Std 1008 is to provide a standard approach to software unit testing. Completed by SESC in 1987 and reaffirmed in 1993, this 24-page standard is intended to be applied as a basis for comparison of current practices, a source of ideas to modify those practices, and a replacement for current practices.

The document provides an integrated approach to systematic unit testing based on requirements, design, and implementation information to determine the completeness of testing. The required testing process is a hierarchy of phases, activities, and tasks. Performance of each activity is required; each of the activity's required tasks must be performed or the results of their prior performance must be available for reverification. The 1008 standard is consistent with IEEE Std 829 on software test documentation and requires the use of the test design specification and the test summary report specified in IEEE Std 829.

The specified unit testing process is applicable to either new or modified code. The standard does not address software debugging, other aspects of comprehensive software verification, or related processes such as configuration management and quality assurance.

Appendixes of the standard include usage guidelines, concepts and assumptions, and references for additional information.

◆ IEEE Std 1219—Software maintenance

SESC has a standard suitable for use in implementing the maintenance process, IEEE Std 1219, approved in 1992 and revised in 1998. The standard describes an iterative process for managing and executing the maintenance activity for software regardless of size, complexity, criticality, or application. It has its own "process model" of "phases," which differ slightly from the activities prescribed by the maintenance process of 12207. Inputs, outputs, and controls are specified for each phase. Metrics for each phase are also provided. Finally, the standard suggests other SESC standards that may be applied in detailing its phase requirements. Annexes to the standard provide an outline of a Maintenance Plan and map that plan to the data provisions of IEEE/EIA 12207.1.

Although the current 1219 standard is not completely reconciled with the 12207 standard, it should be a useful tool in implementing a maintenance process complying with the requirements of 12207.0. The most troublesome misfit of the two is in a basic premise. The 12207.0 maintenance process would execute the development process in order to create a software change and then return to the maintenance process for the remaining work, for example, assuring that the untouched code still works. In the 1219 standard, required development activities are simply subsumed into the maintenance process. This difference is more legalistic than substantive and simply introduces a degree of awkwardness in the explanation of conformance.

Supporting processes

IEEE/EIA 12207.0 provides the following eight supporting processes, which may be invoked by the primary processes in order to accomplish specific goals:

— Documentation
— Configuration management
— Quality assurance
— Verification
— Validation
— Joint review
— Audit
— Problem resolution

The SESC has several standards that may be useful in implementing these processes. They are listed in Table 8.

Table 8—Standards useful in implementing supporting processes

Standard	Title
IEEE Std 730-1998	IEEE Standard for Software Quality Assurance Plans
IEEE Std 730.1-1995	IEEE Guide to Software Quality Assurance Planning
IEEE Std 828-1998	IEEE Standard for Software Configuration Management Plans
IEEE Std 1012-1998	IEEE Standard for Software Verification and Validation
IEEE Std 1012a-1998	Supplement to IEEE Standard for Software Verification and Validation
IEEE Std 1028-1997	IEEE Standard for Software Reviews
IEEE Std 1042-1987	IEEE Guide to Software Configuration Management
IEEE Std 1059-1993	IEEE Guide for Software Verification and Validation Plans

◆ IEEE Stds 730 and 730.1—Software quality assurance plans

IEEE Std 730 has a distinguished history, being the first standard to be approved (in 1979) by the predecessor organization of today's SESC. The current revision was published in 1998. The 52 page guide, IEEE Std 730.1, was completed in 1995.

NOTE—Referring to back-level versions, always risky, is particularly confusing in the case of this document. The current standard was once numbered 730.1, the number now used by the guide, which was itself renumbered from a previous designation as IEEE Std 983.

This standard provides minimum requirements for the content and preparation of a Software Quality Assurance Plan (SQAP) for the development and maintenance of critical software. Although the standard describes the SQAP itself, the requirements for the content of the various sections induce implicit requirements for various Software Quality Assurance (SQA) activities. The 730 standard is most directly applicable to detailing the Quality Assurance Process of 12207. It should be noted, though, that the efforts described in the SQAP could be appropriately applied to any of the other standards prescribing life cycle processes. Annex A maps the SQAP to the data provisions of IEEE/EIA 12207.1.

The purpose of the 730.1 guide is to identify approaches to good SQA practices in support of IEEE 730.

◆ IEEE Stds 828 and 1042—Software configuration management plans

The SESC standard for software CM plans, IEEE Std 828, was originally written in 1983. The 1990 revision was a complete rewrite that, among other changes, reconciled the 16-page standard with the separately written guide, IEEE Std 1042. The 1998 revision reconciles the document with the data provisions of IEEE/EIA 12207.

The concerns of the document are described in its foreword: "Software configuration management (SCM) is a formal engineering discipline that, as part of the overall system configuration management, provides the methods and tools to identify and control the software throughout its development and use. SCM activities include the identification and establishment of baselines; the review, approval, and control of changes; the tracking and reporting of such changes; the audits and reviews of the evolving software product; and the control of interface documentation and project supplier SCM."

The standard is based on the premise that configuration management, at some level of formality, occurs in all software projects. Proper planning of the activity and effective communication of the plan increases its effectiveness. Hence, the standard prescribes the minimum required contents of an SCM plan. Developing the required plan will implicitly induce process requirements on the conduct of the project. Those requirements are intended to be consistent with those of IEEE Std 730 on software quality assurance plans.

The 92-page guide, IEEE Std 1042, was approved in 1987 and reaffirmed in 1993. The guide takes a broader view than the standard and provides a "technical and philosophical overview of the SCM planning process." The main body describes principles, issues for consideration, and lessons learned, all organized around the outline of the plan prescribed by IEEE Std 828. Four appendices provide examples for the application of 828 and a fifth appendix suggests additional references.

◆ IEEE Stds 1012 and 1059—Software verification and validation

IEEE Std 1012 was approved in 1986 and revised in 1998. It has four purposes:

a) To establish a framework for V&V in support of software life cycle processes;
b) To define V&V tasks and the required inputs and outputs;
c) To identify required tasks based upon integrity level; and
d) To define the contents of a Software V&V Plan (SVVP).

The document is intended to be applicable to all primary processes of IEEE/EIA 12207.0 including acquisition, supply, development, operations, and maintenance. It is applicable to any life cycle model.

A key concept in this standard is that of "integrity level." A software developer should assign different integrity levels to the various components of the software depending upon their role in assuring safety or dependability. IEEE Std 1012 defines the V&V activities that would be appropriate to each of four increasingly rigorous integrity levels.

Although IEEE Std 1012 makes no normative references, it is designed to fit well with several other SESC and international standards, notably the IEEE/EIA 12207 series. A total of 18 different standards are listed as informative references. The relationships to them are explained at appropriate points within the body of IEEE Std 1012.

Annex A of IEEE Std 1012 provides a mapping from V&V activities to the provisions of IEEE/EIA 12207.0. A 1998 supplement to the standard, IEEE Std 1012a, describes the relationship of the SVVP to the data provisions of IEEE/EIA 12207.1.

The 87-page IEEE Std 1059 provides extensive guidance for the preparation of the Software V&V Plan prescribed by IEEE Std 1012; it does not provide guidance for the verification and validation processes themselves.

◆ IEEE Std 1028—Software reviews

This SESC standard was originally approved in 1988, corrected in 1989, and revised in 1997 to achieve goals including improved compatibility with 12207.

The standard provides direction to the reviewer on the conduct of management and technical evaluations. Included are activities applicable to both critical and non-critical software and the procedures required for the execution of reviews. The standard specifies the characteristics of five different types of reviews (management review, technical review, inspection, walk-through, audit).

The 12207 standard specifies evaluations intrinsic to the primary processes and specifies joint review and audit processes fundamental to a two-party relationship. IEEE Std 1028 could be applied to implement the intrinsic reviews and, if applied by both parties, could satisfy some of the substantive requirements of the joint review and audit processes.

IEEE Std 1028 is intended to support review and audit requirements of several other IEEE standards including 730, 838, 1012, 1012a, 1058, 1074, 1219, 1220, 1228, 1298, and IEEE/EIA 12207.0.

Process measurement

Most would agree that effective implementation of software processes requires suitable measurement. Table 9 cites an SESC standard suitable for implementing a program of process measurement.

Table 9—Standard useful for implementing process measurement

Standard	Title
IEEE Std 1045-1992	IEEE Standard for Software Productivity Metrics

◆ IEEE Std 1045—Software productivity metrics

The SESC standard for software productivity metrics, IEEE Std 1045, was completed in 1992. Its introduction describes its premise:

> *Although there is more than 20 years of data, consistent productivity indicators for software development have not emerged from this information. The problem is not as much the fault of the metrics being used as it is the inaccuracy and incompleteness of the data being collected. Interpreting productivity based on a single number leaves much unknown about the process being measured. Without knowing the scope and characteristics of the process measured, or the precision of the data used in the calculations, the resulting productivity values are inconclusive.*

To deal with this situation, the 32-page standard is intended to structure the productivity data so that it becomes useful for process improvement. Therefore, it defines a framework for measuring and reporting that data. Separate clauses prescribes data collection for input, data collection for output, and measures that can be obtained from them. Another clause prescribes capturing characteristics of the development process to improve comparability of the data.

References

[Dupuis97] Dupuis, R., Bourque, P., Abran, A., Moore, J. W., "Principes fondamentaux du génie logiciel: Une étude Delphi," presented at Le génie logiciel et ses applications, Dixièmes journées internationales (GL97), Paris, Dec. 1997.

[IEEE95] Institute of Electrical and Electronics Engineers, Inc., *The IEEE Standards Companion*, Piscataway, NJ, 1995.

[IEEE97] Institute of Electrical and Electronics Engineers, Inc., "The IEEE Is...A World of Technology," http://www.ieee.org/ i3e_blb.html, undated, accessed Jan. 8, 1996.

[IEEE97a] Institute of Electrical and Electronics Engineers, Inc., IEEE Standards Operations Manual, Piscataway, NJ, 1997.

[Moore91] James W. Moore, "A National Infrastructure for Defense Reuse," Proc. 4th Ann. Workshop Software Reuse, Reston, VA, Nov. 18–22, 1991. Available at: ftp://gandalf.umcs.maine.edu/pub/WISR/wisr4/proceedings/ps/moore.ps.

[Moore94] James W. Moore, "A Structure for a Defense Software Reuse Marketplace," *SIGAda AdaLetters*, vol. 14, no. 3, May/June 1994.

[Moore97] James W. Moore, *Software Engineering Standards: A User's Road Map*, IEEE Computer Society Press, Los Alamitos, CA, 1998.

[SESC95] SESC Business Planning Group, *Vision 2000 Strategy Statement* (Final Draft), version 0.9, SESC/BPG-002, Aug. 20, 1995.

[SESC96] SESC Business Planning Group, *Overview of Software Engineering Standards of the IEEE Computer Society*, Version 2.2, Oct. 18, 1996.

[SESC96a] SESC Business Planning Group, *Program Plan for 1996–1998* (Review Draft), version 0.6, Aug. 1, 1996.

[SESC96d] SESC Reuse Planning Group, Action Plan, Sept. 17, 1996.

[SESC97] SESC Business Planning Group, *Program Plan for 1997-1999* (Approval Draft), version 0.7, Dec. 23, 1996.

[SESC98] SESC Business Planning Group, *SESC Overview*, version 3.6, June 26, 1998.

[Wegner95] Eberhard Wegner, "Quality of Software Packages: The Forthcoming International Standard," *Computer Standards & Interfaces,* vol. 17, 1995, pp. 115–120.

NOTE—The most recent versions of the SESC documents listed above can be found at the IEEE Computer Society's SESC web site: http://computer.org/standard/sesc/.

IEEE Std 730-1998

(Revision of
IEEE Std 730-1989)

IEEE Standard for Software Quality Assurance Plans

Sponsor

**Software Engineering Standards Committee
of the
IEEE Computer Society**

Approved 25 June 1998

IEEE-SA Standards Board

Abstract: Uniform, minimum acceptable requirements for preparation and content of Software Quality Assurance Plans (SQAPs) are provided. This standard applies to the development and maintenance of critical software. For noncritical software, or for software already developed, a subset of the requirements of this standard may be applied.
Keywords: critical design review, preliminary design review, software configuration management plan, software design description, software quality assurance plan, software requirements review, software requirements specification, software verification and validation plan

The Institute of Electrical and Electronics Engineers, Inc.
345 East 47th Street, New York, NY 10017-2394, USA

Print: ISBN 0-7381-0328-4   SH94650
PDF: ISBN 0-7381-0443-4   SS94650

IEEE Standards documents are developed within the IEEE Societies and the Standards Coordinating Committees of the IEEE Standards Association (IEEE-SA) Standards Board. Members of the committees serve voluntarily and without compensation. They are not necessarily members of the Institute. The standards developed within IEEE represent a consensus of the broad expertise on the subject within the Institute as well as those activities outside of IEEE that have expressed an interest in participating in the development of the standard.

Use of an IEEE Standard is wholly voluntary. The existence of an IEEE Standard does not imply that there are no other ways to produce, test, measure, purchase, market, or provide other goods and services related to the scope of the IEEE Standard. Furthermore, the viewpoint expressed at the time a standard is approved and issued is subject to change brought about through developments in the state of the art and comments received from users of the standard. Every IEEE Standard is subjected to review at least every five years for revision or reaffirmation. When a document is more than five years old and has not been reaffirmed, it is reasonable to conclude that its contents, although still of some value, do not wholly reflect the present state of the art. Users are cautioned to check to determine that they have the latest edition of any IEEE Standard.

Comments for revision of IEEE Standards are welcome from any interested party, regardless of membership affiliation with IEEE. Suggestions for changes in documents should be in the form of a proposed change of text, together with appropriate supporting comments.

Interpretations: Occasionally questions may arise regarding the meaning of portions of standards as they relate to specific applications. When the need for interpretations is brought to the attention of IEEE, the Institute will initiate action to prepare appropriate responses. Since IEEE Standards represent a consensus of all concerned interests, it is important to ensure that any interpretation has also received the concurrence of a balance of interests. For this reason, IEEE and the members of its societies and Standards Coordinating Committees are not able to provide an instant response to interpretation requests except in those cases where the matter has previously received formal consideration.Comments on standards and requests for interpretations should be addressed to:

Secretary, IEEE-SA Standards Board
445 Hoes LaneP.O. Box 1331
Piscataway, NJ 08855-1331
USA

Introduction

(This introduction is not a part of IEEE Std 730-1998, IEEE Standard for Software Quality Assurance Plans.)

This standard assists in the preparation and content of Software Quality Assurance Plans and provides a standard against which such plans can be prepared and assessed. It is directed toward the development and maintenance of critical software, i.e., where failure could impact safety or cause large financial or social losses.

The readers of this document are referred to IEEE Std 730.1-1995 for recommended approaches to good software quality assurance practices in support of this standard. While IEEE Std 730.1-1995 specifically refers to IEEE Std 730-1989, almost all of its content applies directly to this revision.

The readers of this document are referred to Annex A for guidelines for using this document to meet the requirements of IEEE/EIA 12207.1-1997, IEEE/EIA Guide for Information Technology—Software life cycle processes—Life cycle data.

In this standard, firmware is considered to be software and is to be treated as such.

Footnotes are not part of the standard.

There are three groups to whom this standard applies: the user, the developer, and the public.

a) The user, who may be another element of the same organization developing the software, has a need for the product. Further, the user needs the product to meet the requirements identified in the specification. The user thus cannot afford a "hands-off" attitude toward the developer and rely solely on a test to be executed at the end of the software development time period. If the product should fail, not only does the same need still exist, but also a portion of the development time has been lost. Therefore, the user needs to obtain a reasonable degree of confidence that the product is in the process of acquiring required attributes during software development.

b) The developer needs an established standard against which to plan and to be measured. It is unreasonable to expect a complete reorientation from project to project. Not only is it not cost effective, but, unless there exists a stable framework on which to base changes, improvement cannot be made.

c) The public may be affected by the users' use of the product. These users include, for example, depositors at a bank or passengers using a reservation system. Users have requirements, such as legal rights, which preclude haphazard development of software. At some later date, the user and the developer may be required to show that they acted in a reasonable and prudent professional manner to ensure that required software attributes were acquired.

Participants

This standard was prepared by the Life Cycle Data Harmonization Working Group of the Software Engineering Standards Committee of the IEEE Computer Society. At the time this standard was approved, the working group consisted of the following members:

Leonard L. Tripp, *Chair*

Edward Byrne
Paul R. Croll
Perry DeWeese
Robin Fralick
Marilyn Ginsberg-Finner
John Harauz
Mark Henley

Dennis Lawrence
David Maibor
Ray Milovanovic
James Moore
Timothy Niesen
Dennis Rilling

Terry Rout
Richard Schmidt
Norman F. Schneidewind
David Schultz
Basil Sherlund
Peter Voldner
Ronald Wade

The following persons were on the balloting committee:

Syed Ali
Leo Beltracchi
H. Ronald Berlack
Richard E. Biehl
Michael A. Blackledge
Sandro Bologna
Juris Borzovs
Audrey C. Brewer
Kathleen L. Briggs
M. Scott Buck
Michael Caldwell
James E. Cardow
Jaya R. Carl
Enrico A. Carrara
Keith Chan
Antonio M. Cicu
Theo Clarke
Sylvain Clermont
Rosemary Coleman
Virgil Lee Cooper
W. W. Geoff Cozens
Paul R. Croll
Patricia W. Daggett
Gregory T. Daich
Geoffrey Darnton
Taz Daughtrey
Raymond Day
Bostjan K. Derganc
Perry R. DeWeese
Evelyn S. Dow
Charles Droz
Sherman Eagles
Robert G. Ebenau
Leo Egan
Richard L. Evans
William Eventoff
John W. Fendrich
Jay Forster
Kirby Fortenberry
Eva Freund
Richard C. Fries
Roger U. Fujii
Juan Garbajosa-Sopena
Barry L. Garner

Adel N. Ghannam
Marilyn Ginsberg-Finner
John Garth Glynn
Julio Gonzalez-Sanz
L. M. Gunther
David A. Gustafson
John Harauz
Herbert Hecht
William Hefley
Manfred Hein
Debra Herrmann
Umesh P. Hiriyannaiah
John W. Horch
Jerry Huller
Peter L. Hung
George Jackelen
Frank V. Jorgensen
Vladan V. Jovanovic
William S. Junk
George X. Kambic
Ron S. Kenett
Judith S. Kerner
Robert J. Kierzyk
Shaye Koenig
Thomas M. Kurihara
John B. Lane
J. Dennis Lawrence
Stanley H. Levinson
Fang Ching Lim
William M. Lively
John Lord
Stan Magee
David Maibor
Harold Mains
Mike McAndrew
Patrick D. McCray
Sue McGrath
Jerome W. Mersky
Bret Michael
Alan Miller
Celia H. Modell
James W. Moore
Pavol Navrat
Myrna L. Olson
Donald J. Ostrom

Indradeb P. Pal
Lalit M. Patnaik
Alex Polack
Peter T. Poon
Lawrence S. Przybylski
Kenneth R. Ptack
Annette D. Reilly
Dennis Rilling
Terence P. Rout
Andrew P. Sage
Stephen R. Schach
Norman Schneidewind
David J. Schultz
Lisa A. Selmon
Robert W. Shillato
David M. Siefert
Carl A. Singer
Nancy M. Smith
Alfred R. Sorkowitz
Donald W. Sova
Luca Spotorno
Fred J. Strauss
Christine Brown Strysik
Toru Takeshita
Richard H. Thayer
Douglas H. Thiele
Booker Thomas
Patricia Trellue
Mark-Rene Uchida
Theodore J. Urbanowicz
Glenn D. Venables
Andre Villas-Boas
Udo Voges
Dolores Wallace
William M. Walsh
John W. Walz
Camille S. White-Partain
Scott A. Whitmire
P. A. Wolfgang
Paul R. Work
Natalie C. Yopconka
Janusz Zalewski
Geraldine Zimmerman
Peter F. Zoll

When the IEEE-SA Standards Board approved this standard on 25 June 1998, it had the following membership:

Contents

IEEE Standard for Software Quality Assurance Plans

1. Overview

1.1 Scope

The purpose of this standard is to provide uniform, minimum acceptable requirements for preparation and content of Software Quality Assurance Plans (SQAPs).

In considering adoption of this standard, regulatory bodies should be aware that specific application of this standard may already be covered by one or more IEEE standards documents relating to quality assurance, definitions, or other matters. It is not the purpose of this standard to supersede, revise, or amend existing standards directed to specific industries or applications.

This standard applies to the development and maintenance of critical software. For noncritical software, or for software already developed, a subset of the requirements of this standard may be applied.

The existence of this standard should not be construed to prohibit additional content in an SQAP. An assessment should be made for the specific software item to assure adequacy of coverage. Where this standard is invoked for an organization or project engaged in producing several software items, the applicability of the standard should be specified for each of the software items.

2. References

The standards listed below should be used for further information. In using these references, the latest revisions should be obtained. Compliance with this standard does not require nor imply compliance with any of those listed.

ASME NQA-1-1997, Quality Assurance Requirements for Nuclear Facility Applications.[1]

IEEE Std 7-4.3.2-1993, IEEE Standard Criteria for Digital Computers in Safety Systems of Nuclear Power Generating Stations.[2]

---

[1]ASME publications are available from the American Society of Mechanical Engineers, 22 Law Drive, Fairfield, NJ 07007, USA.
[2] IEEE publications are available from the Institute of Electrical and Electronics Engineers, 445 Hoes Lane, P.O. Box 1331, Piscataway, NJ 08855-1331, USA (http://www.standards.ieee.org/).

IEEE Std 603-1998, IEEE Standard Criteria for Safety Systems for Nuclear Power Generating Stations.

IEEE Std 610.12-1990, IEEE Standard Glossary of Software Engineering Terminology.

IEEE Std 730.1-1995, IEEE Guide for Software Quality Assurance Planning.

IEEE Std 828-1998, IEEE Standard for Software Configuration Management Plans.

IEEE Std 829-1998, IEEE Standard for Software Test Documentation.

IEEE Std 830-1998, IEEE Recommended Practice for Software Requirements Specifications.

IEEE Std 982.1-1988, IEEE Standard Dictionary of Measures to Produce Reliable Software.

IEEE Std 982.2-1988, IEEE Guide for the Use of IEEE Standard Dictionary of Measures to Produce Reliable Software.

IEEE Std 1002-1987 (Reaff 1992), IEEE Standard Taxonomy of Software Engineering Standards.

IEEE Std 1008-1987 (Reaff 1993), IEEE Standard for Software Unit Testing.

IEEE Std 1012-1998, IEEE Standard for Software Verification and Validation.

IEEE Std 1012a-1998, IEEE Standard for Software Verification and Validation: Content Map to IEEE/EIA 12207.1-1997.

IEEE Std 1016-1998, IEEE Recommended Practice for Software Design Descriptions.

IEEE Std 1028-1997, IEEE Standard for Software Reviews.

IEEE Std 1033-1985 (Withdrawn), IEEE Recommended Practice for Application of IEEE Std 828 to Nuclear Power Generating Stations.[3]

IEEE Std 1042-1987 (Reaff 1993), IEEE Guide to Software Configuration Management.

IEEE Std 1058-1998, IEEE Standard for Software Project Management Plans.

IEEE Std 1063-1987 (Reaff 1993), IEEE Standard for Software User Documentation.

---

[3]IEEE Std 1033-1985 has been withdrawn; however, copies can be obtained from Global Engineering, 15 Inverness Way East, Englewood, CO 80112-5704, USA, tel. (303) 792-2181.

3. Definitions and acronyms

3.1 Definitions

The definitions listed below establish meaning in the context of this standard. Other definitions can be found in IEEE Std 610.12-1990,[4] or the latest revision thereof. For the purpose of this standard, the term "software" includes firmware, documentation, data, and execution control statements (e.g., command files, job control language).

3.1.1 branch metric: The result of dividing the total number of modules in which every branch has been executed at least once by the total number of modules.[5]

3.1.2 critical software: Software whose failure would impact safety or cause large financial or social losses.

3.1.3 decision point metric: The result of dividing the total number of modules in which every decision point has had 1) all valid conditions, and 2) at least one invalid condition, correctly processed, divided by the total number of modules.[6]

3.1.4 domain metric: The result of dividing the total number of modules in which one valid sample and one invalid sample of every class of input data items (external messages, operator inputs, and local data) have been correctly processed, by the total number of modules.[7]

3.1.5 error message metric: The result of dividing the total number of error messages that have been formally demonstrated, by the total number of error messages.

3.1.6 quality assurance: A planned and systematic pattern of all actions necessary to provide adequate confidence that the item or product conforms to established technical requirements.

3.1.7 requirements demonstration metric: The result of dividing the total number of separately-identified requirements in the software requirements specification (SRS) that have been successfully demonstrated by the total number of separately-identified requirements in the SRS.

3.2 Acronyms

The following alphabetical contractions appear within the text of this standard:

CDR	critical design review
PDR	preliminary design review
SCMP	software configuration management plan
SCMPR	software configuration management plan review
SDD	software design description
SQA	software quality assurance
SQAP	software quality assurance plan
SRR	software requirements review
SRS	software requirements specification
SVV	software verification and validation plan
SVVPR	software verification and validation plan review
SVVR	software verification and validation report
UDR	user documentation review

---

[4]Information on references can be found in Clause 2.
[5]This definition assumes that the modules are essentially the same size.
[6]See Footnote 12.
[7]See Footnote 12.

4. Software Quality Assurance Plan

The Software Quality Assurance Plan shall include the sections listed below to be in compliance with this standard. The sections should be ordered in the described sequence. If the sections are not ordered in the described sequence, then a table shall be provided at the end of the SQAP that provides a cross-reference from the lowest numbered subsection of this standard to that portion of the SQAP where that material is provided. If there is no information pertinent to a section, the following shall appear below the section heading, "This section is not applicable to this plan," together with the appropriate reasons for the exclusion.

   a) Purpose;
   b) Reference documents;
   c) Management;
   d) Documentation;
   e) Standards, practices, conventions, and metrics;
   f) Reviews and audits;
   g) Test;
   h) Problem reporting and corrective action;
   i) Tools, techniques, and methodologies;
   j) Code control;
   k) Media control;
   l) Supplier control;
   m) Records collection, maintenance, and retention;
   n) Training;
   o) Risk management.

Additional sections may be added as required.

Some of the material may appear in other documents. If so, then reference to these documents should be made in the body of the SQAP. In any case, the contents of each section of the plan shall be specified either directly or by reference to another document.

The SQAP shall be approved by the chief operating officer of each unit of the organization having responsibilities defined within this SQAP or their designated representatives.

Details for each section of the SQAP are described in 4.1 through 4.15 of this standard.[8]

4.1 Purpose (Section 1 of the SQAP)

This section shall delineate the specific purpose and scope of the particular SQAP. It shall list the name(s) of the software items covered by the SQAP and the intended use of the software. It shall state the portion of the software life cycle covered by the SQAP for each software item specified.

4.2 Reference documents (Section 2 of the SQAP)

This section shall provide a complete list of documents referenced elsewhere in the text of the SQAP.

---

[8]Guidance in the use of this standard can be found in IEEE Std 730.1-1995. For an expansion of the quality and equipment qualification requirements of IEEE Std 603-1998, to encompass software design, software implementation, and computer systems validation, see IEEE Std 7-4.3.2-1993.

4.3 Management (Section 3 of the SQAP)

This section shall describe organization, tasks, and responsibilities.[9]

4.3.1 Organization

This paragraph shall depict the organizational structure that influences and controls the quality of the software. This shall include a description of each major element of the organization together with the delegated responsibilities. Organizational dependence or independence of the elements responsible for SQA from those responsible for software development and use shall be clearly described or depicted.

4.3.2 Tasks

This paragraph shall describe

a) That portion of the software life cycle covered by the SQAP;
b) The tasks to be performed with special emphasis on software quality assurance activities; and
c) The relationships between these tasks and the planned major checkpoints.

The sequence of the tasks shall be indicated.

4.3.3 Responsibilities

This paragraph shall identify the specific organizational elements responsible for each task.

4.4 Documentation (Section 4 of the SQAP)

4.4.1 Purpose

This section shall perform the following functions:

a) Identify the documentation governing the development, verification and validation, use, and maintenance of the software.
b) State how the documents are to be checked for adequacy. This shall include the criteria and the identification of the review or audit by which the adequacy of each document shall be confirmed, with reference to Section 6 of the SQAP.

4.4.2 Minimum documentation requirements

To ensure that the implementation of the software satisfies requirements, the documentation in 4.4.2.1 through 4.4.2.6 is required as a minimum.

4.4.2.1 Software Requirements Specification (SRS)

The SRS shall clearly and precisely describe each of the essential requirements (functions, performances, design constraints, and attributes) of the software and the external interfaces. Each requirement shall be defined such that its achievement is capable of being objectively verified and validated by a prescribed method (e.g., inspection, analysis, demonstration, or test).[10]

---

[9]See IEEE Std 1002-1987 and IEEE Std 1058-1998.
[10]See IEEE Std 830-1998.

4.4.2.2 Software Design Description (SDD)

The SDD shall depict how the software will be structured to satisfy the requirements in the SRS. The SDD shall describe the components and subcomponents of the software design, including databases and internal interfaces. The SDD shall be prepared first as the Preliminary SDD (also referred to as the top-level SDD) and shall be subsequently expanded to produce the Detailed SDD.[11]

4.4.2.3 Software Verification and Validation Plan (SVVP)

The SVVP shall identify and describe the methods (e.g., inspection, analysis, demonstration, or test) to be used to[12]

a) Verify that
   1) The requirements in the SRS have been approved by an appropriate authority;
   2) The requirements in the SRS are implemented in the design expressed in the SDD; and
   3) The design expressed in the SDD is implemented in the code.
b) Validate that the code, when executed, complies with the requirements expressed in the SRS.

4.4.2.4 Software Verification and Validation Report (SVVR)

The SVVR shall describe the results of the execution of the SVVP.

4.4.2.5 User documentation

User documentation (e.g., manual, guide) shall specify and describe the required data and control inputs, input sequences, options, program limitations, and other activities or items necessary for successful execution of the software. All error messages shall be identified and corrective actions shall be described. A method of describing user-identified errors or problems to the developer or the owner of the software shall be described. (Embedded software that has no direct user interaction has no need for user documentation and is therefore exempted from this requirement.)[13]

4.4.2.6 Software Configuration Management Plan (SCMP)

The SCMP shall document methods to be used for identifying software items, controlling and implementing changes, and recording and reporting change implementation status.[14]

4.4.3 Other

Other documentation may include the following:

a) Software Development Plan;
b) Standards and Procedures Manual;
c) Software Project Management Plan;
d) Software Maintenance Manual.

---

[11]See IEEE Std 1016-1998.
[12]See IEEE Std 829-1998, IEEE Std 1008-1987, IEEE Std 1010-1998, and IEEE Std 1012a-1998.
[13]See IEEE Std 1063-1987.
[14]See IEEE Std 828-1998 and IEEE Std 1042-1987. See also IEEE Std 1033-1985.

4.5 Standards, practices, conventions, and metrics (Section 5 of the SQAP)

4.5.1 Purpose

This section shall

a) Identify the standards, practices, conventions, and metrics to be applied;
b) State how compliance with these items is to be monitored and assured.

4.5.2 Content

The subjects covered shall include the basic technical, design, and programming activities involved, such as documentation, variable and module naming, programming, inspection, and testing. As a minimum, the following information shall be provided:[15]

a) Documentation standards;
b) Logic structure standards;
c) Coding standards;
d) Commentary standards;
e) Testing standards and practices;
f) Selected software quality assurance product and process metrics such as
    1) Branch metric;
    2) Decision point metric;
    3) Domain metric;
    4) Error message metric;
    5) Requirements demonstration metric.

4.6 Reviews and audits (Section 6 of the SQAP)

4.6.1 Purpose

This section shall[16]

a) Define the technical and managerial reviews and audits to be conducted;
b) State how the reviews and audits are to be accomplished;
c) State what further actions are required and how they are to be implemented and verified.

4.6.2 Minimum requirements

As a minimum, the reviews and audits in 4.6.2.1 through 4.6.2.10 shall be conducted.

4.6.2.1 Software Requirements Review (SRR)

The SRR is held to ensure the adequacy of the requirements stated in the SRS.

4.6.2.2 Preliminary Design Review (PDR)

The PDR (also known as the top-level design review) is held to evaluate the technical adequacy of the preliminary design (also known as the top-level design) of the software as depicted in the preliminary software design description.

---

[15] See IEEE Std 990-1987, IEEE Std 982.1-1988, and IEEE Std 982.2-1988.
[16] See IEEE Std 1028-1997.

4.6.2.3 Critical Design Review (CDR)

The CDR (also known as detailed design review) is held to determine the acceptability of the detailed software designs as depicted in the detailed software design description in satisfying the requirements of the SRS.

4.6.2.4 Software Verification and Validation Plan Review (SVVPR)

The SVVPR is held to evaluate the adequacy and completeness of the verification and validation methods defined in the SVVP.

4.6.2.5 Functional audit

This audit is held prior to the software delivery to verify that all requirements specified in the SRS have been met.

4.6.2.6 Physical audit

This audit is held to verify that the software and its documentation are internally consistent and are ready for delivery.

4.6.2.7 In-process audits

In-process audits of a sample of the design are held to verify consistency of the design, including the following:

a) Code versus design documentation;
b) Interface specifications (hardware and software);
c) Design implementations versus functional requirements;
d) Functional requirements versus test descriptions.

4.6.2.8 Managerial reviews

Managerial reviews are held periodically to assess the execution of all of the actions and the items identified in the SQAP. These reviews shall be held by an organizational element independent of the unit being reviewed, or by a qualified third party. This review may require additional changes in the SQAP itself.

4.6.2.9 Software Configuration Management Plan Review (SCMPR)

The SCMPR is held to evaluate the adequacy and completeness of the configuration management methods defined in the SCMP.

4.6.2.10 Post-mortem review

This review is held at the conclusion of the project to assess the development activities implemented on that project and to provide recommendations for appropriate actions.

4.6.3 Other

Other reviews and audits may include the user documentation review (UDR). This review is held to evaluate the adequacy (e.g., completeness, clarity, correctness, and usability) of user documentation.

4.7 Test (Section 7 of the SQAP)

This section shall identify all the tests not included in the SVVP for the software covered by the SQAP and shall state the methods to be used.[17]

4.8 Problem reporting and corrective action (Section 8 of the SQAP)

This section shall

a)   Describe the practices and procedures to be followed for reporting, tracking, and resolving problems identified in both software items and the software development and maintenance process;

b)   State the specific organizational responsibilities concerned with their implementation.

4.9 Tools, techniques, and methodologies (Section 9 of the SQAP)

This section shall identify the special software tools, techniques, and methodologies that support SQA, state their purposes, and describe their use.

4.10 Code control (Section 10 of the SQAP)

This section shall define the methods and facilities used to maintain, store, secure, and document controlled versions of the identified software during all phases of the software life cycle. This may be implemented in conjunction with a computer program library. This may be provided as a part of the SCMP. If so, an appropriate reference shall be made thereto.

4.11 Media control (Section 11 of the SQAP)

This section shall state the methods and facilities to be used to

a)   Identify the media for each computer product and the documentation required to store the media, including the copy and restore process; and

b)   Protect computer program physical media from unauthorized access or inadvertent damage or degradation during all phases of the software life cycle.

This may be provided as a part of the SCMP. If so, an appropriate reference shall be made thereto.

4.12 Supplier control (Section 12 of the SQAP)

This section shall state the provisions for assuring that software provided by suppliers meets established requirements. In addition, this section shall state the methods that will be used to assure that the software supplier receives adequate and complete requirements. For previously developed software, this section shall state the methods to be used to assure the suitability of the product for use with the software items covered by the SQAP. For software that is to be developed, the supplier shall be required to prepare and implement an SQAP in accordance with this standard. This section shall also state the methods to be employed to assure that the developers comply with the requirements of this standard.

---

[17] See IEEE Std 829-1998 and IEEE Std 1008-1987.

4.13 Records collection, maintenance, and retention (Section 13 of the SQAP)

This section shall identify the SQA documentation to be retained; shall state the methods and facilities to be used to assemble, safeguard, and maintain this documentation; and shall designate the retention period.

4.14 Training (Section 14 of the SQAP)

This section shall identify the training activities necessary to meet the needs of the SQAP.

4.15 Risk management (Section 15 of the SQAP)

This section shall specify the methods and procedures employed to identify, assess, monitor, and control areas of risk arising during the portion of the software life cycle covered by the SQAP.

Annex A

Guidelines for compliance with IEEE/EIA 12207.1-1997

(Informative)

A.1 Overview

The Software Engineering Standards Committee (SESC) of the IEEE Computer Society has endorsed the policy of adopting international standards. In 1995, the international standard, ISO/IEC 12207, Information technology—Software life cycle processes, was completed. The standard establishes a common framework for software life cycle processes, with well-defined terminology, that can be referenced by the software industry.

In 1995 the SESC evaluated ISO/IEC 12207 and decided that the standard should be adopted and serve as the basis for life cycle processes within the IEEE Software Engineering Collection. The IEEE adaptation of ISO/IEC 12207 is IEEE/EIA 12207.0-1996. It contains ISO/IEC 12207 and the following additions: improved compliance approach, life cycle process objectives, life cycle data objectives, and errata.

The implementation of ISO/IEC 12207 within the IEEE also includes the following:

— IEEE/EIA 12207.1-1997, IEEE/EIA Guide for Information Technology—Software life cycle processes—Life cycle data;

— IEEE/EIA 12207.2-1997, IEEE/EIA Guide for Information Technology—Software life cycle processes—Implementation considerations; and

— Additions to 11 SESC standards (i.e., IEEE Stds 730, 828, 829, 830, 1012, 1016, 1058, 1062, 1219, 1233, 1362) to define the correlation between the data produced by existing SESC standards and the data produced by the application of IEEE/EIA 12207.1-1997.

NOTE — Although IEEE/EIA 12207.1-1997 is a guide, it also contains provisions for application as a standard with specific compliance requirements. This annex treats 12207.1-1997 as a standard.

A.1.1 Scope and purpose

Both this standard and IEEE/EIA 12207.1-1997 place requirements on an SQAP. The purpose of this annex is to explain the relationship between the two sets of requirements so that users producing documents intended to comply with both standards may do so.

A.2 Correlation

This clause explains the relationship between this standard and IEEE/EIA 12207.0-1996 in the following areas: terminology, process, and life cycle data.

A.2.1 Terminology correlation

The basic term for this standard is quality assurance. The definitions for the term from this standard and IEEE/EIA 12207.0-1996 are presented below:

quality assurance: A planned and systematic pattern of all actions necessary to provide adequate confidence that the item or product conforms to established technical requirements. (IEEE Std 730-1998)

quality assurance: All the planned and systematic activities implemented within the quality system, and demonstrated as needed, to provide adequate confidence that an entity will fulfill requirements for quality. (IEEE/EIA 12207.0-1996)

The two definitions are essentially the same, particularly if it is assumed that "technical requirements" plus quality expectations are the same as "requirements for quality." The remaining terminology in this standard reflects the assumptions prevalent in the 1980s about software engineering, but for the most part this does not affect the use or meaning of terms. There are two exceptions. The first is the use of the term "audit" in 4.6.2.7 in the phrase "in-process audit"; the word "audit" should be placed with "verification." The second is the concept of independence. This standard only requires organizational independence for managerial reviews whereas IEEE/EIA 12207.0-1996 requires "organizational freedom and authority from persons directly responsible for developing the software product or executing the process responsible for the product."

A.2.2 Process correlation

This standard places no explicit requirements on process. However, the information required by its SQAP makes implicit assumptions regarding process, a process that is more prescriptive than that of IEEE/EIA 12207. This standard assumes a set of meetings, events, and audits through which a certain set of documents are developed and evaluated. By contrast, IEEE/EIA 12207.0-1996 requires a certain body of information without stipulating any particular set of events or documents. Generally, fulfilling the implied process requirements of this standard would go beyond the requirements of IEEE/EIA 12207.0-1996, but would not violate its requirements.

A.2.3 Life cycle data correlation

The information required in an SQAP by this standard and the information required in an SQAP by IEEE/EIA 12207.1-1997 are similar. It is reasonable to expect that a single document could comply with both standards. The main difference is that this standard specifies a particular format, while IEEE/EIA 12207.1-1997 does not. Details are provided in the clause below.

A.3 Document compliance

This clause provides details bearing on a claim that an SQAP complying with this standard would also achieve "document compliance" with the SQAP as prescribed in IEEE/EIA 12207.1-1997. The requirements for document compliance are summarized in a single row of Table 1 of IEEE/EIA 12207.1-1997. That row is reproduced in Table A.1 of this standard.

Table A.1—Summary of requirements for an SQAP
excerpted from Table 1 of IEEE/EIA 12207.1-1997

Information item	IEEE/EIA 12207.0-1996 subclause	Kind of documentation	IEEE/EIA 12207.1-1997 subclause	References
Software quality assurance plan	6.3.1.3	Plan	6.20	IEEE Std 730-1998 IEEE Std 730.1-1995 ISO 9000-3: 1997 ISO 9001: 1994 ISO 10005: 1995

The requirements for document compliance are discussed in the following subclauses:

— A.3.1 discusses compliance with the information requirements noted in column 2 of Table A.1 as prescribed by 6.3.1.3 of IEEE/EIA 12207.0-1996.

— A.3.2 discusses compliance with the generic content guideline (the "kind" of document) noted in column 3 of Table A.1 as a "plan." The generic content guidelines for a "plan" appear in 5.2 of IEEE/EIA 12207.1-1997.

— A.3.3 discusses compliance with the specific requirements for an SQAP noted in column 4 of Table A.1 as prescribed by 6.20 of IEEE/EIA 12207.1-1997.

— A.3.4 discusses compliance with the life cycle data objectives of Annex H of IEEE/EIA 12207.0-1996 as described in 4.2 of IEEE/EIA 12207.1-1997.

A.3.1 Compliance with information requirements of IEEE/EIA 12207.0-1996

The information requirements for an SQAP are those prescribed by 6.3.1.3 of IEEE/EIA 12207.0-1996. In this case, those requirements are substantively identical to those considered in A.3.3 of this standard.

A.3.2 Compliance with generic content guidelines of IEEE/EIA 12207.1-1997

The generic content guidelines for a "plan" in IEEE/EIA 12207.1-1997 are prescribed by 5.2 of IEEE/EIA 12207.1-1997. A complying plan shall achieve the purpose stated in 5.2.1 and include the information listed in 5.2.2 of IEEE/EIA 12207.1-1997.

The purpose of a plan is:

> IEEE/EIA 12207.1-1997, subclause 5.2.1: Purpose: Define when, how, and by whom specific activities are to be performed, including options and alternatives, as required.

An SQAP complying with this standard would achieve the stated purpose.

Any plan complying with 12207.1-1997 shall satisfy the generic content requirements provided in 5.2.2 of that standard. Table A.2 of this standard lists the generic content items and, where appropriate, references the clause of this standard that requires the same information. It may be concluded that the information required by this standard is sufficient for compliance except as noted in the third column of Table A.2.

A.3.3 Compliance with specific content requirements of IEEE/EIA 12207.1-1997

The specific content requirements for an SQAP in IEEE/EIA 12207.1-1997 are prescribed by 6.20 of IEEE/EIA 12207.1-1997. A complying SQAP shall achieve the purpose stated in 6.20.1 and include the information listed in 6.20.3 of IEEE/EIA 12207.1-1997.

The purpose of the SQAP is:

— IEEE/EIA 12207.1-1997, subclause 6.20.1: Purpose: Define the software quality assurance activities to be performed during the life cycle of the software. Describe the responsibilities and authorities for accomplishing the planned software quality assurance activities. Identify the required coordination of software quality assurance activities with other activities of the project. Identify the tools and the physical and human resources required for the execution of the plan.

An SQAP complying with this standard and meeting the additional requirements of Table A.2 and Table A.3 of this standard would achieve the stated purpose.

An SQAP complying with 12207.1-1997 shall satisfy the specific content requirements provided in 6.20.3 of that standard. Table A.3 of this standard lists the specific content items and, where appropriate, references the clause of this standard that requires the same information. It may be concluded that the information required by this standard is sufficient for compliance except as noted in the third column of Table A.3.

A.3.4 Compliance with life cycle data objectives

In addition to the content requirements, life cycle data shall be managed in accordance with the objectives provided in Annex H of IEEE/EIA 12207.0-1996.

A.3.5 Conclusion

The analysis documented in this annex suggests that any SQAP complying with this standard and the additions specified in Table A.2 and Table A.3 also complies with the requirements of an SQAP in IEEE/EIA 12207.1-1997. In addition, to comply with IEEE/EIA 12207.1-1997, an SQAP shall support the life cycle data objectives of Annex H of IEEE/EIA 12207.0-1996.

Table A.2—Coverage of generic plan requirements by IEEE Std 730-1998

IEEE/EIA 12207.1-1997 generic content	Corresponding clauses of IEEE Std 730-1998	Additions to requirements of IEEE Std 730-1998
a) Date of issue and status	—	Date of issue and status shall be provided.
b) Scope	4.1 Purpose	—
c) Issuing organization	4.3.1 Organization	Issuing organization shall be identified.
d) References	4.2 Reference documents	—
e) Approval authority	4. Software Quality Assurance Plan	—
f) Planned activities and tasks	4.3.2 Tasks	—
g) Macro references (policies or laws that give rise to the need for this plan)	4.2 Referenced documents	Documents motivating the SQAP shall be referenced.
h) Micro references (other plans or task descriptions that elaborate details of this plan)	4.4.2.3 Software Verification and Validation Plan 4.4.2.6 Software Configuration Management Plan 4.5 Standards, practices, conventions, and metrics 4.8 Problem reporting and corrective action 4.9 Tools, techniques, and methodologies	—
i) Schedules	4.3.2 Tasks 4.6 Reviews and audits	The sequencing and relationships of tasks shall be related to a master schedule.
j) Estimates	—	Estimates of resources to be expended in quality assurance tasks shall be provided or referenced.
k) Resources and their allocation	4.3.1 Organization 4.3.3 Responsibilities 4.9 Tools, techniques, and methodologies	—
l) Responsibilities and authority	4.3.1 Organization 4.3.3 Responsibilities	—
m) Risks	4.15 Risk management	—
n) Quality control measures (NOTE—This includes quality control of the SQAP itself.)	4.4.1 Purpose, item b) 4.8 Problem reporting and corrective action	—
o) Cost	—	The costs of SQA activities and resources shall be provided or referenced.
p) Interfaces among parties involved	4.3 Management	—
q) Environment / infrastructure (including safety needs)	4.5 Standards, practices, conventions, and metrics 4.9 Tools, techniques, and methodologies	Safety needs shall be provided or referenced.
r) Training	4.14 Training	—
s) Glossary	—	A glossary of terms used in the SQAP shall be provided.
t) Change procedures and history (NOTE—This includes the change procedures for the SQAP itself.)	4.13 Records collection, maintenance, and retention	Change procedures and history for the SQAP shall be provided or referenced.

Table A.3—Coverage of specific SQAP requirements by IEEE Std 730-1998

IEEE/EIA 12207.1-1997 specific content	Corresponding clauses of IEEE Std 730-1998	Additions to requirements of IEEE Std 730-1998
a) Generic plan information (see Table A.2)	—	—
b) Quality standards...	4.4.1 Purpose, item b) 4.5 Standards, practices, conventions, and metrics	—
... methodologies, procedures, and tools for performing the quality assurance activities (or their references in the organization's official documentation)	4.9 Tools, techniques, and methodologies	—
c) Procedures for contract review and coordination thereof	4.12 Supplier control	Procedures for reviewing and managing the main development contract between the acquirer and supplier should be added to the plan.
d) Procedures for identification, collection, filing, maintenance, and disposition of quality records	4.10 Code control 4.11 Media control 4.13 Records collection, maintenance, and retention 4.6.2.9 Software Configuration Management Plan Review	—
e) Resources ...	4.3.1 Organization 4.3.3 Responsibilities 4.9 Tools, techniques, and methodologies	—
... schedule(s) ...	4.3.2 Tasks 4.6 Reviews and audits	The sequencing and relationships of tasks shall be related to a master schedule.
... and responsibilities for conducting the quality assurance activities	4.3.3 Responsibilities	—
f) Selected activities and tasks from supporting processes such as Verification, Validation, ...	4.4.2.3 Software Verification and Validation Plan	—
... Joint Review, ...	4.6 Reviews and Audits	—
... Audit, and ...	4.4.1 Purpose, item b) 4.6.2.7 In-process audits 4.6.2.5 Functional audit 4.6.2.6 Physical audit	—
... Problem Resolution	4.6.1 Purpose, item c) 4.8 Problem reporting and corrective action	—

NOTICE TO USERS OF IEEE Std 730.1-1995

IEEE Std 730.1-1995 contains references to clauses in IEEE Std 730-1989.

IEEE Std 730-1989 has been replaced by IEEE Std 730-1998.

The table below is being provided as a cross-referencing tool. The clause numbering has changed as follows:

Clause in IEEE Std 730-1989	Clause in IEEE Std 730-1998
1. Scope and References	1. Overview
1.1 Scope	1.1 Scope
1.2 References	2. References
2. Definitions and Acronyms	3. Definitions and acronyms
2.1 Definitions	3.1 Definitions
2.2 Acronyms	3.2 Acronyms
3. Software Quality Assurance Plan	4. Software Quality Assurance Plan
3.1 Purpose	4.1 Purpose
3.2 Reference Documents	4.2 Reference documents
3.3 Management	4.3 Management
3.4 Documentation	4.4 Documentation
3.5 Standards, Practices, Conventions and Metrics	4.5 Standards, practices, conventions, and metrics
3.6 Reviews and Audits	4.6 Reviews and audits
3.7 Test	4.7 Test
3.8 Problem Reporting and Corrective Action	4.8 Problem reporting and corrective action
3.9 Tools, Techniques, and Methodologies	4.9 Tools, techniques, and methodologies
3.10 Code Control	4.10 Code control
3.11 Media Control	4.11 Media control
3.12 Supplier Control	4.12 Supplier control
3.13 Records Collection, Maintenance, and Retention	4.13 Records collection, maintenance, and retention
3.14 Training	4.14 Training
3.15 Risk Management	4.15 Risk management

IEEE Std 730.1-1995
(Revision and redesignation of
IEEE Std 983-1986)

IEEE Guide for Software Quality Assurance Planning

Sponsor

**Software Engineering Standards Committee
of the
IEEE Computer Society**

Approved December 12, 1995

IEEE Standards Board

Abstract: Approaches to good Software Quality Assurance practices in support of IEEE Std 730-1989, IEEE Standard for Software Quality Assurance Plans, are identified. These practices are directed toward the development and maintenance of critical software, that is, where failure could impair safety or cause large financial losses.
Keywords: software life cycle processes, software metrics, software quality assurance plan

The Institute of Electrical and Electronics Engineers, Inc.
345 East 47th Street, New York, NY 10017-2394, USA

ISBN 1-55937-593-0

IEEE Standards documents are developed within the Technical Committees of the IEEE Societies and the Standards Coordinating Committees of the IEEE Standards Board. Members of the committees serve voluntarily and without compensation. They are not necessarily members of the Institute. The standards developed within IEEE represent a consensus of the broad expertise on the subject within the Institute as well as those activities outside of IEEE that have expressed an interest in participating in the development of the standard.

Use of an IEEE Standard is wholly voluntary. The existence of an IEEE Standard does not imply that there are no other ways to produce, test, measure, purchase, market, or provide other goods and services related to the scope of the IEEE Standard. Furthermore, the viewpoint expressed at the time a standard is approved and issued is subject to change brought about through developments in the state of the art and comments received from users of the standard. Every IEEE Standard is subjected to review at least every five years for revision or reaffirmation. When a document is more than five years old and has not been reaffirmed, it is reasonable to conclude that its contents, although still of some value, do not wholly reflect the present state of the art. Users are cautioned to check to determine that they have the latest edition of any IEEE Standard.

Comments for revision of IEEE Standards are welcome from any interested party, regardless of membership affiliation with IEEE. Suggestions for changes in documents should be in the form of a proposed change of text, together with appropriate supporting comments.

Interpretations: Occasionally questions may arise regarding the meaning of portions of standards as they relate to specific applications. When the need for interpretations is brought to the attention of IEEE, the Institute will initiate action to prepare appropriate responses. Since IEEE Standards represent a consensus of all concerned interests, it is important to ensure that any interpretation has also received the concurrence of a balance of interests. For this reason IEEE and the members of its technical committees are not able to provide an instant response to interpretation requests except in those cases where the matter has previously received formal consideration.

Comments on standards and requests for interpretations should be addressed to:

Secretary, IEEE Standards Board
445 Hoes Lane
P.O. Box 1331
Piscataway, NJ 08855-1331
USA

Introduction

(This introduction is not a part of IEEE Std 730.1-1995, IEEE Guide for Software Quality Assurance Planning.)

The purpose of this guide is to identify approaches to good Software Quality Assurance practices in support of IEEE Std 730-1989, IEEE Standard for Software Quality Assurance Plans. This guide is meant to supplement IEEE Std 730.1-1989 by presenting the current consensus of those in the software development community who have expertise or experience in generating, implementing, evaluating, and modifying Software Quality Assurance Plans. This guide is not offered as a detailed procedures manual for establishing and operating Software Quality Assurance programs. This guide does not constitute further requirements than those stated in IEEE Std 730-1989. An organization can claim compliance with IEEE Std 730-1989 without following this guide completely, or in part. Detailed information regarding specific software quality assurance activities may be found in the other IEEE standards. These are referenced where appropriate. While this guide quotes major portions of IEEE Std 730-1989, the standard is not quoted in its entirety. IEEE Std 730-1989 users are advised to consult that standard directly.

In accordance with IEEE Std 730-1989, the practices herein are directed toward the development and maintenance of critical software, that is, where failure could impair safety or cause large financial losses. Determination of this criticality lies in the "eyes of the beholder." The specific application and situation of each user must be carefully considered. Should there be doubt, it is suggested that the software be considered critical. For software that is definitely noncritical, or software already developed, a subset of the requirements stated in IEEE Std 730-1989 is appropriate.

This guide serves the three groups discussed in the Foreword to IEEE Std 730.1-1989: the user, the developer, and the public.

a) The user, who may be another element of the same organization developing the software, has a need for the product. Further, the user needs the product to meet the requirements identified in the specification. The user thus cannot afford to assume a "hands-off" attitude toward the developer and rely solely on a test to be executed at the end of the software development time period. If the product should fail, not only does the same need still exist, but also a portion of the development time has been lost. Therefore, the user needs to obtain a reasonable degree of confidence that the product is in the process of acquiring required attributes during software development.

b) The developer needs an established standard against which to plan and to be measured. It is unreasonable to expect a complete reorientation from project to project. Not only is it not cost-effective, but, unless there exists a stable framework on which to base changes, improvements cannot be made.

c) The public may be affected by the users' use of the product. These users include, for example, depositors at a bank or passengers using a reservation system. Users have requirements, such as legal rights, which preclude haphazard development of software. At some later date, the user and the developer may be required to show that they acted in a reasonable and prudent professional manner to ensure that required software attributes were acquired.

This guide is addressed to readers who have professional experience in quality assurance, or in software development, but not necessarily in both. For example, this guide should be useful to the following individuals:

a) A quality assurance person with the responsibility for developing or implementing Software Quality Assurance Plan for a project.

b) A software development project manager desiring to initiate Software Quality Assurance procedures on a project.

c) A purchaser or user of a software product who wants to evaluate a seller's Software Quality Assurance Plan or to specify a Software Quality Assurance Plan.

d) An independent evaluator, such as an electronic data processing auditor.

e) The person with accountability for implementation of a Software Quality Assurance Plan.

In the body of this guide, the use of "shall" is to be understood as referring to an item or activity that is mandated by IEEE Std 730-1989. The use of "should" is to be understood as referring to an item or activity for which there is a professional consensus. The use of "may" is to be understood as referring to an item or activity that can be advised under some circumstances, but for which there is not a professional consensus. The use of "could" is to be understood as suggesting the existence of several possibilities, the selection among which will be specific to the project and not driven by specific quality assurance considerations.

At the time this standard was completed, the Working Group on Software Quality Assurance Planning had the following membership:

Camille S. White-Partain, *Chair*
Roger G. Fordham, *First Vice Chair*
Robert B. Kosinski, *Second Vice Chair*
John P. Franklin, *Third Vice Chair*
Pamela Hinds, *Fourth Vice Chair*
Manfred Hein, *Fifth Vice Chair*

Terry L. King provided administrative support. Other individuals who have contributed review and comments include the following:

Fletcher J. Buckley	Leonard L. Tripp	Christer Von Schantz
John W. Horch		R. Jerrold White-Partain

The following persons were on the balloting committee:

Mark Amaya	Caroline L. Evans	Dwayne L. Knirk
Wolf Arfvidson	Richard L. Evans	Roy W. Ko
Theodore K. Atchinson	John W. Fendrich	Shai Koenig
David Avery	Judy Fiala	Robert Kosinski
Motoei Azuma	A. M. Foley	Joan Kundig
Bakul Banerjee	Gordon Force	Thomas M. Kurihara
Richard L. Barrett	Roger G. Fordham	Lak Ming Lam
Mordechai Ben-Menachem	Jay Forster	Robert A. C. Lane
H. Ronald Berlack	Kirby Fortenberry	John B. Lane
B. P. Bhat	Richard C. Fries	J. Dennis Lawrence
Robert V. Binder	Yair Gershkovitch	Mary Leatherman
Michael A. Blackledge	Julio Gonzalez Sanz	Randal Leavitt
William J. Boll	Praveen Gupta	Suzanne Leif
Sandro Bologna	David A. Gustafson	Fang Ching Lim
Damien P. Brignell	Carol J. Harkness	Bertil Lindberg
Fletcher Buckley	Robert T. Harley	John Lindgren
David W. Burnett	Manfred Hein	Ben Livson
W. Larry Campbell	Mark Heinrich	Dieter Look
John P. Chihorek	Daniel E. Hocking	John Lord
Tsun S. Chow	John W. Horch	Joseph Maayan
François Coallier	Jerry Huller	Harold Mains
Peter G. Comer	Peter L. Hung	Ivano Mazza
Christopher Cooke	Lynn D. Ihlenfeldt	Mike McAndrew
Geoff Cozens	Richard Johansson	Patrick McCray
Patricia W. Daggett	Ken Johnson	Russell McDowell
Michael A. Daniels	Russell E. Jones	Jerome W. Mersky
Taz Daughtrey	Frank V. Jorgensen	Dennis E. Nickle
Paul I. Davis	Michael Kalecki	Michael O'Neill
Bostjan K. Derganc	Laurel V. Kaleda	Robert Parys
Rodney Dorville	Myron S. Karasik	Paul G. Petersen
C. Einar Dragstedt	Ron S. Kenett	Donald J. Pfeiffer
Julian Edelman	Judy Kerner	John G. Phippen
Leo G. Egan	Peter Klopfenstein	Peter T. Poon

Contents

IEEE Guide for Software Quality Assurance Planning

1. Overview

This guide is divided into six clauses and one annex. Text extracted from IEEE Std 730-1989 is shown in boxes and is used as the introduction to each subclause of the guide as applicable. Clause 1 provides the document overview, scope, and purpose. Clause 2 lists the specific and general references that are useful in applying this guide. Clause 3 describes the contents of each section in a Software Quality Assurance Plan (SQAP) that satisfies IEEE Std 730-1989.[1] Each subclause of clause 3 quotes the applicable wording from the standard using a box to display the quote. Clause 4 provides guidance for implementing an SQAP on a software project, or within a software development organization. Clause 5 provides guidance for evaluating the contents and the implementation of an SQAP. Clause 6 provides guidance for the procedures used to modify an existing SQAP. The annex presents a summary of the SQAP and related standards. This guide is applicable to the development and maintenance of all software, recognizing that the application of these approaches should be tailored to the specific software item. The user of this guide should be aware that efforts are under way to revise and provide additional standards and guides. Prior to implementation, a check should be made with the Secretary, IEEE Standards Board, for further detailed guidance in this area.

1.1 Scope

This guide explains and clarifies the contents of each section of an SQAP that satisfies the requirements of IEEE Std 730-1989. The guide supersedes IEEE Std 983-1986 and does not constitute further requirements than those stated in IEEE Std 730-1989. An organization can claim compliance with IEEE Std 730-1989 without following this guide completely.

1.2 Purpose

This guide presents the current consensus of those in the software development and maintenance community with expertise or experience in generating, implementing, evaluating, and modifying an SQAP. The SQAP should describe the plans and activities for the Software Quality Assurance (SQA) staff. The SQA staff observes the development process and reports deficiencies observed in the procedures and the resulting products.

---

[1]Information on references can be found in clause 2.

2. References, definitions, and acronyms

2.1 Specific references

This guide shall be used in conjunction with the following publications:

IEEE Std 610.12-1990, IEEE Standard Glossary of Software Engineering Terminology (ANSI).[2]

IEEE Std 730-1989, IEEE Standard for Software Quality Assurance Plans (ANSI).

IEEE Std 828-1990, IEEE Standard for Software Configuration Management Plans (ANSI).

IEEE Std 829-1983 (Reaff 1991), IEEE Standard for Software Test Documentation (ANSI).

IEEE Std 830-1993, IEEE Recommended Practice for Software Requirements Specifications (ANSI).

IEEE Std 982.1-1988, IEEE Standard Dictionary of Measures to Produce Reliable Software (ANSI).

IEEE Std 982.2-1988, IEEE Guide for the Use of IEEE Standard Dictionary of Measures to Produce Reliable Software (ANSI).

IEEE Std 990-1987 (Reaff 1992), IEEE Recommended Practice for Ada as a Program Design Language (ANSI).

IEEE Std 1008-1987 (Reaff 1993), IEEE Standard for Software Unit Testing (ANSI).

IEEE Std 1012-1986 (Reaff 1992), IEEE Standard for Software Verification and Validation Plans (ANSI).

IEEE Std 1016-1987 (Reaff 1993), IEEE Recommended Practice for Software Design Descriptions (ANSI).

IEEE Std 1028-1988, IEEE Standard for Software Reviews and Audits (ANSI).

IEEE Std 1033-1985, IEEE Recommended Practice for Application of IEEE Std 828 to Nuclear Power Generating Stations (ANSI).[3]

IEEE Std 1042-1987 (Reaff 1993), IEEE Guide to Software Configuration Management (ANSI).

IEEE Std 1045-1992, IEEE Standard for Software Productivity Metrics (ANSI).

IEEE Std 1058.1-1987 (Reaff 1993), IEEE Standard for Software Project Management Plans (ANSI).

IEEE Std 1061-1992, IEEE Standard for a Software Quality Metrics Methodology (ANSI).

IEEE Std 1063-1987 (Reaff 1993), IEEE Standard for Software User Documentation (ANSI).

IEEE Std 1074-1995, IEEE Standard for Developing Software Life Cycle Processes.

IEEE Std 1209-1992, IEEE Recommended Practice for the Evaluation and Selection of CASE Tools (ANSI).

---

[2]IEEE publications may be obtained from the IEEE Service Center, 445 Hoes Lane, P.O. Box 1331, Piscataway, NJ 08855-1331 or from the Sales Department, American National Standards Institute, 11 West 42nd Street, New York, NY 10036.

[3]IEEE Std 1033-1985 has been withdrawn; it is, however, available in the *Nuclear Power Standards Collection, 1990 Edition*. Archive copies of withdrawn IEEE standards may also be obtained from Global Engineering, 15 Inverness Way East, Englewood, CO 80112-5704, USA, tel. (303) 792-2181.

IEEE Std 1219-1992, IEEE Standard for Software Maintenance (ANSI).

ISO 9000-1: 1994, Quality management and quality assurance standards—Part 1: Guidelines for selection and use.[4]

2.2 Definitions

The definitions listed below establish meaning in the context of this guide. Other definitions can be found in IEEE Std 610.12-1990 and IEEE Std 730-1989.

2.2.1 conventions: Accepted guidelines employed to prescribe a disciplined, uniform approach to providing consistency in a software item, for example, uniform patterns or forms for arranging data.

2.2.2 guide: Document in which alternative approaches to good practice are suggested but no clear-cut recommendations are made.

2.2.3 practice: Recommended approach, employed to prescribe a disciplined, uniform approach to the software life cycle.

2.2.4 standards: Mandatory requirements employed to prescribe a disciplined, uniform approach to software development, maintenance, and operation.

2.2.5 techniques: Technical and managerial procedures used to achieve a given objective.

2.2.6 software tools: Computer programs used to aid in the development, testing, analysis, or maintenance of a computer program or its documentation.

2.2.7 methodology: A comprehensive, integrated series of techniques or methods creating a general systems theory of how a class of thought-intensive work ought to be performed.

2.3 Abbreviations and acronyms

The following alphabetical contractions appear within the text of this guide:

CASE	Computer-Aided Software Engineering
CCB	Configuration Control Board
CDR	Critical Design Review
CI	Configuration Item
CM	Configuration Management
COTS	Commercial-Off-The-Shelf
ICD	Interface Control Document
PDR	Preliminary Design Review
QA	Quality Assurance
RVTM	Requirements Verification Traceability Matrix
SCM	Software Configuration Management
SCMP	Software Configuration Management Plan
SCMPR	Software Configuration Management Plan Review
SDD	Software Design Description
SDP	Software Development Plan

---

[4]ISO publications are available from the ISO Central Secretariat, Case Postale 56, 1 rue de Varembé, CH-1211, Genève 20, Switzerland/Suisse. ISO publications are also available in the United States from the Sales Department, American National Standards Institute, 11 West 42nd Street, 13th Floor, New York, NY 10036, USA.

SMM	Software Maintenance Manual
SPMP	Software Project Management Plan
SPM	Standards and Procedures Manual
SQA	Software Quality Assurance
SQAP	Software Quality Assurance Plan
SRR	Software Requirements Review
SRS	Software Requirements Specifications
SVVP	Software Verification and Validation Plan
SVVPR	Software Verification and Validation Report
SVVR	Software Verification and Validation Repor
TQM	Total Quality Management
UDR	User Documentation Review
V&V	Verification and Validation

3. Contents of a Software Quality Assurance Plan

NOTE—Original footnotes to the text of IEEE Std 730-1989 appear with updated references beneath the boxes.

The Software Quality Assurance Plan shall include the sections listed below to be in compliance with this standard. The sections should be ordered in the described sequence. If the sections are not ordered in the described sequence, then a table shall be provided at the end of the SQAP that provides a cross-reference from the lowest numbered subsection of this standard to that portion of the SQAP where that material is provided. If there is no information pertinent to a section, the following shall appear below the section heading, "This section is not applicable to this plan," together with the appropriate reasons for the exclusion.

(1) Purpose
(2) Reference documents
(3) Management
(4) Documentation
(5) Standards, practices, conventions, and metrics
(6) Reviews and audits
(7) Test
(8) Problem reporting and corrective action
(9) Tools, techniques, and methodologies
(10) Code Control
(11) Media Control
(12) Supplier Control
(13) Records collection, maintenance, and retention
(14) Training
(15) Risk Management
  Additional sections may be added as required.
  Some of the material may appear in other documents. If so, then reference to these documents should be made in the body of the SQAP. In any case, the contents of each section of the plan shall be specified either directly or by reference to another document.

Some of the SQAP required information may be contained in other documents, such as a separate Software Configuration Management Plan (SCMP), Software Development Plan (SDP), Software Project Management Plan (SPMP), or Software Verification and Validation Plan (SVVP). The required information also may be documented in approved standards and accepted conventions, practices, or procedures. The sections of the SQAP should reference the documents in which the information is contained. The referenced documents should be reviewed to ensure that they provide all the required information.

3.1 Purpose

> **3.1 Purpose (Section 1 of the SQAP).** This section shall delineate the specific purpose and scope of the particular SQAP. It shall list the name(s) of the software items covered by the SQAP and the intended use of the software. It shall state the portion of the software life cycle covered by the SQAP for each software item specified.

The following questions should be addressed in this section:

a) *What is the intended use of the software covered by this SQAP?* How is the software to be used? How critical is this software? Is it part of a larger system? If so, how is it related to the system?

b) *What is the scope of this SQAP?* Who does it apply to? Who is the intended audience?

c) *Why is this SQAP being written?* Is this plan being written in response to an internal (e.g., in-house goals) or external (e.g., legal or contractual) requirement? How will this plan contribute to the success of the project?

d) *Which software items are covered by this SQAP?* Specific names and abbreviations should be supplied for these items.

e) *Which portions of the software life cycle apply to each of the software items mentioned in 3.1a)?* Name the life cycle model to be used by this project. If the reader of the SQAP is unfamiliar with that name, then refer to the document or documents that define the model. For projects enhancing, modifying, and correcting existing products, identify the life cycle stages or phases they will pass through before being integrated into the existing product. Depending upon complexity of the relationship of the software items to the portions of the software life cycle,[5] a matrix may be provided or referenced.

f) *Why were the documents that form the basis of this SQAP chosen?* Describe the extent to which this SQAP is based on IEEE Std 730-1989 and other documents.

g) *What, if any, are the deviations from the documents mentioned in 3.1e)?* Which software items warrant additional, more rigorous, or more relaxed practices or procedures? Record any deviations that reflect the criticality presented in 3.1a). Justify here, or reference a document with the full justification in terms the customer and developers can understand.

3.2 Reference documents

> **3.2 Reference Documents (Section 2 of the SQAP).** This section shall provide a complete list of documents referenced elsewhere in the text of the SQAP.

Documents used to develop the SQAP should be referenced in the text of the SQAP (e.g., military, industry-specific, or corporate quality assurance standards and guidelines).

By definition, these documents originate outside the project. Some may have confidentiality restrictions so only part of the document is available to the project. Some may have different update and version release procedures. Some may be on paper and some electronic. Some may be located with the project and some may be located elsewhere. Identify any special arrangement to obtain the document and to ensure the project uses the most current official version.

---

[5]See IEEE Std 1074-1995.

3.3 Management

> **3.3 Management (Section 3 of the SQAP).** This section shall describe organization, tasks, and responsibilities.

Section 3.3.1 shall describe each major element of the organization that influences the quality of the software. Section 3.3.2 shall list the tasks covered by this plan. Section 3.3.3 shall identify specific organizational responsibilities for each task. This description also should identify the management position that retains overall authority and responsibility for software quality.

3.3.1 Organization

> **3.3.1 Organization.** This paragraph shall depict the organizational structure that influences and controls the quality of the software. This shall include a description of each major element of the organization together with the delegated responsibilities. Organizational dependence or independence of the elements responsible for SQA from those responsible for software development and use shall be clearly described or depicted.

The organizational element(s) responsible for the software quality assurance functions covered by the SQAP may be developers knowledgeable in quality assurance tools, techniques, and methodologies; a dedicated quality assurance element serving a number of projects; or a series of separate organizational elements, each of which implements one or more SQA functional activities. The SQAP should state the organizational and functional boundaries of the SQA organizational element. The SQA element can be distributed over different organizational elements. The SQAP should endeavor to identify all. The relationship between the primary SQA organizational element and the software development element should be delineated and explained. This should not be construed to indicate that a specific SQA organization must be established. The most effective organization is a separate Quality Assurance (QA) team that is responsible to an SQA organization rather than to the manager of the software development organization. SQA independence is necessary because the QA manager must not have development responsibilities that tend to override quality concerns.

Customer management, customer and developer contracts departments, the hands-on operational user, and any independent organization contracted for a specific aspect of the project (e.g., training, technical writers, internal verification and validation, or document publishing) contribute their part with the SQA organizational element and developers in the quality of the deliverables. SQA organizational elements should share quality evaluation records and related information with customer organizations to promote resolution of quality issues.

A pictorial organizational structure should be included with an explanation describing the nature and degree of relationships with all organizational elements responsible for software quality and development. The explanation should include the following:

a) A description of each element that interacts with the SQA element.
b) The organizational element delegating authority and delegated responsibilities of interacting elements.
c) Reporting relationships among the interacting elements identifying dependence/independence.
d) Identification of the organizational element with product release authority.
e) Identification of the organizational element or elements that approve the SQAP.
f) The reporting lines for escalating conflicts and the method by which conflicts are to be resolved among the elements.

The explanations also may include

g) The size of the SQA element and the amount of effort dedicated to the project, where the amount is less than 100%.

h) An explanation of any deviations from the organizational structure outlined in existing SQA policies, procedures, or standards.

The description of the organizational structure should be complete so that all the tasks addressed in the SQAP can be directly related to a responsible organization.

3.3.2 Tasks

> **3.3.2 Tasks.** This paragraph shall describe (a) that portion of the software life cycle covered by the SQAP, (b) the tasks to be performed with special emphasis on software quality assurance activities, and (c) the relationships between these tasks and the planned major check-points. The sequence of the tasks shall be indicated.

The SQA tasks are described in 3.4 through 3.15 of the IEEE Std 730-1989 SQAP. Some of these tasks consist of planning activities while others, such as reviews and tests, are directed towards the software product. All the tasks in these sections may not be applicable to a specific project, in which event they may be omitted from the project SQAP. Any omissions or deviations from IEEE Std 730-1989 should be explained in the appropriate section of the project SQAP. Any additional tasks should be included in the appropriate SQAP sections. Any deviations from corporate software quality assurance policies should be explained in the appropriate SQAP sections.

This section of the SQAP also should identify the tasks associated with the publication, distribution, maintenance, and implementation of the SQAP.

All tasks discussed in 3.4–3.15 are SQA tasks and are to be performed by the SQA function. Some of these tasks have a profound influence on the development element, and such tasks should be performed by, or in close cooperation with, the software development element. This is especially true for the tasks defined by 3.4 and 3.5.

Each task identified should be defined together with entrance and exit criteria required to initiate and terminate the task. The output of each task should be defined in such a way that its achievement or termination can be objectively determined in a prescribed manner. Additionally, this section could include a table indicating the staffing levels required for the listed tasks.

While it is strongly recommended that a Software Development Plan (SDP) or a Software Project Management Plan (SPMP) (see 3.4.3.1 or 3.4.3.3 of this guide, respectively) be prepared, if either document is not available, this section should provide schedule information outlining the development cycle to include the software quality assurance activities. This schedule should define the sequence of tasks to be performed, the major milestones occurring during the development life cycle, and the tasks and deliverables that should be completed prior to each major milestone.[6]

3.3.3 Responsibilities

> **3.3.3 Responsibilities.** This paragraph shall identify the specific organizational elements responsible for each task.

If two or more organizational elements share responsibility for a task, their respective responsibilities should be identified. Describe the procedure for resolving issues between organizational elements sharing responsi-

---

[6]See IEEE Std 1074-1995.

bilities. The management position accountable for overall software quality should be identified. This section of the SQAP should indicate the review and approval cycle, indicating signature authority as required. It should show the number of controlled copies and describe the method of control. It should designate the personnel and organizational element responsible for distributing the SQAP and describe the methods and responsibilities for the approval, distribution, and incorporation of changes (all changes should follow the approved CM procedures). The SQAP should identify the organizational elements responsible for the origination, review, verification, approval, maintenance, and control of the required task documentation as described in 3.4.

A tabular listing or matrix that provides the individual or organizational element responsible for each task described in the SQAP should be provided, including those tasks that are shared. The size and complexity of the project may require the duplication of this information in other plans, especially in the Software Development Plan and the Software Project Management Plan. If duplication exists, reference all documents with duplicate data in order to promote ease of maintenance. In these cases, the data in a responsibility matrix is particularly helpful in clarifying task responsibilities for all aspects of the software project.

3.4 Documentation

> **3.4 Documentation (Section 4 of the SQAP)**
> **3.4.1 Purpose.** This section shall perform the following functions:
> (1) Identify the documentation governing the development, verification and validation, use, and maintenance of the software.
> (2) State how the documents are to be checked for adequacy. This shall include the criteria and the identification of the review or audit by which the adequacy of each document shall be confirmed, with reference to Section 6 of the SQAP.

3.4.1 Purpose

Section 6 of the SQAP is discussed in 3.6 of this guide.

The SQAP shall identify documentation, whether hardcopy or softcopy, that will be prepared during the development, verification and validation, use, and maintenance of the software. If there is no independent verification and validation, then the quality assurance procedures that are to be used on the project should be identified. Also, all required test documentation should be noted. The SQAP also shall identify the specific reviews, audits, and associated criteria required for each document, including references as appropriate to 3.6, Reviews and Audits.

The following clauses of this guide should describe the format and content of each of the documents used. If this information is provided in another document, only a reference should be given. Organizational policies, procedures, and standards may determine additional information requirements.

3.4.2 Minimum documentation requirements

> **3.4.2 Minimum Documentation Requirements.** To ensure that the implementation of the software satisfies requirements, the following documentation is required as a minimum.

IEEE Std 730-1989 requires the following documents:

a) Software Requirements Specifications (SRS)
b) Software Design Description (SDD)
c) Software Verification and Validation Plan (SVVP)

    d)   Software Verification and Validation Report (SVVR)
    e)   User documentation
    f)   Software Configuration Management Plan (SCMP)

This minimum set of documents has been found to be a solid foundation to assure the quality of a software development in supplier-purchaser relationships. These documents are equally usable in in-house developments with an informal contract or with no contract. They are applicable where the customer is the company marketing division representing the marketplace or the business manager reaching for help to achieve business objectives. Other documentation, such as test plans and database design information, should be provided as applicable. Database design information may be incorporated into the SDD if the project is small in size and the database is not a complex structure.

The QA activities associated with each document review must be scheduled in consonance with the development life cycle phases of the project.

Where the development project changes existing software, the required set of documents may be a subset of the documents used for the original development. A brief description of each document follows.

3.4.2.1 Software Requirements Specifications (SRS)

> **3.4.2.1 Software Requirements Specification (SRS).** The SRS shall clearly and precisely describe each of the essential requirements (functions, performances, design constraints, and attributes) of the software and the external interfaces. Each requirement shall be defined such that its achievement is capable of being objectively verified and validated by a prescribed method; for example, inspection, analysis, demonstration, or test.[a]

[a]See IEEE Std 830-1993.

The SRS is usually developed from one or more documents, such as a user requirements statement, operational requirements, preliminary hazard analysis, software product market definition, parent or previous SRS reverse engineering documentation, system-level requirements and design documentation, statement of work, or contract. It specifies in detail the requirements as agreed upon by the developer and the requester or user. The SQAP should identify the governing documents and state the precedence in the event of two or more documents containing contradictory requirements. Where the SRS is produced by the developer, the SQAP should identify what standards or guides apply to the content and format of the SRS as well as the process used to develop it.[7] The SRS may contain a list of references that identify working models (such as prototypes or products) that are part of the requirements and need to be included in the design (software and system), development, testing and operational phases. The SQAP should clearly define the methods to be used by the SQA organizational element to verify and validate the data in the SRS.

The SRS is subject to the Software Requirements Review (SRR) described in 3.6.2.1, which identifies the SQA organizational element's QA activities.

---

[7]See IEEE Std 830-1993 for further guidance on the content of an SRS.

3.4.2.2 Software Design Description (SDD)

> **3.4.2.2 Software Design Description (SDD).** The SDD shall depict how the software will be structured to satisfy the requirements in the SRS. The SDD shall describe the components and subcomponents of the software design, including data bases and internal interfaces. The SDD shall be prepared first as the Preliminary SDD (also referred to as the Top-Level SDD) and shall be subsequently expanded to produce the Detailed SDD.[a]

[a]See IEEE Std 1016-1987 (Reaff 1993).

The SDD is a technical description of how the software will meet the requirements set forth in the SRS. Its most important function is to describe a decomposition of the whole system into components (subsystems, segments, etc.) that are complete and well-bounded. In addition, it should document the rationale for the more important design decisions in order to facilitate the understanding of the system structure.

The SDD describes major system features such as data bases, diagnostics, external and internal interfaces, as well as the overall structure of the design. It involves descriptions of the operating environment, timing, system throughput, tables, sizing, centralized or distributed processing, extent of parallelism, client/server, reusable objects library, program design language (PDL), prototypes, modeling, simulation, etc. The SQAP should identify the standards and conventions that apply to the content and format of the SDD, as well as the process and procedures to be used in developing the SDD. If prototyping, modeling, or simulations are used, the SQA organizational element could observe a demonstration, which is a more efficient way to review and assess written design documentation.

Where the SDD is produced by separate teams, the procedures shall relate to the responsibilities in 3.3.3. The SDD may be an evolving document or a document that is baselined after each significant review. A new version containing a more detailed design description is developed for each subsequent review. The SQAP should identify the number and purpose of the SDD documents. Where one document spawns several others at a more detailed level (e.g., the data base design distinct from the user interface design, distinct from the algorithmic processing) this section should explain the scope and precedence of the sibling documents.

The SDD is subject to the Preliminary Design Review (PDR) and the Critical Design Review (CDR), described in 3.6.2.2 and 3.6.2.3, respectively, which identify the SQA organizational element's QA activities, or equivalent design reviews in the chosen life cycle model.

In addition to the design descriptions noted in IEEE Std 1016-1987 (Reaff 1993), which are applicable to 4GL and object-oriented methodologies, the SDD also should consist of items pertaining to earlier languages and methodologies (e.g., 2GL, 3GL, COBOL, and FORTRAN), if applicable, for each component in the system. The SDD should consist of items such as the following:

a) A textual description of the component's
  1) Inputs
  2) Outputs
  3) Calling sequence
  4) Function or task
  5) Algorithms
b) A list of other components called.
c) A list of all calling components.
d) Allowed and tolerable range of values for all inputs.
e) Allowed and expected range of values for all outputs.
f) Assumptions, limitations, and impacts.

The SQAP should clearly define the methods to be used by the SQA organizational element to verify and validate the data in the SDD.

3.4.2.3 Software verification and validation plan (SVVP)

3.4.2.3 Software Verification and Validation Plan (SVVP). The SVVP shall identify and describe the methods (for example, inspection, analysis, demonstration, or test) to be used:[a]

(1) To verify that (a) the requirements in the SRS have been approved by an appropriate authority, (b) the requirements in the SRS are implemented in the design expressed in the SDD; and (c) the design expressed in the SDD is implemented in the code.

(2) To validate that the code, when executed, complies with the requirements expressed in the SRS.

---

[a]See IEEE Std 829-1983 (Reaff 1991), IEEE Std 1008-1987 (Reaff 1993), and IEEE Std 1012-1986 (Reaff 1992).

The SVVP describes the overall plan for the verification and validation of the software and could be produced and reviewed incrementally. The tasks, methods, and criteria for verification and validation are described. The SVVP might be used for documentation of the testing standards and practices as they are defined in 3.5.2 and 3.5.2.4. In the same way, it might be used to document the procedures to be followed for some of the reviews defined in 3.6. This section should explain the scope of validation testing to ensure the baselined requirements and explain the stages of development that require customer review and the extent of the verification that will precede such a review. The SVVP specifies minimum test documentation requirements. IEEE Std 829-1983 (Reaff 1991) may be consulted.

The SQAP should identify which standards and conventions apply to the content and format of the SVVP. A stand-alone section of the SVVP should include a verification matrix where requirements are listed with their corresponding SVVP section. This matrix, which is dynamic (and must be maintained), is a tool for the SQA staff to use to verify that all system software requirements have been met. The requirements should be mapped to test cases. The SQA organization should audit the matrix for completion (by all the baselined requirements and tests).

The contents of the SVVP will be evaluated at the Software Verification and Validation Plan Review (SVVPR) described in 3.6.2.4.

3.4.2.4 Software Verification and Validation Report (SVVR)

3.4.2.4 Software Verification and Validation Report (SVVR). The SVVR shall describe the results of the execution of the SVVP.

The SVVR summarizes the observed status of the software as a result of the execution of the SVVP. The SVVR should include the following information:

a) Summary of all life cycle V&V tasks.

b) Summary of task results.

c) Summary of anomalies and resolutions.

d) Assessment of overall software quality.

e) Summary from the verification matrix.

f) Recommendations such as whether the software is, or is not, ready for operational use.

The report may be a full report or a subset, such as a certificate, with the limiting extract being a "tested slip" as seen in some customer products. This section should explain why the style of report was chosen and in what way it satisfies the criticality of the product and gives assurances to the customer.

The SQAP should clearly define the methods to be used by the SQA organizational element to assure the correctness and completeness of the data in the SVVR.

3.4.2.5 User documentation

> **3.4.2.5 User Documentation.** User documentation (e.g., manual, guide, etc.) shall specify and describe the required data and control inputs, input sequences, options, program limitations, and other activities or items necessary for successful execution of the software. All error messages shall be identified and corrective actions described. A method of describing user-identified errors or problems to the developer or owner of the software shall be described. (Embedded software that has no direct user interaction has no need for user documentation and is therefore exempted from this requirement.).[a]

[a]See IEEE Std 1063-1987 (Reaff 1993).

The user documentation section of the SQAP (e.g., documents, videotapes, on-line graphic storyboards, and tutorials) should describe the software's operational use and be comprised of the following items:

a) User instructions that contain an introduction, a description of the user's interaction with the system (in the user's terminology), and a description of any required training for using the system (see also Training manual, 3.4.4.6, in this guide).

b) An overview of the system, its purpose, and description.

c) Input/output specifications.

d) Samples of original source documents and examples of all input formats (forms or displays).

e) Samples of all outputs (forms, reports, or displays).

f) Instructions for data preparation, data keying, data verification, data proofing, and error correction. Wherever software is capable of damage to user assets (e.g., data base contents) the user should be forewarned to avoid accidental damage.

g) References to all documents or manuals intended for use by the users.

h) A description of the system's limitations.

i) A description of all the error messages that may be encountered, together with recommended steps to recover from each error.

j) Procedures for reporting and handling problems encountered during the use of a software item.

k) Menuing hierarchy and navigation methods.

l) User administration activities (backup, recovery, batch initiation, access control).

There may be several different types of users (e.g., new; those requiring refresher instructions; salespersons; or maintainers). Different user guides or manuals may be required to suit the intended audiences. In each case, the documentation should define the extent of the material delivered to enable the users to display the software.

The SQAP should clearly define the methods to be used by the SQA organizational element to verify and validate the data in the user documentation and the process used to develop it.

A User Documentation Review (UDR) is described in 3.6.3.1 of this guide, which identifies the SQA organizational element's QA activities.

3.4.2.6 Software Configuration Management Plan (SCMP)

> **3.4.2.6 Software Configuration Management Plan (SCMP).** The SCMP shall document methods to be used for identifying software items, controlling and implementing changes, and recording and reporting change implementation status.[a]

[a]See IEEE Std 828-1990 and IEEE Std 1042-1987 (Reaff 1993). See also IEEE Std 1033-1985.

The SCMP of the SQAP should describe the tasks, methodology, and tools required to assure that adequate Software Configuration Management (SCM) procedures and controls are documented and are being implemented correctly. If the SCMP is not a stand-alone document, and is included in the SQAP, it is not necessary that the SQA organizational element prepare the Software Configuration Management Plan (SCMP); however, it is essential that one exist for each project. It is suggested that the CM organizational element prepare the SCMP so that the SQA organizational element can maintain its independence for CM evaluation purposes.

The SQAP should define the extent to which the project requires configuration management. Where the project is part of a larger system that is employing configuration management, this clause should define how the software CM plan fits with the system CM plan.

The SCMP should describe the methods to be used for

a)   Identifying the software configuration items.
b)   Controlling and implementing changes.
c)   Recording and reporting change and problem reports implementation status.
d)   Conducting configuration audits.
e)   Identifying review and approval cycle as well as signature authority.
f)   Identifying the personnel responsible for maintaining the baselines and distributing the SCMP.

The SQAP should clearly define the methods to be used by the SQA organizational element to verify and validate the data in the SCMP and the process used to develop it.

3.4.3 Other documentation

> **3.4.3 Other.** Other documentation may include the following:
> (1)   Software Development Plan
> (2)   Standards and Procedures Manual
> (3)   Software Project Management Plan
> (4)   Software Maintenance Manual.

3.4.3.1 Software Development Plan (SDP)

The SDP can be used as the highest-level planning document governing a project, or could be subordinate within a larger set of plans. For example, several SDPs may be written in support of a larger project that is governed by an SPMP. The SDP should identify all technical and managerial activities associated with software development. The SDP should specify the following items, which should be reviewed and assessed by the SQA organizational element:

a)   Description of software development.
b)   Software development organization responsibilities and interfaces.
c)   Process for managing the software development (including allocation of resources, project control mechanisms, software metrics, and risk management).
d)   Technical methods, tools, and techniques to be used in support of the software development.

e)   Assignment of responsibility for each software development activity.

f)   Schedule and interrelationships among activities.

g)   Formal qualification testing organization and approach.

h)   Software product evaluation during each life cycle phase including subcontractor products.

When multiple SDPs are required, they should focus on items a) and d). The associated SPMP should cover items b), c), e), f), g), and h) in order to provide a unified approach to design, coding, and testing.

The SQAP should define the procedures for creating the data in the SDP and criteria for updating and assuring its quality. Any deviations from the plan should be reconciled between the SQA staff and the software development manager. The plan should be updated and the latest version clearly identified. Obsolete versions should be maintained according to the organization's policy. Procedures should be defined for the approval and distribution of the SDP.

3.4.3.2 Standards and Procedures Manual (SPM)

The SPM should provide details on all project standards and procedures to be followed. At a minimum, the information described in 3.5 should be included.

The SQAP should clearly define the methods to be used by the SQA organizational element to verify and validate the data in the SPM.

3.4.3.3 Software Project Management Plan (SPMP)

The SPMP can be used in place of an SDP, or as a plan that governs a larger project that has subordinate projects each covered by SDPs. The SPMP should identify all technical and managerial activities associated with an instance of software development.[8] The SPMP should specify the following items, which should be reviewed and assessed by the SQA organizational element:

a)   Description of software development (high-level description if details are contained in an SDP. If there is no SDP, full details are required in the SPMP).

b)   Software development and management organizations responsibilities and interfaces.

c)   Process for managing the software development (including allocation of resources, project control mechanisms, software metrics, and risk management).

d)   Technical methods, tools, and techniques to be used in support of the software development (high-level description if details are provided in SDP).

e)   Assignment of responsibility for each activity (e.g., specific skill assignments, key personnel).

f)   Schedule and interrelationships among activities.

g)   Process improvement activities.

h)   Goals deployment activities.

i)   Strategic quality planning efforts triggered by reviews (e.g., post mortem), and benchmarking.

j)   A list of deliverables.

k)   Subcontractor(s) project management plan(s).

The SQAP should define the procedures for creating the data in the SPMP and criteria for updating and assuring its quality. Any deviations from the plan should be reconciled between the SQA staff and the software project manager. The plan should be updated and the latest version clearly identified. Obsolete versions should be maintained according to the organization's policy. Procedures should be defined for the approval and distribution of the SPMP.

---

[8]See IEEE Std 1058.1-1987 (Reaff 1993).

3.4.3.4 Software Maintenance Manual (SMM)

A maintenance manual should contain instructions for software product support and maintenance, such as procedures for correcting defects, installation of enhancements, and testing of all changes.[9] All hardware and software configuration specifications required to maintain the software should be described in detail. Any unusual settings or known anomalies should be identified in order to aid in efficient maintenance. New versions of software should be thoroughly tested prior to incorporation into operational systems. Version control procedures should be reviewed and approved by SQA and SCM organizational elements. The SQA organizational element should periodically audit and validate the use of the version control procedures as well as the software maintenance process and procedures. The SMM should refer to the Problem Reporting System (3.8) and the SCMP (3.4.2.6) in this guide.

3.4.4 Additional suggested documentation

The attributes, context, and environment of the product could dictate inclusion of additional documents, such as, but not limited to, the following:

a) User requirements statement
b) External interface specifications
c) Internal interface specifications
d) Operations manual
e) Installation manual
f) Training manual
g) Training plan
h) Software metrics plan
i) Software security plan

The SQAP should clearly define the methods to be used by the SQA organizational element to verify and validate the data in the documents described in the following subclauses (3.4.4.1–3.4.4.9).

3.4.4.1 User requirements statement

A user requirements statement can be used as a high-level document preceding the approved SRS for a large development, in place of an SRS in cases where minor changes are made to an operational system that has no SRS, or as a means of passing requirements on to a supplier. The user requirements statement should include, but is not limited to

a) A natural language service request that contains the identity of the requester, the software item name and title, the date the software item was requested and is required, a description of what the software item should do, an abstract of the need for the software item, privacy or security considerations, and a list of potential users of the software item.
b) A list of the objectives that are to be satisfied by the software item, as well as any other needs (e.g., administrative, timing, quality) and restraints the user perceives as necessary.
c) References to and summarized conclusions from any studies done to define resource requirements (e.g., hardware, software, personnel, plant and facilities, or environmental), feasibility, or cost-benefit analyses.

The SQAP should clearly define the methods to be used by the SQA organizational element to verify and validate the data in the user requirements statement.

---

[9]See IEEE Std 1219-1992.

3.4.4.2 External interface specifications

External interface specifications should be contained within the software requirements specifications, the system design document, or an Interface Control Document (ICD). In situations where the detailed external interface specifications are not available in the design documentation or ICD, a separate external interface specifications document may be required that would provide lower-level detail.

The external interface specifications should contain information about files and other connections, such as messages passed, to software items outside the system under development. Consideration should be given to human interfaces, hardware interfaces, environmental constraints (such as weather conditions) and data structures and files or transactions coming from or going to other systems, standards, protocols, timing issues, and throughput or capacity of the interfaces.

3.4.4.3 Internal interface specifications

Internal interface specifications are a subset of the design documentation and may be traced to a software requirement identified in the SRS. In situations where the internal interface specifications are not available in the design documentation, and/or an ICD, a separate internal interface specifications document may be required.

The internal interface specifications should contain information about files and other connections among all the components within the system. Consideration should be given to such subjects as transfer of control between modules, passing of data between modules, physical and logical interfaces, common data, timing and concurrence management techniques.

3.4.4.4 Operations manual

The operations manual should contain at least the following items:

a) Operating instructions that include
   1) An introduction
   2) Run schedules
   3) Setup requirements/procedures
   4) Run control procedures
   5) Error procedures
   6) Security procedures
   7) Distribution procedures
   8) Backup and recovery procedures
   9) Restart procedures
   10) Termination procedures
   11) Tutorial and practice procedures
b) Specifications for the system, including environmental requirements
c) Input/output specifications
d) Auditing controls

3.4.4.5 Installation manual

An installation manual should contain instructions for the installation of the software, for example, file conversion instructions, use of user-controlled installation options, and instructions for performing an installation test. Installation procedures may be performed through an interactive interface (i.e., menu driven).

3.4.4.6 Training manual

The training manual should contain information necessary for training users and operators of the system. It should contain, but is not limited to, the following:

a) An introduction
b) How to use the system
c) How to prepare input
d) Data input descriptions
e) Data control descriptions
f) How to run the system
g) Output distributions
h) Description of output data and interpretations (e.g., error messages)
i) Tutorial and practice exercises
j) How to get help

3.4.4.7 Training plan

The development of software products that require complex or unfamiliar interactions with users and operators should include a comprehensive plan for training. The training plan should include the following:

a) A description of the populations to be trained, the training objectives for each population, and the content to be covered in the training.
b) An estimate of the amount of resources necessary for training development, delivery, and time expenditures.
c) Procedures for evaluating the effectiveness of the training and for making modifications to the training.

3.4.4.8 Software metrics plan

The software metrics plan should address the way product and process metrics will be used to manage the development, delivery, and maintenance processes. (See 3.5.2.7.) The software metrics plan should contain information on the following:

a) The mission and objectives of the software metrics program.
b) The quantitative measures (target levels and acceptable ranges if applicable) of the quality of the software products.[10]
c) How the product or process metrics will be used to identify and measure performance.
d) How remedial action will be taken if product or process metric levels grow worse or exceed established target levels.
e) Improvement goals in terms of the product and process metrics.
f) The quantitative measures (target levels and acceptable ranges, if applicable) of the quality of the software processes.[11]
g) How the metrics will be used to determine how well the development process is being carried out in terms of milestones and in-process quality objectives being met on schedule.
h) How the metrics will be used to determine how effective the development process improvement is at reducing the probability that faults are introduced or that any faults introduced go undetected.
i) Data collection methodology including roles and responsibilities, retention, and validation.
j) A definition of metrics reports that are generated, including their frequency, reporting periods, as well as which element in the software organization uses these reports.
k) How to validate the software quality metric.

---

[10] See IEEE Std 981.1-1988 and 981.2-1988.
[11] See IEEE Std 981.1-1988 and 981.2-1988.

3.4.4.9 Software security plan

The software security plan should address the way in which the software and the data will be protected from unauthorized access or damage. The software security plan should contain information on the following:

a) How the data should be classified and how this will be communicated (e.g., "no trespassing" messages).
b) How the users of the software access the application and how that access is to be controlled.
c) Network design.
d) User identifications, passwords, security logging, and auditing.
e) Super-user password control and protection of path through the system administrator.
f) Physical security.
g) Virus protection.
h) How employees will be trained on security procedures and practices.
i) The method by which this security plan will be audited for compliance.
j) Disaster plan.
k) Whether the system provides file encryption and decryption capability.

3.5 Standards, practices, conventions and metrics

> **3.5 Standards, Practices, Conventions and Metrics (Section 5 of the SQAP).**

3.5.1 Purpose

> **3.5.1 Purpose.** This section shall:
> (1) Identify the standards, practices, conventions and metrics to be applied.
> (2) State how compliance with these items is to be monitored and assured.

This section of the SQAP shall identify the standards (mandatory requirements), practices (recommended approach), conventions (accepted guidelines), and metrics (system of measurement) to be employed by all associated with the project, including management and vendors. It should specify the phases of the life cycle to which they apply. Also, it shall specify how compliance will be monitored and assured (see 3.6).

3.5.2 Content

> **3.5.2 Content.** The subjects covered shall include the basic technical, design, and programming activities involved, such as documentation, variable and module naming, programming, inspection, and testing. As a minimum, the following information shall be provided:[a]
> (1) Documentation standards
> (2) Logic structure standards
> (3) Coding standards
> (4) Commentary standards
> (5) Testing standards and practices
> (6) Selected software quality assurance product and process metrics such as:
>   (a) Branch metric
>   (b) Decision point metric
>   (c) Domain metric
>   (d) Error message metric
>   (e) Requirements demonstration metric.

[a]See IEEE Std 990-1987 (Reaff 1992), IEEE Std 982.1-1988, and IEEE Std 982.2-1988.

The SQAP should identify or reference the standards, practices, conventions, and metrics to be used on the project. As a minimum, the information required by IEEE Std 730-1989 should be addressed in the following life-cycle phases: software requirements, design, implementation, testing, and maintenance. In addition, the standards, practices, and conventions pertaining to software documentation and the use of metrics should be addressed. It is strongly recommended that these issues be resolved in close cooperation with the software development element. The descriptions of the standards, practices, conventions, and metrics are often given in a standards and procedures manual (see 3.4.3.2) or in an SDP. Use of all of the above should state how compliance is assured.

The SQAP should clearly define the methods to be used by the SQA organizational element to verify and validate the data discussed in the following subclauses (3.5.2.1–3.5.2.7).

3.5.2.1 Requirements phase

Identify or reference the standards, practices, conventions, and metrics to be used during the requirements phase. Cite any internal (e.g., project or corporate) or external (e.g., military or contractual) standards with which requirements baselining and traceability must comply. Use formal requirements statement languages, either textual or graphic, whenever possible.[12] Provision should be made for a scheme that uniquely identifies each requirement. This facilitates traceability and compliance during the subsequent phases.

3.5.2.2 Design phase

Identify or reference the standards, practices, conventions, and metrics to be used during the preliminary design phase where the overall structure of the software system is defined. Cite any internal (e.g., project or corporate) or external (e.g., military or contractual) standards with which the design baselining must comply. Top-down design, which is the most acceptable methodology, should be used whenever feasible. Use of graphic techniques and computer-aided software engineering (CASE) tools that aid in compliance verification should be considered. Object-oriented design methodology should be used with appropriately sized hardware and software in those situations where a simpler design is used.

For the detailed design phase, state what standards, practices, conventions, and metrics will be used for specifying the internal structure of each program module and the interfaces among them. Address such matters as naming conventions and argument list standards. Give serious consideration to requiring the use of a program design language.

3.5.2.3 Implementation phase

Identify or reference the standards, practice, conventions, and metrics to be used during the implementation phase. Cite any internal (e.g., project or corporate) or external (e.g., military or contractual) standards with which implementation procedures must comply. Address such topics as the end-use computer, programming language(s), module size, declaration statement conventions, naming and labeling conventions, component layout standards, the use of structured coding techniques (or structuring precompilers) and CASE tools. Consider data conversion techniques for new systems that are replacing old ones. Standards for the inclusion of comment statement should be covered here. Use standard support software and software tools whenever possible or state reasons for the use of nonstandard support software and tools.

3.5.2.4 Test phase

Identify or reference the standards, practices, conventions, and metrics to be used during the testing phase. Cite any internal (e.g., project or corporate) or external (e.g., military or contractual) standards with which all levels of testing must comply. This includes unit, integration, system and acceptance testing, as well as regression testing. Identify the test environment, which should be the same as the targeted environment.

---

[12]See IEEE Std 830-1993.

IEEE Std 829-1983 (Reaff 1991) describes an integrated set of test documents and IEEE Std 1008-1987 (Reaff 1993) defines a systematic approach to unit testing.

Address criteria for test repeatability and test coverage such as testing every requirement, user procedure, and program statement. Specify techniques for tracing the test coverage to the test set. Indicate whether any support software will be required, and state how and from where this software will be obtained. State the method and process for certification of test tools or other support software used for demonstration.

3.5.2.5 Maintenance phase

Identify or reference the standards, practices, conventions, and metrics to be used to maintain the software. Cite any external (e.g., user, customer) requirements or standards with which maintenance practices must comply. Cite any internal standards or conventions, such as those describing design, implementation, test, and documentation requirements, that affect the maintenance process. Specify the methods and techniques (both manual and automated) for controlling and managing the software maintenance process such as requiring formal written change requests, review and evaluation of change requests, prioritizing and scheduling approved change requests, monitoring of the maintenance process through reviews and audits, and the collection and analysis of data affecting and resulting from the maintenance process. IEEE Std 1219-1992 defines a systematic approach to maintenance.

3.5.2.6 Documentation

Identify or reference the standards, practices, conventions, and metrics to be used in preparing and submitting software documentation. Cite any internal (e.g., project, corporate) or external (e.g., military, contractual) standards with which documentation must comply. Cite any document interchange (softcopy) standards that are applicable. The types of documentation that should be addressed may include software plans (e.g., SQAP, SCMP), software development documents (e.g., SRS, SDD), and any software deliverables (e.g., source code, users' manuals, tools).

3.5.2.7 Metrics

Identify or reference the standards, practices, and conventions to be used in the definition, collection and utilizations of software metrics data. Cite any internal (e.g., project, corporate) and external (e.g., user, customer) requirements or standards with which metrics practices must comply. IEEE Std 1045-1992 describes conventions for counting the results of the development processes. IEEE Std 1061-1992 provides a methodology for selecting and implementing process and product metrics. IEEE Std 982.1-1988 and Std 982.2-1988 provide various measures for use in different life cycle phases to gain confidence in the building of reliable software.

3.6 Reviews and audits

3.6 Reviews and Audits (Section 6 of the SQAP)

   3.6.1 Purpose. This section shall:[a]
(1)   Define the technical and managerial reviews and audits to be conducted.
(2)   State how the reviews and audits are to be accomplished.
(3)   State what further actions are required and how they are to be implemented and verified.

---

[a]See IEEE Std 1028-1988.

3.6.1 Purpose

The software items produced during the software life cycle process[13] should be reviewed and audited on a planned basis to determine the extent of progress and to evaluate the technical adequacy of the work and its conformance to software requirements and standards. Technical reviews and audits should be conducted to evaluate the status and quality of the software development effort. "The examination of project issues (both technical and managerial) occurs at various phases during the project life cycle. The results of such examinations are meant to permit improvement of the methods of ensuring software quality and the ability to meet time and cost constraints. The evaluation of software elements occurs during the construction of the element(s) and on its completion. This ensures that the element(s) completely and correctly embodies its baseline specifications" (IEEE Std 1028-1988, Section 3). Completion of reviews provides assurance that design integrity is maintained, technical deficiencies are identified, and necessary changes have been identified and implemented.

This section of the SQAP should identify the specific technical and managerial reviews and audits to be conducted with respect to the software development plans, schedules, and environment. It should describe the procedures to be used in the conduct of reviews and audits, and it should identify the participants (including vendors) and their specific responsibilities. These review and audit procedures should identify specific responsibility for the preparation of a report upon the completion of each review. This section should identify by position or job title who is to prepare these reports, the report format, who is to receive the reports, and associated management responsibilities. The review and audit procedures should describe the follow-up actions to assure that the recommendations made during the reviews and audits are properly implemented. This section should indicate the interval of time between performance of the review or audit and performance of the follow-up. Also, it should identify those responsible for performing follow-up actions.

3.6.2 Minimum requirements

3.6.2 Minimum Requirements. As a minimum, the following reviews shall be conducted:

a) Software Requirements Review (SRR)
b) Preliminary Design Review (PDR)
c) Critical Design Review (CDR)
d) Software Verification and Validation Plan Review (SVVPR)
e) Functional audit
f) Physical audit
g) In-Process audits
h) Managerial reviews
i) Software Configuration Management Plan Review (SCMPR)
j) Post mortem review

Tailoring or inclusion of additional reviews and audits should be made as local, contractual, or project-specific conditions dictate.

---

[13]See IEEE Std 1074-1995.

Table 1 presents an example of the relationships and timing of these reviews and audits to the software development phases.

Table 1—Example of relationships and timing of required reviews and audits

Typical software development phases (per IEEE Std 1074-1995)	Required software development products (documentation per 3.4.2 and 3.7)	Required SQA audits and reviews[a] per 3.6.2
Requirements	SQAP and SCMP[b] SRS SVVP[c] SDP	SRR In-Process audit[d] SVVPR[c] Managerial review[d]
Design	Preliminary SDD SDD User documentation	PDR[e] In-Process audit CDR[e] UDR[e]
Implementation	Software items with documentation	In-Process audit
Test	Test documentation[f]	Functional audit
Installation and checkout[g]	Deliverable items and SVVR	Physical audit
Operation and maintenance[h]	Products depend on scope of maintenance. Major modifications will have some or all of the above products.	Review depends on scope of required products.

[a]Results of these activities are reports that identify what was reviewed, the deficiencies found, and conclusions. A report generated by a review meeting also includes recommendations as to what needs to be done to resolve the deficiencies. (The items subject to review are the software development products as well as the SQAP and process.)

[b]This includes any referenced documents.

[c]The SVVP completion and SVVPR should be accomplished prior to the PDR.

[d]In-process audits and managerial reviews are scheduled as required throughout the software life cycle. For additional assistance, see clause 5.

[e]A UDR may be held independently of other reviews or in conjunction with the PDR and the CDR (a UDR is not an IEEE Std 730-1989 requirement).

[f]Refer to IEEE Std 829-1983 (Reaff 1991).

[g]In the event this phase is not used in the SQAP, move the required products and audit to the test phase.

[h]This phase is in addition to typical software development phases to show that the SQA effort can be an iterative process.

3.6.2.1 Software Requirements Review (SRR)

> **3.6.2.1 Software Requirements Review (SRR).** The SRR is held to ensure the adequacy of the requirements stated in the SRS.

The SRR is an evaluation of the Software Requirements Specifications (SRS). The SRR is conducted to ensure the adequacy, technical feasibility, and completeness of the requirements stated in the SRS. The SRR should evaluate the SRS for the attributes required by IEEE Std 830-1993 (unambiguous, complete, verifiable, consistent, modifiable, traceable, and usable during the operation and maintenance phase). The review ensures that sufficient detail is available to complete the software design.

The SQAP should indicate the organizational element responsible for conducting the SRR. All organizational elements that contribute or are impacted by the requirements should participate. These may include software design, software test, software quality assurance, system engineering, customers, users marketing, manufacturing, security, etc.

The SQAP should specify how, during the SRR, the quality of the following items will be assessed:

a)   Traceability and completeness of the requirement from the next higher level specification (such as a system specification or user requirements specification).

b)   Adequacy of rationale for any derived requirements.

c)   Adequacy and completeness of algorithms and equations.

d)   Correctness and suitability of logic descriptions that may be warranted.

e)   Compatibility of external (hardware and software) interfaces.

f)   Adequacy of the description of and approach to the human-machine interface.

g)   Consistency in the use of symbols and in the specification of all interfaces.

h)   Availability of constants and tables for calculations.

i)   Testability of the software requirements.

j)   Adequacy and completeness of the verification and acceptance requirements.

k)   Completeness and compatibility of interface specification and control documentation.

l)   Freedom from unwarranted design detail.

Additional items to be considered for assessment of the SRR include

m)   Trade-off and design studies that have applicability for decisions on
  1)   Data base design and/or real-time design issues.
  2)   Programming language characteristics and usage.
  3)   Resource allocation (e.g., storage, machine cycles, I/O channel personnel and hardware).
  4)   Operating system or executive design, or both.
  5)   Development versus COTS solution.

n)   The general description of the size and operating characteristics of all support software (e.g., operational program, maintenance and diagnostic programs, compilers, etc.).

o)   A description of requirements for the operation of the software and identification of functional requirements such as functional simulation, performance, environmental recording and analysis, exercise configuration, etc.

The results of the review should be documented in an SRR report that identifies all deficiencies described in the review and provides a plan and schedule for corrective action. Also, a decision about whether or not to proceed should be made based on cost estimates, feasibility studies, and project risk assessments. After the decision to proceed is made and the SRS is updated to correct any deficiencies, it should be placed under configuration control to establish the baseline to be used for the software design effort. The SQA organizational element should use the baselined requirements to develop a Requirements Verification Traceability Matrix (RVTM). This RVTM should be used as a tool by the SQA organizational element to validate satisfaction of requirements in the design, code, test, and functional capabilities of the system being developed.

3.6.2.2 Preliminary Design Review (PDR)

> **3.6.2.2 Preliminary Design Review (PDR).** The PDR (also known as top-level design review) is held to evaluate the technical adequacy of the preliminary design (also known as top-level design) of the software as depicted in the preliminary software design description.

The PDR, the pivotal step in the design phase, is held to evaluate the technical adequacy of the preliminary design, to include architectural design, before the beginning of detailed design. The review assesses the progress, consistency, and technical adequacy of the selected design approach; checks the compatibility of the design with the functional and performance requirements of the SRS; and verifies the existence compatibility of the interfaces between the software, hardware, and end users. The PDR also is conducted to determine that the preliminary SDD defines a suitable software design that fulfills the requirements contained in the SRS. The RVTM should be updated to include the preliminary design mapped to the requirements and verified by the SQA organizational element.

The SQAP should indicate the organizational element responsible for conducting the PDR. All organizational elements that impose requirements or are impacted by the design should participate in the review. These groups could include system engineering, software development, software test, software quality assurance, the customers, users, etc.

The SQAP should specify how, during the PDR, the quality of the following items will be assessed:

a) All detailed functional interfaces with other software, system equipment, communication systems, etc., for adequate identification of interface design and design solution adequacy.

b) The software design as a whole, emphasizing allocation of software components to functions, functional flows, storage requirements and allocations, software operating sequences, and the design of the data base.

c) The human factor requirements and the human-machine interfaces for adequacy and consistency of design.

d) Testability of the design, such as the existence of data stores and process that support behavior and state determination.

e) Test concepts, requirements, documentation, and tools, for adequacy.

Additional items to be considered for assessment of the PDR include

f) An analysis of the design for compatibility with critical system timing requirements, estimated running times, absence of race conditions and deadlock states, and other performance requirements.

g) Technical accuracy and currency of all available test documentation and its compatibility with the test requirements of the SRS.

The results should be documented in a PDR report that identifies all deficiencies discovered during the review and a plan and schedule for corrective action. The updated preliminary SDD document should be placed under configuration control to establish the baseline for the detailed software design effort.

3.6.2.3 Critical Design Review (CDR)

> **3.6.2.3 Critical Design Review (CDR).** The CDR (also known as detailed design review) is held to determine the acceptability of the detailed software designs as depicted in the detailed software design description in satisfying the requirements of the SRS.

The CDR is an evaluation of the completed Software Design Description (SDD), which includes all PDR updates and should provide the low-level details of the design. The CDR is conducted to evaluate the technical adequacy, completeness, and correctness of the detailed design of the software before the start of formal coding (not to include code associated with proof of concept or rapid prototyping activities) or as referenced to the life cycle described in an SDP. The purpose of the CDR is to evaluate the acceptability of the detailed design, to establish that the detailed design satisfies the requirements of the preliminary SDD and the SRS, to review compatibility with the other software and hardware with which the product is required to interact, and to assess the technical, cost, and schedule risks of the product design. The RVTM should be updated to include the detailed design mapped to preliminary design and requirements and verified by the SQA organizational element.

The SQAP should indicate the organizational element responsible for conducting the CDR. All other organizational elements that impose requirements or are impacted by the design should participate. These groups should include system engineering, software development, software test, software quality assurance, customers, users, etc.

The SQAP should specify how, during the CDR, the quality of the following items will be assessed:

a) The compatibility of the detailed design with the SRS.
b) Available data in the forms of logic diagrams, algorithms, storage allocation charts, and detailed design representation (e.g., flow charts, program design language) to establish design integrity.
c) Compatibility and completeness of interface requirements.
d) All external and internal interfaces, including interactions with the data base.
e) Technical accuracy and currency of all available test documentation and its compatibility with the test requirements of the SRS.
f) The requirements for the support and test software and hardware to be used in the development of the product.
g) The final design, including function flow, timing, sizing, storage requirements, memory maps, data base, and other performance factors.

Additional items to be considered for assessment of the CDR include

h) Final report of any trade-off analysis and design studies.
i) Chosen or recommended design tools and design.

The results of the review should be documented in a CDR report that identifies all deficiencies discovered during the review and a plan and schedule for corrective actions. The updated SDD document, when placed under configuration control, establishes the baseline for coding.

3.6.2.4 Software Verification and Validation Plan Review (SVVPR)

> **3.6.2.4 Software Verification and Validation Plan Review (SVVPR).** The SVVPR is held to evaluate the adequacy and completeness of the verification and validation methods defined in the SVVP.

The SVVPR is an evaluation of the completed Software Verification and Validation Plan (SVVP). Since the SVVP may be developed incrementally, multiple reviews may be required. These reviews are held to assure that the verification and validation methods described in the SVVP are adequate and will provide complete evaluation data.

The SQAP should indicate the organizational element responsible for conducting the Software Verification and Validation Plan Review. All organizational elements that impose requirements or are impacted by the SVVP should participate. These groups could include system engineering, software development, software design, software test, software quality assurance, customers, users, etc.

The SQAP should specify how, during the SVVPR, the quality of the following items will be assessed:

a) All verification and validation methods, along with completion criteria to ensure traceability to, and compatibility with, the functional and performance requirements expressed in the SRS.
b) Reports to adequately documents results of all reviews, audits, and tests based on the requirements listed in the SVVP.
c) Adequate descriptions of the software configuration to be tested, including test support software and hardware.
d) Test plans and test designs to assure that all requirements are tested.
e) Test procedures and test cases to assure that test inputs and success criteria are adequately defined and that test instructions are clear and concise.
f) A test schedule identifying which tests are to be done, when, and by whom.
g) Validation of the requirements listed in the SVVP with the baseline and all updates to the SRR list, which should be documented in the RVTM, should be performed by the SQA organizational element.

An additional item to be considered for assessment of the SVVPR could include

h)   If the SVVP was incrementally developed, a review of previous reviews to assess correction of previously noted deficiencies.

The RVTM should be updated to include the tests mapped to the code, design, and requirements and verified by the SQA organizational element.

The results of the review should be documented in an SVVPR report that identifies all deficiencies discovered during the review and provides a plan and schedule for corrective action. The updated SVVP, when placed under configuration control, establishes the baseline for software verification and validation activities.

3.6.2.5 Functional audit

> **3.6.2.5 Functional Audit.** This audit is held prior to the software delivery to verify that all requirements specified in the SRS have been met.

The functional audit compares the software as built (including its executable forms and available documentation) with the software requirements as stated in the baselined SRS. Its purpose is to assure that the code addressed all, and only, the documented requirements and functional capabilities stated in the SRS. The functional capabilities should be added to the RVTM and mapped to the tests, code, design and requirements. The SQA organizational element should validate the updated RVTM by observing a system demonstration.

The SQAP should indicate the organizational element responsible for the functional audit. The results are to be documented in the functional audit report, which identifies all discrepancies found and a plan and schedule for their resolution. Audits are not considered to be complete until all discrepancies have been resolved.

Input to the functional audit should consist of the following:

a)   Software Requirements Specifications (SRS).
b)   Software Verification and Validation Report (SVVR).
c)   Software Verification and Validation Plan Review (SVVPR) report.

3.6.2.6 Physical audit

> **3.6.2.6 Physical Audit.** This audit is held to verify that the software and its documentation are internally consistent and are ready for delivery.

The physical audit compares the code with its supporting documentation. Its purpose is to assure that the documentation to be delivered is consistent and correctly describes the code.

The SQAP should indicate the organizational element responsible for conducting the physical audit. The results of the physical audit are to be documented in the physical audit report, which identifies all discrepancies and the plans for their disposition. Once the plans have been approved and implemented (all dispositions have been completed), the software can be delivered.

Input to the physical audit should consist of the following:

a)   Software Design Description (SDD).
b)   Software products (e.g., code, algorithms, graphical user interfaces).
c)   Associated documentation (e.g., engineering notes, software development files, user documentation).

3.6.2.7 In-Process audits

> **3.6.2.7 In-Process Audits.** In-process audits of a sample of the design are held to verify consistency of the design, including:
> (1) Code versus design documentation
> (2) Interface specifications (hardware and software)
> (3) Design implementation versus functional requirements
> (4) Functional requirements versus test descriptions.

In-Process audits of samples of the product development items are held as required by the SQAP. The SQAP should indicate the organizational element responsible for conducting the in-process audits. Software inspections and design and test documentation reviews should be included as part of the in-process audit activity. The objective is to verify the consistency of the product as it evolves through the development process by determining that

a) Hardware and software interfaces are consistent with design requirements in the SRS.

b) The functional requirements of the SRS are fully validated by the SVVP.

c) The design of the product, as the SDD is evolving, satisfies the functional requirements of the SRS.

d) The code is consistent with the SDD.

The RVTM should be updated to include the software units (code modules) mapped to the design and requirements and verified by the SQA organizational element.

The result of all in-process audits are measures of how well the development process is working. They should be documented in in-process audit reports that identify all discrepancies found and the plans and schedules for their resolution.

3.6.2.8 Managerial reviews

> **3.6.2.8 Managerial Reviews.** Managerial reviews are held periodically to assess the execution of all of the actions and the items identified in the SQAP. These reviews shall be held by an organizational element independent of the unit being reviewed, or by a qualified third party. This review may require additional changes in the SQAP itself.

Managerial reviews are assessments of the execution of the SQAP. All SQA activities are evaluated. The planned frequency and structure of the managerial reviews should be stated in the SQAP. They should be conducted at the direction of an appropriate level of management independent of the organization performing the software activity. The independent organization could be appointed by management as a process review team of peers.

A managerial review results in a statement as to the adequacy of the SQAP and its execution. This should be conducted by an independent element. Each review should be documented by a report summarizing the review findings, including any exceptions to the process stated in the SQAP, and any recommended changes or improvements.

Clause 5 provides guidance for evaluating the contents and the implementation of an SQAP.

3.6.2.9 Software Configuration Management Plan Review (SCMPR)

> **3.6.2.9 Software Configuration Management Plan Review (SCMPR).** The SCMPR is held to evaluate the adequacy and completeness of the configuration management methods defined in the SCMP.

This SCMPR is an evaluation of the completed SCMP. The review is held to assure the software configuration management procedures described in the SCMP are adequate and will provide the necessary control over documentation and code. The SQAP should clearly define the methods to be used by the SQA organizational element to verify and validate the data presented at the SCMPR.

The SQAP should indicate the organizational element responsible for conducting the SCMPR. All organizational elements that impose requirements on or are impacted by the SCMP should participate. These groups could include systems engineering, software development, software test, SQA, etc.

The following items could be specified in the SQAP as a checklist for the SCMPR:

a) A description of the SCM's purpose, scope of application, key terms, and references for the project.
b) SCM management information that identifies the responsibilities and authorities for accomplishing the planned activities (*WHO?*).
c) Information on all SCM activities to be performed during the project (*WHAT?*).
d) SCM schedule that identifies the required coordination of SCM activities.
e) Identification of tools, physical, and human resources required for execution of SCM (*HOW?*).
f) Overview description of the specified software life cycle.
g) Identification of the software CIs.
h) Identification of other software items to be included, such as support or test software.
i) Relationship of SCM to the hardware or system CM activities during the software life cycle.
j) Reviews and audits that are applied to life cycle milestones.
k) Assumptions that might have an impact on the cost, schedules, or ability to perform or define SCM activities such as assumption of the degree of customer participation in the SCM activities or the availability of automated aides.
l) Status reports that identify the configuration at any point in time during the software life cycle.

Once the SCMP methods and procedures are validated as complete and adequate, routine and spot checking reviews should be conducted by an independent SQA reviewer (i.e., independent from the development activity) in order to verify the use of the approved methods and procedures. Each review should be documented by a report summarizing the review findings, including any exceptions to the process, and any recommended changes or improvements. The implementation of all recommended changes should be monitored and the SCMP methods and procedures should be reevaluated once implementation is complete. This would promote the baselining of standard CM procedures, which is an efficient way to conduct business. New program specific requirements may create the need for the tailoring of the SCMP procedures and methods. The size, scope, and complexity of each program is different; therefore, careful in-depth review should be attempted and the SCMP methods and procedures should be updated and rebaselined as appropriate.

3.6.2.10 Post mortem review

> **3.6.2.10 Post Mortem Review.** This review is held at the conclusion of the project to assess the development activities implemented on that project and to provide recommendations for appropriate action.

Upon conclusion of the development project, a non-attribution, lessons-learned (post mortem) review should be conducted. The objective of the post mortem should be to improve the development process and procedures, not to blame or reward the development team. The SQAP should clearly define the methods used by the SQA organizational element to verify and validate the data presented at the post mortem review.

Independent objective coordinators should gather all of the inputs. Inputs could be obtained anonymously on written forms (either blank or questionnaires) and/or during an evaluation meeting. All who had a part in the development (full life cycle—concept through operation) should be asked their opinion. The scope and size of the project as well as resources available determine how many personnel could participate; however, a representative from each phase or group should give input. Technical personnel, staff [Quality Assurance/ Configuration Management (QA/CM)] administration support managers and, if possible, the users of the system should provide comments on problem areas as well as good practices. Whenever possible, all should discuss their observations and make recommendations for correction to the process. A written summary of the observations as well as the recommendations should be documented by the independent evaluators. A system for reporting problems could be based on that described in 3.8; however, the responsibilities may differ between process and software problems. Also refer to 3.13.1b) of this guide on records collection. Corrections to the standards and operating procedures should be implemented during the next development cycle and an appropriate metric (means to evaluate improvement) should be chosen.

3.6.3 Other

> **3.6.3 Other.** Other reviews and audits may include the user documentation review (UDR). This review is held to evaluate the adequacy (e.g., completeness, clarity, correctness, and usability) of user documentation.

Other reviews may be conducted as required by the organizations responsible for the development. The scope and size of the projects may warrant the additional reviews [e.g., a large user community may require a UDR, the Total Quality Management (TQM) organization may require a Quality Assurance Audit].

3.6.3.1 User Documentation Review (UDR)

The UDR is held to determine the technical adequacy of the documentation approach and design as described in draft versions of the user documentation (softcopy or hardcopy).

The SQAP should indicate the organizational element responsible for conducting the UDR. All organizational elements that are affected or impacted by the user documentation should participate in the review. These groups may include system engineering, software development, software test, software quality assurance, customers, users, etc.

The following items should be specified in the SQAP as the UDR requirement criteria to be used by the SQA organizational element:

a)   The methods used to validate that the software product matches the user documentation.
b)   Test plans, test procedures, and test cases to ensure that all user documentation (e.g., users and operators manuals) are tested in conjunction with the software.
c)   The user documentation should be reviewed for compliance with the approved project documentation standard.

The UDR can be held independently or in conjunction with other reviews.

The results of the review should be documented in a UDR report, which identifies all deficiencies discovered during the review and which provides a plan and schedule for corrective action. The updated user documentation should be placed under configuration management prior to the physical audit described in 3.6.2.6.

3.6.3.2 Quality assurance audit

An audit of the SQAP and procedures may be required by management to ensure its adequacy. This could occur whether the SQA organizational element is independent or part of the development group. It would most likely occur if the SQA organizational element were in the same reporting chain as the development group. The SQAP should indicate the independent organizational element(s) responsible for conducting the QA review and for any corrective action.[14]

3.7 Test

> **3.7 Test (Section 7 of the SQAP).** This section shall identify all the tests not included in the SVVP for the software covered by the SQAP and shall state the methods to be used.[a]

[a]See IEEE Std 829-1983 (Reaff 1991) and IEEE Std 1008-1987 (Reaff 1993).

The SQAP shall include the specific software tests and testing not addressed in the SVVP (Section 4.2.3 of the SQAP) or other test documentation. The SQAP should identify and describe the methods, approaches, and techniques to be used (or reference appropriate test documentation that has been developed for the project). Test methods and techniques can be divided into two classifications: static tests and dynamic tests. Static testing evaluates or analyzes the software without executing the code (e.g., desk checking, code walk-throughs). This section addresses only dynamic testing.

Dynamic testing, the execution of software on any computer, encompasses such methods and techniques as unit level testing, white-box testing, black-box testing, integration testing, system level testing, stress testing, security testing, and acceptance testing. IEEE Std 1008-1987 (Reaff 1993) defines a systematic and documented approach to unit testing.

This section of the SQAP should include a description of the test planning, test execution, and evaluation of the results of testing, or include a reference to the appropriate section of the SQAP or to standards and procedures that describe the testing process. The testing process described should adequately address the preparation and review of documentation associated with the testing process, including test plans, test design and test case specifications, test procedures and test instructions, test schedule, test reports, and test incidents and their resolution.

Test documentation not specifically referenced in Section 7.0 of the SQAP should be delineated, or a reference to the appropriate section of the SQAP or to test documentation standards, procedures, or conventions that describe the test documentation to be provided, should be included in this section. IEEE Std 829-1983 (Reaff 1991) describes a set of basic test documentation associated with dynamic testing.

This section should include a description of the management and organizational responsibilities associated with the implementation of the tests described in this section, or a reference to the appropriate section of the SQAP or standards, procedures, or conventions that describe the management and organizational responsibilities.

This section should include a description of the computer-aided software engineering (CASE) tools used in the support of test activities or a reference to the appropriate section of the SQAP.

The SQAP should clearly define the methods to be used by the SQA organizational element to verify and validate the test plans, test data, and test activities.

---

[14]See ISO 9000-1: 1994.

3.8 Problem reporting and corrective action

> **3.8 Problem Reporting and Corrective Action (Section 8 of the SQAP).** This section shall:
> (1) Describe the practices and procedures to be followed for reporting, tracking, and resolving problems identified in both software items and the software development and maintenance process.
> (2) State the specific organizational responsibilities concerned with their implementation.

Problems encountered during software development or operation may result from defects in the software, supporting and development processes, hardware, or operations. Because of their diversity, the determination of the sources of a problem and the appropriate corrective action requires a centrally controlled system for monitoring problems and determining root causes.

The purposes of problem reporting and corrective action systems are to

a) Assure that problems are documented, corrected, and used for process improvement.

b) Assure that problem reports are assessed for their validity.

c) Assume reported problems and their associated corrective actions are implemented in accordance with customer approved solutions.

d) Provide feedback to the developer and the user of problem status.

e) Provide data for measuring and predicting software quality and reliability.

These goals should be satisfied by the problem reporting and corrective action system described in the SQAP.

The SQAP should include methods to be used to assure the reported problems are being properly addressed. The SQAP should describe the organizational element(s), provisions, and timely procedures for documenting, validating, tracking, and reporting the status of problems and the appropriate corrective action.

Validating, tracking, and resolving problems require the coordination of various groups within the organization. The SQAP should specify the groups responsible for authorizing and implementing problem reporting and corrective actions, and submission of unresolved issues to management for resolution. The problem reporting and corrective action system is usually implemented by SCM and documented in the SCMP. Also, it should identify the point in the development process where generation of problem reports is to begin for each class of development result (e.g., plans, SRS, SDD, code, test documentation).

The SQAP should clearly define the methods to be used by the SQA organizational element to verify and validate the use of problem reporting and corrective action practices and procedures.

3.9 Tools, techniques, and methodologies

> **3.9 Tools, Techniques, and Methodologies (Section 9 of the SQAP).** This section shall identify the special software tools, techniques, and methodologies that support SQA, state their purposes, and describe their use.

The SQAP shall identify the tools, techniques, and methodologies to be used to support software quality assurance. It should list or reference those tools, techniques, and methodologies that are available, and those that need to be acquired or developed. The responsible organization(s) also should be identified.

3.9.1 Tools

SQA software tools aid in the evaluation or improvement of software quality. Typical tools include, but are not limited to, operating system utilities, debugging aids, documentation aids, checklists, structuring preprocessors, file comparators, structure analyzers, code analyzers, standards auditors, simulators, execution analyzers, performance monitors, statistical analysis packages, software development folders/files, software traceability matrices, test drivers, test case generators, static or dynamic test tools, and information engineering CASE tools.[15]

3.9.2 Techniques

SQA techniques are technical and managerial procedures that aid in the evaluation and improvement of software quality. Such techniques include review of the use of standards, software inspections, requirements tracing, requirements and design verification, reliability measurements and assessments, and rigorous or formal logic analysis.

3.9.3 Methodologies

SQA methodologies are integrated sets of the above tools and techniques. The methodologies should be well-documented for accomplishing the task or activity and provide a description of the process to be used. For example, if the SQA staff uses an RVTM as a method to verify and validate the requirements, design, and test phases, a sample should be provided in the SQAP. It should describe how and when (at what control gates during the development cycle) it will be used.

3.10 Code control

> **3.10 Code Control (Section 10 of the SQAP).** This section shall define the methods and facilities used to maintain, store, secure and document controlled versions of the identified software during all phases of the software life cycle. This may be implemented in conjunction with a computer program library. This may be provided as a part of the SCMP. If so, an appropriate reference shall be made thereto.

Code control can be interpreted as the ways and means necessary to protect or ensure the validity of completed code. Once an appropriate baseline has been established, the code should be placed under configuration management in a computer program library. The SQAP should specify controls (or reference the CM procedures for software change) and security measures for software change and for protection from inadvertent alteration after the code has been baselined. It should define or reference the CM procedures (e.g., see SCMP or the CM section in the SDP) and organizational responsibility for controlling the developed code.

The SQAP should specify or reference a code control procedure that

    a)   Defines the specific software to be controlled.
    b)   Describes a standard method for identifying, labeling, and cataloging the software.
    c)   Lists the physical location of the software under control.
    d)   Describes the location, maintenance, and use of all backup copies.
    e)   Describes procedures for distributing a copy.
    f)   Identifies the documentation that is affected by changes.
    g)   Describes procedures for implementing a new version.
    h)   Describes how compliance with the above is assured.

---

[15]See IEEE Std 1209-1992.

3.11 Media control

> **3.11 Media Control (Section 11 of the SQAP).** This section shall state the methods and facilities to be used to (a) identify the media for each computer product and the documentation required to store the media, including the copy and restore process, and (b) protect computer program physical media from unauthorized access or inadvertent damage or degradation during all phases of the software life cycle. This may be provided as a part of the SCMP. If so, an appropriate reference shall be made thereto.

Computer program media can be defined as those media on which computer data are stored. Typically, the storage media are CD-ROM, RAM, disks, or tapes, but could include cards, diskettes, listings, or other forms on which the data reside.

The media control methods and facilities should ensure that

a) The software is stored and retrieval is assured.

b) Off-site storage and retrieval are provided for critical software and copies of baselined code.

c) The software is accessible only to those with the need of access.

d) The environment is controlled so that the physical media on which the software is stored do not degrade.

e) A description is provided of how compliance with the above is assured.

The SQAP should reference (e.g., see SCMP or CM section of the SDP) or specify procedures and practices that pertain to the above items. For example, a backup procedure for software could indicate the schedule for backup, the type of media on which it will be placed, the location of the storage, the environment of the storage area, and the method to retrieve the backed-up software. A security system may be in place that allows access to software only through an authorization process. The Software Security Plan (3.4.4.9) should be referenced. The SQAP should delineate the organization elements responsible for administering and reviewing media control methods and facilities. The method for identifying, labeling, and data logging may be the same in both code and media control.

3.11.1 Unauthorized access

Several methods are available that will provide adequate protection from unauthorized access of computer program media. The primary method is to provide a permanent labeling or identification scheme within the storage media. When a disk or tape is used on a computer, this technique can provide adequate password control or access protection. Other methods include a limited access program library, encryption, external markings, and proprietary statements identifying a controlled program. The physical security of all media also must be considered.

SQA activities to verify appropriateness and implementation of access procedures should be documented in the SQAP. Areas of concern include identifying the programs requiring limited access, adherence to label and file restrictions, ensuring use of adequate external labeling restrictions, and providing a controlled environment such as a program library.

3.11.2 Inadvertent damage or degradation

Damage or degradation of the media can be minimized by providing adequate configuration management techniques, safe storage locations such as fireproof vaults, and packaging practices that are antistatic in design. Periodic review to ensure use of controlled environmental and cataloging practices will minimize degradation of the media.

SQA activities to verify appropriateness and implementation of procedures to minimize media damage or degradation should be documented in the SQAP.

3.12 Supplier control

3.12 Supplier Control (Section 12 of the SQAP). This section shall state the provisions for assuring that software provided by suppliers meets established requirements. In addition, this section shall state the methods that will be used to assure that the software supplier receives adequate and complete requirements. For previously-developed software, this section shall state the methods to be used to assure the suitability of the product for use with the software items covered by the SQAP. For software that is to be developed, the supplier shall be required to prepare and implement a SQAP in accordance with this standard. This section shall also state the methods to be employed to assure that the developers comply with the requirements of this standard.

This section of the purchaser's SQAP should specify

a) The purchaser's involvement with the supplier's SQA program.
b) The purchaser's procedures for auditing the supplier's conformance to IEEE Std 730-1989, or equivalent contractually standard, and the supplier's SQAP (an option could be to provide for an independent auditor).
c) The actions available to the purchaser should the supplier not be in conformance with IEEE Std 730-1989 and the supplier's SQAP.

3.13 Records collection, maintenance, and retention

3.13 Records Collection, Maintenance, and Retention (Section 13 of the SQAP). This section shall identify the SQA documentation to be retained, shall state the methods and facilities to be used to assemble, safeguard, and maintain this documentation, and shall designate the retention period.

SQA records collection, maintenance, and retention procedures in the SQAP should conform to the approved SCMP methods. To avoid redundancy, a reference to the SCMP procedures could be noted in the SQAP.

3.13.1 Records collection

The type of records to be collected, whether softcopy or hardcopy, are determined by the overall objectives for record keeping. These objectives should be documented in the SQAP. Possible objectives are

a) To provide contractual evidence that the software development process was performed in conformance with established practice and the customer's requirements:
1) The SQAP is being followed and conforms to the requirements of applicable standards.
2) The software meets design intent and satisfies contractual requirements.
3) Corrective action is effective, timely, and complete (i.e., action items are tracked until resolution).
4) Testing has been performed in accordance with test plans.
b) To provide historical or reference data that could be used to discover long-term trends in the organization's development techniques. The documents collected for historical or reference purposes should be capable of providing data for productivity, quality, and methodology studies. Metrics collected should be reviewed for trends and process improvement. The documents should provide sufficient design, implementation, and testing data so as to be useful for future development.

In addition to SQA documents, records should include program media containing the exact version of programs and materials used in performing tests to assure, test repeatability at any time in the future.

3.13.2 Records maintenance

The SQAP should specify the manner in which records will be kept, that is, softcopy, hardcopy, microfiche, etc. Also, it should state how records will be stored to protect them from fire, theft, or environmental deterioration. The SQAP should provide for historical archiving if applicable.

3.13.3 Records retention

The SQAP should specify the length of retention for each type of record maintained. It is important to state in the SQAP when records should be retained and when they should be destroyed.

3.14 Training

> **3.14 Training (Section 14 of the SQAP).** This section shall identify the training activities necessary to meet the needs of the SQAP.

The need for training of personnel designated to perform the activities defined in the SQAP should be assessed. It is suggested that a matrix be created that defines the task, skill requirement(s) of the task, and the skills of the personnel designated to perform the task. This will allow the rapid identification of training needs for each task and each individual. Considerations for training should include special tools, techniques, methodologies, and computer resources. The SQA organizational element's tasks should include how to evaluate and report quality of the following:

a) Documentation (e.g., SCMP)

b) Standards, practices, conventions, and metrics

c) Reviews and audits

d) Testing

e) Problem reporting and corrective action

f) Code, media, and supplier control

g) Records collection, maintenance, and retention

h) SQAP evaluation

i) SQA management

Once the training need is established, a training plan should be developed that identifies the training activities required to successfully implement the SQAP. Existing training programs should be adapted or new training programs developed to meet these training needs. Training sessions should be scheduled for personnel who will be assigned to carry out the tasks. This training should be compatible with the task schedules discussed in 4.3.2.

If training for non-SQAP related software activities is not covered in other project documentation, the SQA organizational element, upon completion of the other project documentation review, should recommend the development and inclusion of a training matrix into their documentation. This matrix should be used by the SQA organizational element to evaluate all project training. The matrix should be updated (person and course) as training is successfully completed.

3.15 Risk management

> **3.15 Risk Management (Section 15 of the SQAP).** This section shall specify the methods and procedures employed to identify, assess, monitor, and control areas of risk arising during the portion of the software life cycle covered by the SQAP.

Each risk area, whether technical, economic, schedule, managerial, marketing, or any other kind, shall be identified. The risk identification shall be justified. For example: a) Why does the SQA staff believe it to be an area of risk? b) With whom has the SQA staff consulted (identify by job title not name)? c) What information has reached the SQA staff leading them to believe this is a risk area? The risk factors (risk composition) and acceptable results of the risk should be identified. It is essential to identify the level of risk (high, medium, or low) associated with the possible failure of each required task or the unavailability of each resource. The risk assessment should identify the resulting impact on schedules and outline alternative actions available to mitigate the risks.

The risk assessment should quantify the magnitude of each identified risk. Managers should monitor risks in their assigned areas and present periodic reports on their status. Managers also should develop plans for the elimination or reduction of the risks in their assigned areas and report on their progress in implementing these risk control plans. A separate risk management plan may be appropriate for projects that have been identified as having potential high risks. Each risk assessment item should be documented under the headings: a) Description, b) Impact, c) Monitoring, and d) Mitigation.

As the risks change throughout the life cycle, the SQAP should be updated (e.g., a reprioritization of resources, additional prototyping, walkthroughs, testing, or reviews should be conducted).

4. Implementation of a software quality assurance plan

The purpose of this clause is to describe the steps necessary for successfully implementing the SQAP that has been prepared for a specific project. The following items are discussed in this clause:

a)   Acceptance of the SQAP by the software developers and others whose task responsibilities are defined in the SQAP.

b)   Acceptance of the SQAP by management.

c)   Planning and scheduling of resources and tasks for implementation of the SQAP.

d)   Distribution of the SQAP to implementors and interfacing personnel.

e)   Execution of the SQAP.

4.1 Acceptance by development and other personnel

It is essential to foster a spirit of cooperation between the personnel responsible for software development and the SQA activities. An effective method of achieving this is to have all concerned personnel participate in the preparation of the SQAP. This will tend to increase their support of SQA in general, and of the SQAP in particular. Preliminary drafts of the SQAP should be circulated within the development organization for review and comments. Also, it may be useful to hold walkthroughs of the SQAP with all concerned personnel. During this time they will be able to ask questions directly of the authors of the SQAP, and to make their concerns and objections known before the SQAP is officially published. In this manner, the groundwork will be laid for cooperation and mutual support between all organizations responsible for activities required by the SQAP.

4.2 Acceptance by management

Management acceptance and commitment to the SQAP should be obtained. This will provide the support required for implementing the tasks defined. This acceptance should include commitments for the budget and resources required to implement to the SQA activities.

The SQAP should be coordinated with, and agreed to, by each unit of the organization having responsibilities defined within the SQAP. Acceptance of the SQAP should be indicated on the cover page (hardcopy or softcopy) by an approval signature of the person in charge of each unit. Implementation of the SQAP can be effective only if all the actions called for in the SQAP are performed with the full support of management.

4.3 Planning for implementation of the SQAP

Planning for SQAP implementation comprises two aspects:

a)   Identification of required resources.
b)   Scheduling implementation resources.

4.3.1 Resources

The four types of resources required to implement a SQAP are personnel, equipment, facilities, and tools. The quantity and quality of these resources should be made known to the appropriate level of management.

The responsible element should identify the job classifications and skill levels of the personnel required to implement and maintain the SQAP throughout the life of the project. It should identify the hardware needed to implement the SQAP and to support it throughout the project, as well as estimates of computer time and support required. Also, it should identify the facilities needed for storage of media and records. When resources are identified by an element other than the SQA element, the SQA element should verify compliance with this task. The tools required for implementation should have been already identified in the SQAP itself.

4.3.2 Scheduling

Once the resources involved in implementing a SQAP have been identified, the next step is to establish a schedule for the implementation. The SQA schedule should be established in consonance with the development schedule. For each task identified in SQAP, this schedule should identify the starting and completion dates for each required resource. In a similar manner, a schedule should be established for the development or acquisition of any necessary support tools.

The schedule information should be coordinated with the development team and manager. The program manager, development manager, and the QA manager should be using the same schedule for the total program. A copy of the coordinated, approved schedule could be incorporated into this clause as well as in the SDP and/or the SPMP. The SPMP should contain an overall schedule for all measurable milestones.

4.4 Distribution of the SQAP

The following applies whether the SQAP is distributed by softcopy or hardcopy. A distribution list of all personnel who are to receive the final approved copy of the SQAP should be prepared. A copy of the published SQAP should then be distributed (physically or electronically) to each individual listed, with an attached sign-off sheet that is to be initialed by the person receiving the SQAP and returned to the organization responsible for the SQAP's publication and distribution.

Follow-up should be done if the sign-off sheet is incomplete or not returned. This helps to ensure intended recipients have the correct version of the SQAP.

4.5 Execution of the SQAP

Once the SQAP is distributed, the SQA organizational element, or other designated organization, should assure that the tasks (e.g., reviews and audits) documented within the SQAP are performed at the appropriate points in the life cycle. The SQAP should identify the activity to be performed, the organizational element performing the activity, and the results to be achieved. It should reference other documents as necessary. Associated work papers of the reviews and audits should provide sufficient evidence that the steps in the SQAP have been performed and reviewed by the management accountable for the SQAP. This should permit an objective determination of how well the SQA objectives have been met.

5. Evaluation of a software quality assurance plan

5.1 Purpose

The SQA element should make provision for periodic or ongoing evaluation of the SQAP. Evaluating the SQAP involves examining it from two different viewpoints:

a) Evaluating the content of the SQAP (initially and after all revisions).
b) Evaluating the use and management of the SQAP.

The evaluation of the SQAP's content is an assessment of how the SQAP complies with IEEE Std 730-1989, internal development and quality assurance standards, and contractual documents. Evaluation of the completeness and applicability of the SQAP is facilitated by the questions presented in 5.2.1.

These questions provide an overview of the state of the SQAP.

The evaluation of the use and management of the SQAP is an assessment of the specific project's implementation of the SQAP. Some suggestions for this ongoing activity are contained in 5.2.2.

5.2 Methodology

The methodologies used to evaluate the SQAP should include reviewing the documentation and observing the implementation process. A checklist of questions should be developed in accordance with the documentation standards approved for project use.

5.2.1 SQAP evaluation

The following questions should be asked in evaluating the overall approach of the SQAP:

a) Are all mandatory requirements of IEEE Std 730-1989 addressed in the SQAP?
b) Are all contractual and company SQAP standards addressed in the SQAP?
c) Does the SQAP specify compliance with any standards in addition to IEEE Std 730-1989? If so, does the SQAP meet the requirements of those standards?
d) Are all exceptions to mandatory requirements noted and adequately justified?
e) Is the content of the SQAP adequate to achieve its stated objectives?
f) Are the SQA requirements, as stated, enforceable, and measurable?

Additional questions that can be used in support of the evaluation of specific SQAP sections are

g) Purpose
    1) Are the specific purpose and scope of the SQAP described?
    2) Are the software product items covered by the SQAP completely described?
    3) Is the intended use of the software items described?

h) Referenced documents
    1) Are all documents referenced by the SQAP listed in this section?

i) Management
    1) Are the structures of all the organizations that influence the quality of the software depicted?
    2) Are the management activities completely described?
    3) Are the tasks and responsibilities of the organizations that influence the quality of the software listed?

j) Documentation
    1) Does this section describe all necessary software documentation?
    2) Does this section describe the methodologies to be used for checking documentation adequacy with reference to 3.6, Reviews and Audits?
    3) Are the methodologies adequate?

k) Standards, practices, conventions, and metrics
    1) Does this section identify all standards, practices, conventions, and metrics to be applied to the software?
    2) Are compliance and monitoring procedures identified?
    3) Are 1) and 2) adequate?

l) Reviews and audits
    1) Does this section define all necessary reviews and audits for the documentation described in 3.4, Documentation?
    2) Are the methodologies for all reviews and audits described?
    3) Are 1) and 2) adequate?

m) Test
    1) Does this section define additional tests not included in the SVVP?
    2) Are the test methods and techniques described for static and dynamic testing as well as associated QA activities?
    3) Does the test documentation conform to IEEE Std 829-1983 (Reaff 1991)?

n) Problem reporting corrective action
    1) Does this section describe problem reporting and corrective action procedures to be used for this project?
    2) Does this section state specific organizational responsibilities?
    3) Are the procedures adequate?

o) Tools, techniques, and methodologies
    1) Are all tools, techniques, and methodologies to be used for SQA purposes fully described?
    2) Are they adequate?

p) Code control
    1) Does this section contain a description of all methods and facilities to be used for code control?
    2) Are they adequate?
    3) Does this section describe how compliance will be achieved?

q) Media control
    1) Does this section contain a description of all methods and facilities to be used for media control?
    2) Are they adequate?
    3) Does this section describe how compliance will be achieved?

r) Supplier control
    1) Are all procedures for interfacing between each supplier's SQAP and this SQAP fully described?
    2) Are they adequate?

s) Records collection, maintenance, and retention
    1) Are all records collection, maintenance, and retention procedures fully described?
    2) Are they adequate?

t)   Training

   1)   Does this section identify the training activities associated with the requirements of this SQAP?

   2)   Is the training plan complete (i.e., does it address all of the training activities associated with this SQAP)?

u)   Risk management

   1)   Does this section identify the level of risk (high, medium, or low) associated with each task or resource required?

   2)   Are the methods and procedures which identify, assess, monitor, and control areas of risk described in this SQAP?

   3)   Are the identified risks mitigated?

5.2.2 SQAP implementation evaluation

At several points in the product life cycle, usually major project milestones, the SQAP and its implementation should be evaluated by means of a managerial review. This will help assure that the project and its SQAP evolve together. As the project proceeds through the software life cycle, there are likely to be changes in the product scope. As the development plan changes, the SQAP and its implementation also should be reviewed to determine if any changes are required.

The use of the SQAP should be evaluated in terms of the tasks and responsibilities detailed in the SQAP (3.3.2 and 3.3.3). This evaluation should review the status of each task and the adequacy of the actions taken in terms of both product quality results and the schedules actually achieved for the tasks.

5.2.3 SQAP evaluation process relationship

The evaluation process will have a cause-effect relationship as shown in figure 1. An SQAP evaluation, whether formal or informal, may have the effect of causing SQAP modification or causing an implementation evaluation. An SQAP modification may necessitate a corresponding implementation modification. An implementation evaluation may cause an implementation change to bring the use and management of the SQAP into compliance with the SQAP.

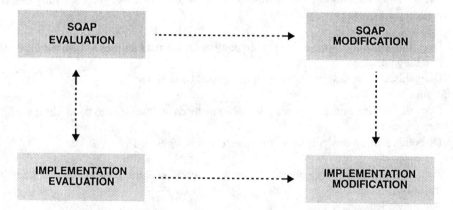

Figure 1—Cause-Effect of SQAP evaluation and modification

6. Modification of a software quality assurance plan

The previous clause addressed the evaluation of an SQAP and the determination of any necessary changes to it. This clause will describe a mechanism for implementing such changes.

6.1 Purpose

The purpose of this subclause is to provide a method for modifying an existing SQAP. Only if there is a provision for systematic modification of an SQAP can its users have confidence in its continued usability.

There are several reasons why an SQAP, once approved and implemented, may subsequently need to be modified. First, the SQAP may contain deficiencies. Second, it may be necessary to adjust to changes in the environment of the SQAP. For example, a new set of system requirements may require more stringent or more detailed testing to assure they are satisfied. Third, changes in the management structure of the project may make portions of the SQAP (e.g., reporting lines of sign-off authorities) obsolete. Finally, the advent of new processes and technology may make modification desirable, as, for example, when new SQAP tools or techniques must be incorporated.

6.2 Scope

This subclause addresses methods for proposing, reviewing, and instituting modifications to an SQAP. It does not cover modifications to the manner in which the SQAP is used, managed, or controlled; provisions for these are made either within the SQAP itself or in project management directives.

6.3 Methodology

There are five steps in the modification of an SQAP:

a) Identify alternative options.
b) Recommend proposed change.
c) Review proposed change.
d) Incorporate approved change.
e) Release and promulgate change.

Steps a) and b) should be followed in all cases. If a project SCM organization exists, then steps c), d), and e) should be accomplished according to that organization's procedures. If there is no project SCM organization, then steps c), d), and e) should be followed as described in the subclauses below.

6.3.1 Identify alternative options

Changes to an SQAP may be proposed from any of several sources, such as project management, software development, system validation, configuration management, quality assurance, or the customer. They could suggest different solutions to the same problem. It is important to provide for the results of the SQAP evaluation process (see clause 5) to be routed through all of these sources in order that each of their proposed solutions may be presented and reviewed.

6.3.2 Recommend proposed change

A Configuration Control Board (CCB) should be organized to review all alternative solutions and to determine a single recommended change (or set of changes) that they believe best addresses the acknowledged requirement. Depending upon the frequency with which SQAP changes are proposed, this CCB may be either a standing or an ad hoc organization. It may be useful to set up such a group as a standing organization at the time the SQAP is first published if numerous change requests are expected. When such requests become fewer and farther between, the CCB may be converted to an ad hoc status.

6.3.3 Review proposed change

Once the CCB has agreed upon a proposed change, it should be sent to all interested or potentially affected parties for their review and comments. This step is necessary to provide agreement before the change is published and distributed. The CCB should have responsibility for evaluation and incorporation of comments received from the reviewers, and for approval or rejection of the proposed change.

6.3.4 Incorporate approved change

If, after studying the reviewers' comments, the CCB approves the proposed change, it is incorporated into the SQAP. Standard document control procedures should be employed here, including editorial review, printing of change pages, use of vertical bars to highlight added or modified text, and control procedures to preserve previous versions of the document.

6.3.5 Release and promulgate change

A management official should be designated who will have sign-off authority on SQAP changes.

Once this official has approved the change page(s) for release, standard document distribution methods may be employed. Then, all that remains is to monitor the implementation of the change. This responsibility should be assigned to the appropriate management official. At this point, the evaluation process begins again (see clause 5).

7. Bibliography

These documents, although not specifically cited in the text of this guide, are related and are provided for information.

ASME NQA-1-1994, Quality Assurance Program Requirements for Nuclear Facilities.[16]

IEEE Std 7-4.3.2-1993, IEEE Standard Criteria for Digital Computers in Safety Systems of Nuclear Power Generating Stations (ANSI).

IEEE Std 603-1991, IEEE Standard Criteria for Safety Systems for Nuclear Power Generating Stations (ANSI).

IEEE Std 1002-1987 (Reaff 1992), IEEE Standard Taxonomy for Software Engineering Standards (ANSI).

---

[16]ASME publications are available from the American Society of Mechanical Engineers, 22 Law Drive, Fairfield, NJ 07007, USA.

Annex A

(informative)

Summary of the SQAP and related standards

Table A.1—Summary of the SQAP and related standards

Item	Shall	Should	May	IEEE Std 730-1989	IEEE Std 730.1-1995	Other standards[a]
—Description of specific scope and purpose of SQAP	X			3.1	3.1	
• Intended use	X			3.1	3.1a)	
• Scope	X				3.1b)	
• Reason for SQAP		X			3.1c)	
• Products covered by the SQAP	X			3.1	3.1d)	
• Software life cycle/products		X			3.1e)	IEEE Std 1074-1995
• Base documents		X			3.1f)	
• Rationale for departures from base documents		X			3.1g)	
—Reference documents list		X		3.2	3.2	
—Description of project and plan management	X			3.3	3.3	
• Organization	X			3.3.1	3.3.1	
• Tasks	X			3.3.2	3.3.2	IEEE Std 1074-1995
• Responsibilities	X			3.3.3	3.3.3	
—Identification of documents to be used for development, verification, use and maintenance of the products covered by SQAP and how they are to be evaluated	X			3.4	3.4	
• SRS	X			3.4.2.1	3.4.2.1	IEEE Std 830-1993
• SDD	X			3.4.2.2	3.4.2.2	IEEE Std 1016-1987
• SVVP	X			3.4.2.3	3.4.2.3	IEEE Std 829-1983, IEEE Std 1008-1987, IEEE Std 1012-1986
• SVVR	X			3.4.2.4	3.4.2.4	
• User documentation	X			3.4.2.5	3.4.2.5	IEEE Std 1063-1987

Table A.1—Summary of the SQAP and related standards *(continued)*

Item	Shall	Should	May	IEEE Std 730-1989	IEEE Std 730.1-1995	Other standards[a]
• SCMP	X			3.4.2.6	3.4.2.6	IEEE Std 828-1990, IEEE Std 1042-1987, IEEE Std 1033-1985
• SDP			X	3.4.3(1)	3.4.3.1	
• SPM			X	3.4.3(2)	3.4.3.2	
• SPMP			X	3.4.3(3)	3.4.3.3	IEEE Std 1058.1-1987
• SMM			X	3.4.3(4)	3.4.3.4	IEEE Std 1219-1992
• User requirements statements			X	—	3.4.4.1	
• External interface specifications			X	—	3.4.4.2	
• Internal interface specifications			X	—	3.4.4.3	
• Operations manual			X	—	3.4.4.4	
• Installation manual			X	—	3.4.4.5	
• Training manual			X	—	3.4.4.6	
• Training plan			X	—	3.4.4.7	
• Software metrics plan			X	—	3.4.4.8	IEEE Std 982.1-1988, IEEE Std 982.2-1988
• Software security plan			X	—	3.4.4.9	
—Identification of standards, practices, conventions, and metrics, and statement of compliance check methods	X			3.5	3.5	
• Documentation standards	X			3.5.2(1)	3.5.2	IEEE Std 830-1993
• Logic structure standards	X			3.2.2(2)	3.5.2	
• Coding standards	X			3.5.2(3)	3.5.2	
• Commentary standards	X			3.5.2(4)	3.5.2	
• Testing standards and practices	X			3.5.2(5)	3.5.2	
• Metrics	X			3.5.2(6)	3.5.2	
• Requirements		X		—	3.5.2.1	
• Design		X		—	3.5.2.2	
• Implementation		X		—	3.5.2.3	

Table A.1—Summary of the SQAP and related standards *(continued)*

Item	Shall	Should	May	IEEE Std 730-1989	IEEE Std 730.1-1995	Other standards[a]
• Test		X		—	3.5.2.4	IEEE Std 829-1983, IEEE Std 1008-1987
• Maintenance		X		—	3.5.2.5	IEEE Std 1219-1992
• Documentation		X		—	3.5.2.6	
• Metrics				—	3.5.2.7	IEEE Std 982.1-1988, IEEE Std 982.2-1988, IEEE Std 1045-1992, IEEE Std 1061-1992
—Reviews and audits	X			3.6	3.6	
—Definition of technical review and audits and means of accomplishment	X			3.6.1	3.6.1	IEEE Std 1028-1988, IEEE Std 1074-1995
—Conduct the following reviews:	X			3.6.2	3.6.2	
• SRR	X			3.6.2.1	3.6.2.1	IEEE Std 830-1993
• PDR	X			3.6.2.2	3.6.2.2	
• CDR	X			3.6.2.3	3.6.2.3	
• SVVPR	X			3.6.2.4	3.6.2.4	
• Functional audit	X			3.6.2.5	3.6.2.5	
• Physical audit	X			3.6.2.6	3.6.2.6	
• In-Process audits	X			3.6.2.7	3.6.2.7	
• Managerial reviews	X			3.6.2.8	3.6.2.8	
• SCMPR	X			3.6.2.9	3.6.2.9	
• Post mortem	X			3.6.2.10	3.6.2.10	
• UDR			X	3.6.3	3.6.3.1	
• Quality assurance audit			X	—	3.6.3.2	ISO 9000-1: 1994
—Test	X			3.7	3.7	IEEE Std 829-1995, IEEE Std 1008-1987
—Describe problem reporting and corrective action	X			3.8	3.8	
—Describe tools, techniques and methodologies to be used	X			3.9	3.9	IEEE Std 1209-1992
—Definition of code control methods and facilities	X			3.10	3.10	

Table A.1—Summary of the SQAP and related standards *(continued)*

Item	Shall	Should	May	IEEE Std 730-1989	IEEE Std 730.1-1995	Other standards[a]
—Definition of media control methods and facilities	X			3.11	3.11	
• Unauthorized access	X			3.11(a)	3.11.1	
• Damage and degradation	X			3.11(b)	3.11.2	
—Provision for supplier quality assurance methods	X			3.12	3.12	
—Identification of SQA records collection, maintenance, and retention	X			3.13	3.13	
—Training	X			3.14	3.14	
—Risk management	X			3.15	3.15	
—Implementing an SQAP		X		—	4	
—Evaluating an SQAP		X		—	5	
—Modifying an SQAP		X		—	6	

[a]Note that reaffirmation dates are not included in this table. For information about references, see clause 2 of the standard.

IEEE Std 828-1998

(Revision of
IEEE Std 828-1990)

IEEE Standard for Software Configuration Management Plans

Sponsor

**Software Engineering Standards Committee
of the
IEEE Computer Society**

Approved 25 June 1998

IEEE-SA Standards Board

Abstract: The minimum required contents of a Software Configuration Management Plan (SCMP) are established, and the specific activities to be addressed and their requirements for any portion of a software product's life cycle are defined.
Keywords: configuration control board, configuration items, software configuration management, software configuration management activities

The Institute of Electrical and Electronics Engineers, Inc.
345 East 47th Street, New York, NY 10017-2394, USA

IEEE Standards documents are developed within the IEEE Societies and the Standards Coordinating Committees of the IEEE Standards Association (IEEE-SA) Standards Board. Members of the committees serve voluntarily and without compensation. They are not necessarily members of the Institute. The standards developed within IEEE represent a consensus of the broad expertise on the subject within the Institute as well as those activities outside of IEEE that have expressed an interest in participating in the development of the standard.

Use of an IEEE Standard is wholly voluntary. The existence of an IEEE Standard does not imply that there are no other ways to produce, test, measure, purchase, market, or provide other goods and services related to the scope of the IEEE Standard. Furthermore, the viewpoint expressed at the time a standard is approved and issued is subject to change brought about through developments in the state of the art and comments received from users of the standard. Every IEEE Standard is subjected to review at least every five years for revision or reaffirmation. When a document is more than five years old and has not been reaffirmed, it is reasonable to conclude that its contents, although still of some value, do not wholly reflect the present state of the art. Users are cautioned to check to determine that they have the latest edition of any IEEE Standard.

Comments for revision of IEEE Standards are welcome from any interested party, regardless of membership affiliation with IEEE. Suggestions for changes in documents should be in the form of a proposed change of text, together with appropriate supporting comments.

Interpretations: Occasionally questions may arise regarding the meaning of portions of standards as they relate to specific applications. When the need for interpretations is brought to the attention of IEEE, the Institute will initiate action to prepare appropriate responses. Since IEEE Standards represent a consensus of all concerned interests, it is important to ensure that any interpretation has also received the concurrence of a balance of interests. For this reason, IEEE and the members of its societies and Standards Coordinating Committees are not able to provide an instant response to interpretation requests except in those cases where the matter has previously received formal consideration.Comments on standards and requests for interpretations should be addressed to:

Secretary, IEEE-SA Standards Board
445 Hoes LaneP.O. Box 1331
Piscataway, NJ 08855-1331
USA

Note: Attention is called to the possibility that implementation of this standard may require use of subject matter covered by patent rights. By publication of this standard, no position is taken with respect to the existence or validity of any patent rights in connection therewith. The IEEE shall not be responsible for identifying patents for which a license may be required by an IEEE standard or for conducting inquiries into the legal validity or scope of those patents that are brought to its attention.

Authorization to photocopy portions of any individual standard for internal or personal use is granted by the Institute of Electrical and Electronics Engineers, Inc., provided that the appropriate fee is paid to Copyright Clearance Center. To arrange for payment of licensing fee, please contact Copyright Clearance Center, Customer Service, 222 Rosewood Drive, Danvers, MA 01923 USA; (508) 750-8400. Permission to photocopy portions of any individual standard for educational classroom use can also be obtained through the Copyright Clearance Center.

Introduction

(This introduction is not part of IEEE Std 828-1998, IEEE Standard for Software Configuration Management Plans.)

This standard is concerned with the activity of planning for software configuration management (SCM). SCM activities, whether planned or not, are performed on all software development projects; planning makes these activities more effective. Good planning results in a document that captures the planning information, makes the information the property of the project, communicates to all who are affected, and provides a basis for ongoing planning.

SCM is a formal engineering discipline that, as part of overall system configuration management, provides the methods and tools to identify and control the software throughout its development and use. SCM activities include the identification and establishment of baselines; the review, approval, and control of changes; the tracking and reporting of such changes; the audits and reviews of the evolving software product; and the control of interface documentation and project supplier SCM.

SCM is the means through which the integrity and traceability of the software system are recorded, communicated, and controlled during both development and maintenance. SCM also supports reduction of overall software life cycle cost by providing a foundation for product and project measurement.

SCM constitutes good engineering practice for all software projects, whether phased development, rapid prototyping, or ongoing maintenance. It enhances the reliability and quality of software by

— Providing a structure for identifying and controlling documentation, code, interfaces, and databases to support all life cycle phases

— Supporting a chosen development/maintenance methodology that fits the requirements, standards, policies, organization, and management philosophy

— Producing management and product information concerning the status of baselines, change control, tests, releases, audits, etc.

The readers of this document are referred to Annex A for guidelines for using this document to meet the requirements of IEEE/EIA 12207.1-1997, IEEE/EIA Guide for Information Technology—Software life cycle processes—Life cycle data.

This standard was prepared by the Life Cycle Data Harmonization Working Group of the Software Engineering Standards Committee of the IEEE Computer Society. At the time this standard was approved, the working group consisted of the following members:

Leonard L. Tripp, *Chair*

Edward Byrne	Dennis Lawrence	Terry Rout
Paul R. Croll	David Maibor	Richard Schmidt
Perry DeWeese	Ray Milovanovic	Norman F. Schneidewind
Robin Fralick	James Moore	David Schultz
Marilyn Ginsberg-Finner	Timothy Niesen	Basil Sherlund
John Harauz	Dennis Rilling	Peter Voldner
Mark Henley		Ronald Wade

The following persons were on the balloting committee:

Syed Ali	Kathleen L. Briggs	Antonio M. Cicu
Theodore K. Atchinson	M. Scott Buck	Theo Clarke
Leo Beltracchi	Michael Caldwell	Sylvain Clermont
H. Ronald Berlack	James E. Cardow	Rosemary Coleman
Richard E. Biehl	Jaya R. Carl	Virgil Lee Cooper
Michael A. Blackledge	Enrico A. Carrara	W. W. Geoff Cozens
Sandro Bologna	Lawrence Catchpole	Paul R. Croll
Juris Borzovs	Keith Chan	Patricia W. Daggett

Contents

IEEE Standard for Software Configuration Management Plans

1. Overview

1.1 Scope

This standard establishes the minimum required contents of a Software Configuration Management (SCM) Plan (the Plan). It is supplemented by IEEE Std 1042-1987,[1] which provides approaches to good software configuration management planning. This standard applies to the entire life cycle of critical software; e.g., where failure would impact safety or cause large financial or social losses. It also applies to noncritical software and to software already developed. The application of this standard is not restricted to any form, class, or type of software.

The Plan documents what SCM activities are to be done, how they are to be done, who is responsible for doing specific activities, when they are to happen, and what resources are required. It can address SCM activities over any portion of a software product's life cycle.

The content of the Plan is identified in Clause 4 of this standard. The required information is indicated by the words "shall" and "required." Additional optional information is also identified as appropriate. The user of this standard, however, is expected to expand and supplement the minimum requirements as necessary for the development environment, specific industry, organization, and project. Tailoring of a plan in conformance with this standard is described in Clause 5.

The primary users of this standard are assumed to be those planning SCM activities or performing SCM audits.

In considering adoption of this standard, regulatory bodies should be aware that specific application of this standard may already be covered by one or more IEEE standards documents relating to quality assurance, definitions, or other matters (see IEEE Std 730-1998). It is not the purpose of this standard to supersede, revise, or amend existing standards directed to specific industries or applications.

---

[1]Information on references can be found in Clause 2.

2. References

This standard shall be used in conjunction with the following publications:

IEEE Std 610.12-1990, IEEE Standard Glossary of Software Engineering Terminology.[2]

IEEE Std 730-1998, IEEE Standard for Software Quality Assurance Plans.

IEEE Std 1042-1987 (Reaff 1993), IEEE Guide to Software Configuration Management.

3. Definitions and acronyms

3.1 Definitions

The definitions below describe specific terms as used within the context of this standard.

3.1.1 control point (project control point): A project agreed on point in time or times when specified agreements or controls are applied to the software configuration items being developed, e.g., an approved baseline or release of a specified document/code.

3.1.2 release: The formal notification and distribution of an approved version.

Additional relevant terms are defined in IEEE Std 610.12-1990 and are as follows: baseline, component, configuration, configuration audit, configuration control, configuration control board, configuration identification, configuration item, configuration management, configuration status accounting, interface, interface control, software, software library, software life cycle, unit, version.

The term "the Plan" is used throughout this standard to refer to the Software Configuration Management Plan.

3.2 Acronyms

The following acronyms appear within the text of this standard:

    CCB   configuration control board
    CI   configuration item
    SCM   software configuration management

4. The Software Configuration Management Plan

SCM planning information shall be partitioned into the six classes described in Table 1. The referenced subclauses of the standard provide the reader with detailed requirements for each class of information.

SCM planning information may be presented in any format, sequence, or location that is meaningful to the intended users of the Plan with the following restrictions:

    a)   A document with the title "Software Configuration Management Plan" shall exist either in stand-alone form or embedded in another project document.

---

[2]IEEE publications are available from the Institute of Electrical and Electronics Engineers, 445 Hoes Lane, P.O. Box 1331, Piscataway, NJ 08855-1331, USA (http://www.standards.ieee.org/).

b) This document shall contain all SCM planning information either by inclusion or by reference to other locations, such as other documents or automated systems.

c) A format for this document shall be defined.

The writer of the Plan shall use the sequence of sections specified in Table 1 unless a different format has been defined in the Introduction of the Plan (see 4.1).

Table 1—SCM classes of information

Class of information	Description	IEEE Std 828-1998 reference	Plan reference
Introduction	Describes the Plan's purpose, scope of application, key terms, and references	4.1	1
SCM management	(Who?) Identifies the responsibilities and authorities for accomplishing the planned activities	4.2	2
SCM activities	(What?) Identifies all activities to be performed in applying to the project	4.3	3
SCM schedules	(When?) Identifies the required coordination of SCM activities with the other activities in the project	4.4	4
SCM resources	(How?) Identifies tools and physical and human resources required for execution of the Plan	4.5	5
SCM plan maintenance	Identifies how the Plan will be kept current while in effect	4.6	6

4.1 Introduction

Introduction information provides a simplified overview of the SCM activities so that those approving, those performing, and those interacting with SCM can obtain a clear understanding of the Plan. The introduction shall include four topics: the purpose of the Plan, the scope, the definition of key terms, and references.

The purpose shall briefly address why the Plan exists and who the intended audience is.

The scope shall address SCM applicability, limitations, and assumptions on which the Plan is based. The following items shall be included:

a) Overview description of the software development project;

b) Identification of the software CI(s) to which SCM will be applied;

c) Identification of other software to be included as part of the Plan (e.g., support or test software);

d) Relationship of SCM to the hardware or system configuration management activities for the project;

e) The degree of formality, depth of control, and portion of the software life cycle for applying SCM on this project;

f) Limitations, such as time constraints, that apply to the Plan;

g) Assumptions that might have an impact on the cost, schedule, or ability to perform defined SCM activities (e.g., assumptions of the degree of customer participation in SCM activities or the availability of automated aids).

Key terms shall be defined as they apply to the Plan in order to establish a common terminology among all users of the Plan.

All references in the Plan to policies, directives, procedures, standards, terminology, and related documents shall be uniquely identified to enable retrieval by users of the Plan.

4.2 SCM management

SCM management information describes the allocation of responsibilities and authorities for SCM activities to organizations and individuals within the project structure.

SCM management information shall include three topics: the project organization(s) within which SCM is to apply, the SCM responsibilities of these organizations, and references to the SCM policies and directives that apply to this project.

4.2.1 Organization

The organizational context, both technical and managerial, within which the planned SCM activities are to be implemented shall be described. The Plan shall identify the following:

a)   All organizational units that participate in or are responsible for any SCM activity on the project;
b)   The functional roles of these organizational units within the project structure;
c)   Relationships between organizational units.

Organizational units may consist of a vendor and customer, a prime contractor and subcontractors, or different groups within one organization. Organization charts, supplemented by statements of function and relationships, can be an effective way of presenting this information.

4.2.2 SCM responsibilities

The allocation of SCM activities to organizational units shall be specified. For each activity listed within SCM activities (see 4.3), the name of the organizational unit or job title to perform this activity shall be provided. A matrix that relates the organizations defined above to the SCM functions, activities, and tasks can be useful for documenting the SCM responsibilities.

For any review board or special organization established for performing SCM activities on this project, the Plan shall describe its

a)   Purpose and objectives;
b)   Membership and affiliations;
c)   Period of effectivity;
d)   Scope of authority;
e)   Operational procedures.

4.2.3 Applicable policies, directives, and procedures

Any external constraints placed on the Plan by other policies, directives, and procedures shall be identified. For each, its impact and effect on the Plan shall be stated.

4.3 SCM activities

SCM activities information identifies all functions and tasks required to manage the configuration of the software system as specified in the scope of the Plan. Both technical and managerial SCM activities shall be identified. General project activities that have SCM implications shall be described from the SCM perspective.

SCM activities are traditionally grouped into four functions: configuration identification, configuration control, status accounting, and configuration audits and reviews. The information requirements for each function are identified in 4.3.1 through 4.3.4.

Due to their high risk nature, the requirements for interface control and subcontractor/vendor control activities are identified separately in 4.3.5 and 4.3.6.

4.3.1 Configuration identification

Configuration identification activities shall identify, name, and describe the documented physical and functional characteristics of the code, specifications, design, and data elements to be controlled for the project. The documents are acquired for configuration control. Controlled items may be intermediate and final outputs (such as executable code, source code, user documentation, program listings, databases, test cases, test plans, specifications, and management plans) and elements of the support environment (such as compilers, operating systems, programming tools, and test beds).

The Plan shall identify the project configuration items (CI) and their structures at each project control point. The Plan shall state how each CI and its versions are to be uniquely named and describe the activities performed to define, track, store, and retrieve CIs. Information required for configuration identification (see Figure 1) is specified in 4.3.1.1 through 4.3.1.3.

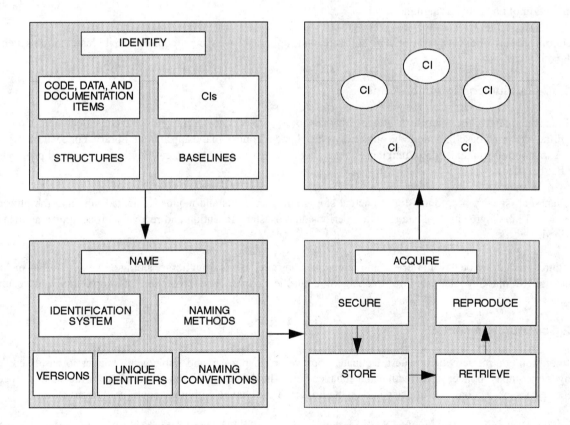

Figure 1—Configuration identification processes

4.3.1.1 Identifying configuration items

The Plan shall record the items to be controlled, the project CIs, and their definitions as they evolve or are selected. The Plan shall also describe how the list of items and the structures are to be maintained for the project. As a minimum, all CIs that are to be delivered shall be listed.

Appropriate baselines shall be defined at control points within the project life cycle in terms of the following:

a) The event that creates the baseline;
b) The items that are to be controlled in the baseline;
c) The procedures used to establish and change the baseline;
d) The authority required to approve changes to the approved baselined documents.

A means of identifying changes and associating them with the affected CIs and the related baseline shall be specified.

4.3.1.2 Naming configuration items

The Plan shall specify an identification system for assigning unique identifiers to each item to be controlled. It shall also specify how different versions of each are to be uniquely identified. Identification methods could include naming conventions and version numbers and letters.

The Plan shall describe the methods for naming controlled items for purposes of storage, retrieval, tracking, reproduction, and distribution. Activities may include version marking, labeling of documentation and executable software, serialization and altered item marking for executable code or data embedded on a microchip, and identification of physical packaging.

Subcontracted software, vendor proprietary software, and support software may require special identification schemes and labeling.

4.3.1.3 Acquiring configuration items

The Plan shall identify the controlled software libraries for the project and describe how the code, documentation, and data of the identified baselines are to be physically placed under control in the appropriate library. For each library the format, location, documentation requirements, receiving and inspection requirements, and access control procedures shall be specified.

The Plan shall specify procedures for the actual storage of documents and magnetic media, including the physical marking and labeling of items. Data retention periods and disaster prevention and recovery procedures may also be described.

Procedures shall describe how to retrieve and reproduce controlled items from library storage. These activities include verification of marking and labeling, tracking of controlled copies, and protection of proprietary and security information.

4.3.2 Configuration control

Configuration control activities request, evaluate, approve or disapprove, and implement changes to baselined CIs. Changes encompass both error correction and enhancement. The degree of formality necessary for the change process depends on the project baseline affected and on the impact of the change within the configuration structure.

For each project software library identified according to 4.3.1.3, the Plan shall describe the change controls imposed on the baselined CIs. The Plan shall define the following sequence of specific steps:

a) Identification and documentation of the need for a change;
b) Analysis and evaluation of a change request;
c) Approval or disapproval of a request;
d) Verification, implementation, and release of a change.

The Plan shall identify the records to be used for tracking and documenting this sequence of steps for each change. Any differences in handling changes based on the origin of the request shall be explicitly documented.

4.3.2.1 Requesting changes

The Plan shall specify the procedures for requesting a change to a baselined CI and the information to be documented for the request. As a minimum, the information recorded for a proposed change shall contain the following:

a) The name(s) and version(s) of the CIs where the problem appears;
b) Originator's name and organization;
c) Date of request;
d) Indication of urgency;
e) The need for the change;
f) Description of the requested change.

Additional information, such as priority or classification, may be included to clarify the significance of the request and to assist in its analysis and evaluation. Other information, such as change request number, status, and disposition, may be recorded for change tracking.

4.3.2.2 Evaluating changes

The Plan shall specify the analysis required to determine the impact of the proposed change and the procedures for reviewing the results of the analysis. Changes should be evaluated according to their effect on the deliverable and their impact on project resources.

4.3.2.3 Approving or disapproving changes

The Plan shall identify each configuration control board (CCB) and its level of authority for approving proposed changes. A CCB may be an individual or a group. Multiple levels of CCBs may be specified, depending upon the degree of system or project complexity and upon the project baseline involved. When multiple CCBs are used, the Plan shall specify how the proper level is determined for a change request, including any variations during the project life cycle.

For any CCB utilized, the Plan shall indicate its level of authority and its responsibilities as defined in 4.2.2.

4.3.2.4 Implementing changes

The Plan shall specify the activities for verifying and implementing an approved change. The information recorded for the completion of a change shall contain the following as a minimum:

a) The associated change request(s);
b) The names and versions of the affected items;
c) Verification date and responsible party;
d) Release or installation date and responsible party;
e) The identifier of the new version.

Additional information, such as software fault metrics or identification of the supporting software used to implement the change, may be included.

The Plan shall also specify activities for release planning and control, i.e., coordinating multiple changes, reconfiguring the CIs, and delivering a new baseline.

4.3.3 Configuration status accounting

Configuration status accounting activities record and report the status of project CIs.

The Plan shall include information on the following:

a) What data elements are to be tracked and reported for baselines and changes;
b) What types of status accounting reports are to be generated and their frequency;
c) How information is to be collected, stored, processed, and reported;
d) How access to the status data is to be controlled.

If an automated system is used for any status accounting activity, its function shall be described or referenced.

The following minimum data elements shall be tracked and reported for each CI: its initial approved version, the status of requested changes, and the implementation status of approved changes. The level of detail and specific data required may vary according to the information needs of the project and the customer.

4.3.4 Configuration audits and reviews

Configuration audits determine to what extent the actual CI reflects the required physical and functional characteristics. Configuration reviews are management tools for establishing a baseline.

The Plan shall identify the configuration audits and reviews to be held for the project. At a minimum, a configuration audit shall be performed on a CI prior to its release.

For each planned configuration audit or review, the Plan shall define the following:

a) Its objective;
b) The CIs under audit or review;
c) The schedule of audit or review tasks;
d) The procedures for conducting the audit or review;
e) The participants by job title;
f) Documentation required to be available for review or to support the audit or review;
g) The procedure for recording any deficiencies and reporting corrective actions;
h) The approval criteria and the specific action(s) to occur upon approval.

4.3.5 Interface control

Interface control activities coordinate changes to the project CIs with changes to interfacing items outside the scope of the Plan. Hardware, system software and support software, as well as other projects and deliverables, should be examined for potential interfacing effects on the project.

The Plan shall identify the external items to which the project software interfaces. For each interface the Plan shall define the following:

a) The nature of the interface;
b) The affected organizations;
c) How the interface code, documentation, and data are to be controlled;
d) How the interface control documents are approved and released into a specified baseline.

For any CCB established to control interfaces, the Plan shall identify its responsibilities and procedures as specified in 4.2.2.

4.3.6 Subcontractor/vendor control

Subcontractor/vendor control activities incorporate items developed outside the project environment into the project CIs. Included are software developed by contract and software acquired in its finished form. Special attention should be directed to these SCM activities due to the added organizational and legal relationships.

For both subcontracted and acquired software, the Plan shall define the activities to incorporate the externally developed items into the project CIs and to coordinate changes to these items with their development organizations.

For subcontracted software, the Plan shall describe the following:

a) What SCM requirements, including an SCM Plan, are to be part of the subcontractor's agreement;
b) How the subcontractor will be monitored for compliance;
c) What configuration audits and reviews of subcontractor items will be held;
d) How external code, documentation, and data will be tested, verified, accepted, and merged with the project software;
e) How proprietary items will be handled for security of information and traceability of ownership (e.g., copyright and royalties);
f) How changes are to be processed, including the subcontractor's participation.

For acquired software, the Plan shall describe how the software will be received, tested, and placed under SCM; how changes to the supplier's software are to be processed; and whether and how the supplier will participate in the project's change management process. Acquired software can come from a vendor, a subcontractor, a customer, another project, or other source.

4.4 SCM schedules

SCM schedule information establishes the sequence and coordination for the identified SCM activities and for all events affecting the Plan's implementation.

The Plan shall state the sequence and dependencies among all SCM activities and the relationship of key SCM activities to project milestones or events. The schedule shall cover the duration of the Plan and contain all major milestones of the project related to SCM activities. SCM milestones shall include establishment of a configuration baseline, implementation of change control procedures, and the start and completion dates for a configuration audit.

Schedule information shall be expressed as absolute dates, as dates relative to either SCM or project milestones, or as a simple sequence of events. Graphic representation can be particularly appropriate for conveying this information.

4.5 SCM resources

SCM resource information identifies the software tools, techniques, equipment, personnel, and training necessary for the implementation of the specified SCM activities.

SCM can be performed by a combination of software tools and manual procedures. Tools can be SCM-specific or embedded in general project aids; they can be standard organizational resources or ones specially acquired or built for this project. Tools can be applied to library structure and access control; documentation development and tracking; code control; baseline system generation; change processing, communication and authorization; change/problem tracking and status reporting; archiving, retention, and retrieval of controlled items; or the SCM planning process itself.

For each type of SCM activity identified, the Plan shall specify what tools, techniques, equipment, personnel, and training are required and bow each resource will be provided or obtained.

For each software tool, whether developed within the project or brought in from outside the project, the Plan shall describe or reference its functions and shall identify the configuration controls to be placed on the tool.

4.6 SCM plan maintenance

SCM plan maintenance information identifies the activities and responsibilities necessary to ensure continued SCM planning during the life cycle of the project. The Plan shall state the following:

a) Who is responsible for monitoring the Plan;
b) How frequently updates are to be performed;
c) How changes to the Plan are to be evaluated and approved;
d) How changes to the Plan are to be made and communicated.

The Plan should be reviewed at the start of each project software phase, changed accordingly, and approved and distributed to the project team.

If the Plan has been constructed with detailed procedures documented elsewhere in appendixes or references, different maintenance mechanisms for those procedures may be appropriate.

5. Tailoring of the plan

This standard permits significant flexibility in preparing an SCM Plan. A successful Plan reflects its project environment. It should be written in terms familiar to its users and should be consistent with the development and procurement processes of the project.

To conform to the requirements set forth in other applicable standards or to accommodate local practices, a Plan may be tailored upward, to add information, or tailored to use a specified format. The Plan may also be tailored downward, omitting information required by this standard, when specific standard requirements are identified as not applicable to this project.

5.1 Upward tailoring

Some information requirements applicable to a particular project may not be stated in this standard due to its scope of establishing the minimum required contents of an SCM Plan. If additional requirements are applicable to the project, the Plan shall so state these additions as part of the Introduction and indicate the reason for their insertion. A cost-benefits analysis should be completed for each additional requirement. Requirements that are additional should be agreed on by all affected project functions and the parties responsible for approval of the plan.

5.2 Downward tailoring

Some information requirements stated in this standard may not apply to a particular project due to the project's limited scope, low complexity, or unusual environment. If a requirement is not applicable to the project, the Plan shall so state this deletion as part of the Introduction and indicate the reason for removal. Requirements that are inapplicable should be agreed upon by all affected project functions and all parties responsible for approval of the Plan.

The Plan shall omit none of the six major classes of information. Detailed information may be omitted as indicated above but within the limits of the consistency criteria stated in Clause 6.

If certain information has not been decided on or is unavailable at the time the Plan is initially approved, the Plan shall mark those areas or sections as "to be determined" and shall indicate, as part of Plan maintenance, information on how and when further information will be provided.

5.3 Format

The information may be presented in the Plan in any sequence or presentation style deemed suitable for the Plan's users. To achieve consistency and convenience within a single organization or industry segment, a standard format for SCM plans is desirable and appropriate. To customize this standard for a particular group of users, a supplement to the standard specifying Plan structure and standard terminology may be used.

6. Conformance to the standard

An SCM Plan shall satisfy the criteria in 6.1 through 6.4 in order to conform with this standard.

6.1 Minimum information

The Plan shall include the six classes of SCM information identified in Clause 4: introduction, management, activities, schedules, resources, and plan maintenance. Within each class, all of the required information stated in Clause 4 of this standard, as indicated by the words "shall" and "required," shall be documented within the Plan. If certain required information is not applicable, the reasons shall be so stated. If a sequence of information other than the sequence of this standard is used, an explicit cross-reference between the Plan and the standard shall be provided.

6.2 Presentation format

One document, section title, or such reference shall exist that is specifically labeled "Software Configuration Management Plan." Within this document, each of the six classes of information shall be included. While the information may be provided in a number of presentation styles, the requirement is to provide all Plan information and references in a single document.

6.3 Consistency criteria

The documented information shall satisfy the following consistency criteria:

a) All activities defined in the Plan (see 4.3.1 through 4.3.6) shall be assigned to an organizational unit (see 4.2.2).
b) All activities defined shall have resources identified to accomplish the activities (see 4.5).
c) All CIs identified in the Plan (see 4.3.1) shall have defined processes for baseline establishment and change control (see 4.3.2).

6.4 Conformance declaration

If the preceding criteria are met, then the conformance of any SCM planning documentation with this standard may be stated accordingly: "This SCM Plan conforms with the requirements of IEEE Std 828-1998."

Annex A

(informative)

Cross-reference to IEEE Std 1042-1987

Clause in IEEE Std 828-1998	Clause in IEEE Std 1042-1987
1. Overview	1. Introduction
—	2. SCM Disciplines in Software Management
4. The Software Configuration Management Plan	3. Software Configuration Management Plans
4.1 Introduction	3.1 Introduction
4.2 SCM management	3.2 Management
4.3 SCM activities	3.3 SCM Activities
4.3.1 Configuration identification	3.3.1 Configuration Identification
4.3.2 Configuration control	3.3.2 Configuration Control
4.3.3 Configuration status accounting	3.3.3 Configuration Status Accounting
4.3.4 Configuration audits and reviews	3.3.4 Audits and Reviews
4.3.5 Interface control	3.2.3 Interface Control
4.3.6 Subcontractor/vendor control	3.5 Supplier Control
4.4 SCM schedules	3.2.4 SCM Plan Implementation
4.5 SCM resources	3.4 Tools, Techniques and Methodologies
4.6 SCM plan maintenance	2.5 The Planning of SCM
5. Tailoring of the plan	2.5 The Planning of SCM
6. Conformance to the standard	2.5 The Planning of SCM

Annex B

(informative)

Guidelines for compliance with IEEE/EIA 12207.1-1997

B.1 Overview

The Software Engineering Standards Committee (SESC) of the IEEE Computer Society has endorsed the policy of adopting international standards. In 1995, the international standard, ISO/IEC 12207, Information technology—Software life cycle processes, was completed. The standard establishes a common framework for software life cycle processes, with well-defined terminology, that can be referenced by the software industry.

In 1995 the SESC evaluated ISO/IEC 12207 and decided that the standard should be adopted and serve as the basis for life cycle processes within the IEEE Software Engineering Collection. The IEEE adaptation of ISO/IEC 12207 is IEEE/EIA 12207.0-1996. It contains ISO/IEC 12207 and the following additions: improved compliance approach, life cycle process objectives, life cycle data objectives, and errata.

The implementation of ISO/IEC 12207 within the IEEE also includes the following:

— IEEE/EIA 12207.1-1997, IEEE/EIA Guide for Information Technology—Software life cycle processes—Life cycle data;

— IEEE/EIA 12207.2-1997, IEEE/EIA Guide for Information Technology—Software life cycle processes—Implementation considerations; and

— Additions to 11 SESC standards (i.e., IEEE Stds 730, 828, 829, 830, 1012, 1016, 1058, 1062, 1219, 1233, 1362) to define the correlation between the data produced by existing SESC standards and the data produced by the application of IEEE/EIA 12207.1-1997.

NOTE — Although IEEE/EIA 12207.1-1997 is a guide, it also contains provisions for application as a standard with specific compliance requirements. This annex treats IEEE/EIA 12207.1-1997 as a standard.

B.1.1 Scope and purpose

Both this standard and IEEE/EIA 12207.1-1997 place requirements on a Software Configuration Management Plan (SCMP). The purpose of this annex is to explain the relationship between the two sets of requirements so that users producing documents intended to comply with both standards may do so.

B.2 Correlation

This clause explains the relationship between this standard and IEEE/EIA 12207.0-1996 in the following areas: terminology, process, and life cycle data.

B.2.1 Terminology correlation

The two standards use similar terms in similar ways. Having first been published in the early 1980s, this standard retains some of the flavor of its time and the assumptions then prevalent about software engineering, but for the most part this does not affect the use or meaning of terms. The major terminology difference is that IEEE/EIA 12207.0-1996 uses the term "configuration evaluation" for what this standard calls "configuration audit." Some of the underlying assumptions may differ between the two standards, but the terms are similar.

B.2.2 Process correlation

This standard places no explicit requirements on process. However, the information required by its SCMP makes implicit assumptions regarding process, a process that is more prescriptive than that of IEEE/EIA 12207.0-1996. IEEE/EIA 12207.0-1996 requires a certain body of information without stipulating any particular sequence of events or documents. Generally, fulfilling the implied process requirements of this standard would go beyond the requirements of IEEE/EIA 12207.0-1996 but would not violate its requirements. IEEE/EIA 12207.0-1996 is more explicit in recognizing release management as an identifiable configuration management activity than is this standard (see Table B-3).

B.2.3 Life cycle data correlation

The information required in an SCMP by this standard and the information required in an SCMP by IEEE/EIA 12207.1-1997 are similar. It is reasonable to expect that a single document could comply with both standards. The main difference is that this standard specifies a particular format, while IEEE/EIA 12207.1-1997 does not. Details are provided in the clause below.

The requirements in IEEE/EIA 12207.1-1997 for change request, software configuration index record, and software configuration management records pertain to records and requests associated with SCM but are not discussed in detail in this annex since they relate to the implementation of SCM plans. The IEEE/EIA 12207.1-1997 requirements for records (see 5.4 of IEEE/EIA 12207.1-1997) should be considered when implementing an SCMP. The IEEE/EIA 12207.1-1997 requirements for change request information are largely the same as those described in this standard.

B.3 Document compliance

This clause provides details bearing on a claim that an SCMP complying with this standard would also achieve "document compliance" with the SCMP as prescribed in IEEE/EIA 12207.1-1997. The requirements for document compliance are summarized in a single row of Table 1 of IEEE/EIA 12207.1-1997. That row is reproduced in Table B-1 of this standard.

**Table B-1—Summary of requirements for an SCMP
excerpted from Table 1 of IEEE/EIA 12207.1-1997**

Information item	IEEE/EIA 12207.0-1996 subclause	Kind of documentation	IEEE/EIA 12207.1-1997 subclause	References
Software configuration management plan	6.2.1.1	Plan	6.14	IEEE Std 828-1998 IEEE Std 1042-1987 ISO 10007: 1995

The requirements for document compliance are discussed in the following subclauses:

— B.3.1 discusses compliance with the information requirements noted in column 2 of Table B-1 as prescribed by 6.2.1.1 of IEEE/EIA 12207.0-1996.

— B.3.2 discusses compliance with the generic content guideline (the "kind" of document) noted in column 3 of Table B-1 as a "plan." The generic content guidelines for a "plan" appear in 5.2 of IEEE/EIA 12207.1-1997.

— B.3.3 discusses compliance with the specific requirements for an SCMP noted in column 4 of Table B-1 as prescribed by 6.14 of IEEE/EIA 12207.1-1997.

— B.3.4 discusses compliance with the life cycle data objectives of Annex H of IEEE/EIA 12207.0-1996 as described in 4.2 of IEEE/EIA 12207.1-1997.

B.3.1 Compliance with information requirements of IEEE/EIA 12207.0-1996

The information requirements for an SCMP are those prescribed by 6.2.1.1 of IEEE/EIA 12207.0-1996. In this case, those requirements are substantively identical to those considered in B.3.3 of this standard.

B.3.2 Compliance with generic content guidelines of IEEE/EIA 12207.1-1997

The generic content guidelines for a "plan" in IEEE/EIA 12207.1-1997 are prescribed by 5.2 of IEEE/EIA 12207.1-1997. A complying plan shall achieve the purpose stated in 5.2.1 and include the information listed in 5.2.2 of IEEE/EIA 12207.1-1997.

The purpose of a plan is as follows:

> IEEE/EIA 12207.1-1997, subclause 5.2.1: Purpose: Define when, how, and by whom specific activities are to be performed, including options and alternatives, as required.

An SCMP complying with this standard would achieve the stated purpose.

Any plan complying with IEEE/EIA 12207.1-1997 shall satisfy the generic content requirements provided in 5.2.2 of that standard. Table B-2 of this standard lists the generic content items and, where appropriate, references the clause of this standard that requires the same information.

B.3.3 Compliance with specific content requirements of IEEE/EIA 12207.1-1997

The specific content requirements for an SCMP in IEEE/EIA 12207.1-1997 are prescribed by 6.14 of IEEE/EIA 12207.1-1997. A complying SCMP shall achieve the purpose stated in 6.14.1 and include the information listed in 6.14.3 of IEEE/EIA 12207.1-1997.

The purpose of the SCMP is as follows:

> IEEE/EIA 12207.1-1997, subclause 6.14.1: Purpose: Define the software configuration management activities to be performed during the life cycle of the software. Describe the responsibilities and authorities for accomplishing the planned software configuration management activities. Identify the required coordination of software configuration management activities with other activities of the project. Identify the tools and the physical and human resources required for the execution of the plan.

An SCMP complying with this standard and meeting the additional requirements of Table B-2 and Table B-3 of this standard would achieve the stated purpose.

An SCMP complying with IEEE/EIA12207.1-1997 shall satisfy the specific content requirements provided in 6.14.3 of that standard. The specific content requirements of 6.14.3 reiterate the generic content requirements and specify the generic requirements that shall be satisfied for each of several activities. Table B-3 of this standard lists the activities along with the reference to the clause of this standard that specifically covers the activity.

B.3.4 Compliance with life cycle data characteristics objectives

In addition to the content requirements, life cycle data shall be managed in accordance with the objectives provided in Annex H of IEEE/EIA 12207.0-1996.

Table B-2—Coverage of generic plan requirements by IEEE Std 828-1998

IEEE/EIA 12207.1-1997 generic content	Corresponding clauses of IEEE Std 828-1998	Additions to requirements of IEEE Std 828-1998
a) Date of issue and status	4.6 SCM plan maintenance and 4.3.1 Configuration identification (by implication, assuming the SCMP is among the documents controlled)	—
b) Scope	4.1 Introduction	—
c) Issuing organization	4.2.2 SCM responsibilities	—
d) References	4.1 Introduction (last paragraph) 4.2.3 Applicable policies, directives, and procedures	—
e) Approval authority	4.6 SCM plan maintenance [item c)]	—
f) Planned activities and tasks	4.3 SCM activities	—
g) Macro references (policies or laws that give rise to the need for this plan)	4.2.3 Applicable policies, directives, and procedures	—
h) Micro references (other plans or task descriptions that elaborate details of this plan)	4.2.3 Applicable policies, directives, and procedures	—
i) Schedules	4.4 SCM schedules	—
j) Estimates	4.5 SCM resources	—
k) Resources and their allocation	4.2.1 Organization 4.5 SCM Resources	—
l) Responsibilities and authority	4.2.2 SCM Responsibilities	—
m) Risks	—	Risks and plans for their abatement shall be provided.
n) Quality control measures (NOTE—This includes quality control of the SCMP itself.)	4.6 SCM plan maintenance and 6.3 Consistency criteria (for the SCM Plan itself) 4.3.2.4 Implementing changes ("The Plan shall specify activities for verifying ... an approved change.") 4.3.4 Configuration audits and reviews ("The procedures for conducting the audit or review.") 4.3.5 Interface control ("How the interface control documents are approved ..." 4.3.6 Subcontractor/vendor control ("How external code, documentation, and data will be tested, verified, and accepted, ...")	—
o) Cost	—	The costs of SCM activities and resources shall be provided or referenced.
p) Interfaces among parties involved	4.2.1 Organization 4.3.6 Subcontractor/vendor control	—
q) Environment / infrastructure (including safety needs)	4.5 SCM resources	In addition, the environment/ infrastructure (including safety needs) shall be provided or referenced.
r) Training	4.5 SCM resources	—
s) Glossary	4.1 Introduction	—
t) Change procedures and history (NOTE—This includes the change procedures for the SCMP itself.)	4.6 SCM plan maintenance	—

Table B-3—Coverage of specific SCMP requirements by IEEE Std 828-1998

IEEE/EIA 12207.1-1997 specific content	Corresponding clauses of IEEE Std 828-1998	Additions to requirements of IEEE Std 828-1998
a) Generic plan information	Table B-2	—
i) Configuration management process implementation	4.2 SCM management	—
ii) Configuration identification	4.3.1 Configuration identification	—
iii) Configuration control	4.3.2 Configuration control	—
iv) Configuration status accounting	4.3.3 Configuration status accounting	—
v) Configuration evaluation	4.3.4 Configuration audits and reviews	—
vi) Release management and delivery	4.3.2.4 Implementing changes	The release and delivery of software products and documentation shall be formally controlled. Master copies of code and documentation shall be maintained for the life of the software product. The code and documentation that contain safety or security critical functions shall be handled, stored, packaged, and delivered in accordance with policies of the organizations involved.
b) Relationship with organizations (such as software development or maintenance)	4.2.1 Organization	—

B.4 Conclusion

Users of this standard will probably find compliance with IEEE/EIA 12207.0-1996 to be a relatively straightforward exercise. The analysis suggests that any SCMP complying with this standard and the additions listed in Table B-2 and Table B-3 also complies with the requirements of an SCMP in IEEE/EIA 12207.1-1997. In addition, to comply with IEEE/EIA 12207.1-1997, an SCMP shall support the life cycle data objectives of Annex H of IEEE/EIA 12207.0-1996.

ANSI/IEEE
Std 1008-1987

An American National Standard

IEEE Standard for Software Unit Testing

Sponsor

**Software Engineering Technical Committee
of the
IEEE Computer Society**

Approved December 11, 1986
Reaffirmed December 2, 1993

IEEE Standards Board

Approved July 28, 1986

American National Standards Institute

Foreword

(This Foreword is not a part of ANSI/IEEE Std 1008-1987, IEEE Standard for Software Unit Testing.)

Objectives

This standard's primary objective is to specify a standard approach to software unit testing that can be used as a basis for sound software engineering practice.

A second objective is to describe the software engineering concepts and testing assumptions on which this standard approach is based. This information is contained in Appendix B. Note that Appendix B is not a part of this standard.

A third objective is to provide guidance and resource information to assist with the implementation and usage of the standard unit testing approach. This information is contained in Appendixes A, C, and D. Note that these Appendixes are not a part of this standard.

Motivation

A consensus definition of sound unit testing provides a baseline for the evaluation of specific approaches. It also aids communication by providing a standard decomposition of the unit testing process.

Audience

The primary audience for this standard is unit testers and unit test supervisors. This standard was developed to assist those who provide input to, perform, supervise, monitor, and evaluate unit testing.

Relationship with Other Software Engineering Standards

ANSI/IEEE Std 829-1983, IEEE Standard for Software Test Documentation, describes the basic information needs and results of software testing. This unit testing standard requires the use of the test design specification and test summary report specified in ANSI/IEEE Std 829-1983.

This standard is one of a series aimed at establishing the norms of professional practice in software engineering. Any of the other software engineering standards in the series may be used in conjunction with it.

Terminology

Terminology in this standard is consistent with ANSI/IEEE Std 729-1983, IEEE Standard Glossary of Software Engineering Terminology. To avoid inconsistency when the glossary is revised, its definitions are not repeated in this standard.

The *test unit* referred to in this standard is a specific case of the *test item* referred to in ANSI/IEEE 829-1983. The term *test unit* is used because of this standard's narrower scope.

The use of the term *specification, description,* or *document* refers to data recorded on either an electronic or paper medium.

The word *must* and imperative verb forms identify mandatory material within the standard. The words *should* and *may* identify optional material.

Overview

The unit testing process is composed of three *phases* that are partitioned into a total of eight basic *activities* as follows:

(1) *Perform the test planning*
   (a) Plan the general approach, resources, and schedule
   (b) Determine features to be tested
   (c) Refine the general plan
(2) *Acquire the test set*
   (a) Design the set of tests
   (b) Implement the refined plan and design

(3) *Measure the test unit*
    (a) Execute the test procedures
    (b) Check for termination
    (c) Evaluate the test effort and unit
The major dataflows into and out of the phases are shown in Fig A.

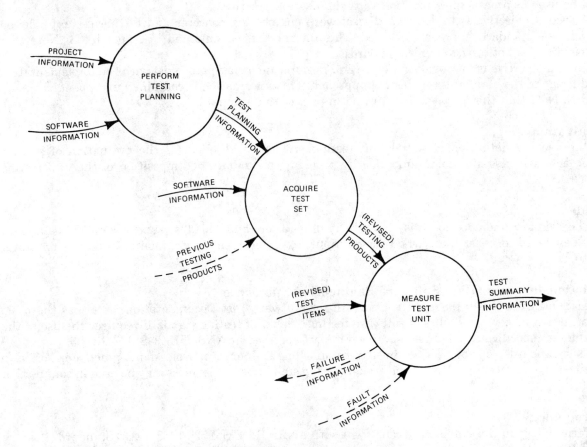

Fig A
Major Dataflows of the Software
Unit Testing Phases

Within a phase, each basic activity is associated with its own set of inputs and outputs and is composed of a series of tasks. The inputs, tasks, and outputs for each activity are specified in the body of this standard.

The set of outputs from all activities must contain sufficient information for the creation of at least two documents—a test design specification and a test summary report. Both documents must conform to the specifications in ANSI/IEEE Std 829-1983.

History

Work on this standard began in February 1983, following announcement of the formation of the task group in the technical and commercial press in late 1982. The project authorization request was approved by the IEEE Standards Board on June 23, 1983 following the second meeting. A total of seven meetings held throughout the United States at three month intervals produced the draft submitted for ballot in March 1985. A total of over 90 persons contributed to the initial development of this standard. Contributors are those individuals who either attended a working-group meeting, submitted written comments on a draft, or both.

This standard was developed by a working group with the following members:

David Gelperin, *Chairperson*   **Pat Wilburn,** *Cochairperson*

A. Frank Ackerman	Ken Foster	John Owens
Craig Adams	John Fox	William Perry
David Adams	Roger Fujii	Gerald Peterson
Jack Barnard	Ross Gagliano	Bob Poston
Wanda Beck	Mark Gerhard	Patricia Powell
Boris Beizer	Ed Gibson	Samuel T. Redwine, Jr
K. Mack Bishop	Therese Gilbertson	Sanford Rosen
Jill E. Boogaard	Gary Girard	Hans Schaefer
Milt Boyd	Keith Gordon	Eric Schnellman
Nathan B. Bradley	Paul Grizenko	Harvey Schock
Martha Branstad	Jeff Grove	Al Sema, Jr
Fletcher Buckley	Ismet Gungor	Harlan Seyfer
John W. Cain	Mark Heinrich	Victor Shtern
Christopher Cooke	Rudolph Hodges	Rick Simkin
L. L. Doc Craddock	R. A. Kessler	Wayne Smith
Palmer Craig	Tom Kurihara	Harry Sneed
Michael Cramer	Costas Labovites	Hugh B. Spillane
Dave Dahlinghaus	Frank LaMonica	Ben Sun
Noah Davids	F. C. Lim	Murray Tabachnick
Henry Davis	Philip C. Marriott	Barbara Taute
Bruce Dawson	Debra L. McCusker	Leonard Tripp
Claudia Dencker	Charlie McCutcheon	William S. Turner III
Michael Deutsch	Rudolf van Megen	John Vance
Judie Divita	Denis Meredith	Guy Vogt
Jim Dobbins	Edward Miller, Jr	Dolores Wallace
David C. Doty	William Milligan	John Walter
Bill Dupras	Marcus Mullins	John C. Wang
Jim Edwards	W. M. Murray	Cheryl Webb
Karen Fairchild	Bruce Nichols	William Wilson
Peter Farrell-Vinay	Dennis Nickle	Ed Yasi
Thom Foote-Lennox	Larry Nitzsche	Natalie C. Yopconka

The following persons were on the balloting committee that approved this document for submission to the IEEE Standards Board:

When the IEEE Standards Board approved this standard on December 11, 1986, it had the following membership:

Contents

An American National Standard

IEEE Standard for
Software Unit Testing

1. Scope and References

1.1 Inside the Scope. Software unit testing is a process that includes the performance of test planning, the acquisition of a test set, and the measurement of a test unit against its requirements. Measuring entails the use of sample data to exercise the unit and the comparison of the unit's actual behavior with its required behavior as specified in the unit's requirements documentation.

This standard defines an integrated approach to systematic and documented unit testing. The approach uses unit design and unit implementation information, in addition to unit requirements, to determine the completeness of the testing.

This standard describes a testing process composed of a hierarchy of phases, activities, and tasks and defines a minimum set of tasks for each activity. Additional tasks may be added to any activity.

This standard requires the performance of each activity. For each task within an activity, this standard requires either that the task be performed, or that previous results be available and be reverified. This standard also requires the preparation of two documents specified in ANSI/IEEE Std 829-1983 [2][1]. These documents are the Test Design Specification and the Test Summary Report.

General unit test planning should occur during overall test planning. This general unit test planning activity is covered by this standard, although the balance of the overall test planning process is outside the scope of this standard.

This standard may be applied to the unit testing of any digital computer software or firmware. However, this standard does *not* specify any class of software or firmware to which it must be applied, nor does it specify any class of software or firmware that must be unit tested. This standard applies to the testing of newly developed and modified units.

This standard is applicable whether or not the unit tester is also the developer.

1.2 Outside the Scope. The results of some overall test planning tasks apply to all testing levels (for example, identify security and privacy constraints). Such tasks are not considered a part of the unit testing process, although they directly affect it.

While the standard identifies a need for failure analysis information and software fault correction, it does not specify a software debugging process.

This standard does not address other components of a comprehensive unit verification and validation process, such as reviews (for example, walkthroughs, inspections), static analysis (for example, consistency checks, data flow analysis), or formal analysis (for example, proof of correctness, symbolic execution).

This standard does not require the use of specific test facilities or tools. This standard does not imply any particular methodology for documentation control, configuration management, quality assurance, or management of the testing process.

1.3 References. This standard shall be used in conjunction with the following publications.

[1] ANSI/IEEE Std 729-1983, IEEE Standard Glossary of Software Engineering Terminology.[2]

[2] ANSI/IEEE Std 829-1983, IEEE Standard for Software Test Documentation.

---

[1] The numbers in brackets correspond to the references listed in 1.3 of this standard.

[2] These publications are available from American National Standards Institute, Sales Department, 1430 Broadway, New York, NY 10018 and from IEEE Service Center, 445 Hoes Lane, Piscataway, NJ 08854.

2. Definitions

This section defines key terms used in this standard but not included in ANSI/IEEE Std 729-1983 [1] or ANSI/IEEE Std 829-1983 [2].

characteristic. *See:* **data characteristic** or **software characteristic.**

data characteristic. An inherent, possibly accidental, trait, quality, or property of data (for example, arrival rates, formats, value ranges, or relationships between field values).

feature. *See:* **software feature.**

incident. *See:* **software test incident.**

nonprocedural programming language. A computer programming language used to express the parameters of a problem rather than the steps in a solution (for example, report writer or sort specification languages). Contrast with **procedural programming language.**

procedural programming language. A computer programming language used to express the sequence of operations to be performed by a computer (for example, COBOL). Contrast with **nonprocedural programming language.**

software characteristic. An inherent, possibly accidental, trait, quality, or property of software (for example, functionality, performance, attributes, design constraints, number of states, lines of branches).

software feature. A software characteristic specified or implied by requirements documentation (for example, functionality, performance, attributes, or design constraints).

software test incident. Any event occuring during the execution of a software test that requires investigation.

state data. Data that defines an internal state of the test unit and is used to establish that state or compare with existing states.

test objective. An identified set of software features to be measured under specified conditions by comparing actual behavior with the required behavior described in the software documentation.

test set architecture. The nested relationships between sets of test cases that directly reflect the hierarchic decomposition of the test objectives.

test unit.[3] A set of one or more computer program modules together with associated control data, (for example, tables), usage procedures, and operating procedures that satisfy the following conditions:

(1) All modules are from a single computer program

(2) At least one of the new or changed modules in the set has not completed the unit test[4]

(3) The set of modules together with its associated data and procedures are the sole object of a testing process

unit. *See:* **test unit.**

unit requirements documentation. Documentation that sets forth the functional, interface, performance, and design constraint requirements for the test unit.

3. Unit Testing Activities

This section specifies the activities involved in the unit testing process and describes the associated input, tasks, and output. The activities described are as follows:

(1) Perform test planning phase

    (a) Plan the general approach, resources, and schedule

    (b) Determine features to be tested

    (c) Refine the general plan

(2) Acquire test set phase

    (a) Design the set of tests

    (b) Implement the refined plan and design

(3) Measure test unit phase

    (a) Execute the test procedures

    (b) Check for termination

    (c) Evaluate the test effort and unit

When more than one unit is to be unit tested (for example, all those associated with a software project), the Plan activity should address the total set of test units and should not be repeated for each test unit. The other activities must be performed at least once for each unit.

Under normal conditions, these activities are sequentially initiated except for the Execute and Check cycle as illustrated in Fig 1. When per-

---

[3] A test unit may occur at any level of the design hierarchy from a single module to a complete program. Therefore, a test unit may be a module, a few modules, or a complete computer program along with associated data and procedures.

[4] A test unit may contain one or more modules that have already been unit tested.

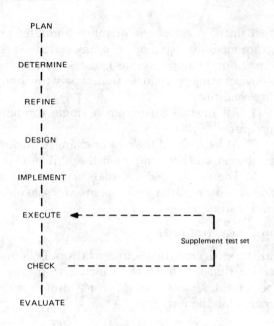

**Fig 1
Unit Testing Activities**

forming any of the activities except Plan, improper performance of a preceding activity or external events (for example, schedule, requirements, or design changes) may result in the need to redo one or more of the preceding activities and then return to the one being performed.

During the testing process, a test design specification and a test summary report must be developed. Other test documents may be developed. All test documents must conform to the ANSI/IEEE Std 829-1983 [2]. In addition, all test documents must have identified authors and be dated.

The test design specification will derive its information from the Determine, Refine, and Design activities. The test summary report will derive its information from all of the activities.

3.1 Plan the General Approach, Resources, and Schedule. General unit test planning should occur during overall test planning and be recorded in the corresponding planning document.

3.1.1 Plan Inputs
(1) Project plans
(2) Software requirements documentation

3.1.2 Plan Tasks
(1) *Specify a General Approach to Unit Testing.* Identify risk areas to be addressed by the testing. Specify constraints on characteristic determination (for example, features that must be

tested), test design, or test implementation (for example, test sets that must be used).

Identify existing sources of input, output, and state data (for example, test files, production files, test data generators). Identify general techniques for data validation. Identify general techniques to be used for output recording, collection, reduction, and validation. Describe provisions for application software that directly interfaces with the units to be tested.

(2) *Specify Completeness Requirements.* Identify the areas (for example, features, procedures, states, functions, data characteristics, instructions) to be covered by the unit test set and the degree of coverage required for each area.

When testing a unit during software development, every software feature must be covered by a test case or an approved exception. The same should hold during software maintenance for any unit testing.

When testing a unit implemented with a procedural language (for example, COBOL) during software development, every instruction that can be reached and executed must be covered by a test case or an approved exception, except for instructions contained in modules that have been separately unit tested. The same should hold during software maintenance for the testing of a unit implemented with a procedural language.

(3) *Specify Termination Requirements.* Specify the requirements for normal termination of the unit testing process. Termination requirements must include satisfying the completeness requirements.

Identify any conditions that could cause abnormal termination of the unit testing process (for example, detecting a major design fault, reaching a schedule deadline) and any notification procedures that apply.

(4) *Determine Resource Requirements.* Estimate the resources required for test set acquisition, initial execution, and subsequent repetition of testing activities. Consider hardware, access time (for example, dedicated computer time), communications or system software, test tools, test files, and forms or other supplies. Also consider the need for unusually large volumes of forms and supplies.

Identify resources needing preparation and the parties responsible. Make arrangements for these resources, including requests for resources that require significant lead time (for example, customized test tools).

Identify the parties responsible for unit testing and unit debugging. Identify personnel requirements including skills, number, and duration.

(5) *Specify a General Schedule.* Specify a schedule constrained by resource and test unit availability for all unit testing activity.

3.1.3 Plan Outputs

(1) General unit test planning information (from 3.1.2(1) through (5) inclusive)

(2) Unit test general resource requests—if produced from 3.1.2(4)

3.2 Determine Features To Be Tested

3.2.1 Determine Inputs

(1) Unit requirements documentation

(2) Software architectural design documentation—if needed

3.2.2 Determine Tasks

(1) *Study the Functional Requirements.* Study each function described in the unit requirements documentation. Ensure that each function has a unique identifier. When necessary, request clarification of the requirements.

(2) *Identify Additional Requirements and Associated Procedures.* Identify requirements other than functions (for example, performance, attributes, or design constraints) associated with software characteristics that can be effectively tested at the unit level. Identify any usage or operating procedures associated only with the unit to be tested. Ensure that each additional requirement and procedure has a unique identifier. When necessary, request clarification of the requirements.

(3) *Identify States of the Unit.* If the unit requirements documentation specifies or implies multiple states (for example, inactive, ready to receive, processing) software, identify each state and each valid state transition. Ensure that each state and state transition has a unique identifier. When necessary, request clarification of the requirements.

(4) *Identify Input and Output Data Characteristics.* Identify the input and output data structures of the unit to be tested. For each structure, identify characteristics, such as arrival rates, formats, value ranges, and relationships between field values. For each characteristic, specify its valid ranges. Ensure that each characteristic has a unique identifier. When necessary, request clarification of the requirements.

(5) *Select Elements to be Included in the Test-ing.* Select the features to be tested. Select the associated procedures, associated states, associated state transitions, and associated data characteristics to be included in the testing. Invalid and valid input data must be selected. When complete testing is impractical, information regarding the expected use of the unit should be used to determine the selections. Identify the risk associated with unselected elements.

Enter the selected features, procedures, states, state transitions, and data characteristics in the *Features to be Tested* section of the unit's Test Design Specification.

3.2.3 Determine Outputs

(1) List of elements to be included in the testing (from 3.2.2(5))

(2) Unit requirements clarification requests—if produced from 3.2.2(1) through (4) inclusive

3.3 Refine the General Plan

3.3.1 Refine Inputs

(1) List of elements to be included in the testing (from 3.2.2(5))

(2) General unit test planning information (from 3.1.2(1) through (5) inclusive)

3.3.2 Refine Tasks

(1) *Refine the Approach.* Identify existing test cases and test procedures to be considered for use. Identify any special techniques to be used for data validation. Identify any special techniques to be used for output recording, collection, reduction, and validation.

Record the refined approach in the *Approach Refinements* section of the unit's test design specification.

(2) *Specify Special Resource Requirements.* Identify any special resources needed to test the unit (for example, software that directly interfaces with the unit). Make preparations for the identified resources.

Record the special resource requirements in the *Approach Refinements* section of the unit's test design specification.

(3) *Specify a Detailed Schedule.* Specify a schedule for the unit testing based on support software, special resource, and unit availability and integration schedules. Record the schedule in the *Approach Refinements* section of the unit's test design specification.

3.3.3 Refine Outputs

(1) Specific unit test planning information (from 3.3.2(1) through (3) inclusive)

(2) Unit test special resource requests—if produced from 3.3.2(2).

3.4 Design the Set of Tests

3.4.1 Design Inputs

(1) Unit requirements documentation

(2) List of elements to be included in the testing (from 3.2.2(5))

(3) Unit test planning information (from 3.1.2(1) and (2) and 3.3.2(1))

(4) Unit design documentation

(5) Test specifications from previous testing—if available

3.4.2 Design Tasks

(1) *Design the Architecture of the Test Set.* Based on the features to be tested and the conditions specified or implied by the selected associated elements (for example, procedures, state transitions, data characteristics), design a hierarchically decomposed set of test objectives so that each lowest-level objective can be directly tested by a few test cases. Select appropriate existing test cases. Associate groups of test-case identifiers with the lowest-level objectives. Record the hierarchy of objectives and associated test case identifiers in the *Test Identification* section of the unit's test design specification.

(2) *Obtain Explicit Test Procedures as Required.* A combination of the unit requirements documentation, test planning information, and test-case specifications may implicitly specify the unit test procedures and therefore minimize the need for explicit specification. Select existing test procedures that can be modified or used without modification.

Specify any additional procedures needed either in a supplementary section in the unit's test design specification or in a separate procedure specification document. Either choice must be in accordance with the information required by ANSI/IEEE Std 829-1983 [2]. When the correlation between test cases and procedures is not readily apparent, develop a table relating them and include it in the unit's test design specification.

(3) *Obtain the Test Case Specifications.* Specify the new test cases. Existing specifications may be referenced.

Record the specifications directly or by reference in either a supplementary section of the unit's test design specification or in a separate document. Either choice must be in accordance with the information required by ANSI/IEEE Std 829-1983 [2].

(4) *Augment, as Required, the Set of Test-Case Specifications Based on Design Information.* Based on information about the unit's design, update as required the test set architecture in accordance with 3.4.2(1). Consider the characteristics of selected algorithms and internal data structures.

Identify control flows and changes to internal data that must be recorded. Anticipate special recording difficulties that might arise, for example, from a need to trace control flow in complex algorithms or from a need to trace changes in internal data structures (for example, stacks or trees). When necessary, request enhancement of the unit design (for example, a formatted data structure dump capability) to increase the testability of the unit.

Based on information in the unit's design, specify any newly identified test cases and complete any partial test case specifications in accordance with 3.4.2(3).

(5) *Complete the Test Design Specification.* Complete the test design specification for the unit in accordance with ANSI/IEEE Std 829-1983 [2].

3.4.3 Design Outputs

(1) Unit test design specification (from 3.4.2(5))

(2) Separate test procedure specifications—if produced from 3.4.2(2)

(3) Separate test-case specifications—if produced from 3.4.2(3) or (4)

(4) Unit design enhancement requests—if produced from 3.4.2(4)

3.5 Implement the Refined Plan and Design

3.5.1 Implement Inputs

(1) Unit test planning information (from 3.1.2(1), (4), and (5) and 3.3.2(1) through (3) inclusive)

(2) Test-case specifications in the unit test design specification or separate documents (from 3.4.2(3) and (4)

(3) Software data structure descriptions

(4) Test support resources

(5) Test items

(6) Test data from previous testing activities—if available

(7) Test tools from previous testing activities—if available

3.5.2 Implement Tasks

(1) *Obtain and Verify Test Data.* Obtain a copy of existing test data to be modified or used without modification. Generate any new data required. Include additional data necessary to ensure data consistency and integrity. Verify all data (including those to be used as is) against

the software data structure specifications. When the correlation between test cases and data sets is not readily apparent, develop a table to record this correlation and include it in the unit's test design specification.

(2) *Obtain Special Resources.* Obtain the test support resources specified in 3.3.2(2).

(3) *Obtain Test Items.* Collect test items including available manuals, operating system procedures, control data (for example, tables), and computer programs. Obtain software identified during test planning that directly interfaces with the test unit.

When testing a unit implemented with a procedural language, ensure that execution trace information will be available to evaluate satisfaction of the code-based completeness requirements.

Record the identifier of each item in the *Summary* section of the unit's test summary report.

3.5.3 Implement Outputs

(1) Verified test data (from 3.5.2(1))

(2) Test support resources (from 3.5.2(2))

(3) Configuration of test items (from 3.5.2(3))

(4) Initial summary information (from 3.5.2(3))

3.6 Execute the Test Procedures

3.6.1 Execute Inputs

(1) Verified test data (from 3.5.2(1))

(2) Test support resources (from 3.5.2(2))

(3) Configuration of test items (from 3.5.2(3))

(4) Test-case specifications (from 3.4.2(3) and (4))

(5) Test procedure specifications (from 3.4.2 (2))—if produced

(6) Failure analysis results (from debugging process)—if produced

3.6.2 Execute Tasks

(1) *Run Tests.* Set up the test environment. Run the test set. Record all test incidents in the *Summary of Results* section of the unit's test summary report.

(2) *Determine Results.* For each test case, determine if the unit passed or failed based on required result specifications in the case descriptions. Record pass or fail results in the *Summary of Results* section of the unit's test summary report. Record resource consumption data in the *Summary of Activities* section of the report. When testing a unit implemented with a procedural language, collect execution trace summary information and attach it to the report.

For each failure, have the failure analyzed and record the fault information in the *Summary of Results* section of the test summary report. Then select the applicable case and perform the associated actions.

Case 1: *A Fault in a Test Specification or Test Data.* Correct the fault, record the fault correction in the *Summary of Activities* section of the test summary report, and rerun the tests that failed.

Case 2: *A Fault in Test Procedure Execution.* Rerun the incorrectly executed procedures.

Case 3: *A Fault in the Test Environment (for example, system software).* Either have the environment corrected, record the fault correction in the *Summary of Activities* section of the test summary report, and rerun the tests that failed OR prepare for abnormal termination by documenting the reason for not correcting the environment in the *Summary of Activities* section of the test summary report and proceed to check for termination (that is, proceed to activity 3.7).

Case 4: *A Fault in the Unit Implementation.* Either have the unit corrected, record the fault correction in the *Summary of Activities* section of the test summary report, and rerun all tests OR prepare for abnormal termination by documenting the reason for not correcting the unit in the *Summary of Activities* section of the test summary report and proceed to check for termination (that is, proceed to activity 3.7).

Case 5: *A Fault in the Unit Design.* Either have the design and unit corrected, modify the test specification and data as appropriate, record the fault correction in the *Summary of Activities* section of the test summary report, and rerun all tests OR prepare for abnormal termination by documenting the reason for not correcting the design in the *Summary of Activities* section of the test summary report and proceed to check for termination (that is, proceed to activity 3.7).

NOTE: The cycle of Execute and Check Tasks must be repeated until a termination condition defined in 3.1.2(3) is satisfied (See Fig 3). Control flow within the Execute activity itself is pictured in Fig 2).

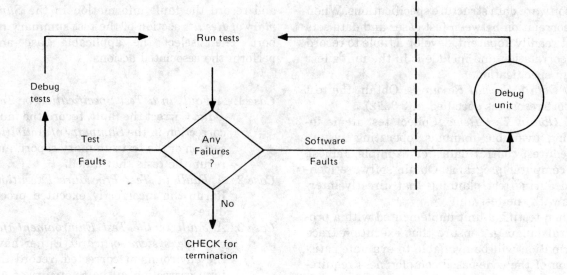

Fig 2
Control Flow Within the Execute Activity

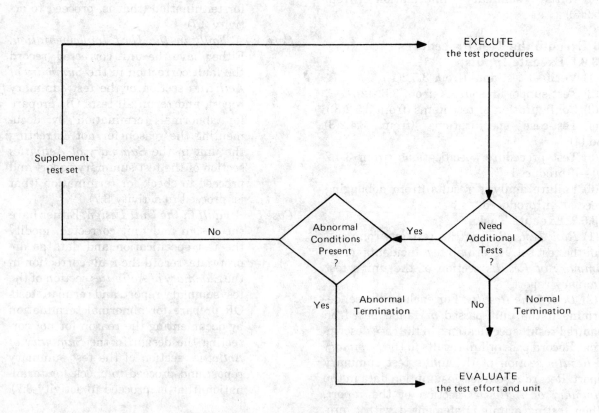

Fig 3
Control Flow Within the Check Activity

3.6.3 Execute Outputs

(1) Execution information logged in the test summary report including test outcomes, test incident descriptions, failure analysis results, fault correction activities, uncorrected fault reasons, resource consumption data and, for procedural language implementations, trace summary information (from 3.6.2(1) and (2))

(2) Revised test specifications—if produced from 3.6.2(2)

(3) Revised test data—if produced from 3.6.2(2)

3.7 Check for Termination
3.7.1 Check Inputs

(1) Completeness and termination requirements (from 3.1.2(2) and (3))

(2) Execution information (from 3.6.2(1) and (2))

(3) Test specifications (from 3.4.2(1) through (3) inclusive)—if required

(4) Software data structure descriptions—if required

3.7.2 Check Tasks

(1) *Check for Normal Termination of the Testing Process*. Determine the need for additional tests based on completeness requirements or concerns raised by the failure history. For procedural language implementations, analyze the execution trace summary information (for example, variable, flow).

If additional tests are *not* needed, then record normal termination in the *Summary of Activities* section of the test summary report and proceed to evaluate the test effort and unit (that is, proceed to activity 3.8).

(2) *Check for Abnormal Termination of the Testing Process*. If an abnormal termination condition is satisfied (for example, uncorrected major fault, out of time) then ensure that the specific situation causing termination is documented in the *Summary of Activities* section of the test summary report together with the unfinished testing and any uncorrected faults. Then proceed to evaluate the test effort and unit (that is, proceed to activity 3.8).

(3) *Supplement the Test Set*. When additional tests are needed and the abnormal termination conditions are not satisfied, supplement the test set by following steps (a) through (e).

(a) Update the test set architecture in accordance with 3.4.2(1) and obtain additional test-case specifications in accordance with 3.4.2(3).

(b) Modify the test procedure specifications in accordance with 3.4.2(2) as required.

(c) Obtain additional test data in accordance with 3.5.2(1).

(d) Record the addition in the *Summary of Activities* section of the test summary report.

(e) Execute the additional tests (that is, return to activity 3.6).

3.7.3 Check Outputs

(1) Check information logged in the test summary report including the termination conditions and any test case addition activities (from 3.7.2(1) through (3) inclusive)

(2) Additional or revised test specifications—if produced from 3.7.2(3)

(3) Additional test data—if produced from 3.7.2(3)

3.8 Evaluate the Test Effort and Unit
3.8.1 Evaluate Inputs

(1) Unit Test Design Specification (from 3.4.2(5)

(2) Execution information (from 3.6.2(1) and (2))

(3) Checking information (from 3.7.2(1) through (3) inclusive)

(4) Separate test-case specifications (from 3.4.2(3) and (4))—if produced

3.8.2 Evaluate Tasks

(1) *Describe Testing Status*. Record variances from test plans and test specifications in the *Variances* section of the test summary report. Specify the reason for each variance.

For abnormal termination, identify areas insufficiently covered by the testing and record reasons in the *Comprehensiveness Assessment* section of the test summary report.

Identify unresolved test incidents and the reasons for a lack of resolution in the *Summary of Results* section of the test summary report.

(2) *Describe Unit's Status*. Record differences revealed by testing between the unit and its requirements documentation in the *Variances* section of the test summary report.

Evaluate the unit design and implementation against requirements based on test results and detected fault information. Record evaluation information in the *Evaluation* section of the test summary report.

(3) *Complete the Test Summary Report*. Complete the test summary report for the unit in accordance with ANSI/IEEE Std 829-1983 [2].

(4) *Ensure Preservation of Testing Products*. Ensure that the testing products are collected,

organized, and stored for reference and reuse. These products include the test design specification, separate test-case specifications, separate test procedure specifications, test data, test data generation procedures, test drivers and stubs, and the test summary report.

3.8.3 Evaluate Outputs

(1) Complete test summary report (from 3.8.2(3))

(2) Complete, stored collection of testing products (from 3.8.2(4))

Appendixes

(These Appendixes are not a part of ANSI / IEEE Std 1008-1987, IEEE Standard for Software Unit Testing, but are included for information only.)

Appendix A

Implementation and Usage Guidelines

This section contains information intended to be of benefit when the standard is being considered for use. It is therefore recommended that this section be read in its entirety before any extensive planning is done.

A1. Use of the Standard

The standard can be used
(1) As a basis for comparison to confirm current practices
(2) As a source of ideas to modify current practices
(3) As a replacement for current practices

A2. Additional Testing Requirements

Requirements such as the amount of additional test documentation (for example, test logs), the level of detail to be included, and the number and types of approvals and reviews must be specified for each project. Factors, such as unit criticality, auditing needs, or contract specifications will often dictate these requirements. The standard leaves it to the user to specify these requirements either by individual project or as organizational standards. If the requirements are project specific, they should appear in the project plan, quality assurance plan, verification and validation plan, or overall test plan.

A3. Additional Test Documentation

The information contained in the test design specification and the test summary report is considered an absolute minimum for process visibility. In addition, it is assumed that any test information need can be satisfied by the set of test documents specified in ANSI / IEEE Std 829-

1983 [2], either by requiring additional content in a required document or by requiring additional documents.

A4. Approvals and Reviews

If more control is desired, the following additional tasks should be considered:
(1) Approval of general approach at the end of Plan
(2) Approval of identified requirements at the end of Determine
(3) Approval of specific plans at the end of Refine
(4) Approval of test specifications at the end of Design
(5) Review of test readiness at the end of Implement
(6) Review of test summary report at the end of Evaluate

A5. Audit Trails

It is assumed that auditing needs are taken into account when specifying control requirements. Therefore, the set of test documents generated together with the reports from test reviews should be sufficient to supply all required audit information.

A6. Configuration Management

Configuration management should be the source of the software requirements, software architectual design, software data structure, and unit requirements documentation. These inputs must be managed to ensure confidence that we have current information and will be notified of any changes.

The final unit testing products should be provided to configuration management. These outputs must be managed to permit thorough and economical regression testing. See ANSI/IEEE Std 828-1983, IEEE Standard for Software Configuration Management Plans, for details.

A7. Determination of Requirements-Based Characteristics

Psychological factors (for example, self-confidence, a detailed knowledge of the unit design) can make it very difficult for the unit developer to determine an effective set of requirements-based elements (for example, features, procedures, state transitions, data characteristics) to be included in the testing. Often, this determination should be made by someone else.

There are several ways to organize this separation.

(1) Developers determine these elements for each other.

(2) Developers fully test each other's code. This has the added advantage that at least two developers will have a detailed knowledge of every unit.

(3) A separate test group should be available The size of the project or the criticality of the software may determine whether a separate group can be justified.

If developers determine requirements-based elements for their own software, they should perform this determination *before* software design begins.

A8. User Involvement

If the unit to be tested interacts with users (for example, menu displays), it can be very effective to involve those users in determining the requirements-based elements to be included in the testing. Asking users about their use of the software may bring to light valuable information to be considered during test planning. For example, questioning may identify the relative criticality of the unit's functions and thus determine the testing emphasis.

A9. Stronger Code-Based Coverage Requirements

Based on the criticality of the unit or a shortage of unit requirement and design information (for example, during maintenance of older software), the code-based coverage requirement specified in 3.1.2(2) could be strengthened. One option is to strengthen the requirement from instruction coverage to branch coverage (that is, the execution of every branch in the unit).

A10. Code Coverage Tools

An automated means of recording the coverage of source code during unit test execution is highly recommended. Automation is usually necessary because manual coverage analysis is unreliable and uneconomical. One automated approach uses a code instrumentation and reporting tool. Such a tool places software probes in the source code and following execution of the test cases provides a report summarizing data and control-flow information. The report identifies unexecuted instructions. Some tools also identify unexecuted branches. This capability is a feature in some compilers.

A11. Process Improvement

To evaluate and improve the effectiveness of unit testing, it is recommended that failure data be gathered from those processes that follow unit testing, such as integration test, system test, and production use. This data should then be analyzed to determine the nature of those faults that should have been detected by unit testing but were not.

A12. Adopting the Standard

Implementing a new technical process is itself a process that requires planning, implementation, and evaluation effort. To successfully implement a testing process based on this standard, one must develop an implementation strategy and tailor the standard. Both activities must reflect the culture and current abilities of the organization. Long-term success will require management commitment, supporting policies, tools, training, and start-up consulting. Management can demonstrate commitment by incorporating the new process into project tracking systems and performance evaluation criteria.

A13. Practicality of the Standard

This standard represents consensus on the definition of good software engineering practice. Some organizations use practices similar to the process specified here while others organize this work quite differently. In any case, it will involve considerable change for many organizations that choose to adopt it. That change involves new policies, new standards and procedures, new tools, and new training programs. If the differences between the standard and current practice are too great, then the changes will need to be phased in. The answer to the question of practicality is basically one of desire. How badly does an organization want to gain control of its unit testing?

Appendix B

Concepts and Assumptions

B1. Software Engineering Concepts

The standard unit testing process specified in this standard is based on several fundamental software engineering concepts which are described in B1.1 through B1.8 inclusive.

B1.1 Relationship of Testing to Verification and Validation. Testing is just one of several complementary verification and validation activities. Other activities include technical reviews (for example, code inspections), static analysis, and proof of correctness. Specification of a comprehensive verification and validation process is outside the scope of this standard.

B1.2 Testing As Product Development. Testing includes a product development process. It results in a *test set* composed of data, test support software, and procedures for its use. This product is documented by test specifications and reports. As with any product development process, test set development requires planning, requirements (test objectives), design, implementation, and evaluation.

B1.3 Composition of Debugging. The debugging process is made up of two major activities. The objective of the first activity, *failure analysis,* is to locate and identify all faults responsible for a failure. The objective of the second, *fault correction,* is to remove all identified faults while avoiding the introduction of new ones. Specification of the process of either failure analysis or fault correction is outside the scope of this standard.

B1.4 Relationship of Testing to Debugging. Testing entails attempts to cause failures in order to detect faults, while debugging entails both failure analysis to locate and identify the associated faults and subsequent fault correction. Testing may need the results of debugging's failure analysis to decide on a course of action. Those actions may include the termination of testing or a request for requirements changes or fault correction.

B1.5 Relationship Between Types of Units. A one-to-one relationship between design units, implementation units, and test units is not necessary. Several design units may make up an implementation unit (for example, a program) and several implementation units may make up a test unit.

B1.6 Need for Design and Implementation Information. Often, requirements information is not enough for effective testing, even though, fundamentally, testing measures actual behavior against required behavior. This is because its usually not feasible to test all possible situations and requirements often do not provide sufficient guidance in identifying situations that have high failure potential. Design and implementation information often are needed, since some of these high-potential situations result from the design and implementation choices that have been made.

B1.7 Incremental Specification of Elements To Be Considered in Testing. Progressively more detailed information about the nature of a test unit is found in the unit requirements documentation, the unit design documentation, and finally in the unit's implementation. As a result, the elements to be considered in testing may be built up incrementally during different periods of test activity.

For procedural language (for example, COBOL) implementations, element specification occurs in three increments. The first group is specified during the Determine activity and is based on the unit requirements documentation. The second group is specified during the Design activity and is based on the unit design (that is, algorithms and data structures) as stated in a software design description. The third group is specified during the Check activity and is based on the unit's code.

For nonprocedural language (for example, report writer or sort specification languages) implementations, specification occurs in two increments. The first is during the Determine activity and is based on requirements and the second is during Design and is based on the non-procedural specification.

An incremental approach permits unit testing to begin as soon as unit requirements are available and minimizes the bias introduced by detailed knowledge of the unit design and code.

B1.8 Incremental Creation of a Test Design Specification. Information recorded in the test design specification is generated during the Determine, Refine, and Design activities. As each of these test activities progress, information is recorded in appropriate sections of the specification. The whole document must be complete at the end of the final iteration of the Design activity.

B1.9 Incremental Creation of the Test Summary Report. Information recorded in the test summary report is generated during all unit testing activities expect Plan. The report is initiated during Implement, updated during Execute and Check, and completed during Evaluate.

B2. Testing Assumptions

The approach to unit testing specified in this standard is based on a variety of economic, psychological, and technical assumptions. The significant assumptions are given in B2.1 through B2.7 inclusive.

B2.1 The objective of unit testing is to attempt to determine the correctness and completeness of an implementation with respect to unit requirements and design documentation by attempting to uncover faults in:

(1) The unit's required features in combination with their associated states (for example, inactive, active awaiting a message, active processing a message)

(2) The unit's handling of invalid input

(3) Any usage or operating procedures associated only with the unit

(4) The unit's algorithms or internal data structures, or both

(5) The decision boundaries of the unit's control logic

B2.2 Testing entails the measurement of behavior against requirements. Although one speaks informally of *interface testing, state testing,* or even *requirement testing,* what is meant is measuring actual behavior associated with an interface, state, or requirement, against the corresponding required behavior. Any verifiable unit testing process must have documented requirements for the test unit. This standard assumes that the documentation of unit requirements exists before testing begins.

B2.3 Unit requirements documentation must be thoroughly reviewed for completeness, testability, and traceability. This standard assumes the requirements have been reviewed either as a normal part of the documentation review process or in a special unit requirements review.

B2.4 There are significant economic benefits in the early detection of faults. This implies that test set development should start as soon as practical following availability of the unit requirements documentation because of the resulting requirements verification and validation. It also implies that as much as practical should be tested at the unit level.

B2.5 The levels of project testing (for example, acceptance, system, integration, unit) are specified in project plans, verification and validation plans, or overall test plans. Also included is the unit test planning information that is applicable to all units being tested (for example, completeness requirements, termination requirements, general resource requirements). Subsequently, based on an analysis of the software design, the test units will be identified and an integration sequence will be selected.

B2.6 The availability of inputs and resources to do a task is the major constraint on the sequencing of activities and on the sequencing of tasks within an activity. If the necessary resources are available, some of the activities and some of the tasks within an activity may be performed concurrently.

B2.7 This standard assumes that it is usually most cost-effective to delay the design of test cases based on source-code characteristics until the set of test cases based on requirements and design characteristics has been executed. This approach minimizes the code-based design task. If code-based design is started before test execution data is available, it should not start until the test cases based on unit requirements and design characteristics have been specified.

Appendix C

Sources for Techniques and Tools

C1. General

Software tools are computer programs and software techniques are detailed methods that aid in the specification, construction, testing, analysis, management, documentation, and maintenance of other computer programs. Software techniques and tools can be used and reused in a variety of development environments. Their effective use increases engineering productivity and software quality.

The references given in C2 of this Appendix contain information on most of the testing techniques and tools in use today. The set of references is not exhaustive, but provides a comprehensive collection of source material. To keep up to date, the reader is encouraged to obtain information on recent IEEE tutorials and recent documents in the Special Publications series of the National Bureau of Standards.[5] Current information on test tools can be obtained from the Federal Software Testing Center[6] and

software tool data bases are accessible through the Data & Analysis Center for Software.[7]

A set of general references on software testing is listed in Appendix D.

C2. References

BEIZER, BORIS. *Software Testing Techniques.* New York: Van Nostrand Reinhold, 1983. This book presents a collection of experience-based test techniques. It describes several test design techniques together with their mathematical foundations. The book describes various techniques (decision tables and formal grammars) that provide a precise specification of the input and software. It also discusses a data-base-driven testing technique. Many techniques are based on the author's first-hand experience as director of testing and quality assurance for a telecommunications software producer. The inclusion of experiences and anecdotes makes this book enjoyable and informative.

HOUGHTON, Jr, RAYMOND C. Software Development Tools: A Profile. *IEEE Computer* vol

[5] The NBS publications and software tools survey may be obtained from Superintendent of Documents, US Government Printing Office, Washington, DC 20402.

[6] Information regarding test tools may be obtained by contacting Federal Software Testing Center, Office of Software Development, General Services Administration, 5203 Leesburg Pike, Suite 1100, Falls Church, VA 22041.

[7] Information regarding the tools data base may be obtained from Data & Analysis Center for Software (DACS), RADC/ISISI, Griffiss AFB NY 13441.

21

16, no 5, May 1983.[8] The Institute of Computer Science and Technology of the National Bureau of Standards studied the software tools available in the early 1980's. This article reports the results of that study and analyzes the information obtained. Various categorizations of the tools are presented, with tools listed by their characteristics. The lists incorporate percentage summaries based on the total number of tools for which information was available.

OSD/DDT & E Software Test and Evaluation Project, Phases I and II, Final Report, vol 2, *Software Test and Evaluation: State-of-the-Art Overview.* School of Information and Computer Science, Georgia Institute of Technology, June 1983, 350 pp.[9] This report contains a concise overview of most current testing techniques and tools. A set of references is provided for each one. A set of test tool data sheets containing implementation details and information contacts is also provided.

POWELL, PATRICIA B. (ed). *Software Validation, Verification, and Testing Technique and Tool Reference Guide.* National Bureau of Standards Special Publication 500–93, 1982. Order from GPO SN-003-003-02422-8.[5] Thirty techniques and tools for validation, verification, and testing are described. Each description includes the basic features of the technique or tool, its input, its output, and an example. Each description also contains an assessment of effectiveness and usability, applicability, an estimate of the learning time and training, an estimate of needed resources, and associated references.

PRESSON, EDWARD. *Software Test Handbook: Software Test Guidebook.* Rome Air Develop-

ment Center RADC-TR-84-53, vol 2 (of two) March 1984. Order from NTIS A147-289. This guidebook contains guidelines and methodology for software testing including summary descriptions of testing techniques, typical paragraphs specifying testing techniques for a Statement of Work, a cross-reference to government and commercial catalogs listing automated test tools, and an extensive bibliography.

REIFER, DONALD J. *Software Quality Assurance Tools and Techniques.* John D. Cooper and Matthew J. Fisher (eds). Software Quality Management, New York: Petrocelli Books, 1979, pp. 209–234. This paper explains how modern tools and techniques support an assurance technology for computer programs. The author first develops categories for quality assurance tools and techniques (aids) and discusses example aids. Material on toolsmithing is presented next. Finally, an assessment is made of the state of the technology and recommendations for improving current practice are offered.

SOFTFAIR 83. *A Conference on Software Development Tools, Techniques, and Alternatives.* IEEE Computer Society Press, 1983.[8] This is the proceedings of the first of what is likely to be a series of conferences aimed at showing the most promising approaches within the field of software tools and environments. It is a collection of 42 papers covering a broad range of software engineering tools from research prototypes to commercial products.

Software Aids and Tools Survey. Federal Software Management Support Center, Office of Software Development, Report OIT/FSMC-86/002, 1985.[6] The purpose of this document is to support management in various government agencies in the identification and selection of software tools. The document identifies and categorizes tools available in the marketplace in mid 1985. Approximately 300 tools are presented with various data concerning each one's function, producer, source language, possible uses, cost, and product description. The survey is expected to be updated periodically.

---

[8] Information regarding IEEE Computer Society publications may be obtained from IEEE Computer Society Order Department, PO Box 80452, Worldway Postal Center, Los Angeles, CA 90080.

[9] The Georgia Technology report may be obtained from Documents Librarian, Software Test and Evaluation Project, School of Information and Computer Science, Georgia Institute of Technology, Atlanta, Georgia 30332.

Appendix D

General References

This section identifies a basic set of reference works on software testing. While the set is not exhaustive, it provides a comprehensive collection of source material. Additional references focusing specifically on testing techniques and tools are contained in Appendix C.

CHANDRASEKARAN, B. and RADICCHI, S., (ed) *Computer Program Testing,* North-Holland, 1981. The following description is from the editors Preface:

"The articles in this volume, taken as a whole, provide a comprehensive, tutorial discussion of the current state of the art as well as research directions in the area of testing computer programs. They cover the spectrum from basic theoretical notions through practical issues in testing programs and large software systems to integrated environments and tools for performing a variety of tests. They are all written by active researchers and practitioners in the field."

DEUTSCH, MICHAEL S. *Software Verification and Validation.* ENGLEWOOD CLIFFS: Prentice-Hall, 1982. The following description is taken from the Preface.

"The main thrust of this book is to describe verification and validation approaches that have been used successfully on contemporary large-scale software projects. Methodologies are explored that can be pragmatically applied to modern complex software developments and that take account of cost, schedule, and management realities in the actual production environment. This book is intended to be tutorial in nature with a 'This is how it's done in the real world' orientation. Contributing to this theme will be observations and recounts from actual software development project experiences in industry."

Guideline for Lifecycle Validation, Verification, and Testing of Computer Software. Federal Information Processing Standards (FIPS) Publication 101.[10] Order from NTIS FIPSPUB101 1983 (See Appendix C). This guideline presents an integrated approach to validation, verification, and testing that should be used throughout the software lifecycle. Also included is a glossary of technical terms and a list of supporting ICST publications. An Appendix provides an outline for formulating a VV & T plan.

HETZEL, WILLIAM, *The Complete Guide to Software Testing.* QED Information Sciences,

1984. This book covers many aspects of software verification and validation with a primary emphasis on testing. It contains an overview of test methods and tools including sample reports from several commercially available tools. The book is especially useful when used for viewing testing from a management perspective and discussing many of the associated management issues. An extensive bibliography is included.

McCABE, THOMAS J. (ed). *Structured Testing.* IEEE Computer Society Press, Cat no EHO 200–6, 1983.[8] This IEEE Tutorial is a collection of papers focusing on the relationship between testing and program complexity. The first two papers define cyclomatic complexity and describe an associated technique for developing program test cases. The third paper describes a systematic approach to the development of system test cases. The fourth paper provides general guidelines for program verification and testing. The balance of the papers deal with complexity and reliability.

MILLER, EDWARD and HOWDEN, WILLIAM E. (ed). Tutorial: *Software Testing & Validation Techniques* (2nd ed) IEEE Computer Society Press, Cat no EHO 180–0, 1981.[8] This IEEE Tutorial is a collection of some significant papers dealing with various aspects of software testing. These aspects include theoretical foundations, static analysis, dynamic analysis, effectiveness assessment, and software management. An extensive bibliography is included.

MYERS, GLENFORD J. *The Art of Software Testing.* New York: Wiley–Interscience, 1979. This book contains practical, *How To Do It* technical information on software testing. The main emphasis is on methodologies for the design of effective test cases. It also covers psychological and economic issues, managerial aspects of testing, test tools, debugging, and code inspections. Comprehensive examples and checklists support the presentation.

---

[10] The FIPS VV & T Guideline may be obtained from National Technical Information Service, 5285 Port Royal Road, Springfield, VA 22161.

POWELL, PATRICIA B. (ed). *Plan for Software Validation, Verification, and Testing.* National Bureau of Standards Special Publication 500–98, 1982.[5] Order from GPO SN-003-003-02449-0 (See Appendix C). This document is for those who direct and those who implement computer projects. It explains the selection and use of validation, verification, and testing (VV & T) tools and techniques. It explains how to develop a plan to meet specific software VV & T goals.

Acknowledgment

Appreciation is expressed to the following companies and organizations for contributing the time of their employees to make possible the development of this text:

- Algoma Steel
- Applied Information Development
- AT & T Bell Labs
- AT & T Information Systems
- Automated Language Processing Systems
- Bank of America
- Bechtel Power
- Bell Canada
- Boeing Computer Services
- Boston University
- Burroughs, Scotland
- CAP GEMINI DASD
- Central Institute for Industrial Research, Norway
- Communications Sciences
- Conoco
- Digital Equipment Corp
- US Department of the Interior
- US Department of Transportation
- Data Systems Analysts
- E-Systems
- K.A. Foster, Inc
- General Dynamics
- Georgia Tech
- General Services Administration
- Honeywell
- Hughes Aircraft
- IBM
- IBM Federal Systems Division
- International Bureau of Software Test
- Johns Hopkins University Applied Physics Laboratory
- Lear Siegler
- Logicon
- Management and Computer Services
- Martin Marietta Aerospace
- McDonald-Douglas
- Medtronic
- Micom
- Mitre
- M. T. Scientific Consulting
- NASA
- National Bureau of Standards
- NCR
- Product Assurances Consulting
- Professional Systems & Technology
- Programming Environments
- Quality Assurance Institute
- RCA
- Reynolds & Reynolds
- Rolm Telecommunications
- Rome Air Development Center
- Sallie Mae
- Seattle—First National Bank
- SHAPE, BELGIUM
- Software Engineering Service, Germany
- Software Quality Engineering
- Software Research Associates
- Solo Systems
- Sperry
- SQS GmbH, Germany
- Tandem Computers
- Tektronix
- Televideo
- Tenn Valley Authority
- Texas Instruments
- Time
- University of DC
- University of Texas, Arlington
- US Army Computer Systems Command
- Warner Robins ALC
- Westinghouse Hanford

IEEE Std 1012-1998
(Revision of IEEE Std 1012-1986)

IEEE Standard for Software Verification and Validation

Sponsor

**Software Engineering Standards Committee
of the
IEEE Computer Society**

Approved 9 March 1998

IEEE-SA Standards Board

Abstract: Software verification and validation (V&V) processes, which determine whether development products of a given activity conform to the requirements of that activity, and whether the software satisfies its intended use and user needs, are described. This determination may include analysis, evaluation, review, inspection, assessment, and testing of software products and processes. V&V processes assess the software in the context of the system, including the operational environment, hardware, interfacing software, operators, and users.
Keywords: software integrity, software life cycle processes, verification and validation

The Institute of Electrical and Electronics Engineers, Inc.
345 East 47th Street, New York, NY 10017-2394, USA

ISBN 0-7381-0196-6

IEEE Standards documents are developed within the IEEE Societies and the Standards Coordinating Committees of the IEEE Standards Association (IEEE-SA) Standards Board. Members of the committees serve voluntarily and without compensation. They are not necessarily members of the Institute. The standards developed within IEEE represent a consensus of the broad expertise on the subject within the Institute as well as those activities outside of IEEE that have expressed an interest in participating in the development of the standard.

Use of an IEEE Standard is wholly voluntary. The existence of an IEEE Standard does not imply that there are no other ways to produce, test, measure, purchase, market, or provide other goods and services related to the scope of the IEEE Standard. Furthermore, the viewpoint expressed at the time a standard is approved and issued is subject to change brought about through developments in the state of the art and comments received from users of the standard. Every IEEE Standard is subjected to review at least every five years for revision or reaffirmation. When a document is more than five years old and has not been reaffirmed, it is reasonable to conclude that its contents, although still of some value, do not wholly reflect the present state of the art. Users are cautioned to check to determine that they have the latest edition of any IEEE Standard.

Comments for revision of IEEE Standards are welcome from any interested party, regardless of membership affiliation with IEEE. Suggestions for changes in documents should be in the form of a proposed change of text, together with appropriate supporting comments.

Interpretations: Occasionally questions may arise regarding the meaning of portions of standards as they relate to specific applications. When the need for interpretations is brought to the attention of IEEE, the Institute will initiate action to prepare appropriate responses. Since IEEE Standards represent a consensus of all concerned interests, it is important to ensure that any interpretation has also received the concurrence of a balance of interests. For this reason, IEEE and the members of its societies and Standards Coordinating Committees are not able to provide an instant response to interpretation requests except in those cases where the matter has previously received formal consideration.

Comments on standards and requests for interpretations should be addressed to:

> Secretary, IEEE-SA Standards Board
> 445 Hoes Lane
> P.O. Box 1331
> Piscataway, NJ 08855-1331
> USA

Note: Attention is called to the possibility that implementation of this standard may require use of subject matter covered by patent rights. By publication of this standard, no position is taken with respect to the existence or validity of any patent rights in connection therewith. The IEEE shall not be responsible for identifying patents for which a license may be required by an IEEE standard or for conducting inquiries into the legal validity or scope of those patents that are brought to its attention.

Introduction

(This introduction is not part of IEEE Std 1012-1998, IEEE Standard for Software Verification and Validation.)

Software verification and validation (V&V) is a technical discipline of systems engineering. The purpose of software V&V is to help the development organization build quality into the software during the software life cycle. The software V&V processes determine if development products of a given activity conform to the requirements of that activity, and if the software satisfies the intended use and user needs. The determination includes assessment, analysis, evaluation, review, inspection, and testing of software products and processes. The software V&V is performed in parallel with the software development, not at the conclusion of the software development.

The software V&V is an extension of the program management and systems engineering team, and undertakes its determination to identify objective data and conclusions (i.e., proactive in its feedback) about software quality, performance, and schedule compliance for the development organization. This feedback consists of anomalies, performance improvements, and quality improvements against not only the expected operating conditions but across the full operating spectrum of the system and its interfaces. Early feedback results allow the development organization to modify the software products in a timely fashion and reduce overall project cost and schedule impacts. Without a proactive approach, the anomalies and the associated software changes are typically delayed to later in the program schedule, resulting in greater program cost and schedule delays.

IEEE Std 1012-1986 was a product standard that defined the contents of the Software Verification and Validation Plan (SVVP). This revision of the standard, IEEE Std 1012-1998, is a process standard that defines the verification and validation processes in terms of specific activities and related tasks. IEEE Std 1012-1998 also defines the contents of the SVVP including example format.

This standard introduces the following key concepts:

— *Software integrity levels.* Defines four software integrity levels to describe the criticality of the software varying from high integrity to low integrity.

— *Minimum V&V tasks for each software integrity level.* Defines the minimum V&V tasks required for each of the four software integrity levels. Includes a table of optional V&V tasks as a method of allowing the user to tailor the V&V effort to address project needs and application specific characteristics.

— *Intensity and rigor applied to V&V tasks.* Introduces the notion that the intensity and rigor applied to the V&V tasks vary according to the software integrity level. Higher software integrity levels require the application of greater intensity and rigor to the V&V task. Intensity includes greater scope of analysis across all normal and abnormal system operating conditions. Rigor includes more formal techniques and recording procedures.

— *Detailed criteria for V&V tasks.* Defines specific criteria for each V&V task including minimum criteria for correctness, consistency, completeness, accuracy, readability, and testability. The V&V task descriptions include a list of the required task inputs and outputs.

— *Systems viewpoint.* Adds minimum V&V tasks to address systems issues. These V&V tasks include Hazard Analysis, Risk Analysis, Migration Assessment, and Retirement Assessment. Specific systems issues are contained in individual V&V task criteria.

— *Compliance with International and IEEE standards.* Defines the V&V processes to be compliant with the life cycle process standards such as ISO/IEC Std 12207, IEEE Std 1074-1997, and IEEE/EIA Std 12207.0-1996, as well as the entire family of IEEE software engineering standards. This standard addresses the full software life cycle processes including acquisition, supply, development, operation, and maintenance.

The following persons were on the working group:

Roger U. Fujii, *Chair* **Delores R. Wallace,** *Vice Chair*

Donald W. Sova, *Secretary*

Richard J. Blauw	Caroline L. Evans	Victor J. Maggioli
Robert Brill	Richard L. Evans	Kartik C. Majumdar
Robert Butler	George Finelli	John R. Matras
John G. Capen	Kirby K. Fortenberry	Tomoo Matsubara
Robert Charette	Eva Freund	Randall May
Hu Cheng	Nicholas P. Ginex	Marco Migliaro
John Chilenski	Stephen Harris	Warren L. Persons
François Coallier	John W. Horch	Ian C. Pyle
Darrell Cooksey	Laura M. Ippolito	W. Jim Rice
Ben Conger	George Jackelen	Paul J. Rodi
Geoff Cozens	William Jackson	Uma D. Satyen
Paul R. Croll	Lisa A. Jensen	John A. Scott
H. Taz Daughtrey	Barry S. Johnson	Grant Shen
Harpal S. Dhama	Q. Leon Jordan	James Stanfield
Lisa J. Downey	Kathryn Kemp	Nancy E. Sunderland
James Dukelow	J. Dennis Lawrence	Gina To
Robert G. Ebenau	Jeffrey Lewis	Leonard L. Tripp
Vera Edelstein		Michael E. Waterman

The following persons were on the balloting committee:

Mikhail Auguston
Dennis Beauchaine
Leo Beltracchi
Mordechai Ben-Menachem
H. Ronald Berlack
Richard E. Biehl
William J. Boll
Juris Borzovs
Edward R. Byrne
James E. Cardow
Keith Chan
John J. Chilenski
Antonio M. Cicu
Theo Clarke
Sylvain Clermont
François Coallier
Rosemary Coleman
Darrell Cooksey
Geoff Cozens
Paul R. Croll
Gregory T. Daich
M. A. Daniels
Taz Daughtrey
Bostjan K. Derganc
Perry R. DeWeese
Harpal Dhama
Sherman Eagles
Robert G. Ebenau
Leo Egan
Richard L. Evans
William Eventoff
Jonathan H. Fairclough
John W. Fendrich
Julian Forster
Kirby K. Fortenberry
Eva Freund
Roger U. Fujii
Simon Gabrihelidis
Barry L. Garner
Adel N. Ghannam
Hiranmay Ghosh
Marilyn Ginsberg-Finner
Eugene A. Glasser
John Garth Glynn

Julio Gonzalez-Sanz
L. M. Gunther
David A. Gustafson
John Harauz
Herbert Hecht
Manfred Hein
Gordon Henley
Mark Henley
John W. Horch
Jerry Huller
Peter L. Hung
George Jackelen
Lisa A. Jensen
Q. Leon Jordan
Vladan V. Jovanovic
William S. Junk
George X. Kambic
Myron S. Karasik
Ron S. Kenett
Robert J. Kierzyk
Shaye Koenig
Thomas M. Kurihara
John B. Lane
J. Dennis Lawrence
Fang Ching Lim
Victor J. Maggioli
David Maibor
Kartik C. Majumdar
Henry A. Malec
John R. Matras
Tomoo Matsubara
Mike McAndrew
Sue McGrath
Jerome W. Mersky
Bret Michael
Lance Miller
Alan Miller
Lisa Ming
Celia H. Modell
Pavol Navrat
Myrna L. Olson
Mike Ottewill
Indradeb P. Pal
Lalit M. Patnaik

Warren L. Persons
John G. Phippen
Alex Polack
Peter T. Poon
Kenneth R. Ptack
Ian C. Pyle
Annette D. Reilly
Christian Reiser
Dennis Rilling
Helmut Sandmayr
Uma D. Satyen
Stephen R. Schach
Hans Schaefer
Norman Schneidewind
David J. Schultz
Gregory D. Schumacher
Carl S. Seddio
Robert W. Shillato
David M. Siefert
Carl A. Singer
James M. Sivak
Alfred R. Sorkowitz
Donald W. Sova
Julia Stesney
Norma Stopyra
Fred J. Strauss
Robert N. Sulgrove
John Swearingen
Booker Thomas
Gina To
Patricia Trellue
T. H. Tse
Theodore J. Urbanowicz
Glenn D. Venables
Udo Voges
Dolores Wallace
Camille S. White-Partain
Scott A. Whitmire
P. A. Wolfgang
Paul R. Work
Kathryn P. Yglesias
Natalie C. Yopconka
Weider D. Yu
Geraldine Zimmerman

When the IEEE-SA Standards Board approved this standard on 19 March 1998, it had the following membership:

Richard J. Holleman, *Chair*   **Donald N. Heirman,** *Vice Chair*

Judith Gorman, *Secretary*

Contents

IEEE Standard for Software Verification and Validation

1. Overview

Software verification and validation (V&V) processes determine whether development products of a given activity conform to the requirements of that activity, and whether the software satisfies its intended use and user needs. This determination may include analysis, evaluation, review, inspection, assessment, and testing of software products and processes. V&V processes assess the software in the context of the system, including the operational environment, hardware, interfacing software, operators, and users.

This V&V standard is a process standard that addresses all software life cycle processes, including acquisition, supply, development, operation, and maintenance. This standard is compatible with all life cycle models. Not all life cycle models use all of the life cycle processes listed in this standard.

The user of this standard may invoke those software life cycle processes and the associated V&V processes that apply to the project. A description of the software life cycle processes may be found in ISO/IEC 12207 [B16][1], IEEE Std 1074-1997 [B12], and IEEE/EIA Std 12207.0-1996 [B13]. Annex A maps ISO/IEC 12207 (Tables A.1 and A.2) and IEEE Std 1074-1997 (Table A.3) to the V&V activities and tasks defined in this standard.

1.1 Purpose

The purpose of this standard is to

1) Establish a common framework for V&V processes, activities, and tasks in support of all software life cycle processes, including acquisition, supply, development, operation, and maintenance processes.

2) Define the V&V tasks, required inputs, and required outputs.

3) Identify the minimum V&V tasks corresponding to software integrity levels using a four-level scheme.

4) Define the content of a Software V&V Plan (SVVP).

---

[1]The numbers in brackets preceded by the letter B correspond to those of the "other references" listed in Annex H.

1.2 Field of application

This standard applies to software being developed, maintained, and reused (See Annex D for a description of V&V of reusable software). The term *software* also includes firmware, microcode, and documentation.

Software is a key component that contributes to system behavior and performance. This relationship requires that software V&V processes must take software interactions with all system components into consideration. The user of this standard should consider V&V as part of the software life cycle processes defined by industry standards such as ISO/IEC 12207 [B16], IEEE Std 1074-1997 [B12], or IEEE/EIA Std 12207.0-1996 [B13].

1.3 V&V objectives

V&V processes provide an objective assessment of software products and processes throughout the software life cycle. This assessment demonstrates whether the software requirements and system requirements (i.e., those allocated to software) are correct, complete, accurate, consistent, and testable. Other objectives of performing V&V are to

1) Facilitate early detection and correction of software errors;
2) Enhance management insight into process and product risk; and
3) Support the software life cycle processes to ensure compliance with program performance, schedule, and budget requirements.

The verification process provides supporting evidence that the software and its associated products

1) Comply with requirements (e.g., for correctness, completeness, consistency, accuracy) for all life cycle activities during each life cycle process (acquisition, supply, development, operation, and maintenance);
2) Satisfy standards, practices, and conventions during life cycle processes; and
3) Establish a basis for assessing the completion of each life cycle activity and for initiating other life cycle activities.

The validation process provides supporting evidence that the software satisfies system requirements allocated to software, and solves the right problem (e.g., correctly models physical laws, or implements system business rules).

V&V support primary life cycle processes. V&V processes are most effective when conducted in parallel with software development processes; otherwise, V&V objectives may not be realized. In this standard, V&V processes are discussed together because the V&V activities and tasks are interrelated and complementary. In some circumstances, the verification process may be viewed as a process separate from the validation process. The V&V task criteria described in Table 1 (starting on page 25) uniquely define the compliance requirements for V&V processes.

1.4 Organization of the standard

This standard is organized into clauses (Clauses 1 through 7), tables (Tables 1 through 3), figures (Figures 1 through 3), and annexes (Annexes A through I). Clause 1, Figures 1, 2, and 3, and Table 3 contain informative material that provides illustrations, examples, and process flow diagrams useful in understanding and using this standard. Clauses 2, 3, 4, 5, 6, and 7 and Tables 1 and 2 contain the mandatory V&V requirements for this standard. All annexes contain informative material except Annex I.

Clause 2 lists normative references. Clause 3 provides a definition of terms, abbreviations, and conventions. Clause 4 explains the concept of using software integrity levels for determining the scope and rigor of V&V

processes. Clause 5 describes each primary software life cycle process and lists the V&V activities and tasks associated with the life cycle process. Clause 6 describes the V&V reporting, administrative, and documentation requirements. Clause 7 outlines the content of a Software Verification and Validation Plan (SVVP).

Tables 1, 2, and 3 are the focal point of this standard, containing detailed V&V process, activity, and task requirements. Table 1 provides V&V task descriptions, inputs, and outputs for each life cycle process. Table 2 lists minimum V&V tasks required for different software integrity levels. Table 3 provides a list of optional V&V tasks and their suggested applications in the life cycle. These optional V&V tasks may be added to the minimum V&V tasks to tailor the V&V effort to project needs and application specific characteristics.

Figure 1 provides an example of an overview of the V&V inputs, outputs, and minimum V&V tasks for the highest software integrity level (Integrity Level 4). Figure 2 provides guidelines for scheduling V&V test planning, execution, and verification activities. An example of a phased life cycle model was used in Figures 1 and 2 to illustrate a mapping of the ISO/IEC 12207 life cycle processes to the V&V activities and tasks described in this standard.

This standard implements the V&V framework using the terminology of process, activity, and task. Figure 3 illustrates how the V&V processes are subdivided into activities, which in turn have associated tasks. Hereafter, the term *V&V effort* is used to refer to the framework of the V&V processes, activities, and tasks.

The annexes contain informative and normative information useful to implementing the requirements of this standard. Annex A (informative) describes the mapping of ISO/IEC 12207 and IEEE Std 1074-1997 V&V requirements to this standard's V&V activities and tasks. Annex B (informative) provides an example of a risk-based, four-level integrity scheme. Annex C (informative) provides a definition of independent verification and validation (IV&V). Annex D (informative) provides guidelines for conducting V&V of reusable software. Annex E (informative) describes V&V metrics for assessing V&V quality, V&V coverage, and software development processes and products. Such V&V metrics support process improvement tasks of project management. Annex F (informative) illustrates an example of the V&V organizational relationship to other project responsibilities. Annex G (informative) describes optional V&V tasks. Annex H (informative) lists standards and guides that may be useful in interpreting and implementing the V&V tasks identified in this standard. Annex I (normative) contains definitions from existing standards.

1.5 Audience

The audience for this standard is software suppliers, acquirers, developers, maintainers, V&V practitioners, operators, and managers in both the supplier and acquirer organizations.

1.6 Compliance

The word *shall* identifies mandatory requirements to claim compliance with this standard. The words *should* or *may* indicate optional tasks that are not required to claim compliance to this standard.

Any software integrity level scheme may be used with this standard. The software integrity level scheme used in this standard is not mandatory, but rather, establishes the minimum V&V tasks for the referenced software integrity scheme. To demonstrate compliance to this standard whenever different software integrity schemes are used, the user should map the project-specific software integrity scheme to the integrity scheme used in this standard. This mapping establishes the minimum V&V tasks that should be assigned to the project. Compliance with this standard requires that this mapping and the associated minimum V&V tasks be documented in the SVVP.

Not all V&V efforts are initiated at the start of the life cycle process of acquisition and continued through the maintenance process. If a project uses only selected life cycle processes, then compliance with this standard is achieved if the minimum V&V tasks are implemented for the associated life cycle processes selected for the project. As in all cases, the minimum V&V tasks are defined by the software integrity level assigned to the software. For life cycle processes that are not used by the project, the V&V requirements and tasks for those life cycle processes are optional V&V tasks invoked as needed at the discretion of the project. Specific software development methods and technologies (such as automated code generation from detailed design) may eliminate development steps or combine several development steps into one. Therefore, a corresponding adaptation of the minimum V&V tasks is permitted.

When this standard is invoked for existing software and the required V&V inputs are not available, then V&V tasks may use other available project input sources or may reconstruct the needed inputs to achieve compliance with this standard.

1.7 Disclaimer

This standard establishes minimum criteria for V&V processes, activities, and tasks. The implementation of these criteria does not, however, automatically ensure compliance to system or mission objectives, or prevent adverse consequences (e.g., loss of life, mission failure, loss of system safety or security, financial or social loss). Compliance with this standard does not absolve any party from any social, moral, financial, or legal obligations.

1.8 Limitations

None.

2. Normative references

This standard does not require the use of any normative references. Other standards considered to be useful in the implementation and interpretation of this standard are listed in Annex H.

3. Definitions, abbreviations, and conventions

3.1 Definitions

The following terms, including those defined in other standards, are used as indicated in this standard. Annex I contains definitions taken from other existing standards.

3.1.1 acceptance testing: Testing conducted in an operational environment to determine whether a system satisfies its acceptance criteria (i.e., initial requirements and current needs of its user) and to enable the customer to determine whether to accept the system.

3.1.2 anomaly: See Annex I.

3.1.3 component testing: Testing conducted to verify the correct implementation of the design and compliance with program requirements for one software element (e.g., unit, module) or a collection of software elements.

3.1.4 criticality: A subjective description of the intended use and application of the system. Software criticality properties may include safety, security, complexity, reliability, performance, or other characteristics.

3.1.5 criticality analysis: A structured evaluation of the software characteristics (e.g., safety, security, complexity, performance) for severity of impact of system failure, system degradation, or failure to meet software requirements or system objectives.

3.1.6 hazard: See Annex I.

3.1.7 hazard analysis: A systematic qualitative or quantitative evaluation of software for undesirable outcomes resulting from the development or operation of a system. These outcomes may include injury, illness, death, mission failure, economic loss, property loss, environmental loss, or adverse social impact. This evaluation may include screening or analysis methods to categorize, eliminate, reduce, or mitigate hazards.

3.1.8 hazard identification: See Annex I.

3.1.9 independent verification and validation (IV&V): V&V processes performed by an organization with a specified degree of technical, managerial, and financial independence from the development organization.

3.1.10 integration testing: An orderly progression of testing of incremental pieces of the software program in which software elements, hardware elements, or both are combined and tested until the entire system has been integrated to show compliance with the program design, and capabilities and requirements of the system.

3.1.11 integrity level: See Annex I.

3.1.12 interface design document (IDD): Documentation that describes the architecture and design of interfaces between system and components. These descriptions include control algorithms, protocols, data contents and formats, and performance.

3.1.13 interface requirement specification (IRS): Documentation that specifies requirements for interfaces between systems or components. These requirements include constraints on formats and timing.

3.1.14 life cycle process: A set of interrelated activities that result in the development or assessment of software products. Each activity consists of tasks. The life cycle processes may overlap one another. For V&V purposes, no process is concluded until its development products are verified and validated according to the defined tasks in the SVVP.

3.1.15 minimum tasks: Those V&V tasks required for the software integrity level assigned to the software to be verified and validated.

3.1.16 optional tasks: Those V&V tasks that may be added to the minimum V&V tasks to address specific application requirements.

3.1.17 required inputs: The set of items necessary to perform the minimum V&V tasks mandated within any life cycle activity.

3.1.18 required outputs: The set of items produced as a result of performing the minimum V&V tasks mandated within any life cycle activity.

3.1.19 risk: See Annex I.

3.1.20 risk analysis: See Annex I.

3.1.21 software design description (SDD): A representation of software created to facilitate analysis, planning, implementation, and decision making. The software design description is used as a medium for communicating software design information, and may be thought of as a blueprint or model of the system.

3.1.22 software integrity levels: See Annex I.

3.1.23 software requirements specification (SRS): Documentation of the essential requirements (i.e., functions, performance, design constraints, and attributes) of the software and its external interfaces. The software requirements are derived from the system specification.

3.1.24 software verification and validation plan (SVVP): A plan describing the conduct of software V&V.

3.1.25 software verification and validation report (SVVR): Documentation of V&V results and software quality assessments.

3.1.26 system testing: The activities of testing an integrated hardware and software system to verify and validate whether the system meets its original objectives.

3.1.27 test case: Documentation that specifies inputs, predicted results, and a set of execution conditions for a test item.

3.1.28 test design: Documentation that specifies the details of the test approach for a software feature or combination of software features and identifying the associated tests.

3.1.29 test plan: Documentation that specifies the scope, approach, resources, and schedule of intended testing activities.

3.1.30 test procedure: Documentation that specifies a sequence of actions for the execution of a test.

3.1.31 validation: See Annex I.

3.1.32 verification: See Annex I.

3.2 Abbreviations

The following abbreviations appear in this standard:

COTS   Commercial-Off-The-Shelf
IDD   Interface Design Document
IEC   International Electrotechnical Commission
IRS   Interface Requirements Specification
ISO   International Organization for Standardization
IV&V   Independent Verification and Validation
RFP   Request for Proposal (-tender)
SDD   Software Design Description
SRS   Software Requirements Specification
SVVP   Software Verification and Validation Plan
SVVR   Software Verification and Validation Report
V&V   Verification and Validation

3.3 Conventions

The term "documentation" refers to information that may exist in several documents or may be embedded within a document addressing more than one subject. "Documentation" includes data in electronic format, and may be in narrative, tabular, or graphic form (e.g., format of Figure 1).

4. V&V software integrity levels

4.1 Software integrity levels

Software exhibits different criticality based upon its intended use and application of the system to critical or noncritical uses. Some software systems affect critical, life-sustaining systems, while other software systems are noncritical, standalone research tools. Software criticality is a description of the intended use and application of a system. This standard uses a software integrity level approach to quantify software criticality. Software integrity levels denote a range of software criticality values necessary to maintain risks within acceptable limits. These software properties may include safety, security, software complexity, performance, reliability, or other characteristics. Critical, high-integrity software typically requires a larger set and more rigorous application of V&V tasks.

For planning the V&V processes, software integrity levels are generally assigned early in the development process, preferably during the system requirements analysis and architecture design activities. The software integrity level can be assigned to software requirements, functions, group of functions, or software components or subsystems. The assigned software integrity levels may vary as the software evolves. Design, coding, procedural, and technology implementation features selected by the development organization can raise or lower the software criticality and the associated software integrity levels assigned to the software. Risk mitigation approaches acceptable to the acquirer also may be used to reduce software criticality, thus allowing the selection of a lower integrity level. The software integrity level assignment is continually updated and reviewed by conducting the V&V criticality analysis task throughout the software development process.

This standard does not mandate the use of the software integrity scheme referenced in this standard. The user of this standard may select any software integrity scheme (such as from existing standards) that defines the requirements for assigning software integrity levels. The software integrity levels established for a project result from agreements among the acquirer, supplier, developer, and independent assurance authorities (e.g., a regulatory body or responsible agency). The V&V effort shall specify a software integrity scheme if one is not already defined. This standard shall use the following four-level software integrity scheme as a method to define the minimum V&V tasks that are assigned to each software integrity level:

Criticality	Description	Level
High	Selected function affects critical performance of the system.	4
Major	Selected function affects important system performance.	3
Moderate	Selected function affects system performance, but workaround strategies can be implemented to compensate for loss of performance.	2
Low	Selected function has noticeable effect on system performance but only creates inconvenience to the user if the function does not perform in accordance with requirements.	1

To identify the minimum V&V tasks that apply to a different selected software integrity level scheme, the user of the standard shall map this standard's software integrity scheme and associated minimum V&V tasks

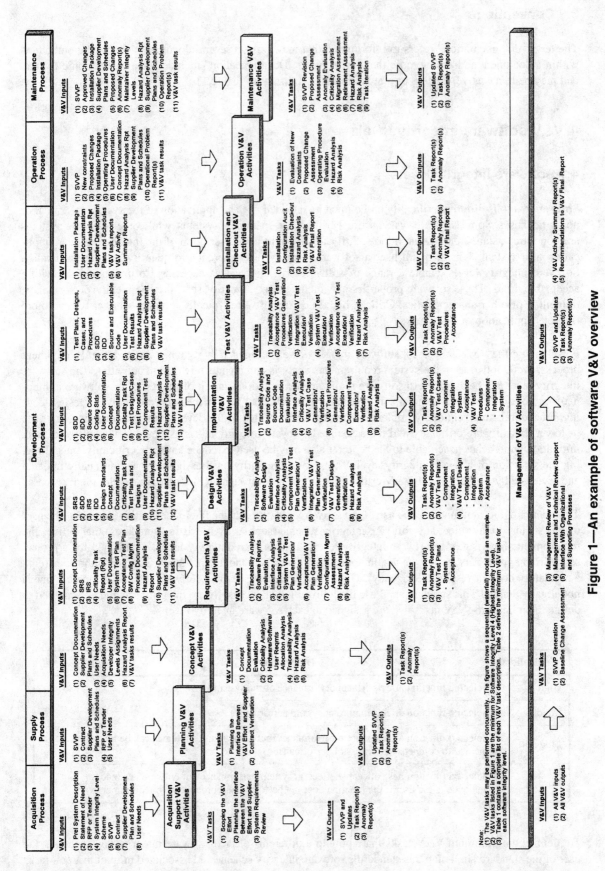

Figure 1—An example of software V&V overview

to their selected software integrity level scheme. The mapping of the software integrity level scheme and the associated minimum V&V tasks shall be documented in the SVVP. An example of a risk-based software integrity level scheme is illustrated in Annex B.

This standard does not apply to those portions of the software for which none of the software integrity criteria apply (i.e., those software portions below level 1). The basis for assigning software integrity levels to software components shall be documented in a V&V Task Report and V&V Final Report.

The integrity level assigned to reusable software shall be in accordance with the integrity level scheme adopted for the project (see Annex D), and the reusable software shall be evaluated for use in the context of its application.

The V&V processes are tailored to specific system requirements and applications through the selection of a software integrity level with its corresponding minimum V&V tasks and the addition of optional V&V tasks. The addition of optional V&V tasks allows the V&V effort to address application specific characteristics of the software.

5. V&V processes

V&V processes support the management process (5.1), acquisition process (5.2), supply process (5.3), development process (5.4), operation process (5.5), and maintenance process (5.6). The minimum V&V activities and tasks supporting the above processes are referenced in the following subclauses and defined in Table 1. This clause's subtitles are the same as subtitles in Table 1 to correlate the requirements of the following subclauses with Table 1 tasks.

The V&V effort shall comply with the task descriptions, inputs, and outputs as described in Table 1. The V&V effort shall perform the minimum V&V tasks as specified in Table 2 for the assigned software integrity level. If the user of this standard has selected a different software integrity level scheme, then the mapping of that integrity level scheme to Table 2 shall define the minimum V&V tasks for each of the user's software integrity levels.

Not all software projects include each of the life cycle processes listed above. To be in compliance with this standard, the V&V processes shall address all those life cycle processes used by the software project.

Some V&V activities and tasks include analysis, evaluations, and tests that may be performed by multiple organizations (e.g., software development, project management, quality assurance, V&V). For example, risk analysis and hazard analysis are performed by project management, the development organization, and the V&V effort. The V&V effort performs these tasks to develop the supporting basis of evidence showing whether the software product satisfies its requirements. These V&V analyses are complementary to other analyses and do not eliminate or replace the analyses performed by other organizations. The degree to which these analyses efforts are coordinated with other organizations shall be documented in the organizational responsibility section of the SVVP.

The user of this standard shall document the V&V processes in the SVVP and shall define the information and facilities necessary to manage and perform these processes, activities, and tasks, and to coordinate those V&V processes with other related aspects of the project. The results of V&V activities and tasks shall be documented in task reports, activity summary reports, anomaly reports, V&V test documents, and the V&V Final Report.

5.1 Process: Management

The management process contains the generic activities and tasks, which may be employed by any party that manages its respective processes. The management tasks are to 1) prepare the plans for execution of the process, 2) initiate the implementation of the plan, 3) monitor the execution of the plan, 4) analyze problems discovered during the execution of the plan, 5) report progress of the processes, 6) ensure products satisfy requirements, 7) assess evaluation results, 8) determine whether a task is complete, and 9) check the results for completeness.

5.1.1 Activity: Management of V&V

The Management of V&V activity is performed in all software life cycle processes and activities. This activity continuously reviews the V&V effort, revises the SVVP as necessary based upon updated project schedules and development status, and coordinates the V&V results with the developer and other supporting processes such as quality assurance, configuration management, and reviews and audits. The Management of V&V assesses each proposed change to the system and software, identifies the software requirements that are affected by the change, and plans the V&V tasks to address the change. For each proposed change, the Management of V&V assesses whether any new hazards or risks are introduced in the software, and identifies the impact of the change to the assigned software integrity levels. V&V task planning is revised by adding new V&V tasks or increasing the scope and intensity of existing V&V tasks if software integrity levels or hazards or risks are changed. The Management of V&V activity monitors and evaluates all V&V outputs. Through the use of V&V metrics and other qualitative and quantitative measures, this V&V activity develops program trend data and possible risk issues that are provided to the developer and acquirer to effect timely notification and resolution. At key program milestones (e.g., requirements review, design review, test readiness), the Management of V&V consolidates the V&V results to establish supporting evidence whether to proceed to the next set of software development activities. Whenever necessary, the Management of V&V determines whether a V&V task needs to be re-performed as a result of developer changes in the software program.

The V&V effort shall perform, as appropriate for the selected software integrity level, the minimum V&V tasks for Management of V&V from the following list:

1)   Task: Software Verification and Validation Plan (SVVP) Generation
2)   Task: Baseline Change Assessment
3)   Task: Management Review of V&V
4)   Task: Management and Technical Review Support
5)   Task: Interface With Organizational and Supporting Processes

5.2 Process: Acquisition

The acquisition process begins with the definition of the need (e.g., statement of need) to acquire a system, software product, or software service. The process continues with the preparation and issuance of a request for proposal (e.g., bid request, tender), selection of a supplier, and management of the acquisition process through to the acceptance of the system, software product, or software service. The V&V effort uses the acquisition process to scope the V&V effort, plan interfaces with the supplier and acquirer, and review the draft systems requirements contained in the request for proposal.

5.2.1 Activity: Acquisition Support V&V

The Acquisition Support V&V activity addresses project initiation, request for proposal, contract preparation, supplier monitoring, and acceptance and completion.

The V&V effort shall perform, as appropriate for the selected software integrity level, the minimum V&V tasks for Acquisition Support V&V from the following list:

1) Task: Scoping the V&V Effort
2) Task: Planning the Interface Between the V&V Effort and Supplier
3) Task: System Requirements Review

5.3 Process: Supply

The supply process is initiated by either a decision to prepare a proposal to answer an acquirer's request for proposal or by signing and entering into a contract with the acquirer to provide the system, software product, or software service. The process continues with the determination of procedures and resources needed to manage the project, including development of project plans and execution of the plans through delivery of the system, software product, or software service to the acquirer. The V&V effort uses the supply process products to verify that the request for proposal requirements and contract requirements are consistent and satisfy user needs. The V&V planning activity uses the contract requirements including program schedules to revise and update the interface planning between the supplier and acquirer.

5.3.1 Activity: Planning V&V

The Planning V&V activity addresses the initiation, preparation of response, contract, planning, execution and control, review and evaluation, and delivery and completion activities.

The V&V effort shall perform, as appropriate for the selected software integrity level, the minimum V&V tasks for Planning V&V from the following list:

1) Task: Planning the Interface Between the V&V Effort and Supplier
2) Task: Contract Verification

5.4 Process: Development

The development process contains the activities and tasks of the developer. The process contains the activities for requirements analysis, design, coding, integration, testing, and installation and acceptance related to software products. The V&V activities verify and validate these software products. The V&V activities are organized into Concept V&V, Requirements V&V, Design V&V, Implementation V&V, Test V&V, and Installation and Checkout V&V.

5.4.1 Activity: Concept V&V

The Concept V&V activity represents the delineation of a specific implementation solution to solve the user's problem. During the Concept V&V activity, the system architecture is selected, and system requirements are allocated to hardware, software, and user interface components. The Concept V&V activity addresses system architectural design and system requirements analysis. The objectives of V&V are to verify the allocation of system requirements, validate the selected solution, and ensure that no false assumptions have been incorporated in the solution.

The V&V effort shall perform, as appropriate for the selected software integrity level, the minimum V&V tasks for Concept V&V from the following list:

1) Task: Concept Documentation Evaluation
2) Task: Criticality Analysis
3) Task: Hardware/Software/User Requirements Allocation Analysis
4) Task: Traceability Analysis

5)   Task: Hazard Analysis
6)   Task: Risk Analysis

5.4.2 Activity: Requirements V&V

The Requirements V&V activity defines the functional and performance requirements, interfaces external to the software, qualification requirements, safety and security requirements, human factors engineering, data definitions, user documentation for the software, installation and acceptance requirements, user operation and execution requirements, and user maintenance requirements. The Requirements V&V activity addresses software requirements analysis. The objectives of V&V are to ensure the correctness, completeness, accuracy, testability, and consistency of the requirements.

The V&V effort shall perform, as appropriate for the selected software integrity level, the minimum V&V tasks for Requirements V&V from the following list:

1)   Task: Traceability Analysis
2)   Task: Software Requirements Evaluation
3)   Task: Interface Analysis
4)   Task: Criticality Analysis
5)   Task: System V&V Test Plan Generation and Verification
6)   Task: Acceptance V&V Test Plan Generation and Verification
7)   Task: Configuration Management Assessment
8)   Task: Hazard Analysis
9)   Task: Risk Analysis

5.4.3 Activity: Design V&V

In the Design V&V activity, software requirements are transformed into an architecture and detailed design for each software component. The design includes databases and interfaces (external to the software, between the software components, and between software units). The Design V&V activity addresses software architectural design and software detailed design. The objectives of V&V are to demonstrate that the design is a correct, accurate, and complete transformation of the software requirements and that no unintended features are introduced.

The V&V effort shall perform, as appropriate for the selected software integrity level, the minimum V&V tasks for Design V&V from the following list:

1)   Task: Traceability Analysis
2)   Task: Software Design Evaluation
3)   Task: Interface Analysis
4)   Task: Criticality Analysis
5)   Task: Component V&V Test Plan Generation and Verification
6)   Task: Integration V&V Test Plan Generation and Verification
7)   Task: V&V Test Design Generation and Verification
8)   Task: Hazard Analysis
9)   Task: Risk Analysis

5.4.4 Activity: Implementation V&V

The Implementation V&V activity transforms the design into code, database structures, and related machine executable representations. The Implementation V&V activity addresses software coding and testing. The objectives of V&V are to verify and validate that these transformations are correct, accurate, and complete.

The V&V effort shall perform, as appropriate for the selected software integrity level, the minimum V&V tasks for Implementation V&V from the following list:

1) Task: Traceability Analysis
2) Task: Source Code and Source Code Documentation Evaluation
3) Task: Interface Analysis
4) Task: Criticality Analysis
5) Task: V&V Test Case Generation and Verification
6) Task: V&V Test Procedure Generation and Verification
7) Task: Component V&V Test Execution and Verification
8) Task: Hazard Analysis
9) Task: Risk Analysis

5.4.5 Activity: Test V&V

The Test V&V activity covers software testing, software integration, software qualification testing, system integration, and system qualification testing. The Test V&V activity and its relationship to the software life cycle is shown in Figure 2. The objectives of V&V are to ensure that the software requirements and system requirements allocated to software are satisfied by execution of integration, system, and acceptance tests.

For software integrity levels 3 and 4, the V&V effort shall generate its own V&V software and system test products (e.g., plans, designs, cases, procedures), execute and record its own tests, and verify those plans, designs, cases, procedures, and test results against software requirements. For software integrity levels 1 and 2, the V&V effort shall verify the development process test activities and products (e.g., test plans, designs, cases, procedures, and test execution results).

The V&V effort shall perform, as appropriate for the selected software integrity level, the minimum V&V tasks for Test V&V from the following list:

1) Task: Traceability Analysis
2) Task: Acceptance V&V Test Procedure Generation and Verification
3) Task: Integration V&V Test Execution and Verification
4) Task: System V&V Test Execution and Verification
5) Task: Acceptance V&V Test Execution and Verification
6) Task: Hazard Analysis
7) Task: Risk Analysis

5.4.6 Activity: Installation and Checkout V&V

The Installation and Checkout V&V activity is the installation of the software product in the target environment and the acquirer's acceptance review and testing of the software product. The Installation and Checkout V&V activity addresses software installation and software acceptance support. The objectives of V&V are to verify and validate the correctness of the software installation in the target environment.

The V&V effort shall perform, as appropriate for the selected software integrity level, the minimum V&V tasks for Installation and Checkout V&V from the following list:

1) Task: Installation Configuration Audit
2) Task: Installation Checkout
3) Task: Hazard Analysis
4) Task: Risk Analysis
5) Task: V&V Final Report Generation

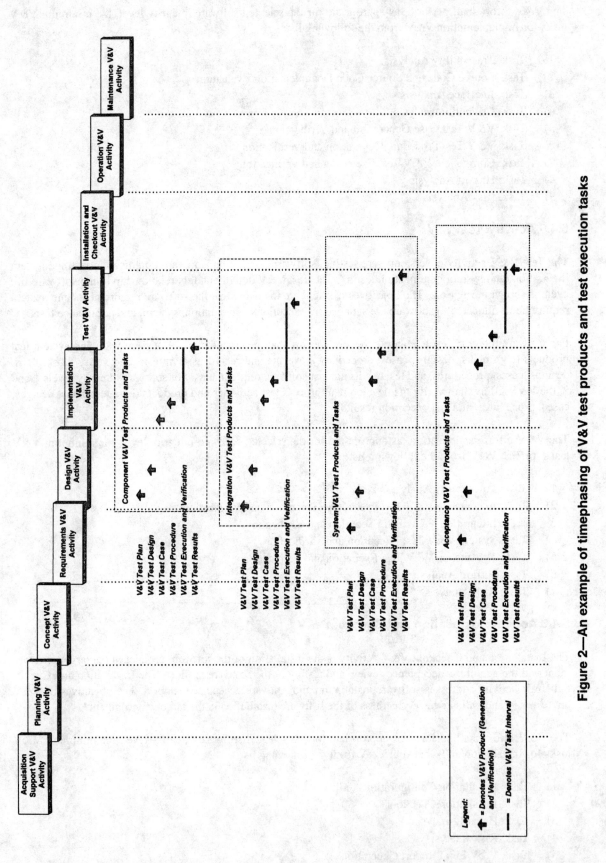

Figure 2—An example of timephasing of V&V test products and test execution tasks

5.5 Process: Operation

The operation process covers the operation of the software product and operational support to users. The Operation V&V activity evaluates the impact of any changes in the intended operating environment, assesses the effect on the system of any proposed changes, evaluates operating procedures for compliance with the intended use, and analyzes risks affecting the user and the system.

5.5.1 Activity: Operation V&V

The Operation V&V activity is the use of the software by the end user in an operational environment. The Operation V&V activity addresses operational testing, system operation, and user support. The objectives of V&V are to evaluate new constraints in the system, assess proposed changes and their impact on the software, and evaluate operating procedures for correctness and usability.

The V&V effort shall perform, as appropriate for the selected software integrity level, the minimum V&V tasks for Operation V&V from the following list:

1) Task: Evaluation of New Constraints
2) Task: Proposed Change Assessment
3) Task: Operating Procedures Evaluation
4) Task: Hazard Analysis
5) Task: Risk Analysis

5.6 Process: Maintenance

The maintenance process is activated when the software product undergoes modifications to code and associated documentation caused by a problem or a need for improvement or adaptation. The Maintenance V&V activity addresses modifications (e.g., enhancements, additions, deletions), migration, or retirement of the software during the operation process.

Modifications of the software shall be treated as development processes and shall be verified and validated as described in 5.1 (management process), and 5.4 (development process) of this standard. Software integrity level assignments shall be assessed during the maintenance process. The software integrity level assignments shall be revised as appropriate to reflect the requirements of the maintenance process. These modifications may be derived from requirements specified to correct software errors (e.g., corrective), to adapt to a changed operating environment (e.g., adaptive), or to respond to additional user requests or enhancements (e.g., perfective).

5.6.1 Activity: Maintenance V&V

The Maintenance V&V activity covers modifications (e.g., corrective, adaptive, and perfective), migration, and retirement of software. Migration of software is the movement of software to a new operational environment. For migrating software, the V&V effort shall verify that the migrated software meets the requirements of 5.4 through 5.5. The retirement of software is the withdrawal of active support by the operation and maintenance organization, partial or total replacement by a new system, or installation of an upgraded system.

If the software was verified under this standard, the standard shall continue to be followed in the maintenance process. If the software was not verified under this standard and appropriate documentation is not available or adequate, the V&V effort shall determine whether the missing or incomplete documentation should be generated. In making this determination of whether to generate missing documentation, the minimum V&V requirements of the assigned software integrity level should be taken into consideration.

The Maintenance V&V activity addresses problem and modification analysis, modification implementation, maintenance review/acceptance, migration, and software retirement. The objectives of V&V are to assess proposed changes and their impact on the software, evaluate anomalies that are discovered during operation, assess migration requirements, assess retirement requirements, and re-perform V&V tasks.

The V&V effort shall perform, as appropriate for the selected software integrity level, the minimum V&V tasks for Maintenance V&V from the following list:

1) Task: SVVP Revision
2) Task: Proposed Change Assessment
3) Task: Anomaly Evaluation
4) Task: Criticality Analysis
5) Task: Migration Assessment
6) Task: Retirement Assessment
7) Task: Hazard Analysis
8) Task: Risk Analysis
9) Task: Task Iteration

6. Software V&V reporting, administrative, and documentation requirements

6.1 V&V reporting requirements

V&V reporting occurs throughout the software life cycle. The SVVP shall specify the content, format, and timing of all V&V reports. The V&V reports shall constitute the Software Verification and Validation Report (SVVR). The V&V reports shall consist of required V&V reports (i.e., V&V Task Reports, V&V Activity Summary Reports, V&V Anomaly Reports, and V&V Final Report). The V&V reports may also include optional reports. Reporting requirements are described in 7.6 of this standard.

6.2 V&V administrative requirements

The SVVP describes the V&V administrative requirements that support the V&V effort. These V&V administrative requirements shall consist of the following:

1) Anomaly Resolution and Reporting
2) Task Iteration Policy
3) Deviation Policy
4) Control Procedures
5) Standards, Practices, and Conventions

V&V administrative requirements are described in 7.7 of this standard.

6.3 V&V documentation requirements

6.3.1 V&V Test documentation

V&V Test documentation requirements shall include the test plans, designs, cases, procedures, and results for component, integration, system, and acceptance testing. The V&V test documentation shall comply with project-defined test document purpose, format, and content (e.g., see IEEE Std 829-1983 [B5]). The V&V task descriptions for component, integration, system, and acceptance testing are described in Table 1.

6.3.2 SVVP documentation

The V&V effort shall generate an SVVP that addresses the topics described in Clause 7 of this standard. If there is no information pertinent to a topic, the SVVP shall contain the phrase, "This topic is not applicable to this plan.", with an appropriate reason for the exclusion. Additional topics may be added to the plan. If some SVVP material appears in other documents, the SVVP may repeat the material or make reference to the material. The SVVP shall be maintained throughout the life of the software.

The SVVP shall include the V&V documentation requirements defined in 6.1, 6.2, and 6.3.1.

7. SVVP outline

The SVVP shall contain the content as described in 7.1 through 7.8 of this standard. The user of this standard may adopt any format and section numbering system for the SVVP. The SVVP section numbers listed in this standard are provided to assist the readability of this standard and are not mandatory to be in compliance with this standard.

An example SVVP outline is shown in the boxed text.

Software V&V plan outline (example)

1. Purpose
2. Referenced Documents
3. Definitions
4. V&V Overview
   4.1 Organization
   4.2 Master Schedule
   4.3 Software Integrity Level Scheme
   4.4 Resources Summary
   4.5 Responsibilities
   4.6 Tools, Techniques, and Methods
5. V&V Processes
   5.1 Process: Management
      5.1.1 Activity: Management of V&V
   5.2 Process: Acquisition
      5.2.1 Activity: Acquisition Support V&V
   5.3 Process: Supply
      5.3.1 Activity: Planning V&V
   5.4 Process: Development
      5.4.1 Activity: Concept V&V
      5.4.2 Activity: Requirements V&V
      5.4.3 Activity: Design V&V
      5.4.4 Activity: Implementation V&V
      5.4.5 Activity: Test V&V
      5.4.6 Activity: Installation and Checkout V&V
   5.5 Process: Operation
      5.5.1 Activity: Operation V&V
   5.6 Process: Maintenance
      5.6.1 Activity: Maintenance V&V
6. V&V Reporting Requirements
7. V&V Administrative Requirements
   7.1 Anomaly Resolution and Reporting
   7.2 Task Iteration Policy
   7.3 Deviation Policy
   7.4 Control Procedures
   7.5 Standards, Practices, and Conventions
8. V&V Documentation Requirements

7.1 (SVVP Section 1) Purpose

The SVVP shall describe the purpose, goals, and scope of the software V&V effort, including waivers from this standard. The software project for which the Plan is being written and the specific software processes and products covered by the software V&V effort shall be identified.

7.2 (SVVP Section 2) Referenced documents

The SVVP shall identify the compliance documents, documents referenced by the SVVP, and any supporting documents supplementing or implementing the SVVP.

7.3 (SVVP Section 3) Definitions

The SVVP shall define or reference all terms used in the SVVP, including the criteria for classifying an anomaly as a critical anomaly. All abbreviations and notations used in the SVVP shall be described.

7.4 (SVVP Section 4) V&V overview

The SVVP shall describe the organization, schedule, software integrity level scheme, resources, responsibilities, tools, techniques, and methods necessary to perform the software V&V.

7.4.1 (SVVP Section 4.1) Organization

The SVVP shall describe the organization of the V&V effort, including the degree of independence required (See Annex C of this standard). The SVVP shall describe the relationship of the V&V processes to other processes such as development, project management, quality assurance, and configuration management. The SVVP shall describe the lines of communication within the V&V effort, the authority for resolving issues raised by V&V tasks, and the authority for approving V&V products. Annex F provides an example organizational relationship chart.

7.4.2 (SVVP Section 4.2) Master Schedule

The SVVP shall describe the project life cycle and milestones. It shall summarize the schedule of V&V tasks and task results as feedback to the development, organizational, and supporting processes (e.g., quality assurance and configuration management). V&V tasks shall be scheduled to be re-performed according to the task iteration policy.

If the life cycle used in the SVVP differs from the life cycle model in this standard, this section shall describe how all requirements of the standard are satisfied (e.g., by cross-referencing to this standard).

7.4.3 (SVVP Section 4.3) Software integrity level scheme

The SVVP shall describe the agreed upon software integrity level scheme established for the system and the mapping of the selected scheme to the model used in this standard. The SVVP shall document the assignment of software integrity levels to individual components (e.g., requirements, detailed functions, software modules, subsystems, or other software partitions), where there are differing software integrity levels assigned within the program. For each SVVP update, the assignment of software integrity levels shall be reassessed to reflect changes that may occur in the integrity levels as a result of architecture selection, detailed design choices, code construction usage, or other development activities.

7.4.4 (SVVP Section 4.4) Resources summary

The SVVP shall summarize the V&V resources, including staffing, facilities, tools, finances, and special procedural requirements (e.g., security, access rights, and documentation control).

7.4.5 (SVVP Section 4.5) Responsibilities

The SVVP shall identify an overview of the organizational element(s) and responsibilities for V&V tasks.

7.4.6 (SVVP Section 4.6) Tools, techniques, and methods

The SVVP shall describe documents, hardware and software V&V tools, techniques, methods, and operating and test environment to be used in the V&V process. Acquisition, training, support, and qualification information for each tool, technology, and method shall be included.

Tools that insert code into the software shall be verified and validated to the same rigor as the highest software integrity level of the software. Tools that do not insert code shall be verified and validated to assure that they meet their operational requirements. If partitioning of tool functions can be demonstrated, only those functions that are used in the V&V processes shall be verified to demonstrate that they perform correctly for their intended use.

The SVVP shall document the metrics to be used by V&V (see Annex E), and shall describe how these metrics support the V&V objectives.

7.5 (SVVP Section 5) V&V processes

The SVVP shall identify V&V activities and tasks to be performed for each of the V&V processes described in Clause 5 of this standard, and shall document those V&V activities and tasks. The SVVP shall contain an overview of the V&V activities and tasks for all software life cycle processes.

7.5.1 (SVVP Sections 5.1 through 5.6) "Software life cycle" [2]

The SVVP shall include sections 5.1 through 5.6 for V&V activities and tasks as shown in SVVP Outline (boxed text).

The SVVP shall address the following eight topics for each V&V activity:

1) *V&V Tasks.* The SVVP shall identify the V&V tasks to be performed. Table 1 describes the minimum V&V tasks, task criteria, and required inputs and outputs. Table 2 specifies the minimum V&V tasks that shall be performed for each software integrity level.

    The minimum tasks for software integrity level 4 are consolidated in graphic form in Figure 1.

    Optional V&V tasks may also be performed to augment the V&V effort to satisfy project needs. Optional V&V tasks are listed in Table 3 and described in Annex G. The list in Table 3 is illustrative and not exhaustive. The standard allows for optional V&V tasks to be used as appropriate.

---

[2]"Software Life Cycle" V&V sections are 5.1 Process: Management; 5.2 Process: Acquisition; 5.3 Process: Supply; 5.4 Process: Development; 5.5 Process: Operation; and 5.6 Process: Maintenance.

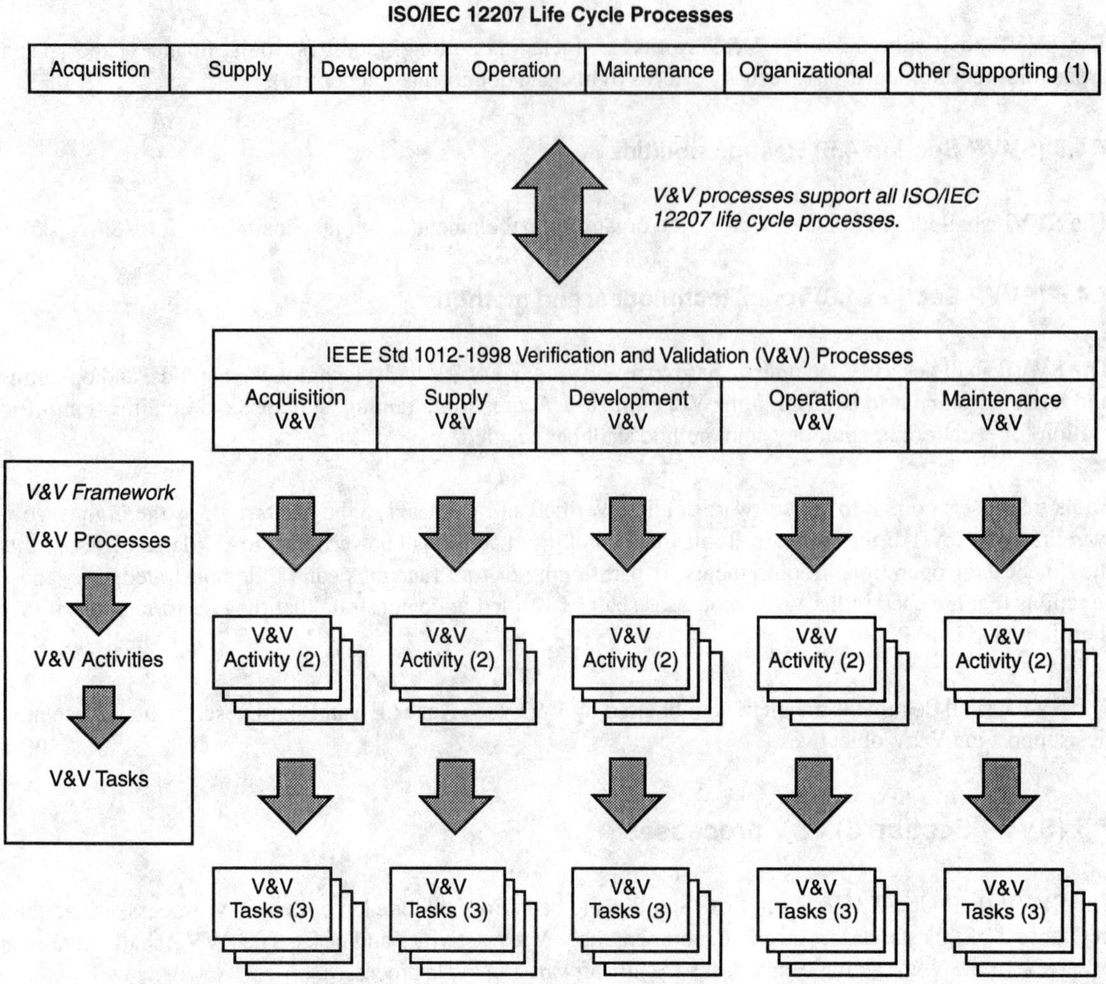

ISO/IEC 12207 Life Cycle Processes

Acquisition	Supply	Development	Operation	Maintenance	Organizational	Other Supporting (1)

V&V processes support all ISO/IEC 12207 life cycle processes.

IEEE Std 1012-1998 Verification and Validation (V&V) Processes

Acquisition V&V	Supply V&V	Development V&V	Operation V&V	Maintenance V&V

V&V Framework

V&V Processes

V&V Activities

V&V Tasks

V&V Activity (2)	V&V Activity (2)	V&V Activity (2)	V&V Activity (2)	V&V Activity (2)

V&V Tasks (3)	V&V Tasks (3)	V&V Tasks (3)	V&V Tasks (3)	V&V Tasks (3)

NOTES

1—"Other Supporting Processes" consist of "Documentation," "Configuration Management," "Quality Assurance," "Joint Review," "Audit," and "Problem Resolution."

2—Management of V&V activity is concurrent with all V&V activities.

3—The task description, inputs, and outputs of all V&V tasks are included in Table 1.

Figure 3—Framework of V&V processes, activities, and tasks hierarchy

Some V&V tasks are applicable to more than one software integrity level. The degree of rigor and intensity in performing and documenting the task should be commensurate with the software integrity level. As the software integrity level decreases, so does the required scope, intensity, and degree of rigor associated with the V&V task. For example, a hazard analysis performed for software integrity level 4 software might be formally documented and consider failures at the module level; a hazard analysis for software integrity level 3 software may consider only significant software failures and be documented informally as part of the design review process.

Testing requires advance planning that spans several development activities. Test documentation and its occurrence at specific processes in the life cycle are shown in Figures 1 and 2.

2) *Methods and Procedures.* The SVVP shall describe the methods and procedures for each task, including on-line access, and conditions for observation/evaluation of development processes. The SVVP shall define the criteria for evaluating the task results.

3) *Inputs.* The SVVP shall identify the required inputs for each V&V task. The SVVP shall specify the source and format of each input. The inputs required for the minimum V&V tasks are identified in Table 1. Other inputs may be used. For any V&V activity and task, all of the required inputs from preceding activities and tasks may be used but for conciseness, only the primary inputs are listed in Table 1.

4) *Outputs.* The SVVP shall identify the required outputs from each V&V task. The SVVP shall specify the purpose, format, and recipients of each output. The required outputs from each of the V&V tasks are identified in Table 1. Other outputs may be produced.

   The outputs of the Management of V&V and of the V&V tasks shall become inputs to subsequent processes and activities, as appropriate.

5) *Schedule.* The SVVP shall describe the schedule for the V&V tasks. The SVVP shall establish specific milestones for initiating and completing each task, for the receipt and criteria of each input, and for the delivery of each output.

6) *Resources.* The SVVP shall identify the resources for the performance of the V&V tasks. The SVVP shall specify resources by category (e.g., staffing, equipment, facilities, travel, and training.)

7) *Risks and Assumptions.* The SVVP shall identify the risks (e.g., schedule, resources, or technical approach) and assumptions associated with the V&V tasks. The SVVP shall provide recommendations to eliminate, reduce, or mitigate risks.

8) *Roles and Responsibilities.* The SVVP shall identify the organizational elements or individuals responsible for performing the V&V tasks.

7.6 (SVVP Section 6) V&V reporting requirements

V&V reporting shall consist of Task Reports, V&V Activity Summary Reports, Anomaly Reports, and the V&V Final Report. Task report(s), V&V activity summary report(s), and anomaly report(s) are provided as feedback to the software development process regarding the technical quality of each software product and process.

V&V reporting may also include optional reports such as special study reports. The format and grouping of the V&V reports are user defined. The required V&V reports shall consist of the following:

1) *Task Reports.* V&V tasks shall document V&V task results and status, and shall be in a format appropriate for technical disclosure. Examples of Task Reports include the following:

   a) Anomaly Evaluation
   b) Baseline Change Assessment
   c) Concept Documentation Evaluation
   d) Configuration Management Assessment
   e) Contract Verification
   f) Criticality Analysis
   g) Evaluation of New Constraints
   h) Hardware/Software/User Requirements Allocation Analysis
   i) Hazard Analysis

j)   Installation Checkout
k)   Installation Configuration Audit
l)   Interface Analysis
m)   Migration Assessment
n)   Operating Procedures Evaluation
o)   Proposed Change Assessment
p)   Recommendations
q)   Review Results
r)   Risk Analysis
s)   Software Design Evaluation
t)   Software Integrity Levels
u)   Software Requirements Evaluation
v)   Source Code and Source Code Documentation Evaluation
w)   System Requirements Review
x)   Test Results
y)   Traceability Analysis

2)   *V&V Activity Summary Reports.* An Activity Summary Report shall summarize the results of V&V tasks performed for each of the following V&V activities: Acquisition Support, Planning, Concept, Requirements, Design, Implementation, Test, and Installation and Checkout. For the Operation activity and Maintenance activity, V&V Activity Summary reports may be either updates to previous V&V activity summary reports or separate documents. Each V&V Activity Summary Report shall contain the following:

a)   Description of V&V tasks performed
b)   Summary of task results
c)   Summary of anomalies and resolution
d)   Assessment of software quality
e)   Identification and assessment of technical and management risks
f)   Recommendations

3)   *Anomaly Report.* An Anomaly Report shall document each anomaly detected by the V&V effort. Each anomaly shall be evaluated for its impact on the software system and assessed as to whether it is a critical anomaly (e.g., IEEE Std 1044-1993 [B9]). The scope and application of V&V activities and tasks shall be revised to address the causes of these anomalies and risks. Each Anomaly Report shall contain the following:

a)   Description and location in document or code
b)   Impact
c)   Cause of the anomaly and description of the error scenario
d)   Anomaly criticality level
e)   Recommendations

4)   *V&V Final Report.* The V&V Final Report shall be issued at the end of the Installation and Checkout activity or at the conclusion of the V&V effort. The V&V Final Report shall include the following:

a)   Summary of all life cycle V&V activities
b)   Summary of task results
c)   Summary of anomalies and resolutions
d)   Assessment of overall software quality
e)   Lessons learned/best practices
f)   Recommendations

Optional reports may include the following:

1) *Special Studies Reports.* These reports shall describe any special V&V studies conducted during the software life cycle. The title of the report may vary according to the subject matter. The reports shall document the results of technical and management tasks and shall include the following:

    a) Purpose and objectives
    b) Approach
    c) Summary of results

2) *Other Reports.* These reports shall describe the results of tasks not defined in the SVVP. The title of the report may vary according to the subject matter. These other task reports may include, for example, quality assurance results, end user testing results, safety assessment report, or configuration and data management status results.

7.7 (SVVP Section 7) V&V administrative requirements

Administrative V&V requirements shall describe anomaly resolution and reporting, task iteration policy, deviation policy, control procedures, and standards, practices, and conventions.

7.7.1 (SVVP Section 7.1) Anomaly resolution and reporting

The SVVP shall describe the method of reporting and resolving anomalies, including the criteria for reporting an anomaly, the anomaly report distribution list, and the authority and time lines for resolving anomalies. The section shall define the anomaly criticality levels. Classification for software anomalies may be found in IEEE Std 1044-1993 [B9].

7.7.2 (SVVP Section 7.2) Task iteration policy

The SVVP shall describe the criteria used to determine the extent to which a V&V task shall be repeated when its input is changed or task procedure is changed. These criteria may include assessments of change, software integrity level, and effects on budget, schedule, and quality.

7.7.3 (SVVP Section 7.3) Deviation policy

The SVVP shall describe the procedures and criteria used to deviate from the Plan. The information required for deviations shall include task identification, rationale, and effect on software quality. The SVVP shall identify the authorities responsible for approving deviations.

7.7.4 (SVVP Section 7.4) Control procedures

The SVVP shall identify control procedures applied to the V&V effort. These procedures shall describe how software products and V&V results shall be configured, protected, and stored.

These procedures may describe quality assurance, configuration management, data management, or other activities if they are not addressed by other efforts. The SVVP shall describe how the V&V effort shall comply with existing security provisions and how the validity of V&V results shall be protected from unauthorized alterations.

7.7.5 (SVVP Section 7.5) Standards, practices, and conventions

The SVVP shall identify the standards, practices, and conventions that govern the performance of V&V tasks including internal organizational standards, practices, and policies.

7.8 (SVVP Section 8) V&V documentation requirements

The SVVP shall define the purpose, format, and content of the test documents. A description of the format for these test documents may be found in IEEE Std 829-1983 [B5]. If the V&V effort uses test documentation or test types (e.g., component, integration, system, acceptance) different from those in this standard, the software V&V effort shall show a mapping of the proposed test documentation and execution to the test items defined in this standard. Test planning tasks defined in Table 1 shall be implemented in the test plan, test design(s), test case(s), and test procedure(s) documentation.

The SVVP shall describe the purpose, format, and content for the following V&V test documents:

1) Test Plan
2) Test Design
3) Test Cases
4) Test Procedures
5) Test Results

All V&V results and findings shall be documented in the V&V Final Report.

Table 1—V&V tasks, inputs, and outputs

V&V tasks	Required inputs	Required outputs
5.1.1 Management of V&V Activity (in parallel with all processes)		
(1) Software Verification and Validation Plan (SVVP) Generation. Generate an SVVP for all life cycle processes. The SVVP may require updating throughout the life cycle. Outputs of other activities are inputs to the SVVP. Establish a baseline SVVP prior to the Requirements V&V activities. Identify project milestones in the SVVP. Schedule V&V tasks to support project management reviews and technical reviews. See Clause 7 for an example SVVP outline and content of the SVVP.	SVVP (previous update) Contract Concept Documentation (e.g., Statement of Need, Advance Planning Report, Project Initiation Memo, Feasibility Studies, System Requirements, Governing Regulations, Procedures, Policies, customer acceptance criteria and requirements, Acquisition Documentation, Business Rules, draft system architecture) Supplier Development Plans and Schedules	SVVP and Updates
(2) Baseline Change Assessment. Evaluate proposed software changes (e.g., anomaly corrections and requirement changes) for effects on previously completed V&V tasks. Plan iteration of affected tasks or initiate new tasks to address software baseline changes or iterative development processes. Verify and validate that the change is consistent with system requirements and does not adversely affect requirements directly or indirectly. An adverse effect is a change that could create new system hazards and risks or impact previously resolved hazards and risks.	SVVP Proposed Changes Hazard Analysis Report Risks identified by V&V Tasks	Updated SVVP Task Report(s) — Baseline Change Assessment Anomaly Report(s)
(3) Management Review of V&V. Review and summarize the V&V effort to define changes to V&V tasks or to redirect the V&V effort. Recommend whether to proceed to the next set of V&V and development life cycle activities, and provide task reports, anomaly reports, and V&V Activity Summary Reports to the organizations identified in the SVVP. Verify that all V&V tasks comply with task requirements defined in the SVVP. Verify that V&V task results have a basis of evidence supporting the results. Assess all V&V results and provide recommendations for program acceptance and certification as input to the V&V Final Report. The management review of V&V may use any review methodology such as provided in IEEE Std 1028-1988 [B8].	SVVP and Updates Supplier Development Plans and Schedules V&V task results [e.g., technical accomplishments, V&V reports, resource utilization, V&V metrics (see Annex E), plans, and identified risks]	Updated SVVP Task Report(s)— Recommendations V&V Activity Summary Reports Recommendations to the V&V Final Report
(4) Management and Technical Review Support. Support project management reviews and technical reviews (e.g., Preliminary Design Review, and Critical Design Review) by assessing the review materials, attending the reviews, and providing task reports and anomaly reports. Verify the timely delivery according to the approved schedule of all software products and documents. The management and technical review support may use any review methodology such as provided in IEEE Std 1028-1988 [B8].	V&V task results Materials for review (e.g., SRS, IRS, SDD, IDD, test documents)	Task Report(s)— Review Results Anomaly Report(s)
(5) Interface With Organizational and Supporting Processes. Coordinate the V&V effort with organizational (e.g., management, improvement) and supporting processes (e.g., quality assurance, joint review, and problem resolution). Identify the V&V data to be exchanged with these processes. Document the data exchange requirements in the SVVP.	SVVP Data identified in the SVVP from organizational and supporting processes	Updated SVVP

Table 1—V&V tasks, inputs, and outputs *(Continued)*

V&V tasks	Required inputs	Required outputs
5.2.1 Acquisition Support V&V Activity (acquisition process)		
(1) Scoping the V&V Effort. Define the project V&V software criticality (e.g., safety, security, mission critical, technical complexity). Assign a software integrity level to the system and the software. Establish the degree of independence (see Annex C), if any, required for the V&V. Provide an estimate of the V&V budget, including test facilities and tools as required. To scope the V&V effort, the following steps shall be performed: (a) Adopt the system integrity scheme assigned to the project. If no system integrity level scheme exists, then one is selected. (b) Determine the minimum V&V tasks for the software integrity level using Table 2 and the selected software integrity level scheme. (c) Augment the minimum V&V tasks with optional V&V tasks, as necessary. (d) Establish the scope of the V&V from the description of V&V tasks, inputs, and outputs defined in Table 1.	Preliminary System Description Statement of Need Request for Proposal (RFP) or tender System Integrity Level Scheme	Updated SVVP
(2) Planning the Interface Between the V&V Effort and Supplier. Plan the V&V schedule for each V&V task. Identify the preliminary list of development processes and products to be evaluated by the V&V processes. Describe V&V access rights to proprietary and classified information. It is recommended that the plan be coordinated with the acquirer. Incorporate the project software integrity level scheme into the planning process.	SVVP RFP or tender Contract Supplier Development Plans and Schedules	Updated SVVP
(3) System Requirements Review. Review the system requirements (e.g., system requirements specification, feasibility study report, business rules description) in the RFP or tender to 1) verify the consistency of requirements to user needs, 2) validate whether the requirements can be satisfied by the defined technologies, methods, and algorithms defined for the project (feasibility), and 3) verify whether objective information that can be demonstrated by testing is provided in the requirements (testability). Review other requirements such as deliverable definitions, listing of appropriate compliance standards and regulations, user needs, etc., for completeness, correctness, and accuracy.	Preliminary System Description Statement of Need User Needs RFP or tender	Task Report(s)— System Requirements Review Anomaly Report(s)
5.3.1 Planning V&V Activity (supply process)		
(1) Planning the Interface Between the V&V Effort and Supplier. Review the supplier development plans and schedules to coordinate the V&V effort with development activities. Establish procedures to exchange V&V data and results with the development effort. It is recommended that the plan be coordinated with the acquirer. Incorporate the project software integrity level scheme into the planning process.	SVVP Contract Supplier Development Plans and Schedules	Updated SVVP
(2) Contract Verification. Verify that 1) system requirements (from RFP or tender, and contract) satisfy and are consistent with user needs; 2) procedures are documented for managing requirement changes and for identifying the management hierarchy to address problems; 3) procedures for interface and cooperation among the parties are documented, including ownership, warranty, copyright, and confidentiality; and 4) acceptance criteria and procedures are documented in accordance with requirements.	SVVP RFP or tender Contract User Needs Supplier Development Plans and Schedules	Updated SVVP Task Report(s)— Contract Verification Anomaly Report(s)

Table 1—V&V tasks, inputs, and outputs *(Continued)*

V&V tasks	Required inputs	Required outputs
5.4.1 Concept V&V Activity (development process)		
(1) Concept Documentation Evaluation. Verify that the concept documentation satisfies user needs and is consistent with acquisition needs. Validate constraints of interfacing systems and constraints or limitations of proposed approach. Analyze system requirements and validate that the following satisfy user needs: 1) system functions; 2) end-to-end system performance; 3) feasibility and testability of the functional requirements; 4) system architecture design; 5) operation and maintenance requirements; and 6) migration requirements from an existing system where applicable.	Concept Documentation Supplier Development Plans and Schedules User Needs Acquisition Needs	Task Report(s)— Concept Documentation Evaluation Anomaly Report(s)
(2) Criticality Analysis. Determine whether software integrity levels are established for requirements, detailed functions, software modules, subsystem, or other software partitions. Verify that the assigned software integrity levels are correct. If software integrity levels are not assigned, then assign software integrity levels to the system requirements. Document the software integrity level assigned to individual software components (e.g., requirements, detailed functions, software modules, subsystems, or other software partitions). For V&V planning purposes, the most critical software integrity level assigned to individual elements shall be the integrity level assigned to the entire software. Verify whether any software component can influence individual software components assigned a higher software integrity level, and if such conditions exist, then assign that software component the same higher software integrity level.	Concept Documentation (system requirements) Developer integrity level assignments	Task Report(s)— Software Integrity Levels Task Report(s)— Criticality Analysis Anomaly Report(s)
(3) Hardware/Software/User Requirements Allocation Analysis. Verify the correctness, accuracy, and completeness of the concept requirement allocation to hardware, software, and user interfaces against user needs. (3.1) Correctness a. Verify that performance requirements (e.g., timing, response time, and throughput) allocated to hardware, software, and user interfaces satisfy user needs. (3.2) Accuracy a. Verify that the internal and external interfaces specify the data formats, interface protocols, frequency of data exchange at each interface, and other key performance requirements to demonstrate compliance with user requirements. (3.3) Completeness a. Verify that application specific requirements such as functional diversity, fault detection, fault isolation, and diagnostic and error recovery satisfy user needs. b. Verify that the user's maintenance requirements for the system are completely specified. c. Verify that the migration from the existing system and replacement of the system satisfy user needs.	User Needs Concept Documentation	Task Report(s)— Hardware/ Software/User Requirements Allocation Analysis Anomaly Report(s)
(4) Traceability Analysis. Identify all system requirements that will be implemented completely or partially by software. Verify that these system requirements are traceable to acquisition needs. Start the software requirements traceability analysis with system requirements.	Concept Documentation	Task Report(s)— Traceability Analysis Anomaly Report(s)

Table 1—V&V tasks, inputs, and outputs *(Continued)*

V&V tasks	Required inputs	Required outputs
5.4.1 Concept V&V Activity (development process) *(Continued)*		
(5) Hazard Analysis. Analyze the potential hazards to and from the conceptual system. The analysis shall 1) identify the potential system hazards; 2) assess the severity of each hazard; 3) assess the probability of each hazard; and 4) identify mitigation strategies for each hazard.	Concept Documentation	Task Report(s)— Hazard Analysis Anomaly Report(s)
(6) Risk Analysis. Identify the technical and management risks. Provide recommendations to eliminate, reduce, or mitigate the risks	Concept Documentation Supplier Development Plans and Schedules Hazard Analysis Report V&V task results	Task Report(s)— Risk Analysis Anomaly Report(s)
5.4.2 Requirements V&V Activity (development process)		
(1) Traceability Analysis. Trace the software requirements (SRS and IRS) to system requirements (Concept Documentation), and system requirements to the software requirements. Analyze identified relationships for correctness, consistency, completeness, and accuracy. The task criteria are as follows: (1.1) Correctness a. Validate that the relationships between each software requirement and its system requirement are correct. (1.2) Consistency a. Verify that the relationships between the software and system requirements are specified to a consistent level of detail. (1.3) Completeness a. Verify that every software requirement is traceable to a system requirement with sufficient detail to show compliance with the system requirement. b. Verify that all system requirements related to software are traceable to software requirements. (1.4) Accuracy a. Validate that the system performance and operating characteristics are accurately specified by the traced software requirements.	Concept Documentation (System requirements) SRS IRS	Task Report(s)— Traceability Analysis Anomaly Report(s)
(2) Software Requirements Evaluation. Evaluate the requirements (e.g., functional, capability, interface, qualification, safety, security, human factors, data definitions, user documentation, installation and acceptance, user operation, and user maintenance) of the SRS and IRS for correctness, consistency, completeness, accuracy, readability, and testability. The task criteria are as follows: (2.1) Correctness a. Verify and validate that the software requirements satisfy the system requirements allocated to software within the assumptions and constraints of the system. b. Verify that the software requirements comply with standards, references, regulations, policies, physical laws, and business rules. c. Validate the sequences of states and state changes using logic and data flows coupled with domain expertise, prototyping results, engineering principles, or other basis. d. Validate that the flow of data and control satisfy functionality and performance requirements. e. Validate data usage and format.	Concept Documentation SRS IRS	Task Report(s)—Software Requirements Evaluation Anomaly Report(s)

Table 1—V&V tasks, inputs, and outputs *(Continued)*

V&V tasks	Required inputs	Required outputs
5.4.2 Requirements V&V Activity (development process) *(Continued)*		

(2.2) Consistency
a. Verify that all terms and concepts are documented consistently.
b. Verify that the function interactions and assumptions are consistent and satisfy system requirements and acquisition needs.
c. Verify that there is internal consistency between the software requirements and external consistency with the system requirements.
 	
(2.3) Completeness
a. Verify that the following elements are in the SRS or IRS, within the assumptions and constraints of the system:
  1. Functionality (e.g., algorithms, state/mode definitions, input/output validation, exception handling, reporting, and logging);
  2. Process definition and scheduling;
  3. Hardware, software, and user interface descriptions.
  4. Performance criteria (e.g., timing sizing, speed, capacity, accuracy, precision, safety, and security);
  5. Critical configuration data; and
  6. System, device, and software control (e.g., initialization, transaction and state monitoring, and self-testing).
b. Verify that the SRS and IRS satisfy specified configuration management procedures.
 	
(2.4) Accuracy
a. Validate that the logic, computational, and interface precision (e.g., truncation and rounding) satisfy the requirements in the system environment.
b. Validate that the modeled physical phenomena conform to system accuracy requirements and physical laws.
 	
(2.5) Readability
a. Verify that the documentation is legible, understandable, and unambiguous to the intended audience.
b. Verify that the documentation defines all acronyms, mnemonics, abbreviations, terms, and symbols.
 	
(2.6) Testability
a. Verify that there are objective acceptance criteria for validating the requirements of the SRS and IRS.		

(3) Interface Analysis. Verify and validate that the requirements for software interfaces with hardware, user, operator, and other systems are correct, consistent, complete, accurate, and testable. The task criteria are as follows: (3.1) Correctness a. Validate the external and internal system and software interface requirements. (3.2) Consistency a. Verify that the interface descriptions are consistent between the SRS and IRS. (3.3) Completeness a. Verify that each interface is described and includes data format and performance criteria (e.g., timing, bandwidth, accuracy, safety, and security).	Concept Documentation SRS IRS	Task Report(s)—Interface Analysis Anomaly Report(s)

Table 1—V&V tasks, inputs, and outputs *(Continued)*

V&V tasks	Required inputs	Required outputs
5.4.2 Requirements V&V Activity (development process) *(Continued)*		
(3.4) Accuracy a. Verify that each interface provides information with the required accuracy. (3.5) Testability a. Verify that there are objective acceptance criteria for validating the interface requirements.		

(4) Criticality Analysis. Review and update the existing criticality analysis results from the prior Criticality Task Report using the SRS and IRS. Implementation methods and interfacing technologies may cause previously assigned software integrity levels to be raised or lowered for a given software element (i.e., requirement, module, function, subsystem, other software partition). Verify that no inconsistent or undesired software integrity consequences are introduced by reviewing the revised software integrity levels.	Task Report(s)—
	    Criticality
	SRS
	IRS
		Task Report(s)—
		    Criticality Analysis
		Anomaly Report(s)

(5) System V&V Test Plan Generation and Verification. *(For Software Integrity Levels 3 and 4)* Plan system V&V testing to validate software requirements. Plan tracing of system requirements to test designs, cases, procedures, and results. Plan documentation of test designs, cases, procedures, and results. The System V&V Test Plan shall address the following: 1) compliance with all system requirements (e.g., functional, performance, security, operation, and maintenance) as complete software end items in the system environment, 2) adequacy of user documentation (e.g., training materials, procedural changes), and 3) performance at boundaries (e.g., data, interfaces) and under stress conditions. Verify that the System V&V Test Plan conform to Project defined test document purpose, format, and content (e.g., see IEEE Std 829-1983 [B5]). Validate that the System Test Plan satisfies the following criteria: 1) test coverage of system requirements; 2) appropriateness of test methods and standards used; 3) conformance to expected results; 4) feasibility of system qualification testing; and 5) feasibility and testability of operation and maintenance requirements.
 	
(For Software Integrity Levels 1 and 2) Verify that developer's System Test Plans conform to Project defined test document purpose, format, and content (e.g., see IEEE Std 829-1983 [B5]). Validate that the System Test Plan satisfies the following criteria: 1) test coverage of system requirements; 2) appropriateness of test methods and standards used; 3) conformance to expected results; 4) feasibility of system qualification testing; and 5) capability to be operated and maintained.
	Concept Documentation
	    (System requirements)
	SRS
	IRS
	User Documentation System
	    Test Plan
		Anomaly Report(s)
		System V&V Test Plan

(6) Acceptance V&V Test Plan Generation and Verification. *(For Software Integrity Levels 3 and 4)* Plan Acceptance V&V testing to validate that software correctly implements system and software requirements in an operational environment. The task criteria are 1) compliance with acceptance requirements in the operational environment, and 2) adequacy of user documentation. Plan tracing of acceptance test requirements to test design, cases, procedures, and execution results. Plan documentation of test tasks and results. Verify that the Acceptance V&V Test Plan complies with Project defined test document purpose, format, and content (e.g., see IEEE Std 829-1983 [B5]). Validate that the Acceptance Test Plan satisfies the following criteria: 1) test coverage of system	Concept Documentation SRS IRS User Documentation Acceptance Test Plan	Acceptance V&V Test Plan Anomaly Report(s)

Table 1—V&V tasks, inputs, and outputs *(Continued)*

V&V tasks	Required inputs	Required outputs
5.4.2 Requirements V&V Activity (development process) *(Continued)*		
requirements; 2) conformance to expected results; and 3) feasibility of operation and maintenance (e.g., capability to be operated and maintained in accordance with user needs). *(For Software Integrity Level 2)* Verify that the developer's Acceptance Test Plan conforms to Project defined test document purpose, format, and content (e.g., see IEEE Std 829-1983 [B5]). Validate that the developer's Acceptance Test Plan satisfies the following criteria: 1) test coverage of system requirements; 2) conformance to expected results; and 3) feasibility of operation and maintenance (e.g., capability to be operated and maintained in accordance with user needs). *(For Software Integrity Level 1, there are no acceptance test requirements.)*		
(7) Configuration Management Assessment. Verify that the Configuration Management process is complete and adequate. The task criteria are as follows: (7.1) Completeness a. Verify that there is a process for describing the software product functionality, tracking program versions, and managing changes. (7.2) Adequacy a. Verify that the configuration management process is adequate for the development complexity, software and system size, software integrity level, project plans, and user needs.	Software Configuration Management Process Documentation	Task Report (s)— Configuration Management Assessment Anomaly Report (s)
(8) Hazard Analysis. Determine software contributions to system hazards. The hazard analysis shall a) identify the software requirements that contribute to each system hazard; and b) validate that the software addresses, controls, or mitigates each hazard.	SRS IRS Hazard Analysis Report	Task Report(s)— Hazard Analysis Anomaly Report(s)
(9) Risk Analysis. Review and update risk analysis using prior task reports. Provide recommendations to eliminate, reduce, or mitigate the risks.	Concept Documentation SRS IRS Supplier Development Plans and Schedules Hazard Analysis Report V&V task results	Task Report(s)— Risk Analysis Anomaly Report(s)
5.4.3 Design V&V Activity (development process)		
(1) Traceability Analysis. Trace design elements (SDD and IDD) to requirements (SRS and IRS), and requirements to design elements. Analyze relationships for correctness, consistency, and completeness. The task criteria are as follows: (1.1) Correctness a Validate the relationship between each design element and the software requirement. (1.2) Consistency a. Verify that the relationship between the design elements and the software requirements are specified to a constant level of detail.	SRS SDD IRS IDD	Task Report(s)— Traceability Analysis Anomaly Report(s)

Table 1—V&V tasks, inputs, and outputs *(Continued)*

V&V tasks	Required inputs	Required outputs
5.4.3 Design V&V Activity (development process) *(Continued)*		

(1.3) Completeness
a. Verify that all design elements are traceable from the software requirements.
b. Verify that all software requirements are traceable to the design elements.
 	
(2) Software Design Evaluation. Evaluate the design elements (SDD and IDD) for correctness, consistency, completeness, accuracy, readability, and testability. The task criteria are as follows:
 	
(2.1) Correctness
a. Verify and validate that the source code component satisfies the software design.
b. Verify that the source code components comply with standards, references, regulations, policies, physical laws, and business rules.
c. Validate the source code component sequences of states and state changes using logic and data flows coupled with domain expertise, prototyping results, engineering principles, or other basis.
d. Validate that the flow of data and control satisfy functionality and performance requirements.
e. Validate data usage and format.
f. Assess the appropriateness of coding methods and standards.
 	
(2.2) Consistency
a. Verify that all terms and code concepts are documented consistently.
b. Verify that there is internal consistency between the source code components.
 	
(2.3) Completeness
a. Verify that the following elements are in the SDD, within the assumptions and constraints of the system:
  1. Functionality (e.g., algorithms, state/mode definitions, input/output validation, exception handling, reporting and logging);
  2. Process definition and scheduling;
  3. Hardware, software, and user interface descriptions;
  4. Performance criteria (e.g., timing, sizing, speed, capacity, accuracy, precision, safety, and security);
  5. Critical configuration data;
  6. System, device, and software control (e.g., initialization, transaction and state monitoring, and self-testing).
b. Verify that the SDD and IDD satisfy specified configuration management procedures.
 	
(2.4) Accuracy
a. Validate that the logic, computational, and interface precision (e.g., truncation and rounding) satisfy the requirements in the system environment.
b. Validate that the modeled physical phenomena conform to system accuracy requirements and physical laws.
 	
(2.5) Readability
a. Verify that the documentation is legible, understandable, and unambiguous to the intended audience.
b. Verify that the documentation defines all acronyms, mnemonics, abbreviations, terms, symbols, and design language, if any.
	SRS
	IRS
	SDD
	IDD
	Design Standards (e.g., standards, practices, and conventions)
		Task Report(s)—
		  Software Design Evaluation
		Anomaly Report(s)

Table 1—V&V tasks, inputs, and outputs *(Continued)*

V&V tasks	Required inputs	Required outputs
5.4.3 Design V&V Activity (development process) *(Continued)*		
(2.6) Testability a. Verify that there are objective acceptance criteria for validating each software design element and the system design. b. Verify that each software design element is testable to objective acceptance criteria.		
(3) Interface Analysis. Verify and validate that the software design interfaces with hardware, user, operator, software, and other systems for correctness, consistency, completeness, accuracy, and testability. The task criteria are as follows: (3.1) Correctness a. Validate the external and internal software interface design in the context of system requirements. (3.2) Consistency a. Verify that the interface design is consistent between the SDD and IDD. (3.3) Completeness a. Verify that each interface is described and includes data format and performance criteria (e.g., timing, bandwidth, accuracy, safety, and security). (3.4) Accuracy a. Verify that each interface provides information with the required accuracy. (3.5) Testability a. Verify that there are objective acceptance criteria for validating the interface design.	Concept Documentation (System requirements) SRS IRS SDD IDD	Task Report(s)—Interface Analysis Anomaly Report(s)
(4) Criticality Analysis. Review and update the existing criticality analysis results from the prior Criticality Task Report using the SDD and IDD. Implementation methods and interfacing technologies may cause previously assigned software integrity levels to be raised or lowered for a given software element (i.e., requirement, module, function, subsystem, other software partition). Verify that no inconsistent or undesired software integrity consequences are introduced by reviewing the revised software integrity levels.	Task Report(s)—Criticality SDD IDD	Task Report(s)—Criticality Analysis Anomaly Report(s)
(5) Component V&V Test Plan Generation and Verification. *(For Software Integrity Levels 3 and 4.)* Plan component V&V testing to validate that the software components (e.g., units, source code modules) correctly implement component requirements. The task criteria are 1) compliance with design requirements; 2) assessment of timing, sizing, and accuracy; 3) performance at boundaries and interfaces and under stress and error conditions; and 4) measures of requirements test coverage and software reliability and maintainability. Plan tracing of design requirements to test design, cases, procedures, and results. Plan documentation of test tasks and results. Verify that the Component V&V Test Plan complies with Project defined test document purpose, format, and content (e.g., see IEEE Std 829-1983 [B5]). Validate that the Component V&V Test Plan satisfies the following criteria: 1) traceable to the software requirements and design; 2) external consistency with the software requirements and design; 3) internal consistency between unit requirements; 4) test coverage of requirements in each unit; 5) feasibility of software	SRS SDD IRS IDD Component Test Plan	Component V&V Test Plan Anomaly Report(s)

Table 1—V&V tasks, inputs, and outputs *(Continued)*

V&V tasks	Required inputs	Required outputs
5.4.3 Design V&V Activity (development process) *(Continued)*		
integration and testing; and 6) feasibility of operation and maintenance (e.g., capability to be operated and maintained in accordance with user needs). *(For Software Integrity Level 2.)* Verify that the developer's Component Test Plan conforms to Project defined test document purpose, format, and content (e.g., see IEEE Std 829-1983). Validate that the developer's Component Test Plan satisfies the following criteria: 1) traceable to the software requirements and design; 2) external consistency with the software requirements and design; 3) internal consistency between unit requirements; 4) test coverage of units; 5) feasibility of software integration and testing; and 6) feasibility of operation and maintenance (e.g., capability to be operated and maintained in accordance with user needs). *(For Software Integrity Level 1, there are no component test requirements.)*		
(6) Integration V&V Test Plan Generation and Verification. *(For Software Integrity Levels 3 and 4.)* Plan integration testing to validate that the software correctly implements the software requirements and design as each software component (e.g., units or modules) is incrementally integrated with each other. The task criteria are 1) compliance with increasingly larger set of functional requirements at each stage of integration; 2) assessment of timing, sizing, and accuracy; 3) performance at boundaries and under stress conditions; and 4) measures of requirements test coverage and software reliability. Plan tracing of requirements to test design, cases, procedures, and results. Plan documentation of test tasks and results. Verify that the Integration V&V Test Plan complies with Project defined test document purpose, format, and content (e.g., see IEEE Std 829-1983 [B5]). Validate that the Integration V&V Test Plan satisfies the following criteria: 1) traceable to the system requirements; 2) external consistency with the system requirements; 3) internal consistency; 4) test coverage of the software requirements; 5) appropriateness of test standards and methods used; 6) conformance to expected results; 7) feasibility of software qualification testing; and 8) feasibility of operation and maintenance (e.g., capability to be operated and maintained in accordance with user needs). *(For Software Integrity Levels 1 and 2.)* Verify that the developer's Integration Test Plan conform to Project defined test document purpose, format, and content (e.g., see IEEE Std 829-1983). Validate that the developer's Integration Test Plan satisfies the following criteria: 1) traceable to the system requirements; 2) external consistency with the system requirements; 3) internal consistency; 4) test coverage of the software requirements; 5) appropriateness of test standards and methods; 6) conformance to expected results; 7) feasibility of software qualification testing; and 8) feasibility of operation and maintenance (e.g., capability to be operated and maintained in accordance with user needs).	SRS IRS SDD IDD Integration Test Plan	Integration V&V Test Plan Anomaly Report(s)
(7) V&V Test Design Generation and Verification. *(For Software Integrity Levels 3 and 4.)* Design tests for: 1) component testing; 2) integration testing; 3) system testing; and 4) acceptance testing. Continue tracing required by the V&V Test Plan. Verify that the V&V Test Designs comply with	SDD IDD User Documentation Test Plans Test Designs	Component V&V Test Design(s) Integration V&V Test Design(s) System V&V Test Design(s) Acceptance V&V Test Design(s) Anomaly Report(s)

Table 1—V&V tasks, inputs, and outputs *(Continued)*

V&V tasks	Required inputs	Required outputs
5.4.3 Design V&V Activity (development process) *(Continued)*		
Project defined test document purpose, format, and content (e.g., see IEEE Std 829-1983 [B5]). Validate that the V&V Test Designs satisfy the criteria in V&V tasks 5.4.3 Task 5; 5.4.3 Task 6; 5.4.2 Task 5; and 5.4.2 Task 6, for component, integration, system, and acceptance testing, respectively. *(For Software Integrity Levels 1 and 2.)* Verify that the developer's Test Designs conform to Project defined test document purpose, format, and content (e.g., see IEEE Std 829-1983). Validate that the developer's Test Designs satisfy the criteria in V&V tasks 5.4.3 Task 5; 5.4.3 Task 6; 5.4.2 Task 5; and 5.4.2 Task 6 for component (level 2 only), integration (levels 1 and 2), system (levels 1 and 2), and acceptance (level 2 only) testing, respectively.		
(8) Hazard Analysis. Verify that logic design and associated data elements correctly implement the critical requirements and introduce no new hazards. Update the hazard analysis.	SDD IDD Hazard Analysis Report	Task Report(s)— Hazard Analysis Anomaly Report(s)

(9) Risk Analysis. Review and update risk analysis using prior task reports. Provide recommendations to eliminate, reduce, or mitigate the risks.	SDD
	IDD
	Supplier Development Plans
	  and Schedules
	Hazard Analysis Report
	V&V task results
		Task Report(s)—
		  Risk Analysis
		Anomaly Report(s)

5.4.4 Implementation V&V Activity (development process)		
(1) Traceability Analysis. Trace the source code components to corresponding design specification(s), and design specification(s) to source code components. Analyze identified relationships for correctness, consistency, and completeness. The task criteria are as follows: (1.1) Correctness a. Validate the relationship between the source code components and design element(s). (1.2) Consistency a. Verify that the relationships between the source code components and design elements are specified to a consistent level of detail. (1.3) Completeness a. Verify that all source code components are traceable from the design elements. b. Verify that all design elements are traceable to the source code components.	SDD IDD Source Code	Task Report(s)— Traceability Analysis Anomaly Report(s)

(2) Source Code and Source Code Documentation Evaluation. Evaluate the source code components (Source Code Documentation) for correctness, consistency, completeness, accuracy, readability, and testability. The task criteria are as follows:
 	
(2.1) Correctness
a. Verify and validate that the source code component satisfies the software design.
b. Verify that the source code components comply with standards, references, regulations, policies, physical laws, and business rules.
	Source Code
	SDD
	IDD
	Coding Standards (e.g.,
	  standards, practices, project
	  restrictions, and
	  conventions)
	User Documentation
		Task Report(s)—
		  Source Code and Source
		  Code Documentation
		  Evaluation
		Anomaly Report(s)

Table 1—V&V tasks, inputs, and outputs (Continued)

V&V tasks	Required inputs	Required outputs
5.4.4 Implementation V&V Activity (development process) (Continued)		

c. Validate the source code component sequences of states and state changes using logic and data flows coupled with domain expertise, prototyping results, engineering principles, or other basis.
d. Validate that the flow of data and control satisfy functionality and performance requirements.
e. Validate data usage and format.
f. Assess the appropriateness of coding methods and standards.
 	
(2.2) Consistency
a. Verify that all terms and code concepts are documented consistently.
b. Verify that there is internal consistency between the source code components.
c. Validate external consistency with the software design and requirements.
 	
(2.3) Completeness
a. Verify that the following elements are in the source code, within the assumptions and constraints of the system:
  1. Functionality (e.g., algorithms, state/mode definitions, input/output validation, exception handling, reporting and logging);
  2. Process definition and scheduling;
  3. Hardware, software, and user interface descriptions;
  4. Performance criteria (e.g., timing, sizing, speed, capacity, accuracy, precision, safety, and security);
  5. Critical configuration data;
  6. System, device, and software control (e.g., initialization, transaction and state monitoring, and self-testing).
b. Verify that the source code documentation satisfies specified configuration management procedures.
 	
(2.4) Accuracy
a. Validate the logic, computational, and interface precision (e.g., truncation and rounding) in the system environment.
b. Validate that the modeled physical phenomena conform to system accuracy requirements and physical laws.
 	
(2.5) Readability
a. Verify that the documentation is legible, understandable, and unambiguous to the intended audience.
b. Verify that the documentation defines all acronyms, mnemonics, abbreviations, terms, and symbols.
 	
(2.6) Testability
a. Verify that there are objective acceptance criteria for validating each source code component.
b. Verify that each source code component is testable against objective acceptance criteria.		

(3) Interface Analysis. Verify and validate that the software source code interfaces with hardware, user, operator, software, and other systems for correctness, consistency, completeness, accuracy, and testability. The task criteria are as follows:
 	
(3.1) Correctness
a. Validate the external and internal software interface code in the context of system requirements.
	Concept Documentation
	  (System requirements)
	SDD
	IDD
	Source Code
	User Documentation
		Task Report(s)—Interface
		  Analysis
		Anomaly Report(s)

Table 1—V&V tasks, inputs, and outputs *(Continued)*

V&V tasks	Required inputs	Required outputs
5.4.4 Implementation V&V Activity (development process) *(Continued)*		
(3.2) Consistency a. Verify that the interface code is consistent between source code components and to external interfaces (i.e., hardware, user, operator, and other software). (3.3) Completeness a. Verify that each interface is described and includes data format and performance criteria (e.g., timing, bandwidth, accuracy, safety, and security). (3.4) Accuracy a. Verify that each interface provides information with the required accuracy. (3.5) Testability a. Verify that there are objective acceptance criteria for validating the interface code.		

(4) Criticality Analysis. Review and update the existing criticality analysis results from the prior Criticality Task Report using the source code. Implementation methods and interfacing technologies may cause previously assigned software integrity levels to be raised or lowered for a given software element (i.e., requirement, module, function, subsystem, other software partition). Verify that no inconsistent or undesired software integrity consequences are introduced by reviewing the revised software integrity levels.	Task Report(s)—
	  Criticality Source Code
		Task Report(s)—Criticality
		  Analysis
		Anomaly Report(s)

(5) V&V Test Case Generation and Verification. *(For Software Integrity Levels 3 and 4.)* Develop V&V Test Cases for 1) component testing; 2) integration testing; 3) system testing; and 4) acceptance testing. Continue tracing required by the V&V Test Plans. Verify that the V&V Test Cases comply with Project defined test document purpose, format, and content (e.g., see IEEE Std 829-1983 [B5]). Validate that the V&V Test Cases satisfy the criteria in V&V tasks 5.4.3 Task 5; 5.4.3 Task 6; 5.4.2 Task 5; and 5.4.2 Task 6 for component, integration, system, and acceptance testing, respectively. *(For Software Integrity Levels 1 and 2.)* Verify that the developer's Test Cases conform to Project defined test document purpose, format, and content (e.g., see IEEE Std 829-1983). Validate that the developer's Test Cases satisfy the criteria in V&V tasks 5.4.3 Task 5; 5.4.3 Task 6; 5.4.2 Task 5; and 5.4.2 Task 6 for component (level 2 only); integration (levels 1 and 2); system (levels 1 and 2); and acceptance (level 2 only) testing, respectively.	SRS IRS SDD IDD User Documentation Test Design Test Cases	Component V&V Test Cases Integration V&V Test Cases System V&V Test Cases Acceptance V&V Test Cases Anomaly Report(s)

(6) V&V Test Procedure Generation and Verification. *(For Software Integrity Levels 3 and 4.)* Develop V&V Test Procedures for 1) component testing; 2) integration testing; and 3) system testing. Continue tracing required by the V&V Test Plans. Verify that the V&V Test Procedures comply with Project defined test document purpose, format, and content (e.g., see IEEE Std 829-1983 [B5]). Validate that the V&V Test Procedures satisfy the criteria in V&V tasks 5.4.3 Task 5; 5.4.3 Task 6; and 5.4.2 Task 5 for component, integration, and system testing, respectively.
 	
(For Software Integrity Levels 1 and 2.) Verify that the developer's Test Procedures conform to Project defined test document purpose, format, and content (e.g., see IEEE Std 829-
	SRS
	IRS
	SDD
	IDD
	User Documentation
	Test Cases
	Test Procedures
		Component V&V Test
		  Procedures
		Integration V&V Test
		  Procedures
		System V&V Test Procedures
		Anomaly Report(s)

Table 1—V&V tasks, inputs, and outputs *(Continued)*

V&V tasks	Required inputs	Required outputs
5.4.4 Implementation V&V Activity (development process) *(Continued)*		
1983). Validate that the developer's Test Procedures satisfy the criteria in V&V tasks 5.4.3 Task 5; 5.4.3 Task 6; and 5.4.2 Task 5 for component (level 2 only); integration (levels 1 and 2); system (levels 1 and 2); and acceptance (level 2 only) testing, respectively.		
(7) Component V&V Test Execution and Verification. *(For Software Integrity Levels 3 and 4.)* Perform V&V component testing. Analyze test results to validate that software correctly implements the design. Validate that the test results trace to test criteria established by the test traceability in the test planning documents. Document the results as required by the Component V&V Test Plan. Use the V&V component test results to validate that the software satisfies the V&V test acceptance criteria. Document discrepancies between actual and expected test results. *(For Software Integrity Level 2.)* Use the developer's component test results to validate that the software satisfies the test acceptance criteria. *(For Software Integrity Level 1, there are no component test requirements.)*	Source Code Executable Code SDD IDD Component Test Plans Component Test Procedures Component Test Results	Task Report(s)— Test Results Anomaly Report(s)
(8) Hazard Analysis. Verify that the implementation and associated data elements correctly implement the critical requirements and introduce no new hazards. Update the hazard analysis.	Source Code SDD IDD Hazard Analysis Report	Task Report(s)— Hazard Analysis Anomaly Report(s)

(9) Risk Analysis. Review and update risk analysis using prior task reports. Provide recommendations to eliminate, reduce or mitigate the risks.	Source Code
	Supplier Development Plans
	   and Schedules
	Hazard Analysis Report
	V&V task results
		Task Report(s)—
		   Risk Analysis
		Anomaly Report(s)

5.4.5 Test V&V Activity (development process)		
(1) Traceability Analysis. Analyze relationships in the V&V Test Plans, Designs, Cases, and Procedures for correctness and completeness. For correctness, verify that there is a valid relationship between the V&V Test Plans, Designs, Cases, and Procedures. For completeness, verify that all V&V Test Procedures are traceable to the V&V Test Plans.	V&V Test Plans V&V Test Designs V&V Test Procedures	Task Report(s)— Traceability Analysis Anomaly Report(s)
(2) Acceptance V&V Test Procedure Generation and Verification. *(For Software Integrity Levels 3 and 4.)* Develop Acceptance V&V Test Procedures. Continue the tracing required by the Acceptance V&V Test Plan. Verify that the V&V Test Procedures comply with Project defined test document purpose, format, and content (e.g., see IEEE Std 829-1983 [B5]). Validate that the Acceptance V&V Test Procedures satisfy the criteria in V&V task 5.4.2 Task 6. *(For Software Integrity Level 2.)* Verify that the developer's Acceptance Test Procedures conform to Project defined test document purpose, format, and content (e.g., see IEEE Std 829-1983). Validate that the developer's Test Procedures satisfy the criteria in V&V task 5.4.2 Task 6. *(For Software Integrity Level 1, there are no acceptance test requirements.)*	SDD IDD Source Code User Documentation Acceptance Test Plan Acceptance Test Procedures	Acceptance V&V Test Procedures Anomaly Report(s)

Table 1—V&V tasks, inputs, and outputs *(Continued)*

V&V tasks	Required inputs	Required outputs
5.4.5 Test V&V Activity (development process) *(Continued)*		
(3) Integration V&V Test Execution and Verification. *(For Software Integrity Levels 3 and 4.)* Perform V&V integration testing. Analyze test results to verify that the software components are integrated correctly. Validate that the test results trace to test criteria established by the test traceability in the test planning documents. Document the results as required by the Integration V&V Test Plan. Use the V&V integration test results to validate that the software satisfies the V&V test acceptance criteria. Document discrepancies between actual and expected test results. *(For Software Integrity Levels 1 and 2.)* Use the developer's integration test results to verify that the software satisfies the test acceptance criteria.	Source Code Executable Code Integration Test Plan Integration Test Procedures Integration Test Results	Task Report(s)—Test Results Anomaly Report(s)
(4) System V&V Test Execution and Verification. *(For Software Integrity Levels 3 and 4.)* Perform V&V system testing. Analyze test results to validate that the software satisfies the system requirements. Validate that the test results trace to test criteria established by the test traceability in the test planning documents. Document the results as required by the System V&V Test Plan. Use the V&V system test results to validate that the software satisfies the V&V test acceptance criteria. Document discrepancies between actual and expected test results. *(For Software Integrity Levels 1 and 2.)* Use the developer's system test results to verify that the software satisfies the test acceptance criteria.	Source Code Executable Code System Test Plan System Test Procedures System Test Results	Task Report(s)—Test Results Anomaly Report(s)
(5) Acceptance V&V Test Execution and Verification. *(For Software Integrity Levels 3 and 4.)* Perform acceptance V&V testing. Analyze test results to validate that the software satisfies the system requirements. Validate that the test results trace to test criteria established by the test traceability in the test planning documents. Document the results as required by the Acceptance V&V Test Plan. Use the acceptance V&V test results to validate that the software satisfies the V&V test acceptance criteria. Document discrepancies between actual and expected test results. *(For Software Integrity Level 2.)* Use the developer's acceptance test results to verify that the software satisfies the test acceptance criteria. *(For Software Integrity Level 1, there are no acceptance test requirements.)*	Source Code Executable Code User Documentation Acceptance Test Plan Acceptance Test Procedures Acceptance Test Results	Task Report(s)—Test Results Anomaly Report(s)
(6) Hazard Analysis. Verify that the test instrumentation does not introduce new hazards. Update the hazard analysis.	Source Code Executable Code Test Results Hazard Analysis Report	Task Report(s)— Hazard Analysis Anomaly Report(s)
(7) Risk Analysis. Review and update risk analysis using prior task reports. Provide recommendations to eliminate, reduce, or mitigate the risks.	Supplier Development Plans and Schedules Hazard Analysis Report V&V task results	Task Report(s)—Risk Analysis Anomaly Report(s)

Table 1—V&V tasks, inputs, and outputs *(Continued)*

V&V tasks	Required inputs	Required outputs
5.4.6 Installation and Checkout V&V Activity (development process)		
(1) Installation Configuration Audit. Verify that all software products required to correctly install and operate the software are present in the installation package. Validate that all site-dependent parameters or conditions to verify supplied values are correct.	Installation Package (e.g., Source Code, Executable Code, User Documentation, SDD, IDD, SRS, IRS, Concept Documentation, Installation Procedures, site-specific parameters, Installation Tests, and Configuration Management Data)	Task Report(s)—Installation Configuration Audit Anomaly Report(s)
(2) Installation Checkout. Conduct analyses or tests to verify that the installed software corresponds to the software subjected to V&V. Verify that the software code and databases initialize, execute, and terminate as specified. In the transition from one version of software to the next, the V&V effort shall validate that the software can be removed from the system without affecting the functionality of the remaining system components. The V&V effort shall verify the requirements for continuous operation and service during transition, including user notification.	User Documentation Installation Package	Task Report(s)—Installation Checkout Anomaly Report(s)
(3) Hazard Analysis. Verify that the installation procedures and installation environment does not introduce new hazards. Update the hazard analysis.	Installation Package Hazard Analysis Report	Task Report(s)— Hazard Analysis Anomaly Report(s)
(4) Risk Analysis. Review and update risk analysis using prior task reports. Provide recommendations to eliminate, reduce, or mitigate the risks.	Installation Package Supplier Development Plans and Schedules V&V task results	Task Report(s)—Risk Analysis Anomaly Report(s)
(5) V&V Final Report Generation. Summarize in the V&V final report the V&V activities, tasks and results, including status and disposition of anomalies. Provide an assessment of the overall software quality and provide recommendations.	V&V Activity Summary Report (s)	V&V Final Report
5.5.1 Operation V&V Activity (operation process)		
(1) Evaluation of New Constraints. Evaluate new constraints (e.g., operational requirements, platform characteristics, operating environment) on the system or software requirements to verify the applicability of the SVVP. Software changes are maintenance activities (see 5.6.1).	SVVP New constraints	Task Report(s)— Evaluation of New Constraints
(2) Proposed Change Assessment. Assess proposed changes (e.g., modifications, enhancements, or additions) to determine the effect of the changes on the system. Determine the extent to which V&V tasks would be iterated.	Proposed Changes Installation Package	Task Report(s)— Proposed Change Assessment
(3) Operating Procedures Evaluation. Verify that the operating procedures are consistent with the user documentation and conform to the system requirements.	Operating Procedures User Documentation Concept Documentation	Task Report(s)— Operating Procedures Evaluation Anomaly Report(s)
(4) Hazard Analysis. Verify that the operating procedures and operational environment does not introduce new hazards. Update the hazard analysis.	Operating Procedures Hazard Analysis Report	Task Report(s)—Hazard Analysis Anomaly Report(s)

Table 1—V&V tasks, inputs, and outputs *(Continued)*

V&V tasks	Required inputs	Required outputs
5.5.1 Operation V&V Activity (operation process) *(Continued)*		
(5) Risk Analysis. Review and update risk analysis using prior task reports. Provide recommendations to eliminate, reduce, or mitigate the risks.	Installation Package Proposed Changes Hazard Analysis Report Supplier Development Plans and Schedules Operation problem reports V&V task results	Task Report(s)—Risk Analysis Anomaly Report(s)
5.6.1 Maintenance V&V Activity (maintenance process)		
(1) SVVP Revision. Revise the SVVP to comply with approved changes. When the development documentation required by this standard is not available, generate a new SVVP and consider the methods in Annex D (V&V of reusable software) for deriving the required development documentation.	SVVP Approved Changes Installation Package Supplier Development Plans and Schedules	Updated SVVP
(2) Proposed Change Assessment. Assess proposed changes (i.e., modifications, enhancements, or additions) to determine the effect of the changes on the system. Determine the extent to which V&V tasks would be iterated.	Proposed Changes Installation Package Supplier Development Plans and Schedules	Task Report(s)— Proposed Change Assessment
(3) Anomaly Evaluation. Evaluate the effect of software operation anomalies.	Anomaly Report(s)	Task Report(s)— Anomaly Evaluation
(4) Criticality Analysis. Determine the software integrity levels for proposed modifications. Validate the integrity levels provided by the maintainer. For V&V planning purposes, the highest software integrity level assigned to the software shall be the software system integrity level.	Proposed Changes Installation Package Maintainer Integrity Levels	Task Report(s)— Criticality Analysis Anomaly Report(s)
(5) Migration Assessment. Assess whether the software requirements and implementation address 1) specific migration requirements, 2) migration tools, 3) conversion of software products and data, 4) software archiving, 5) support for the prior environment, and 6) user notification.	Installation Package Approved Changes	Task Report(s)—Migration Assessment Anomaly Report(s)
(6) Retirement Assessment. For software retirement, assess whether the installation package addresses: 1) software support, 2) impact on existing systems and databases, 3) software archiving, 4) transition to a new software product, and 5) user notification.	Installation Package Approved Changes	Task Report(s)—Retirement Assessment Anomaly Report(s)
(7) Hazard Analysis. Verify that software modifications correctly implement the critical requirements and introduce no new hazards. Update the hazard analysis.	Proposed Changes Installation Package Hazard Analysis Report	Task Report(s)—Hazard Analysis Anomaly Report(s)
(8) Risk Analysis. Review and update risk analysis using prior task reports. Provide recommendations to eliminate, reduce, or mitigate the risks.	Installation Package Proposed Changes Hazard Analysis Report Supplier Development Plans and Schedules Operation problem reports V&V task results	Task Report(s)—Risk Analysis Anomaly Report(s)
(9) Task Iteration. Perform V&V tasks, as needed, to ensure that 1) planned changes are implemented correctly; 2) documentation is complete and current; and 3) changes do not cause unacceptable or unintended system behaviors.	Approved Changes Installation Package	Task Report(s) Anomaly Report(s)

Table 2—Minimum V&V tasks assigned to each software integrity level

Life Cycle Processes →	Acquisition				Supply				Development																								Operation				Maintenance			
V&V Activities →	Acquisition Support V&V Activity				Planning V&V Activity				Concept V&V Activity				Requirements V&V Activity				Design V&V Activity				Implementation V&V Activity				Test V&V Activity				Installation/ checkout V&V Activity				Operation V&V Activity				Maintenance V&V Activity			
Software Integrity Levels / V&V Tasks	4	3	2	1	4	3	2	1	4	3	2	1	4	3	2	1	4	3	2	1	4	3	2	1	4	3	2	1	4	3	2	1	4	3	2	1	4	3	2	1
Acceptance V&V test execution and verification																													X	X	X									
Acceptance V&V test plan generation and verification													X	X	X																									
Acceptance V&V test procedure generation and verification																									X	X	X													
Anomaly evaluation																																					X	X	X	
Component V&V test execution and verification																					X	X	X																	
Component V&V test plan generation and verification																	X	X	X																					
Concept documentation evaluation										X	X																													
Configuration management assessment													X	X																										
Contract verification					X																																			
Criticality analysis									X	X	X		X	X	X		X	X	X		X	X	X																	
Evaluation of new constraints																																	X	X	X		X	X		
Hardware/software/User requirements allocation analysis									X																															

Table 2—Minimum V&V tasks assigned to each software integrity level (Continued)

Life Cycle Processes	Acquisition				Supply				Development																									Installation/checkout				Operation				Maintenance			
V&V Activities	Acquisition Support V&V Activity				Planning V&V Activity				Concept V&V Activity				Requirements V&V Activity				Design V&V Activity				Implementation V&V Activity				Test V&V Activity				Installation/checkout V&V Activity				Operation V&V Activity				Maintenance V&V Activity			
Software Integrity Levels	4	3	2	1	4	3	2	1	4	3	2	1	4	3	2	1	4	3	2	1	4	3	2	1	4	3	2	1	4	3	2	1	4	3	2	1	4	3	2	1
Hazard analysis									X	X			X	X			X	X			X	X			X	X			X	X			X	X			X	X		
Installation checkout																													X	X										
Installation configuration audit																													X	X										
Interface analysis									X	X	X		X	X	X		X	X	X		X	X	X																	
Integration V&V test execution and verification																									X	X	X	X												
Management of V&V																																								
a) Baseline change assessment	X	X							X	X			X	X			X	X			X	X			X	X			X	X			X	X			X	X		
b) Interface with organizational supporting processes	X	X			X	X			X	X			X	X			X	X			X	X			X	X			X	X			X	X			X	X		
c) Management and technical review support									X	X			X	X			X	X			X	X			X	X			X	X			X	X			X	X		
d) Management review of V&V	X	X	X		X	X	X		X	X	X	X	X	X	X	X	X	X	X	X	X	X	X	X	X	X	X	X	X	X	X	X	X	X	X	X	X	X	X	X
e) Software V&V plan (SVVP) generation									X	X	X																										X	X	X	X
Migration assessment																																	X	X						
Operation procedures evaluation									X	X	X																						X	X	X	X				
Planning the interface between the V&V effort and supplier	X	X																																						
Proposed change assessment																																	X	X	X		X	X	X	
Risk analysis	X	X							X	X			X	X			X	X			X	X			X	X			X	X			X	X			X	X		

Table 2—Minimum V&V tasks assigned to each software integrity level (Continued)

Life Cycle Processes → V&V Activities ↓ (Software Integrity Levels)	Acquisition Support V&V Activity 4	3	2	1	Planning V&V Activity 4	3	2	1	Concept V&V Activity 4	3	2	1	Requirements V&V Activity 4	3	2	1	Design V&V Activity 4	3	2	1	Implementation V&V Activity 4	3	2	1	Test V&V Activity 4	3	2	1	Installation/ checkout V&V Activity 4	3	2	1	Operation V&V Activity 4	3	2	1	Maintenance V&V Activity 4	3	2	1
Retirement assessment																																					X	X		
Scoping the V&V effort	X	X	X																																					
Software design evaluation																	X	X	X																					
Software requirements evaluation													X	X	X																									
SVVP revision																																					X	X	X	X
Source code and source code documentation evaluation																					X	X	X																	
System requirements review	X	X	X	X																																				
System V&V test execution and verification																									X	X	X	X												
System V&V test plan generation and verification													X	X	X																									
Task iteration																																								
Traceability analysis									X	X	X		X	X	X		X	X	X		X	X	X		X	X	X										X	X	X	X
V&V final report generation																													X	X	X									
V&V test design generation and verification																																								
a) Component																	X	X	X																					
b) Integration																	X	X	X	X																				
c) System																	X	X	X	X																				
d) Acceptance																	X	X	X																					

IEEE
Std 1012-1998

Table 2—Minimum V&V tasks assigned to each software integrity level *(Continued)*

Life Cycle Processes →	Acquisition				Supply				Development																								Operation				Maintenance			
V&V Activities →	Acquisition Support V&V Activity				Planning V&V Activity				Concept V&V Activity				Requirements V&V Activity				Design V&V Activity				Implementation V&V Activity				Test V&V Activity				Installation/ checkout V&V Activity				Operation V&V Activity				Maintenance V&V Activity			
	Levels				Levels				Levels				Levels				Levels				Levels				Levels				Levels				Levels				Levels			
Software Integrity Levels	4	3	2	1	4	3	2	1	4	3	2	1	4	3	2	1	4	3	2	1	4	3	2	1	4	3	2	1	4	3	2	1	4	3	2	1	4	3	2	1
V&V test case generation and verification																																								
a) Component																					X	X																		
b) Integration																					X	X	X																	
c) System																					X	X	X	X																
d) Acceptance																					X	X	X																	
V&V test procedure generation and verification																																								
a) Component																					X	X																		
b) Integration																					X	X	X	X																
c) System																					X	X	X	X																

Table 3—Optional V&V tasks and suggested applications in the life cycle [a]

Life cycle processes	Acquisition	Supply	Management	Concept	Requirements	Design	Implementation	Test	Installation and Checkout	Operation	Maintenance
Algorithm Analysis					X	X	X				X
Audit Performance					X	X	X	X	X		X
Audit Support			X		X	X	X	X	X		X
Control Flow Analysis					X	X	X				X
Cost Analysis	X	X	X	X	X	X	X	X	X		X
Database Analysis					X	X	X	X			X
Data Flow Analysis					X	X	X				X
Disaster Recovery Plan Assessment				X	X	X	X			X	X
Distributed Architecture Assessment				X	X	X					X
Feasibility Study Evaluation	X	X	X	X	X	X					X
Independent Risk Assessment	X	X	X	X	X	X	X	X	X	X	X
Inspection											
Concept					X	X	X	X	X		X
Design						X					X
Requirements					X						X
Source code							X				X
Test case						X	X	X	X		X
Test design						X	X		X		X
Test plan					X	X	X		X		X
Operational Evaluation										X	
Performance Monitoring					X	X	X	X	X	X	X
Post Installation validation									X	X	X
Project Management Oversight Support	X	X	X	X	X	X	X	X	X	a	X
Qualification Testing								X	X		X
Regression Analysis and Testing					X	X	X	X	X		X
Reusability Assessment	X	X	X	X	X	X					X
Security Assessment	X		X	X	X	X	X	X	X		X
Simulation Analysis				X	X	X	X	X	X	X	X
Sizing and Timing Analysis					X	X	X	X			X
System Software Assessment							X	X	X	X	X
Test Certification								X	X	X	X
Test Evaluation					X	X	X	X	X	X	X
Test Witnessing								X	X	X	X
Training Document Evaluation					X	X	X	X	X	X	X
User Documentation Evaluation			X	X	X	X	X	X	X	X	X

Table 3—Optional V&V tasks and suggested applications in the life cycle *(Continued)*[a]

Life cycle processes	Acquisition	Supply	Management	Concept	Requirements	Design	Implementation	Test	Installation and Checkout	Operation	Maintenance
User training			X					X	X	X	X
V&V tool plan generation	X	X	X								X

Walkthroughs
  Design
  Requirements
  Source code
  Test
					X	X	X	X	X		X
											X
											X
											X

[a]Annex G contains a description of the optional V&V tasks.

Annex A

(informative)

Mapping of ISO/IEC 12207 V&V requirements to IEEE Std 1012 V&V activities and tasks

Table A.1 shows a mapping of all ISO/IEC 12207 [B16] V&V requirements (i.e., processes, activities, and tasks) to the V&V activities and tasks of this standard.

The first column of Table A.1 lists the ISO/IEC 12207 section numbers and titles of V&V processes and activities. The second column of Table A.1 lists the IEEE Std 1012 clauses, subclauses, tables, and annexes that address the topics listed in the first column. Where no subclause titles were assigned, clause titles were created to reflect the clause contents. These derived titles are marked by an [a].

Table A.1—Mapping

ISO/IEC 12207 V&V requirements	IEEE Std 1012 V&V Activities and Tasks	
	Location	**Description**
5.1.4.1 Supplier Monitoring V&V	Subclause 5.2.1 Table 1, Tasks 1, 2, and 3	Activity: Acquisition Support V&V Acquisition Support V&V Tasks
5.2.4.5h) and 5.2.5.5 Interfacing with V&V[a]	Subclause 5.2.1 Table 1, Task 2 Subclause 5.3.1 Table 1, Task 1 Annex C	Activity: Acquisition Support V&V Planning the Interface Between the V&V Effort and Supplier Activity: Planning V&V Planning the Interface Between the V&V Effort and Supplier Definition of IV&V
5.2.6.3 Verification and validation[a]	All clauses, tables, figures, and annexes	Software V&V
5.3.2 System Requirements Analysis	Subclause 5.2.1 Table 1, Task 3 Subclause 5.4.1 Table 1, Tasks 1 and 4	Activity: Acquisition Support V&V System Requirements Review Activity: Concept V&V Concept V&V Tasks (Concept Documentation Evaluation, Traceability Analysis)
5.5.5 and 5.5.6 Migration and Software Retirement	Subclause 5.6.1 Table 1, Task 2	Activity: Maintenance V&V Proposed Change Assessment
6.4.1 Verification Process Implementation[a]	Clause 4 Clauses 6 and 7 Subclauses 6.2 and 7.7	V&V software integrity levels Software V&V reporting, administrative, and documentation requirements; SVVP outline V&V administrative requirements
6.4.1.1 Criticality of Software to be Verified[a]	Clause 4 Table B.1 Table B.2 Annex D	V&V software integrity levels Assignment of software integrity levels Definitions of consequences V&V of reusable software
6.4.1.2 Process for Verification[a]	Clauses 6 and 7	Software V&V reporting, administrative, and documentation requirements; SVVP outline
6.4.1.3 and 6.4.1.4 Extent and Rigor of Verification[a]	Table 2 Annex C	Minimum V&V tasks assigned for each software integrity level Definition of IV&V

Table A.1—Mapping *(Continued)*

ISO/IEC 12207 V&V requirements	IEEE Std 1012 V&V Activities and Tasks	
	Location	Description
6.4.1.5 Verification Plan[a]	Clauses 6 and 7	Software V&V reporting, administrative, and documentation requirements; SVVP outline
6.4.1.6 Problem and Non-conformance Reports[a]	Subclauses 6.2 and 7.7	V&V administrative requirements
6.4.2 Verification	Clause 5	V&V processes
6.4.2.1 Contract Verification	Subclause 5.2.1 Table 1, Task 2	Activity: Planning V&V Contract Verification
6.4.2.2 Process Verification	Subclause 5.2 Subclause 5.3 Subclause 5.4	Process: Acquisition Process: Supply Process: Development
6.4.2.3 Requirements Verification	Subclause 5.2.1 Table 1, Task 3 Subclause 5.4.1 Table 1, Task 1 Subclause 5.4.2 Table 1, Tasks 1–9	Activity: Acquisition Support V&V System Requirements Review Activity: Concept V&V Concept Documentation Evaluation Activity: Requirements V&V Requirements V&V Tasks
6.4.2.4 Design Verification	Subclause 5.4.3 Table 1, Tasks 1–9	Activity: Design V&V Design V&V Tasks
6.4.2.5 Code Verification	Subclause 5.4.4 Table 1, Tasks 1–9	Activity: Implementation V&V Implementation V&V Tasks
6.4.2.6 Integration Verification	Subclause 5.4.5 Table 1, Task 3	Activity: Test V&V Test V&V Tasks
6.4.2.7 Documentation Verification	Subclause 5.2.1 Table 1, Task 3 Subclause 5.3.1 Table 1, Task 2 Subclause 5.4.1 Table 1, Task 1 Subclause 5.4.2 Table 1, Tasks 2 and 3 Subclause 5.4.3 Table 1, Tasks 2 and 3 Subclause 5.4.4 Table 1, Tasks 2 and 3 Subclause 5.4.6 Table 1, Task 1 Subclause 5.5.1 Table 1, Task 3	Activity: Acquisition Support V&V Systems Requirements Review Activity: Planning V&V Contract Verification Activity: Concept V&V Concept Documentation Evaluation Activity: Requirements V&V Software Requirements Evaluation and Interface Analysis Activity: Design V&V Software Design Evaluation and Interface Analysis Activity: Implementation V&V Source Code and Source Code Documentation Evaluation and Interface Analysis Activity: Installation and Checkout Installation Configuration Audit Activity: Operation V&V Operating Procedure Evaluation
6.5.1 Validation Process Implementation[a]	Clause 4 Clauses 6 and 7 Subclauses 6.2 and 7.7 Annexes C, D, and E	V&V software integrity levels Software V&V reporting, administrative, and documentation requirements; SVVP outline V&V administrative requirements Definition of IV&V, V&V of reusable software, and V&V metrics
6.5.1.1 Criticality of Software to be Validated[a]	Clause 4 Table B.1 Table B.2 Annex D	V&V software integrity levels Assignment of software integrity levels Definitions of consequences V&V of reusable software
6.5.1.2 Process for Validation[a]	Clauses 6 and 7	Software V&V reporting, administrative, and documentation requirements; SVVP outline

Table A.1—Mapping *(Continued)*

ISO/IEC 12207 V&V requirements	IEEE Std 1012 V&V Activities and Tasks	
	Location	**Description**
6.5.1.3 Extent and Rigor of Validation[a]	Table 2 Annex C	Minimum V&V tasks assigned for each software integrity level Definition of IV&V
6.5.1.4 Validation Plan[a]	Clauses 6 and 7	Software V&V reporting, administrative, and documentation requirements; SVVP outline
6.5.1.5 Problem and Non-conformance Reports[a]	Subclause 6.2 and 7.7	V&V administrative requirements
6.5.2 Validation	Clause 5	V&V processes
6.5.2.1 Validate Test Preparation[a]	Subclause 5.4.2 Table 1, Tasks 5 and 6 Subclause 5.4.3 Table 1, Tasks 5, 6, and 7 Subclause 5.4.4 Table 1, Tasks 5 and 6 Subclause 5.4.5 Table 1, Task 2	Activity: Requirements V&V System V&V Test Plan Generation and Verification, and Acceptance V&V Test Plan Generation and Verification Activity: Design V&V Component V&V Test Plan Generation and Verification, Integration V&V Test Plan Generation and Verification, and V&V Test Designs Generation and Verification Activity: Implementation V&V V&V Test Cases Generation and Verification, and V&V Test Procedure Generation and Verification Activity: Test V&V Acceptance V&V Test Procedure Generation and Verification
6.5.2.2 Validate Test Traceability[a]	Subclause 5.4.4 Table 1, Task 7 Subclause 5.4.5 Table 1, Tasks 3, 4, and 5	Activity: Implementation V&V Component V&V Test Execution and Verification Activity: Test V&V Test V&V Tasks
6.5.2.3 Validate Test Conduction[a]	Subclause 5.4.4 Table 1, Task 7 Section 5.4.5 Table 1, Tasks 3, 4, and 5	Activity: Implementation V&V Component V&V Test Execution and Verification Activity: Test V&V Test V&V Tasks
6.5.2.4 Validate Software for Intended Use[a]	Subclause 5.4.1 Table 1, Task 1 Subclause 5.4.2 Table 1, Tasks 2 and 3 Subclause 5.4.3 Table 1, Tasks 2 and 3 Subclause 5.4.4 Table 1, Tasks 2 and 3 Subclause 5.4.5 Table 1, Tasks 4 and 5	Activity: Concept V&V Concept Documentation Evaluation Activity: Requirements V&V Software Requirements Evaluation and Interface Analysis Activity: Design V&V Software Design Evaluation and Interface Analysis Activity: Implementation V&V Source Code and Source Code Documentation Evaluation, and Interface Analysis Activity: Test V&V System V&V Test Execution and Verification, and Acceptance V&V Test Execution and Verification
6.5.2.5 Installation Test of Software[a]	Subclause 5.4.6, Table 1, Tasks 1–4	Activity: Installation and Checkout V&V Installation and Checkout V&V Tasks

[a]No ISO/IEC 12207 clause title was listed. For purposes of this mapping, a clause title was assigned to reflect the clause contents.

This standard defines 11 V&V activities, as shown in column 1 of Table A.2, that are part of the V&V processes. Each of the 11 V&V activities supports the ISO/IEC 12207 software life cycle processes and activities shown in columns 2 and 3 of Table A.2.

Table A.2—Mapping of 1012 V&V activities to ISO/IEC 12207 software life cycle processes and activities

| 1012 V&V activities | ISO/IEC 12207 software life cycle | |
	Processes	Activities
Acquisition Support V&V	Acquisition	—Initiation —Request-for-Proposal (-tender) Preparation —Contract Preparation Update —Supplier Monitoring —Acceptance and Completion
Planning V&V	Supply	—Initiation —Preparation of Response —Contract —Planning —Execution and Control —Review and Evaluation —Delivery and Completion
Concept V&V	Development	—Process Implementation —System Requirements Analysis —System Architectural Design
Requirements V&V	Development	—Software Requirements Analysis
Design V&V	Development	—Software Architectural Design —Software Detailed Design
Implementation V&V	Development	—Software Coding and Testing
Test V&V	Development	—Software Integration —Software Qualification Testing —System Integration —System Qualification Testing
Installation and Checkout V&V	Development	—Software Installation —Software Acceptance Support
Operation V&V	Operation	—Process Implementation —Operational Testing —System Operation —User Support
Maintenance V&V	Maintenance	—Process Implementation —Problem and Modification Analysis —Modification Implementation —Maintenance Review/Acceptance —Migration —Software Retirement
Management of V&V	All processes	—All activities

Table A.3 shows a mapping of all IEEE Std 1074-1997 V&V requirements (i.e., processes, activities, and tasks) to the V&V activities and tasks of this standard.

Table A.3—Mapping IEEE Std 1074-1997 V&V requirements to IEEE Std 1012 V&V activities and tasks

IEEE Std 1074-1997 V&V requirements	IEEE 1012 V&V activities and tasks	
	Location	Description
A.1 Project Management Activity	Clause 5, 6, and 7	V&V processes; Software V&V reporting, administrative, and documentation requirements; SVVP outline
A.1.1 Project Initiation Activities A.1.1.1 Create Software Life Cycle Process A.1.1.2 Perform Estimation A.1.1.3 Allocate Project Resources A.1.1.4 Define Metrics	Subclause 5.2.1 Table 1, Task 1 Table 1, Task 2 Subclause 5.3.1 Table 1, Task 1 Subclause 5.1.1 Table 1, Task 1 Subclause 5.6.1 Table 1, Task 1 Subclauses 6.1 and 7.6 Subclauses 6.2 and 7.7 Subclause 6.3.1 and 7.8 Subclauses 6.3.2 and 7 Annex E	Activity: Acquisition Support V&V Scoping the V&V Effort Planning the Interface Between the V&V Effort and Supplier Activity: Planning V&V Planning the Interface Between the V&V Effort and Supplier Activity: Management of V&V SVVP Generation Activity: Maintenance V&V SVVP Revision V&V reporting requirements V&V administrative requirements V&V Test documentation SVVP documentation V&V metrics
A.1.2 Project Planning Activities A.1.2.1 Plan Evaluations A.1.2.2 Plan Configuration Management A.1.2.3 Plan System Transition (if applicable) A.1.2.4 Plan Installation A.1.2.5 Plan Documentation A.1.2.6 Plan Training A.1.2.7 Plan Project Managment	Clauses 5, 6, and 7 Table 1, All Tasks	V&V processes; Software V&V reporting, administrative, and documentation requirements; SVVP outline V&V Tasks
A.1.3 Project Monitoring and Control Activities A.1.3.1 Manage Risks A.1.3.2 Manage the Project A.1.3.3 Identify SLCP Improvement Needs A.1.3.4 Retain Records A.1.3.5 Collect and Analyze Metric Data	Subclause 5.1.1 Table 1, Tasks 1, 2, 3, 4, and 5	Activity: Management of V&V Management of V&V Tasks
A.2 Pre-development Activity	Subclause 5.4.1	Activity: Concept V&V
A.2.1 Concept Exploration Activities A.2.1.1 Identify Ideas or Needs A.2.1.2 Formulate Potential Approaches A.2.1.3 Conduct Feasibility Studies A.2.1.4 Refine and Finalize the Idea or Need	Subclause 5.4.1 Table 1, Tasks 1, 2, 4, 5, and 6	Activity: Concept V&V Tasks: Concept Documentation Evaluation, Criticality Analysis, Traceability Analysis, Hazard Analysis, and Risk Analysis
A.2.2 System Allocation Activities A.2.2.1 Analyze Functions A.2.2.2 Develop System Architecture A.2.2.3 Decompose System Requirements	Subclause 5.4.1 Table 1, Tasks 1 and 3	Activity: Concept V&V Tasks: Concept Documentation Evaluation, and Hardware/Software/User Requirements Allocation Analysis

53

**Table A.3—Mapping IEEE Std 1074-1997 V&V requirements to IEEE Std 1012
V&V activities and tasks** *(Continued)*

IEEE Std 1074-1997 V&V requirements	IEEE 1012 V&V activities and tasks	
	Location	Description
A.2.3 Software Importation Activities A.2.3.1 Identify Imported Software Requirements A.2.3.2 Evaluate Software Imported Source (if applicable) A.2.3.3 Define Software Import Method (if applicable) A.2.3.4 Import Software	Annex D Table 1, All Tasks	V&V of reusable software V&V Tasks
A.3 Development Activity A.3.1 Requirements Activities A.3.1.1 Define and Develop Software Requirements A.3.1.2 Define Interface Requirements A.3.1.3 Prioritize and Integrate Software Requirements	Subclauses 5.4.2, 5.4.3, 5.4.4, and 5.4.5 Subclause 5.4.2 Table 1, Tasks 1–9	Activities: Requirements, Design, Implementation, and Test V&V Activity: Requirements V&V Requirements V&V Tasks
A.3.2 Design Activities A.3.2.1 Perform Architectural Design A.3.2.2 Design Data Base (if applicable) A.3.2.3 Design Interfaces A.3.2.4 Perform Detailed Design	Subclause 5.4.3 Table 1, Tasks 1–9	Activity: Design V&V Design V&V Tasks
A.3.3 Implementation Activities A.3.3.1 Create Executable Code A.3.3.2 Create Operating Documentation A.3.3.3 Perform Integration	Subclause 5.4.4 Table 1, Tasks 1–9 Subclause 5.4.5 Table 1, Tasks 1–7	Activity: Implementation V&V Implementation V&V Tasks Activity: Test V&V Test V&V Tasks
A.4 Post-development Activity	Subclauses 5.4.6, 5.5.1, and 5.6.1	Activities: Installation and Checkout, Operation, and Maintenance V&V
A.4.1 Installation Activities A.4.1.1 Distribute Software A.4.1.2 Install Software A.4.1.3 Accept Software in Operational Environment	Subclause 5.4.6 Table 1, Tasks 1–5	Activity: Installation and Checkout V&V Installation and Checkout V&V Tasks
A.4.2 Operation and Maintenance Activities A.4.2.1 Operate the System A.4.2.2 Provide Technical Assistance and Consulting A.4.2.3 Maintain Support Request Log	Subclause 5.5.1 Table 1, Tasks 1–9	Activity: Operation V&V Operation V&V Tasks
A.4.3 Maintenance Activities A.4.3.3 Reapply Software Life Cycle	Subclause 5.6.1 Table 1, Tasks 1–9	Activity: Maintenance V&V Maintenance V&V Tasks
A.4.4 Retirement Activities A.4.4.2 Conduct Parallel Operations (if applicable) A.4.4.3 Retire System	Subclause 5.6.1	Activity: Maintenance V&V
A.5 Integral Activity A.5.1 Evaluation Activities A.5.1.1 Conduct Reviews A.5.1.2 Create Traceability Matrix A.5.1.3 Conduct Audits A.5.1.4 Develop Test Procedures A.5.1.5 Create Test Data A.5.1.6 Execute Tests A.5.1.7 Report Evaluation Results	Clauses 5, 6, and 7 Table 1, All Tasks	V&V processes; Software V&V reporting, administrative, and documentation requirements; SVVP outline

Annex B

(informative)

A software integrity level scheme

Table B.1 defines four software integrity levels used as an illustration by this standard. Table B.2 describes the consequences of software errors for each of the four software integrity levels. There are overlaps between the software integrity levels to allow for individual interpretations of acceptable risk depending on the application. A software integrity level 0 (zero) may be assigned if there are no consequences associated with a software error that may occur in the system. For software integrity level 0, no V&V tasks are implemented.

Table B.1—Assignment of software integrity levels

Software integrity level	Description
4	An error to a function or system feature that causes catastrophic consequences to the system with reasonable, probable, or occasional likelihood of occurrence of an operating state that contributes to the error; or critical consequences with reasonable or probable likelihood of occurrence of an operating state that contributes to the error.
3	An error to a function or system feature that causes catastrophic consequences with occasional or infrequent likelihood of occurrence of an operating state that contributes to the error; or critical consequences with probable or occasional likelihood of occurrence of an operating state that contributes to the error; or marginal consequences with reasonable or probable likelihood of occurrence of an operating state that contributes to the error.
2	An error to a function or system feature that causes critical consequences with infrequent likelihood of occurrence of an operating state that contributes to the error; or marginal consequences with probable or occasional likelihood of occurrence of an operating state that contributes to the error; or negligible consequences with reasonable or probable likelihood of occurrence of an operating state that contributes to the error.
1	An error to a function or system feature that causes critical consequences with infrequent likelihood of occurrence of an operating state that contributes to the error; or marginal consequences with occasional or infrequent occurrence of an operating state that contributes to the error; or negligible consequences with probable, occasional, or infrequent likelihood of occurrence of an operating state that contributes to the error.

Table B.2—Definitions of consequences

Consequence	Definitions
Catastrophic	Loss of human life, complete mission failure, loss of system security and safety, or extensive financial or social loss.
Critical	Major and permanent injury, partial loss of mission, major system damage, or major financial or social loss.
Marginal	Severe injury or illness, degradation of secondary mission, or some financial or social loss.
Negligible	Minor injury or illness, minor impact on system performance, or operator inconvenience.

Table B.3 illustrates the risk-based scheme shown in Tables B.1 and B.2. Each cell in the table assigns a software integrity level based upon the combination of an error consequence and the likelihood of occurrence of an operating state that contributes to the error. Some table cells reflect more than one software integrity level indicating that the final assignment of the software integrity level can be selected to address the system application and risk mitigation recommendations. For some industry applications, the definition of likelihood of occurrence categories may be expressed as probability figures derived by analysis or from system requirements.

Table B.3—A graphic illustration of the assignment of software integrity levels

Error consequence	Likelihood of occurrence of an operating state that contributes to the error			
	Reasonable	Probable	Occasional	Infrequent
Catastrophic	4	4	4 or 3	3
Critical	4	4 or 3	3	2 or 1
Marginal	3	3 or 2	2 or 1	1
Negligible	2	2 or 1	1	1

Annex C

(informative)

Definition of independent verification and validation (IV&V)

IV&V is defined by three parameters: technical independence, managerial independence, and financial independence.

C.1 Technical independence

Technical independence requires the V&V effort to utilize personnel who are not involved in the development of the software. The IV&V effort must formulate its own understanding of the problem and how the proposed system is solving the problem. Technical independence ("fresh viewpoint") is an important method to detect subtle errors overlooked by those too close to the solution.

For software tools, technical independence means that the IV&V effort uses or develops its own set of test and analysis tools separate from the developer's tools. Sharing of tools is allowable for computer support environments (e.g., compilers, assemblers, utilities) or for system simulations where an independent version would be too costly. For shared tools, IV&V conducts qualification tests on tools to ensure that the common tools do not contain errors that may mask errors in the software being analyzed and tested.

C.2 Managerial independence

This requires that the responsibility for the IV&V effort be vested in an organization separate from the development and program management organizations. Managerial independence also means that the IV&V effort independently selects the segments of the software and system to analyze and test, chooses the IV&V techniques, defines the schedule of IV&V activities, and selects the specific technical issues and problems to act upon. The IV&V effort provides its findings in a timely fashion simultaneously to both the development and program management organizations. The IV&V effort must be allowed to submit to program management the IV&V results, anomalies, and findings without any restrictions (e.g., without requiring prior approval from the development group) or adverse pressures, direct or indirect, from the development group.

C.3 Financial independence

This requires that control of the IV&V budget be vested in an organization independent of the development organization. This independence prevents situations where the IV&V effort cannot complete its analysis or test or deliver timely results because funds have been diverted or adverse financial pressures or influences have been exerted.

C.4 Forms of independence

The extent to which each of the three independence parameters (technical, managerial, and financial) is vested in a V&V organization determines the degree of independence achieved.

Many forms of independence can be adopted for a V&V organization. The four most prevalent are 1) Classical; 2) Modified; 3) Internal; and 4) Embedded. Table C.1 illustrates the degree of independence achieved by these four forms.

Table C.1—Forms of IV&V

Form of IV&V	Technical	Management	Financial
Classical	I[a]	I	I
Modified	I	"I"[b]	I
Internal	"I"	"I"	"I"
Embedded	i[c]	i	i

[a]I = rigorous independence.
[b]"I" = independence with qualifications.
[c]i = minimal maintenance.

C.4.1 Classical IV&V

Classical IV&V embodies all three independence parameters. The IV&V responsibility is vested in an organization that is separate from the development organization. IV&V uses a close working relationship with the development organization to ensure that IV&V findings and recommendations are integrated rapidly back into the development process. Typically, Classical IV&V is performed by one organization (e.g., supplier) and the development is performed by a separate organization (i.e., another vendor). Classical IV&V is generally required for software integrity level 4 (i.e., loss of life, loss of mission, significant social or financial loss) through regulations and standards imposed on the system development.

C.4.2 Modified IV&V

Modified IV&V is used in many large programs where the system prime integrator is selected to manage the entire system development including the IV&V. The prime integrator selects organizations to assist in the development of the system and to perform the IV&V. In the modified IV&V form, the acquirer reduces its own acquisition time by passing this responsibility to the prime integrator. Since the prime integrator performs all or some of the development, the managerial independence is compromised by having the IV&V effort report to the prime integrator. Technical independence is preserved since the IV&V effort formulates an unbiased opinion of the system solution and uses a independent staff to perform the IV&V. Financial independence is preserved since a separate budget is set aside for the IV&V effort. Modified IV&V effort would be appropriate for systems with software integrity level 3 (i.e., an important mission and purpose).

C.4.3 Internal IV&V

Internal IV&V exists when the developer conducts the IV&V with personnel from within its own organization, although not necessarily those personnel involved directly in the development effort. Technical, managerial, and financial independence are compromised. Technical independence is compromised because the IV&V analysis and test is vulnerable to overlooking errors by using the same assumptions or development environment that masked the error from the developers. Managerial independence is compromised because the internal IV&V effort uses the same common tools and corporate analysis procedures as the development group. Peer pressure from the development group may adversely influence how aggressively the software is analyzed and tested by the IV&V effort. Financial independence is compromised because the development group controls the IV&V budget. IV&V funds, resources, and schedules may be reduced as development pressures and needs redirect the IV&V funds into solving development problems. The benefit of an internal IV&V effort is access to staff who know the system and its software. This form of IV&V is used when the degree of independence is not explicitly stated and the benefits of preexisting staff knowledge outweigh the benefits of objectivity.

C.4.4 Embedded V&V

This form is similar to Internal IV&V in that it uses personnel from the development organization who should preferably not be involved directly in the development effort. Embedded V&V is focused on ensuring compliance with the development procedures and processes. The Embedded V&V organization works side by side with the development organization and attends the same inspections, walkthroughs, and reviews as the development staff (i.e., compromise of technical independence). Embedded V&V is not tasked specifically to independently assess the original solution or conduct independent tests (i.e., compromise of managerial independence). Financial independence is compromised because the IV&V staff resource assignments are controlled by the development group. Embedded V&V allows rapid feedback of V&V results into the development process but compromises the technical, managerial, and financial independence of the V&V organization.

Annex D

(informative)

V&V of reusable software

This annex provides guidelines for conducting V&V of reusable software. Reusable software (in part or whole) includes software from software libraries, custom software developed for other applications, legacy software, or commercial-off-the-shelf (COTS) software.

The V&V tasks of Table 1 are applied to reusable software just as they are applied to newly developed software. However, the inputs for these tasks may not be available for reusable software, reducing visibility into the software products and processes. For example, source code may not be available for evaluation, the documentation may be incomplete, or the development process may not be known. The inputs for V&V of reusable software should be obtained from any source available. Some examples of sources for such inputs are provided below.

— Audit results
— Black box testing results
— Design process documentation
— Engineering judgment
— Operational history
— Original developers' interviews
— Prior hazard analysis results
— Prior V&V results
— Product documentation
— Prototyping results
— Reverse engineering results
— Software developer's notebook
— Software integrity level
— Standards complied with
— Static code analysis results
— Test history
— Trial integration results
— User interviews

If V&V of reusable software cannot be carried out at the appropriate level, the reusable software may be used so long as the risk associated with this use is recognized and accounted for in the risk mitigation strategy. Substitution of Table 1 V&V tasks is permitted if equivalent alternative V&V tasks can be shown to satisfy the same criteria as in Table 1.

Annex E

(informative)

V&V metrics

The V&V metrics should consider the software integrity level assigned to the software and system, application domain, project needs, and current industry practices.

This standard considers two categories of metrics: 1) metrics for evaluating software development processes and products; and 2) metrics for evaluating V&V task results, and for improving the quality and coverage of V&V tasks. Values of metrics should be established to serve as indicators as to whether a process, product, or V&V task has been satisfactorily accomplished.

E.1 Metrics for evaluating software development processes and products

The use of metrics should be considered as a V&V approach to evaluating the software development processes and products. By computing evaluation metrics over a period of time, problematic trends can be identified. No standard set of metrics is applicable for all projects so the use of metrics may vary according to the application domain and software development environment.

IEEE Std 1061-1992 [B11] provides a standard definition of available software quality metrics. Other metric-related standards, such as IEEE Std 982.1-1988 [B6] and its corresponding guide, IEEE Std 982.2-1988 [B7], may also be used. The following is a list of metrics that have been found useful. This list is not intended to be exhaustive.

1) Completeness of information (e.g., concept, requirements, design)
2) Software size
3) Requirements traceability
4) Number of changes (e.g., requirements, design, code)
5) Logic and data complexity
6) Analysis or test coverage (type of coverage is based on project and application needs and may consist of requirements, code, functional, module, and test cases)
7) Control and data coupling
8) Status of actual vs. planned progress
9) Number of defects discovered over time
10) Period in the development process when the defect is detected
11) Defect category
12) Severity of defect
13) Systemic or repeated errors having the same cause (such as process deficiencies and tool errors)
14) Time to fix a defect (impact to schedule)

E.2 Metrics for evaluating V&V tasks and for improving the quality and coverage of V&V tasks

No consensus exists on V&V metrics. Candidate metrics to consider fall into two categories:

1) *V&V quality*—to measure the quality and effectiveness of the V&V task (e.g, the ratio of the number of defects identified by V&V to the number of defects missed);

2) *V&V coverage*—to measure the extent or breadth of the application of V&V (e.g., the ratio of the number of software modules verified and validated to the total number of modules).

The Management of V&V activity uses these metric results to change V&V project resources for V&V tasks showing the need for process assistance. These and similar V&V metrics can be used to assess the quality and coverage of V&V tasks. They can be used to provide feedback to the continuous improvement of the V&V processes.

Annex F

(informative)

Example of V&V organizational relationship to other project responsibilities

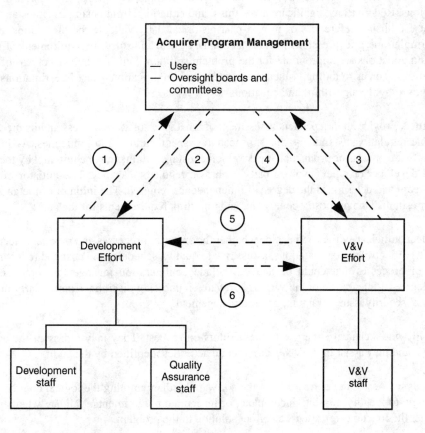

NOTES—The numbered lines represent the flow of control and data as defined below:

1) Submittal of program documentation (e.g., concept, requirements, design, users manuals) source code, program status, program budgets, and development plans and schedules.

2) Approval, denial, and recommendations on development issues and deliverables listed in #1.

3) Submittal of SVVP, V&V task results, anomaly reports, activity summary reports, and other special reports.

4) Approval, denial, and recommendations on V&V issues and deliverables listed in #3.

5) Submittal of V&V task results, anomaly reports, activity summary reports, and special reports as directed by the acquirer program management.

6) Submittal of program documentation (e.g., concept, requirements, design, users manuals, special reports, source code, and program schedules).

Figure F.1—Example of V&V organizational relationship to other project responsibilities

Annex G

(informative)

Optional V&V task descriptions

Algorithm analysis. Verify the correct implementation of algorithms, equations, mathematical formulations, or expressions. Rederive any significant algorithms, and equations from basic principles and theories. Compare against established references or proven past historical data. Validate the algorithms, equations, mathematical formulations, or expressions with respect to the system and software requirements. Ensure that the algorithms and equations are appropriate for the problem solution. Validate the correctness of any constraints or limitations such as rounding, truncation, expression simplifications, best fit estimations, non-linear solutions imposed by the algorithms and equations.

Audit performance. Provide an independent assessment of whether a software process and its products conform to applicable regulations, standards, plans, procedures, specifications and guidelines. Audits may be applied to any software process or product at any development stage. Audits may be initiated by the supplier, the acquirer, the developer or other involved party such as a regulatory agency. The initiator of the audit selects the audit team and determines the degree of independence required. The initiator of the audit and the audit team leader establish the purpose, scope, plan, and reporting requirements for the audit.

The auditors collect sufficient evidence to decide whether the software processes and products meet the evaluation criteria. They identify major deviations, assess risk to quality, schedule, and cost and report their findings. Examples of processes that could be audited include configuration management practices, use of software tools, degree of integration of the various software engineering disciplines particularly in developing an architecture, security issues, training, project management.

Audit support. Provide technical expertise to the auditors on request. They may represent the acquirer at audit proceedings, and may assist in the V&V of remedial activities identified by the audit.

Control flow analysis. Assess the correctness of the software by diagramming the logical control. Examine the flow of the logic to identify missing, incomplete, or inaccurate requirements. Validate whether the flow of control amongst the functions represents a correct solution to the problem.

Cost analysis. Evaluate the cost status of the development processes. Compare budgeted costs against actual costs. Correlate cost expenditures with technical status and schedule progress. Identify program risks if actual costs indicate behind schedule and over cost estimates.

Database analysis. Evaluate database design as part of a design review process could include the following:

1) *Physical Limitations Analysis.* Identify the physical limitations of the database such as maximum number of records, maximum record length, largest numeric value, smallest numeric value, and maximum array length in a data structure and compare them to designed values.

2) *Index vs. Storage Analysis.* Analyze the use of multiple indexes compared to the volume of stored data to determine if the proposed approach meets the requirements for data retrieval performance and size constraints.

3) *Data Structures Analysis.* Some database management systems have specific data structures within a record such as arrays, tables, and date formats. Review the use of these structures for potential impact on requirements for data storage and retrieval.

4) *Backup and Disaster Recovery Analysis.* Review the methods employed for backup against the requirements for data recovery and system disaster recovery and identify deficiencies.

Data flow analysis. Evaluate data flow diagrams as part of a design review process. This could include the following:

1) *Symbology Consistency Check.* The various methods used to depict data flow diagrams employ very specific symbology to represent the actions performed. Verify that each symbol is used consistently.
2) *Flow Balancing.* Compare the output data from each process block to the data inputs and the data derived within the process to ensure the data is available when required. This process does not specifically examine timing or sequence considerations.
3) *Confirmation of Derived Data.* Examine the data derived within a process for correctness and format. Data designed to be entered into a process by operator action should be confirmed to ensure availability.
4) *Keys to Index Comparison.* Compare the data keys used to retrieve data from data stores within a process to the database index design to confirm that no invalid keys have been used and the uniqueness properties are consistent.

Disaster recovery plan assessment. Verify that the disaster recovery plan is adequate to restore critical operation of the system in the case of an extended system outage. The disaster recovery plan should include the following:

1) Identification of the disaster recovery team and a contact list.
2) Recovery operation procedures.
3) Procedure for establishing an alternative site including voice and data communications, mail, and support equipment.
4) Plans for replacement of computer equipment.
5) Establishment of a system backup schedule.
6) Procedures for storage and retrieval of software, data, documentation, and vital records off-site.
7) Logistics of moving staff, data, documentation, etc.

Distributed architecture assessment. Assess the distribution of data and processes in the proposed architecture for feasibility, timing compliance, availability of telecommunications, cost, backup and restore features, downtime, system degradation, and provisions for installation of software updates.

Feasibility study evaluation. Verify that the feasibility study is correct, accurate, and complete. Validate that all logical and physical assumptions (e.g., physical models, business rules, logical processes), constraints, and user requirements are satisfied.

Independent risk assessment. Conduct an independent risk assessment on any aspect of the software project and report on the findings. Such risk assessments will be primarily from a system perspective. Examples of risk assessment include appropriateness of the selected development methodology or tools for the project; and quality risks associated with proposed development schedule alternatives.

Inspection. Inspect the software process to detect defects in the product at each selected development stage to assure the quality of the emerging software. The inspection process may consist of multiple steps for the segregation of the inspection functions of

1) Inspection planning
2) Product overview
3) Inspection preparation
4) Examination meeting
5) Defect rework
6) Resolution follow-up

An inspection is performed by a small team of peer developers and includes, but is not led by, the author. The inspection team usually consists of three to six persons, and in some cases includes personnel from the test group, quality assurance, or V&V. The participants assume specific roles in order to find, classify, report, and analyze defects in the product. Each type of inspection is specifically defined by its intended purpose, required entry criteria, defect classification, checklists, exit criteria, designated participants, and its preparation and examination procedures. Inspections do not debate engineering judgments, suggest corrections, or educate project members; they detect anomalies and problems and verify their resolution by the author.

Inspection (concept). Verify that the system architecture and requirements satisfy customer needs. Verify that the system requirements are complete and correct, and that omissions, defects, and ambiguities in the requirements are detected.

Inspections (design). Verify that the design can be implemented, is traceable to the requirements, and that all interface and procedural logic is complete and correct, and that omissions, defects, and ambiguities in the design are detected.

Inspections (requirements). Verify that the requirements meet customer needs, can be implemented, and are complete, traceable, testable, and consistent so that omissions, defects, and ambiguities in the requirements are detected.

Inspection (source code). Verify that the source code implementation is traceable to the design, and that all interfaces and procedural logic are complete and correct, and that omissions, defects, and ambiguities in the source code are detected.

Inspection—test case (component, integration, system, acceptance). Verify that the (component, integration, system, acceptance) test plan has been followed accurately, that the set of component test cases is complete, and that all component test cases are correct.

Inspection—test design (component, integration, system, acceptance). Verify that the (component, integration, system, acceptance) test design is consistent with the test plan, and that the test design is correct, complete, and readable.

Inspection—test plan (component, integration, system, acceptance). Verify that the scope, strategy, resources, and schedule of the (component, integration, system, acceptance) testing process have been completely and accurately specified, that all items to be tested and all required tasks to be performed have been defined, and to ensure that all personnel necessary to perform the testing have been identified.

Operational evaluation. Assess the deployment readiness and operational readiness of the software. Operational evaluation may include examining the results of operational tests, audit reviews, and anomaly reports. This evaluation verifies that the software is

1) At a suitable point of correctness for mass production of that software
2) Valid and correct for site specific configurations

Performance monitoring. Collect information on the performance of software under operational conditions. Determine whether system and software performance requirements are satisfied. Performance monitoring is a continual process and may include evaluation of the following items:

1) Database transaction rates to determine the need to reorganize or reindex the database.
2) CPU performance monitoring for load balancing.
3) Direct access storage utilization.
4) Network traffic to ensure adequate bandwidth.
5) Critical outputs of a system (e.g., scheduled frequency, expected range of values, scheduled system reports, reports of events).

Post installation validation. Execute a reference benchmark or periodic test for critical software when reliability is crucial or there is a possibility of software corruption. By automatically or manually comparing results with the established benchmark results, the system can be validated prior to each execution of the software. When pre-use benchmark testing is impractical, such as for real time, process control, and emergency-use software, a periodic test, conducted at a pre-determined interval, can be used to ensure continued reliability.

Project management oversight support. Assess project development status for technical and management issues, risks, and problems. Coordinate oversight assessment with the acquirer and development organization. Evaluate project plans, schedules, development processes, and status. Collect, analyze, and report on key project metrics.

Qualification testing. Verify that all software requirements are tested according to qualification testing requirements demonstrating the feasibility of the software for operation and maintenance. Conduct as necessary any tests to verify and validate the correctness, accuracy, and completeness of the qualification testing results. Document the qualification test results together with the expected qualification test results. Planning for qualification testing may begin during the Requirements V&V activity.

Regression analysis and testing. Determine the extent of V&V analyses and tests that must be repeated when changes are made to any previously examined software products. Assess the nature of the change to determine potential ripple or side effects and impacts on other aspects of the system. Rerun test cases based on changes, error corrections, and impact assessment, to detect errors spawned by software modifications.

Reusability assessment. Includes the use of commercial-off-the-shelf (COTS) software, modification of existing software, and the use of code modules specifically designed for reuse. Two important tasks are 1) to identify dependencies on the original hardware or software operating environment, and 2) to verify that the human interface will function correctly in the new target environment. Reuse of existing software can cost-effectively improve the quality of a software product.

Security assessment. Evaluate the security controls on the system to ensure that they protect the hardware and software components from unauthorized use, modifications, and disclosures, and to verify the accountability of the authorized users. Verify that these controls are appropriate for achieving the system's security objectives. A system security assessment should include both the physical components (e.g., computers, controllers, networks, modems, radio frequency, infrared devices) and logical components (e.g., operating systems, utilities, application programs, communication protocols, data, administrative operating policies and procedures).

Simulation analysis. Use a simulation to exercise the software or portions of the software to measure the performance of the software against predefined conditions and events. The simulation can take the form of a manual walkthrough of the software against specific program values and inputs. The simulation can also be another software program that provides the inputs and simulation of the environment to the software under examination. Simulation analysis is used to examine critical performance and response time requirements or the software's response to abnormal events and conditions.

Sizing and timing analysis. Collect and analyze data about the software functions and resource utilization to determine if system and software requirements for speed and capacity are satisfied. The types of software functions and resource utilization issues include, but are not limited to the following:

1) CPU load
2) Random access memory and secondary storage (e.g., disk, tape) utilization
3) Network speed and capacity
4) Input and output speed

Sizing and timing analysis is started at software design and iterated through acceptance testing.

System software assessment. Assess system software (e.g., operating system, computer-aided software engineering tools, data base management system, repository, telecommunications software, graphical user interface) for feasibility, impact on performance and functional requirements, maturity, supportability, adherence to standards, developer's knowledge of and experience with the system software and hardware, and software interface requirements.

Test certification. Certify the test results by verifying that the tests were conducted using baselined requirements, a configuration control process, and repeatable tests, and by witnessing the tests. Certification may be accomplished at a software configuration item level or at a system level.

Test evaluation. Evaluate the tests for requirements coverage and test completeness. Assess coverage by assessing the extent of the software exercised. Assess test completeness by determining if the set of inputs used during test are a fair representative sample from the set of all possible inputs to the software. Assess whether test inputs include boundary condition inputs, rarely encountered inputs, and invalid inputs. For some software it may be necessary to have a set of sequential or simultaneous inputs on one or several processors to test the software adequately.

Test witnessing. Monitor the fidelity of test execution to the specified test procedures, and witness the recording of test results. When a test failure occurs, the testing process can be continued by 1) implementing a "workaround" to the failure; 2) inserting a temporary code patch; or 3) halting the testing process and implementing a software repair. In all cases, assess the test continuation process for test process breakage (e.g., some software is not tested or a patch is left in place permanently), adverse impact on other, tests and loss of configuration control. Regression testing should be done for all the software affected by the test failure.

Training documentation evaluation. Evaluate the training materials and procedures for completeness, correctness, readability, and effectiveness.

User documentation evaluation. Evaluate the user documentation for its completeness, correctness, and consistency with respect to requirements for user interface and for any functionality that can be invoked by the user. The review of the user documentation for its readability and effectiveness should include representative end users who are unfamiliar with the software. Employ the user documentation in planning an acceptance test that is representative of the operational environment.

User training. Assure that the user training includes rules that are specific to the administrative, operational, and application aspects and industry standards for that system. This training should be based on the technical user documentation and procedures provided by the manufacturer of the system. The organization that is responsible for the use of the system should be responsible for providing appropriate user training.

V&V tool plan generation. Prepare a plan that describes the tools needed to support the V&V effort. The plan includes a description of each tool's performance, required inputs, outputs generated, need date, and cost of tool purchase or development. The tool plan should also describe test facilities and integration and system test laboratories supporting the V&V effort. The scope and rigor of the V&V effort as defined by the selected software integrity level should be considered in defining the performance required of each tool.

Walkthrough. Participate in the evaluation processes in which development personnel lead others through a structured examination of a product. Ensure that the participants are qualified to examine the products and are not subject to undue influence. See specific descriptions of the requirement walkthrough, design walkthrough, source code walkthrough, and test walkthrough.

Walkthrough (design). Participate in a walkthrough of the design and updates of the design to ensure completeness, correctness, technical integrity, and quality.

Walkthrough (requirements). Participate in a walkthrough of the requirements specification to ensure that the software requirements are correct, unambiguous, complete, verifiable, consistent, modifiable, traceable, testable, and usable throughout the life cycle.

Walkthrough (source code). Participate in a walkthrough of the source code to ensure that the code is complete, correct, maintainable, free from logic errors, complies with coding standards and conventions, and will operate efficiently.

Walkthrough (test). Participate in a walkthrough of the test documentation to ensure that the planned testing is correct and complete, and that the test results will be correctly analyzed.

Annex H

(informative)

Other references

The following references are considered useful to implement and interpret the V&V requirements contained in this standard. These references are not required to be in compliance with this standard.

[B1] IEC 60300-3-9 (1995), Dependability management—Part 3: Application guide—Section 9: Risk analysis of technological systems.

[B2] IEEE Std 610.12-1990, IEEE Standard Glossary of Software Engineering Terminology.

[B3] IEEE Std 730-1989, IEEE Standard for Software Engineering Quality Assurance Plans.

[B4] IEEE Std 828-1990, IEEE Standard for Software Configuration Management Plans.

[B5] IEEE Std 829-1983 (Reaff 1991), IEEE Standard for Software Test Documentation.

[B6] IEEE Std 982.1-1988, IEEE Standard Dictionary of Measures to Produce Reliable Software.

[B7] IEEE Std 982.2-1988, IEEE Guide for the Use of IEEE Standard Dictionary of Measures to Produce Reliable Software.

[B8] IEEE Std 1028-1997, IEEE Standard for Software Reviews.

[B9] IEEE Std 1044-1993, IEEE Standard for Classification of Software Anomalies.

[B10] IEEE Std 1059-1993, IEEE Guide for Software Verification and Validation Plans.

[B11] IEEE Std 1061-1992, IEEE Standard for a Software Quality Metrics Methodology.

[B12] IEEE Std 1074-1997, IEEE Standard for Developing Software Life Cycle Processes.

[B13] IEEE/EIA 12207.0-1996, IEEE/EIA Standard—Industry Implementation of ISO/IEC 12207 : 1995, Standard for Information Technology—Software life cycle processes.

[B14] IEEE/EIA 12207.1-1997, IEEE/EIA Guide—Industry Implementation of ISO/IEC 12207 : 1995, IEEE/EIA Standard for Information Technology—Software Life Cycle Processes—Life cycle data.

[B15] IEEE/EIA 12207.2-1996, IEEE/EIA Guide—Industry Implementation of ISO/IEC 12207 : 1995, IEEE/EIA Standard for Information Technology—Software Life Cycle Processes—Implementation considerations.

[B16] ISO/IEC 12207: 1995, Information technology—Software life cycle processes.

[B17] ISO/IEC DIS 15026: 1996, Information technology—System and software integrity levels.

[B18] ISO 8402: 1994, Quality Management and Quality Assurance—Vocabulary.

Annex I

(normative)

Definitions from existing standards (normative)

The following are definitions from existing standards as identified in the brackets [ ]. These definitions are placed in this annex so that the body of this standard will not require updating in the event the cited standards and their definitions change.

anomaly: Any condition that deviates from the expected based on requirements, specifications, design, documents, user documents, standards, etc., or from someone's perceptions or experiences. Anomalies may be found during, but not limited to, the review, test, analysis, compilation, or use of software products or applicable documentation. [IEEE Std 1044]

hazard: A source of potential harm or a situation with a potential for harm in terms of human injury, damage to health, property, or the environment, or some combination of these. [IEC 60300-3-9]

hazard identification: The process of recognizing that a hazard exists and defining its characteristics. [IEC 60300-3-9]

integrity level: A denotation of a range of values of a property of an item necessary to maintain system risks within acceptable limits. For items that perform mitigating functions, the property is the reliability with which the item must perform the mitigating function. For items whose failure can lead to a threat, the property is the limit on the frequency of that failure. [ISO/IEC 15026]

risk: The combination of the frequency, or probability, and the consequence of a specified hazardous event. [IEC 60300-3-9]

risk analysis: The systematic use of available information to identify hazards and to estimate the risk to individuals or populations, property or the environment. [IEC 60300-3-9]

software integrity level: The integrity level of a software item. [ISO/IEC 15026]

validation: Confirmation by examination and provisions of objective evidence that the particular requirements for a specific intended use are fulfilled.

NOTES
1—In design and development, validation concerns the process of examining a product to determine conformity with user needs.
2—Validation is normally performed on the final product under defined operating conditions. It may be necessary in earlier stages.
3—"Validated" is used to designate the corresponding status.
4—Multiple validations may be carried out if there are different intended uses. [ISO 8402: 1994]

verification: Confirmation by examination and provisions of objective evidence that specified requirements have been fulfilled.

NOTES
1—In design and development, verification concerns the process of examining the result of a given activity to determine conformity with the stated requirement for that activity.
2—"Verified" is used to designate the corresponding status. [ISO 8402: 1994]

IEEE Std 1012a-1998
(Supplement to
IEEE Std 1012-1998)

Supplement to IEEE Standard for Software Verification and Validation:

Content Map to IEEE/EIA 12207.1-1997

Sponsor
Software Engineering Standards Committee
of the
IEEE Computer Society

Approved 16 September 1998
IEEE-SA Standards Board

Abstract: The relationship between the two sets of requirements on plans for verification and validation of software, found in IEEE Std 1012-1998 and IEEE/EIA 12207.1-1997, is explained so that users may produce documents that comply with both standards.
Keywords: life cycle data plans, qualification test, verification and validation

The Institute of Electrical and Electronics Engineers, Inc.
345 East 47th Street, New York, NY 10017-2394, USA

Print: ISBN 0-7381-1425-1   SH94677
PDF: ISBN 0-7381-1426-X   SS94677

Introduction

(This introduction is not part of IEEE Std 1012a-1998, Supplement to IEEE Standard for Software Verification and Validation: Content Map to IEEE/EIA 12207.1-1997.)

This standard is designed to act as a supplement to IEEE Std 1012-1998, IEEE Standard for Software Verification and Validation. The readers of this docment should use IEEE Std 1012a-1998 in conjunction with IEEE Std 1012-1998.

Participants

This supplement was prepared by the Life Cycle Data Harmonization Working Group of the Software Engineering Standards Committee of the IEEE Computer Society. At the time this supplement was approved, the working group consisted of the following members:

Leonard L. Tripp, *Chair*

Edward Byrne	Dennis Lawrence	Terry Rout
Paul R. Croll	David Maibor	Richard Schmidt
Perry DeWeese	Ray Milovanovic	Norman Schneidewind
Robin Fralick	James Moore	David Schultz
Marilyn Ginsberg-Finner	Timothy Niesen	Basil Sherlund
John Harauz	Dennis Rilling	Peter Voldner
Mark Henley		Ronald Wade

The following persons were on the balloting committee:

Mikhail Auguston
Dennis Beauchaine
Leo Beltracchi
Mordechai Ben-Menachem
H. Ronald Berlack
Richard E. Biehl
William J. Boll
Juris Borzovs
Edward R. Byrne
James E. Cardow
Keith Chan
John J. Chilenski
Antonio M. Cicu
Theo Clarke
Sylvain Clermont
Francois Coallier
Rosemary Coleman
Darrell Cooksey
W. W. Geoff Cozens
Paul R. Croll
Gregory T. Daich
M. A. Daniels
Taz Daughtrey
Bostjan K. Derganc
Perry R. DeWeese
Harpal Dhama
Sherman Eagles
Robert G. Ebenau
Leo Egan
Richard L. Evans
William Eventoff
Jonathan H. Fairclough
John W. Fendrich
Julian Forster
Kirby Fortenberry
Eva Freund
Roger U. Fujii
Simon Gabrihelidis
Barry L. Garner
Adel N. Ghannam
Hiranmay Ghosh
Marilyn Ginsberg-Finner
Eugene A. Glasser
John Garth Glynn

Julio Gonzalez-Sanz
L. M. Gunther
David A. Gustafson
John Harauz
Herbert Hecht
Manfred Hein
Gordon Henley
Mark Henley
John W. Horch
Jerry Huller
Peter L. Hung
George Jackelen
Lisa A. Jensen
Leon Jordan
Vladan V. Jovanovic
William S. Junk
George X. Kambic
Myron S. Karasik
Ron S. Kenett
Robert J. Kierzyk
Shaye Koenig
Thomas M. Kurihara
John B. Lane
J. Dennis Lawrence
Fang Ching Lim
V. J. Maggioli
David Maibor
Kartik C. Majumdar
Henry A. Malec
John R. Matras
Tomoo Matsubara
Mike McAndrew
Sue McGrath
Jerome W. Mersky
Bret Michael
Alan Miller
Lance Miller
Lisa Ming
Celia H. Modell
Pavol Navrat
Myrna L. Olson
Mike Ottewill
Indradeb P. Pal
Lalit M. Patnaik

Warren L. Persons
John G. Phippen
Alex Polack
Peter T. Poon
Kenneth R. Ptack
I. C. Pyle
Annette D. Reilly
Christian Reiser
Dennis Rilling
Helmut Sandmayr
Uma D. Satyen
Stephen R. Schach
Hans Schaefer
Norman Schneidewind
David J. Schultz
Gregory D. Schumacher
Carl S. Seddio
Robert W. Shillato
David M. Siefert
Carl A. Singer
James M. Sivak
Alfred R. Sorkowitz
Donald W. Sova
Julia Stesney
Norma Stopyra
Fred J. Strauss
Robert N. Sulgrove
John Swearingen
Booker Thomas
Gina To
Patricia Trellue
T. H. Tse
Theodore J. Urbanowicz
Glenn D. Venables
Udo Voges
Dolores Wallace
Camille S. White-Partain
Scott A. Whitmire
P. A. Wolfgang
Paul R. Work
Kathryn P. Yglesias
Natalie C. Yopconka
Weider D. Yu
Geraldine Zimmerman

When the IEEE-SA Standards Board approved this supplement on 16 September 1998, it had the following membership:

Contents

Supplement to IEEE Standard for Software Verification and Validation:

Content Map to IEEE/EIA 12207.1-1997

Annex J

(informative)

Guidelines for compliance with IEEE/EIA 12207.1-1997

J.1 Overview

The Software Engineering Standards Committee (SESC) of the IEEE Computer Society has endorsed the policy of adopting international standards. In 1995, the international standard, ISO/IEC 12207, Information technology—Software life cycle processes, was completed. The standard establishes a common framework for software life cycle processes, with well-defined terminology, that can be referenced by the software industry.

In 1995 the SESC evaluated ISO/IEC 12207 and decided that the standard should be adopted and serve as the basis for life cycle processes within the IEEE Software Engineering Collection. The IEEE adaptation of ISO/IEC 12207 is IEEE/EIA 12207.0-1996. It contains ISO/IEC 12207 and the following additions: improved compliance approach, life cycle process objectives, life cycle data objectives, and errata.

The implementation of ISO/IEC 12207 within the IEEE also includes the following:

— IEEE/EIA 12207.1-1997, IEEE/EIA Guide for Information Technology—Software life cycle processes—Life cycle data;
— IEEE/EIA 12207.2-1997, IEEE/EIA Guide for Information Technology—Software life cycle processes—Implementation considerations; and
— Additions to 11 SESC standards (i.e., IEEE Stds 730, 828, 829, 830, 1012, 1016, 1058, 1062, 1219, 1233, 1362) to define the correlation between the data produced by existing SESC standards and the data produced by the application of IEEE/EIA 12207.1-1997.

NOTE—Although IEEE/EIA 12207.1-1997 is a guide, it also contains provisions for application as a standard with specific compliance requirements. This supplement treats IEEE/EIA 12207.1-1997 as a standard.

In order to achieve compliance with both IEEE Std 1012-1998[1] and IEEE/EIA 12207.1-1997, it is essential that the user review and satisfy the data requirements for both standards.

When IEEE Std 1012-1998 is directly referenced, the precedence for conformance is based upon this standard alone. When IEEE Std 1012-1998 is referenced with the IEEE/EIA 12207 standard series, the precedence for conformance is based upon the directly referenced IEEE/EIA 12207 standard, unless there is a statement that this standard has precedence.

J.1.1 Scope and purpose

Both IEEE Std 1012-1998 and IEEE/EIA 12207.1-1997 place requirements on plans for verification of software and validation of software. The purpose of this annex is to explain the relationship between the two sets of requirements so that users producing documents intended to comply with both standards may do so.

J.2 Correlation

This clause explains the relationship between IEEE Std 1012-1998 and IEEE/EIA 12207.0-1996 in the following areas: terminology, process, and life cycle data.

J.2.1 Terminology correlation

The two standards use similar terms in similar ways. Both use the terms test, qualification test, verification, and validation in a similar manner.

J.2.2 Process correlation

Both IEEE Std 1012-1998 and IEEE/EIA 12207.0-1996 use a process-oriented approach for describing the verification process and the validation process. Both documents have the same major processes: acquisition, supply, development, operation, and maintenance. The two, however, differ in the names of the activities of the development process. IEEE Std 1012-1998 uses the following activities:

— Concept;
— Requirements;
— Design;
— Implementation;
— Test;
— Installation and checkout.

IEEE/EIA 12207.0-1996 subdivides the development process into the following activities:

— Process implementation;
— System requirements analysis;
— System architectural design;
— Software requirements analysis;
— Software architectural design;
— Software detailed design;
— Software coding and testing;
— Software integration;

---

[1]For the purpose of this document, it should be assumed that references to IEEE Std 1012-1998 include this supplement, IEEE Std 1012a-1998.

— Software qualification testing;
— System integration;
— System qualification testing;
— Software installation;
— Software acceptance support.

IEEE Std 1012-1998 provides a greater level of detail about what is involved in the verification and validation of software.

J.2.3 Life cycle data correlation for Software Verification and Validation Plans

The information required in a Software Verification and Validation Plan (or V&V plan) by IEEE Std 1012-1998 and the information required in a verification process plan and validation process plan by IEEE/EIA 12207.1-1997 are similar. It is reasonable to expect that a single document could comply with both standards. Details are provided in J.3.

J.2.4 Life cycle data correlation between other data in IEEE/EIA 12207.1-1997 and IEEE Std 1012-1998

Table J.1 correlates the life cycle data other than Software Verification and Validation Plans between IEEE/EIA 12207.1-1997 and IEEE Std 1012-1998. It provides information to users of both standards.

**Table J.1—Life cycle data correlation between other data in
IEEE/EIA 12207.1-1997 and IEEE Std 1012-1998**

Information item	IEEE/EIA 12207.0-1996 subclause(s)	Kind	IEEE/EIA 12207.1-1997 subclause	IEEE Std 1012-1998 subclause(s)
Project management plan	5.2.4.3, 5.2.4.4, and 5.2.4.5	Plan	6.11	5.1 and 7
Software verification report	6.4	Report	6.23	7.6

J.3 Document compliance

This clause provides details bearing on a claim that a Software Verification and Validation Plan complying with IEEE Std 1012-1998 would also achieve "document compliance" with the verification plan and the validation plan specified in IEEE/EIA 12207.1-1997. The requirements for document compliance are summarized in two rows of Table 1 of IEEE/EIA 12207.1-1997. Those rows are reproduced in Table J.2. of this supplement.

Table J.2—Summary of requirements for a Software Verification and Validation Plan excerpted from Table 1 of IEEE/EIA 12207.1-1997

Information item	IEEE/EIA 12207.0-1996 subclause	Kind	IEEE/EIA 12207.1-1997 subclause	References
Verification plan	6.4.1.5	Plan (5.2)	—	IEEE Std 1012-1998 IEEE Std 1059-1993
Validation plan	6.5.1.4	Plan (5.2)	—	IEEE Std 1012-1998 IEEE Std 1059-1993 ISO/IEC 9126: 1991 ISO/IEC 12119: 1994

The requirements for document compliance are discussed in the following subclauses:

— J.3.1. discusses compliance with the generic content guideline (the "kind" of document) noted in column 3 of Table J.2 as a "plan." The generic content guidelines for a "plan" appear in 5.2 of IEEE/EIA 12207.1-1997.
— J.3.2 discusses compliance with the specific content for a verification plan as specified in IEEE/EIA 12207.1-1997.
— J.3.3 discusses compliance with the specific content for a validation plan as specified in IEEE/EIA 12207.1-1997.
— J.3.4 discusses compliance with the life cycle data objectives of Annex H of IEEE/EIA 12207.0-1996 as described in 4.2 of IEEE/EIA 12207.1-1997.

J.3.1 Compliance with generic content guidelines of IEEE/EIA 12207.1-1997

The generic content guidelines for a "plan" in IEEE/EIA 12207.1-1997 are prescribed by 5.2 of IEEE/EIA 12207.1-1997. A complying plan shall achieve the purpose stated in 5.2.1 and include the information listed in 5.2.2 of IEEE/EIA 12207.1-1997.

The purpose of a plan is:

IEEE/EIA 12207.1-1997, subclause 5.2.1: Purpose: Define when, how, and by whom specific activities are to be performed, including options and alternatives, as required.

A software verification and validation plan complying with IEEE Std 1012-1998 would achieve the stated purpose.

Any plan complying with IEEE/EIA 12207.1-1997 shall satisfy the generic content requirements provided in 5.2.2 of that standard. Table J.3 of this supplement lists the generic content items and, where appropriate, references the clause of IEEE Std 1012-1998 that requires the same information. The third column of Table J.3 lists information that shall be added in order to comply with the generic content requirements.

Table J.3—Coverage of generic plan requirements by IEEE Std 1012-1998

IEEE/EIA 12207.1-1997 generic content	Corresponding subclauses of IEEE Std 1012-1998	Additions to requirements of IEEE Std 1012-1998
a) Date of issue and status	7.1 Purpose	Date of issue and status shall be provided.
b) Scope	7.1 Purpose	—
c) Issuing organization	7.1 Purpose	Identification of issuing organization shall be provided.
d) References	7.2 Referenced documents	—
e) Approval authority	7.1 Purpose	Identification of approval authority shall be provided.
f) Planned activities and tasks	7.5 V&V processes	—
g) Macro references (policies or laws that give rise to the need for this plan)	7.2 Referenced documents	—
h) Micro references (other plans or task descriptions that elaborate details of this plan)	7.2 Referenced documents	—
i) Schedules	7.4.2 Master schedule	—
j) Estimates	7.4.4 Resource summary	—
k) Resources and their allocation	7.4.4 Resource summary	—
l) Responsibilities and authority	7.4.5 Responsibilities	—
m) Risks	7.6 V&V reporting requirements	—
n) Quality control measures[a]	7.7.4 Control procedures	—
o) Cost	7.5 Verification and validation processes	The costs of verification and validation activities and resources shall be provided or referenced.
p) Interfaces among parties involved	7.4.1 Organization	—
q) Environment / infrastructure (including safety needs)	7.4.6 Tools, techniques, and methods	—
r) Training	7.4.6 Tools, techniques, and methods	—
s) Glossary	7.3 Definitions	—
t) Change procedures and history	7.7.4 Control procedures	—

[a]This includes quality control of the software verification and validation plan itself.

J.3.2 Compliance with specific verification plan content requirements of IEEE/EIA 12207.1-1997

IEEE/EIA 12207.1-1997 uses the convention that it builds on the content requirements of IEEE/EIA 12207.0-1996 when they exist. Subclause 6.4.1.5 of IEEE/EIA 12207.0-1996 specifies the considerations for software verification plan contents.

Any verification plan complying with IEEE/EIA 12207.1-1997 shall satisfy the specific content requirements provided in 6.4.1.5 of IEEE/EIA 12207.0-1996. Table J.4 of this supplement lists the specific content items and, where appropriate, references the clause of IEEE Std 1012-1998 that requires the same information. The third column of Table J.4 lists information that shall be added in order to comply with the generic content requirements.

Table J.4—Coverage of specific verification plan requirements by IEEE Std 1012-1998

IEEE/EIA 12207.0-1996 information requirement	Corresponding subclauses of IEEE Std 1012-1998	Additions to requirements of IEEE Std 1012-1998[a]
Verification tasks and activities for each life cycle activity	7.5 Verification and validation processes	—
Verification tasks and activities for each software product	7.5 Verification and validation processes	—
Resources for verification	7.4.4 Resource summary	—
Responsibilities for verification	7.4.5 Responsibilities	—
Schedule for verification	7.4.2 Master schedule	—
Procedure for forwarding validation reports to acquirer and other parties	7.6 V&V reporting requirements	—

[a]No additional requirements were identified.

J.3.3 Compliance with specific validation plan content requirements of IEEE/EIA 12207.1-1997

IEEE/EIA 12207.1-1997 uses the convention that it builds on the content requirements of IEEE/EIA 12207.0-1996 when they exist. Subclause 6.5.1.4 of IEEE/EIA 12207.0-1996 specifies the consideration for software validation plan contents.

Any validation plan complying with IEEE/EIA 12207.1-1997 shall satisfy the specific content requirements provided in 6.5.1.4 of IEEE/EIA 12207.0-1996. Table J.5 of this supplement lists the specific content items and, where appropriate, references the clause of IEEE Std 1012-1998 that requires the same information. The third column lists information that shall be added in order to comply with the generic content requirements.

Table J.5—Coverage of specific validation plan requirements by IEEE Std 1012-1998

IEEE/EIA 12207.0-1996 information requirements	Corresponding subclauses of IEEE Std 1012-1998	Additions to requirements of IEEE Std 1012-1998[a]
Items subject to validation	7.1 Purpose	—
Validation tasks to be performed	7.5 Verification and validation processes	—
Resources for validation	7.4.4 Resource summary	—
Responsibilities for validation	7.4.5 Responsibilities	—
Schedule for validation	7.4.2 Master schedule	—
Procedure for forwarding validation reports to acquirer and other parties	7.6 V&V reporting requirements	—

[a]No additional requirements were identified.

J.3.4 Compliance with life cycle data objectives

In addition to the content requirements, life cycle data shall be managed in accordance with the objectives provided in Annex H of IEEE/EIA 12207.0-1996.

NOTE—The information items covered by IEEE Std 1012-1998 include plans and provisions for creating software life cycle data related to the basic types 'test data' and 'management data' in H.4 of IEEE/EIA 12207.0-1996. It provides for the following: (1) test data, such as test strategy and criteria, cases (what to test), procedures (how to carry out tests), test results, and key decision rationale, and (2) management data such as management plans, status reports, management indicators, criteria and key decision rationale, and contract and other procurement information.

J.4 Conclusion

The analysis documented in this annex suggests that any verification and validation plan complying with IEEE Std 1012-1998 and the additions specified in Table J.3, Table J.4, and Table J.5, also complies with the requirements of a verification and validation plan in IEEE/EIA 12207.1-1997. In addition, to comply with IEEE/EIA 12207.1-1997, any verification and validation plan shall support the life cycle data objectives of Annex H of IEEE/EIA 12207.0-1996.

IEEE Standard for Software Reviews

Sponsor

**Software Engineering Standards Committee
of the
IEEE Computer Society**

Approved 9 December 1997

IEEE Standards Board

Abstract: This standard defines five types of software reviews, together with procedures required for the execution of each review type. This standard is concerned only with the reviews; it does not define procedures for determining the necessity of a review, nor does it specify the disposition of the results of the review. Review types include management reviews, technical reviews, inspections, walk-throughs, and audits.

Keywords: audit, inspection, review, walk-through

The Institute of Electrical and Electronics Engineers, Inc.
345 East 47th Street, New York, NY 10017-2394, USA

Introduction

(This introduction is not part of IEEE Std 1028-1997, IEEE Standard for Software Reviews.)

This Introduction provides the user with the rationale and background of the reviews outlined in this standard and their relationships to other IEEE standards.

Purpose

This standard defines five types of software reviews, together with procedures required for the execution of each review type. This standard is concerned only with the reviews; it does not define procedures for determining the necessity of a review, nor does it specify the disposition of the results of the review. Review types include management reviews, technical reviews, inspections, walk-throughs, and audits.

This standard is meant to be used either in conjunction with other IEEE software engineering standards or as a stand-alone definition of software review procedures. In the latter case, local management must determine the events that precede and follow the actual software reviews.

The need for reviews is described in several other IEEE standards, as well as standards prepared by other standards-writing organizations. IEEE Std 1028-1997 is meant to support these other standards. In particular, reviews required by the following standards can be executed using the procedures described herein:

— IEEE Std 730-1989 [B1][a]
— IEEE Std 828-1990 [B2]
— IEEE Std 1012-1986 [B5]
— IEEE Std 1058.1-1987 [B8]
— IEEE Std 1074-1995 [B10]
— IEEE Std 1219-1992 [B11]
— IEEE Std 1220-1994 [B12]
— IEEE Std 1228-1994 B13]
— IEEE Std 1298-1992 (AS 3563.1-1991) [B14]
— ISO/IEC 12207:1995 [B15]

The use of IEEE Std 1044-1993 [B7] is encouraged as part of the reporting procedures for this standard.

General application intent

This standard applies throughout the scope of any selected software life-cycle model and provides a standard against which software review plans can be prepared and assessed. Maximum benefit can be derived from this standard by planning for its application early in the project life cycle.

This standard for software reviews was written in consideration of both the software and its system operating environment. It can be used where software is the total system entity or where it is part of a larger system. Care should be taken to integrate software review activities into any total system life-cycle planning; software reviews should exist in concert with hardware and computer system reviews to the benefit of the entire system.

Reviews carried out in conformance with this standard may include both personnel internal to the project and customers or acquirers of the product, according to local procedures. Subcontractors may also be included if appropriate.

---

[a]The numbers in brackets correspond to those of the bibliography in Annex C.

The information obtained during software reviews (particularly inspections) may be of benefit for improving the user's software acquisition, supply, development, operation, and maintenance processes. The use of review data for process improvement is not required by this standard, but their use is strongly encouraged.

Conformance

Conformance to this standard for a specific review type can be claimed when all mandatory actions (indicated by "shall") are carried out as defined in this standard for the review type used. Claims for conformance should be phrased to indicate the review types used; for example, "conforming to IEEE Std 1028-1997 for inspections."

Development procedure

This standard was developed by the Software Engineering Review Working Group. The entire standards writing procedure was carried out via electronic mail.

Participants

At the time this standard was completed, the Software Engineering Review Working Group had the following membership:

J. Dennis Lawrence, *Chair*
Patricia A. Trellue, *Technical Editor*

Frank Ackerman	Karol Fruehauf	Archibald McKinlay
Leo Beltracchi	Andrew Gabb	Warren L. Persons†
Ron Berlack	Tom Gilb	Peter T. Poon
Antonio Bertolino	Jon Hagar	Christian Reiser
Richard J. Blauw	John Harauz	Helmut Sandmayr
Audrey Brewer	Hans-Ludwig Hausen	Hans Schaefer*
James E. Cardow	Michael Haux	Katsu Shintani
Hu Cheng	Herb Hecht	Mel E. Smyre
Pat Daggett	Chuck Howell	Julia Stesney
Ronald Dean†	Laura Ippolito	Gina To†
Janet Deeney*†	Rikkila Juha	André Villas-Boas
Claude G. Diderich	George X. Kambic	Dolores Wallace
Leo G. Egan	Myron S. Karasik	David A. Wheeler
Martin Elliot	Stanley H. Levinson	Ron Yun
Jon Fairclough*	Michael S. Lines	Tony Zawilski
	Jordan Matejceck	

* Principal writers
† Ballot resolution

The following persons were on the balloting committee:

Leo Beltracchi
Mordechai Ben-Menachem
H. Ronald Berlack
Audrey C. Brewer
Alan L. Bridges
Kathleen L. Briggs
David W. Burnett
Edward R. Byrne
Thomas G. Callaghan
Stuart Ross Campbell
James E. Cardow
Jaya R. Carl
Leslie Chambers
Keith Chan
John P. Chihorek
S. V. Chiyyarath
Antonio M. Cicu
Theo Clarke
Sylvain Clermont
Rosemary Coleman
Darrell Cooksey
Geoff Cozens
Thomas Crowley
Gregory T. Daich
Hillary Davidson
Bostjan K. Derganc
Sanjay Dewal
Michael P. Dewalt
Charles Droz
Robert G. Ebenau
Chrisof Ebert
William Eventoff
Jonathan H. Fairclough
John W. Fendrich
Jay Forster
Kirby Fortenberry
Barry L. Garner
Adel N. Ghannam
Hiranmay Ghosh
Marilyn Ginsberg-Finner
M. Joel Gittleman
John Garth Glynn

Julio Gonzalez-Sanz
Lewis Gray
Lawrence M. Gunther
Jon Hagar
John Harauz
Rob Harker
Herbert Hecht
William Hefley
Manfred Hein
Mark Henley
Umesh P. Hiriyannaiah
John W. Horch
Fabrizio Imelio
George Jackelen
Frank V. Jorgensen
Vladan V. Jovanovic
William S. Junk
George X. Kambic
David W. Kane
Myron S. Karasik
Ron S. Kenett
Judy Kerner
Robert J. Kierzyk
Motti Y. Klein
Dwayne L. Knirk
Shaye Koenig
Joan Kundig
Thomas M. Kurihara
J. Dennis Lawrence
Randal Leavitt
Stanley H. Levinson
Michael Lines
William M. Lively
Dieter Look
David Maibor
Philip P. Mak
Tomoo Matsubara
Scott D. Matthews
Patrick McCray
Sue McGrath
Bret Michael

Alan Miller
Millard Allen Mobley
James W. Moore
Mike Ottewill
Mark Paulk
David E. Peercy
Warren L. Persons
John G. Phippen
Peter T. Poon
Margaretha W. Price
Lawrence S. Przybylski
Kenneth R. Ptack
Terence P. Rout
Andrew P. Sage
Helmut Sandmayr
Stephen R. Schach
Hans Schaefer
David J. Schultz
Gregory D. Schumacher
Robert W. Shillato
Katsutoshi Shintani
Carl A. Singer
James M. Sivak
Alfred R. Sorkowitz
Donald W. Sova
Fred J. Strauss
Michael Surratt
Douglas H. Thiele
Booker Thomas
Carmen J. Trammell
Patricia A. Trellue
Richard D. Tucker
Margaret C. Updike
Theodore J. Urbanowicz
Glenn D. Venables
Dolores Wallace
David A. Wheeler
Camille S. White-Partain
Charles D. Wilson
Paul R. Work
Weider D. Yu
Peter F. Zoll

When the IEEE Standards Board approved this standard on 9 December 1997, it had the following membership:

Donald C. Loughry, *Chair*   **Richard J. Holleman,** *Vice Chair*

Andrew G. Salem, *Secretary*

Clyde R. Camp	Lowell Johnson	Louis-François Pau
Stephen L. Diamond	Robert Kennelly	Gerald H. Peterson
Harold E. Epstein	E. G. "Al" Kiener	John W. Pope
Donald C. Fleckenstein	Joseph L. Koepfinger*	Jose R. Ramos
Jay Forster*	Stephen R. Lambert	Ronald H. Reimer
Thomas F. Garrity	Lawrence V. McCall	Ingo Rüsch
Donald N. Heirman	L. Bruce McClung	John S. Ryan
Jim Isaak	Marco W. Migliaro	Chee Kiow Tan
Ben C. Johnson		Howard L. Wolfman

*Member Emeritus

Also included are the following nonvoting IEEE Standards Board liaisons:

Satish K. Aggarwal
Alan H. Cookson

Paula M. Kelty
IEEE Standards Project Editor

Contents

IEEE Standard for Software Reviews

1. Overview

1.1 Purpose

The purpose of this standard is to define systematic reviews applicable to software acquisition, supply, development, operation, and maintenance. This standard describes how to carry out a review. Other standards or local management define the context within which a review is performed, and the use made of the results of the review. Software reviews can be used in support of the objectives of project management, system engineering (for example, functional allocation between hardware and software), verification and validation, configuration management, and quality assurance. Different types of reviews reflect differences in the goals of each review type. Systematic reviews are described by their defined procedures, scope, and objectives.

1.2 Scope

This standard provides minimum acceptable requirements for systematic software reviews, where "systematic" includes the following attributes:

a) Team participation
b) Documented results of the review
c) Documented procedures for conducting the review

Reviews that do not meet the requirements of this standard are considered to be nonsystematic reviews. This standard is not intended to discourage or prohibit the use of nonsystematic reviews.

The definitions, requirements, and procedures for the following five types of reviews are included within this standard:

a) Management reviews
b) Technical reviews
c) Inspections
d) Walk-throughs
e) Audits

This standard does not establish the need to conduct specific reviews; that need is defined by other software engineering standards or by local procedures. This standard provides definitions, requirements, and proce-

1

dures that are applicable to the reviews of software development products throughout the software life cycle. Users of this standard shall specify where and when this standard applies and any intended deviations from this standard.

It is intended that this standard be used with other software engineering standards that determine the products to be reviewed, the timing of reviews, and the necessity for reviews. This standard is closely aligned with IEEE Std 1012-1986 [B5],[1] but can also be used with IEEE Std 1074-1995 [B10], IEEE Std 730-1989 [B1], ISO/IEC 12207:1995 [B15], and other standards. Use with other standards is described in Annex A. A useful model is to consider IEEE Std 1028-1997 as a subroutine to the other standards. Thus, if IEEE Std 1012-1986 were used to carry out the verification and validation process, the procedure in IEEE Std 1012-1986 could be followed until such time as instructions to carry out a specific review are encountered. At that point, IEEE Std 1028-1997 would be "called" to carry out the review, using the specific review type described herein. Once the review has been completed, IEEE Std 1012-1986 would be returned to for disposition of the results of the review and any additional action required by IEEE Std 1012-1986.

In this model, requirements and quality attributes for the software product are "parameter inputs" to the review and are imposed by the "caller." When the review is finished, the review outputs are "returned" to the "caller" for action. Review outputs typically include anomaly lists and action item lists; the resolution of the anomalies and action items are the responsibility of the "caller."

1.3 Conformance

Conformance to this standard for a specific review type can be claimed when all mandatory actions (indicated by "shall") are carried out as defined in this standard for the review type used. Claims for conformance should be phrased to indicate the review types used; for example, "conforming to IEEE Std 1028-1997 for inspections." The word "shall" is used to express a requirement, "should," to express a recommendation, and "may," to express alternative or optional methods of satisfying a requirement.

1.4 Organization of standard

Clauses 4–8 of this standard provide guidance and descriptions for the five types of systematic reviews addressed by this standard. Each of these clauses contains the following information:

a) *Introduction.* Describes the objectives of the systematic review and provides an overview of the systematic review procedures.
b) *Responsibilities.* Defines the roles and responsibilities needed for the systematic review.
c) *Input.* Describes the requirements for input needed by the systematic review.
d) *Entry criteria.* Describes the criteria to be met before the systematic review can begin, including
   1) Authorization
   2) Initiating event
e) *Procedures.* Details the procedures for the systematic review, including
   1) Planning the review
   2) Overview of procedures
   3) Preparation
   4) Examination/evaluation/recording of results
   5) Rework/follow-up
f) *Exit criteria.* Describes the criteria to be met before the systematic review can be considered complete.
g) *Output.* Describes the minimum set of deliverables to be produced by the systematic review.

---

[1]The numbers in brackets correspond to those of the bibliography in Annex C.

1.5 Application of standard

The procedures and terminology defined in this standard apply to software acquisition, supply, development, operation, and maintenance processes requiring systematic reviews. Systematic reviews are performed on a software product as required by other standards or local procedures.

The term "software product" is used in this standard in a very broad sense. Examples of software products include, but are not limited to, the following:

a) Anomaly reports
b) Audit reports
c) Back up and recovery plans
d) Build procedures
e) Contingency plans
f) Contracts
g) Customer or user representative complaints
h) Disaster plans
i) Hardware performance plans
j) Inspection reports
k) Installation plans
l) Installation procedures
m) Maintenance manuals
n) Maintenance plans
o) Management review reports
p) Operations and user manuals
q) Procurement and contracting methods
r) Progress reports
s) Release notes
t) Reports and data (for example, review, audit, project status, anomaly reports, test data)
u) Request for proposal
v) Risk management plans
w) Software configuration management plans (see IEEE Std 828-1990 [B2])
x) Software design descriptions (see IEEE Std 1016-1987 [B6])
y) Software project management plans (see IEEE Std 1058-1987 [B8])
z) Software quality assurance plans (see IEEE Std 730-1989 [B1])
aa) Software requirements specifications (see IEEE Std 830-1993 [B4])
ab) Software safety plans (see IEEE 1228-1994 [B13])
ac) Software test documentation (see IEEE Std 829-1983 [B3])
ad) Software user documentation (see IEEE Std 1063-1987 [B9])
ae) Software verification and validation plans (see IEEE Std 1012-1986 [B5])
af) Source code
ag) Standards, regulations, guidelines, and procedures
ah) System build procedures
ai) Technical review reports
aj) Vendor documents
ak) Walk-through reports

This standard permits reviews that are held by means other than physically meeting in a single location. Examples include telephone conferences, video conferences, and other means of group electronic communication. In such cases the communication means should be defined in addition to the meeting places, and all other review requirements remain applicable.

In order to make use of this standard to carry out a software review, first decide the objective of the review. Next, select an appropriate review type using the guidance in Annex B or a local procedure. Then follow the procedure described in the appropriate clause (4–8) of this standard.

2. References

This standard shall be used in conjunction with the following publications. If the following publications are superseded by an approved revision, the revision shall apply. (Additional standards that may be used to prepare software products that are the subject of reviews are cited in a bibliography in Annex C.)

IEEE Std 100-1996, The IEEE Standard Dictionary of Electrical and Electronics Terms, Sixth Edition.

IEEE Std 610.12-1990, IEEE Standard Glossary of Software Engineering Terminology.

3. Definitions

For purposes of this standard, the following terms and definitions apply. IEEE Std 610.12-1990[2] and IEEE Std 100-1996 should be consulted for terms not defined in this clause.

Six of the terms given here are defined in other IEEE software engineering standards. The definition of the term "anomaly" is identical to that given in IEEE Std 1044-1993 [B7]. The terms "audit," "inspection," "review," "software product," and "walk-through" are all defined in IEEE Std 610.12-1990; however, some minor modifications have been made to those definitions to more closely match the content of this standard, as explained in the succeeding paragraph.

IEEE Std 610.12-1990 uses different terms for the object of a review: audits and reviews are defined therein in terms of "work products," inspections are defined in terms of "development products," and walk-throughs are defined in terms of "segment of documentation or code." "Work products" are not defined in IEEE Std 610.12-1990. Since "software product" is defined therein, and it is desirable to use a single term in this standard, a change in terminology was made. Since software products being reviewed are not limited to those "designated for delivery to a user," that phrase was dropped from the definition of "software product." The definition of "inspection" has been changed considerably. No other changes to the definitions from IEEE Std 610.12-1990 were made.

3.1 anomaly: Any condition that deviates from expectations based on requirements specifications, design documents, user documents, standards, etc., or from someone's perceptions or experiences. Anomalies may be found during, but not limited to, the review, test, analysis, compilation, or use of software products or applicable documentation.

3.2 audit: An independent examination of a software product, software process, or set of software processes to assess compliance with specifications, standards, contractual agreements, or other criteria.

3.3 inspection: A visual examination of a software product to detect and identify software anomalies, including errors and deviations from standards and specifications. Inspections are peer examinations led by impartial facilitators who are trained in inspection techniques. Determination of remedial or investigative action for an anomaly is a mandatory element of a software inspection, although the solution should not be determined in the inspection meeting.

---

[2]Information on references can be found in Clause 2.

3.4 management review: A systematic evaluation of a software acquisition, supply, development, operation, or maintenance process performed by or on behalf of management that monitors progress, determines the status of plans and schedules, confirms requirements and their system allocation, or evaluates the effectiveness of management approaches used to achieve fitness for purpose.

3.5 review: A process or meeting during which a software product is presented to project personnel, managers, users, customers, user representatives, or other interested parties for comment or approval.

3.6 software product: (A) A complete set of computer programs, procedures, and associated documentation and data. (B) One or more of the individual items in (A).

3.7 technical review: A systematic evaluation of a software product by a team of qualified personnel that examines the suitability of the software product for its intended use and identifies discrepancies from specifications and standards. Technical reviews may also provide recommendations of alternatives and examination of various alternatives.

3.8 walk-through: A static analysis technique in which a designer or programmer leads members of the development team and other interested parties through a software product, and the participants ask questions and make comments about possible errors, violation of development standards, and other problems.

4. Management reviews

4.1 Introduction

The purpose of a management review is to monitor progress, determine the status of plans and schedules, confirm requirements and their system allocation, or evaluate the effectiveness of management approaches used to achieve fitness for purpose. Management reviews support decisions about corrective actions, changes in the allocation of resources, or changes to the scope of the project.

Management reviews are carried out by, or on behalf of, the management personnel having direct responsibility for the system. Management reviews identify consistency with and deviations from plans, or adequacies and inadequacies of management procedures. This examination may require more than one meeting. The examination need not address all aspects of the product.

Examples of software products subject to management review include, but are not limited to

a) Anomaly reports
b) Audit reports
c) Back-up and recovery plans
d) Contingency plans
e) Customer or user representative complaints
f) Disaster plans
g) Hardware performance plans
h) Installation plans
i) Maintenance plans
j) Procurement and contracting methods
k) Progress reports
l) Risk management plans
m) Software configuration management plans
n) Software project management plans
o) Software quality assurance plans
p) Software safety plans

q) Software verification and validation plans
r) Technical review reports
s) Software product analyses
t) Verification and validation reports

4.2 Responsibilities

Management reviews are carried out by, or on behalf of, the management personnel having direct responsibility for the system. Technical knowledge may be necessary to conduct a successful management review. Management reviews shall be performed by the available personnel who are best qualified to evaluate the software product.

The following roles shall be established for the management review:

a) Decision maker
b) Review leader
c) Recorder
d) Management staff
e) Technical staff

The following roles may also be established for the management review:

f) Other team members
g) Customer or user representative
h) Individual participants may act in more than one role

4.2.1 Decision maker

The decision maker is the person for whom the management review is conducted. The decision maker shall determine if the review objectives have been met.

4.2.2 Review leader

The review leader shall be responsible for administrative tasks pertaining to the review, shall be responsible for planning and preparation as described in 4.5.2 and 4.5.4, shall ensure that the review is conducted in an orderly manner and meets its objectives, and shall issue the review outputs as described in 4.7.

4.2.3 Recorder

The recorder shall document anomalies, action items, decisions, and recommendations made by the review team.

4.2.4 Management staff

Management staff assigned to carry out management reviews are responsible for active participation in the review. Managers responsible for the system as a whole have additional responsibilities as defined in 4.5.1.

4.2.5 Technical staff

The technical staff shall provide the information necessary for the management staff to fulfill its responsibilities.

4.2.6 Customer or user representative

The role of the customer or user representative should be determined by the review leader prior to the review.

4.3 Input

Input to the management review shall include the following:

a) A statement of objectives for the management review
b) The software product being evaluated
c) Software project management plan
d) Status, relative to plan, of the software product completed or in progress
e) Current anomalies or issues list
f) Documented review procedures

Input to the management review should also include the following:

g) Status of resources, including finance, as appropriate
h) Relevant review reports
i) Any regulations, standards, guidelines, plans, or procedures against which the software product should be evaluated
j) Anomaly categories (See IEEE Std 1044-1993 [B7])

Additional reference material may be made available by the individuals responsible for the software product when requested by the review leader.

4.4 Entry criteria

4.4.1 Authorization

The need for conducting management reviews should initially be established in the appropriate project planning documents, as listed in 4.1. Under these plans, completion of a specific software product or completion of an activity may initiate a management review. In addition to those management reviews required by a specific plan, other management reviews may be announced and held at the request of software quality management, functional management, project management, or the customer or user representative, according to local procedures.

4.4.2 Preconditions

A management review shall be conducted only when both of the following conditions have been met:

a) A statement of objectives for the review is established by the management personnel for whom the review is being carried out
b) The required review inputs are available

4.5 Procedures

4.5.1 Management preparation

Managers shall ensure that the review is performed as required by applicable standards and procedures and by requirements mandated by law, contract, or other policy. To this end, managers shall

a) Plan time and resources required for reviews, including support functions, as required in IEEE Std 1058.1-1987 [B8] or other appropriate standards
b) Provide funding and facilities required to plan, define, execute, and manage the reviews
c) Provide training and orientation on review procedures applicable to a given project
d) Ensure appropriate levels of expertise and knowledge sufficient to comprehend the software product under review
e) Ensure that planned reviews are conducted
f) Act on review team recommendations in a timely manner

4.5.2 Planning the review

The review leader shall be responsible for the following activities:

a) Identify, with appropriate management support, the review team
b) Assign specific responsibilities to the review team members
c) Schedule and announce the meeting
d) Distribute review materials to participants, allowing adequate time for their preparation
e) Set a timetable for distribution of review material, the return of comments, and forwarding of comments to the author for disposition

4.5.3 Overview of review procedures

A qualified person should present an overview session for the review team when requested by the review leader. This overview may occur as part of the review meeting (see 4.5.6) or as a separate meeting.

4.5.4 Preparation

Each review team member shall examine the software product and other review inputs prior to the review meeting. Anomalies detected during this examination should be documented and sent to the review leader. The review leader should classify anomalies to ensure that review meeting time is used most effectively. The review leader should forward the anomalies to the author of the software product for disposition.

4.5.5 Examination

The management review shall consist of one or more meetings of the review team. The meetings shall accomplish the following goals:

a) Review the objectives of the management review
b) Evaluate the software product under review against the review objectives
c) Evaluate project status, including the status of plans and schedules
d) Review anomalies identified by the review team prior to the review
e) Generate a list of action items, emphasizing risks
f) Document the meeting

The meetings should accomplish the following goals as appropriate:

g) Evaluate the risk issues that may jeopardize the success of the project
h) Confirm software requirements and their system allocation
i) Decide the course of action to be taken or recommendations for action
j) Identify other issues that should be addressed

4.5.6 Rework/follow-up

The review leader shall verify that the action items assigned in the meeting are closed.

4.6 Exit criteria

The management review shall be considered complete when the activities listed in 4.5.5 have been accomplished and the output described in 4.7 exists.

4.7 Output

The output from the management review shall be documented evidence that identifies

   a)   The project being reviewed
   b)   The review team members
   c)   Review objectives
   d)   Software product reviewed
   e)   Specific inputs to the review
   f)   Action item status (open, closed), ownership and target date (if open) or completion date (if closed)
   g)   A list of anomalies identified by the review team that must be addressed for the project to meet its goals

Although this standard sets minimum requirements for the content of the documented evidence, it is left to local procedures to prescribe additional content, format requirements, and media.

5. Technical reviews

5.1 Introduction

The purpose of a technical review is to evaluate a software product by a team of qualified personnel to determine its suitability for its intended use and identify discrepancies from specifications and standards. It provides management with evidence to confirm whether

   a)   The software product conforms to its specifications
   b)   The software product adheres to regulations, standards, guidelines, plans, and procedures applicable to the project
   c)   Changes to the software product are properly implemented and affect only those system areas identified by the change specification

Technical reviews may also provide the recommendation and examination of various alternatives, which may require more than one meeting. The examination need not address all aspects of the product.

Examples of software products subject to technical review include, but are not limited to

   a)   Software requirements specification
   b)   Software design description
   c)   Software test documentation
   d)   Software user documentation
   e)   Maintenance manual
   f)   System build procedures
   g)   Installation procedures
   h)   Release notes

5.2 Responsibilities

The following roles shall be established for the technical review:

a) Decision maker
b) Review leader
c) Recorder
d) Technical staff

The following roles may also be established for the technical review:

e) Management staff
f) Other team members
g) Customer or user representative

Individual participants may act in more than one role.

5.2.1 Decision maker

The decision maker is the person for whom the technical review is conducted. The decision maker shall determine if the review objectives have been met.

5.2.2 Review leader

The review leader shall be responsible for the review. This responsibility includes performing administrative tasks pertaining to the review, ensuring that the review is conducted in an orderly manner, and ensuring that the review meets its objectives. The review leader shall issue the review outputs as described in 5.7.

5.2.3 Recorder

The recorder shall document anomalies, action items, decisions, and recommendations made by the review team.

5.2.4 Technical staffh3

The technical staff shall actively participate in the review and evaluation of the software product.

5.2.5 Management staff

The management staff may participate in the technical review for the purpose of identifying issues that require management resolution.

5.2.6 Customer or user representative

The role of the customer or user representative should be determined by the review leader prior to the review.

5.3 Input

Input to the technical review shall include the following:

a) A statement of objectives for the technical review
b) The software product being examined

c)   Software project management plan
d)   Current anomalies or issues list for the software product
e)   Documented review procedures

Input to the technical review should also include the following:

f)   Relevant review reports
g)   Any regulations, standards, guidelines, plans, and procedures against which the software product is to be examined
h)   Anomaly categories (See IEEE Std 1044-1993 [B7])

Additional reference material may be made available by the individuals responsible for the software product when requested by the review leader.

5.4 Entry criteria

5.4.1 Authorization

The need for conducting technical reviews of a software product shall be defined by project planning documents. In addition to those technical reviews required by a specific plan, other technical reviews may be announced and held at the request of functional management, project management, software quality management, systems engineering, or software engineering according to local procedures. Technical reviews may be required to evaluate impacts of hardware anomalies or deficiencies on the software product.

5.4.2 Preconditions

A technical review shall be conducted only when both of the following conditions have been met:

a)   A statement of objectives for the review is established
b)   The required review inputs are available

5.5 Procedures

5.5.1 Management preparation

Managers shall ensure that the review is performed as required by applicable standards and procedures and by requirements mandated by law, contract, or other policy. To this end, managers shall

a)   Plan time and resources required for reviews, including support functions, as required in IEEE Std 1058.1-1987 [B8] or other appropriate standards
b)   Provide funding and facilities required to plan, define, execute, and manage the reviews
c)   Provide training and orientation on review procedures applicable to a given project
d)   Ensure that review team members possess appropriate levels of expertise and knowledge sufficient to comprehend the software product under review
e)   Ensure that planned reviews are conducted
f)   Act on review team recommendations in a timely manner

5.5.2 Planning the review

The review leader shall be responsible for the following activities:

a)   Identify, with appropriate management support, the review team
b)   Assign specific responsibilities to the review team members

c) Schedule and announce the meeting place
d) Distribute review materials to participants, allowing adequate time for their preparation
e) Set a timetable for distribution of review material, the return of comments and forwarding of comments to the author for disposition

As a part of the planning procedure, the review team shall determine if alternatives are to be discussed at the review meeting. Alternatives may be discussed at the review meeting, afterwards in a separate meeting, or left to the author of the software product to resolve.

5.5.3 Overview of review procedures

A qualified person should present an overview of the review procedures for the review team when requested by the review leader. This overview may occur as a part of the review meeting (see 5.5.6) or as a separate meeting.

5.5.4 Overview of the software product

A technically qualified person should present an overview of the software product for the review team when requested by the review leader. This overview may occur either as a part of the review meeting (see 5.5.6) or as a separate meeting.

5.5.5 Preparation

Each review team member shall examine the software product and other review inputs prior to the review meeting. Anomalies detected during this examination should be documented and sent to the review leader. The review leader should classify anomalies to ensure that review meeting time is used most effectively. The review leader should forward the anomalies to the author of the software product for disposition.

The review leader shall verify that team members are prepared for the technical review. The review leader should gather individual preparation times and record the total. The review leader shall reschedule the meeting if the team members are not adequately prepared.

5.5.6 Examination

During the technical review the review team shall hold one or more meetings. The meetings shall accomplish the following goals:

a) Decide on the agenda for evaluating the software product and anomalies
b) Evaluate the software product
c) Determine if
   1) The software product is complete;
   2) The software product conforms to the regulations, standards, guidelines, plans and procedures applicable to the project;
   3) Changes to the software product are properly implemented and affect only the specified areas;
   4) The software product is suitable for its intended use;
   5) The software product is ready for the next activity;
   6) Hardware anomalies or specification discrepancies exist
d) Identify anomalies
e) Generate a list of action items, emphasizing risks
f) Document the meeting

After the software product has been reviewed, documentation shall be generated to document the meeting, list anomalies found in the software product, and describe any recommendations to management.

When anomalies are sufficiently critical or numerous, the review leader should recommend that an additional review be applied to the modified software product. This, at a minimum, should cover product areas changed to resolve anomalies as well as side effects of those changes.

5.5.7 Rework/follow-up

The review leader shall verify that the action items assigned in the meeting are closed.

5.6 Exit criteria

A technical review shall be considered complete when the activities listed in 5.5.6 have been accomplished, and the output described in 5.7 exists.

5.7 Output

The output from the technical review shall consist of documented evidence that identifies

- a) The project being reviewed
- b) The review team members
- c) The software product reviewed
- d) Specific inputs to the review
- e) Review objectives and whether they were met
- f) A list of resolved and unresolved software product anomalies
- g) A list of unresolved system or hardware anomalies or specification action items
- h) A list of management issues
- i) Action item status (open, closed), ownership and target date (if open), or completion date (if closed)
- j) Any recommendations made by the review team on how to dispose of unresolved issues and anomalies
- k) Whether the software product meets the applicable regulations, standards, guidelines, plans, and procedures without deviations

Although this standard sets minimum requirements for the content of the documented evidence, it is left to local procedures to prescribe additional content, format requirements, and media.

6. Inspections

6.1 Introduction

The purpose of an inspection is to detect and identify software product anomalies. This is a systematic peer examination that

- a) Verifies that the software product satisfies its specifications
- b) Verifies that the software product satisfies specified quality attributes
- c) Verifies that the software product conforms to applicable regulations, standards, guidelines, plans, and procedures
- d) Identifies deviations from standards and specifications
- e) Collects software engineering data (for example, anomaly and effort data) (optional)
- f) Uses the collected software engineering data to improve the inspection process itself and its supporting documentation (for example, checklists) (optional)

Inspections consist of three to six participants. An inspection is led by an impartial facilitator who is trained in inspection techniques. Determination of remedial or investigative action for an anomaly is a mandatory element of a software inspection, although the resolution should not occur in the inspection meeting. Collection of data for the purpose of analysis and improvement of software engineering procedures (including all review procedures) is strongly recommended but is not a mandatory element of software inspections.

Examples of software products subject to inspections include, but are not limited to

a) Software requirements specification
b) Software design description
c) Source code
d) Software test documentation
e) Software user documentation
f) Maintenance manual
g) System build procedures
h) Installation procedures
i) Release notes

6.2 Responsibilities

The following roles shall be established for the inspection:

a) Inspection leader
b) Recorder
c) Reader
d) Author
e) Inspector

All participants in the review are inspectors. The author shall not act as inspection leader and should not act as reader or recorder. Other roles may be shared among the team members. Individual participants may act in more than one role.

Individuals holding management positions over any member of the inspection team shall not participate in the inspection.

6.2.1 Inspection leader

The inspection leader shall be responsible for administrative tasks pertaining to the inspection, shall be responsible for planning and preparation as described in 6.5.2 and 6.5.4, shall ensure that the inspection is conducted in an orderly manner and meets its objectives, should be responsible for collecting inspection data (if appropriate), and shall issue the inspection output as described in 6.7.

6.2.2 Recorder

The recorder shall document anomalies, action items, decisions, and recommendations made by the inspection team. The recorder should record inspection data required for process analysis. The inspection leader may be the recorder.

6.2.3 Reader

The reader shall lead the inspection team through the software product in a comprehensive and logical fashion, interpreting sections of the work (for example, generally paraphrasing groups of 1–3 lines), and highlighting important aspects.

6.2.4 Author

The author shall be responsible for the software product meeting its inspection entry criteria, for contributing to the inspection based on special understanding of the software product, and for performing any rework required to make the software product meet its inspection exit criteria.

6.2.5 Inspector

Inspectors shall identify and describe anomalies in the software product. Inspectors shall be chosen to represent different viewpoints at the meeting (for example, sponsor, requirements, design, code, safety, test, independent test, project management, quality management, and hardware engineering). Only those viewpoints pertinent to the inspection of the product should be present.

Some inspectors should be assigned specific review topics to ensure effective coverage. For example, one inspector may focus on conformance with a specific standard or standards, another on syntax, another for overall coherence. These roles should be assigned by the inspection leader when planning the inspection, as provided in 6.5.2 (b).

6.3 Input

Input to the inspection shall include the following:

a)   A statement of objectives for the inspection
b)   The software product to be inspected
c)   Documented inspection procedure
d)   Inspection reporting forms
e)   Current anomalies or issues list

Input to the inspection may also include the following:

f)   Inspection checklists
g)   Any regulations, standards, guidelines, plans, and procedures against which the software product is
     to be inspected
h)   Hardware product specifications
i)   Hardware performance data
j)   Anomaly categories (see IEEE Std 1044-1993 [B7])

Additional reference material may be made available by the individuals responsible for the software product when requested by the inspection leader.

6.4 Entry criteria

6.4.1 Authorization

Inspections shall be planned and documented in the appropriate project planning documents (for example, the overall project plan, or software verification and validation plan).

Additional inspections may be conducted during acquisition, supply, development, operation, and maintenance of the software product at the request of project management, quality management, or the author, according to local procedures.

6.4.2 Preconditions

An inspection shall be conducted only when both of the following conditions have been met:

a)   A statement of objectives for the inspection is established.
b)   The required inspection inputs are available.

6.4.3 Minimum entry criteria

An inspection shall not be conducted until all of the following events have occurred, unless there is a documented rationale, accepted by management, for exception from these provisions:

a)   The software product that is to be inspected is complete and conforms to project standards for content and format.
b)   Any automated error-detecting tools (such as spell-checkers and compilers) required for the inspection are available.
c)   Prior milestones are satisfied as identified in the appropriate planning documents.
d)   Required supporting documentation is available.
e)   For a re-inspection, all items noted on the anomaly list that affect the software product under inspection are resolved.

6.5 Procedures

6.5.1 Management preparation

Managers shall ensure that the inspection is performed as required by applicable standards and procedures and by requirements mandated by law, contract, or other policy. To this end, managers shall

a)   Plan time and resources required for inspection, including support functions, as required in IEEE Std 1058.1-1987 [B8] or other appropriate standards
b)   Provide funding and facilities required to plan, define, execute, and manage the inspection
c)   Provide training and orientation on inspection procedures applicable to a given project
d)   Ensure that review team members possess appropriate levels of expertise and knowledge sufficient to comprehend the software product under inspection
e)   Ensure that planned inspections are conducted
f)   Act on inspection team recommendations in a timely manner

6.5.2 Planning the inspection

The author shall assemble the inspection materials for the inspection leader.

The inspection leader shall be responsible for the following activities:

a)   Identifying, with appropriate management support, the inspection team
b)   Assigning specific responsibilities to the inspection team members
c)   Scheduling the meeting and selecting the meeting place
d)   Distributing inspection materials to participants, and allowing adequate time for their preparation
e)   Setting a timetable for distribution of inspection material and for the return of comments and forwarding of comments to the author for disposition

As a part of the planning procedure, the inspection team shall determine if alternatives are to be discussed at the inspection meeting. Alternatives may be discussed at the inspection meeting, afterwards in a separate meeting, or left to the authors of the software product to resolve.

6.5.3 Overview of inspection procedures

The author should present an overview of the software product to be inspected. This overview should be used to introduce the inspectors to the software product. The overview may be attended by other project personnel who could profit from the presentation.

Roles shall be assigned by the inspection leader. The inspection leader shall answer questions about any checklists and the role assignments and should present inspection data such as minimal preparation times and the typical number of anomalies found in past similar products.

6.5.4 Preparation

Each inspection team member shall examine the software product and other review inputs prior to the review meeting. Anomalies detected during this examination shall be documented and sent to the inspection leader. The inspection leader should classify anomalies to ensure that inspection meeting time is used effectively. The inspection leader should forward the anomalies to the author of the software product for disposition.

The inspection leader or reader shall specify a suitable order in which the software product will be inspected (such as sequential, hierarchical, data flow, control flow, bottom up, or top down). The reader shall ensure that he or she is able to present the software product at the inspection meeting.

6.5.5 Examination

The inspection meeting shall follow this agenda:

6.5.5.1 Introduce meeting

The inspection leader shall introduce the participants and describe their roles. The inspection leader shall state the purpose of the inspection and should remind the inspectors to focus their efforts toward anomaly detection, not resolution. The inspection leader should remind the inspectors to direct their remarks to the reader and to comment only on the software product, not their author. Inspectors may pose questions to the author regarding the software product. The inspection leader shall resolve any special procedural questions raised by the inspectors.

6.5.5.2 Establish preparedness

The inspection leader shall verify that inspectors are prepared for the inspection. The inspection leader shall reschedule the meeting if the inspectors are not adequately prepared. The inspection leader should gather individual preparation times and record the total in the inspection documentation.

6.5.5.3 Review general items

Anomalies referring to the software product in general (and thus not attributable to a specific instance or location) shall be presented to the inspectors and recorded.

6.5.5.4 Review software product and record anomalies

The reader shall present the software product to the inspection team. The inspection team shall examine the software product objectively and thoroughly, and the inspection leader shall focus this part of the meeting on creating the anomaly list. The recorder shall enter each anomaly, location, description, and classification on the anomaly list. IEEE Std 1044-1993 [B7] may be used to classify anomalies. During this time, the author shall answer specific questions and contribute to anomaly detection based on the author's special understanding of the software product. If there is disagreement about an anomaly, the potential anomaly shall be logged and marked for resolution at the end of the meeting.

6.5.5.5 Review the anomaly list

At the end of the inspection meeting, the inspection leader should have the anomaly list reviewed with the team to ensure its completeness and accuracy. The inspection leader should allow time to discuss every anomaly where disagreement occurred. The inspection leader should not allow the discussion to focus on resolving the anomaly but on clarifying what constitutes the anomaly.

6.5.5.6 Make exit decision

The purpose of the exit decision is to bring an unambiguous closure to the inspection meeting. The exit decision shall determine if the software product meets the inspection exit criteria and shall prescribe any appropriate rework and verification. Specifically, the inspection team shall identify the software product disposition as one of the following:

a) *Accept with no or minor rework.* The software product is accepted as is or with only minor rework (for example, that would require no further verification).
b) *Accept with rework verification.* The software product is to be accepted after the inspection leader or a designated member of the inspection team (other than the author) verifies rework.
c) *Re-inspect.* Schedule a re-inspection to verify rework. At a minimum, a re-inspection shall examine the software product areas changed to resolve anomalies identified in the last inspection, as well as side effects of those changes.

6.5.6 Rework/follow-up

The inspection leader shall verify that the action items assigned in the meeting are closed.

6.6 Exit criteria

An inspection shall be considered complete when the activities listed in 6.5.5 have been accomplished, and the output described in 6.7 exists.

6.7 Output

The output of the inspection shall be documented evidence that identifies

a) The project being inspected
b) The inspection team members
c) The inspection meeting duration
d) The software product inspected
e) The size of the materials inspected (for example, the number of text pages)
f) Specific inputs to the inspection
g) Inspection objectives and whether they were met
h) The anomaly list, containing each anomaly location, description, and classification
i) The inspection anomaly summary listing the number of anomalies identified by each anomaly category
j) The disposition of the software product
k) An estimate of the rework effort and rework completion date

The output of the inspection should include the following documentation:

l) The total preparation time of the inspection team

Although this standard sets minimum requirements for the content of the documented evidence, it is left to local procedures to prescribe additional content, format requirements, and media.

6.8 Data collection recommendations

Inspections should provide data for the analysis of the quality of the software product, the effectiveness of the acquisition, supply, development, operation and maintenance processes, and the efficiency of the inspection itself. In order to maintain the effectiveness of inspections, data should not be used to evaluate the performance of individuals. To enable these analyses, anomalies that are identified at an inspection meeting should be classified in accordance with 6.8.1 through 6.8.3.

Inspection data should contain the identification of the software product, the date and time of the inspection, the inspection leader, the preparation and inspection times, the volume of the materials inspected, and the disposition of the inspected software product. The capture of this information can be used to optimize local guidance for inspections.

The management of inspection data requires a capability to store, enter, access, update, summarize, and report categorized anomalies. The frequency and types of the inspection analysis reports, and their distribution, are left to local standards and procedures.

6.8.1 Anomaly classification

Anomalies may be classified by technical type according to, for example, IEEE Std 1044-1993 [B7].

6.8.2 Anomaly classes

Anomaly classes provide evidence of nonconformance and may be categorized, for example, as

a) Missing
b) Extra (superfluous)
c) Ambiguous
d) Inconsistent
e) Improvement desirable
f) Not conforming to standards
g) Risk-prone, i.e., the review finds that, although an item was not shown to be "wrong," the approach taken involves risks (and there are known safer alternative methods)
h) Factually incorrect
i) Not implementable (e.g., because of system constraints or time constraints)
j) Editorial

6.8.3 Anomaly ranking

Anomalies may be ranked by potential impact on the software product, for example, as

a) *Major.* Anomalies that would result in failure of the software product or an observable departure from specification.
b) *Minor.* Anomalies that deviate from relevant specifications but will not cause failure of the software product or an observable departure in performance.

6.9 Improvement

Inspection data should be analyzed regularly in order to improve the inspection itself, and the software activities used to produce software products. Frequently occurring anomalies may be included in the inspection checklists or role assignments. The checklists themselves should also be inspected regularly for superfluous or misleading questions. The preparation times, meeting times, and number of participants should be analyzed to determine connections between preparation rate, meeting rate, and number and severity of anomalies found.

A "chief inspector" role should exist. The chief inspector acts as the inspection owner, and collects and feeds back data about the inspection. This chief inspector should be responsible for the proposed follow-up on the inspection itself.

7. Walk-throughs

7.1 Introduction

The purpose of a systematic walk-through is to evaluate a software product. A walk-through may be held for the purpose of educating an audience regarding a software product. The major objectives are to

a) Find anomalies
b) Improve the software product
c) Consider alternative implementations
d) Evaluate conformance to standards and specifications

Other important objectives of the walk-through include exchange of techniques and style variations and training of the participants. A walk-through may point out several deficiencies (for example, efficiency and readability problems in the software product, modularity problems in design or code, or untestable specifications).

Examples of software products subject to walk-throughs include, but are not limited to,

a) Software requirements specification
b) Software design description
c) Source code
d) Software test documentation
e) Software user documentation
f) Maintenance manual
g) System build procedures
h) Installation procedures
i) Release notes

7.2 Responsibilities

The following roles shall be established for the walk-through:

a) Walk-through leader
b) Recorder
c) Author
d) Team member

For a review to be considered a systematic walk-through, a team of at least two members shall be assembled. Roles may be shared among the team members. The walk-through leader or the author may serve as the recorder. The walk-through leader may be the author.

Individuals holding management positions over any member of the walk-through team shall not participate in the walk-through.

7.2.1 Walk-through leader

The walk-through leader shall conduct the walk-through, shall handle the administrative tasks pertaining to the walk-through (such as distributing documents and arranging the meeting), and shall ensure that the walk-through is conducted in an orderly manner. The walk-through leader shall prepare the statement of objectives to guide the team through the walk-through. The walk-through leader shall ensure that the team arrives at a decision or identified action for each discussion item, and shall issue the walk-through output as described in 7.7.

7.2.2 Recorder

The recorder shall note all decisions and identified actions arising during the walk-through meeting. In addition, the recorder should note all comments made during the walk-through that pertain to anomalies found, questions of style, omissions, contradictions, suggestions for improvement, or alternative approaches.

7.2.3 Author

The author should present the software product in the walk-through.

7.3 Input

Input to the walk-through shall include the following:

a) A statement of objectives for the walk-through
b) The software product being examined
c) Standards that are in effect for the acquisition, supply, development, operation, and/or maintenance of the software product

Input to the walk-through may also include the following:

d) Any regulations, standards, guidelines, plans, and procedures against which the software product is to be inspected
e) Anomaly categories (see IEEE Std 1044-1993 [B7])

7.4 Entry criteria

7.4.1 Authorization

The need for conducting walk-throughs shall be established in the appropriate project planning documents. Additional walk-throughs may be conducted during acquisition, supply, development, operation, and maintenance of the software product at the request of project management, quality management, or the author, according to local procedures.

7.4.2 Preconditions

A walk-through shall be conducted only when both of the following conditions have been met:

a) A statement of objectives for the review is established by the management personnel for whom the review is being carried out.
b) The required review inputs are available.

7.5 Procedures

7.5.1 Management preparation

Managers shall ensure that the walk-through is performed as required by applicable standards and procedures and by requirements mandated by law, contract, or other policy. To this end, managers shall

a) Plan time and resources required for walk-throughs, including support functions, as required in IEEE Std 1058.1-1987 [B8] or other appropriate standards
b) Provide funding and facilities required to plan, define, execute, and manage the walk-through
c) Provide training and orientation on walk-through procedures applicable to a given project
d) Ensure that walk-through team members possess appropriate levels of expertise and knowledge sufficient to comprehend the software product
e) Ensure that planned walk-throughs are conducted
f) Act on walk-through team recommendations in a timely manner

7.5.2 Planning the walk-through

The walk-through leader shall be responsible for the following activities:

a) Identifying the walk-through team
b) Scheduling the meeting and selecting the meeting place
c) Distributing necessary input materials to participants, and allowing adequate time for their preparation

7.5.3 Overview

An overview presentation should be made by the author as part of the walk-through meeting.

7.5.4 Preparation

The walk-through leader shall distribute the software product and convene a walk-through meeting. Team members shall prepare for the meeting by examining the software product and preparing a list of items for discussion in the meeting. These items should be divided into two categories: general and specific. General items apply to the whole product; specific items apply to a part of it.

Each walk-through team member shall examine the software product and other review inputs prior to the review meeting. Anomalies detected during this examination shall be documented and sent to the walk-through leader. The walk-through leader should classify anomalies to ensure that walk-through meeting time is used effectively. The walk-through leader should forward the anomalies to the author of the software product for disposition.

The author or walk-through leader shall specify a suitable order in which the software product will be inspected (such as sequential, hierarchical, data flow, control flow, bottom up, or top down).

7.5.5 Examination

The walk-through leader shall introduce the participants and describe their roles. The walk-through leader shall state the purpose of the walk-through and should remind the team members to focus their efforts toward anomaly detection, not resolution. The walk-through leader should remind the team members to comment only on the software product, not its author. Team members may pose questions to the author regarding the software product. The walk-through leader shall resolve any special procedural questions raised by the team members.

The author shall present an overview of the software product under review. This is followed by a general discussion during which team members raise their general items. After the general discussion, the author serially presents the software product in detail (hence the name "walk-through"). Team members raise their specific items when the author reaches them in the presentation. New items may be raised during the meeting. The walk-through leader coordinates discussion and guides the meeting to a decision or identified action on each item. The recorder notes all recommendations and required actions.

During the walk-through meeting,

a)   The author or walk-through leader should make an overview presentation of the software product under examination
b)   The walk-through leader shall coordinate a discussion of the general anomalies of concern
c)   The author or walk-through leader shall present the software product, describing every portion of it
d)   Team members shall raise specific anomalies as the author reaches the part of the software product to which the anomalies relate
e)   The recorder shall note recommendations and actions arising out of the discussion upon each anomaly

After the walk-through meeting, the walk-through leader shall issue the walk-through output detailing anomalies, decisions, actions, and other information of interest. Minimum content requirements for the walk-through output are provided in 7.7.

7.5.6 Rework/follow-up

The walk-through leader shall verify that the action items assigned in the meeting are closed.

7.6 Exit criteria

The walk-through shall be considered complete when

a)   The entire software product has been examined
b)   Recommendations and required actions have been recorded
c)   The walk-through output has been completed

7.7 Output

The output of the walk-through shall be documented evidence that identifies

a)   The walk-through team members
b)   The software product being examined
c)   The statement of objectives that were to be accomplished during this walk-through meeting and whether they were met
d)   A list of the recommendations made regarding each anomaly
e)   A list of actions, due dates, and responsible people
f)   Any recommendations made by the walk-through team on how to dispose of deficiencies and unresolved anomalies
g)   Any proposals made by the walk-through team for follow-up walk-throughs

Although this standard sets minimum requirements for the content of the documented evidence, it is left to local procedures to prescribe additional content, format requirements, and media.

7.8 Data collection recommendations

Walk-throughs should provide data for the analysis of the quality of the software product, the effectiveness of the acquisition, supply, development, operation, and maintenance processes, and the efficiency of the walk-through itself. In order to maintain the effectiveness of walk-throughs, data should not be used to evaluate the performance of individuals. To enable these analyses, anomalies that are identified at a walk-through meeting should be classified in accordance with 7.8.1 through 7.8.3.

Walk-through data should contain the identification of the software product, the date and time of the walk-through, the walk-through leader, the preparation and walk-through times, the volume of the materials walked through, and the disposition of the software product. The capture of this information can be used to optimize local guidance for walk-throughs.

The management of walk-through data requires a capability to store, enter, access, update, summarize, and report categorized anomalies. The frequency and types of the walk-through analysis reports, and their distribution, are left to local standards and procedures.

7.8.1 Anomaly classification

Anomalies may be classified by technical type according to, for example, IEEE Std 1044-1993 [B7].

7.8.2 Anomaly classes

Anomaly classes provide evidence of nonconformance, and may be categorized, for example, as

  a) Missing
  b) Extra (superfluous)
  c) Ambiguous
  d) Inconsistent
  e) Improvement desirable
  f) Not conforming to standards
  g) Risk-prone, i.e., the review finds that although an item was not shown to be "wrong," the approach taken involves risks (and there are known safer alternative methods)
  h) Factually incorrect
  i) Not implementable (e.g., because of system constraints or time constraints)
  j) Editorial

7.8.3 Anomaly ranking

Anomalies may be ranked by potential impact on the software product, for example, as

  a) *Major.* Anomalies that would result in failure of the software product or an observable departure from specification
  b) *Minor.* Anomalies that deviate from relevant specifications but will not cause failure of the software product or an observable departure in performance

7.9 Improvement

Walk-through data should be analyzed regularly in order to improve the walk-through itself and to improve the software activities used to produce the software product. Frequently occurring anomalies may be included in the walk-through checklists or role assignments. The checklists themselves should also be inspected regularly for superfluous or misleading questions. The preparation times, meeting times, and number of participants should be analyzed to determine connections between preparation rate, meeting rate, and number and severity of anomalies found.

8. Audits

8.1 Introduction

The purpose of a software audit is to provide an independent evaluation of conformance of software products and processes to applicable regulations, standards, guidelines, plans, and procedures.

Examples of software products subject to audit include, but are not limited to, the following:

a) Back-up and recovery plans
b) Contingency plans
c) Contracts
d) Customer or user representative complaints
e) Disaster plans
f) Hardware performance plans
g) Installation plans
h) Installation procedures
i) Maintenance plans
j) Management review reports
k) Operations and user manuals
l) Procurement and contracting methods
m) Reports and data (for example, review, audit, project status, anomaly reports, test data)
n) Request for proposal
o) Risk management plans
p) Software configuration management plans (see IEEE Std 828-1990 [B2])
q) Software design descriptions (see IEEE Std 1016-1987 [B6])
r) Source code
s) Unit development folders
t) Software project management plans (see IEEE Std. 1058-1987 [B8])
u) Software quality assurance plans (see IEEE Std 730-1989 [B1])
v) Software requirements specifications (see IEEE Std 830-1993 [B4])
w) Software safety plans (see IEEE Std 1228-1994 [B13])
x) Software test documentation (see IEEE Std 829-1983 [B3])
y) Software user documentation (see IEEE Std 1063-1987 [B9])
z) Software verification and validation plans (see IEEE Std 1012-1986 [B5])
aa) Standards, regulations, guidelines, and procedures
ab) System build procedures
ac) Technical review reports
ad) Vendor documents
ae) Walk-through reports
af) Deliverable media (such as tapes and diskettes)

The examination should begin with an overview meeting during which the auditors and audited organization examine and agree upon the arrangements for the audit.

When stipulated in the audit plan, the auditors may make recommendations. These should be reported separately.

8.2 Responsibilities

The following roles shall be established for an audit:

a) Lead auditor
b) Recorder
c) Auditor(s)
d) Initiator
e) Audited organization

The lead auditor may act as recorder. The initiator may act as lead auditor. Additional auditors should be included in the audit team; however, audits by a single person are permitted.

8.2.1 Lead auditor

The lead auditor shall be responsible for the audit. This responsibility includes administrative tasks pertaining to the audit, ensuring that the audit is conducted in an orderly manner, and ensuring that the audit meets its objectives.

a) Preparing the audit plan (see 8.5.2)
b) Assembling the audit team
c) Managing the audit team
d) Making decisions regarding the conduct of the audit
e) Making decisions regarding any audit observations
f) Preparing the audit report (see 8.7)
g) Reporting on the inability or apparent inability of any of individuals involved in the audit to fulfill their responsibilities
h) Negotiating any discrepancies or inconsistencies with the initiator which could impair the ability to satisfy the exit criteria (8.6)
i) Recommending corrective actions

The lead auditor shall be free from bias and influence that could reduce his ability to make independent, objective evaluations.

8.2.2 Recorder

The recorder shall document anomalies, action items, decisions, and recommendations made by the audit team.

8.2.3 Auditor

The auditors shall examine products, as defined in the audit plan. They shall document their observations and recommend corrective actions. All auditors shall be free from bias and influences that could reduce their ability to make independent, objective evaluations, or shall identify their bias and proceed with acceptance from the initiator.

8.2.4 Initiator

The initiator shall be responsible for the following activities:

a) Decide upon the need for an audit
b) Decide upon the purpose and scope of the audit
c) Decide the software products to be audited

d) Decide the evaluation criteria, including the regulations, standards, guidelines, plans, and procedures to be used for evaluation
e) Decide upon who will carry out the audit
f) Review the audit report
g) Decide what follow-up action will be required
h) Distribute the audit report

The initiator may be a manager in the audited organization, a customer or user representative of the audited organization, or a third party.

8.2.5 Audited organization

The audited organization shall provide a liaison to the auditors and shall provide all information requested by the auditors. When the audit is completed, the audited organization should implement corrective actions and recommendations.

8.3 Input

Inputs to the audit shall be listed in the audit plan and shall include the following:

a) Purpose and scope of the audit
b) Background information about the audited organization
c) Software products to be audited
d) Evaluation criteria, including applicable regulations, standards, guidelines, plans, and procedures to be used for evaluation
e) Evaluation criteria: for example, "acceptable," "needs improvement," "unacceptable," "not rated"

Inputs to the audit should also include the following:

f) Records of previous similar audits

8.4 Entry criteria

8.4.1 Authorization

An initiator decides upon the need for an audit. This decision may be prompted by a routine event, such as the arrival at a project milestone, or a non-routine event, such as the suspicion or discovery of a major non-conformance.

The initiator selects an auditing organization that can perform an independent evaluation. The initiator provides the auditors with information that defines the purpose of the audit, the software products to be audited, and the evaluation criteria. The initiator should request the auditors to make recommendations. The lead auditor produces an audit plan and the auditors prepare for the audit.

The need for an audit may be established by one or more of the following events:

a) The supplier organization decides to verify compliance with the applicable regulations, standards, guidelines, plans, and procedures (this decision may have been made when planning the project).
b) The customer organization decides to verify compliance with applicable regulations, standards, guidelines, plans, and procedures.
c) A third party, such as a regulatory agency or assessment body, decides upon the need to audit the supplier organization to verify compliance with applicable regulations, standards, guidelines, plans, and procedures.

In every case, the initiator shall authorize the audit.

8.4.2 Preconditions

An audit shall be conducted only when all of the following conditions have been met:

a) The audit has been authorized by an appropriate authority
b) A statement of objectives of the audit is established
c) The required audit inputs are available

8.5 Procedures

8.5.1 Management preparation

Managers shall ensure that the audit is performed as required by applicable standards and procedures and by requirements mandated by law, contract, or other policy. To this end, managers shall

a) Plan time and resources required for audits, including support functions, as required in IEEE Std 1058.1-1987 [B8], legal or regulatory documents, or other appropriate standards
b) Provide funding and facilities required to plan, define, execute, and manage the audits
c) Provide training and orientation on the audit procedures applicable to a given project
d) Ensure appropriate levels of expertise and knowledge sufficient to comprehend the software product being audited
e) Ensure that planned audits are conducted
f) Act on audit team recommendations in a timely manner

8.5.2 Planning the audit

The audit plan shall describe the

a) Purpose and scope of the audit
b) Audited organization, including location and management
c) Software products to be audited
d) Evaluation criteria, including applicable regulations, standards, guidelines, plans, and procedures to be used for evaluation
e) Auditor's responsibilities
f) Examination activities (for example, interview staff, read and evaluate documents, observe tests)
g) Audit activity resource requirements
h) Audit activity schedule
i) Requirements for confidentiality (for example, company confidential, restricted information, classified information)
j) Checklists
k) Report formats
l) Report distribution
m) Required follow-up activities

Where sampling is used, a statistically valid sampling method shall be used to establish selection criteria and sample size.

The audit plan shall be approved by the initiator. The audit plan should allow for changes based on information gathered during the audit, subject to approval by the initiator.

8.5.3 Opening meeting

An opening meeting between the audit team and audited organization shall occur at the beginning of the examination phase of the audit. The overview meeting agenda shall include

a) Purpose and scope of the audit
b) Software products being audited
c) Audit procedures and outputs
d) Expected contributions of the audited organization to the audit (for example, the number of people to be interviewed, meeting facilities)
e) Audit schedule
f) Access to facilities, information, and documents required

8.5.4 Preparation

The initiator shall notify the audited organization's management in writing before the audit is performed, except for unannounced audits. The notification shall define the purpose and scope of the audit, identify what will be audited, identify the auditors, and identify the audit schedule. The purpose of notification is to enable the audited organization to ensure that the people and material to be examined in the audit are available.

Auditors shall prepare for the audit by studying the

a) Audit plan
b) Audited organization
c) Products to be audited
d) Applicable regulations, standards, guidelines, plans, and procedures to be used for evaluation
e) Evaluation criteria

In addition, the lead auditor shall make the necessary arrangements for

f) Team orientation and training
g) Facilities for audit interviews
h) Materials, documents, and tools required by the audit procedures
i) Examination activities

8.5.5 Examination

Examination shall consist of evidence collection and analysis with respect to the audit criteria, a closing meeting between the auditors and audited organization, and preparing an audit report.

8.5.5.1 Evidence collection

The auditors shall collect evidence of conformance and non-conformance by interviewing audited organization staff, examining documents, and witnessing processes. The auditors should attempt all the examination activities defined in the audit plan. They shall undertake additional investigative activities if they consider such activities required to define the full extent of conformance or non-conformance.

Auditors shall document all observations of non-conformance and exemplary conformance. An observation is a statement of fact made during an audit that is substantiated by objective evidence. Examples of non-conformance are

a) Applicable regulations, standards, guidelines, plans, and procedures not used at all
b) Applicable regulations, standards, guidelines, plans, and procedures not used correctly

Observations should be categorized as major or minor. An observation should be classified as major if the non-conformity will likely have a significant effect on product quality, project cost, or project schedule.

All observations shall be verified by discussing them with the audited organization before the closing audit meeting.

8.5.5.2 Closing meeting

The lead auditor shall convene a closing meeting with the audited organization's management. The closing meeting should review

a) Actual extent of implementation of the audit plan
b) Problems experienced in implementing the audit plan, if any
c) Observations made by the auditors
d) Preliminary conclusions of the auditors
e) Preliminary recommendations of the auditors
f) Overall audit assessment (for example, whether the audited organization successfully passed the audit criteria)

Comments and issues raised by the audited organization should be resolved. Agreements should be reached during the closing audit meeting and must be completed before the audit report is finalized.

8.5.5.3 Reporting

The lead auditor shall prepare the audit report, as described in 8.7. The audit report should be prepared as soon as possible after the audit. Any communication between auditors and the audited organization made between the closing meeting and the issue of the report should pass through the lead auditor.

The lead auditor shall send the audit report to the initiator. The initiator should distribute the audit report within the audited organization.

8.5.6 Follow-up

Rework, if any, shall be the responsibility of the initiator and audited organization and shall include

a) Determining what corrective action is required to remove or prevent a non-conformity
b) Initiating the corrective action

8.6 Exit criteria

An audit shall be considered complete when

a) The audit report has been submitted to the initiator
b) All of the auditing organization's follow-up actions included in the scope of the audit have been performed, reviewed, and approved

8.7 Output

The output of the audit is the audit report. The audit report shall contain the

a) Purpose and scope of the audit
b) Audited organization, including location, liaison staff, and management
c) Identification of the software products audited

    d)   Applicable regulations, standards, guidelines, plans, and procedures used for evaluation
    e)   Evaluation criteria
    f)   Summary of auditor's organization
    g)   Summary of examination activities
    h)   Summary of the planned examination activities not performed
    i)   Observation list, classified as major or minor
    j)   A summary and interpretation of the audit findings including the key items of non-conformance
    k)   The type and timing of audit follow-up activities

Additionally, when stipulated by the audit plan, recommendations shall be provided to the audited organization or the initiator. Recommendations may be reported separately from results.

Although this standard sets minimum requirements for report content, it is left to local standards to prescribe additional content, report format requirements, and media.

Annex A

(informative)

Relationship of this standard to the life cycle processes of other standards

This standard may be used in conjunction with other IEEE or ISO/IEC standards. In particular, IEEE Std 730-1989 [B1], IEEE Std 1012-1986 [B5], IEEE Std 1074-1995 [B10], and ISO/IEC 12207:1995 [B15] all require that software reviews take place during the software life cycle. The following table shows, for each of these standards, a possible mapping to the five review types described in the body of IEEE Std 1028-1997.

Standard	Clause	Review title	Corresponding IEEE Std 1028-1997 review type
IEEE Std 730-1989 [B1]	3.6.2.1	Software requirements review	Technical review
	3.6.2.2	Preliminary design review	Technical review
	3.6.2.3	Critical design review	Technical review
	3.6.2.4	Software V& V plan review	Management review
	3.6.2.5	Functional audit	Audit
	3.6.2.6	Physical audit	Audit
	3.6.2.7	In-process audit	Audit
	3.6.2.8	Managerial reviews	Management review
	3.6.2.9	Software configuration management revIew	Management review
	3.6.2.10	Postmortem review	Management review, technical review
IEEE Std 1012-1986 [B5]	3.5.2	Concept documentation evaluation	Technical review
	3.5.3	Software requirements traceability analysis, requirements evaluation, and interface analysis	Technical review, inspection, walk-through
	3.5.4	Design traceability analysis, design evaluation, and design interface analysis	Technical review, inspection, walk-through
	3.5.5	Source code traceability analysis, evaluation, and interface analysis	Technical review, inspection, walk-through
	3.5.5	Source code documentation evaluation	Technical review, inspection, walk-through

Standard	Clause	Review title	Corresponding IEEE Std 1028-1997 review type
IEEE Std 1012-1986 [B5]	Appendix	Algorithm analysis	Technical review, inspection, walk-through
		Audit performance	Audit
		Configuration control audit	Audit
		Control flow analysis	Technical review, walk-through
		Database analysis	Technical review, inspection, walk-through
		Data flow analysis	Technical review, inspection, walk-through
		Design walk-through	Walk-through
		Feasibility study evaluation	Management review
		Functional audit	Audit
		In-process audit	Audit
		Operational readiness review	Management review, technical review
		Physical audit	Audit
		Requirements walk-through	Walk-through
		Sizing and timing analysis	Technical review, inspection, walk-through
		Source code walk-through	Walk-through
		Test evaluation	Technical review, inspection, audit
		Test readiness review	Management review, technical review
		Test walk-through	Walk-through
		User documentation evaluation	Technical review, audit
IEEE Std 1074-1995 [B10]	7.1.3.2	Plan verification and validation	All types
ISO/IEC 12207:1995 [B15]	5.2.4.5	Project management plan	Management review, technical review, inspection, walk-through, audit
	5.2.6.2	Supplier/acquirer joint reviews	Management review, technical review, inspection, walk-through, audit

Standard	Clause	Review title	Corresponding IEEE Std 1028-1997 review type
ISO/IEC 12207:1995 [B15]	5.3.1.3	Development process	Management review, technical review, inspection, walk-through, audit
	5.3.2.2	System requirements analysis evaluation	Technical review, inspection, walk-through
	5.3.3.2	System architectural design evaluation	Technical review, inspection, walk-through
	5.3.4.2	Software requirements analysis evaluation	Technical review, inspection, walk-through
	5.3.5.6	Software architectural design evaluation	Technical review, inspection, walk-through
	5.3.6.7	Software detailed design evaluation	Technical review, inspection, walk-through
	5.3.7.5	Software code evaluation	Technical review, inspection, walk-through
	5.3.8.5	Software integration evaluation	Technical review, inspection, walk-through
	5.3.9.3	Software qualification testing evaluation	Technical review, inspection, walk-through
	5.3.10.3	System integration evaluation	Technical review, inspection, walk-through
	5.3.11.2	System qualification test evaluation	Technical review, inspection, walk-through
	6.1.2.3	Document review	Management review, technical review, inspection, walk-through, audit
	6.6.2	Project management reviews	Management review
	6.6.3	Technical reviews	Technical review
	6.7	Audit process	Audit
	7.1.4	Review and evaluation	Management review, technical review
	B.3.c	Tailoring—reviews and audits	Inspection, walk-through

Annex B

(informative)

Comparison of review types

The following table compares the five types of reviews in a number of salient characteristics. This is meant to be indicative of the ways in which the review types match with or differ from one another.

Characteristic	Management review	Technical review	Inspection	Walk-through	Audit
Objective	Ensure progress; recommend corrective action; ensure proper allocation of resources	Evaluate conformance to specifications and plans; ensure change integrity	Find anomalies; verify resolution; verify product quality	Find anomalies; examine alternatives; improve product; forum for learning	Independently evaluate compliance with objective standards and regulations
Decision-making	Management team charts course of action; decisions made at the meeting or as a result of recommendations	Review team requests management or technical leadership to act on recommendations	Review team chooses predefined product dispositions; defects must be removed	The team agrees on changes to be made by the author	Audited organization, initiator, acquirer, customer or user
Change verification	Leader verifies that action items are closed; change verification left to other project controls	Leader verifies that action items are closed; change verification left to other project controls	Leader verifies that action items are closed; change verification left to other project controls	Leader verifies that action items are closed; change verification left to other project controls	Responsibility of the audited organization
Recommended group size	Two or more people	Three or more people	Three to six people	Two to seven people	One to five people
Group attendance	Management, technical leadership and peer mix	Technical leadership and peer mix	Peers meet with documented attendance	Technical leadership and peer mix	Auditors, audited organization, management and technical personnel
Group leadership	Usually the responsible manager	Usually the lead engineer	Trained facilitator	Facilitator or author	Lead auditor
Volume of material	Moderate to high, depending on the specific meeting objectives	Moderate to high, depending on the specific meeting objectives	Relatively low	Relatively low	Moderate to high, depending on the specific audit objectives

Characteristic	Management review	Technical review	Inspection	Walk-through	Audit
Presenter	Project representative	Development team representative	A reader	Author	Auditors collect and examine information provided by audited organization
Data collection	As required by applicable policies, standards, or plans	Not a formal project requirement. May be done locally.	Strongly recommended	Recommended	Not a formal project requirement. May be done locally.
Output	Management review documentation	Technical review documentation	Anomaly list, anomaly summary, inspection documentation	Anomaly list, action items, decisions, follow-up proposals	Formal audit report; observations, findings, deficiencies
Formal facilitator training	No	No	Yes	No	Yes (formal auditing training)
Defined participant roles	Yes	Yes	Yes	Yes	Yes
Use of defect checklists	No	No	Yes	No	Yes
Management participates	Yes	Optional	No	No	Yes
Customer or user representative participates	Optional	Optional	Optional	Optional	Optional

Annex C

(informative)

Bibliography

The standards listed here may be useful in the preparation of software products that can be reviewed using the procedure documented in this standard:

[B1] IEEE Std 730-1989, IEEE Standard for Software Quality Assurance Plans.[3]

[B2] IEEE Std 828-1990, IEEE Standard for Software Configuration Management Plans.

[B3] IEEE Std 829-1983 (R1991), IEEE Standard for Software Test Documentation.

[B4] IEEE Std 830-1993, IEEE Recommended Practice for Software Requirements Specifications.

[B5] IEEE Std 1012-1986 (R1992), IEEE Standard for Software Verification and Validation Plans.

[B6] IEEE Std 1016-1987 (R1993), IEEE Recommended Practice for Software Design Descriptions.

[B7] IEEE Std 1044-1993, IEEE Standard Classification for Software Anomalies.

[B8] IEEE Std 1058-1987 (R1993), IEEE Standard for Software Project Management Plans.

[B9] IEEE Std 1063-1987 (R1993), IEEE Standard for Software User Documentation.

[B10] IEEE Std 1074-1995, IEEE Standard for Developing Software Life Cycle Processes.

[B11] IEEE Std 1219-1992, IEEE Standard for Software Maintenance.

[B12] IEEE Std 1220-1994, IEEE Trial-Use Standard for Application and Management of the Systems Engineering Process.

[B13] IEEE Std 1228-1994, IEEE Standard for Software Safety Plans.

[B14] IEEE Std 1298-1992 (AS 3563.1-1991), IEEE Standard for Software Quality Management System, Part 1: Requirements.

[B15] ISO/IEC 12207:1995, Information technology—Software life cycle processes.[4]

[B16] ISO 9001:1994, Quality systems—Model for quality assurance in design/development, production, installation and servicing.

[B17] ISO 10011-1:1990, Guidelines for auditing quality systems—Part 1: Auditing.

---

[3]IEEE publications are available from the Institute of Electrical and Electronics Engineers, 445 Hoes Lane, P.O. Box 1331, Piscataway, NJ 08855-1331, USA.

[4]ISO publications are available from the ISO Central Secretariat, Case Postale 56, 1 rue de Varembé, CH-1211, Genève 20, Switzerland/Suisse. ISO publications are also available in the United States from the Sales Department, American National Standards Institute, 11 West 42nd Street, 13th Floor, New York, NY 10036, USA.

ANSI/IEEE
Std 1042-1987

An American National Standard

IEEE Guide to
Software Configuration Management

Sponsor

**Technical Committee on Software Engineering of the
Computer Society of IEEE**

Approved September 10. 1987
Reaffirmed December 15, 1993

IEEE Standards Board

Approved March 10, 1988

American National Standards Institute

Foreword

(This Foreword is not a part of ANSI/IEEE Std 1042-1987, IEEE Guide for Software Configuration Management.)

The purpose of this guide is to provide guidance in planning software configuration management (SCM) practices that are compatible with ANSI/IEEE Std 828-1983, IEEE Standard for Software Configuration Management Plans. Three groups are served by this guide: developers of software, software management community, and those responsible for preparation of SCM Plans. The developers of software will be interested in the different ways SCM can be used to support the software engineering process. The management community will be interested in how the SCM Plan can be tailored to the needs and resources of a project. Those preparing plans for SCM will be interested in the suggestions and examples for preparation of a Plan.

The introduction of this guide presents a technical and philosophical overview of the SCM planning process. Subsequent paragraphs in the body of the guide contain general statements of principles, commentary on issues to consider, and *lessons learned* for the corresponding paragraph in the outline of the ANSI/IEEE Std 828-1983 Plan. Four Appendixes illustrate how the ANSI/IEEE Std 828-1983 can be used for a variety of different projects. A fifth Appendix lists current references that may be useful in planning SCM.

This guide was prepared by a working group chartered by the Software Engineering Subcommittee of the Technical Committee on Software Engineering of the Computer Society of IEEE. This guide represents a consensus of individual working-group participants with broad expertise in software engineering and configuration management, staffed with both members within the Institute and from other groups that have expertise and interest in participating.

The following individuals contributed to the writing of this guide by attendance to two or more working sessions, or by substantial written commentary, or both.

Richard L. Van Tilburg, *Chairman*   **David Schwartz,** *Cochairman*

Bakul Banerjee	David Gelperin	Brian F. Rospide
H. Ronald Berlack	Curtis F. Jagger	Margaret Rumley
Grazyna Bielecka	Allen T. L. Jin	Edward Showalter
Jack L. Cardiff	Dwayne Knirk	Jean Stanford
Larry Cummings	Nancy Murachanian	William S. Turner, III
Michael A. Daniels	Sarah H. Nash	Albert T. Williams
	Wilma Osborne	

When the IEEE Standards Board approved this standard on September 10, 1987, it had the following membership:

Donald C. Fleckenstein, *Chairman*   **Marco W. Migliaro,** *Vice Chairman*

Andrew G. Salem, *Secretary*

James H. Beall	Leslie R. Kerr	Donald T. Michael*
Dennis Bodson	Jack Kinn	L. John Rankine
Marshall L. Cain	Irving Kolodny	John P. Riganati
James M. Daly	Joseph L. Koepfinger*	Gary S. Robinson
Stephen R. Dillon	Edward Lohse	Frank L. Rose
Eugene P. Fogarty	John May	Robert E. Rountree
Jay Forster	Lawrence V. McCall	William R. Tackaberry
Kenneth D. Hendrix	L. Bruce McClung	William B. Wilkens
Irvin N. Howell		Helen M. Wood

*Member emeritus

The following person were on the balloting committee that approved this document for submission to the IEEE Standards Board:

A. Frank Ackerman
Richard L. Aurbach
Motoei Azuma
H. Jack Barnard
Roy Bass
James Behm
H. R. Berlack
Michael A. Blackledge
Gilles Bracon
Kathleen L. Briggs
A. Winsor Brown
William L. Bryan
Fletcher Buckley
Lorie J. Call
Harry Carl
John Center
T. S. Chow
J. K. Chung
Won L. Chung
Antonio M. Cicu
Francos Coallier
Peter Cond, Jr
Christopher Cook
Richard Cotter
Arthur N. Damask
Taz Daughtrey
Peter A. Denny
Fred M. Discenzo
William P. Dupras
Robert E. Dwyer
Mary L. Eads
W. D. Ehrenberger
L. G. Egan
Walter J. Ellis
Caroline L. Evans
David W. Favor
Joan Feld
John W. Fendrich
Glenn S. Fields
A. M. Foley
Joel J. Forman
Julian Foster
Crespo Fuentes
F. K. Gardner
Leonard B. Gardner
David Gelperin
Anne K. Geraci
Shirley Gloss-Soler
J. G. Glynn

Andrej Grebnec
Benjamin W. Green
Victor M. Guarnera
Lawrence M. Gunther
David A. Gustafson
G. B. Hawthorne
John W. Horch
Cheng Hu
Harry Kalmbach
Myron S. Karasik
Dwayne L. Knirk
Shaye Koenig
George Konstantinow
Joseph A. Krupinski
Joan Kundig
T. M. Kurihara
Lak Ming Lam
John B. Lane
Robert A. C. Lane
Gregory N. Larsen
Ming-Kin Leung
F. C. Lim
Bertil Lindberg
Austin J. Maher
Paulo Cesar Marcondes
C. D. Marsh
Roger J. Martin
John McArdle
Russell McDowell
W. F. Michell
Manijeh Mogh
Charles S. Mooney
George Morrone
D. D. Morton
G. T. Morum
Hironobu Nagano
Gerry Neidhart
Dennis Nickle
Wilma M. Osborne
Thomas D. Parish
David E. Peercy
Michael T. Perkins
John Petraglia
Donald J. Pfeiffer
I. C. Pyle
Thomas S. Radi
Salim Ramji
Jean-Claude Rault

Meir Razy
Donald Reifer
John C. Rowe
Julio Gonzalez Sanz
Stephen R. Schach
Lee O. Schmidt
N. Schneidewind
Wolf A. Schnoege
Robert Schueppert
David J. Schultz
Gregory D. Schumacher
Leonard W. Seagren
Robert W. Shillato
David M. Siefert
Jacob Slonim
Harry M. Sneed
V. Srinivas
Manfred P. Stael
Wayne G. Staley
Franklin M. Sterling
Mary Jane Stoughton
William G. Sutcliffe
Richard H. Thayer
Bob Thibodeau
Paul U. Thompson
Terrence L. Tillmanns
G. R. Treble
Henry J. Trochesset
C. L. Troyanowski
William S. Turner III
W. T. Valentin, Jr
R. I. Van Tilburg
Tom Vollman
Dolores R. Wallace
Martha G. Walsh
John P. Walter
Andrew H. Weigel
Peter J. Weyman
G. Allen Whittaker
Patrick J. Wilson
David L. Winningham
W. M. Wong
Dennis L. Wood
Nancy Yavne
William W. Young
Janusz Zalewski
Donald Zeleny
Hugh Zettel
Peter F. Zoll

Acknowledgment

Appreciation is expressed to the following companies and organizations for contributing the time of their employees to make possible the development of this text:

Boeing
Burroughs
General Dynamics
Hughes Aircraft Co
Intel Corporation
IBM
Goodyear Atomic Corporation
GTE
National Bureau of Standards

MITRE
Motorola
Programming Environments, Inc
RCA Astro Electronics
Sperry
Telos
Texas Instruments
ZTROW Software Inc

Contents

Contents

An American National Standard

IEEE Guide to
Software Configuration Management

1. Introduction

1.1 Scope. This guide describes the application of configuration management (CM) disciplines to the management of software engineering projects. Software configuration management (SCM) consists of two major aspects: planning and implementation. For those planning SCM activities, this guide provides insight into the various factors that must be considered.

Users implementing SCM disciplines will find suggestions and detailed examples of plans in this guide. This guide also presents an interpretation of how ANSI/IEEE Std 828-1983 [2][1] can be used for planning the management of different kinds of computer program development and maintenance activities.

The guide is presented in two parts. The first part, the main body of the guide, presents issues to consider when planning software configuration management for a project or organization. The second part of the guide presents, for those preparing SCM Plans, a series of sample Plans illustrating different concepts discussed in the body of the guide.

The text of the guide introduces the essential concepts of SCM, particularly those of special significance (for example, libraries and tools) to software engineering. It then presents the plan-

---

[1] The numbers in brackets correspond with those of the references in 1.2.

ning for SCM in terms of documenting a Plan following the outline of ANSI/IEEE Std 828-1983 [2] so that a user who is unfamiliar with the disciplines of software configuration management can gain some insight into the issues. For those preparing SCM Plans, the second part of the guide provides sample plans for consideration.

The sample SCM Plans include a variety of software configuration management applications for different types of projects and organizations. Appendix A illustrates a software configuration management plan (SCMP) for a project developing a complex, critical computer system. It describes a Plan for managing a typical software development cycle where the development is contracted to an organization that does not have responsibility for its maintenance or use. Appendix B illustrates a SCMP for a small software development project. It describes a Plan for supporting a prototype development activity where the goal of the project is to demonstrate the feasibility of a concept. Appendix C illustrates a SCMP used by an organization where the emphasis is on maintaining programs developed by other activities or organizations. Appendix D illustrates a SCMP for an organization developing and maintaining computer programs embedded in a hardware product line. It describes a Plan for managing both software development and maintenance of a commercial product line. Some of the different characteristics illustrated are shown in Table 1.

Table 1
Characteristics of Appendixes*

Appendix Number	Emphasis of Control (Life Cycle Phase)	Type of Project	Relative Size (Dollar/Manhour)	SCM Tools Available	Life Span of Plan	Writing for Plan
1	Development	Critical	Medium	Advanced	Short	Highly structured
2	Concept	Prototype	Small	Basic	Short	Informal
3	Operations	Support sw	Large	On-line	Full life cycle	Structured
4	All	Commercial	Small	Integrated	Full life cycle	Organizational Informal

*NOTE: The purpose of the Appendixes is not to provide an illustration for every possible combination of project characteristics but rather to show that the ANSI/IEEE Std 828-1983 [2] can be applied to a wide variety of projects.

1.2 References. This guide shall be used in conjunction with the following publications:

[1] ANSI/IEEE Std 729-1983, IEEE Standard Glossary of Software Engineering Terminology.[2]

[2] ANSI/IEEE Std 828-1983, IEEE Standard for Software Configuration Management Plans.

Additional references useful in understanding software configuration management are given in Appendix E.

1.3 Mnemonics. The following acronyms are used in the text of this guide:

CCB	Configuration Control Board
CDR	Critical Design Review
CI	Configuration Item
CM	Configuration Management
CPC	Computer Program Component
CPCI	Computer Program Configuration Item
CSC	Computer Software Component
CSCI	Computer Software Configuration Item
[EP]ROM	[Electrically Programmable] Read Only Memory
FCA	Functional Configuration Audit
OEM	Original Equipment Manufacturer
PCA	Physical Configuration Audit
PDR	Preliminary Design Review
RAM	Random Access Memory
ROM	Read Only Memory
SCA	System/Software Change Authorization
SCCB	Software Configuration Control Board
SCM	Software Configuration Management
SCMP	Software Configuration Management Plan
SCR	System/Software Change Request
SQA	Software Quality Assurance
VDD	Version Description Document

1.4 Terms. Some terms used in SCM circles have restricted meanings or are not defined in the guide. General statements of the contextual meanings are given to aid in understanding the concepts in the guide. These are not formal definitions, subject to review and approval as in a standard, but contextual definitions serving to augment the understanding of configuration management activities as described within this guide.

As used here, the term **baseline**[3] represents the assignment of a documented identifier to each software product configuration item (CI) and associated entities. That is, the source code, relocatable code, executable code, files controlling the process of generating executable code from source code, documentation, and tools used to support development or maintenance of the software product should all be captured, labeled and somehow denoted or recorded as parts of the same baseline. As computer programs move from an initial idea to the maintenance phase, it is common for a series of developmental baselines of increasing complexity to be established during the various internal and external reviews conducted by management (and customers) to determine progress and technical suitability. The baseline concept is as useful to engineering during development as it is after release for use and maintenance.

The various SCM functions are dependent on the baseline concept. Several valuable uses of the baseline concept include

(1) To distinguish between different internal releases for delivery to a customer (that is, successive variants of the same product baseline)

(2) To help to ensure complete and up-to-date technical product documentation

(3) To enforce standards (SQA)

(4) To be used as a means of promoting (that is, internally releasing) each CI from one phase of development or test to another

(5) To identify customer involvement in internal (developmental) baselies

Since SCM disciplines are an integral part of the engineering process they guide the management of internal developmental baselines as well as the more formal functional, allocated, and product baselines. The SCM disciplines, as applied to developmental baselines, are used (implicitly or explicitly) to coordinate most engineering activities that occur within the context of each baseline. Varying levels of formality provide flexibility and responsiveness to the engineering process, yet maintain the benefits of recognizing SCM disciplines.

---

[2] ANSI/IEEE publications are available from IEEE Service Center, 445 Hoes Lane, Piscataway, NJ 08855-1331 and from the Sales Department, American National Standards Institute, 1430 Broadway, New York, NY 10018.

[3] A specification or product that has been formally reviewed and agreed to by responsible management, that thereafter serves as the basis for further development, and can be changed only through formal change control procedures.

The term **promotion** is used here to indicate a transition in the level of authority needed to approve changes to a controlled entity, such as a baseline CI.

Promotions typically signify a change in a CI's internal development state. The term **release** is used to designate certain promotions of CI that are distributed outside the development organization.

In general, as the development process continues, there are more constraints imposed on the change process (coordination with interfacing hardware, user's adaptations, etc) and correspondingly higher levels of authority are needed for approving the changes. When an entity is finally released as a formal baseline, a high level of authority is needed to approve changes. When internal or developmental baselines are created as a part of the engineering process and entitites are moved or released to another internal activity for additional work, integration, or testing the term **promotion** is used to distinguish this type of release from the more formal releases to users.

Promotion from one developmental baseline to another represents the visibility granted to some organizations for a given baseline. As developmental baselines are promoted within an organization, they tend to become more stable. The more stable a baseline is, the higher the level of visibility it is granted.

The term **version** is used here to indicate a software CI having a defined set of functional capabilities. As functional capabilities are added, modified, or deleted the CI is given a different version identifier. It is common and recommended practice to use a configuration identification scheme that permits easy and automatic identification of particular version labels.

The term **revision** is commonly associated with the notion of *bug fixing*, that is, making changes to a program that corrects only errors in the design logic but does not affect documented functional capabilities since none of the requirements have changed. The configuration identification scheme must provide for clear identification of revisions and versions of each specific promotion and release.

2. SCM Disciplines in Software Management

2.1 The Context of SCM. This guide discusses SCM as a set of management disciplines within the context of the software engineering process rather than as a set of specific activities performed, or as functions within an organization. The reason for this approach is that software CM, as contrasted with hardware CM, tends to be more deeply involved in the software engineering process and, while the same general CM functions are performed, the disciplines are extended to include the process of developing a baseline.

Software CM and release processing are performed within the context of several basic CM functions: configuration identification, baseline management, change control and library control, status accounting, reviews and audits, and release processing. In practice, the ways in which these functions are performed are different for the different kinds of programs being developed (commercial, embedded, OEM, etc), and may vary in the degree of formal documentation required within and across different life-cycle management phases (research phase, product development, operations, and maintenance).

Software CM also provides a common point of integration for all planning, oversight and implementation activities for a project or product line. These functions are performed within the context of a project—providing the framework (labeling and identification) for interfacing different activities and defining the mechanisms (change controls) necessary for coordinating parallel activities of different groups. SCM provides a framework for controlling computer program interfaces with their underlying support hardware, coordinating software changes when both hardware and software may be evolving during development or maintenance activities.

Finally, SCM is practiced within the context of management, providing management with the visibility (through status accounting and audits) of the evolving computer products that it needs to perform effectively.

2.1.1 SCM is a Service Function. Software CM is a support activity that makes technical and managerial activities more effective. Effectiveness of the SCM processes increases in proportion to the degree that its disciplines are an explicit part of the normal day-to-day activities of everyone involved in the development and maintenance efforts, (as opposed to a separate SCM organization or activity). This holds true whether SCM is administered by a separate SCM group, distributed among many projects, or a mixture of both.

2.1.2 SCM is a Part of the Engineering Process. The disciplines of SCM apply to the development of programmed logic, regardless of the form of packaging used for the application. Software engineering technology is effectively used in the generation of stored programmed logic when the complexity of the function is large. SCM disciplines assist in the identification and evolution of changes during the engineering process, even though the final package may be ROM, and managed as a hardware configuration item.

Configuration management is practiced in one form or another as a part of every software engineering activity where several individuals or organizations have to coordinate their activities. Although the basic disciplines of configuration management are common to both hardware and software engineering activities, there are some differences in emphasis due to the nature of the design activity. Software products (as compared to hardware products) are easy to change[4] (little if any lead time is needed for parts procurement and production setup).

Software CM is a discipline for managing the evolution of computer program products, both during the initial stages of development and during all stages of maintenance. The designs of programs are not easily partitioned into independent tasks due to their complexity. Therefore, configuration management disciplines are more valuable during the design (and redesign during maintenance) phases. This is when using techniques of multiple levels of baselines and internal releases (or promotions) to a larger degree than is typically practiced by hardware CM really pays off.

Whether software is released for general use as programs in RAM or embedded in ROM, it is a form of logic. Therefore, SCM disciplines can and should be extended to include development of the computer programs' component parts (for example, source code and executable code) whereas hardware CM focuses mainly on the management of documentation.

The differences between hardware and software CM, of importance to software CM, include

(1) Software CM disciplines are used to simultaneously coordinate configurations of many different representations of the software product (source code, relocatable code and executable code) rather than just their *documentation*. The nature of computer programs requires this extension and the SCM disciplines and related SCM support software adapt readily to this task.

(2) The use of interactive software development environments extends the concepts of software CM to managing evolutionary changes that occur during the routine generation of specifications, designs, and implementation of code, as well as to the more rigidly documented and controlled baselines defined during development and system maintenance.

(3) Software development environments are rapidly becoming automated with interactive tool sets. This modifies many of the traditional methods used in hardware CM but the fundamental concepts of CM still apply.

2.1.3 SCM Manages all Software Entities. Software CM extends the management disciplines of hardware CM to include all of the entities of the product as well as their various representations in documentation. Examples of entities managed in the software engineering process include

(1) Management plans
(2) Specifications (requirements, design)
(3) User documentation
(4) Test design, case and procedure specifications
(5) Test data and test generation procedures
(6) Support software
(7) Data dictionaries and various cross-references
(8) Source code (on machine-readable media)
(9) Executable code (the run-time system)
(10) Libraries
(11) Data bases:
    (a) Data which are processed,
    (b) Data which are part of a program
(12) Maintenance documentation (listings, detail design descriptions, etc)

All supporting software used in development, even though not a part of the product, should also be controlled by configuration management disciplines.

Not all entities are subject to the same SCM disciplines at the same time. When the software product is under development, the documentation entities (baselined specifications and user requirements) are the most important. When coding begins, the documentation representing the design is the most important entity to be

---

[4] Even what is traditionally thought of as *hard* software—that is, firmware, is becoming easier to modify. An example is card edge programming where the programs in a ROM are easily modified, though not under program control during execution.
NOTE: While the time to change a design may be the same for hardware engineering as for software engineering, implementation and installation time is greater and consequently more expensive for hardware configuration items.

managed. Finally, when the product is ready for general use, the source code is the most accurate representation of the real product and the documentation is related so that representation is most important. These transitions of disciplinary focus over time are common to all SCM disciplines and need to be recognized in planning systems for effectively supporting project management.

Firmware[5] raises some special considerations for configuration management. While being developed, the disciplines of software CM apply; but when made a part of the hardware (*burned* into [EP]ROM), the disciplines of hardware CM apply. Testing may vary but the SCM requirements are generally the same. The packaging of [EP]ROM versus RAM code also introduces and necessitates different identification procedures, which are noted in 3.3.1.

2.1.3.2 The issue of what entities are to be managed often arises in the practical context of what gets captured in each library, and when. Consideration need also be given to the hierarchy of entities managed during this process. There are several different ways of looking at this hierarchy of entities; one, for example, is a three-level hierarchy:

(1) Configuration item (CSCI, CPCI, System, System Segment, Program package, module)
(2) Component (CPC, CSC, Subsystem, Unit, Package, Program function)
(3) Unit (Procedure, function Routine, Module)

The configuration control boards (CCB) that are oriented to business type management decisions usually select one level in this hierarchy as the level at which they will control changes. Other CCB may focus on more technical issues and would each select other levels, the module for example, as the control level for reviewing changes. See 2.2.5 for further discussion of control levels.

---

[5]**Firmware.** Computer programs and data loaded in a class of memory that cannot by dynamically modified by the computer during processing. Used here to generically refer to any programmed code implemented in nonvolatile memory such as [EP]ROM, regardless of its function; contrasts with code designed to execute out of volatile memory, such as RAM. There are differences between software intensive firmware and hardware intensive firmware. The key is ease of adaptability or degree with which programmed instructions are used, and the size of the program. Software intensive firmware denotes an activity that has available a set of tools commonly used in software engineering. Hardware intensive firmware denotes a development activity that has available a minimum of tools necessary for creation (*burn in*) of the firmware.

Another way of looking at entities to be managed is in terms of the interrelationships between the computer programs being developed and the other software entities used during development and testing of that program. This hierarchy is illustrated in Table 2.

Table 2
Hierarchy of Controlled Entities

Entity	Layer
Released entities	Product layer
Promoted entities	Test layer
Modifiable unique entities and support software	Invocation layers
Product development environment	Support software layer
Operating system	Run-time software layer

The SCM process should support each of these layers.

2.1.3.3 Still another way of viewing the entities is in terms of the intermediate products generated in the process of building the computer program product. Each of these intermediate products may be viewed as:

(1) *Modifiable entities.* These items are the individually modifiable units that are required to produce the deliverable entities. They are the source code, control files, data descriptions, test data, documents, etc, that constitute the focus of SCM. The entities at this level are referenced as *units* or *components* in this guide.
(2) *The compilation or assembly entities, such as compilers.* These are needed to develop, test and maintain the program throughout the life cycle of the product. These entities are referenced as *support software* in this guide.
(3) *Application-specific entities.* These are the different representations that are created in the process of producing the deliverables. Examples are the results produced by the compilation and assembly entities, and link/load entities, such as a link editor/locator. These culminate in the product that is released for general use. These entities are referenced as *configuration items* (CI) in this guide.

2.2 The Process of SCM

2.2.1 Management Environment of SCM.
Software engineering, and therefore SCM, takes place within an organizational business environment. To be effective, SCM must blend in with and reflect the organization. It must take into account the management style — entrepreneurial, very disciplined, etc. The technical skills of the implementing organization must be taken into account as well as available resources when specifying whether SCM is to be performed by a single organization or distributed among several. The organization must also be responsive to the kinds of controls needed by the organization that will ultimately be using the product.

SCM management provides support to the organization by working within it to define implement policies, techniques, standards, and tools that facilitate their control of the SCM process. These processes assist other managers (and customers as required) by supporting effective configuration identification, change controls, status accounting, audits, and reviews.

2.2.2 Dynamics of SCM.
The cornerstone activity of SCM is managing the change process and tracking changes to ensure that the configuration of the computer program product is accurately known at any given time. The change management is accomplished by completely identifying each baseline and tracking all subsequent changes made to that baseline. This process is used whether the baseline represents preliminary documentation, such as requirements, or a fully documented program including source and object code. All entities (specifications, documents, text data, and source code) are subject to this change management discipline.

Effectively managing baseline changes requires that a scheme for identifying the *structure* of the software product must be established. This structure relates to the hierarchical organization of the computer program and is extended to include all entities or work-products associated with the program. This identification scheme must normally be maintained throughout the full life of the computer program product. Usually a numbering scheme or file name scheme is associated with the structure, and unique and appropriate labels are assigned to each entity of the product.

As new baselines are created in transition by a promotion or release, the aggregate of entities is reviewed or audited to verify consistency with the old baseline, and the identification labeling is modified to reflect the new baseline. Changes to the different versions and revisions of each baseline are maintained. The history of changes to baselined configurations is maintained and made available to engineering and management in status reports. Figure 1 illustrates a model of the SCM process.

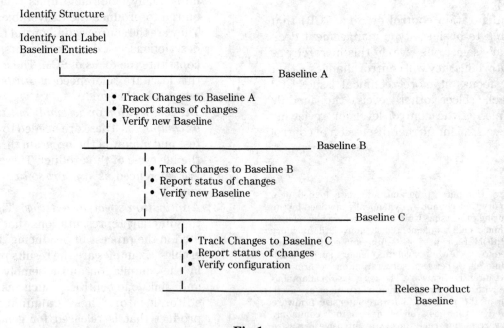

Identify Structure

Identify and Label
Baseline Entities

Baseline A

- Track Changes to Baseline A
- Report status of changes
- Verify new Baseline

Baseline B

- Track Changes to Baseline B
- Report status of changes
- Verify new Baseline

Baseline C

- Track Changes to Baseline C
- Report status of changes
- Verify configuration

Release Product
Baseline

Fig 1
Model of Change Management

2.2.3 Role of Source Code in SCM. A key entity to be managed is the source code, since it is the basic representation in readable form of the product being controlled. Other forms of documentation and data are verified by comparison to this entity. At different phases in a development cycle, source code may not be available and different baselined entities may be defined as the basic representation. However, for most of the software life cycle, the source code provides the key entity for verification. The creation of executable code for the machine is directly derived (in the majority of computer systems) from the source code by various mechanized tools, such as assemblers, compilers, link/loaders, and interpreters. Recreation of source code (and object code) from design documentation can be costly. Therefore, to control only design documentation does not usually fully capture the implementation of the software. If the source code were to be lost because of improper, unreliable, or insufficient controls, the cost of recreating all of the source code would (in the majority of cases) be very expensive because of the typically incomplete state of the documentation.

Design documentation is verified against the product represented by the source code. The test entities (test design, text cases and procedures), test data (including data generation procedures) and test reports, are used to verify that the executable code (produced by the source code) matches the documentation. Documentation needed for maintenance (programming notebooks, etc) and user documentation are also verified against the source code.

Depending on the difficulty of rebuilding a complete set of executable code, the relocatable code may also be identified and considered an entity. However, the source code is generally considered to be the primary, if not sole source in establishing the product configuration.

Since source code can be interpreted differently by different compilers, it is necessary to control the versions of the support software used for a specific released product so as to have full control over the computer program product.

2.2.4 Different Levels of Control. Management delegates the authority for action downward to and including the work done by nonmanagement personnel. Management also selectively delegates aspects of control to nonmanagement personnel. In this guide, the term **levels of control** includes all control exercised by both management and nonmanagement. The term **authority** refers to control reserved by management for

management decisions relative to allocation of resources: schedule, production cost, customer requirements for product cost, performance, delivery, etc. Nonmanagement provides technical data to support these evaluations. Since the SCM Plan must identify all software CI (or classes thereof) that will be covered by the Plan, it must also define the level of management needed to authorize changes to each entity. As the software product evolves, it may be wise or necessary to increase the management authorization level (that is, level of control) needed. This can be accomplished through the internal part promotion hierarchy.

A general-use facility, which has many released software CI as well as CI under development, will often require many separate levels of control, and possibly different levels of authority for approving changes. For example, software CI that are used by several organizations may require change approval by management that is in charge of all those organizations. Not only the CI that will be delivered by the development group but also the level of authority for all vendor-supplied or internally developed software tools, utilities, operating systems, etc, used in the development need to be identified. Software CI used within any intermediate organization may usually require change approval by that organization's management. These intermediate organizations may have unique design or analysis tools for their own use on the project and can have change control authority over these tools.

2.3 The Implementation of SCM

2.3.1 Using Software Libraries. The techniques and methods used for implementing control and status reporting in SCM generally center around the operation of software libraries. Software libraries provide the means for identifying and labeling baselined entities, and for capturing and tracking the status of changes to those entities.

Libraries have been historically composed of documentation on hard copy and software on machine readable media, but the trend today is towards all information being created and maintained on machine-readable media.[6] This trend, which encourages the increased use of automated tools, leads to higher productivity. The trend also

---

[6]There may still be valid *legal* needs for maintaining hard copy versions of all baselined materials. The ability to eliminate hard copy media should not be construed as a necessary or even wise thing for an organization to do.

means that the libraries are a part of the software engineering working environment. The SCM functions associated with the libraries have to become a part of the software engineering environment, making the process of configuration management more transparent to the software developers and maintainers.

The number and kind of libraries will vary from project to project according to variations in the access rights and needs of their users, which are directly related to levels of control. The entities maintained in the libraries may vary in physical form based on the level of technology of the software tooling. When the libraries are automated, the libraries that represent different levels of control may be functionally (logically) different even though they are physically the same. The insertion of entities and changes to entities in a controlled library should produce an auditable authorization trail.

The names of libraries may vary, but fundamentally three kinds should be considered, as outlined in Fig 2.

The **dynamic library**, sometimes called the *programmer's library*, is a library used for holding newly created or modified software entities (units/modules or data files and associated documentation). This is the library used by programmers in developing code. It is freely accessible to the programmer responsible for that unit at any time. It is the programmers' workspace and controlled by the programmers.

The **controlled library**, sometimes called the *master library*, is a library used for managing the current baseline(s) and for controlling changes made to them. This is the library where the units and components of a configuration item that have been promoted for integration are maintained.

Entry is controlled, usually after verification. Copies may be freely made for use by programmers and others. Changes to units or components in this library must be authorized by the responsible authority (which could be a configuration control board or other body with delegated authority).

The **static library**, sometimes called the *software repository*, is a library used to archive various baselines released for general use. This is the library where the master copies plus authorized copies of computer program configuration items that have been released for operational use are maintained. Copies of these masters may be made available to requesting organizations.

2.3.2 Controlling Changes to Libraries. Several possible methods for controlling access to libraries are illustrated in the Appendixes. Appendix B prescribes formal change control of several configuration items at the component level within established baselines. Another approach is having rather informal methods for authorizing changes to configuration items. This method is used for fast integration of changes in a research type environment, as in Appendix B. For libraries having several configuration items including both external (third-party software) and internal (in-house developments) sources of supply, a mixture of formal methods for authorizing changes is applicable, as illustrated in Appendix C. Externally developed computer programs may be controlled at CI levels, whereas internally developed computer programs may be controlled at more discrete component levels. The procedures for authorizing changes may be integrated with the software tools in an integrated environment, as illustrated in Appendix D.

In summary, the levels of control described in each appendix are illustrated in Table 3.

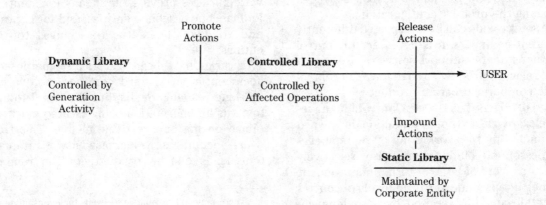

**Fig 2
Three Types of Libraries**

Table 3
Levels of Control in Sample Plans

	Appendix A	Appendix B	Appendix C	Appendix D
Number of CI	Several CI (internal)	3 CI (internal)	Internal CI External CI	2 CI (internal)
Components (CSC)	All components	NA	Internal components	Unit
Type of control	Formal	Informal	Formal	Formal (automated)

2.3.3 Using Configuration Control Boards. Another functional concept of SCM is the extended use of configuration control boards (CCB). This concept provides for implementing change controls at optimum levels of authority. Configuration control boards can exist in a hierarchical fashion (for example, at the program, system design, and program product level), or one such board may be constituted with authority over all levels of the change process. In most projects, the CCB is composed of senior level managers. They include representatives from the major software, hardware, test, engineering, and support organizations. The purpose of the CCB is to control major issues such as schedule, function, and configuration of the system as a whole.

The more technical issues that do not relate to performance, cost, schedule, etc, are often assigned to a software configuration control board (SCCB). The SCCB discusses issues related to specific schedules for partial functions, interim delivery dates, common data structures, design changes and the like. This is the place for decision-making concerning the items that must be coordinated across CI but which do not require the attention of high level management. The SCCB members should be technically well-versed in the details of their area; the CCB members are more concerned with broad management issues facing the project as a whole and with customer issues.

2.4 The Tools of SCM. The SCM software tools selected for use by a project and described in a Plan need to be compatible with the software engineering environment in which the development or maintenance is to take place.

SCM tools are beginning to proliferate and choices have to be made as to the tool set most useful for supporting engineering and management. There are many different ways of examining available SCM tools. One way is to categorize them according to characteristics of their products: a filing system, a data-base management system, and an independent knowledge-based system.[7] Another way is to examine the functions they perform: clerical support, testing and management support, and transformation support.[8] A third way of categorizing the SCM tools is by how they are integrated into the software engineering environment on the project. The current set of available SCM tools is classed in terms of the level of automation they provide to the programming environment on a project.

2.4.1 Basic Tool Set. This set includes:
(1) Basic data-base management systems
(2) Report generators
(3) Means for maintaining separate dynamic and controlled libraries
(4) File system for managing the check-in and check-out of units, for controlling compilations, and capturing the resulting products

This set is compatible with a programming environment that is relatively unsophisticated.

The tools control the information on hard copy regarding a program product. They assume a capability for maintaining machine processable libraries that distinguish between controlled and uncontrolled units or components. The tools simplify and minimize the complexity, time, and methods needed to generate a given baseline. Appendix B illustrates a project using such a tool set.

2.4.2 Advanced Tool Set. This set includes:
(1) Items in the basic tool set
(2) Source code control programs that will maintain version and revision history
(3) Compare programs for identifying (and helping verify) changes

---

[7] Reference: British Alvey Programme.

[8] Reference: *Life Cycle Support in the Ada[9] Environment* by Mc Dermid and Ripken.

[9] Ada is a registered trademark of the US Government, AJPO.

(4) Tools for building or generating executable code

(5) A documentation system (word processing) to enter and maintain the specifications and associated user documentation files

(6) A system/software change request/authorization (SCR/SCA) tracking system that makes requests for changes machine readable

This set provides a capability for a SCM group to perform more efficiently on larger, more complex software engineering efforts. It assumes a programming environment that has more computing resources available.

It provides the means of efficiently managing information about the units or components and associated data items. It also has rudimentary capabilities for managing the configurations of the product (building run-time programs from source code) and providing for more effective control of the libraries. Appendix A illustrates use of such a tool set.

2.4.3 On-Line Tool Set. This set includes:

(1) Generic tools of the advanced tool set integrated so they work from a common data base

(2) An SCR/SCA tracking and control system that brings generation, review, and approval of changes on-line

(3) Report generators working on-line with the common data base, and an SCR/SCA tracking system that enables the SCM group to generate responses to on-line queries of a general nature

This set of tools requires an interactive programming environment available to the project. It also provides an organization with the minimal state-of-the-art SCM capabilities needed to support the typical interactive programming environment currently available in industry. It assumes on-line access to the programming data base and the resources necessary for using the tools. Appendix C illustrates use of such a SCM tool set.

2.4.4 Integrated Tool Set. This set includes:

(1) On-line SCM tools covering all functions

(2) An integrated engineering data base with SCM commands built into the on-line engineering commands commonly used in designing and developing programs (most functions of CM are heavily used during design and development phases)

(3) The integration of the SCM commands with on-line management commands for building and promoting units and components

This set integrates the SCM functions with the software engineering environment so that the SCM functions are transparent to the engineer. The software engineer becomes aware of the SCM functions only when he/she attempts to perform a function or operation that has not been authorized (for example, changing a controlled entity when the engineer does not have the required level of authority or control). Appendix D illustrates a project having such an approach to SCM.

2.5 The Planning of SCM. Planning for SCM is essential to its success. Most of the routine activities associates with SCM are repetitious, clerical-type activities, which can be automated fairly easily. Effective SCM involves planning for how activities are to be performed, and performing these activities in accordance with the Plan. The more important disciplines of SCM, such as defining a scheme for identifying the configuration items, components, and units, or the systematic review of changes before authorizing their inclusion in a program, are management activities that require engineering judgment. Relating engineering judgment with management decisions, while also providing the necessary clerical support without slowing the decision-making process, is the critical role of SCM personnel and tools, or both.

SCM defines the interaction between a number of activities extending throughout the life cycle of the product. The SCM Plan functions as a centralized document for bringing together all these different points of view. The cover sheet of the Plan is usually approved by all of the persons with responsibilities identified in the Plan. This makes the Plan a living document, to be maintained by approved changes throughout the life of the computer programs.

Maintenance of the Plan throughout the life of the software is especially important as the disciplines of identification, status reporting, and record keeping apply throughout the maintenance part of the life cycle. Differences may be expected in how change processing is managed, and these need to be understood by all participants.

It should be clear from the information given above, but it is stated explicitly here, that the application (and thus the planning) of SCM is very sensitive to the context of the project and the organization being served. If SCM is applied as a corporate policy, it must not be done blindly, but rather it should be done in such a way that the details of a particular SCM application are reexamined for each project (or phase for very large projects). It must take into consideration the size, complexity, and criticality of the software system being managed; and the number of individuals, amount of personnel turnover, and organizational form and structure that have to interface during the life of the software system being managed.

This guide provides suggestions as to how ANSI/IEEE Std 828-1983 [2] can be interpreted for specific projects, and items to be considered in preparing a plan. The objective of the planner is to prepare a document that

(1) Clearly states the actions to be performed by software engineering and supporting activities that are required to maintain visibility of the evolving configuration of the computer program products
(2) Supports management in the process of evaluating and implementing changes to each configuration
(3) Assures that the changes have been properly and completely incorporated into each computer program product.

3. Software Configuration Management Plans

3.1 Introduction. Because SCM extends throughout the life cycle of the software product, the SCM Plan is the recommended focal point for integrating and maintaining the necessary details for software CM. Projects do differ in scope and complexity and a single format may not always be applicable. ANSI/IEEE Std 828-1983 [2] describes a minimum format for plans with a maximum amount of flexibility. If a section of the format is not applicable, the sentence *There is no pertinent information for this section* should be inserted to indicate that the section has not been overlooked.

It is desirable to provide a synopsis for users of the Software Configuration Management Plan and for the managers who must approve it. In each Appendix to this guide, a synopsis has been prepared to set the context surrounding the generation of the sample SCM Plan. For purposes of this guide, the viewpoint of each synopsis in the Appendixes is directed towards the user of the guide.

3.1.1 Purpose. The theme here is to inform the reader of the specific purpose of the SCM activity(ies) to be defined in the SCM Plan. It is sufficient to write a brief paragraph identifying

the system to which the particular SCM Plan applies, noting any dependencies on other SCM or CM Plans. For example, Appendix A emphasizes thoroughness of audits and reviews to assure conformance to contractual requirements for a computer program product; the theme is rigorous control of the configuration during development. Appendix B is directed towards low cost, quick response to changes, and documentation of the as-built versions of the computer programs. In Appendix C the theme is maintaining configuration control of many computer program products after development and while they are in use. This is complicated by the necessity to manage third-party software and subcontracted software along with internally developed software. Appendix D is directed towards the complex process of generating computer programs, and includes third-party software and subcontracted software in an environment where changes to configurations are driven by marketing, engineering, vendor changes, and customer demands, as well as the normal iteration of engineering changes.

3.1.2 Scope. The scope of the Plan encompasses the tasks of SCM. The function of the subsection is to

(1) Identify the specific SCM concerns
(2) Define what the Plan will and will not address
(3) Identify the items to be managed.

3.1.2.1 It is also important to identify the

(1) Lowest entity in the hierarchy (the control element) that will be reviewed by the top level project or system management CCB
(2) Smallest useful entity that will be reviewed (a module, a unit, a line of code) by technical management (SCCB)
(3) Deliverable entities or configuration item(s) to be released for use as separate entities

The definition and scope of each entity of the configuration item and the kind of control to be considered for each type of entity is also needed. A short description of relationships among configuration items may be appropriate. The boundary of the SCM activities may be described here with the help of graphics (block diagrams, tables, engineering drawing) as necessary.

**Issues to Consider in Planning
Section 1.2 — Scope**

(1) What are the characteristics of the configuration items to be controlled?

17

(a) Only one application program[10]
(b) Many separate small application programs
(c) An integrated set of application and support programs embedded in a system
(d) Computer programs as an integral part of a hardware system
(2) What are the different high-level interfaces to be managed?
(a) People, organization interfaces
(b) Subcontractor interfaces
(c) Specification interfaces
(d) Contractor interfaces
(e) Hardware interfaces
(f) Life cycle phase interfaces
(g) Software interface
(3) What are the time frames of the project
(a) Life cycle phases
(b) Calendar time
(4) What resources will be available or required for the SCM activities?
(a) Machine resources
(b) Space resources
(c) People resources
(d) Schedule dependencies
(5) What are the software engineering entities to be controlled?
(a) Contractual documents
(b) Specifications
(c) Other documentation
(d) Test procedures, data, verification reports
(e) Source code
(f) Support software

3.1.3 Definitions. Subsection 1.3 of the Plan is used to capture all definitions needed for understanding the Plan or helpful for communication.

**Issues to Consider in Planning
Section 1.3 — Definitions**
(1) Are the definitions easily understood?
(2) Is there a list of definitions that can be easily referenced?
(3) Do you really need to define a new term?
(4) Can a glossary of acronyms be used?

---

[10]Throughout the guide, when lists are added to questions in the *issues to consider* NOTES, the lists are to be considered as suggested items, not an exhaustive checklist as in a standard.

It is best to use standard definitions that are common to the industry. For example, terms defined in ANSI/IEEE Std 729-1983 [1] have been arrived at by a consensus of professionals in the industry; it is a good source to use. Numerous new definitions tend only to make understanding the Plan more difficult. Define only those new terms that have to be defined — usually specific to the computer program product. Also duplicating definitions used elsewhere leads to unnecessary work to maintain them current — another configuration management task.

3.1.4 References. Subsection 1.4 of the Plan lists the documents cited elsewhere in the Plan. References made here refer to existing documents and, when customers are involved, the contractual standards and directives cited in the Plan. Having all the references in one place eliminates duplication of citing different sources. This makes a Plan that is more readable and supports general standardization of work instructions.

**Issues to Consider in Planning
Section 1.4 — References**
(1) Can policies, practices, and procedures that already exist within the organization be referenced?
(2) Is each reference necessary for the Plan?
(3) Are some references a part of the organization's directive system?

Large, critical software developments, such as illustrated in Appendix A, tend to rely on a set of standards that are shared with other projects. This makes for better communication among those using the same general system but at the cost of some flexibility. Smaller projects, such as cited in Appendix B do not need the cross-checks and redundancy of these generalized standards and tend to rely on fewer documented standards.

Referencing helps to reduce the bulk of the document that must be maintained. Care should be taken to reference only those documents that are directly applicable to the Plan. Excessive references will lessen the effectiveness of the more important references. A distinction should be made between references that are necessary for *execution* of the Plan and those documents that are included as *general or supplementary* information.

3.2 Management. Section 2 of the Plan has the theme of relating the elements of the SCM discipline to specific activities of the project's or company's management organization. It also provides an opportunity to specify budgetary, schedule, and resource requirements necessary to carry out the Plan.

3.2.1 Organization. In 2.1 of the Plan, functions are allocated to organizational entities. Interfaces between organizations are handled in a separate section (2.3). The functions of the SCM department itself (if it will exist) are defined in more detail in 2.2. It is not necessary or desirable in most cases to allocate all SCM functions to an SCM department; SCM is a part of the entire software engineering process and as such may best be accomplished by the various organizations actually performing the systems engineering or integration. Software Development, Systems Engineering, Test and Quality Assurance departments all may assume significant roles in carrying out SCM functions. The *Issues to Consider* listed below are designed to provide a starting point in looking at the project's work-flow in relation to the current management structure and to support consideration of how the SCM activities can be best allocated or coordinated.

**Issues to Consider in Planning
Section 2.1—Organization**

(1) What kind of product interfaces have to be supported within the project itself?
  (a) Software—hardware
  (b) Software—software
  (c) Software maintained at multiple sites
  (d) Software developed at different sites
  (e) Dependencies on support software
  (f) Maintenance changes generated from different sites
(2) What are the capabilities of the staff available to perform CM specific activities?
(3) What is the management style of the organization within which the software is being developed or maintained?
(4) Who will be responsible for maintaining the support software?
(5) What organizational responsibilities are likely to change during the life of the Plan?
  (a) Project management organization

  (b) Organizational interfaces
  (c) Configuration management organization
(6) Who has the authority to capture data and information and who has authority to direct implementation of changes?
(7) What are the plans for maintaining current organization charts(s)?
(8) What level of management support is needed forimplementing various portions of the SCM discipline?
(9) Will the project management be confined to a single organization or will it be distributed among several organizations?
(10) Are responsibilities for processing changes to baselines clearly indicated, including who
  (a) Originates changes
  (b) Reviews changes
  (c) Signs-off changes
  (d) Approves changes
  (e) Administers the process
  (f) Validates and checks for completion?
(11) Who has the authority to release any software, data, and associated documents?
(12) Who has the responsibility for various SCM activities?
  (a) Ensuring the integrity of the software system
  (b) Maintaining physical custody of the baselines
  (c) Performing product audits (versus quality audits)
  (d) Library management
  (e) Developing and maintaining specialized SCM tools
(13) How is authority vested for handling exceptional situations and waivers?

If the plan for maintaining organizational charts shows a certain organization or management group (such as the program office or the business management office) assuming this responsibility, it may be wise to reference those charts in the Plan rather than placing the actual chart in the document, which must then be maintained every time another group of charts is updated. Alternatively, the organizational chart may be shown in the initial version of the Plan with a footnote directing readers to the proper official source for updates. It is usually best to include organizational charts that refer only to functional names (such as department names) rather than to individuals responsible for managing them. This information is quite dynamic in most organizations, and it is probably not worth updating a Plan every time a department is assigned a new manager.

Consider advantages of alternative forms of organizing activities. Appendix A illustrates a complex, critical software development where there is a strong need for independence and centralization of SCM duties in a functional type organization. Appendix C also illustrates a functional type organization but for a different reason: in a software maintenance environment, SCM plays a stronger role in managing the change processing, even to the scheduling of work—more so than in a typical development environment.

Another point to consider is the management support for the various SCM disciplines. Note, for example, in Appendix B the management supported some concepts of SCM but wanted the process to be as *painless* as possible for the software developers and customers. The SCM administrator established a method of collecting information necessary to achieve the purpose without interfering with the flow of changes to the sites. Similarly, the other Appendixes illustrate SCM practices that are tailored to the reality of the situations in which they are found.

For ease of reading, organize the tasks and the owners in terms of the classical set of CM functions: identification, configuration control, status accounting, and audits and reviews. The matrix in Appendix A, Table 1 illustrates how this kind of information can easily be presented.

3.2.2 SCM Responsibilities. If a specific SCM department or group is identified in the management structure, this section provides a specific description of the role this organization will play in the overall SCM process.

**Issues to Consider in Planning
Section 2.2—SCM Responsibilities**

(1) Are there any special considerations for this project that require the SCM department to change its standard method of doing business?

(2) What explicit assumptions is the SCM group making in planning their part of the project?

---

(3) Are there specific expectations on the part of the customer or client (such as contractual requirements) for an SCM group that need to be taken into account?

While the major considerations may center on responsibilities of the configuration control boards (CCB), there is the need to consider the responsibilities of other activities such as software quality assurance (SQA), users of the system, other system or hardware configuration control boards, and other management activities.

3.2.3 Interface Control. The theme of subsection 2.3 of the Plan is how SCM disciplines are coordinated and how they are used to manage interfaces throughout the project's life. This is the place to define the roles and composition of the various CCB, SCCB, and other activities and practices used for interface control. All types of interfaces should be considered.

The scope of the SCM Plan (1.2) specifies the boundaries of the CI and the jurisdiction of the Plan, but this boundary is often not as clear as it should be and the control mechanisms are even fuzzier. The definition of interfaces is one of the most important planning elements for ensuring a smooth operation. Every possible effort should be made to reach a common agreement regarding each organization's responsibility regarding the interface(s), and then document them in this subsection. The basic types of interfaces to consider here include organization, phase, software, and hardware.

Organizational interface elements include interfaces between various organizations involved with the product; for example, vendor to buyer, subcontractor to contractor, and co-developer to co-developer. It is typical that different organizations have different views of a product and will apply different expectations to it. Effective SCM disciplines can help minimize and resolve these differences whenever and wherever they may arise.

Phase interface elements include transition interfaces between those life cycle phases of the product that are included in the Plan. They are often coincident with a transition in control of the product between different organizations; for example, promotion from a development group to a formal testing group. Effective SCM disciplines can support these transitions with all the documentation, code, data, tools, and records that are needed for management to smoothly continue SCM on the product.

Software interface elements are the agreements shared between the computer program product and other software entities (for example, operating system, utilities, communication system). These agreements involve the structure and meanings assigned to data passing and operational coordination of the data and the results. The other software may already exist or may be concurrently developed. Effective SCM disciplines can make these agreements generally known and assist management in maintaining the integrity of the product(s).

Hardware interface elements are the agreements shared between the computer program product and characteristics of any hardware in the environment with which the program product interacts. These agreements involve capabilities provided by the hardware and operations defined by the computer programs. Effective SCM disciplines help make these agreements known and support their evaluation for consistency throughout the evolution of both hardware and software.

**Issues to Consider in Planning
Section 2.3 — Interface Control**

(1) What are the organizational interfaces?
(2) What are the important interfaces between adjacent phases of the life cycle?
(3) What are the interfaces between different entities of the computer programs?
(4) What are the dependent hardware interfaces?
(5) Where are the documents defined and maintained that are used in interface control?
(6) What are the procedures for making changes to these interface documents?

Interface control should be extended to include more than just documentation. If the hardware configuration and its supporting software interfaces are complex, then the Plan must also include or reference controls for hardware drawings and equipment as well. The sample Plan in Appendix D illustrates the interface between multiple kinds of computer programs in a variable hardware configuration. In real-time system environments, the interface controls may involve tracking changes to configurations of external sensors, valves, etc. Typically, in a software modification and maintenance situation, human operator interface controls may play a significant role in this section. In

---

some organizations, [EP]ROM are considered hardware, yet the programs residing in them must be explicitly dealt with in this section of the Plan. The guiding principle of SCM is that any proposed changes to the product or to its expected use be considered and evaluated in an open, documented, deliberate, and mutually acceptable fashion.

3.2.4 SCM Plan Implementation. Subsection 2.4 of the Plan has the theme of providing details concerning the implementation of the key SCM milestones identified in the Plan. These details include:

(1) Identification of prerequisites or required activities that affect the Plan and the sequencing of events in the Plan
(2) Schedules for accomplishing these items
(3) Resource requirements (for example, machine time, disk space, specialized tool availability, and staff support)

The implementation section's level of detail and complexity are dependent on the level of complexity of the system being controlled. Small software development activities, particularly those that focus primarily on software and are not currently tied to hardware systems development, may need relatively simple implementation schedules. SCM Plans that support more complex activities, such as software maintenance (Appendix C) or development and maintenance of product line software (Appendix D), will have more complex implementation schedules but will focus more on events such as release for use, new product baselines, audits, and reviews.

**Issues to Consider in Planning
Section 2.4 — SCM Plan Implementation**

(1) Are the resources planned for SCM commensurate with the size and complexity of the system being controlled?
(2) How will the SCM activities be coordinated with other project activities?
(3) How will the different phases (development, maintenance) be managed throughout the software life cycle?

Resource requirements should be carefully considered and included here only when they are important factors in implementing the Plan. If there are any separate project documents that contain the necessary information (for example, department budgets, development laboratory implementation Plans), include them here by reference to avoid unnecessary document maintenance. Items to include are:

(1) People resources
(2) Computer and computer-related resources
(3) Library space
(4) Storage space (including electronic media)

It is usually impractical to put actual dates in the Plan for events. In general, it is better from the maintenance perspective to put actual dates in a schedule chart kept in an appendix or a separate document. In this section it is more appropriate to refer to significant events in terms of their relationships to other milestones (for example, a controlled library for source code will be established following the completion of the critical design review), or in terms of their relationship in time to other events (for example, the physical configuration audit will be held 90 days after the functional qualification test).

Requirements for implementation should be discussed in the same sequence in this section as they are discussed in the body of your Plan (for example, configuration identification is followed by product baselines). This should make correlating the Plan with the implementation considerations easier for the user.

Keep in mind that this section should be updated as the project continues. Consider reviewing this section and making any necessary additions or changes upon the achievement of each major milestone in the system development life cycle (for example, completion of functional design) or on a periodic basis (for example, once per quarter).

Project managers are often asked to provide a budget for SCM separate from the development budget. Little historical data are reported in the literature, primarily because every SCM activity has a slightly different organizational structure. In the example given in Appendix B, the project defined 0.5 full time equivalent man-months. Other types of projects, such as illustrated in Appendix A, will require a larger portion of dedicated SCM personnel. In general, however, as more effective automated tools are deployed and used, the need for dedicated personnel will diminish.

3.2.5 Applicable Policies, Directives, and Procedures. Subsection 2.5 of the Plan has the theme of identifying and defining the degree to which existing and future SCM policies and procedures apply to the Plan. The actual identification of referenced documents, and information on how to obtain them should be cited in Section 1.4 of the Plan. Subsection 2.5 provides the opportunity to *interpret the use* of reference document(s) and to describe any new document(s) that may be planned or are under development (which, obviously, cannot be cited in Section 1.4 of the Plan).

**Issues to Consider in Planning
Section 2.5 — Applicable Policies,
Directives and Procedures**

(1) Are any standard identification procedures available?
  (a) Standard labels for products
  (b) Identification of the hierarchical structure of computer programs
  (c) Component and unit naming conventions and limitations
  (d) Numbering or version level designations
  (e) Media identification methods (including [EP]ROM)
  (f) Data-base identification methods
  (g) Documentation labeling and identification standards
(2) Are any specific procedures existing for interacting with the dynamic libraries?
  (a) Promoting from one type of library to another
  (b) Documentation releases
  (c) Releasing computer program products
  (d) Releasing firmware products
(3) Are there standard procedures for managing the change process?
  (a) Handling change or enhancement requests
  (b) Provisions for accepting changes into a controlled library
  (c) Processing problem reports
  (d) Membership in CCB
  (e) Operating CCB
  (f) Capturing the audit trail of changes
(4) Are any status accounting procedures available?
  (a) Reporting procedures for summarizing problem reports

  (b) Standard reports and other formatted management information
  (c) Distributing status data
 (5) Are there procedures for audits?
  (a) Procedures for functional configuration audits
  (b) Procedures for physical configuration audits
 (6) Are there procedures for other general SCM activities?
  (a) Standards for accessing and controlling libraries, including security provisions, change processing, backups and long-term storage
  (b) Forms or file definitions for problem reports, change requests, documentation change notices, etc

The set of procedures need not be developed at one time; but effort consistently applied over a period of time can generate an adequate set of policies and procedures that are effective. The kinds of policies, directives, and procedures that are part of an organization's general practices and procedures might also be considered a part of the Plan.

3.3 SCM Activities. The SCM organizational descriptions in Section 2 of the Plan describe who has what responsibilities for software configuration management. Section 3 of the Plan describes how these groups accomplish their responsibilities.

3.3.1 Configuration Identification. The theme of this subsection is to document an identification scheme that reflects the structure of the product. This is a critical task of SCM, a most difficult task but one that is necessary for a smoothly running SCM operation. It is critical because the flow of management control must follow the structure of the software being managed. It is important because the identification scheme carries forth through the life of the computer program(s). It is difficult because at the time the identification scheme is constructed, the structure of the product is rarely known to the level of detail required during the development process.

Relating the identification scheme to the structure of the computer programs is complicated because there are generally two levels of identification that SCM has historically kept separate. The first level, the identification of configuration items and components recognized by management and users, is identified traditionally by

documentation. This is the level associated with released programs. The second level, the labeling of files (parts), is more unique to software and is constrained by the support software used in generating code. File nomenclature must support the structure of the product. Typically, these files are identified with mnemonics unique to a project and need to be correlated back to the identification scheme. This is the level associated with the parts of a released program. SCM not only must set identification schemes for both of these levels, but also must devise a method for relating the two different views of the same product.

Project management generally determines the criteria for identifying CI and subordinate control level items. SCM then devises the identification numbering or labeling structure for tracking those entities.

Other kinds of problems that should be considered include legal responsibilities. Some contracts require that all new code added to a program belongs legally to the owner of the original computer programs. Problems of third-party software acquisition must also be considered. The legal status of each program should be accurately identifiable before the computer programs are released for use. Usually some controls must be placed on the number of copies of third-party software *passed through* and delivered to customers as royalty payments might even be required.

**Issues to Consider in Planning
Section 3.1—Configuration Identification**
 (1) What scheme is to be used to relate the identification of files to the formal (document based) identification scheme?
 (2) How does one relate the software identification scheme to the hardware identification scheme when the computer programs are deeply embedded in the system (for example, device controller firmware, code and data split between ROM firmware and loadable RAM image code)?
 (3) How does one identify computer programs embedded in [EP]ROM?
 (4) What specifications and management plans need to be identified and maintained under configuration management?
 (5) What timing is involved in naming documents as CI?

    (a) When does a document enter into controlled status (for example, when presented by author, when reviewed, when rework is verified, or when the document is formally distributed)?

    (b) When and how does a document get removed from the CI status?

(6) Is a separate identification scheme needed to track third-party software?

(7) Is a special scheme needed to identify reusable/reused software as different from other software parts?

(8) Are there differences in identification across projects that have different fiscal accounting?

(9) How does one identify support software such as language translators, linkers, and cross-support tools?

(10) Is a special identification scheme needed to identify test data (transaction files, data-bases, etc) that must be kept for regression testing?

(11) Is there a need to identify tables and files for data driven systems?

One practice for identification of parts of a CI (as illustrated in Appendix A) is to use a version description document to relate the different files to the component or configuration item scheme. A suggested practice for embedding computer programs into hardware systems is illustrated in Appendix D where the system index type of project identification is used.

The management of firmware changes can become difficult when the package becomes a part of the hardware item. The problem remains to relate functional capabilities to physical part identifiers, especially when changes to the firmware are closely coupled to changes in the system or application software (for example, boot loaders, device controllers, and high-level ROM-resident system debuggers).

Third-party software needs to be tracked even though it is not changed in the same manner as other software. This is especially important if you, as a reseller, accept responsibility of collecting and dealing with problem reports generated by your customers for these products. It may be necessary too for compliance with legal restrictions on copies and distribution accounting. Appendix C describes this identification situation.

The successful reuse of pieces of software in a (controlled) production library requires a standardized identification scheme to retrieve packages or units and account for their use in different configurations. Appendix C, 3.1 references identification of reused software. It should be noted that it is important to control the test procedures and test cases needed for regression testing in an environment that maintains such software or has extensive dynamic libraries of reusable software.

The identification scheme needs to reference dependent supporting software. Therefore, provisions must be made for identifying the internal documentation, data, and programs used in the generation of the computer program product(s).

3.3.1.2 Identify Project Baselines. Baselines are an effective mechanism to allow many people to work together at the same time. They are a way of synchronizing people working on the same project. The SCM discipline, as in all CM, focuses its activity around the construction and maintenance of baselines. The modifiable units need an identifying mechanism, and a way of describing what is contained in their aggregates is needed. Even if the program is small, a baseline is used to let the other, nonprogramming people, know what is taking place.

**Issues to Consider in
Defining Baselines**

(1) Are baselines other than, for example, the traditional three required[11] to support the project?

(2) Who is needed to authorize the creation of new baselines?

(3) Who approves a baseline for promotion?

(4) How and where are the baselines created and who is responsible for them?

(5) How will the numbering system account for different baselines?

---

[11] The traditional baselines used in CM (functional, allocated, product) are defined in ANSI/IEEE Std 828-1983 [2] along with the minimal requirements for identifying and establishing those baselines. Additional internal or developmental baselines can be defined and included in the Plan when necessary. For example, in making multiple builds, it is useful to define separate baselines for each build to keep the status of changes straight. The sample SCM Plan in Appendix B illustrates the use of multiple builds. These developmental baselines are very helpful for integrating and testing large software systems.

    (a) Different versions (functional changes)

    (b) Different revisions (something to make the existing functions work)

(6) How are baselines verified?

    (a) Reviews

    (b) Customer approval

    (c) Developer test reports

    (d) Independent verification and validation

(7) Are baselines tied to milestones?

    (a) Developmental milestones

    (b) New versions

Baselines tie documentation, labeling, and the program together. Developmental baselines define a state of the system at a specific point in time, usually relative to an integration level, and serve to synchronize the engineering activity and documentation that occurs at that time.

Promotions are basically a change in the informal authority required to effect changes in developmental baselines. The new authority commonly represents a higher level of engineering management. The programmer cannot change a unit that has been promoted and integrated with other programmer's units without notifying the others involved, and gaining their (explicit or implicit) approval by way of an SCCB (or CCB).

The more formal baselines (functional, allocated, and product) define a product capability associated with performance, cost, and other user interests. These baselines relate the product to contractual commitments.

3.3.1.3 Delineate Project Titling, Labeling, Numbering. This part of the Plan defines the procedures and labels for identifying the CI, components, and units. This is important for identifying and retrieving information, reporting status and for legal protection of data rights.

Issues to Consider in Labeling and Numbering

(1) Is there a (corporate) standard for labeling that must be used?

(2) Does the identification scheme provide for identification of versions and revisions for each release?

(3) How can or will the physical media be identified?

(4) Are specific naming conventions available for all modifiable entities?

---

(5) Does the identification scheme need to identify the hierarchy of links between modifiable entities?

(6) Are there constraints on unit and file names?

    (a) Compiler and file system limitations on name length and composition

    (b) Mnemonic requirements

    (c) Names that cannot be used

It is often useful to have the identification label indicate the level (that is, release, version, and revision) of the product it identifies. Labeling the components or units of computer programs can be accomplished in several ways. Numbering schemes can be devised to identify the components. A hierarchy of names can be devised that organizes and identifies parts using mnemonic or English labels. Naming conventions that are associated with the compilation system and are significant for a project are most easily used.

[EP]ROM labeling has special problems and will require a different scheme than that used for RAM-based packages shipped on disk or tape. In developing embedded computer programs, there is the additional consideration of labeling the media ([EP]ROM) with the correct version of the programs. This means that the identification scheme of some computer program packages must somehow relate to the hardware identification scheme. One possible solution is to use the version description document (VDD) form for relating the computer program identification documents to the altered item drawings conventionally used for identifying the [EP]ROM parts.

3.3.2 Configuration Control. Subsection 3.2 of the Plan describes how the configuration control process is managed. The theme here deals with identifying the procedures used to process changes to known baselines. An appropriate level of authority for controlling changes must be identified or delegated for each baseline. The organizations assigned responsibilities for control in Section 2 of the Plan have to manage changes made to the entities identified as defined in Section 3.1 of the Plan. Procedures for processing the requests for changes and approvals must be defined.

3.3.2.1 Levels of Authority. The levels of authority required to make changes to configuration items under SCM control can vary. The system or contract may often dictate the level of authority needed. For example, internally controlled software tools may require less change controls than man-rated or critical software developed under contract. The levels of authority may vary throughout the life cycle. For example, changes to code in the development cycle usually require a lower level of control to be authorized than changes to the same code after it has been released for general use. The level of authority required can also depend on how broadly the change impacts the system. A change affecting specifications during the requirements analysis phase has less ramifications than a change affecting software in operational use. Likewise, changes to draft versions of documents are less controlled than changes to final versions. Changes to a product distributed to several sites and used by many different users requires a different level of authority than products with a very restricted or minimal user base.

The level of control needed to authorize changes to developmental baselines depends on the level of the element in relation to the system as a whole (for example, a change in logic affecting one or a few units usually has less impact on the system than an interface between CI, especially if the CI are developed by different organizations.

Issues to Consider in Defining Levels of Authority

(1) Is the level of authority consistent with the entities identified in subsection 3.1 of the Plan?

(2) When are levels of control assigned to the modifiable units (parts) of the computer programs during top level and detail design stages (technical engineering phase) for developmental baselines?

(3) Do control levels assigned for developmental baselines (for both components and configuration items) need to be reviewed by management?

(4) Are there significant increases in levels of control for transitions between developmental baselines?
  (a) During design
  (b) For promotion from design to implementation
  (c) For unit testing

  (d) For integration

(5) Does management need to know specifically who requested a change?

(6) Do changes originating from outside the organization, such as customers or general users, require different authority for approval than changes from a technical development group?

(7) Do changes that do not impact formal baselines require coordination and approval by a CCB or can they be authorized by a SCCB?

The Plan should clearly define the level of authority to be applied to the baselined entities throughout the life cycle of the system, and should distinguish between controls applied to processing technical changes that do not impact formal baselines and the authority needed to approve changes to formal baselines. For example, during maintenance or in the latter stages of preparing multiple builds for a project, authority for making changes to all entities at all levels is typically restricted. However, when beginning development of a new version or build, the controls on the dynamic library and testing with the controlled library can be relaxed.

Table 4 suggests some ideas for assigning different levels of change authority to different SCM elements during the life cycle.

3.3.2.2 Processing Changes. The theme of these paragraphs is to describe the methods to be used for processing change requests. Generally, no single procedure can meet the needs of all levels of change management and approval levels. These paragraphs must concentrate on

(1) Defining the information needed for approving a change

(2) Identifying the routing of this information

Table 4
Variable Levels of Control

Element	Internal Coordination	Developmental Baselines	Formal Baselines
Specifications	Supervision	CCB	CCB
Test data	Supervision	SCCB	CCB
Unit code	Supervision	SCCB	CCB
Configuration Item code	SCCB	CCB	CCB

(3) Describe the control of the library(ies) used in processing the changes

(4) Describe or refer to the procedure for implementing each change in the code, in the documentation, and in the released program (for example, field upgrades).

The change initiator should analyze the proposed change to assess its impact on all configuration items (documentation, software, and hardware) and the CCB should satisfy themselves that this has been done and interface with the CCB in the impacted areas (if any).

Another area that is often overlooked (and not specifically covered) is that of the maintenance of design documentation. The documentation hierarchy should be fully defined and a change to any level should be analyzed to ensure that the higher levels of documentation have been considered and that the change is *rippled through* the lower levels to implementation in the code.

Source code changes, and indeed hardware changes, should first be implemented in the highest level of documentation and the change implemented through the subsequent levels. Provisions for backing up of changes and maintaining their history need to be considered.

A more critical issue centers on managing controlled libraries. This configuration management concept grew out of the SCM experience with managing source code and has been expanded to include all of the baseline items (including associated documentation and reports) that relate to the computer programs. One can observe that as the interactive programming environments continue to evolve, most of the procedural controls associated with SCM will probably be integrated into the programming environment. The procedures for processing changes are the same, whether for approval by a designated management authority or approval by a control activity (SCCB) delegated by management. The procedure needs to distinguish the proper channels for making the decisions, defining the flow for changes made to an established formal baseline, and the flow for changes made to developmental baselines. Most of this capability is now available in SCM and software engineering tools in one form or another.

Issues to Consider in Processing Changes

(1) What is the information necessary for processing a software/system change request (SCR) or authorizing a change (SCA)?

(2) What kind of information will a CCB or SCCB need in order to make a decision?

(3) What is the overall processing cycle of changes?

(4) What SCM support is provided by automated tools available in the environment?

(5) Will changes in procedures be required to support different kinds of reviews during each of the phases of the life cycle?

(6) When there are multiple CCB in a hierarchy, what are the procedures for information exchange and approval chains?

(7) Is there a need for dynamic libraries and controlled library interfaces?

(8) Is there a need for controlling all access to a library or just controlling changes made to the information in the libraries?

(9) Does the library system provide an audit trail, such as change histories?

(10) Are back-up and disaster files taken into account?

(11) Are there provisions for archive procedures to provide the static library support to the full life cycle?

(12) How are source items (source code) associated with their derived object (executable code) programs?

(13) What are the provisions for *draw down* or *check out* to get units from the controlled library?

(14) What are the provisions for keeping the data files synchronized with the program(s) using them?

(15) How does the change process itself support or accommodate the development of new versions or revisions?

Some library tools maintain *deltas* to base units of source code. Procedures for maintaining version histories of units as well as derived configuration items need to be established along with archiving maintenance.

A CCB concerned with project management may need information regarding estimated cost and schedules for a change, as illustrated in Appendix B. Other CCB may be interested only in the technical interfaces affected by a change, as illustrated in the sample Plan in Appendix C. Still others may need, in addition, information on proprietary rights and copyrights affected, as illustrated in Appendix D.

Some CCB review a proposed change to validate it (approve it as a necessary change; to expend time and resources for investigating feasibility of the change) while others may simply want completed (programmed and documented) changes to be approved prior to inclusion in released computer programs. There are different functions of SCCB responsibility, extending from coordinating engineering technical changes to allocating the work to a work group. Some organizations design, code and test all proposed changes with preliminary CCB approval before submitting them for final CCB approval. This technique may reduce total time to produce a change. The process for granting change approvals must guarantee that unauthorized changes do not contaminate baselined software.

Some advanced tools provide capabilities for formatting change requests, routing to different sets of individuals for approvals, and authorizing work to be done; reviewing changes and tests while in a holding area; and releasing a baseline to a controlled library for operational use. Others provide only for the recording of change information and a history of past versions of source code.

If secure procedures are not in place or feasible for controlling a library system, the library may necessarily be divided into physical entities that control access.

3.3.2.3 The Configuration Control Board.
The theme of these paragraphs is identifying the authorities needed for granting change approvals. Subsection 2.2 of the management section of the Plan identifies the general role(s) of each CCB. These paragraphs go into detail on the roles and authority. It should be remembered that the CCB has traditionally been concerned with managing changes to established baselines of documented configuration items and the components of those configuration items. There may be other change control bodies (SCCB) that authorize changes subordinate to the CCB described here. The CCB described in these paragraphs of the Plan have the role of authorizing changes to baselined configuration items and components from the point of view of entrepreneurial management. They reflect concerns over the costs, schedules, and resources available to implement changes in response to user desires for change.

Issues to Consider in Identifying Configuration Control Boards

(1) Can the limits of authority be defined?
   (a) Limited to contractual baselines as in Appendix A
   (b) Limited to developmental baselines (noncontractual) as in Appendix D
(2) Will the project mix computer programs that are controlled by other CCB?
(3) Is there a need to limit the CCB tabling actions by setting time limits?
(4) Are there contractual requirements imposed on a CCB that must be reflected in the Plan?
(5) How are the different levels of authority determined?
(6) How are different organizational bodies phased in when transitioning from one phase of the life cycle to another?
(7) How are changes to a baselined product to be batched together for release?
   (a) For a new version
   (b) For a revision
(8) Does the CCB membership reflect the management style of the organization?
   (a) For a functional organization
   (b) For a matrixed organization

Large, complex systems require ongoing configuration control authorities to coordinate the technical work involved in generating specifications and code, and in continuing the work of technical coordination required for maintaining interacting software systems (such as defined in Appendix C). Such projects use the same principles of configuration management and perform the same generic approval and scheduling functions as the CCB concerned with smaller-scale entrepreneurial management, particularly where automated SCM tools are used to support both types of activities.

Large software systems are frequently not completely new. They are often mixtures of software in public domain, vendor-supplied products, vendor supplied but modified by a contractor, subcontracted software, proprietary software, and software paid for on another project but reused or adapted. The procedures of how the CCB handles the special nature of proprietary software and reusable software are important and need to be specifically addressed in a Plan.

It may be noted that the CCB concept is another one of those functional concepts of SCM. On a small project, the CCB could be the *chief programmer* and the system will function quite adequately.

Any other change approval activities, such as the SCCB that supports the CCB, also needs to be identified and their roles defined. In some installations, the CCB may need to have the technical expertise to make the final decision on whether a requested change is technically feasible. Other CCB must be supported by technical experts or be prepared to delegate a level of change authorization to qualified subordinate bodies. *In general, decision making that affects the allocation and scheduling of development or maintenance resources should be separated from decision making motivated by various technical and marketing issues.*

3.3.2.4 Interface With Other CCB. Large or complex systems can have many hardware-software interfaces (as documented in the Interface Control [2.3] subsection of the Plan) that require continued ongoing change coordination. Sometimes these boards are called program change review boards (PCRB). The Plan needs to include a description of how these interfaces are handled and documented so all of the people on the projects know how to get the job done (this will probably involve both formal and informal organizational structures and interfaces).

Issues to Consider in Describing CCB Interfaces

(1) Are there a number of CCB that have to work together, as illustrated in Appendix C, or is there only one that has total responsibility for the software configuration items?

(2) Is there a hierarchy of CCB that have authority for making business-type management decisions such as illustrated in Appendixes A and D?

(3) Who has the responsibility and authority for maintaining communications with these CCB?

(4) What body or authority has been designated to arbitrate deadlocks when two parallel CCB are unable to resolve an issue?

(5) What are the procedures for resolving differences of opinion?

---

(6) What needs to be done to maintain responsive communication and time limits on decision making?

3.3.2.5 Support Software. The theme of these paragraphs has to do with managing all the other software needed to build and maintain the computer program products throughout their life cycle. Specifically, this focus is on describing the necessary controls used to manage support software. Support software, which may be user-furnished, developed in-house, leased from a vendor or purchased off-the-shelf, is the class of software which may or may not be delivered with a product, but yet is necessary for designing, enhancing, or testing the changes made during the life of a delivered computer program product. The developer or maintainer needs to ensure that the support software is available for use for as long as may be necessary. For example, compilers need to be archived for use later *as is* when implementing enhancements to prevent subtle compiler dependencies from turning simple enhancements into major upgrades. Host systems, when used, and utility programs and test drivers are also needed.

Issues to Consider in Planning SCM of Support Software

(1) What is the total set of support software used to design, develop, and test the software controlled under this Plan?

(2) Is this set of software archived and maintained for the full life cycle of the computer program products?

(3) What procedures are to be followed to introduce new versions of support software that impact the software within the scope of the Plan?

(4) How are problems resolved and changes made in the support software that impact the configurability or maintainability of the software within the scope of the Plan?

(5) How is the hardware configuration used to develop and maintain the software product identified and maintained for the full life cycle of the computer program product?

It is necessary to determine the appropriate level of software support needed for maintenance of the product throughout its full life cycle. What is sufficient and necessary for the job but not prohibitive in terms

---

of support software costs for maintenance? In some situations, it can be very costly to actually maintain or enhance some of the support tools. For example, fixing bugs in a compiler may trigger unknown changes in production software after it is simply recompiled. *Whenever a production baseline is established, it is very important to archive all environment and support tools along with the production code.*

3.3.3 Configuration Status Accounting. The theme of this subsection is identifying what information is needed for various activities, obtaining the information and reporting it. The concern is with the acquisition of the right information at the right time so reports may be made when they are needed. In essence, this is a typical data management problem. Status accounting may be literally thought of as an accounting system; many of the concepts used to track the flow of funds through accounts may be used to track the flow of software through its evolution. Using this accounting analogy, separate accounts can be established for each CI. Individual transactions can then be tracked through each account as they occur. The configuration status accounting function, at a minimum, is basically reporting the transactions occurring between SCM-controlled entities.

The functional capabilities of the library system (or the software programming environment), in conjunction with the SCM tools, determine in a large way the capabilities of the status accounting function. As well as providing *live* information regarding the development process, the configuration of each released baseline needs to be documented, together with the exact configuration of the released system (that is, historical records). The definition of the *Build Standard* of systems is an important tool for maintenance teams. Because of its impact on maintaining operational software, support software must be addressed in status accounting.

Status accounting reports need to be addressed in detail in the Plan. The theme should be able to answer queries as to *What is the status of SCR 21, 37, 38, 39 and 50?* when one is not always sure of the query in advance. More sophisticated SCM tools that capture transaction data in the library data base can use data management systems and report generators to provide flexibility. Other systems need to anticipate common queries by capturing information in a form where it is easily accessible.

**Issues to Consider in Planning
Section 3.3 — Configuration
Status Accounting**

(1) What types of information needs to be reported?

(2) What is the degree of control required by the customer (typically management)?

(3) Who are the different audiences for each report?

(4) What is the formality required by the organization's standards and procedures for requesting or obtaining reports, or both?

(5) What kind of reports are needed to support integration of units and the tracing of error sources?

(6) What information is needed to produce reports?

   (a) Any problem report number included in a release or promotion

   (b) Units that have been delivered within a given time to integration and test activity

   (c) Changes made and released as a result of a particular problem report

   (d) Units that have been through various types of testing but have not been promoted or released

   (e) Units that have been promoted as a result of a design change

(7) For large systems, is there a need for handling rollover of identification sequences?

Many different types of reports can and do prove useful. The project's managers may, for example, make use of the status accounting data to keep track of the project's progress. Typically the report requests must evolve over a period of time. For some projects, status reporting can be extended to include the status of data items and reviews that are more strictly management scheduling information rather than just configuration management status.

The basic information needed by a CCB relates to transactions applied to the baseline(s), particularly the operational (product) baselines. The disciplines involved in controlling computer programs complement traditional CM for this process. Information needed for more detailed technical management between baseline events should also be collected somehow. Interfaces with available software engineering tools can provide much of this information.

The procedure for tracking the status of CI should be established early enough in the software development process to allow data gathering when it is most easily generated (that is, at the decision and response points) rather than after the fact. The desirable amount of automation depends in large part on the tools available, the size of the project and the maturity of the existing procedures.

Status accounting for multiple sites represents a more complex reporting procedure. The sample Plan in Appendix B describes this problem. Other general requirements for reporting must anticipate management needs for various combinations of information. An ad hoc query capability is often most useful.

3.3.4 Audits and Reviews. The theme of subsection 3.4 of the Plan involves the procedures used to verify that the software product (executable code) matches the configuration item descriptions in the specifications and documents, and that the package being reviewed is complete. It should be noted that, as a general division of labor, the organization performing quality assurance functions also usually performs the audits that address change processing functions, operation of the library(ies), and other activities associated with the processes of software configuration management. This constrasts with the reviews and audits performed within the scope of a SCM activity or organization that verify that a software or firmware product is a consistent, well-defined collection of parts.

Audits are one means by which an organization can ensure that the developers have done all their work in a way that will satisfy any external obligations. Audits vary in formality and rigor, depending on the legal liability of external obligations. They are a check on the completeness of a computer program product. Any anomalies found during audits should not only be corrected but the root cause of the problem should be identified and corrected to ensure that the problem does not resurface.

Generally, there should be a physical configuration audit (PCA) and a functional configuration audit (FCA) of configuration items prior to the release of a product baseline or an updated version of a product baseline. The PCA portion of the audit consists of determining that all items identified as being part of the configuration are present in the product baseline. The audit must also establish that the correct version and revision of each part are included in the product baseline and that they correspond to information contained in the baseline's configuration status report.

The FCA portion is similar, in that someone acknowledges having inspected or tested each item to determine that it satisfies the functions defined in the specifications or contract(s) for which it was developed. The objectives of a PCA/FCA are for the developers to provide notice that contractual obligations are nearing completion, and to provide sufficient evidence for the clients or user organization to accept the product and initiate the transition into operational usage.

This section of the Plan should define ways to ensure that established configuration management procedures are followed:

(1) Test specifications are maintained current
(2) Test reports are properly prepared
(3) Test procedures explicitly define tests to be conducted
(4) Test results comply with acceptance criteria in the test procedure
(5) Test data package contents are complete and comply with approved formats

---

**Issues to Consider in Planning
Section 3.4 — Audits and Reviews**

(1) Are there needs or provisions for more than one audit of each product baseline?
(2) Is there a single, separate audit trail for each component and for the personnel working on them?
(3) How are subcontractors involved in an audit (if part of project)?
(4) Are provisions made for auditing the SCM process?
(5) Are periodic reviews held to determine the progress and technical quality of a computer program product?

Audits of a configuration as it evolves can prevent massive problems at the time of release for operational use.

A higher-level audit trail for business-type management that reflects the real-time relationships and status of CI changes, component changes and individuals responsible for development is often very useful. When addressing subcontractor audits, reference Section 5, Supplier Control, in the Plan.

When addressing internal audits, the Plan should identify who will be performing these audits and exactly what is to be audited. For example, the SQA group may audit the SCM group's adherence to change control procedures (assuming an SCM group exists — otherwise the general use of tools is audited).

Although SCM functions generally do not initiate or direct reviews, quite often the mechanisms used by SCM to process changes are used to organize and process items in a review conducted by other functions such as software quality assurance (SQA). The mechanisms of status reporting are often useful in maintaining detailed action items from reviews of complex systems. SCM supports reviews in this way as any other support provided to management.

There should always be an audit of the configuration items at the time a product is released. This will vary according to the baseline being released and the criteria for the audit stated in the Plan. At a minimum, when the product baseline is established and whenever it is subsequently changed due to the release of a new version of the computer program, the configuration should be audited. Again, the roles of the SCM organization and its participation in the audit should be established in the Plan.

3.3.5 Release Process. Major releases of software must be described so that the recipient understands what has just been delivered. Often the recipient will need installation instructions and other data concerning the use of the new system. The installation instructions should define the environment on which the software will run. This is to cover both hardware (for example, machine type, peripherals needed, and extra memory required) and software (for example, operating system version, and utilities not provided) environments. SCM verifies that the release package is complete and ready to be handed over to the user.

A short outline of the documentation (often referred to as the version description document, or VDD) typically associated with the release package is given in 3.3.5.1. It may be modified to suit the project. The more critical or the larger the application, the more complete the documentation needs to be.

3.3.5.1 Version Description Document. The version description document describes the tapes, diskettes, or other media used to provide the software.

(1) *Release Media.* List the labels on each tape, diskette or [EP]ROM and provide some guidance as to the contents of each volume. For example, *Tape FG301 contains the executable load unit library required to run FRED.*

When one has a more complex system with many CI and associated data files, it may be necessary to describe each file on the tape in this section.

(2) *Functional Description.* When the release contains any functions not previously released, describe them briefly to inform the users of new capabilities. This is not intended to be a user's manual — just the summation of the new capabilities.

(3) *User Considerations.* If there are any special actions the users must take in using the new release, describe them here. Examples may be changes in the use of a new function key, a special procedure needed to complete a certain action, hardware limitations, etc.

In this section, also list any open problem reports (SCR) against the system. Typically the open reports are listed by short title and number in this section. This is for user reference. It may prevent users from filing duplicate problem reports and will give them a better understanding of the system's status.

(4) *Closed Problem Reports.* List in this section all SCR closed out in this release.

(5) *Inventory.* If necessary, provide in this section an inventory of the source and executable load units and data objects (typically at the file level) that are contained in this release. This inventory is generally necessary for those systems that must be tightly controlled. The units are usually listed in alphabetical order by CI, with a designation of version, revision, and date changed. In some cases, the SCR initiating the change is listed against each unit.

(6) *Installation Instructions.* This section may be used when the installation is made at a remote site, at numerous sites or when there are special actions to be taken. The instructions should be specific for each site.

The most important aspect of writing installation instructions is to walk through each step that the installer will have to perform and ensure that he/she will have the information necessary to perform it.

3.4 Tools, Techniques and Methodologies.

The theme of Section 4 of the Plan is making it all happen — the easy way. A well planned project typically takes advantage of planning tools such as PERT charts and Gantt charts.

The audit trail reports should reflect directly back to milestones and other activities on the planning charts, thus giving management a tool for tracking progress on a project. An automated system for software configuration management may include some way of integrating these classical planning tools with the SCM data base to provide all parties (management, designers, developers, testers, quality assurance, etc) with an on-line tool for creating products and observing their current development status dynamically in real-time, correlated automatically with a predefined Plan to yield a quantitative performance-against-schedule measures. The group that is responsible for specific tools should be identified.

The tools, techniques, and methods used to implement SCM are usually discussed in terms of a (set of) libraries and the methods and techniques used to capture, store, and promote or release the items of each type of library in a controlled manner. The concept of *software library* varies according to the level of technology available for generating software. The degree to which all entities of the product are machine accessible is a rough measure of the level of automation for a particular project.

**Issues to Consider in Planning
Section 4 — Tools, Techniques,
and Methodologies**

(1) What are the number and types of libraries to be established?
   (a) A dynamic library (or programmer's library)
   (b) A controlled library (or master library)
   (c) A static library (or software repository)
   (d) Other libraries
(2) What is the amount of change activity anticipated for the project?
(3) Can the SCM tools in the library be used to manage documentation and source code?

---

(4) What kinds and amounts of training (for example, orientation and learning time) are needed to make the tools and procedures an effective solution for the organization?

Definition and use of a minimal set of libraries are illustrated in Appendix C and in 2.3.1. These libraries can accomplish all of the necessary functions of baseline control but usually need to be supplemented with other kinds of libraries to provide the necessary flexibility for smooth operation on larger projects. The libraries have to be structured in such a way that the source code associated with a given executable unit is promoted at the same time that the executable unit is. The source and executable load unit libraries should **always** be kept in synchronization. There are numerous technical methods for achieving this, depending on the development environment and the tools available.

For run-time efficiency, it may be necessary to merge various CI executable units into an integrated run-time environment. When this is done, it is also advisable to maintain the source separately that created the load units.

Note that the corresponding data files are included in the various levels of libraries. When table driven software is used, it is critical to maintain that data at the same level as the corresponding code. This can be handled by carefully structuring the libraries and using appropriate naming conventions.

Manual SCM methods may be perfectly adequate for a small project. However, if the tools and equipment are already in place, they may well be cost effective. The characteristics of the project must guide tool selection. A small project may not need the detailed planning and overhead supported by a complex set of integrated SCM tools. Problems in turnover of software developers may make automation attractive even though its initial cost is high.

In the selection of SCM tools, one needs to consider the cost effectiveness of their use for the given project, product, or site. New SCM tools and methods may be good, but if the engineering staff does not trust them, understand them, or is unwilling to learn new ways of working, they may hinder rather than support the performing organizations in getting the job done.

Current commercially available SCM tools focus primarily on controlling source code. They are written by programmers and code is the important element in programming. Due consideration should be made to bring documentation under control of the same tools as the code. Good SCM systems work on files, and files can consist of paragraphs of a document as well as code.

The kinds of SCM tools recommended in a Plan should also be considered in relation to the probable availability of the tools for use within the project's environment. That is, one should not make the entire Plan dependent on a tool set that may never materialize.

3.5 Supplier Control. The theme of Section 5 of the Plan is how to place effective CM on the computer programs over which you have no direct CM control. Computer program suppliers are considered to fall into one of two classes:

(1) Subcontracted software, or those contractors that develop unique or dedicated software under contract to a developer
(2) Vendor software, or those contractors that provide privately developed and existing software, and bundled application software such as operating systems, compilers, word processing tools, software configuration management tools, and data-base management systems.

**Issues to Consider in Planning
Section 5 — Supplier Control**

(1) Is the product being procured to be used internally, delivered as part of your organization's product, or both?
(2) What post-delivery defect correction requirements and procedures need to be established?
(3) What changes is the purchaser permitted to make after delivery without invalidating the warranty or violating legal constraints?
(4) When should audits be performed?
   (a) When subcontractor or vendor releases parts to the buyer
   (b) After successful integration in buyer's system
(5) Is there a need to *pass through* SCM tools to a supplier or a vendor?
(6) Consider the use of *software in escrow*[12] as a method of enforcing SCM and quality
(7) What periodic reviews of the subcontractor's work will be needed?

3.5.1 Subcontractor Software. If a portion of a software development project is to be subcontracted to another organization, the responsibility for SCM is generally passed to that organization. However, the subcontractor can only be responsible for the portion of the work that his organization is tasked to perform, not for the integration of the subcontracted work with the final product.

Possible methods for integrating subcontractor SCM include

(1) Specifying or providing a library management tool and monitoring its use
(2) Letting the subcontractor(s) promote code to your software generation system and controlling it in the same fashion as is done in-house.
(3) Obtaining the source for all subcontractor deliveries and recompiling and relinking it using the buyer's software generation tools

To ease integration and maintenance, the subcontractor should be required to implement a system of configuration management based on the buyer's requirements — one that is compatible with the buyer's configuration management system or a subset thereof. Identification schemes should be compatible. A system for effectively managing interfaces should be developed. The subcontractor should have an internal configuration control system that is equivalent to the systems and procedures described by the buyer. The format and frequency of status reports also should be agreed upon.

Not all contractor-subcontractor relationships are easily identifiable. Sometimes, the contractual relationship does not afford the buyers any control over the subcontractor SCM processes and the buyer has to bound the relationship of the subcontracted software by alternate identification and by accepting the configuration as given, verified by testing the delivered product (as illustrated in Appendix C). Generally, it is possible to tailor the SCM requirements passed on to the subcontractor, using specifications or statements of work.

---

[12] If the executable code is the only code obtained, it may be advisable to have the supplier place the source code in *escrow* as a warranty that the source will be available if the supplier goes out of business.

Issues to Consider in Defining Subcontractor Relationships

(1) What SCM concerns need to be added to or removed from the contract?

(2) Who is responsible for auditing versus enforcing SCM for contractual products?

(3) What audits and procedures need to be established where the subcontractor has no documented SCM practices or procedures?

If the buyer's organization is developing the computer programs for a customer, the contract should be reviewed for any specific legal requirements that need to be passed on to the subcontractor, or special actions that have to be taken by the buyer to ensure the performance of the subcontractors' product.

Integration of subcontractor software is very difficult unless communication is kept open. One way is to allow subcontractor representatives to attend SCCB meetings to ensure that they are aware of all important technical issues. It may also be useful to accept incremental versions of the code for integration and test with the rest of the code, rather than waiting until the end of the development cycle.

In specifying delivery, identify all items that are to be a part of the deliverable. Possibilities include

(1) Source code

(2) Executable code

(3) Load units

(4) Data files

(5) Test cases

(6) Any JCL or other procedures used in running or creating the software

(7) Compilation listings or link-edit maps (for debugging)

(8) Documentation

Another concern for SCM is the subcontractor's actual performance to an agreed-upon Plan or statement of work. A preselection or purchase audit of the potential subcontractor's configuration management policies and procedures can provide an indication of the potential for the organization to perform satisfactorily. If possible, the buyer's software configuration management group should perform an in-process SCM audit of all project subcontractors to ensure satisfactory compliance. As part of this audit, a specific approved change should be traced through the subcontractor's system to the point of verifying the implementation.

A critical role for SCM is in the inspection (FCA/PCA) of the product as it is prepared for delivery to the buyer. This is most important as it determines the effort and resources that may be needed to integrate and maintain the product once it has been incorporated in the buyer's system. There are still compatibility problems and problems of error correction, and updates that have to be provided for even if the program is a stand-alone product (as for a compiler). If the program received is not well identified and documented, then the task of maintenance is generally increased.

3.5.2 Vendor Software. Warranties contained in purchase orders may be difficult to enforce. The specific criterion is that the vendor should furnish the computer program *media* as specified by a purchase order or as specified by the supplier's documentation referenced in the purchase order. Test documentation confirming compliance is desirable but often unavailable.

Issues to Consider in Defining Vendor Interfaces

(1) How is the vendor software identified?

(2) How are license agreements and data rights protected and enforced? Are there limitations on

(a) Duplication of documentation

(b) Your customer making copies of the program

(3) How will vendor support be provided over the life cycle of the computer program product being purchased?

(4) How will copyright interests be protected?

(5) How will legal copies of leased software be controlled?

The handling of vendor software can be very complex, particularly in a maintenance environment, such as described in Appendix C, where the vendor software is intermixed with internally developed software. More importantly, if you release the vendor product as a part of your organization's product, your organization may be responsible for ensuring its maintenance as part of your released product. An organization embedding third party software in a product delivered to a customer can be open to financial and legal liabilities if a vendor fails to perform—that is, making required changes in a timely manner. One possible consideration is the use of an escrow account with a vendor agreement tied to performance of his product.

3.6 Records Collection and Retention. The theme of Section 6 of the Plan is to *keep the information necessary only for the time required.* This is another service aspect of configuration management. Good configuration management practices include maintaining copies of released material for backup and disaster protection. Also the liability and warranty provisions and responsibilities make considering the retention of test and approval records a necessity. If a master disaster recovery plan exists for the company, the Plan needs to disclose all information regarding the location of backups and records that are impounded in relation with that plan.

Records collection can also be a part of risk management. Part of the trade-off must consider whether personnel will be available to recover lost software. Trade-offs can be made concerning the cost of capturing and maintaining records versus the potential cost savings for

(1) Recovering programs in the event of a disaster for
   (a) Software developed for internal use
   (b) Delivered products for which warranty is still in effect
   (c) Support software necessary for maintaining computer program products under warranty
(2) Liability for not being able to certify the reliability of delivered products
(3) Information gathered that may lead to performance or productivity improvements in development or maintenance activities.

Record keeping begins in planning the capture of all data that needs to be maintained. In addition to all other considerations, archiving the software should be done in a manner acceptable to any legal contracts that may affect the computer programs. Static libraries, disaster planning, and storage should consider the legal status of the software involved (for example, whether it has trade secret status) and the impact on the provisions made for the care and storage of the software components. Special attention should be given to the retention of support software associated with software on target machines.

**Issues to Consider in Planning
Section 6 — Records Collection
and Retention**

(1) What type of information needs to be retained?
(2) What data need to be maintained over a period of time for trend data analysis?
(3) Is all the information, support software, and equipment needed to recreate the product available from archives?
(4) Is media protected from disaster?
(5) Is there a need to maintain copies of software licensed for use and distribution?
(6) What activities need to be recorded (and data captured) for maintaining a product after the project is completed?
   (a) Copyright records
   (b) Distribution records
   (c) Benchmarks
   (d) Change history (CCB activity, SPR, etc)
   (e) Audits, reviews, status reports
(7) For whose use are the records being maintained?
   (a) Engineering
   (b) Management
   (c) Software Quality Assurance
   (d) Legal, customer
(8) How are the records to be kept?
   (a) On line versus off line
   (b) Media and format (hard copy document versus electronic media, deterioration rate versus time needed)
   (c) Location (preservation conditions, accessibility both off site and on site)
   (d) Tools used on the project that affect data capture
(9) How long will the data be kept?

The information collected need not mirror that collected for hardware bit for bit. For example, serial information on production that is kept to identify configurations in hardware may not be necessary for software. Plan to keep only the data that will be of use in maintenance, disaster recovery, or which has other justification. Is the deterioration rate of the storage medium sufficient for the needed time span? Media can deteriorate in storage; also, work in-progress should be backed-up at specific intervals to protect the investment for projects that have long development periods or are of high cost.

Appendixes

(The following Appendixes are not a part of ANSI/IEEE Std 1042-1987, IEEE Guide to Software Configuration Management, but are included for information only.)

Appendix A

Software Configuration Management Plan for Critical Software for Embedded Systems

Version 1.0

Approved

_____

Mgr, SCM Dept

_____

Project Mgr

_____

Contracts

_____

Customer

Date: ___ /___ /___

Synopsis

This example contains a discussion of a hypothetical contract to provide a medium-sized real-time control system for the management of advanced vehicles. Sensors are used for input of information to the system; displays are used to support a man-machine interface. The contract for the system consists of eight software configuration items being developed concurrently with five new and seven off-the-shelf hardware configuration items. The project is expected to have at most three hundred and fifty-six personnel, with an average of thirty-four and peak of fifty software development personnel over the estimated three and a half year development cycle.

Most of the development work is performed in the contractor's main facility with some work being performed at a nearby subsidiary. Testing and acceptance is performed at the mock-up in the contractor's facility. Some commercial software is procured from a vendor for the support software and the firmware for the vehicle is subcontracted to the builder of the vehicle. This is a turnkey contract. The customer takes over all maintenance of the software after delivery of the first system.

The customer's procurement organization has a large staff for monitoring the contract and is expected to perform frequent audits. The contractor's project office wishes to minimize friction with the customer and is willing to perform most, but not all, of the necessary record keeping and in-process inspections. The configuration management department of the contractor has a long history of involvement in projects with the customer and there is a general familiarity and comfortableness in *doing business* in this manner. The software configuration management activity is relatively new but is strongly supported by the old line configuration management department.

In this environment, the software configuration management activity will be a very disciplined operation, logging and maintaining accurate records of *all* transactions against established baselines.

Contents

ANSI/IEEE
Std 1042-1987

Appendix A

Software Configuration Management Plan for
Critical Software for Embedded Systems

1. Introduction

This document is the Software Configuration Management (SCM) Plan for the *Critical Software for Embedded Systems* (CSES). The CSES system performs functions critical to the life and safety of human beings. The configuration management of this software during development is essential to the delivery of error-free and reliable software configuration items.

1.1 Purpose. This plan provides information on the requirements and procedures necessary for the configuration management activities of the CSES project. It identifies the software configuration management requirements and establishes the methodology for generating configuration identifiers, controlling engineering changes, maintaining status accounting, and performing audits and reviews during the design and development of software configuration items.

1.2 Scope. This plan applies to all software and associated documentation used in the production of computer programs produced under the critical software for embedded systems contract including, but not limited to, source, object, and executable load images. Software configuration items referenced in the contract and controlled by this plan include

CSES Operational System
CSES Training Program
CSES Test Program
CSES Hardware Acceptance Programs

CSES Diagnostic Software
CSES Software Support System
CSES Simulation System
CSES Utilities

The organizations involved in this project are identified in Fig 1.

This plan applies to all phases of the software development life cycle, up to and including the time of delivery to the customer. Maintenance of the software after delivery is covered by another contract.

1.3 Definitions and Mnemonics

1.3.1 Definitions. The definitions used in this plan conform to the company standards as set forth in Vol II of the company *Configuration Practices Manual*. Other definitions will conform to those found in ANSI/IEEE Std 729-1983, IEEE Standard Glossary of Software Engineering Terminology. See specifically: baseline, configuration item, configuration management, configuration control, configuration control board, configuration audit, configuration identification, configuration status accounting, and software library. Unique definitions used in this document include:

interface control. The process of

(1) Identifying all functional and physical characteristics relevant to the interfacing of two or more configuration items provided by one or more organizations.

(2) Ensuring that proposed changes to these characteristics are evaluated and approved prior to implementation.

1.3.2 Mnemonics. The following mnemonics are referred to within the text of this standard:

Fig 1
Program Organization Chart

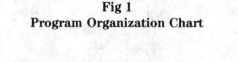

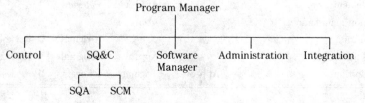

41

CCB	Configuration Control Board
CDR	Critical Design Review
CI	Configuration Item
CM	Configuration Management
CSES	Critical Software in Embedded System
ECN	Engineering Change Notice
FCA	Functional Configuration Audit
I&T	Integration and Test
PCA	Physical Configuration Audit
SCA	Software Change Authorization
SCM	Software Configuration Management
SCMP	Software Configuration Management Plan
SCR	Systems/Software Change Request
SQ&C	Software Quality and Control
SQA	Software Quality Assurance
SQAP	Software Quality Assurance Plan
SRR	System Requirements Review
SSR	Software Specifications Review

1.4 References. The standards listed here will be considered when applying this plan. The latest revisions apply:

[1] ANSI/IEEE Std 729-1983, IEEE Standard Glossary of Software Engineering Terminology.

[2] ANSI/IEEE Std 730-1984, IEEE Standard for Software Quality Assurance Plans.

[3] ANSI/IEEE Std 828-1983, IEEE Standard for Software Configuration Management Plans.

[4] ANSI/IEEE Std 829-1983, IEEE Standard for Software Test Documentation.

[5] Company Standard *Configuration Management Practices Manual*, Vol II.

[6] CSES Software Development Plan

Reference documents are available for use in the company library.

2. Management

2.1 Organization. The critical software for embedded systems program organization is designed to ensure clear lines of authority and to provide a framework within which administrative and technical control of software activities can be cost-effectively integrated into a quality product.

Primary responsibilities for various configuration management tasks are assigned as shown in Table 1. Within the CSES project organization, the program manager has total responsibility for the project. With this project, the program manager will have overall responsibility for configuration management of this project. The program manager serves as the project configuration control board (CCB) chairperson. The SCM project authority from the SCM organization cochairs the CCB. The SCM authority assists the program manager with planning and tailoring of the software configuration management plan (SCMP) and related CM procedures and is responsible for overseeing their implementation. The software configuration management authority reports functionally to the critical software for embedded systems program manager for the implementation of this plan. Administratively, the SCM authority reports to the SCM Department, which performs the necessary activities for the project.

Table 1
Responsibility Assignments

Responsibilities	Program Manager	Software Engineer	SCM Authority	SQA	Drafting
Configuration identification			Originate		
Approve/release tech documentation	Approve	Originate	Review	Review	
Change preparation		Originate			
Change control		Approve			
Change implementation		Approve	Review		Originate
Documentation maintenance		Approve			
Status accounting			Originate	Review	
Formal SCM audits		Approve	Originate	Review	
Baseline definition	Approve	Originate	Review	Review	Review

2.2 SCM Responsibilities. The software configuration management authority has the authority to require changes in practices and procedures that do not meet contract requirements. The general responsibilities of the software configuration management authority are outlined in Table 1. The software configuration management authority's functions include, but are not limited to the following tasks:

(1) Configuration control
(2) Status accounting
(3) Configuration identification
(4) Implementation and maintenance of the software configuration management plan
(5) Configuration control board cochairperson
(6) Establishment and maintenance of engineering baselines
(7) Cochairperson for formal audits
(8) Participation in reviews

2.2.1 Configuration Identification. Configuration identification is applied to all critical software for embedded software, both code and associated documentation. Associated documentation (that is, specifications, design documents, and program/procedure listings) along with the actual produced software makes up the configuration item. The software configuration management authority originates the identification scheme, with the approval of program management.

Configuration identification of computer programs and documentation during the development effort consists of established baselines and releases that are time-phased to the development schedules as described in the CSES software development plan.

2.2.1.1 Baselines. Baselines are established for the control of design, product, and engineering changes and are time-phased to the development effort. Baselines are established by the authority of the program manager. The software configuration management authority administers application of the baselines. Baselines defined for CSES include

(1) Functional baseline
(2) Allocated baseline
(3) Developmental baseline
(4) Product baseline

More details on baselines are presented in 2.4.2.

2.2.1.2 Releases. Throughout the development life cycle, at the discretion of the program manager, software manager, and SCM, baseline releases are performed. The releases fall into one of three categories

(1) Developer release (engineering release)

(2) Release to SCM (preliminary release)
(3) Final release (formal release to customer).

It is the responsibility of SCM to establish the release, version, and update number identifiers.

2.2.1.3 Documentation. All relevant specifications and documentation are given an identifier by SCM.

2.2.2 Configuration Control. All documentation and software entities are released to and maintained by software configuration management in a controlled library. SCM administers the change control process.

2.2.2.1 Systems/Software Change Request (SCR). The SCR is the mechanism by which change requests are presented to the CCB. This action allows a developer to check out software/documentation from SCM controlled libraries. The mechanism for requesting authorization is to present the SCR to the CCB and request approval for work to begin. The SCR form shown in Attachment A is used.

2.2.2.2 Software Change Authorization (SCA). The SCA is used to request SCM to place a new version of software/documentation into the controlled libraries. The approvals necessary are as follows: software manager, software quality assurance, and SCM. The SCA form shown in Attachment B is used.

2.2.3 Status Accounting. A software change authorization data base is used for generating reports that track changes to all of the controlled baselines. At project request, SCM generates reports that track the status of documentation and the software.

2.2.4 Audits. The SCM authority is responsible for cochairing, with the customer, all formal audits.

2.2.4.1 SQA Audits. It is the responsibility of SCM to assist SQA with their audit of the development effort. SCM maintains all documentation and software under strict controls to minimize the effort required by SQA to perform their function.

2.2.5 Configuration Control Board (CCB). The CSES project CCB is established by the program manager and SCM authority.

The program manager is the CCB chairperson and has the final responsibility for CCB actions relative to program SCM policies, plans, procedures, and interfaces. The software configuration management authority acts as cochair. In addition to the chairpersons and the CCB secretary, the CCB may include: development personnel; hardware representative; drafting representative; testing representative; customers; and always will include a representative from software quality assurance. CCB meetings are held on a regular basis determined by the CSES program manager, or when required at the call of the CCB chairperson. The system/software change request that is generated is reviewed by the CCB and one of the following actions taken: approved, disapproved, or tabled.

2.3 Interface Control. Interface control is handled in the same manner as other types of hardware, software, or documentation. Any differences between the SQAP and the SCMP must be resolved prior to the establishment of any baselines.

2.4 SCMP Implementation. The SCMP is implemented as soon as it is signed off by the CSES program manager but prior to holding any formal reviews with the customer. Any unresolved issues found once the SCMP is written must be resolved as soon as possible during the development period and prior to any baselines being established.

2.4.1 Configuration Control Board. The CCB is established at the time of SCMP approval but prior to the establishment of any baselines.

2.4.2 Configuration Baselines. Baselines are established by the following events:

2.4.2.1 Functional Baseline. The functional baselines are established by the acceptance, or customer approval of the CSES system/segment specification. Normally this occurs at the completion of the CSES system requirement review (SRR).

2.4.2.2 Allocated Baseline. The allocated baseline is established with the customer approval of the CSES software requirement specification. Normally this corresponds to the completion of the software specification review (SSR). The specification(s) and associated documentation define the allocated configuration identification.

2.4.2.3 Developmental Baseline. The developmental baseline is established by the approval

of technical documentation that defines the top-level design and detailed design (including documentation of interfaces and data bases for the computer software). Normally, this corresponds to the time frame spanning the preliminary design review (PDR) and the critical design review (CDR).

2.4.2.4 Product Baseline. The product baseline is established upon customer approval of the product specification following completion of the last formal audit (FCA).

2.4.3 Schedules and Procedures for SCM Reviews and Audits. Reviews and audits are held as defined by CSES software development plan.

2.4.4 Configuration Management of Software Development Tools. The configurations of all support software used in development and test on the CSES project software is controlled in the same manner as the critical software. Nondeliverable support software baselines do not need customer approval.

2.5 Applicable Policies, Directives, and Procedures. The complete SCM policies, directives, and procedures that apply to this program are included as part of the procedures section of this document or are part of the referenced documents or one of the appendixes.

3. SCM Activities

3.1 Configuration Identification

3.1.1 Documentation. All supporting documentation generated for this project is identified by the use of the following convention: CSES, an abbreviation for the document nomenclature, a unique four digit number assigned by the CSES software configuration manager, and the product's version-revision-update number.
EXAMPLE: CSES-SDP-0024-1.2.1

**Table 2
Baseline Objectives**

Baseline	Purpose	Reviews & Audits
Functional	Functions established	SRR
Allocated	Requirement defined	SSR
Developmental	Top level design complete	PDR
Developmental	Detailed design complete	CDR
Product	Approval of product spec	FCA/PCA

Document Nomenclature	Mnemonic
Software Configuration Management Plan	SCMP
Software Detailed Design Document	SDD
Software Development Plan	SDP
Software Test Procedures	SPP
Software Product Specification	SPS
Software Quality Assurance Plan	SQAP
Software Requirements Specification	SRS
Software System Specification	SSS
Software Top-Level Design Document	STD
Software Test Plan	STP
Software Test Report	STR

3.1.2 Software Parts. The software configuration items, components, and units are identified by unique identification labels.

3.1.3 Configuration Identification of the Functional Baseline. The functional baseline is identified by the approval of the CSES system segment specification.

3.1.4 Configuration Identification of the Allocated Baseline. The allocated baseline is identified by the approval of the software requirement specification.

3.1.5 Configuration Identification of the Developmental Baselines. The developmental baselines are identified by the approved technical documentation that defines the top level design and detailed designs. The process by which the initial developmental baselines are established is shown in Attachment C, Create Initial Baseline.

3.1.6 Configuration Identification of the Product Baseline. The product baseline is identified by the approval of the CSES software product specification. This baseline specification is made up of the top level specification, detailed design specification, and the computer listings.

3.2 Configuration Control. Software configuration management and change control is applied to all documents and code, including CSES critical operational software and support software. Control is effected through the implementation of configuration identification, the CCB, change control, and status accounting functions.

3.2.1 Function of the Configuration Control Board. The configuration control board reviews proposed changes for assuring compliance with approved specifications and designs, and evaluates impacts on existing software. Each engineering change or problem report that is initiated against a formally identified configuration item is evaluated by the CCB to determine its necessity and impact. The CCB members electronically sign the document to indicate that they have reviewed the changes and provided their recommendations to the chairperson. The CCB approves, disapproves, or tables all changes. The mechanism for submitting changes to the software or documentation is the systems/software change request.

3.2.2 The System/Software Change Request. The SCR system is one of the major tools for identifying and coordinating changes to software and documentation. The SCR system is a minicomputer based tool used to track the status of a change from its proposal to its eventual disposition and assist in documenting important information about the change. The SCR form (Attachment A) contains a narrative description of the change or problem, information to identify the source of the report and some basic information to aid in evaluating the report. SCR is submitted only against baselined software or documentation. SCR may be submitted by anyone associated with the project effort or its products, but usually is submitted by a member of the software development team. SCM provides the single point for receiving and processing SCR. SCM, using the report writer feature of the SCR system, is capable of producing reports that provide change control tracking. A SCR is *closed* when

(1) Integration testing has shown that the changes have been correctly made
(2) No unexpected side-effects have resulted from making the change
(3) Documentation has been updated and reviewed

3.2.3 Software Change Authorization. The software change authorization form (Attachment B) is used to control changes to all documents and software under SCM control and for documents and software that have been released to SCM. The SCA is an on-line form that the software developers use to submit changes to software and documents to SCM for updating the master library. Approvals required for baselining or updating baselined software are as follows. The developer(s) first obtain the manager's signature, I&T signature, and an SCM signature. These approvals can either be written or added electronically. SCM signature testifies that the action has occurred. SQA signature signifies that they have verified that the change has been incorporated. SCM notifies the software developer through the electronic mail system that the change has occurred so the developer can delete extra copies of the changed parts. The SCA data base, along with the SCR data base, is used for status accounting needs.

The process by which changes are made is shown in Attachment D, change procedure.

3.2.4 Change Control Automated SCM Tools.
The libraries of the CSES system are used to control all textual files containing the specifications, documentation, test plans and procedures, and source code. The support software (listed below) is also under configuration management by SCM. The library structure that is used is as follows:

(1) The CSES master library
(2) The program library
(3) The development library

3.2.4.1 For this mini-computer based development effort, the change control tools are as follows:

(1) *The Source Management System* The mechanism for creating and maintaining delta files (changes only) for the CSES master library. Only SCM has access to the CSES master libraries. The CSES master library data base is accessible by the SCM status accounting system.

(2) *The Package Management System* is used to automate the build process and is used to assist SCM with the generation of software.

(3) *SCM Get* is the function invoked by software developers to acquire software modules, or parts from the program libraries.

(4) *SCM Send* is the function invoked by software developers to impound a software module into the SCM program libraries. The use of this function implicitly and automatically generates an SCA.

3.3 Configuration Status Accounting.
The status accounting system is capable of generating the following reports:

(1) *Report 1.* A list of all SCR with a status of *not closed* (that is, the same as *open*)

(2) *Report 2.* A cross-reference of SCA, engineering change notices (ECN), and drawings, per SCA

(3) *Report 3.* A monthly summary of the SCR and SCA data bases

(4) *Report 4.* A total of all SCR submitted per unit within a user-selected range of submittal dates

(5) *Report 5.* A list of all SCR which are *open, closed,* or *all* (selected by the user)

(6) *Report 6.* A summary of all SCR submitted by unit

(7) *Report 7.* A summary of the current approval status of all SCR with a status of *not closed*

(8) *Report 8.* A short summary of all SCR within a particular software component with a status of either open, closed, or all

(9) *Report 9.* A version description document

(10) *Report 10.* A report that gives the status of all documentation under SCM control

(11) *General Report.* Allows the user to define his/her own reports. The user must first specify which fields to include in the report.

(12) *On-Line Inquiry.* Allows the user to interactively view fields within the SCM data bases. The user specifies the fields that he/she wishes displayed and conditions for searching the data base

3.4 Audits and Reviews.
The SCM authority co-chairs, with the customer, the formal CM audits: the functional configuration audit (FCA) and the physical configuration audit (PCA).

3.4.1 Functional Configuration Audit. The functional configuration audit is performed on the software configuration items when the acceptance tests have been completed. Both the functional baseline and the allocated baselines have previously been approved by the customer.

The audit is made on the formal test plans, descriptions, and procedures and compared against the official test data. The results are checked for completeness and accuracy. Deficiencies are documented and made a part of the FCA minutes.

Completion dates for all discrepancies are clearly established and documented. An audit of both draft and final test reports is performed to validate that the reports are accurate and completely describe the development tests.

Preliminary and critical design review minutes are examined to assure that all findings have been incorporated and completed.

3.4.2 Physical Configuration Audit. A physical examination is made of the CI to verify that the first article conforms *as-built* to its technical documentation. The SCM authority assembles and makes available to the PCA team at the time of the audit all data describing the item configuration. This includes a current set of listings and the final draft of the product baseline specifications. Customer acceptance or rejection of the CI and the CI product specification presented for the PCA is furnished to the project manager in writing by the responsible customer representative after completion of the PCA.

3.4.3 Reviews. The SCM authority participates in all formal reviews with the customer.

In addition, the SCM activity conducts two informal audits of the developing CI during the development cycle. The first informal audit is just prior to CDR. The second informal audit is performed at the discretion of the SCM authority midpoint between the CDR and final acceptance test.

4. Tools, Techniques, and Methodologies

4.1 Configuration Control Tools. An integrated set of SCM tools is used for configuration control and status accounting for this project. The particular tools are as follows:

(1) *Source Management System* (SMS). This tool is a file system for checking out vendor-supplied and internal software. A license agreement has been purchased from the vendor of this tool for use on this project.

(2) *Package Management System* (PMS). This tool is a vendor supplied data management tool used to automatically generate software. A license agreement has been secured from the vendor for use on this project.

(3) *Systems/Software Change Request Tool.* This is a proprietary piece of CSES software. This tool has two parts: the input form and its data base.

(4) *Software Change Authorization* (SCA) *Tool.* The SCA is a proprietary piece of CSES software. This tool has two parts: the input form and its data base.

(5) *Status Accounting Report Generator Tool.* This is a proprietary piece of CSES software. This is a report generation tool that gathers input from the following subsystems:
  (a) Source management system
  (b) Package management system
  (c) System/software change request
  (d) Software change authorization

5. Supplier Control

5.1 Vendor-Provided Software. Vendor-provided software that is to be used by this project must conform to *good business practice* SCM. The vendor provides to this project a copy of its SCM Plan for evaluation. This project must ensure that the vendor SCM system is adequate. If the vendor system is found to be inadequate, or if no vendor SCM Plan is available, then at the program manager's discretion, the vendor can be disqualified from providing software for this project.

5.2 Subcontracted Software. Any subcontractor wishing to do business with this project must provide a copy of its SCMP for evaluation by project SCM or agree to follow and abide by this SCMP. If the subcontractor SCMP is found inadequate, all other provisions of this SCMP apply. Any subcontractor not willing to abide by the above provision may be disqualified at the program manager's discretion.

5.3 Vendor and Subcontractor Software. All vendors and subcontractors are audited for compliance with *good business practice* SCM. The frequency and methods of audits are determined by the size, dollar value, and critical nature of the software.

6. Records Collection and Retention

All formal documentation produced for and by this project is retained and safeguarded for 20 years. A second copy of all software and documentation is stored in an off-site facility. This off-site facility is 21 mi from primary storage.

Attachment A
System/Software Change Request

SCR NUM.: _____

1. Submitted by: _____ DATE: _____ / _____ / _____

   Project Name: _____

2. Software Program/Document Name: _____

   Version/Revision _____

3. SCR Type: (1-Development, 2-Problem, 3-Enhancement)

4. Short Task Description:

5. Detail Description:

6. Submitter's Priority [   ]   1=Critical   2=Very Important   3=Important   4=Inconvenient   5=Interesting

7. CCB Action: _____   CCB Priority [   ]

8. Assigned to: _____   Target Release Date_____

9. Solution Comments:

10. Software Programs affected:

11. I&T Approval _____ Date: _____ / _____ / _____

    SCM Approval _____ Date: _____ / _____ / _____

12. Actual Release _____ Date: _____ / _____ / _____

13. Closed by: _____ Date: _____ / _____ / _____

    SCA Reference No: _____

14. SQA Approval: _____ Date: _____ / _____ / _____

Attachment B
Software Change Authorization

SCA Number: XXXXXX
Sheet Number: 1

Submitter:_____ System: _____ Date: _____/_____/_____   Time: _____/_____/_____ 00:00:00

Product Version ID: _____ Computer Name_____

Input Names	Release Names	Module Types	L N	A C	System/Software Change Request Numbers

Comments: _____

_____

_____

_____

_____

Approvals	I & T	SCM	SQA
Signature			
Date			

Attachment C

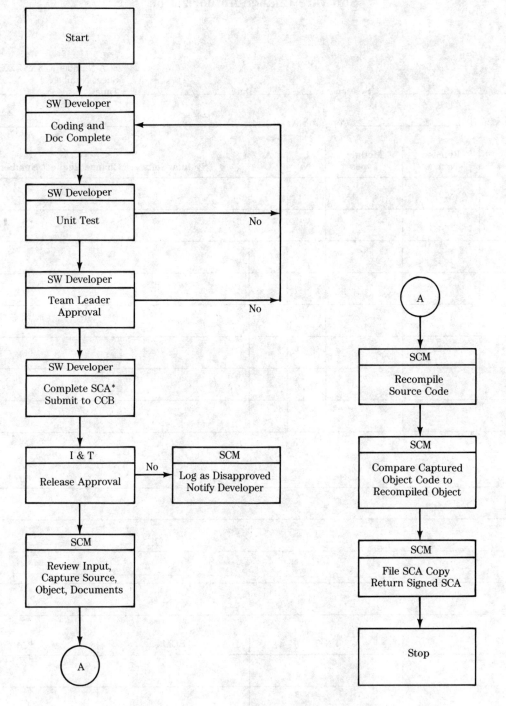

*NOTE: Developer's work files are retained until an approved SCA is received from SCM.

Fig 1
CSES Procedure for Creating Initial Baseline

Attachment D

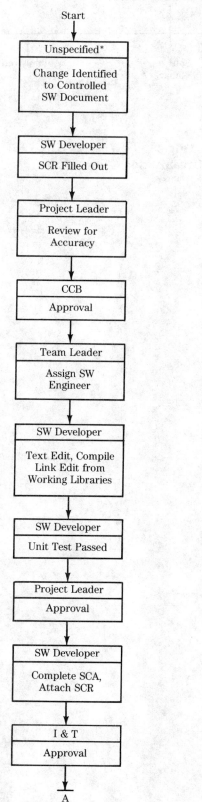

NOTE: If type of change is unspecified, submit SCR to SW Development.

Fig 1
CSES Procedures for Changes to Controlled Software/Documentation

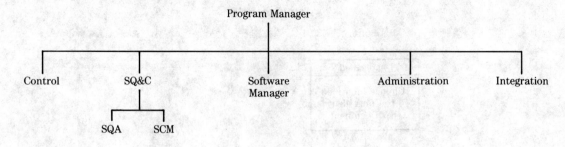

Fig 2
Program Organization Chart

Appendix B

Software Configuration Management Plan for Experimental Development Small System

Version 1.0

Approved

_____

Project Manager

_____

SCM Manager

_____

Customer

Date: ___ / ___ / ___

Synopsis

This example contains a hypothetical contract to provide a prototype minicomputer-based system for a research-oriented customer. The system consists of three software programs, to be developed by a project team of twenty persons (of which ten are programmers) and is considered a prototype for installation in one field site. The software is written in COBOL. If the system is considered successful at that site, it will be expanded to an additional two sites for further evaluation. These sites may be supported by different hardware (for example, a transition may have to be made from hardware configuration A to hardware configuration B) or by different versions of the code (for example, one site may be a data input-processing installation and another a centralized data-gathering installation; each may use slightly different logic or data elements). The development time frame for the prototype system is two years. The expected life of the system is not known as the production system becomes part of a major procurement sometime in the future when the management of the first three sites agree on the requirements.

The contracting company and the customer are very end-user oriented, willing to sacrifice rigor in configuration management and specifications in the interest of speedy delivery of software to the sites and rapid response to changes. Because of this orientation, the configuration control board functions are administered by the project manager alone. All change requests are reviewed by the manager and an immediate ruling is made as to whether and when to implement them. The project manager meets with the customer technical representative regularly to review change requests that require consultation, making disposition of the requests quite rapid.

In this environment, the software configuration management (SCM) activity must be very supportive of the customer and manager or all SCM records will be lost. The SCM coordinator attends meetings between users and the project staff and prepares change requests on the spot. These are provided to the project manager and customer technical representative for resolution. The project emphasis is on intensive support to management in performing SCM — it is literally transparent to management since the SCM organization completes all of the required paperwork. The managers' and customers' responsibility is to review and authorize the resulting documentation.

Contents

Appendix B

Software Configuration Management Plan for
Experimental Development Small System

1. Introduction

This document describes the software configuration management activities to be performed in support of the Experimental Development Small System (EDSS) Project. The EDSS project is charged with developing and demonstrating an advanced data processing concept, which, at a later date, may be converted to a fully functional system for processing special data. The project is considered to be a research/development program.

1.1 Purpose of the Plan. The software configuration management plan (SCMP) for the EDSS system describes how the software development activity supports EDSS management in the rapid iteration of software builds necessary for efficient development of the prototype demonstration software at site A. It also describes how this demonstration baseline is to be captured to provide for adaptation of the operational program to sites B and C and for subsequent up-grade of the software to full production quality for support of operational sites.

1.2 Scope. Three software configuration items (CI) are being developed as part of this contract:
(1) The Operational Program
(2) The Data Reduction Program
(3) The Test Generator Program
The development of these three CI is the responsibility of the contractor's software engineering organization. The internal build testing, the conduct of integration testing and demonstration of the prototype at site A is the responsibility of the contractor's test and control organization. The test and control organization is also responsible for demonstrations at sites B and C under this contract and possible subsequent upgrade testing of the software during later contracts.

The configuration of the operational program is managed at the unit level with all changes reviewed and approved as each unit comes under configuration management in the master library. The configuration of the data reduction program

and test generator program is managed at the component level after being released for use with the operational program.

This SCMP specifically covers the configuration management support provided by the software configuration management department to the EDSS project office for
(1) The development of software used for different builds in test
(2) The prototype demonstration at site A
(3) The demonstrations at sites B and C.

1.3 Definitions and Mnemonics
1.3.1 Standard Definitions. Definitions used are found in ANSI/IEEE Std 729-1983, IEEE Standard Glossary of Software Engineering Terminology. Specifically, attention is called to definitions of
configuration item
configuration identification
configuration status accounting
master library
software library
1.3.2 Other Definitions
prototype system. The software developed for demonstrating the feasibility of the system concept.
1.3.3 Mnemonics. The following mnemonics are used within this document:

AXCESS	Vendor Software Company
CCB	Configuration Control Board
CI	Configuration Item
CM	Configuration Management
DRP	Data Reduction Program
EDSS	Experimental Development Software System
OP	Operational Program
SCA	Software Change Authorization
SCI	Software Configuration Item
SCM	Software Configuration Management
SCMP	Software Configuration Management Plan
SCR	System/Software Change Request
SDG	Software Development Group
SPR	Software Promotion Request
T & CG	Test and Control Group
TGP	Test Generation Program

1.4 References

[1] ANSI/IEEE Std 729-1983, IEEE Standard Glossary of Software Engineering Terminology.[13]

[2] ANSI/IEEE Std 828-1983, IEEE Standard for Software Configuration Management Plans.

[3] Contractor Software Engineering Organization Labeling Standards for EDSS System.

[4] Contractor Test and Control Malfunction Reports.[14]

[5] EDSS Software Development Plan

2. Management

2.1 Organizations. All authority for managing the EDSS system is vested in the EDSS project office. The software engineering organization and the test and control organization provide personnel on loan to the EDSS project office for the duration of the project. The configuration management department provides qualified personnel to the EDSS project office to perform the necessary SCM coordination. Figure 1 illustrates the major organizations.

The working organization is divided into two main groups
(1) EDSS software development group (SDG)
(2) EDSS test and control group (T & CG)

---

[13] IEEE publications are available in the company technical library.

[14] Organizational standards are available from the EDSS project office secretary.

Both groups report to the EDSS project manager. The SCM coordinator is provided by the CM department to the EDSS project office to help support both the software development group and the test and control group.

The EDSS project office has full responsibility for program management functions, including configuration management, until the demonstrations at all three sites are concluded. The SDG has responsibility for preparing and maintaining requirements specifications, designing the software, and performing the unit testing needed for all builds. The T & CG is responsible for integration tests, field installations, and all demonstrations. The SCM coordinator is responsible for processing all changes affecting the documentation (including test data and test procedures) and programs after their release to the T & CG.

The EDSS project manager is responsible for approving/denying all changes to the program, whether originating from the T & CG or from the customer. The project manager functions as the configuration control board (CCB).

2.2 SCM Responsibilities. The general responsibilities of the SCM coordinator are to process the information needed to control changes in the prototype software as it develops and to capture the as-built documentation, test data and reports, and code that represent each successful site demonstration. The emphasis is placed on supporting the project change activities by independently handling all of the required paperwork —making the CM process transparent to management.

Specific organizational responsibilities of the SCM coordinator are as follows:

2.2.1 Identification. Naming conventions are established for

Fig 1
Project Organization Chart

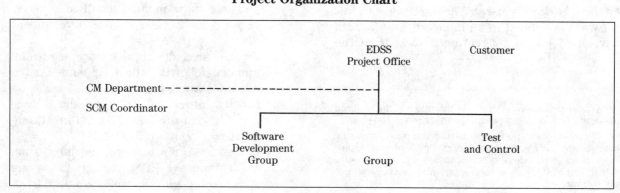

(1) *Unit Names.* These are designed so that unique identification of each item is possible. In addition, the unit naming conventions are structured so that it is possible to determine which SCI each unit belongs to by simply looking at the unit name.

(2) *File Names.* These are designed with the same mnemonic capability as the units.

(3) *Component Names.* These are given unique names so the source code can be matched to the supporting documentation.

(4) *Configuration Item Names.* These are defined in the same manner as in the contract statement of work.

2.2.2 Control. Control of all changes is maintained by

(1) Preparing and tracking approved system/ software change requests (SCR), including all problem reports originatingfrom the customer, throughout implementation and testing

(2) Acting as software librarian, controlling the release of code to

   (a) The integration library for integration and testing by the T & CG at the contractor's development facility

   (b) The master library for installation and demonstrations at the site(s)

2.2.3 Status Accounting. The SCM coordinator provides the necessary status reports to the groups and project management. Typically, the reports cover

(1) SCR opened during period XXXX-XXXX[15]

(2) SCR closed for period XXXX

(3) Major SCR remaining open for three or more weeks

(4) SPR made during period XXXX

(5) SCR included in SPR, by date of promotion

2.2.4 Audits and Reviews. There is no pertinent information for this section.[16]

2.3 Interface Control. The EDSS system interfaces with the *AXCESS* software being developed by the *AXCESS Company.* The interface with this software is defined in an interface specification developed jointly by representatives from the

software development activities of each company. The specification is approved by the responsible project managers of each company.

The EDSS interfaces with the hardware configurations found at customer sites are defined in a memorandum of agreement between the customer and EDSS project manager. Where agreement is not mutual, resolution is reached by contract negotiations. For changes to the EDSS system, the EDSS project manager initiates all change requests. For necessary changes to the *AXCESS* system, the *AXCESS* project manager initiates the change requests.

2.4 SCMP Implementation. The CM Department supports the EDSS project office with the services of a qualified SCM coordinator on the basis of 50% of one person's services per month.

One four-drawer file cabinet in the library is used for storage for the period of time specified in Section 6.

One workstation for execution of the data management system is used for the duration of the project.

Key events in the SCM planning phase are

(1) Establishing the integration library upon release of the first unit to T & CG for integration

(2) Establishing the EDSS master library upon release of the first software system configuration for demonstration at site A

(3) Impounding the master libraries from the three sites, along with the associated documentation and test data and reports, at the end of the final site demonstrations

2.5 Applicable Policies, Directives, and Procedures. The following standards and procedures apply for the duration of the contract:

(1) Labeling standards used for documentation, test data, and software media are in accordance with the standards in the software engineering organization's standards and procedures manual, modified as necessary in the EDSS software development plan.

(2) Version level designations are sequential numbers following a dash, appended to the documentation/media label.

(3) Problem report (SCR) processing is done according to the flow diagram in Attachment B.

(4) Procedures for operating the integration library and the EDSS master library are documented and distributed as a part of

---

[15]The period *XXXX* is left to the discretion of the program manager but is no less frequent than three-week intervals.

[16]No audits are performed as there is no contractual requirements. All reviews are informally conducted. Since there is no formal delivery, the software quality assurance activity is not involved in the configuration management of the software.

the EDSS software development plan prior to establishing the integration library

3. SCM Activities

3.1 Configuration Identification

3.1.1 EDSS Project Baselines. The requirements baseline (functional baseline) is established as the list of functional capabilities set forth in Addendum 2 of the statement of work in the contract.

The design baseline (allocated baseline) is established as the source code and associated design documentation, and all test procedures of the *as built* configuration items are successfully demonstrated to the customer at site A.

The prototype system baseline (product baseline) is established by the current design baseline of site A and versions of the configuration items for sites B and C at the end of the final demonstration.

Integration baselines are used to maintain successive builds during the development of the prototype demonstration at site A. A significant number of software builds at site A can be expected.

3.1.2 EDSS Project Labeling. The basis for labeling is by mnemonic labels assigned to each unit. In addition, each source unit shall have a prologue embedded in it. This prologue shall contain the following elements:

(1) Unit name
(2) Component name or identifier
(3) CI identifier
(4) Programmer name
(5) Brief description of the function of the module
(6) Change history
    (a) Date of each change
    (b) Reason for change (see SCR)
    (c) Change level (version being changed)

For example, the initial version of a unit is A-0, the second is A-1, etc. The change level is incremented each time the code is revised. The change level and the unit name are used to uniquely identify the version of the source code that incorporated a given problem correction, for example, ABC (3) for revision 3 of the unit ABC.

3.2 Configuration Control

3.2.1 Configuration Control Board. The EDSS project manager performs the functions of the change control board. The SCM coordinator supports the project manager by preparing SCR for the manager's review and processing the SCR subsequent to the manager's decision.

3.2.2 Processing SCR. The procedure for handling SCR is described in Attachment B.

3.2.3 CCB Interfaces. The EDSS project manager performs all of the coordination necessary with the customer in reviewing and in accepting, rejecting and negotiating changes. The manager also performs the liaison with the AXCESS vendor. Changes originating from the EDSS project are processed by the SCM coordinator. The two project managers provide coordination between projects and mutually resolve differences.

Changes to a system that result from these agreements are initiated by the responsible project manager.

3.3 Configuration Status Accounting.
Status accounting is accomplished by tracking the changes to units through the use of the SCR form. This manually generated form (reference Attachment C) is updated (upon release) with the version number of each release.

Status of each CI is reported periodically to the project manager or at the manager's request. The status of the revisions to the units and components is reported weekly to the managers of the SDG and T & CG. When a software system is released to a site, the release and version are recorded and the units contained in the system are listed, along with their current change level.

3.4 Audits and Reviews.
No audits are scheduled to be held for the EDSS system. Instead, the system is verified through the customer's functional testing. Parallel operation using the site's previous manual system and the new system is maintained until the users are confident that the system is producing accurate reports and displays. The SCM coordinator attends performance/functional reviews to record action items and change status.

Functional reviews are held periodically during the software development cycle. The principle document used is the *User Interface Guide*. This document contains the layouts of each of the displays and reports the users have available from the system. Each data element in each display or report is defined there, along with the method by which the element is derived (if any).

4. Tools, Techniques, and Methodologies

The primary technique for SCM is the manual processing of SCR, SCA, and SPR. The SCR form (see Attachment C) is used to record all customer requests for changes, their disposition, and eventual implementation. The same form is used to record enhancements or changes requested by the SDG. These forms later become the basis for updating the requirements specifications and for resolving questions concerning the origin of a change or the status of a requirement that arise during implementation, during integration, installation and checkout at site(s) and during the demonstrations.

A set of basic SCM tools is available for use. A data management system is used for recording and reporting status of the units, components, and CI.

The integration library uses a file system to check in and check out units for revision and test. The project master library uses the same system to impound master copies of the units and components.

Release of code to the integration library is made through software promotion requests (SPR) shown in Attachment A. The software is compiled and built into a protected integration package owned by the T & CG. Software successfully demonstrated at the sites is placed in the EDSS master library for future demonstrations and upgrades.

5. Supplier Control

There is no pertinent information for this section.

6. Records Collection and Retention

Copies of each status report are maintained as a historical record for the EDSS project until the project is terminated or the prototype demonstration system is replaced by the production system. These records are transferred to microfiche as they age over six months.

The prototype system baseline code, test data and reports, and documentation shall be maintained at the termination of the project for a period of two years or until replaced by a production system. The software media for retention of this baseline code is magnetic tape. The documentation for this is retained on microfiche.

Test procedures and test data resulting from the successful demonstrations shall be retained as a part of the data for use in defining the production system.

Attachment A

Software Promotion Requests

Table 1 defines the list of data elements included in the Transaction file for release of each unit.

Table 1
Data for Software Release

Element Name	Definition
CI number	Number assigned for CI identification
Sub-application	The name or number assigned to the unit or portion of the CI being released
Release request	Data release was requested
Action requested	The control action requested by the development activity (builds, move to test library)
Members	Names of modules, units to be included in the release
Change level	The change level or version number of the units being released
Justification	The number or the statement of justification concerning the reason for release
From library	The library location of the units before the release
Member type	The type of the unit being released (procedures, macros, test drivers)
Load module	The load module with which the units are linked
Time tag	The time tag for the version of the unit being promoted

Attachment B

IEEE Guide for
Processing System Software Change Requests

System/Software Change Request (SCR) forms are used to document three types of situations:

(1) Requests for changes to the software by the customer (whether these requests result from tests, demonstrations, or from experience at the sites).

(2) Requests for changes by the designers or coders (generated within the company) that affect code already in use at the sites.

(3) Problems or errors in the code in test or at the sites that were clearly not requests for new or different functions—documented *bugs* in the released code

1.1 Processing steps are

(1) All SCR are logged in by the SCM coordinator and assigned a number on receipt. After logging, the SCR is forwarded to appropriate manager for action or resolution.

(2) When an SCR results in a software change (whether a correction or a new function), the software manager annotates the SCR form at the time of release of the new software to the sites and forwards the SCR to the SCM coordinator who then updates the master file.

1.2 SCM Coordinator. The SCM coordinator attends all customer/designer meetings and acts as the recorder of change requests. Signature approvals are obtained at that time.

When a release of software to sites is being prepared, the SCM coordinator meets with the project manager and review all outstanding SCR against the released software.

The SCR closed at that time are documented by the SCM coordinator.

Attachment C

System/Software Change Request Form

The following data elements are included on the SCR form.

Table 1
SCR Data Elements

Element	Values
CI	The name of the configuration item involved
Environment	The hardware site involved (may be more than one as project uses three different types of minicomputers)
Change type	Legal values: new function, error correction, design change
Date requested	DD/MM/YR
Narrative description	Description of the change desired in language as explicit as possible; description of the problem in the case of error reports
Disposition	Final disposition: fixed, accepted but delayed, rejected.
	If fixed, description of changes made are included here
Requester	Person making the request for the change
Requester site	Location of the person making the request
Release and version	The release and version number in which the problem existed
Implementation data	List of modules involved in the change on system/software change request form
Implementation release and version	Release and version number in which change appears
Implementation ship date	Date on which the change is shipped to the sites
Responsible manager signature	
Customer approval signature	(Used only for changes to software already released for field use)

Appendix C

Software Configuration Management Plan for a
Software Maintenance Organization

Version 1.0

Approved

_____

Mgr SPLIT Facility

_____

Mgr SCM Dept

Date: ___ /___ /___

ANSI/IEEE
Std 1042-1987

Synopsis

This example contains a discussion of a hypothetical programming facility that manages the support software systems used in the design, development, test and maintenance of the software systems for a large software engineering company. The company has approximately twenty-seven hundred employees of whom nine hundred are professional software engineers with degrees in computer science, computer systems or electrical engineering. The average experience of the professional engineers is five and one-half years. The software products they build and maintain are primarily real-time systems for many applications, some critical and some not. The company has an extensive investment in software engineering facilities. There are software engineering work stations for a third of the professional programming staff and terminals available for the support staff. The work stations are attached to a local area network that is integrated with a large number of mini-computers and two mainframes.

The programming facility, SPLIT, is staffed with one hundred and thirty-five people. Fifty are systems and maintenance programmers. There is a software configuration management department within the company that performs all of the configuration management activities for the facility and the software engineering groups. Special emphasis is placed on the management of the products in the SPLIT facility since the productivity and reputation of the company directly depends on the efficiency and reliability of the support software used by the engineering groups. A special software configuration management group is permanently assigned to the SPLIT facility with the responsibility for controlling the company's support software. The company management supports this focus—as long as the software engineering activities do not complain too loudly about the service they receive.

In this environment, the software configuration management group in the facility has a direct role in the control of the support software. This group processes all changes made to the support software by the system programmers, builds the run-time systems and performs all the other normal configuration management activities. The role of configuration management in maintenance makes this group a major part of the facility's management team.

Since the company has a considerable investment in the support software and data records, the disaster control practice requires that the support software in the production library have copies in the software archival repository. The company maintains the software repository in a protected shelter thirty-five miles from the main facility.

Contents

Appendix C

Software Configuration Management Plan for a
Software Maintenance Organization

1. Introduction

This plan describes the standard operating procedures for managing the configuration of all the support software available to the users of the SPLIT facility. The SPLIT facility provides the supporting software used in the design, development and maintenance of software products produced by the company. All of the support software products available to the users of the SPLIT facility are maintained under configuration management to ensure that users have continual and reliable service from the software products in the run-time environment, and that errors in the support software and requests for enhancements are handled accurately, completely, and in a timely manner.

1.1 Purpose of the Plan. This operating plan specifies procedures whereby software configuration management supports the entire software change/enhancement process.

1.2 Scope. This plan defines the SCM activities necessary for maintaining all support software items being procured, tested, sustained and kept in the production environment in the facility. The list of the software configuration items will vary over time. The consolidated list of configuration items and their status is maintained by the SCM group within the SPLIT facility and published monthly in the SPLIT configuration summary.

1.3 Definitions and Mnemonics
  1.3.1 Definitions. The terms used in this plan conform to the definitions found in ANSI/IEEE Std 729-1983, IEEE Standard Glossary of Software Engineering Terminology.
  1.3.2 Mnemonics. The following mnemonics are used within this document:

CCB	Configuration Control Board
CCM	Configuration Change Management [system]
CI	Configuration Item
CM	Configuration Management
COMM	Communications Software
EWS	Engineering Work Stations
HW	Hardware
LAN	Local Area Network
SCA	Software Change Authorization
SCM	Software Configuration Management
SCMG	Software Configuration Management Group
SCMP	Software Configuration Management Plan
SSQAG	SPLIT Software Quality Assurance Group
SCR	System/Software Change Request
SQA	Software Quality Assurance
SQAG	Software Quality Assurance Group
STEG	SPLIT Test and Evaluation Group
SDT	Software Development Tools
TFR	Transfer File Request

1.4 References [17]

[1] ANSI/IEEE Std 729-1983, IEEE Standard Glossary of Software Engineering Terminology.

[2] ANSI/IEEE Std 828-1983, IEEE Standard for Software Configuration Management Plans.

[3] GP:25, Software Configuration Management.

[4] GP:26, Software Change Request Processing.

[5] SF:39, Vendor License Identification and Accountability.

[6] SF:27, Inspection and Test of Support Software Products.

[7] SF:15, Test and Evaluation Group Activities.

[8] CMP:13, Identification and Labeling of Software.

[9] CMP:25.3, Unit Naming Conventions.

[10] CMP:25.4, Version Level Designation.

[11] CMP:37, Computer Program Media Identification and Marking.

[12] CMP:12, Software Auditing.

[13] SP:17, Support Software Status Reporting.

---

[17] Referenced documents are available for use in the SPLIT software reference library.

[14] SP:12, Operation of SPLIT Configuration Control Board.

[15] SP:5, User Documentation Maintenance.

[16] SP:7, SPLIT Production Library Maintenance.

[17] SP:95, Work Station Request and Allocation.

[18] SCMG-WP:19, Data Retention—SCR/SCA.

[19] SCMG-WP:1, Software Release Procedures.

2. Management

2.1 Organization. The vice-president managing the SPLIT facility reports to the company president along with the vice-president in charge of the product effectiveness group and the vice-president in charge of the operations division (engineering). The configuration management (CM) department is part of the product effectiveness group. The software configuration management group (SCMG) is administratively a part of the CM department and their activities are responsive to the policies set by the CM department; but, functionally, they report to the manager of the SPLIT facility.

The organizational structure of the SPLIT facility is shown in Fig 1.

2.1.1 Operations Group. The operations group maintains the processing and communications systems, installs and reconfigures hardware installations, and performs the day-to-day operations of the processing environments.

2.1.2 Systems Software Programmers. The systems software programmers perform the maintenance on the support software developed in-house (generally by the engineering division) and subcontracted software acquired by the facility. Third party software acquired from vendors is not maintained by the SPLIT facility.

2.1.3 Test and Evaluation Group. The test and evaluation group performs the acceptance tests for vendor and subcontracted software and also all new releases for in-house support software maintained by the systems software programmers.

2.1.4 User Consultants. The user consultants provide training to that portion of the company that does not include Section 2.1.3 in the use of the support software systems, and consulting services to the software engineers as needed. They are the primary source of change requests for support software.

2.1.5 SPLIT Software Quality Assurance Group. The SSQAG is functionally a part of the product effectiveness group. They perform evaluations of new software as an incoming QA function, and periodic audits of the operations of the facility.

2.1.6 Multiple Configuration Control Boards. There are multiple configuration control boards (CCB) within the facility. The senior CCB, called the SPLIT CCB, has overall responsibility for managing the hardware and software configurations in the facility. This responsibility includes

(1) Allocating SPLIT resources for use on company projects
(2) Setting overall schedules for support software updates and new version releases
(3) Allocating resources to update configurations of mainframe processors, the minicomputer nodes, and the LAN/Hi-Speed data bus configurations.

Fig 1
SPLIT Facility Organization

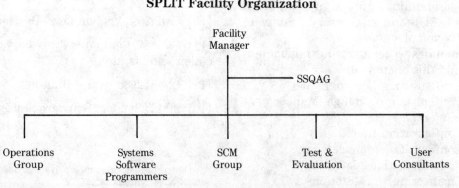

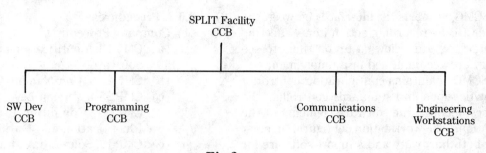

**Fig 2
Structure of CCB**

(4) Providing resources to subordinate CCB that manage software product lines

The manager of the SPLIT facility chairs the SPLIT CCB. The head of the SCMG is the alternate chairman and attends all meetings of the SPLIT CCB.

The in-house software is grouped by function into three separate CCB

    (a) Software development (SWDEV) tools

    (b) Programming environments (PROG)

    (c) Communications (COMM) software

These subordinate CCB have configuration management responsibility for support software developed in-house, and managing the changes approved for software acquired from outside sources. Individual product line CCB are assigned to software products developed by the company, but their operation is independent of the SPLIT facility CCB. When these company software products are used in the SPLIT facility, they are controlled in the same way any product purchased from an outside vendor is controlled. The software used in the engineering work stations has a separate work station CCB for tracking the volatile hardware and software configuration.

Each SPLIT facility CCB is responsible for allocating resources needed for maintaining their assigned software products. Where changes affect interfaces with other hardware or software within the facility, or both, the issue must be brought before the SPLIT facility CCB. The head of the SCMG cochairs the SPLIT facility CCB and work station CCB with their respective managers.

Each project making use of a software product has representation on the CCB controlling that product.

2.2 SCM Responsibilities. The primary SCMG responsibilities involve supporting the change process as it affects existing software product baselines; maintaining an accounting of the status

of *all* the software configuration items in the facility; and auditing physical configurations (CI) received from subcontractors, vendors of commercial software used in the facility, and support software from the company engineering division.

2.2.1 Identification. The SCMG is responsible for maintaining the identification (numbering, labeling, and integrity of documentation) for all the support software in the facility. Responsibility also extends to identifying the configuration items that are acquired from commercial vendors.

2.2.2 Configuration Control. The SCMG is responsible for supporting the change process for all of the support software used in the SPLIT facility.

2.2.3 Configuration Status Accounting. The SCMG maintains the data base used to prepare reports on the status of all support software products and hardware configurations used in the facility.

2.2.4 Audits and Reviews. Audits are performed by two groups

(1) The SCMG performs physical configuration audits of all support software acquired by the facility. Periodic inventory audits of the support software are also performed as directed by the SPLIT facility manager

(2) The SCMG supports SSQAG in performing functional configuration audits of incoming subcontracted and vendor-provided support software. The SCMG also provides SSQAG with summary data on probable causes of failure

The SCMG works directly with the STEG in evaluating software changes being released to the production library.

2.3 Interface Control. One of the most critical activities is controlling the interfaces between the different software systems in the facility and between the software and changing hardware configurations.

The SCMG supports the interfaces between the multiple CCB by recording action items affecting each interface and following up on them to see that they are accomplished in a timely manner.

The SCMG maintains configuration control of the specifications and standards controlling the interfaces between the software elements of the workstations. The workstation configuration must include both hardware and support software for each installation. This includes accounting for leased and licensed software used on personal computers and in workstations.

The SCMG maintains the operating system configuration used in the SPLIT facility as a means for enforcing control of the interfaces with the applications programs.

2.4 SCMP Implementation. The staff of the SCMG is composed of one group head, who acts as coordinator, and one qualified SCM administrator for each separate SPLIT facility CCB (one per CCB). One additional person has the function of tracking the EWS configuration(s).

Computer resources and work space are provided by the SPLIT facility manager for the SCMG.

Milestones for SCMG activity are set by the manager of the SPLIT facility and reflect the on-going continuous support activities required for managing the various support software configurations.

2.5 Applicable Policies, Directives, and Procedures

2.5.1 Policies

(1) Company Policy
   (a) GP:25, Software Configuration Management
   (b) GP:26, Software Change Request Processing
(2) SPLIT Policies
   (a) SF:39, Vendor License Identification and Accountability
   (b) SF:27, Inspection and Test of Support Software Products
   (c) SF:15, Test and Evaluation Group Operations

2.5.2 Directives

(1) Company Bulletin, GB:87, *Use of Licensed Software*
(2) Company Directive, CD:34, *Copyright Protection*
(3) Company Bulletin(s), GB:(various), *CCB Membership*

2.5.3 Procedures

(1) Company Procedures
   (a) CMP:13, Identification and Labeling of Software
   (b) CMP:25.3, Unit Naming Conventions
   (c) CMP:25.4, Version Level Designations
   (d) CMP:37, Computer Program Media Identification and Marking
   (e) CMP:12, Software Auditing
(2) SPLIT Procedures
   (a) SP:17, Support Software Status Reporting
   (b) SP:12, Operation of SPLIT Configuration Control Board
   (c) SP:5, User Documentation Maintenance
   (d) SP:7, SPLIT Production Library Maintenance
   (e) SP:95, Work Station Request and Allocation
(3) SCMG Procedures
   (a) SCMG-WP:19, Data Retention—SCR/SCA
   (b) SCMG-WP:1, Software Release Procedure

3. SCM Activities

3.1 Configuration Identification. Each support software product in the facility is identified by configuration item title, specifications, user documentation, and media labels in accordance with established company procedures.

Since the software being managed has already had a product baseline established, the identification schema is already set. The SCMG uses the identification and labeling standards in the product baseline. In-house software identification follows company procedures CMP-13; 25.3; 25.4; and 37. Third-party software is labeled with company-defined labels for record-keeping purposes.

The elements of software (programs, documentation, test data, etc) in the production library (the library of software released for running on hardware in the facility) is organized as in Table 1.

Table 1
Hierarchy of Elements

Generic Term	Alternate Terms
Configuration item	Package, product
Component	Segment, program
Unit	Module, routine

The level of control applied by the SCMG will generally be to the component level. Components are considered to be the *controlled item* in managing the operation of the SPLIT facility. A given programming library used by systems programmers may have a system for managing configurations of software units previously used in the development and maintenance of other programs. Sometimes the units in these libraries are referred to as packages, following the concepts of *reusable software* being advocated.

3.1.1 Baseline Identification. Support software product baselines are established during incoming inspections of the product at the facility. New releases to a product baseline are labeled in accordance with 2.5.3(1)(c). New releases include changes or updates as necessary to the product package—specifications, user documentation, design documentation (listings), test procedures, and associated test and inspection reports. The procedure 2.5.3(1)(a) is followed for each new release of a support software product.

A new release of a support software product is made in accordance with 2.5.3(3)(b).

The scheduling of a new release is determined by the SPLIT CCB.

3.1.2 Product Baseline Cataloging. Labeling of product CI is in accordance with 2.5.3(1)(a). The SCMG reviews each request to be released for conformance to company procedures. The SCMG then checks the release package against the transfer file and the CCB authorization for completeness and STEG/SSQAG approvals.

3.2 Inspection and Receiving. New products entering into the facility for use are inspected for conformance to 2.5.3(1)(a) by the SCMG. Vendor software parts (configuration items) are given company CI part numbers in the 7000 series for maintaining separate accountability within the status accounting system.

3.3 Configuration Control

3.3.1 Levels of Authority for Approvals. All software is tested by the STEG prior to its promotion into the integration library or the production library. Both STEG approval and SCMG approval is required before the software is promoted to the integration library or production library.

The promotion of changes into the integration library is authorized by the SPLIT facility and work station CCB and approved by the SCMG after design checks by the STEG.

The release of changes to the production library is authorized by the SPLIT CCB. Prior to entering changes into the production library, each change is tested and verified as correct by the STEG, checked for conformance to packaging standards by SSQAG, and administratively approved by the head of the SCMG before being placed into the library.

3.3.2 Change Proposal Processing

3.3.2.1 SCR Processing. Software change requests are prepared using the form C-1049, software/system change request, or use of the SCR ENT command in the interactive configuration change management (CCM) system. Manually prepared forms (C-1049) are entered into the CCM system by the SCMG librarian. The same form used to initiate a problem report is used for requesting an enhancement to the system. All changes are concurrently routed to the SCMG files in the CCM system for administrative checks and to the appropriate product line manager for verification. Each SCR is reviewed by technical personnel and their evaluation is forwarded to the appropriate SPLIT CCB for action.

The SPLIT CCB can approve, reject, or table (with an action date) a request pending further information.

Action in response to a SCR is scheduled by the CCB in response to the severity of the problem reported or the need for enhancement. Problem reports are given priority over change requests not associated with an operating problem. Problem reports (as indicated on the SCR form) are processed on an expedited basis.

Problem reports that are determined to be valid errors in the performance of the system and given priority for solution with temporary fixes are incorporated into the subject system—along with publication of a bulletin notifying all users of the

Table 2
Problem Criteria

Category	Symptom
"C"	A software item cannot be executed by a user
"M"	Users have problems with a program but can work around with temporary fix
"S"	Minor irritation but users can still accomplish work

change in the system. Permanent modifications to correct the error are incorporated with the next upgrade released to all users.

Requests for system enhancements that are valid and within the scope and resources allocated to the software product are scheduled for incorporation in the next scheduled upgrade to that product.

Approvals are incorporated in the maintenance schedule and a release date tentatively identified for a scheduled upgrade or correction to the affected support software product(s). Status of these SCR is indicated as *approved*.

The SCR may be returned to the user when additional clarification is needed or when the results of the design review may necessitate additional design analysis or even modification to the change request. The SCR is held with the status *pending* until a course of action has been determined.

Testing for promotion to the integration library or release to the production library may result in additional design changes or recoding. In that event, the status of the SCR reflects *approved* and the status of the SCA reflects *in-work*. The status of the SCR/SCA action is changed to *implemented* only if the change has been completed, verified, and released into the production library.

3.3.2.2 SCA Processing. Approved SCR are forwarded by the CCM system to the appropriate programming activity for implementation. Similar changes that are grouped together for an upgrade are worked on at the same time. Emergency changes (needed to keep the system in operation) are expedited through the system. The programming activity extracts necessary files for work from the production library and makes the changes. When the supervisor is ready to integrate the file, the SCA and the code are completed and passed to the CCM_HLD/INT area for administrative checks by SCMG before being released to the integration library for integration and test.

STEG performs the integration and testing, requesting modifications from the programming activity as appropriate. When it has been demonstrated that the change package is correct and introduces no additional errors into the system, the SPLIT CCB is informed of the pending update whereby STEG initiates a transaction file request (TFR). Upon approval by the SPLIT CCB, the SCMG enters the change into the production library. The status of the SCR/SCA is then changed to *closed*.

The SCMG performs the systems generation of the run-time programs used in the facility, and

loads, after verification by the STEG, into the necessary hardware configurations.

Failure of the users to accept the changes in the support software system may result in it being returned to a previous step or cancellation of the task.

3.3.2.3 Changes to EWS. The processing of changes to work station support software is the same as the above procedure except that the run-time software generation and allocation to HW configuration is controlled by the EWS CCB network manager.

3.3.2.4 Changes to Supplier Software. Change processing for subcontracted software is performed in the same manner described above when the source code is in-house and maintenance is being performed by the SPLIT systems software programmers. When the software product is under subcontractor warranty, the SCR is passed to the subcontractor and the new version is accepted into the production library in the usual manner. In the event where the subcontractor has a maintenance contract for the product, the SCR is passed on to them for processing.

3.3.2.5 Licensed Software. Licensed software is given a company label with a unique identifier to indicate limited use. Periodic audits are conducted by the SCMG to determine adherence to the license limitations by users.

3.3.2.6 Purchased Commercial Software. Purchased commercial software is relabeled with company identifying numbers and released for use and configuration management in the same manner as in-house developed software.

3.3.3 CCB Roles. The CCB evaluation takes into consideration, among other things, the staff resources available versus the estimated workload of the request; the estimated additional computing resources that are required for the design, test, debug, and operation of the modified system, and the time and cost of updating the documentation.

An essential function of each CCB is to coordinate the flow of information between the users of the software product and the maintenance organization supporting the product. This function is executed when the CCB representatives of the project use the products and monitor the evaluation of the significance of problem reports and requests for enhancements. The result of the CCB review is the assignment of a priority to each request.

3.3.4 Control of Interfaces. There is no pertinent information for this subsection.

3.4 Configuration Status Accounting. The SCMG supports the following reports:

(1) *SPLIT Software Configuration Report.* An accounting of the software and hardware configurations of all the systems within the SPLIT facility. This report is kept current at all times. Weekly reports are made to the SPLIT facility manager, including changes just completed and changes scheduled for the next week.

(2) *SPLIT Performance Summary.* A monthly summary of the up-time of all systems and an analysis of all problems causing unscheduled down-time.

(3) *SCR/SCA Summary.* For each configuration item, a summary of the current status of SCR/SCA activity is given on a weekly basis to the SPLIT facility manager. The SCR summary includes problem type and severity, priority given by the CCB, activity or programmer assigned, and target release date for either the fix or new release.

(4) *EWS Configuration Status.* This configuration status is maintained in a data base for general access. Status and configuration summaries are presented to the SPLIT facility manager on a weekly basis.

3.5 Audits and Reviews. The SCMG performs a physical configuration audit on all incoming third-party software.

The SCMG performs functional and physical configuration audits on each new release of software in the system.

The SCMG performs periodic audits of the software and hardware configurations in the facility to ascertain that no unauthorized changes have been made. Particular attention is paid to licensed software.

4. Tools, Techniques, and Methodologies

4.1 Use of the CCM System. The CCM system is used to manage and track all changes to the software in the SPLIT facility. The system provides for initiating changes, review and approval by management, assigning and monitoring work status, and the testing and releasing of all changes. Status reporting is provided as an output from the CCM data base. This configuration management tool is one of the set of software tools used

in the SPLIT facility by all of the operating activities.

4.2 Inspections. Releases to the production library are inspected to confirm inclusion of scheduled SCR/SCA.

4.3 Library Management. The SCMG makes disciplined use of programming libraries to manage the changes to support software configuration items. The SCMG and the STEG cooperate in promoting software modifications from the development library into the integration library and from there releasing them to the production library.

4.3.1 Development Library. The development library is used by the systems software programmers as they develop their code. The units and components are controlled by the individual programmers. Criteria for allowing promotions into the integration library includes the successful completion of unit testing and approval by the group's supervisor.

4.3.2 Integration Library. The integration library is used by the SCMG to capture and build the code that is designated for promotion to the STEG for integration and test. This library contains the source code and executable load modules created as a result of a system build. The source code is placed in a special controlled library in preparation for a build. Then the code is recompiled and link edited before it is placed in the integration library. Criteria for releasing to the production library includes

(1) Submission of a software release request by the SPLIT CCB

(2) Completion of status accounting audits and resolution of issues by SCMG

(3) Acknowledgment of regression and integration test completion by the STEG and SQA

All test data and routines used to verify software released for use are also maintained under configuration control in the integration library.

4.3.3 Production Library. The production library contains the master copies of all the support software configuration items used in the SPLIT facility. Copies are made from the masters by the SCMG for use on other systems. The production library acts as backup for the run-time configurations used on the systems. Only current master copies of support software configuration items are maintained in the production library.

4.3.4 Software Repository. Current copies of all support software configuration items from the production library are maintained in the software repository. Historical copies of support software released for use outside the facility are maintained in the repository for a period of ten years after release.

5. Supplier Control

Since the SCMG does not have responsibility for supporting the development of subcontracted software, the SCMG has no interface with the support software developed in this way.

The SCMG does participate with the STEG in the receiving inspection of commercial software and subcontracted software to ascertain that

(1) All physical items are available as required by contract
(2) The proper labels are on the media to be placed in the integration library, and subsequently, in the production library

The SCMG is responsible for the physical configuration audit of subcontracted and vendor-supplied software. The SQA activity performs the functional configuration audit.

6. Records Collection and Retention

Records of SCR/SCA processing are retained for a period of five years to support fiscal standards of records. Status reports of the SPLIT facility configurations are also maintained for a period of five years.

Records defining the product baselines of all support software products released for use outside the facility (in conjunction with engineering division sales) are maintained for a period of twenty years to protect product warranties. The product baselines of all other support software products developed in-house but not released for use outside the facility are maintained for a period of ten years.

Records of licensed vendor software integrated, or otherwise used, with internal configurations are maintained for a period of five years after their removal from the system.

Biweekly backups of the systems are archived for a period of six months to protect the data files of the ongoing engineering division development activities. Backups of the systems processing company financial records are archived for a period of seven years, as required by law.

Attachment A

System/Software Change Request
(SPLIT Form C-1049)

Table 1
Definitions of Elements in SCR

Element	Values
Originator	Name of the person making the request
Product	Originator's subject support software product
Date	Date of change request (option: date of anomaly detection for the SCR
SCR number	Sequential number assigned for the product in question
SCR title	A concise descriptive title of the request
SCR type	One of the following types: AR — Anomaly Report SCN — Specification Change Notice ECR — Engineering Change Request ER — Enhancement Request IR — Impound Request
Program	Identification of the support software product for which the change is requested
System version	Version identifier of the system for which the change is requested
Description of change	Originator's description of the need for a change
Disposition	CCB indicates one of the following dispositions: Approved — Date approved and assigned for implementation _____ Deferred — Date deferred to _____ Rejected — Date rejected _____
User class	Indicates organization/activity using the software
Date needed	Indicates date the change is needed in the production system

For those SCR referencing anomalies detected in a product baseline, the CCB must verify that the problem exists and the following data should be added:

Optional Data for Anomaly Reports

Item	Data
1	System configuration on which the anomaly was detected.
2	Performance effect — The effect the anomaly has on the performance of the system [c] critical; [m] major; or [s] small

Attachment B

Software Change Authorization

Table 1 defines the list of data elements included in the SCA file for releasing each unit. The SPLIT facility CCB may add to the list of elements. Deletions are made only with explicit approval of the SPLIT CCB.

Table 1
Definitions of Elements in SCA

Element Name	Definition
CI number	Number assigned for CI identification
Date	(1) Date change was released to the integration library
	(2) Date change was released to the production library
SCR number	The SCR number of the request/authority for making the change
Subapplication	The name or number assigned to the unit or portion of the CI being released
Release request	Date release was requested
Action requested	The control action requested by the development activity (builds, move to integration library, etc)
Programmer(s)	The names of the programmer(s) making the changes
Members	Names of modules, units affected by the change in the release
Change level	The change level or version number of the units being released
Justification	The number or the statement of justification concerning the reason for release
From library	The library location of the units before the release
Member type	The type of the unit being released (procedures, macros, test drivers)
Load module	The load module with which the unit will be linked
Verified by	Name of the person approving the verification
Verified system name	Identification of system used for testing change
Time tag	The time tag for the version of the unit being released

ANSI/IEEE
Std 1042-1987

Appendix D

Software Configuration Management Plan for a
Product Line System

Version 1.0

Approved

_____

Director, Engineering

_____

PLAS Program Manager

Date: ___ / ___ / ___

Synopsis

This example Plan contains a discussion of a hypothetical project in a microelectronics company that makes microprocessors and microprocessor-based systems that are later embedded within other hi-tech electronic systems. The company has approximately nineteen hundred employees, of which one hundred and thirty-four are in the engineering division and the remainder are in the production division, marketing, and administration group. There is an extensive investment in hardware CAD/CAM to make the operation productive and a lesser investment in computer-aided engineering (CAE). Office automation is used to minimize the costly handling of paper; therefore, most of the communication within the company uses electronic media. Customers buy hardware or systems — receiving software products only as part of a system.

There is no independent software development activity. Software technology is considered a basic skill that electronic engineers and system designers use in their day-to-day work. The engineers design software for execution within their system's RAM or ROM with the same ease as they use the silicon compilers to design chips. There are two focal points where the different engineering design technologies interact with the configuration management discipline. The first focal point is in the system's computer aided engineering system where the engineering libraries (where functional logic and piece/part information is maintained) or data bases and VLSI design systems are maintained. The second focal point is in the production computer aided manufacturing system where the programmed logic is transformed from compiled into deliverable products. The two focal points are separate as the mode of implementation demands different interfaces — the production system interfaces directly with the hardware CAD/CAM systems in production; the engineering system with the software/firmware development stations and prototype-testing stations. The configuration management software to support management of these data bases is largely embedded within the program management system, which schedules work and manages the changes to baselines.

In this environment, the software configuration management disciplines are just another one of the tools used by engineering and production management for performing their daily tasks. The software configuration management plan focuses primarily on establishing unique project data base structures in the engineering systems, routing the change management materials to named organizational positions for approvals, and defining data-base baselines. Software configuration management is a service provided by the engineering, production, and management systems to help management more effectively perform their tasks.

Contents

Appendix D

Software Configuration Management Plan for a
Product Line System

1. Introduction

This guide describes the plan for managing the configurations of stored program logic used in manufacturing the product line analysis system (PLAS) module. This module performs the computational, communications, and device-controller functions of a larger system — *The Quick Stretch*, which performs stress analysis for mechanical structures. This system is sold as a proprietary company product to customers and is maintained by field representatives of the company. The company intends that the PLAS module have functional flexibility through its use of computer programs to make the module adaptable to other company proprietary systems and possibly for sale to other systems manufacturers.

1.1 Purpose. This plan identifies the procedures for managing the configurations of the PLAS computer programs during their development and for maintenance of the programs throughout the time period the company sells and has warranty responsibility for the products that incorporate the PLAS as an embedded system.

1.2 Scope. This plan is applicable to the development and maintenance of all the computer programs embedded in ROM, loaded into EPROMS, or loaded into RAM for use in the PLAS module. Configuration management of the hardware associated with the PLAS module is covered in a PLAS hardware configuration management plan— PLAS-CMP. These computer programs, packaged in different media, are collectively managed under the single configuration item *PLAS software configuration item* regardless of their function. The computer programs packaged for ROM or EPROM are managed as hardware components, identified under their prime hardware configuration item identification. The support software used in production and test of the PLAS module components (both hardware and computer programs) is also controlled by this plan.

1.3 Definitions and Mnemonics

1.3.1 Definitions. The terms used in this plan conform to the definitions found in ANSI/IEEE Std 729-1983, *IEEE Standard Glossary of Software Engineering Terminology.*

hard logic. Programmed logic that is embedded as circuit logic in a chip. The logic is developed using the general software engineering tools and disciplines. Packaging of the logic uses silicon compilers for generating the geometry of the chip.

P-CAMS. The product computer aided manufacturing system (P-CAMS) environment that contains
(1) The engineering data bases of hard logic and stored-programmed logic defining the products in the production environment (the controlled libraries)
(2) The support software used in converting the controlled engineering data bases into instructions and data for
    (a) Production of chips, software and firmware
    (b) Test programs and data for verifying that the produced entities have been correctly implemented
User documentation is also produced using P-CAMS. Configuration management disciplines relating to product serialization, change labeling and tracking, and verification tests are a part of this environment.

project-management system (PMS). The PMS provides the capability for management to
(1) Define an identification schema for projects at start-up time and to make changes to the different schemes
(2) Authorize and control the release of project drawings and engineering data bases from the dynamic libraries in systems computer-aided engineering system (SCAES) to the controlled project libraries in P-CAMS

(3) Schedule the production and release of product changes, and coordinate the production schedules within the production division

In general, this system supports the configuration management change control board (CCB) and production scheduling activities.

stored program logic. Computer program instructions and data that are executed out of RAM, ROM, and EPROM in the PLAS module. The instructions and data are developed using general software engineering tools and disciplines. Packaging of the instructions and data uses technology appropriate for the media.

systems computer aided engineering system (SCAES). The SCAES environment is composed of

(1) A variety of engineering support software including different simulators, prototyping tools, modeling programs, engineering design aids, documentation tools, test generators, test simulators, utilities and compilers

(2) Engineering libraries (the **dynamic** libraries) that contain general algorithms that have widespread utility, reusable stored-programmed logic, reusable hard-logic functions, and access to selected product designs

(3) Design data bases representing the dynamic working libraries for product developments that are currently in progress (such as the PLAS module development)

The commands that are used in SCM disciplines for supporting identification of entities relating to a specific project and for tracking current versions of those entities are an integral part of SCAES.

1.3.2 Mnemonics. The following mnemonics are used within this document:

APM	Associate Program Manager
CAD/CAM	Computer-Aided Design/Computer-Aided Manufacturing
CAE	Computer-Aided Engineering
CAES	Computer-Aided Engineering Systems
CCB	Configuration Control Board
CI	Configuration Item
CM	Configuration Management
CMP	Configuration Management Plan
CMS	Change Management System
CSCI	Computer Software Configuration Item
DP&S	Data Processing and Support

EPROM	Erasable Programmable Read Only Memory
EWS	Engineering Work Stations
EWSW	Engineering Work Stations Environment
LSI	Large Scale Integration
MSI	Medium Scale Integration
P-CAM	Product Computer-Aided Manufacturing System
PLAS	Product Line Analysis System
PMS	Project Management System
QC	Quality Control
ROM	Read Only Memory
SCA	System Change Authorization
SCR	System Change Request
SCAES	Systems Computer-Aided Engineering System
TD	Technical Director
VDD	Version Description Document
VLSI	Very Large Scale Integration

1.4 References

[1] PLAS Functional Requirements.[18]

[2] Engineering Work Station and Environment User's Manual.

[3] Programming Standards Manual.

[4] Product Line Identification Numbering Standard.

[5] Software Quality Assurance Policy.

[6] Production Test Standards.

2. Management

2.1 Organization. The PLAS program manager of the product line has financial and administrative responsibility for all PLAS module engineering and production. He is part of the administration and reports directly to the general manager of the company. The company uses a matrix organization for managing projects.

The PLAS program manager has final responsibility for the business success of the program. The project staff consists of the financial staff, the technical director (TD), an associate program manager (APM), and a quality representative from the quality control (QC) department. The PLAS APM is functionally a part of the production division and attends all PLAS project meetings.

---

[18]All referenced documentation is available from the SCAES library.

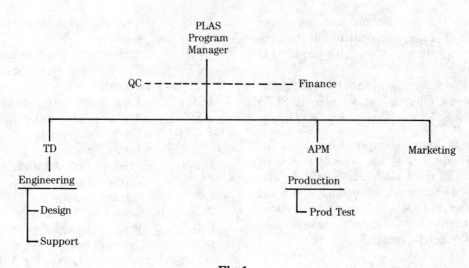

Fig 1
PLAS Organization Chart

The major elements in the administration, engineering division, and production division that support the PLAS product line include

(1) Marketing (administration) provides the sales and marketing support to

    (a) Perform market analyses and prepare functional requirements for the Quick Stretch System that indirectly determine the functional requirements for engineering the PLAS module

    (b) Maintain customer liaison for product maintenance and improvement and

    (c) Sell the Quick Stretch Systems

(2) The PLAS engineering design group (engineering division) is an ad hoc organization under the direction of the PLAS technical director, which provides engineering expertise to

    (a) Manage the overall system design activity

    (b) Develop the hard logic, the stored program logic, and drawings for PLAS assemblies

    (c) Review all proposed changes for feasibility, cost, and design integrity

    (d) Perform all necessary engineering design and logic changes

(3) The PLAS engineering support group (engineering division) provides the technicians and technical resources to

    (a) Maintain the SCAES_PLAS engineering data base

    (b) Perform product engineering based on design prototypes to be released for production

    (c) Support TD and PLAS program manager in verifying design changes prior to release to P-CAMS.

(4) The PLAS production group (production division) activity, under direction of the PLAS APM, provides the capability to

    (a) Manufacture hardware in accordance with PLAS drawings released for production

    (b) Compile, verify, and package programmed logic released as software for PLAS RAM

    (c) Compile, verify, and burn-in programmed logic released as firmware for PLAS EPROM

    (d) Compile, verify, and coordinate mask production or programmed logic released as firmware for PLAS ROM

    (e) Compile, verify, and coordinate production of hard logic released as VLSI chips

    (f) Test complete assemblies of PLAS modules

    (g) Maintain inventories

    (h) Ship PLAS modules to customers as directed by the PLAS program manager

The functions that are generally performed by a separate SCM activity and not supported by SCAES and PMS are shared between the quality control representative and the APM. This is possible because most of the detailed SCM processing activities and library interface management are accomplished by the PMS.

The PLAS technical director is the chairperson of the configuration control board (CCB). The PLAS identification scheme implemented in the SCAES control system is approved by the chairperson of the CCB. The responsibility for reviewing and approving all changes to established baselines and scheduling releases belongs to the CCB chairperson. Release of PLAS engineering data base(s) to P-CAMS and all changes to the P-CAMS data base for PLAS is authorized by the CCB chairperson.

2.2 SCM Responsibilities

(1) The PLAS program manager provides general direction to the TD for establishing the identification scheme, to the APM for production scheduling, and authorizes the establishment of baselines. The PLAS program manager also provides general direction to the TD for CCB actions and issues requests for QC to audit and review the integrity of the SCAES_PLAS engineering data base and the P-CAMS_PLAS production data base.

(2) The PLAS TD establishes the contract identification schema used by the PLAS project engineers and performs (or delegates to engineering support group) the duties of updating the P-CAMS_PLAS production data base when authorized by CCB actions. All changes to the P-CAMS_PLAS production data base are approved by the TD.

(3) The PLAS associate program manager (or a delegated assistant, such as a librarian) has overall responsibility for maintaining the P-CAM PLAS data base, PLAS unit and module tests, and production schedules.

(4) The production test group is responsible for testing the hardware assemblies, including the units containing the packages of programmed logic (ROM and EPROM), and verifying that the correct version of the logic is embedded in the device. The group also verifies that the diskettes containing the dynamically loadable software for the PLAS module is the correct version for shipment. Final assembly tests of these units along with VLSI chips are also conducted by this group.

(5) The PLAS quality control representative is responsible for reviewing the production test group's verification activities, and auditing the integrity and use of SCAES_PLAS engineering data base and P-CAMS_PLAS production data base. The QC representative verifies the physical configuration of the PLAS module, its associated user documentation, and its functional capabilities (review of module acceptance testing) as a part of the quality review prior to shipment.

(6) The engineering support group provides special extractions from the SCAES, P-CAMS and PMS systems data bases showing status of the various baselines when information other than that provided by general project status commands is required.

(7) The marketing organization provides the functional requirements for the system and is the major source of high-level system changes and improvements. In effect, this organization defines the functional baseline. Customers purchasing a PLAS module for their own use or for the PLAS module integration in the Quick Stretch System have no direct interface or review authority over PLAS baseline activities or product capabilities.

2.3 Interface Control. The data bases for the PLAS module are maintained in two different library systems: the SCAES_PLAS engineering data base and the P-CAMS_PLAS production data base. The interface between these two data bases is controlled by PLAS CCB authorizations.

The SCAES_PLAS engineering data base is made up of several parts representing

(1) Top-level drawing of the PLAS module
(2) Detail design representations of the programmed logic as it is to be packaged for implementation in ROM, EPROM, and RAM based software
(3) Detail designs for implementation in chips (LSI and VLSI designs)
(4) Electrical engineering drawings for cards and assemblies and
(5) Mechanical drawings for the module assemblies

The interfaces between these subdata bases are managed as developmental baselines during the engineering development phase of a PLAS module.

The interface with the Quick Stretch System, or with customer defined systems using the PLAS module, is defined by the top-drawing design data base. Changes in this interface are made only with the authority of the TD. In case of conflict, the PLAS program manager negotiates the changes with the appropriate system representative.

Interfaces with the P-CAMS_PLAS production data base and the computer-aided manufacturing software are managed by the APM in production division, as long as the changes do not affect the CAES_PLAS engineering data-base interface.

2.4 SCMP Implementation

2.4.1 PLAS Configuration Baselines. The functional baseline is established when the system level description for the PLAS module is approved by the general manager for prototype development. Marketing surveys and analyses of potential customer applications provide a description of the desired functional capabilities of the proposed system. The functional baseline is documented with the marketing analysis report, supplemented by a preliminary top-level drawing of a proposed system. This baseline is considered obsolete after acceptance of the preproduction baseline.

The allocated baseline is established upon approval of the top-level drawing and preliminary detailed designs, verified by simulation runs, by the PLAS program manager. This baseline is obsoleted after acceptance of the preproduction baseline.

The developmental baselines are established by the TD at his/her discretion as needed for coordinating the changing allocated baselines during development. The developmental baselines represent incremental software builds needed to develop the prototype system and to verify revisions to the production baseline or different models of the production baseline for various customer applications.

The preproduction baseline is established with the successful demonstration of a prototype system and an absence of any priority 1 (emergency) error reports or changes outstanding. The PLAS program manager authorizes development of the preproduction baseline when given the go-ahead by Marketing management.

The production baseline is established with the concurrence of the PLAS APM and PLAS TD that the design is functionally adequate and that the production facilities of the production division can produce the design in an economical way. The production baseline is a formal agreement between the PLAS program manager and the production division manager.

2.4.2 The Configuration Control Board. The PLAS technical director is the chairperson of the PLAS CCB. This review activity is established at the initiation of preproduction model development.

2.4.3 The Support Environment. The SCAES environment consists of a compatible set of engineering and software development tools that can work with the general engineering data base and special data bases set up for different projects, such as PLAS. The configuration of this support software environment is most carefully controlled by the company data processing and support (DP & S) organization. The support software that interfaces with the data-base management system is most rigidly controlled but there is latitude for engineers to develop special programs restricted to engineering work stations (EWS), that do not generate data for entry into the dynamic engineering data bases. Access keys for controlling entry to the SCAES_PLAS engineering data base are assigned to responsible engineers at the onset of allocated baseline development.

The P-CAMS environment interfaces with a wide variety of CAM and computer-aided test (CAT) systems. These interfaces are critical for the reliable management and administration of company operations. The company DP & S organization manages these interfaces. Any changes must be approved (among other approvals) by the PLAS APM. This review activity is initiated with the development of the preproduction baseline.

Vendor software is used extensively in the supporting software environments of CAES and P-CAMS. Vendor software is also used extensively in the EWS environment supporting SCAES. The management of the vendor software in the EWS environment that is not under the control of the company DP & S organization is initiated by the PLAS TD after the preproduction baseline is established.

2.4.4 SCM Resource Requirements. The resources required for providing configuration management of the PLAS module development and production are embedded in the requirements for training, management oversight, computer resources, administrative support from the engineering support group and DP & S maintenance.

(1) *Training requirements.* Approximately two days training is needed for a new hire engineer to become familiar with use of the data bases and control programs relative to managing configurations. This time is allocated as a part of the overall training program for new hires.

(2) *Management oversight.* Approximately two hours a week are spent on CCB reviews and six hours a week using the PMS control program to schedule analysis and imple-

mentation of system change requests (SCR).

(3) *Computer resources.* Storage requirements for configuration data are a small part of the engineering and production data bases for PLAS modules. The requirements for processor time varies from day to day, but generally does not exceed three minutes of CPU time per day for processing each SCR.

(4) *Support software maintenance.* DP & S is budgeted three man-years effort per year for maintaining the software used for PLAS module configuration management.

2.5 Applicable Policies, Directives, and Procedures

2.5.1 Existing Policies and Procedures. The following company policies are used for configuration management on the PLAS subsystem:

(1) Product Line Identification Numbering — Supplement 2

(2) Corporate Software Protection Policy (Rev 3)

(3) Quality Control Policy for Engineering Data Bases

(4) Production Test Standards

(5) Engineering Standards for Detail Design and Drawings

(6) User's Manual for SCAES

(7) User's Manual for EWS

(8) User's Manual for P-CAMS

2.5.2 New Policies and Procedures To Be Written. The following procedure(s) will be developed for the PLAS project:

(1) Managing of Third-Party Software: Proprietary Marking

(2) PLAS Project Naming Standards

3. SCM Activities

3.1 Configuration Identification. The identification scheme for the PLAS project is developed by the engineering support group and approved by the PLAS TD. The numbering and labeling standards are distributed for project use in the *PLAS Project Naming Standards document*.

3.1.1 Naming Conventions. All data in the SCAES_PLAS engineering data base is arranged and retrievable under the collective identifier PLAS-1800000.

All control level items (programmed logic components and hardware assemblies) are identified within a block of numbers beginning with 532000 and ending with 554000. The engineering support group allocates the numbers for the control level items.

Programmed-logic components have a version description document (VDD) associated with their assigned number. Each assigned number has a preceeding letter identifying the media in which the logic is embedded:

ROM = R
EPROM = E
Diskette[19] = S
Gate arrays = G
PLA = P
Programmable microcontrollers = M

Hardware drawing numbers are assigned to a control level drawing. Parts list for the drawing is made up of part numbers assigned from the 700000 series of numbers.

Reprogrammed logic components keep their basic 1000 number assigned to them in the general SCAES engineering data base. Dash numbers, referencing appropriate VDD, tracks embedded CI, and associated SCR.

3.1.2 Implementation. Identification is assigned to each component and unit defined in the top-level drawing. When an engineer defines a unit, he/she indicates to the program the type of component he/she is defining and the system assigns the appropriate number. Programmed login associated with a defined hardware component or unit is linked to that component's identifier in a *packaging list* associated with the top-level drawing.

Components and units are identified by form, fit, and function (data flow). The engineer defining a component or unit is automatically made *owner* of that component or unit. Changes in the form, fit, or function cannot be made without his/her consent and approval of change. The CAES design tools automatically flag conflicts and force resolution before another of the iterative development baselines can be created.

All system entities associated with the design (specifications, drawings, detail documentation, test data, test procedures, etc) are assigned the appropriate component or unit identifier with which they are associated.

The identifiers assigned in the SCAES_PLAS engineering data base are transferred to the P-CAMS_PLAS production data base at the time

---

[19]Used for shipping software that executes out of RAM. Software media characteristics may vary but the implementation designator is always *S*.

the preproduction baseline definition effort is initiated.

3.1.3 Ownership Notification Procedures.

Filing of software copyright notices for proprietary programmed logic developed for the PLAS project will be performed by Marketing.

Notification to users of the PLAS module copyright will be included in the load module of the software released to the user on the PLAS module diskette. Visual indication of ownership and copyright registration will be displayed at the console when the system is booted, in accordance with Revision 3 (current) of the corporate software protection policy.

All documentation released to customers will be marked with a proprietary notice, vendor license number, or both.

3.2 Configuration Control.

Authority for approving changes to baselines varies in accordance with the baseline being changed and the phase of the project.

(1) Authority for approving changes to the *functional baseline* is vested in the PLAS program manager. The PLAS program manager coordinates all changes with the production department manager and with the PLAS TD. This baseline is obsoleted with the initiation of the production baseline.

(2) Authority for approving changes to the *allocated baseline* is vested in the PLAS TD. The PLAS TD coordinates all changes in the allocated baseline with the PLAS program manager and PLAS APM for production. This baseline is shared by SCAES and P-CAMS during the period after the preproduction demonstration is accepted and the production baseline is formally defined.

(3) Authority for approving changes to *developmental baselines* is vested in the PLAS TD. The PLAS TD establishes the developmental baseline criteria, resolves conflicts in allocation and ownership of components or units, and sets schedules for iteration of these baselines.

(4) Authority for approving changes to the *preproduction baseline* is vested in the PLAS TD. The PLAS TD makes changes in allocation and detail design to fit the production facilities on the recommendation of the PLAS APM from production division. Conflicts are resolved by the PLAS program manager.

(5) Authority for approving changes to the *PLAS production baseline* is vested in the PLAS CCB, chaired by the PLAS TD. The PLAS APM and PLAS marketing representative are members of the PLAS CCB. Technical representation from PLAS engineering and PLAS production activities are made when necessary. The PLAS QC representative and production test group representative are permanent members of the PLAS CCB.

Technical review of the system change requests (SCR) is provided by members of the engineering support group who assemble engineering analyses as required, and by members of the PLAS production team who assemble information on the impact of a proposed SCR as required

3.2.1 Change Processing.

Changes to the system may originate from the marketing organization (in response to customer desires), from the test group in the production division, or from within the engineering division. Requests for changes are submitted by way of electronic mail using the SCR format provided in the EWS environment. Changes originating from outside the company are entered into the program management system (PMS) by marketing representatives. Internally originated changes are submitted by way of local engineering work stations.

The PMS control system routes SCR to the originator's supervisor for verification when appropriate, and then queues it for review and disposition by the appropriate change authority for the affected baseline. When change requests require further analysis, the change authority routes the SCR (electronically) to the appropriate support group for gathering information. When the support group has assembled a complete analysis package, it is again queued to the appropriate review authority or CCB for disposition. This authority then disposes of the request by indicating approval (providing a schedule and effectivity date of change), deferring it for further analysis or allocation of resources, or disapproving it with reason(s) for disapproval noted.

Approved changes are electronically routed to the PLAS engineering group for implementation.

The tracking of changes is performed in the PMS control system, based on the SCR approval flow status and system change authorizations (SCA), or by extractions from the PLAS data bases in SCAES or P-CAMS to which it has access.

3.2.2 Production Baseline Changes.

Changes to the production baseline are made only after changes have been verified in a test environment on a test model of the PLAS module, using simulated test drivers or mock-ups to test the system.

Table 1
Processing Approved Changes

Baseline	Entity	Implemented By	Verified By	Scheduled By
Functional	Document	Engineering	Eng check	Various
Allocated	Document	Engineering	Eng check	Various
Developmental	Document	Engineering	Eng check	TD
	Design data	Engineering	Simulation	TD
	Drawings	Engineering	Eng check	TD
Preproduction	Document	Eng or prod	Eng check	TD
	Design data	Engineering	Simulation	TD
	Drawings	Engineering	Eng check	TD
Production	Document	Production	Test Gp	APM
	Design data	Engineering	Test Gp	APM
	Drawings	Engineering	Eng check	APM

The production test group verifies the changes as operational and authorizes release of the change data from the SCAES_PLAS engineering data base to the P-CAMS_PLAS production data base. The transfer of data is performed by the engineering support group.

3.2.3 PLAS Module Release. Each PLAS module version is released for use in a Quick Stretch System or to individual customers for incorporation into their systems, along with a technical data kit containing the top-level drawings of the system, associated parts lists, and the VDD for control level programmed logic components.

Since PLAS software, released on diskettes, provides the most flexible means of adaptation, provisions exist to release the software VDD independently of the rest of the data packages. This way, revisions to the PLAS functions can be made to PLAS modules in systems released previously. This requires that the configuration of all released modules be maintained in an archive, along with an extraction from the P-CAMS configuration environment containing all support software used in the production and test of that delivery.

3.3 Configuration Status Accounting. The following PLAS configuration status reports are regularly available:

(1) *PLAS Module Development Status.* This is a listing of all configuration items, control level items, and units that are being designed or modified by engineering. The report identifies each unit/control-level-item/CI, status of technical work, outstanding SCR, SCA ready for release, and units or changes released since the last reporting period. This report is generated weekly for the PLAS management team.

(2) *PLAS Module Production Status.* This is a listing of all configuration items, control level items and units that are in production. The report identifies all units in production during the period, SCR/SCA incorporated, scheduled release date (by contract number), and schedule variance. The report is generated weekly for the PLAS management team.

(3) *SCR Status Summary.* This report lists all outstanding SCR that have not been resolved or incorporated into delivered modules. The report lists, for each SCR: CCB action date and disposition; group or department presently responsible for action; status of activity; and schedule for completion. The report is prepared weekly but is available any time the PLAS management team requests it.

(4) *Special Queries.* The report generator of the PMS program provides a query capability that allows anyone to extract the status of:

(a) Any one SCR
(b) All open SCR
(c) All SCR in engineering
(d) All SCR in production
(e) PLAS modules in production with associated SCR number

The general query capability for the data-management systems allow formulation of special queries in the PMS control program for interrogating the SCAES_PLAS engineering data base and the P-CAMS_PLAS production data base for information relative to any changes that are in process or that have been released to customers.

3.4 Audits and Reviews

3.4.1 Audits. The PLAS module configuration is audited each time a baseline is established.

(1) *Functional Baseline.* The PLAS program manager is responsible for ascertaining if the reports and design descriptions are complete enough to present to management.

(2) *Allocated Baselines.* The PLAS technical director is responsible for reviewing the designs to ascertain if the designs are complete enough to present to the PLAS program manager. The engineering support group assists the TD in this review.

(3) *Developmental Baselines.* The engineering support group uses the PMS control program to

(a) Generate set/use type analyses of the detailed designs to uncover outstanding discrepancies and

(b) Establish design activity cut-offs for a specific iteration.

This group also supports the changes by modifying access codes to the new baseline to restrict entry of changes. The TD reviews the summaries of design activities to estimate technical progress in the design.

(4) *Preproduction Baseline.* Prior to establishing the preproduction baseline, the configuration is again audited by the engineering support group to ascertain that the design of the demonstration meets all functional requirements established by the functional baseline and that all entities generated in the developmental baselines are present or accounted for in the demonstration. The QC representative assists in the review of entities for this baseline.

(5) *Production Baseline.* The QC representative reviews the entities in the P-CAMS_ PLAS production data base to ascertain that all functional capabilities demonstrated for the preproduction model and all changes stemming from the review of the demonstration are present in the data base. The production test group reviews the entities to verify that all changes and modifications to the preproduction demonstration have been made to the production data base. The engineering support group performs a comparison of the engineering data base with the production data base to verify that the transfer of data is complete. The PLAS TD is responsible for preparing this audit.

(6) *Shipping Review.* The PLAS module and its associated documentation package is audited prior to shipment to a customer, either as a part of the Quick Stretch System or as an independent line item to a customer.

The functional audit is performed by the QC representative who reviews the PLAS module against the appropriate extracted data from the P-CAM_PLAS library for that item. A representative from the PLAS engineering support group reviews the product to ascertain that the physical configuration of the module and its associated documentation represents

(a) The specified configuration ordered by the customer

(b) The corresponding configuration in the P-CAMS_PLAS data base and

(c) Accurately reflects any changes that have been made to the data base by the PLAS CCB

Discrepancies or problems uncovered in reviews and audits are reported to the PLAS program manager for resolution.

4. Tools, Techniques, and Methodologies

The basic configuration management tool used for PLAS module is the change management program (CMP), which is a part of the PMS. This program supports change management by

(1) Providing the means to enter system/software change requests (SCR)

(2) Forcing reviews by appropriate supervision by way of the electronic mail system

(3) Deriving analytical data from each SCR

(4) Providing for supervision or CCB review and approval, as appropriate

(5) Directing authorized changes to engineering or production supervision

(6) Providing for authorizing of changes to the P-CAMS_PLAS data base

(7) Providing for transfering data from the PLAS engineering data base to the production data base

The SCM tool for establishing the identification scheme for PLAS data bases is resident in the SCAES system. This information is transferred to the production data base during the preproduction phase. It is verified when the production baseline is established.

Order information from marketing is entered into the PLAS production schedule by way of the program management system. The detailed configuration is formatted by the configuration management program in CMS, passed on to the P-CAMS_ PLAS data base upon approval of the PLAS program manager, and reviewed for schedule and resource consumption by the PLAS APM. Upon his/her approval, resources are committed to the production configuration. Extractions of this configuration are released for inspection and auditing at time of shipment.

5. Supplier Control

Subcontracted PLAS support software is placed under configuration management after inspection and acceptance by the QC representative.

6. Records Collection and Retention

6.1 Backup Data Base. The engineering data base from SCAES_PLAS is backed-up on a weekly basis and stored in Beskin's storage building during the engineering phase (up to the time the production baseline is established). Following establishment of the production baseline, the engineering data base is backed-up on a monthly basis.

The production data base from P-CAMS_PLAS is backed-up on a weekly basis.

6.2 Archive Data Base. Archive data is maintained for purposes of warranty protection, proprietary data production, and liability insurance. The following data are maintained in on-line optical storage media:

(1) Copies of each baseline data base extracted at the time the baseline is established
(2) Copies of order and configuration data passed from PMS to the production data base for each order and
(3) Copies of each configuration of the data base used for production of customer order
(4) Copies of reviews and audits performed on each production item

Appendix E

References Bibliography

Preface

This Appendix contains selected bibliography pertaining to the subject of software configuration management. The list of publications contains both government and private sector references so users may find material applicable to their situation. Because of the scarcity of literature pertaining to configuration management, and especially to software configuration management, the fullest possible list of references will be useful to the practitioner.

Most of the references contain some information regarding software configuration management. The topic of software configuration management plans is addressed in a subset of these references.

References Bibliography

E1. General Bibliography

[1] BERSOFF, E., HENDERSON, V., and SIEGEL, S. *Software Configuration Management, An Investment in Product Integrity*. Englewood, N.J.: Prentice-Hall, 1980.

[2] BERSOFF, E., HENDERSON, V., and SIEGEL, S. *Software Configuration Management: A Tutorial*. Computer, *IEEE Computer Society Magazine*, vol 12 no 1, Jan 1979.

[3] *Configuration Management Procedures (CMP)*, Global Engineering Documents, 1984.

[4] *IEEE Transactions on Software Engineering*, IEEE Computer Society, vol SE-10, nr 1, Jan 1984.

[5] BUCKLE, J. K. *Software Configuration Management*, New York: The Macmillan Press Ltd, 1982.

[6] DANIELS, M. A. *Principles of Configuration Management*, Advanced Applications Consultants, Inc, 1987.

[7] BABICH, W. A. *Software Configuration Management*: Coordination for Team Productivity, New York: Addison-Wesley, 1986.

E2. Military Standards for SCM[20]

[8] MIL-STD-481A Configuration Control—Engineering Changes, Deviations, and Waivers (Short Form).

[9] MIL-STD-482A Configuration Status Accounting Data Elements and Related Features.

[10] MIL-STD-483A Configuration Management Practices for Systems Equipment, Munitions, and Computer Programs.

[11] MIL-STD-490A Specification Practices.

[12] MIL-STD-499A Engineering Management.

[13] MIL-STD-881A Work Breakdown Structure.

[14] MIL-STD-962A Outline of Forms and Instructions for the Preparation of Military Standards and Military Documents.

[15] MIL-STD-1456 Contractor Configuration Management Plan.

---

[20] Military Standards may be ordered from the Commanding Officer (Code 301) Naval Publications and Forms Center, 5801 Tabor Avenue, Philadelphia, PA 19120.

[16] MIL-STD-1521B Technical Reviews and Audits for Systems, Equipments, and Computer Programs.

E3. Department of Defense Standards

[17] DoD-STD-480 Configuration Control-Engineering Changes, Deviations and Waivers.

[18] DoD-STD-1467 Software Support Environment.

[19] DoD-STD-2167 Defense System Software Development.

[20] DoD-STD-2168 Software Quality Evaluation.

[21] DoD-STD-7935 Automated Data Systems Documentation.

E4. Military Specification

[22] MIL-D-1000B Drawings, Engineering, and Associated List.

[23] MIL-S-83490 Specifications, Types and Forms.

E5. Department of Defense Directives

[24] DoDD 4120.21 Specifications and Standards Applications.

[25] DoDD 5000.1 Major Systems Applications.

[26] DoDD 5000.19L Acquisition Management Systems and Data Requirements Control List.

[27] DoDD 5000.39 Acquisition and Management of Integrated Logistic Support for Systems and Equipment.

[28] DoDD 5010.19 Configuration Management.

[29] DoDD 7920.1 Life Cycle Management of Automated Information Systems (AIS).

E6. Department of Defense Instructions

[30] DoDI 5000.2 Major Systems Acquisition Process.

[31] DoDI 5000.38 Production Readiness Reviews.

[32] DoDI 7045.7 The Planning, Programming and Budgeting System.

[33] DoDI 7935.1 DoD Automated Data Systems Documentation Standards.

E7. US Government Publications[21]

[34] DoD Configuration Management Standardization Program, (CMAM) Plan.

[35] DoD Trusted Computer System Evaluation Criteria, CSC-STD-001-83, 15 Aug 1983.

[36] *NASA Handbook 8040.2.* System Engineering Management Guide, Defense System Management College, 1983. Configuration Management, Management Instruction, GMI8040.1A. NASA Goddard Space Flight Center.

[37] Federal Information Processing Standards (FIPS) *Publication 106.* Guideline on Software Maintenance, National Bureau of Standards. Institute for Computer Sciences and Technology, 1984.

[38] MARTIN, R. and OSBORNE, W. *Special Publication 500-106,* Guidance on Software Maintenance. National Bureau of Standards, Institute for Computer Sciences and Technology, 1983.

[39] McCALL, JIM, HERNDON, MARY, and OSBORNE, WILMA. *Special Publication 500-129,* Software Maintenance Management, National Bureau of Standards, Institute for Computer Sciences and Technology, 1985.

---

[21] Copies of these publications can be obtained from the Superintendent of Documents, US Governmental Printing Office, Washington, DC 20402.

E8. Electronic Industries Association Publications[22]

[40] EIA CMB 4-1a (Sept 1984), Configuration Management Definitions for Digital Computer Programs.

[41] EIA CMB 4-2 (June 1981), Configuration Identification for Digital Computer Programs.

[42] EIA CMB 4-3 (Feb 1981), Computer Software Libraries.

[43] EIA CMB 4-4 (May 1982), Configuration Change Control for Digital Computer Programs.

[44] EIA CMB 5 (April 1973), Subcontractor/Vendor Configuration Management and Technical Data Requirements.

---

[22]EIA publications can be obtained from the Standards Sales Department, Electronics Industries Association, 2001 Eye Street, NW, Washington DC 20006.

E9. American Defense Preparedness Association Publications[23]

[45] Proceedings of the 24th Annual Meeting, Technical Documentation Division, May 1982, Denver, Colorado.

[46] Proceedings of the 25th Annual Meeting, Technical Documentation Division, May 1983, Ft. Monroe, Virginia.

[47] Proceedings of the 26th Annual Meeting, Technical Documentation Division, May 1984, San Antonio, Texas.

---

[23]Copies of these publications can be obtained from the American Defense Preparedness Association, 1700 N. Monroe St, Suite 900, Arlington, VA 22209.

IEEE Standard for Software Productivity Metrics

Sponsor

**Software Engineering Standards Subcommittee
of the
Technical Committee on Software Engineering
of the
IEEE Computer Society**

Approved September 17, 1992

IEEE Standards Board

Abstract: A consistent way to measure the elements that go into computing software productivity is defined. Software productivity metrics terminology are given to ensure an understanding of measurement data for both source code and document production. Although this standard prescribes measurements to characterize the software process, it does not establish software productivity norms, nor does it recommend productivity measurements as a method to evaluate software projects or software developers. This standard does not measure the quality of software. This standard does not claim to improve productivity, only to measure it. The goal of this standard is for a better understanding of the software process, which may lend insight to improving it.
Keywords: attribute, primitive, productivity ratio, source statement, staff-hour

The Institute of Electrical and Electronics Engineers, Inc.
345 East 47th Street, New York, NY 10017-2394, USA

Introduction

(This introduction is not a part of IEEE Std 1045-1992, IEEE Standard for Software Productivity Metrics.)

This introduction is intended to provide the reader with some background into the rationale used to develop the standard. This information is being provided to aid in the understanding and usage of the standard. The introduction is nonbinding.

This standard defines a framework for measuring and reporting software productivity. It focuses on definitions of how to measure software productivity and what to report when giving productivity results. It is meant for those who want to measure the productivity of the software process in order to create code and documentation products.

Past software productivity metrics have not proven as useful as desired to provide insight into the software process. Although there is an accumulation of more than 20 years of data, consistent productivity indicators for software development have not emerged from this information. The problem is not as much the fault of the metrics being used as it is the inaccuracy and incompleteness of the data being collected.

The definition of productivity states that it is the ratio of a unit of output to a unit of input used to produce the output. For this relationship to be useful for software, the data used in it must be accurate and complete. For instance, reported software productivity of 5000 lines of source code per year leaves many questions unanswered, *What is a line of source code? How long, in work hours, was the year? What activities were included? Whose effort was counted?*

Interpreting productivity based on a single number leaves much unknown about the process being measured. Without knowing the scope and characteristics of the process measured, or the precision of the data used in the calculations, the resulting productivity values are inconclusive.

The goal of this standard is to build a foundation to accurately measure software productivity. This is done through a set of precisely defined units of measure. However, not all software processes lend themselves to precise measurement. Software development is a new and rapidly evolving field, and it is strongly influenced by the variability of the people who build the software. In those situations where precise measurement definitions are not possible, this standard requests that descriptions of the processes used and the measurements taken be done in a specified format.

The intention of the standard is to formalize the presentation of productivity data so that it is useful to anyone wishing to improve the software process. This standard is not an end in itself. Instead, it is the beginning of increased precision in collecting and reporting software productivity data. The hope is that this will lead to an improved understanding of the software development process and to improved productivity metrics.

Participants

At the time this standard was completed, the Software Productivity Metrics Working Group had the following membership:

Robert N. Sulgrove, *Chair*   **Christine H. Smith,** *Co-chair*
Eleanor Antreassian, *Past Chair*   **Nicholas L. Marselos,** *Editor*

Bakul Banerjee	John E. Gaffney, Jr.	Jainendra K. Navlakha
Stephen E. Blake	Stuart Glickman	Dennis E. Nickle
Thomas P. Bowen	Lennor Gresham	Richard Reese
David N. Card	Stuart Jeans	Julian Roberts
Thomas J. Carlton	Robert W. Judge	Brian Sakai
Deborah Caswell	Lawrence King	Sylvia Shiroyama
Mike Demshki	Thomas M. Kurihara	Paul Stevens
Sherman Eagles	Arnold W. Kwong	Wolfgang B. Strigel
Ruth S. Euler	Fred Lau	Leonard L. Tripp
Michael Evangelist	Chi Yun Lin	Scott A. Whitmire
Al Freund	Denis C. Meredith	Ron Willis
James T. Fritsch	Lois J. Morton	Paul Wolfgang
	Andrew Najberg	

Contributors

The following individuals also contributed to the development of the standard:

William W. Agresti	Jack Harrington	Randy Paddock
Lowell Jay Arthur	Warren Harrison	Bruce Parker
Jeff A. Aune	Bruce Healton	Bud W. Pezet
Victor R. Basili	Francis B. Herr	Wes Philp
Mordechai Ben-Menachem	Herman Hess	Robert M. Poston
Victor G. Berecz	Geoffrey W. Higgin	Lawrence H. Putnam
Robert C. Birss	John W. Horch	Donald J. Reifer
Bob Bisschoff	David Hurst	Niall Ross
Barry Boehm	Randall W. Jensen	Vince Rupolo
George Bozoki	Bud Jones	Norman F. Schneidewind
Fred Burke	T. Capers Jones	Roger Scholten
Neva Carlson	Bill Junk	David J. Schultz
Sally Cheung	Motti Y. Klein	Suzanne E. Schwab
Rutherford Cooke	Phil Kolton	Carl Seddio
Charles D'Argenio	Steven E. Kreutzer	Al Serna
James B. Dolkas	Walt Kutz	Jean Shaffer
Carl Einar Dragstedt	Robert L. Lanphar, Jr.	Vincent Y. Shen
Christof Ebert	F. C. Lim	Josef Sherif
Violet Foldes	Michael Lyu	David M. Siefert
Andrew S. Fortunak	Andy Mahindru	Vijaya K. Srivastava
Robert Fraley	Jukka Marijarvi	Edwin J. Summers
Jack Fried	Phillip C. Marriott	David Swinney
Jean A. Gilmore	Roger J. Martin	Robert C. Tausworthe
Clell Gladson	Robert F. Martini	C. L. Troyanowski
J. G. Glynn	Joseph F. Mathews	Dolores Wallace
Robert Grady	Bruce Millar	Richard Werling
Dan Grigore	James Miller	John Westergaard
Amal Gupta	Robert C. Natale	Clyde E. Willis
Nash Hair	Stephen R. Neuendorf	William Wong
H. D. Hall	Ken O'Brien	Weider Yu

Sponsoring Organizations

The following persons were on the balloting committee that approved this standard for submission to the IEEE Standards Board:

M. Amaya
B. Banerjee
L. Beltracchi
M. Ben-Menache
R. Birss
S. Blake
W. Boll
R. Both
F. Buckley
D. Card
N. Carlson
W. Chung
F. Coallier
P. Daggett
B. Derganc
C. Ebert
R. Euler
W. Eventoff
F. Frati
R. Fries
J. Gaffney, Jr.
Y. Gershkovitch
A. Godin
D. Gustafson
W. Harrison
W. Hefley
P. Hinds
J. Horch

C. Kemerer
R. Kessler
L. King
T. Kurihara
L. Lam
R. Lamb
J. Lane
J. Lawrence
F.C. Lim
B. Livson
D. Look
M. Lyu
J. Maayan
H. Mains
N. Marselos
R. Martin
T. Matsubara
I. Mazza
L. Miller
A. Najberg
J. Navlakha
D. Nickle
P. Petersen
S. Redwine
R. Reese
D. Reifer
B. Sakai
R. San Roman
J. Sanz

H. Schaefer
N. Schneidewind
G. Schumacher
C. Seddio
R. Shillato
S. Shiroyama
D. Siefert
C. Smith
V. Srivastava
W. Strigel
R. Sulgrove
W. Thetford
G. Trebble
L. Tripp
M. Updike
R. Van Scoy
D. Wallace
J. Walz
S. Whitmire
P. Work
A. Yonda
W. Yu
L. Heselton
C. Hu
W. Perry
I. Trandafir
A. Wainberg
P. Zoll

When the IEEE Standards Board approved this standard on Sept. 17, 1992, it had the following membership:

Marco W. Migliaro, *Chair*   **Donald C. Loughry,** *Vice Chair*
Andrew G. Salem, *Secretary*

Dennis Bodson
Paul L. Borrill
Clyde Camp
Donald C. Fleckenstein
Jay Forster*
David F. Franklin
Ramiro Garcia
Thomas L. Hannan

Donald N. Heirman
Ben C. Johnson
Walter J. Karplus
Ivor N. Knight
Joseph Koepfinger*
Irving Kolodny
D. N. "Jim" Logothetis
Lawrence V. McCall

T. Don Michael*
John L. Rankine
Wallace S. Read
Ronald H. Reimer
Gary S. Robinson
Martin V. Schneider
Terrance R. Whittemore
Donald W. Zipse

*Member Emeritus

Also included are the following nonvoting IEEE Standards Board liaisons:

Satish K. Aggarwal
James Beall
Richard B. Engelman
David E. Soffrin
Stanley Warshaw

Rachel Auslander
IEEE Standards Project Editor

Contents

IEEE Standard for Software Productivity Metrics

1. Overview

This standard describes the data collection process and calculations for measuring software productivity. This standard is divided into eight clauses. Clause 1 provides the scope of this standard. Clause 2 lists references to other standards that are useful in applying this standard. Clause 3 provides an abbreviated set of definitions and acronyms defined more fully in the standard, but provided here as a quick reference. Clause 4 provides an introduction to the standard's measurement approach. Clause 5 describes data collection for measuring output. Clause 6 describes data collection for measuring input. Clause 7 describes productivity results represented by ratios of outputs to inputs. Clause 8 provides a method to capture the characteristics of the software process to better understand their effects on productivity results.

This standard also contains four annexes. These provide additional information for understanding and using this standard, but they are not part of the standard. Annex A is a data collection form for recording quantitative metrics data defined in this standard, and Annex B is a data collection form for recording the characteristics data defined in this standard. Annex C contains a bibliography of some of the many references used in developing this standard. Annex D describes a counting method for the relationships defined in the standard.

1.1 Scope

Measuring software productivity is similar to measuring other forms of productivity; that is, it is measured as the ratio of units of output divided by units of input. The inputs consist of the effort expended to produce a given output. For software, the tangible outputs are source code and documentation. Of course the product of software is a process, an algorithm that drives a computer to do work. Unfortunately, understanding of the functionality incorporated into a software product is still rudimentary. Only by understanding what can be measured will it be possible to understand the essence of the software process.

Toward this end, this document standardizes software productivity metrics terminology to ensure an understanding of measurement data for both code and documentation production. It defines a set of units to measure the output products and input effort.

The lowest level of measurement defined in this standard is called a *primitive*. The output primitives measured are software source statements, documentation pages, and, optionally, function points. The input primitives measure the efforts of those developing the software products. The capacity and capability of automated support tools are not directly measured by this standard, but are indirectly measured by the improvements in the productivity of the people who use them.

This standard prescribes measurements to characterize the software process, and in doing so gives insight for improving it. This standard does not establish software productivity norms, nor does it recommend productivity measurements as a method to evaluate software projects or software developers.

Although the overall value of a product cannot be separated from the quality of what is produced, this standard does not measure the quality of software. The issue of measuring quality is beyond the scope of this standard, because it covers a different aspect of the software process. Nevertheless, productivity metrics should be interpreted in the context of the overall quality of the product. It is left to the user of this standard to look to other standards covering quality metrics for that information.

The definition of productivity as the ratio of product to effort was selected in this standard because it is more stable than value relationships like product to monetary units or production to sales. The effects of inflation on the value of monetary units, or the caprice of the marketplace on sales, cause these measures to vary unpredictably. As a result, they do not offer a stable measure over time. However, the quantity of the product and the effort in hours expended to produce it are more consistent measures, and over time these measures will provide a better gauge of software productivity. Users may wish to translate productivity into monetary equivalents, but results shall be reported in the units specified in this standard.

The metrics in this standard apply equally well to new development and to the enhancement or maintenance of an existing software product. Subsequent releases or changes to a released or delivered software product should be viewed as a new product for the purpose of applying these metrics.

This standard defines a consistent way to measure the elements that go into computing software productivity. A consistent measurement process will lead to a better understanding of the software development process, and a better understanding will lead to improvement. This standard does not claim to improve productivity, only to measure it.

1.2 Terminology

The words *shall*, *must*, and words in the imperative form identify the mandatory (essential) material within this standard. The words *should* and *may* identify optional (conditional) material. As with other IEEE Software Engineering Standards, the terminology in this document is based on the IEEE Std 610.12-1990.[1] To avoid inconsistency when the glossary is revised, the definitions are not repeated in this document. New terms and modified definitions as applied in this standard are included in clause 3.

1.3 Audience

This standard should be of interest to software development managers, software productivity and process assessment personnel, quality assurance personnel, software engineering improvement personnel, and researchers.

2. References

This standard shall be used in conjunction with the following publications:

IEEE Std 610.12-1990, IEEE Standard Glossary of Software Engineering Terminology (ANSI).

IEEE Std 1074-1991, IEEE Standard for Developing Software Life Cycle Processes (ANSI).

---

[1]Information on references can be found in clause 2.

3. Definitions

This clause contains key terms as they are used in this standard.

3.1 activities: Events in the software life cycle for which effort data is collected and reported.

3.2 added source statements: The count of source statements that were created specifically for the software product.

3.3 attributes: Measurable characteristics of a primitive.

3.4 characteristics: Those inherent factors of software development that may have a significant impact on productivity.

3.5 comment source statements: Source statements that provide information to people reading the software source code and are ignored by the compiler.

3.6 compiler directive source statements: Source statements that define macros, or labels, or direct the compiler to insert external source statements (for example, an *include* statement), or direct conditional compilation, or are not described by one of the other type attributes.

3.7 data declaration source statements: Source statements that reserve or initialize memory at compilation time.

3.8 deleted source statements: Source statements that are removed or modified from an existing software product as a new product is constructed.

3.9 delivered source statements: Source statements that are incorporated into the product delivered to the customer.

3.10 developed source statements: Source statements that are newly created for, added to, or modified for a software product.

3.11 direct staff-hour: The amount of effort directly expended in creating a specific output product.

3.12 document page count: The total number of nonblank pages contained in a hard-copy document.

3.13 document screen count: The total number of page images for electronically displayed documents.

3.14 documents: Hard copy, screen images, text, and graphics used to convey information to people.

3.15 executable source statements: Source statements that direct the actions of the computer at run time.

3.16 function point: A measure of the delivered software functionality.

3.17 granularity: The depth or level of detail at which data is collected.

3.18 incremental productivity: The productivity computed periodically during development.

3.19 input primitive: The effort to develop software products, expressed in units of staff-hours.

3.20 logical source statements (LSS): Source statements that measure software instructions independently of the physical format in which they appear.

3

3.21 modified source statements: Original source statements that have been changed.

3.22 new source statements: The sum of the added and modified source statements.

3.23 nondelivered source statements: Source statements that are developed in support of the final product, but not delivered to the customer.

3.24 nondeveloped source statements: Existing source statements that are reused or deleted.

3.25 origin attribute: The classification of software as either developed or nondeveloped.

3.26 original source statements: Source statements that are obtained from an external product.

3.27 output primitives: Primitives that include source statements, function points, and documents.

3.28 page size: The edge-to-edge dimensions of hard-copy documents, or the average characters per line and the number of lines per screen for electronically displayed documents.

3.29 physical source statements (PSS): Source statements that measure the quantity of software in lines of code.

3.30 primitive: The lowest level for which data is collected.

3.31 productivity ratio: The relationship of an output primitive to its corresponding input primitive.

3.32 reused source statements: Unmodified source statements obtained for the product from an external source.

3.33 source statements (SS): The encoded logic of the software product.

3.34 staff-hour: An hour of effort expended by a member of the staff.

3.35 support staff-hour: An hour of effort expended by a member of the staff who does not directly define or create the software product, but acts to assist those who do.

3.36 tokens: The content of a document as characterized by words, ideograms, and graphics.

3.37 type attributes: The classification of each source statement as either executable, data declaration, compiler directive, or comment.

3.38 usage attributes: The classification of software as delivered to a user of the final product, or as nondelivered when created only to support the development process.

4. Software productivity metrics

This standard defines measurement primitives for computing software productivity. A primitive is the lowest level for which data is collected. The output primitives for software are source statements and, optionally, function points. For documentation, the output primitive is the page. The input primitive is the staff-hour.

Primitives are categorized by attributes. An attribute is a measurable characteristic of a primitive. This standard requires that all attributes be measured for each primitive. For example, the source statement primitive may be either new or reused, and it may also be either delivered or nondelivered. Each of these attributes is a different variation of the primitive. Thus, a new delivered source statement differs from a new nondelivered source statement. By using this scheme of primitives and attributes, the elements of productivity are consistently categorized.

Because productivity measurements are only as valid as the primitive data used to calculate them, accuracy and consistency of the data used are essential for the results to be meaningful. The degree of granularity, which is the depth or level of detail at which data is collected, is important in determining the precision and consistency of the data.

Data of fine granularity is obtained when collecting data by staff-hour for each hour worked. Tracking the effort expended at this level reduces the potential for large errors. Estimates, such as those made at the end of a project by best guess approximation of effort, are an example of very coarse granularity. In this situation, large errors may be introduced into the productivity results.

This standard requires the use of the finest degree of granularity obtainable in collecting software productivity data. For the results of this standard to be most useful, the measuring process used shall be both accurate and detailed. Therefore, recording input effort as it is expended is the only acceptable method for this standard.

5. Output primitives

Three categories of output primitives are defined in this standard: source statements, function points, and documents. Source statements are a fundamental part of software, representing the encoded logic of the software product. Function points are a measure of the functional content of software. Production of documents is a significant component of the effort expended in software development, and measuring productivity for it is important. This standard requires reporting productivity results for source statements and documents. The use of function points is optional but recommended.

5.1 Source statement output primitives

This clause defines methods for counting software statements, and methods for categorizing the nature, origin, and disposition of the software.

Two methods are used to count software source statements: the logical source statement (LSS) method, which counts instructions, and the physical source statement (PSS) method, which counts lines of code. Logical source statement counting is the preferred method for this standard. Physical source statement counting is included in this standard because it is commonly found in published data.

Software is categorized by a set of attributes that describe it. Each source statement primitive is defined by three attribute qualifiers. The first of these is the type attribute that classifies each source statement as either executable, data declaration, compiler directive, or comment. The second is the origin attribute that classifies software as either developed or nondeveloped. Developed software is created new, or modified from existing software, for this product. Nondeveloped software is reused or deleted from the existing software. The last attribute is the usage attribute that identifies whether the software was delivered to a user of the final product, or produced only to support the development process and not delivered to the user.

5.1.1 Source statement counting

Source statements in different programming languages shall be counted separately. The programming language used shall be identified for each count along with its software module name. If two languages are used in the development, for example Pascal and C, the quantity of source statements of each language shall be counted and reported separately. Combining counts of different languages into a single count shall not be permitted.

This standard requires that only those source statements written by people be counted. Other counting practices, such as counting compiler derived instructions, program generator output, reuse library output, or machine instructions may be counted in addition to the people-created source statements provided these counts are kept separate and clearly identified. Counts of object code, executable code, and code that is mechanically generated from source code are not required by this standard. It may be most useful to count source statements at the level that the source is maintained. As a minimum, counting shall be done at product completion, when the product is ready for delivery. In all cases, what is counted shall be specifically stated along with the quantity of software measured.

Source statements that are expanded within a software module, for example, macro expansions, or supplied to the program, for example, by an *include* statement, shall be counted only once for all modules being measured. Source statements that invoke, call, or direct inclusion of other source statements in the module shall be counted each time they are used.

Source statements are counted in one of two ways, as logical source statements (LSS) or as physical source statements (PSS):

a) *Logical source statements*. The LSS counting method measures the number of software instructions. When a source statement is the count of instructions irrespective of its relationship to lines, the count shall be stated as being in logical source statements.

The LSS method is used to count software statements independently of the physical format in which they appear. For example, if two instructions appear on a single line, the LSS count would be two. If one instruction spans two lines, the LSS count would be one.

An LSS count shall be accompanied by a description of the procedure for counting the source statements. This description shall define the algorithm used to determine the beginning and end of each source statement, and how embedded source statements are counted.

b) *Physical source statements*. The PSS counting method measures the number of software lines of code. When the end-of-line character or a line of code method is used to count source statements, the count shall be stated as being in physical source statements.

A PSS measurement is line counting where a typical line format is 80 characters. Any deviation from the typical line format shall be noted. A PSS may consist of one LSS, more than one LSS, or part of an LSS.

Blank lines shall be excluded from PSS counts. If desired, blank lines may be counted separately as the number of blank lines.

5.1.2 Source statement attributes

This standard partitions source statements into three attributes: type, origin, and usage. The type attribute consists of executable, data declaration, compiler directive, and comment source statements. The origin attribute consists of developed and nondeveloped source statements. The usage attribute consists of delivered and nondelivered source statements.

Separate counts for each combination of attribute values shall be stated when reporting productivity results. For example, separate counts shall be stated for executable source statements that are developed delivered and for executable source statements that are developed nondelivered.

5.1.2.1 Type attribute

The type attribute classifies all LSS into the categories of executable, data declaration, compiler directive, and comment source statements. Each LSS shall be counted as one of the following:

a) *Executable source statements.* Source statements that direct the actions of the computer at run time shall be counted as executable source statements.

b) *Data declaration source statements.* Source statements that reserve or initialize memory at compilation time; that are directives to the compiler to constrain or check data; or that define the structure of the data that will be reserved, allocated, or created at run time shall be counted as data declaration source statements.

c) *Compiler directive source statements.* Source statements that define macros; are labels; direct the compiler to insert external source statements, for example, *include* statement; direct conditional compilation; or are not described by one of the other type attributes shall be identified as compiler directive source statements.

d) *Comment source statements.* Source statements that provide information to people reading the software source code and are ignored by the compiler shall be counted separately from other source statements and reported as comment source statements.

Physical source statement counting is a count of the number of nonblank lines. This count is expressed as the number of PSS. Physical source statements are further subdivided as follows:

a) *Noncomment lines.* Lines of software that contain either executable, data declaration, or compiler directive source statements.

b) *Comment lines.* Lines that contain only comment source statements.

All counts of LSS and PSS shall be kept by source module, and identified by module name and software language. The counts may be combined for all modules when expressing aggregate results for the software product, but the combined count shall be only of those modules of the same software source language.

5.1.2.2 Origin attribute

Each source statement is designated by a second attribute called the origin attribute. Each source statement can have one of two possible origins:

a) *Developed source statements.* Source statements added or modified for the specific product being measured shall be counted as new source statements. Added source statements are those that did not previously exist and were created specifically for this product. Modified source statements are those taken from another software product to which any changes were made to make the software suitable for this application.

b) *Nondeveloped source statements.* Source statements that were not developed new for this product are counted in two categories: deleted source statements and reused source statements. Deleted source statements shall be the count of all source statements that have been removed or modified from an earlier version of this software product. Reused source statements are unmodified source statements obtained for the product from an external source of software. The size (LSS or PSS) of this external source would be counted as original source statements and could be a previous version of this product, a reuse library, or acquired software. Reused source statements shall be counted as a part of the software module count. Modifying a source statement is considered to be the process of removing one existing source statement and then adding one or more new source statements. When a single source statement is modified, and the result is two or more source statements, all but one source statement shall be counted in added source statements, and one shall be counted as a modified source statement.

The following computations shall be used for calculating the counts of new, reused, and deleted source statements:

Number of New SS = Number of Added SS + Number of Modified SS

Number of Deleted SS = Number of Modified SS + Number of Removed SS

Number of Reused SS = Number of Original SS − Number of Modified SS − Number of Removed SS

The modified source statement count is identical in each relationship above in which it is used.

Pictorially, these relationships can be represented as in figure 1.

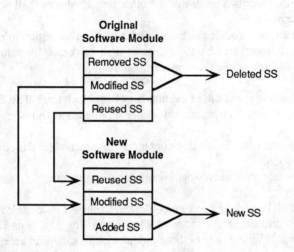

Figure 1—Source statements counts

5.1.2.3 Usage attribute

All source statements shall be divided into two categories based upon their usage:

a) *Delivered source statements*. All source statements incorporated into the final product delivered to the customer, shall be counted as delivered source statements. This includes all source statements that are used directly in the product's designed functions, and all source statements that support the product in its operating environment such as installation, diagnostic, and support utility software.

b) *Nondelivered source statements*. All software developed for the final product but not delivered to the customer shall be counted as nondelivered source statements. This includes all software not counted as delivered source statements that was produced to support development of the final product such as test software, tools, and aids to the developers.

5.2 Function point output primitive

The output primitive used to measure delivered software functionality is the function point. This standard uses the term *function point* to mean Albrecht's definition of function point (see [B1[2]]) or similar methods of measuring functionality.

Measuring function points is not required by this standard. However, those who do measure function points shall also accompany the measurements with source statement counts as defined in clause 5.1. This requirement is meant to enable a better understanding of the relationship between function point and source statement measures of productivity.

5.2.1 Function point counting

Function points are computed from an algorithm that uses various characteristics of the application's functionality expressed as a relationship of function types. Each function type is a variable that defines a characteristic of the application, and is set to a specific value for each application called the function value.

Productivity measurement given in function points shall be accompanied by the following:

a) The function point algorithm shall be stated explicitly. If the algorithm is proprietary, and cannot be stated, then the source and version of the algorithm shall be identified.
b) Each function type used in the function point algorithm shall be specified and defined. The function type definitions shall be complete (see 5.2.2).
c) A listing of the function values used for each function type shall be stated. This is the numeric quantity or factor supplied for each function type in the algorithm.

5.2.2 Function point attributes

The type attribute describes the function types. The origin and usage attributes are not generally used to describe function points since function points are computed only for delivered software.

Function types used in the function point algorithm shall be precisely defined. An example of how a function type definition might be stated is

> *External output type:* Any unique user data or control output type that leaves the boundary of the application being measured. An external output should be considered unique if it has a format different from other external outputs, or if the external (logical) design requires that processing logic be different from other external outputs with the same format. External outputs include reports and messages that leave the application directly for the user, and output files of reports and messages that leave the application boundary for other applications.

A definition is required for each function type used in the function point algorithm.

5.3 Document output primitives

This standard requires measurement of all documents that consume a nontrivial (as determined by the user of the standard) amount of project resources. Documents include hard copy, screen images, text, and graphics used to convey information to people. The effort associated with the preparation of each document measured shall be recorded separately.

---

[2]The numbers in brackets correspond to those of the bibliographical references in Annex C.

All documents that actively support the development or the usage of a software product shall be measured. Typical documents of this type are requirements statements, architectural and design specifications, data definitions, user manuals, reference manuals, tutorials, training guides, installation and maintenance manuals, and test plans.

Documents that are produced, but not preserved beyond the completion of the project should also be measured if they require a significant amount of effort to produce. These include such documents as proposals, schedules, budgets, project plans, and reports.

5.3.1 Document counting

The primitive unit of measure for a document is the page. This is a physical page for hard-copy documents, and a screen or page image for electronically displayed documents. The primary form of the output determines which measure is used.

The document measurement is augmented by reporting the page (or screen) size and the counts of three kinds of tokens: words, ideograms, and graphics. These auxiliary details help to distinguish between different document sizes and densities.

5.3.1.1 Document page count

The document page count is defined to be the total number of nonblank pages contained in a hard-copy document. For documents that are not printed, such as computer displays, a document screen count replaces the document page count.

The document page count is an integer value. Partially filled pages, such as at clause and chapter breaks, are counted as full pages. Blank pages are not counted.

5.3.1.2 Document page size

The page size for the document shall be specified. Both the width and the height dimensions of the document shall be measured in inches or equivalent units. This is the edge-to-edge dimensions, not the margin-to-margin dimensions.

For electronically displayed documents, the screen dimensions shall be specified. The screen width is measured by the average number of characters per line, and the screen height is measured by the number of lines per screen.

5.3.1.3 Document token count

The total number of tokens contained in each document are counted to characterize the document. Three kinds of token counts shall be made: words, ideograms, and graphics. The counting rules for each are as follows:

   a) *Number of words*. When counting words in the text, these rules shall apply:
     — All simple words are counted as single words.
     — Contractions, such as *can't, won't, aren't*, are counted as single words.
     — Numeric values, such as *1234, 12.34*, and *$1 234 567.89*, are counted as single words.
     — Acronyms, Roman numerals, abbreviations, and hyphenated words are counted as single words.
     — Punctuation marks are ignored.
   b) *Number of ideograms*. These are symbols representing ideas rather than words, such as Kanji characters, or equations. When counting ideograms, each type of symbol is counted and reported separately, for example, the number of Kanji characters, and the number of equations.

c) *Number of graphics.* These are the number of graphs, tables, figures, charts, pictures, etc., that are included in the document. When counting graphics, the number of each type of graphic is reported separately, for example, the number of tables, the number of figures, the number of graphs, the number of pictures.

5.3.2 Document attributes

Document attributes define the type, origin, and usage of the documents measured.

5.3.2.1 Document type

Document type is reported with two values: the name of the document and its purpose. The name of the document is the name used by the development organization. The document purpose describes the intention of the document phrased in commonly used terminology.

5.3.2.2 Document origin

The amount of reuse of documents may be specified by the document's percentage reused. This value is computed by dividing the number of tokens in the document that are not modified or added by the total number of tokens in the document. The result is expressed as a percentage of the type of tokens measured. The type of tokens used for calculating the percentage shall be stated. For example, if a document contains 8000 word tokens from the original document that were not modified or added, and the final document size is 10 000 word tokens, then the document would be reported to have a value for the document percentage reused of 80% word tokens (8000/10 000).

5.3.2.3 Document usage

Each document shall be identified as to its usage, delivered or nondelivered. The document usage is delivered if it is provided to the user or to the user's facility. A nondelivered document is one that is not provided to the user.

6. Input primitive

In the productivity relationship for this standard, input represents the effort applied to develop the software product. The principal measure for effort in this standard is labor expressed in units of staff-hour.

6.1 Staff-hour input primitive

Effort shall be measured only in staff-hour units. A staff-hour is an hour of time expended by a member of the staff. The staff-hours collected shall include those directly expended in creating a specific output product for which productivity is calculated.

The accuracy of productivity results depends on how precisely the effort expended to produce an output product is recorded. Recording effort as it is expended is required by this standard.

The staff-hour measure shall include all effort expended on the product, including all overtime hours, both compensated and uncompensated.

Staff-hours are not counted in productivity calculations if they do not directly contribute to the software product. Any time away from the job, such as vacations, holidays, jury duty, and sick leave, are not counted. Also, time expended on something other than the specific product being measured, or time spent on other products or projects is not counted.

Staff-hours may be expressed as larger units for convenience. To express effort in larger units, such as staff-day, staff-month, or staff-year, a conversion factor shall be specified to translate the larger unit into staff-hours. For example, stating results in staff-months, the user would accompany it with a statement similar to "one staff-month = 152 staff-hours for this data."

6.2 Staff-hour attribute

The nature of the effort expended by personnel shall be measured in the following categories:

a) *Direct staff-hour.* The effort expended by those members of the development staff that directly contribute to defining or creating the software product is measured as direct staff-hours. This category should include, but not be limited to, first level supervisors and members of the staff that perform analysis, design, programming, testing, and documentation tasks.

   1) *Direct delivered staff-hour.* All direct staff-hours resulting in the production of output primitives (namely, source statements, function points, or documents) that are delivered to the customer shall be counted as direct delivered staff-hours.

   2) *Direct nondelivered staff-hour.* All direct staff-hours resulting in the production of output primitives (namely, source statements, function points, or documents) that are not delivered to the customer shall be counted as direct nondelivered staff-hours.

b) *Support staff-hour.* The effort expended by those members of the staff who do not directly define or create the software product, but act to assist those who do, shall be collected and recorded as support staff-hours. This category should include, but not be limited to, members of the staff who perform clerical functions or support activities, such as development computer operators or project coordinators. This category also includes those who contribute to the production process but whose efforts are too distributed to allocate their effort directly to a specific product, such as configuration managers and quality assurance personnel.

6.3 Activities

This standard does not specify a standard life cycle, nor does it imply the existence of a standard software life cycle. Users of this software standard shall specify activities of their own life cycle that directly contribute to producing specific output primitives in order to compute the productivity associated with those outputs (see IEEE Std 1074-1991 for life cycle activities). Staff-hours shall be collected and reported for each output primitive by staff-hour attribute.

7. Relationships

This clause describes several types of relationships, using the primitives defined in clauses 5 and 6. These relationships are presented as examples of the way that output and input primitives may be combined. It is left to the users to decide which combinations of primitives are most useful to them.

7.1 Productivity ratios

In this standard, productivity is defined as the ratio of the output product to the input effort that produced it. For a specific product output, such as the number of source statements or the number of document pages, productivity is computed by dividing that product quantity by the effort expended on it.

Productivity is computed using the ratio of output to input for each measured output primitive for which related input effort data is collected. The productivity for product a, which has the quantity of output primitive O_a and which required effort E_a to create, is defined by the relationship

$$\text{Productivity}_a = \frac{O_a}{E_a}$$

The ratio's units of measure are those from the dimensions of the primitives used, for example, source statements per staff-hour, or document page count per staff-hour.

All statements of productivity shall be accompanied by information about the characteristics (see clause 8) and about the activities included in the measurement (see IEEE Std 1074-1991).

The usefulness of productivity values depends on the accuracy of the data used to compute them. Here accuracy refers to the level of detail and precision of the data collection process; estimates are not acceptable. Only recording the input effort as it is worked and counting the output produced are acceptable methods for measuring the primitives.

Only the product quantity and the effort expended to build that product should be used in calculating productivity. Any degree of ambiguity introduced in measuring the output product or capturing the effort diminishes the usefulness of the productivity value. For example, consider computing the productivity of a software module when the effort is not specifically recorded for it. If the effort for writing source statements was not recorded separately, but included in the effort of creating documentation for it, the resulting productivity would be the output of source statements divided by the effort for source statements and documentation. This result would be difficult to interpret because the productivity would not be for source statements alone.

7.1.1 Incremental productivity ratios

Productivity shall be computed at the completion of an output product, that is, when the product is delivered to the user. At the point of delivery, the productivity is

$$\text{Final Productivity} = \frac{O_{\text{Final}}}{E_{\text{Final}}}$$

where O_{Final} is the total quantity of the output product being measured, and E_{Final} is the total effort expended in creating it.

This relationship might also be used during the development process prior to delivery to ascertain accumulated productivity results. In this case the output measured is the quantity of the product at that point in the process, and the input is the effort expended in producing that incremental quantity of output.

During development of a product, it may be useful to measure productivity at intervals to assess trends as it progresses toward final productivity. This periodic sampling of productivity is called the incremental productivity and computed by

$$\text{Incremental Productivity} = \frac{O_{tn} - O_{tn-1}}{E_{tn} - E_{tn-1}}$$

where O_{tn} is the output production and E_{tn} is the direct effort for that output expended through time t_n, and O_{tn-1} and E_{tn-1} are the output production and direct effort through some prior time t_{n-1}.

If the incremental productivity is computed at intervals throughout the development process, it may show productivity fluctuations. It is useful to chart the progress of productivity in order to show trends, or to estimate final productivity based on trend patterns from past projects.

7.1.2 Source statement productivity ratios

The source statement output primitives that may be useful in productivity calculations are:

Delivered New SS

Delivered Reused SS

Nondelivered New SS

Nondelivered Reused SS

Nondelivered Deleted SS

where SS stands for logical source statements or physical source statements.

The input primitives used in productivity relationships are:

Direct Delivered Staff-Hour

Direct Nondelivered Staff-Hour

Support Staff-Hour

Ratios of output primitives to input primitives will show various types of productivity results. For example, the productivity for direct delivered source statements may be computed for the output primitives:

Delivered New SS

Delivered Reused SS

by dividing each by the input primitive for

Direct Delivered Staff-Hours

The productivity for direct nondelivered source statements is computed by taking each of the output primitives:

Nondelivered New SS

Nondelivered Reused SS

Nondelivered Deleted SS

and dividing by the input primitive:

Direct Nondelivered Staff-Hours

The differences between software languages are sufficiently great to make cross-language comparisons of productivity difficult. This standard provides a foundation for collecting accurate productivity data. This may make cross-language comparisons possible in the future.

This standard supports only comparing source statement productivity of identical source languages. When attempting to compare the source statement productivity of two software developments, they shall be in the same software programming languages. This means that the productivity computed for a software product development in a third-generation language shall not be directly compared with the productivity for a software product developed in an assembler-level language, nor should it be compared with a different third-generation language.

7.1.3 Function point productivity ratios

The function point output primitive is the number of function points.

The input primitives used in productivity relationships are:

Direct Delivered Staff-Hour

Direct Nondelivered Staff-Hour

Support Staff-Hour

Dividing the number of function points by each of the above input primitives provides different productivity ratios.

7.1.4 Documentation productivity ratios

Documentation is another form of software output, and document outputs are treated similarly to source statement outputs.

The document output primitives are:

Document Page Count or Screen Count

Number of Words

Number of Ideograms

Number of Graphics

The input primitives used for document productivity are:

Direct Delivered Staff-Hour

Direct Nondelivered Staff-Hour

Support Staff-Hour

All of the productivity ratios described for source statements apply analogously for documents.

7.2 Output-to-output ratios

The following clauses describe some output-to-output ratios. Other combinations of output-to-output ratios will provide additional insights into the process being measured.

7.2.1 Source statement output-to-output ratios

Consider the matrix of the source statement origin to usage attributes in table 1.

Table 1—Source statement origin to usage attribute matrix

		USAGE	
		Delivered	Nondelivered
ORIGIN	Developed	New SS (1)	New SS (2)
	Nondeveloped	Reused SS (3)	Reused SS (4)
		Deleted SS* (5)	Deleted SS (6)

*Measurement data for this variable is not collected, since deleted software is not delivered to the user.

Output source statement primitives in the cells of the preceding table combine to form numerous relationships. Some of these are:

The total number of developed source statements:

Developed SS = (1) + (2)

The total number of delivered source statements:

Delivered SS = (1) + (3)

All source statements contributing to the total product:

Total SS = (1) + (2) + (3) + (4)

The total number of source statements not delivered to the user:

Nondelivered SS = (2) + (4) + (6)

The total number of reused source statements:

Reused SS = (3) + (4)

The total number of source statements deleted from the product prior to delivery to the user:

Deleted SS = (6)

The proportion of delivered source statements to the number of source statements in the total output:

$$\frac{\text{Delivered SS}}{\text{Total SS}} = \frac{(1) + (3)}{(1) + (2) + (3) + (4)}$$

The proportion of reuse in the total product:

$$\frac{\text{Reused SS}}{\text{Total SS}} = \frac{(3) + (4)}{(1) + (2) + (3) + (4)}$$

The proportion of delivered source statements that are new:

$$\frac{\text{New}_{\text{Delv}}\text{SS}}{\text{Delivered SS}} = \frac{(1)}{(1) + (3)}$$

The proportion of delivered source statements that are reused:

$$\frac{\text{Reused}_{\text{Delv}}\text{SS}}{\text{Delivered SS}} = \frac{(3)}{(1) + (3)}$$

The proportion of nondelivered source statements that are reused:

$$\frac{\text{Reused}_{\text{Nondelv}}\text{SS}}{\text{Nondelivered SS}} = \frac{(4)}{(2) + (4) + (6)}$$

Ratios of the type attribute values may prove to be useful. Consider the type attribute values for logical source statements:

Executable LSS   (7)

Data Declaration LSS   (8)

Compiler Directive LSS   (9)

Comment LSS   (10)

A ratio of interest might be the executable LSS to the total LSS for a module:

$$\frac{\text{Executable SS}}{\text{Module's Total LSS}} = \frac{(7)}{(7) + (8) + (9) + (10)}$$

Consider similar ratios for the values of the PSS type attribute:

Noncomment PSS   (11)

Comment PSS   (12)

Finally, consider the ratio of comments to the total number of PSS:

$$\frac{\text{Comment PSS}}{\text{Total PSS}} = \frac{(12)}{(11) + 12}$$

7.2.2 Function point output-to-output ratios

Output-to-output ratios are meaningless for the cases where the function point count is a single number. In other cases, ratios similar to those above can be constructed.

7.2.3 Documentation output-to-output ratios

Three document content ratios are computed to describe the density of a document. These ratios help to distinguish high density documents from low density ones:

Number of Words per Page

Number of Ideograms per Page

Number of Graphics per Page

Document usage ratios are equivalent to the source statement usage ratios. Measurement of delivered documents versus nondelivered documents is at the document level; either the document is delivered or it is nondelivered. Measurement of developed versus nondeveloped documents shall be made at the token level; the page level is inadequate due to page break realignments and changes made to tokens.

Document products are developed in tokens, but often are measured in pages or screens. The origin to usage matrix for document pages is shown in table 2. A similar matrix could be made for screens or for each of the individual tokens, namely, words, ideograms, or graphics.

Table 2—Document origin to usage attribute matrix

		USAGE	
		Delivered	Nondelivered
ORIGIN	Developed	New Pages (1)	New Pages (2)
	Nondeveloped	Reused Pages (3)	Reused Pages (4)
		Deleted Pages* (5)	Deleted Pages (6)

*Measurement data for this variable is not collected, since deleted pages are not delivered to the user.

The document output-to-output terminology and ratio definitions are applied at the token level, and are similar to the terminology and ratio definitions described for source statement output-to-output ratios.

7.2.4 Mixed output primitive ratios

Ratios comparing output primitives of different types may provide insight into the software development process. Two possible combinations are shown here for consideration:

$$\frac{\text{Function Points}}{\text{Total Source Statements}} \quad \text{or} \quad \frac{\text{Document Pages}}{\text{Total Source Statements}}$$

7.3 Input-to-input ratios

Ratios of input primitives to input effort primitives provide insights about the effort expended. The input primitives are

Direct Delivered Staff-Hours   (A)

Direct Nondelivered Staff-Hours   (B)

Support Staff-Hours   (C)

Some meaningful combinations with these primitives are

Total Effort = (A) + (B) + (C)   and   Total Direct Effort = (A) + (B)

The ratio of Direct Effort to Total Effort:

$$\frac{\text{Total Direct Effort}}{\text{Total Effort}} = \frac{(A) + (B)}{(A) + (B) + (C)}$$

The ratio of Support Effort to Total Direct Effort:

$$\frac{\text{Support Effort}}{\text{Total Direct Effort}} = \frac{(C)}{(A) + (B)}$$

The ratio of Direct Delivered to Direct Nondelivered Effort:

$$\frac{\text{Direct Delivered Effort}}{\text{Direct Nondelivered Effort}} = \frac{(A)}{(B)}$$

Many other meaningful combinations are possible. Users of this standard may wish to explore them.

8. Characteristics

Within the context of this document, characteristics are defined as those inherent factors of software development that may have a significant impact on productivity. The purpose of recording measures of characteristics is to ensure consistent comparisons between projects developing software products.

The characteristics are divided into three categories: project characteristics, management characteristics, and product characteristics. Project characteristics describe the people and processes involved in the development effort. Management characteristics describe how a project is managed. Product characteristics reflect the nature of the product itself.

Whenever data is collected to assess software productivity, the characteristics shall be recorded. Comparing productivity data between projects is applicable only if the characteristics are similar. This standard does not attempt to precisely quantify characteristics, but it does require that all characteristics be documented and reported along with productivity data.

Most of the required characteristics data shall be recorded in the early stages of the project. Some data, however, will not be available until the later stages. Characteristics shall be monitored throughout the project and recorded in the characteristics clause as new data is available.

The following is the minimum set of characteristics that shall be recorded.

8.1 Project characteristics

Project characteristics are factors involving the people and the working environment of the development effort. They represent factors that the developer may be able to control or alter. Project characteristic information is recorded in one of two main categories: personnel or software development environment (SDE).

8.1.1 Personnel

The personnel category includes most of the human elements that are involved in a software development project, such as education, experience, expert experience, training, size, and turnover. These personnel characteristics are explained below, and when possible, a metric is included for each characteristic.

8.1.1.1 Education

Education refers to the highest level of education beyond high school.

Level of education:

— No Degree
— Associate's Degree
— Bachelor's Degree
— Master's Degree
— Doctorate Degree

Classify each member of the project team according to the above list. Record this data as an educational profile expressed as a percentage of total team (for example, 10% Associate's, 50% Bachelor's, 30% Master's, 10% Doctorate degrees).

8.1.1.2 Experience

Experience refers to the number of years of relevant experience, and encompasses three aspects:

a) Years of work in software engineering
b) Years of work with specific software applications and technologies relevant to this project (for example, 4GL, graphics, real-time)
c) Years of experience in the organization

Record years of relevant experience as a profile in the three categories for the highest, lowest, and median years (for example, Experience in current job: Highest = 8 yrs, Lowest = <1 yr, Median = 2.5 yrs).

8.1.1.3 Expert assistance

Expert assistance refers to a person, or group of persons, external to the project team who has knowledge and experience in the application being developed by the project team.

Indicate if expert assistance was required on this project. Record expert assistance required as either yes or no.

Indicate if expert assistance was available as needed for this project. Record expert assistance availability as either yes or no.

8.1.1.4 Training

Training refers to all formal professional training. This includes external training courses, such as seminars, and in-house training courses, such as training on company coding standards, software development environment, testing techniques, etc.

Record the average number of days each project employee spends in training per year (for example, an employee receives an average of 6.5 days of training per year).

8.1.1.5 Size

Size refers to the number of direct and support staff involved in the project. Record the number of people on the project at peak and average staff levels.

8.1.1.6 Turnover

Turnover refers to a shift in personnel during a project. Record if turnover was a disruptive factor as either yes or no.

8.1.2 Software development environment

The software development environment (SDE) is the combination of tools, techniques, and administration used during the development. For recording this part of the project characteristics, below is a checklist of the items to be included:

a) On-line documentation with word processing
b) Configuration management techniques and tools
c) Project libraries
d) Formal design techniques
e) Coding standards
f) Format and content standards for documentation
g) Software cost estimation tools
h) Formal project management methods (for example, PERT charts, work breakdown structures, critical path analysis, etc.)
i) Reuse libraries
j) Walkthroughs, code inspections, design reviews, etc.
k) Automated test tools
l) Debugging tools
m) Defect tracking and resolution systems
n) Requirements traceability
o) Other

Record all letters that are used by this project.

8.2 Management characteristics

This clause provides some insight into how the project was managed. The data for this clause should be recorded after the project is completed.

8.2.1 User participation

User participation refers to the level of participation by the user or their representative on the project.

— *High* is user participation in all reviews, as well as commenting on all documentation.
— *Low* is user participation limited to just the start and end of the project.
— *Medium* is all user participation between the levels of *High* and *Low*.
— *N/A* is when user participation is not applicable.

Record the appropriate level of user participation.

8.2.2 Stability of product requirements

Stability of product requirements characterizes the extent that the requirements remained constant throughout development. Record whether instability of product requirements was a disruptive factor as either yes or no.

8.2.3 Constraining factors

Specify the factors that constrained the project. The following is a list of possible constraining factors:

— Fixed cost
— Fixed staff size
— Fixed functionality
— Fixed quality and/or reliability
— Fixed schedule
— Limited accessibility to development system
— Limited accessibility to target system

Record these and any other limiting factors as a checklist (for example, cost, schedule, access to target system).

8.3 Product characteristics

Product characteristics are those factors imposed upon the product. The specific product characteristics that shall be recorded are defined below.

8.3.1 Criticality

The following are product critical characteristics that directly impact productivity.

8.3.1.1 Timing critical

Certain products must work in environments where the real-time behavior, user response, or throughput is critical. Record timing critical as either yes or no.

8.3.1.2 Memory critical

Certain products must fit into a limited amount of memory. Record memory critical as either yes or no.

8.3.1.3 Quality/reliability critical

Certain products must meet very stringent quality or reliability criteria. Record quality/reliability critical as either yes or no.

8.3.2 Degree of innovation

This characteristic represents the technological risk of the project.

0 = Never done before

1 = Previously done by others

2 = Previously done by us

Record the degree of innovation as either 0, 1, or 2.

8.3.3 Complexity

This standard requires a rating for three types of complexities: programming, data, and organizational.

8.3.3.1 Programming complexity

Programming complexity addresses the program control flow of a software product.

— *Low* is straight line code, simple loops and branches, simple calculations.
— *Medium* is simple nesting, simple intermodule communications, moderately difficult calculations.
— *High* is re-entrant/recursive code, data structure control, complex calculations requiring accurate results.

Record programming complexity. Other formal complexity measures may be recorded as well. In this case, the complexity measurement methodology used shall be cited.

8.3.3.2 Data complexity

Data complexity refers to the arrangement, access, and retrieval of stored data.

— *Low* are simple arrays or files in main memory, few inputs/outputs, no restructuring of data.
— *Medium* are multiple inputs/outputs, data typing, restructuring of data, access to other storage media (for example, tape, hard disk, other machines).
— *High* are highly coupled and relational data structures, optimized search algorithms, background data consistency checks.

Record data complexity.

8.3.3.3 Organizational complexity

Organizational complexity refers to the difficulty in coordinating and communicating with all parties on the project team.

SP = Single Person

SD = Single Department/Division

MD = Multiple Departments/Divisions

MS = Multiple Sites

SC = Subcontracted development to third party

Record all levels of organizational complexity that apply (for example, MD, MS).

8.3.4 Development concurrency

Some products require concurrent, that is, parallel development of software (S), hardware (H), and firmware (F).

H-S: hardware and software concurrent

H-F: hardware and firmware concurrent

S-F: software and firmware concurrent

S-S: software and software concurrent

H-S-F: hardware, software, and firmware concurrent

Record which areas were being developed concurrently.

8.3.5 Product description

Provide a brief description of the software application, that is, a brief description of what the product does.

Annexes

(These informative annexes are not a part of IEEE Std 1045-1992, IEEE Standard for Software Productivity Metrics, but are included for information only.)

Annex A
Sample metrics data collection summary list

(informative)

The items listed here are required by the standard. Items inside brackets "[...]" are optional or may be required under special conditions. Numbers in parentheses "(...)" are the clause numbers of this standard that describe that measurement.

A.1 Descriptive fields

This information identifies the source of the measurements.

— Product Name
— Product Release and Version
— Development Organization
— Current Date
— Name of Data Collector

A.2 Software module information (5.1.1)

— Software Module Name
— Software Language

A.3 Type attribute primitives (5.1.2.1)

— Logical Source Statement (LSS) Count:
  • Number of Executable LSS
  • Number of Data Declarations
  • Number of Compiler Directives
  • Number of Comments

— Physical Source Statement (PSS) Count:
  • Number of Noncomment Lines
  • Number of Comment Lines
  • Number of Characters per Line (if different from 80 characters per line)
  • [Number of Blank Lines]

25

A.4 Origin attribute source statement primitives (5.1.2)

— Number of Developed Source Statements
— Number of Nondeveloped Source Statements
— Source Statement Counts:
  • Number of Original SS
  • Number of Added SS
  • Number of Modified SS
  • Number of Removed SS

A.5 Usage attribute source statement primitives (5.1.2.3)

— Number of Delivered Source Statements
— Number of Nondelivered Source Statements

A.6 Function point primitives (5.2.1)

— Number of Function Points
— Function Point Algorithm
— Function Types Description
— Function Type Values for Each Function Type

A.7 Documentation primitives (5.3)

— Document Name
— Document Purpose
— Document Usage (delivered or nondelivered)
— Document Medium (hard copy or screen)
— For Hard-Copy Documents:
  • Document Page Count (blank pages not counted)
  • Page Size (edge-to-edge in inches)
— For Electronically Displayed Documents:
  • Document Screen Count
  • Average Number of Screen Characters per Line
  • Lines per Screen
— Number of Words
— Number of Ideograms
— Number of Graphics (list each type separately)
— [Document Percentage Reused (name the token measured)]

A.8 Input primitives by activity category (6.0)

— Activity Name
— Direct Delivered Staff-Hours
— Direct Nondelivered Staff-Hours
— Support Staff-Hours

Annex B
Characteristics data collection form

(informative)

Project Characteristics (8.1)

Personnel

<u>Education</u>	<u>Percent of Project Team Members</u>
No Degree:	_____ %
Associate's Degree:	_____ %
Bachelor's Degree:	_____ %
Master's Degree:	_____ %
Doctorate Degree:	_____ %

<u>Experience</u>

1) Years in software engineering:	Highest____ Lowest____ Median____
2) Years in specific s/w technology:	Highest____ Lowest____ Median____
3) Years in organization:	Highest____ Lowest____ Median____

Expert Assistance	Required:	_____ YES/NO
	Available:	_____ YES/NO
Training	Average:	_____ days per year
Size	Peak:	_____ number of people
	Average:	_____ number of people
Turnover	Disruptive:	_____ YES/NO

Software Development Environment: _____, _____, _____, _____

Management Characteristics (8.2)

User Participation		_____ H/M/L/NA
Product Requirements Stability	Disruptive:	_____ YES/NO
Constraining Factors		_____, _____, _____, _____

Product Characteristics (8.3)

Criticality

Timing Critical:	_____ YES/NO
Memory Critical:	_____ YES/NO
Quality/Reliability Critical:	_____ YES/NO

Degree of Innovation: _____ 0/1/2

Complexity

Programming:	_____ H/M/L
Data:	_____ H/M/L
Organizational:	____, ____, ____ SP/SD/MD/MS/SC (Record all that apply.)

Development Concurrency: _____ H-S/H-F/S-F/S-S/H-S-F

Product Description:_____

Annex C
Bibliography

(informative)

The following references were used extensively in the development of this standard. Users of this standard may wish to become familiar with these and other software productivity literature to further their understanding of the subject.

[B1] Albrecht, Allan J., and Gaffney, John E., Jr., "Software function, source lines of code, and development effort prediction: a software science validation." *IEEE Transactions on Software Engineering*, vol. SE-9, no. 6, pp. 639–648, Nov. 1983.

[B2] Basili, Victor R., and Weiss, David M., "A methodology for collecting valid software engineering data." *IEEE Transactions on Software Engineering*, vol. SE-10, no. 6, pp. 728–738, Nov. 1984.

[B3] Boehm, Barry W., *Software Engineering Economics,* Prentice Hall, Inc., Englewood Cliffs, NJ, 1981.

[B4] Conte, S. D., Dunsmore, H. E., Shen, V. Y., *Software Engineering Metrics and Models,* Benjamin/Cummings Publishing, Menlo Park, CA, 1986.

[B5] Grady, Robert B., Caswell, Deborah L., *Software Metrics: Establishing a Company-Wide Program,* Prentice Hall, Inc., Englewood Cliffs, NJ, 1987.

[B6] Jones, T. Capers, *Programming Productivity,* McGraw–Hill Book Company, New York, 1986.

[B7] Putnam, Lawrence H., "A general empirical solution to the macro software sizing and estimation problem." *IEEE Transactions on Software Engineering,* vol. SE-4, no. 4, pp. 345–361, Jul. 1978.

Annex D
Software counting relationships

(informative)

Presented here is an example of several relationships among the various categories of source statements included in a software product or application system. Rules relating the counts of each of these categories are also provided.

A new software system may consist of code obtained from an existing one and of new code created specifically for it. The earlier system may be a member of the same family as the new one or may be a member of a different family. Formulas are provided here that relate the source statement counts for the several categories of statements involved in creating a new software system. The formulas and relationships presented apply to both logical and physical statements, with or without comments. However, in any given instance, they are to be applied to only one category of statement (for example, physical statements, without comments). The logical source statement (LSS) count measures the number of software instructions independent of their physical format. It is imperative that LSS counts be accompanied by a description of the way in which they were counted. The physical source statement (PSS) count measures the quantity of software in lines of code.

A system consists of two categories of code: *new* and *reused*. It is expected that the development labor costs for a new application system are to be assigned corresponding to these categories of code. The definitions of *new* and *reused* source statements are as follows:

new source statements: The number of LSS or PSS that were newly created or modified for the application or system.

reused source statements: The number of LSS or PSS incorporated unmodified into the application system. Code that is ported is considered to be reused under the definition here.

When a new system is created in part from an earlier one, some of the statements from the earlier one are deleted. Figure D1 is a Venn diagram that depicts the relationships between the three categories of statements, new, reused, and deleted.

The development of a new software system using some source statements from an existing one employs four types of operations: removal, addition, modification, and reuse of some of the original system's code. The counts of each of the four types of source statements correspond to those operations; removed (re), added (a), modified (m), and reused original (o); are elements of the counts for the more general categories, new (n), reused (r), and deleted (d), related as shown in figure D1.

a) new = added + modified or, $\qquad$ $n = a + m$
b) deleted = modified + removed or, $\qquad$ $d = m + re$
c) reused = original – deleted or, $\qquad$ $r = o - m - re$

Note that *removed* means physically removed. If a source statement is changed in any way, it is called *modified*. Hence, the count of *new* statements is the sum of the *added* and the *modified* counts. Figure D2 is a Venn diagram that depicts the relationships between the sets of source statements of the different categories cited above. It shows the components of the new, reused, and deleted categories depicted in figure D1.

The formulas given above are for the special case of modifying one system to produce another. Note that the generalization works well, that is, incorporating code from several *original systems* into a *new* one. However, it is necessary to carefully define the quantities appropriately when doing so.

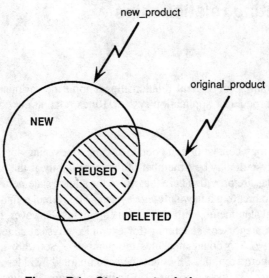

Figure D1—Statement relations

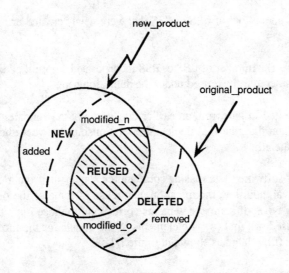

new_file = new $\cup$ reused

old_file = reused $\cup$ deleted

diff_file = new $\cup$ deleted

new = added $\cup$ modified_n

deleted = removed $\cup$ modified_o

NOTE—SS_count(modified_n) = SS_count(modified_o); that is both
of these sets are the same size.

Figure D2—Detailed statement relations

Suppose there are three files of source corresponding to the original system (old_file), the new system (new_file), and the difference between the two (diff_file). The (diff_file) is the set of elements not found in both the (new_file) and the (old_file). The Venn diagram in figure D2 shows them to be the *new* and *deleted* elements. The counts indicated below show this. The counts of the reused source (r), the new source (n), and the deleted source (d), as defined above, can be obtained very simply from the counts of the three files. Let c() mean *count of*. Then the following relationships exist:

    a)   c(old_file) = reused + deleted = r + d.
          By the formulas given above,
          c(old_file) = (o − m − re) + (m + re) = o.

    b)   c(diff_file) = new + deleted = n + d.
          By the formulas given above,
          c(diff_file) = (a + m) + (m + re) = a + 2m + re

    c)   c(new_file) = reused + new = r + n.
          By the formulas given above,
          c(new_file) = (o − m − re) + (a + m) = a + o − re.

Observe that the diff_file count, c(diff_file), includes a factor 2m, twice the number of the modified source statements. The reason for this can be understood by considering the Venn diagram in figure D2. There are actually two sets of *modified* statements, both of size m. The first set is in the original system. The statements in that set are modified or transformed into a somewhat different set of statements in the new system. Note that the original or *old* system may have some statements in it that will be modified or changed and become *new* statements in the new system.

The counts for reused (r), new (n), and deleted (d) statements, as defined above, can be obtained from the counts for the old_file, the diff_file, and the new_file, as now shown. Verifications of the correctness of the formulas are also provided. The formulas are as follows:

    a)   ((c(old_file) + c(new_file)) − c(diff_file))/2 = r
          Verification; ((r + d + r + n) − (n + d))/2 = r,
          or, ((o + (a + o − re)) − (a + 2m + re))/2 = (2o − 2m − 2re)/2 = o − m − re = r,
              by definition.

    b)   c(new_file) − r = n
          Verification; (r + n) − r = n
          or, (a + o − re) − (o − m − re) = a + m = n,
              by definition.

    c)   c(old_file) − r = d
          Verification; (r + d) − r = d
          or, (o − (o − m − re)) = m + re = d,
              by definition.

An example is now provided for applying of the counting rules presented above. In it, a new module is created using some statements obtained from another module developed earlier. The counts for the various categories of statements involved are:

Statement Category	Statement Count
Original module size (o):	100
Statements modified (m):	7

Statements added (a):   3

Statements removed (re):   2

Therefore:

Statements reused = r = o − m − re = 100 − 7 − 2 = 91

Statements new = n = a + m = 3 + 7 = 10

Statements deleted = d = m + re = 7 + 2 = 9.

Consequently, the total product size, which is the sum of the new and the reused statements, is

10 + 91 = 101

The counts of the new (n), reused (r), and deleted statements (d), can be determined very simply using the relationships presented by the three equations in the text immediately preceding this example. Suppose the statement counts for the old_file, the new_file, and the diff_file were as follows:

a) c(old_file) = 100

b) c(new_file) = 101

c) c(diff_file) = 19

Then the desired counts can be determined as follows:

a) count of reused,
    r = (c(old_file) + c(new_file) − c(diff_file))/2 = (100 + 101 − 19)/2 = 91.

b) count of new,
    n = c(new_file) − r = 101 − 91 = 10.

c) count of deleted,
    d = c(old_file) − r = 100 − 91 = 9.

These values are the same as those derived earlier in the example from the counts for modified, added, original, and removed, demonstrating the correctness of the calculations used to obtain them. The example illustrates the simplicity of calculating the number of new, reused, and deleted statements from the counts of the statements in the three files.

IEEE Std 1058-1998
(Revision and redesignation of IEEE Std 1058.1-1987,
incorporating IEEE Std 1058-1998 and
IEEE Std 1058a-1998)

IEEE Standard for Software Project Management Plans

Sponsor

**Software Engineering Standards Committee
of the
IEEE Computer Society**

Approved 8 December 1998

IEEE-SA Standards Board

Abstract: The format and contents of software project management plans, applicable to any type or size of software project, are described. The elements that should appear in all software project management plans are identified.
Keywords: management plans, software project management plans

The Institute of Electrical and Electronics Engineers, Inc.
345 East 47th Street, New York, NY 10017-2394, USA

Introduction

Overview

This standard contains four clauses. Clause 1 defines the scope and purpose of the standard. Clause 2 provides references to other IEEE standards that should be followed when applying this standard. Clause 3 provides definitions of terms that are used throughout the standard. Clause 4 contains an overview and detailed specification of the standard, including required components that shall be included, and optional components that may be included in software project management plans (SPMPs) based on this standard. The sequence of the elements presented in Clause 4 does not imply that SPMPs must be developed in the order of presentation. In most instances, SPMPs based on this standard will be developed by repeated iteration and refinement of the various elements in the plan.

Purpose

This standard specifies the format and content of SPMPs. This standard does not specify the exact techniques to be used in developing an SPMP, nor does it provide examples of SPMPs. Each organization using this standard should develop a set of practices and procedures to provide detailed guidance for preparing and updating of SPMPs based on this standard. These practices and procedures should take into account the environmental, organizational, and political factors that influence application of the standard.

Not all software projects are concerned with development of source code for a new software product. Some software projects consist of a feasibility study and definition of product requirements. Other software projects terminate upon completion of product design, and some projects are concerned with major modifications to existing software products. This standard is applicable to all types of software projects; applicability is not limited to projects that develop source code for new products. Project size or type of software product does not limit application of this standard. Small projects may require less formality in planning than large projects, but all components of the standard should be addressed by every software project.

Software projects are sometimes component parts of larger projects. In these cases, the SPMP may be a separate component of a larger plan or it may be merged into a system-level or business-level project management plan.

Audience

This standard is intended for use by software project managers and other personnel who prepare and update project plans and monitor adherence to those plans.

Evolution of plans

Developing the initial version of the SPMP should be one of the first activities to be completed in a software project. As the project evolves the nature of the work to be done will be better understood and plans will become more detailed. Thus, each version of the plan should be placed under configuration management, and each version should contain a schedule for subsequent updates to the plan.

Terminology

This standard follows the *IEEE Standards Style Manual*. In particular, the word *shall* is used to indicate mandatory requirements to be strictly followed in order to conform to the standard and from which no deviation is permitted.

The word *should* is used to indicate that among several possibilities one is recommended as particularly suitable, without mentioning or excluding others; or that a certain course of action is preferred but not necessarily required; or that (in the negative form) a certain course of action is deprecated but not prohibited.

The word *may* is used to indicate a course of action permissible within the limits of the standard.

The word *can* is used for statements of possibility and capability, whether material, physical, or causal.

History

The project authorization request for development of this standard was approved by the IEEE Standards Board on 13 December 1984. The first version of this standard (IEEE Std 1058.1-1987) was approved on 10 December 1987. The standard was reaffirmed 2 December 1993. IEEE Std 1058a was approved by the IEEE-SA Standards Board on 17 September 1998; the revision of the full standard was approved on 8 December 1998. The changes in this version of the standard are based on comments from users of the 1987 standard and the desire for conformance with IEEE/EIA 12207.0-1996.

Contributors

This standard was developed by the Software Project Management Plans Working Group of the Software Engineering Standards Committee of the Computer Society of the IEEE. The following individuals contributed to the development of this standard:

Richard E. Fairley   John M. Glabas   Richard H. Thayer

The following persons were on the balloting committee of IEEE Std 1058a:

Torben Aabo	Julio Gonzalez-Sanz	Donald J. Ostrom
T. J. Al-Hussaini	Lewis Gray	Mike Ottewill
R. W. Allen	L. M. Gunther	Indradeb P. Pal
Leo Beltracchi	David A. Gustafson	Mark Paulk
H. Ronald Berlack	Jon D. Hagar	John G. Phippen
Richard E. Biehl	John Harauz	Alex Polack
Juris Borzovs	Rob Harker	Peter T. Poon
David W. Burnett	Robert T. Harley	Lawrence S. Przybylski
Edward R. Byrne	Herbert Hecht	Kenneth R. Ptack
Michael Caldwell	William Hefley	Larry K. Reed
Keith Chan	Mark Heinrich	Donald J. Reifer
Antonio M. Cicu	Debra Herrmann	Annette D. Reilly
Theo Clarke	Umesh P. Hiriyannaiah	Dennis Rilling
François Coallier	Peter L. Hung	R. Waldo Roth
Virgil Lee Cooper	George Jackelen	Andrew P. Sage
W. W. Geoff Cozens	David Johnson	Helmut Sandmayr
Paul R. Croll	Frank V. Jorgensen	Stephen R. Schach
Thomas Crowley	Vladan V. Jovanovic	Norman Schneidewind
Geoffrey Darnton	William S. Junk	David J. Schultz
Taz Daughtrey	George X. Kambic	Lisa A. Selmon
Raymond Day	Ron S. Kenett	Robert W. Shillato
Bostjan K. Derganc	Judith S. Kerner	David M. Siefert
Sanjay Dewal	Robert J. Kierzyk	Lynn J. Simms
Perry R. DeWeese	Thomas M. Kurihara	Carl A. Singer
Sherman Eagles	John B. Lane	Melford E. Smyre
Christof Ebert	J. Dennis Lawrence	Alfred R. Sorkowitz
William Eventoff	Mary Leatherman	Julia. Stesney
Jonathan H. Fairclough	Randal Leavitt	Fred J. Strauss
Richard E. Fairley	William M. Lively	Christine Brown Strysik
John W. Fendrich	James J. Longbucco	Toru Takeshita
Jay Forster	Stan Magee	Richard H. Thayer
Kirby Fortenberry	David Maibor	Booker Thomas
Eva Freund	Robert A. Martin	Patricia Trellue
Karol Fruehauf	Mike McAndrew	Mark-Rene Uchida
Barry L. Garner	Patrick D. McCray	Theodore J. Urbanowicz
Marilyn Ginsberg-Finner	James W. Moore	Glenn D. Venables
John Garth Glynn	Pavol Navrat	Delores Wallace

John W. Walz
Camille S. White-Partain
Scott A. Whitmire

P. A. Wolfgang
Paul R. Work
Natalie C. Yopconka

Janusz Zalewski
Geraldine Zimmerman
Peter F. Zoll

The following persons were on the balloting group of IEEE Std 1058.1 (renumbered as 1058):

Syed Ali
Theodore K. Atchinson
H. Ronald Berlack
Richard E. Biehl
Juris Borzovs
David W. Burnett
James E. Cardow
Leslie Chambers
Keith Chan
Antonio M. Cicu
Theo Clarke
Rosemary Coleman
Darrell Cooksey
Virgil Lee Cooper
W. W. Geoff Cozens
Paul R. Croll
Thomas Crowley
Taz Daughtrey
Hillary Davidson
Bostjan K. Derganc
Perry R. DeWeese
Audrey Dorofee
Carl Einar Dragstedt
Jonathan H. Fairclough
Richard E. Fairley
John W. Fendrich
Kirby Fortenberry
Eva Freund
Karol Fruehauf
Roger U. Fujii
Barry L. Garner
Marilyn Ginsberg-Finner
John Garth Glynn
Julio Gonzalez-Sanz

Donald Gotterbarn
L. M. Gunther
Robert T. Harley
William Hefley
Manfred Hein
Debra Herrmann
S. H. Stephen Huang
George Jackelen
Frank V. Jorgensen
Vladan V. Jovanovic
William S. Junk
George X. Kambic
Diana Kang
Ron S. Kenett
Judith S. Kerner
Robert J. Kierzyk
Shaye Koenig
Thomas M. Kurihara
John B. Lane
J. Dennis Lawrence
Randal Leavitt
Michael Lines
Dieter Look
John Lord
Stan Magee
Tomoo Matsubara
Patrick D. McCray
Russell McDowell
Sue McGrath
Jerome W. Mersky
Alan Miller
James W. Moore
Pavol Navrat
Mike Ottewill

David E. Peercy
John G. Phippen
Peter T. Poon
Kenneth R. Ptack
Annette D. Reilly
Andrew P. Sage
Helmut Sandmayr
Norman Schneidewind
David J. Schultz
Lisa A. Selmon
Robert W. Shillato
Lynn J. Simms
Carl A. Singer
James M. Sivak
Alfred R. Sorkowitz
Julia Stesney
Fred J. Strauss
Christine Brown Strysik
Toru Takeshita
Richard H. Thayer
Douglas H. Thiele
Booker Thomas
Patricia Trellue
Leonard L. Tripp
Mark-Rene Uchida
Theodore J. Urbanowicz
Andre Villas-Boas
Udo Voges
Ronald L. Wade
Scott A. Whitmire
P. A. Wolfgang
Paul R. Work
Natalie C. Yopconka
Geraldine Zimmerman

The IEEE-SA Standards Board approved IEEE Std 1058a on 16 September 1998. When it approved IEEE Std 1058 on 8 December 1998, it had the following membership:

Richard J. Holleman, *Chair*

Donald N. Heirman, *Vice Chair*

Judith Gorman, *Secretary*

Satish K. Aggarwal
Clyde R. Camp
James T. Carlo
Gary R. Engmann
Harold E. Epstein
Jay Forster*
Thomas F. Garrity
Ruben D. Garzon

James H. Gurney
Jim D. Isaak
Lowell G. Johnson
Robert Kennelly
E. G. "Al" Kiener
Joseph L. Koepfinger*
Stephen R. Lambert
Jim Logothetis
Donald C. Loughry

L. Bruce McClung
Louis-François Pau
Ronald C. Petersen
Gerald H. Peterson
John B. Posey
Gary S. Robinson
Hans E. Weinrich
Donald W. Zipse

*Member Emeritus

Kristin Dittmann
IEEE Standards Project Editor

Contents

IEEE Standard for Software Project Management Plans

1. Overview

This standard prescribes the format and content of software project management plans (SPMPs). An SPMP is the controlling document for managing a software project; it defines the technical and managerial processes necessary to develop software work products that satisfy the product requirements.

The readers of this document are referred to Annex B for guidelines for using this document to meet the requirements of IEEE/EIA 12207.1-1997, IEEE/EIA Guide for Information Technology—Software life cycle processes—Life cycle data.

This standard may be applied to any type of software project. Use of this standard is not restricted by the size, complexity, or criticality of the software product. This standard is applicable to all forms of product delivery media, including traditional source code, firmware, embedded systems code, programmable logic arrays, and software-in-silicon. This standard can be applied to any, or all, phases of a software product life cycle.

This standard identifies the elements that should appear in all SPMPs. There are two types of compliance to this standard: *format compliance*, in which the exact format and contents of this standard are followed in a project plan; and *content compliance*, in which the contents of this standard are rearranged in a project plan. In the case of content compliance, a mapping should be provided to map the content-compliant project plan into the various clauses and subclauses of this standard. Project plans that conform to the earlier version of this standard, IEEE Std 1058.1-1987, may claim partial content-compliance with this standard; this is the only type of partial content-compliance allowed. All compliant project plans must be titled "Software Project Management Plan."

Project plans based on this standard may incorporate additional elements by appending additional clauses or subclauses. The various clauses and subclauses of an SPMP conformant to this standard may be included in the plan by direct incorporation or by reference to other plans. Access to plans incorporated by reference shall be provided for all project stakeholders.

Some organizations may have generic project plans based on this standard, so that development of a particular project plan will involve tailoring of the generic plan in areas such as the process model, supporting processes, and infrastructure, and adding project-unique elements such as schedule, budget, work activities, and risk management plan.

2. References

This standard shall be used in conjunction with the following publication. When the following standard is superseded by an approved revision, the revision shall apply.

IEEE Std 610.12-1990, IEEE Standard Glossary of Software Engineering Terminology.[1]

3. Definitions

The definitions listed here establish meanings within the context of this standard. Definitions of other terms that may be appropriate within the context of this standard can be found in IEEE Std 610.12-1990.

3.1 acquirer: The individual or organization that specifies requirements for and accepts delivery of a new or modified software product and its documentation. The acquirer may be internal or external to the supplier organization. Acquisition of a software product may involve, but does not necessarily require, a legal contract or a financial transaction between acquirer and supplier.

3.2 baseline: A work product that has been formally reviewed and accepted by the involved parties. A baseline should be changed only through formal configuration management procedures. Some baselines may be project deliverables while others provide the basis for further work.

3.3 milestone: A scheduled event used to measure progress. Examples of major milestones for software projects may include an acquirer or managerial sign-off, baselining of a specification, completion of system integration, and product delivery. Minor milestones might include baselining of a software module or completion of a chapter of the user's manual.

3.4 project agreement: A document or set of documents baselined by the acquirer and the supplier that specifies the conditions under which the project will be conducted. A project agreement may include items such as the scope, objectives, assumptions, management interfaces, risks, staffing plan, resource requirements, price, schedule, resource and budget allocations, project deliverables, and acceptance criteria for the project deliverables. Documents in a project agreement may include some or all of the following: a contract, a statement of work, user requirements, system engineering specifications, software requirements specifications, a software project management plan, supporting process plans, a business plan, a project charter, or a memo of understanding.

3.5 project deliverable: A work product to be delivered to the acquirer. Quantities, delivery dates, and delivery locations are specified in a project agreement. Project deliverables may include the following: operational requirements, functional specifications, design documentation, source code, object code, test results, installation instructions, training aids, user's manuals, product development tools, and maintenance documentation. Project deliverables may be self-contained or may be part of a larger system's deliverables.

3.6 software project: The set of work activities, both technical and managerial, required to satisfy the terms and conditions of a project agreement. A software project should have specific starting and ending dates, well-defined objectives and constraints, established responsibilities, and a budget and schedule. A software project may be self-contained or may be part of a larger project. In some cases, a software project may span only a portion of the software development cycle. In other cases, a software project may span many years and consist of numerous subprojects, each being a well-defined and self-contained software project.

3.7 supplier: An organization that develops some or all of the project deliverables for an acquirer. Suppliers may include organizations that have primary responsibility for project deliverables and subcontractors that deliver some part of the project deliverables to a primary supplier. In the latter case, the primary supplier is also an acquirer.

---

[1]IEEE publications are available from the Institute of Electrical and Electronics Engineers, 445 Hoes Lane, P.O. Box 1331, Piscataway, NJ 08855-1331, USA (http://standards.ieee.org/).

3.8 supporting process: A collection of work activities that span the entire duration of a software project. Examples of supporting processes include software documentation, quality assurance, configuration management, software reviews, audit processes, and problem resolution activities.

3.9 work activity: A collection of work tasks spanning a fixed duration within the schedule of a software project. Work activities may contain other work activities, as in a work breakdown structure. The lowest-level work activities in a hierarchy of activities are work tasks. Typical work activities include project planning, requirements specification, software design, implementation, and testing.

3.10 work package: A specification of the work that must be accomplished to complete a work task. A work package should have a unique name and identifier, preconditions for initiating the work, staffing requirements, other needed resources, work products to be generated, estimated duration, risks factors, predecessor and successor work tasks, any special considerations for the work, and the completion criteria for the work package—including quality criteria for the work products to be generated.

3.11 work product: Any tangible item produced during the process of developing or modifying software. Examples of work products include the project plan, supporting process requirements, design documentation, source code, test plans, meeting minutes, schedules, budgets, and problem reports. Some subset of the work products will be baselined and some will form the set of project deliverables.

3.12 work task: The smallest unit of work subject to management accountability. A work task must be small enough to allow adequate planning and control of a software project, but large enough to avoid micro-management. The specification of work to be accomplished in completing a work task should be documented in a work package. Related work tasks should be grouped to form supporting processes and work activities.

4. Elements of the software project management plan

The individual or organization responsible for a software project shall also be responsible for the software project management plan (hereafter referred to as the SPMP). This clause of the standard describes each of the elements of an SPMP, as shown in Figure 1.

The ordering of elements presented in Figure 1 is not meant to imply that the clauses and subclauses must be developed in that order. The order of elements is intended for ease of reading, presentation, and use, and not as a guide to the order of preparation of the various elements of an SPMP. The various clauses and subclauses of an SPMP may be included by direct incorporation or by reference to other plans and documents.

Detailed descriptions of each clause and subclause in an SPMP are presented in 4.1 through 4.7 of this standard. Certain additional plans may be included in an SPMP. Additional plans are specified in 4.8.

Each version of an SPMP based on this standard shall contain a title page, a signature page, and a change history. The title page shall contain the date of issue, a unique identifier (draft number, baseline version number), and identification of the issuing organization. The signature page shall contain the signature(s) of the persons responsible for approving the SPMP. The change history shall include the project name, version number of the plan, date of release, a list of pages that have been changed in the current version of the plan, a brief statement describing the nature of changes incorporated into this version of the plan, and a list of version numbers and dates of release of all previous versions of the plan.

The preface of the SPMP shall describe the scope and context of the SPMP and identify the intended audience for the SPMP. A table of contents, and lists of figures and tables that appear in the SPMP shall be included, as indicated in Figure 1.

Title page
Signature page
Change history
Preface
Table of contents
List of figures
List of tables
1. Overview
1.1 Project summary
1.1.1 Purpose, scope, and objectives
1.1.2 Assumptions and constraints
1.1.3 Project deliverables
1.1.4 Schedule and budget summary
1.2 Evolution of the plan
2. References
3. Definitions
4. Project organization
4.1 External interfaces
4.2 Internal structure
4.3 Roles and responsibilities
5. Managerial process plans
5.1 Start-up plan
5.1.1 Estimation plan
5.1.2 Staffing plan
5.1.3 Resource acquisition plan
5.1.4 Project staff training plan
5.2 Work plan
5.2.1 Work activities
5.2.2 Schedule allocation
5.2.3 Resource allocation
5.2.4 Budget allocation
5.3 Control plan
5.3.1 Requirements control plan
5.3.2 Schedule control plan
5.3.3 Budget control plan
5.3.4 Quality control plan
5.3.5 Reporting plan
5.3.6 Metrics collection plan
5.4 Risk management plan
5.5 Closeout plan
6. Technical process plans
6.1 Process model
6.2 Methods, tools, and techniques
6.3 Infrastructure plan
6.4 Product acceptance plan
7. Supporting process plans
7.1 Configuration management plan
7.2 Verification and validation plan
7.3 Documentation plan
7.4 Quality assurance plan
7.5 Reviews and audits
7.6 Problem resolution plan
7.7 Subcontractor management plan
7.8 Process improvement plan
8. Additional plans
Annexes
Index

Figure 1—Format of a software project management plan

4.1 Overview (Clause 1 of the SPMP)

This clause of the SPMP shall provide an overview of the purpose, scope, and objectives of the project, the project assumptions and constraints, a list of project deliverables, a summary of the project schedule and budget, and the plan for evolution of the SPMP.

4.1.1 Project summary (Subclause 1.1 of the SPMP)

4.1.1.1 Purpose, scope, and objectives (Subclause 1.1.1 of the SPMP)

This subclause of the SPMP shall define the purpose, scope, and objectives of the project and the products to be delivered. This subclause should also describe any considerations of scope or objectives to be excluded from the project or the resulting product. The statement of scope shall be consistent with similar statements in the project agreement and other relevant system-level or business-level documents.

This subclause of the SPMP shall also provide a brief statement of the business or system needs to be satisfied by the project, with a concise summary of the project objectives, the products to be delivered to satisfy those objectives, and the methods by which satisfaction will be determined. The project statement of purpose shall describe the relationship of this project to other projects, and, as appropriate, how this project will be integrated with other projects or ongoing work processes.

A reference to the official statement of product requirements shall be provided in this subclause of the SPMP.

4.1.1.2 Assumptions and constraints (Subclause 1.1.2 of the SPMP)

This subclause of the SPMP shall describe the assumptions on which the project is based and imposed constraints on project factors such as the schedule, budget, resources, software to be reused, acquirer software to be incorporated, technology to be employed, and product interfaces to other products.

4.1.1.3 Project deliverables (Subclause 1.1.3 of the SPMP)

This subclause of the SPMP shall list the work products that will be delivered to the acquirer, the delivery dates, delivery locations, and quantities required to satisfy the terms of the project agreement. In addition, this subclause shall specify the delivery media and any special instructions for packaging and handling. The list of project deliverables may be incorporated into the SPMP directly or by reference to an external document such as a contract data requirements list (CDRL) or a product parts list (PPL).

4.1.1.4 Schedule and budget summary (Subclause 1.1.4 of the SPMP)

This subclause of the SPMP shall provide a summary of the schedule and budget for the software project. The level of detail should be restricted to an itemization of the major work activities and supporting processes as, for example, those depicted by the top level of the work breakdown structure.

4.1.2 Evolution of the SPMP (Subclause 1.2 of the SPMP)

This subclause of the SPMP shall specify the plans for producing both scheduled and unscheduled updates to the SPMP. Methods of disseminating the updates shall be specified. This subclause shall also specify the mechanisms used to place the initial version of the SPMP under configuration management and to control subsequent changes to the SPMP.

4.2 References (Clause 2 of the SPMP)

This clause of the SPMP shall provide a complete list of all documents and other sources of information referenced in the SPMP. Each document should be identified by title, report number, date, author, path/name for electronic access, and publishing organization. Other sources of information, such as electronic files, shall be identified using unique identifiers such as date and version number. Any deviations from referenced standards or policies shall be identified and justifications shall be provided.

4.3 Definitions (Clause 3 of the SPMP)

This clause of the SPMP shall define, or provide references to, documents containing the definition of all terms and acronyms required to properly understand the SPMP.

4.4 Project organization (Clause 4 of the SPMP)

This clause of the SPMP shall identify interfaces to organizational entities external to the project; describe the project's internal organizational structure; and define roles and responsibilities for the project.

4.4.1 External interfaces (Subclause 4.1 of the SPMP)

This subclause of the SPMP shall describe the organizational boundaries between the project and external entities. This should include, but is not limited to, the following: the parent organization, the acquiring organization, subcontracted organizations, and other organizational entities that interact with the project. Representations such as organizational charts and diagrams may be used to depict the project's external interfaces.

4.4.2 Internal structure (Subclause 4.2 of the SPMP)

This subclause of the SPMP shall describe the internal structure of the project organization to include the interfaces among the units of the software development team. In addition, the organizational interfaces between the project and organizational entities that provide supporting processes, such as configuration management, quality assurance, and verification and validation, shall be specified in this subclause. Graphical devices such as organizational charts or diagrams should be used to depict the lines of authority, responsibility, and communication within the project.

4.4.3 Roles and responsibilities (Subclause 4.3 of the SPMP)

This subclause of the SPMP shall identify and state the nature of each major work activity and supporting process and identify the organizational units that are responsible for those processes and activities. A matrix of work activities and supporting processes vs. organizational units may be used to depict project roles and responsibilities.

4.5 Managerial process plans (Clause 5 of the SPMP)

This clause of the SPMP shall specify the project management processes for the project. This clause shall be consistent with the statement of project scope and shall include the project start-up plan, risk management plan, project work plan, project control plan, and project closeout plan.

4.5.1 Project start-up plan (Subclause 5.1 of the SPMP)

This subclause of the SPMP shall specify the estimation plan, staffing plan, resource acquisition plan, and training plan. Depending on the size and scope of the project, these plans may be incorporated directly or by reference to other plans.

4.5.1.1 Estimation plan (Subclause 5.1.1 of the SPMP)

This subclause of the SPMP shall specify the cost and schedule for conducting the project as well as methods, tools, and techniques used to estimate project cost, schedule, resource requirements, and associated confidence levels. In addition, the basis of estimation shall be specified to include techniques such as analogy, rule of thumb, or local history and the sources of data. This subclause shall also specify the methods, tools, and techniques that will be used to periodically re-estimate the cost, schedule, and resources needed to complete the project. Re-estimation may be done on a monthly basis and aperiodically as necessary.

4.5.1.2 Staffing plan (Subclause 5.1.2 of the SPMP)

This subclause of the SPMP shall specify the number of staff required by skill level, the project phases in which the numbers of personnel and types of skills are needed, and the duration of need. In addition, this subclause shall specify the sources of staff personnel; for example by internal transfer, new hire, or contracted. Resource Gantt charts, resource histograms, spreadsheets, and tables may be used to depict the staffing plan by skill level, by project phase, and by aggregations of skill levels and project phases.

4.5.1.3 Resource acquisition plan (Subclause 5.1.3 of the SPMP)

This subclause of the SPMP shall specify the plan for acquiring the resources in addition to personnel needed to successfully complete the project. The resource acquisition plan should include a description of the resource acquisition process, including assignment of responsibility for all aspects of resource acquisition. The plan should include, but not be limited to, acquisition plans for equipment, computer hardware and software, training, service contracts, transportation, facilities, and administrative and janitorial services. The plan should specify the points in the project schedule when the various acquisition activities will be required. Constraints on acquiring the necessary resources shall be specified. This subclause may be expanded into additional subclauses of the form 5.1.3.x to accommodate acquisition plans for various types of resources to be acquired.

4.5.1.4 Project staff training plan (Subclause 5.1.4 of the SPMP)

This subclause of the SPMP shall specify the training needed to ensure that necessary skill levels in sufficient numbers are available to successfully conduct the software project. The training schedule shall include the types of training to be provided, numbers of personnel to be trained, entry and exit criteria for training, and the training method; for example, lectures, consultations, mentoring, or computer-assisted training. The training plan should include training as needed in both technical and managerial skills.

4.5.2 Work plan (Subclause 5.2 of the SPMP)

This clause of the SPMP shall specify the work activities, schedule, resources, and budget details for the software project.

4.5.2.1 Work activities (Subclause 5.2.1 of the SPMP)

This subclause of the SPMP shall specify the various work activities to be performed in the software project. A work breakdown structure shall be used to depict the work activities and the relationships among work activities. Work activities should be decomposed to a level that exposes all project risk factors and allows accurate estimate of resource requirements and schedule duration for each work activity. Work packages should be used to specify, for each work activity, factors such as the necessary resources, estimated duration, work products to be produced, acceptance criteria for the work products, and predecessor and successor work activities. The level of decomposition for different work activities in the work breakdown structure may be different depending on factors such as the quality of the requirements, familiarity of the work, and novelty of the technology to be used.

4.5.2.2 Schedule allocation (Subclause 5.2.2 of the SPMP)

This subclause of the SPMP shall provide scheduling relationships among work activities in a manner that depicts the time-sequencing constraints and illustrates opportunities for concurrent work activities. Any constraints on scheduling of particular work activities caused by factors external to the project shall be indicated in the work activity schedule. The schedule should include frequent milestones that can be assessed for achievement using objective indicators to assess the scope and quality of work products completed at those milestones. Techniques for depicting schedule relationships may include milestone charts, activity lists, activity Gantt charts, activity networks, critical path networks, and PERT.

4.5.2.3 Resource allocation (Subclause 5.2.3 of the SPMP)

This subclause of the SPMP shall provide a detailed itemization of the resources allocated to each major work activity in the project work breakdown structure. Resources shall include the numbers and required skill levels of personnel for each work activity. Resource allocation may include, as appropriate, personnel by skill level and factors such as computing resources, software tools, special testing and simulation facilities, and administrative support. A separate line item should be provided for each type of resource for each work activity. A summary of resource requirements for the various work activities should be collected from the work packages of the work breakdown structure and presented in tabular form.

4.5.2.4 Budget allocation (Subclause 5.2.4 of the SPMP)

This subclause of the SPMP shall provide a detailed breakdown of necessary resource budgets for each of the major work activities in the work breakdown structure. The activity budget shall include the estimated cost for activity personnel and may include, as appropriate, costs for factors such as travel, meetings, computing resources, software tools, special testing and simulation facilities, and administrative support. A separate line item shall be provided for each type of resource in each activity budget. The work activity budget may be developed using a spreadsheet and presented in tabular form.

4.5.3 Control plan (Subclause 5.3 of the SPMP)

This subclause of the SPMP shall specify the metrics, reporting mechanisms, and control procedures necessary to measure, report, and control the product requirements, the project schedule, budget, and resources, and the quality of work processes and work products. All elements of the control plan should be consistent with the organization's standards, policies, and procedures for project control as well as with any contractual agreements for project control.

4.5.3.1 Requirements control plan (Subclause 5.3.1 of the SPMP)

This subclause of the SPMP shall specify the control mechanisms for measuring, reporting, and controlling changes to the product requirements. This subclause shall also specify the mechanisms to be used in assessing the impact of requirements changes on product scope and quality, and the impacts of requirements changes on project schedule, budget, resources, and risk factors. Configuration management mechanisms shall include change control procedures and a change control board. Techniques that may be used for requirements control include traceability, prototyping and modeling, impact analysis, and reviews.

4.5.3.2 Schedule control plan (Subclause 5.3.2 of the SPMP)

This subclause of the SPMP shall specify the control mechanisms to be used to measure the progress of work completed at the major and minor project milestones, to compare actual progress to planned progress, and to implement corrective action when actual progress does not conform to planned progress. The schedule control plan shall specify the methods and tools that will be used to measure and control schedule progress. Achievement of schedule milestones should be assessed using objective criteria to measure the scope and quality of work products completed at each milestone.

4.5.3.3 Budget control plan (Subclause 5.3.3 of the SPMP)

This subclause of the SPMP shall specify the control mechanisms to be used to measure the cost of work completed, compare planned cost to budgeted cost, and implement corrective action when actual cost does not conform to budgeted cost. The budget control plan shall specify the intervals at which cost reporting will be done and the methods and tools that will be used to manage the budget. The budget plan should include frequent milestones that can be assessed for achievement using objective indicators to assess the scope and quality of work products completed at those milestones. A mechanism such as earned value tracking should be used to report the budget and schedule plan, schedule progress, and the cost of work completed.

4.5.3.4 Quality control plan (Subclause 5.3.4 of the SPMP)

This subclause of the SPMP shall specify the mechanisms to be used to measure and control the quality of the work processes and the resulting work products. Quality control mechanisms may include quality assurance of work processes, verification and validation, joint reviews, audits, and process assessment.

4.5.3.5 Reporting plan (Subclause 5.3.5 of the SPMP)

This subclause of the SPMP shall specify the reporting mechanisms, report formats, and information flows to be used in communicating the status of requirements, schedule, budget, quality, and other desired or required status metrics within the project and to entities external to the project. The methods, tools, and techniques of communication shall be specified in this subclause. The frequency and detail of communications related to project measurement and control shall be consistent with the project scope, criticality, risk, and visibility.

4.5.3.6 Metrics collection plan (Subclause 5.3.6 of the SPMP)

This subclause of the SPMP shall specify the methods, tools, and techniques to be used in collecting and retaining project metrics. The metrics collection plan shall specify the metrics to be collected, the frequency of collection, and the methods to be used in validating, analyzing, and reporting the metrics.

4.5.4 Risk management plan (Subclause 5.4 of the SPMP)

This subclause of the SPMP shall specify the risk management plan for identifying, analyzing, and prioritizing project risk factors. This subclause shall also describe the procedures for contingency planning, and the methods to be used in tracking the various risk factors, evaluating changes in the levels of risk factors, and the responses to those changes. The risk management plan shall also specify plans for assessing initial risk factors and the ongoing identification, assessment, and mitigation of risk factors throughout the life cycle of the project. This plan should describe risk management work activities, procedures and schedules for performing those activities, documentation and reporting requirements, organizations and personnel responsible for performing specific activities, and procedures for communicating risks and risk status among the various acquirer, supplier, and subcontractor organizations. Risk factors that should be considered include risks in the acquirer-supplier relationship, contractual risks, technological risks, risks caused by the size and complexity of the product, risks in the development and target environments, risks in personnel acquisition, skill levels and retention, risks to schedule and budget, and risks in achieving acquirer acceptance of the product.

4.5.5 Project closeout plan (Subclause 5.5 of the SPMP)

This subclause of the SPMP shall contain the plans necessary to ensure orderly closeout of the software project. Items in the closeout plan should include a staff reassignment plan, a plan for archiving project materials, a plan for post-mortem debriefings of project personnel, and preparation of a final report to include lessons learned and analysis of project objectives achieved.

4.6 Technical process plans (Clause 6 of the SPMP)

This clause of the SPMP shall specify the development process model, the technical methods, tools, and techniques to be used to develop the various work products; plans for establishing and maintaining the project infrastructure; and the product acceptance plan.

4.6.1 Process model (Subclause 6.1 of the SPMP)

This subclause of the SPMP shall define the relationships among major project work activities and supporting processes by specifying the flow of information and work products among activities and functions, the timing of work products to be generated, reviews to be conducted, major milestones to be achieved, baselines to be established, project deliverables to be completed, and required approvals that span the duration of the project. The process model for the project shall include project initiation and project termination activities. To describe the process model, a combination of graphical and textual notations may be used. Any tailoring of an organization's standard process model for a project shall be indicated in this subclause.

4.6.2 Methods, tools, and techniques (Subclause 6.2 of the SPMP)

This subclause of the SPMP shall specify the development methodologies, programming languages and other notations, and the tools and techniques to be used to specify, design, build, test, integrate, document, deliver, modify and maintain the project deliverable and nondeliverable work products. In addition, the technical standards, policies, and procedures governing development and/or modification of the work products shall be specified.

4.6.3 Infrastructure plan (Subclause 6.3 of the SPMP)

This subclause of the SPMP shall specify the plan for establishing and maintaining the development environment (hardware, operating system, network, and software), and the policies, procedures, standards, and facilities required to conduct the software project. These resources may include workstations, local area networks, software tools for analysis, design, implementation, testing, and project management, desks, office space, and provisions for physical security, administrative personnel, and janitorial services.

4.6.4 Product acceptance plan (Subclause 6.4 of the SPMP)

This subclause of the SPMP shall specify the plan for acquirer acceptance of the deliverable work products generated by the software project. Objective criteria for determining acceptability of the deliverable work products shall be specified in this plan and a formal agreement of the acceptance criteria shall be signed by representatives of the development organization and the acquiring organization. Any technical processes, methods, or tools required for product acceptance shall be specified in the product acceptance plan. Methods such as testing, demonstration, analysis and inspection should be specified in this plan.

4.7 Supporting process plans (Clause 7 of the SPMP)

This clause of the SPMP shall contain plans for the supporting processes that span the duration of the software project. These plans shall include, but are not limited to, configuration management, verification and validation, software documentation, quality assurance, reviews and audits, problem resolution, and subcontractor management. Plans for supporting processes shall be developed to a level of detail consistent with the other clauses and subclauses of the SPMP. In particular, the roles, responsibilities, authorities, schedule, budgets, resource requirements, risk factors, and work products for each supporting process shall be specified. The nature and types of supporting processes required may vary from project to project; however, the absence of a configuration management plan, verification and validation plan, quality assurance plan, joint acquirer-supplier review plan, problem resolution plan, or subcontractor management plan shall be explicitly justified in any SPMP that does not include them. Plans for supporting processes may be incorporated directly into the SPMP or incorporated by reference to other plans.

4.7.1 Configuration management plan (Subclause 7.1 of the SPMP)

This subclause of the SPMP shall contain the configuration management plan for the software project, to include the methods that will be used to provide configuration identification, control, status accounting, evaluation, and release management. In addition, this subclause shall specify the processes of configuration management to include procedures for initial baselining of work products, logging and analysis of change requests, change control board procedures, tracking of changes in progress, and procedures for notifying concerned parties when baselines are first established or later changed. The configuration management process should be supported by one or more automated configuration management tools.

4.7.2 Verification and validation plan (Subclause 7.2 of the SPMP)

This subclause of the SPMP shall contain the verification and validation plan for the software project to include scope, tools, techniques, and responsibilities for the verification and validation work activities. The organizational relationships and degrees of independence between development activities and verification and validation activities shall be specified. Verification planning should result in specification of techniques such as traceability, milestone reviews, progress reviews, peer reviews, prototyping, simulation, and modeling. Validation planning should result in specification of techniques such as testing, demonstration, analysis, and inspection. Automated tools to be used in verification and validation should be specified.

4.7.3 Documentation plan (Subclause 7.3 of the SPMP)

This subclause of the SPMP shall contain the documentation plan for the software project, to include plans for generating nondeliverable and deliverable work products. Organizational entities responsible for providing input information, generating, and reviewing the various documents shall be specified in the documentation plan. Non-deliverable work products may include items such as requirements specifications, design documentation, traceability matrices, test plans, meeting minutes and review reports. Deliverable work products may include source code, object code, a user's manual, an on-line help system, a regression test suite, a configuration library and configuration management tool, principles of operation, a maintenance guide, or other items specified in subclause 1.1.3 of the SPMP. The documentation plan should include a list of documents to be prepared, the controlling template or standard for each document, who will prepare it, who will review it, due dates for review copy and initial baseline version, and a distribution list for review copies and baseline versions.

4.7.4 Quality assurance plan (Subclause 7.4 of the SPMP)

This subclause of the SPMP shall provide the plans for assuring that the software project fulfills its commitments to the software process and the software product as specified in the requirements specification, the SPMP, supporting plans, and any standards, procedures, or guidelines to which the process or the product must adhere. Quality assurance procedures may include analysis, inspections, reviews, audits, and assessments. The quality assurance plan should indicate the relationships among the quality assurance, verification and validation, review, audit, configuration management, system engineering, and assessment processes.

4.7.5 Reviews and audits plan (Subclause 7.5 of the SPMP)

This subclause of the SPMP shall specify the schedule, resources, and methods and procedures to be used in conducting project reviews and audits. The plan should specify plans for joint acquirer-supplier reviews, management progress reviews, developer peer reviews, quality assurance audits, and acquirer-conducted reviews and audits. The plan should list the external agencies that approve or regulate any product of the project.

4.7.6 Problem resolution plan (Subclause 7.6 of the SPMP)

This subclause of the SPMP shall specify the resources, methods, tools, techniques, and procedures to be used in reporting, analyzing, prioritizing, and processing software problem reports generated during the project. The problem resolution plan should indicate the roles of development, configuration management, the change control board, and verification and validation in problem resolution work activities. Effort devoted to problem reporting, analysis, and resolution should be separately reported so that rework can be tracked and process improvement accomplished.

4.7.7 Subcontractor management plans (Subclause 7.7 of the SPMP)

This subclause of the SPMP shall contain plans for selecting and managing any subcontractors that may contribute work products to the software project. The criteria for selecting subcontractors shall be specified and the management plan for each subcontract shall be generated using a tailored version of this standard. Tailored plans should include the items necessary to ensure successful completion of each subcontract. In particular, requirements management, monitoring of technical progress, schedule and budget control, product acceptance criteria, and risk management procedures shall be included in each subcontractor plan. Additional topics should be added as needed to ensure successful completion of the subcontract. A reference to the official subcontract and prime contractor/subcontractor points of contact shall be specified.

4.7.8 Process improvement plan (Subclause 7.8 of the SPMP)

This subclause of the SPMP shall include plans for periodically assessing the project, determining areas for improvement, and implementing improvement plans. The process improvement plan should be closely related to the problem resolution plan; for example, root cause analysis of recurring problems may lead to simple process improvements that can significantly reduce rework during the remainder of the project. Implementation of improvement plans should be examined to identify those processes that can be improved without serious disruptions to an ongoing project and to identify those processes that can best be improved by process improvement initiatives at the organizational level.

4.8 Additional plans (Clause 8 of the SPMP)

This clause of the SPMP shall contain additional plans required to satisfy product requirements and contractual terms. Additional plans for a particular project may include plans for assuring that safety, privacy, and security requirements for the product are met, special facilities or equipment, product installation plans, user training plans, integration plans, data conversion plans, system transition plans, product maintenance plans, or product support plans.

4.9 Plan annexes

Annexes may be included, either directly or by reference to other documents, to provide supporting details that could detract from the SPMP if included in the body of the SPMP.

4.10 Plan index

An index to the key terms and acronyms used throughout the SPMP is optional, but recommended to improve the usability of the SPMP.

Annex A

(informative)

Bibliography

The standards listed here should be consulted when applying this standard. The latest revisions should be consulted.

[B1] IEEE Std 730-1998, IEEE Standard for Software Quality Assurance Plans.

[B2] IEEE Std 828-1998, IEEE Standard for Software Configuration Management Plans.

[B3] IEEE Std 1012-1998, IEEE Standard for Software Verification and Validation.

[B4] IEEE Std 1074-1997, IEEE Standard for Developing Software Life Cycle Processes.

[B5] IEEE Std 1490-1998, IEEE Guide—Adoption of PMI Standard, A Guide to the Project Management Body of Knowledge.

[B6] IEEE/EIA 12207.0-1996, IEEE/EIA Standard—Industry Implementation of ISO/IEC 12207: 1995, Standard for Information Technology—Software life cycle processes.

[B7] IEEE/EIA 12207.1-1997, IEEE/EIA Guide for Information Technology—Software life cycle processes—Life cycle data.

[B8] IEEE/EIA 12207.2-1997, IEEE/EIA Guide for Information Technology—Software life cycle processes—Implementation considerations.

[B9] ISO/IEC 12119: 1994, Information technology—Software packages—Quality requirements and testing.

[B10] ISO/IEC 9126: 1991, Information technology—Software product evaluation—Quality characteristics and their use.

Annex B

(informative)

Guidelines for compliance with IEEE/EIA 12207.1-1997

B.1 Overview

The Software Engineering Standards Committee (SESC) of the IEEE Computer Society has endorsed the policy of adopting international standards. In 1995, the international standard, ISO/IEC 12207, Information technology—Software life cycle processes, was completed. The standard establishes a common framework for software life cycle processes, with well-defined terminology, that can be referenced by the software industry.

In 1995 the SESC evaluated ISO/IEC 12207 and decided that the standard should be adopted and serve as the basis for life cycle processes within the IEEE Software Engineering Collection. The IEEE adaptation of ISO/IEC 12207 is IEEE/EIA 12207.0-1996. It contains ISO/IEC 12207 and the following additions: improved compliance approach, life cycle process objectives, life cycle data objectives, and errata.

The implementation of ISO/IEC 12207 within the IEEE also includes the following:

— IEEE/EIA 12207.1-1997, IEEE/EIA Guide for Information Technology—Software life cycle processes—Life cycle data;

— IEEE/EIA 12207.2-1997, IEEE/EIA Guide for Information Technology—Software life cycle processes—Implementation considerations; and

— Additions to 11 SESC standards (i.e., IEEE Stds 730, 828, 829, 830, 1012, 1016, 1058, 1062, 1219, 1233, 1362) to define the correlation between the data produced by existing SESC standards and the data produced by the application of IEEE/EIA 12207.1-1997.

NOTE — Although IEEE/EIA 12207.1-1997 is a guide, it also contains provisions for application as a standard with specific compliance requirements. This annex treats IEEE/EIA 12207.1-1997 as a standard.

In order to achieve compliance with both this standard and IEEE/EIA 12207.1-1997, it is essential that the user review and satisfy the data requirements for both standards.

When this standard is directly referenced, the precedence for conformance is based upon this standard alone. When this standard is referenced with the IEEE/EIA 12207.x standard series, the precedence for conformance is based upon the directly referenced IEEE/EIA 12207.x standard, unless there is a statement that this standard has precedence.

B.1.1 Scope and purpose

Both this standard and IEEE/EIA 12207.1-1997 place requirements on an SPMP. The purpose of this annex is to explain the relationship between the two sets of requirements so that users producing documents intended to comply with both standards may do so.

B.2 Correlation

This clause explains the relationship between this standard and IEEE/EIA 12207.0-1996 in the following areas: terminology, process, and life cycle data.

B.2.1 Terminology correlation

The two standards use similar terms in similar ways. The concept of project management is present in IEEE/EIA 12207.0-1996 but it is embedded in two other processes: acquisition and supply. Hence, there is an acquisition project and a supply project that, though related, may be done by different organizations.

B.2.2 Process correlation

This standard places no explicit requirements on process. However, the information required by its SPMP makes implicit assumptions regarding process, similar to that of IEEE/EIA 12207, but limited to a software project. Generally, fulfilling the implied process requirements of this standard would meet the requirements of IEEE/EIA 12207.0-1996 and would not violate its requirements.

B.2.3 Life cycle data correlation and SPMPs

The information required in an SPMP by this standard and the information required in an SPMP by IEEE/EIA 12207.1-1997 are similar. It is reasonable to expect that a single document could comply with both standards. The main difference is that this standard specifies a particular format, while IEEE/EIA 12207.1-1997 does not. Details are provided in Clause B.3 of this standard.

B.2.4 Life cycle data correlation between other data in IEEE/EIA 12207.1-1997 and IEEE Std 1058-1998

Table B.1 correlates the life cycle data other than SPMP between this standard and IEEE/EIA 12207.1-1997. It provides information to users of both standards.

**Table B.1—Life cycle data correlation between other data in
IEEE/EIA 12207.1-1997 and IEEE Std 1058-1998**

Information item(s)	IEEE/EIA 12207.0-1996 subclause	Kind of documentation	IEEE/EIA 12207.1-1997 subclause	Corresponding subclause of IEEE Std 1058-1998
Management process plans	7.1.2.1	Plan	—	4.5
Supplier selection record—Proposal evaluation criteria, Requirements compliance weighting	5.1.3.1	Record	—	4.7.7

B.3 Document compliance

This clause provides details substantiating a claim that an SPMP complying with this standard may achieve document compliance with the SPMP prescribed in IEEE/EIA 12207.1-1997. The requirements for document compliance are summarized in a single row of Table 1 of IEEE/EIA 12207.1-1997. That row is reproduced in Table B.2 of this standard.

**Table B.2—Summary of requirements for an SPMP
excerpted from Table 1 of IEEE/EIA 12207.1-1997**

Information item(s)	IEEE/EIA 12207.0-1996 subclause	Kind of documentation	IEEE/EIA 12207.1-1997 subclause	References
Project management plan	5.2.4.3, 5.2.4.4, 5.2.4.5	Plan	6.11	IEEE Std 1012-1998; IEEE Std 1058-1998; IEEE Std 1074-1997; EIA/IEEE J-STD 016-1995, E.2.1; ISO/IEC 9126: 1991; ISO/IEC 12119: 1994; *SEI Continuous Risk Management Guidebook*

The requirements for document compliance are discussed in the following subclauses:

— B.3.1 discusses compliance with the information requirements noted in column 2 of Table B.2 as prescribed by 6.2.1.1 of IEEE/EIA 12207.0-1996.
— B.3.2 discusses compliance with the generic content guideline (the "kind" of document) noted in column 3 of Table B.2 as a "plan." The generic content guidelines for a "plan" appear in 5.2 of IEEE/EIA 12207.1-1997.
— B.3.3 discusses compliance with the specific requirements for an SPMP noted in column 4 of Table B.2 as prescribed by 6.11 of IEEE/EIA 12207.1-1997.
— B.3.4 discusses compliance with the life cycle data objectives of Annex H of IEEE/EIA 12207.0-1996 as described in 4.2 of IEEE/EIA 12207.1-1997.

B.3.1 Compliance with information requirements of IEEE/EIA 12207.0-1996

The information requirements for an SPMP are those prescribed by 5.2.4.3, 5.2.4.4, and 5.2.4.5 of IEEE/EIA 12207.0-1996. In this case, those requirements are substantively identical with those considered in B.3.3 of this standard.

B.3.2 Compliance with generic content guidelines of IEEE/EIA 12207.1-1997

The generic content guidelines for a "plan" in IEEE/EIA 12207.1-1997 are prescribed by 5.2 of IEEE/EIA 12207.1-1997. A complying plan shall achieve the purpose stated in 5.2.1 and include the information listed in 5.2.2 of IEEE/EIA 12207.1-1997.

The purpose of a plan is as follows:

IEEE/EIA 12207.1-1997, subclause 5.2.1: Purpose: Define when, how, and by whom specific activities are to be performed, including options and alternatives, as required.

Any plan complying with IEEE/EIA 12207.1-1997 shall satisfy the generic content requirements provided in 5.2.2 of that standard. Table B.3 of this standard lists the generic content items and, where appropriate, references the subclause of this standard that requires the same information.

Table B.3—Coverage of generic plan requirements by IEEE Std 1058-1998

IEEE/EIA 12207.1-1997 generic content	Corresponding clause of IEEE Std 1058-1998	Additions to requirements of IEEE Std 1058-1998
a) Date of issue and status	Front pages of outline	—
b) Scope	4.1.1.1 Purpose, scope, and objectives	—
c) Issuing organization	Front pages of outline	—
d) References	4.2 References	—
e) Approval authority	4.6.1 Process model	—
f) Planned activities and tasks	4.5.2 Work plan	—
g) Macro references (policies or laws that give rise to the need for this plan)	4.2 References	
h) Micro references (other plans or task descriptions that elaborate details of this plan)	4.2 References	—
i) Schedules	4.5.2.2 Schedule allocation 4.5.5 Project closeout plan	—
j) Estimates	4.5.2.4 Budget allocation	—
k) Resources and their allocation	4.5.2.3 Resource allocation	—
l) Responsibilities and authority	4.4.3 Roles and responsibilities	—
m) Risks	4.5.4 Risk management plan	—
n) Quality control measures NOTE — This includes quality control of the SPMP itself.	4.1.2 Evolution of the SPMP 4.5.3.1 Requirements control plan 4.5.3.4 Quality control plan	—
o) Cost	4.5.2.4 Budget allocation 4.5.3.3 Budget control plan	—
p) Interfaces among parties involved	4.4.1 External interfaces 4.4.2 Internal structure	—
q) Environment/infrastructure (including safety needs)	4.5.1.3 Resource acquisition plan 4.5.2.3 Resource allocation 4.6.3 Infrastructure plan 4.8 Additional plans	—
r) Training	4.5.1.4 Project staff training plan	—
s) Glossary	4.3 Definitions	—
t) Change procedures and history NOTE — This includes the change procedures for the SPMP itself.	Front pages of outline Evolution of the plan	—

B.3.3 Compliance with specific content requirements of IEEE/EIA 12207.1-1997

The specific content requirements for an SPMP in IEEE/EIA Std 12207.1-1997 are prescribed by 6.11 of IEEE/EIA 12207.1-1997. A compliant SPMP shall achieve the purpose stated in 6.11.1 and include the information listed in 6.11.3 of IEEE/EIA 12207.1-1997.

The purpose of the SPMP is as follows:

> IEEE/EIA 12207.1-1997, subclause 6.11.1: Purpose: Define the technical and managerial processes necessary to satisfy project requirements.

An SPMP complying with IEEE/EIA 12207.1-1997 shall satisfy the specific content requirements provided in 6.11.3 of that standard. The specific content requirements of 6.11.3 of IEEE/EIA 12207.1-1997 reiterate the generic content requirements and specify the generic requirements that must be satisfied for several activities. The activities are listed in Table B.4 of this standard along with the reference to the clause of this standard that specifically deals with the activity.

Table B.4—Coverage of specific SPMP requirements by IEEE Std 1058-1998

IEEE/EIA 12207.1-1997 specific content	Corresponding clauses of IEEE Std 1058-1998	Additions to requirements of IEEE Std 1058-1998
a) Generic plan for managing the project	See Table B.3	—
b) Project organizational structure showing authority and responsibility of each organizational unit, including external organizations	4.4 Project organization	—
c) Engineering environment (for development, operation or maintenance, as applicable), including test environment, library, equipment, facilities, standards, procedures, and tools	4.5.2.3 Resource allocation 4.6.3 Infrastructure plan	—
d) Work breakdown structure of the life cycle processes and activities, including the software products, software services and nondeliverable items to be performed, budgets, staffing, physical resources, software size, and schedules associated with the tasks	4.5.2 Work plan	—
e) Management of the quality characteristics of the software products or services (Separate plans for quality may be developed.)	4.5.3.4 Quality control plan	—
f) Management of safety, security, privacy, and other critical requirements of the software products or services (Separate plans for safety and security may be developed.)	4.5.3.1 Requirements control plan 4.8 Additional plans	—

Table B.4—Coverage of specific SPMP requirements by IEEE Std 1058-1998 *(Continued)*

IEEE/EIA 12207.1-1997 specific content	Corresponding clauses of IEEE Std 1058-1998	Additions to requirements of IEEE Std 1058-1998
g) Subcontractor management, including subcontractor selection and involvement between the subcontractor and the acquirer, if any	4.7.7 Subcontractor management plan	—
h) Quality assurance	4.7.4 Quality assurance plan	—
i) Verification and validation, including the approach for interfacing with the verification and validation agent, if specified	4.7.2 Verification and validation plan	—
j) Acquirer involvement (i.e., joint reviews, audits, informal meetings, reporting, modification and change, implementation, approval, acceptance, access to facilities)	4.4.3 Roles and responsibilities 4.7.5 Reviews and audits	—
k) User involvement (i.e., requirements setting exercises, prototype demonstrations and evaluations)	4.4.3 Roles and responsibilities 4.6.4 Product Acceptance Plan 4.7.5 Reviews and Audits	—
l) Risk management (i.e., the management of the areas of the project that involve technical, cost, and schedule risks)	4.5.4 Risk Management Plan	—
m) Security policy (i.e., the rules for need-to-know and access-to-information at each project organizational level)	4.6.1 Process Model 4.6.2 Infrastructure Plan 4.8 Additional Plans	—
n) Approval required by such means as regulations, required certifications, proprietary, usage, ownership, warranty and licensing rights	4.6.1 Process model 4.7.5 Reviews and audits	—
o) Means for scheduling, tracking, and reporting	4.5.3.2 Schedule control plan 4.5.3.5 Reporting plan	—
p) Training of personnel	4.5.1.4 Project staff training plan	—
q) Software life cycle model	4.6.1 Process model	—
r) Configuration management	4.7.1 Configuration management plan	—

B.3.4 Compliance with life cycle data characteristics objectives

In addition to the content requirements, life cycle data shall be managed in accordance with the objectives provided in Annex H of IEEE/EIA 12207.0-1996.

NOTE — The information items covered by this standard include plans and provisions for creating software life cycle data related to the basic "management data" in H.4 of IEEE/EIA 12207.0-1996. It provides for the following: management data, management plans, status reports, management indicators, criteria and key decision rationale, and contract and other procurement information.

B.4 Conclusion

The analysis documented in this annex suggests that any SPMP complying with this standard will comply with the requirements of an SPMP in IEEE/EIA 12207.1-1997. In addition, to comply with IEEE/EIA 12207.1-1997, an SPMP shall support the life cycle data objectives of Annex H of IEEE/EIA 12207.0-1996.

IEEE Guide for Software Verification and Validation Plans

Sponsor

**Software Engineering Standards Committee
of the
IEEE Computer Society**

Approved December 2, 1993

IEEE Standards Board

Abstract: Guidance in preparing Software Verification and Validation Plans (SVVPs) that comply with IEEE Std 1012-1986 are provided. IEEE Std 1012-1986 specifies the required content for an SVVP. This guide recommends approaches to Verification and Validation (V&V) planning. This guide does not present requirements beyond those stated in IEEE Std 1012-1986.
Keywords: baseline change assessment, life cycle phases, master schedule, V&V tasks

The Institute of Electrical and Electronics Engineers, Inc.
345 East 47th Street, New York, NY 10017-2394, USA

ISBN 1-55937-384-9

Introduction

(This introduction is not a part of IEEE Std 1059-1993, IEEE Guide for Software Verification and Validation Plans.)

The purpose of this guide is to provide guidance in preparing Software Verification and Validation Plans (SVVPs) that comply with IEEE Std 1012-1986[*] (referred to throughout as the Standard). The Standard specifies the required content for an SVVP. This guide recommends approaches to Verification and Validation (V&V) planning. This guide does not present requirements beyond those in the Standard.

When describing specific information to be placed in sections of an SVVP, this guide quotes extensively from the Standard. Not all of the Standard is reproduced. The Standard is a prerequisite for the use of this guide.

This guide does not provide a comprehensive view of the verification and validation process itself. It does provide an overview of the process of creating an SVVP. For each section in a plan, it presents a list of topics that could be addressed when preparing that section. The guide is not specific to any application area.

This guide includes the following:
a) Recommended planning procedures (e.g., criticality analysis) to aid in selecting specific V&V tasks for each phase
b) General guidance on the topics that shall be addressed in the life cycle phase sections of a plan (e.g., task descriptions, methods and criteria, and inputs and outputs)
c) Specific guidance in planning the V&V tasks required by the Standard
d) Samples of V&V planning based on the elevator system, which is described in annex A

As with the Standard, this guide is directed at the development and maintenance of critical software—software in which a failure could affect personal or equipment safety, or could result in a large financial or social loss. The guidance may also be applied to noncritical software. Determination of criticality should be carefully considered.

The Standard and this guide employ a specific life cycle model of the software development process, although plans written in the Standard may make use of a different model.

This guide may be used where software is the system or where software is part of a larger system. When software is part of a larger system, software V&V should be integrated into a system-level V&V effort covering critical hardware, software, and interfaces to operators.

This guide is primarily directed to those preparing SVVPs. This guide may be used by project management, system and software developers, quality assurance organizations, purchasers, end users, maintainers, and those performing V&V.

Neither the Standard nor this guide assumes that the V&V effort is necessarily independent of the development effort. V&V tasks may be performed by personnel doing development tasks, by a separate team within a single organization, by a completely independent organization, or by some combination as assigned within the SVVP.

---

[*]Information on references can be found in clause 2.

At the time this guide was completed, the P1059 working group had the following membership:

Jerome W. Mersky, *Chair* **Dolores Wallace,** *Co-chair*
Kirby Fortenberry, *Secretary*

François Coallier	Caroline L. Evans	Dennis E. Nickle
Cora Carmody	Robert V. Ebenau	S. J. Pasquariello
Michael S. Deutsch	Eva Freund	Lee Perkins
Michael P. Dewalt	Jack Leavenworth	Andrew Vaughan
David C. Doty	George Lee	Natalie C. Yopconka

The following persons were on the balloting committee:

H. R. Berlack	John Harauz	Dennis E. Nickle
William J. Boll, Jr.	John W. Horch	John D. Pope
Fletcher Buckley	Peter L. Hung	Patricia Rodriguez
Geoff Cozens	Myron S. Karasik	Hans Schaefer
Stewart Crawford	Judy S. Kerner	Gregory D. Schumacher
Bostjan K. Derganc	Robert Kosinski	Robert W. Shillato
Einar Dragstedt	Thomas Kurihara	D. M. Siefert
Robert G. Ebenau	Renee Lamb	A. R. Sorkowitz
Caroline L. Evans	Robert Lane	Vijaya Srivastava
John W. Fendrich	Ben Livson	David Terrell
Kirby Fortenberry	Joseph Maayan	Richard Thayer
Eva Freund	Jukka Marijarvi	George D. Tice
Roger Fujii	Roger Martin	Leonard L. Tripp
David Gelperin	Scott D. Matthews	Dolores Wallace
Yair Gershkovitch	Ivano Mazza	William M. Walsh
Julio Ganzalez-Sanz	Michael McAndrew	Natalie C. Yopconka
David A. Gustafson	Sue McGrath	Janusz Zalewski
	Jerome W. Mersky	

When the IEEE Standards Board approved this standard on December 2, 1993, it had the following membership:

Wallace S. Read, *Chair* **Donald C. Loughry,** *Vice Chair*
Andrew G. Salem, *Secretary*

Gilles A. Baril	Jim Isaak	Don T. Michael*
José A. Berrios de la Paz	Ben C. Johnson	Marco W. Migliaro
Clyde R. Camp	Walter J. Karplus	L. John Rankine
Donald C. Fleckenstein	Lorraine C. Kevra	Arthur K. Reilly
Jay Forster*	E. G. "Al" Kiener	Ronald H. Reimer
David F. Franklin	Ivor N. Knight	Gary S. Robinson
Ramiro Garcia	Joseph L. Koepfinger*	Leonard L. Tripp
Donald N. Heirman	D. N. "Jim" Logothetis	Donald W. Zipse

*Member Emeritus

Also included are the following nonvoting IEEE Standards Board liaisons:

Satish K. Aggarwal
James Beall
Richard B. Engelman
David E. Soffrin
Stanley I. Warshaw

Rachel A. Meisel
IEEE Standards Project Editor

Contents

IEEE Guide for Software Verification and Validation Plans

1. Overview

This guide is the explication of IEEE Std 1012-1986[1] (referred to throughout as the Standard). This Standard specified the required content of a Software Verification and Validation Plan (SVVP). This guide provides the guidance and background discussion that a user of the Standard may need in order to write a plan.

This guide is divided into four clauses. Clause 1 provides the overview and scope of this guide. Clause 2 lists references to other standards. Clause 3 defines the terms, conventions, and acronyms used in this guide. Clause 4 provides an overview of software V&V, general planning guidance, and a description of the major V&V activities that continue across more than one life cycle phase (e.g., traceability analysis, evaluation, interface analysis, and testing). Clause 5 provides a sequential review of each of the sections of the SVVP, providing specific guidance for each section. In many cases, the guidance for a section or task is in the form of a list of questions or activities to consider. Note that these lists are not complete because for any given situation there will be other questions or activities that can be addressed. Also, all items in a given list may not be applicable to any given situation.

This guide also contains three annexes. Annex A describes the elevator example that was used to develop sample plan extracts. These sample extracts are also presented in this annex. Annex B describes and overviews software criticality planning analysis. Annex C provides guidance for the seven planning topics that are aimed at V&V tasks in an SVVP.

1.1 Scope

This document provides specific guidance about planning and documenting the tasks required by the Standard so that the user may write an effective plan. Some guidance is in the form of checklists, questions, or activities to consider.

This guide does not present requirements beyond those found in the Standard. Mention of certain methods or activities in this guide does not mean that the user of the Standard must include these in a plan in order for that plan to comply with the Standard. There may be other methods or activities that are relevant to a specific software project or product. The user of this guide is encouraged to survey the standards referenced in clause 2 for additional guidance, particularly guidance for specific tools or techniques.

---

[1]Information on references can be found in clause 2.

2. References

This guide shall be used in conjunction with the following publications:

IEEE Std 610.12-1990, IEEE Glossary of Software Engineering Terminology (ANSI).[2]

IEEE Std 730-1989, IEEE Standard for Software Quality Assurance Plans (ANSI).

IEEE Std 828-1990, IEEE Standard for Software Configuration Management Plans (ANSI).

IEEE Std 829-1983 (Reaff 1991), IEEE Standard for Software Test Documentation (ANSI).

IEEE Std 830-1993, IEEE Recommended Practice for Software Requirements Specifications.

IEEE Std 1008-1987, IEEE Standard for Software Unit Testing (ANSI).

IEEE Std 1012-1986, IEEE Standard for Software Verification and Validation Plans (ANSI).

IEEE Std 1016-1987, IEEE Recommended Practice for Software Design Descriptions (ANSI).

IEEE Std 1042-1987, IEEE Guide to Software Configuration Management (ANSI).

---

[2]IEEE publications are available from the Institute of Electrical and Electronics Engineers, 445 Hoes Lane, P.O. Box 1331, Piscataway, NJ 08855-1331, USA.

3. Conventions, definitions, and acronyms and abbreviations

3.1 Conventions

Below are a number of conventions adopted within the body of this guide.

— *Standard* refers to IEEE Std 1012-1986.
— *Plan* refers to a Software Verification and Validation Plan (SVVP).
— *Shall* or the imperative form indicates an item or activity required by the Standard.
— *Should* indicates a recommended item or activity.
— *May* indicates an item or activity appropriate under some, but not all, conditions; for which there are a number of acceptable alternatives; or for which there is no professional consensus.
— *Life cycle model* is taken from the Standard. As stated in the Standard, a different model of the life cycle may be used, provided the SVVP written for that model includes cross-references to the original model.
— *System* is used to denote the item that will contain the developed software.
— Material quoted from the Standard is indented and italicized and is followed by a reference to the section (or, in some cases, part of a table) of the Standard.

3.2 Definitions

This guide is consistent with other IEEE standards in its use of terms. For a complete list of definitions, refer to IEEE Std 1012-1986.

Note that definitions for the terms *verification* and *validation* may be used differently by other standards organization.

3.3 Acronyms and abbreviations

The following acronyms and abbreviations are used in this guide:

COTS   Commercial-off-the-shelf

CPM   Critical path method

IV&V   Independent verification and validation

PERT   Program evaluation review technique

QA   Quality assurance

SDD   Software design description

SQA   Software quality assurance

SRS   Software requirements specification

SV&V   Software verification and validation

SVVP   Software verification and validation plan

SVVR   Software verification and validation report

TBD   To be determined

V&V   Verification and validation

4. Software verification and validation

Software Verification and Validation (V&V) is a disciplined approach to assessing software products throughout the product life cycle. A V&V effort strives to ensure that quality is built into the software and that the software satisfies user requirements. V&V provides software management with insights into the state of the software project and products, allowing for timely change in the products or in the development and support processes.

Software verification and validation employs review, analysis, and testing techniques to determine whether a software system and its intermediate products comply with requirements. These requirements include both functional capabilities and quality attributes.

These quality attributes will differ from project to project. Quality attributes that are identified serve the user's need for a software product that is capable of meeting its objectives with adequate performance with no unexpected side effects. The following list enumerates quality attributes that may be specified.

— accuracy
— completeness
— consistency
— correctness
— efficiency
— expandability
— flexibility
— interoperability
— maintainability
— manageability
— portability
— readability
— reusability
— reliability
— safety
— security
— survivability
— testability
— usability

The objectives of the V&V effort are to find defects and to determine if required functions and attributes are built into the software system. The activities of V&V operate on the products of software development and support the following:

a) Verification that the products of each software life cycle phase
   1) Comply with previous life cycle phase requirements and products (e.g., for correctness, completeness, consistency, and accuracy)
   2) Satisfy the standards, practices, and conventions of the phase
   3) Establish the proper basis for initiating the next life cycle phase activities
b) Validation that the completed end product complies with established software and system requirements

A V&V effort is typically applied in parallel with software development and support activities. Some V&V tasks may be interleaved with the development and support process. A V&V effort consists of management tasks (e.g., planning, organizing, and monitoring the V&V effort) and technical tasks (e.g., analyzing, evaluating, reviewing, and testing the software development processes and products) to provide information about the engineering, quality, and status of software products throughout the life cycle.

Planning for a V&V effort begins early in the project so as to aid in assessing the scope of the V&V effort as part of the total effort. This is necessary in order to ensure that V&V resource needs are included in the total project planning. The initial SVVP may provide insights to the financial sponsor of the project concerning development or support plans. It also provides enough information for the sponsor to approve the plan and to monitor its implementation.

It is important on each project to clarify how V&V fits into the overall project life cycle and relates to all project entities (e.g., user, developer, buyer, software configuration management, software quality assurance, etc.). Sometimes the V&V effort will be performed by an entirely different organization, often directly for the buyer of the software. This situation is referred to as Independent Verification and Validation (IV&V). V&V tasks may be performed internally by a completely separate organization within the company or perhaps by the systems engineering group or product assurance group. Selection of some tasks may depend on how a project is organized (e.g., consider not only how the V&V tasks serve immediate V&V objectives, but also how they serve the total project).

The first V&V tasks begin early, with concept documentation evaluation, requirements analysis, and acceptance test planning. Planning the V&V should be closely coupled to the planning of the rest of the project. The planner should anticipate and schedule regular updating of the SVVP to reflect changes in the overall development effort.

Software verification and validation tasks support one another and combine to become a powerful tool that does the following:

— Discovers errors as early as feasible in the software life cycle
— Ensures that required software qualities are planned and built into the system
— Predicts how well the interim and final products will result in final products satisfying user requirements
— Assures conformance to standards
— Confirms safety and security functions
— Helps prevent last-minute problems at delivery
— Provides a higher confidence level in the reliability of the software
— Provides management with better decision criteria
— Reduces frequency of operational changes
— Assesses impact of proposed changes on V&V activities

4.1 Software V&V planning guidance

This subclause describes activities required for effective V&V planning. The purpose of planning and plan documentation is to employ the V&V resources efficiently, to monitor and control the V&V process, and to allow the identification of each participant's role and responsibility. Planning results in a well-structured, thorough, and realistic SVVP that provides the foundation for a successful V&V effort. Documentation of the scope and explicit statement of the objectives provides all parties with an understanding of what is going to be achieved and what is not.

Each project needs its own SVVP, based on the generic plan identified in the Standard. The specific plan will be tailored to the project. The plan may be modified at times in response to major changes. While the basic objectives of the V&V effort are not likely to change over time, there may be major changes that require response. These changes may be associated with development activities (e.g., significant delays in schedules, unanticipated technological changes) or V&V tasks (e.g., loss of resources, inability to develop tools in time). Therefore, procedures for modifying the plan should be included in the plan.

V&V planning, which should be thought of as an integrated part of overall project planning, may be broken down into the following steps:

a) *Identify the V&V scope.* Define a set of software tasks as early as possible. The tasks should be tailored and take into consideration several software factors (e.g., criticality, complexity, available resources including development environment and tools). Determining which V&V tasks to perform requires a decision-making methodology. One such methodology, criticality analysis, is presented in annex B.

Before beginning the next step, the recommended V&V tasks should be reviewed by all participants, especially the user and customer. The next step should begin only after agreement is achieved.

b) *Establish specific objectives from the general project scope.* Detailed, measurable, and achievable objectives establish the conditions of satisfaction with the V&V effort. These conditions of satisfaction provide the basis for assessing and enforcing V&V performance. Measurable criteria, such as defined load limits and response time, are desirable because of the objectivity they afford. Also, the discipline and effort required to formulate measurable objectives reveal ambiguities and differences of expectations early in the V&V effort.

It is important to identify only achievable objectives. The presence of unachievable objectives reduces the credibility of a plan, and of the V&V effort itself, before the execution of the plan begins. A realistic plan enhances the motivation of all parties in a project and increases the value of the V&V effort.

c) *Analyze the project input prior to selecting the V&V tools and techniques and preparing the plan.* Input analysis identifies all the specific products, information, and other documentation that will be available during the project phases. Examples of such products are given in figure 1 of the Standard and are reproduced here in figure 1. Input can be divided into two types—the products and information available at project start and the products and information that will become available in the later phases of the development cycle. The items that are available during the planning stage are either project- or product-related. Project-related information includes the budget, manpower and other resources, development schedules and milestones, and any other project-specific considerations, such as contractual requirements. Product-related information includes concept documentation, requirements specifications, or other formal specifications for the product being developed. Note that terminology for these products varies according to the user or developer environment.

Historical defect data from previous versions of the same or similar software, if available, can be a great aid. Such historical data will be available only if planned for (e.g., by archiving and analyzing anomalies). When planning the V&V effort, prediction and analysis of the nature and number of expected defects aid in the selection of V&V tasks and help to determine the resources required to perform the tasks.

d) *Select techniques and tools.* Identify those tools and techniques (such as those that support traceability analysis) that are available and applicable to the project, and gather sufficient information in order to choose among alternatives. For techniques, this information includes input needed, range of applicability, and resources and skills needed. For tools, this information includes availability of tool and associated documentation, applicability, and resource requirements including cost of operation and training.

Specific information about the software development environment, methodology, and tools should be considered when selecting the tools and techniques to be used in V&V. Techniques and tools need to be selected with the format, structure, and schedule of the development products in mind. Also, while in some cases it is appropriate to have separately developed and qualified tools, it may be more cost effective to use a common set of tools for similar functions.

Obtain a subset of tools and techniques that are tailored to the particular constraints and needs of the project. When doing so consider the skills and training of the personnel and the availability of the other necessary resources.

e) *Develop the plan.* Review the results of the previous steps and prepare a detailed set of tasks (addressing the seven topics discussed in 3.5 of the Standard and annex C of this guide) to meet the V&V goals, objectives, and constraints.

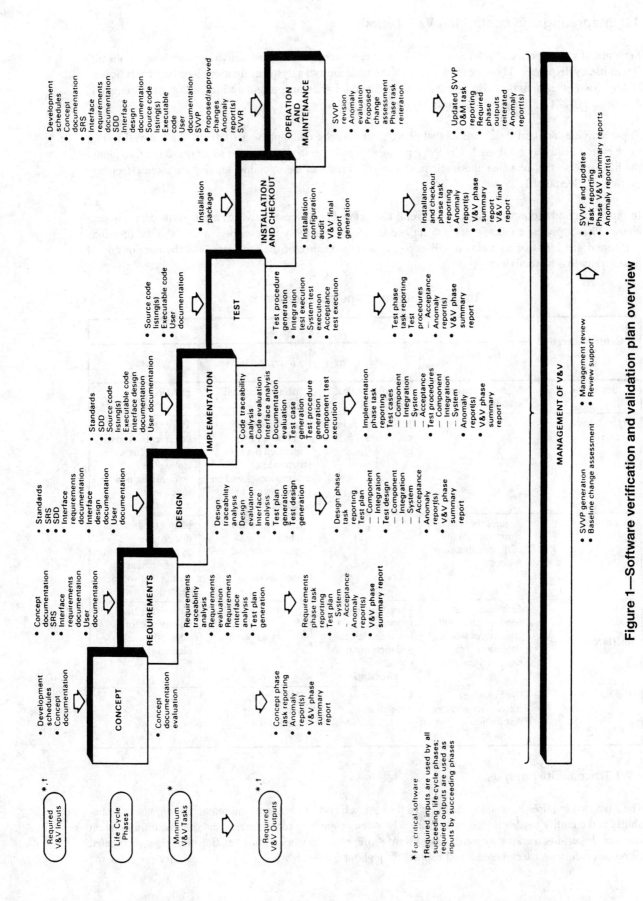

Figure 1—Software verification and validation plan overview

4.2 Integrating and continuing V&V tasks

Several tasks, as described by the Standard, collectively make up continuing activities that go across the different life cycle phases. These general activities are traceability analysis, evaluation, interface analysis, and testing. Two other activities also discussed in the Standard are management and reporting. Management is described in 5.5.1 of this guide. Reporting is described in 5.6.

These activities are horizontal threads that tie together the subsequent phase activities and allow verification to be more effectively conducted. The V&V planner should plan to integrate and share resources throughout the life cycle so that planning and implementation of all tasks of a continuing activity are more effectively performed. See table 1.

In order to avoid redundancy, only the general characteristics of these activities are described in this subclause. Phase-specific applications are described in 5.5. Each activity is described in terms of the functions performed, the kinds of problems it will uncover, the significance of the problems, and the relationship of this activity to other activities.

Table 1—Relationships between tasks

Contribution of Task	Task			
	Traceability Analysis	*Evaluation*	*Interface Analysis*	*Testing*
Criticality Analysis	Identifies critical features for tracing.	Identifies critical areas for evaluation.	Identifies critical interfaces.	Establishes priorities for testing.
Traceability Analysis		Maps the location of each feature to be evaluated.	Identifies where interfaces are required between dependent components, and the information to be passed.	Traces test documents. Assists in developing a test strategy by determining how functions are distributed.
Evaluation	Assures the structural validity of the distribution of function.		Establishes that interfaces are appropriate and are correctly implemented.	Identifies attributes that require dynamic validation, and the extent of testing that will be needed.
Interface Analysis	Establishes the need for traceability, and assures that dependent elements can communicate.	Identifies explicit relationships between elements, and their input and output requirements.		Establishes the framework for integration test planning.
Testing	Confirms the traceability and the distribution of functions.	Confirms the evaluation.	Confirms that interfaces are operational.	

4.2.1 Traceability analysis

The Standard requires traceability analysis in the requirements, design, and implementation phases. Traceability is the ability to identify the relationships between originating requirements and their resulting system features. It permits tracking forward or backward through the network of interrelationships that are created as requirements are decomposed and refined throughout a system's life cycle. Traceability provides the thread that links one element to another. When an element is traced to another, and that element is traced on to another, a chain of cause and effect is formed.

Traceability allows verification of the properties set forth in the concept and that requirement specifications have been

a) Carried forward to the design specifications
b) Implemented in the code
c) Included in the test plan and cases
d) Provided to the customer and user in the resulting system

Traceability, with the aid of forward and backward tracing, facilitates the construction of efficient test plans and permits verification that the resulting test cases have covered the permutations of functional and design requirements/features.

When the trace from all software requirements back to the concept documentation and system requirements is verified, then successive traceability analysis occurs, beginning from the software requirements through all the development representations, user documentation, and test documentation. Each trace is analyzed for consistency, completeness, and correctness to verify that all software requirements are implemented in the software and are associated with the correct design, code, and test information.

In the course of performing traceability analysis, some errors are readily apparent, such as a requirement with no design element, or a design element with no source code, or the converse of these. The analyst examines each trace path to ensure that the connected pieces are the proper ones. To be able to do this the analyst has to understand the intent of both requirements and design.

Traceability analysis can be used to support configuration management, test coverage analysis, analysis of V&V results, regression testing, criticality assessment, and V&V management decisions. Also, traceability analysis is useful in evaluating the software development effort for good software engineering practices.

Traceability analysis is performed to assure that

— Every requirement in the specification is identified correctly
— All traces are continuous from the prior phase through the current phase
— Forward and backward traces between adjoining phases are consistent
— The combined forward traces originating from each specification, fully support that specification
— Each current specification or feature is fully supported by traceable predecessor specifications

4.2.2 Evaluation

Evaluations ascertain the value or worth of an item and help to assure that a system meets its specifications. Evaluations are performed by many persons across all life cycle phases, on both interim and final software products, and may be either a comprehensive or selective assessment of a system.

Evaluations uncover problems in the different products and their relationships. These problems relate to the basic user need for the system to be fit for use in its intended setting. For a product to be fit for use, an evaluation may be used to assure that

— The product conforms to its specifications.
— The product is correct.
— The product is complete, clear, and consistent.
— Appropriate alternatives have been considered.
— The product complies with all appropriate standards.
— The product meets all specified quality attributes.

Evaluations not only identify problems, but may help to determine the progress of software development by recommending that the project

— Continue on to the next stage
— Correct specific items first, then continue
— Go back several steps and correct some problems
— Perform additional evaluations, such as a simulation, before that part of the system is further refined
— Monitor the progress of an item whose quality may be doubtful
— Make changes in methodology or software tools
— Make changes in schedules
— Make staffing decisions, such as additional resources, additional training, or changes in assignment

Evaluations are used through all phases and for all types of software products, including user documents, manuals, and other project documents. These may be of many forms, such as text or graphic representations, and in various media, such as paper, magnetic tape, diskette, and computer files. This range of product types and forms requires a large variety of techniques for performing and managing software evaluations.

When evaluating system products, there will be a change in emphasis from one development stage to the next. As the product progresses from a concept to a final product, its functional requirements are first defined. Next, the organization and structure of design elements are established. Then, all executable procedures are prepared. Questions of "what and why," "what-if," "alternatives," and "better-or-best" will predominate during the earlier development stages, while issues of "how," "correctness," and "conformance" will be more frequent in the later development stages.

When selecting evaluation strategies, the V&V planner first uses the features and characteristics of the system as a guide in the selection of the evaluation techniques. The planner shall question the system's functions, how they will be addressed, and what types of problems might be encountered. Second, the V&V planner derives additional evaluation techniques from quality attributes that may be specified for the system. Third, the V&V planner considers other evaluation methods, based on special V&V concerns and experience.

It may be helpful for the V&V planner to consider these three approaches when selecting techniques for evaluating the product:

a) Static analysis of the specification (e.g., reviews, inspections, structure analysis)
b) Dynamic analysis of expected software behavior (e.g., simulation, prototyping, screen emulation, branch execution analysis)
c) Formal analysis (e.g., mathematical proofs)

All these evaluation types can be used in conjunction with one another to provide a powerful synergism. Selection of a particular type of evaluation depends on the results required, tool availability, and cost trade-offs.

Static analysis detects deficiencies and errors through the examination of the software product, manually or automatically, without executing the software code. For example, static analysis can be applied to evaluate the form and content of the specification. It is usually straightforward. It frequently employs various types of reviews. Applicable to all levels of specification, it is able to detect flaws that could preclude or make meaningless the other forms of analysis, or prevent inadequate testing of the product. Static analysis focuses on the form, structure, and content of the product; its interfaces and dependencies; and on the environment in which it is to be used. Static analysis may be applied at all phases of development, and to all documented deliverables.

Dynamic analysis requires the execution of the software itself, or a model or simplified version of the software, to determine the validity of some of its attributes. Dynamic analysis can produce results that are not available or are more time consuming with the other techniques. Dynamic analysis may also be more tractable than formal analysis, as there are a variety of tools expressly designed to support it.

Formal analysis uses rigorous mathematical proof techniques to analyze the algorithms or properties of the software. It can provide a strong conclusion regarding certain properties of an approach, but it is limited by the difficulty of its application and the general scarcity of automated support. Formal techniques generally require both a formal specification and a formal implementation. For example, the correctness of a natural, English-language requirement could not be proven. Certain assertions could be drawn from the requirement though, and proved to satisfy a set of conditions, thereby increasing the confidence that could be placed in the requirements for those conditions. Formal analysis is frequently used to verify sections of a specification that handle security requirements.

4.2.3 Interface analysis

When information is passed across a boundary (e.g., hardware to software, software to software, software to user) there is always the possibility of losing some information or altering the information content. The task of interface analysis serves to ensure the completeness, accuracy, and consistency of these interfaces. Interface requirements at the design and implementation phases should be identified and analyzed at the functional, physical, and data interface level. The goal of interface analysis is to evaluate the specific software deliverable (e.g., requirements, design, code) for correct, consistent, complete, and accurate interpretation of the interface requirements.

Interface analysis is concerned with data that flows from one part of the system to another. The sources of this information are important in assuring that the intended flow is feasible. Information about the recipient of the interface data is needed to assure that each interface is indeed necessary and sufficient. The correctness of the interface will rely on the use to which it is put, and its form and content will be part of the analysis.

Interface analysis should focus on three interface areas:

a) *User interface.* This should analyze what the human interfaces to the software product are, such as required screen format, protection mechanisms, page layout and content of the reports, relative timing of inputs and outputs, etc.
b) *Hardware interface.* This should analyze what the logical characteristics of each interface are between the software product and the hardware components of the system. Identify electronic devices, firmware, communication devices, and output devices. Then identify applicable standards for these interfaces and verify the current application's interface.
c) *Software interface.* This should analyze what the interfaces to other required software products are (e.g., data management system, operating system, or a library package), and interfaces with other application systems. Identify applicable standards for any other software products and interfaces to other application systems. Verify correct software interfaces to them.

In planning interface analysis consider the following:

— *Are the interface objectives technically adequate and well understood?*
— *Are all data elements well defined?*
— *Are all restrictions and constraints clearly defined?*
— *Were all the different kinds of interfaces taken into account and properly described?*
— *Are all hardware-to-software functional interfaces specified in quantitative terms such as units, bits per second, message formats, priority rules, word length, timelines, and protocols?*
— *Are all software-to-software interfaces functional, and are all data interface levels specified in quantitative terms, such as data timeliness, data definition, data formats, priority rules, message content, and communication protocols?*
— *Are the interface performance requirements well defined, and are the limits specified?*

- *Is the criticality of the interface taken into consideration?*
- *What are impacts if the interface is degraded?*
- *Are the interfaces testable and maintainable?*
- *Have all appropriate standards been identified for the interfaces, including those from the current software application to its environment?*

4.2.4 Testing

> *Testing is the process of analyzing a software item to detect the differences between existing and required conditions (that is, bugs) and to evaluate the features of the software item.*

In the context of software verification and validation, testing can be defined as the testing that is performed in support of the V&V objectives. These objectives may differ from those of the developer. For example, V&V testing may focus on a narrow or critical area or on ensuring compliance to planned testing by the developers.

The scope and organizational responsibilities for the testing defined in an SVVP will depend on project-specific considerations. Once V&V objectives are established, the testing performed is in support of those objectives. Recognize there may be other testing activities beyond those of software verification and validation and there may be other organizations involved. Testing performed as part of V&V may be performed by personnel who generated the software or by personnel independent of the original developers.

The remainder of this subclause provides a description of testing activities performed during software verification and validation. It is not meant to be a guide to testing, but to clarify the concepts and terminology of the Standard, and to be a basis for V&V test planning.

4.2.4.1 Levels of testing

Testing is performed at several points in the life cycle as the product is constructed component by component into a functioning system. These points in the life cycle can be viewed as levels of capabilities that need to be tested. The levels progress from the smallest or single component through combining or integrating the single units into larger components or stages. The Standard describes these levels as component, integration, system, and acceptance. Table 2 further describes these levels of testing.

4.2.4.2 Test planning

V&V test planning is a continuing activity performed throughout the life cycle, starting from the requirements phase up to the test phase. Test plans are developed for each level of testing. These plans correspond to the developed products of the phase. The requirements phase produces the system requirements specification and acceptance and system test plans. The design phase produces the system design document and the component and integration test plans. The implementation phase produces the software product and test cases, test procedures, and component level execution. In the test phase, acceptance test procedures are produced and integration system and acceptance tests executed. An additional benefit of test planning is the additional review of the requirements, design, and interface descriptions.

The Standard provides for the creation of the test plan components in stages at appropriate points and times in the life cycle. Table 3 shows the stages and sequences. Following the table is an explanation of the various test activities.

Table 2—Levels of testing

Testing	Definition in the Standard	Purpose	Traceability
Component Testing	Testing conducted to verify the implementation of the design for one software element (e.g., unit, module) or a collection of software elements.	Ensures program logic is complete and correct. Ensures component works as designed.	From each test to detailed design
Integration Testing	An orderly progression of testing in which software elements, hardware elements, or both are combined and tested until the entire system has been integrated.	Ensures that design objectives are met.	From each test to the high-level design
System Testing	The process of testing an integrated hardware and software system to verify that the system meets its specified requirements.	Ensures that the software as a complete entity complies with its operational requirements.	From each test to the requirements
Acceptance Testing	Formal testing conducted to determine whether or not a system satisfies its acceptance criteria and to enable the customer to determine whether or not to accept the system.	Ensures that customers' requirements objectives are met and that all components are correctly included in a customer package.	From each test to customer-specific requirements

Table 3—Test activities in life cycle phases

Activities	Requirements	Design	Implementation	Test
Test Plan Generation	- System - Acceptance	- Component - Integration		
Test Design Generation		- Component - Integration - System - Acceptance		
Test Case Generation			- Component - Integration - System - Acceptance	
Test Procedure Generation			- Component - Integration - System	- Acceptance
Test Execution			- Component	- Integration - System - Acceptance

4.2.4.2.1 Test plans

A test plan spells out the scope, approach, resources, and schedule of the testing activity. It indicates what is to be tested, what is not to be tested, testing tasks to perform, people responsible, and risks. Key points in planning include

— Transitioning from one phase or level to another
— Estimating the number of test cases and their duration
— Defining the test completion criteria
— Identifying areas of risks
— Allocating resources

The testing tasks performed during the requirements phase involve planning for and generating the system and acceptance test plans. Since these tests attempt to demonstrate that both the operational concept and the requirements are satisfied, planning may begin as soon as the requirements are written, although completion of the test plans shall await finishing other requirements phase V&V tasks. More detailed levels of preparation of test procedures and test cases will be performed in later phases.

The system design document is a key input to planning for component and integration test in the design phase. By developing the test plans early, there is adequate time to put test resources in place and to ensure that any untestable design features are identified prior to implementation.

Identifying methodologies, techniques, and tools is part of planning for testing. Methodologies are derived from the overall testing strategy. Techniques and tools are identified according to the specified methodologies. The specific methodologies, techniques, and tools selected will be determined by the type of software (e.g., application, operating system) to be tested, the test budget, the risk assessment, the skill level of available staff, and the time available.

In planning for verification and validation testing, the V&V planner should answer the following questions:

— *Who is responsible for generating the different levels of test designs, cases, and procedures?*
— *Who is responsible for executing the different levels of tests?*
— *Who is responsible for building and maintaining the test bed?*
— *Who is responsible for configuration management?*
— *What are the criteria for stopping test effort?*
— *What are the criteria for restarting test effort?*
— *When will source code be placed under change control?*
— *Which test designs, cases, and procedures will be placed under change control?*
— *For which level of tests will anomaly reports be written?*

It is often difficult to determine when to stop testing or when a reasonable number of defects have been detected. In fact, it may be unreasonable to expect that all defects will be detected. Therefore, completion criteria should be provided as a guideline for test completion. There are at least two common types of completion criteria. One criterion, test case completion, requires that all resultant test cases are executed without observing defects. A second criterion is fault prediction. For example, since the objective of testing is to find defects, the second criterion might be to test until a predefined number of defects have been found (or, conversely, a number of successful tests has been executed).

4.2.4.2.2 Test design

The test plan is followed by the development of test designs in the design phase. Test designs refine the test plan's approach, identify specific features to be tested by the design, and define its associated test cases and procedures. Whenever possible, tests should be designed to be suitable for regression testing; that is, tests previously executed and verified can then be repeated at a later point in development or during maintenance of the installed system.

Consider the following when developing test designs:

— Required features to be tested
— Specified quality attributes
— Load limits
— Stress tests
— Configurations that the software may need to support
— Compatibility with existent or planned system components
— Security of the system
— Storage limits of the software, and related data
— Performance (such as accuracy) response times, and throughput
— Installability, primarily in the user environment
— Reliability/availability to the specifications
— Recovery from software and data failures
— Serviceability requirements
— Users' guides
— Human factors for usability and acceptability
— Interfaces with other system components
— Hardware interfaces

4.2.4.2.3 Test case

The test cases and test procedures are developed in the implementation phase. A test case specifies actual input values and expected results. The goal in the generation of test cases is to exercise the component's logic and to set up testing scenarios that will expose errors, omissions, and unexpected results. In developing test cases, one desire is to produce the smallest set of cases possible that will still meet the goal. Use of a matrix relating requirements to test cases aids in determining completeness and overlap.

4.2.4.2.4 Test procedure

A test procedure identifies all steps required to operate the system and exercise the specified test cases in order to implement the associated test design. Refer to IEEE Std 829-1983 for a discussion of test procedures.

4.2.4.2.5 Test execution

Test execution is the exercising of the test procedures. Test execution begins at the component level of testing in the implementation phase. The remaining levels of testing (e.g., integration, system, acceptance) are executed in the test phase.

5. SVVP guidance

The following provides detailed information about each section of an SVVP. The information here is organized in the same order as an SVVP and written in accordance with the Standard. In most cases, the following subclauses begin by quoting the requirements of the Standard for that section. Immediately following is the section number or subsection number where this quote can be found in the Standard.

> *The Software Verification and Validation Plan (also referred to as the Plan) shall include the sections shown below to be in compliance with this standard. If there is no information pertinent to a section or a required paragraph within a section, the following shall appear below the section or paragraph heading together with the appropriate reason for the exclusion: This section/paragraph is not applicable to this plan. Additional sections may be added at the end of the plan as required. Some of the material may appear in other documents. If so, reference to those documents shall be made in the body of the Plan. [3]*

When preparing an SVVP, include the following additional information prior to the first section of the plan, when appropriate to the particular project.

a) *Cover or title page.* This will typically include the title of the plan, a document or configuration control identifier, the date, and the identification of the organizations by whom and for whom the SVVP is prepared.

b) *Signature lines or page.* In many cases, the SVVP will require the signature or signatures of the persons responsible for writing or approving the plan.

c) *Revision history.* If the SVVP is updated by issuing change pages, it is helpful to include a list of such pages at the front of the SVVP. A brief history of the document and change bars or some other form of attention to changed material are useful regardless of the distribution method.

d) *Preface or foreword.* This will typically include a brief description of the project and identification of related documents (e.g., project management plan, software quality assurance plan, configuration management plan).

e) *Table of contents.* A table of contents is required if the reader is to make efficient use of the plan.

f) *Lists of figures, tables, or illustrations.* If there are more than a few figures, tables, or illustrations, or if these are referenced at widely-scattered points in the text, reference lists similar to a table of contents should be included. These items are typically listed separately.

g) *Assumptions.* Indicate any assumptions on which the plan is predicated, such as anticipated deliveries, availability of input, or intermediate products.

Include the following material after the last section of the SVVP, when appropriate to the project:

— *Glossary.* Define project-specific terms and acronyms.

— *Procedures.* Provide a clear understanding of the SVVP. In many cases, it is useful to separate the high-level planning information from the detailed procedures. These procedures may also be provided in a separate document referenced in the body of the SVVP.

— *Report formats and standard forms.* Furnish samples of reporting forms that will be useful. If large numbers of standard forms and report formats are to be included, these are best placed in an appendix.

5.1 Purpose

> *(Section 1 of the Plan.) This section shall delineate the specific purpose and scope of the Software Verification and Validation Plan, including waivers from this standard. The software project for which the Plan is being written and the specific software product items covered by the Plan shall be identified. The goals of the verification and validation efforts shall be specified. [3.1]*

See annex A, A.3.1.

The purpose statement of the SVVP provides the highest level description of the software V&V effort. The following topics should be addressed in the purpose statement:

— Identify the project to which the SVVP applies and describe why the plan is written.
— State the goals to be satisfied by the SVVP. For example, a specific V&V effort may intend to validate that all security requirements are satisfied. Another plan may be concerned only with validating performance requirements.
— Clearly summarize the V&V effort and the responsibilities conveyed under this plan.
— Define the extent of the application of the SVVP to the software. Explicitly cite each part of the software to which the SVVP applies and each part not covered by the SVVP. For example, perhaps only two of three subsystems of a computer system will fall under the SVVP (the third component may be unchanged from a previous system), or the SVVP may be invoked only for design verification.
— Identify waivers and changes if the Standard's requirements have been tailored for this SVVP. Examples include items such as addition or removal of sections or use of a different life cycle model. Sufficient detail should be included to demonstrate compliance with the Standard if the SVVP is audited. Descriptions of extensive changes may be placed in an appendix or a separate tailoring document.

5.2 Referenced documents

(Section 2 of the Plan.) This section shall identify the binding compliance documents, documents referenced by this Plan, and any supporting documents required to supplement or implement this Plan. [3.2]

This section of the SVVP should

— Specify documents completely, using any serial or publication numbers available.
— Make certain the correct version of the document is cited.
— Note clearly changes to referenced document list when SVVP is revised.
— List all documents referenced in the plan.
— Be consistent with other referenced document lists in other project documentation or explicitly indicate differences and reasons.

5.3 Definitions

(Section 3 of the Plan.) This section shall define or provide a reference to the definitions of all terms required to properly interpret the Plan. This section shall describe the acronyms and notations used in the Plan. [3.3]

For this section of the SVVP

— Include only terms necessary for understanding the SVVP.
— Keep the list short by referring to lists of definitions in other project documentation.
— If separate lists are maintained in different project documentation, be sure to use the same definitions in each list. It is helpful, to this end, to have a single database of project definitions and acronyms.
— Use definitions from IEEE Std 610.12-1990 and the series of IEEE glossaries where possible.

5.4 Verification and validation overview

(Section 4 of the Plan.) This section shall describe the organization, schedule, resources, responsibilities, tools, techniques, and methodologies necessary to perform the software verification and validation. [3.4]

5.4.1 Organization

(Section 4.1 of the Plan.) This section shall describe the organization of the V&V effort. It shall define the relationship of V&V to other efforts such as development, project management, quality assurance, configuration or data management, or end user. It shall define the lines of communication within the V&V effort, the authority for resolving issues raised by V&V tasks, and the authority for approving V&V products. [3.4.1]

See annex A, figure A.3.

The specific organizational structure of the V&V effort will depend on the nature of the system under development, the developing and acquiring organizations, and the contractual arrangements. Each organization responsible for a V&V effort may want to arrange the V&V effort differently. A V&V effort is simply the set of V&V tasks defined by the SVVP to be performed to achieve a quality product. Organization of the effort is then the assignment of each task to some appropriate person or organizational entity. There is no single, correct organization for all projects.

When planning for the organization of a V&V effort, consider the following:

— Assigning specific responsibility for each task (e.g., accepting the input, performing the task, analyzing the results, reporting the results, making decisions based on the results) where responsibility may be shared
— In the case of overlapping responsibilities, being precise about these assignments
— Using diagrams to show the control and data flow of V&V efforts to clarify responsibilities

5.4.2 Master schedule

(Section 4.2 of the Plan). This section shall describe the project life cycle and milestones, including completion dates. It shall summarize the scheduling of V&V tasks and shall describe how V&V results provide feedback to the development process to support project management functions (for example, comments on design review material).

If the life cycle used in the Plan differs from the life-cycle model in the standard, this section shall show how all requirements of the standard are satisfied (for example, cross reference for life-cycle phases, tasks, inputs, and outputs). When planning V&V tasks, it should be recognized that the V&V process is iterative. The summary of tasks may be in narrative, tabular, or graphic form. [3.4.2]

The master schedule summarizes the various V&V tasks and their relationships within the overall project environment. The objective is to spell out the orderly flow of materials between V&V activities and project tasks. This helps to ensure that V&V tasks are appropriately placed and their deliverables are identified within the larger project environment. Be aware that the development of the master schedule will be an iterative process.

In developing the master schedule, the V&V planner should focus on V&V tasks and their placement within the project schedule and highlight the key V&V tasks, deliverables, and completion dates. If an independent V&V effort is being conducted, the interfaces for delivery of materials, reviews, completion meetings, etc. need to be highlighted. There are many formats for schedule presentation (e.g., Gantt Charts, PERT, CPM) and in some cases analysis of schedule flow. The approach used should be consistent with other project elements.

5.4.3 Resource summary

(Section 4.3 of the Plan.) This section shall summarize the resources needed to perform the V&V tasks, including staffing, facilities, tools, finances, and special procedural requirements such as security, access rights, or documentation control. [3.4.3]

An overview of the resources needed for the V&V effort should be presented. The planner should not repeat the resource requirements of the individual tasks; instead, overall requirements should be summarized and potential conflicts for resources, long-lead items, inefficient uses of resources, and alternative resource options should be identified. For very small plans, all resource information could be placed in this section, rather than in the task discussions. It may be valuable to collect the detailed resource information in an appendix.

Resource types include labor or staffing, facilities, equipment, laboratories, the configuration of the laboratories, tools (both software and hardware), budget and financial requirements, documentation, special procedures and conditions (such as, security, access rights, and/or controls).

— Use graphs and tables as an effective means of presenting resource use. Graphs of resource use versus calendar time or life cycle phase give a quick grasp of the relative amounts of effort involved in the different tasks or phases. Tables of resource use, again by calendar time or life cycle phase, aid in comparing resource use with a budget or with the requirements of other project efforts.
— Include in the equipment and laboratories summary the type of equipment needed, duration needed, particular configurations, and other peripheral facilities that will be needed to perform the total V&V operations.
— In the tools section of the summary list the various tools that are to be used throughout the V&V effort. The tools can be subdivided into software and hardware.
— In the budget and financial requirements, take all the resources into account and allow for additional tools and staff to cope with contingencies.

5.4.4 Responsibilities

(Section 4.4 of the Plan.) This section shall identify the organizational element(s) responsible for performing each V&V task. It shall identify the specific responsibility of each element for tasks assigned to more than one element. This section may be a summary of the roles and responsibilities defined in each of the life-cycle phases. [3.4.4]

See annex A, table A.1.

There are two levels of responsibility for the V&V tasks—general responsibilities assigned to different organizational elements throughout the project and specific responsibilities for the tasks to be performed. A summary of the general responsibilities may be described in this section of the SVVP or in another project-level plan (e.g., a project management plan). If described in another document, this section should contain a summary and a reference to the other document. The specific responsibilities may be described in this section, or this section may summarize the responsibilities defined in the life cycle phase sections of the SVVP.

5.4.5 Tools, techniques, and methodologies

(Section 4.5 of the Plan.) This section shall identify the special software tools, techniques, and methodologies employed by the V&V effort. The purpose and use of each shall be described. Plans for the acquisition, training, support, and qualification for each shall be included. This section may reference a V&V Tool Plan. [3.4.5]

Describe the V&V approach, tools, and techniques and their roles in the V&V effort. This may be in narrative or graphic form. References to technique or tool descriptions should be included. A separate tool plan may be developed for a software tool acquisition, development, or modification. In this case this section of the SVVP should refer to the tool plan. If a tool is to be acquired or developed, its acquisition or development schedule should be included in the V&V schedule. Determine whether sufficient time and appropriate tasks are allowed for tool acquisition or development.

When planning the use of tools, techniques, and methodologies, consider the following:

a) A description of, or reference to, the methodology selected for the V&V approach
b) Staff experience and training needed
c) Special tools and specific techniques for the methodology
d) How each tool and technique enhances the methodology
e) Risks associated with a tool or technique
f) Status of each tool
   1) *Is it a new acquisition?*
   2) *Are changes needed or is it completely ready for use?*
   3) *Is the required quantization available?*
   4) *Is its documentation acceptable?*
   5) *Is the tool proprietary?*
g) Acquisition or development schedule
h) Necessary support (hardware, other software)
i) Alternate approach for a high-risk tool

5.5 Life cycle verification and validation

This subclause parallels 3.5 of the Standard, using the same life cycle model. The Standard points out that any life cycle model can be employed for development and V&V activities. The Standard can then be adapted to it as long as there is a clear mapping from one life cycle model to the other.

While many tasks can be thought of as going across life cycle phases, most SVVPs are likely to be written and managed with tasks assigned to a particular life cycle phase. Each of the following subclauses amplifies the requirements of the Standard. (See 4.2 of this guide for further guidance on planning the tasks that go across life cycle phases.)

Additionally, the Standard defines management as one of the phases. Of course, management is not a single life cycle phase activity, but rather an activity that goes across all of the individual phases and that ties all of the activities together into a coherent, useful program.

5.5.1 Management of V&V

(Section 5.1 of the Plan.) This section of the Plan shall address the seven topics identified in section 3.5 of this standard. The management of V&V spans all life-cycle phases. The software development may be a cyclic or iterative process. The V&V effort shall reperform previous V&V tasks or initiate new V&V tasks to address software changes created by the cyclic or iterative development process. V&V tasks are reperformed if errors are discovered in the V&V inputs or outputs.

For all software, the management of V&V shall include the following minimum tasks:

   1. Software Verification and Validation Plan (SVVP) Generation

   2. Baseline Change Assessment

   3. Management Review of V&V

   4. Review Support [3.5.1]

The primary tasks of V&V management are planning, review, and control. The Standard maps these responsibilities into four fundamental tasks for V&V management—SVVP Generation, Baseline Change Assessment, Management Review, and Review Support. Conceptually, management's responsibility is to ensure the positive, successful interaction between the V&V activities and other software development activities to ensure the creation of defect-free software. The planning of the management tasks shall recognize the iterative nature of V&V tasks (e.g., determining when to reanalyze amended software products, when to revise V&V plans to reflect changes in the development process).

5.5.1.1 Software Verification and Validation Plan (SVVP) generation

Generate SVVP (during Concept Phase) for all life cycle phases in accordance with the standard based upon available documentation Include estimate of anticipated V&V activities for Operation and Maintenance Phase. Update SVVP for each life cycle phase, particularly prior to Operation and Maintenance. Consider SVVP to be a living document, and make changes as necessary. A baseline SVVP should be established prior to the Requirements Phase. [Table 1, 5.1 (1)]

See annex A, A.3.4.

The Standard specifies the required content and format for an SVVP. From this starting point, V&V planners should tailor these requirements to the operating environment and the development environment. Tailoring considerations include the following:

— Software development environment and methodology
— Size and complexity of software being verified and validated
— Risk management considerations
— Organization and number of personnel performing V&V tasks
— Relationship of personnel performing V&V tasks to other development personnel, management, and user
— Approvals required for the SVVP
— Method of configuration control, maintenance, and updating of SVVP
— Special focus of V&V required (e.g., safety or security)

V&V planners may be dependent on things outside of their control. As a consequence, the plan may need to be able to respond to occasional, controlled changes to support the overall project milestones and objectives. At the same time it should remain constant in its quality goals and V&V objectives. Some of the uncertainties that should be considered include the following:

— Timely delivery of products
— Whether the quality of the products will be sufficient to allow meaningful verification and validation
— Availability of staff and resources needed to perform the planned tasks

V&V planning is most effectively performed in conjunction with the overall software development planning. Revisions to the plan are prepared regularly throughout the software development life cycle, usually at the completion or initiation of each life cycle phase. The plan, to be effective as a complete specification of the tasks required to achieve the established V&V objectives, shall be thorough, comprehensive, and specific.

The SVVP is often best developed incrementally. An SVVP will start small, based on an early, perhaps incomplete, view of the project. The SVVP will grow and incorporate changes as the software is developed. Eventually, the SVVP will be completed and serve as a record of the complete and detailed plan for the project's V&V activities.

This should not be taken to mean that the plan should be continually revised throughout the life cycle phases. Only those changes needed to provide further or more detailed task management for the future or to make corrections should be made. Revisions to the plan should not be made retrospectively; that is, as a way of removing deviations from the plan. Deviations that arise during the execution of the plan, necessary for project changes or external factors, are addressed in the Software Verification and Validation Reports (SVVRs).

Incremental planning may be prudent for at least two reasons.

a) *It allows for a more realistic view of what is possible in planning in the early stages of a project.* Too often, much time and attention is spent overplanning future life cycle phases when there is the likelihood of significant changes in those phases. For example, certain design and implementation questions may be unanswerable in the concept phase and, as a consequence, precise planning for design and implementation of V&V may not be possible. As decisions are made and results and products obtained throughout the life cycle, more careful planning of subsequent phases is meaningful.

b) *If a plan is to be effective (e.g., if people are to use it to identify responsibilities, to prepare for future tasks, to measure past performance) it should be realistic and achievable.* It should reflect the changes that are inherent in the other development process activities. It cannot be a static view of the desires of management at the outset of the V&V effort without regard to actual developments. The plan should represent reasonable and achievable objectives.

The SVVP is thus referred to as a living document because it may undergo changes and expansion over time. At its first publication (in most cases at the beginning of the life cycle) it will contain detailed plans about the near-term activities and only cursory descriptions of the later phases. When generating input for the SVVP, be prepared to revise and update the SVVP at fixed points. Most effectively, plan for review and revision at the end of each life cycle phase.

Additionally, during life cycle phases it sometimes may be advisable to incorporate revisions to the plan in response to significant changes in other project plans, and to include references to those revised plans. Plan for the maintenance of the SVVP under configuration identification and control. This can be accommodated by maintaining the SVVP on electronic media or in a hard copy format that can be easily updated.

The SVVP should be an item under configuration management. Plan to establish the baseline SVVP prior to the Requirements Phase if V&V begins early enough. In other cases, baseline the SVVP no later than at the end of the current life cycle phase. The use of a configuration identifier and change notations (such as change bars) will allow effective control of the configuration and status of the document.

5.5.1.2 Baseline change assessment

Evaluate proposed software changes (for example, anomaly corrections, performance enhancements, requirements changes, clarifications) for effects on previously completed V&V tasks. When changes are made, plan iteration of affected tasks which includes reperforming previous V&V tasks or initiating new V&V tasks to address the software changes created by the cyclic or iterative development process. [Table 1, 5.1 (2)]

Baseline change assessment may be the most dynamic task performed during a V&V effort. Any change proposal could affect an unknown amount of previously completed development and V&V work. A V&V task should examine the change to determine the nature and extent of the V&V rework required by the change. Because changes will be proposed asynchronously, the SVVP cannot, before the fact, contain detailed planning for any given change assessment; rather, it shall contain general guidance for allocating resources to change proposals as they occur.

The request for baseline change assessment should be documented in a change proposal. The change proposal should indicate the perceived severity of the anomaly (if any), the immediacy of the change, and the systems affected so that the criticality of the software can be determined.

5.5.1.3 Management review of V&V

Conduct periodic reviews of V&V effort, technical accomplishments, resource utilization, future planning, risk management. Support daily management of V&V phase activities, including technical quality of final and interim V&V reports and results. Review the task and V&V phase summary reports of each life-cycle phase. Evaluate V&V results and anomaly resolution to determine when to proceed to next life-cycle phase and to define changes to V&V tasks to improve the V&V effort. [Table 1, 5.1 (3)]

See annex A, A.3.5.

Management review comprises all of the general responsibilities of management for the monitoring, controlling, and reporting of the V&V effort and, in effect, the managing of this plan. In this task, V&V management is responsible for creating the positive interaction between the V&V activities and the other development activities. V&V management is responsible, in particular, for reviewing on-going efforts, accomplishments, and the use of resources. This section of the SVVP addresses only V&V-specific issues in project management review. While not stated earlier, a manager sufficiently technically expert in the system under development and in the process of software V&V is necessary to make informed and useful decisions throughout the project. This need is most keenly felt in the task of management review.

The results and findings of V&V tasks will have a significant impact on the development effort. (See also 5.7 of this guide for control and administrative procedures relating to the distribution of V&V products.) Early identification and correction of defects is one obvious benefit. The monitoring and reporting of levels and types of defects may identify other quality engineering issues in the development process.

Careful management attention to the technical quality and accuracy of the V&V products is particularly important. It is important that inaccurate or incorrect reports are not distributed to development or management personnel lest unnecessary effort be expended responding to illusory or imprecisely stated anomalies.

When reviewing reports, consider the following:

a) *Is the report complete?*
b) *Is the report technically accurate?*
c) *Is the report judicious in its use of language?*
   1) *Does it restrict itself to the technical issues under discussion?*
   2) *Is it restricted to the tasking direction?*
   3) *Is its tone positive?*
   4) *Does it support development success?*
d) *Does the report support effective management decision-making?*
e) *Does it discriminate between levels of severity?*
f) *Does it clearly identify impact?*
g) *Does it propose alternate approaches?*

Prepare summary documents to make them as useful as possible to development and acquiring organization management. When organizing the results, consider the following:

— Summary assessment
— Itemization of critical outstanding problems and the impact of their not being resolved
— Recommendations about corrective course of action
— Summary of rescheduling impact, V&V, and resource requirements
— Distribution of anomalies according to some predefined categorization scheme and the significance of this distribution

5.5.1.4 Review support

Correlate V&V task results to support management and technical reviews (for example, software requirements review, preliminary design review, critical design review). Identify key review support milestones in SVVP. Schedule V&V tasks to meet milestones. Establish methods to exchange V&V data and results with development effort. [Table 1, 5.1 (4)]

Formal review meetings are a common means of evaluating and approving the products of one life cycle phase before going on to the next phase. V&V can contribute to the effectiveness of management and technical reviews through a variety of functions and tasks. In most cases, these functions and tasks will be similar between one review meeting and the next. As a result, this section of the SVVP need not have a detailed plan for each individual review to be supported; rather, it may contain general guidance when preparing for a review, together with such review-specific information as seems necessary (e.g., listing the contents of the review package for each review).

When planning the review support activities, consider the following:

— Reviewing documentation packages for compliance with specified review requirements; completeness, consistency, and traceability; and identification of open items
— Developing agenda items to cover unresolved anomalies, deficiencies; unresolved open items; and technical alternatives and trade-off studies

Participation in reviews by personnel performing V&V tasks may involve the following:

— Asking questions to clarify points or identify unresolved issues
— Raising issues from prior analysis of review packages
— Assessing impact of V&V on changes under discussion in the review

Note that where an independent V&V agent is used, the developer's contract may need to contain provisions to ensure the availability of necessary materials and access to those performing IV&V.

5.5.2 Concept phase V&V

(Section 5.2 of the Plan.) This section of the Plan shall address the seven topics identified in section 3.5 of this standard. For critical software, Concept Phase V&V shall include the following minimum V&V task: Concept Documentation Evaluation. [3.5.2]

The concept phase establishes the reason for the system. The concept defines the nature of the system that will be developed and enumerates its goals and its risks within technical and business constraints.

Evaluation in the concept phase should establish that the objectives of the system define the user needs to be addressed and the technical and business advantages that are expected. These objectives may be stated in a variety of ways, and may include a statement of need, a business case, feasibility studies, and a system definition.

V&V establishes that risks and constraints enumerate any technical, business, or policy considerations that may impede development of the system. Initial planning should be included and should outline the staffing, time, and cost expected for each alternative. In addition, any regulations and policies that govern the system and its development will be stipulated. Alternative approaches may be included, with their respective advantages and disadvantages.

5.5.2.1 Concept documentation evaluation

Evaluate concept documentation to determine if proposed concept satisfies user needs and project objectives (for example, performance goals). Identify major constraints of interfacing systems and constraints or limitations of proposed approach. Assess allocation of functions to hardware and software items, where appropriate. Assess criticality of each software item. [Table 1, 5.2 (1)]

The actual V&V evaluation performed during the Concept Phase should delineate specific quality goals and areas of risk. These should be reflected in the full-scale development V&V plan in addressing risk mitigation, resource allocation, and selection of methods and criteria. Of particular interest to risk mitigation would be instances where there is a potential imbalance between technical scope and allocated cost and schedule resources for the overall project and the subsequent V&V activities. In addition, the criticality of each software item should be addressed.

5.5.3 Requirements phase V&V

(Section 5.3 of the Plan.) This section of the Plan shall address the seven topics identified in 3.5 of this standard.

For critical software, Requirements Phase V&V shall include the following minimum tasks:

> *(1)   Software Requirements Traceability Analysis*
>
> *(2)   Software Requirements Evaluation*
>
> *(3)   Software Requirements Interface Analysis*
>
> *(4)   Test Plan Generation*
>
> > *(a)   System Test*
> >
> > *(b)   Acceptance Test [3.5.3]*

The requirements phase is the period of time in the software life cycle during which the requirements, such as functional and nonfunctional capabilities for a software product, are defined and documented. The main product of the requirements phase, the Software Requirements Specification (SRS), should accurately state the software mission, that is, what the software is intended to do. The SRS should be traceable back to the user needs and system concept, as defined in concept documentation. It should be traceable forward through successive development phases and representations, into the design, code, and test documentation. It should also be compatible with the operational environment of hardware and software. The requirements should provide both qualitative and quantitative constraints on subsequent design and implementation options. There are five types of requirements—functional, external interfaces, performance, design constraints, and quality attributes.

An SRS typically describes or specifies several of the following:

— *The system boundary.* What is within the required software and what is outside.

— *The software environment.* Conditions of the surroundings that are imposed on the software (e.g., interfaces, response times, availability, size).

— *The software functions.* What the software is to do and how the software should respond to its environment.

— *The software constraints.* Imposed limits that are placed on the software and its stimulation and responses.

— *The software interfaces.* The nature of the information flow across software boundaries, where this information is found, and under what conditions.

— *The software data.* The contents of the information flows with their formats, and relationships.

— *The software algorithms.* Detailed descriptions of the software algorithms and their conditions in the most applicable terms.
— *The software states.* Stable modes that the software may assume, under which conditions, and with what actions.
— *The software error conditions.* What constitutes a departure from the norm, under which conditions, and what actions to take.
— *The software standards.* Those forms of representation and content of the requirements that are required by the development and user organizations.
— *The hardware interfaces.* What the software must do to transfer data across hardware boundaries and The software quality attributes. The conditions that the software must meet in order to be considered fit for use in its intended application. The attributes will always include conformance to specifications, correctness, and compliance with standards. There may be other quality attributes (e.g., reliability, safety) depending on the type of system and its use.

Requirements verification is concerned with assuring that each item in the SRS conforms to what is wanted, correct, complete, clear, consistent, and, as appropriate, measurable and testable. See also IEEE Std 830-1984.

5.5.3.1 Software requirements traceability analysis

Trace SRS requirements to system requirements in concept documentation. Analyze identified relationships for correctness, consistency, completeness, accuracy. [Table 1, 5.3 (1)]

See annex A, A.3.6. See also 4.2.1.

One goal of the requirements traceability analysis is to establish that the SRS completely satisfies all of the capabilities specified in the concept document(s). A second is to determine which requirements satisfy each need in the concept. Another goal is to establish that the SRS is structured so that the requirements may be traced through subsequent development stages. The SRS traceability analysis makes sure that all of the necessary parts of the software system are specified. Further, it determines where those parts are so that they can be followed in later development steps, and that there are no untraceable requirements.

The plan should identify the following:

— The format of the concept, SRS, interface documentation, and their releasing organizations
— Indexing and cross-reference schemes that are established as part of the requirements specification to facilitate traceability analysis
— Criteria for extracting and identifying discrete requirements from narrative documents
— Acceptance conditions for the SRS, including the criteria for release to configuration control

There may be some requirements that are not directly traceable to other documents. It can be expected that each succeeding development phase will present new information that must be traced to following phases, but are not explicitly present, or only hinted at, by preceding specifications (e.g., concurrence of tasks, standard error recovery procedures). Some of these may be called for by the SRS, but may not be present in the concept documents. All derived requirements should be identified and included in the traceability matrix.

Plan to establish the traceability of the SRS prior to completing the other V&V tasks for this phase. If the traceability analysis is incomplete it is inconclusive to evaluate the SRS, or to perform an interface analysis, or to plan testing. Although these other V&V tasks may be performed concurrently with traceability analysis, they cannot be considered finished until assurance is provided that all of the SRS has been traced.

5.5.3.2 Software requirements evaluation

Evaluate SRS requirements for correctness, consistency, completeness, accuracy, readability, and testability. Assess how well SRS satisfies software system objectives. Assess the criticality of requirements to identify key performance or critical areas of software. [Table 1, 5.3 (2)]

See annex A, A.3.7. See also 4.2.2.

The objectives of the software requirements evaluation are to assess the technical merits of the requirements, to determine that the requirements satisfy the software objectives defined in the concept phase, and to assure that the specifications are correct, complete, clear, and consistent. An additional objective is to determine if any requirements are missing. Where there is an absolute measure available for a requirement (e.g., response time), establish the correctness of the requirement with respect to the measure. The evaluation should establish the technical adequacy of the requirements. The SRS should be evaluated to ensure that all requirements are testable against objective criteria.

Depending on the scope and complexity of the SRS, there may be multiple evaluations. Each evaluation will address a specific purpose and may use specialized techniques and specific participants. A policy may need to be defined that coordinates multiple evaluations of an SRS and correlates their results.

In addition, the scheduling of the evaluation may be determined by the availability of specific portions of the SRS that are required by one or another evaluation. In practice, there are usually parallel efforts underway that will use some portion of the SRS, or an uncertified version, to proceed with either a more detailed level of development, such as high level design, or with an interfacing product. In all cases, though, the limits of this work should be defined.

5.5.3.3 Software requirements interface analysis

Evaluate the SRS with hardware, user, operator, and software interface requirements documentation for correctness, consistency, completeness, accuracy, and readability. [Table 1, 5.3 (3)]

See annex A, A.3.8. See also 4.2.3.

The goal of the requirements interface analysis is to assure that all external interfaces to the software and internal interfaces between software functions are completely and correctly specified. As software reuse and standard software components are more frequently used, the importance of internal interface analysis will increase.

Depending on the form of the SRS and on the tools available, manual or automated analysis of the interfaces may be employed. Mechanisms should be provided to ensure the following:

— The sources and recipients of interface data are accurately described.
— Protocols for transferring and receiving data across interfaces are accurate and complete.
— The SRS interfaces are compatible with the interface documentation.

In addition to the SRS, the documents describing the external interfaces, such as interface definition documents, data dictionaries, and related SRS documents, should be included. Techniques for analyzing internal interfaces between individual requirements should also be included.

The acceptance criteria for the interface documents should be specified, including release to configuration control. Criteria include compliance to format guidelines to ensure traceability, complete resolution plans for all incomplete requirements (TBDs), and notice of completion of interface analysis.

5.5.3.4 System test plan generation and acceptance test plan generation

Plan System testing to determine if the software satisfies system objectives. Criteria for this determination are, at a minimum: (a) compliance with all functional requirements as complete software end item in system environment (b) performance at hardware, software, user, and operator interfaces (c) adequacy of user documentation (d) performance at boundaries (for example, data, interface) and under stress conditions. Plan tracing of system end-item requirements to test design, cases, procedures, and execution results. Plan documentation of test tasks and results. [Table 1, 5.3 (4a)]

Plan acceptance testing to determine if software correctly implements system and software requirements in an operational environment. Criteria for this determination are, at a minimum: (a) compliance with acceptance requirements in operational environment (b) adequacy of user documentation. Plan tracing of acceptance test requirements to test design, cases, procedures, and execution results. Plan documentation of test tasks and results. [Table 1, 5.3 (4b)]

See annex A, A.3.9 and A.3.10. See also 4.2.4.

The V&V testing tasks performed during the requirements phase involve planning for and generating the system and acceptance test plans. Since these tests attempt to demonstrate that both the operational concept and the requirements are satisfied, planning may begin as soon as the requirements are written, although completion of the test plans will generally await finishing the other requirements phase V&V tasks. More detailed levels of preparation of test procedures and test cases will be performed in later phases.

System and acceptance test plans will benefit from any matrices or other organized sets of information that are used for traceability and interface analysis. This information should be designed to include references to test plans and test procedure elements. Test plans should be evaluated and verified to assure that all planned conditions and features of the software under development are tested sufficiently to meet the V&V objectives.

For system testing, the primary goal is to validate that there are no defects among and omissions from the software, the concept document, and the system requirements specification. Specific areas of testing (e.g., performance, security, reliability, availability) may need to be planned.

For acceptance testing, the primary goal is user validation that the software complies with expectations, as reflected by the operational concept functional requirements, and quality attributes. Additional goals of acceptance testing are to establish that the software can be successfully installed and operated by the intended user, is appropriately documented, and that it can be maintained. Wherever possible, it is recommended that the user or user representatives be involved in establishing appropriate acceptance test plans. Both the system and acceptance test plans should identify the following, in addition to general testing requirements:

— All the input documentation required for system testing as well as the protocol for transferring these documents to the V&V staff. These documents should include system requirements specifications, interface requirements documents, operational scenarios, and users manuals.
— The stopping criteria for testing. These could include the fraction of requirements covered, number of errors remaining metrics, statistical reliability goals, etc.
— Provisions for witnessing tests.

5.5.4 Design phase V&V

(Section 5.4 of the Plan.) This section of the Plan shall address the seven topics identified in Section 3.5 of this standard. For critical software, Design Phase V&V shall include the following minimum V&V tasks:

(1) *Software Design Traceability Analysis*

(2) *Software Design Evaluation*

(3) *Software Design Interface Analysis*

(4) *Test Plan Generation*

　　(a) *Component Test*

　　(b) *Integration Test*

(5) *Test Design Generation*

　　(a) *Component Test*

　　(b) *Integration Test*

　　(c) *System Test*

　　(d) *Acceptance Test*

Table 1 contains a description of the minimum Design Phase V&V tasks and identifies the required inputs and outputs. The inputs and outputs required to accomplish the minimum V&V tasks shall include, but not be limited to, those listed in Table 1. [3.5.4]

The design phase is the period of time in the software life cycle during which the designs for architecture, software components, interfaces, and data are created, documented, and verified to satisfy requirements. Removing errors from the designs during this phase will substantially reduce the occurrence of defects in the subsequent code, and will lessen both product and project risk later in the life cycle. Design V&V also indirectly provides an opportunity to locate faults not previously detected in the requirements.

Although simple products may be designed in a single step, design frequently occurs as a multiple-step process. The first level of the design specifies architectural features (e.g., major subsystems and their interfaces). Successive design steps evolve by adding detail until the subsystems have been sufficiently specified for coding to begin. Designs may be represented in many forms, including text, graphical descriptions, pseudo-code representation, or combinations of these and others.

In addition to solving the problem of how to organize and build the required system, designers have a wide range of quality objectives that include:

— Tracing the requirements through all design levels, and ensuring that there are no omissions or additions
— Structuring the design so that it is appropriate to the system objectives and the desired product quality attributes
— Describing all hardware, operator, and software interfaces
— Documenting that the design conforms with all applicable standards, practices, and conventions
— Establishing that the design will satisfy the requirements when fully integrated
— Documenting the design so that it is understandable to those who write the source code and later maintain the product
— Including sufficient information in the design to plan, design, and execute tests
— Controlling the design configuration and ensuring that all documentation is completed and delivered, especially when mixed media are used (e.g., graphic charts, text specifications)

Meeting these objectives provides assurance that all the requirements are represented in the design, that the design will satisfy the requirements, and that the design is testable and will lead to testable code. The responsibility of the V&V planner is to select V&V tasks for the design products, including intermediate specifications, to ensure that these objectives are in fact met.

The V&V planner selects the V&V tasks and their accompanying methods that are appropriate for each level of design for the specified features. While the V&V tasks are repeated through each design level, the V&V methods or techniques used may change. For example, where evaluation of the choice of an algorithm may be appropriate at high-level design, mathematical analysis of the algorithm may be more appropriate at detailed design.

The scope of the V&V effort will be determined by the complexity of the design effort. When planning the V&V tasks for the design phase, consider the following:

— Responsibilities levied by the project plan (e.g., to support the critical design review)
— Design methodology
— Design standards
— Critical or difficult sections of the design
— Design assumptions that require proofs (or references to proofs)
— The presence of complex algorithms that may require extensive analysis
— Resource restrictions (e.g., available computer hardware, timing limitations) requiring sizing and performance analysis
— Database privacy and access requirements needing security analysis
— The level of the design (i.e., different V&V tasks and methods may be appropriate for high-level and detail design)
— The different approaches that will be needed for component and integration testing
— The organization performing the design V&V tasks
— The media and format of the design

V&V schedules should accommodate comments and anomalies emerging from the design V&V tasks that will be addressed. Additionally, potential risks may emerge. An updated list of these identified risks should be maintained, and they should then be reflected by the developing test plans.

5.5.4.1 Software design traceability analysis

Trace SDD to SRS and SRS to SDD. Analyze identified relationships for correctness, consistency, completeness, and accuracy. [Table 1, 5.4 (1)]

See annex A, A.3.11. See also 4.2.1.

Whether manual or automated procedures are used, perform the physical trace in both directions between requirements and design. Analyze the trace to ensure that

— No requirements are omitted or designed more than once.
— No extraneous design pieces exist.
— A requirement addressed by more than one design element is completely and consistently satisfied.

Evaluate each of the relationships for correctness, consistency, completeness, and accuracy. Ensure that

— All conditions of a requirement have been designed.
— The technical relationship between a requirement and its design is correct.
— Any multiple relationships that are detected between requirements and design are necessary.

5.5.4.2 Software design evaluation

Evaluate SDD for correctness, consistency, completeness, accuracy, and testability. Evaluate design for compliance with established standards, practices, and conventions. Assess design quality. [Table 1, 5.4 (2)]

See annex A, A.3.12. See also 4.2.2.

Evaluate each element of each level of the design. Some of the optional tasks in the Standard may be used for design evaluation. Consider the project needs and their relationships with other project efforts when selecting V&V methods. The methods and techniques that are selected will depend on characteristics of the project. Examine the total project to select the methods for design evaluation that will locate the design errors that present the most risk to the project's success. The results of criticality analysis can help identify those design elements that require more intense evaluation.

5.5.4.3 Software design interface analysis

Evaluate SDD with hardware, operator, and software interface requirements for correctness, consistency, completeness, and accuracy. At a minimum, analyze data items at each interface. [Table 1, 5.4 (3)]

See annex A, A.3.13. See also 4.2.3.

Perform design interface analysis on each level of the software design. When planning design interface analysis, consider the following:

— *Is the use of the data items (i.e., the inputs and outputs) consistent and complete?*
— *Is the interface correct, complete, and necessary?*
— *Are the data items used correctly in the design element where sent?*
— *Are system resources being used properly in the data transfer (e.g., are calls being made by value that should be made by reference)?*
— *For user interfaces, is the interface design understandable? Will the software provide appropriate help? Will the software detect user errors and provide clear error responses?*
— *Has a prototype been built for a critical interface (particularly the user interface)? If so, has it been thoroughly and independently evaluated? Does it demonstrate the critical features properly?*
— *Are the interfaces designed for effective configuration management?*
— *Is an interface needed where there is none?*

5.5.4.4 Component test plan generation and integration test plan generation

Plan component testing to determine if software elements (for example, units, modules) correctly implement component requirements. Criteria for this determination are, at a minimum: (a) compliance with design requirements (b) assessment of timing, sizing and accuracy (c) performance at boundaries and interfaces and under stress and error conditions (d) measures of test coverage and software reliability and maintainability. Plan tracing of design requirements to test design, cases, procedures, and execution results. Plan documentation of test tasks and results. [Table 1, 5.4 (4a)]

See annex A, A.3.14. See also 4.2.4.

Plan integration testing to determine if software (for example, subelements, interfaces) correctly implements the software requirements and design. Criteria for this determination are, at a minimum: (a) compliance with increasingly larger set of functional requirements at each stage of integration (b) assessment of timing, sizing, and accuracy (c) performance at boundaries and under stress conditions (d) measures of functional test coverage and soft-

ware reliability. Plan tracing of requirements to test design, cases, procedures, and execution results. Plan documentation of test tasks and results. [Table 1, 5.4 (4b)]

See annex A, A.3.15.

Use the SDD to plan for component and integration test. A benefit of test planning in the design phase is that adequate time is allowed to put test resources in place and to ensure that any untestable design features are identified prior to implementation.

Component testing demonstrates the adequacy of the functions and quality attributes of each component of the software design. The focus is on software flow patterns and functionality of individual components. The tests could target on accuracy of solutions, data handling, etc. The coverage of the test cases should be analyzed to determine level of coverage of tests to code statements and paths.

The approach taken for integration testing depends on the system design. Integration testing validates the structure of the design, or how well the components perform with other components and fit into the developing system structure. Once the design has been determined, integration test planning should begin to ensure readiness of all test materials and the adequate allocation of testing resources.

5.5.4.5 Test design generation

Design tests for: (a) component testing (b) integration testing (c) system testing (d) acceptance testing. Continue tracing required by the Test Plan. [Table 1, 5.4 (5)]

See annex A, A.3.16–A.3.19.

All of the functional, performance, and user interface tests can now be designed, but not yet executed. Resulting test designs should be traceable from the concept documentation to the system requirement specification, to the system design document, or to other user documentation as appropriate.

5.5.5 Implementation phase V&V

(Section 5.5 of the Plan.) This section of the Plan shall address the seven topics identified in 3.5 of this Standard.

For critical software, Implementation Phase V&V shall include the following minimum V&V tasks:

(1) Source Code Traceability Analysis

(2) Source Code Evaluation

(3) Source Code Interface Analysis

(4) Source Code Documentation Evaluation

(5) Test Case Generation

    (a) Component Test

    (b) Integration Test

    (c) System Test

    (d) Acceptance Test

(6) Test Procedure Generation

    (a) Component Test

    (b) Integration Test

    (c) System Test

(7) Component Test Execution [3.5.5]

The implementation phase is the period of time in the software life cycle during which a software product is created from design documentation and then debugged. In the implementation phase, the V&V tasks are focused on the code and the determination of how well it conforms to the design specifications and coding standards. The objective of V&V in this phase is to determine the quality of the code.

The quality of the code can be determined in several ways. The design specifications are traced to the corresponding code in the program. Code is traced back to the design requirements. These steps are performed to ensure that no requirements have been added, modified, or missed. The program interfaces are analyzed and compared to the interface documentation. A detailed program evaluation is performed to analyze the program for the correct translation of the design specification and conformance to program coding standards. Another activity in the implementation phase is the generation of test cases and test procedures for the various levels of testing (e.g., component, integration, system, and acceptance). The test procedures for the component level of testing will be executed.

5.5.5.1 Source code traceability analysis

Trace source code to corresponding design specification(s) and design specification(s) to source code. Analyze identified relationships for correctness, consistency, completeness, and accuracy. [Table 1, 5.5 (1)]

See annex A, A.3.20. See also 4.2.1.

The goal of traceability analysis from source code to design components and from design components to source code is to identify possible inconsistencies between design and code. This comparison identifies anomalies such as, source code without antecedent design components, design components that do not clearly associate with the source code, or any other issues or abnormalities that emerge from this process. This forward and backward tracing identifies completeness and accuracy of the code. Plan to perform the physical trace in both directions between design components and code.

Analyze the trace to ensure that:

— No design specifications are omitted or coded more than once
— No extraneous code pieces exist
— A design specification addressed by more than one code element is completely and consistently satisfied

5.5.5.2 Source code evaluation

Evaluate source code for correctness, consistency, completeness, accuracy, and testability. Evaluate source code for compliance with established standards, practices, and conventions. Assess source code quality. [Table 1, 5.5 (2)]

See annex A, A.3.21. See also 4.2.2.

Several evaluation techniques can be used depending on the level of risk or criticality desired (e.g. reviews, walkthroughs and inspections could be used). Refer to 4.2.2 for general discussion of evaluation techniques.

When planning source code evaluations, consider the following:

— Using criticality analysis of the code components to determine which code to evaluate
— Ensuring that the coding standards understood
— Ensuring that coding standards are available to staff before coding begins
— Determining how to evaluate code quality attributes
— Identifying code analysis tools that could be used

5.5.5.3 Source code interface analysis

Evaluate source code with hardware, operator, and software design documentation for correctness, consistency, completeness, and accuracy. At a minimum, analyze data items at each interface. [Table 1, 5.5 (3)]

See annex A, A.3.22. See also 4.2.3.

The goal of source code interface analysis is to assess the information and control flow between and within components. The results of the source code traceability analysis may be used in conjunction with this task. The output of this task describes component interface inconsistencies and errors. Interface analysis is effective at detecting errors that can be difficult to isolate in testing. Examples of these errors are

— Software elements that are referenced but not defined
— Software elements that are defined but not referenced
— Incorrect number of arguments
— Data type mismatches
— Data constraint mismatches
— Other data usage anomalies
— Control flow inconsistencies

When planning source code interface analysis, consider the following:

— Physical units precision
— Coordinates references
— Granularity
— Control flow
— Timing requirements
— Data transfer
— Naming conventions

5.5.5.4 Source code documentation evaluation

Evaluate draft code-related documents with source code to ensure completeness, correctness, and consistency. [Table 1, 5.5 (4)]

See annex A, A.3.23.

The goal of evaluating source code documentation with source code is to ensure that the documentation correctly reflects the actual implementation of the source code. Code-related documents could include program support manuals, user manuals, and operations manuals. Due to the stage of the life cycle, these documents are frequently in draft form and will be modified. When planning for source code documentation evaluation consider the following:

— Reviewing for user functionality in addition to technical accuracy, completeness, and consistency
— Making sure the documentation is written at the appropriate level for the audience
— Making sure usability issues (such as index, table of contents, glossary, heading, format, etc.) are correct
— Seeing if a new user can use the documentation to perform the task/job
— Making sure the documentation can handle error correction processes
— Making sure there is follow-up to complete the draft documents

5.5.5.5 Test case generation

Develop test cases for: (a) component testing (b) integration testing (c) system testing (d) acceptance testing. Continue tracing required by the Test Plan. [Table 1, 5.5 (5)]

See annex A, A.3.24–A.3.27.

A test case documents the actual values used for input along with the anticipated outputs. Test cases are developed for each level of testing (component, integration, system, acceptance).

a) *Component test cases* exercise as many paths through the code as are feasible. The V&V planner shall determine and plan for coverage analysis. A tool may be needed to aid in determining coverage.
b) *Integration test cases* focus on testing the interfaces and interdependencies of the components that have been combined.
c) *System test cases* focus on the combination of tests of the computer programs, manual controls, and procedures as they will exist in the new system environment. System test cases will focus on areas such as performance, security, reliability, and human factors.
d) *Acceptance test cases* demonstrate to the user that the system meets the objectives and performance expectations agreed upon by the developers and users of the system.

Refer to 4.2.4 of this guide for general discussion of test cases. Also, refer to IEEE Std 829-1983 for further discussion of test case generation.

5.5.5.6 Test procedure generation

Develop test procedures for: (a) component testing (b) integration testing (c) system testing. Continue tracing required by the Test Plan. [Table 1, 5.5 (6)]

See annex A, A.3.28–A.3.30.

Refer to 4.2.4 of this guide for general discussion of test procedures. Also, refer to IEEE Std 829-1983 for further discussion of test procedure generation.

5.5.5.7 Component test execution

Perform component testing as required by component test procedures. Analyze results to determine that software correctly implements design. Document and trace results as required by the Test Plan. [Table 1, 5.5 (7)]

See annex A, A.3.31.

The component test should demonstrate the internal integrity and correctness of the component. The tests should exercise paths defined between components, and should exercise the data interfaces supported through shared database elements and components.

The planner needs to consider the following:

a) Scheduling test runs
b) Executing predefined test cases
c) Evaluating test results
d) Issuing status reports

5.5.6 Test phase V&V

(Section 5.6 of the Plan.) This section of the Plan shall address the seven topics identified in 3.5 of this standard.... For critical software, Test Phase V&V shall include the following minimum V&V tasks:

(1)   Acceptance Test Procedure Generation
(2)   Test Execution
      (a)   Integration Test
      (b)   System Test
      (c)   Acceptance Test.[3.5.6]

The test phase is the period of time in the software life cycle when the components of a software product are evaluated and integrated, and the software product is evaluated to determine whether or not requirements have been satisfied. During the Test Phase, V&V activities include

— Generation of acceptance test procedures
— Performance of integration testing according to previously developed test procedures
— Analysis of integration test results
— Performance of system testing according to previously developed test procedures
— Analysis of system test results
— Performance of acceptance testing in accordance with test procedures that have been placed under configuration control
— Generation and resolution of anomaly reports

Planning for the test phase V&V activities should be accomplished within the context of 4.2.4 of this guide. Thus, the planning for test procedures generation, test performance, and results analysis is highly dependent on such factors as organization, schedule, resources, responsibilities, tools, techniques, and methodologies. The nature of the organization and how verification and validation tasking is performed within the organization may determine how successful the test phase will be.

The overall software development schedule will determine when the test phase will begin and approximately how long the test effort will take. The schedule should be evaluated periodically to ensure that enough time is allocated to the test phase. Some practitioners suggest, as a rule of thumb, that enough time includes time to run each test at least three times—the first time the test itself is tested, the second time the source code is tested, and the third time is for regression testing.

Proper coordination and adherence to deadlines are important during this phase. Large projects may involve many people and various organizations. For example, the development organization or third-party vendors may be providing hardware or firmware. Additionally, the client may be providing required information, data, or software. All of them may be working simultaneously, and independently, on complex, interrelated tasks. Because of the interdependencies, it is essential that deadlines be met. It is also important that the entire effort be coordinated through such control mechanisms as change control, configuration management, and reporting.

5.5.6.1 Acceptance test procedure generation

Develop test procedures for acceptance test. Continue tracing required by the Test Plan. [Table 1, 5.6 (1)]

See annex A, A.3.32.

Acceptance test procedures specify the steps for executing a set of test cases or, more generally, the steps used to analyze a software item in order to evaluate a set of features. Refer to 4.2.4 of this guide for general discussion of test procedures. Also, refer to IEEE Std 829-1983 for further explanation of test procedures.

5.5.6.2 Test execution

During the test phase, components are progressively integrated. The integrated components are progressively tested according to the test plan, case, and procedures. At each level of testing, the software is taken from and then returned to a controlled environment under configuration management.

5.5.6.2.1 Integration test execution

Perform integration testing in accordance with test procedures. Analyze results to determine if software implements software requirements and design and that software components function correctly together. Document and trace results as required by the Test Plan. [Table 1, 5.6 (2a)]

See annex A, A.3.33.

Integration testing focuses on testing the interfaces and interdependencies of the components that have been combined. Integration testing validates the structure of the design, that is, how well the components fit into the developing system structure and perform with other components.

5.5.6.2.2 System test execution

Perform system testing in accordance with test procedures. Analyze results to determine if software satisfies system objectives. Document and trace all testing results as required by the Test Plan. [Table 1, 5.6 (2b)]

See annex A, A.3.34.

The system test is a consolidated test of the computer programs, manual controls, and procedures as they will exist in the new system environment. System testing ensures that the procedures work according to the system specifications. The object of the system test is to uncover deviations from the system's business requirements. This means testing the system against its specifications and requirements. System testing focuses on areas such as performance, security, reliability, and human factors.

5.5.6.2.3 Acceptance test execution

Perform acceptance testing in accordance with test procedures under formal configuration control. Analyze results to determine if software satisfies acceptance criteria. Document and trace all testing results as required by the Test Plan. [Table 1, 5.6 (2c)]

See annex A, A.3.35.

Successful completion of acceptance testing demonstrates to the user that the system meets the objectives and performance expectations agreed upon by the developers and users of the system. The acceptance test should not only verify the accuracy and completeness of all software but also ensure that user procedures, user training, and operational considerations have been addressed. A part of the testing will be of the documentation. Publications that accompany the system may also need to be tested.

Before acceptance testing can take place, the following must occur:

a)   Support equipment is in place and ready.
b)   Required personnel are available according to plan.
c)   Test documentation is completed and ready for use.
d)   All application components are tested, integrated, and available.
e)   Data is prepared.

After the acceptance test has been executed, a test report may be written. The test report may include a summary of the acceptance test, an evaluation of the status of the application (pass/fail), a statement of the results of each test, and conclusions and recommendations.

5.5.7 Installation and checkout phase V&V

(Section 5.7 of the Plan.) This section of the Plan shall address the seven topics identified in Section 3.5 of this standard.

For critical software, Installation and Checkout Phase V&V shall include the following minimum V&V tasks:

    (1)   Installation Configuration Audit

    (2)   Final V&V Report Generation. [3.5]

The installation and checkout phase is the period of time in the software life cycle during which a software product is integrated into its operational environment and tested to ensure that it performs as required. Characteristics of installation include the installation staff, the duration of the installation process, the number of installation sites, the number of system versions, and the adequacy of their configurations.

Installation procedures place a completed and tested application into an operations environment in a manner that satisfies user requirements for using the system. Sometimes this process is separate from development and is performed by an organization different from that which developed and tested the application (e.g., by field or customer support engineers). In some cases, installation and its checkout are performed by the software end user. This is typically the case in the personal computer software industry. In many cases, installation occurs in a very short span of time, sometimes in an hour or in a few hours. At that time operation of the software in its production environment is expected to commence. Installation sometimes occurs in installments where one or more subsystems are added to the initial delivery, with a user acceptance testing period occurring after each installation. Each subsystem should be appropriately integrated with previous subsystems before release for acceptance testing.

Installation may be repeated an indefinite number of times, once for each site for each software version. There may be considerable tailoring of a product for each site (e.g., setting site-dependent parameters, building site-dependent command tables); each site may have different installation procedures.

Installation and checkout V&V procedures can ensure that:

— Each site-dependent configuration is correct and complete
— The instructions for installation at each site are an accurate and complete representation of the configuration
— The instructions are appropriately written for the expertise level(s) of the expected installer(s)
— User-oriented checkout tests are adequate to demonstrate satisfactory installation
— The software that has been verified and validated is the same software that has been delivered for installation

Responsibility for installation and checkout V&V may be split between the development and user organizations. The users may take a large role in the installation. Any V&V activities assigned to the user organization should be well defined and documented. Pre-installation V&V establishes and verifies the procedures for user V&V at installation.

Scheduling installation and checkout V&V may be difficult, for all the reasons listed above. If the software is to be installed at a large number of sites, it may be necessary to develop a schedule for a generic installation in advance, to be tailored to each specific installation as required by time or resources. A procedural flowchart or checklist may be valuable.

When planning for installation and checkout V&V, consider the following:

— *Verifying accuracy and completeness.* Ensure the integrity of the data before, during, and after installation with accuracy and completeness controls. For example, if a data file is to be reformatted, plan a test to demonstrate that the integrity of the file is preserved by reformatting. If control totals are maintained, verify the final controls against the initial controls.
— *Maintaining and verifying an installation audit trail.* Verify that all processes and changes that occur during installation are recorded.
— *Assuring the integrity of a previous system.* In many cases, the software being installed is a replacement for an existing system. Verify that the installation process allows the existing system to continue operation until the new system is formally accepted and declared operational. It may be necessary to operate the two systems in parallel for some period of time, or to maintain the old system in case the new system fails.
— *Verifying compliance to installation or checkout standards.* Ensure that the installation and checkout is performed in accordance with appropriate standards, procedures, and guidelines.

Frequently used optional tasks for installation and checkout V&V include, but are not limited to, the following:

a) *Regression analysis and testing.* Changes occurring from installation and test are reviewed. Regression analysis and testing verifies that basic requirement and design assumptions affecting other areas of the program have not been violated.
b) *Simulation.* Operator procedures are tested. Simulation tests also help to isolate any installation problems. This technique may be especially useful before delivery when many site-dependent versions of the software will be delivered.
c) *Test certification.* Test certification is used, especially in critical systems, to demonstrate that the software product is identical to the software product that was subjected to V&V.

It is important that the results of any installation tests be available prior to the completion of installation. The objective of this testing (or checkout) is to determine whether or not the installation is successful. As with other tests, this frequently means that the test results should be predicted before the test starts.

5.5.7.1 Installation configuration audit

Audit installation package to determine that all software products required to correctly install and operate the software are present, including operations documentation. Analyze all site-dependent parameters or conditions to determine that supplied values are correct. Conduct analyses or tests to demonstrate that installed software corresponds to software subjected to V&V. [Table 1, 5.7 (1)]

This task can be divided into three smaller tasks:

a) *Configuration audit.* This determines that all software products required to correctly install and operate the software are present in the installation package. The installation package typically consists of an installation plan with its checkout procedures, cases, and predicted results, source code listings and other development documentation, operator instructions, and end-user documentation.
b) *Site-dependent parameter analysis.* This verifies that the software has been properly tailored for the installation site. This may require analysis and verification of parameter values, command tables, configuration files, or other means of tailoring the software to the site. If site-dependent code is developed, either for installation or as part of the operational system (e.g., device drivers), that software should be verified and validated during its development.
c) *Corroboration analysis.* This verifies that the installed software corresponds to that software subjected to V&V during development. This may require inspection of audit trails, file comparison, or other means of demonstrating that the delivered software matches the verified and validated software.

5.5.7.2 V&V final report generation

Summarize all V&V activities and results, including status and disposition of anomalies in the V&V final report. [Table 1, 5.7 (2)]

Although V&V should be performed for the life of the software, the initial V&V effort may be completed with the installation and checkout of the software. In other cases, different organizations will be performing V&V during maintenance, requiring a hand-off of documentation and responsibility. Whenever V&V is completed, a final report should be prepared to summarize the activities and results of the V&V effort. The format of a final report will be specified in section 6 of the Plan (see 3.6 of the Standard).

This report serves several purposes.

a)   It serves as the starting point for V&V of the maintenance of the system.
b)   It can be a vehicle for lessons learned, or a way for project personnel to improve the development or V&V process for the next project.
c)   It can call attention to outstanding unresolved anomalies from development, installation, or operation.

The final report can typically be written by reviewing and summarizing the task reports, anomaly reports, and phase summary reports, written during the course of the V&V effort.

5.5.8 Operation and maintenance V&V

(Section 5.8 of the Plan.) This section of the Plan shall address the seven topics identified in Section 3.5 of this standard.

Any modifications, enhancements, or additions to software during this phase shall be treated as development activities and shall be verified and validated as described in 3.5.1 through 3.5.7. These modifications may derive from requirements specified to correct software errors (that is, corrective) to adapt to a changed operating environment (that is, adaptive), or to respond to additional user requests (that is, perfective).

If the software was verified under this standard, the standard shall continue to be followed in the Operation and Maintenance Phase. If the software was not verified under this standard, the V&V effort may require documentation that is not available or adequate. If appropriate documentation is not available or adequate, the SVVP shall comply with this standard within cost and schedule constraints. The V&V effort may generate the missing documentation.

For critical software, Operation and Maintenance Phase V&V tasks shall include the following minimum V&V tasks:

(1)   Software Verification and Validation Plan Revision

(2)   Anomaly Evaluation

(3)   Proposed Change Assessment

(4)   Phase Task Iteration [3.5.8]

The operation and maintenance phase is the period of time in the software life cycle during which a software product is employed in its operational environment, monitored for satisfactory performance, and modified, as necessary, to correct problems or respond to changing requirements.

Operation and maintenance is sometimes not so much a phase as sequence of repetitions of subsets of the life cycle. Multiple versions of a software product may be available and supported simultaneously. Each version may be found at several sites, each with installation-specific parameters, device drivers, or other code. Different installations may upgrade versions at different times. The operations and maintenance phase may be further complicated by other considerations that depend strongly on the software product and its application and users.

Given this complexity, it is difficult to provide specific guidance for the V&V tasks of this phase, which are often repetitions of previously described tasks. Instead, guidelines are offered here for V&V planning during operation and maintenance.

There are two primary cases to consider:

a)   The software was verified and validated (possibly under the Standard) when originally developed.
b)   The software was not adequately or formally verified or validated when originally developed.

Planning for V&V during operation and maintenance shall reflect which of these two cases holds true for the software of interest.

The V&V planner has a number of advantages when the software under maintenance was verified and validated during its original development. Complete and current documentation should exist. Verification and validation procedures should be in place and effectively used. Finally, there should be an historical record to use as the basis of future planning.

These advantages can help the V&V planner offset some of the common pitfalls faced during maintenance. Many key development personnel may have left the project, leaving perhaps a reduced maintenance cadre. There may have been a formal transfer from a development organization to a maintenance organization with no connection to the original development. Users will be reporting problems and requesting new functions simultaneously, each with his or her own priority for implementation.

Where the software was not verified or validated before maintenance, the planner faces the above pitfalls as well as some new ones. Documentation may not exist or may not be up to date (this is possibly worse than no documentation at all). Developers and management may not welcome verification and validation. When V&V are being performed for the first time, there may be no basis for planning other than engineering judgment.

Critical software should be verified and validated during maintenance whether or not it was verified or validated during development. If it was verified during development, maintenance is the time where the investment in V&V provides further significant payback. If the software was not previously verified, V&V may be able to bring some order to the possibly perceived chaos, thus easing the lives of the maintenance personnel.

The Standard requires four tasks—software verification and validation plan revision, anomaly evaluation, proposed change assessment, and phase task iteration—specifically for the operation and maintenance phase.

Note that verification and validation without complete, up-to-date documentation can no more be performed in operation and maintenance than in any other phase. Considerable effort in operation and maintenance may be spent in preparing or updating inadequate documentation. When planning V&V for software with missing or inadequate documentation, either include resources for developing necessary documents or ensure that management, developers, and users are aware that the effectiveness of the V&V effort may be seriously compromised. Developing the missing documentation is most worthwhile if extensive new development or thorough understanding of the existing system is required.

5.5.8.1 Software verification and validation plan revision

For software verified and validated under this standard, revise SVVP to comply with new constraints based upon available documentation. For software not verified and validated under this standard, write new SVVP. [Table 1, 5.8 (1)]

Develop a new or revised SVVP regularly during maintenance, since the problems found in the software and the desired new functionality will be constantly changing. Depending on the organization, schedule replanning according to project needs (e.g., revise the SVVP for every major software version) or by time interval (e.g., revise the SVVP every six months).

5.5.8.2 Anomaly evaluation

Evaluate severity of anomalies in software operation. Analyze effect of anomalies on system. [Table 1, 5.8 (2)]

The only fundamental differences between anomalies found during development and those found during operation are the nature of the environment and the nature of the operators. During development, the software is typically operated by personnel technically knowledgeable of the software design and code. Actual operators, in contrast, may be unfamiliar with the design and code and may be operating an active environment with site-specific equipment, parameters, or code.

These differences affect the way anomalies are handled in maintenance. The descriptions of anomalies may be incomplete. Information on the environment is particularly hard to determine remotely. These two differences make it difficult to replicate the anomaly, which in turn makes resolution difficult.

For some systems, anomaly evaluation may be complicated by site-specific configuration and by the potential multiplicity of software versions. The V&V personnel shall determine the version of the software in which the anomaly occurred and in which other versions the same or similar anomaly could occur. An automated tool for recording and tracking anomalies, particularly if the tool is tied into the development documents and to the proposed change assessment process, can greatly assist the anomaly resolution. The anomaly tracking system could collect performance data as well.

When preparing this section of the SVVP, plan for anomaly resolution in general. Describe how V&V resources should be allocated to an anomaly when it occurs and as it is analyzed and resolved. The detailed procedures for recording, analyzing, tracking, and resolving anomalies should be found in section 7 of the plan.

5.5.8.3 Proposed change assessment

Assess all proposed modifications, enhancements, or additions to determine effect each change would have on system. Determine extent to which V&V tasks would be iterated. [Table 1, 5.8 (3)]

Change proposals typically come from one of two sources—maintainers (to correct anomalies, to improve the software, or to adapt to changed operating environments) or users (to provide more functionality). These changes need to be evaluated in different ways. Changes proposed by maintainers should be relatively easy to evaluate, since they can be referenced to existing code, requirements, and design documentation. Changes proposed by users will often require analysis to determine which requirements, design, and code would be changed and to what degree. Describe, in this section of the SVVP, how V&V resources will be allocated to evaluate the proposed changes.

Changes to software systems, particularly large or complex ones, should be carefully managed. This is typically implemented through a configuration management system with a configuration control board. Where such a system is in place, plan V&V participation on the board. If such a system is not in place, consider having V&V act as configuration management. V&V is very difficult and very expensive in an environment of uncontrolled change.

Evaluate proposed changes to

a)   Clarify an ambiguous or poorly worded proposal.
b)   Reveal the true extent of a change.
c)   Help management determine which changes to implement and on what schedule.
d)   Determine how the change fits into the existing or desired system.

This is one area where V&V may perform a systems engineering role for the software development to prevent the uncontrolled growth of the software. Change evaluation is, in many respects, identical to the V&V evaluation of the concept phase, since many of the same planning and execution considerations apply.

Changes may be proposed as object-level patches to existing software, rather than as redesign and recode at the source level. These changes are particularly difficult to evaluate and debug. Where patching is unavoidable, the patches should be tracked (possibly with an automated database) and the source-level redesign and recode undertaken as soon as practical.

5.5.8.4 Phase task iteration

For approved software changes, perform V&V tasks necessary to ensure that: planned changes are implemented correctly; all documentation is complete and up to date; and no unacceptable changes have occurred in software performance. [Table 1, 5.8 (4)]

The implementation of each change may be thought of as following its own life cycle. This life cycle will include a subset of the full life cycle, depending on the nature of the change. In each phase of this reduced life cycle, plan and execute the V&V tasks required by the Standard for that phase (e.g., if the change modifies design documentation, trace and evaluate the design changes and plan appropriate tests).

5.6 Reporting

(Section 6 of the Plan.) This section shall describe how the results of implementing the Plan will be documented. V&V reporting shall occur throughout the software life cycle. This section of the Plan shall specify the content, format, and timing of all V&V reports. These V&V reports shall constitute the Software Verification and Validation Report (SVVR). [3.6]

V&V reporting communicates the status of the V&V effort and its findings among all interested parties. Those concerned with the results of the V&V activities might be quite diverse as a variety of different persons and organizations may be assigned responsibility for performing V&V. The diversity of the audience requires tailoring the distribution, format, and content of the reports. V&V reports can provide added visibility into the development process and more complete understanding of the product, but only to the extent that the participants in the V&V process share the V&V information.

The timing of the V&V reports is geared to their function and audience. The great cost multiplier for software errors is their latency period, the time between the introduction of a defect into a software product and its identification and subsequent removal. The greatest benefit of V&V in being performed in parallel to the development of the software comes from prompt notification to the developers of any problems identified by V&V.

All V&V activities need to be reported. Planning for V&V requires that sufficient time be allocated for reporting, although specific reporting requirements will vary with the activity. V&V reports may have a variety of names and formats, such as memos, presentations, marked-up copies of reviewed documents, minutes of meetings, action items, status reports, assessment and analysis reports, review notations, audit reports, inspection reports, test reports, anomaly reports, failure reports, etc. All of these fall into the broad categories of either being required by the Standard or optional.

5.6.1 Required reports

The hierarchy of the four types of required V&V reports ranges from individual findings about specific deficiencies in the software (anomaly reports) to a comprehensive evaluation of the entire development project (final V&V report). The four types of required V&V reports are as follows:

a) *Anomaly reports.* These reports should be promptly forwarded to developers. Quick turnaround requires established procedures to record and characterize identified anomalies, and then to provide the relevant information to the developers. Details of the anomaly reports include descriptions of each anomaly, a severity scale for each, rework approval mechanics, and required administration of the anomaly. (See also 5.7.1 of this guide.)

b) *V&V task reporting.* These reports follow the performance of each well-defined V&V task. Task reports may be viewed by V&V project management as proof of the progress of the V&V effort. Task reports also provide key insights into the need for any mid-course corrections to the development or V&V plans and are put into the V&V management review (see 5.5.1). The relative efficiencies and difficulties of certain V&V tasks may lead to tactical adjustments, such as choice of methodologies and tools. Further, the actual task results may call for strategic changes as well, including reallocation of V&V resources or alteration of schedules. Task reporting, its content and scheduling, should address the needs of one task requiring the outputs of another as input (for example, when test planning requires the results of traceability analysis), and be scheduled to allow an orderly and timely progression of the V&V tasks.

c) *V&V phase summary reports.* These reports serve to summarize and consolidate the results of the V&V activities performed by different organizations for each life cycle phase. The phase summary report may be an extensive formal document or a brief informal notification, depending on the span and depth of the V&V activities performed within a particular phase. The report may also be a briefing delivered as part of a phase review such as a preliminary design review. If the information is too critical to await reporting at the conclusion of the entire phase, interim reports may be generated in a more timely fashion.

d) *V&V final report.* This report summarizes and consolidates the results of the software anomalies, V&V tasks, and all V&V phase reports. The V&V Final Report is prepared at the conclusion of the V&V effort and will provide an assessment of overall software quality and any recommendations for the product and/or the development process.

5.6.2 Optional reports

Frequently, a need arises for more than the four required reports. These optional reports are either the result of some special V&V study or some other, unanticipated activity. Given the unique nature of these reports, there are no specific guidelines for their format or contents. As with all V&V reports, though, the optional reports need to be timely and properly distributed. They should identify the purpose of the V&V activity and describe the approach used, and report their results at an appropriate level.

5.7 Verification and validation administrative procedures

(Section 7 of the Plan.) This section of the Plan shall describe, at a minimum, the V&V administrative procedures described in 3.7.1 through 3.7.5. [3.7]

For a V&V effort to make its maximum contribution to the overall project, it should function in an unambiguous way with a controlled flow of information, orderly processes, and an ability to adapt to unanticipated situations. Clear, well-defined administrative procedures are an essential ingredient of a successful V&V plan. This section of the SVVP should specify such procedures in sufficient detail to allow for their successful implementation.

At a minimum, the administrative procedures shall address anomaly reporting and resolution, task iteration policy, deviation policy and control procedures, as well as standards, practices, and conventions. The necessary procedures can often be adopted, or tailored for the specific V&V effort, from established procedures, policies, standards, conventions, and practices.

This section of the SVVP should identify any existing administrative procedures that are to be implemented as part of this V&V plan, and any procedures that are to be written and implemented as part of the V&V effort. Existing procedures will also be identified as references in 2 of the SVVP. This section provides the opportunity to interpret the use of the referenced procedures, and to describe any new ones that may be planned or under development.

This section should identify the life cycle phase(s) and V&V task(s) to which each procedure will be applied. The degree of implementation of each procedure should be stated. This section should also indicate which individual or organizational element will be responsible for the enforcement, evaluation, and maintenance of each procedure, and specify how compliance will be monitored and assured.

Diagrams may be provided to show the relationships among the various responsible organizations. To be effective, the administrative procedures should be consistent with the organization and responsibilities defined elsewhere in the SVVP.

A V&V effort consists of both management and technical tasks, and at least three audiences can be identified for the information generated during the project—personnel performing V&V tasks, personnel performing development tasks, and management. In order to assure that the different information needs of each audience are satisfied, the administrative procedures may include one or more distribution lists. Information flow can be facilitated, and many misunderstandings avoided, if the appropriate distribution of development documentation, formal V&V documentation, memos, meeting minutes, status reports, etc., is established in advance.

5.7.1 Anomaly reporting and resolution

(Section 7.1 of the Plan.) This section shall describe the method of reporting and resolving anomalies, including the criteria for reporting an anomaly, the anomaly report distribution list, and the authority and time lines for resolving anomalies. This section shall define the anomaly criticality levels. Each critical anomaly shall be resolved satisfactorily before the V&V effort can formally proceed to the next life-cycle phase. [3.7.1]

The Standard defines an *anomaly* as anything observed in the documentation or operation of software that deviates from expectations based on previous verified software products or reference documents.

The SVVP should describe clear and unambiguous procedures for anomaly reporting and resolution, so that each participants can determine their roles in the process. Reporting and resolving anomalies as early in the development process as possible is one obvious benefit. Specific methods for documenting anomalies and their resolution, including the use of anomaly report forms, should be provided.

In addition to anomaly reporting and resolution tracking, the anomaly reporting process can be a primary means of data collection for the software verification and validation effort. The number and criticality level of the anomalies may determine whether the effort can formally proceed to the next life cycle phase. Data for process monitoring activities such as root-cause analysis also rely on data from the anomaly reporting process.

5.7.1.1 Methods and criteria for reporting

The Standard requires that the SVVP include criteria for reporting an anomaly. The circumstances under which the anomalies will be formally reported should be clearly defined. Disruption of the development process by unnecessary notification should be avoided. Anomaly reporting processes vary from informal to formal and from manual to fully automated reporting and tracking. Project size and criticality issues determine the sophistication of the system.

V&V planning should address the role of informal comments in the anomaly reporting process. Issues may include whether informal comments are to be allowed at all. If informal comments are allowed, the following should be addressed:

— The form in which the informal comments should be (e.g., memo, telephone call)
— When to use informal comments (e.g., for early notification, with anomaly reports to follows)
— The classes of problems (e.g., minor or out of current scope) for which informal comments are sufficient and formal notification is not required

While informal comments are often useful, care should be taken to assure that all significant problems are documented formally and brought to the attention of the appropriate personnel. All anomalies should be documented and reported.

V&V planning should specify

— Who is responsible for recording anomalies and analyzing their impact, criticality, etc.
— Who has the responsibility and authority for approving anomaly reports for issue

In some cases, V&V activities are performed in conjunction with software quality assurance activities, e.g., V&V personnel provide audit support, attend review meetings, monitor tests. In these cases, the SVVP should specify whether V&V anomaly reports are required to duplicate reporting of problems by other groups. For example, if V&V personnel monitor tests and find the testing organization's test incident reports to be adequate, there may be no need for separate V&V anomaly reports for the testing. Any instances of inadequate reporting by the testers would, however, be the subject of V&V anomaly reports in this case.

5.7.1.2 Anomaly report distribution

According to the Standard, the SVVP is to include an anomaly report distribution list. The planned distribution of anomaly reports should be clearly defined, including specification of who gets each report, under what circumstances, and for what reasons.

Reports should be distributed where needed for information and for tracking, as well as for action. If reports are to be distributed on a priority basis, the priority levels should be defined and the distribution criteria established.

The distribution list will depend on the organization and degree of independence of the V&V effort. For example, if the personnel performing V&V tasks are independent of the development group, anomaly reports should be distributed to both the development group and the user (or the development group's higher level management).

5.7.1.3 Methods and criteria for anomaly resolution

The resolution of an anomaly may result in a change to documentation, software, or hardware. The resolution of an anomaly can be a complicated, subjective, and resource-consuming task. The Standard requires that

> *Each critical anomaly shall be resolved satisfactorily before the V&V effort can formally proceed to the next life cycle phase.*

The plan shall specify the procedures for determining the criticality of the anomaly, determining the impact of the anomaly, and for resolving differences between the originator of the anomaly report and personnel responsible for resolving the anomaly.

Responsibility and authority with respect to anomaly reporting should be specified in the SVVP. These should include the following:

— Responsibility for responding to anomaly reports
— Authority for evaluating responses and resolving anomalies
— Responsibility for tracking the status (open vs. resolved) of anomaly reports

To be effective, the specification of responsibility and authority in this area shall be consistent with the organization and responsibilities defined elsewhere in the SVVP. (See also 5.4.1, 5.4.4, and C.7 of this guide.)

5.7.1.4 Timing

V&V planning should address timing considerations for reporting anomalies, as well as for their resolution. As indicated in 5.6 of this guide, anomaly reports should be forwarded promptly. Daily or even more frequent reports may be provided in some instances. Early identification and correction of defects is one obvious benefit of timely notification. Early notification of V&V results should be balanced against possible disruption of the development process.

Effective procedures are needed to assure that anomaly reports are valid and necessary as well as timely. The SVVP may require that anomalies be grouped and held for distribution according to some predefined categorization scheme, so that relationships among anomalies are more easily seen. If so, the maximum allowable hold time should be specified, which may be different for the different categories.

According to the Standard, the SVVP is to include time lines for resolving anomalies. A normal assumption is timely response to informal comments (if applicable) and anomaly reports. The SVVP should indicate the time frame that can be considered to be timely.

5.7.2 Task iteration policy

> *(Section 7.2 of the Plan.) This section shall describe the criteria used to determine the extent to which a V&V task shall be reperformed when its input is changed. These criteria may include assessments of change, criticality, and cost, schedule, or quality effects. [3.7.2]*

The software products that are input to the V&V effort are often changed as, for example, the results of anomaly corrections, performance enhancements, requirements changes, and clarifications. When changes are made, V&V tasks are iterated by repeating previous tasks or initiating new ones. V&V task iteration is needed to ensure that planned changes are implemented correctly, all documentation is complete and up to date, and no unacceptable changes in software performance have occurred.

Administrative procedures should include criteria for appropriate allocation of V&V resources as changes are evaluated. Without such procedures resources might be overextended in one or more areas, to the detriment of the project as a whole.

The criteria used to determine the extent to which V&V tasks are to be repeated when their inputs change may include assessments of change; criticality; and cost, schedule, or quality effects. Historical data may also be helpful in this planning.

Issues to be considered in selecting criteria may include the following:

a) *What portion(s) of development documentation will be re-evaluated in response to a change? For example, would revision of the Software Requirements Specification require review of the entire document, or of only those portions identified by the developers as revised in response to anomaly reports?*

b) *What degree of regression testing will be necessary when the software is changed? (Component? Integration? System? Acceptance?)*

c) *Is it necessary to repeat the V&V tasks until all anomalies are resolved?* (For noncritical anomalies, this may not be necessary or practical.)

d) *Will this V&V effort be continued into operations and maintenance? If not, at what point are changes considered to be maintenance and beyond the current V&V scope?*

5.7.3 Deviation policy

(Section 7.3 of the Plan.) This section shall describe the procedures and forms used to deviate from the Plan. The information required for deviations shall include task identification, deviation rationale, and effect on software quality. This section shall define the authorities responsible for approving deviations. [3.7.3]

Project changes or external factors may make it necessary to deviate from the SVVP. Any such deviations should be documented and approved before they are allowed to occur.

A standard form may be prepared, including task identification, deviation rationale, and effect on software quality. Tracking information may also be included. The personnel preparing and approving the deviation request should be identified. For smaller, less formal projects, it may be sufficient to document the required information in memo form.

Authority for preparing and approving requests for deviation from the SVVP should be comparable to those for writing and approving the SVVP itself. Consider software criticality when defining the necessary levels of authority.

Deviations in the execution of the SVVP are reported in the SVVRs. The approved deviations may be documented in the V&V final report by including copies of the forms or memos, or by listing forms or memos available separately for reference. Deviations that apply to a given task or phase should also be documented in the corresponding V&V task report or phase summary report.

It is not appropriate to remove past deviations by retroactive revision of the SVVP. However, some deviations affect the V&V tasks that are planned for the future. If a deviation is expected to occur again, or if it will have a significant effect on remaining activities, consider revising the SVVP. Subclauses 4.1 and 5.5.1.1 include guidance on revising the SVVP.

5.7.4 Control procedures

(Section 7.4 of the Plan.) This section shall identify control procedures applied to the V&V effort. These procedures shall describe how software products and results of software V&V shall be configured, protected, and stored.

These procedures may describe quality assurance, configuration management, data management, or other activities if they are not addressed by other efforts. At a minimum, this section shall describe how SVVP materials shall comply with existing security provisions and how the validity of V&V results shall be protected from accidental or deliberate compromise. [3.7.4]

Well-defined procedures are necessary for effective control of the software products (inputs for V&V evaluation) and the results of the software V&V efforts (V&V outputs). These procedures, especially those used in software quality assurance and configuration and data management, are similar to those used in software development. In many cases, the same procedures can be employed here. If so, those procedures may be incorporated by reference. The degree to which they are to be implemented should be identified, along with any necessary amendments. New procedures that are planned or under development should also be identified.

The set of procedures should describe how software products and results of software V&V shall be configured, protected, and stored. At a minimum, they should describe how SVVP materials shall comply with existing security provisions, and how the validity of V&V results shall be protected from accidental or deliberate compromise.

The Standard lists configuration management as an optional V&V task. Ideally, effective software configuration management procedures for development will have already been implemented. If not, their implementation as part of the V&V is recommended. Configuration management of the V&V products is also important if the validity of V&V results is to be protected. Additional guidance on effective control procedures can be found in IEEE Std 828-1990 and IEEE Std 1042-1987.

In order to ensure valid results, control procedures should include methods for identifying software items (including documentation), controlling and implementing changes, and recording and reporting change implementation status. These configuration management processes are needed if the V&V results are to be correctly linked with the products that were evaluated and the V&V tasks that were performed. Reviews and audits may be useful in assuring that these processes are effective. Code and media control are also needed, and may be part of configuration management. Finally, records collection, maintenance and retention should be addressed.

The first step in control is the identification of the items to be controlled. The various V&V inputs and outputs should be listed, along with provisions for unique identification of each (e.g., name, version/revision, date). Annex C.3 of this guide discusses V&V inputs and outputs. As is pointed out in annex C, V&V inputs include the V&V plan and procedures as well as the development products that are to be verified and validated.

Items to control include the following:

a) Computer files as well as documents
b) Applications software, operating system software, libraries, test drivers, test data, etc.
c) Any automated tools used as resources in obtaining the V&V results, so that those results will be reproducible if necessary

Identification of the V&V inputs and outputs includes the form (e.g., paper, 5.25" floppy disk) and format (e.g., pure ASCII text, IEEE Std 1012-1986). The state (e.g., draft or official releases only, TBDs) should be considered. Criteria for release of input documents to V&V, and for release of V&V results, should be defined.

The procedures should specify the means of controlling and implementing changes to the computer files and documentation. Effective change control is needed to avoid attempting V&V on a moving target. Considerations include the following:

— Change review authority and responsibility
— Preparation, routing and approval of change proposals
— Methods of implementing approved change proposals
— Software library control procedures, e.g., access control, read/write protection, change history, archival

See also the discussion of change proposals in 5.5.1.2 of this guide.

Status accounting procedures are needed, for recording and reporting change implementation status. Information on the current status of each item should be known, and periodic reports may be issued. Examples of information that may be collected are

— Latest version/revision of each computer file and document
— Status of change proposals related to each item (e.g., pending vs. issued vs. approved)
— Status of anomaly reports for each item (e.g., open vs. resolved)
— V&V tasks completed for each item
— Review/audit history of each item
— Approved deviations applicable to latest SVVP version/revision

Reviews and audits should be considered, to monitor the effectiveness of the control procedures. Organizational roles in such reviews and audits should be defined. The points in the life cycle at which the reviews and audits will occur, and the items to be covered in each, should be specified. Methods for identifying and resolving problems should be stated.

Code control can be interpreted as the ways and means necessary to protect or ensure the validity of a completed code. Code control may be performed as part of the configuration management process. The procedures described above can be used to cover many of the elements of code control such as specification of code to be controlled, code identification, use of a software library, and code change control. In order to comply with existing security provisions, procedures may also be needed to describe the physical location of the software under control; the requirements for obtaining copies; and the location, maintenance, and use of backup copies.

Media control is concerned with protection of the physical media on which computer files are stored, including storage and retrieval (including off-site storage), access restrictions, and environmental control to avoid physical degradation. Here, as in code control, existing security provisions should be addressed.

Provisions for records collection, maintenance, and retention should include identification of records to be retained, specification of the manner in which they will be maintained (e.g, hard copy, microfiche), and specification of the length of retention for each type of record addressed. Organizational responsibilities in this area include originating, collecting, maintaining, sorting, and protecting records. Authority for accessing, changing, purging, or destroying records should also be considered.

5.7.5 Standards, practices, and conventions

(Section 7.5 of the Plan.) This section shall identify the standards, practices, and conventions that govern the performance of V&V tasks, including internal organizational standards, practices, and policies. [3.7.5]

This section of the plan identifies the standards, practices, and conventions that govern the actual performance of the V&V tasks. New and existing standards, practices, and conventions are to be identified here. These may include documents that direct the V&V tasks and documents against which software products are to be evaluated during those tasks. Both internal and external documents should be considered.

The following are general examples of standards, practices, and conventions that may be applicable.

— Standards for software requirements, design, implementation, test, and documentation, against which the software is to be evaluated
— Detailed procedures for V&V tasks
— Detailed checklists for use in software evaluation
— Standards for reviews and audits
— Quality assurance requirements for the V&V program
— Any standards, practices, and conventions required by the contract

Depending on the project environment, specific standards, practices, and conventions like the following may be required

— Industry standards
— Professional standards
— Government standards
— Regulatory standards

Annex A

(informative)

Extracts from a sample Software Verification and Validation Plan

A.1 Overview

Extracts from a sample software verification and validation plan are provided to represent an SVVP that complies with IEEE Std 1012-1986. The material is intended to show an example of the development of an SVVP. The example is based on a planned software development effort for an elevator system from a fictitious manufacturer, the U&D Elevator Company. The elevator example represents a software application that is meaningful and is easily understood by a wide audience.

The purpose of providing this material is to illustrate

— Realistic planning decisions
— Details and specific requirements in a plan
— Relationship of tasks

The rest of this annex is divided into two sections—elevator reference material and extracts from a sample SVVP.

The extracts from the sample SVVP are presented in a format that explicitly identifies the following seven topics the Standard requires (see also annex C):

a) *Task*. Identify task and how it applies.
b) *Method*. Describe specific method and procedure for each task.
c) *Inputs/Outputs*. Identify inputs and outputs for each task.
d) *Schedule*. Identify schedule for each task.
e) *Resources*. Identify resources for performance of task.
f) *Risks*. Identify risks associated with task.
g) *Roles*. Identify organization or individual responsible for task.

It is important to understand the timing of writing this SVVP in context with the timing of a software development project supporting the elevator example.

The first set of extracts for the sample plan were developed as if the SVVP was being written at the end of the concept phase. These extracts address the V&V effort as a whole as well as specific tasks for the requirements and design phases.

The extracts from 3.5.5 of the SVVP were written as if the plans were being updated and expanded at the end of the design phase. Similarly, the extracts from 3.5.6 of the SVVP represent updates made at the end of the implementation phase.

NOTE—The extracts illustrate a few of the components of an SVVP but are not complete, nor do they represent the only approach to the development of an SVVP.

A.2 Elevator system reference material

**OUTLINE OF CONCEPT
for the
U&D Elevator Control System—UDC.100**

Project No. 466-A
Prepared for the:
Department of Elevators
By the:
Elevator Design Group

I. SCOPE

A. Identification

The concept document establishes the computer software and hardware configuration items of the U&D Elevator Control System, UDC.100.

B. Purpose

The U&D Elevator Control System, UDC.100, is a distributed system of computer hardware and software, operating as a local area network (LAN) for the control and scheduling of a modular, large-scale elevator installation. It handles all operator control, user requests, elevator scheduling, event logging, monitoring, reporting, maintenance, and security. The Elevator Control System will control up to 16 banks of elevators, with each bank having up to 16 elevators. Up to 256 vertical levels can be served by the UDC.100 elevator system.

II. SOFTWARE DESCRIPTION

Four major subsystems will comprise the Elevator Control System:

a)   Master control
b)   Bank control
c)   Motion control
d)   Elevator database

There is a control computer, UDC.HS1100, for each elevator in the system, providing backup and redundancy. The bank control subsystem software, UDC.S1101, and motion control software, UDC.S1102, are both resident in each elevators' control computer. Only one bank controller, though, will be active at any time for each bank. The other idle bank controllers are in standby mode, and can each assume control of their respective elevator banks upon command from master control. The master control computer will be duplexed and the database will be mirrored for backup. These elements and their data relationships are illustrated in figures A.1 and A.2.

A. Elevator master control subsystem—UDC.S110

The master control subsystem will initiate and terminate all operations of the elevator system, and will allow the system operator to direct any elevator to a specific level and to set its mode to either *in-service* or *out-of-service*. The master control subsystem will set the scheduling of each bank controller independently, with either predetermined (e.g., morning arrivals, evening departures, etc.) or custom scheduling scripts (e.g., skip floors 6–10). The master control subsystem will report status information for the operator about all elevators, and log all activity into the elevator database. The master control subsystem will produce analysis reports of elevator activity on request. In addition, the master control subsystem will assist maintenance by controlling diagnostic services for any bank controller and/or motion controller in the system.

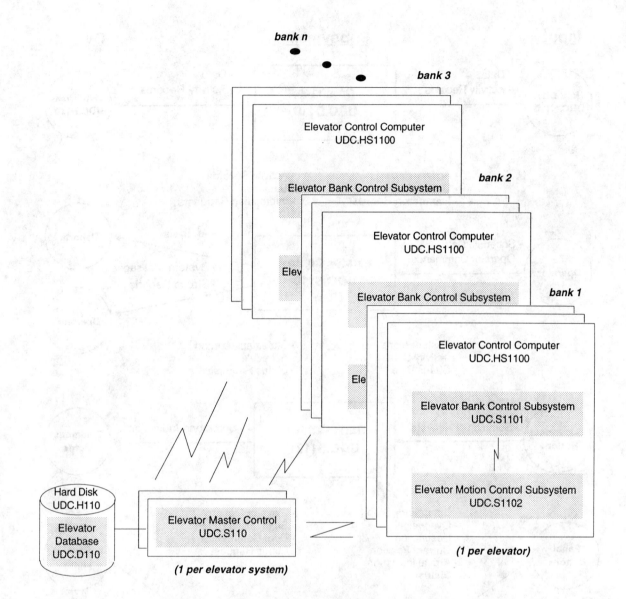

Figure A.1—U&D elevator control system UDC.100

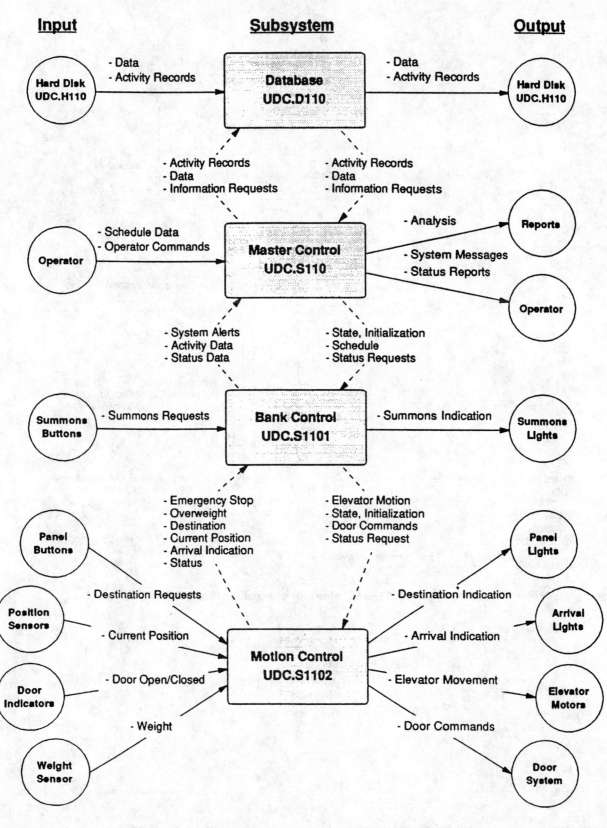

Figure A.2—Elevator control system UDC.100 data flow

The master control subsystem will direct each elevator bank controller, UDC.S1101, and will issue scheduling and operating commands, will request real-time operating status, and will receive and log all elevator command and operating history into the elevator system database, UDC.D110.

The master control subsystem will designate which will be the active bank control subsystem for each bank. This designation can be either directed by the operator, or occur in response to a time-out condition between the master control subsystem and the current bank control subsystem. The operator will be notified if a change of bank controller occurs in response to a time-out condition. In all cases, the change will be logged.

The master control subsystem will include the necessary operator support for entering and updating all elevator system database files. This will include the preparation of scheduling scripts, status reports, and analytical and historical reports.

B. Elevator bank control subsystem—UDC.S1101

Each elevator will have a microcomputer, UDC.HS1100, that will house both the bank control subsystem program, UDC.S1101, and the elevator motion control subsystem program, UDC.S1102. The bank control subsystem of only one of the elevators in a bank will be active at a time and will control the entire bank of elevators, comprising all of their individual motion controllers.

Each in-service elevator control unit will be able to take over as the bank controller, that is, activate its dormant bank control subsystem program, UDC.S1101, if the original bank controller does not respond to a transmission with the master controller in a specified period of time. The master control subsystem will assign the new bank controller from one of the dormant bank controllers within that bank of elevators.

The bank control subsystem will schedule each elevator in the bank according to the scheduling script provided to it by the master control subsystem. It keeps current information on the status of all elevators in the bank and determines which car will respond to each summons.

The bank controller will do the following:

— Schedule passenger requests (from interior panels)
— Schedule responses to summonses from floors
— Command elevator motion
— Set floor summons lights
— Monitor position (parked/in-transit/arrived)
— Monitor emergency stop condition
— Log all elevator activity to the master controller

The bank control subsystem will respond to all master controller commands, such as:

— Activate/deactivate
— Provide status information
— Update scheduling scripts
— Initiate maintenance procedures

In addition, the bank control subsystem will detect, notify the master controller, and remove from service any failing motion controller. In the event of the failure of a motion controller, the associated elevator will be stopped at the next floor and placed out of service.

C. Elevator motion control subsystem—UDC.S1102

There is one motion control subsystem for each elevator car, resident in the elevator control unit, UDC.HS1100, which is the same microcomputer used by the bank control program. The motion controller receives commands for its elevator car's operation from passengers, from its bank controller, and from sensors for the elevator position, door status, and weight. A motion controller will be active concurrently for each in-service elevator, and will do the following:

— Load elevator operations parameter tables

— Control lift motor operation
— Control door operation
— Respond to weight sensor
— Respond to emergency stop switch
— Set interior request (panel) lights
— Set arrival indicators (audible, visual)
— Set progress lights

If a motion controller fails, the elevator car will revert to a fail-safe mechanical operating mode and stop at the next level in its direction. The car can be further directed by the bank controller, if one is serviceable, to perform other operations.

D. Elevator system database—UDC.D110

The database will maintain files for elevator operations, scheduling, status, history, maintenance, and security.

1. Elevator operations files

The operating parameters of each elevator, such as its velocity and acceleration characteristics, door open/close specifications, weight limits, and manual control modes are individually determined. The operating parameters are provided to each elevator's motion controller by the master controller (through the bank controller) during an elevator initialization procedure.

2. Scheduling Files

These files contain the various scheduling scripts that are supplied by the master controller to the bank controller. Scheduling files are generally used by all of the elevators of a bank, although they can be targeted to individual elevators.

3. Status Files

The current elevator system operating environment is recorded, such as assigned schedules, in-service/out-of-service elevators, operators, and timed events (e.g., schedule changes).

4. History Files

They record a history of all elevator movements, schedule changes, and operating modes by date, time, bank, and elevator for a period of up to one year. These files are continuously recorded, and are purged by command. Analysis routines will produce operational history reports for determining scheduling and use patterns.

5. Maintenance Files

A record of the maintenance status and history of every elevator and system component will be recorded.

6. Security Files

A file of passwords and permissions will be maintained for allowed operating personnel.

III. HARDWARE DESCRIPTION

A. Elevator system master control center

A duplex computer, UDC.H4000, with touch-screen color displays, keyboards, audible alarms, two printers, removable disk media, backup tape drives, token-ring LAN telecommunications, and 12–16 MB of memory (see also II, D, Elevator system database—UDC.D110).

B. Elevator control computer

A microcomputer, UDC.HS1100, with 8 MB of memory, and a token-ring LAN port. Removable storage is provided for maintenance. Analog to digital ports will provide control signals for destination requests and indicators, elevator movement, summons requests and indicators, position sensors, door open/close signals, weight sensors, emergency call/stop signals, and manual mode key.

Keyboard, printer, and display may be connected for maintenance, but are not normally present. There is an elevator control computer for each elevator, and both the bank control subsystem and motion control subsystem will be resident.

C. Elevator hard disk

A mirrored set of hard disks, each with 1 GB (1 000 000 000 B) of storage, and 12 ms access time, UDC.H110. This disk subsystem will be accessible from each of the duplexed master control computers, UDC.H4000. Backup will be via streaming tape, and be performed each 24 h. All operating software, utilities, and databases will be stored on-line on this disk.

IV. DEVELOPMENT ENVIRONMENT

A development environment is outlined in which the V&V plan examples are defined.

The software is being produced by a fictitious manufacturer, the U&D Elevator Company. Software development is governed by the manufacturer's standards, which are tailored versions of the IEEE software standards. Tailoring of these standards has incorporated the requirements of the different regulatory agencies controlling the licensing and certification of elevator systems. (Note that fictitious standards and references will be cited by the examples as they are needed.)

The software development methodology can be characterized as being an iterative waterfall process employing real-time structured design methods, using data flow diagrams, data relationship diagrams, module hierarchy diagrams (structure charts), and state transition diagrams. There will be two levels of design, high level and detail. It is assumed that the resulting program code will be written in C language, and will be approximately 250 000 lines of source code. A significant part of this code will be available from reused modules, or commercial sources (e.g., door control, hoist motor control). The schedule calls for software development to be completed in 12 months.

Software testing will be divided into these four categories:

a) *Software component test.* Defined and performed by software development.
b) *Software integration test.* Defined and performed by systems engineering, with quality assurance review.
c) *System test.* Defined by quality assurance, executed and reviewed by systems engineering.
d) *Acceptance test.* Defined and executed by quality assurance, and reviewed by marketing.

Quality assurance has the responsibility defining system testing of hardware and software, and for writing the SVVP. Portions of the plan may be generated by software development. Final approval for the SVVP will reside with project management. There is assumed to be monthly project management meetings, and that marketing will attend for concept and user representation.

The plan will be administered and executed by quality assurance. Specific tasks within the plan may also be executed by other organizations. Hardware development will participate in the execution of the SVVP for interfaces with the hardware components during systems and acceptance testing. Similarly, quality assurance will develop a hardware verification and validation plan (HVVP), and hardware development and systems engineering will assist with its execution.

A.3 Extracts from a sample SVVP

A.3.1 Example for 5.1 Purpose

Purpose

This SVVP specifies the tasks to be performed for the U&D Elevator Control System UDC.100, project 466A-SVVP 1.0. This SVVP is written in accordance with IEEE Std 1012-1986.

Scope

The scope of this SVVP is to verify and validate all UDC.100 developed software and to validate all packaged and embedded software components for conformance to requirements for safety factors, response time, expandability, and external interfaces. Until a customer is under contract, the acceptance testing activities will not be included.

Objectives

The objectives of this SVVP are to verify and validate all developed software and interfaces for conformance with UDC.100 requirements for response time, expandability, and safety factors.

Applicability

This SVVP applies to the products of the requirements, design, implementation, and test phases of the UDC.100 software development cycle.

Waivers

This SVVP deviates from IEEE Std 1012-1986 in that it will not be applied to the following phases:

a) Concept phase
b) Installation and checkout phase
c) Operation and maintenance phase

This SVVP has been developed during the concept phase and applies to subsequent phases. The V&V planning for the installation and checkout phase, and the operation and maintenance phase will be deferred until a customer installation has been identified for UDC.100.

A.3.2 Example for 5.4.1 Organization

See figure A.3.

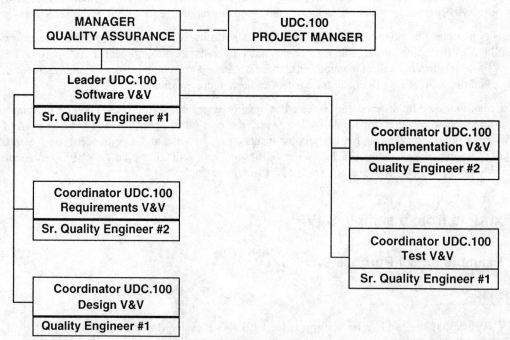

Figure A.3—Software V&V organization—UDC.100 project organization

A.3.3 Example for 5.4.4 Responsibilities

See table A.1.

Table A.1—UDC.100 software V&V project responsibilities

Position	Responsibilities
Sr. Quality Engineer #1	Coordinator—Software V&V Coordinator—Test V&V Management Acceptance Test Plan Generation Acceptance Test Design Generation
Sr. Quality Engineer #2	Coordinator—Requirements V&V Criticality Analysis Requirements Traceability Analysis
Quality Engineer #1	Coordinator—Design V&V Design Traceability Analysis Acceptance Test Procedure Generation
Quality Engineer #2	Coordinator—Implementation V&V Requirements Evaluation System Test Plan Generation Design Evaluation System Test Design Generation Source Code Traceability Analysis Acceptance Test Case Generation Acceptance Test Execution
Quality Engineer #3	Source Code Evaluation System Test Case Generation System Test Procedure Generation
Associate Quality Engineer #1	Requirements Interface Analysis Design Interface Analysis Source Code Interface Analysis Source Code Documentation Evaluation
Software Engineer #1	Source Code Evaluation Component Test Plan Generation Component Test Design Generation Integration Test Execution
Software Engineer #2	Component Test Case Generation Component Test Procedure Generation System Test Execution
Software Engineer #3	Component Test Execution
Sr. Systems Engineer #1	Integration Test Plan Generation Test Design Generation Integration Test Design Generation
Systems Engineer #1	Integration Test Case Generation Integration Test Procedure Generation Integration Test Execution

A.3.4 Example for 5.5.1.1 SVVP generation

a) Task: Update the SVVP at the completion of the Design Phase.

b) Method: Review the output products of Requirements and Design phases. Assess for changes and impacts. Revise plan accordingly.

c) Inputs/Outputs:

   1) Inputs

      i) Current SVVP

      ii) Design phase summary report

      iii) Component test plans and test designs

      iv) Integration test plans and test designs

      v) System test plans and test designs

      vi) Current development plans

   2) Output: Revised SVVP

d) Schedule: Initiate within two weeks of the publication of the Design Phase V&V Summary Report and complete in five days.

e) Resources: Senior quality engineer for four staff days.

f) Risks: There are no identified risks.

g) Roles: Senior quality engineer #1 will update the SVVP. The manager and quality assurance will approve.

A.3.5 Example for 5.5.1.3 Management review of V&V

NOTE—The example represents one component of management review. Other activities that must be planned include periodic review, daily management, and evaluation of results.

a) Task: Review Design Phase task reports.

b) Method: Review and evaluate intermediate products for overall assessment of quality and adherence to plan. Identify key findings and deviations from plan. Make specific recommendations as appropriate.

c) Inputs/Outputs:

   1) The inputs are all SVV outputs

   2) The output is the design phase summary report

d) Schedule: Initiate at the completion of the other design phase V&V activities and complete within two weeks.

e) Resources: Senior quality engineer for one staff day.

f) Risks: There are no identified risks.

g) Roles: Senior quality engineer # 1 will prepare the report.

A.3.6 Example for 5.5.3.1 Software requirements traceability analysis

a) Task: Trace the functions for the Elevator Master Control Subsystem that are specified in the concept for U&D UDC.100 to the requirements for component UDC.HS1100, and trace backward to the concept for UDC.100. Identify the response time, safety factors, and expandability requirements.

b) Method: Perform a manual trace, both backward and forward, to determine functional and data relationships, and any functions and data not defined in the UDC.100 concept or requirements for

UDC.HS1100. Indicate where either functions or data cannot be traced from the concept to the requirements, or back from the requirements to the concept for UDC.HS1100.

c) Inputs/Outputs:

    1) Inputs

        i) UDC.100 concept document

        ii) UDC.HS1100 requirements

    2) Outputs

        i) Trace table of the requirements for UDC.HS1100

        ii) Traceability discrepancy report for UDC.HS1100

d) Schedule: Initiate at the completion of the requirements for UDC.HS1100, planned for three months after project initiation and complete within three weeks.

e) Resources: The traceability analysis will require ten staff-days to perform. Reproduction facilities and clerical support are required for three days.

f) Risks: The traceability analysis must be completed prior to the initiation of the design of UDC.HS1100.

g) Roles: The traceability analysis will be performed by senior quality engineer # 2.

A.3.7 Example for 5.5.3.2 Software requirements evaluation

a) Task: Evaluate that the specified response time requirements for service of an elevator bank do not exceed the capabilities of the specified equipment parameters.

b) Method: Use the Lipoff-Craig queuing model, tailored for the UDC development workstation.

c) Inputs/Outputs:

    1) Inputs

        i) Distribution and maximum service wait times

        ii) Specified by the requirements for UDC.HS1100

        iii) Configuration of the UDC.100 elevator bank (operational parameters are included within the model)

        iv) Distribution of the expected service requests

    2) Output: Expected service distribution report produced by the model

d) Schedule: Initiate at the completion of the requirements for UDC.HS1100, planned for three months after project initiation, and complete within four weeks.

e) Resources: The Lipoff-Craig queuing model software is required, and a quality engineer for one staff week has been allocated for this task. Access to an engineering workstation with the standard network capabilities will be required for 40 hours.

f) Risks: The Lipoff-Craig model has not been validated for the Ockerman hoist motor, UDC.H2620 door retractor, and requests greater than 25 per minute.

g) Roles: Quality engineer # 2, trained in the use of the Lipoff-Craig model.

A.3.8 Example for 5.5.3.3 Software requirements interface analysis

a) Task: Analyze the interfaces between the Bank Control, UDC.S1101, and Motion Control, UDC.S1102, subsystems.

b) Method: The interfaces between UDC.S1101 and UDC.S1102 will be verified by an interface inspection.

c) Inputs/Outputs:

   1) Inputs

      i) UDC.100 data dictionary

      ii) Data flow diagrams for the UDC.HS1100 Control Computer

      iii) The interface between UDC.S1101 and UDC.S1102

      iv) Elevator motion timing parameters

   2) Outputs

      i) Series of inspection defect lists

      ii) Summary reports

      iii) Inspection report detailing the inspection findings

d) Schedule: Initiate at completion of the requirements for UDC.HS1100, planned for three months after project initiation, and complete within two weeks.

e) Resources: Assigned moderator (16 staff hours), inspectors (one other beside the author for 5 hours each), and inspection meeting room and clerk (4 hours) are also required.

f) Risks: There are no identified risks, except that the interface inspection and the resolution of all identified anomalies must occur prior to design of the two components.

g) Roles: Associate quality engineer # 1, trained in the inspection technique, as moderator, with the participation of the author of the UDC.HS1100 requirements, and an experienced systems engineer as one of the inspectors.

A.3.9 Example for 5.5.3.4 System test plan generation

a) Task: Generate the system test plan for the Elevator Control System UDC.100.

b) Method: Cast the operations for the Elevator Control System UDC.100 as a series of matrices of operations, one matrix for each operational state. These matrices will be used to define test conditions for UDC.100. Test will focus on elevator response and safety features.

c) Inputs/Outputs:

   1) Inputs

      i) Concept document

      ii) SRS

      iii) Trace analysis (from the software requirements traceability analysis task in A.3.6)

      iv) Interface data flow diagrams for UDC.100

   2) Output: Elevator Control System UDC.100 system test plan

d) Schedule: Initiate at the completion of the SRS for UDC.100 and complete before initiating integration test design.

e) Resources: A quality engineer for two months.

f) Risks: There are no identified risks.

g) Roles: Quality engineer # 2, experienced in system test planning for U&D software control systems.

A.3.10 Example for 5.5.3.4 Acceptance test plan generation

Task: Generate a draft acceptance test plan for the Elevator Control System UDC.100 to be installed in a large office building for a customer not yet specified.

Method: Cast the operations for the Elevator Control System UDC.100 as a series of matrices of ary values, one matrix for each operational state. These matrices will be used to define acceptance conditions for UDC.100. Develop an operation suite reflecting expected customer usage conditions. Test will focus on elevator response and safety features.

 c) Inputs/Outputs:

  1) Inputs

   i) Concept document

   ii) SRS

   iii) Trace for the SRS

   iv) Interface analysis

   v) Expected customer usage patterns and conditions.

  2) Outputs

   i) Acceptance test plan matrices

   ii) Plans for providing the input conditions for the UDC.100 customer installation

 d) Schedule: Integrate at completion of the SRS for UDC.100 and complete before initiating acceptance test design.

 e) Resources: A senior quality engineer for two months.

 f) Risks: The Elevator Control System UDC.100 is new, without an identified customer. Specific customer demands may require changes to the draft plan.

 g) Roles: Senior quality engineer # 1 trained in acceptance test planning.

A.3.11 Example for 5.5.4.1 Software design traceability analysis

 a) Task: Trace requirements in the SRS to each of the high level design components of the SDD for the Elevator Master Control, UDC.S110; Bank Control, UDC.S1101; Motion Control, UDC.S1102; and Elevator Database, UDC.D110. The reverse trace, from each high level design component of the SDD back to the SRS, shall also be performed. Identify the response time, safety factors, and expandability requirements.

 b) Method: The U&D Trace Tool 1 analytic tracing program shall associate each high level design component with the appropriate requirements to identify any possible inconsistencies between requirements and design. Anomalies will be identified.

 c) Inputs/Outputs:

  1) Inputs

   i) SRS for the Elevator Master Control, UDC.S110; Bank Control, UDC.S1101; Motion Control, UDC.S1102; and Elevator Database, UDC.D110

   ii) Draft software high level design description

   iii) UDC.S110 requirements trace table (from the software requirements traceability analysis task in A.3.6)

    [Both the requirements and high level design shall be in standard ASCII format, written respectively to requirements standard REQ-1.2 and high level design standard HLD-1.4.]

  2) Outputs

   i) Design traceability table

   ii) Anomalies list produced by U&D Trace Tool 1

 d) Schedule: Initiate at the release of the draft high level design descriptions and complete within five days.

 e) Resources: The U&D Trace Tool 1 support tool is required, and 16 staff hours for a quality engineer have been allocated for this task. Access to an engineering workstation with the standard network capabilities will be required for 8 hours.

 f) Risks: U&D Trace Tool 1 is a newly released tool offering improved capabilities, but has not yet been qualified on an operational project. Should unforeseen problems arise, the proven U&D TRACER tool can be utilized, but with more limited capabilities.

 g) Roles: This task will be performed by quality engineer # 1.

A.3.12 Example for 5.5.4.2 Software design evaluation

a) Task: Evaluate that the response time for service for each elevator bank will not exceed the specified limit.

b) Method: Use the UDC Elevator System Simulator. Verify that the scheduling algorithms provide designed response times.

c) Inputs/Outputs:

1) Inputs

    i) Hardware response times of the UDC.100 components (motor acceleration and deceleration characteristics, car door open and close times, etc.)

    ii) Expected request patterns for each scheduling mode (maximum up, maximum down, normal, etc.)

    iii) Scheduling algorithms

    iv) State transition diagrams

2) Outputs

    i) Response time report

    ii) Service time distributions

    iii) Anomalies report

d) Schedule: Initiate at the receipt of high level SDD and complete within six weeks.

e) Resources: The UDC Elevator System Simulator is required, and one staff month for a quality engineer (with previous UDC Elevator System Simulator experience) has been allocated for this task. Access to an engineering workstation with the standard network capabilities will be required for 160 hours.

f) Risks: The updated parameters for the UDC Elevator System Simulator shall have been calibrated and certified.

g) Roles: Quality engineer # 2 familiar with the use of the UDC Elevator System Simulator will perform the analysis. Results will be provided to the UDC.100 project manager. Any modifications to the scheduling algorithms will be re-evaluated.

A.3.13 Example for 5.5.4.3 Software design interface analysis

a) Task: Analyze the interfaces between the high level design of the Bank Control Subsystem UDC.S1101, and the Motion Control Subsystem UDC.S1102.

b) Method: The specifications for the interface formats, parameters, queuing, tasking, timing, and expected responses will be verified by design interface inspections.

c) Inputs/Outputs:

1) Inputs (for both subsystems UDC.S1101 and UDC.S1102)

    i) Design traceability table (from the software design traceability analysis in A.3.11)

    ii) Subsystem data flow diagrams

    iii) Data entity charts

    iv) Subsystem message lists

    v) SDD interface standards and conventions

2) Outputs

    i) Inspection defect lists

    Inspection database reports

    Inspection management reports

    Anomaly reports

d) Schedule: Initiate at completion of both UDC.S1101 and UDC.S1102 high level design interface specifications and complete within two weeks.

e) Resources: Each inspection will consist of a team of four persons, including the developer of the specification. It is estimated that there will be two high level design interface inspections of two hours each. Thirty staff hours are estimated for the inspections, expected rework, and inspection data analysis and reporting.

f) Risks: There are no identified risks.

g) Roles: Associate quality engineer # 2 as moderator for each interface inspection. The moderator will certify inspection of the interface specifications for UDC.S1101 and UDC.S1102. The UDC.100 project manager and a lead software engineer will receive the inspection management reports and the inspection database summaries.

A.3.14 Example for 5.5.4.4 Component test plan generation

a) Task: Generate the component test plan for the Motion Control Subsystem UDC.S1102 components.

NOTE—There will be a series of four component test plans for each of the subsystems.

b) Method: Develop a plan for testing each component of the Motion Control Subsystem UDC.S1102, using IEEE Std 1008-1987 and document according to IEEE Std 829-1983. Specify use of U&D Code Coverage analyzer to achieve 100% statement coverage for each component. The test will be conducted with hardware and software simulators in the UDC Elevator Testing Lab. The test results will be compared to the expected results for each test case.

c) Inputs/Outputs:

   1) Inputs

      i) SRS

      ii) SDD

      iii) Design traceability table (from the software design traceability analysis in A.3.11)

      iv) Interface design specifications

      v) Hardware and software simulators user's guide

      vi) Draft user documentation

      vii) UDC code coverage analyzer specifications

   2) Output: UDC.S1102 component test plan

d) Schedule: Initiate at completion of interface analysis and complete prior to final design approval.

e) Resources: The component test plan will be prepared by a UDC.100 software engineer and is estimated as requiring two staff weeks of effort.

f) Risks: There are no identified risks.

g) Roles: Software engineer # 1 will prepare the component test plan. A lead software engineer will approve it.

A.3.15 Example for 5.5.4.4 Integration test plan generation

a) Task: Generate the Elevator Control System UDC.100 Integration Test Plan.

b) Method: Develop an integration test plan for UDC.100, which will comprise integrating test plans for the four individual subsystem's integration test plans as well as a integration test plan for the total UDC.100 system.

c) Inputs/Outputs:

   1) Inputs

     i)   SDD

     ii)   Design traceability table (from the software design traceability analysis in A.3.11)

     iii) Interface design specifications

     iv) Interface analysis report

     v)   Criticality analysis report

     vi) Draft operating documentation

     vii) Draft maintenance documentation

  2)   Output: UDC.100 integration test plan

d)   Schedule: Initiate one month following the start of the design and complete within four weeks.

e)   Resources: Integration test planning is estimated as requiring three staff weeks of effort.

f)   Risks: There are no identified risks.

g)   Roles: Systems engineer # 1 will prepare the integration test plan. The manager of quality assurance will approve the integration test plan.

A.3.16 Example for 5.5.4.5 Test design generation—Component testing

a)   Task: Design component tests for the Motion Control Subsystem UDC.S1102.

    NOTE—It is expected that the component test plan will specify that the generation of test designs be done for each subsystem.

b)   Method: Develop test designs in accordance with the Component Test Plans for the Motion Control System. In addition, design the necessary interfaces and support for the use of the UDC code coverage analyzer.

c)   Inputs/Outputs:

  1)   The inputs are:

     i)   Component test plans

     ii)   SDD

     iii) Interface design specifications

     iv) Draft operating documentation

     v)   Hardware and software simulators setup procedures

     vi) UDC code coverage analyzer operations manual

  2)   Output: Test designs for the Motion Control Subsystem UDC.S1102

d)   Schedule: Initiate two weeks after the component test plan is started, and complete within four weeks.

e)   Resources: Three staff weeks are estimated for a software engineer.

f)   Risks: There are no identified risks.

g)   Roles: Software engineer # 1 will design the Motion Control Subsystem tests.

A.3.17 Example for 5.5.4.5 Test design generation—Integration testing

Task: Design integration tests for the four subsystems and integration of the four subsystems into the UDC.100.

     thod: Develop the test designs for the four subsystems and integration of the four subsystems into
       'DC.100. Design for the recording of the test results.

       utputs:

    i)   UDC.100 integration test plan

    ii)   SDD

    iii) Interface specifications

  2)   Output: Test designs for the four subsystems and integration of the four subsystems into the UDC.100.

d)   Schedule: Initiate two weeks after the integration test plan is started, and complete within twelve weeks.

e)   Resources: Two staff months are estimated for a software engineer.

f)   Risks: Integration test cases for distributed architecture such as UDC.100 have not been developed before. Schedule estimates are based on past experience. Earlier integration test activities and initial test case development times will be monitored to validate the schedule estimates.

g)   Roles: Senior systems engineer # 1 will design integration tests. The designs must be approved by the manager of quality assurance.

A.3.18 Example for 5.5.4.5 Test design generation—System testing

a)   Task: Design system tests for the Elevator Control System UDC.100.

b)   Method: Develop test designs in accordance with UDC.100 system test plan (from the system test plan generation task in A.3.9). Test Elevator Tower will be used. Design for the recording of the test results.

c)   Inputs/Outputs:

  1)   Inputs

    i)   UDC.100 system test plan

    ii)   SDD

    iii) Interface specifications

    iv) Draft operating documentation

    v)   Maintenance documentation

    vi) Test elevator tower configurations

  2)   Output: UDC.100 system test designs

d)   Schedule: Initiate two weeks after the system test plan is started and complete within six weeks.

e)   Resources: A staff month is estimated for a software engineer for the design of system test for the UDC Elevator Control System.

f)   Risks: System tests haven't been designed before for distributed systems such as UDC.100. Estimates for the schedule are tentative. A margin of 100% schedule and resource overrun needs to be considered for this activity. System test design may be critical to the UDC.100 project.

g)   Roles: Quality engineer # 2 will design system tests. The design must be approved by the manager of quality assurance.

A.3.19 Example for 5.5.4.5 Test design generation—Acceptance testing

a)   Task: To be developed when a customer is identified and when the acceptance test plan generation task in A.3.10 is completed.

b)   Method: Pending

c)   Inputs/Outputs:

  1)   The inputs are pending.

  2)   The outputs are pending.

d)   Schedule: Pending

e)   Resources: Pending

f)   Risks: Pending

g)   Roles: Pending

(Reminder—The extracts from 5.5.5 of the SVVP were written as if the plans were being updated and expanded at the end of the design phase.)

A.3.20 Example for 5.5.5.1 Source code traceability analysis

a)   Task: Trace each of the design requirements in the SDD to the Bank Control Subsystem UDC.S1101 source code. The reverse trace shall also be performed. Identify the response time, safety factor, and expandability design requirements.

b)   Method: The U&D Trace Tool 1 analytic tracing program shall associate the design requirements to the individual section of source code where they are implemented to identify any possible inconsistencies between design and code. Anomalies will be defined and categorized.

c)   Inputs/Outputs:

   1)   Inputs

      i)   SDD for Bank Control Subsystem UDC.S1101

      ii)   The source code from configuration controlled libraries

      iii) Design Traceability Table for UDC.S1101

   2)   Outputs

      i)   Source code traceability table

      ii)   List of anomalies

d)   Schedule: Initiate at the acceptance of components by configuration management and complete within five calendar days of acceptance of last component.

e)   Resources: A quality engineer for 10 staff days.

f)   Risks: There are no identified risks.

g)   Roles: This task will be performed by quality engineer # 2.

A.3.21 Example for 5.5.5.2 Source code evaluation

a)   Task: Evaluate the Bank Control Subsystem scheduling algorithm requirements.

b)   Method: Use Monte Carlo simulation to evaluate the scheduling algorithm requirements to ensure conformance with real time response requirements.

c)   Inputs/Outputs:

   1)   Inputs

      i)   Bank Control program specifications

      ii)   Source code

      iii) Scheduling algorithm design specifications

      iv)   Monte Carlo simulation software

   2)   Output: Scheduling algorithm performance characteristic

d)   Schedule: Initiate at acceptance of components by configuration management and complete within two weeks.

e)   Resources: One software engineer experienced in Monte Carlo simulations for three staff days.

f)   Risks: The Monte Carlo simulation has not been used for elevator banks in excess of eight elevators. This task will be performed immediately upon release of code to allow time for necessary recalibration.

g)   Roles: Software engineer #1 experienced in Monte Carlo simulation will perform this task. Quality engineer # 3 will review the results.

A.3.22 Example for 5.5.5.3 Source code interface analysis

a) Task: Analyze the source code interfaces for the Bank Control Subsystem UDC.S1101 and Motion Control Subsystem UDC.S1102.

b) Method: The source code for the interface formats, parameters, timing, and expected responses will be verified by interface inspections. The analysis will focus on the complete and correct transfer of data across the interfaces.

c) Inputs/Outputs:

   1) Inputs

      i) Interface design specification for UDC.S1101 & UDC.S1102

      ii) The program specification for UDC.S1101 and UDC.S1102

      iii) The UDC.S1101 and UDC.S1102 source code

   2) Outputs

      i) Inspection defect lists

      ii) Inspection database reports

      iii) Inspection management reports

      iv) Anomaly reports

d) Schedule: Initiate at acceptance of code by configuration management and complete within two weeks.

e) Resources: Each inspection will consist of a team of three persons, including the developer of the code. It is estimated that there will be two code inspections of two hours each. Thirty staff hours are estimated for the inspections, expected rework, and inspection data analysis and reporting.

f) Risks: There are no identified risks.

g) Roles: Associate quality engineer # 1 will be moderator for each interface inspection. The lead software engineer will receive a copy of inspection reports.

A.3.23 Example for 5.5.5.4 Source code documentation evaluation

a) Task: Evaluate operating manual documentation to ensure consistency with the UDC.S110 Master Control Subsystem specifications.

b) Method: Use a document walkthrough to ensure the operating documentation to the source code of the UDC.S110 Master Control Subsystem. Evaluation of the procedures for entering and updating all elevator system database files will be emphasized. Consistency of the operating documentation instructions and error messages will be checked.

c) Inputs/Outputs:

   1) Inputs

      i) UDC.S110 source code

      ii) UDC.S110 operating documentation

      iii) UDC.S110 specification

   2) Output: List of discrepancies

d) Schedule: Initiate at receipt of the UDC.S110 source code and the draft of the operator manual. Prior review of documentation is expected. Complete within two weeks.

e) Resources: The evaluation process will include author of documentation and representatives from quality engineering and systems engineering. Estimated that three walkthrough sessions of four hours each will be scheduled. Fifty staff hours are estimated for the walkthroughs and expected rework.

f) Risks: There are no identified risks.

g) Roles: Associate quality engineer # 1 will be moderator for each walkthrough session.

A.3.24 Example for 5.5.5.5 Test case generation—Component testing

a) Task: Generate test cases for component testing of the Motion Control Subsystem UDC.S1102.

NOTE—It is expected that the component test plan will specify that the generation of test cases be done for each subsystem.

b) Method: Develop test case specifications to support the test designs previously defined for the Motion Control Subsystem UDC.S1102. Cases will state actual input and expected results of each test to be run.

c) Inputs/Outputs:

1) Inputs

i) Component test plan

ii) Test design document for Motion Control Subsystem UDC.S1102

iii) Hardware interface specifications

iv) Hardware and hardware simulators documentation

v) Motion Control Subsystem UDC.S1102 source code

vi) UDC code coverage analyzer manual

2) Output: Test case specifications documents

d) Schedule: Initiate after the component test designs are started and complete within four weeks.

e) Resources: Three staff weeks are estimated for a software engineer for developing test cases for UDC.S1102.

f) Risks: There are no identified risks.

g) Roles: Software engineer # 2 will develop the component test cases.

A.3.25 Example for 5.5.5.5 Test case generation—Integration testing

a) Task: Generate test cases for integration testing of the UDC.100.

b) Method: Develop test case specifications for the four subsystems and the integration of the four subsystems into the UDC.100. Cases will state actual input and expected results of each test to be run.

c) Inputs/Outputs:

1) Inputs

i) Integration test plan document

ii) Integration test design document

iii) Hardware and hardware simulators documentation

iv) UDC.100 source code

2) Output: Integration test case specifications

d) Schedule: Initiate after the integration test designs are started and complete within twelve weeks.

e) Resources: Two staff months are estimated for a systems engineer.

f) Risks: Integration test cases for distributed architecture such as UDC.100 have not been developed before. Schedule estimates are based on past experience. Earlier integration test activities and initial test case development times will be monitored to validate the schedule estimates.

g) Roles: Systems engineer # 1 will develop the integration test cases.

A.3.26 Example for 5.5.5.5 Test case generation—System testing

a) Task: Generate test cases for system testing of the Elevator Control System UDC.100.

b) Method: Develop system test case specifications in accordance with UDC.100 test designs from the test design generation—system testing task in A.3.18. Cases will state actual input and expected results of each test to be run.

c) Inputs/Outputs:

   1) Inputs

      i) System test plan document

      ii) System test design document

      iii) UDC.100 subsystem's source code

      iv) Operating manuals

   2) Output: System test case specifications

d) Schedule: Initiate after the system test designs are started and complete within fourteen weeks.

e) Resources: Two staff months are estimated for a quality engineer for developing test cases for UDC.100.

f) Risks: System test cases for distributed architecture such as UDC.100 have not been developed before. Schedule estimates are based on past experience. Earlier system test activities and initial test case generation development times will be monitored to validate the schedule estimates.

g) Roles: Quality engineer # 3 will develop the system test cases.

A.3.27 Example for 5.5.5.5 Test case generation—Acceptance testing

NOTE—This is to be determined when a customer is identified and the test design generation—system testing task in A.3.18 is completed.

a) Task: Generate test cases for acceptance testing of the Elevator Control System UDC.100.

b) Method: Pending

c) Inputs/Outputs:

   1) The inputs are pending.

   2 The outputs are pending.

d) Schedule: Pending

e) Resources: Pending

f) Risks: Pending

g) Roles: Pending

A.3.28 Example for 5.5.5.6 Test procedure generation—Component testing

a) Task: Generate test procedures for component test cases developed for Motion Control Subsystem UDC.S1102.

b) Method: Develop steps and actions required to execute each test case defined for component testing of the Motion Control Subsystem UDC.S1102. Procedures are needed for hardware and software simulators and monitors.

c) Inputs/Outputs:

   1) Inputs

      i) Component test plan designs

      ii) Component test cases for Motion Control Subsystem UDC.S1102

     iii)   Hardware interface specifications

     iv)   Hardware set-up procedures

     v)   Hardware simulators operating procedures

     vi)   Motion Control Subsystem UDC.S1102 source code

     vii) UDC code coverage analyzer manual

  2)   Output: Component test procedures document

d)   Schedule: Initiate one week after component test cases are started. Complete within two weeks after receipt of final component test cases.

e)   Resources: One staff week is estimated for a software engineer for developing test procedures for UDC.S1102.

f)   Risks: There are no identified risks.

g)   Roles: Software engineer # 2 will develop the component test procedures.

A.3.29 Example for 5.5.5.6 Test procedure generation—Integration testing

a)   Task: Generate integration test procedures for Elevator Control System UDC.100.

b)   Method: Develop steps and actions required to execute each test case defined for the four subsystems and the integration of the four subsystems into the UDC.100.

c)   Inputs/Outputs:

  1)   Inputs

     i)   Integration test plan designs

     ii)   Integration test cases specifications

     iii)   Hardware interface specifications

     iv)   Hardware set-up procedures

     v)   Hardware simulators operating procedures

     vi)   UDC.100 source code

  2)   Output: Integration test procedures

d)   Schedule: Initiate one week after integration test case generation starts. Complete within two weeks after receipt of final integration test cases.

e)   Resources: One staff month is estimated for a systems engineer.

f)   Risks: Integration test procedures for distributed architecture such as UDC.100 have not been developed before. Schedule estimates are based on past experience. Earlier integration test activities and initial test procedure development times will be monitored to validate the schedule estimates.

g)   Roles: Systems engineer # 1 will develop the integration test procedures.

A.3.30 Example for 5.5.5.6 Test procedure generation—System testing

a)   Task: Generate test procedures for system testing of the Elevator Control System UDC.100.

b)   Method: Develop test procedures required to execute each test case defined for system test of the Elevator Control System UDC.100.

c)   Inputs/Outputs:

  1)   Inputs

     i)   System test designs

     ii)   System test case specifications for Elevator Control System UDC.100

     iii)   Test elevator tower set-up procedures

    iv) Hardware timing monitors set-up procedures

    v) UDC.100 source code

    vi) Operating manuals

   2) Output: Test procedures documentation

d) Schedule: Initiate after test case generation starts. Complete within two weeks after receipt of final system test cases.

e) Resources: One staff month is estimated for a quality engineer for developing test procedures for UDC.100.

f) Risks: System test procedures for distributed systems such as UDC.100 have not been developed before. Schedule estimates are based on past experience. Earlier system test activities and initial system test procedure development times will be monitored to validate the schedule estimates.

g) Roles: Quality engineer # 3 will develop the system test procedures. Software quality engineer will approve.

A.3.31 Example for 5.5.5.7 Component test execution

a) Task: Execute test procedures and cases for Motion Control components.

b) Method: Follow the test procedures for Motion Control components test. Procedures define the equipment set-up, initialization procedures, and execution steps. Analyze the results of testing to determine success or failure for each test.

c) Inputs/Outputs:

   1) Inputs

    i) Component test designs

    ii) Component test cases

    iii) Component test procedures

    iv) User documentation and the source code

   2) The outputs are:

    i) Component test reports

    ii) Anomaly reports

d) Schedule: Initiate after completion of component test procedures and acceptance of code by configuration management. Complete within two weeks.

e) Resources: One staff week is estimated for a software engineer.

f) Risks: There are no identified risks.

g) Roles: Software engineer # 3 will execute the component tests.

(Reminder—The extracts from 5.5.6 of the SVVP represent updates made at the end of the implementation phase.)

A.3.32 Example for 5.5.6.1 Acceptance test procedure generation

a) Task: Generate test procedures for acceptance testing of the Elevator Control System UDC.100.

  NOTE—This is to be developed when a customer is identified and the test case generation—acceptance testing task in A.3.27 is completed.

b) Method: Pending

c) Inputs/Outputs:

   1) The inputs are pending.

   2) The outputs are pending.

d) Schedule: Pending

e) Resources: Pending

f) Risks: Pending

g) Roles: Pending

A.3.33 Example for 5.5.6.2.1 Integration test execution

a) Task: Execute integration test procedures and cases for Elevator Control System UDC.100.

b) Method: Follow the integration test procedures for UDC.100. Procedures define the equipment set-up, initialization procedures, and execution steps. The test execution will be for the four subsystems and integration of the four subsystems into UDC.100. Analyze the results of testing to determine success or failure for each test.

c) Inputs/Outputs:

   1) Inputs

      i) Integration test designs

      ii) Integration test cases

      iii) Integration test procedures

      iv) User documentation

      v) Source and executable code

   2) Outputs

      i) Integration test reports

      ii) Anomaly reports

d) Schedule: Initiate at completion of integration test procedures, component test execution and acceptance of the code by configuration management. Complete within ten weeks.

e) Resources: Two staff months are estimated for a software engineer.

f) Risks: Integration test execution for distributed systems such as UDC.100 has not been performed before. Schedule estimates are based on past experience. Earlier integration test activities and initial integration test execution times will be monitored to validate the schedule estimates.

g) Roles: Software engineer # 1 will execute the integration tests.

A.3.34 Example for 5.5.6.2.2 System test execution

a) Task: Execute system test procedures and cases for Elevation Control System UDC.100.

b) Method: Follow the system test procedures for UDC.100. Procedures define the equipment setup, initialization procedures, and execution steps. Analyze the results of testing to determine success or failure for each test.

c) Inputs/Outputs:

   1) Inputs

      i) System test designs

      ii) System test cases

      iii) System test procedures

      iv) User documentation

      v) Source and executable code

   2) Outputs

      i) System test reports

      ii) Anomaly reports

d) Schedule: Initiate after completion of system test procedures, completion of integration test execution and acceptance of the code by configuration management. Complete within six weeks.

e) Resources: One staff month is estimated for a software engineer.

f) Risks: System test execution for distributed systems such as UDC.100 has not been performed before. Schedule estimates are based on past experience. Earlier system test activities and initial system test execution times will be monitored to validate the schedule estimates.

g) Roles: Software engineer # 2 will execute the system tests.

A.3.35 Example for 5.5.6.2.3 Acceptance test execution

a) Task: Execute acceptance test cases for Elevator Control System UDC.100.

NOTE—This is to be developed when a customer is identified and the acceptance test procedure generation task in A.3.32 is completed.

b) Method: Pending

c) Inputs/Outputs:

1) The inputs are pending.

2) The outputs are pending.

d) Schedule: Pending

e) Resources: Pending

f) Risks: Pending

g) Roles: Pending

Annex B

(informative)

Critical software and criticality analysis

Criticality analysis is a methodology for allocating V&V resources to individual elements of the software. The goal of criticality analysis is to ensure the cost-effective use of these resources, especially when the resources available are insufficient to analyze all areas of the system at a uniformly thorough level. Simply stated, criticality analysis is a systematic methodology for applying V&V resources to the most important (critical) areas of the software.

Criticality analysis is related to the concept of critical software. Critical software, according to the Standard, is software *in which a failure could have an impact on safety or could cause large financial or social losses.* If a system satisfies that definition of criticality, the Standard requires that a specified minimum set of tasks be performed. The level to which these tasks should be performed is not, however, described in the Standard. In criticality analysis, a more systematic approach is taken in making decisions about critical software.

Criticality analysis is performed in four steps:

a) *Establish criticality levels to be applied to the system under development.* Criticality levels may be assigned values of High and Low; High, Medium, and Low; or one of a range of numerical values from 1 to N. In most cases the use of two or three levels is sufficient for planning purposes.

There are frequently several different types of criticality relevant to a given system. Impact on safety, impact on the system mission, financial risk, and technical complexity are examples of types of criticality.

Develop definitions for each level and type of criticality. For example, in the case of safety, the level High may be assigned if failure could result in personal injury, loss of life, or loss of property; Medium if failure would result merely in damage to equipment; and Low if failure would impact neither persons nor property. Similar levels are developed for each criticality type. These levels should be defined clearly and unambiguously, so that different analysts would reach the same criticality assignment independently. This goal is sometimes difficult to achieve.

b) *Identify a set of requirements sufficient to characterize the system.* This step should be part of the development process. Sometimes, however, a complete or useful set does not exist and must be developed. Agreement on what comprises a complete and faithful high-level representation should be reached with the developers, users, V&V agents, and overall program management. The actual level of detail will depend on the complexity of the system. Each identified requirement is then assigned a number and is cross-referenced to the paragraph number within a requirements specification document in which it is found.

c) *For each criticality type, assign a criticality level to each requirement, resolving multiple ratings into a single criticality level.* If the requirements are ambiguous or not quantitative, there may be different assessments of criticality level by separate analysts. This may indicate that the requirements need refinement or revision. In the case of simple differences, a conservative approach (especially for designated critical software) is to assign a higher (more critical) value.

When there are multiple types of criticality, different ratings may be assigned for the different types. For example, suppose there are several criticality types including technical complexity, safety, and financial risk. In this example, suppose the criticality level for technical complexity is Low, safety is Medium, and financial risk is High. These different ratings may be resolved into a common rating in one of two ways.

The first method is the more conservative and is recommended for systems designated "critical." In this case, the criticality level of the requirement is the highest of the criticality levels for the different types. The second approach is to average the ratings for the different types. Weighted averages can also be used. Rounding up is the conservative approach to resolve fractional averages. In the example above, straight averaging would result in a rating of Medium. If technical complexity were twice as important as each of the other two, Medium would again result because of rounding.

d) *Use the criticality level of each requirement to determine the V&V method and level of intensity appropriate for that requirement.* Depending on the criticality of a requirement, more thorough analysis may be required. For a high-criticality requirement, for example, an exhaustive technique might be selected and a specialized software tool developed for this technique. A low-criticality requirement may receive only low-level analysis, or none at all if resources are severely limited.

V&V planning is a subjective process. Criticality analysis is a methodology that guides the planner through this process in a way that allocates the most thorough analysis to the most critical requirements. It reduces the chance that significant requirements will be overlooked or insufficiently analyzed. Because of the step-wise nature of the process the decisions and trade-offs made in the planning process are more visible. This visibility allows review and critique of the plan to be made in a constructive way since individual planning assumptions and decisions may be identified and analyzed.

Annex C

(informative)

The seven planning topics

The Standard calls for seven topics to be addressed for each task or activity. There is no requirement to address each of the seven topics individually. The intent of the Standard is to indicate topics that should be covered. The structure and means of addressing these topics is left to the planner. This annex is intended to provide insight into what is meant by each of the topics and guidance for addressing them.

C.1 V&V Tasks

Identify the V&V tasks for the phase. Describe how each task contributes to the accomplishment of the project V&V goals. For all critical software, the SVVP shall include all minimum V&V tasks for the management of V&V and for each life-cycle phase. Any or all of these minimum tasks may be used for noncritical software.

Optional V&V tasks may also be selected to tailor the V&V effort to project needs for critical or noncritical software.... The optional V&V tasks ... may be applicable to some, but not all, critical software. These tasks may require the use of specific tools or techniques.... The standard allows for the optional V&V tasks and any others identified by the planner to be used as appropriate. [3.5, (1)]

When describing V&V tasks, include the name of the task, the task objectives with respect to the project V&V goals, and any task features that may affect a project goal or the V&V effort. The task descriptions establish specific objectives for the life cycle phase V&V.

When planning the V&V tasks, consider the following:

a) *The scope of each task.* Determine whether the entire software system is addressed or some subset of that system (i.e., identify to what products it applies and the selection criteria, if application is less than 100%).

b) *The V&V objective(s) served by each task.* Determine whether verification, validation, or some combination of these is to be addressed. Each task selected should demonstrably satisfy (in whole or in part) a project-level V&V or quality assurance goal. V&V tasks customarily have the following objectives:

   1) To verify that the software specifications and the outputs of each life cycle activity are complete, correct, clear, consistent, and accurately represent the prior specification

   2) To evaluate the technical adequacy of the products of each life cycle activity (e.g., assessing alternate solutions), and to cause iteration of the activity until a suitable solution is achieved

   3) To trace the specifications developed during this life cycle phase to prior specifications

   4) To prepare and execute tests to validate that the software products fulfill all applicable requirements

c) *The dependency relationships between the V&V tasks and other tasks* (e.g., from what task does this task take input or to what task does it provide output).

d) *The criticality of the software.* Determine the level of criticality of the software. The Standard defines a set of minimum tasks for critical software (see annex B for more detailed guidance on this consideration).

e) *The project environment.* Review and evaluate project plans, including schedule, change control, configuration management, and resources. These resources may be a limiting factor in choosing tasks that require the development of new tools or methods.

f) *The complexity of the product and development activity.* Estimate or evaluate product complexity, product risks, and development complexity (e.g., project size and organization).

g) *The number and types of expected defects.* If possible, estimate the number and types of expected defects. This information can often be determined theoretically or empirically. This information can be used to evaluate the feasibility and benefit of a V&V task.

h) *The experience and expertise of the staff.* An important factor to consider is the time and training required to competently execute V&V tasks.

C.2 Methods and criteria

Identify the methods and criteria used in performing the V&V tasks. Describe the specific methods and procedures for each task. Define the detailed criteria for evaluating the task results. [3.5 (2)]

Identify the methods used in performing the V&V tasks. A V&V task may use more than one method (e.g., code inspections and algorithm analysis for source code evaluation). A particular method may be used for more than one task (e.g., timing analysis for both design and source code evaluation). A chart, table, or other graphic representation may be used to show the relationships of V&V methods to tasks.

When selecting the methods, consider the following:

a) Critical features of the system
b) Integration of methods to achieve task goals
c) The organization and personnel performing the method
d) The project budget, schedule, and resources
e) The inputs to the task, such as
   1) Standards under which the inputs were developed
   2) Level of abstraction of the input
   3) Form of the input
   4) Expected content of the input
f) The outputs from the task; the purpose and destination of each; and the form, format, and expected content
g) Defects the method can be expected to uncover (e.g., misuse of a standard, an algorithm, a new technology, or a difficult feature)

Describe each method and its procedures. State how the method satisfies all or part of the goals of a V&V task required by the SVVP. State any unique information contributing to the selection of the method (e.g., the method is known to uncover a specific type of error common in such engineering problems.) If the method is applied only to some of the input required for the V&V task, identify the appropriate sections. When several methods will be applied to a task, describe the relationships between the methods and the procedures to be followed to ensure that the entire task is performed.

Identify the criteria for evaluating task results. These could include criteria for considering the execution of a task complete (e.g., unit structural testing will continue until 75% of the paths and 100% of the decisions have been tested).

C.3 Inputs and outputs

Identify the inputs required for each V&V task. Specify the source and format of each input...
Identify the outputs from each V&V task. Specify the purpose and format for each output.
[3.5 (3)]

Identify the inputs to each task. There are two types of inputs for V&V tasks the development products to be verified and validated and V&V plans, procedures, and previous results. The development products are the objects of verification or validation. The V&V plans, procedures, and results guide the V&V activities. The V&V planner shall consider both types of input. It may be that specific forms or formats of the inputs are required when V&V is performed. In many cases, there may be contractual requirements for the format (e.g., IEEE standards, military standards), form (e.g., storage medium, specific word processor), and delivery of the inputs.

When specifying the inputs to the tasks, consider the following (where additional description is needed):

a) The source of each input. That is, the specific organizational element or person.
b) The delivery schedule for each input. If V&V planning is not integrated with other planning, inputs may not be received in a timely fashion. The schedule shall include sufficient time for reproduction and distribution as needed.
c) The temporal or logical relationships between the inputs when several inputs are required for a given task or method. For example, a task may begin without product A, but absolutely require product B and product C.
d) The state of the inputs (e.g., draft or official releases only). The evaluation of draft material is sometimes recommended to detect and correct errors early. This may not always be possible (e.g., for contractual or political reasons) and may often be undesirable (the material may change too rapidly).
e) The form (e.g., paper, 5.25" floppy disk) and format (e.g., pure ASCII text) of the input. As with any other software specification, this must be unambiguous (e.g., floppy disks may be 3.5", 5.25", or 8", and may be in a large number of recording and word-processing formats).

Identify the outputs from each task. The outputs of a V&V task will be used by (at least) three audiences personnel performing other V&V tasks (including tasks in other phases of the life cycle), personnel performing other development tasks, and management. These audiences require technical feedback on the status of the products to determine how development should proceed. These audiences may have different specific information requirements to be satisfied.

a) Personnel performing other V&V tasks need detailed technical information to perform those tasks.
b) Development personnel require feedback about the development products verified or validated.
c) Management requires summary information about schedule, resource usage, product status, and identified risks.

V&V outputs include task reports, anomaly reports, test documentation, plans, and phase summary reports. V&V outputs are the tangible products of the V&V effort, and should be planned with care.

When specifying the outputs from the V&V tasks, consider the following:

— The form and format of each output (The same criteria may apply to output as to input, e.g., standards, media.)
— The destination of each output (specific personnel or organizational elements)
— The delivery schedule for each output (Output shall be provided in a timely fashion.)
— The state of each output (i.e., will drafts of an output or only official versions be released)
— The lifetime of each output (i.e., will a given report be used by later phases as input, or will it be an archived document for reference)
— The requirements for the configuration management of the output

C.4 Schedule

Identify the schedule for the V&V tasks. Establish specific milestones for initiating and completing each task, for the receipt of each input, and for the delivery of each output. [3.5, (4)]

This section shall describe the project life cycle and milestones, including completion dates. ...describe how V&V results provide feedback to the development process to support project management functions.... When planning V&V tasks, it should be recognized that the V&V process is iterative. [3.4.2]

The purpose of scheduling is to establish and organize resources to meet defined objectives under the specified constraints of time and events. To be successful, the plan writer shall recognize that the schedule for V&V tasks is part of a larger schedule for an entire project. The available resources and constraints of time and events from the other interfacing parts of the project shall be determined prior to starting the scheduling. After the external environment has been established, the specific requirements for the V&V tasks shall be determined. Any resulting conflicts with the overall schedule shall then be resolved. The iterative nature of the schedule is a factor in planning during initial schedule creation as well as during the lifetime of the project. Most projects involving software encounter substantial change activity prior to release of the initial products. Although the extent of this change is rarely known at project initiation, the schedule should have mechanisms to respond to changes.

The V&V tasks are involved with all life cycle phases. The V&V planner should establish what organizational, schedule, and documentation interfaces are required with the organization responsible for each life cycle phase. Keep in mind at all times that the V&V tasks will be synchronized with the respective project activity (e.g., requirements analysis cannot begin until the requirements documents have been produced).

When scheduling a V&V task with an organization responsible for a specific life cycle phase, consider the following:

a) Due dates for required inputs, such as specification, detailed descriptions, source code, or other data
    1) Establish completion criteria for each input (e.g., requirements released to configuration control) as well as the media and format for transmittal
    2) Schedule for any conversion required (e.g., entering requirements into electronic format, transferring between different formats)
b) Scheduling of participation in internal reviews of particular life cycle phases to ensure that V&V concerns, such as testability, are addressed during product creation
c) Due dates of the results of each task to project management to be responsive to program needs
d) Access to key personnel from the interfacing organization for consultation

Once the requirements from other organizations have been established, the specific V&V tasks for each of the life cycle phases should be determined. For each V&V task selected, the completion criteria should be specified before the resources required for that task can be determined. Estimating required resources can be accomplished by using results of previous projects, various automated tools based on product and project parameters, or outside consultants. These estimates can be effected by the use of tools. Although these estimates will have a degree of uncertainty at the beginning of the project, they can and should be updated throughout the project as better information is available.

When scheduling V&V tasks within a specific life cycle phase, consider the following:

a) Scheduling of V&V outputs and reports to provide timely and effective feedback to development personnel
b) Allowing for the evaluation and internal review of results by V&V management
c) Defining explicit V&V task stopping criteria
d) Defining criteria for establishing the amount of regression testing required due to changes

As with general project scheduling there are many formats for schedule presentation (e.g., Gantt Charts, PERT, CPM) and in some cases analysis of schedule flow. The approach used should be consistent with other project elements. Use of automated tools is encouraged. The criteria and approval process for implementing schedule changes should be specified.

C.5 Resources

Identify the resources for the performance of the V&V tasks. Specify resources by category (for example, staffing, equipment, facilities, schedule, travel, training). If tools are used in the V&V tasks, specify the source of the tools, their availability, and other usage requirements (for example, training). [3.5 (5)]

Resources may be defined as sources of supply or support, in (perhaps artificial) contrast to inputs, which are the objects of verification or validation. Resources typically required for V&V tasks are personnel, manual or automated tools, and finances. Other resources may be required for specific projects (e.g., security controls, travel resources).

Specify staffing resources by identifying the people who are responsible for the given task, either by name or in more general terms (e.g., by job title or classification). In the latter case, provide sufficient detail to insure the selection of personnel capable of adequately performing the task.

When planning the staff for the V&V tasks, consider the following:

— The number of persons or full-time equivalents (e.g., two people half-time). Where staff support is readily available, this may be a statement of expected personnel use. Where staff is in short supply, this may be a key constraint on the tasks and methods selected, or on the schedule or coverage of the selected tasks.
— The required skill level and specific experience. Clearly identify unique requirements (e.g., senior analyst with experience using method X to perform requirements tracing for secure operating systems). Consider staff experience and expertise when predicting the effectiveness of V&V tasks, and when evaluating the relevance of historical data. An inexperienced staff can be expected to introduce (or fail to detect) more defects than a staff of experts. Exercise care not to overspecify skill levels; descriptions should specify the minimum levels necessary to perform the tasks. This allows maximum flexibility in staffing each task. If individuals with requisite experience are likely not to be available, plan for training (or acquiring) skilled staff. Indicate the lead time required for staff development. Identify other credentials (e.g., security clearances, bonding) required, and plan appropriately.

Identify any manual or automated tools that are to be used in performing a task. Checklists and documented, standardized V&V procedures are examples of manual or nonautomated tools. When planning for the use of a manual tool, consider the following:

— The tool should be sufficiently applicable to the task that it produces meaningful, specific results. Otherwise the adaptation of the tool to the project should be planned. For example, generic checklists should be tailored to the needs of the project.
— The tool should either have been qualified or evaluated prior to its use in the given task.

Automated tools include software tools, simulations (hardware, software, or hybrid), test environments, test beds, and the use of electronic communications. As with manual tools, explicit description of their use is essential to good planning and to obtain their benefit to the project.

When planning the use of an automated tool, consider the following:

— Identifying the specific tool (including version identifier, if available) and any actions necessary to prepare for its use (e.g., development, tailoring, adaptation, qualification)
— Identifying special resources needed for its use, including computers and other hardware, databases, test beds, facilities and access to them, training, and maintenance
— Planning for licensing or other contractual arrangements necessary for use
— Planning for achieving task objectives if usable tools are not available

Financial resources may be addressed, although this is usually not done on a task-by-task basis within the SVVP. Special financial considerations, such as trade-offs that might be made during the execution of a given task, could be included.

Include travel requirements for a task (e.g., to attend design review meetings), and cross-reference travel plans to the schedules. Other resources that could be addressed are special procedures, such as security controls. In general, these and other topics should be included at the task level only when they are specific to the task and differ from the procedures in place for the project as a whole.

C.6 Risks and assumptions

Identify the risks and assumptions associated with the V&V tasks, including schedule, resources, or approach. Specify a contingency plan for each risk. [3.5 (6)]

Any plan is based on a number of assumptions. These assumptions create elements of risk in the plan. If the assumptions are violated, the project will not proceed as planned. In many cases, the risks may be mitigated if the assumptions are documented explicitly and contingency plans prepared.

Contingency plans should be realistic. They need not be spelled out in detail unless warranted by the level of risk and the criticality of the V&V task. If the only alternative is a general slip of the project schedule, this should be stated. When documenting risks and assumptions, consider the following:

a) *The software project schedule.* A normal assumption is that all software or system components and deliverables will be delivered on schedule and that the deliverables will be complete, controlled, and up-to-date. By documenting which tasks depend on other tasks for input or for resources, the potential disruption of the project because of late deliveries may be minimized.

b) *The software project complexity.* When the software architecture, components, or deliverables are technically complex, there is a risk that the software will be insufficiently evaluated in early phases, leading to increased errors in later phases. When the software project organization is complex, there is a risk of miscommunication between the elements, leading to interface and documentation errors. When the V&V tasks are complex, particularly in relation to available personnel and other resources, there is a risk that the schedule will not be met.

c) *The availability of adequate resources.* When there are insufficient human resources (e.g., skills, experience) or inadequate material resources (e.g., computing resources, test beds, load generators, code exercisers, code static analyzers), there is a risk that the V&V tasks will be performed inadequately.

d) *The presence of adequate product development processes (e.g., configuration management, reviews, standards).* This affects the number of expected defects, which will affect any V&V effort prediction. A normal assumption is that there will be timely response to informal comments (if applicable) and anomaly reports.

Additional risks possibly present in software verification and validation efforts include

— Development and first use of software tools
— Use of COTS
— First applications of V&V techniques to larger or more complex applications
— Changes in life cycle models

C.7 Roles and responsibilities

Identify the organizational elements or individuals responsible for performing the V&V tasks. Assign specific responsibilities for each task to one or more organizational elements. [3.5 (7)]

Define specific roles and responsibilities for each task, including individually specifying planning, performing, reporting, evaluating, coordinating, and administering if meaningful. Assign each of the roles to specific individuals or organizational elements. In many cases, some roles will be defined by the required inputs and outputs for the task. For example, for a source code walkthrough, some person will supply the code, someone else may distribute the code to the review team, and others may make up the review team. More than one role may be assigned to an individual or organizational element.

Identifying, by name, the personnel who are responsible for a task makes the construction and coordination of a master schedule simpler. For example, periods of overcommitment or underuse of a given person can be more readily identified. Individual participants in a project may easily identify and prepare for their roles by reading the SVVP.

On the other hand, identification by name alone has shortcomings. If personnel change, the rationale for selecting a specific individual for a task may be lost. For large or long projects, there may be too many individuals and too many uncertainties to identify in a reasonably sized plan. For these reasons, it is often a good idea to identify personnel by organization or job classification.

A matrix, table, or chart may be used to assign V&V tasks to organizational elements and to job classifications or individuals within the effort. The plan should be as specific as possible (e.g., specify the number of people for a task). When appropriate, in a proposal for example, the biographies of personnel may be included (perhaps in an appendix). For large projects, the assignment of responsibilities to individuals may be placed in an appendix or in subsidiary documents.

IEEE Std 1074-1997
(Revision of IEEE Std 1074-1995;
Replaces IEEE Std 1074.1-1995)

IEEE Standard for Developing Software Life Cycle Processes

Sponsor

**Software Engineering Standards Committee
of the
IEEE Computer Society**

Approved 9 December 1997

IEEE Standards Board

Abstract: A process for creating a software life cycle process is provided. Although this standard is directed primarily at the process architect, it is useful to any organization that is responsible for managing and performing software projects.
Keywords: software life cycle, software life cycle model, software life cycle process

The Institute of Electrical and Electronics Engineers, Inc.
345 East 47th Street, New York, NY 10017-2394, USA

Print: ISBN 1-55937-993-6   SH94600
PDF: ISBN 0-7381-0532-5   SS94600

IEEE Standards documents are developed within the IEEE Societies and the Standards Coordinating Committees of the IEEE Standards Association (IEEE-SA) Standards Board. Members of the committees serve voluntarily and without compensation. They are not necessarily members of the Institute. The standards developed within IEEE represent a consensus of the broad expertise on the subject within the Institute as well as those activities outside of IEEE that have expressed an interest in participating in the development of the standard.

Use of an IEEE Standard is wholly voluntary. The existence of an IEEE Standard does not imply that there are no other ways to produce, test, measure, purchase, market, or provide other goods and services related to the scope of the IEEE Standard. Furthermore, the viewpoint expressed at the time a standard is approved and issued is subject to change brought about through developments in the state of the art and comments received from users of the standard. Every IEEE Standard is subjected to review at least every five years for revision or reaffirmation. When a document is more than five years old and has not been reaffirmed, it is reasonable to conclude that its contents, although still of some value, do not wholly reflect the present state of the art. Users are cautioned to check to determine that they have the latest edition of any IEEE Standard.

Comments for revision of IEEE Standards are welcome from any interested party, regardless of membership affiliation with IEEE. Suggestions for changes in documents should be in the form of a proposed change of text, together with appropriate supporting comments.

Interpretations: Occasionally questions may arise regarding the meaning of portions of standards as they relate to specific applications. When the need for interpretations is brought to the attention of IEEE, the Institute will initiate action to prepare appropriate responses. Since IEEE Standards represent a consensus of all concerned interests, it is important to ensure that any interpretation has also received the concurrence of a balance of interests. For this reason, IEEE and the members of its societies and Standards Coordinating Committees are not able to provide an instant response to interpretation requests except in those cases where the matter has previously received formal consideration.

Comments on standards and requests for interpretations should be addressed to:

> Secretary, IEEE-SA Standards Board
> 445 Hoes Lane
> P.O. Box 1331
> Piscataway, NJ 08855-1331
> USA

Note: Attention is called to the possibility that implementation of this standard may require use of subject matter covered by patent rights. By publication of this standard, no position is taken with respect to the existence or validity of any patent rights in connection therewith. The IEEE shall not be responsible for identifying patents for which a license may be required by an IEEE standard or for conducting inquiries into the legal validity or scope of those patents that are brought to its attention.

Introduction

(This introduction is not part of IEEE Std 1074-1997, IEEE Standard for Developing Software Life Cycle Processes.)

This introduction is intended to provide the reader with some background into the rationale used to develop this standard. This information is being provided to aid in the understanding and usage of this standard. This introduction is nonbinding.

Background

This is a standard for the generation of the process that governs software development and maintenance for a project. This standard requires the definition of a user's software life cycle and shows mapping into typical software life cycles. It is not intended to define or imply a software life cycle of its own.

This standard applies to the management and support activities that continue throughout the entire life cycle, as well as all aspects of the software life cycle from concept exploration through retirement.

The utilization of these Activities maximizes the benefits to the user when the use of this standard is initiated early in the software life cycle. Software that has proceeded past the initialization phase when this standard is invoked should gradually move into compliance with this standard.

This standard was written for any organization that is responsible for managing and conducting software projects. It will be useful to project managers, software developers, quality assurance organizations, purchasers, users, and maintainers. It can be used where software is the total system or where software is embedded into a larger system.

This standard allows for continuing harmonization with IEEE/EIA 12207.0-1996 and EIA/IEEE J-STD-016-1995 and their successors.

Terminology

The word *shall* and the imperative verb form identify the mandatory material within this standard. The words *should* and *may* identify optional material. As with other IEEE Software Engineering Standards, the terminology in this document is based on IEEE Std 610.12-1990, IEEE Standard Glossary of Software Engineering Terminology. To avoid inconsistency when the Glossary is revised, the definitions are not repeated in this document. New terms and modified definitions are included.

History

Since the original publication of this standard, considerable worldwide attention has been paid to software life cycle processes. Use of IEEE Std 1074-1991, IEEE Std 1074-1995, and other quality system and life cycle standards activity has been carefully considered in preparing this substantive revision of this standard. (The 1995 version of this standard was a minor revision to correct specific errors found in the 1991 version.)

The following changes are among those that are included in this current version:

— Activities are rearranged into more logical groupings (called Activity Groups), such as placing all planning Activities into the new Project Planning Activities Activity Group, collecting all Project Initiation Activities, and collecting and expanding all Review Activities.
— The term "Process," as was used in earlier versions of this Standard, was replaced with the term "Activity Group" to identify collections of Activities. Some users of this standard were misinterpret-

ing the collections as actual "processes" and were trying to execute them as such. The term "Activity Groups" should eliminate this misconception.

— The importance of risk management led to the addition of a new Activity, Manage Risks.
— The recognition that software can be acquired from other sources, for use in the system being developed, led to the addition of the Software Importation Activity Group.

Participants

This standard was developed by a working group consisting of the following members who attended two or more meetings, provided text, or submitted comments on more than two drafts of this standard:

David J. Schultz, *Chair* **Dennis E. Nickle,** *Vice Chair*
Susan M. Burgess, *Configuration Manager* **John W. Horch,** *Editor*

David W. Burnett	Daniel Gray	Pat Marcinko
Ron Dean	Lynn Ihlenfeldt	Keith Middleton
Jean A. Gilmore	Robert J. Kierzyk	Robert W. Shillato
Arthur Godin		Diane Switzer

The following individuals also contributed to the development of this standard by attending one meeting or providing comments on one or two drafts:

Alan Braaten	Sam Godfrey	David Pepper
W. Larry Campbell	Rob Harker	James Shimp
Bostjan K. Derganc	John Jenkins	David Smith
Dorothy Deutch	Denis Meredith	John Swearingen
Leo Egan	Noritoshi Murakami	Allan Willey
Michael Frehse	Christopher Neubert	Natalie Yopconka
John Garth Glynn	John Pellegrin	Janusz Zalewski

The following persons were on the balloting committee:

Jeremy A. Adams
Syed Ali
Mikhail Auguston
Leo Beltracchi
H. Ronald Berlack
Richard E. Biehl
William J. Boll
Alan L. Bridges
M. Scott Buck
David W. Burnett
Edward R. Byrne
Leslie Chambers
Keith Chan
Theo Clarke
Sylvain Clermont
Francois Coallier
Virgil Lee Cooper
Geoff Cozens
Gregory T. Daich
Bostjan K. Derganc
Perry R. DeWeese
Sherman Eagles
Leo Egan
Richard L. Evans
William Eventoff
Jonathan H. Fairclough
John W. Fendrich
Jon J. Fineman
Jay Forster
Simon Gabrihelidis
Hiranmay Ghosh
Marilyn Ginsberg-Finner
John Garth Glynn
Lawrence M. Gunther
David A. Gustafson
John Harauz
Rob Harker
Carol J. Harkness
William Hefley
Manfred Hein
Mark Heinrich

Mark Henley
John W. Horch
Jerry Huller
Peter L. Hung
Fabrizio Imelio
George Jackelen
John O. Jenkins
Frank V. Jorgensen
Vladan V. Jovanovic
William S. Junk
George X. Kambic
Diana Kang
Myron S. Karasik
Ron S. Kenett
Judy Kerner
Robert J. Kierzyk
Dwayne L. Knirk
Shaye Koenig
Thomas M. Kurihara
John B. Lane
J. Dennis Lawrence
Michael Lines
David Maibor
Robert Martin
Tomoo Matsubara
Sue McGrath
Bret Michael
Alan Miller
James W. Moore
R. Muralidharan
Pavol Navrat
Dennis E. Nickle
Myrna L. Olson
Mike Ottewill
Gerald L. Ourada
Indradeb P. Pal
Mark Paulk
Warren L. Persons
John G. Phippen
Alex Polack

Peter T. Poon
Margaretha W. Price
Lawrence S. Przybylski
Kenneth R. Ptack
Ann Reedy
Annette D. Reilly
Dennis Rilling
Patricia Rodriguez
Andrew P. Sage
Helmut Sandmayr
Stephen R. Schach
Norman Schneidewind
David J. Schultz
Gregory D. Schumacher
Robert W. Shillato
Carl A. Singer
James M. Sivak
Alfred R. Sorkowitz
Donald W. Sova
Luca Spotorno
Julia Stesney
Fred J. Strauss
Christine Brown Strysik
Robert N. Sulgrove
Toru Takeshita
Patricia A. Trellue
Leonard L. Tripp
T. H. Tse
Margaret C. Updike
Theodore J. Urbanowicz
Glenn D. Venables
Udo Voges
Ronald L. Wade
Dolores Wallace
John W. Walz
Scott A. Whitmire
Paul A. T. Wolfgang
Natalie C. Yopconka
Weider D. Yu
Janusz Zalewski
Geraldine Zimmerman

Contents

IEEE Standard for Developing Software Life Cycle Processes

1. Overview

This clause presents an overview of this standard.

1.1 Scope

This standard provides a process for creating a software life cycle process (SLCP). It is primarily directed at the process architect for a given software project. It is the function of the process architect to create the SLCP.

This methodology begins with the selection of an appropriate software life cycle model (SLCM) for use on the specific project. It continues through the creation of the software life cycle (SLC), using the selected SLCM and the Activities provided in Annex A. The methodology concludes with the augmentation of the SLC with Organizational Process Assets (OPAs) to create the SLCP.

The Activities that are provided in Annex A cover the entire life cycle of a software project, from concept exploration through the eventual retirement of the software system. This standard does not address non-software activities, such as contracting, purchasing, or hardware development. It also does not mandate the use of a specific SLCM, nor does it provide a selection of, or a tutorial on, SLCMs. This standard presumes that the process architect is already familiar with a variety of SLCMs, with the criteria for choosing among them, and with the criteria for determining the attributes and constraints of the desired end system and the development environment that affects this selection. Finally, this standard does not prescribe how to perform the software Activities in Annex A.

1.2 Purpose

This standard defines the process by which an SLCP is created. It is useful to any organization that is responsible for managing and performing software projects. It can be used where software is the total system or where software is part of a larger system.

1.3 Product of standard

The product of this standard is the SLCP that is required for a specific software project. The SLCP is based on the following:

a) An SLCM that is selected for the project
b) The Activities that are provided in Annex A
c) The OPAs that are selected for the project

While this standard describes the creation of a single, overall SLCP that is to be used for a project, the user of this standard should recognize that an SLCP can itself include lower-level SLCPs. This is the same concept as in configuration management, in which a particular Configuration Item can include subordinate Configuration Items. This standard applies equally to the development of SLCPs at any level.

1.4 Intended audiences

This standard is written to provide direction and guidance to those individuals who are responsible for determining the implementation of this standard's Activities.

1.4.1 Process architect

The primary audience for this standard is the process architect. The process architect is expected to have

a) The authority to develop SLCPs
b) A knowledge of the OPAs
c) A knowledge of SLCMs
d) An understanding of the Activities that are presented in Annex A of this standard

1.4.2 Other interested parties

This standard also can be of use to the performers of the Activities that are presented in Annex A.

1.5 Relationship to other key standards

No standard exists isolated from its associated standards. This standard is related to ISO 9001 : 1994 [B38][1] and IEEE/EIA 12207.0-1996 [B35].

1.5.1 Relationship to ISO 9001 : 1994 [B38] and ISO 9000-3 : 1994 [B39]

ISO 9001 : 1994 [B38], as interpreted by the guidance in Clause 5.1 of ISO 9000-3 : 1994 [B39], recommends organizing a software development project in accordance with a selected life cycle model. It is intended that a conforming application of this standard would satisfy this recommendation; however, it would be the responsibility of the applier to ensure that the created SLCPs satisfy the specific requirements of ISO 9001 : 1994 [B38] and other applicable standards.

1.5.2 Relationship to IEEE/EIA 12207.0-1996 [B35]

Clause 5.1.2.2 of IEEE/EIA 12207.0-1996 [B35] requires an acquirer to "determine which processes, activities, and tasks of (IEEE/EIA 12207.0-1996 [B35]) are appropriate for the project and tailor them accordingly." Clause 5.2.4.2 of IEEE/EIA 12207.0-1996 [B35] requires a supplier to "define or select a software

---

[1]The numbers in brackets preceded by the letter B correspond to those of the bibliography in Annex D.

life cycle model" and map the processes, activities, and tasks of IEEE/EIA 12207.0-1996 [B35] onto that model. Clause 5.3.1.1 places a similar requirement upon a developer in some situations. It is intended that a conforming application of this standard would satisfy any of these requirements; however, it would be the responsibility of the applier to ensure that the created SLCPs satisfy the other specific requirements of IEEE/ EIA 12207.0-1996 [B35] and other applicable standards.

1.6 Relationship to process improvement

While process improvement is outside the scope of this standard, this standard can be integrated into an organization's process improvement program through its use as the framework for the OPAs.

Building the OPAs around this standard's structure of Activities and Input and Output Information can

a)   Minimize the effort needed to create an SLCP
b)   Facilitate the reuse of existing OPAs
c)   Lead to the improvement of the OPAs by incorporating lessons that were learned from the use of the OPAs in projects

The SLCP for a project, in part or as a whole, can become part of the OPAs for use by future projects.

1.7 Organization of this standard

Clauses 1, 2, and 3 of this standard contain required, introductory information. Clause 4 provides a brief discussion of the key concepts that are beneficial to the understanding and use of this standard. Clause 5 provides the requirements for the creation of an SLCP. Requirements for the content of an SLCP are presented in Annex A, which is normative. Annexes B, C, and D are informative and include useful information, but no requirements. Table 1 presents the organization of this standard.

Table 1—Organization of this standard

Element	Title
Clause 1	Overview
Clause 2	References
Clause 3	Definitions and acronyms
Clause 4	Key concepts
Clause 5	Implementation of the standard
Annex A (normative)	Activities
Annex B (informative)	Mapping example
Annex C (informative)	Information mapping template
Annex D (informative)	Bibliography

The components of the SLCP consist of 65 Activities. These Activities are included in Annex A, and are organized into 17 Activity Groups. The Activities cover the entire life cycle of a software project, from concept exploration through the eventual retirement of the software system. The Activity Groups are further grouped into five sections, as shown in Table 2.

Table 2—Activity grouping

Section Title	Clause	Activity Groups
Project Management	A.1	Project Initiation Project Planning Project Monitoring and Control
Pre-Development	A.2	Concept Exploration System Allocation Software Importation
Development	A.3	Requirements Design Implementation
Post-Development	A.4	Installation Operation and Support Maintenance Retirement
Integral	A.5	Evaluation Software Configuration Management Documentation Development Training

The Integral section (Clause A.5) includes those Activity Groups that are necessary to ensure the successful completion of a project, but are considered as support Activities, rather than those Activities that are directly oriented to the development effort. The Integral Activity Groups contain the following two types of Activities:

a) Activities that are performed discretely and are therefore mapped into an SLCM
b) Activities that are invoked (see 4.3.3) by other Activities

2. References

No other publications are required for the use of this standard. A list of standards, which can be consulted for additional guidance, is given in Annex D. Although this standard does not require adherence to any other standard, a knowledge of the principles and concepts that are described in the standards listed in Annex D can be helpful.

3. Definitions and acronyms

This clause defines the terms and identifies the acronyms that are used within the context of this standard.

3.1 Definitions

The definitions listed in this subclause establish meanings within the context of this standard. Definitions of the other terms that are used in this document can be found in IEEE Std 610.12-1990 [B2].

3.1.1 Activity: A defined body of work to be performed, including its required Input and Output Information. *See also:* **Activity Group.**

3.1.2 Activity Group: A set of related Activities. *See also:* **Activity.**

3.1.3 constraint: A restriction on software life cycle process (SLCP) development. *See also:* **software life cycle process (SLCP).**

3.1.4 external: An Input Information source or Output Information destination that is outside the scope of this standard and, therefore, may or may not exist.

3.1.5 Instance: The mapping of an Activity that processes all of its Input Information and generates all of its Output Information. *Contrast with:* **Invocation; Iteration.** *See also:* **mapping.**

3.1.6 Integral Activity Group: An Activity Group that is needed to complete project Activities, but is outside the management and development Activity Groups.

3.1.7 Invocation: The mapping of a parallel initiation of Activities of an Integral Activity Group that perform a distinct function and return to the initiating Activity. *Contrast with:* **Instance; Iteration.** *See also:* **mapping.**

3.1.8 Iteration: The mapping of any execution of an Activity where at least some Input Information is processed and some Output Information is created. One or more Iterations comprise an Instance. *Contrast with:* **Instance; Invocation.** *See also:* **mapping.**

3.1.9 mapping: Establishing a sequence of the Activities in this standard according to a selected software life cycle model (SLCM). *See also:* **Instance; Invocation; Iteration; software life cycle model (SLCM).**

3.1.10 Organizational Process Asset (OPA): An artifact that defines some portion of an organization's software project environment.

3.1.11 process architect: The person or group that has primary responsibility for creating and maintaining the software life cycle process (SLCP). *See also:* **software life cycle process (SLCP).**

3.1.12 product: Any output of the software development Activities (e.g., document, code, or model). *See also:* **Activity.**

3.1.13 software life cycle (SLC): The project-specific sequence of Activities that is created by mapping the Activities of this standard onto a selected software life cycle model (SLCM). *Contrast with:* **software life cycle model (SLCM); software life cycle process (SLCP).**

3.1.14 software life cycle model (SLCM): The framework, selected by each using organization, on which to map the Activities of this standard to produce the software life cycle (SLC). *Contrast with:* **software life cycle (SLC); software life cycle process (SLCP).**

3.1.15 software life cycle process (SLCP): The project-specific description of the process that is based on a project's software life cycle (SLC) and the Organizational Process Assets (OPA). *Contrast with:* **software life cycle (SLC); software life cycle model (SLCM).** *See also:* **Organizational Process Asset (OPA).**

3.2 Acronyms

The following acronyms appear within the text of this standard:

CI	Configuration Item
OPA	Organizational Process Asset
PR&RPI	Problem Reporting and Resolution Planned Information
SCMPI	Software Configuration Management Planned Information
SLC	software life cycle
SLCM	software life cycle model
SLCP	software life cycle process
SPMPI	Software Project Management Planned Information

4. Key concepts

This clause provides an explanation of the key concepts that are used throughout this standard.

4.1 Activities

An Activity is a defined body of work that is to be performed, including its required Input and Output Information. Thus, it is a description of the required transformation of Input Information into Output Information. The performance of an Activity is complete when all Input Information has been processed and all Output Information has been generated.

4.1.1 Format

An Activity consists of three parts:

a) *Input Information*—A list of the required information to be transformed and its source(s)
b) *Description*—A discussion of the value-added actions to be performed in order to accomplish the transformation
c) *Output Information*—A list of the information that is required to be generated by the transformation, and its destination(s)

4.1.2 Entry and exit criteria

To "enter," or start, an Activity, at least one element of the specified Input Information must be present. To "exit," or complete, an Activity, all Input Information shall have been processed and all Output Information shall be generated. Each project is expected to determine information flow requirements during the mapping of Activities to the SLCM.

4.1.3 "If Applicable" Activities

Activities are categorized as either mandatory or "If Applicable." "If Applicable" Activities are marked "If Applicable" in the Activity title. All other Activities are mandatory. Each "If Applicable" Activity contains an explanation of the cases to which it will apply. For example, A.3.2.2, Design Data Base (If Applicable), applies when a data base is to be created as a part of the project. When an "If Applicable" Activity is used, its Output Information becomes "Available" for use by other Activities.

4.1.4 Organizational structure

This standard does not presume or dictate an organizational structure for a software project. Therefore, it is neither implied nor required that Activities within an Activity Group be performed by the same organizational entity, nor that an organizational entity's involvement be concentrated in only one Activity Group. This standard does, however, presume that persons will be assigned accountability for the performance of the Activities and for the quality of the Input and Output Information sets.

4.2 Elements of the SLCP

Figure 1 depicts the key concepts involved in the development of an SLCP.

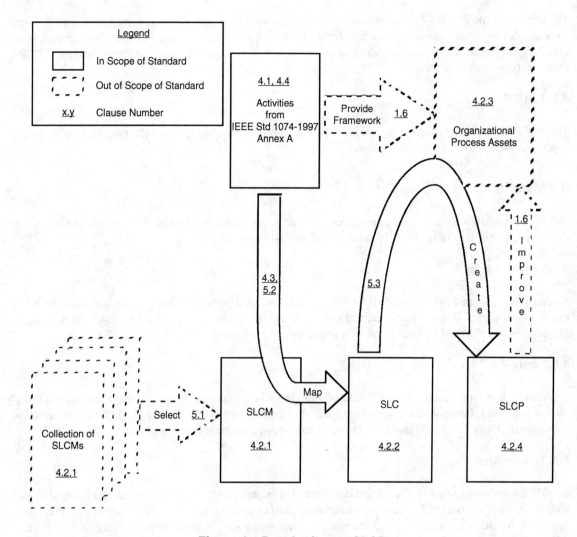

Figure 1—Developing an SLCP

4.2.1 SLCM

The SLCM is the framework on which the Activities of this standard will be mapped to produce the SLC for a project. To use this standard, a SLCM shall be selected for a project. This selection is based on project attributes and organizational capabilities.

This standard does not provide a collection of SLCMs. Providing such a collection of SLCMs is outside the scope of this standard.

4.2.2 SLC

The SLC is the executable sequence of Activities that are to be performed during a project. The SLC is created by mapping the Activities provided in Annex A of this standard onto the SLCM selected for the project.

4.2.3 OPAs

OPAs are the artifacts that define the environment of an organization for software projects. These artifacts are selected and adapted for a particular project.

The content of the Process Assets collection of an organization will vary from organization to organization. Definition of the collection of OPAs is the responsibility of the using organization. It is recommended, however, that the organization consider including assets such as policies, standards, procedures, existing SLCPs, metrics, tools, methodologies, etc.

4.2.4 SLCP

The SLCP is created by augmenting the SLC with the OPAs that are selected for the project. It provides the specific approach to be used for the project.

4.3 Mapping

Mapping establishes the executable sequence of the Activities in this standard onto a selected SLCM. Activities can be mapped in three ways: Instance, Iteration, and Invocation.

4.3.1 Instance

An Activity is mapped as an Instance if it takes all of its specified inputs, processes them, and produces all of its specified outputs. It is mapped once, and appears as a single event in the SLC. Activity A.1.1.3, Allocate Project Resources, could be an example of a single Instance mapping.

4.3.2 Iteration

An Activity is mapped as an Iteration if at least some Input Information is processed and some Output Information is created. Iterations are mapped until all Input Information is processed and all Output Information is created. Activity A.1.3.2, Manage the Project, could require multiple Iterations.

4.3.3 Invocation

In addition to the Activities that are discretely mapped, there are groups of Activities that are invoked in parallel from many Activities. An Activity is invoked to further process specific information before that information is considered complete and permitted to be output by the creating Activity. When invoked, these Activities perform a distinct function and then return to the invoking Activity.

The following example is taken from Activity A.1.2.7, Plan Project Management, with notes added. In this example, the Software Project Management Planned Information (SPMPI) shall be "sent" to the three Activities listed.

"Prior to distribution of the SPMPI[2], the following Activities shall be invoked[3]:

a)   A.5.1.1, Conduct Reviews [4]
b)   A.5.2.2, Perform Configuration Control
c)   A.5.3.1, Implement Documentation"

---

[2]The specified Output Information on which the invoked Activities are to be performed. That is, not all of the Output Information of this Activity is required to be documented, controlled, and evaluated, just the SPMPI.

[3]Initiate a parallel task that is necessary to complete the required invoked Activities and return here, before this Activity can be considered complete.

[4]The Activity to which Output Information is sent. In this example, the SPMPI shall be "sent" to the three named Activities. The evaluated, controlled, and documented information is then returned to Activity A.1.2.7, Plan Project Management.

4.4 Input Information and Output Information

The Input and Output tables show the flow of Information among the Activities in Annex A. Where Information flows among Activities, it can be traced from its original Activity to the receiving Activity through the Input Information and Output Information tables.

Figure 2 depicts the conceptual flow of Input Information and Output Information into and out from an Activity, respectively.

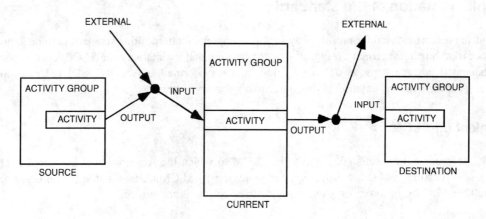

Figure 2—Information flow

4.4.1 Conventions

The Input Information and Output Information for each Activity are listed (in Annex A) in a three-column format. The Input or Output Information name is listed in the left-hand column. The source or destination of the Information (both Activity Group and Activity) is shown in the two right-hand columns.

As a convention of this document, Input and Output Information names are capitalized in the description of an Activity.

4.4.2 External Information

External Information sources and destinations are outside the scope of this standard.

External Input Information sources may or may not exist. If an External Input does not exist, the processing listed for it is not required for completion of the Activity. When an External Input does exist, it shall be used.

External Output Information destinations will receive the information sent, if they exist. No assumption about the use of the Output Information by external destinations is made by this standard.

External sources and destinations are denoted by "External" in the Activity Group column, and a blank in the Activity column of the affected Input or Output table.

4.4.3 Generic Information

In most cases, the Input Information and Output Information columns of the tables designate the specific Information that enters or exits the Activity. However, since many Activities have Output Information whose destination is A.1.3.4, Retain Records, the various Input Information to Retain Records is collected under the term "Records." The corresponding Activity Group and Activity columns refer simply to the originating Activity Group and originating Activity. A.1.3.5, Metric Data, is received in the same way.

4.4.4 Information vs. documents

This standard prescribes the Activities of the SLC, not the products of that life cycle. Therefore, this standard does not require the creation of specific documents. The information that results from the execution of the Activities is expected to be collected in whatever manner and form are consistent with the selected SLCM and OPAs.

5. Implementation of the standard

This clause presents a description of the way in which implementation of this standard is to be approached. The process architect has primary responsibility for creating and maintaining the SLCP. This responsibility is implemented in three steps, as described below, and is performed as Activity A.1.1.1, Create SLCP, in Annex A. A sample implementation of this standard appears in Annex B.

5.1 Select an SLCM

Initially, the process architect shall identify the SLCM to which the Activities will be mapped. This step encompasses locating, evaluating, selecting, and acquiring an SLCM. It is possible for an organization to have multiple SLCMs; however, only one model is to be selected for a project.

The process architect shall follow the following five steps in order to evaluate and select an SLCM:

a) Identify all the SLCMs that are available to the development project.
b) Identify the attributes that apply to the desired end system and the development environment.
c) Identify any constraints that might be imposed on the selection.
d) Evaluate the various SLCMs based on past experience and organizational capabilities.
e) Select the SLCM that will best satisfy the project attributes and constraints.

5.2 Create an SLC

The Activities identified in Annex A shall be mapped onto the SLCM. Note that the selected SLCM, or the project itself, could include or require Activities that are not included in Annex A. Additional Activities are acceptable in the SLC. It should be noted, however, that failure to map one or more of the mandatory Activities in Annex A will result in an SLC and, therefore, an SLCP that are not compliant with this standard. The components of mapping are as follows.

5.2.1 Place the Activities in executable sequence

The order in which Activities will be performed will be determined by three major factors:

a) The selected SLCM will dictate an initial ordering of Activities. As mapping progresses, the actual order in which Activities will be performed will be established.
b) Schedule constraints may require the overlapping of Activities in the SLCM and may thus impact the ordering. In this case, Activities may be mapped for parallel execution rather than for serial execution.
c) The ordering of Activities may be impacted by the entry and exit criteria of associated Activities. The availability of Output Information from one Activity could affect the start of another Activity. The second Activity may require, as inputs, one or more of the outputs of the first Activity. For example, no software design of any kind can be done unless some minimum information is available about software requirements. Another example is that no Evaluation Activities can be performed unless there is some output product upon which to work.

5.2.2 Develop and justify a List of Activities Not Used

All "If Applicable" Activities that do not apply to this project shall be identified and explained in the List of Activities Not Used.

5.2.3 Verify the map

The process architect shall ensure that the Activities are fully mapped onto the selected SLCM and that the resulting SLC contains all of the Activities that are necessary to successfully complete a software project.

The process architect shall also verify that the information flow into and out of the Activities will support the relative order into which they have been mapped.

5.3 Establish an SLCP

The preceding steps develop the SLC. As the next step, the available OPAs shall be applied to the SLC Activities, and the known constraints shall be reconciled. The Output Information that is generated by each Activity shall be assigned to the appropriate document(s). (The Information mapping template in Annex C can be used for assistance in the assignment of information to documents.) The result is the established SLCP.

Annex A

(normative)

Activities

This annex contains the mandatory and "If Applicable" Activities that are to be mapped onto the selected SLCM.

A.1 Project Management Activity Groups

These Activity Groups initiate, monitor, and control a software project throughout its life cycle.

A.1.1 Project Initiation Activities

Project Initiation Activities are those Activities that create and update the infrastructure of a software development or maintenance project. They build the base for the full SLCP.

Project Initiation Activities are

a) A.1.1.1, Create Software Life Cycle Process
b) A.1.1.2, Perform Estimations
c) A.1.1.3, Allocate Project Resources
d) A.1.1.4, Define Metrics

A.1.1.1 Create SLCP

A.1.1.1.1 Input Information

Input Information	Source	
	Activity Group	Activity
Attributes	External	—
Available SLCMs	External	—
Constraints	External	—
Contractual Requirements	External	—
IEEE Std 1074-1997	External	—
OPAs	External	—
Environmental Improvement Needs	Project Monitoring and Control	Identify SLCP Improvement Needs (A.1.3.3)
Statement of Need	Concept Exploration	Refine and Finalize the Idea or Need (A.2.1.4)
Maintenance Recommendations	Maintenance	Reapply SLC (A.4.3.3)

A.1.1.1.2 Description

Using the Input Information, the process architect shall create the SLCP as described in the three steps of Clause 5 of this standard. Any mandatory Activities not used shall be included in the List of Activities Not Used. Exclusion of any mandatory Activity, however, will preclude compliance with this standard.

Prior to the distribution of the SLCP, the following Activities shall be invoked:

a)   A.5.1.1, Conduct Reviews
b)   A.5.2.2, Perform Configuration Control
c)   A.5.3.1, Implement Documentation
d)   A.5.4.1, Develop Training Materials

A.1.1.1.3 Output information

Output Information	Destination	
	Activity Group	Activity
SLCP	Project Initiation	Perform Estimations (A.1.1.2)
		Allocate Project Resources (A.1.1.3)
		Define Metrics (A.1.1.4)
	Project Planning	Plan Documentation (A.1.2.5)
		Plan Training (A.1.2.6)
		Plan Project Management (A.1.2.7)
	Project Monitoring and Control	Manage Risks (A.1.3.1)
		Manage the Project (A.1.3.2)
		Identify SLCP Improvement Needs (A.1.3.3)
List of Activities Not Used	Project Monitoring and Control	Manage Risks (A.1.3.1)

A.1.1.2 Perform Estimations

A.1.1.2.1 Input Information

Input Information	Source	
	Activity Group	Activity
Historical Project Records	External	—
SLCP	Project Initiation	Create SLCP (A.1.1.1)
Statement of Need	Concept Exploration	Refine and Finalize the Idea or Need (A.2.1.4)
System Functional Software Requirements	System Allocation	Decompose System Requirements (A.2.2.3)

A.1.1.2.2 Description

Based on the project requirements that are documented in the Statement of Need and the System Functional Software Requirements, size estimates of work products to be created (both deliverable and nondeliverable) shall be derived. The work products shall be decomposed to the level of granularity that is needed to plan and track the project. Based on these size estimates, effort and cost estimates shall be created for all of the Activities of the SLC. In addition, target computer resource usage shall be estimated.

Historical Project Records shall be used as the basis of estimation, when available. All Estimation Assumptions that were made in deriving the estimates shall be specified. Project Estimates should be reaffirmed and revised throughout the SLCP.

Prior to the distribution of project estimates, the following Activities shall be invoked:

a)   A.5.1.1, Conduct Reviews
b)   A.5.2.2, Perform Configuration Control
c)   A.5.3.1, Implement Documentation

A.1.1.2.3 Output Information

Output Information	Destination	
	Activity Group	Activity
Project Estimates	Project Initiation	Allocate Project Resources (A.1.1.3)
	Project Planning	Plan Project Management (A.1.2.7)
	Project Monitoring and Control	Manage Risks (A.1.3.1)
		Manage the Project (A.1.3.2)
Estimation Assumptions	Project Monitoring and Control	Manage Risks (A.1.3.1)

A.1.1.3 Allocate Project Resources

A.1.1.3.1 Input Information

Input Information	Source	
	Activity Group	Activity
Historical Project Records	External	—
Resources	External	—
SLCP	Project Initiation	Create SLCP (A.1.1.1)
Project Estimates	Project Initiation	Perform Estimations (A.1.1.2)
Statement of Need	Concept Exploration	Refine and Finalize the Idea or Need (A.2.1.4)
System Functional Software Requirements	System Allocation	Decompose System Requirements (A.2.2.3)
Software Requirements	Requirements	Prioritize and Integrate Software Requirements (A.3.1.3)

A.1.1.3.2 Description

Resource Allocations shall be identified at the Activity level of the SLC. Resources that are to be allocated include budget, personnel, equipment, space, and computer resources.

Historical Project Records, if available, and the Statement of Need can provide valuable insight into Resource Allocations.

A.1.1.3.3 Output Information

Output Information	Destination	
	Activity Group	Activity
Resource Allocations	Project Planning	Plan Project Management (A.1.2.7)
	Project Monitoring and Control	Manage Risks (A.1.3.1)
		Manage the Project (A.1.3.2)

14

A.1.1.4 Define Metrics

A.1.1.4.1 Input Information

Input Information	Source	
	Activity Group	**Activity**
SLCP	Project Initiation	Create SLCP (A.1.1.1)
Evaluation Planned Information	Project Planning	Plan Evaluations (A.1.2.1)
SPMPI	Project Planning	Plan Project Management (A.1.2.7)
Software Requirements	Requirements	Prioritize and Integrate Software Requirements (A.3.1.3)

A.1.1.4.2 Description

The metrics for the project, based on the SLC, SPMPI, and Software Requirements, shall be defined. Metrics shall be applied to the products of the project, and to the processes that affect the project, throughout the SLC. For each Defined Metric, Collection and Analysis Methods shall be specified.

Further information related to this Activity can be found in IEEE Std 982.1-1988 [B8], IEEE Std 982.2-1988 [B9], IEEE Std 1044-1993 [B19], IEEE Std 1045-1992 [B21], and IEEE Std 1061-1998 [B24].

Prior to distributing the Defined Metrics, Activity A.5.1.1, Conduct Reviews, should be invoked.

A.1.1.4.3 Output Information

Output Information	Destination	
	Activity Group	**Activity**
Defined Metrics	Project Planning	Plan Evaluations (A.1.2.1)
	Project Monitoring and Control	Collect and Analyze Metric Data (A.1.3.5)
Collection and Analysis Methods	Project Planning	Plan Evaluations (A.1.2.1)
	Project Monitoring and Control	Collect and Analyze Metric Data (A.1.3.5)

A.1.2 Project Planning Activities

Project Planning Activities address the planning for all project management, including contingencies. These Activities can be done as needed (mapped in several Iterations), e.g., at every phase review.

Project Planning Activities are

a) A.1.2.1, Plan Evaluations
b) A.1.2.2, Plan Configuration Management
c) A.1.2.3, Plan System Transition (If Applicable)
d) A.1.2.4, Plan Installation
e) A.1.2.5, Plan Documentation
f) A.1.2.6, Plan Training
g) A.1.2.7, Plan Project Management
h) A.1.2.8, Plan Integration

A.1.2.1 Plan Evaluations

A.1.2.1.1 Input Information

Input Information	Source	
	Activity Group	Activity
Defined Metrics	Project Initiation	Define Metrics (A.1.1.4)
Collection and Analysis Methods	Project Initiation	Define Metrics (A.1.1.4)
SPMPI	Project Planning	Plan Project Management (A.1.2.7)
Integration Planned Information	Project Planning	Plan Integration (A.1.2.8)
Risk Management Reported Information	Project Monitoring and Control	Manage Risks (A.1.3.1)
Imported Software Requirements	Software Importation	Identify Imported Software Requirements (A.2.3.1)
Preliminary Software Requirements	Requirements	Define and Develop Software Requirements (A.3.1.1)
Software Requirements	Requirements	Prioritize and Integrate Software Requirements (A.3.1.3)
Software Detailed Design	Design	Perform Detailed Design (A.3.2.4)

A.1.2.1.2 Description

This Activity shall identify and describe the evaluation tasks that are necessary to ensure that the software product and development efforts meet their goals, as specified in the SPMPI and their requirements. Evaluation methods that are to be considered in this planning Activity include audits, reviews, and testing. The Activities and Activity Output Information that are to be evaluated shall be identified; and the evaluation method, purpose, and scope of the evaluation for each of those Activities and Activity Output Information shall be defined. The size, complexity, and criticality of the software should dictate the minimum reviews, audits, and testing.

Reviews that are to be planned include peer reviews, management reviews, technical reviews, operational reviews, process improvement reviews, and post-implementation reviews. More information on reviews can be found in Activity A.5.1.1, Conduct Reviews.

Audits shall be planned to provide an independent examination of software products and processes in order to assess their compliance with requirements and standards. More information on audits can be found in Activity A.5.1.3, Conduct Audits.

Test planning shall be used to define the generic levels of testing and the basic test environment and structure that are needed to support the required levels of testing. The types of testing to be planned include unit/module/component, integration, acceptance, regression, and system tests. Each planned test shall identify the items to be tested, the requirements to be tested, and the test pass-or-fail criteria. Test planning shall also identify the test coverage criteria. Test planning shall be coordinated with Activity A.1.2.8, Integration Planning.

The evaluation planning information shall include the evaluation teams' organization and responsibilities, and the tools, techniques, and methodologies that will be used to perform the evaluations. The planning shall include developing schedules, estimating resources, identifying special resources, staffing, and establishing exit or acceptance criteria. Evaluation planning shall also define the management controls and reporting procedures, as well as the risks and contingencies. Special attention should be given to minimizing business and technical risks. This planning shall be documented in the Evaluation Planned Information.

Further information on planning evaluations can be found in IEEE Std 730-1998 [B3], IEEE Std 828-1998 [B5], IEEE Std 829-1998 [B6], IEEE Std 982.1-1988 [B8], IEEE Std 982.2-1988 [B9], IEEE Std 1008-1987 [B12], IEEE Std 1012-1998 [B13], IEEE Std 1028-1997 [B17], IEEE Std 1042-1987 [B18], IEEE Std 1044-1993 [B19], IEEE Std 1045-1992 [B21], and IEEE Std 1059-1993 [B23].

Prior to the distribution of the Evaluation Planned Information, the following Activities shall be invoked:

a) A.5.1.1, Conduct Reviews
b) A.5.2.2, Perform Configuration Control
c) A.5.3.1, Implement Documentation

A.1.2.1.3 Output Information

Output Information	Destination	
	Activity Group	Activity
Evaluation Planned Information	Project Initiation	Define Metrics (A.1.1.4)
	Project Planning	Plan Integration (A.1.2.8)
	Project Monitoring and Control	Manage Risks (A.1.3.1)
		Manage the Project (A.1.3.2)
		Collect and Analyze Metric Data (A.1.3.5)
	Maintenance	Identify Software Improvement Needs (A.4.3.1)
	Evaluation	Conduct Reviews (A.5.1.1)
		Conduct Audits (A.5.1.3)
		Develop Test Procedures (A.5.1.4)
		Create Test Data (A.5.1.5)
		Execute Tests (A.5.1.6)

A.1.2.2 Plan Configuration Management

A.1.2.2.1 Input Information

Input Information	Source	
	Activity group	Activity
Deliverable List	External	—
SPMPI	Project Initiation	Plan Project Management (A.1.2.7)
Imported Software Requirements	Software Importation	Identify Imported Software Requirements (A.2.3.1)

A.1.2.2.2 Description

This Activity shall plan and document specific software configuration management organizations and responsibilities, procedures, tools, techniques, and methodologies in the Software Configuration Management Planned Information (SCMPI). The SCMPI shall also describe how and when such procedures are to be performed.

Overall software configuration management objectives are derived using internal guidelines as well as contractual or other agreed-upon requirements from the SPMPI. The software configuration management approach should be compatible with the approaches that are being used on associated systems.

Items that are to be managed should include code, documentation, plans, specifications, and other work products. The configuration identification defined in Activity A.5.2.1, Develop Configuration Identification, should be included in the planned information once it is developed.

The configuration management planning shall include developing schedules, estimating resources, identifying special resources, and staffing, defining management controls and reporting procedures, and the risks and contingencies.

Further information related to this Activity can be found in IEEE Std 828-1998 [B5] and IEEE Std 1042-1987 [B18].

Prior to the distribution of the SCMPI, the following Activities shall be invoked:

a) A.5.1.1, Conduct Reviews
b) A.5.2.2, Perform Configuration Control
c) A.5.3.1, Implement Documentation

A.1.2.2.3 Output Information

Output Information	Destination	
	Activity Group	Activity
SCMPI	Project Monitoring and Control	Manage the Project (A.1.3.2)
		Retain Records (A.1.3.4)
	Software Configuration Management	All Software Configuration Management Activities (A.5.2)

A.1.2.3 Plan System Transition (If Applicable)

A.1.2.3.1 Input Information

Input Information	Source	
	Activity Group	Activity
Retirement Planned Information (for the system being replaced)	External	—
Preliminary Statement of Need	Concept Exploration	Identify Ideas or Needs (A.2.1.1)
Recommendations	Concept Exploration	Conduct Feasibility Studies (A.2.1.3)
Imported Software Requirements	Software Importation	Identify Imported Software Requirements (A.2.3.1)

A.1.2.3.2 Description

This Activity is applicable only when an existing system (automated or manual) is being replaced with a new system. The transition shall be planned and documented in accordance with the Retirement Planned Information of the system being replaced, the Preliminary Statement of Need, and the recommended solutions. Transition strategies and tools shall be part of the Transition Planned Information. A Transition Impact Statement shall also be produced.

The transition planning information shall include the transition team's organization and responsibilities, as well as the tools, techniques, and methodologies that are needed to perform the transition.

The planning shall include developing schedules, estimating resources, identifying special resources, and staffing. Transition planning shall also define management controls and reporting procedures, as well as the risks and contingencies. Special attention should be given to minimizing operational risks. This planning shall be documented in the Transition Planned Information.

Prior to the distribution of the Transition Planned Information, the following Activities should be invoked:

a)   A.5.1.1, Conduct Reviews
b)   A.5.2.2, Perform Configuration Control
c)   A.5.3.1, Implement Documentation

A.1.2.3.3 Output Information

Output Information	Destination	
	Activity Group	Activity
Transition Planned Information	Project Planning	Plan Installation (A.1.2.4)
	Project Monitoring and Control	Manage the Project (A.1.3.2)
Transition Impact Statement	Project Monitoring and Control	Manage Risks (A.1.3.1)
	Concept Exploration	Refine and Finalize the Idea or Need (A.2.1.4)

A.1.2.4 Plan Installation

A.1.2.4.1 Input Information

Input Information	Source	
	Activity Group	Activity
Transition Planned Information (If Available)	Project Planning	Plan System Transition (A.1.2.3)
SPMPI	Project Planning	Plan Project Management (A.1.2.7)
Imported Software Requirements	Software Importation	Identify Imported Software Requirements (A.2.3.1)
Installation Requirements	Requirements	Define and Develop Software Requirements (A.3.1.1)
Operating Documentation	Implementation	Create Operating Documentation (A.3.3.2)

A.1.2.4.2 Description

The tasks to be performed during installation shall be described in the Software Installation Planned Information. The Installation Requirements and the other Input Information are analyzed in order to guide the development of the Software Installation Planned Information. This Planned Information, the associated documentation, and the developed software are used to install the software product.

The Software Installation Planned Information shall include the required hardware and other constraints (e.g., minimum memory requirements, color monitor), detailed instructions for the installer, and any additional steps that are required prior to the operation of the system (e.g., registering the software). The type of software to be installed, and the expected level of expertise of the installer, shall be considered when writing installation instructions.

In some cases, the installation planning shall include defining the order of installation at several sites. It could also define one or more configurable options that are to be handled in the installation process.

Prior to the distribution of the Software Installation Planned Information, the following Activities shall be invoked:

a) A.5.1.1, Conduct Reviews
b) A.5.2.2, Perform Configuration Control
c) A.5.3.1, Implement Documentation
d) A.5.4.1, Develop Training Materials

A.1.2.4.3 Output Information

Output Information	Destination	
	Activity Group	Activity
Software Installation Planned Information	Project Monitoring and Control	Manage the Project (A.1.3.2)
	Installation	Distribute Software (A.4.1.1)

A.1.2.5 Plan Documentation

A.1.2.5.1 Input Information

Input Information	Source	
	Activity Group	Activity
Contractual Requirements	External	—
SLCP	Project Initiation	Create SLCP (A.1.1.1)
SPMPI	Project Planning	Plan Project Management (A.1.2.7)
Imported Software Requirements	Software Importation	Identify Imported Software Requirements (A.2.3.1)

A.1.2.5.2 Description

In this Activity, information such as the SCMPI, product descriptions, schedules, and resource constraints shall be assimilated to create a consistent and disciplined approach to achieving the required documentation. The approach shall identify the required documents, the document production and delivery schedules, and the documentation standards. Responsible organizations, information sources, and intended audiences shall be defined for each document. The approach shall be documented in the Documentation Planned Information. The Documentation Planned Information shall include resource allocations for this Activity.

Additional guidance for the development of user documentation can be found in IEEE Std 1063-1987 [B26].

Prior to the distribution of the Documentation Planned Information, the following Activities shall be invoked:

a) A.5.1.1, Conduct Reviews
b) A.5.3.1, Implement Documentation

Activity A.5.2.2, Perform Configuration Control, should also be invoked.

A.1.2.5.3 Output Information

Output Information	Destination	
	Activity Group	Activity
Documentation Planned Information	Project Monitoring and Control	Manage the Project (A.1.3.2)
		Retain Records (A.1.3.4)
	Implementation	Create Operating Documentation (A.3.3.2)
	Documentation Development	All Document Development Activities (A.5.3)

A.1.2.6 Plan Training

A.1.2.6.1 Input Information

Input Information	Source	
	Activity Group	Activity
Applicable Information	External	—
Skills Inventory	External	—
SLCP	Project Initiation	Create SLCP (A.1.1.1)
SPMPI	Project Planning	Plan Project Management (A.1.2.7)
Imported Software Requirements	Software Importation	Identify Imported Software Requirements (A.2.3.1)
Software Requirements	Requirements	Prioritize and Integrate Software Requirements (A.3.1.3)
Training Feedback	Training	Validate the Training Program (A.5.4.2)
		Implement the Training Program (A.5.4.3)

A.1.2.6.2 Description

This Activity shall identify the needs for different types of training and the categories of people that require training for each need. Customer and project information shall be reviewed, along with existing personnel inventories. Both internal (e.g., project team, sales force) and external (e.g., customers, users, dealers) training needs shall be identified. Responsible organizations, information sources, and the intended audiences shall be defined for each type of training. Training tools, techniques, and methodologies shall be specified.

The planning shall include developing schedules, estimating resources, identifying special resources, staffing, and establishing exit or acceptance criteria. This planning shall be documented in the Training Planned Information.

Additional guidance for training can be found in IEEE Std 1298-1992 [B33].

Prior to the distribution of the Training Planned Information, the following Activities shall be invoked:

a) A.5.1.1, Conduct Reviews
b) A.5.2.2, Perform Configuration Control
c) A.5.3.1, Implement Documentation

A.1.2.6.3 Output Information

Output Information	Destination	
	Activity Group	Activity
Training Planned Information	Project Monitoring and Control	Manage the Project (A.1.3.2)
	Maintenance	Identify Software Improvement Needs (A.4.3.1)
	Training	All Training Activities (A.5.4)

A.1.2.7 Plan Project Management

A.1.2.7.1 Input Information

Input Information	Source	
	Activity Group	Activity
Contractual Requirements	External	—
SLCP	Project Initiation	Create SLCP (A.1.1.1)
Project Estimates	Project Initiation	Perform Estimations (A.1.1.2)
Resource Allocations	Project Initiation	Allocate Project Resources (A.1.1.3)
Risk Management Reported Information	Project Monitoring and Control	Manage Risks (A.1.3.1)
Project Management Reported Information	Project Monitoring and Control	Manage the Project (A.1.3.2)
Preliminary Statement of Need	Concept Exploration	Identify Ideas or Needs (A.2.1.1)
Recommendations	Concept Exploration	Conduct Feasibility Studies (A.2.1.3)
Statement of Need	Concept Exploration	Refine and Finalize the Idea or Need
Imported Software Requirements	Software Importation	Identify Imported Software Requirements (A.2.3.1)

A.1.2.7.2 Description

Project management planning requires the collection and synthesis of a great deal of information into a coherent and organized SPMPI based on the SLCP. This Activity shall initially define, and subsequently update, the SPMPI using the Input Information. This Activity shall detail the project organization and assign responsibilities. Standards, methodologies, and tools for configuration management, quality, evaluation, training, documentation, and development shall be specified. This Activity shall apportion the project budget and staffing, and define schedules, using the applicable Input Information. It also shall define procedures for scheduling, tracking, and reporting. It shall address considerations such as regulatory approvals, required certifications, user involvement, subcontracting, and security.

This Activity shall include planning for support, problem reporting, risk management, and retirement. Support planning shall include methods for supporting the software in the operational environment. Problem Reporting and Resolution Planning Information (PR&RPI) shall include, at a minimum, a definition of the method for logging, routing, and handling problem reports; categories of severity; and the method for verifying problem resolution. Planning for managing risks includes identifying risk factors, analyzing those risks, and developing threshold conditions and contingency action plans. Retirement Planned Information shall address issues such as probable retirement date, archiving, replacement, and residual support issues.

As new or revised Input Information is received in this Activity, project plans shall be updated and further project planning shall be based upon these updated plans.

Additional guidance for SPMPIs can be found in IEEE Std 1058-1998 [B22] and IEEE Std 1220-1998 [B30].

Prior to the distribution of the SPMPI, the following Activities shall be invoked:

a) A.5.1.1, Conduct Reviews
b) A.5.2.2, Perform Configuration Control
c) A.5.3.1, Implement Documentation

A.1.2.7.3 Output Information

Output Information	Destination	
	Activity Group	Activity
SPMPI	Most Activity Groups	Most Activities
PR&RPI	Project Monitoring and Control	Manage Risks (A.1.3.1)
		Manage the Project (A.1.3.2)
	Maintenance	Implement Problem Reporting Method (A.4.3.2)
		Reapply SLC (A.4.3.3)
Retirement Planned Information	Project Monitoring and Control	Manage the Project (A.1.3.2)
	Retirement	Notify User (A.4.4.1)
		Conduct Parallel Operations (If Applicable) (A.4.4.2)
		Retire System (A.4.4.3)
Support Planned Information	Project Monitoring and Control	Manage Risks (A.1.3.1)
		Manage the Project
	Operation and Support	Operation and Support Activities (A.4.2)

A.1.2.8 Plan Integration

Input Information	Source	
	Activity Group	Activity
Evaluation Planned Information	Project Planning	Plan Evaluations (A.1.2.1)
SPMPI	Project Planning	Plan Project Management (A.1.2.7)
Imported Software Requirements	Software Importation	Identify Imported Software Requirements (A.2.3.1)
Software Requirements	Requirements	Prioritize and Integrate Software Requirements (A.3.1.3)
Software Detailed Design	Design	Perform Detailed Design (A.3.2.4)

A.1.2.8.1 Description

During the Plan Integration Activity, the Software Requirements and the Software Detailed Design are analyzed to determine the order for combining software components into an overall system. The SLCP, as defined in the SPMPI, shall be considered when planning integration. The integration methods shall be documented in the Integration Planned Information. The Integration Planned Information shall be coordinated with the Test Planned Information.

The integration planning information shall include the tools, techniques, and methodologies needed to perform the integrations. The planning shall include developing schedules, estimating resources, identifying special resources, staffing, and establishing exit or acceptance criteria.

Prior to the distribution of the Integration Planned Information, the following Activities shall be invoked:

a) A.5.1.1, Conduct Reviews
b) A.5.2.2, Perform Configuration Control
c) A.5.3.1, Implement Documentation

A.1.2.8.2 Output Information

Output Information	Destination	
	Activity Group	Activity
Integration Planned Information	Project Planning	Plan Evaluations (A.1.2.1)
	Project Monitoring and Control	Manage Risks (A.1.3.1)
		Manage the Project (A.1.3.2)
	Implementation	Perform Integration (A.3.3.3)

A.1.3 Project Monitoring and Control Activities

These Activities are used to track and manage the project. During the Project Monitoring and Control Activities, actual project performance is tracked, reported, and managed against the planned performance. Special consideration is given to the management of risk.

In addition, Project Monitoring and Control encompasses the collection and analysis of the software metrics of the project, the retention of project records, and the identification of SLCP Improvement Opportunities.

Project Monitoring and Control Activities are

a) A.1.3.1, Manage Risks
b) A.1.3.2, Manage the Project
c) A.1.3.3, Identify SLCP Improvement Needs
d) A.1.3.4, Retain Records
e) A.1.3.5, Collect and Analyze Metric Data

A.1.3.1 Manage Risks

A.1.3.1.1 Input Information

Input Information	Source	
	Activity Group	Activity
Procurement/Lease Data	External	—
System Constraints	External	—
Historical Project Records	External	—
SLCP	Project Initiation	Create SLCP (A.1.1.1)
List of Activities Not Used	Project Initiation	Create SLCP (A.1.1.1)
Project Estimates	Project Initiation	Perform Estimations (A.1.1.2)
Estimation Assumptions	Project Initiation	Perform Estimations (A.1.1.2)
Resource Allocations	Project Initiation	Allocate Project Resources (A.1.1.3)
Evaluation Planned Information	Project Planning	Plan Evaluations (A.1.2.1)
Transition Impact Statement (If Available)	Project Planning	Plan System Transition (A.1.2.3)
SPMPI	Project Planning	Plan Project Management (A.1.2.7)
Support Planned Information	Project Planning	Plan Project Management (A.1.2.7)
PR&RPI	Project Planning	Plan Project Management (A.1.2.7)
Integration Planned Information	Project Planning	Plan Integration (A.1.2.8)
Project Management Reported Information	Project Monitoring and Control	Manage the Project (A.1.3.2)
Analysis Reported Information	Project Monitoring and Control	Collect and Analyze Metric Data (A.1.3.5)
Statement of Need	Concept Exploration	Refine and Finalize Idea or Need (A.2.1.4)
Imported Software Requirements	Software Importation	Identify Imported Software Requirements (A.2.3.1)
Software Interface Requirements	Requirements	Define Interface Requirements (A.3.1.2)
Software Requirements	Requirements	Prioritize and Integrate Software Requirements (A.3.1.3)
Software Detailed Design	Design	Perform Detailed Design (A.3.2.4)
Evaluation Reported Information	Evaluation	Report Evaluation Results (A.5.1.7)

A.1.3.1.2 Description

This activity shall iteratively analyze and mitigate business, technical, managerial, economic, safety, schedule, and security risks. Factors that could impair or prevent the accomplishment of project objectives, or could require technical trade-offs for accomplishing the technical objectives of the project or product, shall be identified and analyzed. Technical factors can include such items as real-time performance, safety considerations, security considerations, implementation considerations, usability considerations, testability, and maintainability. Analytical approaches for technical risk assessment can include static and dynamic modeling and simulation, prototyping, independent reviews, and audits.

Cost, resource factors, earnings, liabilities, or any other economic measures involved in the project shall be identified and analyzed. The objective of this analysis is to identify potential economic opportunities, losses, and trade-offs. Analytical approaches for economic risk assessment can include financial analysis, such as return on investment and possible incentive and penalty contract clauses.

Operational support risk analysis shall determine the probability that the delivered software will meet the users' requirements. Operational support requirements such as interoperability, security, performance, installability, and maintainability shall be considered. Both the completeness of, and the conformance to, these requirements shall be analyzed. The risks to the safety and reliability of the software, due to software requirements and requirement changes, shall be assessed.

Cost, resource, technical, and other requirements shall be evaluated for their impact on project schedules. This analysis should consider project interdependence and the effect of critical path analysis and resource leveling techniques.

Using the Input Information, this Activity shall also define alternative actions to reduce the cost or likelihood of risks occurring and actions to take in the event that a given risk materializes. Actions shall include resource planning and the establishment of trigger conditions that would invoke a contingency action. Contingency actions can include the consideration of revised requirements, delay, or the cancellation of the project. The threshold conditions that are determined shall be tracked against actual conditions. When a threshold condition is met, the contingency response shall be activated to address the risk.

Project Estimates and their corresponding Estimation Assumptions shall also be analyzed by the Manage Risks Activity. The results of the analyses that are conducted during this Activity shall be included in the Risk Management Reported Information.

Further information on risk management can be found in IEEE Std 1228-1994 [B31].

Prior to the distribution of the Risk Management Reported Information, the following Activities shall be invoked:

a) A.5.1.1, Conduct Reviews
b) A.5.2.2, Perform Configuration Control
c) A.5.3.1, Implement Documentation

Activity A.5.1.3, Conduct Audits, should be invoked.

A.1.3.1.3 Output Information

Output Information	Destination	
	Activity Group	Activity
Risk Management Reported Information	Project Planning	Plan Evaluations (A.1.2.1)
		Plan Project Management (A.1.2.7)
	Project Monitoring and Control	Manage the Project (A.1.3.2)
	Requirements	Define and Develop Software Requirements (A.3.1.1)
		Prioritize and Integrate Software Requirements (A.3.1.3)

A.1.3.2 Manage the Project

A.1.3.2.1 Input Information

Input Information	Source	
	Activity Group	Activity
Feedback Data	External	—
SLCP	Project Initiation	Create SLCP (A.1.1.1)
Project Estimates	Project Initiation	Perform Estimations (A.1.1.2)
Resource Allocations	Project Initiation	Allocate Project Resources (A.1.1.3)
Evaluation Planned Information	Project Planning	Plan Evaluations (A.1.2.1)
SCMPI	Project Planning	Plan Configuration Management Program (A.1.2.2)
Transition Planned Information (If Available)	Project Planning	Plan System Transition (A.1.2.3)
Software Installation Planned Information	Project Planning	Plan Installation (A.1.2.4)
Documentation Planned Information	Project Planning	Plan Documentation (A.1.2.5)
Training Planned Information	Project Planning	Plan Training (A.1.2.6)
SPMPI	Project Planning	Plan Project Management (A.1.2.7)
Retirement Planned Information	Project Planning	Plan Project Management (A.1.2.7)
Support Planned Information	Project Planning	Plan Project Management (A.1.2.7)
PR&RPI	Project Planning	Plan Project Management (A.1.2.7)
Integration Planned Information	Project Planning	Plan Integration (A.1.2.8)
Risk Management Reported Information	Project Monitoring and Control	Manage Risks (A.1.3.1)
Analysis Reported Information	Project Monitoring and Control	Collect and Analyze Metric Data (A.1.3.5)
Selected Software Import Sources	Software Importation	Evaluate Software Import Sources (A.2.3.2)
Installation Reported Information	Installation	Install Software (A.4.1.2)
Software Improvement Recommendations	Maintenance	Identify Software Improvement Needs (A.4.3.1)
Evaluation Reported Information	Evaluation	Report Evaluation Results (A.5.1.7)
Status Reported Information	Software Configuration Management	Perform Status Accounting (A.5.2.3)

A.1.3.2.2 Description

This Activity shall manage the execution of all Activities in the SLCP, according to the plans set forth in the Project Planning Activities. The progress of the project shall be reviewed and measured against the established estimates and plans (e.g., estimated vs. actual cost, estimated vs. actual effort, and planned vs. actual progress). The Input Information shall be tracked and analyzed; any additional pertinent data shall be gathered and analyzed in order to enable the status of the project to be reported. Any Anomalies encountered shall also be reported. This Activity also encompasses the day-to-day management of the project that is needed to ensure successful project completion.

This Activity may invoke Activity A.5.1.1, Conduct Reviews, or Activity A.5.1.3, Conduct Audit, in order to verify compliance to the SLCP and/or Project Planning plans.

Prior to the distribution of the Project Management Reported Information, Activity A.5.1.1, Conduct Reviews, should be invoked.

A.1.3.2.3 Output Information

Output Information	Destination	
	Activity Group	Activity
Project Management Reported Information	External	—
	Project Planning	Plan Project Management (A.1.2.7)
	Project Monitoring and Control	Manage Risks (A.1.3.1)
		Identify SLCP Improvement Needs (A.1.3.3)
Anomalies	Maintenance	Implement Problem Reporting Method (A.4.3.2)

A.1.3.3 Identify SLCP Improvement Needs

A.1.3.3.1 Input Information

Input Information	Source	
	Activity Group	Activity
Historical Project Records	External	—
SLCP	Project Initiation	Create SLCP (A.1.1.1)
Project Management Reported Information	Project Monitoring and Control	Manage the Project (A.1.3.2)
Analysis Reported Information	Project Monitoring and Control	Collect and Analyze Metric Data (A.1.3.5)
Software Improvement Recommendations	Maintenance	Identify Software Improvement Needs (A.4.3.1)
Post-Operation Review Reported Information	Retirement	Retire System (A.4.4.3)
Evaluation Reported Information	Evaluation	Report Evaluation Results (A.5.1.7)

A.1.3.3.2 Description

This activity shall analyze Project Management Reported Information, project metrics from Analysis Reported Information, Evaluation Reported Information, and the other inputs to determine instances in which SLCP improvements could be beneficial. These analyses could be accomplished by using techniques such as Pareto analysis, control charts, fishbone diagrams, and process capability measurements.

Historical Project Records might provide the historical information that is needed to analyze the information from the project.

Environment Improvement Needs shall describe the requested change and shall contain objective criteria to be used to determine if the implemented change produced a positive result. Environment Improvement Needs can point to improvement opportunities that are outside the scope of the project.

Further information on process improvement can be found in IEEE Std 1045-1992 [B21] and IEEE Std 1061-1998 [B24].

A.1.3.3.3 Output Information

Output Information	Destination	
	Activity Group	Activity
Environment Improvement Needs	External	—
	Project Initiation	Create SLCP (A.1.1.1)
	Maintenance	Implement Problem Reporting Method (A.4.3.2)

A.1.3.4 Retain Records

A.1.3.4.1 Input Information

Input Information	Source	
	Activity Group	Activity
Information Retention Standards	External	—
Records	Originating Activity Group	Originating Activity

A.1.3.4.2 Description

This Activity accepts project records from each Activity Group. The Records shall be retained in accordance with pertinent planning information and any external Information Retention Standards. The Records become part of the Historical Project Records of the organization. Uses for these records can include project audits, future project planning, and corporate accounting.

Further information on record retention can be found in IEEE Std 1298-1992 [B33].

A.1.3.4.3 Output Information

Output Information	Destination	
	Activity Group	Activity
Historical Project Records	External	—

A.1.3.5 Collect and Analyze Metric Data

A.1.3.5.1 Input Information

Input Information	Source	
	Activity Group	Activity
Customer Input Information	External	—
Support Personnel Reported Information	External	—
Historical Project Records	External	—
Metric Data	Originating Activity Group	Originating Activity
Defined Metrics	Project Initiation	Define Metrics (A.1.1.4)
Collection and Analysis Methods	Project Initiation	Define Metrics (A.1.1.4)
Evaluation Planned Information	Project Planning	Plan Evaluations (A.1.2.1)
Correction Problem Reported Information	Maintenance	Implement Problem Reporting Method (A.4.3.2)
Enhancement Problem Reported Information	Maintenance	Implement Problem Reporting Method (A.4.3.2)
Report Log	Maintenance	Implement Problem Reporting Method (A.4.3.2)
Resolved Problem Reported Information	Maintenance	Reapply SLC (A.4.3.3)
Updated Report Log	Maintenance	Reapply SLC (A.4.3.3)
Evaluation Reported Information	Evaluation	Report Evaluation Results (A.5.1.7)

A.1.3.5.2 Description

This Activity collects and analyzes project-generated Metric Data, Evaluation Reported Information, Customer Input Information, and Support Personnel Reported Information, as defined in the Collection and Analysis Methods. The Customer Input Information should also be used to obtain a customer point-of-view of the project and to gauge the customer's satisfaction with the software. Historical Project Records can prove to be valuable in the analysis of the metric(s) for the purposes of comparison and for obtaining trend information.

Analysis Reported Information shall be generated that contains the resulting metric(s) and describes the metric(s) analysis.

Further information related to this Activity can be found in IEEE Std 982.1-1988 [B8], IEEE Std 982.2-1988 [B9], IEEE Std 1044-1993 [B19], IEEE Std 1045-1992 [B21], and IEEE Std 1061-1998 [B24].

Prior to the distribution of the Analysis Reported Information, the following Activities should be invoked:

a) A.5.1.1, Conduct Reviews
b) A.5.2.2, Perform Configuration Control
c) A.5.3.1, Documentation Development

A.1.3.5.3 Output Information

Output Information	Destination	
	Activity Group	Activity
Analysis Reported Information	Project Monitoring and Control	Manage Risks (A.1.3.1)
		Manage the Project (A.1.3.2)
		Identify SLCP Improvement Needs (A.1.3.3)
	Maintenance	Identify Software Improvement Needs (A.4.3.1)

A.2 Pre-Development Activity Groups

These are the Activity Groups that explore concepts and allocate system requirements before software development can begin.

A.2.1 Concept Exploration Activities

A development effort is initiated with the identification of an idea or need for a system to be developed, whether it is a new effort or a change to all or part of an existing application. The Concept Exploration Activity Group examines the requirements at the system level, thus producing a Statement of Need that initiates the System Allocation or Requirements Activity Group. The Concept Exploration Activity Group includes the identification of an idea or need, the evaluation and refinement of the idea or need, and, once boundaries are placed around it, the generation of a Statement of Need for developing a system.

Concept Exploration Activities are

- a) A.2.1.1, Identify Ideas or Needs
- b) A.2.1.2, Formulate Potential Approaches
- c) A.2.1.3, Conduct Feasibility Studies
- d) A.2.1.4, Refine and Finalize the Idea or Need

A.2.1.1 Identify Ideas or Needs

A.2.1.1.1 Input Information

Input Information	Source	
	Activity Group	Activity
Changing Software Requirements	External	—
Customer Requests	External	—
Ideas from Within the Development Organization	External	—
Marketing Information Sources	External	—
User Requests	External	—
Enhancement Problem Reported Information	Maintenance	Implement Problem Reporting Method (A.4.3.2)
Maintenance Recommendations	Maintenance	Reapply SLC (A.4.3.3)

A.2.1.1.2 Description

An idea or a need for a new or modified system is generated from one or more of the sources identified in the table above. Input Information to the Preliminary Statement of Need shall be documented, outlining the function and performance needs. Changing Software Requirements can come from legislation, regulations, national and international standards, maintenance, etc.

Prior to the distribution of the Preliminary Statement of Need, the Activity A.5.1.1, Conduct Reviews, may be invoked.

A.2.1.1.3 Output Information

Output Information	Destination	
	Activity Group	Activity
Preliminary Statement of Need	Project Planning	Plan System Transition (If Applicable) (A.1.2.3)
		Plan Project Manager (A.1.2.7)
	Concept Exploration	Formulate Potential Approaches (A.2.1.2)
		Conduct Feasibility Studies (A.2.1.3)
		Refine and Finalize the Idea or Need (A.2.1.4)

A.2.1.2 Formulate Potential Approaches

A.2.1.2.1 Input Information

Input Information	Source	
	Activity Group	Activity
Development Resources and Budget	External	—
Market Availability Data	External	—
Resource Information	External	—
Preliminary Statement of Need	Concept Exploration	Identify Ideas or Needs (A.2.1.1)

A.2.1.2.2 Description

Using Resource Information, budget data, and the availability of third party or existing reusable software products, Potential Approaches shall be developed that are based upon the Preliminary Statement of Need and any data that is pertinent to the decision to develop or acquire the system. The Formulate Potential Approaches Activity shall also produce the Constraints and Benefits with regard to the development of the software. The Constraints and Benefits should include all aspects of the life cycle.

Prior to the distribution of the Constraints and Benefits and the Potential Approaches, the following Activities may be invoked:

a)   A.5.1.1, Conduct Reviews
b)   A.5.2.2, Perform Configuration Control

A.2.1.2.3 Output Information

Output Information	Destination	
	Activity Group	Activity
Constraints and Benefits	Concept Exploration	Conduct Feasibility Studies (A.2.1.3)
		Refine and Finalize the Idea or Need (A.2.1.4)
Potential Approaches	Concept Exploration	Conduct Feasibility Studies (A.2.1.3)
		Refine and Finalize the Idea or Need (A.2.1.4)

A.2.1.3 Conduct Feasibility Studies

A.2.1.3.1 Input Information

Input Information	Source	
	Activity Group	Activity
Preliminary Statement of Need	Concept Exploration	Identify Ideas or Needs (A.2.1.1)
Constraints and Benefits	Concept Exploration	Formulate Potential Approaches (A.2.1.2)
Potential Approaches	Concept Exploration	Formulate Potential Approaches (A.2.1.2)

A.2.1.3.2 Description

The feasibility study shall include the analysis of the idea or need, the Potential Approaches, and all life cycle Constraints and Benefits. Modeling and prototyping techniques might also be considered. In conducting the feasibility study, there could be a need to decide whether to make or buy the system, in part or in total. Justification for each Recommendation shall be fully documented and formally approved by all concerned organizations (including the user and the developer).

Prior to the distribution of the Recommendations, Activity A.5.1.1, Conduct Reviews, may be invoked.

A.2.1.3.3 Output Information

Output Information	Destination	
	Activity Group	Activity
Recommendations	Project Planning	Plan System Transition (If Applicable) (A.1.2.3)
		Plan Project Management (A.1.2.7)
	Concept Exploration	Refine and Finalize the Idea or Need (A.2.1.4)
	System Allocation	Analyze Functions (A.2.2.1)

A.2.1.4 Refine and Finalize the Idea or Need

A.2.1.4.1 Input Information

Input Information	Source	
	Activity Group	Activity
Preliminary Statement of Need	Concept Exploration	Identify Ideas or Needs (A.2.1.1)
Constraints and Benefits	Concept Exploration	Formulate Potential Approaches (A.2.1.2)
Potential Approaches	Concept Exploration	Formulate Potential Approaches (A.2.1.2)
Recommendations	Concept Exploration	Conduct Feasibility Studies (A.2.1.3)
Transition Impact Statement (If Available)	Project Planning	Plan System Transition (A.1.2.3)

A.2.1.4.2 Description

The idea or need shall be refined by analyzing the Preliminary Statement of Need, the Potential Approaches, the Recommendations, and the Transition Impact Statement (If Available). An approach shall be selected and documented that refines the initial idea or need.

Based upon the refined ideas or needs, a Statement of Need shall be generated that identifies the software idea, need, or desire; the recommended approach for its implementation; and any data that is pertinent to a management decision concerning the initiation of the described development effort.

Prior to the distribution of the Statement of Need, the following Activities may be invoked:

a) A.5.1.1, Conduct Reviews
b) A.5.2.2, Perform Configuration Control
c) A.5.3.1, Implement Documentation

A.2.1.4.3 Output Information

Output Information	Destination	
	Activity Group	Activity
Statement of Need	Project Initiation	Create SLCP (A.1.1.1)
		Perform Estimations (A.1.1.2)
		Allocate Project Resources (A.1.1.3)
	Project Planning	Plan Project Management (A.1.2.7)
	Project Monitoring and Control	Manage Risks (A.1.3.1)
	System Allocation	Analyze Functions (A.2.2.1)
		Develop System Architecture (A.2.2.2)

A.2.2 System Allocation Activities

The System Allocation Activity Group is the bridge between Concept Exploration and the definition of software requirements. This Activity Group maps the required functions to software and, when applicable, to hardware and people.

The Statement of Need forms the basis for the analysis of the system, thus resulting in system requirements. These requirements determine the inputs to the system, the processing to be applied to the inputs, and the required outputs. The software and hardware (if required) operational functions are also identified in these definitions.

The architecture of the system shall be developed through the System Allocation Activity Group. The system functions are derived from system requirements, and the hardware, software, and operational requirements are identified. These requirements are analyzed to produce System Functional Software Requirements and System Functional Human and Hardware Requirements (If Applicable). The hardware, software, and operational interfaces shall be defined and closely monitored. No hardware requirements analysis is discussed in this document; it is beyond the scope of this standard.

System Allocation Activities are

a)   A.2.2.1, Analyze Functions
b)   A.2.2.2, Develop System Architecture
c)   A.2.2.3, Decompose System Requirements

A.2.2.1 Analyze Functions

A.2.2.1.1 Input Information

Input Information	Source	
	Activity Group	**Activity**
Recommendations	Concept Exploration	Conduct Feasibility Studies (A.2.1.3)
Statement of Need	Concept Exploration	Refine and Finalize the Idea or Need (A.2.1.4)

A.2.2.1.2 Description

The Statement of Need and Recommendations for solution shall be analyzed to identify the functions of the total system. Once the functions have been identified, they are delineated in the Functional Description of the System and are used to develop the system architecture and to identify the software and (if applicable) hardware functions.

Prior to the distribution of the Functional Description of the System, the following Activities shall be invoked:

a)   A.5.1.1, Conduct Reviews
b)   A.5.2.2, Perform Configuration Control

A.2.2.1.3 Output Information

Output Information	Destination	
	Activity Group	**Activity**
Functional Description of the System	System Allocation	Develop System Architecture (A.2.2.2)
		Decompose System Requirements (A.2.2.3)
	Requirements	Define Interface Requirements (A.3.1.2)

A.2.2.2 Develop System Architecture

A.2.2.2.1 Input Information

Input Information	Source	
	Activity Group	**Activity**
SPMPI	Project Planning	Plan Project Management (A.1.2.7)
Statement of Need	Concept Exploration	Refine and Finalize the Idea or Need (A.2.1.4)
Functional Description of the System	System Allocation	Analyze Functions (A.2.2.1)

A.2.2.2.2 Description

The Statement of Need and the Functional Description of the System shall be transformed into the System Architecture using the methodology, standards, and tools that are established by the organization. The System Architecture becomes the basis for the Design Activity Group and for the determination of the software functions and the hardware functions, if any.

A.2.2.2.3 Output Information

Output Information	Destination	
	Activity Group	**Activity**
System Architecture	System Allocation	Decompose System Requirements (A.2.2.3)
	Design	Perform Architectural Design (A.3.2.1)

A.2.2.3 Decompose System Requirements

A.2.2.3.1 Input Information

Input Information	Source	
	Activity Group	**Activity**
Functional Description of the System	System Allocation	Analyze Functions (A.2.2.1)
System Architecture	System Allocation	Develop System Architecture (A.2.2.2)

A.2.2.3.2 Description

The system functions that are documented in the Functional Description of the System shall be divided according to the System Architecture in order to form software requirements, human and hardware requirements (if applicable), and the System Interface Requirements (if available). The System Interface Requirements define the interfaces that are external to the system and the interfaces between configuration items that comprise the system. Note that any hardware requirements go to an external destination because they are beyond the scope of this standard. The decomposition of the system could result in requirements for more than one project. Each software project shall be managed individually.

Further information on system requirements can be found in IEEE Std 1233, 1998 Edition [B32].

Prior to the distribution of Software Functional Requirements and System Interface Requirements, the following Activities shall be invoked:

a)   A.5.1.1, Conduct Reviews
b)   A.5.2.2, Perform Configuration Control

c) A.5.3.1, Implement Documentation
d) A.5.4.1, Develop Training Materials

A.2.2.3.3 Output Information

Output Information	Destination	
	Activity Group	**Activity**
System Functional Human and Hardware Requirements (If Applicable)	External	—
System Functional Software Requirements	Project Initiation	Perform Estimations (A.1.1.2)
		Allocate Project Resources (A.1.1.3)
	Requirements	Define and Develop Software Requirements (A.3.1.1)
		Define Interface Requirements (A.3.1.2)
System Interface Requirements (If Available)	External	—
	Requirements	Define and Develop Software Requirements (A.3.1.1)
		Define Interface Requirements (A.3.1.2)

A.2.3 Software Importation Activities

Some or all of the software requirements may best be satisfied by reusing existing software or by acquiring software from outside the project. This software may or may not belong to the developing organization. Imported Software can consist of code libraries, device drivers, various utilities, or even fully functional systems that are to be integrated into the current development project. Software Importation Activities provide the means to extract the software requirements that will be satisfied through importation, to evaluate candidate sources from which the imported software might be obtained, to determine the method of importation, and to import the software, including documentation, into the project.

Software Importation Activities are

a) A.2.3.1, Identify Imported Software Requirements
b) A.2.3.2, Evaluate Software Import Sources (If Applicable)
c) A.2.3.3, Define Software Import Method (If Applicable)
d) A.2.3.4, Import Software (If Applicable)

A.2.3.1 Identify Imported Software Requirements

A.2.3.1.1 Input Information

Input Information	Source	
	Activity Group	**Activity**
SPMPI	Project Planning	Plan Project Management (A.1.2.7)
Software Requirements	Requirements	Prioritize and Integrate Software Requirements (A.3.1.3)

A.2.3.1.2 Description

The Identify Imported Software Requirements Activity extracts those Software Requirements that can best be satisfied with existing or acquired software. The resulting requirements for imported software (Imported Software Requirements) cover all categories of requirements, including schedule and budget constraints.

Further information related to this Activity can be found in IEEE Std 1062, 1998 Edition [B25].

Prior to the distribution of the Imported Software Requirements, Activity A.5.1.1, Conduct Reviews, shall be invoked.

A.2.3.1.3 Output Information

Output Information	Destination	
	Activity Group	Activity
Imported Software Requirements	Project Planning	Project Planning Activities (A.1.2)
	Project Monitoring and Control	Manage Risks (A.1.3.1)
	Software Importation	Evaluate Software Import Sources (A.2.3.2)
	Design	All Design Activities (A.3.2)
	Evaluation	Conduct Reviews (A.5.1.1)
		Create Test Data (A.5.1.5)

A.2.3.2 Evaluate Software Import Sources (If Applicable)

A.2.3.2.1 Input Information

Input Information	Source	
	Activity Group	Activity
Imported Software Requirements	Software Importation	Identify Imported Software Requirements (A.2.3.1)

A.2.3.2.2 Description

The Evaluate Software Import Sources Activity applies when software is to be imported for use on the project. This Activity is the mechanism to determine if the Imported Software Requirements are to be satisfied using software from another project within the organization, including items from a reuse library, or if the requirements are to be satisfied by a source outside the organization. Software outside the organization can include public domain software, freeware, shareware, subcontracted development, or purchased commercial software. The available sources shall be evaluated with respect to the compliance of the available software with the requirements, availability, schedule, cost, and the software quality program of the source. The effects on overall project budget, cost, and risk shall be considered in this evaluation and shall be communicated to project management.

For the Selected Software Import Sources, Candidate Software Import Methods by which the software will actually be acquired shall be determined. For example, in the case of software that is to be purchased off the shelf, methods could include site licensing, limited individual licenses, bulk purchase, etc. In the case of software that is to be contractually acquired, methods could include turn-key development, development in the target system's physical project location, various forms of test conduct, contractual clauses dealing with quality programs and configuration management, etc.

Further information related to this Activity can be found in IEEE Std 1063-1987 [B26].

A.2.3.2.3 Output Information

Output Information	Destination	
	Activity Group	Activity
Selected Software Import Sources	Project Monitoring and Control	Manage the Project (A.1.3.2)
	Software Importation	Decline Software Import Method (A.2.3.3)
		Import Software (A.2.3.4)
Candidate Software Import Methods	Software Importation	Define Software Import Method (A.2.3.3)

A.2.3.3 Define Software Import Method (If Applicable)

A.2.3.3.1 Input Information

Input Information	Source	
	Activity Group	Activity
Selected Software Import Sources	Software Importation	Evaluate Software Import Sources (A.2.3.2)
Candidate Software Import Methods	Software Importation	Evaluation Software Import Sources (A.2.3.2)

A.2.3.3.2 Description

The Define Software Import Method Activity applies when software is to be imported for use on the project. Using the listed Input Information, this Activity shall select the most appropriate methods by which the Selected Software Import Sources will provide the imported software. Consideration should be given to the integration of the software importation with the overall project schedule, configuration management, budget and personnel resource requirements, imported software testing requirements, etc.

Further information related to this Activity can be found in IEEE Std 1062, 1998 Edition [B25].

A.2.3.3.3 Output Information

Output Information	Destination	
	Activity Group	Activity
Selected Software Import Methods	Software Importation	Import Software (A.2.3.4)

A.2.3.4 Import Software (If Applicable)

A.2.3.4.1 Input Information

Input Information	Source	
	Activity Group	Activity
Selected Software Import Sources	Software Importation	Evaluate Software Import Sources (A.2.3.2)
Selected Software Import Methods	Software Importation	Define Software Import Method (A.2.3.3)

A.2.3.4.2 Description

The Import Software Activity applies when software is to be imported for use on the project. This Activity brings the imported components into the software project in a controlled manner that ensures their orderly integration into the total software system. The imported software shall be integrated into the design as well as the implementation.

Further information related to this Activity can be found in IEEE Std 1062, 1998 Edition [B25].

Prior to the distribution of the Imported Software, the following Activity Groups shall be invoked:

a)   A.5.1.6, Execute Tests
b)   A.5.2.2, Perform Configuration Control
c)   A.5.4.1, Develop Training Materials

A.2.3.4.3 Output Information

Output Information	Destination	
	Activity Group	Activity
Imported Software	Implementation	Perform Integration (A.3.3.3)
	Evaluation	Execute Tests (A.5.1.6)
Imported Software Documentation	Design	Perform Detailed Design (A.3.2.4)
	Evaluation	Conduct Reviews (A.5.1.1)
	Documentation Development	Implement Documentation (A.5.3.1)
	Training	Develop Training Materials (A.5.4.1)

A.3 Development Activity Groups

These are the Activity Groups that are performed during the development of a software product.

A.3.1 Requirements Activities

This Activity Group includes those Activities that are directed toward the development of software requirements. In the development of a system that contains hardware, human, and software components, the Requirements Activity Group follows the development of total system requirements, and the functional allocation of those system requirements to hardware, humans, and software.

Requirements Activities are

a)   A.3.1.1, Define and Develop Software Requirements
b)   A.3.1.2, Define Interface Requirements
c)   A.3.1.3, Prioritize and Integrate Software Requirements

A.3.1.1 Define and Develop Software Requirements

A.3.1.1.1 Input Information

Input Information	Source	
	Activity Group	Activity
Installation Support Requirements	External	—
System Constraints	External	—
SPMPI	Project Initiation	Plan Project Management (A.1.2.7)
Risk Management Reported Information	Project Monitoring and Control	Manage Risks (A.1.3.1)
System Functional Software Requirements	System Allocation	Decompose System Requirements (A.2.2.3)
System Interface Requirements (If Available)	System Allocation	Decompose System Requirements (A.2.2.3)

A.3.1.1.2 Description

The first Activity in this Activity Group, defining the software requirements, is usually iterative in nature. Whether the software development constitutes the entire project or is part of a system (e.g., hardware, humans, and software), software requirements, including constraints, shall be generated from Input Information documents and the results of modeling, prototyping, or other techniques.

Using the above Input Information, the developer shall analyze the software functional and performance requirements to determine traceability, clarity, validity, testability, safety, and any other project-specific characteristics. The use of a comprehensive methodology is recommended to ensure that requirements are complete and consistent. Techniques such as structured analysis, modeling, prototyping, or transaction analysis are helpful in this Activity. When needed, the requirements for a data base shall be included in the requirements.

The Preliminary Software Requirements and Installation Requirements determination shall include the consideration of System Constraints such as timing, sizing, language, marketing restrictions, and technology.

Further information related to this Activity can be found in IEEE Std 830-1998 [B7].

Prior to the distribution of the Preliminary Software Requirements and Installation Requirements, the following Activities shall be invoked:

a) A.5.1.1, Conduct Reviews
b) A.5.2.2, Perform Configuration Control
c) A.5.3.1, Implement Documentation

A.3.1.1.3 Output Information

Output Information	Destination	
	Activity Group	Activity
Preliminary Software Requirements	Project Planning	Plan Evaluations (A.1.2.1)
	Requirements	Define Interface Requirements (A.3.1.2)
		Prioritize and Integrate Software Requirements (A.3.1.3)
Installation Requirements	Project Planning	Plan Installation (A.1.2.4)

A.3.1.2 Define Interface Requirements

A.3.1.2.1 Input Information

Input Information	Source	
	Activity Group	Activity
System Constraints	External	—
SPMPI	Project Planning	Plan Project Management (A.1.2.7)
Functional Description of the System	System Allocation	Analyze Functions (A.2.2.1)
System Functional Software Requirements	System Allocation	Decompose System Requirements (A.2.2.3)
Preliminary Software Requirements	Requirements	Define and Develop Software Requirements (A.3.1.1)
System Interface Requirements (If Available)	System Allocation	Decompose System Requirements (A.2.2.3)

A.3.1.2.2 Description

All user, software, and hardware interfaces shall be defined using the applicable Input Information. These interfaces shall be defined either as requirements or as constraints, and shall be reviewed by all involved parties.

The user interface is critical in determining the usability of the system. The user interface definition shall specify not only the information flow between the user and the system, but also the manner in which a user goes about using the system.

The Software Interface Requirements shall specify all software interfaces that are required to support the development and execution of the software system. Software interfaces can be affected by System Constraints including operating system, data base management system, language compiler, tools, utilities, network protocol drivers, and hardware interfaces.

Further information related to this Activity can be found in IEEE Std 830-1998 [B7] and IEEE Std 1175-1991 [B27].

Prior to the distribution of the Software Interface Requirements, the following Activities shall be invoked:

a) A.5.1.1, Conduct Reviews
b) A.5.2.2, Perform Configuration Control
c) A.5.3.1, Implement Documentation

A.3.1.2.3 Output Information

Output Information	Destination	
	Activity Group	Activity
Software Interface Requirements	Project Monitoring and Control	Manage Risks (A.1.3.1)
	Requirements	Prioritize and Integrate Software Requirements (A.3.1.3)

A.3.1.3 Prioritize and Integrate Software Requirements

A.3.1.3.1 Input Information

Input Information	Source	
	Activity Group	Activity
Risk Management Reported Information	Project Monitoring and Control	Manage Risks (A.1.3.1)
Preliminary Software Requirements	Requirements	Define and Develop Software Requirements (A.3.1.1)
Software Interface Requirements	Requirements	Define Interface Requirements (A.3.1.2)

A.3.1.3.2 Description

The functional and performance requirements shall be reviewed, and a prioritized list of requirements shall be produced that addresses any trade-offs that may be needed. The organization of the emerging Software Requirements shall be reviewed and revised as necessary. While completing the requirements, a particular design shall not be imposed (i.e., design decisions are made in the Design Activity Group). The Software Requirements shall describe the functional, interface, and performance requirements, and shall also define operational support environments.

Further information related to this Activity can be found in IEEE Std 830-1998 [B7].

Prior to the distribution of the Software Requirements, the following Activities shall be invoked:

a) A.5.1.1, Conduct Reviews
b) A.5.2.2, Perform Configuration Control
c) A.5.3.1, Implement Documentation

A.3.1.3.3 Output Information

Output Information	Destination	
	Activity Group	Activity
Software Requirements	Project Initiation	Allocate Project Resources (A.1.1.3)
		Define Metrics (A.1.1.4)
	Project Planning	Plan Evaluations (A.1.2.1)
		Plan Training (A.1.2.6)
		Plan Integration (A.1.2.8)
	Project Monitoring and Control	Manage Risks (A.1.3.1)
	Software Importation	Identify Imported Software Requirements (A.2.3.1)
	Design	Design Activities (A.3.2)
	Implementation	Create Operating Documentation (A.3.3.2)
	Evaluation	Conduct Reviews (A.5.1.1)
		Create Traceability Matrix (A.5.1.2)
		Develop Test Procedures (A.5.1.4)
		Create Test Data (A.5.1.5)

A.3.2 Design Activities

The objective of the Design Activity Group is to develop a coherent, well-organized representation of the software system that meets the Software Requirements. At the architectural design level, the focus is on the software components that comprise the software system, and the structure and interfacing of those components. At the detailed design level, the emphasis is on the data structures and algorithms for each software component.

The Perform Architectural Design and Perform Detailed Design Activities are usually carried out in sequence because detailed design is largely dependent on the architectural design. They differ from each other in the level of design detail. Other Design Activity Group Activities can be carried out in parallel with these Activities.

Design Activities are

a) A.3.2.1, Perform Architectural Design
b) A.3.2.2, Design Data Base (If Applicable)
c) A.3.2.3, Design Interfaces
d) A.3.2.4, Perform Detailed Design

A.3.2.1 Perform Architectural Design

A.3.2.1.1 Input Information

Input Information	Source	
	Activity Group	Activity
SPMPI	Project Planning	Plan Project Management (A.1.2.7)
System Architecture	System Allocation	Develop System Architecture (A.2.2.2)
Imported Software Requirements	Software Importation	Identify Imported Software Requirements (A.2.3.1)
Software Requirements	Requirements	Prioritize and Integrate Software Requirements (A.3.1.3)

A.3.2.1.2 Description

The Perform Architectural Design Activity transforms the Software Requirements and the System Architecture into high-level design concepts. During this Activity, the software components that constitute the software system and their structures are identified. Purchased software and the contents of the software libraries can influence the architectural design. Techniques such as modeling and prototyping could be used to evaluate alternative designs.

By the end of the Perform Architectural Design Activity, the description of the design of each software component shall have been completed. The data, relationships, and constraints shall be specified. All internal interfaces (among components) shall be defined. This Activity shall create the Software Architectural Design.

Prior to the distribution of the Software Architectural Design, the following Activities shall be invoked:

a) A.5.1.1, Conduct Reviews
b) A.5.2.2, Perform Configuration Control
c) A.5.3.1, Implement Documentation

A.3.2.1.3 Output Information

Output Information	Destination	
	Activity Group	Activity
Software Architectural Design	Design	Perform Detailed Design (A.3.2.4)

A.3.2.2 Design Data Base (If applicable)

A.3.2.2.1 Input Information

Input Information	Source	
	Activity Group	Activity
SPMPI	Project Planning	Plan Project Management (A.1.2.7)
Imported Software Requirements	Software Importation	Identify Imported Software Requirements (A.2.3.1)
Software Requirements	Requirements	Prioritize and Integrate Software Requirements (A.3.1.3)

A.3.2.2.2 Description

The Design Data Base Activity applies when a data base is to be created or modified as a part of the project. This Activity shall specify the information structure that is outlined in the Software Requirements and its characteristics within the software system. The Design Data Base Activity involves three separate but related steps: conceptual data base design, logical data base design, and physical data base design. It does not involve designing or developing the Data Base Management System.

Techniques such as data dictionary, data base optimization, and data modeling should be considered. Requirements are molded into an external schema that describes data entities, attributes, relationships, and constraints. The various external schemata are integrated into a single conceptual schema. The conceptual schema is then mapped into an implementation-dependent logical schema. Finally, the physical data structures and access paths are defined. The result of this Activity is the generation of the Data Base Design.

Prior to the distribution of the Data Base Design, the following Activities shall be invoked:

a) A.5.1.1, Conduct Reviews
b) A.5.2.2, Perform Configuration Control
c) A.5.3.1, Implement Documentation

A.3.2.2.3 Output Information

Output Information	Destination	
	Activity Group	Activity
Data Base Design	Design	Perform Detailed Design (A.3.2.4)

A.3.2.3 Design Interfaces

A.3.2.3.1 Input Information

Input Information	Source	
	Activity Group	Activity
Imported Software Requirements	Software Importation	Identify Imported Software Requirements (A.2.3.1)
Software Requirements	Requirements	Prioritize and Integrate Software Requirements (A.3.1.3)

A.3.2.3.2 Description

The Design Interfaces Activity shall be concerned with the user, software, and hardware interfaces of the software system that is contained in the Software Requirements. This Activity shall consolidate these interface descriptions into a single Interface Design for the software system.

Prior to the distribution of the Interface Design, the following Activities shall be invoked:

a) A.5.1.1, Conduct Reviews
b) A.5.2.2, Perform Configuration Control
c) A.5.3.1, Implement Documentation

A.3.2.3.3 Output Information

Output Information	Destination	
	Activity Group	**Activity**
Interface Design	Design	Perform Detailed Design (A.3.2.4)

A.3.2.4 Perform Detailed Design

A.3.2.4.1 Input Information

Input Information	Source	
	Activity Group	**Activity**
SPMPI	Project Planning	Plan Project Management (A.1.2.7)
Imported Software Requirements	Software Importation	Identify Imported Software Requirements (A.2.3.1)
Imported Software Documentation	Software Importation	Import Software (A.2.3.4)
Software Requirements	Requirements	Prioritize and Integrate Software Requirements (A.3.1.3)
Software Architectural Design	Design	Perform Architectural Design (A.3.2.1)
Data Base Design (If Available)	Design	Design Data Base (If Applicable) (A.3.2.2)
Interface Design	Design	Design Interfaces (A.3.2.3)

A.3.2.4.2 Description

In this Activity, design alternatives shall be chosen for implementing the functions that are specified for each software component. By the end of this Activity, the data structure, algorithm, and control information of each software component shall be specified. The Software Detailed Design contains the consolidated data for all of the above Input Information. The details of the interfaces shall be identified within the Software Detailed Design.

For further information on this topic, see IEEE Std 1016-1998 [B15] and IEEE Std 1016.1-1993 [B16].

Prior to the distribution of the Software Detailed Design, the following Activities shall be invoked:

a) A.5.1.1, Conduct Reviews
b) A.5.2.2, Perform Configuration Control
c) A.5.3.1, Implement Documentation

A.3.2.4.3 Output Information

Output Information	Destination	
	Activity Group	**Activity**
Software Detailed Design	Project Planning	Plan Evaluations (A.1.2.1)
		Plan Integration (A.1.2.8)
	Project Monitoring and Control	Manage Risks (A.1.3.1)
	Implementation	Create Executable Code (A.3.3.1)
		Create Operating Documentation (A.3.3.2)
	Evaluation	Develop Test Procedures (A.5.1.4)
		Create Test Data (A.5.1.5)
	Training	Develop Training Materials (A.5.4.1)

A.3.3 Implementation Activities

The Activities included in the Implementation Activity Group result in the transformation of the Detailed Design representation of a software product into a programming language realization. This Activity Group produces the Executable Code, the Data Base (if applicable), and the documentation that constitutes the physical manifestation of the design. In addition, the code and data base are integrated. Care must also be taken during the Implementation Activity Group to apply the appropriate coding standards.

The code and data base, along with the documentation that was produced within previous Activity Groups, are the first complete representation of the software product.

Implementation Activities are

a)   A.3.3.1, Create Executable Code
b)   A.3.3.2, Create Operating Documentation
c)   A.3.3.3, Perform Integration

A.3.3.1 Create Executable Code

A.3.3.1.1 Input Information

Input Information	Source	
	Activity Group	Activity
SPMPI	Project Planning	Plan Project Management (A.1.2.7)
Software Detailed Design	Design	Perform Detailed Design (A.3.2.4)

A.3.3.1.2 Description

The Source Code, including suitable comments, shall be generated using the SLCP, as found in the SPMPI and the Software Detailed Design. If the Source Code is required for integration, it shall be made available to Activity A.3.3.3, Perform Integration. If the Source Code is going to be used to create test data, it shall be made available to Activity A.5.1.5, Create Test Data.

The code shall be grouped into processable units. (This will be dictated by the selected language and design information.) All units shall be transformed into Executable Code and debugged. Syntactically incorrect code, as identified by the transform output, shall be reworked until the Source Code can be processed free of syntactical errors.

Further information related to this Activity can be found in IEEE Std 1008-1987 [B12].

Prior to the distribution of the Source Code, Executable Code, and Data Base, the following Activities shall be invoked:

a)   A.5.1.1, Conduct Reviews
b)   A.5.1.6, Execute Tests
c)   A.5.2.2, Perform Configuration Control

A.3.3.1.3 Output Information

Output Information	Destination	
	Activity Group	**Activity**
Source Code (When Required)	Implementation	Perform Integration (A.3.3.3)
Source Code (When Required)	Evaluation	Create Test Data (A.5.1.5)
Executable Code	Implementation	Perform Integration (A.3.3.3)
	Evaluation	Execute Tests (A.5.1.6)
Data Base (If Available)	Implementation	Perform Integration (A.3.3.3)
	Evaluation	Create Test Data (A.5.1.5)

A.3.3.2 Create Operating Documentation

A.3.3.2.1 Input Information

Input Information	Source	
	Activity Group	**Activity**
Documentation Planned Information	Project Planning	Plan Documentation (A.1.2.5)
Software Requirements	Requirements	Prioritize and Integrate Software Requirements (A.3.1.3)
Software Detailed Design	Design	Perform Detailed Design (A.3.2.4)

A.3.3.2.2 Description

This Activity shall produce the software project's operating documentation from the Software Detailed Design and the Software Interface Requirements, in accordance with the Documentation Planned Information. The Operating Documentation is required for installing, operating, and supporting the system throughout the life cycle.

For further information, IEEE Std 1063-1987 [B26] can be used.

Prior to the distribution of the Operating Documentation, the following Activities shall be invoked:

a) A.5.1.1, Conduct Reviews
b) A.5.2.2, Perform Configuration Control
c) A.5.3.1, Implement Documentation

A.3.3.2.3 Output Information

Output Information	Destination	
	Activity Group	**Activity**
Operating Documentation	Project Planning	Plan Installation (A.1.2.4)
	Installation	Distribute Software (A.4.1.1)

A.3.3.3 Perform Integration

A.3.3.3.1 Input Information

Input Information	Source	
	Activity Group	**Activity**
System Components	External	—
SPMPI	Project Initiation	Plan Project Management (A.1.2.7)
Integration Planned Information	Project Planning	Plan Integration (A.1.2.8)
Imported Software	Software Importation	Import Software (A.2.3.4)
Source Code (When Required)	Implementation	Create Executable Code (A.3.3.1)
Executable Code	Implementation	Create Executable Code (A.3.3.1)
Tested Software	Evaluation	Execute Tests (A.5.1.6)
Data Base (If Available)	Implementation	Create Executable Code (A.3.3.1)
Stubs and Drivers (If Available)	Evaluation	Create Test Data (A.5.1.5)

A.3.3.3.2 Description

This Activity shall integrate the Data Base, Source Code (if required), Executable Code, and Stubs and Drivers, as specified in the Integration Planned Information, into the Integrated Software. Other necessary Executable Code, from the SLCP as defined in the SPMPI, shall also be integrated. If a system includes both hardware and software components, the system integration could be included as part of this Activity.

Prior to the distribution of the Integrated Software, the following Activities shall be invoked:

a) A.5.1.1, Conduct Reviews
b) A.5.1.6, Execute Tests
c) A.5.2.2, Perform Configuration Control

A.3.3.3.3 Output Information

Output Information	Destination	
	Activity Group	**Activity**
Integrated Software	Evaluation	Execute Tests (A.5.1.6)

A.4 Post-Development Activity Groups

These are the Activity Groups that are performed to install, operate, support, maintain, and retire a software product.

A.4.1 Installation Activities

Installation consists of the transportation and installation of a software system from the development environment to the target environment(s). It includes the necessary software modifications, checkout in the target environment(s), and customer acceptance. If a problem arises, it shall be identified and reported. If necessary and possible, a temporary "work-around" may be applied.

In the Installation Activity Group, the software to be delivered is installed, operationally checked out, and monitored. This effort culminates in formal customer acceptance. The scheduling of turnover and customer acceptance is defined in the SPMPI.

Installation Activities are

a)   A.4.1.1, Distribute Software
b)   A.4.1.2, Install Software
c)   A.4.1.3, Accept Software in Operational Environment

A.4.1.1 Distribute Software

A.4.1.1.1 Input Information

Input Information	Source	
	Activity Group	**Activity**
Data Base Data	External	—
Software Installation Planned Information	Project Planning	Plan Installation (A.1.2.4)
SPMPI	Project Planning	Plan Project Management (A.1.2.7)
Operating Documentation	Implementation	Create Operating Documentation (A.3.3.2)
Tested Software	Evaluation	Execute Tests (A.5.1.6)

A.4.1.1.2 Description

During this Activity, the Tested Software, Data Base Data, Operating Documentation, and Software Installation Planned Information shall be packaged onto their respective media as designated in the SPMPI. The Packaged Software is distributed to the appropriate site(s) for installation efforts. The Packaged Installation Planned Information is distributed, as appropriate, to the site(s) to instruct the installation efforts. The Packaged Operating Documentation shall be available for the operation of the system.

Prior to the distribution of the Packaged Information, Software, and Documentation, the following Activities shall be invoked:

a)   A.5.1.1, Conduct Reviews
b)   A.5.1.3, Conduct Audits
c)   A.5.2.2, Perform Configuration Control
d)   A.5.3.1, Implement Documentation

A.4.1.1.3 Output Information

Output Information	Destination	
	Activity Group	**Activity**
Packaged Installation Planned Information	Installation	Install Software (A.4.1.2)
Packaged Software	Installation	Install Software (A.4.1.2)
Packaged Operating Documentation	Installation	Install Software (A.4.1.2)
	Operation and Support	Operate the System (A.4.2.1)

A.4.1.2 Install Software

A.4.1.2.1 Input Information

Input Information	Source	
	Activity Group	Activity
Data Base Data	External	—
Packaged Installation Planned Information	Installation	Distribute Software (A.4.1.1)
Packaged Operating Documentation	Installation	Distribute Software (A.4.1.1)
Packaged Software	Installation	Distribute Software (A.4.1.1)

A.4.1.2.2 Description

The Packaged Software, and any required Data Base Data, shall be installed in the target environment according to the procedures in the Packaged Installation Planned Information. This could include tailoring by the customer. The Installation Reported Information shall document the installation and any problems that are encountered.

A.4.1.2.3 Output Information

Output Information	Destination	
	Activity Group	Activity
Installation Reported Information	Project Monitoring and Control	Manage the Project (A.1.3.2)
Installed Software	Installation	Accept Software in Operational Environment (A.4.1.3)

A.4.1.3 Accept Software in Operational Environment

A.4.1.3.1 Input Information

Input Information	Source	
	Activity Group	Activity
User Acceptance Planned Information	External	—
Installed Software	Installation	Install Software (A.4.1.2)
Evaluation Reported Information	Evaluation	Report Evaluation Results (A.5.1.7)

A.4.1.3.2 Description

The software acceptance shall consist of an analysis of the Evaluation Reported Information, according to the User Acceptance Planned Information, to ensure that the Installed Software performs as expected. When the results of the analysis satisfy the requirements of the User Acceptance Planned Information, the Installed Software System is accepted by the user.

Prior to the completion of the acceptance of the software in the operational environment, the following Activities should be invoked:

a) A.5.1.1, Conduct Reviews
b) A.5.2.2, Perform Configuration Control

A.4.1.3.3 Output Information

Output Information	Destination	
	Activity Group	**Activity**
Customer Acceptance	External	—
Installed Software System	Operation and Support	Operate the System (A.4.2.1)
	Retirement	Conduct Parallel Operations (If Applicable) (A.4.4.2)

A.4.2 Operation and Support Activities

The Operation and Support Activity Group involves user operation of the system and ongoing support. Support includes providing technical assistance, consulting with the user, and recording user support requests by maintaining a Support Request Log. Thus, the Operation and Support Activity Group can trigger maintenance activities via the ongoing Project Monitoring and Control Activity Group, which will provide information that re-enters the SLCP.

Operation and Support Activities are

a)   A.4.2.1, Operate the System
b)   A.4.2.2, Provide Technical Assistance and Consulting
c)   A.4.2.3, Maintain Support Request Log

A.4.2.1 Operate the System

A.4.2.1.1 Input Information

Input Information	Source	
	Activity Group	**Activity**
Feedback Data	External	—
Support Planned Information	Project Planning	Plan Project Management (A.1.2.7)
Packaged Operating Documentation	Installation	Distribute Software (A.4.1.1)
Installed Software System	Installation	Accept Software in Operational Environment (A.4.1.3)

A.4.2.1.2 Description

During this Activity, the Installed Software System shall be utilized in the intended environment and in accordance with the operating instructions. Feedback Data are collected for product and documentation improvement and system tuning. The user shall analyze the Feedback Data and identify Anomalies (which may include desired enhancements). Anomalies are then reported.

Prior to the distribution of the Operation Logs, the following Activities shall be invoked:

a)   A.5.1.1, Conduct Reviews
b)   A.5.2.2, Perform Configuration Control

A.4.2.1.3 Output Information

Output Information	Destination	
	Activity Group	Activity
Operation Logs	External	—
Anomalies	Maintenance	Implement Problem Reporting Method (A.4.3.2)

A.4.2.2 Provide Technical Assistance and Consulting

A.4.2.2.1 Input Information

Input Information	Source	
	Activity Group	Activity
Request for Support	External	—
Support Planned Information	Project Planning	Plan Project Management (A.1.2.7)

A.4.2.2.2 Description

This Activity applies after the user has accepted the software. The support function shall include providing responses to the user's technical questions or problems. A Support Response is generated to the Maintain Support Request Log so that feedback can be provided to other Activity Groups.

A.4.2.2.3 Output Information

Output Information	Destination	
	Activity Group	Activity
Support Response	External	—
	Operation and Support	Maintain Support Request Log (A.4.2.3)

A.4.2.3 Maintain Support Request Log

A.4.2.3.1 Input Information

Input Information	Source	
	Activity Group	Activity
Support Planned Information	Project Planning	Plan Project Management (A.1.2.7)
Support Response	Operation and Support	Provide Technical Assistance and Consulting (A.4.2.2)

A.4.2.3.2 Description

This Activity shall record support requests in the Support Request Log. The methodology regarding management of this Activity shall be as identified in the Support Planned Information. Anomalies that are reported shall be reported to the Maintenance Activity Group.

Prior to the release of the Support Request Log, Activity A.5.1.1, Conduct Reviews, shall be invoked.

A.4.2.3.3 Output Information

Output Information	Destination	
	Activity Group	Activity
Anomalies	Maintenance	Implement Problem Reporting Method (A.4.3.2)
Support Request Log	Evaluation	Conduct Reviews (A.5.1.1)

A.4.3 Maintenance Activities

The Maintenance Activity Group is concerned with the identification of enhancements and the resolution of software errors, faults, and failures. The requirement for software maintenance initiates SLCP changes. The SLCP is remapped and executed, thereby treating the Maintenance Activity Group as iterations of development.

Maintenance Activities are

a)   A.4.3.1, Identify Software Improvement Needs
b)   A.4.3.2, Implement Problem Reporting Method
c)   A.4.3.3, Reapply SLC

A.4.3.1 Identify Software Improvement Needs

A.4.3.1.1 Input Information

Input Information	Source	
	Activity Group	Activity
Evaluation Planned Information	Project Planning	Plan Evaluations (A.1.2.1)
Training Planned Information	Project Planning	Plan Training (A.1.2.6)
SPMPI	Project Planning	Plan Project Management (A.1.2.7)
Analysis Reported Information	Project Monitoring and Control	Collect and Analyze Metric Data (A.1.3.5)
Post-Operation Review Reported Information	Retirement	Retire System (A.4.4.3)
Evaluation Reported Information	Evaluation	Report Evaluation Results (A.5.1.7)

A.4.3.1.2 Description

This Activity identifies lessons learned and needs for software improvements, and outputs the Software Improvement Recommendations in accordance with the SPMPI. This is accomplished by using the Input Information. These recommendations shall include their impact on the quality of the software that is delivered. In addition, applicable tools, techniques, and methods for the implementation of these recommendations should be identified.

Further information related to this Activity can be found in IEEE Std 1219-1998 [B29].

A.4.3.1.3 Output Information

Output Information	Destination	
	Activity Group	Activity
Software Improvement Recommendations	External	—
	Project Monitoring and Control	Manage the Project (A.1.3.2)
	Project Monitoring and Control	Identify SLCP Improvement Needs (A.1.3.3)
	Maintenance	Implement Problem Reporting Method (A.4.3.2)

A.4.3.2 Implement Problem Reporting Method

A.4.3.2.1 Input Information

Input Information	Source	
	Activity Group	Activity
Anomalies	External	—
	Creating Activity Group	Creating Activity
PR&RPI	Project Planning	Plan Project Management (A.1.2.7)
Environment Improvement Needs	Project Monitoring and Control	Identify SLCP Improvement Needs (A.1.3.3)
Software Improvement Recommendations	Maintenance	Identify Software Improvement Needs (A.4.3.1)
Evaluation Reported Information	Evaluation	Report Evaluation Results (A.5.1.7)
Controlled Item	Software Configuration Management	Perform Configuration Control (A.5.2.2)

A.4.3.2.2 Description

This Activity accepts Anomalies from any source and prepares a problem report. The problem report shall contain information as specified in the PR&RPI. Possible problem solutions can be suggested by the problem reporter. Problems can be resolved through corrections or enhancements (as defined in the PR&RPI). Corrections are documented in the Correction Problem Reported Information for further consideration. Enhancements may be documented in the Enhancement Problem Reported Information, and are possible candidates for new projects. A Report Log shall be maintained to ensure that all problems are tracked until they are resolved and the resolution has been approved.

This Activity shall also analyze the problem including the Controlled Item, the problem report, and the Report Log to make the following determinations:

a)   What the Anomalies are
b)   Source and cause of product or process problem
c)   Product(s) or process(es) presumed to contain the error, including documentation
d)   Problem severity
e)   Course of corrective action
f)   Impact on customer, cost, schedule, and risk

Anomalies that originate from outside the scope of this standard are noted as resolved within this Activity and are forwarded for appropriate action to the responsible authority.

Further information related to this Activity can be found in IEEE Std 1044-1993 [B19] and IEEE Std 1219-1998 [B29].

Prior to the distribution of the Problem Reported Information or the Report Log, Activity A.5.2.2, Perform Configuration Control, should be invoked.

A.4.3.2.3 Output Information

Output Information	Destination	
	Activity Group	Activity
Out of Scope Anomalies	External	—
Report Log	Project Monitoring and Control	Collect and Analyze Metric Data (A.1.3.5)
	Maintenance	Reapply SLC (A.4.3.3)
Enhancement Problem Reported Information	Project Monitoring and Control	Collect and Analyze Metric Data (A.1.3.5)
	Concept Exploration	Identify Ideas or Needs (A.2.1.1)
	Maintenance	Reapply SLC (A.4.3.3)
Correction Problem Reported Information	Project Monitoring and Control	Collect and Analyze Metric Data (A.1.3.5)
	Maintenance	Reapply SLC (A.4.3.3)

A.4.3.3 Reapply SLC

A.4.3.3.1 Input Information

Input Information	Source	
	Activity Group	Activity
SPMPI	Project Planning	Plan Project Management (A.1.2.7)
PR&RPI	Project Planning	Plan Project Management (A.1.2.7)
Enhancement Problem Reported Information	Maintenance	Implement Problem Reporting Method (A.4.3.2)
Correction Problem Reported Information	Maintenance	Implement Problem Reporting Method (A.4.3.2)
Report Log	Maintenance	Implement Problem Reporting Method (A.4.3.2)

A.4.3.3.2 Description

The information that is provided by the Correction Problem Reported Information, Enhancement Problem Reported Information, and current SPMPI shall result in the generation of Maintenance Recommendations. These Maintenance Recommendations will then enter the SLCP at the Concept Exploration Activity Group in order to improve the quality of the software system. When the estimate is greater than a predefined threshold of person-days, it may be appropriate to plan a separate project to complete the recommendations. In this case, the Maintenance Recommendations will go to External.

This Activity shall monitor the problem correction efforts that are performed by the responsible Activity Group, shall determine (according to the Enhancement and Correction Problem Reported Information) that the implementation of the solution by the responsible Activity Group has been completed, and shall then record the resolution of the problem in the Resolved Problem Reported Information. The Resolved Problem Reported Information shall be distributed as specified in the SPMPI. The Resolved Problem Reported Information should be made available to the Activity Group or to the external source that reported the problem.

The Report Log should be updated to reflect the corrective action taken.

A.4.3.3.3 Output Information

Output Information	Destination	
	Activity Group	Activity
Maintenance Recommendations	External	—
	Project Initiation	Create SLCP (A.1.1.1)
	Concept Exploration	Identify Ideas or Needs (A.2.1.1)
Resolved Problem Reported Information	External	—
	Creating Activity Group	Creating Activity
	Project Monitoring and Control	Collect and Analyze Metric Data (A.1.3.5)
	Evaluation	Conduct Reviews (A.5.1.1)
		Create Test Data (A.5.1.5)
		Report Evaluation Results (A.5.1.7)
Updated Report Log	Project Monitoring and Control	Collect and Analyze Metric Data (A.1.3.5)

A.4.4 Retirement Activities

The Retirement Activity Group involves the removal of an existing system from its active support or use, either by ceasing its operation or support, or by replacing it with a new system or an upgraded version of the existing system.

Retirement Activities are

a)   A.4.4.1, Notify User
b)   A.4.4.2, Conduct Parallel Operations (If Applicable)
c)   A.4.4.3, Retire System

A.4.4.1 Notify User

A.4.4.1.1 Input Information

Input Information	Source	
	Activity Group	Activity
Retirement Planned Information	Project Planning	Plan Project Management (A.1.2.7)

A.4.4.1.2 Description

This Activity shall be the formal notification to any user (including both internal and external customers) of an operating software system that is to be removed from active support or use. This notification can take any of several forms, as appropriate for the individual environment. It is important that all users of the outgoing system are made aware that it will become unsupported. The actual dates of the removal of support are to be clearly specified and must allow time for current users to make whatever arrangements are necessary to respond to this notification. Included in the user notification should be one or more of the following:

a)   A description of the replacement system, including its date of availability
b)   A statement as to why the system is not being supported
c)   A description of possible other support

Prior to the distribution of the Official Notification, Activity A.5.3.1, Implement Documentation, shall be invoked.

A.4.4.1.3 Output Information

Output Information	Destination	
	Activity Group	Activity
Official Notification	External	—
	Project Monitoring and Control	Retain Records (A.1.3.4)

A.4.4.2 Conduct Parallel Operations (If Applicable)

A.4.4.2.1 Input Information

Input Information	Source	
	Activity Group	Activity
Transition Planned Information (for the replacing system)	External	—
Retirement Planned Information	Project Planning	Plan Project Management (A.1.2.7)
Installed Software System	Installation	Accept Software in Operational Environment (A.4.1.3)

A.4.4.2.2 Description

If the outgoing system is being replaced by a new system, this Activity may apply. This Activity shall involve a period of dual operation that utilizes the retiring system for official results, while completing the preparation of the new system for formal operation. It is a period of user training on the new system and validation of the new system. The Retirement Planned Information, as well as the Transition Planned Information, can be used to provide information to conduct parallel operations for the replacing system.

Prior to the distribution of the Parallel Operations Log, the following Activities shall be invoked:

a)   A.5.1.1, Conduct Reviews
b)   A.5.2.2, Perform Configuration Control
c)   A.5.4.1, Develop Training Materials

A.4.4.2.3 Output Information

Output Information	Destination	
	Activity Group	Activity
Parallel Operations Log	Project Monitoring and Control	Retain Records (A.1.3.4)

A.4.4.3 Retire System

A.4.4.3.1 Input Information

Input Information	Source	
	Activity Group	Activity
Retirement Planned Information	Project Planning	Plan Project Management (A.1.2.7)

A.4.4.3.2 Description

This Activity shall consist of the actual removal and archiving of the retiring system from regular usage according to the Retirement Planned Information. It could be spread over a period of time and take the form of a phased removal, or it could be the simple removal of the entire system from the active software library. Prior to retirement, users shall be notified of the event. Any preparations for the use of a replacement system should have been completed. The Post-Operation Review Reported Information is generated at this time. The Retire System Activity shall be documented in an Archive Reported Information.

Prior to the distribution of the Post-Operation Review Reported Information or Archive Reported Information, the following Activities shall be invoked:

a) A.5.1.1, Conduct Reviews
b) A.5.2.2, Perform Configuration Control
c) A.5.3.1, Implement Documentation

A.4.4.3.3 Output Information

Output Information	Destination	
	Activity Group	Activity
Archive Reported Information	External	—
Post-Operation Review Reported Information	External	—
	Project Monitoring and Control	Identify SLCP Improvement Needs (A.1.3.3)
		Retain Records (A.1.3.4)
	Maintenance	Identify Software Improvement Needs (A.4.3.1)

A.5 Integral Activity Groups

These are the Activities that are needed to successfully complete project Activities. These Activities are utilized to ensure the completion and quality of project functions.

A.5.1 Evaluation Activities

Evaluation Activities are those Activities performed during the SLCP that are designed to uncover defects in the product or the processes that are used to develop the product. This includes review and audit activities, traceability analysis, test preparation and execution, and the reporting of the results of all the Evaluation Activities.

Because exacting details of these Evaluation Activities can be found in other IEEE software standards, many of the traditional evaluation functions of software development are not specifically called out in this standard. They are placed into more generic groupings. For example, performing in-process reviews, process improvement reviews, etc., are grouped under the generic Activity of "Conduct Reviews." This clause also discusses other topics such as traceability, testing, auditing, and evaluation reporting.

Each Evaluation Activity needs to be applied to each of its Instances in the SLCP. Consider, for example, an SLCP that has six phases, with a requirement for an in-process review at the end of each phase. The "Conduct Reviews" Activity would be mapped for each Instance of a completed phase. Figure A.1 depicts this situation.

Evaluation Activities are

a)   A.5.1.1, Conduct Reviews
b)   A.5.1.2, Create Traceability Matrix
c)   A.5.1.3, Conduct Audits
d)   A.5.1.4, Develop Test Procedures
e)   A.5.1.5, Create Test Data
f)   A.5.1.6, Execute Tests
g)   A.5.1.7, Report Evaluation Results

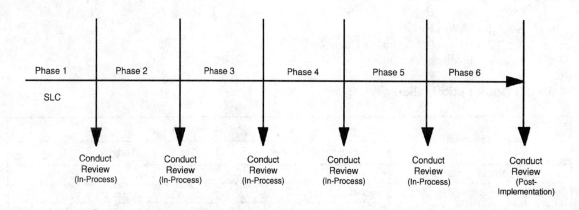

Figure A.1—Mapping reviews

A.5.1.1 Conduct Reviews

A.5.1.1.1 Input Information

Input Information	Source	
	Activity Group	**Activity**
Review Standards and Guidelines	External	—
Item to be Reviewed	Creating Activity Group	Creating Activity
Evaluation Planned Information	Project Planning	Plan Evaluations (A.1.2.1)
SPMPI	Project Planning	Plan Project Management (A.1.2.7)
Imported Software Requirements	Software Importation	Identify Imported Software Requirements (A.2.3.1)
Imported Software Documentation	Software Importation	Import Software (A.2.3.4)
Support Request Log	Operation and Support	Maintain Support Request Log (A.4.2.3)
Resolved Problem Reported Information	Maintenance	Reapply SLC (A.4.3.3)
Traceability Matrix	Evaluation	Create Traceability Matrix (A.5.1.2)
Audit Results Information	Evaluation	Conduct Audits (A.5.1.3)

A.5.1.1.2 Description

Reviews are to be performed throughout the life cycle. They fall into the following four broad categories:

a) *In-Process Reviews*—This type of review shall be held to remove defects from software requirements, preliminary designs, detailed designs, code, and documentation. The reviews are sometimes referred to as peer reviews or technical reviews. They can be formal and structured, following a strict set of rules, roles, and procedures, or informal. They can utilize traceability analysis, walk-through, and inspection techniques. Using these reviews, the functional and performance requirements shall also be reviewed constantly throughout the life cycle to ensure they are being fully addressed in the work products of each phase. Traceability Analysis Reported Information and In-Process Review Results are produced as a result of these various reviews.

b) *Management Reviews*—A review of the products and quality system shall be held at periodic intervals to determine if there is a need to implement corrective action and contingency plans, continue the effort, or cancel the effort. The progress of the effort is reviewed and measured against project milestones that are established in the SPMPI. Each review shall also reconfirm the need for each requirement and its system allocation. If there are changes, System Allocation Change Reported Information shall be generated. Since these reviews are usually held at or near the end of an SLCP phase, they are also referred to as phase-end reviews. Management Status Reported Information is produced after these reviews.

c) *Process Improvement Reviews*—These reviews shall be held to evaluate metrics from the development effort in order to determine if processes need to be modified to prevent or reduce quality related problems in the future of the effort or in new efforts. The reviews can be part of the development schedule or they can be ad-hoc (i.e., driven by the results of one of the other types of reviews). Process Improvement Recommendations are generated as a result of this type of review.

d) Post-Implementation Review—This review shall be held after the completion, or cancellation, of a development effort. It shall compare all planning information with the actual results, and shall use the resulting analysis to determine any improvements needed in such areas as resource utilization, return on investment, quality system, etc. Post-Implementation Review Reported Information is generated at this time.

Further information related to this Activity can be found in IEEE Std 730-1998 [B3], IEEE Std 1012-1998 [B13], IEEE Std 1028-1997 [B17], and IEEE Std 1059-1993 [B23].

Prior to the distribution of the Output Information or Archive Reported Information, Activity A.5.2.2, Perform Configuration Control, may be invoked.

A.5.1.1.3 Output Information

Output Information	Destination	
	Activity Group	**Activity**
In-Process Review Results	Evaluation	Report Evaluation Results (A.5.1.7)
Post-Implementation Review Reported Information	Evaluation	Report Evaluation Results (A.5.1.7)
Process Improvement Recommendations	Evaluation	Report Evaluation Results (A.5.1.7)
Management Status Reported Information	Evaluation	Report Evaluation Results (A.5.1.7)
Traceability Analysis Reported Information	Evaluation	Report Evaluation Results (A.5.1.7)
System Allocation Change Reported Information	Software Configuration Management	Perform Configuration Control (A.5.2.2)

A.5.1.2 Create Traceability Matrix

A.5.1.2.1 Input Information

Input Information	Source	
	Activity Group	**Activity**
Project-Specific Technical Require-ments	External	—
Software Requirements	Requirements	Prioritize and Integrate Software Requirements (A.3.1.3)

A.5.1.2.2 Description

A traceability matrix shall be developed showing, as a minimum, each requirement, the source of the requirement, the life cycle phases that are utilized by this project, and an associated requirement item identi-fication. This shall allow the matrix to be reviewed during each in-process or management review in order to ensure that each requirement is addressed by the output products of each phase. The matrix will allow phase-to-phase and end-to-end review. A reviewer will be able to trace requirements through the development life cycle, forwards or backwards.

Further information related to this Activity can be found in IEEE Std 1012-1998 [B13] and IEEE Std 1059-1993 [B23].

Prior to the distribution of the Traceability Matrix, the following Activities shall be invoked:

a) A.5.1.1, Conduct Reviews
b) A.5.2.2, Perform Configuration Control
c) A.5.3.1, Implement Documentation

A.5.1.2.3 Output Information

Output Information	Destination	
	Activity Group	**Activity**
Traceability Matrix	Evaluation	Conduct Reviews (A.5.1.1)
	Software Configuration Management	Develop Configuration Identification (A.5.2.1)

A.5.1.3 Conduct Audits

A.5.1.3.1 Input Information

Input Information	Source	
	Activity Group	**Activity**
Evaluation Planned Information	Project Planning	Plan Evaluations (A.1.2.1)
SPMPI	Project Planning	Plan Project Management (A.1.2.7)
Auditable Products and Processes	Creating Activity Group	Creating Activity

A.5.1.3.2 Description

Audits shall be performed by independent examiner(s) on software products or processes. The purpose is to assess the compliance of the products or processes with specification requirements, various SLCP plans, standards, the quality system, and any contractual or other agreed-upon requirements. The audits are performed in accordance with the Evaluation Planned Information. Audit results, items of noncompliance, and recommendations are reported in the Audit Results Information. Audits may be conducted in concert with in-process, management, and process improvement reviews.

Two specific types of audits, functional and physical configuration audits, can be performed.

Further information related to this Activity can be found in IEEE Std 730-1998 [B3], IEEE Std 1012-1998 [B13], IEEE Std 1028-1997 [B17], and IEEE Std 1059-1993 [B23].

A.5.1.3.3 Output Information

Output Information	Destination	
	Activity Group	Activity
Audit Results Information	Creating Activity Group	Creating Activity
	Evaluation	Conduct Reviews (A.5.1.1)
		Report Evaluation Results (A.5.1.7)

A.5.1.4 Develop Test Procedures

A.5.1.4.1 Input Information

Input Information	Source	
	Activity Group	Activity
Evaluation Planned Information	Project Planning	Plan Evaluations (A.1.2.1)
Software Requirements	Requirements	Prioritize and Integrate Software Requirements (A.3.1.3)
Software Detailed Design	Design	Perform Detailed Design (A.3.2.4)

A.5.1.4.2 Description

Test Procedures for each level of testing (i.e., unit/module/component, integration, acceptance, regression, and system) shall be developed in order to refine the test approach from the Evaluation Planned Information to the item-specific test procedures used for test execution. The Test Procedures shall define what type of tests are to be conducted (i.e., white box, black box, destructive, noninvasive, etc.), what is to be tested, the data to be used in testing, the expected results, the test environment components, and the procedures to be followed in testing. Information from the Software Requirements, the Software Detailed Design, and the Evaluation Planned Information is used to generate the Test Procedures.

Further information related to this Activity can be found in IEEE Std 829-1998 [B6], IEEE Std 1008-1987 [B12], IEEE Std 1012-1998 [B13], and IEEE Std 1059-1993 [B23].

Prior to the distribution of the Test Procedures, the following Activities shall be invoked:

a) A.5.1.1, Conduct Reviews
b) A.5.2.2, Perform Configuration Control
c) A.5.3.1, Implement Documentation

A.5.1.4.3 Output Information

Output Information	Destination	
	Activity Group	Activity
Test Procedures	Evaluation	Create Test Data (A.5.1.5)
		Execute Tests (A.5.1.6)

A.5.1.5 Create Test Data

A.5.1.5.1 Input Information

Input Information	Source	
	Activity Group	Activity
Evaluation Planned Information	Project Planning	Plan Evaluations (A.1.2.1)
Imported Software Requirements	Software Importation	Identify Imported Software Requirements (A.2.3.1)
Software Requirements	Requirements	Prioritize and Integrate Software Requirements (A.3.1.3)
Software Detailed Design	Design	Perform Detailed Design (A.3.2.4)
Source Code (When Required)	Implementation	Create Executable Code (A.3.3.1)
Data Base (If Available)	Implementation	Create Executable Code (A.3.3.1)
Resolved Problem Reported Information	Maintenance	Reapply SLC (A.4.3.3)
Test Procedures	Evaluation	Develop Test Procedures (A.5.1.4)

A.5.1.5.2 Description

Using the Software Requirements, the Software Detailed Design, and the Source Code (when required), Test Data shall be generated for unit/module/component, integration, acceptance, regression, and system tests. In the case of regression testing, defect scenarios and data from previously failed tests and users in the field are also used and integrated into the regression test data. For each type of test, the Evaluation Planned Information describes the test environment. Test Procedures define the type of test data to be used. To support the testing effort, test Stubs and Drivers may be generated at this time for each item to be tested. The Stubs and Drivers allow the execution of software tests on an individual or integrated basis.

Further information can be found in IEEE Std 829-1998 [B6] and IEEE Std 1008-1987 [B12].

A.5.1.5.3 Output Information

Output Information	Destination	
	Activity Group	Activity
Stubs and Drivers (If Available)	Implementation	Perform Integration (A.3.3.3)
	Evaluation	Execute Tests (A.5.1.6)
Test Data	Evaluation	Execute Tests (A.5.1.6)

A.5.1.6 Execute Tests

A.5.1.6.1 Input Information

Input Information	Source	
	Activity Group	**Activity**
Test Environment Components	External	—
Evaluation Planned Information	Project Planning	Plan Evaluations (A.1.2.1)
Imported Software	Software Importation	Import Software (A.2.3.4)
Executable Code	Implementation	Create Executable Code (A.3.3.1)
Integrated Software	Implementation	Perform Integration (A.3.3.3)
Test Procedures	Evaluation	Develop Test Procedures (A.5.1.4)
Test Data	Evaluation	Create Test Data (A.5.1.5)
Stubs and Drivers (If Available)	Evaluation	Create Test Data (A.5.1.5)

A.5.1.6.2 Description

This Activity shall configure the Test Environment Components as required by the Test Procedures. Tests shall be conducted on Executable Code units/modules/components, Integrated Software, and the full system using Test Data and the associated Test Procedures, in accordance with the Evaluation Planned Information.

This Activity could be iterative, with several Instances performed during the life of the software. Not all Input Information and Output Information are required for a given Iteration. The presence of any Input Information is sufficient as an entry criterion, and the creation of any Output Information is sufficient as an exit criterion.

Based on a comparison of the actual results with the expected results, and according to the pass-fail criteria in the Evaluation Planned Information, a pass-fail determination shall be made and recorded in a test log. Each Anomaly that occurs during test execution that requires further investigation shall be reported. The impact on the validity of the test should also be noted.

Test Summary Reported Information shall summarize the results of a test based on its Test Procedures and test log. Tested Software is that software that has successfully passed all tests at the appropriate level and has met the specified criteria and requirements. Tested Software may then be further integrated with other software or sent for installation.

Further information related to this Activity can be found in IEEE Std 829-1998 [B6] and IEEE Std 1008-1987 [B12].

Prior to the distribution of the Test Summary Reported Information, the following Activities shall be invoked:

a) A.5.1.1, Conduct Reviews
b) A.5.2.2, Perform Configuration Control
c) A.5.3.1, Implement Documentation

A.5.1.6.3 Output Information

Output Information	Destination	
	Activity Group	Activity
Test Summary Reported Information	External	—
	Evaluation	Report Evaluation Results (A.5.1.7)
Tested Software	Implementation	Perform Integration (A.3.3.3)
	Installation	Distribute Software (A.4.1.1)
Anomalies	Maintenance	Implement Problem Reporting Methods (A.4.3.2)
	Evaluation	Report Evaluation Results (A.5.1.7)

A.5.1.7 Report Evaluation Results

A.5.1.7.1 Input Information

Input Information	Source	
	Activity Group	Activity
Basis or Bases for Evaluation	External	—
	Creating Activity Group	Creating Activity
Anomalies	External	—
	Creating Activity Group	Creating Activity
	Evaluation	Execute Tests (A.5.1.6)
SPMPI	Project Planning	Plan Project Management (A.1.2.7)
Resolved Problem Reported Information	Maintenance	Reapply SLC (A.4.3.3)
In-Process Review Results	Evaluation	Conduct Reviews (A.5.1.1)
Post-Implementation Review Reported Information	Evaluation	Conduct Reviews (A.5.1.1)
Process Improvement Recommendations	Evaluation	Conduct Reviews (A.5.1.1)
Management Status Reported Information	Evaluation	Conduct Reviews (A.5.1.1)
Traceability Analysis Reported Information	Evaluation	Conduct Reviews (A.5.1.1)
Audit Results Information	Evaluation	Conduct Audits (A.5.1.3)
Test Summary Reported Information	Evaluation	Execute Tests (A.5.1.6)

A.5.1.7.2 Description

This Activity shall gather the information, recommendations, and data supplied by the Input Information, and shall formulate the results as specified in the SPMPI. The results shall be provided in the Evaluation Reported Information. Anomalies that are identified during the performance of these tasks shall be reported.

Prior to the distribution of the Evaluation Reported Information, Activity A.5.1.1, Conduct Reviews, may be invoked.

A.5.1.7.3 Output Information

Output Information	Destination	
	Activity Group	Activity
Evaluation Reported Information	Creating Activity Group	Creating Activity
	Project Monitoring and Control	Manage Risks (A.1.3.1)
		Manage the Project (A.1.3.2)
		Identify SLCP Improvement Needs (A.1.3.3)
		Collect and Analyze Metric Data (A.1.3.5)
	Installation	Accept Software in Operational Environment (A.4.1.3)
	Maintenance	Identify Software Improvement Needs (A.4.3.1)
		Implement Problem Reporting Method (A.4.3.2)
Anomalies	Maintenance	Implement Problem Reporting Method (A.4.3.2)

A.5.2 Software Configuration Management Activities

Software Configuration Management identifies the items in a software development project and provides both for control of the identified items and for the generation of Status Reported Information for management visibility and accountability throughout the SLC. Items to be managed are those that are defined in the SCMPI. Examples to be considered for inclusion in the SCMPI are code, documentation, plans, and specifications. Configuration audits, if required by the project, should be addressed in the Evaluation Activity Group. The Software Configuration Management approach for a given project should be compatible with the configuration management approach that is being used on associated systems.

Configuration Activities are

a)   A.5.2.1, Develop Configuration Identification
b)   A.5.2.2, Perform Configuration Control
c)   A.5.2.3, Perform Status Accounting

A.5.2.1 Develop Configuration Identification

A.5.2.1.1 Input Information

Input Information	Source	
	Activity Group	Activity
Deliverable List	External	—
SCMPI	Project Planning	Plan Configuration Management (A.1.2.2)
SPMPI	Project Planning	Plan the Project (A.1.2.7)
Traceability Matrix	Evaluation	Create Traceability Matrix (A.5.1.2)

A.5.2.1.2 Description

This Activity shall define the software Configuration Identification including project baseline definition, titling, labeling, and numbering to reflect the structure of the product for tracking. The SCMPI identifies those Configuration Items that are to be addressed by the Configuration Identification. The identification shall support the software throughout the SLC, and shall be documented in the SCMPI. The Configuration Identification shall also define the documentation that is required in order to record the functional and physical characteristics of each Configuration Item.

A series of baselines, based on the Traceability Matrix, shall be established as the product moves from the initial idea to the maintenance phase as required by the SPMPI.

Further information related to this Activity can be found in IEEE Std 828-1998 [B5] and IEEE Std 1028-1997 [B17].

Prior to the distribution of the Configuration Identification, the following Activities shall be invoked:

a) A.5.1.1, Conduct Reviews
b) A.5.2.2, Perform Configuration Control
c) A.5.3.1, Implement Documentation

A.5.2.1.3 Output Information

Output Information	Destination	
	Activity Group	Activity
Configuration Identification	Software Configuration Management	Perform Configuration Control (A.5.2.2)
		Perform Status Accounting (A.5.2.3)

A.5.2.2 Perform Configuration Control

A.5.2.2.1 Input Information

Input Information	Source	
	Activity Group	Activity
Items to be Controlled	Creating Activity Group	Creating Activity
Proposed Change	Creating Activity Group	Creating Activity
SCMPI	Project Planning	Plan Configuration Management (A.1.2.2)
System Allocation Change Reported Information	Evaluation	Conduct Reviews (A.5.1.1)
Configuration Identification	Software Configuration Management	Develop Configuration Identification (A.5.2.1)

A.5.2.2.2 Description

This Activity controls the configuration of products according to the SCMPI and the Configuration Identification. Changes to controlled products shall be tracked to ensure that the configuration of the product is known at all times. All items specified in the SCMPI are subject to this change management discipline.

Changes to Controlled Items shall be allowed only with the approval of the responsible authority. This can result in the establishment of a formal software configuration control board. Controlled Items shall be maintained in a software library.

Further information related to this Activity can be found in IEEE Std 828-1998 [B5] and IEEE Std 1042-1987 [B18].

A.5.2.2.3 Output Information

Output Information	Destination	
	Activity Group	Activity
Controlled Item	Creating Activity Group	Creating Activity
	Maintenance	Implement Problem Reporting Method (A.4.3.2)
Change Status	Software Configuration Management	Perform Status Accounting (A.5.2.3)

A.5.2.3 Perform Status Accounting

A.5.2.3.1 Input Information

Input Information	Source	
	Activity Group	Activity
SCMPI	Project Planning	Plan Configuration Management (A.1.2.2)
Configuration Identification	Software Configuration Management	Develop Configuration Identification (A.5.2.1)
Change Status	Software Configuration Management	Perform Configuration Control (A.5.2.2)

A.5.2.3.2 Description

This Activity shall receive Configuration Identification and Change Status and shall create and update the Status Reported Information to reflect the status and history of Controlled Items. The history of changes to each Controlled Item shall be maintained throughout the SLC as required by the SCMPI.

Status Reported Information may include such data as the number of changes to date for the project, the number of releases, and the latest version and revision identifiers.

Each baseline shall be established as required by the SCMPI, and all subsequent changes shall be tracked relative to it.

Further information related to this Activity can be found in IEEE Std 828-1998 [B5] and IEEE Std 1042-1987 [B18].

Prior to the distribution of the Status Reported Information, the following Activities shall be invoked:

a) A.5.1.1, Conduct Reviews
b) A.5.2.2, Perform Configuration Control

A.5.2.3.3 Output Information

Output Information	Destination	
	Activity Group	Activity
Controlled Item	Creating Activity Group	Creating Activity
Status Reported Information	External	—
	Project Monitoring and Control	Manage the Project (A.1.3.2)

A.5.3 Documentation Development Activities

The Documentation Development Activity Group for software development and usage is the set of Activities that plan, design, implement, edit, produce, distribute, and maintain those documents that are needed by developers and users. The purpose of the Documentation Development Activity Group is to provide timely software documentation to those who need it, based on Input Information from the invoking Activity Groups.

This Activity Group covers both product-oriented and procedure-oriented documentation for internal and external users. Examples of internal users include those who plan, design, implement, or test software. External users can include those who install, operate, apply, or maintain the software.

The Documentation Development Activity Group occurs over various phases of the SLCP, depending on the individual document and the timing of its development. Typically, there will be multiple documents, each at a different stage of development.

Documentation Activities are

a)   A.5.3.1, Implement Documentation
b)   A.5.3.2, Produce and Distribute Documentation

A.5.3.1 Implement Documentation

A.5.3.1.1 Input Information

Input Information	Source	
	Activity group	Activity
Input Information for Document	Creating Activity Group	Creating Activity
Documentation Planned Information	Project Planning	Plan Documentation (A.1.2.5)
SPMPI	Project Planning	Plan Project Management (A.1.2.7)
Imported Software Documentation	Software Importation	Import Software (A.2.3.4)

A.5.3.1.2 Description

This Activity includes the design, preparation, and maintenance of documentation. Those documents that are identified in the Documentation Planned Information shall be formulated in terms of audience, approach, content, structure, and graphics. Arrangements may be made with word or text processing and graphics facilities for their support.

Input Information shall be used to produce the document, including any related graphics.

Following a documentation review, any changes shall be incorporated to produce a technically correct document. Organizational format, style, and production rules shall be applied to produce a final document.

Prior to the distribution of the Document, the following Activities should be invoked:

a)   A.5.1.1, Conduct Reviews
b)   A.5.2.2, Perform Configuration Control

A.5.3.1.3 Output Information

Output Information	Destination	
	Activity Group	Activity
Document	Documentation Development	Produce and Distribute Documentation (A.5.3.2)

A.5.3.2 Produce and Distribute Documentation

A.5.3.2.1 Input Information

Input Information	Source	
	Activity Group	Activity
Documentation Planned Information	Project Planning	Plan Documentation (A.1.2.5)
Document	Documentation Development	Implement Documentation (A.5.3.1)

A.5.3.2.2 Description

This Activity shall provide the intended audience with the needed information that is collected in the document, as specified in the Documentation Planned Information. Document production and distribution can involve electronic file management, paper document reproduction and distribution, or other media handling techniques.

A.5.3.2.3 Output Information

Output Information	Destination	
	Activity Group	Activity
Published Document	External	—
	Creating Activity Group	Creating Activity
	Project Monitoring and Control	Retain Records (A.1.3.4)

A.5.4 Training Activities

The development of quality software products is largely dependent upon knowledgeable and skilled people. These include the developer's technical staff and management. Customer personnel may also need to be trained to install, operate, and maintain the software. It is essential that the Training Planned Information be completed early in the SLC, prior to the time when personnel would be expected to apply required expertise to the project. Plans for customer training should be prepared and reviewed with the customer.

Training Activities are

a) A.5.4.1, Develop Training Materials
b) A.5.4.2, Validate the Training Program
c) A.5.4.3, Implement the Training Program

A.5.4.1 Develop Training Materials

A.5.4.1.1 Input Information

Input Information	Source	
	Activity Group	Activity
Applicable Information	External	—
	Creating Activity Group	Creating Activity
Training Planned Information	Project Planning	Plan Training (A.1.2.6)
SPMPI	Project Planning	Plan Project Management (A.1.2.7)
Imported Software Documentation	Software Importation	Import Software (A.2.3.4)
Software Detailed Design	Design	Perform Detailed Design (A.3.2.4)

A.5.4.1.2 Description

This Activity shall consist of the identification and review of all available materials and Input Information that is pertinent to the training objectives. Included in the Develop Training Materials Activity shall be the development of the substance of the training, training manual, and materials that are to be used in presenting the training, such as outlines, text, exercises, case studies, visuals, and models. Instructors shall review the training materials and develop the actual presentations that are to be based on the developed materials. Instructors are expected to be competent in up-to-date educational methods and effective presentation techniques.

Prior to the distribution of the Training Manual and Training Materials, the following Activities shall be invoked:

a)   A.5.1.1, Conduct Reviews
b)   A.5.3.1, Implement Documentation

Activity A.5.2.2, Perform Configuration Control, should also be invoked.

A.5.4.1.3 Output Information

Output Information	Destination	
	Activity Group	Activity
Training Manual	Training	Validate the Training Program (A.5.4.2)
Training Materials	Training	Validate the Training Program (A.5.4.2)
Prepared Presentations	Training	Validate the Training Program (A.5.4.2)

A.5.4.2 Validate the Training Program

A.5.4.2.1 Input Information

Input Information	Source	
	Activity Group	Activity
Training Planned Information	Project Planning	Plan Training (A.1.2.6)
Training Manual	Training	Develop Training Materials (A.5.4.1)
Training Materials	Training	Develop Training Materials (A.5.4.1)
Prepared Presentations	Training	Develop Training Materials (A.5.4.1)

A.5.4.2.2 Description

This Activity shall consist of competent instructors who present the training to a class of evaluators using the preliminary training manual and materials. The evaluators shall assess the training presentation and materials in detail. The purpose is to evaluate the effectiveness of the delivery and to validate the material presented. Lessons learned in the test of the training program shall be incorporated into the material prior to a general offering. All training manuals and materials shall be evaluated and, if necessary, updated at this time.

Prior to the distribution of the Updated Training Manuals and Materials, the following Activities shall be invoked:

a)   A.5.1.1, Conduct Reviews
b)   A.5.3.1, Implement Documentation

Activity A.5.2.2, Perform Configuration Control, should be also invoked.

A.5.4.2.3 Output Information

Output Information	Destination	
	Activity Group	Activity
Training Feedback	Project Planning	Plan Training (A.1.2.6)
Updated Training Manual	Training	Implement the Training Program (A.5.4.3)
Updated Training Materials	Training	Implement the Training Program (A.5.4.3)

A.5.4.3 Implement the Training Program

A.5.4.3.1 Input Information

Input Information	Source	
	Activity Group	Activity
Staff Participants	External	—
Students	External	—
Training Planned Information	Project Planning	Plan Training (A.1.2.6)
Updated Training Manual	Training	Validate the Training Program (A.5.4.2)
Updated Training Materials	Training	Validate the Training Program (A.5.4.2)

A.5.4.3.2 Description

This Activity shall ensure the provision of all necessary materials, the arrangement of the locations and facilities for training, and the delivery of the training. Included in this Activity shall be the enrolling of students and the monitoring of the course effectiveness.

Lessons learned and the information that is needed for updating the materials for the next training cycle shall be fed back into the Training Activity Group.

A.5.4.3.3 Output Information

Output Information	Destination	
	Activity Group	Activity
Updated Skills Inventory	External	—
Trained Personnel	Creating Activity Group	Creating Activity
Training Feedback	Project Planning	Plan Training (A.1.2.6)

Annex B

(informative)

Mapping example

This annex provides an example of mapping the Activities of this standard onto a selected SLCM.

The purpose of this example is to show the mapping process without constraining the reader to any specific methodologies or tools.

For purposes of illustration, an oversimplified, four-phase waterfall SLCM has been selected. It is understood that any SLCM could be interactive and iterative in the real world, which would cause the expansion of the mapped SLC to reflect multiple Instances of Activities.

At each step, constraints should be identified that impact the development of the SLCP. In the example that follows, common constraints require consideration while verifying information flows, mapping information into deliverable documents, and adding actual dates and times to the SLCP.

Once the SLCP is in place, the experience of the project might dictate necessary modifications to the SLCP. In this case, some or all of steps 1–8 may need to be repeated.

B.1 Step 1: Select SLCM

This first step, as specified by Clause 5 of this standard, is to identify the SLCM to which the Activities will be mapped. This step could mean that the whole process of locating, evaluating, selecting, and acquiring an SLCM shall be performed (see 5.1). For this example, a four-phase waterfall SLCM is selected. During this step, the process architect reviews the SLCM to ensure that it is appropriate for the specific project.

I. Project Initiation/Concept Development

I.A　　Δ
　　　　Project Kick-off
I.B　　Δ_____Δ
　　　　Project Plan
I.C　　Δ_____Δ
　　　　System Level Concepts
I.D　　　　Δ_____Δ
　　　　　User (System) Requirements
I.E　　　　　　Δ_____Δ
　　　　　　System Design (Hardware/Software Allocation)

II. Definition and Design

II.A　　　　　　Δ_____Δ
　　　　　　　Define Software Requirements
II.B　　　　　　　Δ_____Δ
　　　　　　　Define Software Design
II.C　　　　　　　　Δ_____Δ
　　　　　　　　Design User Interface
II.D　　　　　　Δ_____Δ
　　　　　　　Plan Testing

III. System Development

III.A
             Δ_____Δ
              Coding

III.B
         Δ_____Δ
          Test Data Creation

III.C
            Δ_____Δ
             Integration

III.D
             Δ_____Δ
              Testing
             Δ
          Test Readiness Review (TRR)

III.E
        Δ_____Δ
        Preparation of User Documentation

III.F
                  Δ
                Ship Software

    Time ============>

IV. Installation and Operation

IV.A Δ__Δ
    Install Software

IV.B Δ___Δ
    Acceptance Testing

IV.C Δ_____Δ
    User Training

IV.D Δ_____...Δ
    Operation

IV.E Δ_____...Δ
    Maintenance

IV.F Δ_____...Δ
    Support

IV.G   Δ
       Abandon
    Time ============>

B.2 Step 2: Compare Activities to SLC

Having selected an SLCM, perform a detailed mapping of the Activities of this standard against the SLCM. This involves the matching of the Activities against the requirements of the SLCM. This step provides a checklist to ensure that all Activities are mapped and that all SLCM requirements are covered by one or more Activities. Activities that are not mapped will be noted in step 3 (Clause B.3).

NOTE—The Define Software Requirements (II.A) sub-phase, within the Definition and Design phase, will be used to illustrate mapping details.

For this example, the following matrix can be generated:

	I.A	I.B	I.C	I.D	I.E	II.A	II.B	II.C	II.D	III.A	III.B	III.C	III.D	III.E	III.F	IV.A	IV.B	IV.C	IV.D	IV.E	IV.F	IV.G
A.1.1.1	X																					
A.1.1.2		X																				
A.1.1.3		X																				
A.1.1.4		X					X															
A.1.2.1		X																				
A.1.2.2		X																				
A.1.2.3																						
A.1.2.4		X																				
A.1.2.5		X																				
A.1.2.6		X																				
A.1.2.7		X																				
A.1.2.8		X																				
A.1.3.1		X	X	X	X	X	X	X	X	X	X	X	X	X	X	X	X	X	X	X	X	X
A.1.3.2	X	X	X	X	X	X	X	X	X	X	X	X	X	X	X	X	X	X	X	X	X	X
A.1.3.3		X	X	X	X	X	X	X	X	X	X	X	X	X		X	X	X	X	X	X	
A.1.3.4	X	X	X	X	X	X	X	X	X	X	X	X	X	X	X	X	X	X	X	X	X	X
A.1.3.5		X	X	X	X	X	X	X	X	X	X	X	X	X		X	X	X	X	X	X	
A.2.1.1	X		X	X	X																	
A.2.1.2	X		X	X	X																	
A.2.1.3			X	X	X																	
A.2.1.4			X	X	X																	
A.2.2.1			X	X																		
A.2.2.2			X	X																		
A.2.2.3			X																			
A.2.3.1				X		X																
A.2.3.2																						
A.2.3.3																						
A.2.3.4																						
A.3.1.1						X																
A.3.1.2						X																
A.3.1.3						X																
A.3.2.1							X															
A.3.2.2																						
A.3.2.3							X	X														
A.3.2.4							X															
A.3.3.1									X													
A.3.3.2														X								

	I.A	I.B	I.C	I.D	I.E	II.A	II.B	II.C	II.D	III.A	III.B	III.C	III.D	III.E	III.F	IV.A	IV.B	IV.C	IV.D	IV.E	IV.F	IV.G
A.3.3.3												X										
A.4.1.1															X							
A.4.1.2																X						
A.4.1.3																	X					
A.4.2.1																			X			
A.4.2.2																				X	X	
A.4.2.3																					X	
A.4.3.1																			X	X	X	
A.4.3.2		X	X	X	X	X	X	X	X	X	X	X	X	X	X	X	X	X	X	X	X	
A.4.3.3																					X	
A.4.4.1																			X		X	X
A.4.4.2																			X		X	X
A.4.4.3																						X
A.5.1.1		X	X	X	X	X								X								
A.5.1.2			X	X	X	X	X	X	X													
A.5.1.3				X											X						X	
A.5.1.4							X				X						X					
A.5.1.5							X				X							X				
A.5.1.6													X				X					
A.5.1.7					X			X			X		X		X		X				X	
A.5.2.1		X			X						X											
A.5.2.2	X	X	X	X	X	X	X	X	X	X	X	X	X	X	X	X	X	X	X	X	X	X
A.5.2.3	X	X	X	X	X	X	X	X	X	X	X	X	X	X	X	X	X	X	X	X	X	
A.5.3.1	X	X	X	X	X	X	X	X						X								
A.5.3.2														X								
A.5.4.1																						
A.5.4.2														X				X				
A.5.4.3														X				X				

B.3 Step 3: Develop and justify List of Activities Not Used

The following Activities are not used:

a) A.1.2.3—No system transition is needed or planned for.

b) A.2.3.2, A.2.3.3, and A.2.3.4—No imported software will be used.

c) A.3.2.2—No data base design will be needed. The existing structure will be utilized.

B.4 Step 4: List Activities and Invocations

List each Activity and Invocation for all the pieces of the SLCM. This listing will be used in the next step to develop the initial ordering. In the example, the Activities and Invocations that are contained in sub-phase II.A are listed in numerical order.

The initial listing would look like this:

II. Definition and Design
II.A   Δ_____Δ

     Define Software Requirements
     A.1.3.1
       A.5.1.1
       A.5.1.3
       A.5.2.2
       A.5.3.1
     A.1.3.2
       A.5.1.1
     A.1.3.3
     A.1.3.4
     A.1.3.5
       A.5.1.1
       A.5.2.2
       A.5.3.1
     A.2.3.1
       A.5.1.1
       A.5.1.6
     A.3.1.1
       A.5.1.1
       A.5.2.2
       A.5.3.1
     A.3.1.2
       A.5.1.1
       A.5.2.2
       A.5.3.1
     A.3.1.3
       A.5.1.1
       A.5.2.2
       A.5.3.1
     A.4.3.2
       A.5.2.2

B.5 Step 5: Place Activities in executable sequence

This step further organizes the Activities within the SLCM sub-phases to refine executable order relationships.

The result, for sub-phase II.A, would look like this:

II. Definition and Design
II.A Δ_____Δ

Define Software Requirements
A.3.1.1
  A.5.3.1
  A.5.2.2
  A.5.1.1
A.3.1.2
   A.5.3.1
   A.5.2.2
   A.5.1.1
A.2.3.1
   A.5.1.1
   A.5.1.6
A.3.1.3
   A.5.3.1
   A.5.2.2
   A.5.1.1
A.4.3.2
  A.5.2.2
A.1.3.1
   A.5.3.1
   A.5.2.2
   A.5.1.1
   A.5.1.3
A.1.3.2
   A.5.1.1
A.1.3.5
    A.5.3.1
    A.5.2.2
    A.5.1.1
A.1.3.3
A.1.3.4

B.6 Step 6: Verify information flow

The Input and Output Information tables in this standard specify the information that is to be used and generated by each Activity. This step verifies that the information flow into and out of the Activities will support the relative order into which they have been mapped. While it is unlikely that this will cause a major rearrangement or modification of the mapping from step 5 (Clause B.5), it is a necessary check to be sure that all information will be available to the Activities that need it, when they need it.

A check of the information flow for this example could result in remapping. In this example, A.2.3.1, Identify Imported Software Requirements, was moved after A.3.1.3, Prioritize and Integrate Software Requirements, as A.2.3.1 needs the output of A.3.1.3. Additionally, A.1.3.5, Collect and Analyze Metric Data, was moved before A.1.3.1, Manage Risks, as A.1.3.1 uses the output of A.1.3.5.

II.   **Definition and Design**
II.A   Δ_____Δ
                              Define Software Requirements
                    A.3.1.1
                        A.5.3.1
                        A.5.2.2
                        A.5.1.1
                    A.3.1.2
                        A.5.3.1
                        A.5.2.2
                        A.5.1.1
                    A.2.3.1
                        A.5.1.1
                        A.5.1.6
                    A.3.1.3
                        A.5.3.1
                        A.5.2.2
                        A.5.1.1
                A.4.3.2
                    A.5.2.2
                    A.1.3.1
                        A.5.3.1
                        A.5.2.2
                        A.5.1.1
                        A.5.1.3
                    A.1.3.2
                        A.5.1.1
                    A.1.3.5
                        A.5.3.1
                        A.5.2.2
                        A.5.1.1
                    A.1.3.3
                    A.1.3.4

B.7 Step 7: Map information into deliverable documents

Each SLCM requires, and defines the formatted content of, its own set of output products. These products are, for the most part, the specific documents that the SLCM delivers. Note that the term "document" does not imply any particular medium. This step compares the Output Information that is generated by each Activity with the SLCM-required document(s) into which it must go.

Once again, the order of the mapping, this time from step 6 (Clause B.6), might have to be modified. If a particular document, as specified by the selected SLCM, is to be created at a particular point in the development schedule, all of the Activities that contribute information to be recorded in that document must have had an opportunity to generate it.

For this project, the mapping of deliverable documents will occur as follows:

a) A.3.1.1, A.3.1.2, A.3.1.3, A.1.4.1, and A.5.1.2 will be delivered as a Software Requirements Specification.
b) A.1.3.1, A.1.3.2, A.1.3.5, and A.1.3.3 will be delivered as a Project Management Report.
c) A.4.3.2 will be delivered as Problem Reports.
d) No other documentation will be generated.

The information was checked in the mapping of sub-phase II.A to ensure that all required information from it would be available for the SLCM-defined documentation that was detailed in the previous paragraph. No changes to sub-phase II.A were necessary.

B.8 Step 8: Add OPAs

OPAs are now added to the fully mapped Activities and deliverable documents at the appropriate points in the SLCP. Adding the OPAs expands the SLCP beyond the minimum set of Activities that are specified in the standard, and produces a fully robust SLCP for the development project. For this example, the project will use organizational standards for the content and format of the Software Requirements Specification and Project Management Report. The methodology and tools that will be used to create the Software Requirements Specification are also decided.

B.9 Step 9: Add project planning information

Throughout these steps, the project manager could be adding planning specifics to the evolving SLCP. Additions are normally identified during the continuing audit and review process.

Annex C

(informative)

Information mapping template

This annex provides an information mapping template that is designed to assist project managers in identifying project-critical deliverables and ensuring their completion as needed.

This template can be used to assist in the project-specific mapping of information into the required project documentation.

Table C.1—Information mapping template

Activity Group or Activity name	Clause	Output Information	Mapped deliverables
PROJECT MANAGEMENT ACTIVITIES	**A.1.1**		
Project Initiation Activities	**A.1.1**		
Create SLCP	A.1.1.1	SLCP	
		List of Activities Not Used	
Perform Estimation	A.1.1.2	Project Estimates	
		Estimation Assumptions	
Allocate Project Resources	A.1.1.3	Resource Allocations	
Define Metrics	A.1.1.4	Defined Metrics	
		Collection and Analysis Methods	
Project Planning Activities	**A.1.2**		
Plan Evaluations	A.1.2.1	Evaluation Planned Information	
Plan Configuration Management	A.1.2.2	SCMPI	
Plan System Transition (If Applicable)	A.1.2.3	Transition Planned Information	
		Transition Impact Statement	
Plan Installation	A.1.2.4	Software Installation Planned Information	
Plan Documentation	A.1.2.5	Documentation Planned Information	
Plan Training	A.1.2.6	Training Planned Information	
Plan Project Management	A.1.2.7	PR&RPI	
		Retirement Planned Information	
		SPMPI	
		Support Planned Information	
Plan Integration	A.1.2.8	Integration Planned Information	
Project Monitoring and Control Activities	**A.1.3**		
Manage Risks	A.1.3.1	Risk Management Reported Information	
Manage the Project	A.1.3.2	Project Management Reported Information	
		Anomalies	
Identify SLCP Improvement Needs	A.1.3.3	Environment Improvement Needs	
Retain Records	A.1.3.4	Historical Project Records	
Collect and Analyze Metric Data	A.1.3.5	Analysis Reported Information	

Table C.1—Information mapping template *(continued)*

Activity Group or Activity name	Clause	Output Information	Mapped deliverables
PRE-DEVELOPMENT ACTIVITY GROUPS	**A.2**		
Concept Exploration Activities	**A.2.1**		
Identify Ideas or Needs	A.2.1.1	Preliminary Statement of Need	
Formulate Potential Approaches	A.2.1.2	Constraints and Benefits	
		Potential Approaches	
Conduct Feasibility Studies	A.2.1.3	Recommendations	
Refine and Finalize the Idea or Need	A.2.1.4	Statement of Need	
System Allocation Activities	**A.2.2**		
Analyze Functions	A.2.2.1	Functional Description of the System	
Develop System Architecture	A.2.2.2	System Architecture	
Decompose System Requirements	A.2.2.3	System Functional Hardware Requirements (If Applicable)	
		System Functional Software Requirements	
		System Interface Requirements (If Applicable)	
Software Importation Activities	**A.2.3**		
Identify Imported Software Requirements	A.2.3.1	Imported Software Requirements	
Evaluate Software Import Sources (If Applicable)	A.2.3.2	Selected Software Import Source	
		Candidate Software Import Methods	
Define Software Import Method (If Applicable)	A.2.3.3	Selected Software Import Method	
Import Software (If Applicable)	A.2.3.4	Imported Software	
		Imported Software Documentation	
DEVELOPMENT ACTIVITY GROUPS	**A.3**		
Requirements Activities	**A.3.1**		
Define and Develop Software Requirements	A.3.1.1	Preliminary Software Requirements	
		Installation Requirements	
Define Interface Requirements	A.3.1.2	Software Interface Requirements	
Prioritize and Integrate Software Requirements	A.3.1.3	Software Requirements	
Design	**A.3.2**		
Perform Architectural Design	A.3.2.1	Software Architectural Design	
Design Data Base (If Applicable)	A.3.2.2	Data Base Design	
Design Interfaces	A.3.2.3	Interface Design	
Perform Detailed Design	A.3.2.4	Software Detailed Design	
Implementation Activities	**A.3.3**		
Create Executable Code	A.3.3.1	Data Base (If Applicable)	
		Source Code	
		Executable Code	
		Source Code (If Required)	
Create Operating Documentation	A.3.3.2	Operating Documentation	
Perform Integration	A.3.3.3	Integrated Software	

Table C.1—Information mapping template *(continued)*

Activity Group or Activity name	Clause	Output Information	Mapped deliverables
POST-DEVELOPMENT ACTIVITY GROUPS	**A.4**		
Installation Activities	**A.4.1**		
Distribute Software	A.4.1.1	Packaged Installation Planned Information	
		Packaged Software	
		Packaged Operating Documentation	
Install Software	A.4.1.2	Installation Reported Information	
		Installed Software	
Accept Software in Operational Environment	A.4.1.3	Customer Acceptance	
		Installed Software System	
Operation and Support Activities	**A.4.2**		
Operate the System	A.4.2.1	Operation Logs	
		Anomalies	
Provide Technical Assistance and Consulting	A.4.2.2	Support Response	
Maintain Support Request Log	A.4.2.3	Anomalies	
		Support Request Log	
Maintenance Activities	**A.4.3**		
Identify Software Improvement Needs	A.4.3.1	Software Improvement Recommendations	
Implement Problem Reporting Method	A.4.3.2	Out of Scope Anomalies	
		Report Log	
		Enhancement Problem Reported Information	
		Correction Problem Reported Information	
Reapply SLC	A.4.3.3	Maintenance Recommendations	
		Resolved Problem Reported Information	
		Updated Report Log	
Retirement Activities	**A.4.4**		
Notify User	A.4.4.1	Official Notification	
Conduct Parallel Operations (If Applicable)	A.4.4.2	Parallel Operations Log	
Retire System	A.4.4.3	Archive Reported Information	
		Post-Operation Review Reported Information	

Table C.1—Information mapping template *(continued)*

Activity Group or Activity name	Clause	Output Information	Mapped deliverables
INTEGRAL ACTIVITY GROUPS	**A.5**		
Evaluation Activities	**A.5.1**		
Conduct Reviews	A.5.1.1	In-Process Review Results	
		Post-Implementation Review Reported Information	
		Process Improvement Recommendations	
		Management Status Reported Information	
		System Allocation Change Reported Information	
Create Traceability Matrix	A.5.1.2	Traceability Matrix	
Conduct Audits	A.5.1.3	Audit Results Information	
Develop Test Procedures	A.5.1.4	Test Procedures	
Create Test Data	A.5.1.5	Stubs and Drivers (If Applicable)	
		Test Data	
Execute Tests	A.5.1.6	Test Summary Reported Information	
		Tested Software	
		Anomalies	
Report Evaluation Results	A.5.1.7	Evaluation Reported Information	
		Anomalies	
Software Configuration Management Activities	**A.5.2**		
Develop Configuration Identification	A.5.2.1	Configuration Identification	
Perform Configuration Control	A.5.2.2	Change Status	
		Controlled Item	
Perform Status Accounting	A.5.2.3	Status Reported Information	
Documentation Development Activities	**A.5.3**		
Implement Documentation	A.5.3.1	Document	
Produce and Distribute Documentation	A.5.3.2	Published Document	
Training Activities	**A.5.4**		
Develop Training Materials	A.5.4.1	Training Manual	
		Training Materials	
		Prepared Presentations	
Validate the Training Program	A.5.4.2	Training Feedback	
		Updated Training Manual	
		Updated Training Materials	
Implement the Training Program	A.5.4.3	Updated Skills Inventory	
		Trained Personnel	
		Training Feedback	

Annex D

(informative)

Bibliography

This Informative Annex provides a listing of potentially helpful software engineering standards. The standards listed below, and any subsequent standards should be consulted when using this document. Compliance with this standard, however, neither requires nor implies compliance with the listed standards.

[B1] EIA/IEEE J-STD-016-1995, EIA/IEEE Interim Standard for Information Technology—Software Life Cycle Processes—Software Development: Acquirer–Supplier Agreement.[5]

[B2] IEEE Std 610.12-1990, IEEE Standard Glossary of Software Engineering Terminology.[6]

[B3] IEEE Std 730-1998, IEEE Standard for Software Quality Assurance Plans.

[B4] IEEE Std 730.1-1995, IEEE Guide for Software Quality Assurance Planning.

[B5] IEEE Std 828-1998, IEEE Standard for Software Configuration Management Plans.

[B6] IEEE Std 829-1998, IEEE Standard for Software Test Documentation.

[B7] IEEE Std 830-1998, IEEE Recommended Practice for Software Requirements Specifications.

[B8] IEEE Std 982.1-1988, IEEE Standard Dictionary of Measures to Procedure Reliable Software.

[B9] IEEE Std 982.2-1988, IEEE Guide for the Use of IEEE Standard Dictionary of Measures to Procedure Reliable Software.

[B10] IEEE Std 990-1987 (Reaff 1992), IEEE Recommended Practice for Ada as a Program Design Language.

[B11] IEEE Std 1002-1987 (Reaff 1992), IEEE Standard Taxonomy for Software Engineering Standards.

[B12] IEEE Std 1008-1987 (Reaff 1993), IEEE Standard for Software Unit Testing.

[B13] IEEE Std 1012-1998, IEEE Standard for Software Verification and Validation.

[B14] IEEE Std 1012a-1998, IEEE Standard for Software Verification and Validation: Content Map to IEEE/EIA 12207.1-1997.

[B15] IEEE Std 1016-1998, IEEE Recommended Practice for Software Design Descriptions.

[B16] IEEE Std 1016.1-1993, IEEE Guide to Software Design Descriptions.

[B17] IEEE Std 1028-1997, IEEE Standard for Software Reviews.

[B18] IEEE Std 1042-1987 (Reaff 1993), IEEE Guide to Software Configuration Management.

---

[5]This document is available from the Institute of Electrical and Electronics Engineers, 445 Hoes Lane, P.O. Box 1331, Piscataway, NJ 08855-1331, USA (http://www.standards.ieee.org/).
[6]IEEE publications are available from the Institute of Electrical and Electronics Engineers, 445 Hoes Lane, P.O. Box 1331, Piscataway, NJ 08855-1331, USA (http://www.standards.ieee.org/).

[B19] IEEE Std 1044-1993, IEEE Standard for Classification of Software Anomalies.

[B20] IEEE Std 1044.1-1995, IEEE Guide to Classification for Software Anomalies

[B21] IEEE Std 1045-1992, IEEE Standard for Software Productivity Metrics.

[B22] IEEE Std 1058-1998, IEEE Standard for Software Project Management Plans.

[B23] IEEE Std 1059-1993, IEEE Guide for Software Verification and Validation Plans.

[B24] IEEE Std 1061-1998, IEEE Standard for a Software Quality Metrics Methodology.

[B25] IEEE Std 1062, 1998 Edition, IEEE Recommended Practice for Software Acquisition.

[B26] IEEE Std 1063-1987 (Reaff 1993), IEEE Standard for Software User Documentation.

[B27] IEEE Std 1175-1991, IEEE Standard Reference Model for Computing System Tool Interconnections.

[B28] IEEE Std 1209-1992, IEEE Recommended Practice for the Evaluation and Selection of CASE Tools.

[B29] IEEE Std 1219-1998, IEEE Standard for Software Maintenance.

[B30] IEEE Std 1220-1998, IEEE Standard for Application and Management of the Systems Engineering Process.

[B31] IEEE Std 1228-1994, IEEE Standard for Software Safety Plans.

[B32] IEEE Std 1233, 1998 Edition, IEEE Guide for Developing System Requirements Specifications.

[B33] IEEE Std 1298-1992 (AS 3563.1-1991), IEEE Standard for Software Quality Management System, Part 1: Requirements.

[B34] IEEE Std 1348-1995, IEEE Recommended Practice for the Adoption of Computer-Aided Software Engineering (CASE) Tools.

[B35] IEEE/EIA 12207.0-1996, IEEE/EIA Standard—Industry Implementation of ISO/IEC 12207: 1995, Standard for Information Technology—Software life cycle processes.

[B36] IEEE/EIA 12207.1-1997, IEEE/EIA Guide for Information Technology--Software life cycle processes—Life cycle data.

[B37] IEEE/EIA 12207.2-1997, IEEE/EIA Guide for Information Technology—Software life cycle processes—Implementation considerations.

[B38] ISO 9001 : 1994, Quality systems — Model for quality assurance in design, development, production, installation and servicing.[7]

[B39] ISO 9003 : 1994, Quality systems — Model for quality assurance in final inspection and test.

---

[7]ISO publications are available from the ISO Central Secretariat, Case Postale 56, 1 rue de Varembé, CH-1211, Genève 20, Switzer-land/Suisse. ISO publications are also available in the United States from the Sales Department, American National Standards Institute, 11 West 42nd Street, 13th Floor, New York, NY 10036, USA.

IEEE Std 1219-1998
(Revision of
IEEE Std 1219-1992)

IEEE Standard for Software Maintenance

Sponsor

**Software Engineering Standards Committee
of the
IEEE Computer Society**

Approved 25 June 1998

IEEE-SA Standards Board

Abstract: The process for managing and executing software maintenance activities is described.
Keywords: life cycle, maintenance, software, software maintenance

The Institute of Electrical and Electronics Engineers, Inc.
345 East 47th Street, New York, NY 10017-2394, USA

Copyright © 1998 by the Institute of Electrical and Electronics Engineers, Inc.
All rights reserved. Published 21 October 1998. Printed in the United States of America.

Print: ISBN 0-7381-0336-5   SH94568
PDF: ISBN 0-7381-0448-5   SS94568

Introduction

(This introduction is not a part of IEEE Std 1219-1998, IEEE Standard for Software Maintenance.)

This standard describes the process for managing and executing software maintenance activities. Clause 2 lists references to other standards useful in applying this standard. Clause 3 provides a set of definitions and acronyms that are either not found in other standards, or have been modified for use with this standard. Clause 4 contains required information pertaining to the software maintenance process. In order to be in compliance with this standard, Clause 4 must be adhered to.

Annex A, Maintenance guidelines, contains additional information that is not required for compliance. Topics in this annex include: the source of maintenance forms discussed in the standard, validation and verification (V&V), software quality assurance, risk assessment, safety, security, software configuration management (SCM), metrics, software replacement policy, and the maintenance process. Annex B, Supporting maintenance technology, includes the topics of re-engineering, reverse engineering, reuse, maintenance planning, impact analysis, and software tools.

The readers of this standard are referred to Annexes C and D for guidelines for using this standard to meet the requirements of IEEE/EIA 12207.1-1997, IEEE/EIA Guide for Information Technology—Software life cycle processes—Life cycle data.

The audience for which this standard is intended consists of software development managers, maintainers, software quality assurance personnel, SCM personnel, programmers, and researchers.

Participants

This standard was prepared by the Life Cycle Data Harmonization Working Group of the Software Engineering Standards Committee of the IEEE Computer Society. At the time this standard was approved, the working group consisted of the following members:

Leonard L. Tripp, *Chair*

Edward Byrne	Dennis Lawrence	Terry Rout
Paul R. Croll	David Maibor	Richard Schmidt
Perry DeWeese	Ray Milovanovic	Norman F. Schneidewind
Robin Fralick	James Moore	David Schultz
Marilyn Ginsberg-Finner	Timothy Niesen	Basil Sherlund
John Harauz	Dennis Rilling	Peter Voldner
Mark Henley		Ronald Wade

The following persons were on the balloting committee:

Syed Ali	W. W. Geoff Cozens	Richard L. Evans
Theodore K. Atchinson	Paul R. Croll	William Eventoff
Leo Beltracchi	Patricia W. Daggett	Richard E. Fairley
H. Ronald Berlack	Gregory T. Daich	John W. Fendrich
Richard E. Biehl	Geoffrey Darnton	Jay Forster
Juris Borzovs	Taz Daughtrey	Roger U. Fujii
Audrey C. Brewer	Raymond Day	Adel N. Ghannam
M. Scott Buck	Bostjan K. Derganc	Marilyn Ginsberg-Finner
James E. Cardow	Perry R. DeWeese	John Garth Glynn
Enrico A. Carrara	James Do	Julio Gonzalez-Sanz
Keith Chan	Evelyn S. Dow	L. M. Gunther
Antonio M. Cicu	Carl Einar Dragstedt	David A. Gustafson
Theo Clarke	Charles Droz	Jon D. Hagar
Rosemary Coleman	Sherman Eagles	John Harauz
Virgil Lee Cooper	Leo Egan	Robert T. Harley

Contents

IEEE Standard for Software Maintenance

1. Overview

1.1 Scope

This standard describes an iterative process for managing and executing software maintenance activities. Use of this standard is not restricted by size, complexity, criticality, or application of the software product. This standard uses the process model, depicted in Table 2, to discuss and depict each phase of software maintenance. The criteria established apply to both the planning of maintenance for software while under development, as well as the planning and execution of software maintenance activities for existing software products. Ideally, maintenance planning should begin during the stage of planning for software development (see A.3 for guidance).

This standard prescribes requirements for process, control, and management of the planning, execution, and documentation of software maintenance activities. In totality, the requirements constitute a minimal set of criteria that are necessary and sufficient conditions for conformance to this standard. Users of this standard may incorporate other items by reference or as text to meet their specific needs.

The basic process model includes input, process, output, and control for software maintenance. Metrics/ measures captured for maintenance should enable the manager to manage the process and the implementor to implement the process (see Table 3). This standard does not presuppose the use of any particular development model (e.g., waterfall, spiral, etc.).

This standard provides additional software maintenance guidance on associated topics in Annex A and tools/ technology assistance in Annex B. Maintenance plan guidelines are provided in Annex C and guidelines for compliance with IEEE/EIA 12207.1-1997 are provided in Annex D.

1.2 Terminology

The words *shall* and *must* identify the mandatory (essential) material within this standard. The words *should* and *may* identify optional (conditional) material. The terminology in this standard is based on IEEE Std 610.12-1990. [1] New terms and modified definitions as applied in this standard are included in Clause 3.

---

[1] Information on references can be found in Clause 2.

1.3 Conventions

The conventions used in each figure depicting a maintenance phase are shown in Figure 1.

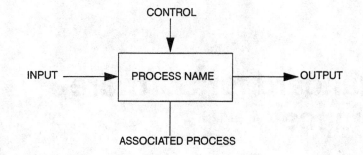

CONTROL

INPUT → PROCESS NAME → OUTPUT

ASSOCIATED PROCESS

Figure 1—Conventions

The term *associated processes* refers to external processes that are defined in other standards; i.e., software quality assurance (SQA), software configuration management (SCM), and verification and validation (V&V). The term *associated processes* also refers to the metrics process illustrated within this standard.

2. References

Table 1 provides a cross-reference of IEEE standards that address various topics related to software maintenance. This standard shall be used in conjunction with the following publications. When the following standards are superseded by an approved revision, the revision shall apply.

IEEE Std 610.12-1990, IEEE Standard Glossary of Software Engineering Terminology.[2]

IEEE Std 730-1998, IEEE Standard for Software Quality Assurance Plans.

IEEE Std 730.1-1995, IEEE Guide for Software Quality Assurance Planning.

IEEE Std 828-1998, IEEE Standard for Software Configuration Management Plans.

IEEE Std 829-1998, IEEE Standard for Software Test Documentation.

IEEE Std 982.1-1988, IEEE Standard Dictionary of Measures to Produce Reliable Software.

IEEE Std 982.2-1988, IEEE Guide for the Use of IEEE Standard Dictionary of Measures to Produce Reliable Software.

IEEE Std 1012-1998, IEEE Standard for Software Verification and Validation.

IEEE Std 1012a-1998, IEEE Standard for Software Verification and Validation: Content Map to IEEE/EIA 12207.1-1997.

IEEE Std 1028-1997, IEEE Standard for Software Reviews.

IEEE Std 1042-1987 (Reaff 1993), IEEE Guide to Software Configuration Management.

IEEE Std 1058-1998, IEEE Standard for Software Project Management Plans.

IEEE Std 1074-1997, IEEE Standard for Developing Software Life Cycle Processes.

---

[2]IEEE publications are available from the Institute of Electrical and Electronics Engineers, 445 Hoes Lane, P.O. Box 1331, Piscataway, NJ 08855-1331, USA (http://www.standards.ieee.org/).

Table 1—The relationship of IEEE software engineering standards to IEEE Std 1219-1998

Relationship		IEEE standard
Process	Problem ID/classification	—
	Analysis	830-1998, 1074-1997
	Design	830-1998, 1016-1998, 1074-1997
	Implementation	1008-1987, 1074-1997
	System test	829-1998, 1012-1998, 1012a-1998, 1028-1988, 1074-1997
	Acceptance testing	1012-1998, 1012a-1998, 1074-1997
	Delivery	—
Control	Problem ID/classification	—
	Analysis	830-1998
	Design	830-1998, 1016-1998
	Implementation	829-1998, 1008-1987
	System test	829-1998, 1012-1998, 1012a-1998, 1028-1988
	Acceptance testing	829-1998, 1012-1998, 1012a-1998, 1028-1988
	Delivery	1063-1987
Management	Configuration management	828-1998, 1042-1987
	Measurement/metrics	982.1-1988, 982.2-1988
	Planning	829-1998, 1012-1998, 1012a-1998, 1058-1998
	Tools/techniques	—
	Quality Assurance	730-1998, 730.1-1995
	Risk assessment	730-1998, 982.2-1988
	Safety	—
	Security	—

3. Definitions and acronyms

3.1 Definitions

The definitions listed below establish meaning in the context of this standard. These are contextual definitions serving to augment the understanding of software maintenance activities as described within this standard. Other definitions can be found in IEEE Std 610.12-1990.

3.1.1 adaptive maintenance: Modification of a software product performed after delivery to keep a computer program usable in a changed or changing environment.

3.1.2 corrective maintenance: Reactive modification of a software product performed after delivery to correct discovered faults.

3.1.3 customer: The person, or persons, for whom the product is intended, and usually (but not necessarily) who decides the requirements.

3.1.4 emergency maintenance: Unscheduled corrective maintenance performed to keep a system operational.

3.1.5 interoperability testing: Testing conducted to ensure that a modified system retains the capability of exchanging information with systems of different types, and of using that information.

3.1.6 modification request (MR): A generic term that includes the forms associated with the various trouble/problem-reporting documents (e.g., incident report, trouble report) and the configuration change control documents [e.g., software change request (SCR)].

3.1.7 perfective maintenance: Modification of a software product after delivery to improve performance or maintainability.

3.1.8 project: A subsystem that is subject to maintenance activity.

3.1.9 regression test: Retesting to detect faults introduced by modification.

3.1.10 repository: (A) A collection of all software-related artifacts (e.g., the software engineering environment) belonging to a system. (B) The location/format in which such a collection is stored.

3.1.11 reverse engineering: The process of extracting software system information (including documentation) from source code.

3.1.12 software maintenance: Modification of a software product after delivery to correct faults, to improve performance or other attributes, or to adapt the product to a modified environment.

3.1.13 system: A set of interlinked units organized to accomplish one or several specific functions.

3.1.14 user: The person or persons operating or interacting directly with the system.

3.2 Acronyms

The following acronyms are referred to in this standard:

CARE	computer-assisted re-engineering
CASE	computer-aided software engineering
CM	configuration management
CPU	central processing unit
CSA	configuration status accounting
FCA	functional configuration audit
FR	feasibility report
I/O	input/output
LC	linear circuit
MP	maintenance plan
MR	modification request
PCA	physical configuration audit
PDL	program design language
SCA	software change authorization
SCM	software configuration management
SCR	system/software change request
SE	software engineering
SLOC	source lines of code
SQA	software quality assurance
V&V	verification and validation
VDD	version description document

4. Software maintenance

This standard defines changes to the software process through a defined maintenance process that includes the following phases:

a) Problem/modification identification, classification, and prioritization;
b) Analysis;
c) Design;
d) Implementation;
e) Regression/system testing;
f) Acceptance testing; and
g) Delivery.

These phases are graphically depicted in Table 2. Software maintenance factors in Table 3 are the entities qualified by the associated metrics/measures identified for each phase.

4.1 Problem/modification identification, classification, and prioritization

In this phase, software modifications are identified, classified, and assigned an initial priority ranking. Each modification request (MR) shall be evaluated to determine its classification and handling priority. Classification shall be identified from the following maintenance types:

a) Corrective;
b) Adaptive;
c) Perfective; and
d) Emergency.

Metrics/measures and associated factors identified for this phase should be collected and reviewed at appropriate intervals (see Table 3 and IEEE Std 982.1-1988 and IEEE Std 982.2-1988).

4.1.1 Input

Input for the problem/modification identification and classification phase shall be an MR.

4.1.2 Process

If a modification to the software is required, the following determinative activities shall occur within the maintenance process:

a) Assign an identification number;
b) Classify the type of maintenance;
c) Analyze the modification to determine whether to accept, reject, or further evaluate;
d) Make a preliminary estimate of the modification size/magnitude;
e) Prioritize the modification; and
f) Assign an MR to a block of modifications scheduled for implementation.

Table 2—Process model for software maintenance

	Problem identification	Analysis	Design	Implementation	System test	Acceptance test	Delivery
Input	MR	Project/system document Repository information Validated MR	Project/system document Source code Databases Analysis phase output	Source code Product/system document Results of design phase	Updated software documentation Test-readiness review report Updated system	Test-readiness review report Fully integrated system	Tested/ accepted system
Process	Assign change number Classify Accept or reject change Preliminary magnitude estimate Prioritize	Feasibility analysis Detailed analysis Redocument, if needed	Create test cases Revise • Requirements • Implementation plan	Code Unit test Test-readiness review	Functional test Interface testing Regression testing Test-readiness review	Acceptance test Interoperability test	PCA Install Training
Control	Uniquely identify MR Enter MR into repository	Conduct technical review Verify • Test strategy • Documentation is updated Identify safety and security issues	Software inspection/review Verify design	Software inspection/ review Verify • CM control of software • Traceability of design	CM control of • Code • Listings • MR • Test documentation	Acceptance test Functional audit Establish baseline	PCA VDD
Output	Validated MR Process determinations	Feasibility report (FR) Detailed analysis report Updated requirements Preliminary modification list Implementation plan Test strategy	Revised • Modification list • Detail analysis • Implementation plan Updated • Design baseline • Test plans	Updated • Software • Design documents • Test documents • User documents • Training material Test-readiness review report	Tested system Test reports	New system baseline Acceptance test report FCA report	PCA report VDD
Metrics		See Table 3					

IEEE
Std 1219-1998

Table 3—Process model metrics for software maintenance

	Problem identification	Analysis	Design	Implementation	System test	Acceptance test	Delivery
Factors	Correctness Maintainability	Flexibility Traceability Reusability Usability Maintainability Comprehensibility	Flexibility Traceability Reusability Testability Maintainability Comprehensibility Reliability	Flexibility Traceability Maintainability Comprehensibility Reliability	Flexibility Traceability Verifiability Testability Interoperability Comprehensibility Reliability	Flexibility Traceability Interoperability Testability Comprehensibility Reliability	Completeness Reliability
Metrics	No. of omissions on MR No. of MR submittals No. of duplicate MRs Time expended for problem validation	Requirement changes Documentation error rates Effort per function area (SQA, SE, etc.) Elapsed time (schedule) Error rates generated by priority and type	Software complexity Design changes Effort per function area Elapsed time Test plans and procedure changes Error rates generated by priority and type Number of lines of code added, deleted, modified, tested Number of applications	Volume/functionality (function points or source lines of code) Error rates generated by priority and type	Error rates by priority and type • Generated • Corrected	Error rates by priority and type • Generated • Corrected	Documentation changes (i.e., VDDs, training manuals, operation guidelines)

Figure 2 summarizes the input, process, control, and output for the problem/modification identification and classification phase of maintenance. For additional information, see also A.4.1.

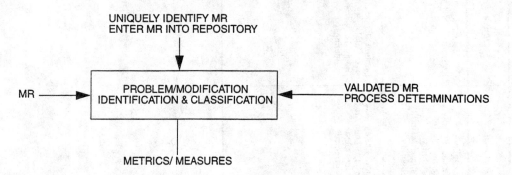

Figure 2—Problem/modification identification and classification phase

4.1.3 Control

MR and process determinations shall be uniquely identified and entered into a repository. See also A.11.1 for guidance.

4.1.4 Output

The output of this process shall be the validated MR and the process determinations that were stored in a repository. The repository shall contain the following items:

a) Statement of the problem or new requirement;
b) Problem or requirement evaluation;
c) Classification of the type of maintenance required;
d) Initial priority;
e) Verification data;
f) Initial estimate of resources required to modify the existing system.

4.2 Analysis

The analysis phase shall use the repository information and the MR validated in the modification identification and classification phase, along with system and project documentation, to study the feasibility and scope of the modification and to devise a preliminary plan for design, implementation, test, and delivery. Metrics/ measures and associated factors identified for this phase should be collected and reviewed at appropriate intervals (see Table 3 and IEEE Std 982.1-1988 and IEEE Std 982.2-1988).

Figure 3 summarizes the input, process, control, and output for the analysis phase of maintenance. For additional guidance, see A.4.2.

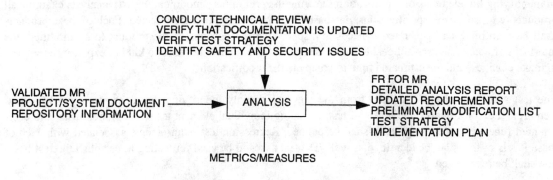

CONDUCT TECHNICAL REVIEW
VERIFY THAT DOCUMENTATION IS UPDATED
VERIFY TEST STRATEGY
IDENTIFY SAFETY AND SECURITY ISSUES

VALIDATED MR
PROJECT/SYSTEM DOCUMENT
REPOSITORY INFORMATION

ANALYSIS

FR FOR MR
DETAILED ANALYSIS REPORT
UPDATED REQUIREMENTS
PRELIMINARY MODIFICATION LIST
TEST STRATEGY
IMPLEMENTATION PLAN

METRICS/MEASURES

Figure 3—Analysis phase

4.2.1 Input

The input to the analysis phase of the maintenance process shall include the following:

a) Validated MR;
b) Initial resource estimate and other repository information;
c) Project and system documentation, if available.

4.2.2 Process

Analysis is an iterative process having at least two components:

a) A feasibility analysis; and
b) A detailed analysis.

If the documentation is not available or is insufficient and the source code is the only reliable representation of the software system, reverse engineering is recommended (see Annex B for guidance).

4.2.2.1 Feasibility analysis

A feasibility analysis shall be performed for an MR and an FR shall be prepared. This FR should contain the following:

a) Impact of the modification;
b) Alternate solutions, including prototyping;
c) Analysis of conversion requirements;
d) Safety and security implications;
e) Human factors;
f) Short-term and long-term costs;
g) Value of the benefit of making the modification.

4.2.2.2 Detailed analysis

Detailed analysis shall include the following:

a) Define firm requirements for the modification;
b) Identify the elements of modification;
c) Identify safety and security issues (see also A.9 and A.10 for guidance);
d) Devise a test strategy;
e) Develop an implementation plan.

In identifying the elements of modification (creating the preliminary modification list), analysts examine all products (e.g., software, specifications, databases, documentation) that are affected. Each of these products shall be identified, and generated if necessary, specifying the portions of the product to be modified, the interfaces affected, the user-noticeable changes expected, the relative degree and kind of experience required to make changes, and the estimated time to complete the modification.

The test strategy is based on input from the previous activity identifying the elements of modification. Requirements for at least three levels of test, including individual element tests, integration tests, and user-oriented functional acceptance tests shall be defined. Regression test requirements associated with each of these levels of test shall be identified as well. The test cases to be used for testing to establish the test base-line shall be revalidated.

A preliminary implementation plan shall state how the design, implementation, testing, and delivery of the modification is to be accomplished with a minimal impact to current users.

4.2.3 Control

Control of analysis shall include the following:

a)   Retrieval of the relevant version of project and system documentation from the configuration control function of the organization;
b)   Review of the proposed changes and engineering analysis to assess technical and economic feasibility, and assess correctness;
c)   Identification of safety and security issues;
d)   Consideration of the integration of the proposed change within the existing software;
e)   Verification that all appropriate analysis and project documentation is updated and properly controlled;
f)   Verification that the test function of the organization is providing a strategy for testing the change(s), and that the change schedule can support the proposed test strategy;
g)   Review of the resource estimates and schedules and verification of their accuracy;
h)   Technical review to select the problem reports and proposed enhancements to be implemented in the new release. The list of changes shall be documented.

Consult A.6, A.7, and A.11.2 for guidance on activities related to V&V, SQA, and SCM.

At the end of the analysis phase, a risk analysis shall be performed (see also A.8 for guidance). Using the output of the analysis phase, the preliminary resource estimate shall be revised, and a decision, that includes the customer, is made on whether to proceed to the design phase.

4.2.4 Output

The output of the maintenance process analysis phase shall include the following:

a)   FR for MRs;
b)   Detailed analysis report;
c)   Updated requirements (including traceability list);
d)   Preliminary modification list;
e)   Test strategy;
f)   Implementation plan.

4.3 Design

In the design phase, all current system and project documentation, existing software and databases, and the output of the analysis phase (including detailed analysis, statements of requirements, identification of elements affected, test strategy, and implementation plan) shall be used to design the modification to the system. Metrics/measures and associated factors identified for this phase should be collected and reviewed at appropriate intervals (see Table 3 and IEEE Std 982.1-1988 and IEEE Std 982.2-1988).

Figure 4 summarizes the input, process, control, and output for the design phase of maintenance. (For additional guidance, see also A.4.3.)

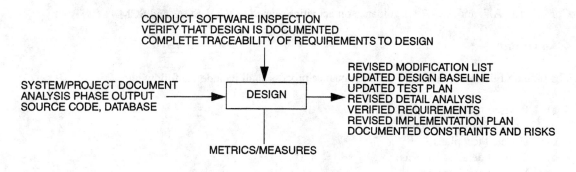

Figure 4—Design phase

4.3.1 Input

Input to the design phase of the maintenance process shall include the following:

a) Analysis phase output, including
    1) Detailed analysis
    2) Updated statement of requirements
    3) Preliminary modification list
    4) Test strategy
    5) Implementation plan
b) System and project documentation
c) Existing source code, comments, and databases

4.3.2 Process

The process steps for design shall include the following:

a) Identify affected software modules;
b) Modify software module documentation [e.g., data and control flow diagrams, schematics, program design language (PDL), etc.];
c) Create test cases for the new design, including safety and security issues (for guidance, see also A.9 and A.10);
d) Identify/create regression tests;
e) Identify documentation (system/user) update requirements;
f) Update modification list.

4.3.3 Control

The following control mechanism shall be used during the design phase of a change:

a)   Conduct software inspection of the design in compliance with IEEE Std 1028-1997.
b)   Verify that the new design/requirement is documented as a software change authorization (SCA), as per IEEE Std 1042-1987.
c)   Verify the inclusion of new design material, including safety and security issues.
d)   Verify that the appropriate test documentation has been updated.
e)   Complete the traceability of the requirements to the design.

Consult A.6, A.7, and A.11.2 for guidance on activities related to V&V, SQA, and SCM.

4.3.4 Output

The output of the design phase of the maintenance process shall include the following:

a)   Revised modification list;
b)   Updated design baseline;
c)   Updated test plans;
d)   Revised detailed analysis;
e)   Verified requirements;
f)   Revised implementation plan;
g)   A list of documented constraints and risks (for guidance, see A.8).

4.4 Implementation

In the implementation phase, the results of the design phase, the current source code, and project and system documentation (i.e., the entire system as updated by the analysis and design phases) shall be used to drive the implementation effort, Metrics/measures and associated factors identified for this phase should be collected and reviewed at appropriate intervals (see Table 3 and IEEE Std 982.1-1988 and IEEE Std 982.2-1988).

Figure 5 summarizes the input, process, control, and output for the implementation phase of maintenance. For additional guidance, see also A.4.4.

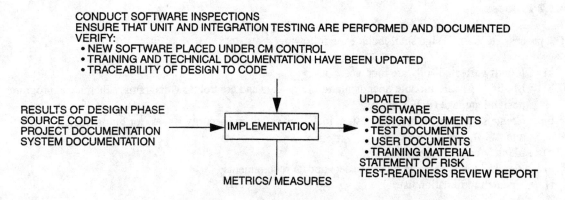

Figure 5—Implementation phase

4.4.1 Input

The input to the implementation phase shall include the following:

a) Results of the design phase;
b) Current source code, comments, and databases;
c) Project and system documentation.

4.4.2 Process

The implementation phase shall include the following four subprocesses, which may be repeated in an incremental, iterative approach:

a) Coding and unit testing;
b) Integration;
c) Risk analysis;
d) Test-readiness review.

Metrics/measures and associated factors identified for this phase should be collected and reviewed at appropriate intervals (see Table 3 and IEEE Std 982.1-1988 and IEEE Std 982.2-1988).

4.4.2.1 Coding and unit testing

The change shall be implemented into the code, and unit testing and other appropriate SQA and V&V processes shall be performed.

4.4.2.2 Integration

After the modifications are coded and unit-tested, or at appropriate intervals during coding, the modified software shall be integrated with the system and integration and regression tests shall be refined and performed. All effects (e.g., functional, performance, usability, safety) of the modification on the existing system shall be assessed. Any unacceptable impacts shall be noted. A return to the coding and unit-testing subprocess shall be made to remedy these.

4.4.2.3 Risk analysis and review

In the implementation phase, risk analysis and review shall be performed periodically during the phase rather than at its end, as in the design and analysis phases. Metrics/measurement data should be used to quantify risk analysis. For additional guidance, see A.8.

4.4.2.4 Test-readiness review

To assess preparedness for system test, a test-readiness review shall be held in accordance with IEEE Std 1028-1997.

4.4.3 Control

The control of implementation shall include the following:

a) Conduct software inspections of the code in compliance with IEEE Std 1028-1997.
b) Ensure that unit and integration testing are performed and documented in a software development folder.
c) Ensure that test documentation (e.g., test plan, test cases, and test procedures) are either updated or created.
d) Identify, document, and resolve any risks exposed during software and test-readiness reviews.

e) Verify that the new software is placed under SCM control.
f) Verify that the training and technical documentation have been updated.
g) Verify the traceability of the design to the code.

Consult A.6, A.7, and A.11.2 for guidance on activities related to V&V, SQA, and SCM.

4.4.4 Output

The output of the implementation phase shall include the following:

a) Updated software;
b) Updated design documentation;
c) Updated test documentation;
d) Updated user documentation;
e) Updated training material;
f) A statement of risk and impact to users;
g) Test-readiness review report (see IEEE Std 1028-1997).

4.5 System test

System testing, as defined in IEEE Std 610.12-1990, shall be performed on the modified system. Regression testing is a part of system testing and shall be performed to validate that the modified code does not introduce faults that did not exist prior to the maintenance activity. Metrics/measures and associated factors identified for this phase should be collected and reviewed at appropriate intervals (see Table 3 and IEEE Std 982.1-1988 and IEEE Std 982.2-1988).

Figure 6 summarizes the input, process, control, and output for the system test phase of maintenance. For additional guidance, see also A.4.5.

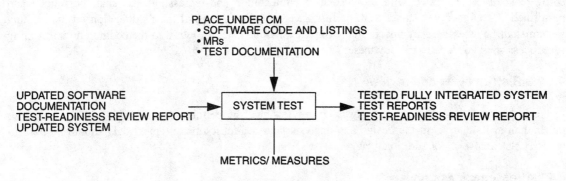

Figure 6—System test phase

4.5.1 Input

Input to the system test phase of maintenance shall include the following:

a) Test-readiness review report
b) Documentation, which includes:
   1) System test plans (IEEE Std 829-1998)
   2) System test cases (IEEE Std 829-1998)
   3) System test procedures (IEEE Std 829-1998)
   4) User manuals
   5) Design
c) Updated system

4.5.2 Process

System tests shall be conducted on a fully integrated system. Testing shall include the following:

a) System functional test;
b) Interface testing;
c) Regression testing;
d) Test-readiness review to assess preparedness for acceptance testing.

NOTE—Results of tests conducted prior to the test-readiness review should not be used as part of the system test report to substantiate requirements at the system level. This is necessary to ensure that the test organization does not consider that testing all parts (one at a time) of the system constitutes a "system test."

4.5.3 Control

System tests shall be conducted by an independent test function, or by the SQA function. Prior to the completion of system testing, the test function shall be responsible for reporting the status of the criteria that had been established in the test plan for satisfactory completion of system testing. The status shall be reported to the appropriate review committee prior to proceeding to acceptance testing. Software code listings, MRs, and test documentation shall be placed under SCM. The customer shall participate in the review to ascertain that the maintenance release is ready to begin acceptance testing.

Consult A.6, A.7, and A.11.2 for guidance on activities related to V&V, SQA, and SCM.

4.5.4 Output

The output for this phase of maintenance shall include the following:

a) Tested and fully integrated system;
b) Test report;
c) Test-readiness review report.

4.6 Acceptance test

Acceptance tests shall be conducted on a fully integrated system. Acceptance tests shall be performed by either the customer, the user of the modification package, or a third party designated by the customer. An acceptance test is conducted with software that is under SCM in accordance with the provisions of IEEE Std 828-1998, and in accordance with the IEEE Std 730-1998. Acceptance testing, as defined in IEEE Std 610.12-1990, shall be performed on the modified system. Metrics/measures and associated factors identified for this phase should be collected and reviewed at appropriate intervals (see Table 3 of this standard, and IEEE Std 982.1-1988 and IEEE Std 982.2-1988).

Figure 7 summarizes the input, process, control, and output for the acceptance test phase of maintenance. For additional guidance, see also A.4.6.

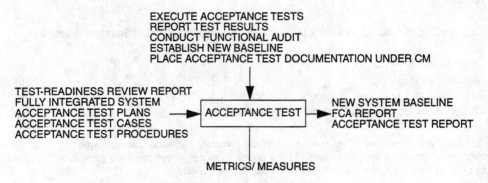

EXECUTE ACCEPTANCE TESTS
REPORT TEST RESULTS
CONDUCT FUNCTIONAL AUDIT
ESTABLISH NEW BASELINE
PLACE ACCEPTANCE TEST DOCUMENTATION UNDER CM

TEST-READINESS REVIEW REPORT
FULLY INTEGRATED SYSTEM
ACCEPTANCE TEST PLANS → ACCEPTANCE TEST → NEW SYSTEM BASELINE
ACCEPTANCE TEST CASES → FCA REPORT
ACCEPTANCE TEST PROCEDURES → ACCEPTANCE TEST REPORT

METRICS/ MEASURES

Figure 7—Acceptance test phase

4.6.1 Input

The input for acceptance testing shall include the following:

a) Test-readiness review report;
b) Fully integrated system;
c) Acceptance test plans;
d) Acceptance test cases;
e) Acceptance test procedures.

4.6.2 Process

The following are the process steps for acceptance testing:

a) Perform acceptance tests at the functional level;
b) Perform interoperability testing;
c) Perform regression testing.

4.6.3 Control

Control of acceptance tests shall include the following:

a) Execute acceptance tests;
b) Report test results for the functional configuration audit (FCA);
c) Conduct functional audit;
d) Establish the new system baseline;
e) Place the acceptance test documentation under SCM control.

Consult A.6, A.7, and A.11.2 for guidance on activities related to V&V, SQA, and SCM.

4.6.4 Output

The output for the acceptance phase shall include the following:

a) New system baseline;
b) FCA report (see IEEE Std 1028-1997);
c) Acceptance test report (see IEEE Std 1042-1987).

NOTE—The customer shall be responsible for the acceptance test report.

4.7 Delivery

This subclause describes the requirements for the delivery of a modified software system. Metrics/measures and associated factors identified for this phase should be collected and reviewed at appropriate intervals (see Table 3 and IEEE Std 982.1-1988 and IEEE Std 982.2-1988).

Figure 8 summarizes the input, process, control, and output for the delivery phase of maintenance. For additional guidance, see also A.4.7.

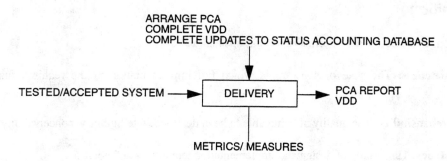

Figure 8—Delivery phase

4.7.1 Input

The input to this phase of the maintenance process shall be the fully tested version of the system as represented in the new baseline.

4.7.2 Process

The process steps for delivery of a modified product shall include the following:

a) Conduct a physical configuration audit (PCA);
b) Notify the user community;
c) Develop an archival version of the system for backup;
d) Perform installation and training at the customer facility.

4.7.3 Control

Control for delivery shall include the following:

a) Arrange and document a PCA;
b) Provide system materials for access to users, including replication and distribution;
c) Complete the version description document (VDD) (IEEE Std 1042-1987);
d) Complete updates to status accounting database;
e) Place contents of the delivery under SCM control.

Consult A.6, A.7, and A.11.2 for guidance on activities related to V&V, SQA, and SCM.

4.7.4 Output

Output for delivery shall include the following:

a) PCA report (IEEE Std 1028-1997);
b) VDD.

Annex A

(informative)

Maintenance guidelines

A.1 Definitions

The definitions listed below define terms as used in this annex.

A.1.1 completeness: The state of software in which full implementation of the required functions is provided.

A.1.2 comprehensibility: The quality of being able to be understood; intelligibility, conceivability.

A.1.3 consistency: Uniformity of design and implementation techniques and notation.

A.1.4 correctness: The state of software in which traceability, consistency, and completeness are provided.

A.1.5 instrumentation: The attributes of software that provide for the measurement of usage or identification of errors.

A.1.6 modularity: Being provided with a structure of highly independent modules.

A.1.7 preventive maintenance: Maintenance performed for the purpose of preventing problems before they occur.

A.1.8 safety: The ability of a system to avoid catastrophic behavior.

A.1.9 self-descriptiveness: The extent of a software's ability to provide an explanation of the implementation of a function or functions.

A.1.10 simplicity: The provision of implementation of functions in the most understandable manner (usually avoidance of practices that increase complexity).

A.1.11 software risk: The potential loss due to failure during a specific time period.

A.1.12 testability: The ability of a software to provide simplicity, modularity, instrumentation, and self-descriptiveness.

A.1.13 traceability: The ability of a software to provide a thread from the requirements to the implementation, with respect to the specific development and operational environment.

A.1.14 verifiability: The capability of a software to be verified, proved, or confirmed by examination or investigation.

A.2 References

The following standards are directly referenced in this annex. Table 1 provides a cross-reference of IEEE standards that address various topics related to software maintenance. These standards are binding to the extent specified within the text of this standard and are referenced to avoid duplication of requirements.

IEEE Std 730-1998, IEEE Standard for Software Quality Assurance Plans.[3]

IEEE Std 730.1-1995, IEEE Guide for Software Quality Assurance Planning.

IEEE Std 828-1998, IEEE Standard for Software Configuration Management Plans.

IEEE Std 829-1998, IEEE Standard for Software Test Documentation.

IEEE Std 982.1-1988, IEEE Standard Dictionary of Measures to Produce Reliable Software.

IEEE Std 982.2-1988, IEEE Guide for the Use of IEEE Standard Dictionary of Measures to Produce Reliable Software.

IEEE Std 1012-1998, IEEE Standard for Software Verification and Validation.

IEEE Std 1012a-1998, IEEE Standard for Software Verification and Validation: Content Map to IEEE/EIA 12207.1-1997.

IEEE Std 1028-1997, IEEE Standard for Software Reviews.

IEEE Std 1042-1987 (Reaff 1993), IEEE Guide to Software Configuration Management.

IEEE Std 1058-1998, IEEE Standard for Software Project Management Plans.

IEEE Std 1228-1994, IEEE Standard for Software Safety Plans.

NIST FIPS Pub. No. 106, Guideline on Software Maintenance, 1984.[4]

A.3 Maintenance planning

Planning for maintenance may include: determining the maintenance effort, determining the current maintenance process, quantifying the maintenance effort, projecting maintenance requirements, and developing a maintenance plan. IEEE Std 1058-1998 may also be used for guidance in maintenance planning.

A.3.1 Determine maintenance effort

The first step in the maintenance planning process is an analysis of current service levels and capabilities. This includes an analysis of the existing maintenance portfolio and the state of each system within that portfolio. At the system level, each system should be examined to determine the following:

— Age since being placed in production;
— Number and type of changes during life;
— Usefulness of the system;

---

[3] IEEE publications are available from the Institute of Electrical and Electronics Engineers, 445 Hoes Lane, P.O. Box 1331, Piscataway, NJ 08855-1331, USA (http://www.standards.ieee.org/).
[4] This publication is available from Global Engineering, 1990 M Street NW, Suite 400, Washington, DC, 20036, USA.

— Types and number of requests received for changes;
— Quality and timeliness of documentation;
— Any existing performance statistics (CPU, disk I/O, etc.).

Descriptions at the portfolio level can assist in describing the overall effort and needs of the maintenance area. This includes the amount and kinds of functional system overlap and gaps within the portfolio architecture.

The reviews of the maintenance staff and the maintenance procedures are also necessary to determine the overall maintenance effort. The analysis at this stage is simply to gather those measures needed to determine the following:

— The number of maintainers, their job descriptions, and their actual jobs;
— The experience level of the maintenance staff, both industry-wide and for the particular application;
— The rate of turnover and possible reasons for leaving;
— Current written maintenance methods at the systems and program level;
— Actual methods used by programming staff;
— Tools used to support the maintenance process and how they are used.

Information at this stage is used to define the baseline for the maintenance organization and provide a means of assessing the necessary changes.

A.3.2 Determine current maintenance process

The maintenance process is a natural outgrowth of many of the baseline measures. Once those measures have been collected, the actual process needs to be determined. In some organizations, the process is tailored to the type of maintenance being performed and can be divided in several different ways. This can include different processes for corrections vs. enhancements, small changes vs. large changes, etc. It is helpful to classify the maintenance approaches used before defining the processes.

Each process will then be described by a series of events. In general, the flow of work is described from receipt of a request to its implementation and delivery.

A.3.3 Quantify maintenance effort

Each step in the process needs to be described numerically in terms of volume or time. These numbers can then be used as a basis to determine the actual performance of the maintenance organization.

A.3.4 Project maintenance requirements

At this stage, the maintenance process needs to be coupled to the business environment. A review of future expectations should be completed and may include the following:

a) Expected external or regulatory changes to the system;
b) Expected internal changes to support new requirements;
c) Wish-list of new functions and features;
d) Expected upgrades for performance, adaptability, connectivity, etc.;
e) New lines of business that need to be supported;
f) New technologies that need to be incorporated.

These need to be quantified (or sized) to determine the future maintenance load for the organization.

A.3.5 Develop maintenance plan

The information collected will provide a basis for a new maintenance plan. The plan should cover the following four main areas:

a) Maintenance process;
b) Organization;
c) Resource allocations;
d) Performance tracking.

Each of these issues are addressed and embedded in the final maintenance plan. The actual process should be described in terms of its scope, the sequence of the process, and the control of the process.

A.3.5.1 Process scope

The plan needs to define the boundaries of the maintenance process. The process begins at some point (receipt of the request) and will end with some action (delivery and sign-off). In addition, the difference between maintenance and development should be addressed at this point. Is an enhancement considered to be a new development, or maintenance? At what point does a newly developed system enter the maintenance process?

Another issue that should be defined within the scope is whether and how the maintenance process will be categorized. Will there be differences between reporting and other types of maintenance? Will adaptations and enhancements be considered within the same process or will they be handled differently?

A.3.5.2 Process sequence

The overall flow of work (and paper) needs to be described. This should include the following:

a) Entry into automated SCM and project management systems;
b) Descriptions of each process step and their interfaces;
c) The data flow between processes.

The sequence should use the process described in this standard.

A.3.5.3 Process control

Each step in the process should be controlled and measured. Expected levels of performance should be defined. The control mechanisms should be automated, if possible. The control process should follow the standards set forth in this document.

A.3.5.4 Organization

Staff size can be estimated from the current work load and estimates of future needs. This estimate may also be based on the expected productivity of each step in the process.

A.3.5.5 Resource allocation

An important part of the maintenance plan is an analysis of the hardware and software most appropriate to support the organization's needs. The development, maintenance, and target platforms should be defined and differences between the environments should be described. Tool sets that enhance productivity should be identified and provided. The tools should be accessible to all who need them, and sufficient training should be provided so that their use is well understood.

A.3.5.6 Tracking

Once the process is in place, it should be tracked and evaluated to judge its effectiveness. If each step in the process has measurement criteria, it should be a straightforward process to collect measurements and evaluate performance over time.

A.3.5.7 Implementation of plan

Implementing a maintenance plan is accomplished in the same way that any organizational change is performed. It is important to have as much technical, professional, and managerial input as possible when the plan is being developed.

A.4 Maintenance process

The phases presented herein mirror those in the main body of this standard.

A.4.1 Problem/modification identification and classification

Each system/software and MR should be evaluated to determine its classification and handling priority and assignment for implementation as a block of modifications that will be released to the user. A suggested method for this is to hold a periodic review of all submitted items. This provides a regular, focused forum and helps prevent the review/analyze/design/implement/test process (which may be iterative) from stalling due to lack of direction. It also increases awareness of the most requested and most critical items. An agenda should be distributed prior to the meeting listing the items to be classified and prioritized.

The frequency and duration for modification classification review meetings should be project-dependent. A guideline might be to consider them as status reviews rather than as technical reviews. Using this guideline, if, after the first few sessions, the reviews take more than an hour or so, their frequency should be increased to as often as weekly. If review time still seems insufficient, determine whether one of the following cases applies and handle accordingly:

— Discussion is focused on major system enhancements (perfective maintenance). This may require analysis/review cycles of a development magnitude, rather than at a sustaining maintenance level.

— The system is new, and design/implementation problems require a significant maintenance effort immediately following delivery. A suggested strategy, to be used where the impact to operations is acceptable, is to classify the MRs as corrective/adaptive/perfective/preventive and integrate them into sets that share the same design areas. Then, rather than prioritizing by individual MR, prioritize by set. This minimizes repetition of design, code, test, and delivery tasks for the same code modules. In this case, review meetings may be longer and more frequent until the system is stabilized. A long-term plan should have a goal of gradually reducing the review meeting overhead.

— The system is aging, and system replacement or reverse engineering and redesign are under consideration.

These are not the only possible cases. They are described to highlight the importance of understanding the goals for classifying modifications as they apply to a particular system.

MRs should be assigned a priority from

— The MR author or a designated representative;
— A knowledgeable user;
— A domain expert;

— Software engineers (depending on the project, this may include representatives of system analysis and design, development, integration, test, maintenance, quality control, and SCM); or

— Project management.

The following criteria should be considered:

a) Rough resource estimate, which may be derived from

1) Relative ease/difficulty of implementation
2) Approximate time to implement (given available human and system resources)

b) Expected impact to current and future users

1) General statement of benefits
2) General statement of drawbacks

c) Assignment to an implementation of a block of modifications that are scheduled to minimize the impact on the user

Detailed cost and impact studies should be performed in the analysis phase, but general cost estimates and statements of impact are desirable for initial classification. Since this is an iterative process, it is likely that handling priority may change during the phases that follow.

A.4.2 Analysis

An MR may generate several system-level functional, performance, usability, reliability, and maintainability requirements. Each of these may be further decomposed into several software, database, interface, documentation, and hardware requirements. Involvement of requesters, implementors, and users is necessary to ensure that requirement(s) are unambiguous statements of the request.

Software change impact analysis should

— Identify potential ripple effects;
— Allow trade-offs between suggested software change approaches to be considered;
— Be performed with the help of documentation abstracted from the source code;
— Consider the history of prior changes, both successful and unsuccessful.

The following should be included in a detailed analysis:

— Determine if additional problem analysis/identification is required;
— Record acceptance or rejection of the proposed change(s);
— Develop an agreed-upon project plan;
— Evaluate any software or hardware constraints that may result from the changes and that need consideration during the design phase;
— Document any project or software risks resulting from the analysis to be considered for subsequent phases of the change life cycle;
— Recommend the use of existing designs, if applicable.

A.4.3 Design

Actual implementation should begin during this phase, while keeping in mind the continued feasibility of the proposed change. For example, the engineering staff may not fully understand the impact and magnitude of a change until the design is complete, or the design of a specific change may be too complex to implement.

The vehicles for communicating the updated design are project/organization-dependent and may include portions of a current design specification, software development files, and entries in computer-aided software engineering (CASE) tool databases. Other items that may be generated during this phase include a revised analysis, revised statements of requirements, a revised list of elements affected, a revised plan for implementation, and a revised risk analysis.

The specifics of the design process may vary from one project to the next and are dependent on such variables as tool use, size of modification, size of existing system, availability of a development system, and accessibility to users and requesting organizations. Product characteristics should also be evaluated when developing the design so that decisions on how modules of software will be changed will take into consideration the reliability and future maintainability of the total system, rather than focusing on expediency.

A.4.4 Implementation

The primary inputs to this phase are the results of the design phase. Other inputs required for successful control of this phase include the following:

— Approved and controlled requirements and design documentation;
— An agreed-upon set of coding standards to be used by the maintenance staff;
— Any design metrics/measurements that may be applicable to the implementation phase (these metrics/measures may provide insight into code that may be complex to develop or maintain);
— A detailed implementation schedule, noting how many code reviews will take place and at what level;
— A set of responses to the defined risks from the previous phase that are applicable to the testing phase.

Risk analysis and review should be performed periodically during this phase rather than at its end, as in the design and analysis phases. This is recommended because a high percentage of design, cost, and performance problems and risks are exposed while modifying the system. Careful measurement of this process is necessary, and becomes especially important if the number of iterations of the coding, unit testing, and integration subprocesses is out of scope with the modification. If this is found true, the feasibility of the design and/or MR may need reassessment, and a return to the design, analysis, or even the modification identification and classification phase may be warranted.

Prior to a review, the following information may be prepared and provided to attendees:

— Entry criteria for system test;
— Resource allocation and need schedule;
— Detailed test schedule;
— Test documentation forms;
— Anomaly resolution procedures;
— SCM procedures;
— Exit criteria for system test;
— Lower-level test results.

Attendees may include the following:

— The MR author, a designated representative, or a knowledgeable user;
— A domain expert;
— Software engineers (depending on the project, this may include representatives of system analysis and design, development, integration, test, maintenance, quality control, and SCM);
— Project management.

A.4.5 System test

It is essential to maintain management controls over the execution of system tests to ensure that the non-technical issues concerning budget and schedule are given the proper attention. This function also ensures that the proper controls are in place to evaluate the product during testing for completeness and accuracy.

System tests should be performed by an independent test organization, and may be witnessed by the customer and the end-user. System test is performed on software that is under SCM in accordance with the provisions of IEEE Std 828-1998.[5] SQA is conducted in accordance with the provisions of IEEE Std 730-1998. The system test is performed with as complete a system as is possible, using simulation/stimulation to the smallest degree possible. Functions are tested from input to output.

For maintenance releases, it is possible that other testing may have to be done to satisfy requirements to interact with other systems or subsystems. It may also be necessary to conduct testing to validate that faults are not introduced as a result of changes.

System tests should be conducted on a fully integrated system. Simulation may be used in cases where it is not possible to have the completely integrated system in the test facility. However, its use should be minimized. If utilized, it should be identified and justified.

The organization that is responsible for system tests should be independent of the software developers and designers, but these organizations may be used as a resource of test personnel. Control of software builds, and all pertinent files (source, object, libraries, etc.) during a system test should be done by the SCM function. Controls to ensure product integrity are executed by the SQA function. They should ensure that the changes to the products that are submitted are in fact authorized and technically correct.

If changes have been made to the software, or test cases, since the software has been delivered, then it may be necessary to run regression and unit tests during the analysis phase in order to establish the product baseline.

A.4.6 Acceptance test

The acceptance test is performed to ensure that the products of the modification are satisfactory to the customer. The products include the software system and the documentation necessary to support it. The culmination of the acceptance test is usually the completion of a functional audit and a physical audit (see IEEE Std 1028-1997).

For maintenance releases, it is possible that other testing may have to be done to satisfy requirements to interact with other systems or subsystems. It may also be necessary to conduct testing to validate that faults are not introduced as a result of changes.

Acceptance tests should be conducted on a fully integrated system. Simulation may be used in cases where it is not possible to have the completely integrated system in the test facility. However, its use should be minimized. This requirement may be modified to include the case where lower-level testing is performed. The customer, or the customer's representative, is responsible for determining the facility requirements that are necessary. These requirements are documented by the developer in the modification plan. Acceptance test facilities may be provided by either the developer or the customer, or a combination of both.

Results of tests conducted prior to the acceptance test-readiness review may be used by the customer to reduce the scope of acceptance tests. If this is done, the customer should document, in the acceptance test report, which results were taken from previous tests.

---

[5] Information on annex references can be found in A.2.

Prior to the completion of acceptance testing, the test organization should be responsible for reporting the status of the criteria that had been established in the test plan for satisfactory completion of acceptance testing. The status should be reported to the appropriate review committee. The customer, or the customer's representative, should chair the review group and evaluate the exit criteria to ensure that the maintenance release is ready for delivery to the end-user.

A.4.7 Delivery

Based on how the users access the system, the delivery may entail replacing the existing system with the new version, duplication of the configuration controlled master for delivery to remote users, or digital transmission.

To reduce the risks associated with installation of the new version of a software system, project management should plan for and document alternative installation procedures that may ensure minimal impact on the system users due to unforeseen software failures not detected during testing. The planning should address time-critical factors (e.g., date/times available for installation, critical milestones of the users, etc.) and restoration/recovery procedures.

When a system modification affects user interfaces or is a significant modification of functionality, user training may be necessary. This can include formal (classroom) and nonformal methods. When the modifications result in significant documentation changes, user training should be considered.

SCM is responsible for backing up the system. To ensure recovery, the backup should consist of the existing system version as well as the new version. To facilitate disaster recovery, complete copies of the system backup should be archived at an off-site location. The backup should consist of source code, requirement documentation, design documentation, test documentation (including test case data), and the support environment [i.e., operating system, compiler, assembler, test driver(s), and other tools].

A.5 Maintenance forms

Recording, tracking, and implementing software maintenance requires that various forms be completed and managed. The following is a list of forms that may be used to perform maintenance, and the IEEE standard that explains their format and usage.

Form	Standard
Test log	IEEE Std 829-1998
Test incident report	IEEE Std 829-1998
Test summary report	IEEE Std 829-1998
Test design specification	IEEE Std 829-1998
System/software change request	IEEE Std 1042-1987
Software change authorization	IEEE Std 1042-1987

A.6 Verification and validation

IEEE Std 1012-1998 should be used to verify and validate that all maintenance requirements are met.

A.7 Software quality assurance

Software quality assurance should be considered when any modifications are made to an existing system. A modification to one segment of the system can cause errors to appear somewhere else. Other concerns can include version control, new documentation release, etc. To ensure that quality is maintained for all modifications, standards as stated in IEEE Std 730-1998, and IEEE Std 983-1986 should be adhered to.

Continuing product quality assurance includes the following:

a) Adherence to the maintenance plan and approach;
b) Testing (including regression testing);
c) Revalidation activities;
d) Recertification activities.

The same types and levels of assurance practices (e.g., inspections, reviews, audits, V&V, evaluation of metric data, records) should be conducted as were performed during development; the degree and conduct of these activities is specified in the software maintenance plan. Special care should be given to ensuring that the original system documentation continues to describe the actual product; during operational use, the time criticality of effecting a repair to the product often results in the lack of related changes to the documentation, with accompanying loss of configuration control. Similarly, the operational facility should be able to maintain the distinction between proposed fixes to the software product needed to provide an immediate resolution of a critical problem; adopted fixes that, due to time criticality, should be utilized prior to having been authorized; and those corrections that, through testing, revalidation, and recertification, have been officially authorized.

A.8 Risk assessment

Software maintenance activities consume considerable resources to implement software changes in existing systems. Traditionally, systems are tested to detect defects in the software. Since defects in various software workproducts cause failures with different consequences, the significance (or risk) of each failure/defect varies.

Software risk is defined as the potential loss due to failure during a specific time period. Risk is measured as a product of the frequency or likelihood of loss and the magnitude or level of exposure. Risk assessment begins with an analysis of external exposure-determination of the magnitude of loss that can result from invalid actions. The external exposure is mapped onto the system to determine the magnitude of loss caused by faults in individual software workproducts. The likelihood of failure for each workproduct is based on its use, verification, validation, adaptability, and size characteristics.

In the context of maintenance, the failure can be product- or process-oriented. That is, the failure of the product (i.e., errors in function and performance) and process (i.e., inaccurate estimates) have the potential of increasing costs of the product and are therefore considered risks. Risk abatement techniques for product risks include testing and maintainability measurement. Risk abatement for the process includes software change impact analysis.

To measure software risk, several functions should be performed: external exposure identification, structural exposure analysis, and software failure likelihood estimation. The following is an outline of these functions as they pertain to software maintenance risk assessment.

A.8.1 External exposure identification

The external exposure identification function has two primary objectives. The first objective is to determine what actions in the environment outside of the software can contribute to loss. The second objective is to assess the significance of the loss.

To this end, the procedure involves the following steps:

a) *Definition of environmental hazards.* Determine how the organization intends to use the software system, and potential hazards such as financial troubles, explosions, incorrect patient treatment, misinformation, loss of life, and like accidents.

b) *Identification of accident sequences.* Investigate how accidents can occur and record them in event trees, scenarios, or annotated event-sequence diagrams.

c) *Failure mode analysis.* Identify failure modes from accident sequences and record them in fault trees. Key failure areas are identified by working backwards in the fault tree.

d) *Consequence analysis.* Determine the consequence of the faults by weighting the loss estimated for each accident scenario. Since this has a wide range of factors and conditions, care should be taken to focus on the key failures.

A.8.2 Structural exposure analysis

Structural exposure analysis is performed to discover how and where software faults can contribute to losses identified in the external exposure assessment. The objective of this function is to assign exposure levels to individual workproducts based on their capability to cause failures. The procedure includes the following activities:

a) *Identify software failure modes.* Indicate where erroneous information can contribute to loss and investigate how the software can fail as a result.

b) *Determine workproduct fault potential.* Locate the potential faults related to the fault modes and identify associated relationships between faults and losses.

c) *Analyze mode use.* Locate where potentially faulty workproducts are used.

d) *Compute workproduct exposure.* Estimate the module exposure by summing its potential loss for all accident scenarios to which it is related.

A.8.3 Software failure likelihood

The objective of the software failure likelihood function is to predict failure likelihood from workproduct and maintenance process characteristics. As software testing proceeds, information about the testing process is used to update or confirm initial estimates of failure likelihood. The likelihood of software failure depends on the number of faults in a workproduct and the probability that the fault will be encountered in the operation of the system, i.e., failure likelihood depends on the number of faults and the probability that the faults will cause failures. Risks for each workproduct are determined by the probability of each type of failure times the costs of that failure.

A.9 Safety

Safety is the ability of a system to avoid catastrophic behavior. Safety requirements may identify critical functions whose failure may be hazardous to people or property. The results of the procedure described in A.8.1 may also be applicable. IEEE Std 1228-1994 contains information that may be used to create and maintain systems with software that have safety aspects.

A.10 Security

The degree to which the system and information access needs to be protected can have an effect on the manner in which the system is maintained. A system is secure if unauthorized personnel cannot get at protected information and to the system itself.

Security during the maintenance process should ensure the following:

a) The integrity of the system is preserved by ensuring that only authorized personnel have access to the system and only authorized changes are implemented. This is accomplished in cooperation with SCM and SQA.
b) Security features implemented during system development are not compromised, either by inadvertent action or failure to comply with the existing security requirements.
c) New functions added to the system are compatible with the existing security features.

A.11 Software configuration management

SCM is a critical element of the software maintenance process. Conformance to IEEE Std 828-1998 and IEEE Std 1042-1987 should be adhered to. SCM, a procedure-driven process, depends on sound, workable, and repeatable procedures to implement the software engineering release function. The procedures should provide for the verification, validation, and certification of each step required to identify, authorize, implement, and release the software product. These procedures should also define the methods used to track the change throughout the maintenance process, to provide the required traceability, to ensure the integrity of the product, to keep project management informed with periodic reports, and to document all the activities involved. During the implementation of the software engineering release process, SCM has responsibilities in each of the major categories of SCM; i.e., configuration identification, configuration audits, change control, and status accounting.

SCM of documentation during system test should be done by the SCM function. The documents to be managed are

a) System documentation;
b) Software code and listings;
c) MRs;
d) Test documentation.

Although SCM is not very involved during the initial phases of traditional software development, SCM should be actively pursued throughout the entire software maintenance process. Failure to provide rigorous SCM can result in chaos during the maintenance process. A11.1 through A.11.7 address the SCM requirements that should prevail during each phase of the maintenance process.

A.11.1 Problem/modification identification and classification

The SCM process is the principal element of the problem identification phase of software maintenance. SCM is responsible for receiving and logging the problem (corrective, adaptive, corrective) into the configuration status accounting (CSA) system (IEEE Std 1042-1987). SCM personnel are responsible for routing the problem to the proper personnel (e.g., system/software engineering, test) for validation and evaluation of the problem. SCM provides tracking and coordination of the problem documentation during this phase.

A.11.2 Analysis

During the analysis phase, it is an SCM responsibility to provide up-to-date documentation to the personnel performing the analysis (e.g., systems/software engineering). SCM should also provide up-to-date listings of the source code and accurate CSA reports showing the current status of the problem.

At the completion of the analysis phase, it is an SCM responsibility to ensure that the analysis results are presented to a review board (an SCM activity). The review board provides visibility and tracking into the problem resolution since it is responsible for authorizing further analysis or implementation. The review board assigns the problems approved for implementation to a software engineering release (block change) package. Although each problem is implemented independently, control is performed on a block of problems associated via the software engineering release. SCM is responsible for documenting the proceedings of the review board and updating the CSA records associated with the problem.

A.11.3 Design

During the design phase, SCM is responsible for ensuring that the design personnel have up-to-date documentation from the system library. It is crucial that design personnel receive any changes to documentation as soon as possible after receipt of a change. It is an SCM responsibility to archive and safeguard software inspection/review results and other design data provided by the design personnel. In an automated design environment (e.g., CASE), SCM may be required to provide assistance to the design personnel in maintaining version control. SCM is expected to provide assistance and guidance to design personnel in the selection and use of consistent naming conventions.

At the completion of the design phase, it is a configuration management responsibility to ensure that design documentation is placed in safekeeping and receives SCM control to protect the integrity of the design product. In automated systems, configuration management is responsible for ensuring rigorous version control.

A.11.4 Implementation

During implementation, SCM is responsible for providing the programmers with copies of the modules to be changed and ensuring rigorous version control. In situations where multiple changes are made to a single module, SCM is responsible for ensuring proper staging to prevent losing changes. This requires complete cooperation and coordination between SCM and the maintenance team. SCM should notify the maintenance team when updated requirement or design data becomes available.

SCM is responsible for maintaining configuration control over all of the support tools used in the software maintenance process. Control of the tools (i.e., compilers, assemblers, operating systems, link editors) is crucial to avoid major impacts to the maintenance schedule and in preventing unnecessary rework.

At the completion of the implementation phase, SCM is responsible for collecting all of the modules that have been changed and placing them in secure library facilities. If a software development folder concept is used, SCM should ensure that each folder is placed under configuration control. SCM is often responsible for regenerating the system (compile, link, etc.) and making it available for the test personnel. This is a good practice that ensures consistent results and products for the test group. The librarian of a chief programmer team may perform this SCM task.

SCM is responsible for ensuring that all the scheduled changes are included in the release package and made available for systems testing. The entire release package is subjected to a physical audit by SCM and validated by SQA. The audit verifies and validates that all the items (e.g., document updates, test plans/procedures, version descriptions, etc.) are complete. After the successful completion of the audit, the release package is presented to a review board for approval to proceed with system testing. This approval process helps reduce wasting system resources for testing when a product is not ready, and provides a substantial cost/schedule benefit.

SCM updates the CSA database with the results of the review board decisions and provides updated status reports to management and the maintenance team. The results and reports generated by the audit are archived and become a permanent part of the release package documentation.

A.11.5 System testing

During the system test phase, SCM is responsible for ensuring the integrity of

a) Test-case data;
b) The software product on suitable media;
c) Other test material.

SCM provides the test group with up-to-date test material as requested. In test environments that are automated, SCM is responsible for maintaining version control over the test material (e.g., test-case drivers, regression test-case data, etc.).

When system test is complete, SCM is responsible for archiving test material for the test group. SCM adds the test-report data to the archived release package documentation. Problems encountered during testing are documented and entered into the CSA database by SCM.

A.11.6 Acceptance testing

SCM provides total control of all the material made available to support acceptance testing. This material is returned to SCM at the completion of acceptance testing. SCM adds the acceptance test-report data to the archived release package documentation. Problems encountered during testing are documented and entered into the CSA database by SCM.

The review board is presented with all the test results, along with recommendations from each group in the maintenance team to allow an informed decision on the suitability of the system for delivery to the user community. SCM updates the CSA database with the results of the review board decision and provides current status reports to management.

A.11.7 Delivery

After approval by the review board and concurrence by project management, SCM is responsible for delivery of the system to the user community. Based on how the users access the system, the delivery may entail replacing the existing system with the new version, duplication from a master for delivery to remote users, or digital transmission to the users. Irrespective of the method, SCM is responsible for preparing and disseminating the system.

In addition to the physical delivery of the system, SCM is responsible for updating the configuration index records to reflect the new version and archiving the complete system, including all release package data. SCM should provide copies of the entire system for disaster recovery storage.

A.12 Metrics/measures

Establishing and implementing a metrics plan is critical for providing insight regarding an organization's level of productivity as well as the quality of the software maintained by that organization. Additional guidance in the form of definitions, methodologies, and rationale for implementing a metrics plan is provided in IEEE Std 982.1-1988 and IEEE Std 982.2-1988. Metrics/measures captured for maintenance should enable the manager to manage the process and the implementor to implement the process.

To initialize a metrics process, management needs to identify technical factors that reflect the technical quality as well as management quality (i.e., effective use of schedule and resources) of the software being maintained. Once these factors are identified as indicators, then measures should be developed that correspond to the technical factors and quantify those technical factors. It is suggested that the selection of the technical factors and their corresponding metrics/measures be optimized such that only the factors that are most pertinent to the specific phase of the maintenance process are addressed during that respective phase of the maintenance process.

Once these are identified, a cost-benefit analysis should be performed to determine the best value that can be achieved by the organization (in terms of increased productivity and overall better management of the process) in exchange for the effort expended to collect and analyze the metrics/measurement data. At the very minimum, effort in terms of work hours should be collected and converted to cost using the organization's internal labor rate. Additionally, some measure of functionality as well as the error rates generated and classified by priority and type should be collected.

Some common measures of functionality are source lines of code (SLOC), function points, and feature points. Whatever method is chosen, it should be well-defined and agreed upon within the organization. Tools used for metrics/measurement collection, analysis, and assessment should be validated, calibrated, and used consistently throughout the organization.

In the world of software maintenance there are three major cost drivers that dominate the effort expended during the software maintenance process. These are documentation, communication and coordination, and testing. Therefore, any software maintenance metrics plan should include metrics/measures that accurately track performance based on these cost drivers, such as documentation change pages, efforts to negotiate the scope of the work to be included in the change package, and classification of the error rates by priority and type. Furthermore, any measure of functionality used should be tied to the complexity of the software as well as the application type (i.e., enhancement, repair, etc.).

A complexity profile of each program may be comprised of but not limited to the following:

a) Size of program (number of statements or instructions);
b) Number of modules in programs;
c) Number of variables in programs;
d) Number of global variables in programs;
e) Average module size (in statements);
f) Average number of compares per module;
g) Average number of modules accessing a global variable;
h) List of common modules;
i) List of modules that access more than the average number of global variables;
j) List of modules that exceed the module size limit of 50 statements or exceed the module compare limit of 10 compares.

The primary data source for the initial metrics/measurement input to the application profile is the software configuration library. Once the initial data are captured, an on-going maintenance metrics repository should be established. This repository should be directly interfaced with the organization's modification control system. The modification control system is a primary data source for the continuing update of the applications inventory profiles.

A.13 Software replacement policy

Planning for maintenance should be considered for all systems, even those under initial development. Although all systems eventually need maintenance, there comes a time when maintenance to an existing system is not technically or fiscally possible. Trade-offs as to resources, funds, priorities, etc., may dictate that a system should be replaced rather than changed. The management policy that can help in making a correct decision includes determination of the following:

a) System outages or failure rate;
b) Code > n years old;
c) Complex system structure or logic;
d) New hardware;
e) Excessive resource requirements;
f) Missing or deficient documentation or design specifications.

Additional information can be found in NIST FIPS Pub. No. 106.

Annex B

(informative)

Supporting maintenance technology

B.1 Definitions

The definitions listed below define terms as used in this annex.

B.1.1 adaptive maintenance: Reactive modification of a software product performed after delivery to make a computer program usable in a changed environment.

B.1.2 emergency maintenance: Unscheduled corrective maintenance performed to keep a system operational.

B.1.3 formal unit: In reverse engineering, a unit of a system identified only by its links with other units.

B.1.4 functional unit: In reverse engineering, a unit of a system defined by its function; a functional unit may include one or several formal units, or be a part of a formal unit.

B.1.5 jump: Transfer of control.

B.1.6 re-engineering: A system-changing activity that results in creating a new system that either retains or does not retain the individuality of the initial system.

B.1.7 restructuring: The translation of an unstructured program into a functionally and semantically equivalent structured program. Restructuring transforms unstructured code into structured code to make the code more understandable, and thus more maintainable.

B.1.8 schematic: In reverse engineering, a description of links between system units; links are represented by jumps.

B.2 Re-engineering

Software maintenance is a significant part of the software engineering process. New code inevitably requires change: new regulations, changes to functions or the rules that compose functions, corrections to problems, extensions to functions, etc. These changes are typically treated as a minor part of the development process and delegated to "less experienced" programmers. It was generally assumed that these newly developed systems would have a short life span and be rebuilt once the mass of changes needed by the system became too costly to undertake. However, these systems have continued to be of significant value to the organization, and hence, the revitalization of these aging systems has become a practical option. As a subset of software maintenance, re-engineering has received a significant amount of recent attention. Redevelopment of key systems has become extremely costly in both dollars and disruption. A critical analysis of the software portfolio and selective re-engineering is a more evolutionary way of bringing old systems up to current standards and supporting newer technologies. A sound approach to re-engineering can not only revitalize a system, but also provide reusable material for future systems and form the functional framework for an object-oriented environment. The techniques to do this have always been available within other engineering disciplines. However, their application to software is a recent trend, and consequently, the tools to support software re-engineering are just now emerging.

Re-engineering as an approach is generally composed of two components: reverse engineering, and forward engineering. Reverse engineering does not change the system. It provides an alternate view of the system at a different level of abstraction. This generally means redocumenting code as schematics, structure charts, or flow diagrams to assist in understanding the logic of the code. Additionally, the process offers opportunities for measurement, problem identification, and the formulation of corrective procedures. Forward engineering is the process of system-building. This process begins with an existing system structure that is the framework for changes and enhancements.

Toolsets to support re-engineering are available and are evolving along the lines of CASE tools; single-function tools have begun to evolve to component toolsets that will evolve to integrated sets. These computer assisted re-engineering (CARE) environments will provide seamless reverse and forward engineering tools that are repository-based. In addition, measurement will play an increasingly important role in problem identification and resolution.

B.3 Reverse engineering

Many systems have the source code as the only reliable representation. This is true for a large long-lived system that has undergone many changes during its lifetime. These systems have substantially overgrown the initial base system, and have poorly updated documentation.

This is where reverse engineering is a recommended technique for redocumenting the system.

The first document that is needed to easily navigate in a system and to find the location of a problem at the analysis stage of system maintenance is a program schematic. A program schematic is similar to an electrical schematic, which is the first document required for maintaining an electrical system.

Parallel definitions of schematic documentation are cited in Table B.1.

Table B.1—Parallel definitions for schematic documentation

Electrical engineering	Software engineering
electrical schematic. A description of links between units of a device (links are represented by wires).	**program schematic.** A description of links between units of a program (links are represented by jumps, i.e., transfers of control).
Schematics "in-the-small" — for local analysis on a unit level	
I/O electrical schematic. A description of all wires connecting an individual electrical unit to other units.	**I/O program schematic.** A description of all transfers of control to and from an individual program unit.
Schematics "in-the-large" — for global analysis on a system level	
linear electrical circuit. A succession of consecutively connected electrical units.	**linear program circuit.** A succession of consecutively connected program units.
electrical application. A family of linear circuits (LCs) executing a specific task of an electrical device.	**program application.** A family of LCs executing a specific task of a program.
electrical system anatomy. A list of all applications with relevant electrical circuits.	**program system anatomy.** A list of all applications with relevant program circuits.

The process of reverse engineering evolves through the following six steps:

"In-the-small"-for local analysis on a unit level

— Dissection of source code into formal units;
— Semantic description of formal units and declaration of functional units;
— Creation of input/output (I/O) schematics of units.

"In-the-large"-for global analysis on a system level

— Declaration and semantic description of LCs;
— Declaration and semantic description of system applications;
— Creation of anatomy of the system.

Steps and products of reverse-engineering a computer program are cited in Table B.2.

B.4 Holistic reusing

A functioning reliable system during its lifetime can give birth to a new, stand-alone system that has its own individuality. The functioning system then becomes a "parent" system. The newborn system is as reliable as the parent system (at least at the time of birth). The parent and the offspring systems concurrently exist and evolve. The process of "delivery" of a new system from the parent system is called *holistic reusing*. This differs from system maintenance activity, which occurs within the bounds of one system.

Holistic reusing is also a powerful tool for maintaining a system that cannot be interrupted except for quick corrective emergency maintenance (to take the bugs out) while the work load is low. Perfective or adaptive maintenance may need a lot of system time that may not be available in the real world of a running business.

B.5 Software tools

Typical methods and tools that can be used during the maintenance process are listed in Table B.3. Information on the tools listed can be found in technical and vendor literature.

Table B.2—Process and products of reverse engineering program schematics

Process steps	Products

1. Formally describe all links (transfers of control) in the program.	Formal units:
	
	unit entrance. A statement to which control is transferred from another unit, or the first program line.
	
	unit output (exit). A statement from which control is transferred to another unit.
	
	unit end. A statement preceding the entrance of another unit.
	
	subroutine unit. A unit that ends with a RETURN-like command.
	
	nonsubroutine units:
	
	    transiting. A one-to-one unit
	
	    branching. A one-to-many unit.
	
	    rooting. A many-to-one unit.
	
	    starting. A none-to-one unit.
	
	    ending. A one-to-none unit.
	
	unit number. A number assigned to a unit from two sets of consecutive numbers—one set for subroutine units, another for nonsubroutine units.

2. Semantically describe function for each formal unit, and create functional units.	A functional unit consisting of one or several formal units or being a part of a formal unit.
3. Describe links for each unit.	An I/O schematic that is combined with a segment of code belonging to a unit.
4. Create a map of all units.	Program LC **FIRST unit.** A unit from which LC starts. **LAST unit.** A unit at which LC ends.
5. Create a map of all FIRST and LAST units.	Program applications
6. Create a list of all applications with relevant LCs.	Program anatomy

Table B.3—Methods and tools for maintenance

Activities/methods	Tools	Manual	Auto
I. Problem/modification identification			
1. Problem/modification reproduction	Automatic test equipment		X
II. Analysis			
1. Code beautifying	Beautifiers		X
2. Reverse engineering program schematic			
a. "In the small"			
– Declaring formal units	Diagrammer	X	X
– Declaring functional units via dissecting/ combining formal units	Expert system	X	X
– Mapping I/O schematic for each functional unit	Mapper		X
b. "In the large"			
– Mapping functional units, and declaring program LCs	Mapper	X	X
– Mapping program LCs, and declaring program applications (families of LCs)	Mapper	X	X
– Creating anatomy of program		X	
– System metrics/measures	Metric analyzer	X	X
3. Code restructuring	Structure analyzer	X	X
III. Design			
1. Reverse engineering design documentation			
a. Flow-charting	Diagrammer	X	X
b. Data-flow diagramming	Diagrammer	X	X
2. Visualizing	Visualizers	X	X
3. Documenting changes (large)	Documenter	X	X
4. Documenting changes (small)	Documenter	X	X
IV. Implementation			
1. Code generation	Code generator		X
2. Code analyzing	Code analyzer	X	X
3. Simulation/emulation	Simulators and emulators	X	X
4. Test analyzing	Test analyzers	X	X
5. Test data generation	Test data generators		X
6. Profiling	Profilers	X	X
V. System/acceptance testing			
1. Stress testing		X	X
2. Performance testing	Performance monitors	X	X
3. Function testing		X	X
VI. Delivery			
1. Media duplication/verification	Media duplicators/verifiers	X	X

Annex C

(normative)

Maintenance plan guidelines

The purpose of this annex is to provide a template to guide the preparation of a software maintenance plan based on this standard.

The maintenance plan (MP) should contain the content as described in C.1 through C.8. The user of this annex may adopt any format and numbering system for the MP. The MP section numbers listed in this annex are provided to assist in the readability of this annex and are not mandatory for the user.

1. Introduction
2. References
3. Definitions
4. Software Maintenance Overview
    4.1 Organization
    4.2 Scheduling Priorities
    4.3 Resource Summary
    4.4 Responsibilities
    4.5 Tools, Techniques, and Methods
5. Software Maintenance Process
    5.1 Problem/modification identification/classification, and prioritization
    5.2 Analysis
    5.3 Design
    5.4 Implementation
    5.5 System Testing
    5.6 Acceptance Testing
    5.7 Delivery
6. Software Maintenance Reporting Requirements
7. Software Maintenance Administrative Requirements
    7.1 Anomaly Resolution and Reporting
    7.2 Deviation Policy
    7.3 Control Procedures
    7.4 Standards, Practices, and Conventions
    7.5 Performance Tracking
    7.6 Quality Control of Plan
8. Software Maintenance Documentation Requirements

Figure C.1—Example software maintenance plan outline

C.1 (MP Section 1) Introduction

The MP should describe the specific purpose, goals, and scope of the software maintenance effort, including deviations from this standard. The software maintenance effort for which the plan is being written and the specific software processes and products covered by the software maintenance effort should be identified. Date of plan issue and status should be provided. Plan issuing organization and approval authority should be identified. (See A.3.1.)

C.2 (MP Section 2) References

The MP should identify the documents placing constraints on the maintenance effort, documents referenced by the MP, and any supporting documents supplementing or implementing the MP including other plans or task descriptions that elaborate details of this plan.

C.3 (MP Section 3) Definitions

The MP should define or reference all terms required to understand the MP. All abbreviations and notations used in the MP should be described.

C.4 (MP Section 4) Software maintenance overview

The MP should describe organization, scheduling priorities, resources, responsibilities, tools, techniques, and methods necessary to perform the software maintenance process. (See A.3, A.4, A.5, A.12, and Annex B.)

C.4.1 (MP Section 4.1) Organization

The MP should describe the organization of the software maintenance effort. The MP should describe the lines of communication with the software maintenance effort including external organizations, the authority for resolving issues raised in the software maintenance effort, and the authority for approving software maintenance products.

C.4.2 (MP Section 4.2) Scheduling priorities

The MP should describe how the maintenance activity will be grouped into work packages, the factors that determine the organizational maintenance priorities, and the process for assigning a priority to a work package and how the resources are assigned to prioritized work packages. The schedule estimating method should be described.

C.4.3 (MP Section 4.3) Resource summary

The MP should summarize the software maintenance resources, including staffing, facilities, tools, finances, and special procedural requirements (e.g., security, access rights, and documentation control). The cost estimating method should be described.

C.4.4 (MP Section 4.4) Responsibilities

The MP should identify an overview of the organizational element(s) and responsibilities for maintenance activities.

C.4.5 (MP Section 4.5) Tools, techniques, and methods

The MP should describe the special documents, software maintenance tools, techniques, methods, and operating and test environment to be used in the maintenance process. Acquisition, training, support, and qualification information for each tool, technology, and methodology should be included. The MP should document the measurements and metrics to be used by the maintenance process and should describe how these measurements and metrics support the maintenance process.

C.5 (MP Section 5) Software maintenance process

The MP should identify actions to be performed for each of the software maintenance phases described in Clause 4, and should document those actions. The MP should contain an overview of the maintenance phases. (See 4.1 through 4.7, and A.4.)

C.5.1 (MP Sections 5.1 through 5.7) Software maintenance process

The MP should include sections 5.1 through 5.7 for software maintenance phases as shown in the MP outline (see Figure C.1).

The MP shall address the following topics for each software maintenance phase:

a) *Phase input.* What is needed to perform the phase.
b) *Phase output.* What results when the phase is performed.
c) *Phase process.* The details of what a phase is expected to do.
d) *Phase controls.* What is to be performed to control the results of the phase.

NOTE—The user of this template should examine 4.1 through 4.7 for process details.

C.6 (MP Section 6) Software maintenance reporting requirements

The MP should describe how information will be collected and provided for each reporting period, including: work packages completed, work packages in-work, work packages received, and backlog. Also, risks should be identified along with their mitigation approach. (See A.7, A.8, and A.11.)

C.7 (MP Section 7) Software maintenance control requirements

The MP should describe the anomaly resolution and reporting; deviation policy; control procedures; and standards, practices, and conventions. (See A.11.)

C.7.1 (MP Section 7.1) Anomaly resolution and reporting

The MP should describe the method of reporting and resolving anomalies, including the criteria for reporting an anomaly, the anomaly distribution list, and authority for resolving anomalies.

C.7.2 (MP Section 7.2) Deviation policy

The MP should describe the procedures and forms used to deviate from the plan. The MP should identify the authorities responsible for approving deviations.

C.7.3 (MP Section 7.3) Control procedures

The MP should identify control procedures applied during the maintenance effort. These procedures should describe how software products and maintenance results should be configured, protected, and stored.

C.7.4 (MP Section 7.4) Standards, practices, and conventions

The MP should identify the standards, practices, and conventions that govern the performance of maintenance actions including internal organizational standards, practices, and policies.

C.7.5 (MP Section 7.5) Performance tracking

The MP should describe the procedures for tracking performance through all software maintenance phases for each work item.

C.7.6 (MP Section 7.6) Quality control of plan

The MP should describe how the plan is reviewed, updated, and approved to ensure plan correctness and currency.

C.8 (MP Section 8) Software maintenance documentation requirements

The MP should describe the procedures to be followed in recording and presenting the outputs of the maintenance process as specified in 4.1.4, 4.2.4, 4.3.4, 4.4.4, 4.5.4, 4.6.4, and 4.7.4. (See A.5.)

Annex D

(informative)

Guidelines for compliance with IEEE/EIA 12207.1-1997

D.1 Overview

The Software Engineering Standards Committee (SESC) of the IEEE Computer Society has endorsed the policy of adopting international standards. In 1995, the international standard, ISO/IEC 12207, Information technology—Software life cycle processes, was completed. The standard establishes a common framework for software life cycle processes, with well-defined terminology, that can be referenced by the software industry.

In 1995 the SESC evaluated ISO/IEC 12207 and decided that the standard should be adopted and serve as the basis for life cycle processes within the IEEE Software Engineering Collection. The IEEE adaptation of ISO/IEC 12207 is IEEE/EIA 12207.0-1996. It contains ISO/IEC 12207 and the following additions: improved compliance approach, life cycle process objectives, life cycle data objectives, and errata.

The implementation of ISO/IEC 12207 within the IEEE also includes the following:

— IEEE/EIA 12207.1-1997, IEEE/EIA Guide for Information Technology—Software life cycle processes—Life cycle data;

— IEEE/EIA 12207.2-1997, IEEE/EIA Guide for Information Technology—Software life cycle processes—Implementation considerations; and

— Additions to 11 SESC standards (i.e., IEEE Stds 730, 828, 829, 830, 1012, 1016, 1058, 1062, 1219, 1233, 1362) to define the correlation between the data produced by existing SESC standards and the data produced by the application of IEEE/EIA 12207.1-1997.

NOTE—Although IEEE/EIA 12207.1-1997 is a guide, it also contains provisions for application as a standard with specific compliance requirements. This annex treats 12207.1-1997 as a standard.

D.1.1 Scope and purpose

Both this standard and IEEE/EIA 12207.1-1997 place requirements on a Software Maintenance Plan. The purpose of this annex is to explain the relationship between the two sets of requirements so that users producing documents intended to comply with both standards may do so.

D.2 Correlation

This clause explains the relationship between this standard and IEEE/EIA 12207.0-1996 in the following areas: terminology, process, and life cycle data.

D.2.1 Terminology correlation

The two standards use similar terms in similar ways. This standard discusses a Software Maintenance Plan whereas IEEE/EIA 12207.0-1996 uses a broader term, maintenance plan, though the focus of 12207.0-1996 is software.

D.2.2 Process correlation

Both this standard and IEEE/EIA 12207.0-1996 use a process-oriented approach for describing the maintenance process. The difference is that this standard is focused on maintenance, whereas IEEE/EIA 12207.0-1996 provides an overall life cycle view. This standard does not use the activity and task model for a process used by IEEE/EIA 12207.0-1996. It describes maintenance in terms of phases and steps. This standard provides a greater level of detail about what is involved in the maintenance of software.

D.2.3 Life cycle data correlation

The information required in a Software Maintenance Plan by this standard and the information required in a Maintenance Plan by IEEE/EIA 12207.1-1997 are similar. It is reasonable to expect that a single document could comply with both standards.

D.3 Document compliance

This clause provides details bearing on a claim that a Software Maintenance Plan complying with this standard would also achieve "document compliance" with a Maintenance Plan as prescribed in IEEE/EIA 12207.1-1997. The requirements for document compliance are summarized in a single row of Table 1 of IEEE/EIA 12207.1-1997. That row is reproduced in Table D.1 of this standard.

**Table D.1—Summary of requirements for a Software Maintenance Plan
excerpted from Table 1 of IEEE/EIA 12207.1-1997**

Information item	IEEE/EIA 12207.0-1996 subclause	Kind of documentation	IEEE/EIA 12207.1-1997 subclause	References
Maintenance plan	5.5.1.1	Plan	6.8	EIA/IEEE J-STD 016-1995, E.2.4 IEEE Std 1219-1998

The requirements for document compliance are discussed in the following subclauses:

— D.3.1 discusses compliance with the information requirements noted in column 2 of Table D. 1 as prescribed by 5.5.1.1 of IEEE/EIA 12207.0-1996.

— D.3.2 discusses compliance with the generic content guideline (the "kind" of document) noted in column 3 of Table D. 1 as a "plan". The generic content guidelines for a "plan" appear in 5.2 of IEEE/EIA 12207.1-1997.

— D.3.3 discusses compliance with the specific requirements for a Software Maintenance Plan noted in column 4 of Table D. 1 as prescribed by 6.8 of IEEE/EIA 12207.1-1997.

— D.3.4 discusses compliance with the life cycle data objectives of Annex H of IEEE/EIA 12207.0-1996 as described in 4.2 of IEEE/EIA 12207.1-1997.

D.3.1 Compliance with information requirements of IEEE/EIA 12207.0-1996

The information requirements for a Software Maintenance Plan are prescribed by 5.5.1.1 of IEEE/EIA 12207.0-1996. In this case, those requirements are substantively identical to those considered in D.3.3 of this standard.

D.3.2 Compliance with generic content guidelines of IEEE/EIA 12207.1-1997

The generic content guidelines for a "plan" in IEEE/EIA 12207.1-1997 are prescribed by 5.2 of IEEE/EIA 12207.1-1997. A complying plan shall achieve the purpose stated in 5.2.1 and include the information listed in 5.2.2 of IEEE.EIA 12207.1-1997.

The purpose of a plan is as follows:

> IEEE/EIA 12207.1-1997, subclause 5.2.1: Purpose: Define when, how, and by whom specific activities are to be performed, including options and alternatives, as required.

A Software Maintenance Plan complying with this standard would achieve the stated purpose.

Any plan complying with 12207.1-1997 shall satisfy the generic content requirements provided in 5.2.2 of that standard. Table D.2 of this standard lists the generic content items and, where appropriate, references the clause of this standard that requires the same information.

Table D.2—Coverage of generic plan requirements by IEEE Std 1219-1998

IEEE/EIA 12207.1-1997 generic content	Corresponding clauses of IEEE Std 1219-1998	Additions to requirements of IEEE Std 1219-1998
a) Date of issue and status	C.1. Introduction	—
b) Scope	C.1. Introduction	—
c) Issuing organization	C.1. Introduction	—
d) References	C.2. References	—
e) Approval authority	C.1. Introduction	—
f) Planned activities and tasks	C.5. Software maintenance process	—
g) Macro references (policies or laws that give rise to the need for this plan)	C.2. References	—
h) Micro references (other plans or task descriptions that elaborate details of this plan)	C.2. References	—
i) Schedules	C.4.2 Scheduling priorities	—
j) Estimates	C.4.3 Resource summary	—
k) Resources and their allocation	C.4.3 Resource summary	—
l) Responsibilities and authority	C.4.4 Responsibilities	—
m) Risks	C.6. Software maintenance reporting requirements	—
n) Quality control measures (NOTE—This includes quality control of the Software Maintenance Plan itself.)	C.7.6 Quality control of plan	—

Table D.2—Coverage of generic plan requirements by IEEE Std 1219-1998 *(continued)*

IEEE/EIA 12207.1-1997 generic content	Corresponding clauses of IEEE Std 1219-1998	Additions to requirements of IEEE Std 1219-1998
o) Cost	C.4.3 Resource summary	—
p) Interfaces among parties involved	C.4.1 Organization	—
q) Environment / infrastructure (including safety needs)	C.4.5 Tools, techniques, and methods	—
r) Training	C.4.5 Tools, techniques, and methods	—
s) Glossary	C.3. Definitions	—
t) Change procedures and history (NOTE—This includes the change procedures for the Software Maintenance Plan itself.)	C.7.3 Control procedures	—

D.3.3 Compliance with specific content requirements of IEEE/EIA 12207.1-1997

The specific content requirements for a Software Maintenance Plan in IEEE/EIA 12207.1-1997 are prescribed by 6.8 of IEEE/EIA 12207.1-1997. A complying Software Maintenance Plan shall achieve the purpose stated in 6.8.1 and include the information listed in 6.8.3 of IEEE/EIA 12207.1-1997.

The purpose of a Software Maintenance Plan is as follows:

IEEE/EIA 12207.1-1997, subclause 6.8.1: Purpose: Define the objectives, standards, and procedures to be used in the software maintenance process.

A Software Maintenance Plan complying with this standard and meeting the additional requirements of Table D.2 and Table D.3 would achieve the stated purpose.

A Software Maintenance Plan complying with 12207.1-1997 shall satisfy the specific content requirements provided in 6.8.3 of that standard. The specific content requirements of 6.8.3 reiterate the generic content requirements and specify that the generic requirements shall be satisfied for several activities. The activities are listed in Table D.3 of this standard along with reference to the clauses of this standard that specifically deal with the activity.

D.3.4 Compliance with life cycle data objectives

In addition to the content requirements, life cycle data shall be managed in accordance with the objectives provided in Annex H of IEEE/EIA 12207.0-1996.

**Table D.3—Coverage of specific Software Maintenance Plan requirements
by IEEE Std 1219-1998**

IEEE/EIA 12207.1-1997 specific content	Corresponding clauses of IEEE Std 1219-1998	Additions to requirements of IEEE Std 1219-1998
a) i) Maintenance process implementation	A.3 Maintenance planning	
a) ii) Problem and modification analysis	4.1 Problem/modification identification, classification, and prioritization 4.2 Analysis	
a) iii) Modification implementation	4.3 Design 4.4 Implementation	
a) iv) Maintenance review/acceptance	4.5 System testing 4.6 Acceptance testing	
a) v) Migration	—	Discussion of migration where appropriate
a) vi) Software retirement	A.13 Software replacement policy	
b) Standards, tools, etc.	C.4.5 Tools, techniques, and methods	

D.4 Conclusion

Users of this standard will probably find compliance with IEEE/EIA 12207.0-1996 to be a relatively straightforward exercise. The analysis suggests that any Software Maintenance Plan complying with IEEE this standard would with the additions listed in Table D.3 also comply with the requirements of a Maintenance Plan in IEEE/EIA 12207.1-1997 In addition, to comply with IEEE/EIA 12207.1-1997, a Software Maintenance Plan shall support the life cycle data objectives of Annex H of IEEE/EIA 12207.0-1996.

IEEE Guide

Adoption of PMI Standard

A Guide to the Project Management Body of Knowledge

Sponsor

**Software Engineering Standards Committee
of the
IEEE Computer Society**

Approved 25 June 1998

IEEE-SA Standards Board

Abstract: The subset of the Project Management Body of Knowledge that is generally accepted is identified and described in this guide. "Generally accepted" means that the knowledge and practices described are applicable to most projects most of the time, and that there is widespread consensus about their value and usefulness. It does not mean that the knowledge and practices should be applied uniformly to all projects without considering whether they are appropriate.
Keywords: body of knowledge, project, project management

Introduction

(This introduction is not part of IEEE Std 1490-1998, IEEE Guide—Adoption of PMI Standard—A Guide to the Project Management Body of Knowledge.)

Participants

The following persons were on the Software Engineering Standards balloting committee at the time this standard was adopted:

Man K. Au
Leo Beltracchi
Mordechai Ben-Menachem
H. Ronald Berlack
Richard E. Biehl
William J. Boll
M. Scott Buck
James E. Cardow
Leslie Chambers
Keith Chan
John P. Chihorek
Antonio M. Cicu
Theo Clarke
Sylvain Clermont
Rosemary Coleman
Virgil Lee Cooper
W. W. Geoff Cozens
Gregory T. Daich
Bostjan K. Derganc
Perry R. DeWeese
Audrey Dorofee
Carl Einar Dragstedt
Sherman Eagles
Leo Egan
Richard L. Evans
William Eventoff
Jonathan H. Fairclough
Richard E. Fairley
John W. Fendrich
Jay Forster
Kirby Fortenberry
Patty Franck
Simon Gabrihelidis
Barry L. Garner
David Gelperin
Hiranmay Ghosh

Marilyn Ginsberg-Finner
M. Joel Gittleman
John Garth Glynn
Julio Gonzalez-Sanz
Donald Gotterbarn
L. M. Gunther
John Harauz
William Hefley
Manfred Hein
Mark Henley
Peter L. Hung
George Jackelen
John O. Jenkins
Frank V. Jorgensen
Vladan V. Jovanovic
William S. Junk
George X. Kambic
Ron S. Kenett
Robert J. Kierzyk
Shaye Koenig
Thomas M. Kurihara
John B. Lane
J. Dennis Lawrence
Randal Leavitt
Michael Lines
David Maibor
Robert A. Martin
Tomoo Matsubara
Russell McDowell
Sue McGrath
Glen A. Meldrum
Jerome W. Mersky
Alan Miller
James W. Moore
Andrew C. Murphy
Pavol Navrat
Myrna L. Olson

Mike Ottewill
Gerald L. Ourada
Indradeb P. Pal
Mark Paulk
John G. Phippen
Alex Polack
Peter T. Poon
Kenneth R. Ptack
Ann E. Reedy
Annette D. Reilly
Andrew P. Sage
Helmut Sandmayr
Stephen R. Schach
Gregory D. Schumacher
Robert W. Shillato
Katsutoshi Shintani
David M. Siefert
Carl A. Singer
James M. Sivak
Alfred R. Sorkowitz
Donald W. Sova
Julia Stesney
Fred J. Strauss
Robert N. Sulgrove
Toru Takeshita
Booker Thomas
Patricia Trellue
Leonard L. Tripp
Theodore J. Urbanowicz
Tom Vaiskunas
Glenn D. Venables
Ronald L. Wade
Dolores Wallace
John W. Walz
Camille S. White-Partain
Scott A. Whitmire

When the IEEE-SA Standards Board approved this standard on 25 June 1998, it had the following membership:

Richard J. Holleman, *Chair*   **Donald N. Heirman,** *Vice Chair*

Judith Gorman, *Secretary*

Contents

IEEE Guide

Adoption of PMI Standard

A Guide to the Project Management Body of Knowledge

Overview

IEEE Std 1490-1998 is an adoption of PMI, A Guide to the Project Management Body of Knowledge (Guide to PMBOK).

References

This standard shall be used in conjunction with the following publications. When the following standards are superseded by an approved revision, the revision shall apply.

IEEE Std 610.12-1990, IEEE Standard Glossary of Software Engineering Terminology.[1]

IEEE Std 1028-1997, IEEE Standard for Software Reviews.

IEEE Std 1044-1993, IEEE Standard for Classification of Software Anomalies.

IEEE Std 1044.1-1995, IEEE Guide to Classification for Software Anomalies.

IEEE Std 1045-1992, IEEE Standard for Software Productivity Metrics.

IEEE Std 1058, 1998 Edition, IEEE Standard for Software Project Management Plans.

IEEE Std 1074-1995, IEEE Standard for Developing Software Life Cycle Processes.

IEEE Std 12207.0-1996, IEEE/EIA Standard—Industry Implementation of ISO/IEC 12207: 1995, Standard for Information Technology—Software life cycle processes.

---

[1]IEEE publications are available from the Institute of Electrical and Electronics Engineers, 445 Hoes Lane, P.O. Box 1331, Piscataway, NJ 08855-1331, USA.

1

IEEE Std 12207.1-1997, IEEE/EIA Guide—Industry Implementation of ISO/IEC 12207: 1995, Standard for Information Technology—Software life cycle processes—Life cycle data.

IEEE Std 12207.2-1997, IEEE/EIA Guide—Industry Implementation of ISO/IEC 12207: 1995, Standard for Information Technology—Software life cycle processes—Implementation considerations.

IEEE adoption implementation considerations

Terminology correlation

The purpose of this clause is to correlate key terminology in the Guide to PMBOK and IEEE software engineering standards. Three key terms are examined: life cycle, process, and project.

Life cycle

project life cycle: A collection of generally sequential project phases whose name and number are determined by the control needs of the organization or organizations involved in the project. (PMI, Guide to PMBOK)

software life cycle: The period of time that begins when a software product is conceived and ends when the software is no longer available for use. (IEEE Std 610.12-1990)

Both definitions have a time dimension. The scope of the PMI definition is limited to a specific project. The PMI definition focuses on the control aspect of the project, whereas the scope of the IEEE definition includes the entire life of the software product. The IEEE definition focuses on the software product and its role.

Process

process: A series of actions bringing about a result. (PMI, Guide to PMBOK)

process: A set of interrelated activities, which transforms inputs into outputs. (IEEE Std 12207.0-1996)
Note–The term "activities" covers use of resources.

Conceptually, the two definitions are the same.

Project

project: A temporary endeavor undertaken to create a unique product or service. (PMI, Guide to PMBOK)

software project: The set of work activities, both technical and managerial, required to satisfy the terms and conditions of a project agreement. A software project should have specific starting and ending dates, well-defined objectives and constraints, established responsibilities, and a budget and schedule. A software project may be self-contained or may be part of a larger project. In some cases, a software project may span only a portion of the software development cycle. In other cases, a software project may span many years and consist of numerous subprojects, each being a well-defined and self-contained software project. (IEEE Std 1058, 1998 Edition)

At the conceptual level both terms have similar semantics. The PMI definition focuses on the essence of a project. The IEEE definition includes a description of the characteristics of a project.

Errata

Page 11: In Section. 2.1.1, change "text" in the third paragraph to "test."

Page 13: In Figure 2-2 and Section 2.1.3, change the reference to DoD5000.2 dated 26 February 1993 and the terminology used for the phases and milestones. The current document is DoD5000.2-R dated 15 March 1996, and the terminology is:

Milestone 0:   Approval to Conduct Concept Studies
Milestone I: Approval to Begin a New Acquisition Program
Milestone II: Approval to Enter Engineering and Manufacturing Development
Milestone III: Production or Fielding/Deployment Approval
Phase 0:   Concept Exploration (CE)
Phase I: Program Definition and Risk Reduction (PDRR)
Phase II: Engineering and Manufacturing Development (EMD)
Phase III: Production, Fielding/Deployment, and Operational Support

Pages 15 and 16: In Figure 2-5 and Section 2.1.3, a preferred reference is:

Boehm, Barry W., "A Spiral Model of Software Development and Enhancement," IEEE Computer, vol. 215, pp. 61–72, May 1988.

Page 27: In Section 3.1, the second sentence should read as follows:

Project processes are performed by people or machines, and generally fall into one of two major categories:

Page 27: In Section 3.1, the first paragraph, second bulleted item, delete reference to Appendix F.

Page 29: In Section 3.2, last paragraph, delete italics for phrase "rolling wave planning."

Page 110: In Figure 10-3, replace the table with the following:

WBS Element	Budget ($)	Earned Value ($)	Actual Cost ($)	Cost Variance		Schedule Variance	
				($)	(%)	($)	(%)
1.0 Pre-pilot planning	63,000	58,000	62,500	–4,500	–7.8	–5,000	–7.9
2.0 Draft checklists	64,000	48,000	46,800	1,200	2.5	–16,000	–25.0
3.0 Curriculum design	23,000	20,000	23,500	–3,500	–17.5	–3,000	–13.0
4.0 Mid-term evaluation	68,000	68,000	72,500	–4,500	–6.6	0	0.0
5.0 Implementation support	12,000	10,000	10,000	0	0.0	–2,000	–16.7
6.0 Manual of practice	7,000	6,200	6,000	200	3.2	–800	–11.4
7.0 Roll-out plan	20,000	13,500	18,100	–4,600	–34.1	–6,500	–32.5
Totals	257,000	223,700	239,400	–15,700	–7.0	–33,300	–13.0
Note: All figures are project-to-date.							

A GUIDE TO THE PROJECT MANAGEMENT BODY OF KNOWLEDGE

A GUIDE TO THE PROJECT MANAGEMENT BODY OF KNOWLEDGE

PMI Standards Committee

William R. Duncan, Director of Standards

Project Management Institute
Four Campus Boulevard
Newtown Square, PA 19073-3299 USA

Library of Congress Cataloging-in-Publication Data

A guide to the project management body of knowledge.
    p.   cm.
   "1996 ed."—Pref.
   "This ... supersedes PMI's Project Management Body of Knowledge
(PMBOK) document that was published in 1987"—Pref.
   Includes index.
   ISBN: 1-880410-12-5 (pbk. : alk. paper)
   ISBN: 1-880410-13-3 (hdbk)
   1. Industrial project management. I. Project Management
Institute. II. Project management body of knowledge (PMBOK)
HD69.P75G845   1996
658.4'04—dc20   95-39934
                                                CIP

PMI Publishing Division welcomes corrections and comments on its documents. In addition to comments directed to PMI about the substance of *A Guide to the Project Management Body of Knowledge*, please feel free to send comments on typographical, formatting, or other errors. Simply make a copy of the relevant page of the *PMBOK™ Guide*, mark the error, and send it to: PMI Publishing Division, Forty Colonial Square, Sylva, North Carolina 28779 USA, phone: 828/586-3715, fax: 828/586-4020, e-mail: pmihq@pmi.org.

PMI publications are available at special quantity discounts. For more information, please write to the Business Manager, PMI Publishing Division, Forty Colonial Square, Sylva, North Carolina 28779 USA or contact your local bookstore.

CONTENTS

C

LIST OF FIGURES

©1996 Project Management Institute, Four Campus Boulevard, Newtown Square, PA 19073-3299 USA

PREFACE TO THE 1996 EDITION

This document supersedes PMI's *Project Management Body of Knowledge (PMBOK)* document that was published in 1987. To assist users of this document who may be familiar with its predecessor, we have summarized the major differences here.

1. *We changed the title to emphasize that this document is* not *the PMBOK.* The 1987 document defined the PMBOK as "all those topics, subject areas and intellectual processes which are involved in the application of sound management principles to … projects." Clearly, one document will never contain the entire PMBOK.

2. *We have completely rewritten the Framework section.* The new section consists of three chapters:
   - *Introduction*, which sets out the purpose of the document and defines at length the terms "project" and "project management."
   - *The Project Management Context*, which covers the context in which projects operate—the project life cycle, stakeholder perspectives, external influences, and key general management skills.
   - *Project Management Processes*, which describes how the various elements of project management interrelate.

3. *We have developed a revised definition of "project."* We wanted a definition that was both inclusive (it should not be possible to identify any undertaking generally thought of as a project that does not fit the definition) and exclusive (it should not be possible to describe any undertaking which satisfies the definition and is not generally thought of as a project). We reviewed many of the definitions of project in the existing literature and found all of them unsatisfactory in some way. The new definition is driven by the unique characteristics of a project: *a project is a temporary endeavor undertaken to create a unique product or service.*

4. *We have developed a revised view of the project life cycle.* The 1987 document defined project phases as subdivisions of the project life cycle. We have reordered this relationship and defined the project life cycle as a collection of phases whose number and names are determined by the control needs of the performing organization.

5. *We have changed the name of the major sections from "function" to "knowledge area."* The term "function" had been frequently misunderstood to mean an element of a functional organization. The name change should eliminate this misunderstanding.

6. *We formally recognized the existence of a ninth knowledge area.* There has been widespread consensus for some time that project management is an integrative process. Chapter 4, Project Integration Management, recognizes the importance of this subject.

7. *We have added the word "project" to the title of each knowledge area.* Although this may seem redundant, it helps to clarify the scope of the document. For example, Project Human Resource Management covers only those aspects of managing human resources that are unique or nearly unique to the project context.

8. *We have chosen to describe the knowledge areas in terms of their component process-es.* The search for a consistent method of presentation led us to completely restructure the 1987 document into 37 "project management processes." Each process is described in terms of its inputs, outputs, and tools and techniques. Inputs and outputs are documents (e.g., a scope statement) or documentable items (e.g., activity dependencies). Tools and techniques are the mechanisms applied to the inputs to create the outputs. In addition to its fundamental simplicity, this approach offers several other benefits:
   - It emphasizes the interactions among the knowledge areas. Outputs from one process become inputs to another.
   - The structure is flexible and robust. Changes in knowledge and practice can be accommodated by adding a new process, by resequencing processes, by subdividing processes, or by adding descriptive material within a process.
   - Processes are at the core of other standards. For example, the International Organization for Standardization's quality standards (the ISO 9000 series) are based on identification of business processes.

9. *We added some illustrations.* When it comes to work breakdown structures, network diagrams, and S-curves, a picture is worth a thousand words.

10. *We have significantly reorganized the document.* The following table provides a comparison of the major headings of the 1987 document and this one:

1987 Number and Name	1996 Number and Name
0. PMBOK Standards	B. Evolution of PMI's *A Guide to the Project Management Body of Knowledge*
1. Framework: The Rationale	1. Introduction (basic definitions)
	2. The Project Context (life cycles)
2. Framework: An Overview	1. Various portions
	2. Various portions
	3. Various portions
3. Framework: An Integrative Model	3. Project Management Processes
	4. Project Integration Management
4. Glossary of General Terms	IV. Glossary
A. Scope Management	5. Project Scope Management
B. Quality Management	8. Project Quality Management
C. Time Management	6. Project Time Management
D. Cost Management	7. Project Cost Management
E. Risk Management	11. Project Risk Management
F. Human Resource Management	9. Project Human Resource Management
G. Contract/Procurement Management	12. Project Procurement Management
H. Communications Management	10. Project Communications Management

11. *"To classify" has been removed from the list of purposes.* Both this document and the 1987 version provide a structure for organizing project management knowledge, but neither is particularly effective as a classification tool. First, the topics included are not comprehensive—they do not include innovative or unusual practices. Second, many elements have relevance in more than one knowledge area or process such that the categories are not unique.

We plan to update this document regularly. Your comments are both welcome and requested. Please send them to:

PMI Standards Committee   Phone: 610/356-4600
Four Campus Boulevard   Fax: 610/356-4647
Newtown Square, PA 19073-3299   E-mail: pmihq@pmi.org
USA   World Wide Web: http://www.pmi.org

THE PROJECT MANAGEMENT FRAMEWORK

1. Introduction

2. The Project Management Context

3. Project Management Processes

i

INTRODUCTION

The *Project Management Body of Knowledge* (PMBOK) is an inclusive term that describes the sum of knowledge within the profession of project management. As with other professions such as law, medicine, and accounting, the body of knowledge rests with the practitioners and academics who apply and advance it. The full PMBOK includes knowledge of proven, traditional practices which are widely applied as well as knowledge of innovative and advanced practices which have seen more limited use.

This chapter defines and explains several key terms and provides an overview of the rest of the document. It includes the following major sections:

1.1 Purpose of this Document
1.2 What is a Project?
1.3 What is Project Management?
1.4 Relationship to Other Management Disciplines
1.5 Related Endeavors

1.1 PURPOSE OF THIS DOCUMENT

The primary purpose of this document is to identify and describe that subset of the PMBOK which is *generally accepted*. Generally accepted means that the knowledge and practices described are applicable to most projects most of the time, and that there is widespread consensus about their value and usefulness. Generally accepted does *not* mean that the knowledge and practices described are or should be applied uniformly on all projects; the project management team is always responsible for determining what is appropriate for any given project.

This document is also intended to provide a common lexicon within the profession for talking about project management. Project management is a relatively young profession, and while there is substantial commonality around what is done, there is relatively little commonality in the terms used.

This document provides a basic reference for anyone interested in the profession of project management. This includes, but is not limited to:

- Project managers and other project team members.
- Managers of project managers.
- Project customers and other project stakeholders.
- Functional managers with employees assigned to project teams.
- Educators teaching project management and related subjects.
- Consultants and other specialists in project management and related fields.
- Trainers developing project management educational programs.

As a basic reference, this document is neither comprehensive nor all-inclusive. Appendix E discusses application area extensions while Appendix F lists sources of further information on project management.

This document is also used by the Project Management Institute to provide a consistent structure for its professional development programs including:
- Certification of Project Management Professionals (PMPs).
- Accreditation of degree-granting educational programs in project management.

1.2 WHAT IS A PROJECT?

Organizations perform work. Work generally involves either *operations* or *projects*, although the two may overlap. Operations and projects share many characteristics; for example, they are:
- Performed by people.
- Constrained by limited resources.
- Planned, executed, and controlled.

Operations and projects differ primarily in that operations are ongoing and repetitive while projects are temporary and unique. A project can thus be defined in terms of its distinctive characteristics—*a project is a temporary endeavor undertaken to create a unique product or service*. *Temporary* means that every project has a definite beginning and a definite end. *Unique* means that the product or service is different in some distinguishing way from all similar products or services.

Projects are undertaken at all levels of the organization. They may involve a single person or many thousands. They may require less than 100 hours to complete or over 10,000,000. Projects may involve a single unit of one organization or may cross organizational boundaries as in joint ventures and partnering. Projects are often critical components of the performing organization's business strategy. Examples of projects include:
- Developing a new product or service.
- Effecting a change in structure, staffing, or style of an organization.
- Designing a new transportation vehicle.
- Developing or acquiring a new or modified information system.
- Constructing a building or facility.
- Running a campaign for political office.
- Implementing a new business procedure or process.

1.2.1 Temporary

Temporary means that every project has a definite beginning and a definite end. The end is reached when the project's objectives have been achieved, or when it becomes clear that the project objectives will not or cannot be met and the project is terminated. Temporary does not necessarily mean short in duration; many projects last for several years. In every case, however, the duration of a project is finite; projects are not ongoing efforts.

In addition, temporary does not generally apply to the product or service created by the project. Most projects are undertaken to create a lasting result. For example, a project to erect a national monument will create a result expected to last centuries.

Many undertakings are temporary in the sense that they will end at some point. For example, assembly work at an automotive plant will eventually be discontinued, and the plant itself decommissioned. Projects are fundamentally different because the project *ceases* when its declared objectives have been attained, while non-project undertakings adopt a new set of objectives and *continue* to work.

The temporary nature of projects may apply to other aspects of the endeavor as well:

- The opportunity or market window is usually temporary—most projects have a limited time frame in which to produce their product or service.
- The project team, as a team, seldom outlives the project—most projects are performed by a team created for the sole purpose of performing the project, and the team is disbanded and members reassigned when the project is complete.

1.2.2 Unique Product or Service

Projects involve doing something which has not been done before and which is, therefore, *unique*. A product or service may be unique even if the category it belongs to is large. For example, many thousands of office buildings have been developed, but each individual facility is unique—different owner, different design, different location, different contractors, and so on. The presence of repetitive elements does not change the fundamental uniqueness of the overall effort. For example:

- A project to develop a new commercial airliner may require multiple prototypes.
- A project to bring a new drug to market may require thousands of doses of the drug to support clinical trials.
- A real estate development project may include hundreds of individual units.

Because the product of each project is unique, the characteristics that distinguish the product or service must be progressively elaborated. *Progressively* means "proceeding in steps; continuing steadily by increments" while *elaborated* means "worked out with care and detail; developed thoroughly" [1]. These distinguishing characteristics will be broadly defined early in the project and will be made more explicit and detailed as the project team develops a better and more complete understanding of the product.

Progressive elaboration of product characteristics must be carefully coordinated with proper project scope definition, particularly if the project is performed under contract. When properly defined, the scope of the project—the work to be done—should remain constant even as the product characteristics are progressively elaborated. The relationship between product scope and project scope is discussed further in the introduction to Chapter 5.

The following two examples illustrate progressive elaboration in two different application areas.

Example 1. A chemical processing plant begins with process engineering to define the characteristics of the process. These characteristics are used to design the major processing units. This information becomes the basis for engineering design which defines both the detail plant layout and the mechanical characteristics of the process units and ancillary facilities. All of these result in design drawings which are elaborated to produce fabrication drawings (construction isometrics). During construction, interpretations and adaptations are made as needed and subject to proper approval. This further elaboration of the characteristics is captured by "as built" drawings. During test and turnover, further elaboration of the characteristics is often made in the form of final operating adjustments.

Example 2. The product of a biopharmaceutical research project may initially be defined as "clinical trials of XYZ" since the number of trials and the size of each is not known. As the project proceeds, the product may be described more explicitly as "three Phase I trials, four Phase II trials, and two Phase III trials." The next round of progressive elaboration might focus exclusively on the protocol for the Phase I trials—how many patients get what dosages and how frequently. In the project's final stages, the Phase III trials would be explicitly defined based on information gathered and analyzed during the Phase I and Phase II trials.

1.3 WHAT IS PROJECT MANAGEMENT?

Project management is the application of knowledge, skills, tools, and techniques to project activities in order to meet or exceed stakeholder needs and expectations from a project. Meeting or exceeding stakeholder needs and expectations invariably involves balancing competing demands among:

- Scope, time, cost, and quality.
- Stakeholders with differing needs and expectations.
- Identified requirements (needs) and unidentified requirements (expectations).

The term *project management* is sometimes used to describe an organizational approach to the management of ongoing operations. This approach, more properly called *management by projects*, treats many aspects of ongoing operations as projects in order to apply project management to them. Although an understanding of project management is obviously critical to an organization that is managing by projects, a detailed discussion of the approach itself is outside the scope of this document.

Knowledge about project management can be organized in many ways. This document has two major sections and 12 chapters as described below.

1.3.1 The Project Management Framework

Part I, The Project Management Framework, provides a basic structure for understanding project management.

Chapter 1, **Introduction**, defines key terms and provides an overview of the rest of the document.

Chapter 2, **The Project Management Context**, describes the environment in which projects operate. The project management team must understand this broader context—managing the day-to-day activities of the project is necessary for success but not sufficient.

Chapter 3, **Project Management Processes**, describes a generalized view of how the various project management processes commonly interact. Understanding these interactions is essential to understanding the material presented in Chapters 4 through 12.

1.3.2 The Project Management Knowledge Areas

Part II, The Project Management Knowledge Areas, describes project management knowledge and practice in terms of its component processes. These processes have been organized into nine knowledge areas as described below and as illustrated in **Figure 1-1**.

Chapter 4, **Project Integration Management**, describes the processes required to ensure that the various elements of the project are properly coordinated. It consists of project plan development, project plan execution, and overall change control.

Chapter 5, **Project Scope Management**, describes the processes required to ensure that the project includes all the work required, and only the work required, to complete the project successfully. It consists of initiation, scope planning, scope definition, scope verification, and scope change control.

Chapter 6, **Project Time Management**, describes the processes required to ensure timely completion of the project. It consists of activity definition, activity sequencing, activity duration estimating, schedule development, and schedule control.

Chapter 7, **Project Cost Management**, describes the processes required to ensure that the project is completed within the approved budget. It consists of resource planning, cost estimating, cost budgeting, and cost control.

Chapter 8, **Project Quality Management**, describes the processes required to ensure that the project will satisfy the needs for which it was undertaken. It consists of quality planning, quality assurance, and quality control.

FIGURE 1–1

Figure 1–1. Overview of Project Management Knowledge Areas and Project Management Processes

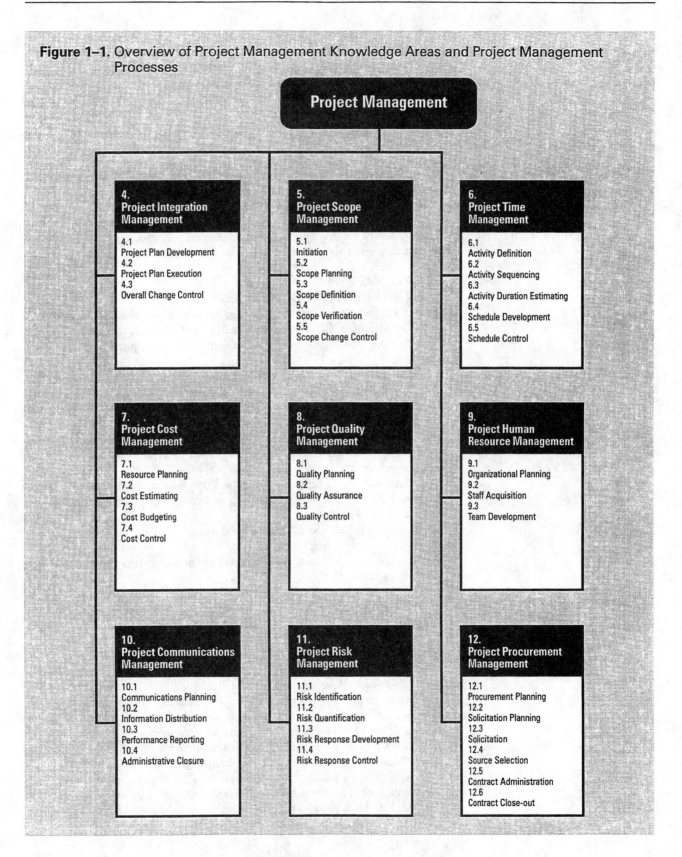

Chapter 9, **Project Human Resource Management**, describes the processes required to make the most effective use of the people involved with the project. It consists of organizational planning, staff acquisition, and team development.

Chapter 10, **Project Communications Management**, describes the processes required to ensure timely and appropriate generation, collection, dissemination, storage, and ultimate disposition of project information. It consists of communications planning, information distribution, performance reporting, and administrative closure.

Chapter 11, **Project Risk Management**, describes the processes concerned with identifying, analyzing, and responding to project risk. It consists of risk identification, risk quantification, risk response development, and risk response control.

Chapter 12, **Project Procurement Management**, describes the processes required to acquire goods and services from outside the performing organization. It consists of procurement planning, solicitation planning, solicitation, source selection, contract administration, and contract close-out.

1.4 RELATIONSHIP TO OTHER MANAGEMENT DISCIPLINES

Much of the knowledge needed to manage projects is unique or nearly unique to project management (e.g., critical path analysis and work breakdown structures). However, the PMBOK does overlap other management disciplines as illustrated in **Figure 1–2**.

General management encompasses planning, organizing, staffing, executing, and controlling the operations of an ongoing enterprise. General management also includes supporting disciplines such as computer programming, law, statistics and probability theory, logistics, and personnel. The PMBOK overlaps general management in many areas—organizational behavior, financial forecasting, and planning techniques to name just a few. Section 2.4 provides a more detailed discussion of general management.

Application areas are categories of projects that have common elements significant in such projects but not needed or present in all projects. Application areas are usually defined in terms of:

- Technical elements, such as software development, pharmaceuticals, or construction engineering.
- Management elements, such as government contracting or new product development.
- Industry groups, such as automotive, chemicals, or financial services.

Appendix E includes a more detailed discussion of project management application areas.

1.5 RELATED ENDEAVORS

Certain types of endeavors are closely related to projects. These related undertakings are described below.

Programs. A *program* is a group of projects managed in a coordinated way to obtain benefits not available from managing them individually [2]. Many programs also include elements of ongoing operations. For example:

- The "XYZ airplane program" includes both the project or projects to design and develop the aircraft as well as the ongoing manufacturing and support of that craft in the field.
- Many electronics firms have "program managers" who are responsible for both individual product releases (projects) and the coordination of multiple releases over time (an ongoing operation).

FIGURE 1–2

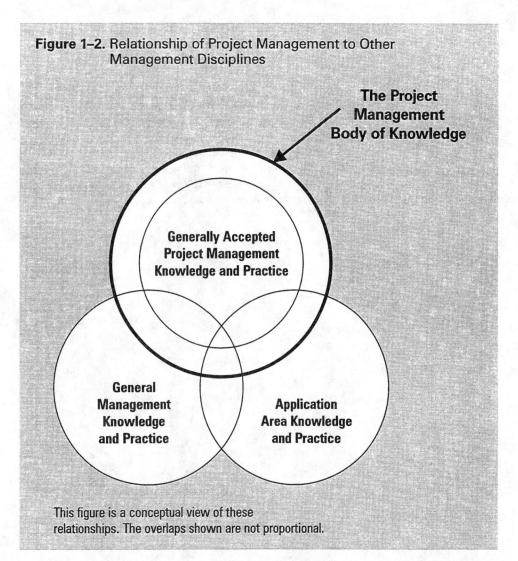

Figure 1–2. Relationship of Project Management to Other Management Disciplines

This figure is a conceptual view of these relationships. The overlaps shown are not proportional.

Programs may also involve a series of repetitive or cyclical undertakings, for example:

- Utilities often speak of an annual "construction program," a regular, ongoing operation which involves many projects.
- Many non-profit organizations have a "fundraising program," an ongoing effort to obtain financial support that often involves a series of discrete projects such as a membership drive or an auction.
- Publishing a newspaper or magazine is also a program—the periodical itself is an ongoing effort, but each individual issue is a project.

In some application areas, program management and project management are treated as synonyms; in others, project management is a subset of program management. Occasionally, program management is considered a subset of project management. This diversity of meaning makes it imperative that any discussion of program management versus project management be preceded by agreement on a clear and consistent definition of each term.

Subprojects. Projects are frequently divided into more manageable components or *subprojects*. Subprojects are often contracted out to an external enterprise or to another functional unit in the performing organization. Examples of subprojects include:

- A single project phase (project phases are described in Section 2.1).
- The installation of plumbing or electrical fixtures on a construction project.
- Automated testing of computer programs on a software development project.
- High-volume manufacturing to support clinical trials of a new drug during a pharmaceutical research and development project.

However, from the perspective of the performing organization, a subproject is often thought of more as a service than as a product, and the service is unique. Thus subprojects are typically referred to as projects and managed as such.

THE PROJECT
MANAGEMENT CONTEXT

2

Projects and project management operate in an environment broader than that of the project itself. The project management team must understand this broader context—managing the day-to-day activities of the project is necessary for success but not sufficient. This chapter describes key aspects of the project management context not covered elsewhere in this document. The topics included here are:

2.1 Project Phases and the Project Life Cycle
2.2 Project Stakeholders
2.3 Organizational Influences
2.4 Key General Management Skills
2.5 Socioeconomic Influences

2.1 PROJECT PHASES AND THE PROJECT LIFE CYCLE

Because projects are unique undertakings, they involve a degree of uncertainty. Organizations performing projects will usually divide each project into several *project phases* to provide better management control and appropriate links to the ongoing operations of the performing organization. Collectively, the project phases are known as the *project life cycle*.

2.1.1 Characteristics of Project Phases

Each project phase is marked by completion of one or more *deliverables*. A deliverable is a tangible, verifiable work product such as a feasibility study, a detail design, or a working prototype. The deliverables, and hence the phases, are part of a generally sequential logic designed to ensure proper definition of the product of the project.

The conclusion of a project phase is generally marked by a review of both key deliverables and project performance in order to (a) determine if the project should continue into its next phase and (b) detect and correct errors cost effectively. These phase-end reviews are often called *phase exits*, *stage gates,* or *kill points*.

Each project phase normally includes a set of defined work products designed to establish the desired level of management control. The majority of these items are related to the primary phase deliverable, and the phases typically take their names from these items: requirements, design, build, text, start-up, turnover, and others as appropriate. Several representative project life cycles are described in Section 2.1.3.

2.1.2 Characteristics of the Project Life Cycle

The project life cycle serves to define the beginning and the end of a project. For example, when an organization identifies an opportunity that it would like to respond to, it will often authorize a feasibility study to decide if it should undertake a project. The project life cycle definition will determine whether the feasibility study is treated as the first project phase or as a separate, stand-alone project.

©1996 Project Management Institute, Four Campus Boulevard, Newtown Square, PA 19073-3299 USA

FIGURE 2–1   A GUIDE TO THE PROJECT MANAGEMENT BODY OF KNOWLEDGE

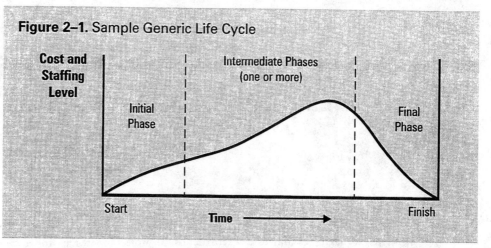

Figure 2–1. Sample Generic Life Cycle

The project life cycle definition will also determine which transitional actions at the end of the project are included and which are not. In this manner, the project life cycle definition can be used to link the project to the ongoing operations of the performing organization.

The phase sequence defined by most project life cycles generally involves some form of technology transfer or hand-off such as requirements to design, construction to operations, or design to manufacturing. Deliverables from the preceding phase are usually approved before work starts on the next phase. However, a subsequent phase is sometimes begun prior to approval of the previous phase deliverables when the risks involved are deemed acceptable. This practice of overlapping phases is often called *fast tracking*.

Project life cycles generally define:
- What technical work should be done in each phase (e.g., is the work of the architect part of the definition phase or part of the execution phase?).
- Who should be involved in each phase (e.g., concurrent engineering requires that the implementors be involved with requirements and design).

Project life cycle descriptions may be very general or very detailed. Highly detailed descriptions may have numerous forms, charts, and checklists to provide structure and consistency. Such detailed approaches are often called project management methodologies.

Most project life cycle descriptions share a number of common characteristics:
- Cost and staffing levels are low at the start, higher towards the end, and drop rapidly as the project draws to a conclusion. This pattern is illustrated in **Figure 2–1**.
- The probability of successfully completing the project is lowest, and hence risk and uncertainty are highest, at the start of the project. The probability of successful completion generally gets progressively higher as the project continues.
- The ability of the stakeholders to influence the final characteristics of the project product and the final cost of the project is highest at the start and gets progressively lower as the project continues. A major contributor to this phenomenon is that the cost of changes and error correction generally increases as the project continues.

Care should be taken to distinguish the *project* life cycle from the *product* life cycle. For example, a project undertaken to bring a new desktop computer to market is but one phase or stage of the product life cycle.

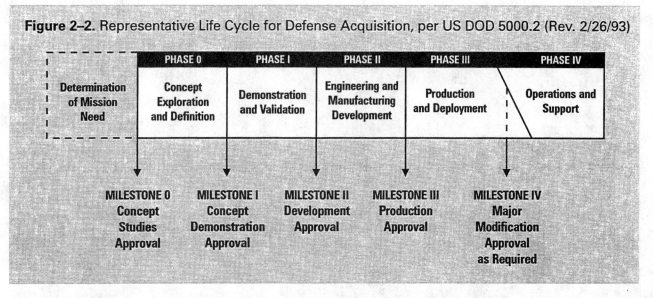

Figure 2–2. Representative Life Cycle for Defense Acquisition, per US DOD 5000.2 (Rev. 2/26/93)

Although many project life cycles have similar phase names with similar work products required, few are identical. Most have four or five phases, but some have nine or more. Even within a single application area there can be significant variations—one organization's software development life cycle may have a single design phase while another's has separate phases for functional and detail design.

Subprojects within projects may also have distinct project life cycles. For example, an architectural firm hired to design a new office building is first involved in the owner's definition phase when doing the design and in the owner's implementation phase when supporting the construction effort. The architect's design project, however, will have its own series of phases from conceptual development through definition and implementation to closure. The architect may even treat designing the facility and supporting the construction as separate projects with their own distinct phases.

2.1.3 Representative Project Life Cycles

The following project life cycles have been chosen to illustrate the diversity of approaches in use. The examples shown are typical; they are neither recommended nor preferred. In each case, the phase names and major deliverables are those described by the author.

Defense acquisition. The U.S. Department of Defense directive 5000.2, as revised February 1993, describes a series of acquisition milestones and phases as illustrated in **Figure 2–2.**

- Determination of Mission Need—ends with Concept Studies Approval.
- Concept Exploration and Definition—ends with Concept Demonstration Approval.
- Demonstration and Validation—ends with Development Approval.
- Engineering and Manufacturing Development—ends with Production Approval.
- Production and Deployment—overlaps ongoing Operations and Support.

FIGURE 2–3   A GUIDE TO THE PROJECT MANAGEMENT BODY OF KNOWLEDGE

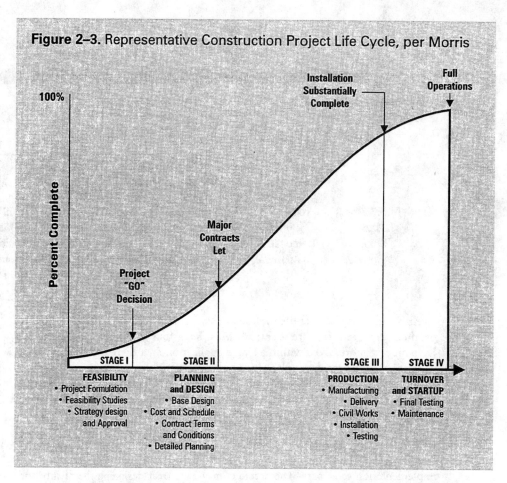

Figure 2–3. Representative Construction Project Life Cycle, per Morris

Construction. Morris [1] describes a construction project life cycle as illustrated in **Figure 2–3**:

- Feasibility—project formulation, feasibility studies, and strategy design and approval. A go/no-go decision is made at the end of this phase.
- Planning and Design—base design, cost and schedule, contract terms and conditions, and detailed planning. Major contracts are let at the end of this phase.
- Production—manufacturing, delivery, civil works, installation, and testing. The facility is substantially complete at the end of this phase.
- Turnover and Start-up—final testing and maintenance. The facility is in full operation at the end of this phase.

Pharmaceuticals. Murphy [2] describes a project life cycle for pharmaceutical new product development in the United States as illustrated in **Figure 2–4**:

- Discovery and Screening—includes basic and applied research to identify candidates for preclinical testing.
- Preclinical Development—includes laboratory and animal testing to determine safety and efficacy as well as preparation and filing of an Investigational New Drug (IND) application.
- Registration(s) Workup—includes Clinical Phase I, II, and III tests as well as preparation and filing of a New Drug Application (NDA).
- Postsubmission Activity—includes additional work as required to support Food and Drug Administration review of the NDA.

14

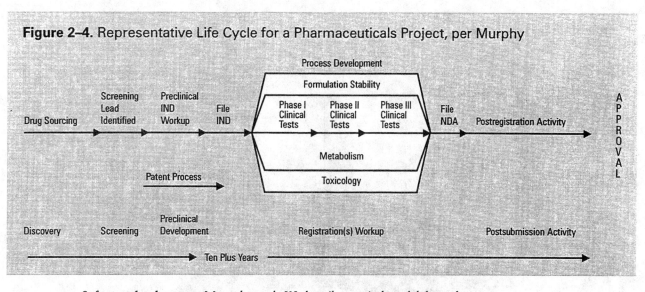

Figure 2–4. Representative Life Cycle for a Pharmaceuticals Project, per Murphy

Software development. Muench, et al. [3] describe a spiral model for software development with four cycles and four quadrants as illustrated in **Figure 2–5**:

- Proof-of-concept cycle—capture business requirements, define goals for proof-of-concept, produce conceptual system design, design and construct the proof-of-concept, produce acceptance test plans, conduct risk analysis and make recommendations.
- First build cycle—derive system requirements, define goals for first build, produce logical system design, design and construct the first build, produce system test plans, evaluate the first build and make recommendations.
- Second build cycle—derive subsystem requirements, define goals for second build, produce physical design, construct the second build, produce system test plans, evaluate the second build and make recommendations.
- Final cycle—complete unit requirements, final design, construct final build, perform unit, subsystem, system, and acceptance tests.

2.2 PROJECT STAKEHOLDERS

Project stakeholders are individuals and organizations who are actively involved in the project, or whose interests may be positively or negatively affected as a result of project execution or successful project completion. The project management team must identify the stakeholders, determine what their needs and expectations are, and then manage and influence those expectations to ensure a successful project. Stakeholder identification is often especially difficult. For example, is an assembly line worker whose future employment depends on the outcome of a new product design project a stakeholder?

Key stakeholders on every project include:

- Project manager—the individual responsible for managing the project.
- Customer—the individual or organization who will use the project product. There may be multiple layers of customers. For example, the customers for a new pharmaceutical product may include the doctors who prescribe it, the patients who take it, and the insurers who pay for it.
- Performing organization—the enterprise whose employees are most directly involved in doing the work of the project.
- Sponsor—the individual or group within the performing organization who provides the financial resources, in cash or in kind, for the project.

Figure 2–5. Representative Software Development Life Cycle, per Muench

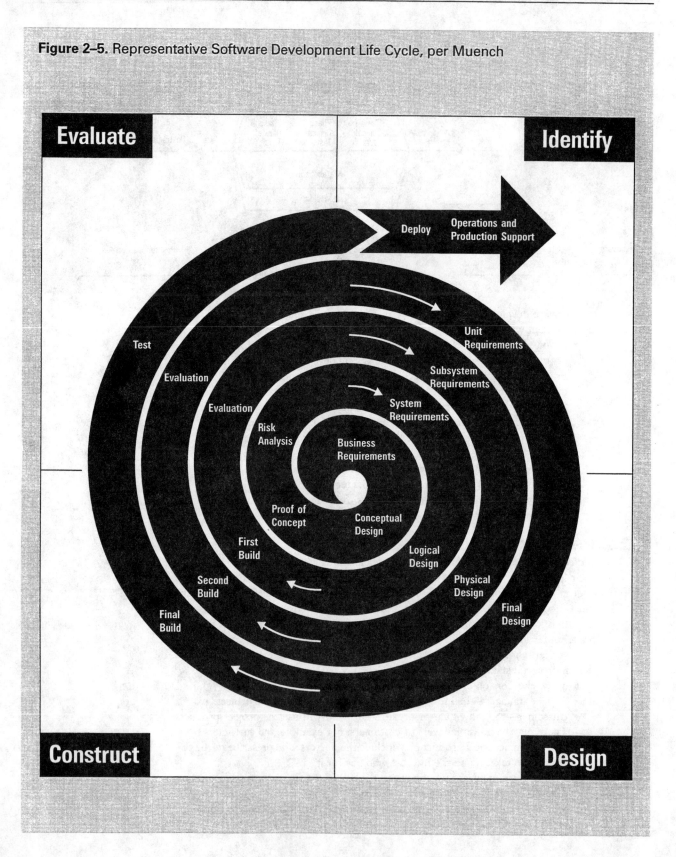

In addition to these there are many different names and categories of project stakeholders—internal and external, owners and funders, suppliers and contractors, team members and their families, government agencies and media outlets, individual citizens, temporary or permanent lobbying organizations, and society at large. The naming or grouping of stakeholders is primarily an aid to identifying which individuals and organizations view themselves as stakeholders. Stakeholder roles and responsibilities may overlap, as when an engineering firm provides financing for a plant it is designing.

Managing stakeholder expectations may be difficult because stakeholders often have very different objectives that may come into conflict. For example:

- The manager of a department that has requested a new management information system may desire low cost, the system architect may emphasize technical excellence, and the programming contractor may be most interested in maximizing its profit.
- The vice president of research at an electronics firm may define new product success as state-of-the-art technology, the vice president of manufacturing may define it as world-class practices, and the vice president of marketing may be primarily concerned with the number of new features.
- The owner of a real estate development project may be focused on timely performance, the local governing body may desire to maximize tax revenue, an environmental group may wish to minimize adverse environmental impacts, and nearby residents may hope to relocate the project.

In general, differences between or among stakeholders should be resolved in favor of the customer. This does not, however, mean that the needs and expectations of other stakeholders can or should be disregarded. Finding appropriate resolutions to such differences can be one of the major challenges of project management.

2.3 ORGANIZATIONAL INFLUENCES

Projects are typically part of an organization larger than the project—corporations, government agencies, health care institutions, international bodies, professional associations, and others. Even when the project is the organization (joint ventures, partnering), the project will still be influenced by the organization or organizations that set it up. The following sections describe key aspects of these larger organizational structures that are likely to influence the project.

2.3.1 Organizational Systems

Project-based organizations are those whose operations consist primarily of projects. These organizations fall into two categories:

- Organizations that derive their revenue primarily from performing projects for others—architectural firms, engineering firms, consultants, construction contractors, government contractors, etc.
- Organizations that have adopted *management by projects* (see Section 1.3).

These organizations tend to have management systems in place to facilitate project management. For example, their financial systems are often specifically designed for accounting, tracking, and reporting on multiple simultaneous projects.

Non–project-based organizations—manufacturing companies, financial service firms, etc.—seldom have management systems designed to support project needs efficiently and effectively. The absence of project-oriented systems usually makes project management more difficult. In some cases, non–project-based organizations will have departments or other sub-units that operate as project-based organizations with systems to match.

FIGURE 2–6   A GUIDE TO THE PROJECT MANAGEMENT BODY OF KNOWLEDGE

Figure 2–6. Organizational Structure Influences on Projects

Project Characteristics \ Organization Type	Functional	Matrix			Projectized
		Weak Matrix	Balanced Matrix	Strong Matrix	
Project Manager's Authority	Little or None	Limited	Low to Moderate	Moderate to High	High to Almost Total
Percent of Performing Organization's Personnel Assigned Full-time to Project Work	Virtually None	0–25%	15–60%	50–95%	85–100%
Project Manager's Role	Part-time	Part-time	Full-time	Full-time	Full-time
Common Titles for Project Manager's Role	Project Coordinator/ Project Leader	Project Coordinator/ Project Leader	Project Manager/ Project Officer	Project Manager/ Program Manager	Project Manager/ Program Manager
Project Management Administrative Staff	Part-time	Part-time	Part-time	Full-time	Full-time

The project management team should be acutely aware of how the organization's systems affect the project. For example, if the organization rewards its functional managers for charging staff time to projects, the project management team may need to implement controls to ensure that assigned staff are being used effectively on the project.

2.3.2 Organizational Cultures and Style

Most organizations have developed unique and describable cultures. These cultures are reflected in their shared values, norms, beliefs, and expectations; in their policies and procedures; in their view of authority relationships; and in numerous other factors. Organizational cultures often have a direct influence on the project. For example:

- A team proposing an unusual or high-risk approach is more likely to secure approval in an aggressive or entrepreneurial organization.
- A project manager with a highly participative style is apt to encounter problems in a rigidly hierarchical organization, while a project manager with an authoritarian style will be equally challenged in a participative organization.

2.3.3 Organizational Structure

The structure of the performing organization often constrains the availability of or terms under which resources become available to the project. Organizational structures can be characterized as spanning a spectrum from *functional* to *projectized*, with a variety of matrix structures in between. **Figure 2–6** details key project-related characteristics of the major types of enterprise organizational structures. Project organization is discussed in Section 9.1, Organizational Planning.

The classic *functional organization* shown in **Figure 2–7** is a hierarchy where each employee has one clear superior. Staff are grouped by specialty, such as production, marketing, engineering, and accounting at the top level, with engineering further subdivided into mechanical and electrical. Functional organizations still have projects, but the perceived scope of the project is limited to the boundaries of

Figure 2–7. Functional Organization

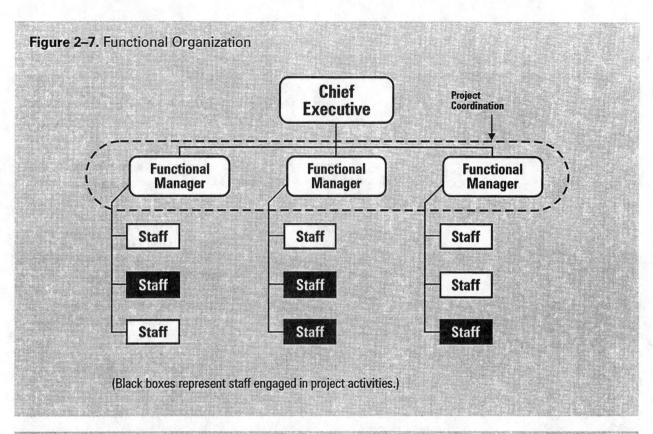

(Black boxes represent staff engaged in project activities.)

Figure 2–8. Projectized Organization

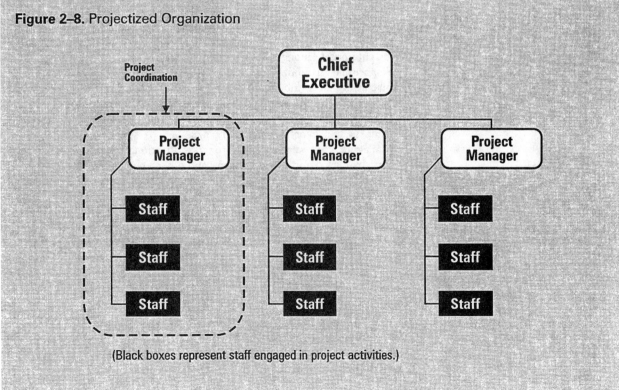

(Black boxes represent staff engaged in project activities.)

the function: the engineering department in a functional organization will do its work independent of the manufacturing or marketing departments. For example, when a new product development is undertaken in a purely functional organization, the design phase is often called a "design project" and includes only engineering department staff. If questions about manufacturing arise, they are passed up the hierarchy to the department head who consults with the head of the manufacturing department. The engineering department head then passes the answer back down the hierarchy to the engineering project manager.

At the opposite end of the spectrum is the *projectized organization* shown in Figure 2–8. In a projectized organization, team members are often collocated. Most of the organization's resources are involved in project work, and project managers have a great deal of independence and authority. Projectized organizations often have organizational units called departments, but these groups either report directly to the project manager or provide support services to the various projects.

Matrix organizations as shown in **Figures 2–9** through **2–11** are a blend of functional and projectized characteristics. Weak matrices maintain many of the characteristics of a functional organization and the project manager role is more that of a coordinator or expediter than that of a manager. In similar fashion, strong matrices have many of the characteristics of the projectized organization—full-time project managers with considerable authority and full-time project administrative staff.

Most modern organizations involve all these structures at various levels as shown in **Figure 2–12**. For example, even a fundamentally functional organization may create a special project team to handle a critical project. Such a team may have many of the characteristics of a project in a projectized organization: it may include full-time staff from different functional departments, it may develop its own set of operating procedures, and it may operate outside the standard, formalized reporting structure.

2.4 KEY GENERAL MANAGEMENT SKILLS

General management is a broad subject dealing with every aspect of managing an ongoing enterprise. Among other topics, it includes:
- Finance and accounting, sales and marketing, research and development, manufacturing and distribution.
- Strategic planning, tactical planning, and operational planning.
- Organizational structures, organizational behavior, personnel administration, compensation, benefits, and career paths.
- Managing work relationships through motivation, delegation, supervision, team building, conflict management, and other techniques.
- Managing oneself through personal time management, stress management, and other techniques.

General management skills provide much of the foundation for building project management skills. They are often essential for the project manager. On any given project, skill in any number of general management areas may be required. This section describes key general management skills that are *highly likely to affect most projects* and that are not covered elsewhere. These skills are well documented in the general management literature and their application is fundamentally the same on a project.

There are also many general management skills that are relevant only on certain projects or in certain application areas. For example, team member safety is critical on virtually all construction projects and of little concern on most software development projects.

FIGURE 2–10

Figure 2–9. Weak Matrix Organization

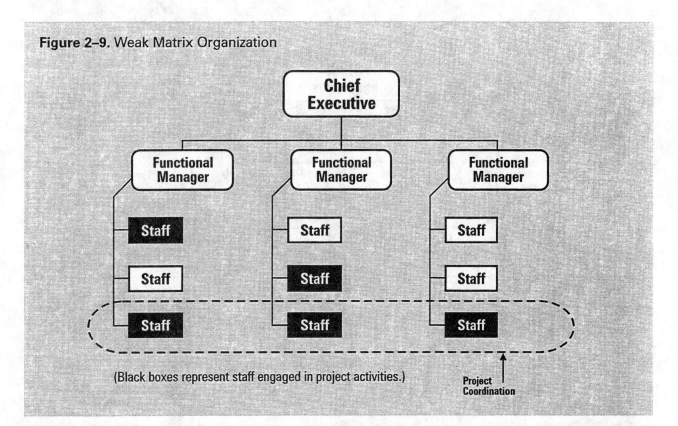

(Black boxes represent staff engaged in project activities.)

Project Coordination

Figure 2–10. Balanced Matrix Organization

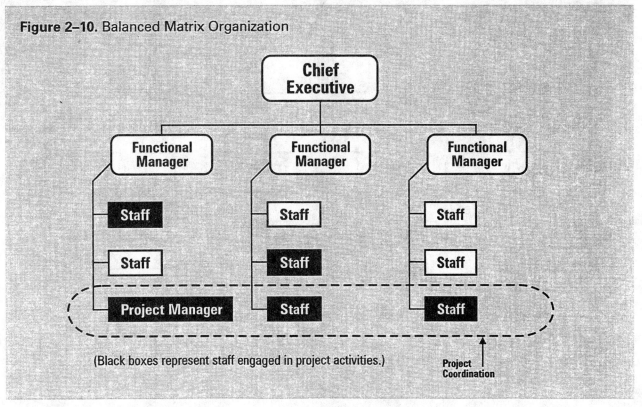

(Black boxes represent staff engaged in project activities.)

Project Coordination

FIGURE 2–11   A GUIDE TO THE PROJECT MANAGEMENT BODY OF KNOWLEDGE

Figure 2–11. Strong Matrix Organization

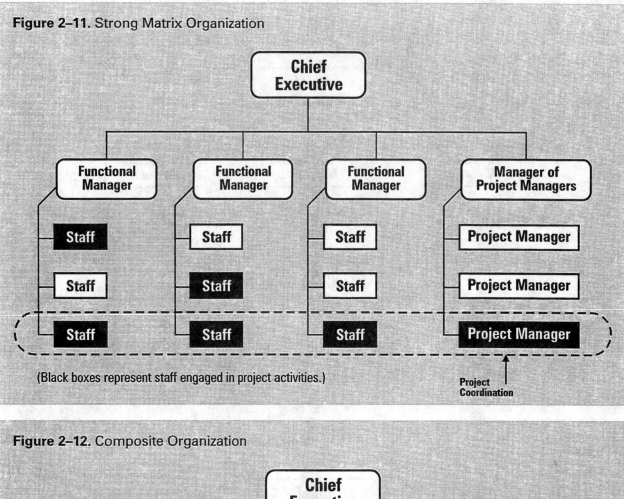

(Black boxes represent staff engaged in project activities.)

Figure 2–12. Composite Organization

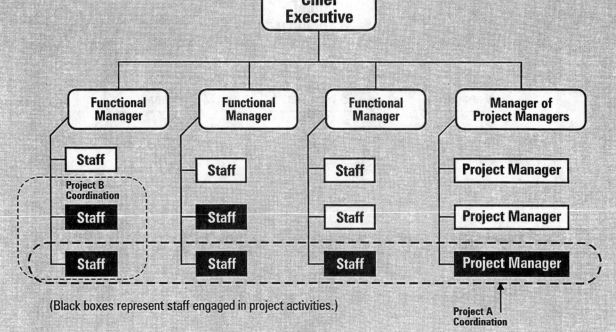

(Black boxes represent staff engaged in project activities.)

2.4.1 Leading

Kotter [4] distinguishes between *leading* and *managing* while emphasizing the need for both: one without the other is likely to produce poor results. He says that managing is primarily concerned with "consistently producing key results expected by stakeholders," while leading involves:

- Establishing direction—developing both a vision of the future and strategies for producing the changes needed to achieve that vision.
- Aligning people—communicating the vision by words and deeds to all those whose cooperation may be needed to achieve the vision.
- Motivating and inspiring—helping people energize themselves to overcome political, bureaucratic, and resource barriers to change.

On a project, particularly a larger project, the project manager is generally expected to be the project's leader as well. Leadership is not, however, limited to the project manager: it may be demonstrated by many different individuals at many different times during the project. Leadership must be demonstrated at all levels of the project (project leadership, technical leadership, team leadership).

2.4.2 Communicating

Communicating involves the exchange of information. The sender is responsible for making the information clear, unambiguous, and complete so that the receiver can receive it correctly. The receiver is responsible for making sure that the information is received in its entirety and understood correctly. Communicating has many dimensions:

- Written and oral, listening and speaking.
- Internal (within the project) and external (to the customer, the media, the public, etc.).
- Formal (reports, briefings, etc.) and informal (memos, ad hoc conversations, etc.).
- Vertical (up and down the organization) and horizontal (with peers).

The general management skill of communicating is related to, but not the same as, Project Communications Management (described in Chapter 10). Communicating is the broader subject and involves a substantial body of knowledge that is not unique to the project context, for example:

- Sender-receiver models—feedback loops, barriers to communications, etc.
- Choice of media—when to communicate in writing, when to communicate orally, when to write an informal memo, when to write a formal report, etc.
- Writing style—active vs. passive voice, sentence structure, word choice, etc.
- Presentation techniques—body language, design of visual aids, etc.
- Meeting management techniques—preparing an agenda, dealing with conflict, etc.

Project Communications Management is the application of these broad concepts to the specific needs of a project; for example, deciding how, when, in what form, and to whom to report project performance.

2.4.3 Negotiating

Negotiating involves conferring with others in order to come to terms or reach an agreement. Agreements may be negotiated directly or with assistance; mediation and arbitration are two types of assisted negotiation.

Negotiations occur around many issues, at many times, and at many levels of the project. During the course of a typical project, project staff are likely to negotiate for any or all of the following:

- Scope, cost, and schedule objectives.
- Changes to scope, cost, or schedule.
- Contract terms and conditions.
- Assignments.
- Resources.

2.4.4 Problem Solving

Problem solving involves a combination of problem definition and decision making. It is concerned with problems that have already occurred (as opposed to risk management that addresses potential problems).

Problem definition requires distinguishing between causes and symptoms. Problems may be internal (a key employee is reassigned to another project) or external (a permit required to begin work is delayed). Problems may be technical (differences of opinion about the best way to design a product), managerial (a functional group is not producing according to plan), or interpersonal (personality or style clashes).

Decision making includes analyzing the problem to identify viable solutions, and then making a choice from among them. Decisions can be made or obtained (from the customer, from the team, or from a functional manager). Once made, decisions must be implemented. Decisions also have a time element to them—the "right" decision may not be the "best" decision if it is made too early or too late.

2.4.5 Influencing the Organization

Influencing the organization involves the ability to "get things done." It requires an understanding of both the formal and informal structures of all the organizations involved—the performing organization, the customer, contractors, and numerous others as appropriate. Influencing the organization also requires an understanding of the mechanics of power and politics.

Both power and politics are used here in their positive senses. Pfeffer [5] defines power as "the potential ability to influence behavior, to change the course of events, to overcome resistance, and to get people to do things that they would not otherwise do." In similar fashion, Eccles [6] says that "politics is about getting collective action from a group of people who may have quite different interests. It is about being willing to use conflict and disorder creatively. The negative sense, of course, derives from the fact that attempts to reconcile these interests result in power struggles and organizational games that can sometimes take on a thoroughly unproductive life of their own."

2.5 SOCIOECONOMIC INFLUENCES

Like general management, *socioeconomic influences* include a wide range of topics and issues. The project management team must understand that current conditions and trends in this area may have a major effect on their project: a small change here can translate, usually with a time lag, into cataclysmic upheavals in the project itself. Of the many potential socioeconomic influences, several major categories that frequently affect projects are described briefly below.

2.5.1 Standards and Regulations

The International Organization for Standardization (ISO) differentiates between standards and regulations as follows [7]:

- A *standard* is a "document approved by a recognized body, that provides, for common and repeated use, rules, guidelines, or characteristics for products, processes or services with which compliance is not mandatory." There are numerous standards in use covering everything from thermal stability of hydraulic fluids to the size of computer diskettes.
- A *regulation* is a "document which lays down product, process or service characteristics, including the applicable administrative provisions, with which compliance is mandatory." Building codes are an example of regulations.

Care must be used in discussing standards and regulations since there is a vast gray area between the two, for example:

- Standards often begin as guidelines that describe a preferred approach, and later, with widespread adoption, become *de facto* regulations (e.g., the use of the Critical Path Method for scheduling major construction projects).
- Compliance may be mandated at different levels (e.g., by a government agency, by the management of the performing organization, or by the project management team).

For many projects, standards and regulations (by whatever definition) are well known and project plans can reflect their effects. In other cases, the influence is unknown or uncertain and must be considered under Project Risk Management.

2.5.2 Internationalization

As more and more organizations engage in work which spans national boundaries, more and more projects span national boundaries as well. In addition to the traditional concerns of scope, cost, time, and quality, the project management team must also consider the effect of time zone differences, national and regional holidays, travel requirements for face-to-face meetings, the logistics of teleconferencing, and often volatile political differences.

2.5.3 Cultural Influences

Culture is the "totality of socially transmitted behavior patterns, arts, beliefs, institutions, and all other products of human work and thought" [8]. Every project must operate within a context of one or more cultural norms. This area of influence includes political, economic, demographic, educational, ethical, ethnic, religious, and other areas of practice, belief, and attitudes that affect the way people and organizations interact.

PROJECT MANAGEMENT PROCESSES

3

Project management is an integrative endeavor—an action, or failure to take action, in one area will usually affect other areas. The interactions may be straightforward and well-understood, or they may be subtle and uncertain. For example, a scope change will almost always affect project cost, but it may or may not affect team morale or product quality.

These interactions often require trade-offs among project objectives—performance in one area may be enhanced only by sacrificing performance in another. Successful project management requires actively managing these interactions.

To help in understanding the integrative nature of project management, and to emphasize the importance of integration, this document describes project management in terms of its component processes and their interactions. This chapter provides an introduction to the concept of project management as a number of interlinked processes and thus provides an essential foundation for understanding the process descriptions in Chapters 4 through 12. It includes the following major sections:

3.1 Project Processes
3.2 Process Groups
3.3 Process Interactions
3.4 Customizing Process Interactions

3.1 PROJECT PROCESSES

Projects are composed of processes. A *process* is "a series of actions bringing about a result" [1]. Project processes are performed by people and generally fall into one of two major categories:

- *Project management processes* are concerned with describing and organizing the work of the project. The project management processes that are applicable to most projects, most of the time, are described briefly in this chapter and in detail in Chapters 4 through 12.
- *Product-oriented processes* are concerned with specifying and creating the project product. Product-oriented processes are typically defined by the project life cycle (discussed in Section 2.1) and vary by application area (discussed in Appendix F).

Project management processes and product-oriented processes overlap and interact throughout the project. For example, the scope of the project cannot be defined in the absence of some basic understanding of how to create the product.

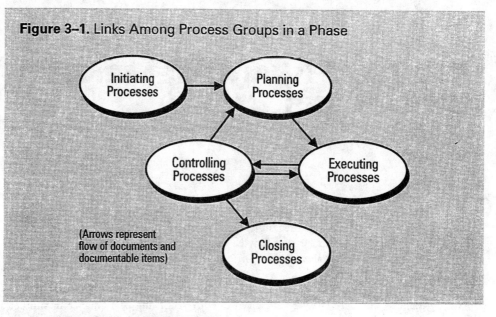

Figure 3–1. Links Among Process Groups in a Phase

3.2 PROCESS GROUPS

Project management processes can be organized into five groups of one or more processes each:

- Initiating processes—recognizing that a project or phase should begin and committing to do so.
- Planning processes—devising and maintaining a workable scheme to accomplish the business need that the project was undertaken to address.
- Executing processes—coordinating people and other resources to carry out the plan.
- Controlling processes—ensuring that project objectives are met by monitoring and measuring progress and taking corrective action when necessary.
- Closing processes—formalizing acceptance of the project or phase and bringing it to an orderly end.

The process groups are linked by the results they produce—the result or outcome of one becomes an input to another. Among the central process groups, the links are iterated—planning provides executing with a documented project plan early on, and then provides documented updates to the plan as the project progresses. These connections are illustrated in **Figure 3–1.** In addition, the project management process groups are not discrete, one-time events; they are overlapping activities which occur at varying levels of intensity throughout each phase of the project. **Figure 3–2** illustrates how the process groups overlap and vary within a phase.

Finally, the process group interactions also cross phases such that closing one phase provides an input to initiating the next. For example, closing a design phase requires customer acceptance of the design document. Simultaneously, the design document defines the product description for the ensuing implementation phase. This interaction is illustrated in **Figure 3–3.**

Repeating the initiation processes at the start of each phase helps to keep the project focused on the business need it was undertaken to address. It should also help ensure that the project is halted if the business need no longer exists or if the project is unlikely to satisfy that need. Business needs are discussed in more detail in the introduction to Section 5.1, Initiation.

Figure 3–2. Overlap of Process Groups in a Phase

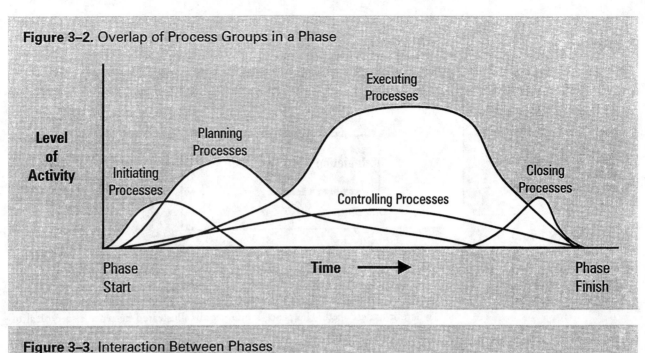

Figure 3–3. Interaction Between Phases

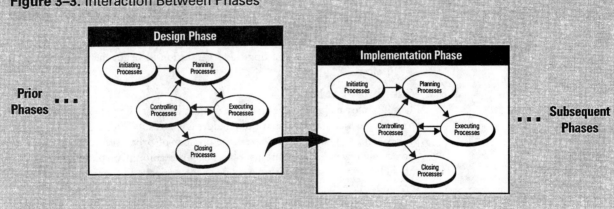

Although **Figure 3–3** is drawn with discrete phases and discrete processes, in an actual project there will be many overlaps. The planning process, for example, must not only provide details of the work to be done to bring the current phase of the project to successful completion but must also provide some preliminary description of work to be done in later phases. This progressive detailing of the project plan is often called *rolling wave planning*.

3.3 PROCESS INTERACTIONS

Within each process group, the individual processes are linked by their inputs and outputs. By focusing on these links, we can describe each process in terms of its:

- Inputs—documents or documentable items that will be acted upon.
- Tools and techniques—mechanisms applied to the inputs to create the outputs.
- Outputs—documents or documentable items that are a result of the process.

FIGURE 3–4   A GUIDE TO THE PROJECT MANAGEMENT BODY OF KNOWLEDGE

Figure 3–4. Relationships Among the Initiating Processes

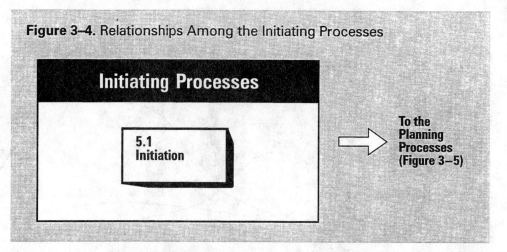

The project management processes common to most projects in most application areas are listed here and described in detail in Chapters 4 through 12. The numbers in parentheses after the process names identify the chapter and section where it is described. The process interactions illustrated here are also typical of most projects in most application areas. Section 3.4 discusses customizing both process descriptions and interactions.

3.3.1 Initiating Processes

Figure 3–4 illustrates the single process in this process group.
- Initiation (5.1)—committing the organization to begin the next phase of the project.

3.3.2 Planning Processes

Planning is of major importance to a project because the project involves doing something which has not been done before. As a result, there are relatively more processes in this section. However, the number of processes does not mean that project management is primarily planning—the amount of planning performed should be commensurate with the scope of the project and the usefulness of the information developed.

The relationships among the project planning processes are shown in **Figure 3–5** (this chart is an explosion of the ellipse labeled "planning processes" in **Figure 3–1**). These processes are subject to frequent iterations prior to completing the plan. For example, if the initial completion date is unacceptable, project resources, cost, or even scope may need to be redefined. In addition, planning is not an exact science—two different teams could generate very different plans for the same project.

Core processes. Some planning processes have clear dependencies that require them to be performed in essentially the same order on most projects. For example, activities must be defined before they can be scheduled or costed. These *core planning processes* may be iterated several times during any one phase of a project. They include:
- Scope Planning (5.2)—developing a written scope statement as the basis for future project decisions.
- Scope Definition (5.3)—subdividing the major project deliverables into smaller, more manageable components.
- Activity Definition (6.1)—identifying the specific activities that must be performed to produce the various project deliverables.

Figure 3–5. Relationships Among the Planning Processes

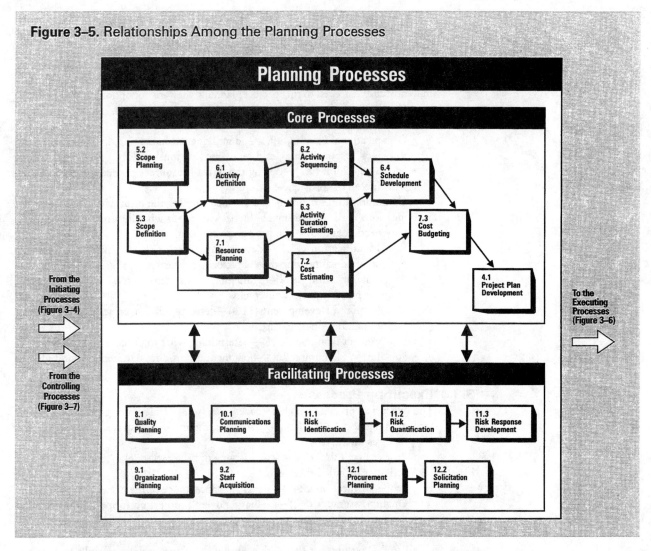

- Activity Sequencing (6.2)—identifying and documenting interactivity dependencies.
- Activity Duration Estimating (6.3)—estimating the number of work periods which will be needed to complete individual activities.
- Schedule Development (6.4)—analyzing activity sequences, activity durations, and resource requirements to create the project schedule.
- Resource Planning (7.1)—determining what resources (people, equipment, materials) and what quantities of each should be used to perform project activities.
- Cost Estimating (7.2)—developing an approximation (estimate) of the costs of the resources needed to complete project activities.
- Cost Budgeting (7.3)—allocating the overall cost estimate to individual work items.
- Project Plan Development (4.1)—taking the results of other planning processes and putting them into a consistent, coherent document.

Facilitating processes. Interactions among the other planning processes are more dependent on the nature of the project. For example, on some projects there may be little or no identifiable risk until after most of the planning has been done and the team recognizes that the cost and schedule targets are extremely aggressive and thus involve considerable risk. Although these *facilitating processes* are performed intermittently and as needed during project planning, they are not optional. They include:

- Quality Planning (8.1)—identifying which quality standards are relevant to the project and determining how to satisfy them.
- Organizational Planning (9.1)—identifying, documenting, and assigning project roles, responsibilities, and reporting relationships.
- Staff Acquisition (9.2)—getting the human resources needed assigned to and working on the project.
- Communications Planning (10.1)—determining the information and communications needs of the stakeholders: who needs what information, when will they need it, and how will it be given to them.
- Risk Identification (11.1)—determining which risks are likely to affect the project and documenting the characteristics of each.
- Risk Quantification (11.2)—evaluating risks and risk interactions to assess the range of possible project outcomes.
- Risk Response Development (11.3)—defining enhancement steps for opportunities and responses to threats.
- Procurement Planning (12.1)—determining what to procure and when.
- Solicitation Planning (12.2)—documenting product requirements and identifying potential sources.

3.3.3 Executing Processes

The executing processes include core processes and facilitating processes as described in Section 3.3.2, Planning Processes. **Figure 3–6** illustrates how the following processes interact:

- Project Plan Execution (4.2)—carrying out the project plan by performing the activities included therein.
- Scope Verification (5.4)—formalizing acceptance of the project scope.
- Quality Assurance (8.2)—evaluating overall project performance on a regular basis to provide confidence that the project will satisfy the relevant quality standards.
- Team Development (9.3)—developing individual and group skills to enhance project performance.
- Information Distribution (10.2)—making needed information available to project stakeholders in a timely manner.
- Solicitation (12.3)—obtaining quotations, bids, offers, or proposals as appropriate.
- Source Selection (12.4)—choosing from among potential sellers.
- Contract Administration (12.5)—managing the relationship with the seller.

3.3.4 Controlling Processes

Project performance must be measured regularly to identify variances from the plan. Variances are fed into the control processes in the various knowledge areas. To the extent that significant variances are observed (i.e., those that jeopardize the project objectives), adjustments to the plan are made by repeating the appropriate project planning processes. For example, a missed activity finish date may require adjustments to the current staffing plan, reliance on overtime, or trade-offs between budget and schedule objectives. Controlling also includes taking preventive action in anticipation of possible problems.

Figure 3–6. Relationships Among the Executing Processes

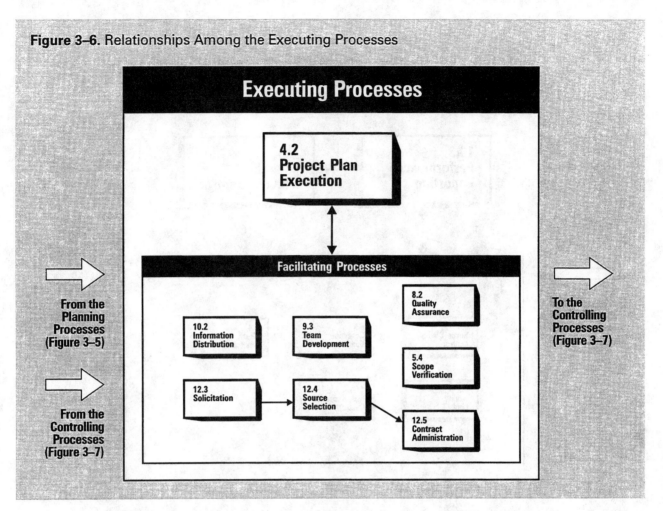

The controlling process group contains core processes and facilitating processes as described in Section 3.3.2, Planning Processes.

Figure 3–7 illustrates how the following processes interact:

- Overall Change Control (4.3)—coordinating changes across the entire project.
- Scope Change Control (5.5)—controlling changes to project scope.
- Schedule Control (6.5)—controlling changes to the project schedule.
- Cost Control (7.4)—controlling changes to the project budget.
- Quality Control (8.3)—monitoring specific project results to determine if they comply with relevant quality standards and identifying ways to eliminate causes of unsatisfactory performance.
- Performance Reporting (10.3)—collecting and disseminating performance information. This includes status reporting, progress measurement, and forecasting.
- Risk Response Control (11.4)—responding to changes in risk over the course of the project.

FIGURE 3–7   A GUIDE TO THE PROJECT MANAGEMENT BODY OF KNOWLEDGE

Figure 3–7. Relationships Among the Controlling Processes

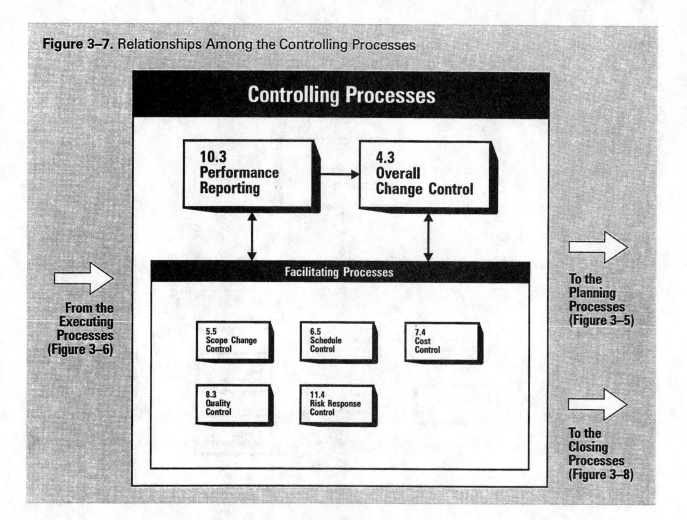

3.3.5 Closing Processes

Figure 3–8 illustrates how the following processes interact:

- Administrative Closure (10.4)—generating, gathering, and disseminating information to formalize phase or project completion.
- Contract Close-out (12.6)—completion and settlement of the contract, including resolution of any open items.

3.4 CUSTOMIZING PROCESS INTERACTIONS

The processes identified and the interactions illustrated in Section 3.3 meet the test of general acceptance—they apply to most projects most of the time. However, not all of the processes will be needed on all projects, and not all of the interactions will apply to all projects. For example:

- An organization that makes extensive use of contractors may explicitly describe where in the planning process each procurement process occurs.
- The absence of a process does not mean that it should not be performed. The project management team should identify and manage all the processes that are needed to ensure a successful project.

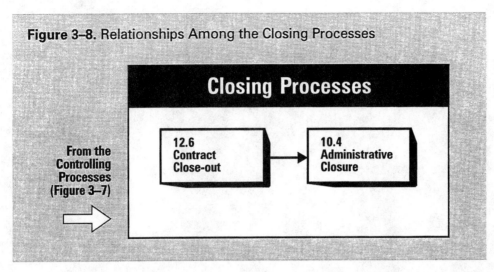

Figure 3–8. Relationships Among the Closing Processes

- Projects which are dependent on unique resources (commercial software development, biopharmaceuticals, etc.) may define roles and responsibilities prior to scope definition since what can be done may be a function of who will be available to do it.
- Some process outputs may be predefined as constraints. For example, management may specify a target completion date rather than allowing it to be determined by the planning process.
- Larger projects may need relatively more detail. For example, risk identification might be further subdivided to focus separately on identifying cost risks, schedule risks, technical risks, and quality risks.
- On subprojects and smaller projects, relatively little effort will be spent on processes whose outputs have been defined at the project level (e.g., a subcontractor may ignore risks explicitly assumed by the prime contractor) or on processes that provide only marginal utility (there may be no formal communications plan on a four-person project).

When there is a need to make a change, the change should be clearly identified, carefully evaluated, and actively managed.

THE PROJECT MANAGEMENT KNOWLEDGE AREAS

ii

4. Project Integration Management

5. Project Scope Management

6. Project Time Management

7. Project Cost Management

8. Project Quality Management

9. Project Human Resource Management

10. Project Communications Management

11. Project Risk Management

12. Project Procurement Management

PROJECT INTEGRATION MANAGEMENT

4

Project Integration Management includes the processes required to ensure that the various elements of the project are properly coordinated. It involves making trade-offs among competing objectives and alternatives in order to meet or exceed stakeholder needs and expectations. While all project management processes are integrative to some extent, the processes described in this chapter are *primarily* integrative. **Figure 4–1** provides an overview of the following major processes:

4.1 **Project Plan Development**—taking the results of other planning processes and putting them into a consistent, coherent document.

4.2 **Project Plan Execution**—carrying out the project plan by performing the activities included therein.

4.3 **Overall Change Control**—coordinating changes across the entire project.

These processes interact with each other and with the processes in the other knowledge areas as well. Each process may involve effort from one or more individuals or groups of individuals based on the needs of the project. Each process generally occurs at least once in every project phase.

Although the processes are presented here as discrete elements with well-defined interfaces, in practice they may overlap and interact in ways not detailed here. Process interactions are discussed in detail in Chapter 3.

The processes, tools, and techniques used to integrate *project management* processes are the focus of this chapter. For example, project integration management comes into play when a cost estimate is needed for a contingency plan or when risks associated with various staffing alternatives must be identified. However, for a project to be completed successfully, integration must also occur in a number of other areas as well. For example:

• The work of the project must be integrated with the ongoing operations of the performing organization.

• Product scope and project scope must be integrated (the difference between product and project scope is discussed in the introduction to Chapter 5).

• Deliverables from different functional specialties (such as civil, electrical, and mechanical drawings for an engineering design project) must be integrated.

4.1 PROJECT PLAN DEVELOPMENT

Project plan development uses the outputs of the other planning processes to create a consistent, coherent document that can be used to guide both project execution and project control. This process is almost always iterated several times. For example, the initial draft may include generic resources and undated durations while the final plan reflects specific resources and explicit dates. The project plan is used to:

• Guide project execution.

• Document project planning assumptions.

- Document project planning decisions regarding alternatives chosen.
- Facilitate communication among stakeholders.
- Define key management reviews as to content, extent, and timing.
- Provide a baseline for progress measurement and project control.

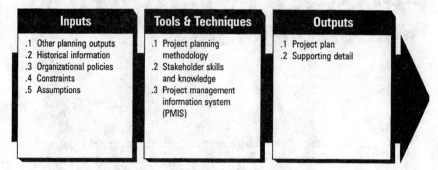

Inputs	Tools & Techniques	Outputs
.1 Other planning outputs .2 Historical information .3 Organizational policies .4 Constraints .5 Assumptions	.1 Project planning methodology .2 Stakeholder skills and knowledge .3 Project management information system (PMIS)	.1 Project plan .2 Supporting detail

4.1.1 Inputs to Project Plan Development

   .1 *Other planning outputs.* All of the outputs of the planning processes in the other knowledge areas (Section 3.3 provides a summary of these project planning processes) are inputs to developing the project plan. Other planning outputs include both base documents such as the work breakdown structure as well as the supporting detail. Many projects will also require application area-specific inputs (e.g., most construction projects will require a cash flow forecast).

   .2 *Historical information.* The available historical information (e.g., estimating databases, records of past project performance) should have been consulted during the other project planning processes. This information should also be available during project plan development to assist with verifying assumptions and assessing alternatives that are identified as part of this process.

   .3 *Organizational policies.* Any and all of the organizations involved in the project may have formal and informal policies whose effects must be considered. Organizational policies which typically must be considered include, but are not limited to:

- Quality management—process audits, continuous improvement targets.
- Personnel administration—hiring and firing guidelines, employee performance reviews.
- Financial controls—time reporting, required expenditure and disbursement reviews, accounting codes, standard contract provisions.

   .4 *Constraints.* Constraints are factors that will limit the project management team's options. For example, a predefined budget is a constraint that is highly likely to limit the team's options regarding scope, staffing, and schedule.

      When a project is performed under contract, contractual provisions will generally be constraints.

   .5 *Assumptions.* Assumptions are factors that, for planning purposes, will be considered to be true, real, or certain. For example, if the date that a key person will become available is uncertain, the team may assume a specific start date. Assumptions generally involve a degree of risk.

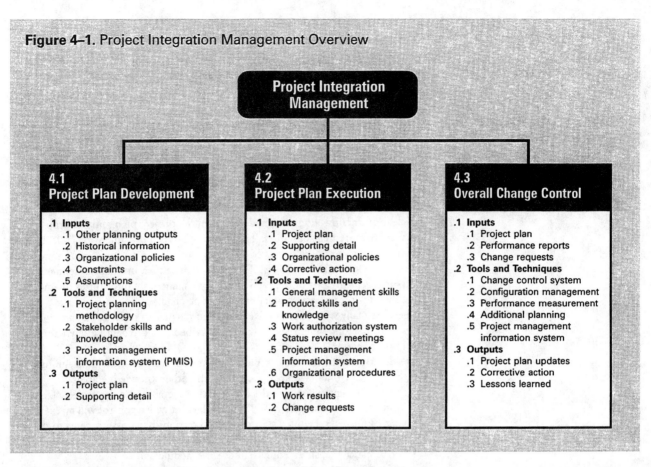

Figure 4–1. Project Integration Management Overview

4.1.2 Tools and Techniques for Project Plan Development

.1 Project planning methodology. A project planning methodology is any structured approach used to guide the project team during development of the project plan. It may be as simple as standard forms and templates (whether paper or electronic, formal or informal) or as complex as a series of required simulations (e.g., Monte Carlo analysis of schedule risk). Most project planning methodologies make use of a combination of "hard" tools such as project management software and "soft" tools such as facilitated start-up meetings.

.2 Stakeholder skills and knowledge. Every stakeholder has skills and knowledge which may be useful in developing the project plan. The project management team must create an environment in which the stakeholders can contribute appropriately (see also Section 9.3, Team Development). Who contributes, what they contribute, and when will vary. For example:

- On a construction project being done under a lump sum contract, the professional cost engineer will make a major contribution to the profitability objective during proposal preparation when the contract amount is being determined.
- On a project where staffing is defined in advance, the individual contributors may contribute significantly to meeting cost and schedule objectives by reviewing duration and effort estimates for reasonableness.

.3 *Project management information system (PMIS).* A project management information system consists of the tools and techniques used to gather, integrate, and disseminate the outputs of the other project management processes. It is used to support all aspects of the project from initiating through closing and generally includes both manual and automated systems.

4.1.3 Outputs from Project Plan Development

.1 *Project plan.* The project plan is a formal, approved document used to manage and control project execution. It should be distributed as defined in the communications management plan (e.g., management of the performing organization may require broad coverage with little detail, while a contractor may require complete details on a single subject). In some application areas, the term *integrated project plan* is used to refer to this document.

A clear distinction should be made between the project plan and the project performance measurement baselines. The project plan is a document or collection of documents that should be expected to change over time as more information becomes available about the project. The performance measurement baselines represent a *management control* that will generally change only intermittently and then generally only in response to an approved scope change.

There are many ways to organize and present the project plan, but it commonly includes all of the following (these items are described in more detail elsewhere):
- Project charter.
- A description of the project management approach or strategy (a summary of the individual management plans from the other knowledge areas).
- Scope statement, which includes the project deliverables and the project objectives.
- Work breakdown structure (WBS) to the level at which control will be exercised.
- Cost estimates, scheduled start dates, and responsibility assignments to the level of the WBS at which control will be exercised.
- Performance measurement baselines for schedule and cost.
- Major milestones and target dates for each.
- Key or required staff.
- Key risks, including constraints and assumptions, and planned responses for each.
- Subsidiary management plans, including scope management plan, schedule management plan, etc.
- Open issues and pending decisions.

Other project planning outputs should be included in the formal plan based upon the needs of the individual project. For example, the project plan for a large project will generally include a project organization chart.

.2 *Supporting detail.* Supporting detail for the project plan includes:
- Outputs from other planning processes that are not included in the project plan.
- Additional information or documentation generated during development of the project plan (e.g., constraints and assumptions that were not previously known).
- Technical documentation such as requirements, specifications, and designs.
- Documentation of relevant standards.

This material should be organized as needed to facilitate its use during project plan execution.

4.2 PROJECT PLAN EXECUTION

Project plan execution is the primary process for carrying out the project plan—the vast majority of the project's budget will be expended in performing this process. In this process, the project manager and the project management team must coordinate and direct the various technical and organizational interfaces that exist in the project. It is the project process that is most directly affected by the project application area in that the product of the project is actually created here.

Inputs	Tools & Techniques	Outputs
.1 Project plan	.1 General management skills	.1 Work results
.2 Supporting detail	.2 Product skills and knowledge	.2 Change requests
.3 Organizational policies	.3 Work authorization system	
.4 Corrective action	.4 Status review meetings	
	.5 Project management information system	
	.6 Organizational procedures	

4.2.1 Inputs to Project Plan Execution

.1 *Project plan*. The project plan is described in Section 4.1.3.1. The subsidiary management plans (scope management plan, risk management plan, procurement management plan, etc.) and the performance measurement baselines are key inputs to project plan execution.

.2 *Supporting detail*. Supporting detail is described in Section 4.1.3.2.

.3 *Organizational policies*. Organizational policies are described in Section 4.1.1.3. Any and all of the organizations involved in the project may have formal and informal policies which may affect project plan execution.

.4 *Corrective action*. Corrective action is anything done to bring expected future project performance into line with the project plan. Corrective action is an output of the various control processes—as an input here it completes the feedback loop needed to ensure effective project management.

4.2.2 Tools and Techniques for Project Plan Execution

.1 *General management skills*. General management skills such as leadership, communicating, and negotiating are essential to effective project plan execution. General management skills are described in Section 2.4.

.2 *Product skills and knowledge*. The project team must have access to an appropriate set of skills and knowledge about the project product. The necessary skills are defined as part of planning (especially in resource planning, Section 7.1) and are provided through the staff acquisition process (described in Section 9.2).

.3 *Work authorization system*. A work authorization system is a formal procedure for sanctioning project work to ensure that work is done at the right time and in the proper sequence. The primary mechanism is typically a written authorization to begin work on a specific activity or work package.

The design of a work authorization system should balance the value of the control provided with the cost of that control. For example, on many smaller projects, verbal authorizations will be adequate.

.4 *Status review meetings*. Status review meetings are regularly scheduled meetings held to exchange information about the project. On most projects, status review meetings will be held at various frequencies and on different levels (e.g., the project management team may meet weekly by itself and monthly with the customer).

.5 *Project management information system*. The project management information system is described in Section 4.1.2.3.

.6 *Organizational procedures.* Any and all of the organizations involved in the project may have formal and informal procedures useful during project execution.

4.2.3 Outputs from Project Plan Execution

.1 *Work results.* Work results are the outcomes of the activities performed to accomplish the project. Information on work results—which deliverables have been completed and which have not, to what extent quality standards are being met, what costs have been incurred or committed, etc.—is collected as part of project plan execution and fed into the performance reporting process (see Section 10.3 for a more detailed discussion of performance reporting).

.2 *Change requests.* Change requests (e.g., to expand or contract project scope, to modify cost or schedule estimates, etc.) are often identified while the work of the project is being done.

4.3 OVERALL CHANGE CONTROL

Overall change control is concerned with (a) influencing the factors which create changes to ensure that changes are beneficial, (b) determining that a change has occurred, and (c) managing the actual changes when and as they occur. Overall change control requires:

- Maintaining the integrity of the performance measurement baselines—all approved changes should be reflected in the project plan, but only project scope changes will affect the performance measurement baselines.
- Ensuring that changes to the product scope are reflected in the definition of the project scope (the difference between product and project scope is discussed in the introduction to Chapter 5).
- Coordinating changes across knowledge areas as illustrated in Figure 4–2. For example, a proposed schedule change will often affect cost, risk, quality, and staffing.

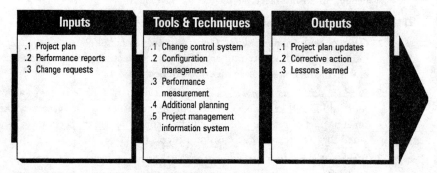

Inputs	Tools & Techniques	Outputs
.1 Project plan .2 Performance reports .3 Change requests	.1 Change control system .2 Configuration management .3 Performance measurement .4 Additional planning .5 Project management information system	.1 Project plan updates .2 Corrective action .3 Lessons learned

4.3.1 Inputs to Overall Change Control

.1 *Project plan.* The project plan provides the baseline against which changes will be controlled (see Section 4.1.3.1).

.2 *Performance reports.* Performance reports (described in Section 10.3) provide information on project performance. Performance reports may also alert the project team to issues which may cause problems in the future.

.3 *Change requests.* Change requests may occur in many forms—oral or written, direct or indirect, externally or internally initiated, and legally mandated or optional.

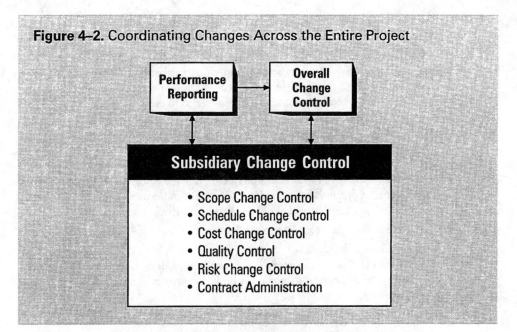

Figure 4–2. Coordinating Changes Across the Entire Project

4.3.2 Tools and Techniques for Overall Change Control

.1 *Change control system.* A change control system is a collection of formal, documented procedures that defines the steps by which official project documents may be changed. It includes the paperwork, tracking systems, and approval levels necessary for authorizing changes.

In many cases, the performing organization will have a change control system that can be adopted "as is" for use by the project. However, if an appropriate system is not available, the project management team will need to develop one as part of the project.

Many change control systems include a change control board (CCB) responsible for approving or rejecting change requests. The powers and responsibilities of a CCB should be well-defined and agreed upon by key stakeholders. On large, complex projects, there may be multiple CCBs with different responsibilities.

The change control system must also include procedures to handle changes which may be approved without prior review; for example, as the result of emergencies. Typically, a change control system will allow for "automatic" approval of defined categories of changes. These changes must still be documented and captured so that they do not cause problems later in the project.

.2 *Configuration management.* Configuration management is any documented procedure used to apply technical and administrative direction and surveillance to:

- Identify and document the functional and physical characteristics of an item or system.
- Control any changes to such characteristics.
- Record and report the change and its implementation status.
- Audit the items and system to verify conformance to requirements [1].

In many application areas, configuration management is a subset of the change control system and is used to ensure that the description of the project product is correct and complete. However, in some application areas, the term *configuration management* is used to describe any rigorous change control system.

.3 *Performance measurement.* Performance measurement techniques such as earned value (described in Section 10.3.2.4) help to assess whether variances from the plan require corrective action.

.4 *Additional planning.* Projects seldom run exactly according to plan. Prospective changes may require new or revised cost estimates, modified activity sequences, analysis of risk response alternatives, or other adjustments to the project plan.

.5 *Project management information system.* Project management information systems are described in Section 4.1.2.3.

4.3.3 Outputs from Overall Change Control

.1 *Project plan updates.* Project plan updates are any modification to the contents of the project plan or the supporting detail (described in Sections 4.1.3.1 and 4.1.3.2, respectively). Appropriate stakeholders must be notified as needed.

.2 *Corrective action.* Corrective action is described in Section 4.2.1.4.

.3 *Lessons learned.* The causes of variances, the reasoning behind the corrective action chosen, and other types of lessons learned should be documented so that they become part of the historical database for both this project and other projects of the performing organization.

PROJECT SCOPE MANAGEMENT

5

Project Scope Management includes the processes required to ensure that the project includes all the work required, and only the work required, to complete the project successfully [1]. It is primarily concerned with defining and controlling what is or is not included in the project. **Figure 5–1** provides an overview of the major project scope management processes:

5.1 **Initiation**—committing the organization to begin the next phase of the project.

5.2 **Scope Planning**—developing a written scope statement as the basis for future project decisions.

5.3 **Scope Definition**—subdividing the major project deliverables into smaller, more manageable components.

5.4 **Scope Verification**—formalizing acceptance of the project scope.

5.5 **Scope Change Control**—controlling changes to project scope.

These processes interact with each other and with the processes in the other knowledge areas as well. Each process may involve effort from one or more individuals or groups of individuals based on the needs of the project. Each process generally occurs at least once in every project phase.

Although the processes are presented here as discrete elements with well-defined interfaces, in practice they may overlap and interact in ways not detailed here. Process interactions are discussed in detail in Chapter 3.

In the project context, the term "scope" may refer to:

• Product scope—the features and functions that are to be included in a product or service.

• Project scope—the work that must be done in order to deliver a product with the specified features and functions.

The processes, tools and techniques used to manage *project* scope are the focus of this chapter. The processes, tools, and techniques used to manage *product* scope vary by application area and are usually defined as part of the project life cycle (the project life cycle is discussed in Section 2.1).

A project consists of a single product, but that product may include subsidiary elements, each with their own separate but interdependent product scopes. For example, a new telephone system would generally include four subsidiary elements—hardware, software, training, and implementation.

Completion of the *product* scope is measured against the requirements while completion of the *project* scope is measured against the plan. Both types of scope management must be well integrated to ensure that the work of the project will result in delivery of the specified product.

5.1
Initiation

5.2
Scope Planning

5.3
Scope Definition

5.4
Scope Verification

5.5
Scope Change Control

FIGURE 5–1   A GUIDE TO THE PROJECT MANAGEMENT BODY OF KNOWLEDGE

Figure 5–1. Project Scope Management Overview

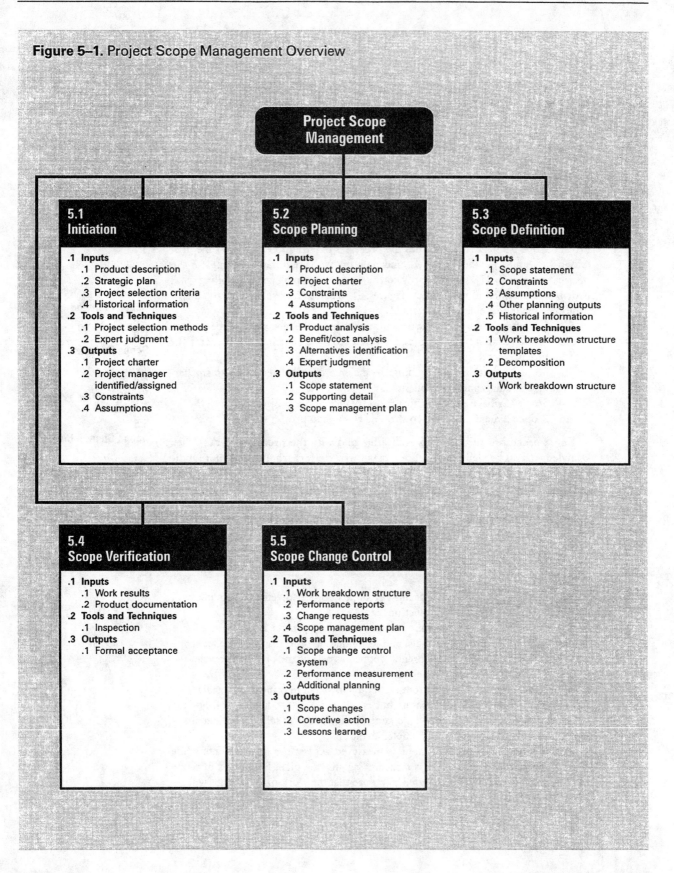

©1996 Project Management Institute, Four Campus Boulevard, Newtown Square, PA 19073-3299 USA

5.1 INITIATION

Initiation is the process of formally recognizing that a new project exists or that an existing project should continue into its next phase (see Section 2.1 for a more detailed discussion of project phases). This formal initiation links the project to the ongoing work of the performing organization. In some organizations, a project is not formally initiated until after completion of a feasibility study, a preliminary plan, or some other equivalent form of analysis which was itself separately initiated. Some types of projects, especially internal service projects and new product development projects, are initiated informally and some limited amount of work is done in order to secure the approvals needed for formal initiation. Projects are typically authorized as a result of one or more of the following:

- A market demand (e.g., an oil company authorizes a project to build a new refinery in response to chronic gasoline shortages).
- A business need (e.g., a training company authorizes a project to create a new course in order to increase its revenues).
- A customer request (e.g., an electric utility authorizes a project to build a new substation to serve a new industrial park).
- A technological advance (e.g., an electronics firm authorizes a new project to develop a video game player after the introduction of the video cassette recorder).
- A legal requirement (e.g., a paint manufacturer authorizes a project to establish guidelines for the handling of toxic materials).

These stimuli may also be called problems, opportunities, or business requirements. The central theme of all these terms is that management generally must make a decision about how to respond.

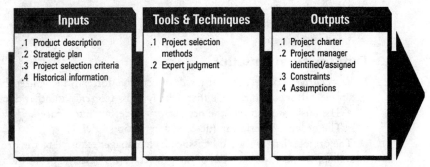

Inputs	Tools & Techniques	Outputs
.1 Product description .2 Strategic plan .3 Project selection criteria .4 Historical information	.1 Project selection methods .2 Expert judgment	.1 Project charter .2 Project manager identified/assigned .3 Constraints .4 Assumptions

5.1.1 Inputs to Initiation

.1 Product description. The product description documents the characteristics of the product or service that the project was undertaken to create. The product description will generally have less detail in early phases and more detail in later ones as the product characteristics are progressively elaborated.

The product description should also document the relationship between the product or service being created and the business need or other stimulus that gave rise to the project (see list above). While the form and substance of the product description will vary, it should always be detailed enough to support later project planning.

Many projects involve one organization (the seller) doing work under contract to another (the buyer). In such circumstances, the initial product description is usually provided by the buyer. If the buyer's work is itself a project, the buyer's product description is a statement of work as described in Section 12.1.3.2.

.2 Strategic plan. All projects should be supportive of the performing organization's strategic goals—the strategic plan of the performing organization should be considered as a factor in project selection decisions.

.3 *Project selection criteria.* Project selection criteria are typically defined in terms of the product of the project and can cover the full range of possible management concerns (financial return, market share, public perceptions, etc.).

.4 *Historical information.* Historical information about both the results of previous project selection decisions and previous project performance should be considered to the extent it is available. When initiation involves approval for the next phase of a project, information about the results of previous phases is often critical.

5.1.2 Tools and Techniques for Initiation

.1 *Project selection methods.* Project selection methods generally fall into one of two broad categories [2]:

- Benefit measurement methods—comparative approaches, scoring models, benefit contribution, or economic models.
- Constrained optimization methods—mathematical models using linear, non-linear, dynamic, integer, and multi-objective programming algorithms.

These methods are often referred to as *decision models*. Decision models include generalized techniques (decision trees, forced choice, and others) as well as specialized ones (Analytic Hierarchy Process, Logical Framework Analysis, and others). Applying complex project selection criteria in a sophisticated model is often treated as a separate project phase.

.2 *Expert judgment.* Expert judgment will often be required to assess the inputs to this process. Such expertise may be provided by any group or individual with specialized knowledge or training and is available from many sources including:

- Other units within the performing organization.
- Consultants.
- Professional and technical associations.
- Industry groups.

5.1.3 Outputs from Initiation

.1 *Project charter.* A project charter is a document that formally recognizes the existence of a project. It should include, either directly or by reference to other documents:

- The business need that the project was undertaken to address.
- The product description (described in Section 5.1.1.1).

The project charter should be issued by a manager external to the project and at a level appropriate to the needs of the project. It provides the project manager with the authority to apply organizational resources to project activities.

When a project is performed under contract, the signed contract will generally serve as the project charter for the seller.

.2 *Project manager identified/assigned.* In general, the project manager should be identified and assigned as early in the project as is feasible. The project manager should always be assigned prior to the start of project plan execution (described in Section 4.2) and preferably before much project planning has been done (the project planning processes are described in Section 3.3.2).

.3 *Constraints.* Constraints are factors that will limit the project management team's options. For example, a predefined budget is a constraint that is highly likely to limit the team's options regarding scope, staffing, and schedule.

When a project is performed under contract, contractual provisions will generally be constraints.

.4 Assumptions. Assumptions are factors that, for planning purposes, will be considered to be true, real, or certain. For example, if the date that a key person will become available is uncertain, the team may assume a specific start date. Assumptions generally involve a degree of risk. They may be identified here or they may be an output of risk identification (described in Section 11.1).

5.2 SCOPE PLANNING

Scope planning is the process of developing a written scope statement as the basis for future project decisions including, in particular, the criteria used to determine if the project or phase has been completed successfully. A written scope statement is necessary for both projects and subprojects. For example, an engineering firm contracted to design a petroleum processing plant must have a scope statement defining the boundaries of its work on the design subproject. The scope statement forms the basis for an agreement between the project team and the project customer by identifying both the project objectives and the major project deliverables.

If all the elements of the scope statement are already available (e.g., a request for proposal may identify the major deliverables, the project charter may define the project objectives), this process may involve little more than physically creating the written document.

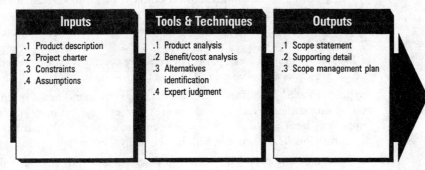

Inputs	Tools & Techniques	Outputs
.1 Product description	.1 Product analysis	.1 Scope statement
.2 Project charter	.2 Benefit/cost analysis	.2 Supporting detail
.3 Constraints	.3 Alternatives	.3 Scope management plan
.4 Assumptions	identification	
	.4 Expert judgment	

5.2.1 Inputs to Scope Planning

.1 Product description. The product description is discussed in Section 5.1.1.1.

.2 Project charter. The project charter is described in Section 5.1.3.1.

.3 Constraints. Constraints are described in Section 5.1.3.3.

.4 Assumptions. Assumptions are described in Section 5.1.3.4.

5.2.2 Tools and Techniques for Scope Planning

.1 Product analysis. Product analysis involves developing a better understanding of the product of the project. It includes techniques such as systems engineering, value engineering, value analysis, function analysis, and quality function deployment.

.2 Benefit/cost analysis. Benefit/cost analysis involves estimating tangible and intangible costs (outlays) and benefits (returns) of various project alternatives, and then using financial measures such as return on investment or payback period to assess the relative desirability of the identified alternatives.

.3 Alternatives identification. This is a catchall term for any technique used to generate different approaches to the project. There are a variety of general management techniques often used here, the most common of which are brainstorming and lateral thinking.

.4 Expert judgment. Expert judgment is described in Section 5.1.2.2.

5.2.3 Outputs from Scope Planning

.1 *Scope statement.* The scope statement provides a documented basis for making future project decisions and for confirming or developing common understanding of project scope among the stakeholders. As the project progresses, the scope statement may need to be revised or refined to reflect changes to the scope of the project. The scope statement should include, either directly or by reference to other documents:

- Project justification—the business need that the project was undertaken to address. The project justification provides the basis for evaluating future trade-offs.
- Project product—a brief summary of the product description (the product description is discussed in Section 5.1.1.1).
- Project deliverables—a list of the summary level sub-products whose full and satisfactory delivery marks completion of the project. For example, the major deliverables for a software development project might include the working computer code, a user manual, and an interactive tutorial. When known, exclusions should be identified, but anything not explicitly included is implicitly excluded.
- Project objectives—the quantifiable criteria that must be met for the project to be considered successful. Project objectives must include, at least, cost, schedule, and quality measures. Project objectives should have an attribute (e.g., cost), a yardstick (e.g., U.S. dollars), and an absolute or relative value (e.g., less than 1.5 million). Unquantified objectives (e.g., "customer satisfaction") entail high risk.

In some application areas, project deliverables are called project objectives while project objectives are called critical success factors.

.2 *Supporting detail.* Supporting detail for the scope statement should be documented and organized as needed to facilitate its use by other project management processes. Supporting detail should always include documentation of all identified assumptions and constraints. The amount of additional detail varies by application area.

.3 *Scope management plan.* This document describes how project scope will be managed and how scope changes will be integrated into the project. It should also include an assessment of the expected stability of the project scope (i.e., how likely is it to change, how frequently, and by how much). The scope management plan should also include a clear description of how scope changes will be identified and classified (this is particularly difficult—and therefore absolutely essential—when the product characteristics are still being elaborated).

A scope management plan may be formal or informal, highly detailed or broadly framed based on the needs of the project. It is a subsidiary element of the overall project plan (described in Section 4.1.3.1).

5.3 SCOPE DEFINITION

Scope definition involves subdividing the major project deliverables (as identified in the scope statement) into smaller, more manageable components in order to:

- Improve the accuracy of cost, time, and resource estimates.
- Define a baseline for performance measurement and control.
- Facilitate clear responsibility assignments.

Proper scope definition is critical to project success. "When there is poor scope definition, final project costs can be expected to be higher because of the inevitable changes which disrupt project rhythm, cause rework, increase project time, and lower the productivity and morale of the workforce" [3].

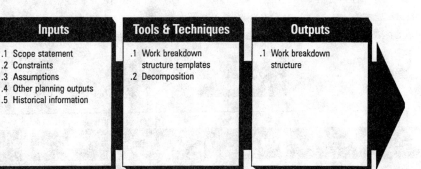

Inputs	Tools & Techniques	Outputs

.1 Scope statement
.2 Constraints
.3 Assumptions
.4 Other planning outputs
.5 Historical information
	.1 Work breakdown
	   structure templates
	.2 Decomposition
		.1 Work breakdown
		   structure

5.3.1 Inputs to Scope Definition

.1 *Scope statement.* The scope statement is described in Section 5.2.3.1.

.2 *Constraints.* Constraints are described in Section 5.1.3.3. When a project is done under contract, the constraints defined by contractual provisions are often important considerations during scope definition.

.3 *Assumptions.* Assumptions are described in Section 5.1.3.4.

.4 *Other planning outputs.* The outputs of the processes in other knowledge areas should be reviewed for possible impact on project scope definition.

.5 *Historical information.* Historical information about previous projects should be considered during scope definition. Information about errors and omissions on previous projects should be especially useful.

5.3.2 Tools and Techniques for Scope Definition

.1 *Work breakdown structure templates.* A work breakdown structure (WBS, described in Section 5.3.3.1) from a previous project can often be used as a template for a new project. Although each project is unique, WBSs can often be "reused" since most projects will resemble another project to some extent. For example, most projects within a given organization will have the same or similar project life cycles and will thus have the same or similar deliverables required from each phase.

Many application areas have standard or semi-standard WBSs that can be used as templates. For example, the U.S. Department of Defense has defined standard WBSs for Defense Materiel Items. A portion of one of these templates is shown as **Figure 5–2**.

.2 *Decomposition.* Decomposition involves subdividing the major project deliverables into smaller, more manageable components until the deliverables are defined in sufficient detail to support future project activities (planning, executing, controlling, and closing). Decomposition involves the following major steps:

(1) Identify the major elements of the project. In general, the major elements will be the project deliverables and project management. However, the major elements should always be defined in terms of how the project will actually be managed. For example:

- The phases of the project life cycle may be used as the first level of decomposition with the project deliverables repeated at the second level, as illustrated in **Figure 5–3**.
- The organizing principle within each branch of the WBS may vary, as illustrated in **Figure 5–4**.

(2) Decide if adequate cost and duration estimates can be developed at this level of detail for each element. The meaning of *adequate* may change over the course of the project—decomposition of a deliverable that will be produced far in the future may not be possible. For each element, proceed to Step 4 if there is adequate detail and to Step 3 if there is not—this means that different elements may have differing levels of decomposition.

FIGURE 5–2   A GUIDE TO THE PROJECT MANAGEMENT BODY OF KNOWLEDGE

Figure 5–2. Sample Work Breakdown Structure for Defense Materiel Items

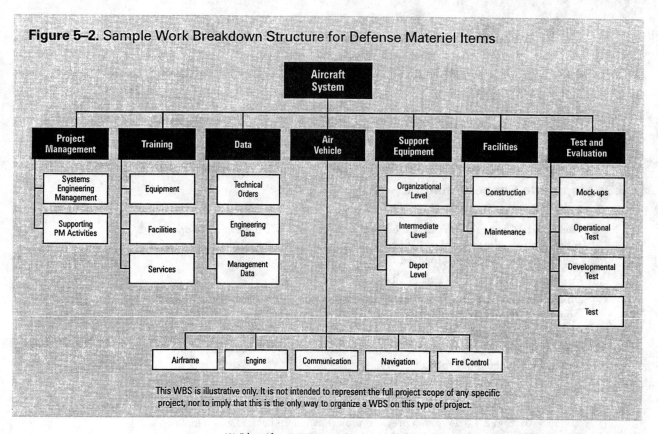

This WBS is illustrative only. It is not intended to represent the full project scope of any specific project, nor to imply that this is the only way to organize a WBS on this type of project.

(3) Identify constituent elements of the deliverable. Constituent elements should be described in terms of tangible, verifiable results in order to facilitate performance measurement. As with the major elements, the constituent elements should be defined in terms of how the work of the project will actually be accomplished. Tangible, verifiable results can include services as well as products (e.g., *status reporting* could be described as *weekly status reports*; for a manufactured item, constituent elements might include several individual components plus *final assembly*). Repeat Step 2 on each constituent element.

(4) Verify the correctness of the decomposition:

- Are the lower-level items both necessary and sufficient for completion of the item decomposed? If not, the constituent elements must be modified (added to, deleted from, or redefined).
- Is each item clearly and completely defined? If not, the descriptions must be revised or expanded.
- Can each item be appropriately scheduled? Budgeted? Assigned to a specific organizational unit (e.g., department, team, or person) who will accept responsibility for satisfactory completion of the item? If not, revisions are needed to provide adequate management control.

5.3.3 Outputs from Scope Definition

.1 *Work breakdown structure.* A work breakdown structure is a deliverable-oriented grouping of project elements that organizes and defines the total scope of the project: work not in the WBS is outside the scope of the project. As with the scope statement, the WBS is often used to develop or confirm a common understanding of project scope. Each descending level represents an increasingly detailed description of the project elements. Section 5.3.2.2 describes the most common approach

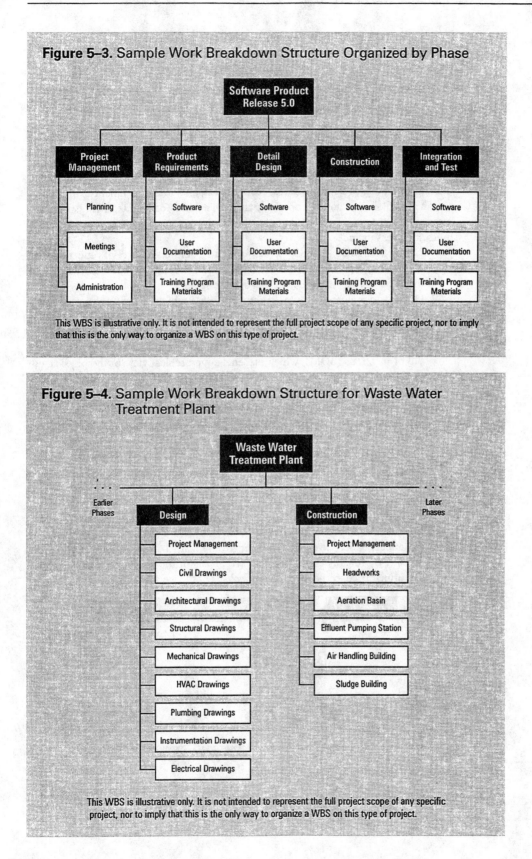

Figure 5–3. Sample Work Breakdown Structure Organized by Phase

This WBS is illustrative only. It is not intended to represent the full project scope of any specific project, nor to imply that this is the only way to organize a WBS on this type of project.

Figure 5–4. Sample Work Breakdown Structure for Waste Water Treatment Plant

This WBS is illustrative only. It is not intended to represent the full project scope of any specific project, nor to imply that this is the only way to organize a WBS on this type of project.

for developing a WBS. A WBS is normally presented in chart form as illustrated in **Figures 5–2, 5–3,** and **5–4;** however, the WBS should not be confused with the method of presentation—drawing an unstructured activity list in chart form does not make it a WBS.

Each item in the WBS is generally assigned a unique identifier; these identifiers are often known collectively as the *code of accounts.* The items at the lowest level of the WBS are often referred to as *work packages.* These work packages may be further decomposed as described in Section 6.1, Activity Definition.

Work element descriptions are often collected in a *WBS dictionary.* A WBS dictionary will typically include work package descriptions as well as other planning information such as schedule dates, cost budgets, and staff assignments.

The WBS should not be confused with other kinds of "breakdown" structures used to present project information. Other structures commonly used in some application areas include:

- Contractual WBS (CWBS), which is used to define the level of reporting that the seller will provide the buyer. The CWBS generally includes less detail than the WBS used by the seller to manage the seller's work.
- Organizational breakdown structure (OBS), which is used to show which work elements have been assigned to which organizational units.
- Resource breakdown structure (RBS), which is a variation of the OBS and is typically used when work elements are assigned to individuals.
- Bill of materials (BOM), which presents a hierarchical view of the physical assemblies, subassemblies, and components needed to fabricate a manufactured product.
- Project breakdown structure (PBS), which is fundamentally the same as a properly done WBS. The term PBS is widely used in application areas where the term WBS is incorrectly used to refer to a BOM.

5.4 SCOPE VERIFICATION

Scope verification is the process of formalizing acceptance of the project scope by the stakeholders (sponsor, client, customer, etc.). It requires reviewing work products and results to ensure that all were completed correctly and satisfactorily. If the project is terminated early, the scope verification process should establish and document the level and extent of completion. Scope verification differs from quality control (described in Section 8.3) in that it is primarily concerned with *acceptance* of the work results while quality control is primarily concerned with the *correctness* of the work results.

Inputs	Tools & Techniques	Outputs
.1 Work results .2 Product documentation	.1 Inspection	.1 Formal acceptance

5.4.1 Inputs to Scope Verification

.1 Work results. Work results—which deliverables have been fully or partially completed, what costs have been incurred or committed, etc.—are an output of project plan execution (discussed in Section 4.2).

.2 *Product documentation.* Documents produced to describe the project's products must be available for review. The terms used to describe this documentation (plans, specifications, technical documentation, drawings, etc.) vary by application area.

5.4.2 Tools and Techniques for Scope Verification

.1 *Inspection.* Inspection includes activities such as measuring, examining, and testing undertaken to determine whether results conform to requirements. Inspections are variously called reviews, product reviews, audits, and walk-throughs; in some application areas, these different terms have narrow and specific meanings.

5.4.3 Outputs from Scope Verification

.1 *Formal acceptance.* Documentation that the client or sponsor has accepted the product of the project or phase must be prepared and distributed. Such acceptance may be conditional, especially at the end of a phase.

5.5 SCOPE CHANGE CONTROL

Scope change control is concerned with (a) influencing the factors which create scope changes to ensure that changes are beneficial, (b) determining that a scope change has occurred, and (c) managing the actual changes when and if they occur. Scope change control must be thoroughly integrated with the other control processes (time control, cost control, quality control, and others as discussed in Section 4.3).

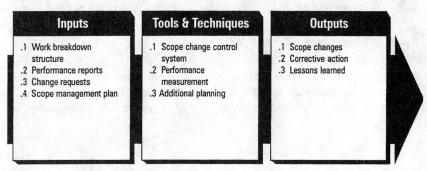

Inputs	Tools & Techniques	Outputs
.1 Work breakdown structure .2 Performance reports .3 Change requests .4 Scope management plan	.1 Scope change control system .2 Performance measurement .3 Additional planning	.1 Scope changes .2 Corrective action .3 Lessons learned

5.5.1 Inputs to Scope Change Control

.1 *Work breakdown structure.* The WBS is described in Section 5.3.3.1. It defines the project's scope baseline.

.2 *Performance reports.* Performance reports discussed in Section 10.3.3.1 provide information on scope performance such as which interim products have been completed and which have not. Performance reports may also alert the project team to issues which may cause problems in the future.

.3 *Change requests.* Change requests may occur in many forms—oral or written, direct or indirect, externally or internally initiated, and legally mandated or optional. Changes may require expanding the scope or may allow shrinking it. Most change requests are the result of:

- An external event (e.g., a change in a government regulation).
- An error or omission in defining the scope of the product (e.g., failure to include a required feature in the design of a telecommunications system).
- An error or omission in defining the scope of the project (e.g., using a bill of materials instead of a work breakdown structure).
- A value-adding change (e.g., an environmental remediation project is able to reduce costs by taking advantage of technology that was not available when the scope was originally defined).

.4 *Scope management plan.* The scope management plan is described in Section 5.2.3.3.

5.5.2 Tools and Techniques for Scope Change Control

.1 *Scope change control system.* A scope change control system defines the procedures by which the project scope may be changed. It includes the paperwork, tracking systems, and approval levels necessary for authorizing changes. The scope change control system should be integrated with the overall change control system described in Section 4.3 and, in particular, with any system or systems in place to control *product* scope. When the project is done under contract, the scope change control system must also comply with all relevant contractual provisions.

.2 *Performance measurement.* Performance measurement techniques, described in Section 10.3.2, help to assess the magnitude of any variations which do occur. An important part of scope change control is to determine what is causing the variance and to decide if the variance requires corrective action.

.3 *Additional planning.* Few projects run exactly according to plan. Prospective scope changes may require modifications to the WBS or analysis of alternative approaches.

5.5.3 Outputs from Scope Change Control

.1 *Scope changes.* A scope change is any modification to the agreed-upon project scope as defined by the approved WBS. Scope changes often require adjustments to cost, time, quality, or other project objectives.

Scope changes are fed back through the planning process, technical and planning documents are updated as needed, and stakeholders are notified as appropriate.

.2 *Corrective action.* Corrective action is anything done to bring expected future project performance into line with the project plan.

.3 *Lessons learned.* The causes of variances, the reasoning behind the corrective action chosen, and other types of lessons learned from scope change control should be documented so that this information becomes part of the historical database for both this project and other projects of the performing organization.

PROJECT TIME MANAGEMENT

6

Project Time Management includes the processes required to ensure timely completion of the project. Figure 6–1 provides an overview of the following major processes:

    6.1   **Activity Definition**—identifying the specific activities that must be performed to produce the various project deliverables.

    6.2   **Activity Sequencing**—identifying and documenting interactivity dependencies.

    6.3   **Activity Duration Estimating**—estimating the number of work periods which will be needed to complete individual activities.

    6.4   **Schedule Development**—analyzing activity sequences, activity durations, and resource requirements to create the project schedule.

    6.5   **Schedule Control**—controlling changes to the project schedule.

These processes interact with each other and with the processes in the other knowledge areas as well. Each process may involve effort from one or more individuals or groups of individuals based on the needs of the project. Each process generally occurs at least once in every project phase.

Although the processes are presented here as discrete elements with well-defined interfaces, in practice they may overlap and interact in ways not detailed here. Process interactions are discussed in detail in Chapter 3.

On some projects, especially smaller ones, activity sequencing, activity duration estimating, and schedule development are so tightly linked that they are viewed as a single process (e.g., they may be performed by a single individual over a relatively short period of time). They are presented here as distinct processes because the tools and techniques for each are different.

At present, there is no consensus within the project management profession about the relationship between *activities* and *tasks*:

- In many application areas, activities are seen as being composed of tasks. This is the most common usage and also the preferred usage.
- In others, tasks are seen as being composed of activities.

However, the important consideration is not the term used, but whether or not the work to be done is described accurately and understood by those who must do the work.

6.1 ACTIVITY DEFINITION

Activity definition involves identifying and documenting the specific activities that must be performed in order to produce the deliverables and sub-deliverables identified in the work breakdown structure. Implicit in this process is the need to define the activities such that the project objectives will be met.

6.1
Activity Definition

6.2
Activity Sequencing

6.3
Activity Duration Estimating

6.4
Schedule Development

6.5
Schedule Control

FIGURE 6–1   A GUIDE TO THE PROJECT MANAGEMENT BODY OF KNOWLEDGE

Figure 6–1. Project Time Management Overview

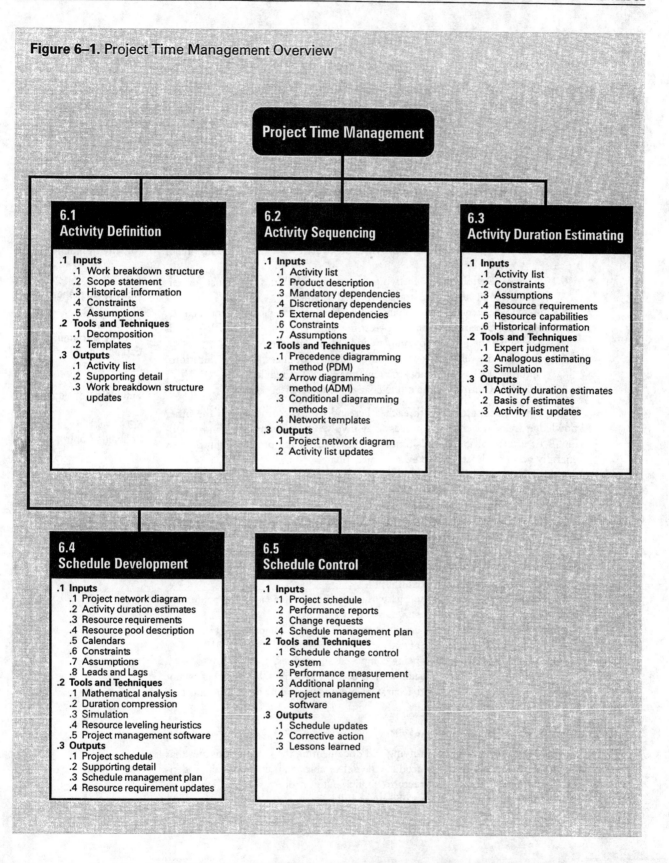

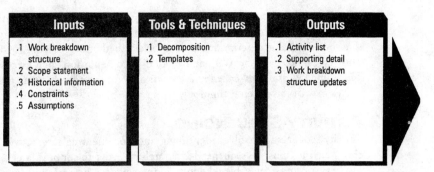

Inputs	Tools & Techniques	Outputs
.1 Work breakdown structure .2 Scope statement .3 Historical information .4 Constraints .5 Assumptions	.1 Decomposition .2 Templates	.1 Activity list .2 Supporting detail .3 Work breakdown structure updates

6.1.1 Inputs to Activity Definition

.1 *Work breakdown structure.* The work breakdown structure is the primary input to activity definition (see Section 5.3.3.1 for a more detailed discussion of the WBS).

.2 *Scope statement.* The project justification and the project objectives contained in the scope statement must be considered explicitly during activity definition (see Section 5.2.3.1 for a more detailed discussion of the scope statement).

.3 *Historical information.* Historical information (what activities were actually required on previous, similar projects) should be considered in defining project activities.

.4 *Constraints.* Constraints are factors that will limit the project management team's options.

.5 *Assumptions.* Assumptions are factors that, for planning purposes, will be considered to be true, real, or certain. Assumptions generally involve a degree of risk and will normally be an output of risk identification (described in Section 11.1).

6.1.2 Tools and Techniques for Activity Definition

.1 *Decomposition.* Decomposition involves subdividing project elements into smaller, more manageable components in order to provide better management control. Decomposition is described in more detail in Section 5.3.2.2. The major difference between decomposition here and in Scope Definition is that the final outputs here are described as activities (action steps) rather than as deliverables (tangible items). In some application areas, the WBS and the activity list are developed concurrently.

.2 *Templates.* An activity list (described in Section 6.1.3.1), or a portion of an activity list from a previous project, is often usable as a template for a new project. In addition, the activity list for a WBS element from the current project may be usable as a template for other, similar WBS elements.

6.1.3 Outputs from Activity Definition

.1 *Activity list.* The activity list must include all activities which will be performed on the project. It should be organized as an extension to the WBS to help ensure that it is complete and that it does not include any activities which are not required as part of the project scope. As with the WBS, the activity list should include descriptions of each activity to ensure that the project team members will understand how the work is to be done.

.2 *Supporting detail.* Supporting detail for the activity list should be documented and organized as needed to facilitate its use by other project management processes. Supporting detail should always include documentation of all identified assumptions and constraints. The amount of additional detail varies by application area.

.3 Work breakdown structure updates. In using the WBS to identify which activities are needed, the project team may identify missing deliverables or may determine that the deliverable descriptions need to be clarified or corrected. Any such updates must be reflected in the WBS and related documentation such as cost estimates. These updates are often called *refinements* and are most likely when the project involves new or unproven technology.

6.2 ACTIVITY SEQUENCING

Activity sequencing involves identifying and documenting interactivity dependencies. Activities must be sequenced accurately in order to support later development of a realistic and achievable schedule. Sequencing can be performed with the aid of a computer (e.g., by using project management software) or with manual techniques. Manual techniques are often more effective on smaller projects and in the early phases of larger ones when little detail is available. Manual and automated techniques may also be used in combination.

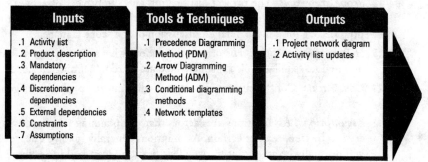

Inputs	Tools & Techniques	Outputs
.1 Activity list	.1 Precedence Diagramming Method (PDM)	.1 Project network diagram
.2 Product description	.2 Arrow Diagramming Method (ADM)	.2 Activity list updates
.3 Mandatory dependencies	.3 Conditional diagramming methods	
.4 Discretionary dependencies	.4 Network templates	
.5 External dependencies		
.6 Constraints		
.7 Assumptions		

6.2.1 Inputs to Activity Sequencing

.1 Activity list. The activity list is described in Section 6.1.3.1.

.2 Product description. The product description is discussed in Section 5.1.1.1. Product characteristics often affect activity sequencing (e.g., the physical layout of a plant to be constructed, subsystem interfaces on a software project). While these effects are often apparent in the activity list, the product description should generally be reviewed to ensure accuracy.

.3 Mandatory dependencies. Mandatory dependencies are those which are inherent in the nature of the work being done. They often involve physical limitations (on a construction project it is impossible to erect the superstructure until after the foundation has been built; on an electronics project, a prototype must be built before it can be tested). Mandatory dependencies are also called *hard logic*.

.4 Discretionary dependencies. Discretionary dependencies are those which are defined by the project management team. They should be used with care (and fully documented) since they may limit later scheduling options. Discretionary dependencies are usually defined based on knowledge of:
- "Best practices" within a particular application area.
- Some unusual aspect of the project where a specific sequence is desired even though there are other acceptable sequences.

Discretionary dependencies may also be called *preferred logic*, *preferential logic*, or *soft logic*.

.5 External dependencies. External dependencies are those that involve a relationship between project activities and non-project activities. For example, the testing activity in a software project may be dependent on delivery of hardware from an exter-

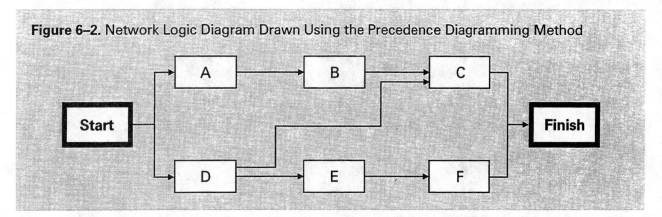

Figure 6–2. Network Logic Diagram Drawn Using the Precedence Diagramming Method

nal source, or environmental hearings may need to be held before site preparation can begin on a construction project.

.6 *Constraints.* Constraints are described in Section 6.1.1.4.

.7 *Assumptions.* Assumptions are described in Section 6.1.1.5.

6.2.2 Tools and Techniques for Activity Sequencing

.1 *Precedence diagramming method (PDM).* This is a method of constructing a project network diagram using nodes to represent the activities and connecting them with arrows that show the dependencies (see also Section 6.2.3.1). **Figure 6–2** shows a simple project network diagram drawn using PDM. This technique is also called *activity-on-node* (AON) and is the method used by most project management software packages. PDM can be done manually or on a computer.

It includes four types of dependencies or precedence relationships:
- Finish-to-start—the "from" activity must finish before the "to" activity can start.
- Finish-to-finish—the "from" activity must finish before the "to" activity can finish.
- Start-to-start—the "from" activity must start before the "to" activity can start.
- Start-to-finish—the "from" activity must start before the "to" activity can finish.

In PDM, finish-to-start is the most commonly used type of logical relationship. Start-to-finish relationships are rarely used, and then typically only by professional scheduling engineers. Using start-to-start, finish-to-finish, or start-to-finish relationships with project management software can produce unexpected results since these types of relationships have not been consistently implemented.

.2 *Arrow diagramming method (ADM).* This is a method of constructing a project network diagram using arrows to represent the activities and connecting them at nodes to show the dependencies (see also Section 6.2.3.1). **Figure 6–3** shows a simple project network diagram drawn using ADM. This technique is also called *activity-on-arrow* (AOA) and, although less prevalent than PDM, is still the technique of choice in some application areas. ADM uses only finish-to-start dependencies and may require the use of dummy activities to define all logical relationships correctly. ADM can be done manually or on a computer.

.3 *Conditional diagramming methods.* Diagramming techniques such as GERT (Graphical Evaluation and Review Technique) and System Dynamics models allow for nonsequential activities such as loops (e.g., a test that must be repeated more than once) or conditional branches (e.g., a design update that is only needed if the inspection detects errors). Neither PDM nor ADM allow loops or conditional branches.

FIGURE 6-3   A GUIDE TO THE PROJECT MANAGEMENT BODY OF KNOWLEDGE

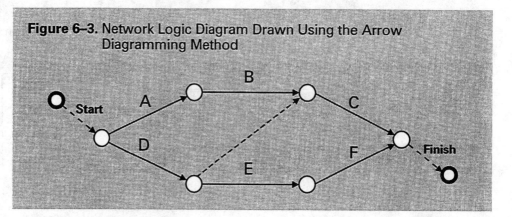

Figure 6–3. Network Logic Diagram Drawn Using the Arrow Diagramming Method

.4 *Network templates.* Standardized networks can be used to expedite the preparation of project network diagrams. They can include an entire project or only a portion of it. Portions of a network are often referred to as *subnets* or *fragnets*. Subnets are especially useful where a project includes several identical or nearly identical features such as floors on a high-rise office building, clinical trials on a pharmaceutical research project, or program modules on a software project.

6.2.3 Outputs from Activity Sequencing

.1 *Project network diagram.* A project network diagram is a schematic display of the project's activities and the logical relationships (dependencies) among them. **Figures 6–2 and 6–3** illustrate two different approaches to drawing a project network diagram. A project network diagram may be produced manually or on a computer. It may include full project details or have one or more summary activities (hammocks). The diagram should be accompanied by a summary narrative that describes the basic sequencing approach. Any unusual sequences should be fully described.

The project network diagram is often incorrectly called a *PERT chart* (for Program Evaluation and Review Technique). A PERT chart is a specific type of project network diagram that is seldom used today.

.2 *Activity list updates.* In much the same manner that the activity definition process may generate updates to the WBS, preparation of the project network diagram may reveal instances where an activity must be divided or otherwise redefined in order to diagram the correct logical relationships.

6.3 ACTIVITY DURATION ESTIMATING

Activity duration estimating involves assessing the number of work periods likely to be needed to complete each identified activity. The person or group on the project team who is most familiar with the nature of a specific activity should make, or at least approve, the estimate.

Estimating the number of work periods required to complete an activity will often require consideration of elapsed time as well. For example, if "concrete curing" will require four days of elapsed time, it may require from two to four work periods based on (a) which day of the week it begins on and (b) whether or not weekend days are treated as work periods. Most computerized scheduling software will handle this problem automatically.

Overall project duration may also be estimated using the tools and techniques presented here, but it is more properly calculated as the output of schedule development (described in Section 6.4).

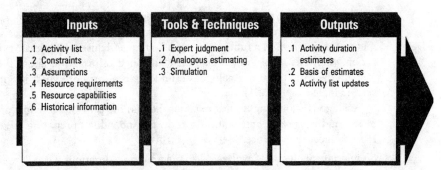

Inputs	Tools & Techniques	Outputs
.1 Activity list	.1 Expert judgment	.1 Activity duration
.2 Constraints	.2 Analogous estimating	estimates
.3 Assumptions	.3 Simulation	.2 Basis of estimates
.4 Resource requirements		.3 Activity list updates
.5 Resource capabilities		
.6 Historical information		

6.3.1 Inputs to Activity Duration Estimating

.1 Activity list. The activity list is described in Section 6.1.3.1.

.2 Constraints. Constraints are described in Section 6.1.1.4.

.3 Assumptions. Assumptions are described in Section 6.1.1.5.

.4 Resource requirements. Resource requirements are described in Section 7.1.3.1. The duration of most activities will be significantly influenced by the resources assigned to them. For example, two people working together may be able to complete a design activity in half the time it takes either of them individually, while a person working half-time on an activity will generally take at least twice as much time as the same person working full-time.

.5 Resource capabilities. The duration of most activities will be significantly influenced by the capabilities of the humans and material resources assigned to them. For example, if both are assigned full-time, a senior staff member can generally be expected to complete a given activity in less time than a junior staff member.

.6 Historical information. Historical information on the likely durations of many categories of activities is often available from one or more of the following sources:

- Project files—one or more of the organizations involved in the project may maintain records of previous project results that are detailed enough to aid in developing duration estimates. In some application areas, individual team members may maintain such records.
- Commercial duration estimating databases—historical information is often available commercially. These databases tend to be especially useful when activity durations are not driven by the actual work content (e.g., how long does it take concrete to cure; how long does a government agency usually take to respond to certain types of requests).
- Project team knowledge—the individual members of the project team may remember previous actuals or estimates. While such recollections may be useful, they are generally far less reliable than documented results.

6.3.2 Tools and Techniques for Activity Duration Estimating

.1 Expert judgment. Expert judgment is described in Section 5.1.2.2. Durations are often difficult to estimate because of the number of factors which can influence them (e.g., resource levels, resource productivity). Expert judgment guided by historical information should be used whenever possible. If such expertise is not available, the estimates are inherently uncertain and risky (see Chapter 11, Project Risk Management).

.2 *Analogous estimating.* Analogous estimating, also called *top-down estimating*, means using the actual duration of a previous, similar activity as the basis for estimating the duration of a future activity. It is frequently used to estimate project duration when there is a limited amount of detailed information about the project (e.g., in the early phases). Analogous estimating is a form of expert judgment (described in Section 6.3.2.1).

Analogous estimating is most reliable when (a) the previous activities are similar in fact and not just in appearance, and (b) the individuals preparing the estimates have the needed expertise.

.3 *Simulation.* Simulation involves calculating multiple durations with different sets of assumptions. The most common is Monte Carlo Analysis in which a distribution of probable results is defined for each activity and used to calculate a distribution of probable results for the total project (see also Section 11.2.2.3, Schedule Simulation).

6.3.3 Outputs from Activity Duration Estimating

.1 *Activity duration estimates.* Activity duration estimates are quantitative assessments of the likely number of work periods that will be required to complete an activity.

Activity duration estimates should always include some indication of the range of possible results. For example:
- 2 weeks ± 2 days to indicate that the activity will take at least 8 days and no more than 12.
- 15 percent probability of exceeding 3 weeks to indicate a high probability—85 percent—that the activity will take 3 weeks or less.

Chapter 11 on Project Risk Management includes a more detailed discussion of estimating uncertainty.

.2 *Basis of estimates.* Assumptions made in developing the estimates must be documented.

.3 *Activity list updates.* Activity list updates are described in Section 6.2.3.2.

6.4 SCHEDULE DEVELOPMENT

Schedule development means determining start and finish dates for project activities. If the start and finish dates are not realistic, the project is unlikely to be finished as scheduled. The schedule development process must often be iterated (along with the processes that provide inputs, especially duration estimating and cost estimating) prior to determination of the project schedule.

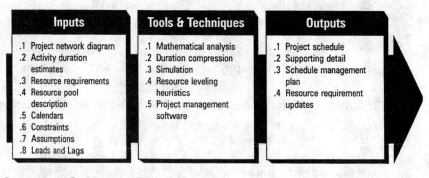

Inputs	Tools & Techniques	Outputs
.1 Project network diagram .2 Activity duration estimates .3 Resource requirements .4 Resource pool description .5 Calendars .6 Constraints .7 Assumptions .8 Leads and Lags	.1 Mathematical analysis .2 Duration compression .3 Simulation .4 Resource leveling heuristics .5 Project management software	.1 Project schedule .2 Supporting detail .3 Schedule management plan .4 Resource requirement updates

6.4.1 Inputs to Schedule Development

.1 *Project network diagram.* The project network diagram is described in Section 6.2.3.1.

.2 *Activity duration estimates.* Activity duration estimates are described in Section 6.3.3.1.

.3 *Resource requirements.* Resource requirements are described in Section 6.3.1.4.

.4 *Resource pool description.* Knowledge of what resources will be available at what times and in what patterns is necessary for schedule development. For example, shared resources can be especially difficult to schedule since their availability may be highly variable.

The amount of detail and the level of specificity in the resource pool description will vary. For example, for preliminary schedule development of a consulting project one need only know that two consultants will be available in a particular timeframe. The final schedule for the same project, however, must identify which specific consultants will be available.

.5 *Calendars.* Project and resource calendars identify periods when work is allowed. *Project calendars* affect all resources (e.g., some projects will work only during normal business hours while others will work a full three shifts). *Resource calendars* affect a specific resource or category of resources (e.g., a project team member may be on vacation or in a training program; a labor contract may limit certain workers to certain days of the week).

.6 *Constraints.* Constraints are described in Section 6.1.1.4. There are two major categories of constraints that must be considered during schedule development:
- Imposed dates. Completion of certain deliverables by a specified date may be *required* by the project sponsor, the project customer, or other external factors (e.g., a market window on a technology project; a court-mandated completion date on an environmental remediation project).
- Key events or major milestones. Completion of certain deliverables by a specified date may be *requested* by the project sponsor, the project customer, or other stakeholders. Once scheduled, these dates become expected and often may be moved only with great difficulty.

.7 *Assumptions.* Assumptions are described in Section 6.1.1.5.

.8 *Leads and lags.* Any of the dependencies may require specification of a lead or a lag in order to accurately define the relationship (e.g., there might be a two-week delay between ordering a piece of equipment and installing or using it).

6.4.2 Tools and Techniques for Schedule Development

.1 *Mathematical analysis.* Mathematical analysis involves calculating theoretical early and late start and finish dates for all project activities without regard for any resource pool limitations. The resulting dates are not the schedule, but rather indicate the time periods within which the activity *should* be scheduled given resource limits and other known constraints. The most widely known mathematical analysis techniques are:
- Critical Path Method (CPM)—calculates a single, deterministic early and late start and finish date for each activity based on specified, sequential network logic and a single duration estimate. The focus of CPM is on calculating *float* in order to determine which activities have the least scheduling flexibility. The underlying CPM algorithms are often used in other types of mathematical analysis.
- Graphical Evaluation and Review Technique (GERT)—allows for probabilistic treatment of both network logic and activity duration estimates (i.e., some activities may not be performed at all, some may be performed only in part, and others may be performed more than once).
- Program Evaluation and Review Technique (PERT)—uses sequential network logic and a weighted average duration estimate to calculate project duration. Although there are surface differences, PERT differs from CPM primarily in that it uses the distribution's mean (expected value) instead of the most likely estimate originally used in CPM (see **Figure 6–4**). PERT itself is seldom used today although PERT-like estimates are often used in CPM calculations.

FIGURE 6–4   A GUIDE TO THE PROJECT MANAGEMENT BODY OF KNOWLEDGE

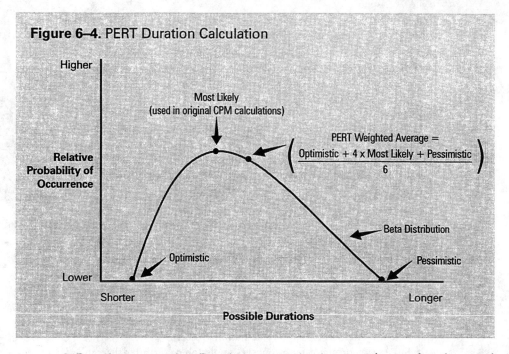

Figure 6–4. PERT Duration Calculation

.2 Duration compression. Duration compression is a special case of mathematical analysis that looks for ways to shorten the project schedule without changing the project scope (e.g., to meet imposed dates or other schedule objectives). Duration compression includes techniques such as:

- Crashing—in which cost and schedule trade-offs are analyzed to determine how to obtain the greatest amount of compression for the least incremental cost. Crashing does not always produce a viable alternative and often results in increased cost.
- Fast tracking—doing activities in parallel that would normally be done in sequence (e.g., starting to write code on a software project before the design is complete, or starting to build the foundation for a petroleum processing plant before the 25 percent of engineering point is reached). Fast tracking often results in rework and usually increases risk.

.3 Simulation. Simulation is described in Section 6.3.2.3.

.4 Resource leveling heuristics. Mathematical analysis often produces a preliminary schedule that requires more resources during certain time periods than are available, or requires changes in resource levels that are not manageable. Heuristics such as "allocate scarce resources to critical path activities first" can be applied to develop a schedule that reflects such constraints. Resource leveling often results in a project duration that is longer than the preliminary schedule. This technique is sometimes called the "Resource-based Method," especially when implemented with computerized optimization.

Resource constrained scheduling is a special case of resource leveling where the heuristic involved is a limitation on the quantity of resources available.

.5 Project management software. Project management software is widely used to assist with schedule development. These products automate the calculations of mathematical analysis and resource leveling and thus allow for rapid consideration of many schedule alternatives. They are also widely used to print or display the outputs of schedule development.

Figure 6–5. Project Network Diagram with Scheduled Dates

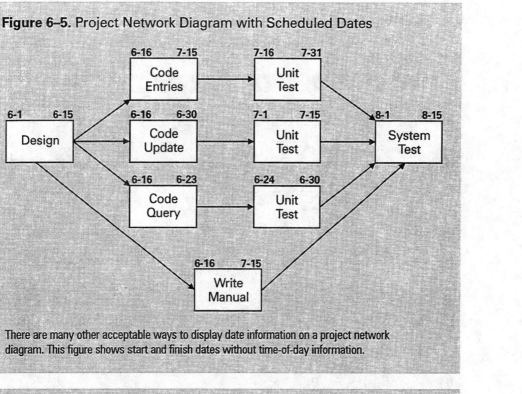

There are many other acceptable ways to display date information on a project network diagram. This figure shows start and finish dates without time-of-day information.

Figure 6–6. Bar (Gantt) Chart

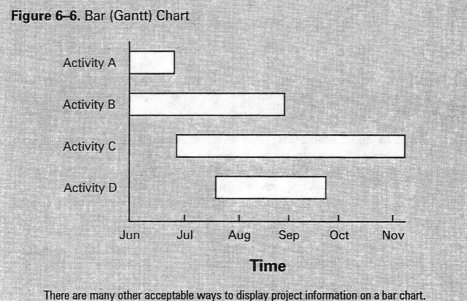

There are many other acceptable ways to display project information on a bar chart.

6.4.3 Outputs from Schedule Development

.1 *Project schedule.* The project schedule includes at least planned start and expected finish dates for each detail activity. (Note: the project schedule remains preliminary until resource assignments have been confirmed. This would usually happen no later than the completion of Project Plan Development, Section 4.1).

FIGURE 6–7   A GUIDE TO THE PROJECT MANAGEMENT BODY OF KNOWLEDGE

Figure 6–7. Milestone Chart

Data Date

Event	Jan	Feb	Mar	Apr	May	Jun	Jul	Aug
Subcontracts Signed			△▼					
Specifications Finalized				△▽				
Design Reviewed					△			
Subsystem Tested						△		
First Unit Delivered							△	
Production Plan Completed								△

There are many other acceptable ways to display project information on a milestone chart.

Figure 6–8. Time-Scaled Network Diagram

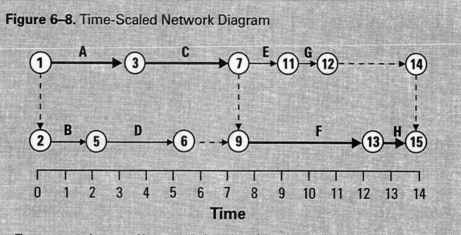

There are many other acceptable ways to display project information on a time-scaled network diagram.

The project schedule may be presented in summary form (the "master schedule") or in detail. Although it can be presented in tabular form, it is more often presented graphically using one or more of the following formats:

- Project network diagrams with date information added (see **Figure 6–5**). These charts usually show both the project logic and the project's critical path activities (see Section 6.2.3.1 for more information on project network diagrams).
- Bar charts, also called Gantt charts (see **Figure 6–6**), show activity start and end dates as well as expected durations, but do not usually show dependencies. They are relatively easy to read and are frequently used in management presentations.
- Milestone charts (see **Figure 6–7**), similar to bar charts, but identifying the scheduled start or completion of major deliverables and key external interfaces.
- Time-scaled network diagrams (see **Figure 6–8**) are a blend of project network diagrams and bar charts in that they show project logic, activity durations, and schedule information.

.2 *Supporting detail.* Supporting detail for the project schedule includes at least documentation of all identified assumptions and constraints. The amount of additional detail varies by application area. For example:

- On a construction project, it will most likely include such items as resource histograms, cash flow projections, and order and delivery schedules.
- On an electronics project, it will most likely include resource histograms only.

Information frequently supplied as supporting detail includes, but is not limited to:

- Resource requirements by time period, often in the form of a resource histogram.
- Alternative schedules (e.g., best case or worst case, resource leveled or not, with or without imposed dates).
- Schedule reserves or schedule risk assessments (see Section 11.3.3).

.3 *Schedule management plan.* A schedule management plan defines how changes to the schedule will be managed. It may be formal or informal, highly detailed or broadly framed based on the needs of the project. It is a subsidiary element of the overall project plan (see Section 4.1).

.4 *Resource requirement updates.* Resource leveling and activity list updates may have a significant effect on preliminary estimates of resource requirements.

6.5 SCHEDULE CONTROL

Schedule control is concerned with (a) influencing the factors which create schedule changes to ensure that changes are beneficial, (b) determining that the schedule has changed, and (c) managing the actual changes when and as they occur. Schedule control must be thoroughly integrated with the other control processes as described in Section 4.3, Overall Change Control.

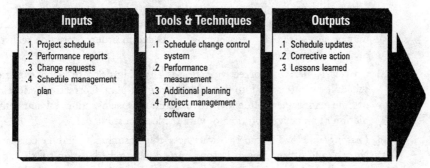

Inputs	Tools & Techniques	Outputs
.1 Project schedule .2 Performance reports .3 Change requests .4 Schedule management plan	.1 Schedule change control system .2 Performance measurement .3 Additional planning .4 Project management software	.1 Schedule updates .2 Corrective action .3 Lessons learned

6.5.1 Inputs to Schedule Control

.1 *Project schedule.* The project schedule is described in Section 6.4.3.1. The approved project schedule, called the schedule baseline, is a component of the overall project plan described in Section 4.1.3.1. It provides the basis for measuring and reporting schedule performance.

.2 *Performance reports.* Performance reports, discussed in Section 10.3.3.1, provide information on schedule performance such as which planned dates have been met and which have not. Performance reports may also alert the project team to issues which may cause problems in the future.

.3 *Change requests.* Change requests may occur in many forms—oral or written, direct or indirect, externally or internally initiated, and legally mandated or optional. Changes may require extending the schedule or may allow accelerating it.

.4 *Schedule management plan.* The schedule management plan is described in Section 6.4.3.3.

6.5.2 Tools and Techniques for Schedule Control

.1 *Schedule change control system.* A schedule change control system defines the procedures by which the project schedule may be changed. It includes the paperwork, tracking systems, and approval levels necessary for authorizing changes. Schedule change control should be integrated with the overall change control system described in Section 4.3.

.2 *Performance measurement.* Performance measurement techniques such as those described in Section 10.3.2 help to assess the magnitude of any variations which do occur. An important part of schedule control is to decide if the schedule variation requires corrective action. For example, a major delay on a non-critical activity may have little effect on the overall project while a much shorter delay on a critical or near-critical activity may require immediate action.

.3 *Additional planning.* Few projects run exactly according to plan. Prospective changes may require new or revised activity duration estimates, modified activity sequences, or analysis of alternative schedules.

.4 *Project management software.* Project management software is described in Section 6.4.2.5. The ability of project management software to track planned dates versus actual dates and to forecast the effects of schedule changes, real or potential, makes it a useful tool for schedule control.

6.5.3 Outputs from Schedule Control

.1 *Schedule updates.* A schedule update is any modification to the schedule information which is used to manage the project. Appropriate stakeholders must be notified as needed. Schedule updates may or may not require adjustments to other aspects of the overall project plan.

    *Revision*s are a special category of schedule updates. Revisions are changes to the scheduled start and finish dates in the approved project schedule. These dates are generally revised only in response to scope changes. In some cases, schedule delays may be so severe that "rebaselining" is needed in order to provide realistic data to measure performance.

.2 *Corrective action.* Corrective action is anything done to bring expected future schedule performance into line with the project plan. Corrective action in the area of time management often involves expediting: special actions taken to ensure completion of an activity on time or with the least possible delay.

.3 *Lessons learned.* The causes of variances, the reasoning behind the corrective action chosen, and other types of lessons learned from schedule control should be documented so that they become part of the historical database for both this project and other projects of the performing organization.

PROJECT COST MANAGEMENT

7

Project Cost Management includes the processes required to ensure that the project is completed within the approved budget. **Figure 7–1** provides an overview of the following major processes:

7.1 **Resource Planning**—determining what resources (people, equipment, materials) and what quantities of each should be used to perform project activities.

7.2 **Cost Estimating**—developing an approximation (estimate) of the costs of the resources needed to complete project activities.

7.3 **Cost Budgeting**—allocating the overall cost estimate to individual work items.

7.4 **Cost Control**—controlling changes to the project budget.

These processes interact with each other and with the processes in the other knowledge areas as well. Each process may involve effort from one or more individuals or groups of individuals based on the needs of the project. Each process generally occurs at least once in every project phase.

Although the processes are presented here as discrete elements with well-defined interfaces, in practice they may overlap and interact in ways not detailed here. Process interactions are discussed in detail in Chapter 3.

Project cost management is primarily concerned with the cost of the resources needed to complete project activities. However, project cost management should also consider the effect of project decisions on the cost of using the project product. For example, limiting the number of design reviews may reduce the cost of the project at the expense of an increase in the customer's operating costs. This broader view of project cost management is often called *life-cycle costing*.

In many application areas predicting and analyzing the prospective financial performance of the project product is done outside the project. In others (e.g., capital facilities projects), project cost management also includes this work. When such predictions and analysis are included, project cost management will include additional processes and numerous general management techniques such as return on investment, discounted cash flow, payback analysis, and others.

Project cost management should consider the information needs of the project stakeholders—different stakeholders may measure project costs in different ways and at different times. For example, the cost of a procurement item may be measured when committed, ordered, delivered, incurred, or recorded for accounting purposes.

When project costs are used as a component of a reward and recognition system (reward and recognition systems are discussed in Section 9.3.2.3), controllable and uncontrollable costs should be estimated and budgeted separately to ensure that rewards reflect actual performance.

7.1
Resource Planning

7.2
Cost Estimating

7.3
Cost Budgeting

7.4
Cost Control

Figure 7–1. Project Cost Management Overview

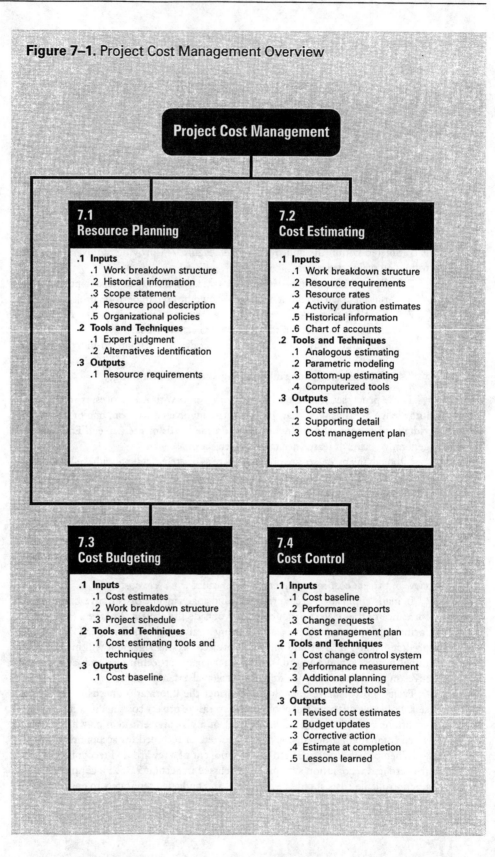

On some projects, especially smaller ones, resource planning, cost estimating, and cost budgeting are so tightly linked that they are viewed as a single process (e.g., they may be performed by a single individual over a relatively short period of time). They are presented here as distinct processes because the tools and techniques for each are different.

7.1 RESOURCE PLANNING

Resource planning involves determining what physical resources (people, equipment, materials) and what quantities of each should be used to perform project activities. It must be closely coordinated with cost estimating (described in Section 7.2). For example:

- A construction project team will need to be familiar with local building codes. Such knowledge is often readily available at virtually no cost by using local labor. However, if the local labor pool lacks experience with unusual or specialized construction techniques, the additional cost for a consultant might be the most effective way to secure knowledge of the local building codes.
- An automotive design team should be familiar with the latest in automated assembly techniques. The requisite knowledge might be obtained by hiring a consultant, by sending a designer to a seminar on robotics, or by including someone from manufacturing as a member of the team.

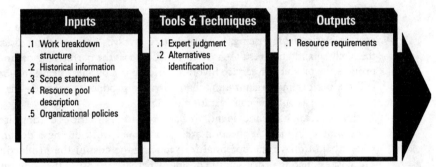

Inputs	Tools & Techniques	Outputs
.1 Work breakdown structure .2 Historical information .3 Scope statement .4 Resource pool description .5 Organizational policies	.1 Expert judgment .2 Alternatives identification	.1 Resource requirements

7.1.1 Inputs to Resource Planning

.1 Work breakdown structure. The work breakdown structure (WBS, described in Section 5.3.3.1) identifies the project elements that will need resources and thus is the primary input to resource planning. Any relevant outputs from other planning processes should be provided through the WBS to ensure proper control.

.2 Historical information. Historical information regarding what types of resources were required for similar work on previous projects should be used if available.

.3 Scope statement. The scope statement (described in Section 5.2.3.1) contains the project justification and the project objectives, both of which should be considered explicitly during resource planning.

.4 Resource pool description. Knowledge of what resources (people, equipment, material) are potentially available is necessary for resource planning. The amount of detail and the level of specificity of the resource pool description will vary. For example, during the early phases of an engineering design project, the pool may include "junior and senior engineers" in large numbers. During later phases of the same project, however, the pool may be limited to those individuals who are knowledgeable about the project as a result of having worked on the earlier phases.

.5 Organizational policies. The policies of the performing organization regarding staffing and the rental or purchase of supplies and equipment must be considered during resource planning.

7.1.2 Tools and Techniques for Resource Planning

.1 *Expert judgment.* Expert judgment will often be required to assess the inputs to this process. Such expertise may be provided by any group or individual with specialized knowledge or training and is available from many sources including:
- Other units within the performing organization.
- Consultants.
- Professional and technical associations.
- Industry groups.

.2 *Alternatives identification.* Alternatives identification is discussed in Section 5.2.2.3.

7.1.3 Outputs from Resource Planning

.1 *Resource requirements.* The output of the resource planning process is a description of what types of resources are required and in what quantities for each element of the work breakdown structure. These resources will be obtained either through staff acquisition (described in Section 9.2) or procurement (described in Chapter 12).

7.2 COST ESTIMATING

Cost estimating involves developing an approximation (estimate) of the costs of the resources needed to complete project activities.

When a project is performed under contract, care should be taken to distinguish cost estimating from pricing. Cost estimating involves developing an assessment of the likely quantitative result—how much will it cost the performing organization to provide the product or service involved. Pricing is a business decision—how much will the performing organization charge for the product or service—that uses the cost estimate as but one consideration of many.

Cost estimating includes identifying and considering various costing alternatives. For example, in most application areas, additional work during a design phase is widely held to have the potential for reducing the cost of the production phase. The cost estimating process must consider whether the cost of the additional design work will offset the expected savings.

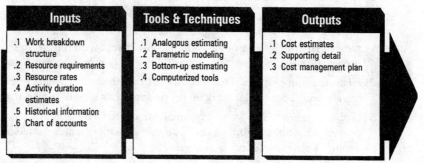

Inputs	Tools & Techniques	Outputs
.1 Work breakdown structure	.1 Analogous estimating	.1 Cost estimates
.2 Resource requirements	.2 Parametric modeling	.2 Supporting detail
.3 Resource rates	.3 Bottom-up estimating	.3 Cost management plan
.4 Activity duration estimates	.4 Computerized tools	
.5 Historical information		
.6 Chart of accounts		

7.2.1 Inputs to Cost Estimating

.1 *Work breakdown structure.* The WBS is described in Section 5.3.3.1. It will be used to organize the cost estimates and to ensure that all identified work has been estimated.

.2 *Resource requirements.* Resource requirements are described in Section 7.1.3.1.

.3 *Resource rates.* The individual or group preparing the estimates must know the unit rates (e.g., staff cost per hour, bulk material cost per cubic yard) for each resource in order to calculate project costs. If actual rates are not known, the rates themselves may have to be estimated.

©1996 Project Management Institute, Four Campus Boulevard, Newtown Square, PA 19073-3299 USA

.4 *Activity duration estimates*. Activity duration estimates (described in Section 6.3) will affect cost estimates on any project where the project budget includes an allowance for the cost of financing (i.e., interest charges).

.5 *Historical information*. Information on the cost of many categories of resources is often available from one or more of the following sources:
  • Project files—one or more of the organizations involved in the project may maintain records of previous project results that are detailed enough to aid in developing cost estimates. In some application areas, individual team members may maintain such records.
  • Commercial cost estimating databases—historical information is often available commercially.
  • Project team knowledge—the individual members of the project team may remember previous actuals or estimates. While such recollections may be useful, they are generally far less reliable than documented results.

.6 *Chart of accounts*. A chart of accounts describes the coding structure used by the performing organization to report financial information in its general ledger. Project cost estimates must be assigned to the correct accounting category.

7.2.2 Tools and Techniques for Cost Estimating

.1 *Analogous estimating*. Analogous estimating, also called *top-down estimating*, means using the actual cost of a previous, similar project as the basis for estimating the cost of the current project. It is frequently used to estimate total project costs when there is a limited amount of detailed information about the project (e.g., in the early phases). Analogous estimating is a form of expert judgment (described in Section 7.1.2.1).

Analogous estimating is generally less costly than other techniques, but it is also generally less accurate. It is most reliable when (a) the previous projects are similar in fact and not just in appearance, and (b) the individuals or groups preparing the estimates have the needed expertise.

.2 *Parametric modeling*. Parametric modeling involves using project characteristics (parameters) in a mathematical model to predict project costs. Models may be simple (residential home construction will cost a certain amount per square foot of living space) or complex (one model of software development costs uses 13 separate adjustment factors each of which has 5–7 points on it).

Both the cost and accuracy of parametric models varies widely. They are most likely to be reliable when (a) the historical information used to develop the model was accurate, (b) the parameters used in the model are readily quantifiable, and (c) the model is scalable (i.e., it works as well for a very large project as for a very small one).

.3 *Bottom-up estimating*. This technique involves estimating the cost of individual work items, then summarizing or rolling-up the individual estimates to get a project total.

The cost and accuracy of bottom-up estimating is driven by the size of the individual work items: smaller work items increase both cost and accuracy. The project management team must weigh the additional accuracy against the additional cost.

.4 *Computerized tools*. Computerized tools such as project management software and spreadsheets are widely used to assist with cost estimating. Such products can simplify the use of the tools described above and thereby facilitate rapid consideration of many costing alternatives.

7.2.3 Outputs from Cost Estimating

.1 *Cost estimates.* Cost estimates are quantitative assessments of the likely costs of the resources required to complete project activities. They may be presented in summary or in detail.

Costs must be estimated for all resources that will be charged to the project. This includes, but is not limited to, labor, materials, supplies, and special categories such as an inflation allowance or cost reserve.

Cost estimates are generally expressed in units of currency (dollars, francs, yen, etc.) in order to facilitate comparisons both within and across projects. Other units such as staff hours or staff days may be used, unless doing so will misstate project costs (e.g., by failing to differentiate among resources with very different costs). In some cases, estimates will have to be provided using multiple units of measure in order to facilitate appropriate management control.

Cost estimates may benefit from being refined during the course of the project to reflect the additional detail available. In some application areas, there are guidelines for when such refinements should be made and what degree of accuracy is expected. For example, AACE International has identified a progression of five types of estimates of construction costs during engineering: order of magnitude, conceptual, preliminary, definitive, and control.

.2 *Supporting detail.* Supporting detail for the cost estimates should include:
- A description of the scope of work estimated. This is often provided by a reference to the WBS.
- Documentation of the basis for the estimate, i.e., how it was developed.
- Documentation of any assumptions made.
- An indication of the range of possible results, for example, $10,000 ± $1,000 to indicate that the item is expected to cost between $9,000 and $11,000.

The amount and type of additional detail varies by application area. Retaining even rough notes may prove valuable by providing a better understanding of how the estimate was developed.

.3 *Cost management plan.* The cost management plan describes how cost variances will be managed (e.g., different responses to major problems than to minor ones). A cost management plan may be formal or informal, highly detailed or broadly framed based on the needs of the project stakeholders. It is a subsidiary element of the overall project plan (discussed in Section 4.1.3.1).

7.3 COST BUDGETING

Cost budgeting involves allocating the overall cost estimates to individual work items in order to establish a cost baseline for measuring project performance.

Inputs	Tools & Techniques	Outputs
.1 Cost estimates .2 Work breakdown structure .3 Project schedule	.1 Cost estimating tools and techniques	.1 Cost baseline

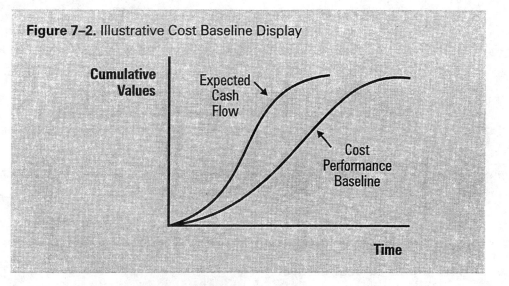

Figure 7–2. Illustrative Cost Baseline Display

7.3.1 Inputs to Cost Budgeting

.1 Cost estimates. Cost estimates are described in Section 7.2.3.1.

.2 Work breakdown structure. The work breakdown structure (described in Section 5.3.3.1) identifies the project elements that costs will be allocated to.

.3 Project schedule. The project schedule (described in Section 6.4.3.1) includes planned start and expected finish dates for the project elements that costs will be allocated to. This information is needed in order to assign costs to the time period when the cost will be incurred.

7.3.2 Tools and Techniques for Cost Budgeting

.1 Cost estimating tools and techniques. The tools and techniques described in Section 7.2.2 for developing project cost estimates are used to develop budgets for work items as well.

7.3.3 Outputs from Cost Budgeting

.1 Cost baseline. The cost baseline is a time-phased budget that will be used to measure and monitor cost performance on the project. It is developed by summing estimated costs by period and is usually displayed in the form of an S-curve, as illustrated in **Figure 7–2**.

Many projects, especially larger ones, may have multiple cost baselines to measure different aspects of cost performance. For example, a spending plan or cash flow forecast is a cost baseline for measuring disbursements.

7.4 COST CONTROL

Cost control is concerned with (a) influencing the factors which create changes to the cost baseline to ensure that changes are beneficial, (b) determining that the cost baseline has changed, and (c) managing the actual changes when and as they occur. Cost control includes:

- Monitoring cost performance to detect variances from plan.
- Ensuring that all appropriate changes are recorded accurately in the cost baseline.
- Preventing incorrect, inappropriate, or unauthorized changes from being included in the cost baseline.
- Informing appropriate stakeholders of authorized changes.

Cost control includes searching out the "whys" of both positive and negative variances. It must be thoroughly integrated with the other control processes (scope change control, schedule control, quality control, and others as discussed in Section 4.3). For example, inappropriate responses to cost variances can cause quality or schedule problems or produce an unacceptable level of risk later in the project.

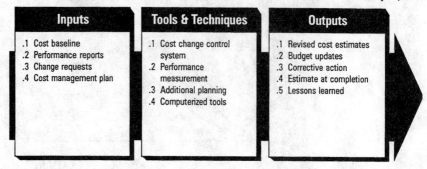

Inputs	Tools & Techniques	Outputs
.1 Cost baseline .2 Performance reports .3 Change requests .4 Cost management plan	.1 Cost change control system .2 Performance measurement .3 Additional planning .4 Computerized tools	.1 Revised cost estimates .2 Budget updates .3 Corrective action .4 Estimate at completion .5 Lessons learned

7.4.1 Inputs to Cost Control

.1 *Cost baseline.* The cost baseline is described in Section 7.3.3.1.

.2 *Performance reports.* Performance reports (discussed in Section 10.3.3.1) provide information on cost performance such as which budgets have been met and which have not. Performance reports may also alert the project team to issues which may cause problems in the future.

.3 *Change requests.* Change requests may occur in many forms—oral or written, direct or indirect, externally or internally initiated, and legally mandated or optional. Changes may require increasing the budget or may allow decreasing it.

.4 *Cost management plan.* The cost management plan is described in Section 7.2.3.3.

7.4.2 Tools and Techniques for Cost Control

.1 *Cost change control system.* A cost change control system defines the procedures by which the cost baseline may be changed. It includes the paperwork, tracking systems, and approval levels necessary for authorizing changes. The cost change control system should be integrated with the overall change control system discussed in Section 4.3.

.2 *Performance measurement.* Performance measurement techniques, described in Section 10.3.2, help to assess the magnitude of any variations which do occur. Earned value analysis, described in Section 10.3.2.4, is especially useful for cost control. An important part of cost control is to determine what is causing the variance and to decide if the variance requires corrective action.

.3 *Additional planning.* Few projects run exactly according to plan. Prospective changes may require new or revised cost estimates or analysis of alternative approaches.

.4 *Computerized tools.* Computerized tools such as project management software and spreadsheets are often used to track planned costs vs. actual costs, and to forecast the effects of cost changes.

7.4.3 Outputs from Cost Control

.1 *Revised cost estimates.* Revised cost estimates are modifications to the cost information used to manage the project. Appropriate stakeholders must be notified as needed. Revised cost estimates may or may not require adjustments to other aspects of the overall project plan.

.2 *Budget updates.* Budget updates are a special category of revised cost estimates. Budget updates are changes to an approved cost baseline. These numbers are generally revised only in response to scope changes. In some cases, cost variances may be so severe that "rebaselining" is needed in order to provide a realistic measure of performance.

.3 *Corrective action.* Corrective action is anything done to bring expected future project performance into line with the project plan.

.4 *Estimate at completion.* An estimate at completion (EAC) is a forecast of total project costs based on project performance. The most common forecasting techniques are some variation of:

- EAC = Actuals to date plus the remaining project budget modified by a performance factor, often the cost performance index described in Section 10.3.2.4. This approach is most often used when current variances are seen as typical of future variances.
- EAC = Actuals to date plus a new estimate for all remaining work. This approach is most often used when past performance shows that the original estimating assumptions were fundamentally flawed, or that they are no longer relevant due to a change in conditions.
- EAC = Actuals to date plus remaining budget. This approach is most often used when current variances are seen as atypical and the project management team's expectation is that similar variances will not occur in the future.

Each of the above approaches may be the correct approach for any given work item.

.5 *Lessons learned.* The causes of variances, the reasoning behind the corrective action chosen, and other types of lessons learned from cost control should be documented so that they become part of the historical database for both this project and other projects of the performing organization.

PROJECT QUALITY MANAGEMENT

Project Quality Management includes the processes required to ensure that the project will satisfy the needs for which it was undertaken. It includes "all activities of the overall management function that determine the quality policy, objectives, and responsibilities and implements them by means such as quality planning, quality control, quality assurance, and quality improvement, within the quality system" [1]. Figure 8–1 provides an overview of the following major project quality management processes:

8.1 **Quality Planning**—identifying which quality standards are relevant to the project and determining how to satisfy them.

8.2 **Quality Assurance**—evaluating overall project performance on a regular basis to provide confidence that the project will satisfy the relevant quality standards.

8.3 **Quality Control**—monitoring specific project results to determine if they comply with relevant quality standards and identifying ways to eliminate causes of unsatisfactory performance.

These processes interact with each other and with the processes in the other knowledge areas as well. Each process may involve effort from one or more individuals or groups of individuals based on the needs of the project. Each process generally occurs at least once in every project phase.

Although the processes are presented here as discrete elements with well-defined interfaces, in practice they may overlap and interact in ways not detailed here. Process interactions are discussed in detail in Chapter 3, Project Management Processes.

The basic approach to quality management described in this section is intended to be compatible with that of the International Organization for Standardization (ISO) as detailed in the ISO 9000 and 10000 series of standards and guidelines. This generalized approach should also be compatible with (a) proprietary approaches to quality management such as those recommended by Deming, Juran, Crosby, and others, and (b) non-proprietary approaches such as Total Quality Management (TQM), Continuous Improvement, and others.

Project quality management must address both the management of the project and the product of the project. Failure to meet quality requirements in either dimension can have serious negative consequences for any or all of the project stakeholders. For example:

• Meeting customer requirements by overworking the project team may produce negative consequences in the form of increased employee turnover.

• Meeting project schedule objectives by rushing planned quality inspections may produce negative consequences when errors go undetected.

8.1
Quality Planning

8.2
Quality Assurance

8.3
Quality Control

FIGURE 8–1   A GUIDE TO THE PROJECT MANAGEMENT BODY OF KNOWLEDGE

Figure 8–1. Project Quality Management Overview

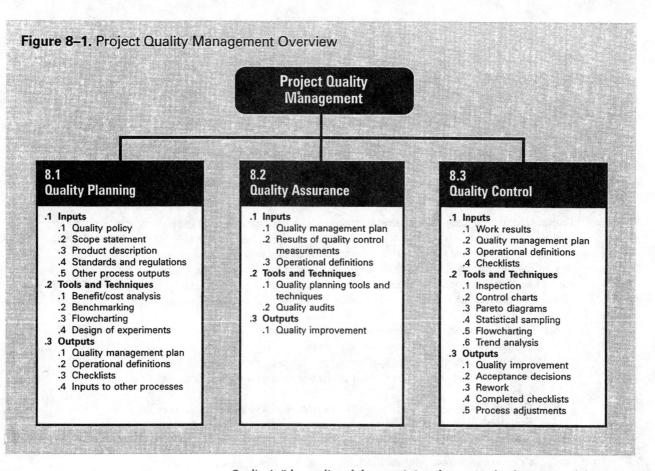

Quality is "the totality of characteristics of an entity that bear on its ability to satisfy stated or implied needs" [2]. A critical aspect of quality management in the project context is the necessity to turn implied needs into stated needs through project scope management, which is described in Chapter 5.

The project management team must be careful not to confuse *quality* with *grade*. Grade is "a category or rank given to entities having the same functional use but different requirements for quality" [3]. Low quality is always a problem; low grade may not be. For example, a software product may be of high quality (no obvious bugs, readable manual) and low grade (a limited number of features), or of low quality (many bugs, poorly organized user documentation) and high grade (numerous features). Determining and delivering the required levels of both quality and grade are the responsibilities of the project manager and the project management team.

The project management team should also be aware that modern quality management complements modern project management. For example, both disciplines recognize the importance of:

- Customer satisfaction—understanding, managing, and influencing needs so that customer expectations are met or exceeded. This requires a combination of *conformance to specifications* (the project must produce what it said it would produce) and *fitness for use* (the product or service produced must satisfy real needs).
- Prevention over inspection—the cost of avoiding mistakes is always much less than the cost of correcting them.

- Management responsibility—success requires the *participation* of all members of the team, but it remains the *responsibility* of management to provide the resources needed to succeed.
- Processes within phases—the repeated plan-do-check-act cycle described by Deming and others is highly similar to the combination of phases and processes discussed in Chapter 3, Project Management Processes.

In addition, quality improvement initiatives undertaken by the performing organization (e.g., TQM, Continuous Improvement, and others) can improve the quality of the project management as well as the quality of the project product.

However, there is an important difference that the project management team must be acutely aware of—the temporary nature of the project means that investments in product quality improvement, especially defect prevention and appraisal, must often be borne by the performing organization since the project may not last long enough to reap the rewards.

8.1 QUALITY PLANNING

Quality planning involves identifying which quality standards are relevant to the project and determining how to satisfy them. It is one of the key facilitating processes during project planning (see Section 3.3.2, Planning Processes) and should be performed regularly and in parallel with the other project planning processes. For example, the desired management quality may require cost or schedule adjustments, or the desired product quality may require a detailed risk analysis of an identified problem. Prior to development of the ISO 9000 Series, the activities described here as *quality planning* were widely discussed as part of *quality assurance*.

The quality planning techniques discussed here are those used most frequently on projects. There are many others that may be useful on certain projects or in some application areas.

The project team should also be aware of one of the fundamental tenets of modern quality management—quality is planned in, not inspected in.

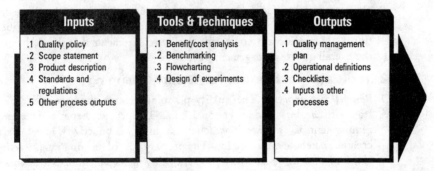

Inputs	Tools & Techniques	Outputs
.1 Quality policy	.1 Benefit/cost analysis	.1 Quality management plan
.2 Scope statement	.2 Benchmarking	.2 Operational definitions
.3 Product description	.3 Flowcharting	.3 Checklists
.4 Standards and regulations	.4 Design of experiments	.4 Inputs to other processes
.5 Other process outputs		

8.1.1 Inputs to Quality Planning

.1 *Quality policy*. Quality policy is "the overall intentions and direction of an organization with regard to quality, as formally expressed by top management" [4]. The quality policy of the performing organization can often be adopted "as is" for use by the project. However, if the performing organization lacks a formal quality policy, or if the project involves multiple performing organizations (as with a joint venture), the project management team will need to develop a quality policy for the project.

Regardless of the origin of the quality policy, the project management team is responsible for ensuring that the project stakeholders are fully aware of it (e.g., through appropriate information distribution, as described in Section 10.2).

FIGURE 8–2   A GUIDE TO THE PROJECT MANAGEMENT BODY OF KNOWLEDGE

Figure 8–2. Cause-and-Effect Diagram

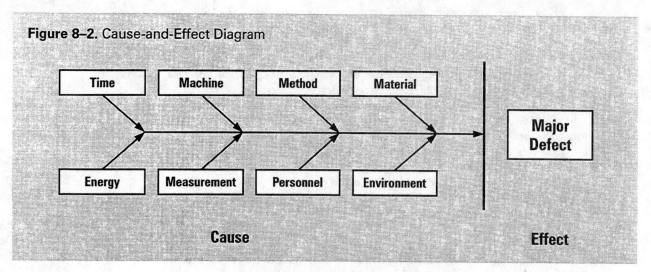

.2 *Scope statement.* The scope statement (described in Section 5.2.3.1) is a key input to quality planning since it documents major project deliverables as well as the project objectives which serve to define important stakeholder requirements.

.3 *Product description.* Although elements of the product description (described in Section 5.1.1.1) may be embodied in the scope statement, the product description will often contain details of technical issues and other concerns that may affect quality planning.

.4 *Standards and regulations.* The project management team must consider any application-area-specific standards or regulations that may affect the project. Section 2.5.1 discusses standards and regulations.

.5 *Other process outputs.* In addition to the scope statement and product description, processes in other knowledge areas may produce outputs that should be considered as part of quality planning. For example, procurement planning (described in Section 12.1) may identify contractor quality requirements that should be reflected in the overall quality management plan.

8.1.2 Tools and Techniques for Quality Planning

.1 *Benefit/cost analysis.* The quality planning process must consider benefit/cost trade-offs, as described in Section 5.2.2.2. The primary benefit of meeting quality requirements is less rework, which means higher productivity, lower costs, and increased stakeholder satisfaction. The primary cost of meeting quality requirements is the expense associated with project quality management activities. It is axiomatic of the quality management discipline that the benefits outweigh the costs.

.2 *Benchmarking.* Benchmarking involves comparing actual or planned project practices to those of other projects in order to generate ideas for improvement and to provide a standard by which to measure performance. The other projects may be within the performing organization or outside of it, and may be within the same application area or in another.

.3 *Flowcharting.* A flowchart is any diagram which shows how various elements of a system relate. Flowcharting techniques commonly used in quality management include:
  - *Cause-and-effect diagrams,* also called *Ishikawa diagrams* or *fishbone diagrams,* which illustrate how various causes and subcauses relate to create potential problems or effects. **Figure** 8–2 is an example of a generic cause-and-effect diagram.

Figure 8–3. Sample Process Flowchart

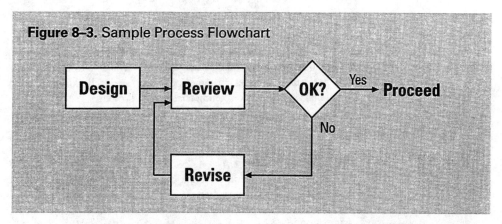

- *System* or *process flowcharts*, which show how various elements of a system interrelate. **Figure 8–3** is an example of a process flowchart for design reviews.

Flowcharting can help the project team anticipate what and where quality problems might occur and thus can help to develop approaches to dealing with them.

.4 **Design of experiments.** Design of experiments is an analytical technique which helps identify which variables have the most influence on the overall outcome. The technique is applied most frequently to product of the project issues (e.g., automotive designers might wish to determine which combination of suspension and tires will produce the most desirable ride characteristics at a reasonable cost).

However, it can also be applied to project management issues such as cost and schedule trade-offs. For example, senior engineers will cost more than junior engineers, but can also be expected to complete the assigned work in less time. An appropriately designed "experiment" (in this case, computing project costs and durations for various combinations of senior and junior engineers) will often allow determination of an optimal solution from a relatively limited number of cases.

8.1.3 Outputs from Quality Planning

.1 *Quality management plan.* The quality management plan should describe how the project management team will implement its quality policy. In ISO 9000 terminology, it should describe the *project quality system*: "the organizational structure, responsibilities, procedures, processes, and resources needed to implement quality management" [5].

The quality management plan provides input to the overall project plan (described in Section 4.1, Project Plan Development) and must address quality control, quality assurance, and quality improvement for the project.

The quality management plan may be formal or informal, highly detailed, or broadly framed, based on the needs of the project.

.2 *Operational definitions.* An operational definition describes, in very specific terms, what something is, and how it is measured by the quality control process. For example, it is not enough to say that meeting the planned schedule dates is a measure of management quality; the project management team must also indicate whether every activity must start on time, or only finish on time; whether individual activities will be measured or only certain deliverables, and if so, which ones. Operational definitions are also called *metrics* in some application areas.

.3 *Checklists.* A checklist is a structured tool, usually industry- or activity-specific, used to verify that a set of required steps has been performed. Checklists may be simple or complex. They are usually phrased as imperatives ("Do this!") or interrogatories ("Have you done this?"). Many organizations have standardized checklists available to ensure consistency in frequently performed activities. In some application areas, checklists are also available from professional associations or commercial service providers.

.4 *Inputs to other processes.* The quality planning process may identify a need for further activity in another area.

8.2 QUALITY ASSURANCE

Quality assurance is all the planned and systematic activities implemented within the quality system to provide confidence that the project will satisfy the relevant quality standards [6]. It should be performed throughout the project. Prior to development of the ISO 9000 Series, the activities described under *quality planning* were widely included as part of quality assurance.

Quality assurance is often provided by a Quality Assurance Department or similarly titled organizational unit, but it does not have to be.

Assurance may be provided to the project management team and to the management of the performing organization (internal quality assurance) or it may be provided to the customer and others not actively involved in the work of the project (external quality assurance).

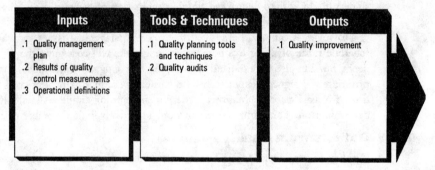

Inputs	Tools & Techniques	Outputs
.1 Quality management plan .2 Results of quality control measurements .3 Operational definitions	.1 Quality planning tools and techniques .2 Quality audits	.1 Quality improvement

8.2.1 Inputs to Quality Assurance

.1 *Quality management plan.* The quality management plan is described in Section 8.1.3.1.

.2 *Results of quality control measurements.* Quality control measurements are records of quality control testing and measurement in a format for comparison and analysis.

.3 *Operational definitions.* Operational definitions are described in Section 8.1.3.2.

8.2.2 Tools and Techniques for Quality Assurance

.1 *Quality planning tools and techniques.* The quality planning tools and techniques described in Section 8.1.2 can be used for quality assurance as well.

.2 *Quality audits.* A quality audit is a structured review of other quality management activities. The objective of a quality audit is to identify lessons learned that can improve performance of this project or of other projects within the performing organization. Quality audits may be scheduled or random, and they may be carried out by properly trained in-house auditors or by third parties such as quality system registration agencies.

©1996 Project Management Institute, Four Campus Boulevard, Newtown Square, PA 19073-3299 USA

8.2.3 Outputs from Quality Assurance

.1 Quality improvement. Quality improvement includes taking action to increase the effectiveness and efficiency of the project to provide added benefits to the project stakeholders. In most cases, implementing quality improvements will require preparation of change requests or taking of corrective action and will be handled according to procedures for overall change control, as described in Section 4.3.

8.3 QUALITY CONTROL

Quality control involves monitoring specific project results to determine if they comply with relevant quality standards and identifying ways to eliminate causes of unsatisfactory results. It should be performed throughout the project. Project results include both *product* results such as deliverables and *management* results such as cost and schedule performance. Quality control is often performed by a Quality Control Department or similarly titled organizational unit, but it does not have to be.

The project management team should have a working knowledge of statistical quality control, especially sampling and probability, to help them evaluate quality control outputs. Among other subjects, they should know the differences between:

- Prevention (keeping errors out of the process) and inspection (keeping errors out of the hands of the customer).
- Attribute sampling (the result conforms or it does not) and variables sampling (the result is rated on a continuous scale that measures the degree of conformity).
- Special causes (unusual events) and random causes (normal process variation).
- Tolerances (the result is acceptable if it falls within the range specified by the tolerance) and control limits (the process is in control if the result falls within the control limits).

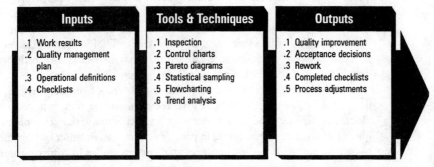

Inputs	Tools & Techniques	Outputs
.1 Work results	.1 Inspection	.1 Quality improvement
.2 Quality management plan	.2 Control charts	.2 Acceptance decisions
.3 Operational definitions	.3 Pareto diagrams	.3 Rework
.4 Checklists	.4 Statistical sampling	.4 Completed checklists
	.5 Flowcharting	.5 Process adjustments
	.6 Trend analysis	

8.3.1 Inputs to Quality Control

.1 Work results. Work results (described in Section 4.2.3.1) include both *process* results and *product* results. Information about the planned or expected results (from the project plan) should be available along with information about the actual results.

.2 Quality management plan. The quality management plan is described in Section 8.1.3.1.

.3 Operational definitions. Operational definitions are described in Section 8.1.3.2.

.4 Checklists. Checklists are described in Section 8.1.3.3.

FIGURE 8–4   A GUIDE TO THE PROJECT MANAGEMENT BODY OF KNOWLEDGE

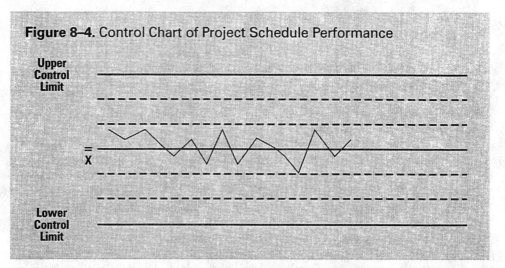

Figure 8–4. Control Chart of Project Schedule Performance

8.3.2 Tools and Techniques for Quality Control

.1 Inspection. Inspection includes activities such as measuring, examining, and testing undertaken to determine whether results conform to requirements. Inspections may be conducted at any level (e.g., the results of a single activity may be inspected or the final product of the project may be inspected). Inspections are variously called reviews, product reviews, audits, and walk-throughs; in some application areas, these terms have narrow and specific meanings.

.2 Control charts. Control charts are a graphic display of the results, over time, of a process. They are used to determine if the process is "in control" (e.g., are differences in the results created by random variations or are unusual events occurring whose causes must be identified and corrected?). When a process is in control, the process should not be adjusted. The process may be *changed* in order to provide improvements but it should not be adjusted when it is in control.

Control charts may be used to monitor any type of output variable. Although used most frequently to track repetitive activities such as manufactured lots, control charts can also be used to monitor cost and schedule variances, volume and frequency of scope changes, errors in project documents, or other management results to help determine if the "project management process" is in control. **Figure 8–4** is a control chart of project schedule performance.

.3 Pareto diagrams. A Pareto diagram is a histogram, ordered by frequency of occurrence, that shows how many results were generated by type or category of identified cause (see **Figure 8–5**). Rank ordering is used to guide corrective action—the project team should take action to fix the problems that are causing the greatest number of defects first. Pareto diagrams are conceptually related to Pareto's Law, which holds that a relatively small number of causes will typically produce a large majority of the problems or defects.

.4 Statistical sampling. Statistical sampling involves choosing part of a population of interest for inspection (e.g., selecting ten engineering drawings at random from a list of 75). Appropriate sampling can often reduce the cost of quality control. There is a substantial body of knowledge on statistical sampling; in some application areas, it is necessary for the project management team to be familiar with a variety of sampling techniques.

.5 Flowcharting. Flowcharting is described in Section 8.1.2.3. Flowcharting is used in quality control to help analyze how problems occur.

Figure 8–5. Pareto Diagram

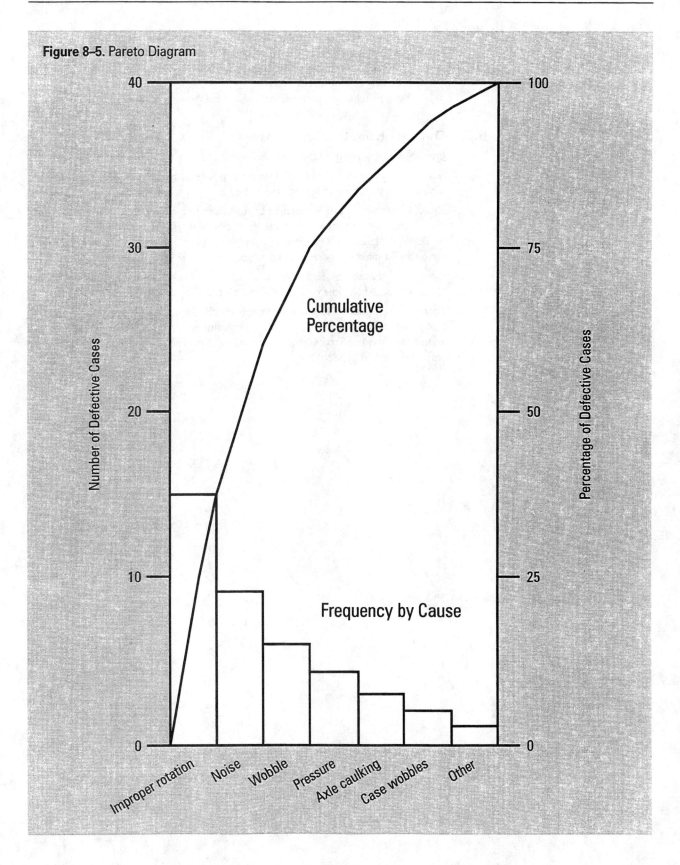

.6 *Trend analysis.* Trend analysis involves using mathematical techniques to forecast future outcomes based on historical results. Trend analysis is often used to monitor:

- Technical performance—how many errors or defects have been identified, how many remain uncorrected.
- Cost and schedule performance—how many activities per period were completed with significant variances.

8.3.3 Outputs from Quality Control

.1 *Quality improvement.* Quality improvement is described in Section 8.2.3.1.

.2 *Acceptance decisions.* The items inspected will be either accepted or rejected. Rejected items may require rework (described in Section 8.3.3.3).

.3 *Rework.* Rework is action taken to bring a defective or non-conforming item into compliance with requirements or specifications. Rework, especially unanticipated rework, is a frequent cause of project overruns in most application areas. The project team should make every reasonable effort to minimize rework.

.4 *Completed checklists.* See Section 8.1.3.3. When checklists are used, the completed checklists should become part of the project's records.

.5 *Process adjustments.* Process adjustments involve immediate corrective or preventive action as a result of quality control measurements. In some cases, the process adjustment may need to be handled according to procedures for overall change control, as described in Section 4.3.

PROJECT HUMAN RESOURCE MANAGEMENT

9

Project Human Resource Management includes the processes required to make the most effective use of the people involved with the project. It includes all the project stakeholders—sponsors, customers, individual contributors, and others described in Section 2.2. **Figure 9–1** provides an overview of the following major processes:

- 9.1 **Organizational Planning**—identifying, documenting, and assigning project roles, responsibilities, and reporting relationships.
- 9.2 **Staff Acquisition**—getting the human resources needed assigned to and working on the project.
- 9.3 **Team Development**—developing individual and group skills to enhance project performance.

These processes interact with each other and with the processes in the other knowledge areas as well. Each process may involve effort from one or more individuals or groups of individuals based on the needs of the project. Although the processes are presented here as discrete elements with well-defined interfaces, in practice they may overlap and interact in ways not detailed here. Process interactions are discussed in detail in Chapter 3, Project Management Processes.

There is a substantial body of literature about dealing with people in an operational, ongoing context. Some of the many topics include:

- Leading, communicating, negotiating, and others discussed in Section 2.4, Key General Management Skills.
- Delegating, motivating, coaching, mentoring, and other subjects related to dealing with individuals.
- Team building, dealing with conflict, and other subjects related to dealing with groups.
- Performance appraisal, recruitment, retention, labor relations, health and safety regulations, and other subjects related to administering the human resource function.

Most of this material is directly applicable to leading and managing people on projects, and the project manager and project management team should be familiar with it. However, they must also be sensitive as to how this knowledge is applied on the project. For example:

- The temporary nature of projects means that the personal and organizational relationships will generally be both temporary and new. The project management team must take care to select techniques that are appropriate for such transient relationships.

FIGURE 9–1   A GUIDE TO THE PROJECT MANAGEMENT BODY OF KNOWLEDGE

Figure 9–1. Project Human Resource Management Overview

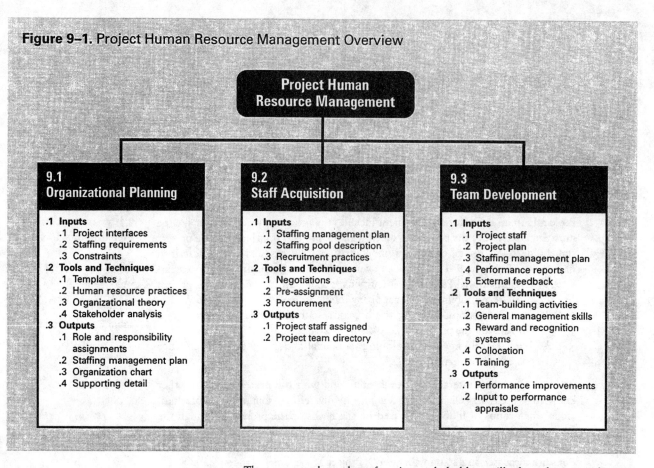

- The nature and number of project stakeholders will often change as the project moves from phase to phase of its life cycle. As a result, techniques that are effective in one phase may not be effective in another. The project management team must take care to use techniques that are appropriate to the current needs of the project.
- Human resource administrative activities are seldom a direct responsibility of the project management team. However, the team must be sufficiently aware of administrative requirements to ensure compliance.

9.1 ORGANIZATIONAL PLANNING

Organizational planning involves identifying, documenting, and assigning project roles, responsibilities, and reporting relationships. Roles, responsibilities, and reporting relationships may be assigned to individuals or to groups. The individuals and groups may be part of the organization performing the project or they may be external to it. Internal groups are often associated with a specific functional department such as engineering, marketing, or accounting.

On most projects, the majority of organizational planning is done as part of the earliest project phases. However, the results of this process should be reviewed regularly throughout the project to ensure continued applicability. If the initial organization is no longer effective, it should be revised promptly.

Organizational planning is often tightly linked with communications planning (described in Section 10.1) since the project's organizational structure will have a major effect on the project's communications requirements.

94

©1996 Project Management Institute, Four Campus Boulevard, Newtown Square, PA 19073-3299 USA

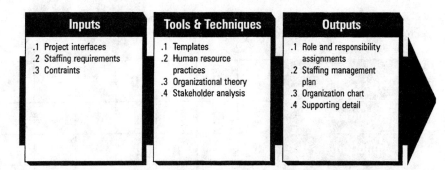

Inputs	Tools & Techniques	Outputs
.1 Project interfaces .2 Staffing requirements .3 Contraints	.1 Templates .2 Human resource practices .3 Organizational theory .4 Stakeholder analysis	.1 Role and responsibility assignments .2 Staffing management plan .3 Organization chart .4 Supporting detail

9.1.1 Inputs to Organizational Planning

.1 Project interfaces. Project interfaces generally fall into one of three categories:

- Organizational interfaces—formal and informal reporting relationships among different organizational units. Organizational interfaces may be highly complex or very simple. For example, developing a complex telecommunications system may require coordinating numerous subcontractors over several years, while fixing a programming error in a system installed at a single site may require little more than notifying the user and the operations staff upon completion.
- Technical interfaces—formal and informal reporting relationships among different technical disciplines. Technical interfaces occur both within project phases (e.g., the site design developed by the civil engineers must be compatible with the superstructure developed by the structural engineers) and between project phases (e.g., when an automotive design team passes the results of its work along to the retooling team that must create the manufacturing capability for the vehicle).
- Interpersonal interfaces—formal and informal reporting relationships among different individuals working on the project.

These interfaces often occur simultaneously, as when an architect employed by a design firm explains key design considerations to an unrelated construction contractor's project management team.

.2 Staffing requirements. Staffing requirements define what kinds of skills are required from what kinds of individuals or groups and in what time frames. Staffing requirements are a subset of the overall resource requirements identified during resource planning (described in Section 7.1).

.3 Constraints. Constraints are factors that limit the project team's options. A project's organizational options may be constrained in many ways. Common factors that may constrain how the team is organized include, but are not limited to, the following:

- Organizational structure of the performing organization—an organization whose basic structure is a *strong matrix* means a relatively stronger role for the project manager than one whose basic structure is a *weak matrix* (see Section 2.3.3 for a more detailed discussion of organizational structures).
- Collective bargaining agreements—contractual agreements with unions or other employee groups may require certain roles or reporting relationships (in essence, the employee group is a stakeholder).
- Preferences of the project management team—if members of the project management team have had success with certain structures in the past, they are likely to advocate similar structures in the future.
- Expected staff assignments—how the project is organized is often influenced by the skills and capabilities of specific individuals.

FIGURE 9–2   A GUIDE TO THE PROJECT MANAGEMENT BODY OF KNOWLEDGE

Figure 9–2. Responsibility Assignment Matrix

PHASE \ PERSON	A	B	C	D	E	F	...
Requirements	S	R	A	P	P		
Functional	S		A	P		P	
Design	S		R	A	I		P
Development		R	S	A		P	P
Testing			S	P	I	A	P

P = Participant   A = Accountable   R = Review required
I = Input required   S = Sign-off required

9.1.2 Tools and Techniques for Organizational Planning

.1 *Templates.* Although each project is unique, most projects will resemble another project to some extent. Using the role and responsibility definitions or reporting relationships of a similar project can help expedite the process of organizational planning.

.2 *Human resource practices.* Many organizations have a variety of policies, guidelines, and procedures that can help the project management team with various aspects of organizational planning. For example, an organization that views managers as "coaches" is likely to have documentation on how the role of "coach" is to be performed.

.3 *Organizational theory.* There is a substantial body of literature describing how organizations can and should be structured. Although only a small subset of this body of literature is specifically targeted at project organizations, the project management team should be generally familiar with the subject of organizational theory so as to be better able to respond to project requirements.

4. *Stakeholder analysis.* The needs of the various stakeholders should be analyzed to ensure that their needs will be met. Section 10.1.2.1 discusses stakeholder analysis in more detail.

9.1.3 Outputs from Organizational Planning

.1 *Role and responsibility assignments.* Project roles (who does what) and responsibilities (who decides what) must be assigned to the appropriate project stakeholders. Roles and responsibilities may vary over time. Most roles and responsibilities will be assigned to stakeholders who are actively involved in the work of the project, such as the project manager, other members of the project management team, and the individual contributors.

The roles and responsibilities of the project manager are generally critical on most projects but vary significantly by application area.

Project roles and responsibilities should be closely linked to the project scope definition. A Responsibility Assignment Matrix (or RAM, see **Figure 9–2**) is often used for this purpose. On larger projects, RAMs may be developed at various levels. For example, a high-level RAM may define which group or unit is responsible for each

Figure 9–3. Illustrative Resource Histogram

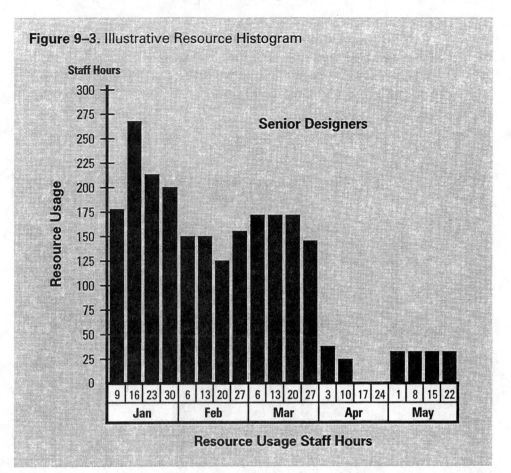

element of the work breakdown structure while lower-level RAMs are used within the group to assign roles and responsibilities for specific activities to particular individuals.

.2 *Staffing management plan.* The staffing management plan describes when and how human resources will be brought onto and taken off the project team. The staffing plan may be formal or informal, highly detailed or broadly framed, based on the needs of the project. It is a subsidiary element of the overall project plan (see Section 4.1, Project Plan Development).

The staffing management plan often includes resource histograms, as illustrated in **Figure 9–3.**

Particular attention should be paid to how project team members (individuals or groups) will be released when they are no longer needed on the project. Appropriate reassignment procedures may:

- Reduce costs by reducing or eliminating the tendency to "make work" to fill the time between this assignment and the next.
- Improve morale by reducing or eliminating uncertainty about future employment opportunities.

.3 *Organization chart.* An organization chart is any graphic display of project reporting relationships. It may be formal or informal, highly detailed or broadly framed, based on the needs of the project. For example, the organization chart for a three- to four-person internal service project is unlikely to have the rigor and detail of the organization chart for a 3,000-person nuclear power plant outage.

An Organizational Breakdown Structure (OBS) is a specific type of organization chart that shows which organizational units are responsible for which work items.

.4 Supporting detail. Supporting detail for organizational planning varies by application area and project size. Information frequently supplied as supporting detail includes, but is not limited to:

- Organizational impact—what alternatives are precluded by organizing in this manner.
- Job descriptions—written outlines by job title of the skills, responsibilities, knowledge, authority, physical environment, and other characteristics involved in performing a given job. Also called *position descriptions*.
- Training needs—if the staff to be assigned is not expected to have the skills needed by the project, those skills will need to be developed as part of the project.

9.2 STAFF ACQUISITION

Staff acquisition involves getting the human resources needed (individuals or groups) assigned to and working on the project. In most environments, the "best" resources may not be available, and the project management team must take care to ensure that the resources which are available will meet project requirements.

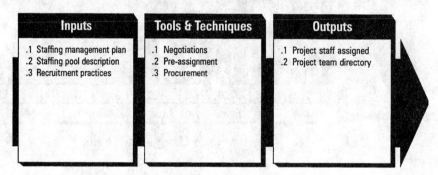

Inputs	Tools & Techniques	Outputs
.1 Staffing management plan	.1 Negotiations	.1 Project staff assigned
.2 Staffing pool description	.2 Pre-assignment	.2 Project team directory
.3 Recruitment practices	.3 Procurement	

9.2.1 Inputs to Staff Acquisition

.1 Staffing management plan. The staffing management plan is described in Section 9.1.3.2. It includes the project's staffing requirements as described in Section 9.1.1.2.

.2 Staffing pool description. When the project management team is able to influence or direct staff assignments, it must consider the characteristics of the potentially available staff. Considerations include, but are not limited to:

- Previous experience—have the individuals or groups done similar or related work before? Have they done it well?
- Personal interests—are the individuals or groups interested in working on this project?
- Personal characteristics—are the individuals or groups likely to work well together as a team?
- Availability—will the most desirable individuals or groups be available in the necessary time frames?

.3 Recruitment practices. One or more of the organizations involved in the project may have policies, guidelines, or procedures governing staff assignments. When they exist, such practices act as a constraint on the staff acquisition process.

9.2.2 Tools and Techniques for Staff Acquisition

.1 Negotiations. Staff assignments must be negotiated on most projects. For example, the project management team may need to negotiate with:

- Responsible functional managers to ensure that the project receives appropriately skilled staff in the necessary time frame.
- Other project management teams within the performing organization to assign scarce or specialized resources appropriately.

The team's influencing skills (see Section 2.4.5, Influencing the Organization) play an important role in negotiating staff assignments as do the politics of the organizations involved. For example, a functional manager may be rewarded based on staff utilization. This creates an incentive for the manager to assign available staff who may not meet all of the project's requirements.

.2 **Pre-assignment.** In some cases, staff may be pre-assigned to the project. This is often the case when (a) the project is the result of a competitive proposal and specific staff were promised as part of the proposal, or (b) the project is an internal service project and staff assignments were defined within the project charter.

.3 **Procurement.** Project procurement management (described in Chapter 12) can be used to obtain the services of specific individuals or groups of individuals to perform project activities. Procurement is required when the performing organization lacks the in-house staff needed to complete the project (e.g., as a result of a conscious decision not to hire such individuals as full-time employees, as a result of having all appropriately skilled staff previously committed to other projects, or as a result of other circumstances).

9.2.3 Outputs from Staff Acquisition

.1 **Project staff assigned.** The project is staffed when appropriate people have been reliably assigned to work on it. Staff may be assigned full-time, part-time, or variably, based on the needs of the project.

.2 **Project team directory.** A project team directory lists all the project team members and other key stakeholders. The directory may be formal or informal, highly detailed or broadly framed, based on the needs of the project.

9.3 TEAM DEVELOPMENT

Team development includes both enhancing the ability of stakeholders to contribute as individuals as well as enhancing the ability of the team to function as a team. Individual development (managerial and technical) is the foundation necessary to develop the team. Development as a team is critical to the project's ability to meet its objectives.

Team development on a project is often complicated when individual team members are accountable to both a functional manager and to the project manager (see Section 2.3.3 for a discussion of matrix organizational structures). Effective management of this dual reporting relationship is often a critical success factor for the project and is generally the responsibility of the project manager.

Although team development is positioned in Chapter 3 as one of the executing processes, team development occurs throughout the project.

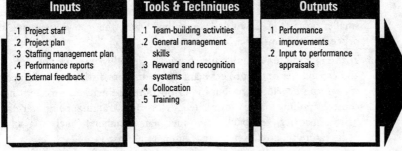

Inputs	Tools & Techniques	Outputs
.1 Project staff	.1 Team-building activities	.1 Performance improvements
.2 Project plan	.2 General management skills	.2 Input to performance appraisals
.3 Staffing management plan	.3 Reward and recognition systems	
.4 Performance reports	.4 Collocation	
.5 External feedback	.5 Training	

9.3.1 Inputs to Team Development

.1 *Project staff.* Project staffing is described in Section 9.2.3.1. The staff assignments implicitly define the individual skills and team skills available to build upon.

.2 *Project plan.* The project plan is described in Section 4.1.3.1. The project plan describes the technical context within which the team operates.

.3 *Staffing management plan.* The staffing management plan is described in Section 9.1.3.2.

.4 *Performance reports.* Performance reports (described in Section 10.3.3.1) provide feedback to the project team about performance against the project plan.

.5 *External feedback.* The project team must periodically measure itself against the performance expectations of those outside the project.

9.3.2 Tools and Techniques for Team Development

.1 *Team-building activities.* Team-building activities include management and individual actions taken specifically and primarily to improve team performance. Many actions, such as involving non–management-level team members in the planning process, or establishing ground rules for surfacing and dealing with conflict, may enhance team performance as a secondary effect. Team-building activities can vary from a five-minute agenda item in a regular status review meeting to an extended, off-site, professionally facilitated experience designed to improve interpersonal relationships among key stakeholders.

There is a substantial body of literature on team building. The project management team should be generally familiar with a variety of team-building activities.

.2 *General management skills.* General management skills (discussed in Section 2.4) are of particular importance to team development.

.3 *Reward and recognition systems.* Reward and recognition systems are formal management actions which promote or reinforce desired behavior. To be effective, such systems must make the link between performance and reward clear, explicit, and achievable. For example, a project manager who is to be rewarded for meeting the project's cost objective should have an appropriate level of control over staffing and procurement decisions.

Projects must often have their own reward and recognition systems since the systems of the performing organization may not be appropriate. For example, the willingness to work overtime in order to meet an aggressive schedule objective *should* be rewarded or recognized; needing to work overtime as the result of poor planning *should not* be.

Reward and recognition systems must also consider cultural differences. For example, developing an appropriate team reward mechanism in a culture that prizes individualism may be very difficult.

.4 *Collocation.* Collocation involves placing all, or almost all, of the most active project team members in the same physical location to enhance their ability to perform as a team. Collocation is widely used on larger projects and can also be effective for smaller projects (e.g., with a "war room" where the team congregates or leaves in-process work items).

.5 *Training.* Training includes all activities designed to enhance the skills, knowledge, and capabilities of the project team. Some authors distinguish among training, education, and development, but the distinctions are neither consistent nor widely accepted. Training may be formal (e.g., classroom training, computer-based training) or informal (e.g., feedback from other team members). There is a substantial body of literature on how to provide training to adults.

If the project team members lack necessary management or technical skills, such skills must be developed as part of the project, or steps must be taken to restaff the project appropriately. Direct and indirect costs for training are generally paid by the performing organization.

9.3.3 Outputs from Team Development

.1 *Performance improvements.* The primary output of team development is improved project performance. Improvements can come from many sources and can affect many areas of project performance, for example:

- Improvements in individual skills may allow a specific person to perform their assigned activities more effectively.
- Improvements in team behaviors (e.g., surfacing and dealing with conflict) may allow project team members to devote a greater percentage of their effort to technical activities.
- Improvements in either individual skills or team capabilities may facilitate identifying and developing better ways of doing project work.

.2 *Input to performance appraisals.* Project staff should generally provide input to the performance appraisals of any project staff members that they interact with in a significant way.

PROJECT COMMUNICATIONS MANAGEMENT

10

Project Communications Management includes the processes required to ensure timely and appropriate generation, collection, dissemination, storage, and ultimate disposition of project information. It provides the critical links among people, ideas, and information that are necessary for success. Everyone involved in the project must be prepared to send and receive communications in the project "language" and must understand how the communications they are involved in as individuals affect the project as a whole. **Figure 10–1** provides an overview of the following major processes:

10.1 **Communications Planning**—determining the information and communications needs of the stakeholders: who needs what information, when will they need it, and how will it be given to them.

10.2 **Information Distribution**—making needed information available to project stakeholders in a timely manner.

10.3 **Performance Reporting**—collecting and disseminating performance information. This includes status reporting, progress measurement, and forecasting.

10.4 **Administrative Closure**—generating, gathering, and disseminating information to formalize phase or project completion.

These processes interact with each other and with the processes in the other knowledge areas as well. Each process may involve effort from one or more individuals or groups of individuals based on the needs of the project. Each process generally occurs at least once in every project phase.

Although the processes are presented here as discrete elements with well-defined interfaces, in practice they may overlap and interact in ways not detailed here. Process interactions are discussed in detail in Chapter 3.

The general management skill of communicating (discussed in Section 2.4.2) is related to, but not the same as, project communications management. Communicating is the broader subject and involves a substantial body of knowledge that is not unique to the project context. For example:

- Sender-receiver models—feedback loops, barriers to communications, etc.
- Choice of media—when to communicate in writing versus when to communicate orally, when to write an informal memo versus when to write a formal report, etc.
- Writing style—active versus passive voice, sentence structure, word choice, etc.
- Presentation techniques—body language, design of visual aids, etc.
- Meeting management techniques—preparing an agenda, dealing with conflict, etc.

FIGURE 10–1   A GUIDE TO THE PROJECT MANAGEMENT BODY OF KNOWLEDGE

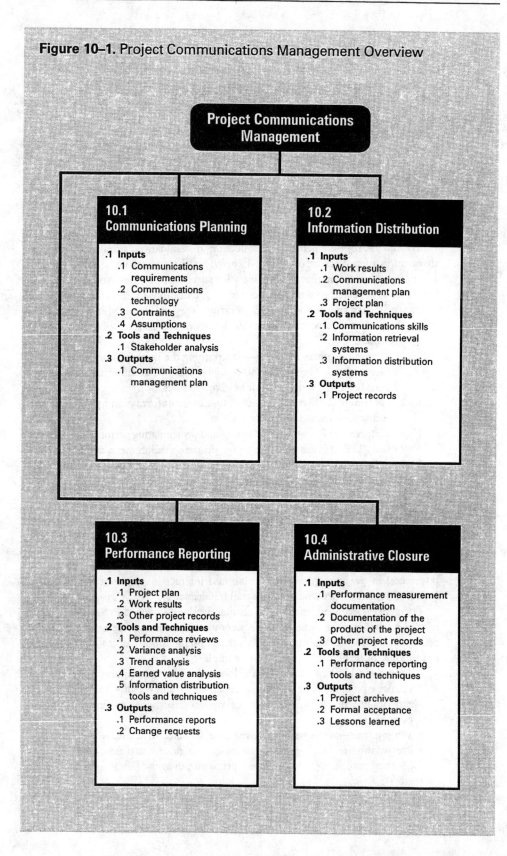

Figure 10–1. Project Communications Management Overview

10.1 COMMUNICATIONS PLANNING

Communications planning involves determining the information and communications needs of the stakeholders: who needs what information, when will they need it, and how will it be given to them. While all projects share the need to communicate project information, the informational needs and the methods of distribution vary widely. Identifying the informational needs of the stakeholders and determining a suitable means of meeting those needs is an important factor for project success.

On most projects, the majority of communications planning is done as part of the earliest project phases. However, the results of this process should be reviewed regularly throughout the project and revised as needed to ensure continued applicability.

Communications planning is often tightly linked with organizational planning (described in Section 9.1) since the project's organizational structure will have a major effect on the project's communications requirements.

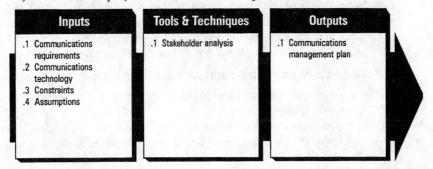

Inputs	Tools & Techniques	Outputs
.1 Communications requirements .2 Communications technology .3 Constraints .4 Assumptions	.1 Stakeholder analysis	.1 Communications management plan

10.1.1 Inputs to Communications Planning

.1 Communications requirements. Communications requirements are the sum of the information requirements of the project stakeholders. Requirements are defined by combining the type and format of information required with an analysis of the value of that information. Project resources should be expended only on communicating information which contributes to success or where lack of communication can lead to failure. Information typically required to determine project communications requirements includes:

- Project organization and stakeholder responsibility relationships.
- Disciplines, departments, and specialties involved in the project.
- Logistics of how many individuals will be involved with the project and at which locations.
- External information needs (e.g., communicating with the media).

.2 Communications technology. The technologies or methods used to transfer information back and forth among project elements can vary significantly: from brief conversations to extended meetings, from simple written documents to immediately accessible on-line schedules and databases. Communications technology factors which may affect the project include:

- The immediacy of the need for information—is project success dependent upon having frequently updated information available on a moment's notice, or would regularly issued written reports suffice?
- The availability of technology—are the systems that are already in place appropriate, or do project needs warrant change?
- The expected project staffing—are the communications systems proposed compatible with the experience and expertise of the project participants, or will extensive training and learning be required?
- The length of the project—is the available technology likely to change before the project is over in a manner that would warrant adopting the newer technology?

.3 *Constraints.* Constraints are factors that will limit the project management team's options. For example, if substantial project resources will be procured, more consideration will need to be given to handling contract information.

When a project is performed under contract, there are often specific contractual provisions that affect communications planning.

.4 *Assumptions.* Assumptions are factors that, for planning purposes, will be considered to be true, real, or certain. Assumptions generally involve a degree of risk. They may be identified here or they may be an output of risk identification (described in Section 11.1).

10.1.2 Tools and Techniques for Communications Planning

.1 *Stakeholder analysis.* The information needs of the various stakeholders should be analyzed to develop a methodical and logical view of their information needs and sources to meet those needs (project stakeholders are discussed in more detail in Sections 2.2 and 5.1). The analysis should consider methods and technologies suited to the project that will provide the information needed. Care should be taken to avoid wasting resources on unnecessary information or inappropriate technology.

10.1.3 Outputs from Communications Planning

.1 *Communications management plan.* A communications management plan is a document which provides:

- A collection and filing structure which details what methods will be used to gather and store various types of information. Procedures should also cover collecting and disseminating updates and corrections to previously distributed material.
- A distribution structure which details to whom information (status reports, data, schedule, technical documentation, etc.) will flow, and what methods (written reports, meetings, etc.) will be used to distribute various types of information. This structure must be compatible with the responsibilities and reporting relationships described by the project organization chart.
- A description of the information to be distributed, including format, content, level of detail, and conventions/definitions to be used.
- Production schedules showing when each type of communication will be produced.
- Methods for accessing information between scheduled communications.
- A method for updating and refining the communications management plan as the project progresses and develops.

The communications management plan may be formal or informal, highly detailed or broadly framed, based on the needs of the project. It is a subsidiary element of the overall project plan (described Section 4.1).

10.2 INFORMATION DISTRIBUTION

Information distribution involves making needed information available to project stakeholders in a timely manner. It includes implementing the communications management plan as well as responding to unexpected requests for information.

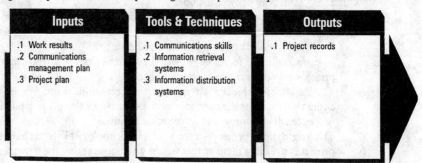

Inputs	Tools & Techniques	Outputs
.1 Work results .2 Communications management plan .3 Project plan	.1 Communications skills .2 Information retrieval systems .3 Information distribution systems	.1 Project records

10.2.1 Inputs to Information Distribution

.1 *Work results.* Work results are described in Section 4.2.3.1.

.2 *Communications management plan.* The communications management plan is described in Section 10.1.3.1.

.3 *Project plan.* The project plan is described in Section 4.1.3.1.

10.2.2 Tools and Techniques for Information Distribution

.1 *Communications skills.* Communications skills are used to exchange information. The sender is responsible for making the information clear, unambiguous, and complete so that the receiver can receive it correctly and for confirming that it is properly understood. The receiver is responsible for making sure that the information is received in its entirety and understood correctly. Communicating has many dimensions:
- Written and oral, listening and speaking.
- Internal (within the project) and external (to the customer, the media, the public, etc.).
- Formal (reports, briefings, etc.) and informal (memos, ad hoc conversations, etc.).
- Vertical (up and down the organization) and horizontal (with peers).

.2 *Information retrieval systems.* Information can be shared by team members through a variety of methods including manual filing systems, electronic text databases, project management software, and systems which allow access to technical documentation such as engineering drawings.

.3 *Information distribution systems.* Project information may be distributed using a variety of methods including project meetings, hard copy document distribution, shared access to networked electronic databases, fax, electronic mail, voice mail, and video conferencing.

10.2.3 Outputs from Information Distribution

.1 *Project records.* Project records may include correspondence, memos, reports, and documents describing the project. This information should, to the extent possible and appropriate, be maintained in an organized fashion. Project team members may often maintain personal records in a project notebook.

10.3 PERFORMANCE REPORTING

Performance reporting involves collecting and disseminating performance information in order to provide stakeholders with information about how resources are being used to achieve project objectives. This process includes:
- Status reporting—describing where the project now stands.
- Progress reporting—describing what the project team has accomplished.
- Forecasting—predicting future project status and progress.

Performance reporting should generally provide information on scope, schedule, cost, and quality. Many projects also require information on risk and procurement. Reports may be prepared comprehensively or on an exception basis.

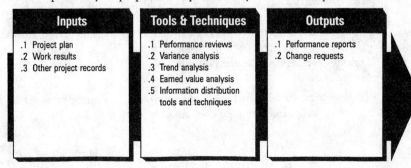

Inputs	Tools & Techniques	Outputs
.1 Project plan	.1 Performance reviews	.1 Performance reports
.2 Work results	.2 Variance analysis	.2 Change requests
.3 Other project records	.3 Trend analysis	
	.4 Earned value analysis	
	.5 Information distribution tools and techniques	

10.3.1 Inputs to Performance Reporting

.1 Project plan. The project plan is discussed in Section 4.1.3.1. The project plan contains the various baselines that will be used to assess project performance.

.2 Work results. Work results—which deliverables have been fully or partially completed, what costs have been incurred or committed, etc.—are an output of project plan execution (discussed in Section 4.2.3.1). Work results should be reported within the framework provided by the communications management plan. Accurate, uniform information on work results is essential to useful performance reporting.

.3 Other project records. Project records are discussed in Section 10.2.3.1. In addition to the project plan and the project's work results, other project documents often contain information pertaining to the project context that should be considered when assessing project performance.

10.3.2 Tools and Techniques for Performance Reporting

.1 Performance reviews. Performance reviews are meetings held to assess project status or progress. Performance reviews are typically used in conjunction with one or more of the performance reporting techniques described below.

.2 Variance analysis. Variance analysis involves comparing actual project results to planned or expected results. Cost and schedule variances are the most frequently analyzed, but variances from plan in the areas of scope, quality, and risk are often of equal or greater importance.

.3 Trend analysis. Trend analysis involves examining project results over time to determine if performance is improving or deteriorating.

.4 Earned value analysis. Earned value analysis in its various forms is the most commonly used method of performance measurement. It integrates scope, cost, and schedule measures to help the project management team assess project performance. Earned value involves calculating three key values for each activity:

- The budget, also called the budgeted cost of work scheduled (BCWS), is that portion of the approved cost estimate planned to be spent on the activity during a given period.
- The actual cost, also called the actual cost of work performed (ACWP), is the total of direct and indirect costs incurred in accomplishing work on the activity during a given period.
- The earned value, also called the budgeted cost of work performed (BCWP), is a percentage of the total budget equal to the percentage of the work actually completed. Many earned value implementations use only a few percentages (e.g., 30 percent, 70 percent, 90 percent, 100 percent) to simplify data collection. Some earned value implementations use only 0 percent or 100 percent (done or not done) to help ensure objective measurement of performance.

These three values are used in combination to provide measures of whether or not work is being accomplished as planned. The most commonly used measures are the cost variance (CV = BCWP − ACWP), the schedule variance (SV = BCWP − BCWS), and the cost performance index (CPI = BCWP/ACWP). The cumulative CPI (the sum of all individual BCWPs divided by the sum of all individual ACWPs) is widely used to forecast project cost at completion. In some application areas, the schedule performance index (SPI = BCWP/BCWS) is used to forecast the project completion date.

.5 Information distribution tools and techniques. Performance reports are distributed using the tools and techniques described in Section 10.2.2.

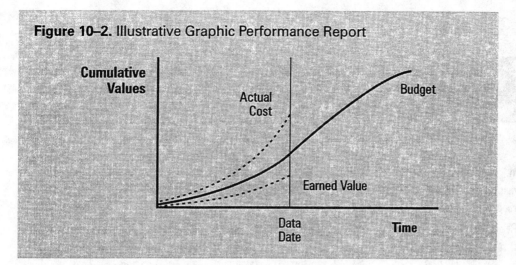

Figure 10–2. Illustrative Graphic Performance Report

10.3.3 Outputs from Performance Reporting

.1 Performance reports. Performance reports organize and summarize the information gathered and present the results of any analysis. Reports should provide the kinds of information and the level of detail required by various stakeholders as documented in the communications management plan.

Common formats for performance reports include bar charts (also called Gantt charts), S-curves, histograms, and tables. **Figure 10–2** uses S-curves to display cumulative earned value analysis data while **Figure 10–3** displays a different set of earned value data in tabular form.

.2 Change requests. Analysis of project performance often generates a request for a change to some aspect of the project. These change requests are handled as described in the various change control processes (e.g., scope change management, schedule control, etc.).

10.4 ADMINISTRATIVE CLOSURE

The project or phase, after either achieving its objectives or being terminated for other reasons, requires closure. Administrative closure consists of verifying and documenting project results to formalize acceptance of the product of the project by the sponsor, client, or customer. It includes collection of project records, ensuring that they reflect final specifications, analysis of project success and effectiveness, and archiving such information for future use.

Administrative closure activities should not be delayed until project completion. Each phase of the project should be properly closed to ensure that important and useful information is not lost.

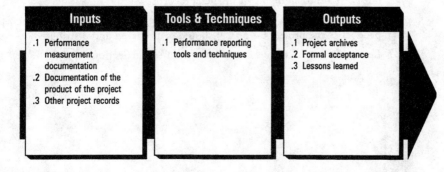

Inputs	Tools & Techniques	Outputs
.1 Performance measurement documentation .2 Documentation of the product of the project .3 Other project records	.1 Performance reporting tools and techniques	.1 Project archives .2 Formal acceptance .3 Lessons learned

FIGURE 10–3   A GUIDE TO THE PROJECT MANAGEMENT BODY OF KNOWLEDGE

Figure 10–3. Illustrative Tabular Performance Report

WBS Element	Budget ($) (BCWS)	Earned Value ($) (BCWP)	Actual Cost ($) (ACWP)	Cost Variance ($) (BCWP–ACWP)	Cost Variance (%) (BCWP÷ACWP)	Schedule Variance ($) (BCWP–BCWS)	Schedule Variance (%) (BCWP÷BCWS)
1.0 Pre-pilot planning	63,000	58,000	62,500	–4,500	–7.8	–5,000	–7.9
2.0 Draft checklists	64,000	48,000	46,800	1,200	2.5	–16,000	–25.0
3.0 Curriculum design	23,000	20,000	23,500	–3,500	–17.5	–3,000	–13.0
4.0 Mid-term evaluation	68,000	68,000	72,500	–4,500	–6.6	0	0.0
5.0 Implementation support	12,000	10,000	10,000	0	0.0	–2,000	–16.7
6.0 Manual of practice	7,000	6,200	6,000	200	3.2	–800	–11.4
7.0 Roll-out plan	20,000	13,500	18,100	–4,600	–34.1	–6,500	–32.5
Totals	**257,000**	**223,700**	**239,400**	**–15,700**	**–7.0**	**–33,300**	**–13.0**

Note: All figures are project-to-date.

10.4.1 Inputs to Administrative Closure

.1 *Performance measurement documentation.* All documentation produced to record and analyze project performance, including the planning documents which established the framework for performance measurement, must be available for review during administrative closure.

.2 *Documentation of the product of the project.* Documents produced to describe the product of the project (plans, specifications, technical documentation, drawings, electronic files, etc.—the terminology varies by application area) must also be available for review during administrative closure.

.3 *Other project records.* Project records are discussed in Section 10.2.3.1.

10.4.2 Tools and Techniques for Administrative Closure

.1 *Performance reporting tools and techniques.* Performance reporting tools and techniques are discussed in Section 10.3.2.

10.4.3 Outputs from Administrative Closure

.1 *Project archives.* A complete set of indexed project records should be prepared for archiving by the appropriate parties. Any project-specific or program-wide historical databases pertinent to the project should be updated. When projects are done under contract or when they involve significant procurement, particular attention must be paid to archiving of financial records.

.2 *Formal acceptance.* Documentation that the client or sponsor has accepted the product of the project (or phase) should be prepared and distributed.

.3 *Lessons learned.* Lessons learned are discussed in Section 4.3.3.3.

©1996 Project Management Institute, Four Campus Boulevard, Newtown Square, PA 19073-3299 USA

PROJECT RISK MANAGEMENT

11

Project Risk Management includes the processes concerned with identifying, analyzing, and responding to project risk. It includes maximizing the results of positive events and minimizing the consequences of adverse events. **Figure 11–1** provides an overview of the following major processes:

11.1 **Risk Identification**—determining which risks are likely to affect the project and documenting the characteristics of each.

11.2 **Risk Quantification**—evaluating risks and risk interactions to assess the range of possible project outcomes.

11.3 **Risk Response Development**—defining enhancement steps for opportunities and responses to threats.

11.4 **Risk Response Control**—responding to changes in risk over the course of the project.

These processes interact with each other and with the processes in the other knowledge areas as well. Each process may involve effort from one or more individuals or groups of individuals based on the needs of the project. Each process generally occurs at least once in every project phase.

Although the processes are presented here as discrete elements with well-defined interfaces, in practice they may overlap and interact in ways not detailed here. Process interactions are discussed in detail in Chapter 3.

Different application areas often use different names for the processes described here. For example:

- Risk identification and risk quantification are sometimes treated as a single process, and the combined process may be called risk analysis or risk assessment.
- Risk response development is sometimes called response planning or risk mitigation.
- Risk response development and risk response control are sometimes treated as a single process, and the combined process may be called risk management.

11.1 RISK IDENTIFICATION

Risk identification consists of determining which risks are likely to affect the project and documenting the characteristics of each. Risk identification is not a one-time event; it should be performed on a regular basis throughout the project.

Risk identification should address both internal and external risks. Internal risks are things that the project team can control or influence, such as staff assignments and cost estimates. External risks are things beyond the control or influence of the project team, such as market shifts or government action.

Strictly speaking, risk involves only the possibility of suffering harm or loss. In the project context, however, risk identification is also concerned with opportunities (positive outcomes) as well as threats (negative outcomes).

FIGURE 11–1   A GUIDE TO THE PROJECT MANAGEMENT BODY OF KNOWLEDGE

Figure 11–1. Project Risk Management Overview

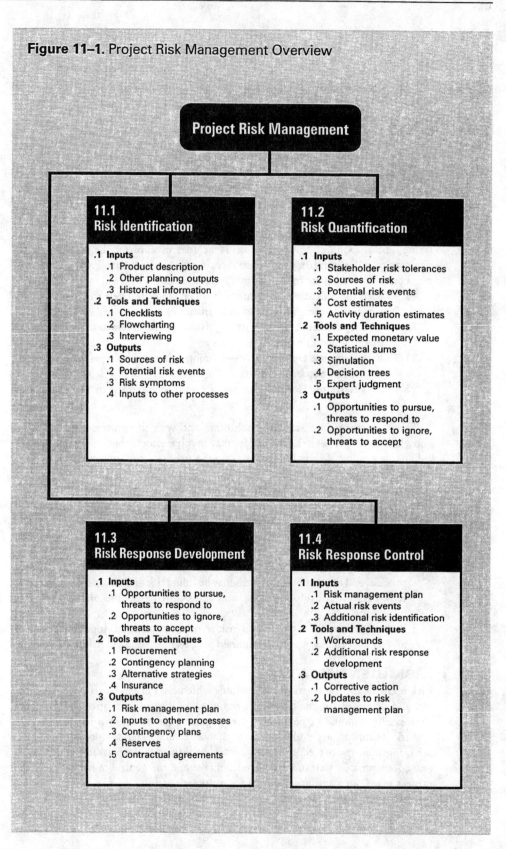

Risk identification may be accomplished by identifying causes-and-effects (what could happen and what will ensue) or effects-and-causes (what outcomes are to be avoided or encouraged and how each might occur).

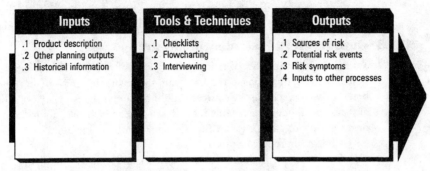

Inputs	Tools & Techniques	Outputs
.1 Product description	.1 Checklists	.1 Sources of risk
.2 Other planning outputs	.2 Flowcharting	.2 Potential risk events
.3 Historical information	.3 Interviewing	.3 Risk symptoms
		.4 Inputs to other processes

11.1.1 Inputs to Risk Identification

.1 Product description. The nature of the product of the project will have a major effect on the risks identified. Products that involve proven technology will, all other things being equal, involve less risk than products which require innovation or invention. Risks associated with the product of the project are often described in terms of their cost and schedule impact. Section 5.1.1.1 has additional information about the product description.

.2 Other planning outputs. The outputs of the processes in other knowledge areas should be reviewed to identify possible risks. For example:

- Work breakdown structure—non-traditional approaches to detail deliverables may offer opportunities that were not apparent from the higher-level deliverables identified in the scope statement.
- Cost estimates and duration estimates—aggressive estimates and estimates developed with a limited amount of information entail more risk.
- Staffing plan—identified team members may have unique skills that would be hard to replace or may have other commitments that make their availability tenuous.
- Procurement management plan—market conditions such as a sluggish local economy may offer opportunities to reduce contract costs.

.3 Historical information. Historical information about what actually happened on previous projects can be especially helpful in identifying potential risks. Information on historical results is often available from the following sources:

- Project files—one or more of the organizations involved in the project may maintain records of previous project results that are detailed enough to aid in risk identification. In some application areas, individual team members may maintain such records.
- Commercial databases—historical information is available commercially in many application areas.
- Project team knowledge—the individual members of the project team may remember previous occurrences or assumptions. While such recollections may be useful, they are generally less reliable than documented results.

11.1.2 Tools and Techniques for Risk Identification

.1 Checklists. Checklists are typically organized by source of risk. Sources include the project context (see Chapter 2), other process outputs (see Section 11.1.1.2), the product of the project or technology issues, and internal sources such as team member skills (or the lack thereof). Some application areas have widely used classification schemes for sources of risk.

2. *Flowcharting.* Flowcharting (described in Section 8.1.2.3) can help the project team better understand the causes and effects of risks.

.3 *Interviewing.* Risk-oriented interviews with various stakeholders may help identify risks not identified during normal planning activities. Records of pre-project interviews (e.g., those conducted during a feasibility study) may also be available.

11.1.3 Outputs from Risk Identification

.1 *Sources of risk.* Sources of risk are categories of possible risk events (e.g., stakeholder actions, unreliable estimates, team turnover) that may affect the project for better or worse. The list of sources should be comprehensive, i.e., it should generally include all identified items regardless of frequency, probability of occurrence, or magnitude of gain or loss. Common sources of risk include:
   • Changes in requirements.
   • Design errors, omissions, and misunderstandings.
   • Poorly defined or understood roles and responsibilities.
   • Poor estimates.
   • Insufficiently skilled staff.

   Descriptions of the sources of risk should generally include estimates of (a) the probability that a risk event from that source will occur, (b) the range of possible outcomes, (c) expected timing, and (d) anticipated frequency of risk events from that source.

   Both probabilities and outcomes may be specified as continuous functions (an estimated cost between $100,000 and $150,000) or as discrete ones (a patent either will or will not be granted). In addition, estimates of probabilities and outcomes made during early project phases are likely to have a broader range than those made later in the project.

.2 *Potential risk events.* Potential risk events are discrete occurrences such as a natural disaster or the departure of a specific team member that may affect the project. Potential risk events should be identified in addition to sources of risk when the probability of occurrence or magnitude of loss is relatively large ("relatively large" will vary by project). While potential risk events are seldom application-area-specific, a list of *common* risk events usually is. For example:
   • Development of new technology that will obviate the need for a project is common in electronics and rare in real estate development.
   • Losses due to a major storm are common in construction and rare in biotechnology.

   Descriptions of potential risk events should generally include estimates of (a) the probability that the risk event will occur, (b) the alternative possible outcomes, (c) expected timing of the event, and (d) anticipated frequency (i.e., can it happen more than once).

   Both probabilities and outcomes may be specified as continuous functions (an estimated cost between $100,000 and $150,000) or as discrete ones (a patent either will or will not be granted). In addition, estimates of probabilities and outcomes made during early project phases are likely to have a broader range than those made later in the project.

.3 *Risk symptoms.* Risk symptoms, sometimes called triggers, are indirect manifestations of actual risk events. For example, poor morale may be an early warning signal of an impending schedule delay or cost overruns on early activities may be indicative of poor estimating.

.4 *Inputs to other processes.* The risk identification process may identify a need for further activity in another area. For example, the work breakdown structure may not have sufficient detail to allow adequate identification of risks.

   Risks are often input to the other processes as constraints or assumptions.

11.2 RISK QUANTIFICATION

Risk quantification involves evaluating risks and risk interactions to assess the range of possible project outcomes. It is primarily concerned with determining which risk events warrant response. It is complicated by a number of factors including, but not limited to:

- Opportunities and threats can interact in unanticipated ways (e.g., schedule delays may force consideration of a new strategy that reduces overall project duration).
- A single risk event can cause multiple effects, as when late delivery of a key component produces cost overruns, schedule delays, penalty payments, and a lower-quality product.
- Opportunities for one stakeholder (reduced cost) may be threats to another (reduced profits).
- The mathematical techniques used can create a false impression of precision and reliability.

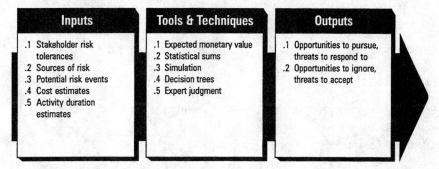

Inputs	Tools & Techniques	Outputs
.1 Stakeholder risk tolerances .2 Sources of risk .3 Potential risk events .4 Cost estimates .5 Activity duration estimates	.1 Expected monetary value .2 Statistical sums .3 Simulation .4 Decision trees .5 Expert judgment	.1 Opportunities to pursue, threats to respond to .2 Opportunities to ignore, threats to accept

11.2.1 Inputs to Risk Quantification

.1 Stakeholder risk tolerances. Different organizations and different individuals have different tolerances for risk. For example:

- A highly profitable company may be willing to spend $500,000 to write a proposal for a $1 billion contract, while a company operating at break-even is not.
- One organization may perceive an estimate that has a 15 percent probability of overrunning as high risk, while another perceives it as low risk.

Stakeholder risk tolerances provide a screen for both inputs and outputs to risk quantification.

.2 Sources of risk. Sources of risk are described in Section 11.1.3.1.

.3 Potential risk events. Potential risk events are described in Section 11.1.3.2.

.4 Cost estimates. Cost estimates are described in Section 7.2.3.1.

.5 Activity duration estimates. Activity duration estimates are described in Section 6.3.3.1.

11.2.2 Tools and Techniques for Risk Quantification

.1 Expected monetary value. Expected monetary value, as a tool for risk quantification, is the product of two numbers:

- Risk event probability—an estimate of the probability that a given risk event will occur.
- Risk event value—an estimate of the gain or loss that will be incurred if the risk event does occur.

The risk event value must reflect both tangibles and intangibles. For example, Project A and Project B both identify an equal probability of a tangible loss of $100,000 as an outcome of an aggressively priced proposal. If Project A predicts little or no intangible effect, while Project B predicts that such a loss will put its performing organization out of business, the two risks are not equivalent.

FIGURE 11–2   A GUIDE TO THE PROJECT MANAGEMENT BODY OF KNOWLEDGE

Figure 11–2. Summing Probability Distributions

Activity Name	Low	Most Likely	High	Mean	Sigma	Variance
	a	m	b	$\bar{x}$	σ	σ^2
Triangular Distribution						
Initial draft						
Gather information	40	45	80	55.0	8.9	79.2
Write sections	35	50	100	61.7	13.9	193.1
Review informally	10	15	30	18.3	4.2	18.1
Inspection						
Inspectors inspect	18	25	50	31.0	6.9	47.2
Prepare defects/issues list	10	20	40	23.3	6.2	38.9
Resolve defects/issues	10	25	60	31.7	10.5	109.7
Make necessary changes	15	20	40	25.0	5.4	29.2
Estimated Project Totals:		200		246.0	22.7 ←	515.2

Mean = (a + m + b) / 3   Variance = [(b − a)^2 + (m − a)(m − b)] / 18

Beta Distribution (using PERT approximations)

Activity Name	Low	Most Likely	High	Mean	Sigma	Variance
Initial draft						
Gather information	40	45	80	50.0	6.7	44.4
Write sections	35	50	100	55.8	10.8	117.4
Review informally	10	15	30	16.7	3.3	11.1
Inspection						
Inspectors inspect	18	25	50	28.0	5.3	28.4
Prepare defects/issues list	10	20	40	21.7	5.0	25.0
Resolve defects/issues	10	25	60	28.3	8.3	69.4
Make necessary changes	15	20	40	22.5	4.2	17.4
Estimated Project Totals:		200		223.0	17.7 ←	313.2

Mean = (a + 4m + b) / 6   Variance = [(b − a) /6]^2

When summing probability distributions:
- If the distributions are skewed to the left as in this illustration, the project mean will always be significantly higher than the sum of the most likely estimates.
- Distributions can be mixed and matched at will. The same distribution was used for all activities to simplify this illustration.

In order to sum probability distributions, calculate:
- The mean, sigma (standard deviation), and variance for each individual activity based on the formula for that distribution (i.e., beta, triangular, flat, etc.).
- The project mean as the sum of the individual activity means.
- The project variance as the sum of the individual activity variances.
- The project sigma (standard deviation) as the square root of the project variance.

In similar fashion, failure to include intangibles in this calculation can severely distort the result by equating a small loss with a high probability to a large loss with a small probability.

The expected monetary value is generally used as input to further analysis (e.g., in a decision tree) since risk events can occur individually or in groups, in parallel or in sequence.

.2 *Statistical sums.* Statistical sums can be used to calculate a range of total project costs from the cost estimates for individual work items. (Calculating a range of probable project completion dates from the activity duration estimates requires simulation as described in Section 11.2.2.3).

The range of total project costs can be used to quantify the relative risk of alternative project budgets or proposal prices. **Figure 11–2** illustrates the use of the "method of moments" technique to calculate project range estimates.

.3 *Simulation.* Simulation uses a representation or model of a system to analyze the behavior or performance of the system. The most common form of simulation on a project is schedule simulation using the project network as the model of the project. Most schedule simulations are based on some form of Monte Carlo analysis. This technique, adapted from general management, "performs" the project many times to provide a statistical distribution of the calculated results as illustrated in **Figure 11–3**.

The results of a schedule simulation may be used to quantify the risk of various schedule alternatives, different project strategies, different paths through the network, or individual activities.

Schedule simulation should be used on any large or complex project since traditional mathematical analysis techniques such as the Critical Path Method (CPM) and the Program Evaluation and Review Technique (PERT) do not account for path convergence (see **Figure 11–4**) and thus tend to underestimate project durations.

Monte Carlo analysis and other forms of simulation can also be used to assess the range of possible cost outcomes.

.4 *Decision trees.* A decision tree is a diagram that depicts key interactions among decisions and associated chance events as they are understood by the decision maker. The branches of the tree represent either decisions (shown as boxes) or chance events (shown as circles). **Figure 11–5** is an example of a decision tree.

.5 *Expert judgment.* Expert judgment can often be applied in lieu of or in addition to the mathematical techniques described above. For example, risk events could be described as having a high, medium, or low probability of occurrence and a severe, moderate, or limited impact.

11.2.3 Outputs from Risk Quantification

.1 *Opportunities to pursue, threats to respond to.* The major output from risk quantification is a list of opportunities that should be pursued and threats that require attention.

.2 *Opportunities to ignore, threats to accept.* The risk quantification process should also document (a) those sources of risk and risk events that the project management team has consciously decided to accept or ignore and (b) who made the decision to do so.

FIGURE 11–3   A GUIDE TO THE PROJECT MANAGEMENT BODY OF KNOWLEDGE

Figure 11–3. Results from a Monte Carlo Simulation of a Project Schedule

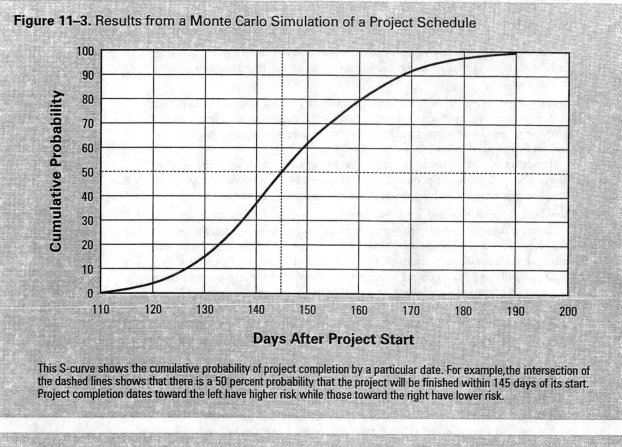

This S-curve shows the cumulative probability of project completion by a particular date. For example, the intersection of the dashed lines shows that there is a 50 percent probability that the project will be finished within 145 days of its start. Project completion dates toward the left have higher risk while those toward the right have lower risk.

Figure 11–4. Path Convergence

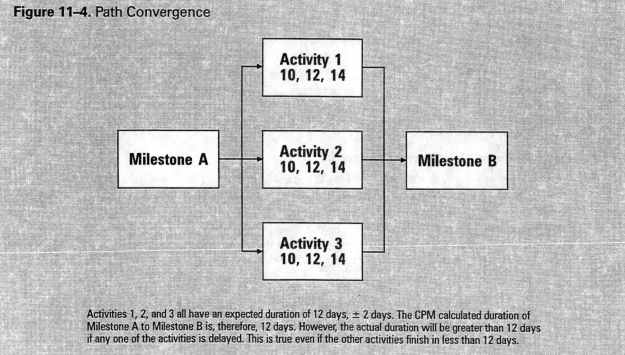

Activities 1, 2, and 3 all have an expected duration of 12 days, ± 2 days. The CPM calculated duration of Milestone A to Milestone B is, therefore, 12 days. However, the actual duration will be greater than 12 days if any one of the activities is delayed. This is true even if the other activities finish in less than 12 days.

Figure 11–5. Decision Tree

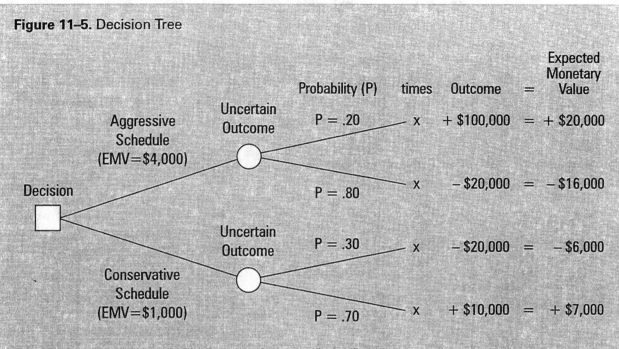

- Expected monetary value (EMV) of result = Outcome x Probability of that outcome.
- Expected monetary value of a decision = sum of EMVs of all Outcomes stemming from that decision.
- Aggressive schedule has expected monetary value of $4,000 and is "preferred" over conservative schedule with expected monetary value of $1,000.

11.3 RISK RESPONSE DEVELOPMENT

Risk response development involves defining enhancement steps for opportunities and responses to threats. Responses to threats generally fall into one of three categories:

- Avoidance—eliminating a specific threat, usually by eliminating the cause. The project management team can never eliminate all risk, but specific risk events can often be eliminated.
- Mitigation—reducing the expected monetary value of a risk event by reducing the probability of occurrence (e.g., using proven technology to lessen the probability that the product of the project will not work), reducing the risk event value (e.g., buying insurance), or both.
- Acceptance—accepting the consequences. Acceptance can be active (e.g., by developing a contingency plan to execute should the risk event occur) or passive (e.g., by accepting a lower profit if some activities overrun).

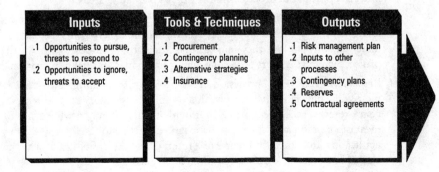

Inputs	Tools & Techniques	Outputs
.1 Opportunities to pursue, threats to respond to .2 Opportunities to ignore, threats to accept	.1 Procurement .2 Contingency planning .3 Alternative strategies .4 Insurance	.1 Risk management plan .2 Inputs to other processes .3 Contingency plans .4 Reserves .5 Contractual agreements

©1996 Project Management Institute, Four Campus Boulevard, Newtown Square, PA 19073-3299 USA

11.3.1 Inputs to Risk Response Development

.1 *Opportunities to pursue, threats to respond to.* These are described in Section 11.2.3.1.

.2 *Opportunities to ignore, threats to accept.* These are described in Section 11.2.3.2. These items are input to the risk response development process because they should be documented in the risk management plan (described in Section 11.3.3.1).

11.3.2 Tools and Techniques for Risk Response Development

.1 *Procurement.* Procurement, acquiring goods or services from outside the immediate project organization, is often an appropriate response to some types of risk. For example, risks associated with using a particular technology may be mitigated by contracting with an organization that has experience with that technology.

Procurement often involves exchanging one risk for another. For example, mitigating cost risk with a fixed price contract may create schedule risk if the seller is unable to perform. In similar fashion, trying to transfer all technical risk to the seller may result in an unacceptably high cost proposal.

Project Procurement Management is described in Chapter 12.

.2 *Contingency planning.* Contingency planning involves defining action steps to be taken if an identified risk event should occur (see also the discussion of workarounds in Section 11.4.2.1).

.3 *Alternative strategies.* Risk events can often be prevented or avoided by changing the planned approach. For example, additional design work may decrease the number of changes which must be handled during the implementation or construction phase. Many application areas have a substantial body of literature on the potential value of various alternative strategies.

.4 *Insurance.* Insurance or an insurance-like arrangement such as bonding is often available to deal with some categories of risk. The type of coverage available and the cost of coverage varies by application area.

11.3.3 Outputs from Risk Response Development

.1 *Risk management plan.* The risk management plan should document the procedures that will be used to manage risk throughout the project. In addition to documenting the results of the risk identification and risk quantification processes, it should cover who is responsible for managing various areas of risk, how the initial identification and quantification outputs will be maintained, how contingency plans will be implemented, and how reserves will be allocated.

A risk management plan may be formal or informal, highly detailed or broadly framed, based on the needs of the project. It is a subsidiary element of the overall project plan (described in Section 4.1).

.2 *Inputs to other processes.* Selected or suggested alternative strategies, contingency plans, anticipated procurements, and other risk-related outputs must all be fed back into the appropriate processes in the other knowledge areas.

.3 *Contingency plans.* Contingency plans are pre-defined action steps to be taken if an identified risk event should occur. Contingency plans are generally part of the risk management plan, but they may also be integrated into other parts of the overall project plan (e.g., as part of a scope management plan or quality management plan).

.4 *Reserves.* A reserve is a provision in the project plan to mitigate cost and/or schedule risk. The term is often used with a modifier (e.g., management reserve, contingency reserve, schedule reserve) to provide further detail on what types of risk are meant to be mitigated. The specific meaning of the modified terms often varies by application area. In addition, use of a reserve, and the definition of what may be included in a reserve, is also application-area-specific.

.5 *Contractual agreements.* Contractual agreements may be entered into for insurance, services, and other items as appropriate in order to avoid or mitigate threats. Contractual terms and conditions will have a significant effect on the degree of risk reduction.

11.4 RISK RESPONSE CONTROL

Risk response control involves executing the risk management plan in order to respond to risk events over the course of the project. When changes occur, the basic cycle of identify, quantify, and respond is repeated. It is important to understand that even the most thorough and comprehensive analysis cannot identify all risks and probabilities correctly; control and iteration are required.

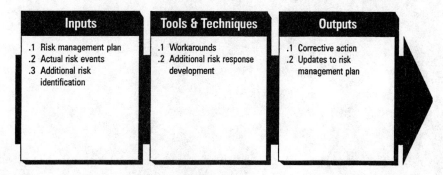

Inputs	Tools & Techniques	Outputs
.1 Risk management plan	.1 Workarounds	.1 Corrective action
.2 Actual risk events	.2 Additional risk response	.2 Updates to risk
.3 Additional risk identification	development	management plan

11.4.1 Inputs to Risk Response Control

.1 *Risk management plan.* The risk management plan is described in Section 11.3.3.1.

.2 *Actual risk events.* Some of the identified risk events will occur, others will not. The ones that do are actual risk events or sources of risk, and the project management team must recognize that one has occurred so that the response developed can be implemented.

.3 *Additional risk identification.* As project performance is measured and reported (discussed in Section 10.3), potential risk events or sources of risk not previously identified may surface.

11.4.2 Tools and Techniques for Risk Response Control

.1 *Workarounds.* Workarounds are unplanned responses to negative risk events. Workarounds are unplanned only in the sense that the response was not defined in advance of the risk event occurring.

.2 *Additional risk response development.* If the risk event was not anticipated, or the effect is greater than expected, the planned response may not be adequate, and it will be necessary to repeat the response development process and perhaps the risk quantification process as well.

11.4.3 Outputs from Risk Response Control

.1 *Corrective action.* Corrective action consists primarily of performing the planned risk response (e.g., implementing contingency plans or workarounds).

.2 *Updates to risk management plan.* As anticipated risk events occur or fail to occur, and as actual risk event effects are evaluated, estimates of probabilities and value, as well as other aspects of the risk management plan, should be updated.

PROJECT PROCUREMENT MANAGEMENT

12

Project Procurement Management includes the processes required to acquire goods and services from outside the performing organization. For simplicity, goods and services, whether one or many, will generally be referred to as a "product." **Figure 12–1** provides an overview of the following major processes:

12.1 **Procurement Planning**—determining what to procure and when.

12.2 **Solicitation Planning**—documenting product requirements and identifying potential sources.

12.3 **Solicitation**—obtaining quotations, bids, offers, or proposals as appropriate.

12.4 **Source Selection**—choosing from among potential sellers.

12.5 **Contract Administration**—managing the relationship with the seller.

12.6 **Contract Close-out**—completion and settlement of the contract, including resolution of any open items.

These processes interact with each other and with the processes in the other knowledge areas as well. Each process may involve effort from one or more individuals or groups of individuals based on the needs of the project. Although the processes are presented here as discrete elements with well-defined interfaces, in practice they may overlap and interact in ways not detailed here. Process interactions are discussed in detail in Chapter 3, Project Management Processes.

Project Procurement Management is discussed from the perspective of the buyer in the buyer-seller relationship. The buyer-seller relationship can exist at many levels on one project. Depending on the application area, the seller may be called a contractor, a vendor, or a supplier.

The *seller* will typically manage their work as a project. In such cases:

• The *buyer* becomes the customer and is thus a key stakeholder for the seller.

• The *seller's* project management team must be concerned with all the processes of project management, not just with those of this knowledge area.

• The terms and conditions of the contract become a key input to many of the seller's processes. The contract may actually contain the input (e.g., major deliverables, key milestones, cost objectives) or it may limit the project team's options (e.g., buyer approval of staffing decisions is often required on design projects).

This chapter assumes that the seller is external to the performing organization. Most of the discussion, however, is equally applicable to *formal* agreements entered into with other units of the performing organization. When informal agreements are involved, the processes described in Project Human Resource Management, Chapter 9, and Project Communications Management, Chapter 10, are more likely to apply.

12.1
Procurement Planning

12.2
Solicitation Planning

12.3
Solicitation

12.4
Source Selection

12.5
Contract Administration

12.6
Contract Close-out

FIGURE 12–1   A GUIDE TO THE PROJECT MANAGEMENT BODY OF KNOWLEDGE

Figure 12–1. Project Procurement Management Overview

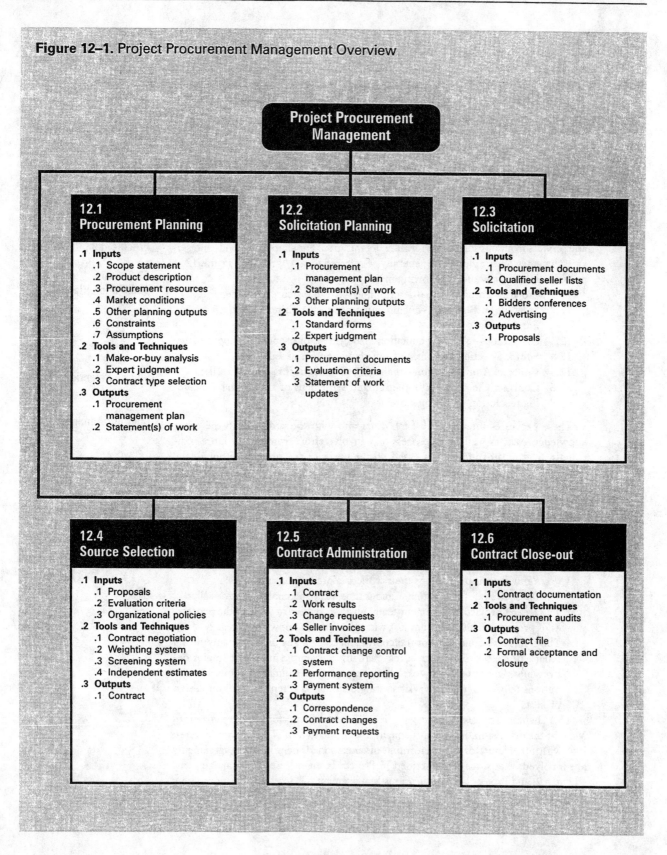

12.1 PROCUREMENT PLANNING

Procurement planning is the process of identifying which project needs can be best met by procuring products or services outside the project organization. It involves consideration of whether to procure, how to procure, what to procure, how much to procure, and when to procure it.

When the project obtains products and services from outside the performing organization, the processes from solicitation planning (Section 12.2) through contract close-out (Section 12.6) would be performed once for each product or service item. The project management team should seek support from specialists in the disciplines of contracting and procurement when needed.

When the project does not obtain products and services from outside the performing organization, the processes from solicitation planning (Section 12.2) through contract close-out (Section 12.6) would *not* be performed. This often occurs on research and development projects when the performing organization is reluctant to share project technology, and on many smaller, in-house projects when the cost of finding and managing an external resource may exceed the potential savings.

Procurement planning should also include consideration of potential subcontracts, particularly if the buyer wishes to exercise some degree of influence or control over subcontracting decisions.

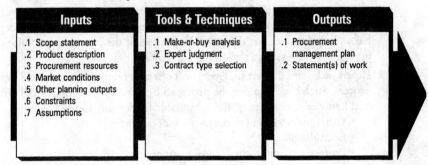

Inputs	Tools & Techniques	Outputs
.1 Scope statement .2 Product description .3 Procurement resources .4 Market conditions .5 Other planning outputs .6 Constraints .7 Assumptions	.1 Make-or-buy analysis .2 Expert judgment .3 Contract type selection	.1 Procurement management plan .2 Statement(s) of work

12.1.1 Inputs to Procurement Planning

.1 *Scope statement.* The scope statement (see Section 5.2.3.1) describes the current project boundaries. It provides important information about project needs and strategies that must be considered during procurement planning.

.2 *Product description.* The description of the product of the project (described in Section 5.1.1.1) provides important information about any technical issues or concerns that would need to be considered during procurement planning.

The product description is generally broader than a statement of work. A product description describes the ultimate end-product of the project; a statement of work (discussed in Section 12.1.3.2) describes the portion of that product to be provided by a seller to the project. However, if the performing organization chooses to procure the entire product, the distinction between the two terms becomes moot.

.3 *Procurement resources.* If the performing organization does not have a formal contracting group, the project team will have to supply both the resources and the expertise to support project procurement activities.

.4 *Market conditions.* The procurement planning process must consider what products and services are available in the marketplace, from whom, and under what terms and conditions.

.5 *Other planning outputs.* To the extent that other planning outputs are available, they must be considered during procurement planning. Other planning outputs which must often be considered include preliminary cost and schedule estimates, quality management plans, cash flow projections, the work breakdown structure, identified risks, and planned staffing.

.6 *Constraints.* Constraints are factors that limit the buyer's options. One of the most common constraints for many projects is funds availability.

.7 *Assumptions.* Assumptions are factors that, for planning purposes, will be considered to be true, real, or certain.

12.1.2 Tools and Techniques for Procurement Planning

.1 *Make-or-buy analysis.* This is a general management technique which can be used to determine whether a particular product can be produced cost-effectively by the performing organization. Both sides of the analysis include indirect as well as direct costs. For example, the "buy" side of the analysis should include both the actual out-of-pocket cost to purchase the product as well as the indirect costs of managing the purchasing process.

A make-or-buy analysis must also reflect the perspective of the performing organization as well as the immediate needs of the project. For example, purchasing a capital item (anything from a construction crane to a personal computer) rather than renting it is seldom cost effective. However, if the performing organization has an ongoing need for the item, the portion of the purchase cost allocated to the project may be less than the cost of the rental.

.2 *Expert judgment.* Expert judgment will often be required to assess the inputs to this process. Such expertise may be provided by any group or individual with specialized knowledge or training and is available from many sources including:
- Other units within the performing organization.
- Consultants.
- Professional and technical associations.
- Industry groups.

.3 *Contract type selection.* Different types of contracts are more or less appropriate for different types of purchases. Contracts generally fall into one of three broad categories:
- Fixed price or lump sum contracts—this category of contract involves a fixed total price for a well-defined product. To the extent that the product is not well-defined, both the buyer and seller are at risk—the buyer may not receive the desired product or the seller may need to incur additional costs in order to provide it. Fixed price contracts may also include incentives for meeting or exceeding selected project objectives such as schedule targets.
- Cost reimbursable contracts—this category of contract involves payment (reimbursement) to the seller for its actual costs. Costs are usually classified as *direct* costs or *indirect* costs. Direct costs are costs incurred for the exclusive benefit of the project (e.g., salaries of full-time project staff). Indirect costs, also called overhead costs, are costs allocated to the project by the performing organization as a cost of doing business (e.g., salaries of corporate executives). Indirect costs are usually calculated as a percentage of direct costs. Cost reimbursable contracts often include incentives for meeting or exceeding selected project objectives such as schedule targets or total cost.
- Unit price contracts—the seller is paid a preset amount per unit of service (e.g., $70 per hour for professional services or $1.08 per cubic yard of earth removed), and the total value of the contract is a function of the quantities needed to complete the work.

12.1.3 Outputs from Procurement Planning

.1 *Procurement management plan.* The procurement management plan should describe how the remaining procurement processes (from solicitation planning through contract close-out) will be managed. For example:

- What types of contracts will be used?
- If independent estimates will be needed as evaluation criteria, who will prepare them and when?
- If the performing organization has a procurement department, what actions can the project management team take on its own?
- If standardized procurement documents are needed, where can they be found?
- How will multiple providers be managed?
- How will procurement be coordinated with other project aspects such as scheduling and performance reporting?

A procurement management plan may be formal or informal, highly detailed or broadly framed, based on the needs of the project. It is a subsidiary element of the overall project plan described in Section 4.1, Project Plan Development.

.2 *Statement(s) of work.* The statement of work (SOW) describes the procurement item in sufficient detail to allow prospective sellers to determine if they are capable of providing the item. "Sufficient detail" may vary based on the nature of the item, the needs of the buyer, or the expected contract form.

Some application areas recognize different types of SOW. For example, in some government jurisdictions, the term SOW is reserved for a procurement item that is a clearly specified product or service, and the term Statement of Requirements (SOR) is used for a procurement item that is presented as a problem to be solved.

The statement of work may be revised and refined as it moves through the procurement process. For example, a prospective seller may suggest a more efficient approach or a less costly product than that originally specified. Each individual procurement item requires a separate statement of work. However, multiple products or services may be grouped as one procurement item with a single SOW.

The statement of work should be as clear, as complete, and as concise as possible. It should include a description of any collateral services required, such as performance reporting or post-project operational support for the procured item. In some application areas, there are specific content and format requirements for a SOW.

12.2 SOLICITATION PLANNING

Solicitation planning involves preparing the documents needed to support solicitation (the solicitation process is described in Section 12.3).

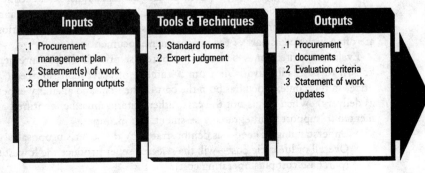

Inputs	Tools & Techniques	Outputs
.1 Procurement management plan .2 Statement(s) of work .3 Other planning outputs	.1 Standard forms .2 Expert judgment	.1 Procurement documents .2 Evaluation criteria .3 Statement of work updates

12.2.1 Inputs to Solicitation Planning

.1 Procurement management plan. The procurement management plan is described in Section 12.1.3.1.

.2 Statement(s) of work. The statement of work is described in Section 12.1.3.2.

.3 Other planning outputs. Other planning outputs (see Section 12.1.1.5), which may have been modified from when they were considered as part of procurement planning, should be reviewed again as part of solicitation. In particular, solicitation planning should be closely coordinated with the project schedule.

12.2.2 Tools and Techniques for Solicitation Planning

.1 Standard forms. Standard forms may include standard contracts, standard descriptions of procurement items, or standardized versions of all or part of the needed bid documents (see Section 12.2.3.1). Organizations that do substantial amounts of procurement should have many of these documents standardized.

.2 Expert judgment. Expert judgment is described in Section 12.1.2.2.

12.2.3 Outputs from Solicitation Planning

.1 Procurement documents. Procurement documents are used to solicit proposals from prospective sellers. The terms "bid" and "quotation" are generally used when the source selection decision will be price-driven (as when buying commercial items), while the term "proposal" is generally used when non-financial considerations such as technical skills or approach are paramount (as when buying professional services). However, the terms are often used interchangeably and care should be taken not to make unwarranted assumptions about the implications of the term used. Common names for different types of procurement documents include: Invitation for Bid (IFB), Request for Proposal (RFP), Request for Quotation (RFQ), Invitation for Negotiation, and Contractor Initial Response.

Procurement documents should be structured to facilitate accurate and complete responses from prospective sellers. They should always include the relevant statement of work, a description of the desired form of the response, and any required contractual provisions (e.g., a copy of a model contract, non-disclosure provisions). Some or all of the content and structure of procurement documents, particularly for those prepared by a government agency, may be defined by regulation.

Procurement documents should be rigorous enough to ensure consistent, comparable responses, but flexible enough to allow consideration of seller suggestions for better ways to satisfy the requirements.

.2 Evaluation criteria. Evaluation criteria are used to rate or score proposals. They may be objective (e.g., "the proposed project manager must be a certified Project Management Professional") or subjective (e.g., "the proposed project manager must have documented, previous experience with similar projects"). Evaluation criteria are often included as part of the procurement documents.

Evaluation criteria may be limited to purchase price if the procurement item is known to be readily available from a number of acceptable sources ("purchase price" in this context includes both the cost of the item and ancillary expenses such as delivery). When this is not the case, other criteria must be identified and documented to support an integrated assessment. For example:

- Understanding of need—as demonstrated by the seller's proposal.
- Overall or life cycle cost—will the selected seller produce the lowest total cost (purchase cost plus operating cost)?
- Technical capability—does the seller have, or can the seller be reasonably expected to acquire, the technical skills and knowledge needed?

- Management approach—does the seller have, or can the seller be reasonably expected to develop, management processes and procedures to ensure a successful project?
- Financial capacity—does the seller have, or can the seller reasonably be expected to obtain, the financial resources needed?

.3 Statement of work updates. The statement of work is described in Section 12.1.3.2. Modifications to one or more statements of work may be identified during solicitation planning.

12.3 SOLICITATION

Solicitation involves obtaining information (bids and proposals) from prospective sellers on how project needs can be met. Most of the actual effort in this process is expended by the prospective sellers, normally at no cost to the project.

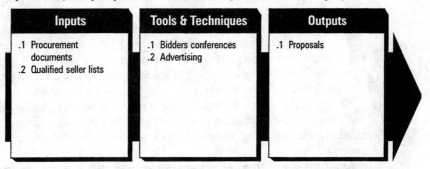

Inputs	Tools & Techniques	Outputs
.1 Procurement documents .2 Qualified seller lists	.1 Bidders conferences .2 Advertising	.1 Proposals

12.3.1 Inputs to Solicitation

.1 Procurement documents. Procurement documents are described in Section 12.2.3.1.

.2 Qualified seller lists. Some organizations maintain lists or files with information on prospective sellers. These lists will generally have information on relevant experience and other characteristics of the prospective sellers.

If such lists are not readily available, the project team will have to develop its own sources. General information is widely available through library directories, relevant local associations, trade catalogs, and similar sources. Detailed information on specific sources may require more extensive effort, such as site visits or contact with previous customers.

Procurement documents may be sent to some or all of the prospective sellers.

12.3.2 Tools and Techniques for Solicitation

.1 Bidder conferences. Bidder conferences (also called contractor conferences, vendor conferences, and pre-bid conferences) are meetings with prospective sellers prior to preparation of a proposal. They are used to ensure that all prospective sellers have a clear, common understanding of the procurement (technical requirements, contract requirements, etc.). Responses to questions may be incorporated into the procurement documents as amendments.

.2 Advertising. Existing lists of potential sellers can often be expanded by placing advertisements in general circulation publications such as newspapers or in specialty publications such as professional journals. Some government jurisdictions require public advertising of certain types of procurement items; most government jurisdictions require public advertising of subcontracts on a government contract.

12.3.3 Outputs from Solicitation

.1 Proposals. Proposals (see also discussion of bids, quotations, and proposals in Section 12.2.3.1) are seller-prepared documents that describe the seller's ability and willingness to provide the requested product. They are prepared in accordance with the requirements of the relevant procurement documents.

12.4 SOURCE SELECTION

Source selection involves the receipt of bids or proposals and the application of the evaluation criteria to select a provider. This process is seldom straightforward:

- Price may be the primary determinant for an off-the-shelf item, but the lowest proposed *price* may not be the lowest *cost* if the seller proves unable to deliver the product in a timely manner.
- Proposals are often separated into technical (approach) and commercial (price) sections with each evaluated separately.
- Multiple sources may be required for critical products.

The tools and techniques described below may be used singly or in combination. For example, a weighting system may be used to:

- Select a single source who will be asked to sign a standard contract.
- Rank order all proposals to establish a negotiating sequence.

On major procurement items, this process may be iterated. A short list of qualified sellers will be selected based on a preliminary proposal, and then a more detailed evaluation will be conducted based on a more detailed and comprehensive proposal.

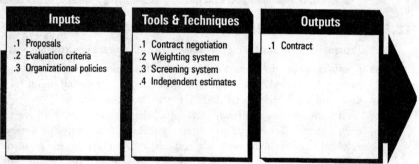

Inputs	Tools & Techniques	Outputs
.1 Proposals .2 Evaluation criteria .3 Organizational policies	.1 Contract negotiation .2 Weighting system .3 Screening system .4 Independent estimates	.1 Contract

12.4.1 Inputs to Source Selection

.1 Proposals. Proposals are described in Section 12.3.3.1.

.2 Evaluation criteria. Evaluation criteria are described in Section 12.2.3.2.

.3 Organizational policies. Any and all of the organizations involved in the project may have formal or informal policies that can affect the evaluation of proposals.

12.4.2 Tools and Techniques for Source Selection

.1 Contract negotiation. Contract negotiation involves clarification and mutual agreement on the structure and requirements of the contract prior to the signing of the contract. To the extent possible, final contract language should reflect all agreements reached. Subjects covered generally include, but are not limited to, responsibilities and authorities, applicable terms and law, technical and business management approaches, contract financing, and price.

For complex procurement items, contract negotiation may be an independent process with inputs (e.g., an issues or open items list) and outputs (e.g., memorandum of understanding) of its own.

Contract negotiation is a special case of the general management skill called "negotiation." Negotiation tools, techniques, and styles are widely discussed in the general management literature and are generally applicable to contract negotiation.

.2 **Weighting system.** A weighting system is a method for quantifying qualitative data in order to minimize the effect of personal prejudice on source selection. Most such systems involve (1) assigning a numerical weight to each of the evaluation criteria, (2) rating the prospective sellers on each criterion, (3) multiplying the weight by the rating, and (4) totaling the resultant products to compute an overall score.

.3 **Screening system.** A screening system involves establishing minimum requirements of performance for one or more of the evaluation criteria. For example, a prospective seller might be required to propose a project manager who is a Project Management Professional (PMP) before the remainder of their proposal would be considered.

.4 **Independent estimates.** For many procurement items, the procuring organization may prepare its own estimates as a check on proposed pricing. Significant differences from these estimates may be an indication that the SOW was not adequate or that the prospective seller either misunderstood or failed to respond fully to the SOW. Independent estimates are often referred to as "should cost" estimates.

12.4.3 Outputs from Source Selection

.1 **Contract.** A contract is a mutually binding agreement which obligates the seller to provide the specified product and obligates the buyer to pay for it. *A contract is a legal relationship subject to remedy in the courts.* The agreement may be simple or complex, usually (but not always) reflecting the simplicity or complexity of the product. It may be called, among other names, a contract, an agreement, a subcontract, a purchase order, or a memorandum of understanding. Most organizations have documented policies and procedures defining who can sign such agreements on behalf of the organization.

Although all project documents are subject to some form of review and approval, the legally binding nature of a contract usually means that it will be subjected to a more extensive approval process. In all cases, a primary focus of the review and approval process should be to ensure that the contract language describes a product or service that will satisfy the need identified. In the case of major projects undertaken by public agencies, the review process may even include public review of the agreement.

12.5 CONTRACT ADMINISTRATION

Contract administration is the process of ensuring that the seller's performance meets contractual requirements. On larger projects with multiple product and service providers, a key aspect of contract administration is managing the interfaces among the various providers. *The legal nature of the contractual relationship makes it imperative that the project team be acutely aware of the legal implications of actions taken when administering the contract.*

Contract administration includes application of the appropriate project management processes to the contractual relationship(s) and integration of the outputs from these processes into the overall management of the project. This integration and coordination will often occur at multiple levels when there are multiple sellers and multiple products involved. The project management processes which must be applied include:

- Project plan execution, described in Section 4.2, to authorize the contractor's work at the appropriate time.
- Performance reporting, described in Section 10.3, to monitor contractor cost, schedule, and technical performance.

- Quality control, described in Section 8.3, to inspect and verify the adequacy of the contractor's product.
- Change control, described in Section 4.3, to ensure that changes are properly approved and that all those with a need to know are aware of such changes.

Contract administration also has a financial management component. Payment terms should be defined within the contract and should involve a specific linkage between progress made and compensation paid.

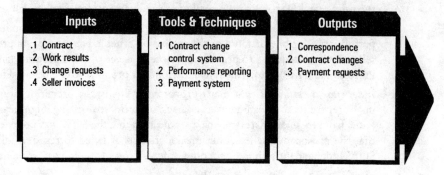

Inputs	Tools & Techniques	Outputs
.1 Contract	.1 Contract change control system	.1 Correspondence
.2 Work results	.2 Performance reporting	.2 Contract changes
.3 Change requests	.3 Payment system	.3 Payment requests
.4 Seller invoices		

12.5.1 Inputs to Contract Administration

.1 Contract. Contracts are described in Section 12.4.3.1.

.2 Work results. The seller's work results—which deliverables have been completed and which have not, to what extent are quality standards being met, what costs have been incurred or committed, etc.—are collected as part of project plan execution (Section 4.2 provides more detail on project plan execution).

.3 Change requests. Change requests may include modifications to the terms of the contract or to the description of the product or service to be provided. If the seller's work is unsatisfactory, a decision to terminate the contract would also be handled as a change request. Contested changes, those where the seller and the project management team cannot agree on compensation for the change, are variously called claims, disputes, or appeals.

.4 Seller invoices. The seller must submit invoices from time to time to request payment for work performed. Invoicing requirements, including necessary supporting documentation, are usually defined in the contract.

12.5.2 Tools and Techniques for Contract Administration

.1 Contract change control system. A contract change control system defines the process by which the contract may be modified. It includes the paperwork, tracking systems, dispute resolution procedures, and approval levels necessary for authorizing changes. The contract change control system should be integrated with the overall change control system (Section 4.3 describes the overall change control system).

.2 Performance reporting. Performance reporting provides management with information about how effectively the seller is achieving the contractual objectives. Contract performance reporting should be integrated with the overall project performance reporting described in Section 10.3.

.3 Payment system. Payments to the seller are usually handled by the accounts payable system of the performing organization. On larger projects with many or complex procurement requirements, the project may develop its own system. In either case, the system must include appropriate reviews and approvals by the project management team.

©1996 Project Management Institute, Four Campus Boulevard, Newtown Square, PA 19073-3299 USA

12.5.3 Outputs from Contract Administration

.1 *Correspondence.* Contract terms and conditions often require written documentation of certain aspects of buyer/seller communications, such as warnings of unsatisfactory performance and contract changes or clarifications.

.2 *Contract changes.* Changes (approved and unapproved) are fed back through the appropriate project planning and project procurement processes, and the project plan or other relevant documentation is updated as appropriate.

.3 *Payment requests.* This assumes that the project is using an external payment system. If the project has its own internal system, the output here would simply be "payments."

12.6 CONTRACT CLOSE-OUT

Contract close-out is similar to administrative closure (described in Section 10.4) in that it involves both product verification (Was all work completed correctly and satisfactorily?) and administrative close-out (updating of records to reflect final results and archiving of such information for future use). The contract terms and conditions may prescribe specific procedures for contract close-out. Early termination of a contract is a special case of contract close-out.

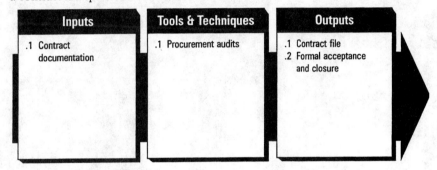

Inputs	Tools & Techniques	Outputs
.1 Contract documentation	.1 Procurement audits	.1 Contract file .2 Formal acceptance and closure

12.6.1 Inputs to Contract Close-out

.1 *Contract documentation.* Contract documentation includes, but is not limited to, the contract itself along with all supporting schedules, requested and approved contract changes, any seller-developed technical documentation, seller performance reports, financial documents such as invoices and payment records, and the results of any contract-related inspections.

12.6.2 Tools and Techniques for Contract Close-out

.1 *Procurement audits.* A procurement audit is a structured review of the procurement process from procurement planning through contract administration. The objective of a procurement audit is to identify successes and failures that warrant transfer to other procurement items on this project or to other projects within the performing organization.

12.6.3 Outputs from Contract Close-out

.1 *Contract file.* A complete set of indexed records should be prepared for inclusion with the final project records (see Section 10.4.3.1 for a more detailed discussion of administrative closure).

.2 *Formal acceptance and closure.* The person or organization responsible for contract administration should provide the seller with formal written notice that the contract has been completed. Requirements for formal acceptance and closure are usually defined in the contract.

APPENDICES

A. The Project Management Institute Standards-Setting Process

B. Evolution of PMI's *A Guide to the Project Management Body of Knowledge*

C. Contributors and Reviewers

D. Notes

E. Application Area Extensions

F. Additional Sources of Information on Project Management

G. Summary of Project Management Knowledge Areas

iii

THE PROJECT MANAGEMENT INSTITUTE STANDARDS-SETTING PROCESS

a

The following procedure was established as Institute policy by a vote of the Project Management Institute (PMI) Board of Directors at its October 1993 meeting.

A.1 PMI Standards Documents

PMI Standards Documents are those developed or published by PMI that describe generally accepted practices of project management, specifically:

- *A Guide to the Project Management Body of Knowledge* (PMBOK).
- Project Management Body of Knowledge Handbooks.

Additional documents may be added to this list by the Director of Standards subject to the advice and consent of PMI's Professional Development Group (PDG). Standards Documents may be original works published by PMI or they may be publications of other organizations or individuals.

Standards Documents will be developed in accordance with the "Code of Good Practice for Standardization" developed by the International Organization for Standardization (ISO).

A.2 Development of Original Works

Standards Documents that are original works to be published by PMI will be developed as follows:

- Prospective developer(s) will submit a proposal to the Director of Standards. The Director may also request such proposals. The Director will accept or reject such proposals and will inform the proposer as to the rationale for the decision. If the proposal requires funding in excess of that budgeted for standards development, the Director will submit the proposal to the PMI Board before approving it.
- The Director will support the developer's efforts so as to maximize the probability that the end product will be accepted.
- When the proposed material has been completed to the satisfaction of the developer, the developer will submit the material to the Director of Standards. The Director will appoint at least three knowledgeable individuals to review and comment on the material. Based on comments received, the Director will decide whether to accept the material as an *Exposure Draft*. Developer(s) will be required to sign PMI's standard copyright release prior to publication of the Exposure Draft.
- Exposure Drafts will be published under the aegis of the PMI Publications Board and must meet the standards of that group regarding typography and style.
- Exposure Drafts will be generally available to anyone who wishes to review the material. The Director of Standards will define a review period of not less than six months for all Exposure Drafts. Each Exposure Draft will include a notice asking for comments to be sent to the Director and noting the expiration of the review period.

- At the conclusion of the review period, the Director of Standards will review comments received and will work with the developer(s) and others as needed to incorporate appropriate comments. If the comments are major, the Director may elect to repeat the Exposure Draft review process. The Director will promptly submit proposed Standards Documents to the PDG for review and approval. The PDG may (a) approve the document as submitted; (b) reject the document; or (c) require a repetition of the Exposure Draft review process.

A.3 Adoption of Non-Original Works as Standards

Standards Documents that are the work of other organizations or individuals will be handled as follows:

- Anyone may submit a request to the Director of Standards to consider a non-PMI publication as a PMI Standard. The Director will appoint at least three knowledgeable individuals to consider the material. If the comments received are positive, the Director will prepare a proposal for the PDG to consider regarding a prospective relationship with the owner(s) of the material.
- The Director's proposal shall address the review and approval process, possible effects on Certification and Accreditation, whether or not PMI Board action is needed, and any financial considerations.

EVOLUTION OF PMI'S
A GUIDE TO THE
PROJECT MANAGEMENT
BODY OF KNOWLEDGE

b

B.1 Initial Development

PMI was founded in 1969 on the premise that there were many management practices that were common to projects in application areas as diverse as construction and pharmaceuticals. By the time of the Montreal Seminar/Symposium in 1976, the idea that such common practices might be documented as "standards" began to be widely discussed. This led in turn to consideration of project management as a distinct profession.

It was not until 1981, however, that the PMI Board of Directors approved a project to develop the procedures and concepts necessary to support the profession of project management. The project proposal suggested three areas of focus:

- The distinguishing characteristics of a practicing professional (ethics).
- The content and structure of the profession's body of knowledge (standards).
- Recognition of professional attainment (accreditation).

The project team thus came to be known as the Ethics, Standards and Accreditation Management Group (ESA). The ESA Management Group consisted of the following individuals:

- Matthew H. Parry, Chair
- David C. Aird
- Frederick R. Fisher
- David Haeney
- Harvey Kolodney
- Charles E. Oliver
- William H. Robinson
- Douglas J. Ronson
- Paul Sims
- Eric W. Smythe

This group was assisted by more than 25 volunteers in several local chapters. The Ethics statement was developed and submitted by a committee in Washington, D.C., chaired by Lew Ireland. The Time Management statement was developed through extensive meetings of a group in Southern Ontario, including Dave MacDonald, Dave Norman, Bob Spence, Bob Hall and Matt Parry. The Cost Management statement was developed through extensive meetings within the cost department of Stelco under the direction of Dave Haeney and Larry Harrison. Other statements were developed by the ESA Management Group. Accreditation was taken up by John Adams and his group at Western Carolina University, which resulted in the development of accreditation guidelines and a program for the certification of Project Management Professionals under the guidance of Dean Martin.

The results of the ESA Project were published in a Special Report in the *Project Management Journal* in August 1983. The report included:

- A Code of Ethics plus a procedure for code enforcement.
- A standards baseline consisting of six major knowledge areas: Scope Management, Cost Management, Time Management, Quality Management, Human Resources Management, and Communications Management.
- Guidelines for both accreditation (recognition of the quality of programs provided by educational institutions) and certification (recognition of the professional qualifications of individuals).

This report subsequently served as the basis for PMI's initial Accreditation and Certification programs. Western Carolina University's Masters Degree in Project Management was accredited in 1983 and the first Project Management Professionals (PMPs) were certified in 1984.

B.2 1986–87 Update

Publication of the ESA Baseline Report gave rise to much discussion within PMI about the adequacy of the standards. In 1984, the PMI Board of Directors approved a second standards-related project "to capture the knowledge applied to project management ... within the existing ESA framework." Six committees were then recruited to address each of the six identified knowledge areas. In addition, a workshop was scheduled as part of the 1985 Annual Seminar/Symposium.

As a result of these efforts, a revised document was approved in principle by the PMI Board of Directors and published for comment in the *Project Management Journal* in August 1986. The primary contributors to this version of the document were:

- R. Max Wideman, Chair (during development)
- John R. Adams, Chair (when issued)
- Joseph R. Beck
- Peter Bibbes
- Jim Blethen
- Richard Cockfield
- Peggy Day
- William Dixon
- Peter C. Georgas
- Shirl Holingsworth
- William Kane
- Colin Morris
- Joe Muhlberger
- Philip Nunn
- Pat Patrick
- David Pym
- Linn C. Stuckenbruck
- George Vallance
- Larry C. Woolslager
- Shakir Zuberi

In addition to expanding and restructuring the original material, the revised document included three new sections:

- **Project Management Framework** was added to cover the relationships between the project and its external environment and between project management and general management.
- **Risk Management** was added as a separate knowledge area in order to provide better coverage of this subject.
- **Contract/Procurement Management** was added as a separate knowledge area in order to provide better coverage of this subject.

Subsequently, a variety of editorial changes and corrections were incorporated into the material, and the PMI Board of Directors approved it in March 1987. The final manuscript was published as a stand-alone document titled *The Project Management Body of Knowledge* in August 1987.

B.3 1996 Update

Discussion about the proper form, content, and structure of PMI's key standards document continued after publication of the 1987 version. In August 1991, PMI's Director of Standards, Alan Stretton, initiated a project to update the document based on comments received from the membership. The revised document was developed over several years through a series of widely circulated working drafts and through workshops at the PMI Seminars/Symposia in Dallas, Pittsburgh, and San Diego.

In August 1994, the PMI Standards Committee issued an Exposure Draft of the document that was distributed for comment to all 10,000 PMI members and to more than 20 other professional and technical associations.

This document represents the completion of the project initiated in 1991. Contributors and reviewers are listed in Appendix C. A summary of the differences between the 1987 document and the 1996 document is included in the Preface of the 1996 edition.

CONTRIBUTORS AND REVIEWERS

C

The following individuals contributed in many different ways to various drafts of this document. PMI is indebted to them for their support.

C.1 Standards Committee

The following individuals served as members of the PMI Standards Committee during development of this update of the PMBOK document:

- William R. Duncan, Duncan•Nevison, Director of Standards
- Frederick Ayer, Defense Systems Management College
- Cynthia Berg, Medtronic Micro-Rel
- Mark Burgess, KnowledgeWorks
- Helen Cooke, Cooke & Cooke
- Judy Doll, Searle
- Drew Fetters, PECO Energy Company
- Brian Fletcher, ABRINN Project Management Services
- Earl Glenwright, A.S.S.I.S.T.
- Eric Jenett, Consultant
- Deborah O'Bray, Manitoba Telephone System
- Diane Quinn, Eastman Kodak Co.
- Anthony Rizzotto, Miles Diagnostics
- Alan Stretton, University of Technology, Sydney
- Douglas E. Tryloff, TASC

C.2 Contributors

In addition to the members of the Standards Committee, the following individuals provided original text or key concepts for one or more sections in the chapters indicated:

- John Adams, Western Carolina University (Chapter 3, Project Management Processes)
- Keely Brunner, Ball Aerospace (Chapter 7, Project Cost Management)
- Louis J. Cabano, Pathfinder, Inc. (Chapter 5, Project Scope Management)
- David Curling, Loday Systems (Chapter 12, Project Procurement Management)
- Douglas Gordon, Special Projects Coordinations (Chapter 7, Project Cost Management)
- David T. Hulett, D.T. Hulett & Associates (Chapter 11, Project Risk Management)
- Edward Ionata, Bechtel/Parsons Brinckerhoff (Chapter 10, Project Communications Management)
- John M. Nevison, Duncan•Nevison (Chapter 9, Project Human Resource Management)
- Hadley Reynolds, Reynolds Associates (Chapter 2, The Project Management Context)

- Agnes Salvo, CUNA Mutual Insurance (Chapter 11, Project Risk Management)
- W. Stephen Sawle, Consultants to Management, Inc. (Chapter 5, Project Scope Management)
- Leonard Stolba, Parsons, Brinckerhoff, Douglas & Quade (Chapter 8, Project Quality Management)
- Ahmet Taspinar, MBP Network (Chapter 6, Project Time Management)
- Francis M. Webster (Chapter 1, definition of project)

C.3 Reviewers

In addition to the Standards Committee and the contributors, the following individuals provided comments on various drafts of this document:

- Edward L. Averill, Edward Averill & Associates
- A.C. "Fred" Baker, Scott, Madden & Associates
- F.J. "Bud" Baker, Wright State University
- Tom Belanger, The Sterling Planning Group
- John A. Bing, Coastline Community College
- Brian Bock, Ziff Desktop Information
- Paul Bosakowski, Fluor Daniel
- Dorothy J. Burton, Management Systems Associates, Ltd.
- Cohort '93, University of Technology, Sydney
- Cohort '94, University of Technology, Sydney
- Kim Colenso, Applied Business Technologies
- Samuel K. Collier, Mead Corporation
- Karen Condos-Alfonsi, PMI Executive Office
- E.J. Coyle, VDO Yazaki
- Darlene Crane, Crane Consulting
- Russ Darnall, Fluor Daniel
- Maureen Dougherty, GPS Technologies
- John J. Downing, Digital Equipment Corporation
- Daniel D. Dudek, Optimum Technologies, Inc.
- Lawrence East, Westinghouse
- Quentin W. Fleming, Primavera Systems, Inc.
- Rick Fletcher, Acres
- Greg Githens, Maxicomm Project Services, Inc.
- Leo Giulianeti, Keane Inc.
- Martha D. Hammonds, AMEX TSG Systems
- Abdulrazak Hajibrahim, Bombardier
- G. Alan Hellawell, Eastman Kodak
- Paul Hinkley, Meta Consultants
- Wayne L. Hinthorn, PMI Orange Co.
- Mark E. Hodson, Eli Lilly & Company
- Lew Ireland, L.R. Ireland Associates
- Elvin Isgrig, North Dakota State University
- Murray Janzen, Procter & Gamble
- Frank Jenes
- Walter Karpowski, Management Assoc.
- William F. Kerrigan, Bechtel International, Inc.

- Harold Kerzner, Baldwin-Wallace College
- Robert L. Kimmons, Kimmons-Asaro Group Ltd., Inc.
- Richard King, AT&T
- J.D. "Kaay" Koch, Koch Associates
- Lauri Koskela, VTT Building Technology
- Richard E. Little, Project Performance Management
- Lyle W. Lockwood, Universal Technology Inc.
- Lawrence Mack, PMI Pittsburgh
- Christopher Madigan, Sandia National Laboratories
- Michael L. McCauley, Integrated Project Systems
- Hugh McLaughlin, Broadstar Inc.
- Frank McNeely, National Contract Management Association
- Pierre Menard, University of Quebec at Montreal
- Rick Michaels
- Raymond Miller, AT&T
- Alan Minson, A&R Minson
- Colin Morris, Delcan Hatch
- R. Bruce Morris
- David J. Mueller, Westinghouse
- Gary Nelson, Athena Consulting Inc.
- John P. Nolan, AACE International
- Louise C. Novakowski, Cominco Engineering Services, Ltd.
- James O'Brien, O'Brien-Kreitzberg
- JoAnn C. Osmer, Arbella Mutual Insurance Co.
- Jon V. Palmquist, Allstate Insurance
- Matthew Parry, Target Consultants
- John G. Phippen, JGP Quality Services
- Hans E. Picard, P&A Consultants Corporation
- Serge Y. Piotte, Cartier Group
- PMI, Houston Chapter
- PMI, Manitoba Chapter
- PMI, New Zealand Chapter
- Charles J. Pospisil, Procon, Inc.
- Janice Y. Preston, Pacifica Companies
- Mark T. Price, GE Nuclear Energy
- Christopher Quaife, Symmetric Resources
- Peter E. Quinn, Canadian Air Force
- Steven F. Ritter, Mead Corporation
- William S. Ruggles, Ruggles & Associates
- Ralph B. Sackman, Levi Strauss & Co.
- Alice Sapienza, Simmons College
- Darryl M. Selleck
- Melvin Silverman, Atrium Associates, Inc.
- Roy Smith, Decision Planning Corp.
- Craig T. Stone, Management Counseling Corp.

- Hiroshi Tanaka, JGC Corporation
- Robert Templeton, MW Kellogg
- Dick Thiel, King County (WA) DPW
- Saul Thomashow, Andersen Consulting
- J. Tidhar, Oranatech Management Systems Ltd.
- Vijay K. Verma, TRIUMF
- Janet Toepfer, Business Office Systems
- Alex Walton, Harris Corporation
- Jack Way, Simetra, Inc.
- R. Max Wideman, AEW Services
- Rebecca Winston, EG&G Idaho Inc.
- Hugh M. Woodward, Proctor & Gamble
- Robert Youker, Management Planning & Control Systems
- Shakir H. Zuberi, ICF Kaiser Engineers Hanford
- Dirk Zwart, Computer Sciences Corp.

C.4 Production Staff

Special mention is due to the following employees of PMI Communications:

- Jeannette M. Cabanis, Editor, Book Division
- Misty N. Dillard, Administrative Assistant
- Linda V. Gillman, Office Administrator
- Bobby R. Hensley, Publications Coordinator
- Jonathan Hicks, Systems Administrator
- Sandy Jenkins, Associate Editor
- Mark S. Parker, Production Coordinator
- Dewey L. Messer, Managing Editor
- Danell Moses, Marketing Promotion Coordinator
- Shirley B. Parker, Business/Marketing Manager
- Melissa Pendergast, Information Services Coordinator
- James S. Pennypacker, Publisher/Editor-In-Chief
- Michelle Triggs, Graphic Designer
- Lisa Woodring, Administrative Assistant

NOTES

d

Chapter 1. Introduction

1. *The American Heritage Dictionary of the English Language*, Third Edition. 1992. Boston, Mass.: Houghton Mifflin Company.

2. Turner, J. Rodney. 1992. *The Handbook of Project-Based Management*. New York, N.Y.: McGraw-Hill.

Chapter 2. The Project Management Context

1. Morris, Peter W.G. 1981. Managing Project Interfaces: Key Points for Project Success. In Cleland and King, *Project Management Handbook*, Second Edition. Englewood Cliffs, N.J.: Prentice-Hall.

2. Murphy, Patrice L. 1989. Pharmaceutical Project Management: Is It Different? *Project Management Journal* (September).

3. Muench, Dean. 1994. *The Sybase Development Framework*. Oakland, Calif.: Sybase Inc.

4. Kotter, John P. 1990. *A Force for Change: How Leadership Differs from Management*. New York, N.Y.: The Free Press.

5. Pfeffer, Jeffrey. 1992. *Managing with Power: Politics and Influence in Organizations*. HBS Press. Quoted in [6].

6. Eccles, Robert, et al. 1992. *Beyond the Hype*. Cambridge, Mass.: Harvard University Press.

7. International Organization for Standardization. 1994. *Code of Good Practice for Standardization (Draft International Standard)*. Geneva, Switzerland: ISO Press.

8. *The American Heritage Dictionary of the English Language*, Third Edition. 1992. Boston, Mass.: Houghton Mifflin Company.

Chapter 3. Project Management Processes

1. *The American Heritage Dictionary of the English Language*, Third Edition. 1992. Boston, Mass.: Houghton Mifflin Company.

Chapter 4. Project Integration Management

No notes for this chapter.

Chapter 5. Project Scope Management

1. Turner, J. Rodney, *op cit*, Ch. 1.

2. İyigün, M. Güven. 1993. A Decision Support System for R&D Project Selection and Resource Allocation Under Uncertainty. *Project Management Journal* (December).

3. Scope Definition and Control, Publication 6–2, p. 45. 1986 (July). Austin, Tex.: Construction Industry Institute

Chapter 6. Project Time Management

No notes for this chapter.

Chapter 7. Project Cost Management

No notes for this chapter.

Chapter 8. Project Quality Management

1. International Organization for Standardization. 1993. *Quality—Vocabulary (Draft International Standard 8402)*. Geneva, Switzerland: ISO Press.
2. *Ibid.*
3. *Ibid.*
4. *Ibid.*
5. *Ibid.*

Chapter 9. Project Human Resource Management

No notes for this chapter.

Chapter 10. Project Communications Management

No notes for this chapter.

Chapter 11. Project Risk Management

No notes for this chapter.

Chapter 12. Project Procurement Management

No notes for this chapter.

APPLICATION AREA
EXTENSIONS

e

E.1 Need for Application Area Extensions

Application area extensions are necessary when there are generally accepted practices for a category of projects (an application area) that are not generally accepted across the full range of project types. Application area extensions reflect:

- Unique or unusual aspects of the project environment that the project management team must be aware of in order to manage the project efficiently and effectively.
- Common practices which, if followed, will improve the efficiency and effectiveness of the project (e.g., standard work breakdown structures).

Application area-specific practices can arise as a result of many factors, including, but not limited to—differences in cultural norms, technical terminology, societal impact, or project life cycles. For example:

- In construction, where virtually all work is accomplished under contract, there are common practices related to procurement that do not apply to all categories of projects.
- In biosciences, there are common practices driven by the regulatory environment that do not apply to all categories of projects.
- In government contracting, there are common practices driven by government acquisition regulations that do not apply to all categories of projects.
- In consulting, there are common practices created by the project manager's sales and marketing responsibilities that do not apply to all categories of projects.

Application area extensions are additions to the core material of Chapters 1 through 12, not substitutes for it. Extensions are expected to be organized in a fashion similar to this document, i.e., by identifying and describing the project management processes unique to that application area. In different application areas, there may be a need to identify additional processes, to subdivide common processes, to define different sequences or process interactions, or to add elements to the common process definitions.

E.2 Criteria for Development

Extensions will be developed for those application areas that meet the following criteria:

- There is a substantial body of knowledge for the application area that is both project-oriented and unique or nearly unique to that area.
- There is an identifiable organization (e.g., a PMI Specific Interest Group or another professional or technical association) willing to commit the necessary resources to support the PMI Standards Committee with developing and maintaining the material.
- The additional material developed is able to pass the same level of rigorous review as the core material.

ADDITIONAL SOURCES OF INFORMATION ON PROJECT MANAGEMENT

f

Project management is a growing, dynamic field with books and articles on the subject published regularly. The entities listed below provide a variety of products and services that may be of use to those interested in project management.

F.1 Professional and Technical Organizations

This document was developed and published by the Project Management Institute. PMI can be contacted at:

Project Management Institute   Phone: 610/356-4600
Four Campus Boulevard   Fax: 610/356-4647
Newtown Square, PA 19073-3299   E-mail: pmihq@pmi.org
USA   World Wide Web: www.pmi.org

PMI currently has cooperative agreements with the following organizations:

AACE International
Phone: 304/296-8444   Fax: 304/291-5728

Australian Institute of Project Management (AIPM)
Phone: +61-02-9960-0058   Fax: +61-02-9960-0052

Construction Management Association of America (CMAA)
Phone: 703/356-2622   Fax: 703/356-6388

Engineering Advancement Association of Japan (ENAA)
Phone: +81-3-3502-4441   Fax: +81-3-3502-5500

Institute of Industrial Engineers (IIE)
Phone: 770/449-0460   Fax: 770/263-8532

Institute of Project Management (IPM-Ireland)
Phone: +353-1-661-4677   Fax: +353-1-661-3588

International Project Management Association (IPMA)
Phone: +45-45-76-46-76   Fax: +45-45-76-80-20

Korean Institute of Project Management and Technology (PROMAT)
Phone: +822-510-5835   Fax: +822-510-5380

Performance Management Association (PMA)
Phone: 703/370-7885   Fax: 703/461-7328

Project Management Association (PMA-India)
Phone: +91-11-852-6673   Fax: +91-11-646-4481

Project Management Institute of Canada
Phone: Fax: 403/281-3068

Russian Project Management Association (SOVNET)
Phone: +7-095-133-24-41   Fax: +7-095-131-85-29

Western Australian Project Management Association, Inc. (WAPMA)
Phone: 619/383-3849   Fax: 619/383-3849

In addition, there are numerous other organizations in related fields that may be able to provide additional information about project management. For example:

American Society for Quality Control
Construction Industry Institute
National Association for Purchasing Management
National Contract Management Association
Society for Human Resource Management
American Society of Civil Engineers

Current contact information for these and other professional and technical organizations worldwide can generally be found in your local library.

F.2 Commercial Publishers

Many commercial publishers produce books on project management and related fields. Commercial publishers that regularly produce such materials include:

Addison-Wesley
AMACOM
Gower Press
John Wiley & Sons
Marcel Dekker
McGraw-Hill
Prentice-Hall
Probus
Van Nostrand Reinhold

Most project management books from these publishers are available from PMI. Many of the books available from these sources include extensive bibliographies or lists of suggested readings.

F.3 Product and Service Vendors

Companies that provide software, training, consulting, and other products and services to the project management profession often provide monographs or reprints. PMI publishes an annual directory of such vendors in *PM Network* and similar lists are often available from the other organizations listed in F.1.

F.4 Educational Institutions

Many universities, colleges, and junior colleges offer continuing education programs in project management and related disciplines. Some of these institutions also offer graduate or undergraduate degree programs. PMI publishes an annual directory of such programs in *PM Network*.

SUMMARY OF PROJECT MANAGEMENT KNOWLEDGE AREAS

g

Project Integration Management
A subset of project management that includes the processes required to ensure that the various elements of the project are properly coordinated. It consists of:
- Project plan development—taking the results of other planning processes and putting them into a consistent, coherent document.
- Project plan execution—carrying out the project plan by performing the activities included therein.
- Overall change control—coordinating changes across the entire project.

Project Scope Management
A subset of project management that includes the processes required to ensure that the project includes all the work required, and only the work required, to complete the project successfully. It consists of:
- Initiation—committing the organization to begin the next phase of the project.
- Scope planning—developing a written scope statement as the basis for future project decisions.
- Scope definition—subdividing the major project deliverables into smaller, more manageable components.
- Scope verification—formalizing acceptance of the project scope.
- Scope change control—controlling changes to project scope.

Project Time Management
A subset of project management that includes the processes required to ensure timely completion of the project. It consists of:
- Activity definition—identifying the specific activities that must be performed to produce the various project deliverables.
- Activity sequencing—identifying and documenting interactivity dependencies.
- Activity duration estimating—estimating the number of work periods which will be needed to complete individual activities.
- Schedule development—analyzing activity sequences, activity durations, and resource requirements to create the project schedule.
- Schedule control—controlling changes to the project schedule.

Project Cost Management

A subset of project management that includes the processes required to ensure that the project is completed within the approved budget. It consists of:

- Resource planning—determining what resources (people, equipment, materials) and what quantities of each should be used to perform project activities.
- Cost estimating—developing an approximation (estimate) of the costs of the resources needed to complete project activities.
- Cost budgeting—allocating the overall cost estimate to individual work items.
- Cost control—controlling changes to the project budget.

Project Quality Management

A subset of project management that includes the processes required to ensure that the project will satisfy the needs for which it was undertaken. It consists of:

- Quality planning—identifying which quality standards are relevant to the project and determining how to satisfy them.
- Quality assurance—evaluating overall project performance on a regular basis to provide confidence that the project will satisfy the relevant quality standards.
- Quality control—monitoring specific project results to determine if they comply with relevant quality standards and identifying ways to eliminate causes of unsatisfactory performance.

Project Human Resource Management

A subset of project management that includes the processes required to make the most effective use of the people involved with the project. It consists of:

- Organizational planning—identifying, documenting, and assigning project roles, responsibilities, and reporting relationships.
- Staff acquisition—getting the human resources needed assigned to and working on the project.
- Team development—developing individual and group skills to enhance project performance.

Project Communications Management

A subset of project management that includes the processes required to ensure timely and appropriate generation, collection, dissemination, storage, and ultimate disposition of project information. It consists of:

- Communications planning—determining the information and communications needs of the stakeholders: who needs what information, when will they need it, and how will it be given to them.
- Information distribution—making needed information available to project stakeholders in a timely manner.
- Performance reporting—collecting and disseminating performance information. This includes status reporting, progress measurement, and forecasting.
- Administrative closure—generating, gathering, and disseminating information to formalize phase or project completion.

©1996 Project Management Institute, Four Campus Boulevard, Newtown Square, PA 19073-3299 USA

Project Risk Management

A subset of project management that includes the processes concerned with identifying, analyzing, and responding to project risk. It consists of:

- Risk identification—determining which risks are likely to affect the project and documenting the characteristics of each.
- Risk quantification—evaluating risks and risk interactions to assess the range of possible project outcomes.
- Risk response development—defining enhancement steps for opportunities and responses to threats.
- Risk response control—responding to changes in risk over the course of the project.

Project Procurement Management

A subset of project management that includes the processes required to acquire goods and services from outside the performing organization. It consists of:

- Procurement planning—determining what to procure and when.
- Solicitation planning—documenting product requirements and identifying potential sources.
- Solicitation—obtaining quotations, bids, offers, or proposals as appropriate.
- Source selection—choosing from among potential sellers.
- Contract administration—managing the relationship with the seller.
- Contract close-out—completion and settlement of the contract, including resolution of any open items.

GLOSSARY AND INDEX

GLOSSARY

1. Inclusions and Exclusions
This glossary includes terms that are:
- Unique or nearly unique to project management (e.g., scope statement, work package, work breakdown structure, critical path method).
- Not unique to project management, but used differently or with a narrower meaning in project management than in general everyday usage (e.g., early start date, activity, task).

This glossary generally does not include:
- Application area-specific terms (e.g., project prospectus as a legal document—unique to real estate development).
- Terms whose use in project management do not differ in any material way from everyday use (e.g., contract).
- Compound terms whose meaning is clear from the combined meanings of the component parts.
- Variants when the meaning of the variant is clear from the base term (e.g., *exception report* is included, *exception reporting* is not).

As a result of the above inclusions and exclusions, this glossary includes:
- A preponderance of terms related to Project Scope Management and Project Time Management, since many of the terms used in these two knowledge areas are unique or nearly unique to project management.
- Many terms from Project Quality Management, since these terms are used more narrowly than in their everyday usage.
- Relatively few terms related to Project Human Resource Management, Project Risk Management, and Project Communications Management, since most of the terms used in these knowledge areas do not differ significantly from everyday usage.
- Relatively few terms related to Project Cost Management and Project Procurement Management, since many of the terms used in these knowledge areas have narrow meanings that are unique to a particular application area.

2. Common Acronyms

ACWP	Actual Cost of Work Performed
AD	Activity Description
ADM	Arrow Diagramming Method
AF	Actual Finish date
AOA	Activity-On-Arrow
AON	Activity-On-Node
AS	Actual Start date
BAC	Budget At Completion
BCWP	Budgeted Cost of Work Performed

BCWS	Budgeted Cost of Work Scheduled
CCB	Change Control Board
CPFF	Cost Plus Fixed Fee
CPIF	Cost Plus Incentive Fee
CPI	Cost Performance Index
CPM	Critical Path Method
CV	Cost Variance
DD	Data Date
DU	DUration
EAC	Estimate At Completion
EF	Early Finish date
ES	Early Start date
ETC	Estimate (or Estimated) To Complete (or Completion)
EV	Earned Value
FF	Free Float or Finish-to-Finish
FFP	Firm Fixed Price
FPIF	Fixed Price Incentive Fee
FS	Finish-to-Start
GERT	Graphical Evaluation and Review Technique
IFB	Invitation For Bid
LF	Late Finish date
LOE	Level Of Effort
LS	Late Start date
MPM	Modern Project Management
OBS	Organization(al) Breakdown Structure
PC	Percent Complete
PDM	Precedence Diagramming Method
PERT	Program Evaluation and Review Technique
PF	Planned Finish date
PM	Project Management or Project Manager
PMBOK	Project Management Body of Knowledge
PMP	Project Management Professional
PS	Planned Start date
QA	Quality Assurance
QC	Quality Control
RAM	Responsibility Assignment Matrix
RDU	Remaining DUration
RFP	Request For Proposal
RFQ	Request For Quotation
SF	Scheduled Finish date or Start-to-Finish
SOW	Statement Of Work
SPI	Schedule Performance Index
SS	Scheduled Start date or Start-to-Start
SV	Schedule Variance
TC	Target Completion date
TF	Total Float or Target Finish date
TS	Target Start date
TQM	Total Quality Management
WBS	Work Breakdown Structure

3. Definitions

Many of the words defined here have broader, and in some cases different, dictionary definitions.

The definitions use the following conventions:

- Terms used as part of the definitions, and are defined in the glossary, are shown in *italics*.
- When synonyms are included, no definition is given and the reader is directed to the preferred term (ie., see *preferred term*).
- Related terms that are not synonyms are cross-referenced at the end of the definition (ie., see also *related term*).

Accountability Matrix. See *responsibility assignment matrix*.

Activity. An element of work performed during the course of a project. An activity normally has an expected duration, an expected cost, and expected resource requirements. Activities are often subdivided into tasks.

Activity Definition. Identifying the specific activities that must be performed in order to produce the various project deliverables.

Activity Description (AD). A short phrase or label used in a project network diagram. The activity description normally describes the scope of work of the activity.

Activity Duration Estimating. Estimating the number of work periods which will be needed to complete individual activities.

Activity-On-Arrow (AOA). See *arrow diagramming method*.

Activity-On-Node (AON). See *precedence diagramming method*.

Actual Cost of Work Performed (ACWP). Total costs incurred (direct and indirect) in accomplishing work during a given time period. See also *earned value*.

Actual Finish Date (AF). The point in time that work actually ended on an activity. (Note: in some application areas, the activity is considered "finished" when work is "substantially complete.")

Actual Start Date (AS). The point in time that work actually started on an activity.

Administrative Closure. Generating, gathering, and disseminating information to formalize project completion.

Application Area. A category of projects that have common elements not present in all projects. Application areas are usually defined in terms of either the product of the project (i.e., by similar technologies or industry sectors) or the type of customer (e.g., internal vs. external, government vs. commercial). Application areas often overlap.

Arrow. The graphic presentation of an activity. See also *arrow diagramming method*.

Arrow Diagramming Method (ADM). A network diagramming technique in which activities are represented by arrows. The tail of the arrow represents the start and the head represents the finish of the activity (the length of the arrow does *not* represent the expected duration of the activity). Activities are connected at points called nodes (usually drawn as small circles) to illustrate the sequence in which the activities are expected to be performed. See also *precedence diagramming method*.

As-of Date. See *data date*.

Backward Pass. The calculation of late finish dates and late start dates for the uncompleted portions of all network activities. Determined by working backwards through the network logic from the project's end date. The end date may be calculated in a *forward pass* or set by the customer or sponsor. See also *network analysis*.

Bar Chart. A graphic display of schedule-related information. In the typical bar chart, activities or other project elements are listed down the left side of the chart, dates are shown across the top, and activity durations are shown as date-placed horizontal bars. Also called a *Gantt chart*.

Baseline. The original plan (for a project, a work package, or an activity), plus or minus approved changes. Usually used with a modifier (e.g., cost baseline, schedule baseline, performance measurement baseline).

Baseline Finish Date. See *scheduled finish date*.

Baseline Start Date. See *scheduled start date*.

Budget At Completion (BAC). The estimated total cost of the project when done.

Budget Estimate. See *estimate*.

Budgeted Cost of Work Performed (BCWP). The sum of the approved cost estimates (including any overhead allocation) for activities (or portions of activities) completed during a given period (usually project-to-date). See also *earned value*.

Budgeted Cost of Work Scheduled (BCWS). The sum of the approved cost estimates (including any overhead allocation) for activities (or portions of activities) scheduled to be performed during a given period (usually project-to-date). See also *earned value*.

Calendar Unit. The smallest unit of time used in scheduling the project. Calendar units are generally in hours, days, or weeks, but can also be in shifts or even in minutes. Used primarily in relation to *project management software*.

Change Control Board (CCB). A formally constituted group of stakeholders responsible for approving or rejecting changes to the project *baselines*.

Change in Scope. See *scope change*.

Chart of Accounts. Any numbering system used to monitor project costs by category (e.g., labor, supplies, materials). The project chart of accounts is usually based upon the corporate chart of accounts of the primary performing organization. See also *code of accounts*.

Charter. See *project charter*.

Code of Accounts. Any numbering system used to uniquely identify each element of the *work breakdown structure*. See also *chart of accounts*.

Communications Planning. Determining the information and communications needs of the project stakeholders.

Concurrent Engineering. An approach to project staffing that, in its most general form, calls for implementors to be involved in the design phase. Sometimes confused with *fast tracking*.

Contingencies. See *reserve* and *contingency planning*.

Contingency Allowance. See *reserve*.

Contingency Planning. The development of a management plan that identifies alternative strategies to be used to ensure project success if specified risk events occur.

Contingency Reserve. A separately planned quantity used to allow for future situations which may be planned for only in part (sometimes called "known unknowns"). For example, rework is certain, the amount of rework is not. Contingency reserves may involve cost, schedule, or both. Contingency reserves are intended to reduce the impact of missing cost or schedule objectives. Contingency reserves are normally included in the project's cost and schedule baselines.

Contract. A contract is a mutually binding agreement which obligates the seller to provide the specified product and obligates the buyer to pay for it. Contracts generally fall into one of three broad categories:

- Fixed price or lump sum contracts—this category of contract involves a fixed total price for a well-defined product. Fixed price contracts may also include incentives for meeting or exceeding selected project objectives such as schedule targets.
- Cost reimbursable contracts—this category of contract involves payment (reimbursement) to the contractor for its actual costs. Costs are usually classified as direct costs (costs incurred directly by the project, such as wages for members of the project team) and indirect costs (costs allocated to the project by the performing organization as a cost of doing business, such as salaries for corporate executives). Indirect costs are usually calculated as a percentage of direct costs. Cost reimbursable contracts often include incentives for meeting or exceeding selected project objectives such as schedule targets or total cost.
- Unit price contracts—the contractor is paid a preset amount per unit of service (e.g., $70 per hour for professional services or $1.08 per cubic yard of earth removed) and the total value of the contract is a function of the quantities needed to complete the work.

Contract Administration. Managing the relationship with the seller.

Contract Close-out. Completion and settlement of the contract, including resolution of all outstanding items.

Control. The process of comparing actual performance with planned performance, analyzing variances, evaluating possible alternatives, and taking appropriate *corrective action* as needed.

Control Charts. Control charts are a graphic display of the results, over time and against established control limits, of a process. They are used to determine if the process is "in control" or in need of adjustment.

Corrective Action. Changes made to bring expected future performance of the project into line with the plan.

Cost Budgeting. Allocating the cost estimates to individual project components.

Cost Control. Controlling changes to the project budget.

Cost Estimating. Estimating the cost of the resources needed to complete project activities.

Cost of Quality. The costs incurred to ensure quality. The cost of quality includes quality planning, quality control, quality assurance, and rework.

Cost Performance Index (CPI). The ratio of budgeted costs to actual costs (BCWP/ACWP). CPI is often used to predict the magnitude of a possible cost overrun using the following formula: original cost estimate/CPI = projected cost at completion. See also *earned value*.

Cost Plus Fixed Fee (CPFF) Contract. A type of *contract* where the buyer reimburses the seller for the seller's allowable costs (allowable costs are defined by the contract) plus a fixed amount of profit (fee).

Cost Plus Incentive Fee (CPIF) Contract. A type of *contract* where the buyer reimburses the seller for the seller's allowable costs (allowable costs are defined by the contract), and the seller earns its profit if it meets defined performance criteria.

Cost Variance (CV). (1) Any difference between the estimated cost of an activity and the actual cost of that activity. (2) In *earned value*, BCWP less ACWP.

Crashing. Taking action to decrease the total project duration after analyzing a number of alternatives to determine how to get the maximum duration compression for the least cost.

Critical Activity. Any activity on a *critical path*. Most commonly determined by using the *critical path method*. Although some activities are "critical" in the dictionary sense without being on the critical path, this meaning is seldom used in the project context.

Critical Path. In a *project network diagram*, the series of activities which determines the earliest completion of the project. The critical path will generally change from time to time as activities are completed ahead of or behind schedule. Although normally calculated for the entire project, the critical path can also be determined for a *milestone* or *subproject*. The critical path is usually defined as those activities with float less than or equal to a specified value, often zero. See *critical path method*.

Critical Path Method (CPM). A *network analysis* technique used to predict project duration by analyzing which sequence of activities (which *path*) has the least amount of scheduling flexibility (the least amount of *float*). Early dates are calculated by means of a *forward pass* using a specified start date. Late dates are calculated by means of a *backward pass* starting from a specified completion date (usually the forward pass's calculated project *early finish date*).

Current Finish Date. The current estimate of the point in time when an activity will be completed.

Current Start Date. The current estimate of the point in time when an activity will begin.

Data Date (DD). The point in time that separates actual (historical) data from future (scheduled) data. Also called *as-of date*.

Definitive Estimate. See *estimate*.

Deliverable. Any measurable, tangible, verifiable outcome, result, or item that must be produced to complete a project or part of a project. Often used more narrowly in reference to an *external deliverable*, which is a deliverable that is subject to approval by the project sponsor or customer.

Dependency. See *logical relationship*.

Dummy Activity. An activity of zero duration used to show a *logical relationship* in the *arrow diagramming method*. Dummy activities are used when logical relationships cannot be completely or correctly described with regular activity arrows. Dummies are shown graphically as a dashed line headed by an arrow.

Duration (DU). The number of work periods (not including holidays or other non-working periods) required to complete an activity or other project element. Usually expressed as workdays or workweeks. Sometimes incorrectly equated with elapsed time. See also *effort*.

Duration Compression. Shortening the project schedule without reducing the project scope. Duration compression is not always possible and often requires an increase in project cost.

Early Finish Date (EF). In the *critical path method*, the earliest possible point in time on which the uncompleted portions of an activity (or the project) can finish based on the network logic and any schedule constraints. Early finish dates can change as the project progresses and changes are made to the project plan.

Early Start Date (ES). In the *critical path method*, the earliest possible point in time on which the uncompleted portions of an activity (or the project) can start, based on the network logic and any schedule constraints. Early start dates can change as the project progresses and changes are made to the project plan.

©1996 Project Management Institute, Four Campus Boulevard, Newtown Square, PA 19073-3299 USA

Earned Value (EV). (1) A method for measuring project performance. It compares the amount of work that was planned with what was actually accomplished to determine if cost and schedule performance is as planned. See also *actual cost of work performed*, *budgeted cost of work scheduled*, *budgeted cost of work performed*, *cost variance*, *cost performance index*, *schedule variance*, and *schedule performance index*. (2) The *budgeted cost of work performed* for an activity or group of activities.

Earned Value Analysis. See definition (1) under *earned value*.

Effort. The number of labor units required to complete an activity or other project element. Usually expressed as staffhours, staffdays, or staffweeks. Should not be confused with *duration*.

Estimate. An assessment of the likely quantitative result. Usually applied to project costs and durations and should always include some indication of accuracy (e.g., ± x percent). Usually used with a modifier (e.g., preliminary, conceptual, feasibility). Some application areas have specific modifiers that imply particular accuracy ranges (e.g., order-of-magnitude estimate, budget estimate, and definitive estimate in engineering and construction projects).

Estimate At Completion (EAC). The expected total cost of an activity, a group of activities, or of the project when the defined scope of work has been completed. Most techniques for forecasting EAC include some adjustment of the original cost estimate based on project performance to date. Also shown as "estimated at completion." Often shown as EAC = Actuals-to-date + ETC. See also *earned value* and *estimate to complete*.

Estimate To Complete (ETC). The expected additional cost needed to complete an activity, a group of activities, or the project. Most techniques for forecasting ETC include some adjustment to the original estimate based on project performance to date. Also called "estimated to complete." See also *earned value* and *estimate at completion*.

Event-on-Node. A network diagramming technique in which events are represented by boxes (or nodes) connected by arrows to show the sequence in which the events are to occur. Used in the original *Program Evaluation and Review Technique*.

Exception Report. Document that includes only major variations from plan (rather than all variations).

Expected Monetary Value. The product of an event's probability of occurrence and the gain or loss that will result. For example, if there is a 50 percent probability that it will rain, and rain will result in a $100 loss, the expected monetary value of the rain event is $50 (.5 x $100).

Fast Tracking. Compressing the project schedule by overlapping activities that would normally be done in sequence, such as design and construction. Sometimes confused with *concurrent engineering*.

Finish Date. A point in time associated with an activity's completion. Usually qualified by one of the following: actual, planned, estimated, scheduled, early, late, baseline, target or current.

Finish-to-Finish (FF). See *logical relationship*.

Finish-to-Start (FS). See *logical relationship*.

Firm Fixed Price (FFP) Contract. A type of *contract* where the buyer pays the seller a set amount (as defined by the contract) regardless of the seller's costs.

Fixed Price Contract. See *firm fixed price contract*.

Fixed Price Incentive Fee (FPIF) Contract. A type of *contract* where the buyer pays the seller a set amount (as defined by the contract), and the seller can earn an additional amount if it meets defined performance criteria.

Float. The amount of time that an activity may be delayed from its early start without delaying the project finish date. Float is a mathematical calculation and can change as the project progresses and changes are made to the project plan. Also called slack, total float, and path float. See also *free float*.

Forecast Final Cost. See *estimate at completion*.

Forward Pass. The calculation of the early start and early finish dates for the uncompleted portions of all network activities. See also *network analysis* and *backward pass*.

Fragnet. See *subnet*.

Free Float (FF). The amount of time an activity can be delayed without delaying the *early start* of any immediately following activities. See also *float*.

Functional Manager. A manager responsible for activities in a specialized department or function (e.g., engineering, manufacturing, marketing).

Functional Organization. An organization structure in which staff are grouped hierarchically by specialty (e.g., production, marketing, engineering, and accounting at the top level; with engineering, further divided into mechanical, electrical, and others).

Gantt Chart. See *bar chart*.

Grade. A category or rank used to distinguish items that have the same functional use (e.g., "hammer") but do not share the same requirements for quality (e.g., different hammers may need to withstand different amounts of force).

Graphical Evaluation and Review Technique (GERT). A *network analysis* technique that allows for conditional and probabilistic treatment of *logical relationships* (i.e., some activities may not be performed).

Hammock. An aggregate or summary activity (a group of related activities is shown as one and reported at a summary level). A hammock may or may not have an internal sequence. See also *subproject* and *subnet*.

Hanger. An unintended break in a *network path*. Hangers are usually caused by missing *activities* or missing *logical relationships*.

Information Distribution. Making needed information available to project stakeholders in a timely manner.

Initiation. Committing the organization to begin a project phase.

Integrated Cost/Schedule Reporting. See *earned value*.

Invitation for Bid (IFB). Generally, this term is equivalent to *request for proposal*. However, in some application areas it may have a narrower or more specific meaning.

Key Event Schedule. See *master schedule*.

Lag. A modification of a *logical relationship* which directs a delay in the successor task. For example, in a finish-to-start dependency with a 10-day lag, the successor activity cannot start until 10 days after the predecessor has finished. See also *lead*.

Late Finish Date (LF). In the *critical path method*, the latest possible point in time that an activity may be completed without delaying a specified milestone (usually the project finish date).

Late Start Date (LS). In the *critical path method*, the latest possible point in time that an activity may begin without delaying a specified milestone (usually the project finish date).

Lead. A modification of a *logical relationship* which allows an acceleration of the successor task. For example, in a finish-to-start dependency with a 10-day lead, the successor activity can start 10 days before the predecessor has finished. See also *lag*.

Level of Effort (LOE). Support-type activity (e.g., vendor or customer liaison) that does not readily lend itself to measurement of discrete accomplishment. It is generally characterized by a uniform rate of activity over a specific period of time.

Leveling. See *resource leveling*.

Life-cycle Costing. The concept of including acquisition, operating, and disposal costs when evaluating various alternatives.

Line Manager. (1) The manager of any group that actually makes a product or performs a service. (2) A *functional manager*.

Link. See *logical relationship*.

Logic. See *network logic*.

Logic Diagram. See *project network diagram*.

Logical Relationship. A dependency between two project activities, or between a project activity and a milestone. See also *precedence relationship*. The four possible types of logical relationships are:
- Finish-to-start—the "from" activity must finish before the "to" activity can start.
- Finish-to-finish—the "from" activity must finish before the "to" activity can finish.
- Start-to-start—the "from" activity must start before the "to" activity can start.
- Start-to-finish—the "from" activity must start before the "to" activity can finish.

Loop. A *network path* that passes the same node twice. Loops cannot be analyzed using traditional *network analysis* techniques such as *CPM* and *PERT*. Loops are allowed in *GERT*.

Management Reserve. A separately planned quantity used to allow for future situations which are impossible to predict (sometimes called "unknown unknowns"). Management reserves may involve cost or schedule. Management reserves are intended to reduce the risk of missing cost or schedule objectives. Use of management reserve requires a change to the project's cost baseline.

Master Schedule. A *summary-level schedule* which identifies the major activities and key milestones. See also *milestone schedule*.

Mathematical Analysis. See *network analysis*.

Matrix Organization. Any organizational structure in which the project manager shares responsibility with the functional managers for assigning priorities and for directing the work of individuals assigned to the project.

Milestone. A significant event in the project, usually completion of a major deliverable.

Milestone Schedule. A summary-level schedule which identifies the major milestones. See also *master schedule*.

Mitigation. Taking steps to lessen risk by lowering the probability of a risk event's occurrence or reducing its effect should it occur.

Modern Project Management (MPM). A term used to distinguish the current broad range of project management (scope, cost, time, quality, risk, etc.) from narrower, traditional use that focused on cost and time.

Monitoring. The capture, analysis, and reporting of project performance, usually as compared to plan.

Monte Carlo Analysis. A schedule risk assessment technique that performs a project simulation many times in order to calculate a distribution of likely results.

Near-Critical Activity. An *activity* that has low total *float*.

Network. See *project network diagram*.

Network Analysis. The process of identifying early and late start and finish dates for the uncompleted portions of project activities. See also *Critical Path Method, Program Evaluation and Review Technique*, and *Graphical Evaluation and Review Technique*.

Network Logic. The collection of activity dependencies that make up a *project network diagram*.

Network Path. Any continuous series of connected activities in a *project network diagram*.

Node. One of the defining points of a network; a junction point joined to some or all of the other dependency lines. See also *arrow diagramming method* and *precedence diagramming method*.

Order of Magnitude Estimate. See *estimate*.

Organizational Breakdown Structure (OBS). A depiction of the project organization arranged so as to relate *work packages* to organizational units.

Organizational Planning. Identifying, documenting, and assigning project roles, responsibilities, and reporting relationships.

Overall Change Control. Coordinating changes across the entire project.

Overlap. See *lead*.

Parametric Estimating. An estimating technique that uses a statistical relationship between historical data and other variables (e.g., square footage in construction, lines of code in software development) to calculate an estimate.

Pareto Diagram. A histogram, ordered by frequency of occurrence, that shows how many results were generated by each identified cause.

Path. A set of sequentially connected activities in a *project network diagram*.

Path Convergence. In mathematical analysis, the tendency of parallel paths of approximately equal duration to delay the completion of the milestone where they meet.

Path Float. See *float*.

Percent Complete (PC). An estimate, expressed as a percent, of the amount of work which has been completed on an activity or group of activities.

Performance Reporting. Collecting and disseminating information about project performance to help ensure project progress.

Performing Organization. The enterprise whose employees are most directly involved in doing the work of the project.

PERT Chart. A specific type of *project network diagram*. See *Program Evaluation and Review Technique*.

Phase. See *project phase*.

Planned Finish Date (PF). See *scheduled finish date*.

Planned Start Date (PS). See *scheduled start date*.

Precedence Diagramming Method (PDM). A network diagramming technique in which activities are represented by boxes (or nodes). Activities are linked by *precedence relationships* to show the sequence in which the activities are to be performed.

Precedence Relationship. The term used in the *precedence diagramming method* for a *logical relationship*. In current usage, however, precedence relationship, logical relationship, and dependency are widely used interchangeably regardless of the diagramming method in use.

Predecessor Activity. (1) In the *arrow diagramming method*, the activity which enters a *node*. (2) In the *precedence diagramming method*, the "from" activity.

Procurement Planning. Determining what to procure and when.

Program. A group of related projects managed in a coordinated way. Programs usually include an element of ongoing activity.

Program Evaluation and Review Technique (PERT). An event-oriented *network analysis* technique used to estimate project duration when there is a high degree of uncertainty with the individual activity duration estimates. PERT applies the *critical path method* to a weighted average duration estimate. Also given as *Program Evaluation and Review Technique.*

Project. A temporary endeavor undertaken to create a unique product or service.

Project Charter. A document issued by senior management that provides the project manager with the authority to apply organizational resources to project activities.

Project Communications Management. A subset of project management that includes the processes required to ensure proper collection and dissemination of project information. It consists of *communications planning, information distribution, performance reporting,* and *administrative closure.*

Project Cost Management. A subset of project management that includes the processes required to ensure that the project is completed within the approved budget. It consists of *resource planning, cost estimating, cost budgeting,* and *cost control.*

Project Human Resource Management. A subset of project management that includes the processes required to make the most effective use of the people involved with the project. It consists of *organizational planning, staff acquisition,* and *team development.*

Project Integration Management. A subset of project management that includes the processes required to ensure that the various elements of the project are properly coordinated. It consists of *project plan development, project plan execution,* and *overall change control.*

Project Life Cycle. A collection of generally sequential *project phases* whose name and number are determined by the control needs of the organization or organizations involved in the project.

Project Management (PM). The application of knowledge, skills, tools, and techniques to project activities in order to meet or exceed stakeholder needs and expectations from a project.

Project Management Body of Knowledge (PMBOK). An inclusive term that describes the sum of knowledge within the profession of project management. As with other professions such as law, medicine, and accounting, the body of knowledge rests with the practitioners and academics who apply and advance it. The PMBOK includes proven, traditional practices which are widely applied as well as innovative and advanced ones which have seen more limited use.

Project Management Professional (PMP). An individual certified as such by the Project Management Institute.

Project Management Software. A class of computer applications specifically designed to aid with planning and controlling project costs and schedules.

Project Management Team. The members of the project team who are directly involved in project management activities. On some smaller projects, the project management team may include virtually all of the *project team members.*

Project Manager (PM). The individual responsible for managing a project.

Project Network Diagram. Any schematic display of the logical relationships of project activities. Always drawn from left to right to reflect project chronology. Often incorrectly referred to as a "PERT chart."

Project Phase. A collection of logically related project activities, usually culminating in the completion of a major *deliverable.*

Project Plan. A formal, approved document used to guide both project execution and project control. The primary uses of the project plan are to document planning assumptions and decisions, to facilitate communication among stakeholders, and to document approved scope, cost, and schedule baselines. A project plan may be summary or detailed.

Project Plan Development. Taking the results of other planning processes and putting them into a consistent, coherent document.

Project Plan Execution. Carrying out the project plan by performing the activities included therein.

Project Planning. The development and maintenance of the *project plan*.

Project Procurement Management. A subset of project management that includes the processes required to acquire goods and services from outside the performing organization. It consists of *procurement planning, solicitation planning, solicitation, source selection, contract administration,* and *contract close-out.*

Project Quality Management. A subset of project management that includes the processes required to ensure that the project will satisfy the needs for which it was undertaken. It consists of *quality planning, quality assurance,* and *quality control.*

Project Risk Management. A subset of project management that includes the processes concerned with identifying, analyzing, and responding to project risk. It consists of *risk identification, risk quantification, risk response development,* and *risk response control.*

Project Schedule. The planned dates for performing activities and the planned dates for meeting milestones.

Project Scope Management. A subset of project management that includes the processes required to ensure that the project includes all of the work required, and only the work required, to complete the project successfully. It consists of *initiation, scope planning, scope definition, scope verification,* and *scope change control.*

Project Team Members. The people who report either directly or indirectly to the project manager.

Project Time Management. A subset of project management that includes the processes required to ensure timely completion of the project. It consists of *activity definition, activity sequencing, activity duration estimating, schedule development,* and *schedule control.*

Projectized Organization. Any organizational structure in which the project manager has full authority to assign priorities and to direct the work of individuals assigned to the project.

Quality Assurance (QA). (1) The process of evaluating overall project performance on a regular basis to provide confidence that the project will satisfy the relevant quality standards. (2) The organizational unit that is assigned responsibility for quality assurance.

Quality Control (QC). (1) The process of monitoring specific project results to determine if they comply with relevant quality standards and identifying ways to eliminate causes of unsatisfactory performance. (2) The organizational unit that is assigned responsibility for quality control.

Quality Planning. Identifying which quality standards are relevant to the project and determining how to satisfy them.

Remaining Duration (RDU). The time needed to complete an activity.

Request for Proposal (RFP). A type of bid document used to solicit proposals from prospective sellers of products or services. In some application areas it may have a narrower or more specific meaning.

Request for Quotation (RFQ). Generally, this term is equivalent to *request for proposal*. However, in some application areas it may have a narrower or more specific meaning.

Reserve. A provision in the project plan to mitigate cost and/or schedule risk. Often used with a modifier (e.g., *management reserve, contingency reserve*) to provide further detail on what types of risk are meant to be mitigated. The specific meaning of the modified term varies by *application area*.

Resource Leveling. Any form of *network analysis* in which scheduling decisions (start and finish dates) are driven by resource management concerns (e.g., limited resource availability or difficult-to-manage changes in resource levels).

Resource-Limited Schedule. A project schedule whose start and finish dates reflect expected resource availability. The final project schedule should always be resource-limited.

Resource Planning. Determining what resources (people, equipment, materials) are needed in what quantities to perform project activities.

Responsibility Assignment Matrix (RAM). A structure which relates the project organization structure to the *work breakdown structure* to help ensure that each element of the project's scope of work is assigned to a responsible individual.

Responsibility Chart. See *responsibility assignment matrix*.

Responsibility Matrix. See *responsibility assignment matrix*.

Retainage. A portion of a contract payment that is held until contract completion in order to ensure full performance of the contract terms.

Risk Event. A discrete occurrence that may affect the project for better or worse.

Risk Identification. Determining which risk events are likely to affect the project.

Risk Quantification. Evaluating the probability of risk event occurrence and effect.

Risk Response Control. Responding to changes in risk over the course of the project.

Risk Response Development. Defining enhancement steps for opportunities and mitigation steps for threats.

S-Curve. Graphic display of cumulative costs, labor hours, or other quantities, plotted against time. The name derives from the S-like shape of the curve (flatter at the beginning and end, steeper in the middle) produced on a project that starts slowly, accelerates, and then tails off.

Schedule. See *project schedule*.

Schedule Analysis. See *network analysis*.

Schedule Compression. See *duration compression*.

Schedule Control. Controlling changes to the project schedule.

Schedule Development. Analyzing activity sequences, activity durations, and resource requirements to create the project schedule.

Schedule Performance Index (SPI). The ratio of work performed to work scheduled (BCWP/BCWS). See *earned value*.

Schedule Variance (SV). (1) Any difference between the scheduled completion of an activity and the actual completion of that activity. (2) In *earned value*, BCWP less BCWS.

Scheduled Finish Date (SF). The point in time work was scheduled to finish on an activity. The scheduled finish date is normally within the range of dates delimited by the *early finish date* and the *late finish date*.

Scheduled Start Date (SS). The point in time work was scheduled to start on an activity. The scheduled start date is normally within the range of dates delimited by the *early start date* and the *late start date*.

Scope. The sum of the products and services to be provided as a project.

Scope Baseline. See *baseline*.

Scope Change. Any change to the project scope. A scope change almost always requires an adjustment to the project cost or schedule.

Scope Change Control. Controlling changes to project scope.

Scope Definition. Decomposing the major deliverables into smaller, more manageable components to provide better control.

Scope Planning. Developing a written scope statement that includes the project justification, the major deliverables, and the project objectives.

Scope Verification. Ensuring that all identified project deliverables have been completed satisfactorily.

Should-Cost Estimates. An *estimate* of the cost of a product or service used to provide an assessment of the reasonableness of a prospective contractor's proposed cost.

Slack. Term used in *PERT* for *float*.

Solicitation. Obtaining quotations, bids, offers, or proposals as appropriate.

Solicitation Planning. Documenting product requirements and identifying potential sources.

Source Selection. Choosing from among potential contractors.

Staff Acquisition. Getting the human resources needed assigned to and working on the project.

Stakeholder. Individuals and organizations who are involved in or may be affected by project activities.

Start Date. A point in time associated with an activity's start, usually qualified by one of the following: actual, planned, estimated, scheduled, early, late, target, baseline, or current.

Start-to-Finish. See *logical relationship*.

Start-to-Start. See *logical relationship*.

Statement of Work (SOW). A narrative description of products or services to be supplied under contract.

Subnet. A subdivision of a *project network diagram* usually representing some form of subproject.

Subnetwork. See *subnet*.

Successor Activity. (1) In the *arrow diagramming method*, the activity which departs a node. (2) In the *precedence diagramming method*, the "to" activity.

Target Completion Date (TC). An imposed date which constrains or otherwise modifies the *network analysis*.

Target Schedule. See *baseline*.

Task. See *activity*.

Team Development. Developing individual and group skills to enhance project performance.

Team Members. See *project team members*.

Time-Scaled Network Diagram. Any *project network diagram* drawn in such a way that the positioning and length of the activity represents its duration. Essentially, it is a bar chart that includes *network logic*.

Target Finish Date (TF). The date work is planned (targeted) to finish on an activity.

Target Start Date (TS). The date work is planned (targeted) to start on an activity.

Total Float (TF). See *float*.

Total Quality Management (TQM). A common approach to implementing a quality improvement program within an organization.

Workaround. A response to a negative risk event. Distinguished from *contingency plan* in that a workaround is not planned in advance of the occurrence of the risk event.

Work Breakdown Structure (WBS). A deliverable-oriented grouping of project elements which organizes and defines the total scope of the project. Each descending level represents an increasingly detailed definition of a project component. Project components may be products or services.

Work Item. See *activity*.

Work Package. A deliverable at the lowest level of the *work breakdown structure*. A work package may be divided into activities.

INDEX

©1996 Project Management Institute, Four Campus Boulevard, Newtown Square, PA 19073-3299 USA

©1996 Project Management Institute, Four Campus Boulevard, Newtown Square, PA 19073-3299 USA